Economics of the Environment

Selected Readings

SIXTH EDITION

Economics of the Environment

Selected Readings

SIXTH EDITION

Edited by

Robert N. Stavins

HARVARD KENNEDY SCHOOL

W. W. Norton & Company

New York   London

W. W. Norton & Company has been independent since its founding in 1923, when William Warder Norton and Mary D. Herter Norton first published lectures delivered at the People's Institute, the adult education division of New York City's Cooper Union. The firm soon expanded its program beyond the Institute, publishing books by celebrated academics from America and abroad. By mid-century, the two major pillars of Norton's publishing program—trade books and college texts—were firmly established. In the 1950s, the Norton family transferred control of the company to its employees, and today—with a staff of four hundred and a comparable number of trade, college, and professional titles published each year—W. W. Norton & Company stands as the largest and oldest publishing house owned wholly by its employees.

The text of this book is composed in New Aster
with the display set in Frutiger and Europa Arabesque.
Composition by Westchester.
Manufacturing by Courier.
Book design by Joan Greenfield.
Project editor: Rachel Mayer.
Production manager: Sean Mintus.

Library of Congress Cataloging-in-Publication Data

Economics of the environment : selected readings / edited by
Robert N. Stavins. — 6th ed.
p. cm.
Includes bibliographical references.
ISBN 978-0-393-91340-8 (pbk.)
1. Pollution—Economic aspects.   2. Environmental policy—Costs.
I. Stavins, R. N. (Robert N.), 1948–
HC79.P55D65 2012
363.7—dc23
2011046723

W. W. Norton & Company, Inc., 500 Fifth Avenue,
New York, N.Y. 10110-0017
www.wwnorton.com

W. W. Norton & Company Ltd., Castle House, 75/76 Wells Street,
London W1T 3QT

1 2 3 4 5 6 7 8 9 0

For Daniel, Julia, and Rudy

Contents

Preface

Environmental and natural-resource problems are both more widespread and more important today than they were one hundred years ago, when the discipline of economics was marking its emergence with the publication of the first volume of the *American Economic Review*. A century of economic growth and globalization have brought unparalleled improvements in societal well-being but also unprecedented challenges to the carrying capacity of the planet. Increases in income and population that would have been inconceivable one hundred years ago have greatly heightened pressures on the natural environment.

The stocks of a variety of renewable natural resources—including water, forests, fish, and numerous other plant and animal species—have been depleted below socially efficient levels, principally because of specific market failures. Likewise, market failures of open access—whether characterized as externalities or public goods—have led to the degradation of air and water quality, inappropriate disposal of hazardous waste, depletion of stratospheric ozone, and the atmospheric accumulation of greenhouse gases linked with global climate change.

Over this same century, economics as a discipline has gradually come to focus increasingly on these problems, first with regard to natural resources and more recently with regard to environmental quality. Economic research in academia and in think tanks has improved our understanding of the causes and consequences of excessive resource depletion and inefficient environmental degradation, thereby helping identify sensible policy solutions.

Overall, the problems have not diminished, and the lag between understanding and action can be long. Although some environmental problems have been addressed successfully, others continue to emerge. Some—such as the threat of global climate change—are both more important and more difficult than problems of the past. Fortunately, economics is well positioned to offer better understanding and better policies to address these new and ongoing challenges. As the second decade of the twenty-first century begins, environmental economics has emerged as a productive field within the discipline and one that shows even greater promise for the future.

Approximately six years have passed since the previous (fifth) edition of this volume was published, and it is now well over three decades since the first edition appeared, edited by Robert and Nancy Dorfman. Environmental economics continues to evolve from its origins as an obscure application of welfare economics to a prominent field in its own right that combines elements from public finance, industrial organization, microeconomic theory, and many other areas of economics. The number of articles on the environment appearing in mainstream economics periodicals continues to increase, and more and more economics journals are dedicated exclusively to environmental and resource topics.

There has also been a proliferation of environmental economics textbooks. Many are excellent, but none can be expected to provide direct access to timely and original contributions by the field's leading scholars. As most teachers of economics recognize, it is valuable to supplement the structure and rigor of a text with original readings from the literature. This new edition has been prepared with that in mind. It consists of thirty-four chapters that instructors will find to be of tremendous value as a complement to their chosen text and their lectures. The scope is comprehensive, the list of authors is a veritable who's who of environmental economics, and the articles are timely, with more than 90 percent published since 1990 and half since 2005. There are two completely new sections of the book, "Economics of Natural Resources" and "Corporate Social Responsibility." All of the chapters in the section on global climate change are new to this edition.

In order to make these readings accessible to students at all levels, one criterion used in the selection process is that articles should not only be original and well written—and meet the highest standards of economic scholarship—but should also be nontechnical in their presentations. Hence, readers will find virtually no formal mathematics in the chapters that follow.

Part I of this volume provides an overview of the field and a review of its foundations. Don Fullerton and I start things off with a brief essay about how economists think about the environment. This is followed by the classic treatment of social costs and bargaining by Ronald Coase and a new article by Jason Shogren and Laura Taylor on the important, emerging field of behavioral environmental economics.

Part II examines the costs of environmental protection, which might seem to be without controversy or current analytical interest. This is not, however, the case. We begin with a survey article by Carl Pasurka that reviews the theory and empirical evidence on the relationship between environmental regulation and so-called competitiveness. A revisionist view is provided by Michael Porter and Class van der Linde, who suggest that the conventional approach to thinking about the costs of environmental protection is fundamentally flawed. Karen Palmer, Wallace Oates, and Paul Portney provide a careful response.

In Part III, the focus turns to the other side of the analytic ledger—the benefits of environmental protection. This area has been even more contentious, both in the policy world and among scholars. Here the core questions are whether and how environmental amenities can be valued in economic terms for analytical purposes. We feature a provocative debate on the stated-preference method known as "contingent valuation." Paul Portney outlines the structure and importance of the debate, Michael Hanemann makes the affirmative case, and Peter Diamond and Jerry Hausman provide the critique. In the final article in Part III, we turn to a concept that is both very important in assessments of the benefits of environmental regulations and very widely misunderstood—the value of a statistical life. In an insightful essay, Trudy Cameron seeks to set the record straight.

Two principal policy questions need to be addressed in the environmental realm: how much environmental protection is desirable; and how that degree of environmental protection should be achieved. The first of these questions is addressed in Part IV and the second in Part V.

In Part IV, the criterion of economic efficiency and the analytical tool of benefit-cost analysis are considered as ways of judging the goals of environmental policy. In an introductory essay, Kenneth Arrow and his coauthors ask whether benefit-cost analysis can play a role in environmental, health, and safety regulation. Then, Lawrence Goulder and I focus on an ingredient of benefit-cost analysis that noneconomists seem to find particularly confusing or even troubling—intertemporal discounting. Next, Robert Pindyck examines a subject of fundamental importance, the role of uncertainty in environmental economics. Steven Kelman provides an ethically based critique of benefit-cost analysis, which is followed by a set of responses. Part IV concludes with an up-to-date essay by John Graham on the critical role of the U.S. Office of Management and Budget in federal regulatory impact analysis.

Part V examines the policy instruments—the means—that can be employed to achieve environmental targets or goals. The study of such policy instruments is an area where economists have made their greatest inroads of influence in the policy world. Tremendous changes have taken place over the past twenty years in the reception politicians and policy makers give to so-called market-based or economic-incentive instruments for environmental protection. Lawrence Goulder and Ian Parry start things off with a broad-ranging essay on instrument choice in environmental policy. Following this, I examine lessons that can be learned from the innovative sulfur dioxide allowance-trading program, set up by the Clean Air Act Amendments of 1990. Finally, Michael Sandel provides a critique of market-based instruments, with responses offered by Eric Maskin, Steven Shavell, and others.

Part VI consists of three essays on a new topic for this book—the economics of natural resources. First, John Livernois examines the empirical significance of a central tenet in natural resource economics, namely the

Hotelling rule—the proposition that under conditions of efficiency, the scarcity rent (price minus marginal extraction cost) of natural resources will rise over time at the rate of interest. Essays by Leonardo Maugeri and Sheila Olmstead examine two particularly important resources: petroleum and water.

The next four sections of the book treat some timely and important topics and problems. Part VII examines corporate social responsibility and the environment, discussion of which has too often been characterized by more heat than light. Forest Reinhardt, Richard Vietor, and I provide an overview of this realm from the perspective of economics, examining the notion that firms voluntarily sacrifice profits in the social interest. In a second essay, Paul Portney provides a valuable empirical perspective.

Part VIII is dedicated to investigations of the economic dimensions of global climate change, which may in the long term prove to be the most significant environmental problem that has ever arisen, in terms of both its potential damages and the costs of addressing it. First, a broad overview of the topic is provided in a survey article by Joseph Aldy, Alan Krupnick, Richard Newell, Ian Parry, and William Pizer. Next, William Nordhaus critiques the well-known *Stern Review on the Economics of Climate Change*, and Nicholas Stern and Chris Taylor respond. In the final essay in this section, Gilbert Metcalf examines market-based policy instruments that can be used to address greenhouse gas emissions.

Part IX examines another important area of analysis in environmental economics: sustainability, the commons, and globalization. Robert Solow begins with an economic perspective on sustainability. This is followed by Elinor Ostrom's development of a general framework for analyzing sustainability and my own historical view of economic analysis of problems associated with open-access resources. Then, Jeffrey Frankel draws on diverse sources of empirical evidence to examine whether globalization is good or bad for the environment.

The final section of the book, Part X, departs from the normative concerns of much of the rest of the volume to examine some interesting and important questions of political economy. It turns out that an economic perspective can provide useful insights into questions that might at first seem to be fundamentally political. Nathaniel Keohane, Richard Revesz, and I utilize an economic framework to ask why our political system has produced the particular set of environmental policy instruments it has. Myrick Freeman reflects on the benefits that U.S. environmental policies have brought about since the first Earth Day in 1970. Last, Robert Hahn addresses the question that many of the articles in this volume raise: What impact has economics actually had on environmental policy?

Environmental economics is a rapidly evolving field. Not only do new theoretical models and improved empirical methods appear on a regular basis but entirely new areas of investigation open up when the natural sciences indicate new concerns or the policy world turns to new issues. Therefore, this volume of collected essays remains a work in progress. I owe a great debt of gratitude to the teachers and students of previous editions who have sent their comments and suggestions for revisions. Thanks are also due to Jason Chapman, Susan Lynch, Matthew Ranson, and Robert Stowe for valuable assistance in producing this sixth edition. Looking to future editions, I invite all readers—whether teachers, students, or practitioners—to send me any thoughts or suggestions for improvement.

Robert Stavins
Cambridge, Massachusetts

I

Overview and Principles

1   How Economists See the Environment*

Don Fullerton

Robert N. Stavins

Don Fullerton is Gutgsell Professor of Finance and Institute of Government and Public Affairs at the University of Illinois at Urbana-Champaign. Robert N. Stavins is Albert Pratt Professor of Business and Government at Harvard Kennedy School, Research Associate at the National Bureau of Economics Research, and University Fellow at Resources for the Future.

On a topic such as the environment, communication among those from different disciplines in the natural and social sciences is both important and difficult. Economists themselves may have contributed to some misunderstandings about how they think about the environment, perhaps through enthusiasm for market solutions, perhaps by neglecting to make explicit all the necessary qualifications, and perhaps simply by the use of jargon.

There are several prevalent myths about how economists think about the environment. By examining them here, we hope to explain how economists really do think about the natural environment.

Myth of the Universal Market

The first myth is that economists believe that the market solves all problems. The "first theorem of welfare economics," as taught to generations of economics students, is that private markets are perfectly efficient on their own, with no interference from government, provided certain conditions are met.

This theorem, easily proved, is exceptionally powerful, because it means that no one needs to tell producers of goods and services what to sell to which consumers. Instead, self-interested producers and consumers meet in the market-place, engage in trade, and thereby achieve the greatest good for the greatest number, as if "guided by an invisible hand."[1] This maximum general welfare is what economists mean by the "efficiency" of

---

"How Economists See the Environment" by Don Fullerton and Robert Stavins. *Nature*, Vol. 395. Oct. 1, 1998. Pp. 433–434.

*The authors are grateful for suggestions from Robert Frosch, Robert Hahn, Gilbert Metcalf, Richard Revesz, and Thomas Schelling.

[1]Smith, A. *An Inquiry into the Nature and Causes of the Wealth of Nations* (Whitestone, Dublin, 1776).

competitive markets. Economists in business schools are particularly fond of identifying markets where the necessary conditions are met, such as the stock market, where many buyers and sellers operate with good information and low transaction costs to trade well-defined commodities with enforced rights of ownership.

Other economists, especially those in public policy schools, have a different approach to this theorem. By clarifying the conditions under which markets are efficient, the theorem also identifies the conditions under which they are not. Private markets are perfectly efficient only if there are no public goods, no externalities, no monopoly buyers or sellers, no increasing returns to scale, no information problems, no transaction costs, no taxes, no common property and no other "distortions" between the costs paid by buyers and the benefits received by sellers. Those conditions are obviously very restrictive, and they are usually not all satisfied simultaneously in the real world.

When a market thus fails, this same theorem offers guidance. For any particular market, it asks whether the number of sellers is sufficiently small to warrant antitrust action, whether the returns to scale are great enough to justify tolerating a single producer in a regulated market, or whether the benefits from the good are public in a way that might justify outright government provision of it. A public good, like the light from a lighthouse, benefits additional users at no cost to society.

Environmental economists are interested in pollution and other externalities, where some consequences of producing or consuming a good or service are external to the market (not considered by producers or consumers). With a negative externality, such as environmental pollution, the total

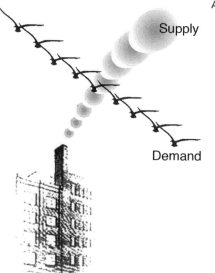

An economist's view of the environment.

Supply

Demand

social cost of production may exceed the value to consumers. If the market is left to itself, too many pollution-generating products are made.

Similarly, natural-resource economists are interested in common property, or open-access resources, where anyone can extract or harvest the resource freely and no one recognizes the full cost of using the resource. Extractors consider only their own direct and immediate costs, not the costs to others of increased scarcity ("user cost" or "scarcity rent"). The result is that the resource is depleted too quickly.

So, the market by itself demonstrably does not solve all problems. Indeed, in the environmental domain, perfectly functioning markets are the exception rather than the rule. Governments can try to correct these market failures, for example by restricting pollutant emissions or limiting access to open-access resources, which can improve welfare and lead to greater efficiency.

Myth of Market Solutions

A second common myth is that economists always recommend a market solution to a market problem. Economists tend to search for instruments of public policy that can fix one market essentially by introducing another, allowing each to operate efficiently on its own. If pollution imposes large external costs, for example, the government can establish a market for rights to emit a limited amount of that pollutant. Such a market for tradable emission permits will work if there are many buyers and sellers, all are well informed, and the other conditions of the "first theorem" are met. In this case, the government's role is to enforce the rights and responsibilities of permit ownership, so that each unit of emissions is matched by the ownership of one emission permit. Then the market for the output will also work, as the producer has to pay a price for each permit that reflects the social cost of the associated pollution. Equivalently, producers can be required to pay a tax on their emissions that reflects the external social cost. Either way, the result in theory will be the efficient amount of pollution abatement, undertaken at minimum aggregate abatement cost.

This tradable-permit approach has much to recommend it, and can be just the right solution in some cases, but it is still a "market." Therefore the outcome will be efficient only if certain conditions are met. But these conditions are not always met.[2] Could the sale of permits be monopolized by a small number of buyers or sellers? Do problems arise from inadequate information or significant transaction costs? Will the government find it too costly to measure emissions? If the answer to any such question is yes, the permit market may work less than optimally. The environmental goal may still be met, but at more than minimum cost.

---

[2]Hahn, R. W. & Hester, G. L. *Ecol. Law Q.* 16, 361–406 (1989).

As an example, to reduce acid rain in the United States, amendments to the Clean Air Act of 1990 require electricity generators to hold a permit for each tonne of SO_2 they emit. A robust market for the permits has emerged, in which well-defined prices are broadly known to many potential buyers and sellers. Through continuous emissions monitoring, the government can track SO_2 emissions from each plant. Equally important, penalties are significantly greater than incremental abatement costs and hence are sufficient to ensure compliance. Overall, this market works; acid rain deposition is being reduced by 50 per cent in a cost-effective manner.[3]

A permit market achieves this efficiency through trades because any company that has high abatement costs can buy permits from another that has low costs, so reducing the total cost of abating pollution. These trades also switch the source of the pollution from one company to another, which is unimportant when any emissions equally affect the whole trading area. This "perfect mixing" assumption is certainly valid for global problems such as greenhouse gases or the effect of chlorofluorocarbons on the stratospheric ozone layer. It may also work reasonably well for a regional problem such as acid rain, because acid deposition in downwind states of New England is about equally affected by SO_2 emissions that were traded among upwind sources in Ohio, Indiana or Illinois. But it does not work perfectly, as acid rain in New England may increase if a plant there sells permits to a plant in the mid-west.

At the other extreme, many environmental problems might not be addressed appropriately by tradable-permit systems or other market-based policy instruments.[4] One example is a hazardous air pollutant such as benzene that does not mix in the airshed and so can cause localized "hotspots." Because a company can buy permits and increase local emissions, permit trading does not ensure that each location will meet a specific standard. Moreover, the damages caused by local concentrations may increase nonlinearly. If so, then even a permit system that reduces total emissions might allow trades that move those emissions to a high-impact location and thus increase total damages.

The bottom line is that no specific policy instrument, or even set of policy instruments, is a panacea. Market instruments do not always provide the best solutions, and sometimes not even satisfactory solutions.

Myth of Market Prices

The next myth is that, when non-market solutions are considered, economists still use only market prices to evaluate them. No matter what policy instrument is chosen, the environmental goal of that policy must be identified. For example, should vehicle emissions be reduced by 10, 20 or 50 per

---

[3]Schmalensee, R. *et al. J. Econ. Perspect.* 12 No. 3 (Summer 1998).
[4]Hahn, R. W. & Stavins, R. N. *Am. Econ. Rev.* 82, 464–468 (1992).

cent? Economists frequently try to identify the most efficient degree of control that provides the greatest net benefit. This means, of course, that both benefits and costs need to be evaluated. True enough, economists typically favour using market prices, whenever possible, to carry out such evaluations, because these prices reveal how members of society actually value the scarce amenities and resources under consideration.

Economists are wary of asking people how much they value something, as respondents may not provide honest assessments of their own valuations. Instead, actions may reveal their preferences, as when individuals pay more for a house in a neighbourhood with cleaner air, all else being equal.[5]

This is not to suggest that economists are concerned only with the financial value of things. Far from it. The financial flows that make up the gross national product represent only a fraction of all economic flows. The scope of economics encompasses the allocation and use of all scarce resources. For example, the economic value of the human-health damages of environmental pollution is greater than the sum of health-care costs and lost wages (or lost productivity), as it includes what lawyers would call "pain and suffering." Economists might use a market price indirectly to measure revealed rather than stated preferences, but the goal is to measure the total value of the loss that individuals incur.

To take another example, the economic value of part of the Amazon rainforest is not limited to its financial value as a repository of future pharmaceutical products or as a location for ecotourism. That "use" value may only be a small part of the properly defined economic valuation. For decades, economists have recognized the importance of "non-use" value of environmental amenities such as wilderness areas or endangered species. The public nature of these goods make [sic] it particularly difficult to quantify these values empirically, as we cannot use market prices! The important fact is that benefit-cost analysis of environmental policies, virtually by definition, cannot rely exclusively on market prices.[6]

Economists insist on trying to convert all these disparate values into monetary terms because a common unit of measure is needed to be able to add them up. How else can we combine the benefits of ten extra miles of visibility plus some amount of reduced morbidity, and then compare these total benefits with the total cost of installing scrubbers to clean stack gases at coal-fired power plants? Money, after all, is simply a medium of exchange, a convenient way to add together or compare disparate goods and services.

Myth of Efficiency

The last myth we address here is that these economic analyses are concerned only with efficiency rather than distribution. Many economists do

---

[5]Smith, V. K. &. Huang, J.-C. *J. Polit. Econ.* 103, 209–227 (1995).
[6]Arrow, K. *et al. Science* 272, 221–222 (1996).

give more attention to measures of aggregate social welfare than to measures of the distribution of the benefits and costs of policies among members of society. The reason is that an improvement in economic efficiency can be determined by a simple and unambiguous criterion—an increase in total net benefits. What constitutes an improvement in distributional equity, on the other hand, is inevitably the subject of considerable dispute. Nevertheless, many economists do analyse distributional issues thoroughly. The more difficult problem, not yet solved in a satisfactory manner, is how to combine efficiency and distributional issues in a unified analysis.

Available data often permit reliable estimates of the impacts of environmental policies on important subgroups of the population.[7] On the other hand, environmental regulations are neither effective nor efficient tools for achieving redistributional goals. The best economic analyses recognize the contributions and limitations of efficiency and distributional measures.

Where Does This Leave Us?

To summarize, economists do not necessarily believe that the market solves all problems. Indeed, many economists, ourselves included, make a living out of analysing market failures such as environmental pollution in which laissez-faire policy leads not to social efficiency, but to inefficiency. When economists identify market problems, their tendency is first to consider the feasibility of market solutions because of their potential cost-effectiveness, but market-based approaches to environmental protection are no panacea. When market or non-market solutions to environmental problems are being assessed, economists do not limit their analysis to financial considerations but use money as a unit of measurement in the absence of a more convenient unit. And although the efficiency criterion is by definition aggregate in nature, economic analysis can reveal much about the distribution of the benefits and costs of environmental policy.

Having identified and sought to dispel four prevalent myths about how economists think about the natural environment, we acknowledge that our profession bears some responsibility for the existence of such misunderstandings. Like their colleagues in other social and natural sciences, academic economists focus their greatest energies on communicating to their peers within their own discipline. Greater effort can certainly be made to improve communication across disciplinary boundaries.

---

[7]Christiansen, G. B. & Tietenberg, T. H. in *Handbook of Natural Resource and Energy Economics* Vol. 1 (eds Kneese, A. V. & Sweeney, J. L.) 345–393 (North-Holland, Amsterdam, 1985).

2   *The Problem of Social Cost* *

Ronald Coase

Ronald Coase is Clifton R. Musser Professor Emeritus of Economics at the University of Chicago Law School

I. The Problem to Be Examined

This paper is concerned with those actions of business firms which have harmful effects on others. The standard example is that of a factory the smoke from which has harmful effects on those occupying neighbouring properties. The economic analysis of such a situation has usually proceeded in terms of a divergence between the private and social product of the factory, in which economists have largely followed the treatment of Pigou in *The Economics of Welfare*. The conclusion to which this kind of analysis seems to have led most economists is that it would be desirable to make the owner of the factory liable for the damage caused to those injured by the smoke, or alternatively, to place a tax on the factory owner varying with the amount of smoke produced and equivalent in money terms to the damage it would cause, or finally, to exclude the factory from residential districts (and presumably from other areas in which the emission of smoke would have harmful effects on others). It is my contention that the suggested courses of action are inappropriate, in that they lead to results which are not necessarily, or even usually, desirable.

II. The Reciprocal Nature of the Problem

The traditional approach has tended to obscure the nature of the choice that has to be made. The question is commonly thought of as one in which

"The Problem of Social Cost" by Ronald Coase. *Journal of Legal Studies*, Vol. 3, 1960. Pp.1–44. Reprinted by permission of the University of Chicago Press.

*This article, although concerned with a technical problem of economic analysis, arose out of the study of the Political Economy of Broadcasting which I am now conducting. The argument of the present article was implicit in a previous article dealing with the problem of allocating radio and television frequencies ("The Federal Communications Commission," 2 *J. Law & Econ.* [1959]) but comments which I have received seemed to suggest that it would be desirable to deal with the question in a more explicit way and without reference to the original problem for the solution of which the analysis was developed.

A inflicts harm on B and what has to be decided is: how should we restrain A? But this is wrong. We are dealing with a problem of a reciprocal nature. To avoid the harm to B would inflict harm on A. The real question that has to be decided is: should A be allowed to harm B or should B be allowed to harm A? The problem is to avoid the more serious harm. I instanced in my previous article[1] the case of a confectioner the noise and vibrations from whose machinery disturbed a doctor in his work. To avoid harming the doctor would inflict harm on the confectioner. The problem posed by this case was essentially whether it was worthwhile, as a result of restricting the methods of production which could be used by the confectioner, to secure more doctoring at the cost of a reduced supply of confectionery products. Another example is afforded by the problem of straying cattle which destroy crops on neighbouring land. If it is inevitable that some cattle will stray, an increase in the supply of meat can only be obtained at the expense of a decrease in the supply of crops. The nature of the choice is clear: meat or crops. What answer should be given is, of course, not clear unless we know the value of what is obtained as well as the value of what is sacrificed to obtain it. To give another example, Professor George J. Stigler instances the contamination of a stream.[2] If we assume that the harmful effect of the pollution is that it kills the fish, the question to be decided is: is the value of the fish lost greater or less than the value of the product which the contamination of the stream makes possible? It goes almost without saying that this problem has to be looked at in total *and* at the margin.

III. The Pricing System with Liability for Damage

I propose to start my analysis by examining a case in which most economists would presumably agree that the problem would be solved in a completely satisfactory manner: when the damaging business has to pay for all damage caused *and* the pricing system works smoothly (strictly this means that the operation of a pricing system is without cost).

A good example of the problem under discussion is afforded by the case of straying cattle which destroy crops growing on neighbouring land. Let us suppose that a farmer and cattle-raiser are operating on neighbouring properties. Let us further suppose that, without any fencing between the properties, an increase in the size of the cattle-raiser's herd increases the total damage to the farmer's crops. What happens to the marginal damage as the size of the herd increases is another matter. This depends on whether the cattle tend to follow one another or to roam side by side, on whether they tend to be more or less restless as the size of the herd increases and on other similar factors. For my immediate purpose, it is immaterial

---

[1]Coase, "The Federal Communications Commission," 2 *J. Law & Econ.* 26–27 (1959).
[2]G. J. Stigler, *The Theory of Price*, 105 (1952).

what assumption is made about marginal damage as the size of the herd increases.

To simplify the argument, I propose to use an arithmetical example. I shall assume that the annual cost of fencing the farmer's property is $9 and the price of the crop is $1 per ton. Also, I assume that the relation between the number of cattle in the herd and the annual crop loss is as follows:

Number in Herd (Steers)	Annual Crop Loss (Tons)	Crop Loss per Additional Steer (Tons)
1	1	1
2	3	2
3	6	3
4	10	4

Given that the cattle-raiser is liable for the damage caused, the additional annual cost imposed on the cattle-raiser if he increased his herd from, say, 2 to 3 steers is $3 and in deciding on the size of the herd, he will take this into account along with his other costs. That is, he will not increase the size of the herd unless the value of the additional meat produced (assuming that the cattle-raiser slaughters the cattle) is greater than the additional costs that this will entail, including the value of the additional crops destroyed. Of course, if, by the employment of dogs, herdsmen, aeroplanes, mobile radio and other means, the amount of damage can be reduced, these means will be adopted when their cost is less than the value of the crop which they prevent being lost. Given that the annual cost of fencing is $9, the cattle-raiser who wished to have a herd with 4 steers or more would pay for fencing to be erected and maintained, assuming that other means of attaining the same end would not do so more cheaply. When the fence is erected, the marginal cost due to the liability for damage becomes zero, except to the extent that an increase in the size of the herd necessitates a stronger and therefore more expensive fence because more steers are liable to lean against it at the same time. But, of course, it may be cheaper for the cattle-raiser not to fence and to pay for the damaged crops, as in my arithmetical example, with 3 or fewer steers.

It might be thought that the fact that the cattle-raiser would pay for all crops damaged would lead the farmer to increase his planting if a cattle-raiser came to occupy the neighbouring property. But this is not so. If the crop was previously sold in conditions of perfect competition, marginal cost was equal to price for the amount of planting undertaken and any expansion would have reduced the profits of the farmer. In the new situation, the existence of crop damage would mean that the farmer would sell less on the open market but his receipts for a given production would remain the same, since the cattle-raiser would pay the market price for any crop damaged. Of course, if cattle-raising commonly involved the destruction of crops, the coming into existence of a cattle-raising industry might raise the price of the crops involved and farmers would then extend their planting. But I wish to confine my attention to the individual farmer.

I have said that the occupation of a neighbouring property by a cattle-raiser would not cause the amount of production, or perhaps more exactly the amount of planting, by the farmer to increase. In fact, if the cattle-raising has any effect, it will be to decrease the amount of planting. The reason for this is that, for any given tract of land, if the value of the crop damaged is so great that the receipts from the sale of the undamaged crop are less than the total costs of cultivating that tract of land, it will be profitable for the farmer and the cattle-raiser to make a bargain whereby that tract of land is left uncultivated. This can be made clear by means of an arithmetical example. Assume initially that the value of the crop obtained from cultivating a given tract of land is $12 and that the cost incurred in cultivating this tract of land is $10, the net gain from cultivating the land being $2. I assume for purposes of simplicity that the farmer owns the land. Now assume that the cattle-raiser starts operations on the neighbouring property and that the value of the crops damaged is $1. In this case $11 is obtained by the farmer from sale on the market and $1 is obtained from the cattle-raiser for damage suffered and the net gain remains $2. Now suppose that the cattle-raiser finds it profitable to increase the size of his herd, even though the amount of damage rises to $3; which means that the value of the additional meat production is greater than the additional costs, including the additional $2 payment for damage. But the total payment for damage is now $3. The net gain to the farmer from cultivating the land is still $2. The cattle-raiser would be better off if the farmer would agree not to cultivate his land for any payment less than $3. The farmer would be agreeable to not cultivating the land for any payment greater than $2. There is clearly room for a mutually satisfactory bargain which would lead to the abandonment of cultivation.[3] But the same argument applies not only to the whole tract cultivated by the farmer but also to any subdivision of it. Suppose, for example, that the cattle have a well-defined route, say, to a brook or to a shady area. In these circumstances, the amount of damage to the crop along the route may well be great and if so, it could be that the farmer and the cattle-raiser would find it profitable to make a bargain whereby the farmer would agree not to cultivate this strip of land.

---

[3]The argument in the text has proceeded on the assumption that the alternative to cultivation of the crop is abandonment of cultivation altogether. But this need not be so. There may be crops which are less liable to damage by cattle but which would not be as profitable as the crop grown in the absence of damage. Thus, if the cultivation of a new crop would yield a return to the farmer of $1 instead of $2, and the size of the herd which would cause $3 damage with the old crop would cause $1 damage with the new crop, it would be profitable to the cattle-raiser to pay any sum less than $2 to induce the farmer to change his crop (since this would reduce damage liability from $3 to $1) and it would be profitable for the farmer to do so if the amount received was more than $1 (the reduction in his return caused by switching crops). In fact, there would be room for a mutually satisfactory bargain in all cases in which change of crop would reduce the amount of damage by more than it reduces the value of the crop (excluding damage)—in all cases, that is, in which a change in the crop cultivated would lead to an increase in the value of production.

But this raises a further possibility. Suppose that there is such a well-defined route. Suppose further that the value of the crop that would be obtained by cultivating this strip of land is $10 but that the cost of cultivation is $11. In the absence of the cattle-raiser, the land would not be cultivated. However, given the presence of the cattle-raiser, it could well be that if the strip was cultivated, the whole crop would be destroyed by the cattle. In which case, the cattle-raiser would be forced to pay $10 to the farmer. It is true that the farmer would lose $1. But the cattle-raiser would lose $10. Clearly this is a situation which is not likely to last indefinitely since neither party would want this to happen. The aim of the farmer would be to induce the cattle-raiser to make a payment in return for an agreement to leave this land uncultivated. The farmer would not be able to obtain a payment greater than the cost of fencing off this piece of land nor so high as to lead the cattle-raiser to abandon the use of the neighbouring property. What payment would in fact be made would depend on the shrewdness of the farmer and the cattle-raiser as bargainers. But as the payment would not be so high as to cause the cattle-raiser to abandon this location and as it would not vary with the size of the herd, such an agreement would not affect the allocation of resources but would merely alter the distribution of income and wealth as between the cattle-raiser and the farmer.

I think it is clear that if the cattle-raiser is liable for damage caused and the pricing system works smoothly, the reduction in the value of production elsewhere will be taken into account in computing the additional cost involved in increasing the size of the herd. This cost will be weighed against the value of the additional meat production and, given perfect competition in the cattle industry, the allocation of resources in cattle-raising will be optimal. What needs to be emphasized is that the fall in the value of production elsewhere which would be taken into account in the costs of the cattle-raiser may well be less than the damage which the cattle would cause to the crops in the ordinary course of events. This is because it is possible, as a result of market transactions, to discontinue cultivation of the land. This is desirable in all cases in which the damage that the cattle would cause, and for which the cattle-raiser would be willing to pay, exceeds the amount which the farmer would pay for use of the land. In conditions of perfect competition, the amount which the farmer would pay for the use of the land is equal to the difference between the value of the total production when the factors are employed on this land and the value of the additional product yielded in their next best use (which would be what the farmer would have to pay for the factors). If damage exceeds the amount the farmer would pay for the use of the land, the value of the additional product of the factors employed elsewhere would exceed the value of the total product in this use after damage is taken into account. It follows that it would be desirable to abandon cultivation of the land and to release the factors employed for production elsewhere. A procedure which merely provided for payment for damage to the crop caused by the cattle but which did not allow for the possibility of cultivation being discontinued would result in too small an employment of factors of production in cattle-raising and too large an employment of factors in cultivation of the crop. But given the possibility of market transactions, a situation in which damage to crops exceeded the rent of the land would not endure. Whether the cattle-raiser pays the farmer to leave the land uncultivated or himself rents the land by paying the land-owner an amount slightly greater than the farmer would pay (if the farmer was himself renting the land), the final result would be the same and would maximise the value of production. Even when the farmer is induced to plant crops which it would not be profitable to cultivate for sale on the market, this will be a purely short-term phenomenon and may be expected to lead to an agreement under which the planting will cease. The cattle-raiser will remain in that location and the marginal cost of meat production will be the same as before, thus having no long-run effect on the allocation of resources.

IV. The Pricing System with No Liability for Damage

I now turn to the case in which, although the pricing system is assumed to work smoothly (that is, costlessly), the damaging business is not liable for any of the damage which it causes. This business does not have to make a payment to those damaged by its actions. I propose to show that the allocation of resources will be the same in this case is it was when the damaging business was liable for damage caused. As I showed in the previous case that the allocation of resources was optimal, it will not be necessary to repeat this part of the argument.

I return to the case of the farmer and the cattle-raiser. The farmer would suffer increased damage to his crop as the size of the herd increased. Suppose that the size of the cattle-raiser's herd is 3 steers (and that this is the size of the herd that would be maintained if crop damage was not taken into account). Then the farmer would be willing to pay up to $3 if the cattle-raiser would reduce his herd to 2 steers, up to $5 if the herd were reduced to 1 steer and would pay up to $6 if cattle-raising was abandoned. The cattle-raiser would therefore receive $3 from the farmer if he kept 2 steers instead of 3. This $3 foregone is therefore part of the cost incurred in keeping the third steer. Whether the $3 is a payment which the cattle-raiser has to make if he adds the third steer to his herd (which it would be if the cattle-raiser was liable to the farmer for damage caused to the crop) or whether it is a sum of money which he would have received if he did not keep a third steer (which it would be if the cattle-raiser was not liable to the farmer for damage caused to the crop) does not affect the final result. In both cases $3 is part of the cost of adding a third steer, to be included along with the other costs. If the increase in the value of production in cattle-raising through increasing the size of the herd from 2 to 3 is greater than the additional costs that have to be incurred (including the $3 damage to crops), the size of the herd will be increased. Otherwise, it will not. The size of the herd will be the same whether the cattle-raiser is liable for damage caused to the crop or not.

It may be argued that the assumed starting point—a herd of 3 steers—was arbitrary. And this is true. But the farmer would not wish to pay to avoid crop damage which the cattle-raiser would not be able to cause. For example, the maximum annual payment which the farmer could be induced to pay could not exceed $9, the annual cost of fencing. And the farmer would only be willing to pay this sum if it did not reduce his earnings to a level that would cause him to abandon cultivation of this particular tract of land. Furthermore, the farmer would only be willing to pay this amount if he believed that, in the absence of any payment by him, the size of the herd maintained by the cattle-raiser would be 4 or more steers. Let us assume that this is the case. Then the farmer would be willing to pay up to $3 if the cattle-raiser would reduce his herd to 3 steers, up to $6 if the herd were reduced to 2 steers, up to $8 if one steer only were kept and up to $9 if cattle-raising were abandoned. It will be noticed that the change in the starting point has not altered the amount which would accrue to the cattle-raiser if he reduced the size of his herd by any given amount. It is still true that the cattle-raiser could receive an additional $3 from the farmer if he agreed to reduce his herd from 3 steers to 2 and that the $3 represents the value of the crop that would be destroyed by adding the third steer to the herd. Although a different belief on the part of the farmer (whether justified or not) about the size of the herd that the cattle-raiser would maintain in the absence of payments from him may affect the total payment he can be induced to pay, it is not true that this different belief would have any effect on the size of the herd that the cattle-raiser will actually keep. This will be the same as it would be if the cattle-raiser had to pay for damage caused by his cattle, since a receipt foregone of a given amount is the equivalent of a payment of the same amount.

It might be thought that it would pay the cattle-raiser to increase his herd above the size that he would wish to maintain once a bargain had been made, in order to induce the farmer to make a larger total payment. And this may be true. It is similar in nature to the action of the farmer (when the cattle-raiser was liable for damage) in cultivating land on which, as a result of an agreement with the cattle-raiser, planting would subsequently be abandoned (including land which would not be cultivated at all in the absence of cattle-raising). But such manoeuvres are preliminaries to an agreement and do not affect the long-run equilibrium position, which is the same whether or not the cattle-raiser is held responsible for the crop damage brought about by his cattle.

It is necessary to know whether the damaging business is liable or not for damage caused since without the establishment of this initial delimitation of rights there can be no market transactions to transfer and recombine them. But the ultimate result (which maximises the value of production) is independent of the legal position if the pricing system is assumed to work without cost.

V. The Problem Illustrated Anew

The harmful effects of the activities of a business can assume a wide variety of forms. An early English case concerned a building which, by obstructing currents of air, hindered the operation of a windmill.[4] A recent case in Florida concerned a building which cast a shadow on the cabana, swimming pool and sunbathing areas of a neighbouring hotel.[5] The problem of straying cattle and the damaging of crops which was the subject of detailed examination in the two preceding sections, although it may have appeared to be rather a special case, is in fact but one example of a problem which arises in many different guises. To clarify the nature of my argument and to demonstrate its general applicability, I propose to illustrate it anew by reference to four actual cases.

Let us first reconsider the case of *Sturges v. Bridgman*[6] which I used as an illustration of the general problem in my article on "The Federal Communications Commission." In this case, a confectioner (in Wigmore Street) used two mortars and pestles in connection with his business (one had been in operation in the same position for more than 60 years and the other for more than 26 years). A doctor than came to occupy neighbouring premises (in Wimpole Street). The confectioner's machinery caused the doctor no harm until, eight years after he had first occupied the premises, he built a consulting room at the end of his garden right against the confectioner's kitchen. It was then found that the noise and vibration caused by the confectioner's machinery made it difficult for the doctor to use his new consulting room. "In particular . . . the noise prevented him from examining his patients by auscultation[7] for diseases of the chest. He also found it impossible to engage with effect in any occupation which required thought and attention." The doctor therefore brought a legal action to force the confectioner to stop using his machinery. The courts had little difficulty in granting the doctor the injunction he sought. "Individual cases of hardship may occur in the strict carrying out of the principle upon which we found our judgment, but the negation of the principle would lead even more to individual hardship, and would at the same time produce a prejudicial effect upon the development of land for residential purposes."

The court's decision established that the doctor had the right to prevent the confectioner from using his machinery. But, of course, it would have been possible to modify the arrangements envisaged in the legal ruling by means of a bargain between the parties. The doctor would have been willing to waive his right and allow the machinery to continue in

---

[4] See Gale on *Easements* 237–39 (13th ed. M. Bowles 1959).

[5] See *Fontainebleu Hotel Corp. v. Forty-Five Twenty-Five, Inc.*, 114 So. 2d 357 (1959).

[6] 11 Ch. D. 852 (1879).

[7] Auscultation is the act of listening by ear or stethoscope in order to judge by sound the condition of the body.

operation if the confectioner would have paid him a sum of money which was greater than the loss of income which he would suffer from having to move to a more closely or less convenient location or from having to curtail his activities at this location or, as was suggested as a possibility, from having to build a separate wall which would deaden the noise and vibration. The confectioner would have been willing to do this if the amount he would have to pay the doctor was less than the fall in income he would suffer if he had to change his mode of operation at this location, abandon his operation or move his confectionery business to some other location. The solution of the problem depends essentially on whether the continued use of the machinery adds more to the confectioner's income than it subtracts from the doctor's.[8] But now consider the situation if the confectioner had won the case. The confectioner would then have had the right to continue operating his noise and vibration-generating machinery without having to pay anything to the doctor. The boot would have been on the other foot: the doctor would have had to pay the confectioner to induce him to stop using the machinery. If the doctor's income would have fallen more through continuance of the use of this machinery than it added to the income of the confectioner, there would clearly be room for a bargain whereby the doctor paid the confectioner to stop using the machinery. That is to say, the circumstances in which it would not pay the confectioner to continue to use the machinery and to compensate the doctor for the losses that this would bring (if the doctor had the right to prevent the confectioner's using his machinery) would be those in which it would be in the interest of the doctor to make a payment to the confectioner which would induce him to discontinue the use of the machinery (if the confectioner had the right to operate the machinery). The basic conditions are exactly the same in this case as they were in the example of the cattle which destroyed crops. With costless market transactions, the decision of the courts concerning liability for damage would be without effect on the allocation of resources. It was of course the view of the judges that they were affecting the working of the economic system—and in a desirable direction. Any other decision would have had "a prejudicial effect upon the development of land for residential purposes," an argument which was elaborated by examining the example of a forge operating on a barren moor, which was later developed for residential purposes. The judges' view that they were settling how the land was to be used would be true only in the case in which the costs of carrying out the necessary market transactions exceeded the gain which might be achieved by any rearrangement of rights. And it would be desirable to preserve the areas (Wimpole Street or the moor) for residential or professional use (by giving non-industrial users the right to stop the noise, vibration, smoke, etc., by injunction) only if the value of the additional

---

[8]Note that what is taken into account is the change in income after allowing for alterations in methods of production, location, character of product, etc.

residential facilities obtained was greater than the value of cakes or iron lost. But of this the judges seem to have been unaware.

———————————

The reasoning employed by the courts in determining legal rights will often seem strange to an economist because many of the factors on which the decision turns are, to an economist, irrelevant. Because of this, situations which are, from an economic point of view, identical will be treated quite differently by the courts. The economic problem in all cases of harmful effects is how to maximise the value of production. In the case of *Bass v. Gregory* fresh air was drawn in through the well which facilitated the production of beer but foul air was expelled through the well which made life in the adjoining houses less pleasant. The economic problem was to decide which to choose: a lower cost of beer and worsened amenities in adjoining houses or a higher cost of beer and improved amenities. In deciding this question, the "doctrine of lost grant" is about as relevant as the colour of the judge's eyes. But it has to be remembered that the immediate question faced by the courts is *not* what shall be done by whom *but* who has the legal right to do what. It is always possible to modify by transactions on the market the initial legal delimitation of rights. And, of course, if such market transactions are costless, such a rearrangement of rights will always take place if it would lead to an increase in the value of production.

VI. *The Cost of Market Transactions Taken into Account*

The argument has proceeded up to this point on the assumption (explicit in Sections III and IV and tacit in Section V) that there were no costs involved in carrying out market transactions. This is, of course, a very unrealistic assumption. In order to carry out a market transaction it is necessary to discover who it is that one wishes to deal with, to inform people that one wishes to deal and on what terms, to conduct negotiations leading up to a bargain, to draw up the contract, to undertake the inspection needed to make sure that the terms of the contract are being observed and so on. These operations are often extremely costly, sufficiently costly at any rate to prevent many transactions that would be carried out in a world in which the pricing system worked without cost.

In earlier sections, when dealing with the problem of the rearrangement of legal rights through the market, it was argued that such a rearrangement would be made through the market whenever this would lead to an increase in the value of production. But this assumed costless market transactions. Once the costs of carrying out market transactions are taken into account it is clear that such a rearrangement of rights will only be undertaken when the increase in the value of production consequent upon the rearrangement is greater than the costs which would be involved in bringing it about. When it is less, the granting of an injunction (or the knowledge that it would be granted) or the liability to pay damages may result in an activity being discontinued (or may prevent its being started) which would be undertaken if market transactions were costless. In these conditions the initial delimitation of legal rights does have an effect on the efficiency with which the economic system operates. One arrangement of rights may bring about a greater value of production than any other. But unless this is the arrangement of rights established by the legal system, the costs of reaching the same result by altering and combining rights through the market may be so great that this optimal arrangement of rights, and the greater value of production which it would bring, may never be achieved. The part played by economic considerations in the process of delimiting legal rights will be discussed in the next section. In this section, I will take the initial delimitation of rights and the costs of carrying out market transactions as given.

It is clear that an alternative form of economic organisation which could achieve the same result at less cost than would be incurred by using the market would enable the value of production to be raised. As I explained many years ago, the firm represents such an alternative to organising production through market transactions.[9] Within the firm individual bargains between the various cooperating factors of production are eliminated and for a market transaction is substituted an administrative decision. The rearrangement of production then takes place without the need for bargains between the owners of the factors of production. A landowner who has control of a large tract of land may devote his land to various uses taking into account the effect that the interrelations of the various activities will have on the net return of the land, thus rendering unnecessary bargains between those undertaking the various activities. Owners of a large building or of several adjoining properties in a given area may act in much the same way. In effect, using our earlier terminology, the firm would acquire the legal rights of all the parties and the rearrangement of activities would not follow on a rearrangement of rights by contract, but as a result of an administrative decision as to how the rights should be used.

It does not, of course, follow that the administrative costs of organising a transaction through a firm are inevitably less than the costs of the market transactions which are superseded. But where contracts are peculiarly difficult to draw up and an attempt to describe what the parties have agreed to do or not to do (e.g. the amount and kind of a smell or noise that they may make or will not make) would necessitate a lengthy and highly involved document, and, where, as is probable, a long-term contract would be desirable,[10] it would be hardly surprising if the emergence of a firm or the extension of the activities of an existing firm was not the solution adopted on many occasions to

---

[9]See Coase, "The Nature of the Firm," 4 *Economica*, New Series, 386 (1937). Reprinted in *Readings in Price Theory*, 331 (1952).

[10]For reasons explained in my earlier article, see *Readings in Price Theory*, n. 14 at 337.

deal with the problem of harmful effects. This solution would be adopted whenever the administrative costs of the firm were less than the costs of the market transactions that it supersedes and the gains which would result from the rearrangement of activities greater than the firm's costs of organising them. I do not need to examine in great detail the character of this solution since I have explained what is involved in my earlier article.

But the firm is not the only possible answer to this problem. The administrative costs of organising transactions within the firm may also be high, and particularly so when many diverse activities are brought within the control of a single organisation. In the standard case of a smoke nuisance, which may affect a vast number of people engaged in a wide variety of activities, the administrative costs might well be so high as to make any attempt to deal with the problem within the confines of a single firm impossible. An alternative solution is direct government regulation. Instead of instituting a legal system of rights which can be modified by transactions on the market, the government may impose regulations which state what people must or must not do and which have to be obeyed. Thus, the government (by statute or perhaps more likely through an administrative agency) may, to deal with the problem of smoke nuisance, decree that certain methods of production should or should not be used (e.g. that smoke preventing devices should be installed or that coal or oil should not be burned) or may confine certain types of business to certain districts (zoning regulations).

The government is, in a sense, a superfirm (but of a very special kind) since it is able to influence the use of factors of production by administrative decision. But the ordinary firm is subject to checks in its operations because of the competition of other firms, which might administer the same activities at lower cost and also because there is always the alternative of market transactions as against organisation within the firm if the administrative costs become too great. The government is able, if it wishes, to avoid the market altogether, which a firm can never do. The firm has to make market agreements with the owners of the factors of production that it uses. Just as the government can conscript or seize property, so it can decree that factors of production should only be used in such-and-such a way. Such authoritarian methods save a lot of trouble (for those doing the organising). Furthermore, the government has at its disposal the police and the other law enforcement agencies to make sure that its regulations are carried out.

It is clear that the government has powers which might enable it to get some things done at a lower cost than could a private organisation (or at any rate one without special governmental powers). But the governmental administrative machine is not itself costless. It can, in fact, on occasion be extremely costly. Furthermore, there is no reason to suppose that the restrictive and zoning regulations, made by a fallible administration subject to political pressures and operating without any competitive check, will necessarily always be those which increase the efficiency with which the economic system operates. Furthermore, such general regulations which must apply to a wide variety of cases will be enforced in some cases in which they are clearly inappropriate. From these considerations it follows that direct governmental regulation will not necessarily give better results than leaving the problem to be solved by the market or the firm. But equally there is no reason why, on occasion, such governmental administrative regulation should not lead to an improvement in economic efficiency. This would seem particularly likely when, as is normally the case with the smoke nuisance, a large number of people are involved and in which therefore the costs of handling the problem through the market or the firm may be high.

There is, of course, a further alternative which is to do nothing about the problem at all. And given that the costs involved in solving the problem by regulations issued by the governmental administrative machine will often be heavy (particularly if the costs are interpreted to include all the consequences which follow from the government engaging in this kind of activity), it will no doubt be commonly the case that the gain which would come from regulating the actions which give rise to the harmful effects will be less than the costs involved in government regulation.

The discussion of the problem of harmful effects in this section (when the costs of market transactions are taken into account) is extremely inadequate. But at least it has made clear that the problem is one of choosing the appropriate social arrangement for dealing with the harmful effects. All solutions have costs and there is no reason to suppose that government regulation is called for simply because the problem is not well handled by the market or the firm. Satisfactory views on policy can only come from a patient study of how, in practice, the market, firms and governments handle the problem of harmful effects. Economists need to study the work of the broker in bringing parties together, the effectiveness of restrictive covenants, the problems of the large-scale real-estate development company, the operation of government zoning and other regulating activities. It is my belief that economists, and policy-makers generally, have tended to overestimate the advantages which come from governmental regulation. But this belief, even if justified, does not do more than suggest that government regulation should be curtailed. It does not tell us where the boundary line should be drawn. This, it seems to me, has to come from a detailed investigation of the actual results of handling the problem in different ways. But it would be unfortunate if this investigation were undertaken with the aid of a faulty economic analysis. The aim of this article is to indicate what the economic approach to the problem should be.

VII. The Legal Delimitation of Rights and the Economic Problem

The discussion in Section V not only served to illustrate the argument but also afforded a glimpse at the legal approach to the problem of harmful effects. The cases considered were all English but a similar selection of American cases could easily be made and the character of the reasoning would have been the same. Of course, if market transactions were costless, all that matters (questions of equity apart) is that the rights of the various parties should be well-defined and the results of legal actions easy to forecast. But as we have seen, the situation is quite different when market transactions are so costly as to make it difficult to change the arrangement of rights established by the law. In such cases, the courts directly influence economic activity. It would therefore seem desirable that the courts should understand the economic consequences of their decisions and should, insofar as this is possible without creating too much uncertainty about the legal position itself, take these consequences into account when making their decisions. Even when it is possible to change the legal delimitation of rights through market transactions, it is obviously desirable to reduce the need for such transactions and thus reduce the employment of resources in carrying them out.

A thorough examination of the presuppositions of the courts in trying such cases would be of great interest but I have not been able to attempt it. Nevertheless it is clear from a cursory study that the courts have often recognized the economic implications of their decisions and are aware (as many economists are not) of the reciprocal nature of the problem. Furthermore, from time to time, they take these economic implications into account, along with other factors, in arriving at their decisions. The American writers on this subject refer to the question in a more explicit fashion than do the British. Thus, to quote Prosser on Torts, a person may

> make use of his own property or . . . conduct his own affairs at the expense of some harm to his neighbors. He may operate a factory whose noise and smoke cause some discomfort to others, so long as he keeps within reasonable bounds. It is only when his conduct is unreasonable, *in the light of its utility and the harm which results* [italics added], that it becomes a nuisance. . . . As it was said in an ancient case in regard to candle-making in a town, "Le utility del chose excusera le noisomeness del stink."
>
> The world must have factories, smelters, oil refineries, noisy machinery and blasting, even at the expense of some inconvenience to those in the vicinity and the plaintiff may be required to accept some not unreasonable discomfort for the general good.[11]

The standard British writers do not state as explicitly as this that a comparison between the utility and harm produced is an element in deciding whether a harmful effect should be considered a nuisance. But similar views, if less strongly expressed, are to be found.[12] The doctrine that the harmful effect must be substantial before the court will act is, no doubt, in

---

[11]See W. L. Prosser, *The Law of Torts* 398–99, 412 (2d ed. 1955). The quotation about the ancient case concerning candle-making is taken from Sir James Fitzjames Stephen, *A General View of the Criminal Law of England* 106 (1890). Sir James Stephen gives no reference. He perhaps had in mind *Rex. v. Ronkett*, included in Seavey, Keeton and Thurston, *Cases on Torts* 604 (1950). A similar view to that expressed by Prosser is to be found in F. V. Harper and F. James, *The Law of Torts* 67–74 (1956); *Restatement, Torts* §§826, 827 and 828.

[12]See Winfield on *Torts* 541–48 (6th ed. T. E. Lewis 1954); Salmond on the *Law of Torts* 181–90 (12th ed. R. F. V. Heuston 1957); H. Street, *The Law of Torts* 221–29 (1959).

part a reflection of the fact that there will almost always be some gain to offset the harm. And in the reports of individual cases, it is clear that the judges have had in mind what would be lost as well as what would be gained in deciding whether to grant an injunction or award damages. Thus, in refusing to prevent the destruction of a prospect by a new building, the judge stated:

> I know no general rule of common law, which . . . says, that building so as to stop another's prospect is a nuisance. Was that the case, there could be no great towns; and I must grant injunctions to all the new buildings in this town. . . . [13]

The problem which we face in dealing with actions which have harmful effects is not simply one of restraining those responsible for them. What has to be decided is whether the gain from preventing the harm is greater than the loss which would be suffered elsewhere as a result of stopping the action which produces the harm. In a world in which there are costs of rearranging the rights established by the legal system, the courts, in cases rearranging to nuisance, are, in effect, making a decision on the economic problem and determining how resources are to be employed. It was argued that the courts are conscious of this and that they often make, although not always in a very explicit fashion, a comparison between what would be gained and what lost by preventing actions which have harmful effects. But the delimitation of rights is also the result of statutory enactments. Here we also find evidence of an appreciation of the reciprocal nature of the problem. While statutory enactments add to the list of nuisances, action is also taken to legalize what would otherwise be nuisances under the common law. The kind of situation which economists are prone to consider as requiring corrective government action is, in fact, often the result of government action. Such action is not necessarily unwise. But there is a real danger that extensive government intervention in the economic system may lead to the protection of those responsible for harmful effects being carried too far.

VIII. Pigou's Treatment in "The Economics of Welfare"

The fountainhead for the modern economic analysis of the problem discussed in this article is Pigou's *Economics of Welfare* and, in particular, that section of Part II which deals with divergences between social and private net products which come about because

---

[13]*Attorney General v. Doughty*, 2 Ves. Sen. 453, 28 Eng. Rep. 290 (Ch. 1752). Compare in this connection the statement of an American judge, quoted in Prosser, *op. cit. supra* n. 16 at 413 n. 54: "Without smoke, Pittsburgh would have remained a very pretty village," Musmanno, J., in *Versailles Borough v. McKeesport Coal & Coke Co.*, 1935, 83 Pitts. Leg. J. 379, 385.

one person A, in the course of rendering some service, for which payment is made, to a second person B, incidentally also renders services or disservices to other persons (not producers of like services), or such a sort that payment cannot be exacted from the benefited parties or compensation enforced on behalf of the injured parties.[14]

Pigou tells us that his aim in Part II of *The Economics of Welfare* is

to ascertain how far the free play of self-interest, acting under the existing legal system, tends to distribute the country's resources in the way most favorable to the production of a large national dividend, and how far it is feasible for State action to improve upon 'natural' tendencies.[15]

To judge from the first part of this statement, Pigou's purpose is to discover whether any improvements could be made in the existing arrangements which determine the use of resources. Since Pigou's conclusions [sic] is that improvements could be made, one might have expected him to continue by saying that he proposed to set out the changes required to bring them about. Instead, Pigou adds a phrase which contrasts "natural" tendencies with State action, which seems in some sense to equate the present arrangements with "natural" tendencies and to imply that what is required to bring about these improvements is State action (if feasible). That this is more or less Pigou's position is evident from Chapter I of Part II.[16] Pigou starts by referring to "optimistic followers of the classical economists"[17] who have argued that the value of production would be maximised if the government refrained from any interference in the economic system and the economic arrangements were those which came about "naturally." Pigou goes on to say that if self-interest does promote economic welfare, it is because human institutions have been devised to make it so. (This part of Pigou's argument, which he develops with the aid of a quotation from Cannan, seems to me to be essentially correct.) Pigou concludes:

But even in the most advanced States there are failures and imperfections. . . . there are many obstacles that prevent a community's resources from being distributed . . . in the most efficient way. The study of these constitutes our present problem. . . . Its purpose is essentially practical. It seeks to bring into clearer light some of the ways in which it now is, or eventually may become, feasible for governments to control the play of economic forces in such ways as to promote the economic welfare, and through that, the total welfare, of their citizens as a whole.[18]

---

[14]A. C. Pigou, *The Economics of Welfare* 183 (4th ed. 1932). My references will all be to the fourth edition but the argument and examples examined in this article remained substantially unchanged from the first edition in 1920 to the fourth in 1932. A large part (but not all) of this analysis had appeared previously in *Wealth and Welfare* (1912).

[15]*Id.* at xii.

[16]*Id.* at 127–30.

[17]In *Wealth and Welfare*, Pigou attributes the "optimism" to Adam Smith himself and not to his followers. He there refers to the "highly optimistic theory of Adam Smith that the national dividend, in given circumstances of demand and supply, tends 'naturally' to a maximum" (p. 104).

[18]Pigou, *op. cit. supra* n. 35 at 129–30.

Pigou's underlying thought would appear to be: Some have argued that no State action is needed. But the system has performed as well as it has because of State action. Nonetheless, there are still imperfections. What additional State action is required?

If this is a correct summary of Pigou's position, its inadequacy can be demonstrated by examining the first example he gives of a divergence between private and social products.

> It might happen . . . that costs are thrown upon people not directly concerned, through, say, uncompensated damage done to surrounding woods by sparks from railway engines. All such effects must be included—some of them will be positive, others negative elements—in reckoning up the social net product of the marginal increment of any volume of resources turned into any use or place.[19]

The example used by Pigou refers to a real situation. In Britain, a railway does not normally have to compensate those who suffer damage by fire caused by sparks from an engine. Taken in conjunction with what he says in Chapter 9 of Part II, I take Pigou's policy recommendations to be, first, that there should be State action to correct this "natural" situation and, second, that the railways should be forced to compensate those whose woods are burnt. If this is a correct interpretation of Pigou's position, I would argue that the first recommendation is based on a misapprehension of the facts and that the second is not necessarily desirable.

Let us consider the legal position. Under the heading "Sparks from engines," we find the following in Halsbury's *Laws of England*:

> If railway undertakers use steam engines on their railway without express statutory authority to do so, they are liable, irrespective of any negligence on their part, for fires caused by sparks from engines. Railway undertakers are, however, generally given statutory authority to use steam engines on their railway; accordingly, if an engine is constructed with the precautions which science suggests against fire and is used without negligence, they are not responsible at common law for any damage which may be done by sparks. . . . In the construction of an engine the undertaker is bound to use all the discoveries which science has put within its reach in order to avoid doing harm, provided they are such as it is reasonable to require the company to adopt, having proper regard to the likelihood of the damage and to the cost and convenience of the remedy; but it is not negligence on the part of an undertaker if it refuses to use an apparatus the efficiency of which is open to bona fide doubt.

To this general rule, there is a statutory exception arising from the Railway (Fires) Act, 1905, as amended in 1923. This concerns agricultural land or agricultural crops.

> In such a case the fact that the engine was used under statutory powers does not affect the liability of the company in an action for the damage. . . . These provisions, however, only apply where the claim for damage . . . does not exceed £200 [£100 in the 1905 Act], and where written notice of the occurrence of the fire and

---

[19]*Id.* at 134.

the intention to claim has been sent to the company within seven days of the occurrence of the damage and particulars of the damage in writing showing the amount of the claim in money not exceeding £200 have been sent to the company within twenty-one days.

Agricultural land does not include moorland or buildings and agricultural crops do not include those led away or stacked.[20] I have not made a close study of the parliamentary history of this statutory exception, but to judge from debates in the House of Commons in 1922 and 1923, this exception was probably designed to help the smallholder.[21]

Let us return to Pigou's example of uncompensated damage to surrounding woods caused by sparks from railway engines. This is presumably intended to show how it is possible "for State action to improve on 'natural' tendencies." If we treat Pigou's example as referring to the position before 1905, or as being an arbitrary example (in that he might just as well have written "surrounding buildings" instead of "surrounding woods"), then it is clear that the reason why compensation was not paid must have been that the railway had statutory authority to run steam engines (which relieved it of liability for fires caused by sparks). That this was the legal position was established in 1860, in a case, oddly enough, which concerned the burning of surrounding woods by a railway,[22] and the law on this point has not been changed (apart from the one exception) by a century of railway legislation, including nationalisation. If we treat Pigou's example of "uncompensated damage done to surrounding woods by sparks from railway engines" literally, and assume that it refers to the period after 1905, then it is clear that the reason why compensation was not paid must have been that the damage was more than £100 (in the first edition of *The Economics of Welfare*) or more than £200 (in later editions) or that the owner of the wood failed to notify the railway in writing within seven days of the fire or did not send particulars of the damage, in writing, within twenty-one days. In the real world, Pigou's example could only exist as a result of a deliberate choice of the legislature. It is not, of course, easy to imagine the construction of a railway in a state of nature. The nearest one can get to this is presumably a railway which uses steam engines "without express statutory authority." However, in this case the railway would be obliged to compensate those whose woods it burnt down. That is to say, compensation would be paid in the absence of Government action. The only circumstances in which compensation would not be paid would be those in which there had been Government action. It is strange that Pigou, who clearly thought it desirable that compensation should be paid, should have chosen this particular example to demonstrate how it is possible "for State action to improve on 'natural' tendencies."

Pigou seems to have had a faulty view of the facts of the situation. But it also seems likely that he was mistaken in his economic analysis. It is not

---

[20]See 31 Halsbury, *Laws of England* 474–75 (3d ed. 1960), Article on Railways and Canals, from which this summary of the legal position, and all quotations, are taken.

[21]See 152 H.C. Deb. 2622–63 (1922); 161 H.C. Deb. 2935–55 (1923).

[22]*Vaughan v. Taff Railway Co.*, 3 H. and N. 743 (Ex. 1858) and 5 H. and N. 679 (Ex. 1860).

necessarily desirable that the railway should be required to compensate those who suffer damage by fires caused by railway engines. I need not show here that, if the railway could make a bargain with everyone having property adjoining the railway line and there were no costs involved in making such bargains, it would not matter whether the railway was liable for damage caused by fires or not. This question has been treated at length in earlier sections. The problem is whether it would be desirable to make the railway liable in conditions in which it is too expensive for such bargains to be made. Pigou clearly thought it was desirable to force the railway to pay compensation and it is easy to see the kind of argument that would have led him to this conclusion. Suppose a railway is considering whether to run an additional train or to increase the speed of an existing train or to install spark-preventing devices on its engines. If the railway were not liable for fire damage, then, when making these decisions, it would not take into account as a cost the increase in damage resulting from the additional train or the faster train or the failure to install spark-preventing devices. This is the source of the divergence between private and social net products. It results in the railway performing acts which will lower the value of total production—and which it would not do if it were liable for the damage. This can be shown by means of an arithmetical example.

Consider a railway, which is *not* liable for damage by fires caused by sparks from its engines, which runs two trains per day on a certain line. Suppose that running one train per day would enable the railway to perform services worth $150 per annum and running two trains a day would enable the railway to perform services worth $250 per annum. Suppose further that the cost of running one train is $50 per annum and two trains $100 per annum. Assuming perfect competition, the cost equals the fall in the value of production elsewhere due to the employment of additional factors of production by the railway. Clearly the railway would find it profitable to run two trains per day. But suppose that running one train per day would destroy by fire crops worth (on an average over the year) $60 and two trains a day would result in the destruction of crops worth $120. In these circumstances running one train per day would raise the value of total production but the running of a second train would reduce the value of total production. The second train would enable additional railway services worth $100 per annum to be performed. But the fall in the value of production elsewhere would be $110 per annum; $50 as a result of the employment of additional factors of production and $60 as a result of the destruction of crops. Since it would be better if the second train were not run and since it would not run if the railway were liable for damage caused to crops, the conclusion that the railway should be made liable for the damage seems irresistible. Undoubtedly it is this kind of reasoning which underlies the Pigovian position.

The conclusion that it would be better if the second train did not run is correct. The conclusion that it is desirable that the railway should be made liable for the damage it causes is wrong. Let us change our assumption concerning the rule of liability. Suppose that the railway is liable for damage from fires caused by sparks from the engine. A farmer on lands adjoining the railway is then in the position that, if his crop is destroyed by fires caused by the railway, he will receive the market price from the railway; but if his crop is not damaged, he will receive the market price by sale. It therefore becomes a matter of indifference to him whether his crop is damaged by fire or not. The position is very different when the railway is *not* liable. Any crop destruction through railway-caused fires would then reduce the receipts of the farmer. He would therefore take out of cultivation any land for which the damage is likely to be greater than the net return of the land (for reasons explained at length in Section III). A change from a regime in which the railway is *not* liable for damage to one in which it *is* liable is likely therefore to lead to an increase in the amount of cultivation on lands adjoining the railway. It will also, of course, lead to an increase in the amount of crop destruction due to railway-caused fires.

Let us return to our arithmetical example. Assume that, with the changed rule of liability, there is a doubling in the amount of crop destruction due to railway-caused fires. With one train per day, crops worth $120 would be destroyed each year and two trains per day would lead to the destruction of crops worth $240. We saw previously that it would not be profitable to run the second train if the railway had to pay $60 per annum as compensation for damage. With damage at $120 per annum the loss from running the second train would be $60 greater. But now let us consider the first train. The value of the transport services furnished by the first train is $150. The cost of running the train is $50. The amount that the railway would have to pay out as compensation for damage is $120. It follows that it would not be profitable to run any trains. With the figures in our example we reach the following result: if the railway is not liable for fire-damage, two trains per day would be run; if the railway is liable for fire-damage, it would cease operations altogether. Does this mean that it is better that there should be no railway? This question can be resolved by considering what would happen to the value of total production if it were decided to exempt the railway from liability for fire-damage, thus bringing it into operation (with two trains per day).

The operation of the railway would enable transport services worth $250 to be performed. It would also mean the employment of factors of production which would reduce the value of production elsewhere by $100. Furthermore it would mean the destruction of crops worth $120. The coming of the railway will also have led to the abandonment of cultivation of some land. Since we know that, had this land been cultivated, the value of the crops destroyed by fire would have been $120, and since it is unlikely that the total crop on this land would have been destroyed, it seems reasonable to suppose that the value of the crop yield on this land would have been higher than this. Assume it would have been $160. But the abandonment of cultivation would have released factors of production for employment elsewhere. All we know is that the amount by which the value of production elsewhere will increase will be less than $160. Suppose that it is $150. Then the gain from operating the railway would be $250 (the value of the transport services) minus $100 (the cost of the factors of production) minus $120 (the value of crops destroyed by fire) minus $160 (the fall in the value of crop production due to the abandonment of cultivation) plus $150 (the value of production elsewhere of the released factors of production). Overall, operating the railway will increase the value of total production by $20. With these figures it is clear that it is better that the railway should not be liable for the damage it causes, thus enabling it to operate profitably. Of course, by altering the figures, it could be shown that there are other cases in which it would be desirable that the railway should be liable for the damage it causes. It is enough for my purpose to show that, from an economic point of view, a situation in which there is "uncompensated damage done to surrounding woods by sparks from railway engines" is not necessarily undesirable. Whether it is desirable or not depends on the particular circumstances.

How is it that the Pigovian analysis seems to give the wrong answer? The reason is that Pigou does not seem to have noticed that his analysis is dealing with an entirely different question. The analysis as such is correct. But it is quite illegitimate for Pigou to draw the particular conclusion he does. The question at issue is not whether it is desirable to run an additional train or a faster train or to install smoke-preventing devices; the question at issue is whether it is desirable to have a system in which the railway has to compensate those who suffer damage from the fires which it causes or one in which the railway does not have to compensate them. When an economist is comparing alternative social arrangements, the proper procedure is to compare the total social product yielded by these different arrangements. The comparison of private and social products is neither here nor there. A simple example will demonstrate this. Imagine a town in which there are traffic lights. A motorist approaches an intersection and stops because the light is red. There are no cars approaching the intersection on the other street. If the motorist ignored the red signal, no accident would occur and the total product would increase because the motorist would arrive earlier at his destination. Why does he not do this? The reason is that if he ignored the light he would be fined. The private product from crossing the street is less than the social product. Should we conclude from this that the total product would be greater if there were no fines for failing to obey traffic signals? The Pigovian analysis shows us that it is possible to conceive of better worlds than the one in which we live. But the problem is to devise practical arrangements which will correct defects in one part of the system without causing more serious harm in other parts.

I have examined in considerable detail one example of a divergence between private and social products and I do not propose to make any further examination of Pigou's analytical system. But the main discussion of the problem considered in this article is to be found in that part of Chapter 9 in Part II which deals with Pigou's second class of divergence and it is of interest to see how Pigou develops his argument. Pigou's own description of this second class of divergence was quoted at the beginning of this section. Pigou distinguishes between the case in which a person renders services for which he receives no payment and the case in which a person renders disservices and compensation is not given to the injured parties. Our main attention has, of course, centered on this second case. It is therefore rather astonishing to find, as was pointed out to me by Professor Francesco Forte, that the problem of the smoking chimney—the "stock instance"[23] or "classroom example"[24] of the second case—is used by Pigou as an example of the first case (services rendered without payment) and is never mentioned, at any rate explicitly, in connection with the second case.[25] Pigou points out that factory owners who devote resources to preventing their chimneys from smoking render services for which they receive no payment. The implication, in the light of Pigou's discussion later in the chapter, is that a factory owner with a smokey chimney should be given a bounty to induce him to install smoke-preventing devices. Most modern economists would suggest that the owner of the factor with the smokey chimney should be taxed. It seems a pity that economists (apart from Professor Forte) do not seem to have noticed this feature of Pigou's treatment since a realisation that the problem could be tackled in either of these two ways would probably have led to an explicit recognition of its reciprocal nature.

In discussing the second case (disservices without compensation to those damaged), Pigou says that they are rendered "when the owner of a site in a residential quarter of a city builds a factory there and so destroys a great part of the amenities of neighbouring sites; or, in a less degree, when he uses his site in such a way as to spoil the lighting of the house opposite; or when he invests resources in erecting buildings in a crowded centre, which by contracting the air-space and the playing room of the neighbourhood, tend to injure the health and efficiency of the families living there."[26] Pigou is, of course, quite right to describe such actions as "uncharged disservices." But he is wrong when he describes these actions as "anti-social."[27] They may or may not be. It is necessary to weigh the harm against the good that will result. Nothing could be more "anti-social" than to oppose any action which causes any harm to anyone.

Indeed, Pigou's treatment of the problems considered in this article is extremely elusive and the discussion of his views raises almost insuperable difficulties of interpretation. Consequently it is impossible to be sure that one has understood what Pigou really meant. Nevertheless, it is difficult to resist the conclusion, extraordinary though this may be in an economist of Pigou's stature, that the main source of this obscurity is that Pigou had not thought his position through.

------

[23]Sir Dennis Robertson, I *Lectures on Economic Principles* 162 (1957).

[24]E. J. Mishan, "The Meaning of Efficiency in Economics," 189, *The Bankers' Magazine* 482 (June 1960).

[25]Pigou, *op. cit. supra* n. 35 at 184.

[26]*Id.* at 185–86.

[27]*Id.* at 186 n. 1. For similar unqualified statements see Pigou's lecture "Some Aspects of the Housing Problem" in B. S. Rowntree and A. C. Pigou, "Lectures on Housing," in 18 *Manchester Univ. Lectures* (1914).

IX. *The Pigovian Tradition*

It is strange that a doctrine as faulty as that developed by Pigou should have been so influential, although part of its success has probably been due to the lack of clarity in the exposition. Not being clear, it was never clearly wrong. Curiously enough, this obscurity in the source has not prevented the emergence of a fairly well-defined oral tradition. What economists think they learn from Pigou, and what they tell their students, which I term the Pigovian tradition, is reasonably clear. I propose to show the inadequacy of this Pigovian tradition by demonstrating that both the analysis and the policy conclusions which it supports are incorrect.

I do not propose to justify my view as to the prevailing opinion by copious references to the literature. I do this partly because the treatment in the literature is usually so fragmentary, often involving little more than a reference to Pigou plus some explanatory comment, that detailed examination would be inappropriate. But the main reason for this lack of reference is that the doctrine, although based on Pigou, must have been largely the product of an oral tradition. Certainly economists with whom I have discussed these problems have shown a unanimity of opinion which is quite remarkable considering the meagre treatment accorded this subject in the literature. No doubt there are some economists who do not share the usual view but they must represent a small minority of the profession.

The approach to the problems under discussion is through an examination of the value of physical production. The private product is the value of the additional product resulting from a particular activity of a business. The social product equals the private product minus the fall in the value of production elsewhere for which no compensation is paid by the business. Thus, if 10 units of a factor (and no other factors) are used by a business to make a certain product with a value of $105; and the owner of this factor is not compensated for their use, which he is unable to prevent; and these 10 units of the factor would yield products in their best alternative use worth $100; then, the social product is $105 minus $100 or $5. If the business now pays for one unit of the factor and its price equals the value of its marginal product, then the social product rises to $15. If two units are paid for, the social product rises to $25 and so on until it reaches $105 when all units of the factor are paid for. It is not difficult to see why economists have so readily accepted this rather odd procedure. The analysis focusses on the individual business decision and since the use of certain resources is not allowed for in costs, receipts are reduced by the same amount. But, of course, this means that the value of the social product has no social significance whatsoever. It seems to me preferable to use the opportunity cost concept and to approach these problems by comparing the value of the product yielded by factors in alternative uses or by alternative arrangements. The main advantage of a pricing system is that it leads to the employment of factors in places where the value of the product yielded is greatest and does so at less cost than alternative systems (I leave aside that a pricing system also eases the problem of the redistribution of income). But if through some God-given natural harmony factors flowed to the places where the value of the product yielded was greatest without any use of the pricing system and consequently there was no compensation, I would find it a source of surprise rather than a cause for dismay.

The definition of the social product is queer but this does not mean that the conclusions for policy drawn from the analysis are necessarily wrong. However, there are bound to be dangers in an approach which diverts attention from the basic issues and there can be little doubt that it has been responsible for some of the errors in current doctrine. The belief that it is desirable that the business which causes harmful effects should be forced to compensate those who suffer damage (which was exhaustively discussed in section VIII in connection with Pigou's railway sparks example) is undoubtedly the result of not comparing the total product obtainable with alternative social arrangements.

The same fault is to be found in proposals for solving the problem of harmful effects by the use of taxes or bounties. Pigou lays considerable stress on this solution although he is, as usual, lacking in detail and qualified in his support.[28] Modern economists tend to think exclusively in terms of taxes and in a very precise way. The tax should be equal to the damage done and should therefore vary with the amount of the harmful effect. As it is not proposed that the proceeds of the tax should be paid to those suffering the damage, this solution is not the same as that which would force a business to pay compensation to those damaged by its actions, although economists generally do not seem to have noticed this and tend to treat the two solutions as being identical.

Assume that a factory which emits smoke is set up in a district previously free from smoke pollution, causing damage valued at $100 per annum. Assume that the taxation solution is adopted and that the factory-owner is taxed $100 per annum as long as the factory emits the smoke. Assume further that a smoke-preventing device costing $90 per annum to run is available. In these circumstances, the smoke-preventing device would be installed. Damage of $100 would have been avoided at an expenditure of $90 and the factory-owner would be better off by $10 per annum. Yet the position achieved may not be optimal. Suppose that those who suffer the damage could avoid it by moving to other locations or by taking various precautions which would cost them, or be equivalent to a loss in income of, $40 per annum. Then there would be a gain in the value of production of $50 if the factory continued to emit its smoke and those now in the district moved elsewhere or made other adjustments to avoid the damage. If the factory owner is to be made to pay a tax equal to the damage caused, it would clearly be desirable to institute a double tax system and to make residents of the district pay an amount equal to the additional cost incurred by the factory-owner (or the consumers of his products) in order to avoid the damage. In these conditions, people would not stay in the district or would take

---

[28]*Id.*192–4, 381 and *Public Finance* 94–100 (3d ed. 1947).

other measures to prevent the damage from occurring, when the costs of doing so were less than the costs that would be incurred by the producer to reduce the damage (the producer's object, of course, being not so much to reduce the damage as to reduce the tax payments). A tax system which was confined to a tax on the producer for damage caused would tend to lead to unduly high costs being incurred for the prevention of damage. Of course this could be avoided if it were possible to base the tax, not on the damage caused, but on the fall in the value of production (in its widest sense) resulting from the emission of smoke. But to do so would require a detailed knowledge of individual preferences and I am unable to imagine how the data needed for such a taxation system could be assembled. Indeed, the proposal to solve the smoke pollution and similar problems by the use of taxes bristles with difficulties: the problem of calculation, the difference between average and marginal damage, the interrelations between the damage suffered on different properties, etc. But it is unnecessary to examine these problems here. It is enough for my purpose to show that, even if the tax is exactly adjusted to equal the damage that would be done to neighbouring properties as a result of the emission of each additional puff of smoke, the tax would not necessarily bring about optimal conditions. An increase in the number of people living or of businesses operating in the vicinity of the smoke-emitting factory will increase the amount of harm produced by a given emission of smoke. The tax that would be imposed would therefore increase with an increase in the number of those in the vicinity. This will tend to lead to a decrease in the value of production of the factors employed by the factory, either because a reduction in production due to the tax will result in factors being used elsewhere in ways which are less valuable, or because factors will be diverted to produce means for reducing the amount of smoke emitted. But people deciding to establish themselves in the vicinity of the factory will not take into account this fall in the value of production which results from their presence. This failure to take into account costs imposed on others is comparable to the action of a factory owner in not taking into account the harm resulting from his emission of smoke. Without the tax, there may be too much smoke and too few people in the vicinity of the factory; but with the tax there may be too little smoke and too many people in the vicinity of the factory. There is no reason to suppose that one of these results is necessarily preferable.

I need not devote much space to discussing the similar error involved in the suggestion that smoke-producing factories should, by means of zoning regulations, be removed from the districts in which the smoke causes harmful effects. When the change in the location of the factory results in a reduction in production, this obviously needs to be taken into account and weighed against the harm which would result from the factory remaining in that location. The aim of such regulation should not be to eliminate smoke pollution but rather to secure the optimum amount of smoke pollution, this being the amount which will maximise the values of production.

X. A Change of Approach

It is my belief that the failure of economists to reach correct conclusions about the treatment of harmful effects cannot be ascribed simply to a few slips in analysis. It stems from basic defects in the current approach to problems of welfare economics. What is needed is a change of approach.

Analysis in terms of divergencies between private and social products concentrates attention on particular deficiencies in the system and tends to nourish the belief that any measure which will remove the deficiency is necessarily desirable. It diverts attention from those other changes in the system which are inevitably associated with the corrective measure, changes which may well produce more harm than the original deficiency. In the preceding sections of this article, we have seen many examples of this. But it is not necessary to approach the problem in this way. Economists who study problems of the firm habitually use an opportunity cost approach and compare the receipts obtained from a given combination of factors with alternative business arrangements. It would seem desirable to use a similar approach when dealing with questions of economic policy and to compare the total product yielded by alternative social arrangements. In this article, the analysis has been confined, as is usual in this part of economics, to comparisons of the value of production, as measured by the market. But it is, of course, desirable that the choice between different social arrangements for the solution of economic problems should be carried out in broader terms than this and that the total effect of these arrangements in all spheres of life should be taken into account. As Frank H. Knight has so often emphasized, problems of welfare economics must ultimately dissolve into a study of aesthetics and morals.

A second feature of the usual treatment of the problems discussed in this article is that the analysis proceeds in terms of a comparison between a state of laissez faire and some kind of ideal world. This approach inevitably leads to a looseness of thought since the nature of the alternatives being compared is never clear. In a state of laissez faire, is there a monetary, a legal or a political system and if so, what are they? In an ideal world, would there be a monetary, a legal or a political system and if so, what would they be? The answers to all these questions are shrouded in mystery and every man is free to draw whatever conclusions he likes. Actually very little analysis is required to show that an ideal world is better than a state of laissez faire, unless the definitions of a state of laissez faire and an ideal world happen to be the same. But the whole discussion is largely irrelevant for questions of economic policy since whatever we may have in mind as our ideal world, it is clear that we have not yet discovered how to get to it from where we are. A better approach would seem to be to start our analysis with a situation approximating that which actually exists, to examine the effects of a proposed policy change and to attempt to decide whether the new situation would be, in total, better or worse than the original one. In this way, conclusions for policy would have some relevance to the actual situation.

A final reason for the failure to develop a theory adequate to handle the problem of harmful effects stems from a faulty concept of a factor of production. This is usually thought of as a physical entity which the businessman acquires and uses (an acre of land, a ton of fertiliser) instead of as a right to perform certain (physical) actions. We may speak of a person owning land and using it as a factor of production but what the land-owner in fact possesses is the right to carry out a circumscribed list of actions. The rights of a land-owner are not unlimited. It is not even always possible for him to remove the land to another place, for instance, by quarrying it. And although it may be possible for him to exclude some people from using "his" land, this may not be true of others. For example, some people may have the right to cross the land. Furthermore, it may or may not be possible to erect certain types of buildings or to grow certain crops or to use particular drainage systems on the land. This does not come about simply because of Government regulation. It would be equally true under the common law. In fact it would be true under any system of law. A system in which the rights of individuals were unlimited would be one in which there were no rights to acquire.

If factors of production are thought of as rights, it becomes easier to understand that the right to do something which has a harmful effect (such as the creation of smoke, noise, smells, etc.) is also a factor of production. Just as we may use a piece of land in such a way as to prevent someone else from crossing it, or parking his car, or building his house upon it, so we may use it in such a way as to deny him a view or quiet or unpolluted air. The cost of exercising a right (of using a factor of production) is always the loss which is suffered elsewhere in consequence of the exercise of that right—the inability to cross land, to park a car, to build a house, to enjoy a view, to have peace and quiet or to breathe clean air.

It would clearly be desirable if the only actions performed were those in which what was gained was worth more than what was lost. But in choosing between social arrangements within the context of which individual decisions are made, we have to bear in mind that a change in the existing system which will lead to an improvement in some decisions may well lead to a worsening of others. Furthermore we have to take into account the costs involved in operating the various social arrangements (whether it be the working of a market or of a government department), as well as the costs involved in moving to a new system. In devising and choosing between social arrangements we should have regard for the total effect. This, above all, is the change in approach which I am advocating.

3 On Behavioral-Environmental Economics*

Jason F. Shogren and Laura O. Taylor

Jason F. Shogren is the Stroock Professor of Natural Resource Conservation and Management, Department of Economics and Finance, University of Wyoming, and the King Carl XVI Gustaf Professor of Environmental Sciences, Umeå University. E-mail: JRamses@uwyo.edu. Laura O. Taylor is Professor, Department of Agricultural and Resource Economics, and Director, Center for Environmental and Resource Economic Policy, North Carolina State University.

Introduction

This article examines how behavioral economics might advance the science of environmental and resource economics. Behavioral economics explores, catalogues, and rationalizes systematic deviations from rational choice theory. Mullainathan and Thaler (2000) have distilled these deviations or limits on human behavior down to three general categories: bounded rationality, bounded willpower, and bounded self-interest. Based on Simon's (1957) ideas, bounded rationality implies that people do not have unlimited abilities to process all the information needed to make rational choices. Rather, they have inherent behavioral biases and use rules of thumb and shortcuts to make decisions (Mazzotta and Opaluch 1995). Bounded willpower reflects the idea that people lack self-control sometimes—we consume too much, save too little, make rash decisions, procrastinate, and so on. Bounded self-interest captures the other face of Adam Smith—that people can be selfless. People are concerned about other people too (Bergstrom 1989; Smith 1998). They have social preferences for emotive ideas like reciprocity, altruism, paternalism, and aversion to inequality.

In contrast to the argument that the formalism of rational choice theory provides the "necessary fiction" for guiding decisions, behavioral economists continue to strive toward reintroducing more psychology into economics (see Rabin 1998; Sent 2004). Some researchers have gone a step further to develop

"On Behavioral Environmental Economics" by Jason Shogren and Laura Taylor. *Review of Environmental Economics and Policy* 2. 2008. Pp. 26–44. Reprinted with permission.

*Shogren thanks the Norwegian University of Life Sciences, GREQAM, and the University of Paris I-Sorbonne for their hospitality. This review draws from many discussions over the years with our colleagues: thanks to T. Cherry, T. Crocker, P. Ferraro, G. Hollard, T. Hurley, D. Hayes, G. Harrison, N. Hanley, B. Kriström, S. Kroll, S. Luchini, G. Parkhurst, C. Plott, E. Romstad, V. K. Smith, and V. L. Smith.

the so-called *neuroeconomics*—the study of brain imaging during decision-making—to gain more insight into the biological and psychological underpinnings of behavior (see, for example, Weber et al. 2007). They work to categorize and catalog the ever-expanding list of deviations from rational choice theory. Examples of anomalous behavior are numerous, including the status quo bias and endowment effect, loss aversion, framing effects, anchoring, preference reversals, the willingness-to-accept (WTA) willingness-to-pay (WTP) gap, self-control, time inconsistency, and coherent arbitrariness.[1] McFadden (1999) provides a useful catalogue of these and other biases. While appreciating that all economics is about "behavior," this area of behavioral economics identifies and rationalizes empirical pattern recognition to help challenge existing ideas of rational choice and guide the foundations of new theories of choice (see Starmer 2000).

The field of behavioral economics has developed its own taxonomy of behavioral biases and general rules of thumb that we group together for rhetorical ease as *behavioral failures*. We use the term *behavioral failures* to parallel the familiar idea of market failures. For our discussion, behavioral failure means a person fails to behave as predicted by rational choice theory. A behavioral failure is also referred to as an anomaly, paradox, bias, heuristic misperception, fallacy, illusion, or paradigm.

Using recent research as illustrative examples, this article explores four questions concerning behavioral failures and environmental economics. First, how can behavioral failures affect thinking about environmental policy? Second, when are behavioral failures relevant to the science of environmental and resource economics? Third, is behavioral failure just another form of market failure? And lastly, our most speculative question, do we have a new behavioral-environmental second-best problem?

We address these four questions within the following context. When thinking about protecting nature, environmental economics has traditionally focused on the idea that market failure is the critical source of economic inefficiency (see Arrow 1969). More specifically, without well-defined property rights and well-functioning exchange institutions that move goods and services from low- to high-value uses, a society's ability to allocate resources efficiently is constrained. Environmental market failure is grouped into the taxonomy of externalities, nonrival goods, nonexcludable benefits and costs, nonconvexities, and asymmetric information. Economists use this taxonomy to design and evaluate policies for environmental protection, which include collective sharing rules, Pigovian taxes, marketable permits, liability rules, and mechanism designs (see, e.g., Kolstad 1999).

---

[1] An endowment effect suggests people become overly attached to some goods; loss aversion is when people are risk averse for potential gains, but risk seeking for potential losses; framing effects suggest that how a question is asked matters as much as what question is asked; anchoring implies that people lock on to the external prices or information given to them; time inconsistency implies that people make a choice today about tomorrow, but when tomorrow comes, they change their minds; and coherent arbitrariness means people will focus on an arbitrary starting point, but will then make coherent choices. See McFadden (1999) for more explanation.

The idea that economic theory can reverse market failure through the creation of new markets or market-like incentives rests on the presumption of rational behavior—that people facing these new incentives will act with purpose and make consistent choices that take into account the consequences of their choices. But relying on rational choice theory to guide environmental policy makes sense only if people make, or act as if they make, consistent and systematic choices. Here lies the rub. Numerous empirical studies over the last four decades reveal that rational choice might, in some circumstances, be a poor guide for economics in general, and for environmental economics in particular (see Tversky and Kahneman 2000). The problem is that rationality in economics is a social construct based on active market exchange, not an individual construct based on isolated introspection (Arrow 1987). Assuming rational behavior for environmental policy decisions may be problematic because nature's goods and services frequently lack the active market-like arbitrage needed to encourage consistent choice (Crocker, Shogren, and Turner 1998). So-called "anomalous behavior" may arise in private and public decisions, undercutting the rational underpinning of environmental policy.

Using their persistent rhetoric, behavioral economists continue to point out the limits to human nature, both in scholarly articles and now in popular books, e.g., *The Economic Naturalist; Why Smart People Make Big Money Mistakes; Why Smart People Do Dumb Things; How We Know What Isn't So; Decision Traps.* As noted by Vernon Smith (2003), however, behavioral failure is about looking for and finding unexpected behavior out in the tails of the distribution of rational behavior. How fat or thin these behavioral distribution tails actually are remains the most contentious aspect of the debate about how much we need to change current practices and methods in economics, environmental and otherwise.

How Can Behavioral Economics Affect Thinking about Environmental Policy?

Some researchers in environmental economics have always been interested in what behavioral economics has to say about economic decisions relevant to environmental policy. For instance, read Kahneman's (1986) comments on the state of the art of contingent valuation from two decades ago; the public goods experiments run by Brookshire, Coursey, and Schulze (1990); work on behavior and the Coase theorem by Hoffman and Spitzer (1982) and Harrison and McKee (1985); or the earlier work of Bohm (1972) on the behavioral regularities in alternative institutions to elicit values for public goods. But this research is the exception, not the rule. Models of agent behavior in environmental and resource applications have almost universally conformed with the standard neoclassical framework. Jack Knetsch has long advocated for more behavioral economics in environmental economics. A decade ago,

Knetsch (1997, p. 209) argued that "in view of the evidence, the seemingly quite deliberate avoidance of any accounting of these [behavioral] findings in the design of environmental policy or in debates over environmental values, does not appear to be the most productive means to improvement."

Economists who criticize behavioral economics argue that people can learn to be rational from a combination of market forces and evolution. The common view is that the market is more rational than the individual, and makes better allocation decisions concerning what people should specialize in and where resources should go. To illustrate this common market-orientated perspective, consider Nobel laureate Gary Becker's opinion about behavioral economics and the experimental methods used for pattern recognition. Becker notes that "there is a heck of a difference between demonstrating something in a laboratory, in experiments, even highly sophisticated experiments, and showing that they are important in the marketplace. Economists have a theory of behavior in markets, not in labs, and the relevant theories can be very different. One reason is the division of labor in markets. . . . . I am dubious about behavior that won't survive in an exchange economy with an extensive division of labor" (Becker 2002).

A behavioral economist's response to this market-oriented criticism is to point out that the strict market-like arbitrage necessary to motivate more rational behavior and the ideal division of labor do not always exist for many genuine economic decisions. This observation holds with greater force for environmental goods and services in which direct exchange within active market institutions usually does not exist. The needed markets are missing— which is why we need environmental economics in the first place. In cases of missing markets, or constructed markets, it becomes possible for behavioral failures to affect policy outcomes. To illustrate this point, we discuss four examples where behavioral failures may well affect the way researchers and decision-makers think about environmental policy: nonmarket valuation, risk, conflict/cooperation, and control.

Non-Market Valuation

Behavioral economics has probably had the biggest impact on environmental economics through research on the nonmarket valuation for environmental goods. Here, behavioral and environmental economists have documented empirical deviations between theory and behavior. This work has chipped away at the idea that rational choice theory and welfare economics should remain the unchallenged analytical foundation for environmental valuation. People sometimes do not seem as if they have core preferences for the environment, or that they can articulate these into consistent monetary values. If people do not follow rational choice theory, and instead state values that are momentary declarations, one becomes concerned that preferences and stated values are transient artifacts of context, which undercuts the whole foundation of rational valuation.

The longest and the most visible research in this area concerns the oft-found disparity between the willingness-to-pay (WTP) and the willingness-to-accept (WTA) compensation measures of economic value. With small income effects and many available substitutes, the willingness to pay for a commodity and the willingness to accept compensation to sell the same commodity should be about equal. But evidence suggests a significant gap can exit between WTP and WTA, which the behavioral economics literature has argued could be due to a fundamental endowment effect (Knetsch and Sinden 1984; Knetsch 1989).

An endowment effect exists when people are more eager to retain something that they already own than to acquire something new (e.g., when people offer to sell a commonly available good in their possession at a substantially higher rate than they will pay for the identical good when it is not in their possession). One experiment run by Knetsch (1989) gave half of the participants a candy bar and the other half a coffee mug of approximately the same value. Subjects were then offered the opportunity to trade for the other commodity. Preferences for the mug over the candy bar varied from 10 to 89 percent, depending purely on which commodity the person was given first (also see Borges and Knetsch 1998). Kahneman, Knetsch, and Thaler (1990) further argue that the endowment effect explains why WTP diverges from WTA. They conduct experiments using an incentive-compatible auction mechanism where each individual can do no better than to reveal his/her true value for a good. Their results make a case for the existence of the endowment effect—WTA exceeded WTP in all treatments over all iterations. People's preferences seemed to depend on their initial endowments of resources.

If revealed preferences are context-dependent, then the core of benefit-cost analysis is on shaky ground (see Kahneman and Knetsch 1992 and Tversky and Simonson 1993). But until researchers offer up a viable theoretical alternative to welfare economics, others will continue to rely on rational choice as the benchmark to guide benefit-cost analyses. Interested readers should consult the recent work of Sugden (2005), who defines a benefit-cost framework that is immune from preference anomalies. He relaxes the presumption of coherent and consistent preferences and replaces it with a weaker assumption of price sensitivity as the way to measure economic surplus (i.e., buyers prefer to pay less money than more; sellers prefer to receive more money than less). But whether one can operationalize this new framework for environmental and resource questions remains unresolved.

Not surprisingly, this behavioral challenge to fundamental welfare theory triggered many responses over the last two decades. Coursey, Hovis, and Schulze (1987) argued that the WTA-WTP gap was an illusion that will disappear with repeated experience with market exchange mechanisms. This market-driven rationality idea was supported by Shogren et al. (1994, 2001), who compared stated values with repeated market interactions. Loomes, Starmer, and Sugden (2003) have an alternative view and argue that seemingly rational bidders are actually using a behavioral rule of thumb in that they are "anchoring" on the posted price such that they are being led by the nose, so to speak. This is not inconsistent with the idea that people learn to be rational with market experience. Plott and Zeiler (2005a, b) take this argument a step further. They contend that the endowment effect can be turned on and off, depending on which experimental protocols are used. They contend that the WTA-WTP gap is less about a fundamental bias than about a subject's misunderstanding of the valuation task. They run a series of experiments with alternative protocols to illustrate how it is possible for poorly understood experimental procedures to be confounded with fundamental behavioral biases (also see Braga and Starmer 2005).

Other behavioral anomalies that could affect nonmarket valuation (e.g., preference reversals, ambiguity aversion, anchoring) have been discussed in the literature (see Shogren 2006a or Flachaire and Hollard 2007 for more discussion). The debate, however, about whether researchers should be concerned about preference anomalies in nonmarket valuation is far from over. Moreover, among the topics studied by environmental and resource economists, behavioral economics may very well have the greatest implications for stated preference valuation research, where individuals are typically asked to make judgments and report economic values in isolated, unfamiliar decision situations.

Choice under Risk

Since nearly all environmental policy can be defined as a lottery, the second example focuses on choice under risk. No environmental policy makes an outcome happen with certainty, rather, it substitutes a baseline lottery for another lottery, hopefully with better odds of good health and a clean environment. Policy-as-lottery implies people think about a combination of probabilities and consequences that define the risks to human and environmental health. Researchers need to better understand how people react to the baseline lottery and how they respond to changes from this baseline due to private and collective risk reduction investments.

The expected utility model is the basis for many environmental economists' thinking about how to value and control risks to health and nature. In contrast, behavioral economists have provided substantial evidence to suggest that expected utility might not be the best model to guide good environmental risk policy. A good example of behavioral failure is when an outcome is potentially very bad, but the probability of its realization is low, i.e. [sic], climate induced shift in the Gulf Stream. Experience tells people little about how to react to these low-probability, high-consequence risks. Behavioral studies reveal that people tend to overestimate the chance they might suffer from such a risk, or they seem to have loss aversion—they tend to deal differently with potential losses than with equivalent gains. Here, a descriptive model might be a better guide to behavior than expected utility.

To illustrate, consider Mason et al.'s (2005) experiment designed to test the behavioral accuracy of the expected utility model over low-probability/ high-loss scenarios such as those found in environmental policy. These experiments ask people to make choices between a pair of risky lotteries defined over potential losses. Mason et al.'s results support the behavioral economics literature, finding that for risks in which the probabilities of both the best and worst outcomes are relatively small, expected utility theory performed poorly. Their results suggest that policy based on expected benefits and costs could underestimate the real WTP to reduce environmental risk.

Incorporation of nonexpected utility models into the environmental economics literature has been relatively slow (see Shaw and Woodward 2007). One example is Ranjan and Shogren (2006), who construct a behavioral model to explain the sluggish development of water markets. Farmers have been reluctant to participate in water markets because they fear that their participation today will lead to a loss of water rights to urban users tomorrow. A farmer assigns greater weight to low probabilities of future water rights loss and lower weights to high probabilities. Their results suggest that subjective weighting of probabilities leads to discounting of resources when farmers overestimate probabilities of loss. When farmers have idiosyncratic time preferences, total water supply in the market depends on the level of heterogeneity in the population.

The next question then is whether misestimation of value or behavioral outcomes due to mismodeling of preferences is significant enough to change policy decisions. If people act as if they have a nonexpected-value utility function, can the expected utility still be close enough if the predictions fall within a reasonable approximation error? But this immediately leads to the next thorny behavioral question—do people form coherent beliefs over uncertain events, so we can define a probabilistic threshold to separate a reasonable from an unreasonable error (see, for example, Grether 1980)? These are underexplored questions.

Environmental Conflict and Cooperation

The third example considers the role of behavioral game theory for environmental conflict and cooperation. Game theory has been the breakthrough method for exploring likely equilibrium outcomes when two or more groups have strategic interactions. The behavioral economics literature has found that people frequently violate game theory assumptions (see Camerer 2003). First, people do not always perceive the game clearly and consistently. Evidence suggests that people's behavior changes when the description of the game changes, even though outcomes do not change. Second, the literature suggests that players are overconfident about their own relative skill. In addition, strategic reasoning principles that underpin game theory seem to be irrelevant to the average person.

Behavioral economics has advocated looking for a more pragmatic approach to environmental conflict policy that takes observed behavior, rational or otherwise, and reconstructs incentives to improve the efficiency of some program. To illustrate, consider the behavioral economics discussion of conflict in common property or public good games (see Ledyard 1995; Ostrom 2006). International environmental treaties between sovereign nations frequently suffer from weak enforcement and nonbinding voting rules, e.g., the Kyoto Protocol for climate change. Under rational game theory, free riding should dominate the behavior of the people in the group because there is no punishment for deviation. Evidence suggests that one can introduce an enforcement regime that emerges endogenously from the participants themselves (see Ostrom, Walker, and Gardner 1994). But the problem here is that endogenous enforcement is costly to each person. A person who chooses to punish a violator bears all the marginal costs himself, but earns only a fraction of the marginal benefits, which are shared throughout the group. No one individual should be willing to expend his own resources to punish violators, since his net benefits at the margin are negative.

Behavioral research has revealed that such people—the willing punishers—do exist in experimental settings, along with rational egoists and conditional cooperators (those who initiate cooperation when they expect others to reciprocate). These willing punishers will pick up the tab to punish violators even though they know they will not recoup all the benefits of their actions. By "taking one for the team," they can increase the overall efficiency of the institution designed to reduce the costs of noncooperative behavior. Fehr and Gächter (2000) observed that cooperation rates increased when the willing punishers could police the collective. The simple threat to punish was enough to coerce others to cooperate. For example, Kroll, Cherry, and Shogren (2007) created a nonbinding voting public goods game with and without punishment. They found that willing punishers seem to drive the other players to increase their contributions, leading to increased cooperation and greater social efficiency. Including behavioral factors in institutional design suggests that one can correct for a global public goods problem more effectively by accounting for the behavioral failure of these willing punishers (also see Noussair and Tucker 2005).

Resolving environmental conflict frequently requires researchers to understand how people cooperate and negotiate a solution. Some people see collaboration as the future of environmental policy. The effectiveness of collaboration can be facilitated by a better understanding of the Coase theorem and transaction costs (Coase 1960). The Coase theorem says that disputing parties will bargain until they reach an efficient private agreement, regardless of which party initially holds the unilateral property rights. As long as these legal entitlements can be freely exchanged and transaction costs are zero, government intervention is relegated to designating and enforcing well-defined property rights. But Coase was not promoting a world of zero transaction costs. Instead, Coase said that since a zero-transaction-costs world does not exist, we need to study the world that does exist—the one with transaction costs. A behavioral economist might say we also need to study the world of cognitive bounds (see Sunstein 2000).

Policy-makers should be interested in how different bargaining rules and protocols affect behavior and outcomes. Concerning environmental collaboration, behavioral economics has explored how rules affect or are affected by bounded self-interest (entitlements and fairness) and bounded rationality (endowment effects; self-serving bias leading to an impasse). The first behavioral-style paper exploring the Coase theorem (Hoffman and Spitzer 1982) observed efficient outcomes, but found that bargainers were rather selfless, splitting outcomes equally rather than rationally. This suggested that other-regarding, or altruistic, behavior was affected by the institutional context of policy. In response, Harrison and McKee (1985) revisited the design, and showed that a person's selflessness could be manipulated by the order in which he or she was exposed to property right structures. Because bargainers who are first asked to bargain without property rights grasp the legitimate nature of unilateral property rights, these bargains were both efficient and mutually advantageous.

Since then, behavioral economics has, with limited success, pushed bargaining models to the limit in an effort to isolate and identify selfless versus selfish behavior in bargaining games. The Dictator game is the extreme example of a bargaining game. Self-interested strategic behavior is controlled by giving a person complete control over the distribution of wealth. While theory predicts that people with complete control will offer up nothing to others, Hoffman, McCabe, and Smith (1996) found that they still share the wealth in about 40 percent of the observed bargains. Such other-regarding choice is another example of behavior that differs from what is predicted by standard game theory models. The results in Cherry, Frykblom, and Shogren (2002), however, suggest other-regarding behavior arises from strategic concerns, not altruism.

Using Mechanism Design to Control for Market Failure

The final example considers how behavioral failure can affect mechanism design to control for market failure. Mechanism design imposes constraints on individual rationality, and assumes rational responses to incentive-based menus (see, e.g., Bénabou and Tirole 2003). But as discussed throughput this article, people do not always react as predicted if their rationality and willpower are bounded. The general economics literature contains a few attempts to account for such behavioral failures in mechanism design. Esteban and Miyagawa (2006) construct a mechanism in which a person suffers from self-control problems and temptation. Within this mechanism, this person prefers to choose from a smaller rather than a larger menu, even if the tempting alternatives are off the equilibrium path. This smaller-is-better finding also emerges in Gruber and Mullainathan (2005), who argue that US and Canadian smokers are happier with higher cigarette taxes. Another example is Aronsson and Thunström (2006), who construct an optimal tax-subsidy scheme for people who suffer from self-control problems that lead to obesity and poor health (also see the optimal sin tax discussion in O'Donoghue and Rabin 2006).

Few such examples exist in the environmental literature. One exception is Johansson (1997), who considers how bounded selfishness—altruism—affects the design of a Pigovian tax. In general, he finds that the existence of altruism itself is insufficient to generate a lower Pigovian tax. Another exception is Löfgren's (2003) work on optimal green taxation given addictive behavior, rational and otherwise. Using the theory of rational addiction, she considers how myopic and time-inconsistent addictive behavior might affect the design of an optimal environmental tax, given that consumption of the addictive good causes a harmful externality (e.g., car driving releases pollution). Her results suggest that the optimal environmental tax should exceed the standard Pigovian tax.

Interestingly, we found no papers (as of September 2007) that examine the existence or implications of behavioral failure within a marketable permit system. This may be because we did not look hard enough or because no one has written much about it; or, potentially more fascinating, it may be because the tradable permit mechanism designed to correct market failure also works to correct behavioral failure. We will return to this point.

When Are Behavioral Failures Relevant?

The previous examples illustrate why behavioral economics could well play a bigger role in how we think about environmental and resource economics. This conclusion, however, has not been accepted by all researchers. For instance, Rubinstein (2006) and Harrison (2005) provide biting assessments of the power and science that underlie many of the popular works in behavioral economics. They warn readers new to the field to read the literature more critically and to look out for the selling (or overselling) of scientific ideas, experimental control (or lack of it), the match (or mismatch) of theory and design, the muddling of concepts and terms, and the lack of critical peer oversight.

But the issue is not whether behavioral failure exists; it does. Rather, the issue is whether such behavioral failures exist only in the tails of the distribution, or whether these failures are robust to institutional designs and result in nontrivial deviations from efficiency (see Smith 1991, 2003). The key is to separate anecdotes from systematic behavior, and to understand the context of market experience and exchange institutions, which serve to push behavior more toward the *"Homo Economicus"* fiction we assume in our models. Before environmental economists sign up for the behavioralist union card, researchers should ask two related questions: Are these behavioral failures *relevant* to the markets of interest? Are these behavioral failures *relevant* to the policies prescribed to correct for missing markets?

Robustness and Order of Importance

When defining relevance, there are two issues one must consider—robustness and order of importance. First, an anomaly is relevant if it remains robust to the environment(s) of interest. An anomaly may be consistently observed in laboratory or field experiments, but this does not imply it will be robust to naturally occurring contexts of interest. There will always be a question about whether the constructed environment is sufficiently rich to elicit behavior that is consistent with what would be expressed in natural economic environments with real economic commitments. Empirical testing and observation from naturally occurring situations and data are necessary to establish relevance. We recognize this is not an easy charge, but it is a necessary condition to fully understand the relevance of any behavioral bias to economic phenomena.

Consider, for example, the case of altruistic behavior, which has been explored within a laboratory context for over thirty years (e.g., Guth, Schmittberger, and Schwarze 1982; Hoffman and Spitzer 1982). A recent study by Laury and Taylor (2006) suggests that even if altruistic behavior is observed in the lab, one cannot necessarily use it to predict behavior in naturally occurring environments. Laury and Taylor explored whether the selfless behavior in the lab would spill over to how people made contributions to a real public good. They found that purely selfish players (zero contributions) were less likely to give to the naturally occurring public good. But, using their measure of altruism, they could not predict with any degree of confidence the other subjects' level of contributions toward the naturally occurring public good.

Even if an anomaly is robust to policy-relevant environments, the next question is whether the phenomenon is of first-order or second-order importance. An anomaly must be nontrivial to be relevant for policy-making. An anomaly can be defined as nontrivial if it results in identifiable and significant reallocation of resources compared to the economic outcome that would occur without the anomalous behavior. If there is no detectable change in resource allocation due to a behavioral bias on the part of any agents involved, then the bias is irrelevant. But efficiency losses need not occur for a bias to be relevant.[2] The comparison to a "bias-free" counterfactual may be of interest for equity, fairness, or other social concerns.

Identifying Relevant Anomalies

Identification of a relevant anomaly is a nontrivial task in itself. No single experiment or empirical paper can accomplish such a task; this is a long-term exercise based on replication across alternative contexts. Recall the idea of inductive inference, and Platt's (1964, p. 347) description of a strong inference approach to scientific inquiry:

Strong inference consists of applying the following steps to every problem in science, formally, explicitly, and regularly:

---

[2]A comparison can be made to the classic case of the perfect-price discriminating monopoly in which no loss in market efficiency occurs. This market structure is of interest, and has important normative concerns, even if it does not result in an efficiency loss.

1. Devising alternative hypotheses.
2. Devising a crucial experiment (or several of them), with alternative possible outcomes, each of which will, as nearly as possible, exclude one or more of the hypotheses.
3. Carrying out the experiment so as to get a clean result.
4. Recycling the procedure, making subhypotheses or sequential hypotheses to refine the possibilities that remain; and so on.

Why restate a classic of modern hypothesis testing? Because much criticism within the profession has been aimed at the behavioral economics literature (and vice versa) with a seeming "you're with us, or you're against us" mentality (e.g., see Rubenstein 2006). This is certainly not new in economics or scientific inquiry. Again, Platt (1964) offers this insight (p. 146): "The conflict and exclusion of alternatives that is necessary to sharp inductive inference has been all too often a conflict between men, each with his single Ruling Theory." He also offers this solution:

> But whenever each man begins to have multiple working hypotheses, it becomes purely a conflict between ideas. It becomes much easier then for each of us to aim every day at conclusive disproofs—at *strong* inference—without either reluctance or combativeness.

If a research program is to become convincing evidence of the relevance of behavioral anomalies for naturally occurring economic phenomena, particularly for environmental and resource economics problems, it should begin with a strong inference approach. Vigilant hypothesis design, experimentation, and empirical investigation will move the field forward and reduce the number of studies reporting results that fail to reject a *just so story*.[3]

A key feature of social science research is that convincing evidence is only secured when we include empirical evidence from the naturally occurring world. Laboratory or field experiments alone cannot establish the relevance of a behavioral bias. They may strongly indicate relevance as the body of evidence grows, but such experiments are unlikely to stand on their own without empirical investigation. Within a market context, the work by DellaVigna and Malmendier (2004) is an example of research that seeks nonexperimental evidence of behavioral biases. They approach the question of behavioral biases from a background in contract theory. Their opening paragraph reiterates these points:

> A growing body of laboratory and field evidence documents deviations from standard preferences and biases in decision-making. If deviations are systematic and persistent, profit-maximizing firms should respond to them and

---

[3]Playing off the title of Rudyard Kipling's *Just So Stories for Little Children*, a "just so story" is a term used in social sciences to refer to narrative explanations about natural phenomena that are not falsifiable.

tailor their contracts and pricing schemes in response. (DellaVigna and Malmendier, p. 354).

They further note (p. 357) that "[t]he design of contracts is a key test for the relevance of deviations. Firms would not respond to consumer deviations that are not systematic or limited to small stakes." DellaVigna and Malmendier develop a model of firm behavior in a market in which firms are assumed to be rational, and consumers are assumed to be time-inconsistent. Their model leads to competing hypotheses regarding a firm's optimal contract design when consumers are time-inconsistent (and who are naïve about their time inconsistency) versus when they are time-consistent. While their empirical testing is more anecdotal than formal, their overall approach is the most important message—if behavioral biases are relevant, evidence in naturally occurring contexts should be discernable.

The search for relevance within the context of environmental and resource economics places a substantial burden on researchers, but it is a challenge that must be met before existing tools and prescriptions are discarded. DellaVigna and Malmendier had the luxury of looking at well-developed, naturally occurring markets for common private goods (credit cards, cellular phones, health clubs). But resource and environmental economists rarely have such luxury. Problems of interest typically involve missing markets and diffuse, largely undocumented economic behaviors. The effects of policy intervention on these diffuse economic activities are difficult to test using naturally occurring data, and constructed markets may lead to erroneous conclusions.

Most experimental results presented in the literature do not have naturally occurring markets against which we can shine a light on experimental methods and results—including field experiments.[4] This holds especially true for research on environmental and resource economics problems, in which by definition real markets are missing. The relevance of past and present laboratory and field experiments for environmental decision-making is not necessarily clear-cut; social context matters, institutional design matters, and economic circumstances matter.

---

[4]An exception is a well-cited study by Gneezy and Rustichini (2000), who tested the deterrence hypothesis using a field experiment to examine changes in behavior after a fine is imposed. The authors imposed a flat fine of about $2 per child on parents who picked up their children late from daycare centers in Israel and found that, contrary to predictions that might result from a standard deterrence model, late pickups actually increased after the fine was imposed. In contrast, we found that standard fines for late pickups at daycare centers in the southeastern United States are $1 to $2 *per minute, per child*, and that late pickups are infrequent events at these centers. While the Gneezy-Rustichini field experiment suggests that at some low prices, a perverse effect may arise, the bigger issue is whether those field experiment prices are relevant to naturally occurring and evolving markets.

Is Behavioral Failure Market Failure in Disguise?

The answer to this question depends on whom you ask. If repeated market experience pushes people toward more rational behavior, the answer is "yes"; if you believe that these behavioral failures are hardwired into our genetics, the answer is "no." The issue is how behavioral failures and market failures affect each other. Market experience affects behavioral failure by focusing on poor choices with high opportunity costs; behavioral failure affects the creation of new markets if behavioral biases prevent policy-makers and people from realizing how to capture potential gains. Two circular questions arise in the context of environmental policy: Does market failure lead to behavioral failure, which leads to continued market failure? Does behavioral failure prevent the creation of new markets that would eliminate the behavioral failure?

People are not always isolated decision-makers—they make decisions within, outside, and alongside the markets and social rules that punish and reward rational and consistent decision-making (see Bowles 1998). This view argues that tests of rational behavior should not be separated from the interactive experience provided by an exchange institution. These institutions matter because they provide a social context that rewards or punishes rational or irrational choices. The institution makes rationality a social, rather than an individual, construct—a key condition that separates economic rules from psychological rules of thumb. As noted by Tversky and Kahneman (2000, p. 223): "[t]he claim that the market can be trusted to correct the effect of individual irrationalities cannot be made without supporting evidence, and the burden of specifying a plausible corrective mechanism should rest on those who make the claim." In light of this perspective, researchers interested in environmental policy might want to think more about the power and the limits of the ideas of rationality spillovers and rationality crossovers.

Recent research shows that people quickly respond to the feedback and discipline of an active exchange institution by adjusting their behavior to more closely match rational choice theory (see, e.g., Chu and Chu 1990). Cherry, Crocker, and Shogren (2003) show that this result can extend beyond the exchange institution. They find that arbitrage increases rational behavior, and that it is not limited to the decisions within that institution, but spills over to parallel decisions that lack any discipline or exchange.[5] Cherry and Shogren (2007) take the idea one step further and examine whether rationality crossovers exist—to what degree the arbitrage-induced rationality can cross over to different decisions. They find that rationality crossovers do exist, but not always.

---

[5]Additional evidence supporting the idea of a rationality spillover is found in List (2004). While not referring to it as a rationality spillover, he finds that experienced sports card traders have fewer tendencies to exhibit the endowment effect for both sports cards *and* different goods like chocolates and mugs.

From a rationality spillover perspective, behavioral failure is a form of market failure. That said, even if markets exist, arbitrage does not guarantee the elimination of all behavioral failures from all choices and all people. If a market does not exist, behavioral failure is not guaranteed either—some spillovers could occur via other markets. Understanding this better will impact how researchers think about the elicitation of individual preferences and values in isolated and undisciplined settings. Given that most environmental policy questions fall within this messy confluence of market choices and missing markets, we need to learn more about the power of market-like arbitrage to remove behavioral failures. Understanding the institutions and contexts when and where rationality emerges seems most relevant for environmental economics and policy.

Do We Have a New Behavioral-Environmental Second-Best Problem?

We conclude with a discussion of our most speculative question about the interaction between behavioral failure and market failure. Recall that the theory of second-best says if you have two imperfections, correcting only one failure does not guarantee that social welfare will increase. One could conjecture that if behavioral and market failures exist simultaneously for some environmental good or service, correcting one failure without correcting the other could actually reduce overall welfare. This argument could hold whether or not one believes behavioral failure is hardwired into our genetics.

Think for a minute about the challenges that would likely arise if environmental and resource policy had to be designed to simultaneously correct for both market failure and behavioral failure. In the world of *ex-ante* policy design, where natural experiments are prohibited and *ex-post* policy changes are difficult if not impossible in the near-term, constructing policies or markets that promote efficiency without consideration of relevant behavioral failures would likely result in inefficient outcomes. For example, if a policy-maker introduces a Pigovian tax/subsidy to address climate change externalities without accounting for the fact that people overestimate low probability/high severity events, he could create a behaviorally ineffective tax that reduces total welfare. In theory, the policy-maker might be able to resolve this problem by adjusting the tax to account for the probability weighting issue, which would generate a behavioral first best out of a market failure. But then he or she would need more information than is normally assumed about the representative person, i.e., what is the curvature of the probability weighting function.

We find the idea of avoiding a behavioral second-best problem through creative incentive design to be a somewhat staggering proposition. Consider five sources of market failure commonly considered by resource and environmental economists: externalities, nonrival goods, nonexcludable goods, nonconvexities, and asymmetric information. Currently, well over twenty-five behavioral failures have been identified as relevant to economic decision-making. With only five sources of market failure, this means there are 125 possible failure-interactions, and this is only if the behavioral failures are all independent of each other.

Our question is this: would policies designed to affect each market failure also need to be differentiated to correct for each interactive behavioral failure? For example, when considering corrective policies for externality problems, might we also have to correct for loss aversion (i.e., people are risk averse for potential gains, and risk seeking for potential losses)? Perhaps this would be doable by redesigning our marketable permit system or the Pigovian tax. But that is only part of the story. What if our agent also suffers from coherent arbitrariness by anchoring on a random point and then acting relatively rationally? Now the Pigovian tax needs to account for both behavioral failures. But what if our agent is also prone to reversing preferences, is time-inconsistent, or exhibits other behavioral failures?

Moreover, our previous discussion assumes that there is some form of separability across these behavioral failures—that we can correct for each one independently within each market failure context. But what if there is some behavioral complementarity or substitutability across these biases? Do economists know whether the marginal impact of loss aversion is attenuated or accentuated by an increase in the degree of coherent arbitrariness? Or whether the incremental effects of time inconsistency are increased with a greater tendency toward preference reversal? We have not seen these types of results documented in the economics literature because researchers usually focus on only one behavioral failure at a time. The preferred research strategy is to add the one degree of freedom needed to capture the behavior ignored by rational choice theory (Shogren 2006b). Granted, it is an excellent research strategy to start simple and add complexity, but for policy decisions, the separability assumption seems rather *ad hoc*. And if one works out the logic to the total number of behavioral failures thus far identified in the behavioral literature, there are thousands of potential interactions between biases to be explored. Would we need behaviorally differentiated taxes, with each tax targeted to each agent's particular failing? If so, the sheer magnitude of the task implies policy impasse. Policy-makers might be able to reduce the number of relevant interactive biases based on *ex-ante* intuition, but these choices would still be subject to *ex-post* evaluation. Or researchers might be able to reduce the number of relevant biases by identifying irrelevant behavioral failures, in which case policy design might become more tractable.

Our arguments might not convince the reader to completely rethink economic analysis on account of the identified behavioral-environmental second-best problem. But analysts should be aware of instances in which the evidence points to a problem, and they should rigorously address these realities to advance the science of economics. Considering all possible simultaneous behavioral-market failure combinations in *ex-ante* policy design is surely too costly to undertake in meaningful policy settings. This suggests the use of adaptive regulatory schemes in which policy-makers adjust market-failure regulation for behavioral failures that may arise. Researchers need to explore options for flexible institutional design that could be used to account for key failures—market, behavioral, or both. Perhaps this is all pointing to marketable permits as the best institution to avoid the behavioral second-best problem in environmental policy. Marketable permit systems, provided they are active exchange institutions, could be the most effective behavioral disciplining device, or at a minimum, the institutional design least affected by behavioral failures.

Conclusions

In some settings, individuals make isolated choices that are not accountable to others. If there are no consequences, an individual can change risk attitudes at will, reverse his or her choices on a whim, or make seemingly random choices based on unobservable fancy. In such cases, rational choice assertions about how people behave seem less relevant. Rational choice theory does not describe or predict such inconsistent behavior for environmental goods and services. Here, the standard model is simply "too thin" because it implicitly assumes individual decisions are being made within some (nonexistent) market that is making its own rational allocation and specialization decisions. As discussed earlier, environmental and resource economics may suffer if it relies on the standard model, since the model does not address the behavioral failures of human nature that are no longer attenuated by a well-functioning market.

Behavioral failures have prompted some researchers to argue that government intervention can be justified beyond the standard market failure motivation. The argument goes that government intervention in private decision-making is justified—even in a full functioning market—when people know what is good for them, but still cannot make those "correct" choices. This new form of intervention has been called *soft paternalism, libertarian paternalism*, or *paternalism for conservatives* (see Thaler and Sunstein 2003). This new paternalism captures the notion that people need sin taxes and outright bans to protect themselves from their own self-destructive biases and lack of self-control. If this new paternalism has merit, environmental policy-makers will have to consider how the taxonomy of behavioral failures might affect the design of efficiency-promoting rules and regulations.[6] This means that environmental policy-makers might

---

[6] The soft paternalism idea has not gained widespread acceptance among most economists. Smith (2007), for instance, offers a skeptical account of a paternalistic approach to guiding individual decision-making when the person is deemed incapable of improving his own welfare due to a behavioral failure. Who decides what choices are actually welfare improving for individuals? Experts? Policy-makers? And who says these people or groups are not without their own set of behavioral limitations—workaholism, procrastination, myopia, and so on?

have to think about correcting for both market failure and behavioral failure, and doing so simultaneously.

Environmental economics has a long history of developing solutions to market failures. To the credit of environmental policy over the past 40 years, its focus on markets and market incentives is likely to attenuate the problems behavioral failure might present in the environmental policy process. That said, environmental and resource economics still must address questions of environmental lotteries, environmental valuation, and decisions made outside the confines of repeated market interactions. In these contexts, behavioral failures might lead to inefficient policy design. The first step must be identifying those behavioral failures that are the most relevant for environmental policy. With the relevance of behavioral anomalies identified, or at least given a preponderance of evidential support, the search for solutions should begin in earnest.

While we applaud the challenge that behavioral economics presents to the economist's modeling norm, we conclude that the evidence from behavioral economics remains insufficient to support the wholesale rejection of rational choice theory within environmental and resource economics. This does not mean, however, that anomalous behavior is nonexistent; as discussed above, nature's goods and services frequently lack the active market-like arbitrage needed to encourage consistent and rational choice. We believe it is crucial to identify the economic circumstances, institutional designs, and social contexts in which rational choice theory works and those where it fails to capture observed behavior. Explicitly incorporating the idea of behavioral failures into the research agenda for environmental policy seems like a step worth pursuing, if only to rule some of them out as second-order effects. We also urge the reader to keep open a cautious eye—critical review of new evidence is necessary and the evidence should be germane to the questions and the policy contexts that resource and environmental economists think about.

REFERENCES

Aronsson, T., and L. Thunström. 2006. Optimal paternalism: Sin taxes and health subsidies. *Umeå Economic Studies*, No. 662, Umeå University.

Arrow, K. 1969. The organization of economic activity: Issues pertinent to the choice of market versus nonmarket allocation. *The Analysis and Evaluation of Public Expenditures: The PPB System*. Washington, DC: Joint Economic Committee, 91st Congress, pp. 47–64.

———. 1987. Rationality of self and others in an economic system. In *Rational Choice: The Contrast between Economics and Psychology*, ed. R. Hogarth and M. Reder. Chicago: University of Chicago Press.

Becker, G. 2002. Interview. *The Region*. Federal Reserve Bank of Minneapolis. Available at [www.minneapolisfed.org/publications papers/pub display.cfm?id=3407 (accessed 6/6/11)].

Bénabou, R., and J. Tirole. 2003. Intrinsic and extrinsic motivation. *Review of Economic Studies* 70:489–520.

Bergstrom, T. 1989. Love and spaghetti: The opportunity cost of virtue. *Journal of Economic Perspectives* 3:165–73.

Bohm, P. 1972. Estimating demand for public goods: An experiment. *European Economic Review* 3:111–30.

Borges, B., and J. Knetsch. 1998. Tests of market outcomes with asymmetric valuations of gains and losses: Smaller gains, fewer trades, and less value. *Journal of Economic Behavior and Organization* 33:185–93.

Bowles, S. 1998. Endogenous preferences: The cultural consequences of markets and other economic institutions. *Journal of Economic Literature* 36:75–111.

Braga, J., and C. Starmer. 2005. Preference anomalies, preference elicitation, and the discovered preference hypothesis. *Environmental and Resource Economics* 32:55–89.

Brookshire, D., D. Coursey, and W. Schulze. 1990. Experiments in the solicitation of private and public values: An overview. In *Advances in Behavioral Economics*, ed. L. Green and J. Kagel. Norwood, NJ: Ablex Publishing Corporation; 2:173–90.

Camerer, C. 2003. *Behavioral Game Theory*. Princeton, NJ: Princeton University Press.

Cherry, T., T. Crocker, and J. Shogren. 2003. Rationality spillovers. *Journal of Environmental Economics and Management* 45:63–84.

Cherry, T., P. Frykblom, and J. Shogren. 2002. Hardnose the dictator. *American Economic Review* 92:1218–21.

Cherry, T., and J. Shogren. 2007. Rationality crossovers. *Journal of Economic Psychology* 28:261–77.

Chu, Y.-P., and R.-L. Chu. 1990. The subsidence of preference reversals in simplified and market-like experimental settings: A note. *American Economic Review* 80:902–11.

Coase, R. 1960. The problem of social cost. *Journal of Law and Economics* 3:1–44.

Coursey, D., J. Hovis, and W. Schulze. 1987. The disparity between willingness to accept and willingness to pay measures of value. *Quarterly Journal of Economics* 102:679–90.

Crocker, T., J. Shogren, and P. Turner. 1998. Incomplete beliefs and nonmarket valuation. *Resources and Energy Economics* 20:139–62.

DellaVigna, S., and U. Malmendier. 2004. Contract design and self-control: Theory and evidence. *Quarterly Journal of Economics* 119:353–402.

Esteban, S., and E. Miyagawa. 2006. Temptation, self-control, and competitive nonlinear pricing. *Economics Letters* 90:348–55.

Fehr, E., and S. Gächter. 2000. Cooperation and punishment in public goods experiments. *American Economic Review* 90:980–94.

Flachaire, E., and G. Hollard. 2007. Starting point bias and respondent uncertainty in dichotomous choice contingent valuation surveys. *Resources and Energy Economics* 29:183–94.

Gneezy, U., and A. Rustichini. 2000. A fine is a price. *Journal of Legal Studies* 29:1–17.

Grether, D. 1980. Bayes's rule as a descriptive model: The representative heuristic. *Quarterly Journal of Economics* 95:537–57.

Gruber, J., and S. Mullainathan. 2005. Do cigarette taxes make smokers happier? *Advances in Economic Analysis and Policy* 5: Art. 4. [Available at http://www.bepress.com/bejeap/advances/vol5/iss1/art4 (accessed 6/6/11)].

Guth, W., R. Schmittberger, and B. Schwarze. 1982. An experimental analysis of ultimatum bargaining. *Journal of Economic Behavior and Organization* 3:367–88.

Harrison, G. 2005. Review of advances in behavioral economics. *Journal of Economic Psychology* 26:793–95.

Harrison, G., and M. McKee. 1985. Experimental evaluation of the Coase theorem. *Journal of Law and Economics* 28:653–70.

Hoffman, E., K. McCabe, and V. Smith. 1996. Social distance and other-regarding behavior in dictator games. *American Economic Review* 86:653–60.

Hoffman, E., and M. Spitzer. 1982. The Coase theorem: Some experimental tests. *Journal of Law and Economics* 25:73–98.

Johansson, O. 1997. Optimal Pigovian taxes under altruism. *Land Economics* 73:297–308.

Kahneman, D. 1986. *Comments. In Valuing Environmental Goods: An Assessment of the Contingent Valuation Method*, ed. R. Cummings, D. Brookshire, and W. Schulze. Totowa, NJ: Rowman and Allenheld, pp. 185–94.

Kahneman, D., and J. Knetsch. 1992. Valuing public goods: The purchase of moral satisfaction. *Journal of Environmental Economics and Management* 22:57–70.

Kahneman, D., J. Knetsch, and R. Thaler. 1990. Experimental tests of the endowment effect and the Coase theorem. *Journal of Political Economy* 98:1325–48.

Knetsch, J. 1989. The endowment effect and evidence of non-reversible indifference curves. *American Economic Review* 79:1277–84.

———. 1997. Evaluation and environmental policies: Recent behavioural findings and further implications. In *Sustainability and Global Environmental Policy: New Perspectives*, ed. A. Dragun and K. Jakobsson. Cheltenham, UK: Edward Elgar Publishing, pp. 193–212.

Knetsch, J., and J. Sinden. 1984. Willingness to pay and compensation demanded: Experimental evidence of an unexpected disparity in measures of values. *Quarterly Journal of Economics* 99:507–21.

Kolstad, C. 1999. *Environmental Economics*. New York: Oxford University Press.

Kroll, S., T. Cherry, and J. Shogren. 2007. Voting, punishment, and public goods. *Economic Inquiry* 45:557–70.

Laury, S., and L. Taylor. 2006. Altruism spillovers: Are behaviors in context-free experiments predictive of altruism toward a naturally occurring public good? *Journal of Economic Behavior and Organization* [65(1): 9–29. Available at www.sciencedirect.com/science/article/pii/S0167268106001107 (accessed 6/6/11)].

Ledyard, J. O. 1995. Public goods: A survey of experimental research. In *Handbook of Experimental Economics*, ed. J. Kagel and A. Roth. Princeton, NJ: Princeton University Press, pp. 111–94.

List, J. 2004. Neoclassical theory versus prospect theory: Evidence from the marketplace. *Econometrica* 72:615–25.

Löfgren, Å. 2003. The effect of addiction on environmental taxation in a first- and second-best world. Working Papers in Economics No. 91, Department of Economics, Göteborg University. [Available at http://swopec.hhs.se/gunwpe/abs/gunwpe0091.htm (accessed 6/6/11)].

Loomes, G., C. Starmer, and R. Sugden. 2003. Do anomalies disappear in repeated markets? *Economic Journal* 113:C153–66.

Mason, C, J. Shogren, C. Settle, and J. List. 2005. Investigating risky choices over losses using experimental data. *Journal of Risk and Uncertainty* 31:187–215.

Mazzotta, M., and J. Opaluch. 1995. Decision making when choices are complex: A test of Heiner's hypothesis. *Land Economics* 71:500–15.

McFadden, D. 1999. Rationality for economists? *Journal of Risk and Uncertainty* 19:73–105.

Mullainathan, S., and R. Thaler. 2000. Behavioral economics. MIT Department of Economics Working Paper No. 00–27.

Noussair, C., and S. Tucker. 2005. Combining monetary and social sanctions to promote cooperation. *Economic Inquiry* 43:649–60.

O'Donoghue, T., and M. Rabin. 2006. Optimal sin taxes. *Journal of Public Economics* 90:1825–49.

Ostrom, E. 2006. The value-added of laboratory experiments for the study of institutions and common-pool resources. *Journal of Economic Behavior and Organization* 61(2):149–63.

Ostrom, E., J. Walker, and R. Gardner. 1994. *Rules, Games, and Common-Pool Resources.* Ann Arbor, MI: University of Michigan Press.

Platt, J. 1964. Strong inference. *Science* 146:347–53.

Plott, C, and K. Zeiler. 2005a. The willingness to pay–willingness to accept gap, the "endowment effect": Subject misperceptions and experimental procedures for eliciting valuations. *American Economic Review* 95:530–45.

———. [2007]. Asymmetries in exchange behavior incorrectly interpreted as prospect theory. [*American Economic Review* 97(4): 1449–66. Available at www .aeaweb.org/articles.php?doi=10.1257/aer.97.4.1449 (accessed 6/6/11)].

Rabin, M. 1998. Psychology and economics. *Journal of Economic Literature* 36:11–46.

Ranjan, R., and J. Shogren. 2006. How probability weighting affects participation in water markets. *Water Resources Research* 42:262–82.

Rubinstein, A. 2006. Comments on behavioral economics. In *Advances in Economic Theory (2005 World Congress of the Econometric Society)*, ed. R. Blundell, W. K. Newey, and T. Persson, Vol. II. Cambridge: Cambridge University Press, pp. 246–54.

Sent, E.-M. 2004. Behavioral economics: How psychology made its (limited) way back into economics. *History of Political Economy* 36: 735–60.

Shaw, W. D., and R. Woodward. [2008]. Why environmental and resource economists should care about non-expected utility models. *Resource and Energy Economics* [30(1): 66–89. Available at www.sciencedirect.com/science/article/ pii/S092876550700019X (accessed 6/6/11)].

Shogren, J. 2006a. Experimental methods and valuation. In *Handbook of Environmental Economics*, ed. K. G. Mäler and J. R. Vincent, Vol. 2. Amsterdam: Elsevier, pp. 969–1027.

———. 2006b. A rule of one. *American Journal of Agricultural Economics* 88:1147–59.

Shogren, J., S. Cho, C. Koo, J. List, C. Park, P. Polo, and R. Wilhelmi. 2001. Auction mechanisms and the measurement of WTP and WTA. *Resource and Energy Economics* 23:97–109.

Shogren, J., S. Shin, D. Hayes, and J. Kliebenstein. 1994. Resolving differences in willingness to pay and willingness to accept. *American Economic Review* 84: 255–70.

Simon, H. 1957. *A Behavioral Model of Rational Choice, in Models of Man, Social and Rational: Mathematical Essays on Rational Human Behavior in a Social Setting.* New York: Wiley.

Smith, V. K. 2007. Reflections on the literature. *Review of Environmental Economics and Policy* 1(1):152–65.

Smith, V. L. 1991. Rational choice: The contrast between economics and psychology. *Journal of Political Economy* 99:877–97.

———. 1998. The two faces of Adam Smith. *Southern Economic Journal* 65:1–19.

———. 2003. Constructivist and ecological rationality in economics. *American Economic Review* 93:465–508.

Starmer, C. 2000. Developments in non-expected utility theory: The hunt for a descriptive theory of choice under risk. *Journal of Economic Literature* 38:332–82.

Sugden, R. 2005. Coping with preference anomalies in benefit-cost analysis: A market-simulation approach. *Environmental and Resource Economics* 32:129–60.

Sunstein, C., ed. 2000. *Behavioral Law and Economics*. Cambridge: Cambridge University Press.

Thaler, R., and C. Sunstein. 2003. Libertarian paternalism is not an oxymoron. *University of Chicago Law Review* 70:1159–1202.

Tversky, A., and D. Kahneman. 2000. Rational choice and the framing of decisions. In *Choices, Values, and Frames,* ed. D. Kahneman and A. Tversky. Cambridge: Cambridge University Press, pp. 209–23.

Tversky, A., and I. Simonson. 1993. Context-dependent preferences. *Management Science* 39:1179–89.

Weber, B., A. Holt, C. Neuhaus, P. Trautner, C. Elger, and T. Teichert. 2007. Neural evidence for reference-dependence in real-market transactions. *NeuroImage* 35:441–47.

Yun-Peng, C., and C. Ruey-Ling. 1990. The Subsidence of Preference Reversals in Simplified and Market-Like Experimental Settings: A note. *American Economic Review* 80:902–11.

II

The Costs of Environmental Protection

4 Perspectives on Pollution Abatement and Competitiveness: Theory, Data, and Analyses*

Carl Pasurka

Carl Pasurka is an economist in the Office of Policy, Economics and Innovation, US Environmental Protection Agency

Introduction

In recent decades, there has been a growing interest in reducing the undesirable by-products (i.e., emissions of pollutants) associated with producing and consuming marketed goods and services. Such reductions in emissions are achieved by reallocating inputs from producing marketed goods and services to pollution abatement. However, as government regulations restricting emissions have been implemented, concerns have emerged about how this real-location of inputs to pollution abatement affects the economic health of nations, industries, and firms.[1]

Probably, the earliest manifestation of concern about the effect of pollution abatement on competitiveness can be found in the OECD's establishment in 1972 of the "Polluter Pays Principle" (PPP), which states that "the polluter should bear the expenses of carrying out (pollution prevention and control) measures decided by public authorities to ensure that the environment is in an acceptable state. In other words, the cost of these measures should be reflected in the cost of goods and services which cause pollution in production and/or consumption. Such measures should not be accompanied by subsidies that would create significant distortions in international trade and investment" (OECD 2002). Although the PPP discouraged government subsidies for pollution abatement, it did not mandate identical levels

"Perspectives on Pollution Abatement and Competitiveness: Theory, Data, and Analyses" by Carl Pasurka. *Review of Environmental Economics and Policy* 2. 2008. Pp. 194–218. Reprinted with permission.

*The author wishes to thank Ian Lange and an anonymous referee for helpful comments on earlier drafts of this study, and Yenmeng Li, Graeme Oakley, Carsten Stahmer, Kimio Uno, and Taiwan's Directorate General of Budget, Accounting, and Statistics (DGBAS) for assistance with data acquisition. All views expressed in this article are those of the author and do not reflect the opinions of the US Environmental Protection Agency. Of course, any errors are the sole responsibility of the author.

[1]For surveys of the link between pollution abatement and competitiveness, see Jaffe et al. (1995); SQW—Economic Development Consultants (2006); and the United Nations (2006).

of regulatory intensity across countries. While variations in regulatory stringency across jurisdictions may represent optimal behavior, it does little to ease the anxiety of groups adversely affected by changes in relative competitiveness. This has resulted in continuing interest in studying the links between differences in regulatory stringency and competitiveness.

The purpose of this article is to present existing national- and industry-level data on pollution abatement costs and emissions and discuss and summarize the theoretical and empirical literature on the link between pollution abatement and competitiveness. In the next section, competitiveness is defined and alternative theoretical perspectives on pollution abatement and competitiveness are presented. The following section reviews and compares national- and industry-level data on the cost of inputs assigned to pollution abatement. The fourth section briefly discusses emissions data that are currently available. The fifth section reviews empirical studies of pollution abatement and indicators of competitiveness. The main findings of the article are summarized in the final section.

Theoretical Perspectives on Competitiveness and Pollution Abatement

Competitiveness is an elusive concept whose definition remains subject to debate. At least some of the difficulty stems from uncertainty over whether competitiveness should be viewed from the perspective of a nation, an industry, or a firm. An early, widely adopted definition of national competitiveness is "the degree to which it can, under free and fair market conditions, produce goods and services that meet the test of international markets, while at the same time maintaining or expanding the real incomes of its citizens" (President's Commission on Industrial Competitiveness 1985, p. 6). Lawrence (2007) sets forth three questions to guide an assessment of national competitiveness:

1. How well is an economy performing relative to other economies?
2. How well has an economy performed in international trade?
3. Is the economy doing the best it can?

While acknowledging that his definition fails to incorporate factors such as environmental quality, Lawrence argues that a country's living standard (i.e., gross domestic product per capita) is the most important indicator of its economy's performance. Because productivity growth is the primary factor associated with improving material living standards, it is possible to trace the link between pollution abatement and the material standard of living through the link between pollution abatement and productivity.

Because pollution abatement reallocates inputs from producing marketed goods and services measured by GDP to activities excluded from

GDP (i.e., reduced levels of emissions that result in a cleaner environment), there is likely to be reduced production of marketed goods and services used to satisfy household consumption. While a short-run (i.e., fixed technology and inputs) analysis finds that pollution abatement results in a decline in the material living standard of a society, pollution abatement also positively affects the standard of living via improved environmental quality. Thus, if we adopt a definition of competitiveness that embraces "sustainable development," GDP represents an unsatisfactory measure of a country's standard of living.[2]

Although national competitiveness remains a popular concept (World Economic Forum 2006), some scholars (e.g., Krugman 1994) have expressed concerns about referring to the competitiveness of a nation. As a result, competitiveness is often discussed from the perspective of a firm or industry. According to the President's Commission on Industrial Competitiveness (1985, p. 6), a firm demonstrates its competitiveness by producing "products or services of superior quality or lower costs than domestic and international competitors. Competitiveness is then synonymous with a firm's long-run profit performance and its ability to compensate its employees and provide superior returns to its owners." Firms within an industry can be inefficient, while the industry overall enjoys a comparative advantage relative to competitors in other countries. Nevertheless, it follows that the extent to which an industry is competitive is at least in part a reflection of the competitiveness of firms comprising that industry. While changes in a firm's productivity are an indicator of the effect of pollution abatement on its competitiveness, changes in trade balances and foreign direct investment (FDI) are also frequently used to indicate an industry's competitiveness.

Pollution Abatement

When regulating a technology that produces emissions, abatement costs can be identified by decomposing the technology into two components (see Fare, Grosskopf, and Pasurka 2006).[3] The first component employs inputs to produce a marketed good or service (e.g., electricity) and at least one pollutant (e.g., SO_2 emissions). The marketed good output can be consumed as a final output (e.g., sold to households) or used as an intermediate input by the second component (e.g., an end-of-pipe, EOP, abatement technology such as a flue gas desulfurization system). Emissions generated by the first component, which represent gross pollution, reflect quantities produced after change-in-process (CIP) abatement activities (i.e., pollution abatement integrated into the production process) or no treatment at all. These pollutants can be discharged from the plant or sent to the EOP abatement technology that combines inputs, including emissions sent for treatment, to produce net pollution. In this model, reallocating inputs from the first to

---

[2]Some studies, including the World Bank (2006), incorporate environmental factors into adjusted measures of national wealth.

[3]Pizer and Kopp (2005) survey the literature on calculating pollution abatement costs.

the second component reduces production of both marketed goods and emissions. Hence, abatement costs can be determined by calculating either the cost of inputs assigned to pollution abatement or the production value of the marketed good that is foregone.

Because the information required to simultaneously model both components is rarely available, two methodologies have evolved to measure the productivity effects of pollution abatement. The "assigned input" model constitutes the basis for surveys that collect information on the costs of inputs assigned to pollution abatement. While this model requires information on production of marketed goods plus the quantities of inputs assigned to both production of marketed goods and pollution abatement, it requires no information on emissions. Although this remains a popular strategy for calculating abatement costs, concerns have been expressed about the quality of information generated by these surveys. Initially, EOP technologies were the preferred strategy for reducing emissions. This is because EOP technologies are separate technologies, which simplifies the task of determining which input costs are assigned to pollution abatement. Over time, producers have shifted from EOP strategies to CIP strategies. But because it is more difficult to determine the share of an integrated technology that should be assigned to pollution abatement, estimates of CIP costs are more problematic.

The second methodology models the joint production of marketed goods plus emissions (Färe et al. 1989). The "joint production model" only requires information on total inputs and the quantities of marketed goods produced plus emissions. Hence, the technology can be represented by a production possibilities frontier, in which a producer chooses between different combinations of marketed goods and emissions. As inputs are assigned to pollution abatement, the opportunity cost of abatement is revealed as the value of the reduced production of marketed goods.

Shifts in a production possibilities frontier reflect the combined effect of invention, innovation, and technology diffusion (see Jaffe, Newell, and Stavins 2003). While an invention represents the development of a new product or process, it must be brought to market to constitute an innovation. Hence, one interpretation of "best practice" frontiers is that they represent production possibilities if all innovations are fully diffused, while inefficient production (production inside the frontier) occurs when innovations are not fully diffused (see Jaffe, Newell, and Stavins 2003, p. 468). There are two perspectives on calculating inefficiency and technical change (i.e., shifts in the frontier) in the presence of emissions. The traditional perspective credits a producer for expanding production of marketed goods but ignores emissions (see Färe, Grosskopf, and Pasurka 2007). In contrast, the "evolutionary" perspective credits a producer for simultaneously expanding production of marketed goods and contracting emissions (see Chung, Färe, and Grosskopf 1997 for an example of one approach).

The Link between Pollution Abatement
and Competitiveness: Traditional Perspective

The traditional perspective emphasizes optimizing firms that confront trade-offs between producing marketed goods and environmental quality. While reducing emissions may improve the overall welfare of a nation, the traditional perspective argues that a unilateral increase in pollution abatement costs (PAC) results in some firms and industries becoming less competitive (see Palmer, Oates, and Portney 1995). For a polluting firm or industry that is producing on its production possibilities frontier, pollution abatement reduces both emissions and production of marketed goods as inputs are moved from production of marketed goods to pollution abatement. As a result, for a given technology, pollution abatement is associated with declining productivity and increasing opportunity costs of reducing emissions. If the model is extended to allow for "induced innovation," the change in the price (i.e., the opportunity cost) of emissions resulting from environmental regulations relative to the price of marketed goods spurs expenditures on R&D, with the goal of developing products and processes that reduce emissions while also increasing production of marketed goods.

Extending the framework to allow interactions among producers (i.e., a general equilibrium model) yields a more complicated picture. Changes in production costs associated with introducing environmental regulations result in the movement of primary inputs (e.g., labor and capital) among industries. The direct effect of environmental regulations is a decline in productivity as inputs are reassigned from producing marketed goods to pollution abatement. The reduction in an industry's output that is associated with the productivity decline may be offset or exacerbated depending on whether there is an increase or decrease in the demand for the industry's output from other industries. Some of the demand for an industry's output may be associated with environmental related activities. These activities are sometimes referred to as the environmental protection (EP) industry, which is composed of firms that produce the goods and services purchased by regulated producers in order to meet environmental regulations.[4]

Closely related to productivity concerns are concerns about the effect of pollution abatement on employment. While one direct effect of decreasing output in regulated industries is declining employment in those industries, these declines are offset by employment increases in other sectors of the economy if production occurs on the frontier. Some of these employment increases are associated with activities of the EP industry.

The effect of pollution abatement on economy-wide employment depends on whether existing unemployment is involuntary or voluntary. If the labor

---

[4]More specifically, according to the OECD (1999, p. 9), the EP industry "consists of activities which produce goods and services to measure, prevent, limit, minimize or correct environmental damage to water, air, and soil, as well as problems related to waste, noise and eco-systems. This includes cleaner technologies, products and services that reduce environmental risk and minimize pollution and resource use."

market is in disequilibrium (i.e., involuntary unemployment exists), there is the possibility of employment increases if the appropriate environmental policies are implemented. If the labor market is in equilibrium (i.e., all unemployment is voluntary), then environmental policies must induce workers to substitute work for leisure in order for employment to increase as a result of environmental policies.

Finally, as pollution abatement increases unit production costs, a country's export industries and import competing industries become less competitive. In addition, increased production costs associated with pollution abatement may discourage FDI in the domestic economy and encourage an outflow of FDI to economies with less stringent regulations.

The Link between Pollution Abatement and Competitiveness: Porter Hypothesis Perspective

The "evolutionary" perspective offers an alternative approach to the link between pollution abatement and competitiveness—satisficing firms whose objective is not profit maximization. This perspective provides a theoretical rationale for the win-win situation sometimes referred to as the Porter Hypothesis (see Porter and van der Linde 1995). Here, unlike under the traditional perspective, an increase in regulatory stringency can trigger innovation and improve competitiveness, which opens the possibility of a win-win situation—an increase in both social welfare and the firm's profits.

There are several circumstances in which a firm may benefit from increased regulatory stringency. First, environmental regulations can lead to increased competitiveness of firms in the EP industry. Second, environmental regulations can stimulate product innovations leading to competitive gains for producers of "green" goods and services via improvements in either processes or product performance and quality. Finally, the most provocative claim is that regulations can stimulate regulated entities to undertake process innovation to become more efficient than they would have been without the regulations.

Validation of the Porter Hypothesis requires conditions where there is a decline in emissions and an increase in firm profits. The Porter Hypothesis says this can be achieved because firm inefficiencies are revealed through increasingly stringent environmental regulations.[5] However, while there is ample evidence of the existence of technical inefficiency and technical change, the extent to which increased regulatory stringency reduces inefficiency or triggers technical progress remains unresolved.

According to Jaffe, Newell, and Stavins (2003, p. 488), areas of agreement between the "win-win" Porter Hypothesis perspective and neoclassical economics (i.e., the traditional perspective) include: (1) environmental regulation is likely to stimulate innovation and (2) first adopters may gain a competitive advantage if domestic regulations anticipate world-wide trends in

---

[5]Wagner (2003); and Ambec and Barla (2006) summarize theoretical models of the Porter Hypothesis.

regulation. Areas of disagreement include: (1) the opportunity cost of R&D and management effort makes a true "win-win" outcome unlikely when cost-reducing innovation occurs and (2) the extent to which existing productivity studies capture innovation offsets (i.e., lower costs).

Comparing Pollution Abatement Costs across Countries

Investigations of pollution abatement and competitiveness make frequent use of national and industry pollution abatement cost (PAC) data.[6] This section summarizes national- and industrial-level PAC estimates from several international surveys. Although there are concerns about the accuracy of survey estimates of input costs assigned to pollution abatement, they represent the most readily available information on pollution abatement costs.

National Data

Plooy (1985), who compares industrial PAC in the Netherlands with Denmark, Germany, Sweden, and the United States, represents the first effort to assess the difficulties associated with comparing abatement costs across countries.[7] Next, the Organization for Economic Co-operation and Development (OECD) published four reports entitled *Pollution Control and Abatement Expenditure in OECD Countries* that reported PAC for the years between 1972 and 2000.[8] Based in part on the OECD studies, which show that historically the United States has reported some of the highest spending on pollution abatement as a share of GDP and as a share of business capital expenditures, Leonard (2003) concluded that US producers bear a higher regulatory burden than producers in other countries. However, starting in 1990, Austria, the Czech Republic, and Poland reported the largest shares of GDP assigned to pollution abatement. Similarly, the Czech Republic and Poland assigned the largest shares of business capital expenditures to pollution abatement during the 1990s.

Another OECD (2003a) report presented estimates of PAC as a percent of GDP between 1996 and 2001 for countries in Eastern Europe, the Caucasus, and Central Asia (see Appendix Table 3). These data show some republics of the former Soviet Union reporting values that are similar to those for Germany during this time period. However, the values for Germany and Portugal in this report differ dramatically from those in the OECD reports described above. This illustrates the difficulties associated with making

---

[6]Environmental taxes are excluded from the discussion of pollution abatement costs.

[7]Other efforts to compare pollution abatement cost surveys include Bouman (1998) (for Germany, the Netherlands, and the United States) and EuroStat (1994) for selected European countries.

[8]Appendix Tables 1 and 2 present a sample of the OECD data.

cross-country comparisons of PAC, and indicates that caution must be exercised when using these data.

Industry Data

National data are useful for making initial comparisons of regulatory burdens across countries, but they can obscure variations in costs across industries. Hence, industry-level PAC data may provide some useful insights.

From the early 1970s through the early 1980s, McGraw-Hill (various issues) published data on the percent of capital expenditures assigned to pollution abatement by US industrial firms, in both their US and overseas operations (see Appendix Table 4). The data reveal that during this time period, a larger share of American firms' capital expenditures on pollution abatement was assigned to domestic activities than to foreign operations.

As more countries collected industry-level information on PAC, Euro-Stat (2001a, 2002a, b) assembled these data[9] for EU-15 countries plus the ten accession countries.[10] Later, EuroStat (2005) provided summary statistics on pollution abatement costs for the mining, manufacturing, and electricity and water supply industries for 1997–2002. Most recently, the United Nations (2006, pp. 7–8) compared industry-level current account PAC expenditures as a share of gross output for seven European countries and the United States during the late 1990s. The PAC incurred by the US manufacturing sector (0.41 percent in 1999) was comparable to Finland (0.4 percent in 1998), but less than the burden on the manufacturing sectors of Austria (0.7 percent in 1998), Hungary (0.6 percent in 1999), and the United Kingdom (0.7 percent in 1997).

Comparison of Industrial-Level PAC Data for Nine Countries

There are no recent comparisons of industry-level PAC data for nations outside Europe and the United States. To fill this gap, PAC data for nine economies in different regions of the world are discussed and compared here.[11] For Europe, the countries are Germany, the Netherlands, Sweden, and the United Kingdom. For North America, the countries are Canada and the United States. For Asia and the Pacific, the countries are Australia, Japan, and Taiwan.

---

[9]The environmental accounts at [http://unstats.un.org/unsd/envaccounting/ceea/archive/EPEA/KS-39-01-320-EN.pdf (accessed 6/6/11)] provide industry-level emission and environmental protection expenditure data for EU countries.

[10]The EU-15 refers to the fifteen member countries of the EU prior to its 1 May 2004 expansion: Austria, Belgium, Denmark, Finland, France, Germany, Greece, Ireland, Italy, Luxembourg, the Netherlands, Portugal, Spain, Sweden, and the United Kingdom. The ten countries that acceded to the EU on 1 May 2004 were Cyprus, the Czech Republic, Estonia, Hungary, Latvia, Lithuania, Malta, Poland, Slovakia, and Slovenia.

[11]Information on the data sources, assumptions, and concordances between national classification systems and the International Standard Industrial Classification codes (ISIC, Rev. 3) used for this comparison appears in the online Supplementary Materials for this article.

In order to develop comparable measures of PAC, three issues must be addressed. First, industry definitions that are comparable across economies require the development of concordances between national classification systems and the International Standard Industrial Classification codes. Second, the costs associated with abating emissions for each media must be identified. Because the United States collected cost data for air, water, and solid waste, these media categories are used in the comparison of abatement costs. Third, it is necessary to use similar expenditure categories. For example, with the exception of Germany, whose capital expenditure data from 1996 to 2002 consist solely of end-of-pipe expenditures, capital expenditure data include both end-of-pipe and change-in-process expenditures. Efforts to reconcile current account expenditures face similar challenges. For example, the US survey includes estimates of depreciation costs, while the Canadian survey does not. No attempt is made to adjust the data to compensate for these and other differences.

Abatement operating costs per dollar of output and the share of capital expenditures assigned to pollution abatement for 1990, 1995, and 2000 are used to compare PAC for the mining sector, manufacturing sector, chemicals, rubber, and plastics industry, and metal products industry (see Appendix Tables 5 and 6).[12] For abatement operating costs, the Netherlands was the only country reporting values for the mining sector in 1990, while Germany reported the highest values in 1995 and 2000. For 1990, the United States reported the highest expenditures for the manufacturing sector, while Germany reported the highest expenditures in 1995 and 2000. However, the values for Germany's manufacturing sector in both 1995 and 2000 exceeded the value in 1990 for the United States. For capital expenditures in the mining sector, the data reveal that Germany reported the highest share in 1990, the United States reported the highest share in 1995, and Japan reported the highest share in 2000. For manufacturing, Taiwan reported the largest share in 1990, with Canada reporting the highest shares in 1995 and 2000. As shown in Figure 1, the US share of manufacturing capital expenditures assigned to pollution abatement was similar to the shares reported for Germany and Sweden in 2000, but substantially less than the shares reported for most other economies.[13] For the chemical, rubber, and plastics industry, the Netherlands reported the highest share of capital expenditures in 1990 and 2000, and the United States reported the highest share in 1995. Taiwan assigned the highest share of capital expenditures to pollution abatement in the metal products industry in 1990, while Germany and Australia reported the highest shares in 1995 and 2000, respectively.

---

[12]Additional pollution abatement cost data are reported for these sectors and additional manufacturing industries in the online Supplemental Materials.

[13]Becker and Shadbegian (2005) discuss how differences in survey methodology (e.g., excluding pollution prevention costs) might account for lower cost estimates found by the 1999 survey relative to the 1994 survey of abatement expenditures by US manufacturers.

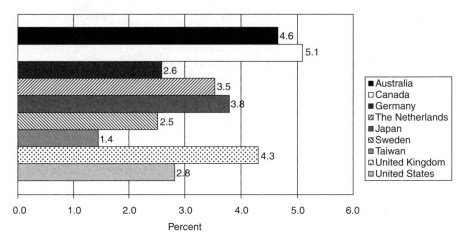

Figure 1 Percentage of manufacturing capital expenditures assigned to pollution abatement in 2000.

Source: Australian Bureau of Statistics, Federal Republic of Germany, Federal Statistical Office, Ministry of Economy, Trade and Industry (formerly Ministry of International Trade and Industry), Japan, the Netherlands, Centraal bureau voor de Statistiek, Statistics Canada, Environment Accounts and Statistics Division, Statistics Sweden, China, Directorate-General of Budget, Accounting, and Statistics, United Kingdom, Department for Environment, Food, and Rural Affairs, US Department of Commerce, Bureau of the Census.

Figure 2 Percentage of manufacturing capital expenditures assigned to pollution abatement (1975–2004).

Note: The annual survey of US manufacturers was halted after 1994, and the only recent data are from the 1999 and 2005 surveys. Because of the break in the time series, the 1999 observation is not included in Figure 2.
Source: Federal Republic of Germany, Federal Statistical Office, Ministry of Economy, Trade and Industry (formerly Ministry of International Trade and Industry), Japan, the Netherlands, Centraal bureau voor de Statistiek, US Department of Commerce, Bureau of the Census.

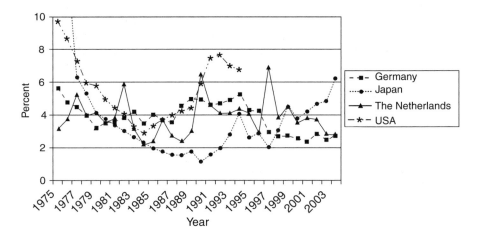

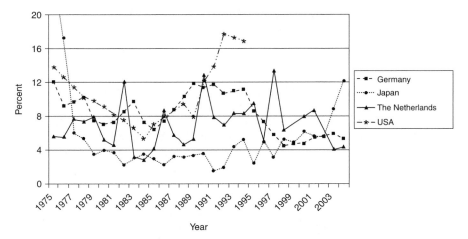

Year

Figure 3 Percentage of chemical industry ISIC (23–25) capital expenditures assigned to pollution abatement (1975–2004).

Note: The annual survey of US manufacturers was halted after 1994, and the only recent data are from the 1999 and 2005 surveys. Chemical industry cost data after 1994 are not reported because of concordance issues between the old and new industry classification systems.
Source: Federal Republic of Germany, Federal Statistical Office, Ministry of Economy, Trade and Industry (formerly Ministry of International Trade and Industry), Japan, the Netherlands, Centraal bureau voor de Statistiek, US Department of Commerce, Bureau of the Census.

Germany, Japan, the Netherlands, and the United States began collecting data on capital expenditures assigned to pollution abatement prior to 1980. Trends for the manufacturing sector for these countries from 1975 to 2004 are shown in Figure 2, and trends for the chemical industry are shown in Figure 3. In both figures, a spike in capital expenditures in Japan and the United States during the early stages of regulation implementation was followed by a fairly pronounced downward trend among the four countries over the 1975–1985 period. This was followed by a slight upward trend until the early 1990s. With the exception of Japan, since the early 1990s, there has been a gradual decline in the share of capital expenditures assigned to pollution abatement.

Comparing Emissions across Countries

This section discusses the country- and industry-level emissions data that are currently available. The US toxic release inventory (TRI) and the World Bank's Industrial Pollution Projection System (IPPS), whose estimates draw on the US TRI data, are the primary sources of emissions data used in empirical studies. However, there are also ongoing efforts to develop emissions estimates within the National Accounting Matrix, including the Environmental Accounts (NAMEA) framework.[14]

National Data

OECD estimates of SO_x and NO_x emissions indicate a 56-percent decline in SO_x and a 38-percent reduction in NOx intensities per unit of GDP for all OECD countries between 1990 and 2002 (see Appendix Table 7). Interestingly, 2002 SO_x and NO_x emission intensities for the United States exceeded the OECD average, while the percent change in SO_x and NO_x emission intensities between 1990 and 2002 was near the OECD average.[15]

Industry Data

Unfortunately, there are no industry-level emissions estimates associated with the 1990–2002 national emission estimates discussed above and presented in Appendix Table 7. However, the adoption of the NAMEA framework, which is part of the environmental accounting framework used by some countries, has led to the development of industry-level time-series data on emissions linked to economic accounts. Of the undesirable by-products associated with production and consumption activities, air emissions are typically the first to be included in NAMEAs. For example, EuroStat (2001b) provides estimates of air emissions by industry for selected European countries from 1990–1998. More recently, the Commission for Environmental Cooperation (CEC) (2007), which was established by the North American Agreement on Environmental Cooperation, has also assembled information on chemical releases and transfers by North American industrial facilities.

Empirical Analyses of Pollution Abatement and Competitiveness

This section reviews studies of the empirical association between pollution abatement and productivity, employment, international trade flows, and FDI, and whether environmental regulations appear to significantly affect indicators of competitiveness.

---

[14]A NAMEA (EuroStat 2001b, p. 11) is a framework that organizes data on economic activity and the undesirable by-products (e.g., emissions of air pollutants) resulting from that activity. In recent years, NAMEAs have been compiled by members of the EU and Japan.

[15]Because values for PAC reported in Appendix Table 1 include costs associated with abating air, water, and solid waste residuals, they are not directly comparable with the changes in SO_x and NO_x emissions reported in Appendix Table 7. Nevertheless, it is interesting that substantial declines in total SO_x and NO_x emissions and emission intensities were apparently achieved without substantial increases in PAC.

Pollution Abatement and Productivity

Traditionally, analyses of the association between pollution abatement and productivity ignore the reduced emissions that result from pollution abatement and focus instead on the association between PAC and production of marketed goods. Using information on the cost of inputs assigned to pollution abatement, these studies compare the levels of marketed goods production when emissions are and are not regulated.

The results of some early studies are summarized by the Congressional Budget Office (1985) and Pearce and Palmer (2001, pp. 420–423). Overall, these studies reported that pollution abatement had negative effects on productivity. The studies surveyed by the CBO (1985) found changes in the US productivity growth rate ranging from no change for 1973–1979 (Siegel 1979) to a 0.25 percent annual decline during 1974–1979 (Data Resources Inc. 1981). Among the studies reviewed by Pearce and Palmer (2001), both Josni, Krishnan, and Lave (2001) and Gray and Shadbegian (2002) found that each $1 of environmental expenditures increased costs by more than $1. In contrast, Morgenstern, Pizer, and Shih (2001) found some evidence of cost savings associated with environmental expenditures. Results of studies not summarized by the Congressional Budget Office (1985) or Pearce and Palmer (2001) are presented in Appendix Table 8. Most of these studies (e.g., Gray and Shadbegian 2003) also found negative effects on productivity. However, some studies did find a positive association between pollution abatement and productivity (e.g., Berman and Bui 2001).

Environmental Protection Industry

There have been numerous efforts to determine employment, output, and international trade in the goods and services produced by the EP industry (e.g., OECD 2004; European Commission, 2006). Using data from 1997 to 2000, the OECD (2004, p. 14) found that direct employment in the EP industry in twenty OECD countries ranged from 0.4 percent (Portugal) to 3.2 percent (Germany) of total employment, with most countries falling in the 1.0 to 1.5 percent range. In 2004, the EP industry in the EU-25 (European Commission 2006, p. 21 and 28) constituted 2.2 percent of GDP with a range of less than 1 percent (Ireland) to 4.5 percent (Denmark). The output of the EP industry serves as intermediate inputs and capital inputs in pollution abatement activities. The cost of these purchased goods and services combined with the cost of labor assigned to pollution abatement yields total pollution abatement costs. As a result, changes in the demand for goods and services produced by the EP industry should mirror changes in pollution abatement costs.

Pollution Abatement and Employment

Closely related to productivity are concerns about the association between pollution abatement and employment. Pollution abatement can reduce employment in an industry by decreasing its competitiveness, while increasing employment in other industries either in response to changes in relative prices or as a result of increases in labor assigned to pollution abatement. Morgenstern, Pizer, and Shih (2002) used plant-level data from four US manufacturing industries and found that pollution abatement expenditures are generally not associated with significant employment changes. Using data from the United Kingdom, Cole and Elliott (2007) also found no evidence that pollution abatement costs have an adverse effect on employment. These results fit nicely into the standard general equilibrium view that pollution abatement has no net effect on employment. Instead, differences in pollution abatement intensities among industries result in factor movements among industries until factor markets clear.

Computable General Equilibrium Models

By modeling the flow of goods and services among industries, computable general equilibrium (CGE) models provide a picture of the economy-wide effects of environmental regulations. For example, in one of the best-known retrospective environmental CGE studies, Jorgenson and Wilcoxen (1990) found a 0.19-percent reduction in the annual growth rate of the US economy between 1973 and 1985 as a result of environmental regulations. Conrad (2002) and Bergman (2005) provide the most recent surveys of applications of general equilibrium models to environmental issues. In recent years, applications of CGE models to environmental issues have focused less on *ex post* analyses of regulations and more on the potential effects of greenhouse gas regulations, which has led to an increased interest in modeling environmental taxes.

Pollution Abatement and Pollution Havens

The main focus of empirical work on pollution abatement and competitiveness has been the intersection of environmental concerns and international trade. The extent of the interest in this topic is indicated by the fact that there are no fewer than two meta-analyses (Jeppesen, List, and Folmer 2002; Mulatu, Florax, and Withagen 2003) and three surveys (Brunnermeier and Levinson 2004, Copeland and Taylor 2004, and Taylor 2004) on the topic of international trade and the environment.

The pollution haven hypothesis examines whether differences in regulatory stringency can affect trade or investment flows across economies. Copeland and Taylor (2004, p. 9) distinguish between the pollution haven *effect*, in which stricter environmental regulations affect trade and investment flows, and the stronger pollution haven *hypothesis*, in which trade liberalization results in pollution-intensive industries relocating from high-income countries with strict regulations to low-income countries with weaker regulations. Copeland and Taylor conclude that while there is evidence of a pollution haven effect, there is little evidence supporting the pollution haven hypothesis. Because the pollution haven *effect* is most relevant to competitiveness, the empirical evidence on pollution havens is generally assessed from this perspective.

In a meta-analysis using data from eleven studies of the link between new plant location and environmental regulations, Jeppesen, List, and Folmer (2002) found that results are sensitive to the methodology employed. They also found that environmental regulations have a greater influence on foreign firms in the United States than on domestic firms, and that smaller geographic areas lead to larger estimated effects of environmental regulations on new plant location. Finally, they found mixed results about whether examining only pollution-intensive industries produces different results than the pooling of pollution-intensive industries with nonpollution-intensive industries.

Mulatu, Florax, and Withagen (2003) undertook a meta-analysis of pollution abatement and international trade using data from thirteen studies. They concluded that the typical study found a negative relationship between environmental regulations and trade flows. While including developing countries increased the chance of finding a negative relationship between regulations and trade flows, including PAC as a measure of regulatory stringency reduced the likelihood of finding a negative relationship. They also found that more recent studies identified fewer negative effects of environmental regulations on trade flows.

The studies surveyed by Brunnermeier and Levinson (2004) used net exports, foreign direct investment, plant openings or closures, employment, and output as proxies for economic activity. Brunnermeier and Levinson found that early studies, that used primarily cross-section data, concluded that environmental regulations had statistically insignificant affects on firm location, while later studies, that relied on panel data, found statistically significant pollution haven effects. Similar to Jeppesen, List, and Folmer (2002), Brunnermeier and Levinson found that models using panel data produced more evidence of a pollution haven effect than cross-sectional studies.

Taylor (2004) reviewed the findings of a collection of papers on the topic of pollution havens and concluded that while environmental regulation affects trade and investment flows, it is only one of a number of factors— including a country's factor abundance, an industry's factor intensity, and the socio-economic characteristics of the country—that determines [sic] trade flows.

At least eleven articles on the existence of pollution havens have been published since the publication of the meta-analyses and surveys discussed above.[16] These publications reflect the continuing move from cross-sectional

---

[16]Appendix Table 9 summarizes these recently published articles.

to panel studies. It is also interesting to note, that of the five studies that find little evidence supporting the existence of pollution havens, only one used FDI data. In contrast, three of the six studies providing support for the existence of pollution havens used FDI data.

Concluding Observations

This article has reviewed theory, data, and empirical analyses on the link between pollution abatement and indicators of competitiveness. National- and industry-level data on inputs assigned to pollution abatement and emissions indicate that the burden borne by US producers relative to other OECD countries in the 1970s had largely disappeared by the 1990s. The higher US emission intensity ratios can be explained partly by some countries' heavier reliance on nuclear power for electricity generation (e.g., France). However, the United Kingdom obtains approximately the same share of its electricity from nuclear power as the United States and still reports lower emission intensities and higher percent declines in its emission intensities than the United States.

While most productivity studies that ignore the reduced emissions from pollution abatement find that pollution abatement has an adverse effect on productivity, some studies yield a less pessimistic result. Productivity studies will continue to produce conflicting results until a formal unification of the underlying theoretical models is achieved and the same data sets are used.

Although more countries started to collect information on PAC and emissions during the 1990s, empirical studies continued to rely on US PAC and emissions data. Only in recent years have empirical studies started to use non-US data to investigate pollution abatement and competitiveness. As environmental accounting efforts expand in the future, more non-US data will become available.

Appendix

Table 1A Pollution control expenditures (excluding household expenditures) as percentage of GDP

Country	1975	1980	1985	1990	1995	2000
Canada					1.2	
United States	1.6	1.6	1.4	1.4	1.6[b]	
Japan					1.3	1.4[d]
Korea					1.6	1.5
Australia				0.6[a]	0.8	
Austria				2.1	2.0	2.4[d]
Belgium					1.3[c]	1.5
Czech Republic				1.0	2.3	1.7
Finland		1.3	1.3		1.0	0.8[d]
France			0.8	1.2	1.4	1.6
Germany	1.4	1.45	1.5	1.6	1.3	1.6[d]
Hungary				0.4[a]	0.7[b]	
Netherlands		1.1	1.5	1.6	1.8	
Norway				1.2		
Poland				0.7	1.0	2.0
Portugal				0.8	0.7[b], 0.9[c]	0.8
Slovak Republic						0.8
Sweden				1.1[a]		0.8[d]
United Kingdom			1.3	0.7		0.7

[a]Indicates 1991 data. [b]Indicates 1994 data. [c]Indicates 1996 data. [d]Indicates 1999 data.
Source: *Pollution control and abatement expenditure in OECD countries* (OECD, various issues). The 1975 and 1980 data are from OECD (1990, p. 40), and 1985 data are from OECD (1993, p. 11) except for Finland which is from OECD (1990). The 1990–2000 data are from OECD (2003a, p. 32). Pre-1991 data for Germany are for West Germany.

Table 2A Percentage of business capital expenditures assigned to pollution abatement

Country	1985	1990	1995	2000
Canada		0.9	1.5	1.1
United States	2.0	1.7	2.2[b]	0.3[d]
Japan	0.5	0.3	0.6	0.6[d]
Korea			1.0	0.6
Australia		0.5[a]	0.3	
Austria		2.5	0.7	0.5[d]
Belgium			0.8[c]	0.4
Czech Republic			4.7	1.9
Finland			1.7	0.6[d]
France	0.4	0.5	0.6	0.5
Germany	1.6	1.4	0.6	0.4
Hungary		1.3[a]	0.9	
Netherlands	1.0	1.7	1.1	
Norway				0.3
Poland		2.5	3.8	1.9
Portugal			0.7	0.8
Slovak Republic				1.0
Sweden	0.8	0.7[a]		0.7
United Kingdom		0.7	1.1[b]	0.8

[a]Indicates 1991 data. [b]Indicates 1994 data. [c]Indicates 1996 data. [d]Indicates 1999 data.
Source: *Pollution control and abatement expenditure in OECD countries* (OECD, various issues). The 1985 data are from OECD (1993, p. 12). The 1990–2000 data are from OECD (2003a, pp. 36–37). Pre-1991 data for Germany are for West Germany. Because 1990 values for Germany and Japan are not reported in OECD (2003a), values are from (OECD 1993).

Table 3A Percent of GDP assigned to pollution abatement in Europe, the Caucasus, and Central Asia

Country	1996	1997	1998	1999	2000	2001
Armenia	0.4	0.4	0.4	0.5	0.6	0.2
Azerbaijan	0.8	0.5	0.5	0.4	0.3	0.3
Georgia						1.0
Kazakhstan	0.9	0.9	1.5	1.8	2.3	1.8
Kyrgyz Republic	0.3	0.4	0.4	0.7	0.4	
Moldova	2.9	2.8	3.0	3.1	2.4	3.1
Russian Fed.	2.5	2.2	2.3	1.6	1.6	1.5
Turkmenistan	0.5	0.5	0.5	0.4	0.5	0.3
Ukraine	0.5	0.4	2.2	2.1	1.9	1.9
Uzbekistan	1.3	1.8	1.7	1.4	0.7	
Bulgaria	1.7	1.6	2.1	2.8	2.6	
Hungary						1.8
Lithuania	1.2	1.4	2.2	2.2	1.8	
Romania	1.7	2.8	2.9	3.4	2.7	
Germany	2.0	2.0	2.3	2.2		
Portugal	1.2	1.2	1.2	1.7	1.8	

Note: Data should be compared with care, as definitions and sectors coverage vary across countries. To enhance comparisons, data on water supply expenditure of the industry sector have been included in total environmental protection expenditure of OECD and Central and Eastern European (CEE) countries.
Source: OECD (2003b, p. 43).

Table 4A Percent of capital expenditures assigned to pollution abatement by US companies

	1972		1977		1982	
	Overseas	*United States*	*Overseas*	*United States*	*Overseas*	*United States*
Primary metals	9.4	13.6	12.0	21.6	4	6
Machinery	0.9	3.8	2.1	6.6	1	2
Electrical machinery	5.8	2.8	3.9	2.7	1	2
Autos, trucks parts	1.9	6.6	3.9	3.8	0	1
Other transportation equipment	1.0	4.5	1.0	3.3	a	a
Fabricated metals and instruments	2.3	6.0	2.1	4.9	b	b
Chemicals	7.6	10.9	4.8	10.5	3	7
Paper	8.0	23.3	8.0	13.0		
Rubber	1.2	5.8	2.2	11.8		
Stone, clay, and glass	4.7	9.6	7.5	7.3		
Food and beverages	2.2	5.2	2.3	5.2	2	7
Textiles and misc. manufacturing	4.1	4.4	4.3	5.2		
Other manufacturing					6	5
All Manufacturing			3.9	8.7	2	4
Petroleum	8.3	10.7	3.7	8.3	2	5
Mining	1.5	5.1				
All Industry	5.5	8.0	3.8	9.2	2	4

[a]In 1982, other transportation equipment is included in autos, trucks and parts. [b]In 1982, fabricated metals and instruments is included in primary metals.
Source: McGraw-Hill (various issues).

Table 5A Air, water, and solid waste abatement operating costs per dollar of output

Country	Mining sector (ISIC 10–14)			Manufacturing sector (ISIC 15–36)			Chemicals, rubber, and plastics industry (ISIC 23–25)			Metal products industry (ISIC 27–28)		
	1990	1995	2000	1990	1995	2000	1990	1995	2000	1990	1995	2000
Australia				0.18			0.19			0.43		
Canada		0.56	0.34	0.25	0.26		0.26	0.34		0.65	0.69	
Germany		3.81[b]	2.25	0.86[b]	0.68		2.42[b]	1.80		1.22[b]	1.00	
Netherlands	0.29	0.40	0.31[d]	0.36	0.43	0.46[d]	0.91	1.07		0.77	0.66	0.53
Sweden		0.46[c]			0.23[c]			0.38[c]				0.30[c]
Taiwan				0.23	0.23	0.19	0.30	0.41	0.23	0.32	0.21	0.23
United Kingdom		0.37			0.45			0.68				0.45
United States				0.59	0.57[a]	0.25[c]	1.26	1.32[a]		0.92	0.86[a]	

[a] Indicates 1994 data. [b] Indicates 1996 data. [c] Indicates 1999 data. [d] Indicates 2001 data.
Source: Australian Bureau of Statistics, Statistics Canada, Environment Accounts and Statistics Division, Federal Republic of Germany, Federal Statistical Office, Netherlands, Centraal bureau voor de Statistiek, Statistics Sweden, United Kingdom, Department for Environment, Food, and Rural Affairs, US Department of Commerce, Bureau of the Census.

Table 6A Percent of capital expenditures assigned to air, water, and solid waste pollution abatement

Country	Mining sector (ISIC 10–14)			Manufacturing sector (ISIC 15–36)			Chemicals, rubber, and plastics industry (ISIC 23–25)			Metal products industry (ISIC 27–28)		
	1990	1995	2000	1990	1995	2000	1990	1995	2000	1990	1995	2000
Australia		0.80	1.72[c]		1.44	4.65[c]		1.31	7.10[c]		4.58	10.78[c]
Canada		1.81	1.97		6.63	5.09		7.29	6.60		6.21	3.12
Germany	14.70	3.22	2.92	4.94	4.24	2.56	11.41	8.66	4.79	9.59	8.59	5.53
Japan	1.80	1.84	10.09	1.17	2.61	3.78	3.62	2.41	6.23	3.42	2.58	7.27
The Netherlands	1.40	3.24		6.47	4.12	3.53	12.91	9.53	8.02	5.61	2.87	1.34
Sweden			4.11			2.50			1.26			4.15
Taiwan				7.90	3.73	1.41	9.15	6.10	2.68	12.42	4.72	1.50
United Kingdom			4.25			4.30			5.26			3.73
United States	2.55	3.86[a]		5.92	6.72[a]	2.80[b]	12.08	16.93[a]		6.36	4.61[a]	

[a] Indicates 1994 data. [b] Indicates 1999 data. [c] Indicates 2001 data.
Sources: Australian Bureau of Statistics, Federal Republic of Germany, Federal Statistical Office, Ministry of Economy, Trade and Industry (formerly Ministry of International Trade and Industry), Japan, the Netherlands, Centraal bureau voor de Statistiek, Statistics Canada, Environment Accounts and Statistics Division, Statistics Sweden, China, Directorate-General of Budget, Accounting, and Statistics, United Kingdom, Department for Environment, Food, and Rural Affairs, US Department of Commerce, Bureau of the Census.

Table 7A Changes in SO$_x$ and NO$_x$ total emissions and intensities (1990–2002)

Country	Total SO$_x$ emissions		SO$_x$ intensities per unit of GDP		Total NO$_x$ emissions		NO$_x$ intensities per unit of GDP		Fossil fuel supply GDP	
	1000 tonnes (2002)	%change since 1990	kg/1000 USD (2002)	%change since 1990	1000 tonnes (2002)	%change since 1990	kg/1000 USD (2002)	%change since 1990	%change since 1990	%change since 1990
Canada	2394	−27	2.6	−48	2459	−6	2.6	−33	22	40
United States	13847	−34	1.4	−53	18833	−18	1.9	−42	19	42
Japan	857	−14	0.3	−26	2018	−2	0.6	−15	12	16
Korea	501		0.6		1106		1.3		116	97
Australia	2803	71	5.3	15	1691	20	3.2	−19	27	49
New Zealand	68	10	0.8	−22	204	48	2.4	4	40	42
Austria	36	−55	0.2	−66	200	−3	0.9	−26	17	31
Belgium	151	−57	0.6	−66	290	−20	1.1	−37	16	26
Czech Republic	237	−87	1.5	−88	318	−42	2.1	−45	−16	7
Denmark	24	−86	0.2	−89	191	−31	1.2	−46	10	29
Finland	85	−64	0.6	−71	211	−32	1.6	−46	17	24
France	537	−60	0.3	−67	1350	−29	0.9	−43	6	25
Germany	611	−89	0.3	−91	1417	−48	0.7	−58	−7	22
Greece	509	4	2.7	−24	318	11	1.7	−19	30	36
Hungary	359	−64	2.8	−69	180	−24	1.4	−35	−11	16
Iceland	10	22	1.3	−7	26	−2	3.3	−26	22	32
Ireland	96	−48	0.8	−77	121	5	1.0	−53	44	125
Italy	665	−63	0.5	−69	1267	−34	0.9	−45	11	20
Luxembourg	3	−80	0.1	−89	17	−27	0.8	−59	15	78
Netherlands	85	−58	0.2	−69	430	−28	1.0	−47	16	36

Norway	22	−58	0.1	−72	213	−5	1.3	−37	29	50
Poland	1455	−55	3.6	−69	796	−38	2.0	−58	−13	46
Portugal	295	−9	1.6	−32	288	13	1.6	−16	56	34
Slovak Republic	102	−81	1.6	−84	102	−53	1.6	−60	−24	18
Spain	1541	−29	1.8	−48	1432	14	1.7	−17	52	37
Sweden	58	−45	0.2	−57	242	−25	1.0	−41	7	26
Switzerland	19	−58	0.1	−62	90	−46	0.4	−52	1	13
Turkey	2112	33	4.7	−7	951	48	2.1	4	50	42
United Kingdom	1003	−73	0.6	−80	1587	−43	1.0	−57	4	32
OECD	31654	−41	1.1	−56	39500	−17	1.4	−38	17	34

Source: OECD (2005, pp. 54, 56).

Table 8A Results of studies on productivity effects of pollution abatement

Study	Years	Industries/geographic area	Results
US Congressional Budget Office (1985)	1968–1982	Manufacturing sector in Canada, West Germany, Japan, and the United States.	Although statistically insignificant, PAC was associated with reduced output; decline in average annual growth rate of the United States of 0.28 for 1973–1982.
Conrad and Wastl (1995)	1975–1991	10 manufacturing industries in West Germany.	TFP declines ranging from 0.3 percent to 2.5 percent, with a median decline of approximately 0.7 percent.
Dufour, Lanoie, and Patry (1998)	1985–1988	19 manufacturing industries in Quebec.	TFP reduced by 0.1 percent (significant).
Berman and Bui (2001)	1979–1992	Plant-level data for oil refineries (SIC 2911) in the United States.	During 1982–1992, productivity at heavily regulated South Coast (Los Angeles) refineries was 5 percentage points higher than the (declining) national average.
Tsai (2002)	1987–1997	15 manufacturing industries in Taiwan.	TFP increases ranging from 2.5 to 4.0 percent.
Millimet and Osang (2003)	1984–1993	48 3-digit SIC manufacturing industries in the United States.	Average decline in productivity growth across all industries of 0.3 percent.
Gray and Shadbegian (2003)	1979–1990	Plant-level data for 116 pulp and paper mills in the United States.	Plants with higher PAC have significantly lower productivity.
Shadbegian and Gray (2005)	1979–1990	Plant-level data for 68 pulp and paper mills, 55 oil refineries, and 27 steel mills in the United States.	Inputs assigned to pollution abatement have little effect on production of marketed goods.
Shadbegian and Gray (2006)	1990–2000	Plant-level data for 327 pulp and paper mills, 121 oil refineries, and 83 steel mills in the United States.	Plants spending more on pollution abatement tend to have lower technical efficiency.
Aiken et al. (2006)	1987–2001	Manufacturing sector and 8 manufacturing industries in Japan, the Netherlands, Germany, and the United States.	There were negligible effects for the manufacturing sectors in Japan and the Netherlands, annual productivity growth declined by 0.11 percent in the United States and increased by 0.24 percent in Germany.

Table 9A Recent studies of trade and FDI effects of pollution abatement

Study	Countries; (Years)	Industry categories (if applicable)	Dependent variable	Environmental regulatory variable(s)	Results
No evidence for existence of pollution havens					
Harris, Kónya, and Mátyás (2002)	24 OECD countries; (1990–1996)	N/A	Bilateral total imports and imports of "dirty" industries	Six measures of regulatory stringency (based on energy supply and consumption).	Strictness measures seem unimportant in preferred specifications of model.
Cole and Elliott (2003)	60 developed and developing countries that produced 630 trade pairs; (1995)	Iron and steel, chemicals, pulp and paper, nonferrous metals	Net exports	Two measures of regulatory stringency.	Environmental regulations are not statistically significant determinants of net exports.
Eskeland and Harrison (2003)	Mexico (1984–1990), Morocco (1985–1990), Côte d'Ivoire (1977–1987), and Venezuela (1983–1988)	Plant-level data from manufacturing plants	Inward FDI	US PA operating costs per dollar of industry value added.	Some evidence of FDI being drawn to industries with high levels of air pollution; however, no evidence of FDI by the United States to avoid PAC.
Grether and de Melo (2004)	52 countries; (1981–1998)	3-digit ISIC industries classified as "dirty" or "clean"	Revealed comparative advantage, bilateral trade	Index of emissions per unit of output.	Although most developing countries increase their comparative advantage in polluting products, there is little evidence of regulatory gaps affecting trade flows.

(continued)

Table 9A (Continued)

Study	Countries; (Years)	Industry categories (if applicable)	Dependent variable	Environmental regulatory variable(s)	Results
Cole, Elliott, and Shimamoto (2005)	United States; (1978–1994)	96 3-digit SIC manufacturing industries	Revealed comparative advantage, Michaely index, net exports	US PA operating costs per unit of value added.	US specialization in "dirty" industries is neither lower nor declining more rapidly (or increasing more slowly) than other sectors.
Evidence for existence of pollution havens					
Fredriksson, List, and Millimet (2003)	US state-level data; (1977–1987)	Aggregate manufacturing, chemicals, metals, and food and kindred products	Total inbound FDI for each state in a given year	Index of state environmental abatement costs.	Corruption and regulatory stringency play a significant role in the allocation of foreign investment among states.
Mulatu, Florax, and Withagen (2004)	Germany (1975–1992), the Netherlands (1972–1992), and the United States (1973–1991)	9 two-digit ISIC manufacturing industries classified as "dirty" or "clean"	Net exports	Share of gross fixed new capital formation assigned to pollution abatement.	Trade patterns in "dirty" commodities are jointly determined by relative factor endowments and environmental stringency differentials.
Cole and Elliott (2005)	Brazil, Mexico, the United States; (1989–1994)	31 industries in Brazil and 36 industries in Mexico	US FDI stocks in Brazil and Mexico	US PA operating costs per dollar of industry value added.	Level of PAC in US industry is a statistically significant determinant of its FDI.

Study	Sample	Industries	Dependent variable	Independent variable	Finding
Jug and Mirza (2005)	12 importing countries from EU-15 and 19 exporting countries from EU-15 and Central and Eastern Europe; (1996–1999)	9 two-digit ISIC manufacturing industries classified as "dirty" or "clean"	Total imports and relative imports of country i from country j	Current account environmental expenditures as share of production.	Environmental regulations are an important variable in the determination of trade flows (i.e., they have a negative effect on exports).
Cole, Elliott, and Fredriksson (2006)	13 OECD and 20 developing countries; (1982–1992)	N/A	Environmental regulations (lead content per gallon of gasoline)	Lead content per gallon of gasoline.	With higher (lower) levels of corruption, FDI is associated with less (more) stringent environmental regulations; FDI contributes to (mitigates) formation of pollution haven.
Levinson and Taylor (2008)	Canada, Mexico, and the United States; (1977–1986)	130 3-digit manufacturing industries in the United States	US net imports scaled by domestic production	US PAC operating costs per dollar of value added.	US PAC had a significant effect on its trade with Canada and Mexico.

Supplementary Data

Supplementary data for this article are available online at http://www.reep .oxfordjournals.org.

REFERENCES

Aiken, Deborah Vaughn, Rolf Färe, Shawna Grosskopf, and Carl Pasurka. 2006. Pollution abatement activities and traditional productivity growth in Germany, Japan, the Netherlands and the United States. Mimeo.

Ambec, Stefan, and Philippe Barla. 2006. Can environmental regulation be good for business? An assessment of the porter hypothesis. *Energy Studies Review* 14(2):42–62.

Australian Bureau of Statistics. Various issues. *Cost of Environmental Protection, Australia—Selected Statistics.*

Becker, Randy A., and Ronald J. Shadbegian. 2005. A change of pace: A comparison of the 1994 and 1999 pollution abatement costs and expenditures survey. *Journal of Economic and Social Measurement* 30(1):63–95.

Bergman, Lars. 2005. CGE modeling of environmental policy and resource management. In *Handbook of Environmental Economics*, ed. Karl-Göran Mäler and Jeffrey Vincent, Vol. 3., Chapter 24. New York, NY: North-Holland, pp. 1273–1306.

Berman, Eli, and Linda Bui. 2001. Environmental regulation and productivity. Evidence from oil refineries. *Review of Economics and Statistics* 83(3):498–510.

Bouman, Mathijs. 1998. *Environmental Costs and Capital Flight.* Tinbergen Institute Research Series, no. 177. Amsterdam: Thesis Publishers.

Brunnermeier, Smita B., and Arik Levinson. 2004. Examining the evidence on environmental regulations and industry location. *Journal of Environment and Development* 13:6–41.

China, Directorate-General of Budget, Accounting, and Statistics. Various issues. *Statistical Yearbook of the Republic of China.* Taipei.

Chung, Yangho H., Rolf Färe, and Shawna Grosskopf. 1997. Productivity and undesirable outputs: A directional distance function approach. *Journal of Environmental Management* 51:229–40.

Cole, Mathew A., and Robert J. R. Elliott. 2003. Do environmental regulations influence trade patterns? Testing old and new trade theories. *World Economy* 26(8):1163–86.

———. 2005. FDI and the capital intensity of "dirty" sectors: A missing piece of the pollution haven puzzle. *Review of Development Economics* 9:530–48.

———. 2007. Do environmental regulations cost jobs? An industry-level analysis of the UK. *B.E. Journal of Economic Analysis and Policy* 7(1) (Topics), Article 28. [Available at www.bepress.com/bejeap/vol7/iss1/art28 (accessed 6/6/11)].

Cole, Mathew A., Robert J. R. Elliott, and Per G. Fredriksson. 2006. Endogenous pollution havens: Does FDI influence environmental regulations? *Scandinavian Journal of Economics* 108:157–78.

Cole, Mathew A., Robert J. R. Elliott, and K. Shimamoto. 2005. Why the grass is not always greener: The competing effects of environmental regulations and factor intensities on US specialization. *Ecological Economics* 54(1):95–109.

Commission for Environmental Cooperation. 2007. *Taking Stock: 2004 North American Pollutant Releases and Transfers.* Montreal: Commission for

Environmental Cooperation. [Available at www.cec.org/Storage/61/5338_ CEC%TakingStock-Web.pdf (accessed 6/6/11)].

Congressional Budget Office, US Congress. 1985. *Environmental Regulation and Economic Efficiency.* Washington, DC: US Government Printing Office.

Conrad, Klaus. 2002. Computable general equilibrium models in environmental and resource economics. In *The International Yearbook of Environmental and Resource Economics 2002/2003: A Survey of Current Issues,* ed. T. H. Tietenberg and H. Folmer. Northampton, MA: Edward Elgar Publishers, pp. 66–114.

Conrad, Klaus, and Dieter Wastl. 1995. The impact of environmental regulation on productivity in German industries. *Empirical Economics* 20(4):615–33.

Copeland, Brian, and M. Scott Taylor. 2004. Trade, growth, and the environment. *Journal of Economic Literature* 42(1):7–71.

Data Resources Inc. 1981. Macroeconomic impact of federal pollution control programs: 1981 assessment. Submitted to the US Environmental Protection Agency.

Dufour, Charles, Paul Lanoie, and Michel Patry. 1998. Regulation and productivity. *Journal of Productivity Analysis* 9(3):233–47.

Eskeland, G. S., and A. E. Harrison. 2003. Moving to greener pastures? Multinationals and the pollution haven hypothesis. *Journal of Development Economics* 70:1–23.

European Commission. 2006. *Eco-Industry, Its Size, Employment, Perspectives and Barriers to Growth in an Enlarged EU.* Luxembourg: Office for Official Publications of the European Communities. Available at [http://ec.europe.eu/environment/enveco/eco_industry/pdf/ecoindustry2006.pdf (accessed 6/6/11)].

EuroStat. 1994. *Environmental Protection Expenditure: Data Collection Methods in the Public Sector and Industry.* Luxembourg: Office for Official Publications of the European Communities.

———. 2001a. *Environmental Protection Expenditure in Europe, Data 1990–99.* Luxembourg: Office for Official Publications of the European Communities.

———. 2001b. *NAMEAs for Air Emissions, Results of Pilot Studies.* Luxembourg: Office for Official Publications of the European Communities.

———. 2002a. *Environmental Protection Expenditure Account—Results of Pilot Applications.* Luxembourg: Office for Official Publications of the European Communities.

———. 2002b. *Environmental Protection Expenditure in Accession Countries, Data 1996–2000.* Luxembourg: Office for Official Publications of the European Communities.

———. 2005. Environmental Protection Expenditure by Industry in the European Community. *Statistics in Focus,* Energy and Environment, 2005. Luxembourg: Office for Official Publications of the European Communities.

Färe, Rolf, Shawna Grosskopf, Knox Lovell, and Carl Pasurka. 1989. Multilateral productivity comparisons when some outputs are undesirable. *Review of Economics and Statistics* 71(1):90–98.

Färe, Rolf, Shawna Grosskopf, and Carl Pasurka. 2006. Modeling pollution abatement technologies and traditional productivity within a network technology. Paper presented at the 2007 Southern Economic Association Conference in Charleston, SC.

———. 2007. Pollution abatement activities and traditional measures of productivity. *Ecological Economics* 62(3–4):673–82.

Federal Republic of Germany, Federal Statistical Office. Various issues. *Umwelt* Fachserie 19, Reihe 3, "Investitionen für Umweltschutz im Produzierenden Gewerbe."

————. Various issues. *Unwelt* Fachserie 19, Reihe 3.2, "Laufende Aufwendungen für den Umweltschutz im Produzierenden Gewerbe."

Fredriksson, P. G., J. A. List, and D. L. Millimet. 2003. Bureaucratic corruption, environmental policy and inbound US FDI: Theory and evidence. *Journal of Public Economics* 87(7–8):1407–30.

Gray, Wayne B., and Ronald J. Shadbegian. 2002. Pollution abatement costs, regulation, and plant-level productivity. In *Economic Costs and Consequences of Environmental Regulation*, ed. Wayne B. Gray. Aldershot, UK: Ashgate Publishing.

————. 2003. Plant vintage, technology, and environmental regulation. *Journal of Environmental Economics and Management* 46(3):384–402.

Grether, J. M., and J. de Melo. 2004. Globalization and dirty industries: Do pollution havens matter? In *Challenges to Globalization: Analyzing the Economics*, ed. R. E. Baldwin and L. A. Winters. Chicago, IL: University of Chicago Press.

Harris, M. N., L. Kónya, and L. Mátyás. (2002). Modelling the impact of environmental regulations on bilateral trade flows: OECD, 1990–1996. *World Economy* 25(3):387–405.

Jaffe, Adam B., Richard G. Newell, and Robert N. Stavins. 2003. Technological change and the environment. In *Handbook of Environmental Economics*, ed. Karl-Göran Mäler and Jeffrey Vincent, Vol. 1., Chapter 11. New York: North-Holland, pp. 461–516.

Jaffe, Adam B., Steven R. Peterson, Paul R. Portney, and Robert R. Stavins. 1995. Environmental regulation and the competitiveness of U.S. manufacturing: What does the evidence tell us?. *Journal of Economic Literature* 33(1):132–63.

Jeppesen, T., J. A. List, and H. Folmer. 2002. Environmental regulations and new plant location decisions: Evidence from a meta-analysis. *Journal of Regional Science* 42(1):19–49.

Jorgenson, Dale W., and Peter J. Wilcoxen. 1990. Environmental regulation and U.S. economic growth. *Rand Journal of Economics* 21:314–40.

Joshi, Satishi, Ranjani Krishnan, and Lester Lave. 2001. Estimating the hidden costs of environmental regulation. *Accounting Review* 76(2):171–98.

Jug, Jerneja, and Daniel Mirza. 2005. Environmental regulations in gravity equations: Evidence from Europe. *World Economy* 28(11):1591–1615.

Krugman, Paul. 1994. Competitiveness: A dangerous obsession. *Foreign Affairs* 73(2):28–44.

Lawrence, Robert Z. 2007. Competitiveness. In *The Concise Encyclopedia of Economics*, ed. David R. Henderson. Liberty Fund, Inc. Library of Economics and Liberty. Available at [www.econlib.org/library/Enc1/Competitiveness.html (accessed 6/6/11)].

Leonard, Jeremy A. 2003. *How Structural Costs Imposed on U.S. Manufacturers Harm Workers and Threaten Competitiveness.* Manufacturers Alliance/MAPI and the National Association of Manufacturers.

Levinson, Arik, and M. Scott Taylor. 2008. Unmasking the pollution haven effect. *International Economic Review* 49:223–54.

McGraw Hill. Various issues. *Overseas Operations of U.S. Industrial Companies.*

Millimet, Daniel L., and Thomas Osang. 2003. Environmental regulation and productivity growth: An analysis of US manufacturing industries. In *Empirical Modeling of the Economy and the Environment* (ZEW Economic Studies), ed. C. Böehringer and A Löeschel. Heidelberg: Physica Verlag.

Ministry of Economy, Trade and Industry (formerly Ministry of International Trade and Industry), Japan. Various issues. Survey results of investments for industrial pollution control facilities. In *Plant and Equipment Investment Plans in Major Industries* (Shuyō Sangyō no Setsubi Tōshi Keikaku). Tokyo: Ministry of Finance Printing Bureau.

Morgenstern, R. D., W. A. Pizer, and J. S. Shih. 2001. The cost of environmental protection. *Review of Economics and Statistics* 83(4):732–38.

———. 2002. Jobs versus the environment: An industry-level perspective. *Journal of Environmental Economics and Management* 43:412–36.

Mulatu, Abay, Raymond J. G. M. Florax, and Cees Withagen. 2003. Environmental regulation and competitiveness: An exploratory meta-analysis. In *Empirical Modeling of the Economy and the Environment* (ZEW Economic Studies), ed. C. Böehringer and A. Löeschel. Heidelberg: Physica Verlag.

———. 2004. Environmental regulation and international trade: Empirical results for Germany, the Netherlands and the US, 1977–1992. *Contributions to Economic Analysis and Policy* 3(2):1–28, Article 5. [Available at www.bepress.com/bejeap/contributions/vol3/iss2/art5 (accessed 6/6/11)].

Netherlands, Centraal Bureau voor de Statistiek. Various issues. *Milieukosten van Bedrijven.* 's Gravenhage: Staaatsuitgeverij. Data from 1997 to the present are available via StatLine at www.cbs.nl/ [accessed 6/6/11].

Organization for Economic Co-operation and Development. 1999. *The Environmental Goods and Services Industry: Manual for Data Collection and Analysis.* Paris: OECD.

———. 2004. *Environment and Employment: An Assessment.* Paris: OECD.

———. 2005. *Environment at a Glance: OECD Environmental Indicators.* Paris: OECD.

Organization for Economic Co-operation and Development, Environment Directorate. 1990. Pollution control and abatement expenditure in OECD countries: A statistical compendium. OECD Environment Monographs, No. 38.

———. 1993. Pollution control and abatement expenditure in OECD countries. OECD Environment Monographs, No. 75.

———. 2002. Polluter-pays-principle as it relates to international trade. Paris: OECD. [Available at www.oecd.org/officialdocuments/displaydocumentpdf?cote=com/env/td(2001)44/final&doclanguage=en (accessed 6/6/11)].

———. 2003a. Trends in environmental expenditure and international commitments for the environment in Eastern Europe, Caucasus and Central Asia, 1996–2001. Fifth Ministerial Conference, Environment for Europe, Kiev, Ukraine, May 21–23.

———. 2003b. *Pollution Control and Abatement Expenditure in OECD Countries.* Available at http://www.oecd.org/dataoecd/41/57/4704311.pdf.

Palmer, Karen, Wallace E. Oates, and Paul R. Portney. 1995. Tightening environmental standards: The benefit-cost or the no-cost paradigm? *Journal of Economic Perspectives* 9(4):119–32.

Pearce, David, and Charles Palmer. 2001. Public and private spending for environmental protection: A cross-country policy analysis. *Fiscal Studies* 22(4):403–56.

Pizer, William, and Raymond Kopp. 2005. Calculating the costs of environmental regulations. In *Handbook of Environmental Economics*, ed. Karl-Göran Mäler and Jeffrey Vincent, Vol. 3, Chapter 25. New York: North-Holland, pp. 1307–71.

Plooy, L. H. E. C. 1985. International comparison of industrial pollution control costs. *Statistical Journal of the United Nations Economic Commission for Europe* 3:55–68.

Porter, Michael E., and Claas van der Linde. 1995. Toward a new conception of the environment-competitiveness relationship. *Journal of Economic Perspectives* 9(4):97–118.

President's Commission on Industrial Competitiveness. 1985. *Global Competition: The New Reality*, Vol. 2. Washington, DC: US Government Printing Office.

Shadbegian, Ronald J., and Wayne B. Gray. 2005. Pollution abatement expenditures and plant-level productivity: A production function approach. *Ecological Economics* 54:196–208.

———. 2006. Assessing multi-dimensional performance: Environmental and economic outcomes. *Journal of Productivity Analysis* 26(4):213–34.

Siegel, R. 1979. Why has productivity slowed down so much? *Data Resources US Rev* 1: 1.59–1.65.

SQW—Economic Development Consultants. 2006. Exploring the relationship between environmental regulation and competitiveness: A literature review. A research report completed for Department for Environment, Food, and Rural Affairs (DEFRA), United Kingdom.

Statistics Canada, Environment Accounts and Statistics Division. Various issues. *Environmental Protection Expenditures in the Business Sector*.

Statistics Sweden. Various issues. *Miljöskyddskostnader i industrin*.

Taylor, M. Scott. 2004. Unbundling the pollution haven hypothesis. *Advances in Economic Analysis and Policy* 4(2):1–26, Article 8. [Available at www.bepress.com/bejeap/advances/vol4/iss2/art8 (accessed 6/6/11)].

Tsai, Diana H. 2002. Environmental policy and technological innovation: Evidence from Taiwan manufacturing industries. Paper presented at the 5th Annual Conference on Global Economic Analysis, Taipei. Available at [https://www.gtap.agecon.purdue.edu/resources/download/952.pdf (accessed 6/6/11)].

United Kingdom, Department for Environment, Food, and Rural Affairs. Various issues. *Environmental Protection Expenditure by Industry*.

United Nations, Economic Commission for Europe. 2006. Environmental policy and international competitiveness: Can we afford a better environment in a globalizing world? Committee on Environmental Policy, Thirteenth Session, October 9–11, Geneva, Switzerland. [Available at http://unece.org/env/cep/13%20CEP/ECE_CEP_2006_4%20e%20policy%20issues.pdf (accessed 6/6/11)].

US Department of Commerce, Bureau of the Census. Various issues. *Pollution Abatement Costs and Expenditures*. Current Industrial Reports, MA200, Washington, DC: US Government Printing Office.

Wagner, Marcus. 2003. The Porter hypothesis revisited: A literature review of theoretical models and empirical tests. Centre for Sustainable Management, Universität Lüneburg. Available at [http://129.3.20.41/eps/pe/papers/0407/0407014.pdf (accessed 6/6/11)].

World Bank. 2006. *Where Is the Wealth of Nations? Measuring Capital for the 21st Century*. Washington, DC: World Bank.

World Economic Forum. 2006. *Global Competitiveness Report: 2006–2007*. Oxford: Oxford University Press.

5 Toward a New Conception of the Environment-Competitiveness Relationship*

Michael E. Porter

Claas van der Linde

Michael E. Porter is the Bishop William Lawrence Professor, Harvard Business School; and Claas van der Linde was on the faculty of the International Management Research Institute of St. Gallen University, Switzerland.

The relationship between environmental goals and industrial competitiveness has normally been thought of as involving a tradeoff between social benefits and private costs. The issue was how to balance society's desire for environmental protection with the economic burden on industry. Framed this way, environmental improvement becomes a kind of arm-wrestling match. One side pushes for tougher standards; the other side tries to beat the standards back.

Our central message is that the environmental-competitiveness debate has been framed incorrectly. The notion of an inevitable struggle between ecology and the economy grows out of a static view of environmental regulation, in which technology, products, processes and customer needs are all fixed. In this static world, where firms have already made their cost-minimizing choices, environmental regulation inevitably raises costs and will tend to reduce the market share of domestic companies on global markets.

However, the paradigm defining competitiveness has been shifting, particularly in the last 20 to 30 years, away from this static model. The new paradigm of international competitiveness is a dynamic one, based on innovation. A body of research first published in *The Competitive Advantage of Nations* has begun to address these changes (Porter, 1990). Competitiveness at the industry level arises from superior productivity, either in terms

"Toward a New Conception of the Environment-Competitiveness Relationship" by Michael E. Porter and Claas van der Linde. *Journal of Economic Perspectives* 9. 1995. Pp. 97–118. Reprinted by permission from the American Economic Association.

*The authors are grateful to Alan Auerbach, Ben Bonifant, Daniel C. Esty, Ridgway M. Hall, Jr., Donald B. Matron, Jan Rivkin, Nicolaj Siggelkow, R. David Simpson and Timothy Taylor for extensive valuable editorial suggestions. We are also grateful to Reed Hundt for ongoing discussions that have greatly benefitted our thinking.

of lower costs than rivals or the ability to offer products with superior value that justify a premium price.[1] Detailed case studies of hundreds of industries, based in dozens of countries, reveal that internationally competitive companies are not those with the cheapest inputs or the largest scale, but those with the capacity to improve and innovate continually. (We use the term innovation broadly, to include a product's or service's design, the segments it serves, how it is produced, how it is marketed and how it is supported.) Competitive advantage, then, rests not on static efficiency nor on optimizing within fixed constraints, but on the capacity for innovation and improvement that shift the constraints.

This paradigm of dynamic competitiveness raises an intriguing possibility: in this paper, we will argue that properly designed environmental standards can trigger innovation that may partially or more than fully offset the costs of complying with them. Such "innovation offsets," as we call them, can not only lower the net cost of meeting environmental regulations, but can even lead to absolute advantages over firms in foreign countries not subject to similar regulations. Innovation offsets will be common because reducing pollution is often coincident with improving the productivity with which resources are used. In short, firms can actually benefit from properly crafted environmental regulations that are more stringent (or are imposed earlier) than those faced by their competitors in other countries. By stimulating innovation, strict environmental regulations can actually enhance competitiveness.

There is a legitimate and continuing controversy over the social benefits of specific environmental standards, and there is a huge benefit-cost literature. Some believe that the risks of pollution have been overstated; others fear the reverse. Our focus here is not on the social benefits of environmental regulation, but on the private costs. Our argument is that whatever the level of social benefits, these costs are far higher than they need to be. The policy focus should, then, be on relaxing the tradeoff between competitiveness and the environment rather than accepting it as a given.

The Link from Regulation to Promoting Innovation

It is sometimes argued that companies must, by the very notion of profit seeking, be pursuing all profitable innovations. In the metaphor economists often cite, $10 bills will never be found on the ground because someone would have already picked them up. In this view, if complying with environ-

---

[1]At the industry level, the meaning of competitiveness is clear. At the level of a state or nation, however, the notion of competitiveness is less clear because no nation or state is, or can be, competitive in everything. The proper definition of competitiveness at the aggregate level is the average *productivity* of industry or the value created per unit of labor and per dollar of capital invested. Productivity depends on both the quality and features of products (which determine their value) and the efficiency with which they are produced.

mental regulation can be profitable, in the sense that a company can more than offset the cost of compliance, then why is such regulation necessary?

The possibility that regulation might act as a spur to innovation arises because the world does not fit the Panglossian belief that firms always make optimal choices. This will hold true only in a static optimization framework where information is perfect and profitable opportunities for innovation have already been discovered, so that profit-seeking firms need only choose their approach. Of course, this does not describe reality. Instead, the actual process of dynamic competition is characterized by changing technological opportunities coupled with highly incomplete information, organizational inertia and control problems reflecting the difficulty of aligning individual, group and corporate incentives. Companies have numerous avenues for technological improvement, and limited attention.

Actual experience with energy-saving investments illustrates that in the real world, $10 bills are waiting to be picked up. As one example, consider the "Green Lights" program of the Environmental Protection Agency. Firms volunteering to participate in this program pledge to scrutinize every avenue of electrical energy consumption. In return, they receive advice on efficient lighting, hearing and cooling operations. When the EPA collected data on energy-saving lighting upgrades reported by companies as part of the Green Lights program, it showed that nearly 80 percent of the projects had paybacks of two years or less (DeCanio, 1993). Yet only after companies became part of the program, and benefitted from information and cajoling from the EPA, were these highly profitable projects carried out. This paper will present numerous other examples of where environmental innovation produces net benefits for private companies.[2]

We are currently in a transitional phase of industrial history where companies are still inexperienced in dealing creatively with environmental issues. The environment has not been a principal area of corporate or technological emphasis, and knowledge about environmental impacts is still rudimentary in many firms and industries, elevating uncertainty about innovation benefits. Customers are also unaware of the costs of resource inefficiency in the packaging they discard, the scrap value they forego and the disposal costs they bear. Rather than attempting to innovate in every direction at once, firms in fact make choices based on how they perceive their competitive situation and the world around them. In such a world, regulation can be an important influence on the discretion of innovation, either for better or for worse. Properly crafted environmental regulation can serve at least six purposes.

First, regulation signals companies about likely resource inefficiencies and potential technological improvements. Companies are still inexperi-

---

[2]Of course, there are many nonenvironmental examples of where industry has been extremely slow to pick up available $10 bills by choosing new approaches. For example, total quality management programs only came to the United States and Europe decades after they had been widely diffused in Japan, and only after Japanese firms had devastated U.S. and European competitors in the marketplace. The analogy between searching for product quality and for environmental protection is explored later in this paper.

enced in measuring their discharges, understanding the full costs of incomplete utilization of resources and toxicity, and conceiving new approaches to minimize discharges or eliminate hazardous substances. Regulation rivets attention on this area of potential innovation.[3]

Second, regulation focused on information gathering can achieve major benefits by raising corporate awareness. For example, Toxics Release Inventories, which are published annually as part of the 1986 Superfund reauthorization, require more than 20,000 manufacturing plants to report their releases of some 320 toxic chemicals. Such information gathering often leads to environmental improvement without mandating pollution reductions, sometimes even at lower costs.

Third, regulation reduces the uncertainty that investments to address the environment will be valuable. Greater certainty encourages investment in any area.

Fourth, regulation creates pressure that motivates innovation and progress. Our broader research on competitiveness highlights the important role of outside pressure in the innovation process, to overcome organizational inertia, foster creative thinking and mitigate agency problems. Economists are used to the argument that pressure for innovation can come from strong competitors, demanding customers or rising prices of raw materials; we are arguing that properly crafted regulation can also provide such pressure.

Fifth, regulation levels the transitional playing field. During the transition period to innovation-based solutions, regulation ensures that one company cannot opportunistically gain position by avoiding environmental investments. Regulations provide a buffer until new technologies become proven and learning effects reduce their costs.

Sixth, regulation is needed in the case of incomplete offsets. We readily admit that innovation cannot always completely offset the cost of compliance, especially in the short term before learning can reduce the cost of innovation-based solutions. In such cases, regulation will be necessary to improve environmental quality.

Stringent regulation can actually produce greater innovation and innovation offsets than lax regulation. Relatively lax regulation can be dealt with incrementally and without innovation, and often with "end-of-pipe" or secondary treatment solutions. More stringent regulation, however, focuses greater company attention on discharges and emissions, and compliance requires more fundamental solutions, like reconfiguring products and processes. While the cost of compliance may rise with stringency, then, the potential for innovation offsets may rise even faster. Thus the *net* cost of compliance can fall with stringency and may even turn into a net benefit.

---

[3]Regulation also raises the likelihood that product and process in general will incorporate environmental improvements.

How Innovation Offsets Occur

Innovation in response to environmental regulation can take two broad forms. The first is that companies simply get smarter about how to deal with pollution once it occurs, including the processing of toxic materials and emissions, how to reduce the amount of toxic or harmful material generated (or convert it into salable forms) and how to improve secondary treatment. Molten Metal Technology, of Waltham, Massachusetts, for example, has developed a catalytic extraction process to process many types of hazardous waste efficiently and effectively. This sort of innovation reduces the cost of compliance with pollution control, but changes nothing else.

The second form of innovation addresses environmental impacts while simultaneously improving the affected product itself and/or related processes. In some cases, these "innovation offsets" can exceed the costs of compliance. This second sort of innovation is central to our claim that environmental regulation can actually increase industrial competitiveness.

Innovation offsets can be broadly divided into product offsets and process offsets. Product offsets occur when environmental regulation produces not just less pollution, but also creates better-performing or higher-quality products, safer products, lower product costs (perhaps from material substitution or less packaging), products with higher resale or scrap value (because of ease in recycling or disassembly) or lower costs of product disposal for users. Process offsets occur when environmental regulation not only leads to reduced pollution, but also results in higher resource productivity such as higher process yields, less downtime through more careful monitoring and maintenance, materials savings (due to substitution, reuse or recycling of production inputs), better utilization of by-products, lower energy consumption during the production process, reduced material storage and handling costs, conversion of waste into valuable forms, reduced waste disposal costs or safer workplace conditions. These offsets are frequently related, so that achieving one can lead to the realization of several others.

As yet, no broad tabulation exists of innovation offsets. Most of the work done in this area involves case studies, because case studies are the only vehicle currently available to measure compliance costs and both direct and indirect innovation benefits. This journal is not the place for a comprehensive listing of available case studies. However, offering some examples should help the reader to understand how common and plausible such effects are.

Innovation to comply with environmental regulation often improves product performance or quality. In 1990, for instance, Raytheon found itself required (by the Montreal Protocol and the U.S. Clean Air Act) to eliminate ozone-depleting chlorofluorocarbons (CFCs) used for cleaning printed electronic circuit boards after the soldering process. Scientists at Raytheon initially thought that complete elimination of CFCs would be impossible. However, they eventually adopted a new semiaqueous, terpene-based cleaning agent that could be reused. The new method proved to result in an increase in average product quality, which had occasionally been compromised by the old CFC-based cleaning agent, as well as lower operating costs (Raytheon, 1991, 1993). It would not have been adopted in the absence of environmental regulation mandating the phase-out of CFCs. Another example is the move by the Robbins Company (a jewelry company based in Attleboro, Massachusetts) to a closed-loop, zero-discharge system for handling the water used in plating (Berube, Nash, Maxwell and Ehrenfeld, 1992). Robbins was facing closure due to violation of its existing discharge permits. The water produced by purification through filtering and ion exchange in the new closed-loop system was 40 times cleaner than city water and led to higher-quality plating and fewer rejects. The result was enhanced competitiveness.

Environmental regulations may also reduce product costs by showing how to eliminate costly materials, reduce unnecessary packaging or simplify designs. Hitachi responded to a 1991 Japanese recycling law by redesigning products to reduce disassembly time. In the process, the number of parts in a washing machine fell 16 percent, and the number of parts on a vacuum cleaner fell 30 percent. In this way, moves to redesign products for better recyclability can lead to fewer components and thus easier assembly.

Environmental standards can also lead to innovation that reduces disposal costs (or boosts scrap or resale value) for the user. For instance, regulation that requires recyclability of products can lead to designs that allow valuable materials to be recovered more easily after disposal of the product. Either the customer or the manufacturer who takes back used products reaps greater value.

These have all been examples of product offsets, but process offsets are common as well. Process changes to reduce emissions frequently result in increases in product yields. At Ciba-Geigy's dyestuff plant in New Jersey, the need to meet new environmental standards caused the firm to reexamine its wastewater streams. Two changes in its production process—replacing iron with a different chemical conversion agent that did not result in the formation of solid iron sludge and process changes that eliminated the release of potentially toxic product into the wastewater stream—not only boosted yield by 40 percent but also eliminated wastes, resulting in annual cost savings of $740,000 (Dorfman, Muir and Miller, 1992).[4]

Similarly, 3M discovered that in producing adhesives in batches that were transferred to storage tanks, one bad batch could spoil the entire contents of a tank. The result was wasted raw materials and high costs of hazardous waste disposal. 3M developed a new technique to run quality tests more rapidly on new batches. The new technique allowed 3M to reduce hazardous wastes by 10 tons per year at almost no cost, yielding an annual savings of more than $200,000 (Sheridan, 1992).

Solving environmental problems can also yield benefits in terms of reduced downtime. Many chemical production processes at DuPont, for

---

[4]We should note that this plant was ultimately closed. However, the example described here does illustrate the role of regulatory pressure in process innovation.

example, require start-up time to stabilize and bring output within specifications, resulting in an initial period during which only scrap and waste is produced. Installing higher-quality monitoring equipment has allowed DuPont to reduce production interruptions and the associated wasteful production start-ups, thus reducing waste generation as well as downtime (Parkinson, 1990).

Regulation can trigger innovation offsets through substitution of less costly materials or better utilization of materials in the process. For example, 3M faced new regulations that will force many solvent users in paper, plastic and metal coatings to reduce its solvent emissions 90 percent by 1995 (Boroughs and Carpenter, 1991). The company responded by avoiding the use of solvents altogether and developing coating products with safer, water-based solutions. At another 3M plant, a change from a solvent-based to a water-based carrier, used for coating tablets, eliminated 24 tons per year of air emissions. The $60,000 investment saved $180,000 in unneeded pollution control equipment and created annual savings of $15,000 in solvent purchases (Parkinson, 1990). Similarly, when federal and state regulations required that Dow Chemical close certain evaporation ponds used for storing and evaporating wastewater resulting from scrubbing hydrochloric gas with caustic soda, Dow redesigned its production process. By first scrubbing the hydrochloric acid with water and then caustic soda, Dow was able to eliminate the need for evaporation ponds, reduce its use of caustic soda, and capture a portion of the waste stream for reuse as a raw material in other parts of the plant. This process change cost $250,000 to implement. It reduced caustic waste by 6,000 tons per year and hydrochloric acid waste by 80 tons per year, for a savings of $2.4 million per year (Dorfman, Muir and Miller, 1992).

The Robbins Company's jewelry-plating system illustrates similar benefits. In moving to the closed-loop system that purified and recycled water, Robbins saved over $115,000 per year in water, chemicals, disposal costs, and lab fees and reduced water usage from 500,000 gallons per week to 500 gallons per week. The capital cost of the new system, which completely eliminated the waste, was $220,000, compared to about $500,000 for a wastewater treatment facility that would have brought Robbins' discharge into compliance only with current regulations.

At the Tobyhanna Army Depot, for instance, improvements in sandblasting, cleaning, plating and painting operations reduced hazardous waste generation by 82 percent between 1985 and 1992. That reduction saved the depot over $550,000 in disposal costs, and $400,000 in material purchasing and handling costs (PR Newswire, 1993).

Innovation offsets can also be derived by converting waste into more valuable forms. The Robbins Company recovered valuable precious metals in its zero discharge plating system. At Rhone-Poulenc's nylon plant in Chalampe, France, diacids (by-products that had been produced by an adipic acid process) used to be separated and incinerated. Rhone-Poulenc invested Fr 76 million and installed new equipment to recover and sell them as dye and tanning additives or coagulation agents, resulting in annual revenues of about Fr 20.1 million. In the United States, similar by-products from a Monsanto Chemical Company plant in Pensacola, Florida, are sold to utility companies who use them to accelerate sulfur dioxide removal during flue gas desulfurization (Basta and Vagi, 1988).

A few studies of innovation offsets do go beyond individual cases and offer some broader-based data. One of the most extensive studies is by INFORM, an environmental research organization. INFORM investigated activities to prevent waste generation—so-called source reduction activities—at 29 chemical plants in California, Ohio and New Jersey (Dorfman, Muir and Miller, 1992). Of the 181 source-reduction activities identified in this study, only one was found to have resulted in a net cost increase. Of the 70 activities for which the study was able to document changes in product yield, 68 reported yield increases; the average yield increase for the 20 initiatives with specific available data was 7 percent. These innovation offsets were achieved with surprisingly low investments and very short payback periods. One-quarter of the 48 initiatives with detailed capital cost information required no capital investment at all; of the 38 initiatives with payback period data, nearly two-thirds were shown to have recouped their initial investments in six months or less. The annual savings per dollar spent on source reduction averaged $3.49 for the 27 activities for which this information could be calculated. The study also investigated the motivating factors behind the plant's source-reduction activities. Significantly, it found that waste disposal costs were the most often cited, followed by environmental regulation.

To build a broader base of studies on innovation offsets to environmental regulation, we have been collaborating with the Management Institute for Environment and Business on a series of international case studies, sponsored by the EPA, of industries and entire sectors significantly affected by environmental regulation. Sectors studied include pulp and paper, paint and coatings, electronics manufacturing, refrigerators, dry cell batteries and printing inks (Bonifant and Ratcliffe, 1994; Bonifant 1994a,b; van der Linde, 1995a,b,c). Some examples from that effort have already been described here.

A solid body of case study evidence, then, demonstrates that innovation offsets to environmental regulation are common.[5] Even with a generally hostile regulatory climate, which is not designed to encourage such innovation, these offsets can sometimes exceed the cost of compliance. We expect that such examples will proliferate as companies and regulators become more sophisticated and shed old mindsets.

---

[5]Of course, a list of case examples, however long, does not prove that companies can always innovate or substitute for careful empirical testing in a large cross-section of industries. Given our current ability to capture the true costs and often multifaceted benefits of regulatory-induced innovation, reliance on the weight of case study evidence is necessary. As we discuss elsewhere, there is no countervailing set of case studies that shows that innovation offsets are unlikely or impossible.

Early-Mover Advantage in International Markets

World demand is moving rapidly in the direction of valuing low-pollution and energy-efficient products, not to mention more resource-efficient products with higher resale or scrap value. Many companies are using innovation to command price premiums for "green" products and open up new market segments. For example, Germany enacted recycling standards earlier than in most other countries, which gave German firms an early-mover advantage in developing less packaging-intensive products, which have been warmly received in the marketplace. Scandinavian pulp and paper producers have been leaders in introducing new environmentally friendly production processes, and thus Scandinavian pulp and paper equipment suppliers such as Kamyr and Sunds have made major gains internationally in selling innovative bleaching equipment. In the United States, a parallel example is the development by Cummins Engine of low-emissions diesel engines for trucks, buses and other applications in response to U.S. environmental regulations. Its new competence is allowing the firm to gain international market share.

Clearly, this argument only works to the extent that national environmental standards anticipate and are consistent with international trends in environmental protection, rather than break with them. Creating expertise in cleaning up abandoned hazardous waste sites, as the U.S. Superfund law has done, does little to benefit U.S. suppliers if no other country adopts comparable toxic waste cleanup requirements. But when a competitive edge is attained, especially because a company's home market is sophisticated and demanding in a way that pressures the company to further innovation, the economic gains can be lasting.

Answering Defenders of the Traditional Model

Our argument that strict environmental regulation can be fully consistent with competitiveness was originally put forward in a short *Scientific American* essay (Porter, 1991; see also van der Linde, 1993). This essay received far more scrutiny than we expected. It has been warmly received by many, especially in the business community. But it has also had its share of critics, especially among economists (Jaffe, Peterson, Portney and Stavins, 1993, 1994; Oates, Palmer and Portney, 1993; Palmer and Simpson, 1993; Simpson, 1993; Schmalensee, 1993).

One criticism is that while innovation offsets are theoretically possible, they are likely to be rare or small in practice. We disagree. Pollution is the emission or discharge of a (harmful) substance or energy form into the environment. Fundamentally, it is a manifestation of economic waste and involves unnecessary, inefficient or incomplete utilization of resources, or resources not used to generate their highest value. In many cases, emissions are a sign of inefficiency and force a firm to perform non-value-creating activities such as handling, storage and disposal. Within the company itself, the costs of poor resource utilization are most obvious in incomplete material utilization, but are also manifested in poor process control, which generates unnecessary stored material, waste and defects. There are many other hidden costs of resource inefficiencies later in the life cycle of the product. Packaging discarded by distributors or customers, for example, wastes resources and adds costs. Customers bear additional costs when they use polluting products or products that waste energy. Resources are also wasted when customers discard products embodying unused materials or when they bear the costs of product disposal.[6]

As the many examples discussed earlier suggest, the opportunity to reduce cost by diminishing pollution should thus be the rule, not the exception. Highly toxic materials such as heavy metals or solvents are often expensive and hard to handle, and reducing their use makes sense from several points of view. More broadly, efforts to reduce pollution and maximize profits share the same basic principles, including the efficient use of input, substitution of less expensive materials and the minimization of unneeded activities.[7]

A corollary to this observation is that scrap or waste or emissions can carry important information about flaws in product design or the production process. A recent study of process changes in 10 printed circuit board manufacturers, for example, found that 13 of 33 major changes were initiated by pollution control personnel. Of these, 12 resulted in cost reduction, eight in quality improvements and five in extension of production capabilities (King, 1994).

Environmental improvement efforts have traditionally overlooked the systems cost of resource inefficiency. Improvement efforts have focused on *pollution control* through better identification, processing and disposal of discharges or waste, an inherently costly approach. In recent years, more advanced companies and regulators have embraced the concept of *pollution prevention*, sometimes called source reduction, which uses material substitution, closed-loop processes and the like to limit pollution before it occurs.

But although pollution prevention is an important step in the right direction, ultimately companies and regulators must learn to frame environmental improvement in terms of *resource productivity*, or the efficiency and effectiveness with which companies and their customers use

---

[6]At its core, then, pollution is a result of an intermediate state of technology or management methods. Apparent exceptions to the resource productivity thesis often prove the rule by highlighting the role of technology. Paper made with recycled fiber was once greatly inferior, but new de-inking and other technologies have made its quality better and better. Apparent tradeoffs between energy efficiency and emissions rest on incomplete combustion.

[7]Schmalensee (1993) counters that NO_x emissions often result from thermodynamically efficient combustion. But surely this is an anomaly, not the rule, and may represent an intermediate level of efficiency.

resources.[8] Improving resource productivity within companies goes beyond eliminating pollution (and the cost of dealing with it) to lowering true economic cost and raising the true economic value of products. At the level of resource productivity, environmental improvement and competitiveness come together. The imperative for resource productivity rests on the private costs that companies bear because of pollution, not on mitigating pollution's social costs. In addressing these private costs, it highlights the opportunity costs of pollution—wasted resources, wasted efforts and diminished product value to the customer—not its actual costs.

This view of pollution as unproductive resource utilization suggests a helpful analogy between environmental protection and product quality measured by defects. Companies used to promote quality by conducting careful inspections during the production process, and then by creating a service organization to correct the quality problems that turned up in the field. This approach has proven misguided. Instead, the most cost-effective way to improve quality is to build it into the entire process, which includes design, purchased components, process technology, shipping and handling techniques and so forth. This method dramatically reduces inspection, rework and the need for a large service organization. (It also leads to the oft-quoted phrase, "quality is free.") Similarly, there is reason to believe that companies can enjoy substantial innovation offsets by improving resource productivity throughout the value chain instead of through dealing with the manifestations of inefficiency like emissions and discharges.

Indeed, corporate total quality management programs have strong potential also to reduce pollution and lead to innovation offsets.[9] Dow Chemical, for example, has explicitly identified the link between quality improvement and environmental performance, by using statistical process control to reduce the variance in processes and lower waste (Sheridan, 1992).

A second criticism of our hypothesis is to point to the studies finding high costs of compliance with environmental regulation, as evidence that there is a fixed tradeoff between regulation and competitiveness. But these studies are far from definitive.

Estimates of regulatory compliance costs prior to enactment of a new rule typically exceed the actual costs. In part, this is because such estimates are often self-reported by industries who oppose the rule, which creates a tendency to inflation. A prime example of this type of thinking was a statement by Lee Iacocca, then vice president at the Ford Motor Company, during the debate on the 1970 Clean Air Act. Iacocca warned that compliance with the new regulations would require huge price increases for automobiles, force U.S. automobile production to a halt after January 1, 1975, and "do irreparable damage to the U.S. economy" (Smith, 1992). The

---

[8]One of the pioneering efforts to see environmental improvement this way is Joel Makower's (1993) book. *The E-Factor. The Bottom-Line Approach to Environmentally Responsible Business.*

[9]A case study of pollution prevention in a large multinational firm showed those units with strong total quality management programs in place usually undertake more effective pollution prevention efforts than units with less commitment to total quality management. See Rappaport (1992), cited in U.S. Congress, Office of Technology Assessment (1994).

1970 Clean Air Act was subsequently enacted, and Iacocca's predictions turned out to be wrong. Similar dire predictions were made during the 1990 Clean Air Act debate; industry analysts predicted that burdens on the U.S. industry would exceed $100 billion. Of course, the reality has proven to be far less dramatic. In one study in the pulp and paper sector, actual costs of compliance were $4.00 to $5.50 per ton compared to original industry estimates of $16.40 (Bonson, McCubbin and Sprague, 1988).

Early estimates of compliance cost also tend to be exaggerated because they assume no innovation. Early cost estimates for dealing with regulations concerning emission of volatile compounds released during paint application held everything else constant, assuming only the addition of a hood to capture the fumes from paint lines. Innovation that improved the paint's transfer efficiency subsequently allowed not only the reduction of fumes but also paint usage. Further innovation in waterborne paint formulations without any VOC-releasing solvents made it possible to eliminate the need for capturing and treating the fumes altogether (Bonifant, 1994b). Similarly, early estimates of the costs of complying with a 1991 federal clean air regulation calling for a 98 percent reduction in atmospheric emissions of benzene from tar-storage tanks used by coal tar distillers initially assumed that tar-storage tanks would have to be covered by costly gas blankets. While many distillers opposed the regulations, Pittsburgh-based Aristech Chemical, a major distiller of coal tar, subsequently developed an innovative way to remove benzene from tar in the first processing step, thereby eliminating the need for the gas blanket and resulting in a saving of $3.3 million instead of a cost increase (PR Newswire, 1993).

Prices in the new market for trading allowances to emit SO_2 provide another vivid example. At the time the law was passed, analysts projected that the marginal cost of SO_2 controls (and, therefore, the price of an emission allowance) would be on the order of $300 to $600 (or more) per ton in Phase I and up to $1000 or more in Phase II. Actual Phase I allowance prices have turned out to be in the $170 to $250 range, and recent trades are heading lower, with Phase II estimates only slightly higher (after adjusting for the time value of money). In case after case, the differences between initial predictions and actual outcomes—especially after industry has had time to learn and innovate—are striking.

Econometric studies showing that environmental regulation raises costs and harms competitiveness are subject to bias, because net compliance costs are overestimated by assuming away innovation benefits. Jorgenson and Wilcoxen (1990), for example, explicitly state that they did not attempt to assess public or private benefits. Other often-cited studies that solely focus on costs, leaving out benefits, are Hazilla and Kopp (1990) and Gray (1987). By largely assuming away innovation effects, how could economic studies reach any other conclusion than they do?

Internationally competitive industries seem to be much better able to innovate in response to environmental regulation than industries that were uncompetitive to begin with, but no study measuring the effects of environmental regulation on industry competitiveness has taken initial competitiveness into account. In a study by Kalt (1988), for instance, the sectors where high environmental costs were associated with negative trade performance were ones such as ferrous metal mining, nonferrous mining, chemical and fertilizer manufacturing, primary iron and steel and primary nonferrous metals, industries where the United States suffers from dwindling raw material deposits, very high relative electricity costs, heavily subsidized foreign competitors and other disadvantages that have rendered them uncompetitive quite apart from environmental costs.[10] Other sectors identified by Kalt as having incurred very high environmental costs can actually be interpreted as supporting our hypothesis. Chemicals, plastics and synthetics, fabric, yarn and thread, miscellaneous textiles, leather tanning, paints and allied products, and paperboard containers all had high environmental costs but displayed positive trade performance.

A number of studies have failed to find that stringent environmental regulation hurts industrial competitiveness. Meyer (1992, 1993) tested and refuted the hypothesis that U.S. states with stringent environmental policies experience weak economic growth. Leonard (1988) was unable to demonstrate statistically significant offshore movements by U.S. firms in pollution-intensive industries. Wheeler and Mody (1992) failed to find that environmental regulation affected the foreign investment decisions of U.S. firms. Repetto (1995) found that industries heavily affected by environmental regulations experienced slighter reductions in their share of world exports than did the entire American industry from 1970 to 1990. Using U.S. Bureau of Census Data of more than 200,000 large manufacturing establishments, the study also found that plants with poor environmental records are generally not more profitable than cleaner ones in the same industry, even controlling for their age, size and technology. Jaffe, Peterson, Portney and Stavins (1993) recently surveyed more than 100 studies and concluded there is little evidence to support the view that U.S. environmental regulation had a large adverse effect on competitiveness.

Of course, these studies offer no proof for our hypothesis, either. But it is striking that so many studies find that even the poorly designed environmental laws presently in effect have little adverse effect on competitiveness. After all, traditional approaches to regulation have surely worked to stifle potential innovation offsets and imposed unnecessarily high costs of compliance on industry (as we will discuss in greater detail in the next section). Thus, studies using actual compliance costs to regulation are heavily biased

---

[10]It should be observed that a strong correlation between environmental costs and industry competitiveness does not necessarily indicate causality. Omitting environmental benefits from regulation, and reporting obvious (end-of-pipe) costs but not more difficult to identify or quantify innovation benefits can actually obscure a reverse causal relationship: industries that were uncompetitive in the first place may well be less able to innovate in response to environmental pressures, and thus be prone to end-of-pipe solutions whose costs are easily measured. In contrast, competitive industries capable of addressing environmental problems in innovative ways may report a lower compliance cost.

toward finding that such regulation has a substantial cost.[11] In no way do such studies measure the potential of well-crafted environmental regulations to stimulate competitiveness.

A third criticism of our thesis is that even if regulation fosters innovation, it will harm competitiveness by crowding out other potentially more productive investments or avenues for innovation. Given incomplete information, the limited attention many companies have devoted to environmental innovations and the inherent linkage between pollution and resource productivity described earlier, it certainly is not obvious that this line of innovation has been so thoroughly explored that the marginal benefits of further investment would be low. The high returns evident in the studies we have cited support this view. Moreover, environmental investments represent only a small percentage of overall investment in all but a very few industries.[12]

A final counterargument, more caricature than criticism, is that we are asserting that any strict environmental regulation will inevitably lead to innovation and competitiveness. Of course, this is not our position. Instead, we believe that if regulations are properly crafted and companies are attuned to the possibilities, then innovation to minimize and even offset the cost of compliance is likely in many circumstances.

Designing Environmental Regulation to Encourage Innovation

If environmental standards are to foster the innovation offsets that arise from new technologies and approaches to production, they should adhere to three principles. First, they must create the maximum opportunity for innovation, leaving the approach to innovation to industry and not the standard-setting agency. Second, regulations should foster continuous improvement, rather than locking in any particular technology. Third, the regulatory process should leave as little room as possible for uncertainty at every stage. Evaluated by these principles, it is clear that U.S. environmental regulations have often been crafted in a way that deters innovative solutions,

---

[11]Gray and Shadbegian (1993), another often-mentioned study, suffers from several of the problems discussed here. The article uses industry-reported compliance costs and does not control for plant technology vintage or the extent of other productivity-enhancing investments at the plant High compliance costs may well have been borne in old, inefficient plants where firms opted for secondary treatment rather than innovation. Moreover, U.S. producers may well have been disadvantaged in innovating given the nature of the U.S. regulatory process—this seems clearly to have been the case in pulp and paper, one of the industries studied by the Management Institute for Environment and Business (MEB).

[12]In paints and coatings, for example, environmental investments were 3.3 percent of total capital investment in 1989. According to Department of Commerce (1991) data (self-reported by industry), capital spending for pollution control and abatement outside of the chemical, pulp and paper, petroleum and coal, and primary metal sectors made up just 3.15 percent of total capital spending in 1991.

or even renders them impossible. Environmental laws and regulations need to take three substantial steps: phrasing environmental rules as goals that can be met in flexible ways; encouraging innovation to reach and exceed those goals; and administering the system in a coordinated way.

Clear Goals, Flexible Approaches

Environmental regulation should focus on outcomes, not technologies.[13] Past regulations have often prescribed particular remediation technologies—like catalysts or scrubbers to address air pollution—rather than encouraging innovative approaches. American environmental law emphasized phrases like "best available technology," or "best available control technology." But legislating as if one particular technology is always the "best" almost guarantees that innovation will not occur.

Regulations should encourage product and process changes to better utilize resources and avoid pollution early, rather than mandating end-of-pipe or secondary treatment, which is almost always more costly. For regulators, this poses a question of where to impose regulations in the chain of production from raw materials, equipment, the producer of the end product, to the consumer (Porter, 1985). Regulators must consider the technological capabilities and resources available at each stage, because it affects the likelihood that innovation will occur. With that in mind, the governing principle should be to regulate as late in the production chain as practical, which will normally allow more flexibility for innovation there and in upstream stages.

The EPA should move beyond the single medium (air, water and so on) as the principal way of thinking about the environment, toward total discharges or total impact.[14] It should reorganize around affected industry clusters (including suppliers and related industries) to better understand a cluster's products, technologies and total set of environmental problems. This will foster fundamental rather than piecemeal solutions.[15]

---

[13]There will always be instances of extremely hazardous pollution requiring immediate action, where imposing a specific technology by command and control may be the best or only viable solution. However, such methods should be seen as a last resort.

[14]A first step in this direction is the EPA's recent adjustment of the timing of its air rule for the pulp and paper industry so that it will coincide with the rule for water, allowing industry to see the dual impact of the rules and innovate accordingly.

[15]The EPA's regulatory cluster team concept, under which a team from relevant EPA offices approaches particular problems for a broader viewpoint, is a first step in this direction. Note, however, that of the 17 cluster groups formed, only four were organized around specific industries (petroleum refining, oil and gas production, pulp and paper, printing), while the remaining 13 focused on specific chemicals or types of pollution (U.S. Congress, Office of Technology Assessment, 1994).

Seeding and Spreading Environmental Innovations

Where possible, regulations should include the use of market incentives, including pollution taxes, deposit-refund schemes and tradable permits.[16] Such approaches often allow considerable flexibility, reinforce resource productivity, and also create incentives for ongoing innovation. Mandating outcomes by setting emission levels, while preferable to choosing a particular technology, still fails to provide incentives for continued and ongoing innovation and will tend to freeze a status quo until new regulations appear. In contrast, market incentives can encourage the introduction of technologies that exceed current standards.

The EPA should also promote an increased use of preemptive standards by industry, which appear to be an effective way of dealing with environmental regulation. Preemptive standards, agreed to with EPA oversight to avoid collusion, can be set and met by industry to avoid government standards that might go further or be more restrictive on innovation. They are not only less costly, but allow faster change and leave the initiative for innovation with industry.

The EPA should play a major role in collecting and disseminating information on innovation offsets and their consequences, both here and in other countries. Limited knowledge about opportunities for innovation is a major constraint on company behavior. A good start can be the "clearinghouse" of information on source-reduction approaches that EPA was directed to establish by the Pollution Prevention Act (PPA) of 1990. The Green Lights and Toxics Release Inventories described at the start of this paper are other programs that involve collecting and spreading information. Yet another important initiative is the EPA program to compare emissions rates at different companies, creating methodologies to measure the full internal costs of pollution and ways of exchanging best practices and learning on innovative technologies.

Regulatory approaches can also function by helping create demand pressure for environmental innovation. One example is the prestigious German "Blue Angel" eco-label, introduced by the German government in 1977, which can be displayed only by products meeting very strict environmental criteria. One of the label's biggest success stories has been in oil and gas heating appliances: the energy efficiency of these appliances improved significantly when the label was introduced, and emissions of sulfur dioxide, carbon monoxide and nitrogen oxides were reduced by more than 30 percent.

---

[16]Pollution taxes can be implemented as effluent charges on the quantity of pollution discharges, as user charges for public treatment facilities, or as product charges based on the potential pollution of a product. In a deposit-refund system, such product charges may be rebated if a product user disposes of it properly (for example, by returning a lead battery for recycling rather than sending it to a landfill). Under a tradable permit system, like that included in the recent Clean Air Act Amendments, a maximum amount of pollution is set, and rights equal to that cap are distributed to firms. Firms must hold enough rights to cover their emissions; firms with excess rights can sell them to firms who are short.

Another point of leverage on the demand side is to harness the role of government as a demanding buyer of environmental solutions and environmentally friendly products. While there are benefits of government procurement of products such as recycled paper and retreaded tires, the far more leveraged role is in buying specialized environmental equipment and services.[17] One useful change would be to alter the current practice of requiring bidders in competitive bid processes for government projects to only bid with "proven" technologies, a practice sure to hinder innovation.

The EPA can employ demonstration projects to stimulate and seed innovative new technologies, working through universities and industry associations. A good example is the project to develop and demonstrate technologies for super-efficient refrigerators, which was conducted by the EPA and researchers in government, academia and the private sector (United States Environmental Protection Agency, 1992). An estimated $1.7 billion was spent in 1992 by the federal government on environmental technology R&D, but only $70 million was directed toward research on pollution prevention (U.S. Congress, Office of Technology Assessment, 1994).

Incentives for innovation must also be built into the regulatory process itself. The current permitting system under Title V of the Clean Air Act Amendments, to choose a negative example, requires firms seeking to change or expand their production process in a way that might impact air quality to revise their permit extensively, *no matter how little the potential effect on air quality may be.* This not only deters innovation, but drains the resources of regulators away from timely action on significant matters. On the positive side, the state of Massachusetts has initiated a program to waive permits in some circumstances, or promise an immediate permit, if a company takes a zero-discharge approach.

A final priority is new forums for settling regulatory issues that minimize litigation. Potential litigation creates enormous uncertainty; actual litigation burns resources. Mandatory arbitration, or rigid arbitration steps before litigation is allowed, would benefit innovation. There is also a need to rethink certain liability issues. While adequate safeguards must be provided against companies that recklessly harm citizens, there is a pressing need for liability standards that more clearly recognize the countervailing health and safety benefits of innovations that lower or eliminate the discharge of harmful pollutants.

Regulatory Coordination

Coordination of environmental regulation can be improved in at least three ways: between industry and regulators, between regulators at different levels and places in government, and between U.S. regulators and their international counterparts.

---

[17]See Marron (1994) for a demonstration of the modest productivity gains likely from government procurement of standard items, although in a static model.

In setting environmental standards and regulatory processes to encourage innovation, substantive industry participation in setting standards is needed right from the beginning, as is common in many European countries. An appropriate regulatory process is one in which regulations themselves are clear, who must meet them is clear, and industry accepts the regulations and begins innovating to address them, rather than spending years attempting to delay or relax them. In our current system, by the time standards are finally settled and clarified, it is often too late to address them fundamentally, making secondary treatment the only alternative. We need to evolve toward a regulatory regime in which the EPA and other regulators make a commitment that standards will be in place for, say, five years, so that industry is motivated to innovate rather than adopt increment solutions.

Different parts and levels of government must coordinate and organize themselves so that companies are not forced to deal with multiple parties with inconsistent desires and approaches. As a matter of regulatory structure, the EPA's proposed new Innovative Technology Council, being set up to advocate the development of new technology in every field of environmental policy, is a step in the right direction. Another unit in the EPA should be responsible for continued reengineering of the process of regulation to reduce uncertainty and minimize costs. Also, an explicit strategy is needed to coordinate and harmonize federal and state activities.[18]

A final issue of coordination involves the relationship between U.S. environmental regulations and those in other countries. U.S. regulations should be in sync with regulations in other countries and, ideally, be slightly ahead of them. This will minimize possible competitive disadvantages relative to foreign competitors who are not yet subject to the standard, while at the same time maximizing export potential in the pollution control sector. Standards that lead world developments provide domestic firms with opportunities to create valuable early-mover advantages. However, standards should not be too far ahead of, or too different in character from, those that are likely to apply to foreign competitors, for this would lead industry to innovate in the wrong directions.

Critics may note, with some basis, that U.S. regulators may not be able to project better than firms what type of regulations, and resultant demands for environmental products and services, will develop in other nations. However, regulators would seem to possess greater resources and information than firms for understanding the path of regulation in other countries.

---

[18]The cluster-based approach to regulation discussed earlier should also help eliminate the practice of sending multiple EPA inspectors to the same plant who do not talk to one another, make conflicting demands and waste time and resources. The potential savings from cluster- and multimedia-oriented permitting and inspection programs appear to be substantial. During a pilot multimedia testing program called the Blackstone Project, the Massachusetts Department of Environmental Protection found that multimedia inspections required 50 percent less time than conventional inspections—which at that time accounted for nearly one-fourth of the department's operating budget (Roy and Dillard, 1990).

Moreover, U.S. regulations influence the type and stringency of regulations in other nations, and as such help define demand in other world markets.

Imperatives for Companies

Of course, the regulatory reforms described here also seek to change how companies view environmental issues.[19] Companies must start to recognize the environment as a competitive opportunity—not as an annoying cost or a postponable threat. Yet many companies are ill-prepared to carry out a strategy of environmental innovation that produces sizable compensating offsets.

For starters, companies must improve their measurement and assessment methods to detect environmental costs and benefits.[20] Too often, relevant information is simply lacking. Typical is the case of a large producer of organic chemicals that retained a consulting firm to explore opportunities for reducing waste. The client thought it had 40 waste streams, but a careful audit revealed that 497 different waste streams were actually present (Parkinson, 1990). Few companies analyze the true cost of toxicity, waste, discharges and the second-order impacts of waste and discharges on other activities. Fewer still look beyond the out-of-pocket costs of dealing with pollution to investigate the opportunity costs of the wasted resources or foregone productivity. How much money is going up the smokestack? What percentage of inputs are wasted? Many companies do not even track environmental spending carefully, or subject it to evaluation techniques typical for "normal" investments.

Once environmental costs are measured and understood, the next step is to create a presumption for innovation-based solutions. Discharges, scrap and emissions should be analyzed for insights about beneficial product design or process changes. Approaches based on treatment or handling of discharges should be accepted only after being sent back several times for reconsideration. The responsibility for environmental issues should not be delegated to lawyers or outside consultants except in the adversarial regulatory process, or even to internal specialists removed from the line organization, residing in legal, government or environmental affairs departments. Instead, environmental strategies must become a general management

---

[19]For a more detailed perspective on changing company mindsets about competitiveness and environmentalism, see Porter and van der Linde (1995) in the *Harvard Business Review*.

[20]Accounting methods that are currently being discussed in this context include "full cost accounting," which attempts to assign all costs to specific products or processes, and "total cost accounting," which goes a step further and attempts both to allocate costs more specifically and to include cost items beyond traditional concerns, such as indirect or hidden costs (like compliance costs, insurance, on-site waste management, operation of pollution control and future liability) and less tangible benefits (like revenue from enhanced company image). See White, Becker and Goldstein (1991), cited in U.S. Congress, Office of Technology Assessment (1994).

issue if the sorts of process and product redesigns needed for true innovation are to even be considered, much less be proposed and implemented.

Conclusion

We have found that economists as a group are resistant to the notion that even well-designed environmental regulations might lead to improved competitiveness. This hesitancy strikes us as somewhat peculiar, given that in other contexts, economists are extremely willing to argue that technological change has overcome predictions of severe, broadly defined environmental costs. A static model (among other flaws) has been behind many dire predictions of economic disaster and human catastrophe: from the predictions of Thomas Malthus that population would inevitably outstrip food supply; to the *Limits of Growth* (Meadows and Meadows, 1972), which predicted the depletion of the world's natural resources; to *The Population Bomb* (Ehrlich, 1968), which predicted that a quarter of the world's population would starve to death between 1973 and 1983. As economists are often eager to point out, these models failed because they did not appreciate the power of innovations in technology to change old assumptions about resource availability and utilization.

Moreover, the static mindset that environmentalism is inevitably costly has created a self-fulfilling gridlock, where both regulators and industry battle over every inch of territory. The process has spawned an industry of litigators and consultants, driving up costs and draining resources away from real solutions. It has been reported that four out of five EPA decisions are currently challenged in court (Clay, 1993, cited in U.S. Congress, Office of Technology Assessment, 1994). A study by the Rand Institute for Civil Justice found that 88 percent of the money paid out between 1986 and 1989 by insurers on Superfund claims went to pay for legal and administrative costs, while only 12 percent were used for actual site cleanups (Acton and Dixon, 1992).

The United States and other countries need an entirely new way of thinking about the relationship between environment and industrial competitiveness—one closer to the reality of modern competition. The focus should be on relaxing the environment-competitiveness tradeoff rather than accepting and, worse yet, steepening it. The orientation should shift from pollution control to resource productivity. We believe that no lasting success can come from policies that promise that environmentalism will triumph over industry, nor from policies that promise that industry will triumph over environmentalism. Instead, success must involve innovation-based solutions that promote both environmentalism and industrial competitiveness.

REFERENCES

Acton, Jan Paul, and Lloyd S. Dixon, *Superfund and Transaction Costs: The Experiences of Insurers and Very Large Industrial Firms*. Santa Monica: Rand Institute for Civil Justice, 1992.

Amoco Corporation and United States Environmental Protection Agency, "Amoco--U.S. EPA Pollution Prevention Project: Yorktown, Virginia, Project Summary," Chicago and Washington, D.C., 1992.

Basta, Nicholas and David Vagi, "A Casebook of Successful Waste Reduction Projections," *Chemical Engineering*, August 15, 1988, 95:11, 37.

Berube, M., J. Nash, J. Maxwell, and J. Ehrenfeld, "From Pollution Control to Zero Discharge: How the Robbins Company Overcame the Obstacles," *Pollution Prevention Review*, Spring 1992, 2:2, 189–207.

Bonifant, B., "Competitive Implications of Environmental Regulation in the Electronics Manufacturing Industry," Management Institute for Environment and Business, Washington, D.C., 1994a.

——, "Competitive Implications of Environmental Regulation in the Paint and Coatings Industry," Management Institute for Environment and Business, Washington, D.C., 1994b.

Bonifant, B., and I. Ratcliffe, "Competitive Implications of Environmental Regulation in the Pulp and Paper Industry," Management Institute for Environment and Business, Washington, D.C., 1994.

Bonson, N. C, Neil McCubbin, and John B. Sprague, "Kraft Mill Effluents in Ontario." Report prepared for the Technical Advisory Committee, Pulp and Paper Sector of MISA, Ontario Ministry of the Environment, Toronto, Ontario, Canada, March 29, 1988, Section 6, p. 166.

Boroughs, D. L., and B. Carpenter, "Helping the Planet and the Economy," *U.S. News & World Report*, March 25, 1991, 110:11, 46.

Clay, Don, "New Environmentalist: A Cooperative Strategy," *Forum for Applied Research and Public Policy*, Spring 1993, 8, 125–28.

DeCanio, Stephen J., "Why Do Profitable Energy-Saving Investment Projects Languish?" Paper presented at the Second International Research Conference of the Greening of Industry Network, Cambridge, Mass., 1993.

Department of Commerce, "Pollution Abatement Costs and Expenditures," Washington, D.C., 1991.

Dorfman, Mark H., Warren R. Muir, and Catherine G. Miller, *Environmental Dividends: Cutting More Chemical Wastes*. New York INFORM, 1992.

Ehrlich, Paul, *The Population Bomb*. New York: Ballantine Books, 1968.

Freeman, A. Myrick, III, "Methods for Assessing the Benefits of Environmental Programs." In Kneese, A. V., and J. L. Sweeney, eds., *Handbook of Natural Resource and Energy Economics*. Vol. 1. Amsterdam: North-Holland, 1985, pp. 223–70.

Gray, Wayne B., "The Cost of Regulation: OSHA, EPA, and the Productivity Slowdown," *American Economic Review*, 1987, 77:5, 998–1006.

Gray, Wayne B., and Ronald J. Shadbegian, "Environmental Regulation and Productivity at the Plant Level," discussion paper, U.S. Department of Commerce, Center for Economic Studies, Washington, D.C., 1993.

Hartwell, R. V., and L. Bergkamp, "Eco-Labelling in Europe: New Market-Related Environmental Risks?," *BNA International Environment Daily*, Special Report, Oct. 20, 1992.

Hazilla, Michael, and Raymond J. Kopp, "Social Cost of Environmental Quality Regulations: A General Equilibrium Analysis," *Journal of Political Economy*, 1990, *98*:4, 853–73.

Jaffe, Adam B., S. Peterson, Paul Portney, and Robert N. Stavins, "Environmental Regulations and the Competitiveness of U.S. Industry," Economics Resource Group, Cambridge, Mass., 1993.

Jaffe, Adam B., S. Peterson, Paul Portney, and Robert N. Stavins, "Environmental Regulation and International Competitiveness: What Does the Evidence Tell Us," draft, January 13, 1994.

Jorgenson, Dale W., and Peter J. Wilcoxen, "Environmental Regulation and U.S. Economic Growth," *Rand Journal of Economics*, Summer 1990, *21*:2, 314–40.

Kalt, Joseph P., "The Impact of Domestic Environmental Regulatory Policies on U.S. International Competitiveness." In Spence, A. M., and H. Hazard, eds., *International Competitiveness*, Cambridge, Mass: Harper and Row, Ballinger, 1988, pp. 221–62.

King, A., "Improved Manufacturing Resulting from Learning-From-Waste: Causes, Importance, and Enabling Conditions," working paper, Stern School of Business, New York University, 1994.

Leonard, H. Jeffrey, *Pollution and the Struggle for World Product*. Cambridge, U.K.: Cambridge University Press, 1988.

Makower, Joel, *The E-Factor: The Bottom-Line Approach to Environmentally Responsible Business*. New York: Times Books, 1993.

Marron, Donald B., "Buying Green: Government Procurement as an Instrument of Environmental Policy," mimeo, Massachusetts Institute of Technology, 1994.

Massachusetts Department of Environmental Protection, Daniel S. Greenbaum, Commissioner, interview, Boston, August 8, 1993.

Meadows, Donella H., and Dennis L. Meadows, *The Limits of Growth*. New York: New American Library, 1972.

Meyer, Stephen M., *Environmentalism and Economic Prosperity: Testing the Environmental Impact Hypothesis*. Cambridge, Mass.: Massachusetts Institute of Technology, 1992.

Meyer, Stephen M., *Environmentalism and Economic Prosperity: An Update*. Cambridge, Mass.: Massachusetts Institute of Technology, 1993.

National Paint and Coatings Association, *Improving the Superfund: Correcting a National Public Policy Disaster*. Washington, D.C., 1992.

Oates, Wallace, Karen L. Palmer, and Paul Portney, "Environmental Regulation and International Competitiveness: Thinking About the Porter Hypothesis." Resources for the Future Working Paper 94–02, 1993.

Palmer, Karen L., and Ralph David Simpson, "Environmental Policy as Industrial Policy," *Resources*, Summer 1993, *112*, 17–21.

Parkinson, Gerald, "Reducing Wastes Can Be Cost-Effective," *Chemical Engineering*, July 1990, *97*:7, 30.

Porter, Michael E., *Competitive Advantage: Creating and Sustaining Superior Performance*. New York: Free Press, 1985.

———, *The Competitive Advantage of Nations*. New York: Free Press, 1990.

———, "America's Green Strategy," *Scientific American*, April 1991, *264*, 168.

Porter, Michael E., and Claas van der Linde, "Green *and* Competitive: Breaking the Stalemate," *Harvard Business Review*, September–October 1995.

PR Newswire, "Winners Announced for Governor's Waste Minimization Awards," January 21, 1993, State and Regional News Section.

Rappaport, Ann, "Development and Transfer of Pollution Prevention Technology Within a Multinational Corporation," dissertation, Department of Civil Engineering. Tufts University, May 1992.

Raytheon Inc., "Alternative Cleaning Technology." Technical Report Phase II. January–October 1991.

Raytheon Inc., J. R. Pasquariello, Vice President Environmental Quality; Kenneth J. Tierney, Director Environmental and Energy Conservation; Frank A. Marino, Senior Corporate Environmental Specialist; interview, Lexington, Mass., April 4, 1993.

Repetto, Robert, "Jobs, Competitiveness, and Environmental Regulation: What Are the Real Issues?," Washington, D.C.: World Resources Institute, 1995.

Roy, M., and L. A. Dillard, "Toxics Use in Massachusetts: The Blackstone Project," *Journal of Air and Waste Management Association*, October 1990, *40*:10, 1368–71.

Schmalensee, Richard, "The Costs of Environmental Regulation." Massachusetts Institute of Technology, Center for Energy and Environmental Policy Research Working Paper 93–015, 1993.

Sheridan, J. H., "Attacking Wastes and Saving Money . . . Some of the Time," *Industry Week*, February 17, 1992, *241*:4, 43.

Simpson, Ralph David, "Taxing Variable Cost: Environmental Regulation as Industrial Policy." Resources for the Future Working Paper ENR93–12, 1993.

Smith, Zachary A, *The Environmental Policy Paradox*. Englewood Cliffs, N.J.: Prentice-Hall, 1992.

United States Environmental Protection Agency, "Multiple Pathways to Super Efficient Refrigerators," Washington, D.C., 1992.

U.S. Congress, Office of Technology Assessment, "Industry, Technology, and the Environment: Competitive Challenges and Business Opportunities," OTA-ITE-586, Washington, D.C., 1994.

van der Linde, Claas, "The Micro-Economic Implications of Environmental Regulation: A Preliminary Framework." In *Environmental Policies and Industrial Competitiveness*. Paris: Organization of Economic Cooperation and Development, 1993, pp. 69–77.

———, "Competitive Implications of Environmental Regulation in the Cell Battery Industry," Hochschule St. Gallen, St. Gallen, forthcoming 1995a.

———, "Competitive Implications of Environmental Regulation in the Printing Ink Industry," Hochschule St. Gallen, St. Gallen, forthcoming 1995b.

———, "Competitive Implications of Environmental Regulation in the Refrigerator Industry," Hochschule St. Gallen, St. Gallen, forthcoming 1995c.

Wheeler, David, and Ashoka Mody, "International Investment Location Decisions: The Case of U.S. Firms," *Journal of International Economics*, August 1992, *33*, 57–76.

White, A. L., M. Becker, and J. Goldstein, "Alternative Approaches to the Financial Evaluation of Industrial Pollution Prevention Investments," prepared for the New Jersey Department of Environmental Protection, Division of Science and Research, November 1991.

6   *Tightening Environmental Standards: The Benefit-Cost or the No-Cost Paradigm?**

Karen Palmer

Wallace E. Oates

Paul R. Portney

Karen Palmer is Senior Fellow at Resources for the Future; Wallace Oates is Professor of Economics at the University of Maryland, and University Resources for the Future; and Fellow Paul R. Portney is Professor of Economics, Halle Chair in Leadership and Dean, Eller College of Management at the University of Arizona.

Michael Porter and Claas van der Linde have written a paper that is interesting and, to us at least, somewhat astonishing. It is a defense of environmental regulation—indeed, an invitation to more stringent regulation—that makes essentially no reference to the *social* benefits of such regulation. This approach contrasts starkly with the methods that economists and other policy analysts have traditionally used when assessing environmental or other regulatory programs.

The traditional approach consists of comparing the beneficial effects of regulation with the costs that must be borne to secure these benefits. For environmental regulation, the social benefits include the reductions in morbidity or premature mortality that can accompany cleaner air, the enhanced recreational opportunities that can result from water-quality improvements, the increased land values that might attend the cleanup of a hazardous waste site, the enhanced vitality of aquatic ecosystems that might follow reductions in agricultural pesticide use or any of the other potentially significant benefits associated with tighter standards. From this benefit-cost approach emerges the standard tradeoff discussed in virtually every economics textbook.

Porter and van der Linde deny the validity of this approach to the analysis of environmental regulation, claiming it to be an artifact of what

"Tightening Environmental Standards: The Benefit-Cost or the No-Cost Paradigm?" by Karen Palmer, Wallace E. Oates, and Paul R. Portney. *Journal of Economic Perspectives* 9. 1995. Pp. 119–132. Reprinted by permission of the American Economic Association.

*We are grateful for helpful comments on earlier drafts to Albert McGartland, Richard Schmalensee and the editors of this journal. We wish to thank the Environmental Protection Agency, the National Science Foundation and the Sloan Foundation for support that made this work possible.

they see as a "static mindset." In their view, economists have failed to appreciate the capacity of stringent environmental regulations to induce innovation, and this failure has led them to a fundamental misrepresentation of the problem of environmental regulation. There is no tradeoff, Porter and van der Linde suggest; instead, environmental protection, properly pursued, often presents a free or even a paid lunch. As they put it, there are lots of $10 bills lying around waiting to be picked up.

We take strong issue with their view. If this were simply a matter of intellectual sparring, it would be inconsequential outside academe. But their view has found a ready audience in some parts of the policymaking community. For example, Vice President Gore (1992, p. 342) writes that "3M, in its Pollution Prevention Pays program, has reported significant profit improvement as a direct result of its increased attention to shutting off all the causes of pollution it could find." If environmental regulations are essentially costless (or even carry a negative cost!), then it is unnecessary to justify and measure with care the presumed social benefits of environmental programs. Stringent environmental measures (of the right kind) are good for business as well as the environment; in the Washington parlance, we have ourselves a "win-win situation." Not surprisingly, this view has also been warmly received by environmentalists and by regulators eager to avoid being seen as imposing unwanted costs on businesses or lower levels of government. At a time of burgeoning interest in Congress in the economic justification for federal regulations, Porter and van der Linde suggest the cost of environmental regulation may be negligible or even nonexistent.

To clarify the points that are in dispute, we should state at the outset that we agree with Porter and van der Linde on a number of matters. First, we share their enthusiasm for a heavier reliance on incentive-based regulation in lieu of command-and-control. Early returns suggest, for example, that tradable permits for sulfur dioxide emissions will reduce the cost of the 1990 acid rain control program by at least 50 percent when measured against the most likely command-and-control alternative (Burtraw, 1995; U.S. General Accounting Office, 1994; Rico, 1995). Second, we agree that early estimates of regulatory compliance costs are likely to be biased upward because of unforeseen technological advances in pollution control or prevention. Third, we accept that providing information, such as in EPA's "Green Lights" program (through which the agency provides technical assistance concerning energy-efficient lighting), may well help disseminate new technologies. Fourth, we acknowledge that regulations have sometimes led to the discovery of cost-saving or quality-improving innovation; in other words, we do *not* believe that firms are ever-vigilantly perched on their efficiency frontiers.

On this last point, however, we do not find Porter and van der Linde at all convincing concerning the pervasiveness of inefficiencies. The major empirical evidence that they advance in support of their position is a series of case studies. With literally hundreds of thousands of firms subject to environmental regulation in the United States alone, it would be hard *not* to find instances where regulation has seemingly worked to a polluting firm's advantage. But collecting cases where this has happened in no way establishes a general presumption in favor of this outcome. It would be an easy matter for us to assemble a matching list where firms have found their costs increased and profits reduced as a result of (even enlightened) environmental regulations, not to mention cases where regulation has pushed firms over the brink into bankruptcy.

What is needed, we believe, is a more systematic approach to the issue. Following a general observation to put things in context, we begin with a model in which increasing the stringency of incentive-based environmental regulations *must* result in reduced profits for the firm. This model is incomplete in various ways, but it provides a useful baseline for the succeeding discussion. From this baseline, we can then explore the sorts of changes in the model that could produce the result that regulation leads to higher profits—the outcome that Porter and van der Linde seem to suggest is the norm. We are then in a better position to assess the evidence and the weight of their case.

Innovation and Environmental Regulation: An Observation

Porter and van der Linde accuse mainstream environmental economics, with its "static mindset," of having neglected innovation. This charge is puzzling. For several decades now, environmental economists have made their case for incentive-based policy instruments (such as effluent charges or tradable emission permits) precisely by emphasizing the incentives that these measures provide for innovation in abatement technology (Kneese and Bower, 1968, p. 139). Virtually every standard textbook in environmental economics makes the point that incentive-based approaches are perhaps more attractive for reasons of dynamic efficiency than for their ability to minimize the costs of attaining environmental standards at any particular point in time. A substantial literature has developed in recent years that explores the effects of various policy instruments on research and development decisions concerning abatement technology, a literature on which we shall draw in this discussion.[1]

What distinguishes the Porter and van der Linde perspective from neoclassical environmental economics is *not* the "static mindset" of the latter. It is two other presumptions. First, they see a private sector that systematically overlooks profitable opportunities for innovation.[2] Second, and equally important, they envision a regulatory authority that is in a position to correct

---

[1]The reader interested in exploring this literature might begin with Magat (1978), Downing and White (1986), Malueg (1989), Milliman and Prince (1989), Parry (1992), Biglaiser and Horowitz (1995) and Simpson (1995).

[2]This, incidentally, seems a rather odd and sad commentary on the private sector to be coming from one of the country's eminent business professors and consultants.

this "market failure."[3] With properly designed measures, regulators can set in motion innovative activities through which firms can realize these over-looked opportunities. Their vision thus suggests a new role for regulatory activity in bringing about dynamic efficiency: enlightened regulators provide the needed incentives for cost-saving and quality-improving innovations that competition apparently fails to provide. Regulators can, as Porter and van der Linde put it, help firms "to overcome organizational inertia and to foster creative thinking," thereby increasing their profits.[4] We find this view hard to swallow, and suspect that most regulated firms would share our difficulty.

Environmental Regulation and Competitiveness: A Proposition

Drawing on some of the early literature on innovation in abatement technology, we now present a model in which even incentive-based environmental regulation results in reduced profits for the regulated firm. The model essentially formalizes the basic point that the addition (or tightening) of constraints on a firm's set of choices cannot be expected to result in an increased level of profits. Readers uninterested in the analytics may wish to skip to the next section.

We emphasize that this model is static in character and fails to address the inherent uncertainty in research and development (R&D) decisions. In this sense, it is subject to precisely the sort of criticism that Porter and van der Linde level in their paper. However, for the same reason, it provides a useful point of entry into the issue. The model is premised on the assumption that the polluting firm maximizes profits and operates in a perfectly competitive market; the firm takes competitors' outputs and R&D expenditures as given and also takes any regulations as exogenously determined. Given these assumptions, the model does not allow for any sort of strategic interaction. The possible effects of relaxing these assumptions and allowing game-theoretic strategic interactions among firms, or between the polluting firm and the regulator, will be discussed in the next section of this paper.

---

[3]This "market failure," incidentally, is quite different in character from the usual public goods argument that private firms underinvest in research and development because they will have difficulty appropriating enough of the social benefits. What Porter and van der Linde have in mind is a failure of private decision makers to respond to *private* profit opportunities.

[4]It is unclear whether Porter and van der Linde view this expanded role for regulation as a general proposition, or whether it is limited to environmental regulation. They appear to suggest the latter when they contend that as waste emissions into the environment, "[Pollution] is a manifestation of economic waste and involves unnecessary, inefficient or incomplete utilization of resources. . . ." This we also find puzzling. Whether it is efficient to recycle wastes, to discharge them into the environment or to adopt an entirely new technology that employs fewer polluting inputs depends on the costs (meaning, of course, the full social costs) of the various alternatives.

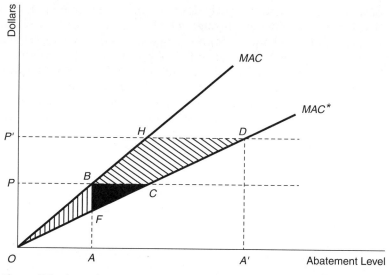

Figure 1 The Incentive to Innovate under an emission fee

Figure 1 depicts the polluting firm's options. The horizontal axis shows the "abatement level," so that the reduction in pollution increases as one moves from left to right. The vertical axis is measured in dollars, which means that one can graph both the firm's cost of various levels of pollution abatement and compare those costs with market-oriented effluent charges imposed by environmental regulators. The MAC curve (without a star) is the firm's present "marginal abatement cost" function; it indicates the marginal cost incurred by the firm to reduce pollution by an additional unit. The upward slope of the curve implies that the marginal cost of reducing pollution is rising.

Let us now assume that the firm could, if it chooses, reduce its marginal abatement cost function from the curve MAC to MAC*. Notice that with MAC*, a given marginal expenditure has a greater effect on pollution abatement than it would have with MAC. However, to move from MAC to MAC*, the firm must spend money to research and develop new pollution abatement technology. To simplify the problem, we will assume that the R&D expenditure necessary to move from MAC to MAC* is known completely—there is no risk or uncertainty.

This model will presume market-oriented regulators who use effluent charges to encourage pollution abatement. As long as a profit-maximizing firm can abate pollution itself for less than the effluent charge, it will choose to do so. However, after the point where the cost of abating pollution exceeds the effluent charge, the firm will prefer to pay the charge. Let us assume that the firm is initially confronted by an effluent charge of P. It chooses its profit-maximizing level of abatement activity, A, corresponding to the point *B*, where marginal abatement cost equals the effluent charge.

If the firm has been operating at abatement level *A*, an implication is that the (annualized) cost of the R&D effort to reduce MAC to MAC* must exceed the gains to the firm. The R&D investment in additional pollution-abatement technology won't pay off; thus outcome *B* must produce more profits for the firm than does the attainable point *C*. Figure 1 also depicts the gains to the polluting firm from undertaking the R&D effort, which can be divided into two parts. The source of the first part is that the earlier level of abatement activity becomes cheaper; the amount of gain here is given by the triangle *OFB*. The second part comes from the new technology. The company will choose to abate a greater amount of pollution and thus avoid paying the pollution charge on that additional pollution; the gain here is the triangle *BCF*.

The total gains to the polluting firm from innovation would thus be the area bounded by *OFCB*. Since the firm has not chosen this option, it must be that the cost of the R&D program that would move the firm from MAC to MAC* exceeds the area of the profit that would be gained, *OFCB*.

Now, assume that the environmental authority introduces a new, more stringent market-oriented environmental standard, taking the form of an increase in the effluent fee to *P′*. Without further assumptions, one cannot say whether the firm will respond to the higher effluent charge by sticking with the old technology and ending up at *H* or by investing in the new one and ending up at *D*.[5] But we will prove that both *H* and *D* generate lower profits than *B*. Therefore, it will be unambiguously true in this model that the higher effluent standard reduces profits for the firm.

It is straightforward to show that if the firm sticks with its old technology, the higher effluent charge must reduce its profits. In this case, the firm moves from *B* to *H*, and while this higher level of pollution abatement may be better for society, the firm is unambiguously worse off. It is paying the same amount to abate pollution up to *B* as it was before. Between *B* and *H*, it is paying more to abate pollution than under the previous, lower effluent charge. And above *H*, it is paying the higher effluent charge rather than the previously lower one.[6]

---

[5]What are some of the factors determining whether the firm chooses to respond to a higher effluent charge by investing in new technology? Overall, of course, the question is whether the cost-savings from the new technology exceed the R&D expenditures. Recent work offers some further insights. Ulph (1994) shows that an increase in an emission tax rate may increase a firm's incentive to engage in environmental R&D, but is likely to decrease its incentive to engage in R&D of a general unit-cost-reducing nature, leading to an ambiguous effect on overall R&D expenditures and on the firm's costs. Simpson (1995) suggests that when R&D is both cost reducing and emission reducing, the incentive effects of an increase in the emissions tax for R&D are lower the more R&D reduces marginal cost and the more competitive are rival firms.

[6]This is an application of a more general principle that for a given technology, profit is decreasing in input prices. In the environmental economics literature, waste emissions are typically treated as an input (along with labor, capital and so on) in the production function. This is reasonable, since attempts to cut back on waste emissions will involve the diversion of other inputs to abatement activities, thereby reducing the availability of these other inputs for the production of goods. Reduc-

It is only a bit trickier to demonstrate that profits at D, where the firm faces a higher effluent charge with the new technology, must be lower than profits at B, where the firm chose to face the lower effluent charge with its existing technology. Notice first that along the MAC* frontier, profits at choice D (given the higher effluent charge) must be lower than profits at point C, given the lower previous effluent charge. As already explained, if technology is constant, the higher effluent charge unambiguously reduces profits. But the basis of this model was that at the lower effluent charge, the firm didn't find it worthwhile to invest in the new technology; that is, profits were lower at C than at B. By transitivity, if profits at B exceed C, and profits at C exceed D, then it must be true that the higher effluent charge reduces profits for the firm, even if it adopts a new technology.

Thus, in this model of innovation in abatement technology, an increase in the stringency of environmental regulations unambiguously makes the polluting firm worse off. Even if the firm can invest and adopt a new, more efficient abatement technology, if that technology wasn't worth investing in before, its benefits won't be enough to raise the company's profits after the environmental standards are raised, either.

This leads us naturally to ask how one might amend the simple model to alter this basic result. We point out that simply making the model dynamic and/or introducing uncertainty will not overturn this result. It is straightforward to show that our basic proposition likewise applies to a firm that maximizes the expected present value of future profits. What elements, then, are missing from this simplified model that could give rise to an *increase* in profits following the imposition of tighter standards?

We can identify two such elements of potential importance. One possibility is strategic behavior, perhaps involving interactions between polluting firms, or between these firms and the regulating agency, or between regulatory agencies in different countries. The second possibility (the one emphasized by Porter and van der Linde) is the existence of opportunities for profitable innovation in the production of the firm's output that for some reason have been overlooked and that would be realized in the wake of new and tougher environmental regulations. The next two sections take up these extensions to the basic model and present some of the relevant empirical evidence.

Strategic Interaction among Polluters and Regulators

In the basic model, the polluting firm was operating in a competitive environment, taking as given both the behavior of competing firms and the

---

tions in emissions, in short, result in reduced output Moreover, given the reasonable assumption of rising marginal abatement costs, it makes sense to assume the usual curvature properties so that we can legitimately construct isoquants in emissions and another input and treat them in the usual way. In this framework, the emissions fee becomes simply the price of an input called "waste emissions."

standards set by the regulator. One important line of extension of the analysis is the introduction of strategic interaction among the various participants. There is some recent and ongoing work along these lines. For example, Barrett (1994) has explored a series of models in which regulators and polluting firms behave strategically. He finds that, in the spirit of the Porter–van der Linde thesis, there are indeed cases in which the government can actually improve the international competitive position of domestic exporters by imposing environmental standards upon them. One such case occurs if each firm takes the price of its competitor as fixed and then competes by setting its own profit-maximizing price. If the government sets a strong emission standard—by which Barrett means a standard beyond the point where the marginal benefits of pollution control equal marginal abatement costs—the domestic firm's marginal cost, and therefore its price, will rise. Recognizing that the domestic firm must charge a higher price to comply with the new standard, foreign competitors raise their prices without fear of retaliation. However, an increase in the foreign price raises demand for the output of the domestic firm with a resulting increase in its profits. This result holds when the domestic industry is an oligopoly as well as when it is a monopoly competing in an oligopolistic international market. It *may* also hold under Cournot competition—where each firm takes the quantity produced by its competitors as given and competes by altering the quantity it produces—if the domestic industry is an oligopoly, although this need not be the case.

In general, however, this result is not robust to other changes in the nature of the strategic behavior. For instance, if the domestic firm is a monopolist in its home country and the domestic and foreign firm are Cournot competitors, then the home government can improve the domestic firm's competitive position by reducing its environmental standards below the efficient level. Kennedy (1994) obtains a similar finding in a model with Cournot competition.

In another treatment of the issue, Simpson and Bradford (1996) develop a strategic trade model that explicitly includes R&D expenditures by firms. In this model, firms behave strategically both in setting levels of spending on R&D and in selecting output levels. The government regulates pollution through an emission fee. Simpson and Bradford find that for certain specifications of the cost and demand functions, increasing the emission fee can increase domestic R&D investment, reduce foreign R&D spending and increase domestic welfare (composed of domestic profits plus pollution fee revenues). However, they note that slight variations in the form of the cost function can reverse these results. Ulph (1994) surveys a number of recent papers that explicitly incorporate strategic R&D investment behavior by firms. This body of work indicates that the effect of environmental regulation on R&D is ambiguous and that even in the cases where higher emissions standards lead to higher domestic R&D spending, governments may still be better off selecting a lower-than-social-cost emission tax rate to shift profits from foreign firms to domestic firms.

Overall, this literature suggests that while it is possible to get results like those that Porter and van der Linde suggest are the norm from models that incorporate strategic behavior, such results are special cases. In many instances, these same strategic trade models suggest that the domestic authority should employ *weak* environmental regulations to promote international competitiveness. Moreover, as Barrett (1994) and Simpson and Bradford (1996) suggest, there are typically other sorts of measures that are more effective at improving international competitiveness than strategic environmental regulatory policy. This bottom line does not deny the Porter–van der Linde argument entirely; certain kinds of strategic models can produce outcomes of the type they describe. But it does seem to us that strategic models are unlikely to establish anything close to a general presumption that stringent environmental measures will enhance competitiveness. In addition, such strategic behavior is not what Porter and van der Linde have in mind. We turn to their basic contention now.

Regulation and "Offsets"

Their claim is that technologies exist of which the firm is unaware until prodded into discovering them by stringent environmental regulations. They go on to contend that such regulation will spur firms to innovate and that the newly discovered technologies will generally offset, or more than offset, the costs of pollution abatement or prevention. Our response takes two very different tacks.

First, we spoke with the vice presidents or corporate directors for environmental protection at Dow, 3M, Ciba-Geigy and Monsanto—all firms mentioned by Porter and van der Linde in their discussion of innovation or process offsets. While each manager acknowledged that in certain instances a particular regulatory requirement may have cost less than had been expected, or perhaps even paid for itself, each also said quite emphatically that, on the whole, environmental regulation amounted to a significant *net* cost to his company.

We have little doubt about the general applicability of this conclusion. Fortunately, we need not confine ourselves to speculation and anecdotes about the pervasiveness or the significance of pollution or innovation offsets. There are data available on this matter, and they indicate that such offsets pale in comparison to expenditures for pollution abatement and control.

Each year the Environmental Economics Division of the Commerce Department's Bureau of Economic Analysis (BEA) makes estimates of pollution abatement and control expenditures in the United States. One source for these estimates are Bureau of the Census surveys of manufacturing establishments, state and local governments, electric utilities, petroleum refiners and mining operations. Other information is gathered on federal government expenditures on pollution control, the cost of solid waste disposal, individual spending for motor vehicle pollution control equipment and operating costs and other environmental spending, as well. In 1992, according to BEA, pollution abatement and control expenditures in the United States came to $102 billion (Rutledge and Vogan, 1994, p. 47).

In addition to estimates of environmental spending, BEA also estimates the magnitude of the "offsets" that Porter and van der Linde claim are so pervasive. In fact, the Census Bureau survey of manufacturers (upon which BEA relies for most of its information about offsets) specifically asks respondents to report "cost offsets," which are defined in such a way as seemingly to encompass both the "product" and "process" offsets that Porter and van der Linde describe (U.S. Commerce Department, 1994).[7] For 1992, BEA estimates that cost offsets for the U.S. amounted to $1.7 billion, less than 2 percent of estimated environmental expenditures. This implies *net* spending for environmental protection in excess of $100 billion in 1992.

Net spending on protecting the environment may be greater than that, however, because there is reason to believe that the BEA estimates of environmental costs are on the low side. According to the Environmental Protection Agency (1990), the total cost associated with federal environmental regulation in the United States in 1992 was $135 billion.[8] EPA's estimates differ from those of BEA for a variety of reasons, some of which are difficult to discern. But some of the difference is due to the fact that EPA counts certain expenditures that BEA ignores (like those associated with measures to improve indoor air quality); because EPA apparently includes some opportunity costs in addition to out-of-pocket expenditures; and because the two agencies use different approaches occasionally even when focusing on the same category of pollution control. Some of the additional costs the EPA includes may give rise to their own offsets, but it is unlikely they will increase in proportion to these added costs. This is especially true where the difference between EPA's estimates and BEA's estimates involve imputed or opportunity costs.

One possible criticism of these estimates of offsets is that certain kinds of offsets in response to more stringent environmental regulation are not easily reportable on the Census Bureau survey form, and hence do not find

---

[7]It is worth including one of the examples from the Census Bureau survey to illustrate how closely the survey conforms to the Porter and van der Linde vision of offsets. The survey (U.S. Commerce Department, 1994, p. A-11) contains the following wording: "A manufacturer installs a closed loop recovery system in the production process so as to prevent the dumping of the chemicals into the water system. Since the closed loop recovery system recaptures and reuses the chemicals in the production process, it reduces expenses for chemicals. The pollution abatement portion of the capital expenditure pertaining to the closed loop recovery system is reported in Item 7 [the section of the survey where new capital expenditures are reported]. The operating expenses to maintain the system are reported in Item 3 [the analogous section for operating costs]. The value of recovered chemicals is reported as a cost offset." This example matches perfectly the example of the Robbins Company given by Porter and van der Linde, hence suggesting a close connection between the "offsets" described by Porter and van der Linde and the BEA estimates of offsets based on the Census Bureau survey.

[8]To this must be added the costs of additional control measures introduced by states (like California) that have, in some instances, gone beyond the federal statutes. We know of no estimates of these additional costs, but they may be substantial.

their way into the Census or BEA estimates. For instance, a manufacturing firm that dropped a product line altogether because it wished to avoid environmental regulations, and entered what instead turned out to be a more profitable product line, would be hard-pressed to report this as an "offset" according to the definition provided in the Census Bureau survey. But even if one doubled or tripled or even quadrupled the estimated offsets that are reported by Census and included in BEA's estimates, the total offsets would be less than $10 billion per year, leaving net annual environmental compliance costs in the range of $100 billion or more.

It is impossible to escape the conclusion that the U.S. devotes significant resources, *net of cost savings*, to environmental protection each year. Moreover, we reach this conclusion without making reference to the work of either Jorgenson and Wilcoxen (1990) or Hazilla and Kopp (1990), both of whom showed that the social costs of environmental regulation are *greater* when viewed in a dynamic general equilibrium context than in a static, partial equilibrium setting, because of the manner in which environmental regulations depress "productive" investment and the consequent reduction in the rate of economic growth. Porter and van der Linde deny the validity of this work on the grounds that it fails to factor offsets into account. Since these offsets appear to be quite small—based on both the reports of those who make environmental investments, as well as on hard data—this is hardly a liability of the general equilibrium approach.

One more word about offsets. Suppose that every single dollar a firm spent on pollution control or prevention was matched by a dollar of savings in the form of product or process offsets described by Porter and van der Linde. Would it then be the case that environmental regulation is free? Of course not. The sacrifice would be measured by other opportunities foregone. Firms can and do invest in changing the size and skill mix of their labor force, in their capital base, in the sources and term structure of their financing, their research and development strategies and other things, as well. Each of these investments is expected to do more than return one dollar for each dollar spent—typically firms must project returns that exceed a "hurdle rate" of 20 percent or more before undertaking an investment. Thus, even if environmental compliance produced offsets on a dollar-for-dollar basis—rather than one dollar for every 50 spent, as the data suggest—the foregone return on invested capital would still be a significant cost of regulation.

The International Setting

The original question prompting this debate concerned the impact of environmental regulations on the competitiveness of U.S. industry in the international arena. In a much shorter essay that appeared several years ago in *Scientific American*, Porter (1991) argued that the perverse command-and-control character of most U.S. regulation has seriously handicapped American firms in competitive with foreign rivals. Making the case (with which we enthusiastically agree) for incentive-based policy measures, Porter argued that U.S. firms were losing out to competition from German and Japanese companies, which benefit from more enlightened regulatory regimes.[9]

However, we believe the truth of the matter is rather different. It is not the case that other countries, including Germany or Japan, have made better use of incentive-based approaches than the United States. While other countries appear to have put in place regulatory programs that are less adversarial (and therefore less time consuming) than certain U.S. programs, most environmental regulation in Europe looks every bit as proscriptive as does the U.S. version. In fact, visitors from OECD and developing countries pour through Washington on a regular basis, trying to learn about the sulfur dioxide trading program put in place here five years ago.

Moreover, it is not clear that environmental regulation is harming the competitiveness of U.S. firms. In fact, Porter and van der Linde acknowledge as much, citing Jaffe et al. (1995, p. 157), who conclude in their survey paper that "overall, there is relatively little evidence to support the hypothesis that environmental regulations have had a large adverse effect on competitiveness, however that elusive term is defined."

This finding is important, but it has little to do with innovation offsets. As Jaffe et al. (1995) point out, there are several reasons why the relative stringency of U.S. environmental regulation to date has not been found to have adverse effects on competitiveness. First, for all but the most heavily polluting industries, the cost of complying with federal environmental regulations is a small fraction of total costs, sufficiently small (in most instances) to be swamped by international differentials in labor and material costs, capital costs, swings in exchange rates and so on. Second, although U.S. environmental regulations are arguably the most stringent in the world, the *differentials* between U.S. standards and those of our major industrialized trading partners are not very great, especially for air and water pollution control. Third, U.S. firms (as well as other multinationals) appear inclined to build modern, state-of-the-art facilities abroad, irrespective of the stringency of environmental statutes in the host country. Thus, even a significant difference in environmental standards between, say, the United States and a developing country will mean little to firms not willing to take advantage of lax standards.[10]

This is not to say that cost differentials stemming from international variations in environmental regulations are nonexistent. But as Jaffe et al.

---

[9]For a more detailed treatment of these particular issues, see our response (Oates et al., 1993) to the Porter (1991) paper.

[10]The rationale for this behavior appears to be two-fold. First, there is a widespread perception that tighter environmental regulations in the developing countries are inevitable, and that it is less expensive to invest initially in state-of-the-art abatement technology than it will be to retrofit later. Second, the aftermath of certain disasters, notably the Union Carbide catastrophe in Bhopal, India, has made management aware of the dangers inherent in the adoption of less than state-of-the-art control technologies in developing countries.

(1995, p. 159) conclude, these differentials "pose insufficient threats to U.S. industrial competitiveness to justify substantial cutbacks in domestic environmental regulations." More basically, the case for redesigning environmental programs to make more effective use of market incentives has little to do with international competitiveness; it's a much more straightforward issue of getting environmental value for the expenditures of social resources.

Conclusion

The underlying message from Porter and van der Linde about environmental regulation is not to worry, because it really won't be all that expensive. But it will. Annual U.S. expenditures for environmental protection, net of any offsets, currently are at least $100 billion, and probably considerably more. From *society's* standpoint, with the benefits of a cleaner environment figures into the balance, every dime of this money may be well spent; the literature is replete with examples of environmental programs that pass a benefit-cost test. But a comparison of the benefits and costs is exactly how one should determine the economic attractiveness of specific programs— not on the false premise of cost-free controls.

REFERENCES

Barrett, Scott, "Strategic Environmental Policy and International Trade," *Journal of Public Economics*, 1994, *54*:3, 325–38.

Biglaiser, Gary, and John K. Horowitz, "Pollution Regulation and Incentives for Pollution-Control Research," *Journal of Economics and Management Strategy*, Winter 1995, *3*, 663–840.

Burtraw, Dallas, "Efficiency Sans Allowance Traders?: Evaluating the SO2 Emission Trading Program to Date." Resources for the Future Discussion Paper No. 95–30, 1995.

Downing, Paul B., and Lawrence J. White, "Innovation in Pollution Control," *Journal of Environmental Economics and Management*, March 1986, *13*, 18–29.

Gore, Albert, *Earth in the Balance*. Boston: Houghton Mifflin Co., 1992.

Hazilla, Michael, and Raymond Kopp, "Social Cost of Environmental Quality Regulations: A General Equilibrium Analysis," *Journal of Political Economy*, August 1990, *98*, 853–73.

Jaffe, Adam B., Steven R. Peterson, Paul R. Portney, and Robert N. Stavins, "Environmental Regulations and the Competitiveness of U.S. Manufacturing: What Does the Evidence Tell Us?," *Journal of Economic Literature*, March 1995, *33*, 132–63.

Jorgenson, Dale W., and Peter J. Wilcoxen, "Environmental Regulation and U.S. Economic Growth," *Rand Journal of Economics*, Summer 1990, *21*, 314–40.

Kennedy, Peter, "Equilibrium Pollution Taxes in Open Economies with Imperfect Competition," *Journal of Environmental Economics and Management*, July 1994, *27*, 49–63.

Kneese, Allen V., and Blair T. Bower, *Managing Water Quality: Economics, Technology, Institutions*. Baltimore, Md.: Johns Hopkins University Press, 1968.

Magat, Wesley A., "Pollution Control and Technological Advance: A Dynamic Model of the Firm," *Journal of Environmental Economics and Management*, March 1978, *5*, 1–25.

Malueg, David A., "Emission Credit Trading and the Incentive to Adopt New Pollution Abatement Technology," *Journal of Environmental Economics and Management*, January 1989, *16*, 52–7.

Milliman, Scott R., and Raymond Prince, "Firm Incentives to Promote Technological Change in Pollution Control," *Journal of Environmental Economics and Management*, November 1989, *17*, 247–65.

Oates, Wallace E., Karen Palmer, and Paul R. Portney, "Environmental Regulation and International Competitiveness: Thinking About the Porter Hypothesis." Resources for the Future Discussion Paper No. 94–02, 1993.

Parry, Ian, "Environmental R&D and the Choice Between Pigouvian Taxes and Marketable Emissions Permits," unpublished Ph.D. dissertation, University of Chicago, 1992.

Porter, Michael E., "America's Green Strategy," *Scientific American*, April 1991, *264*, 168.

Rico, Renee, "The U.S. Allowance Trading System for Sulfer Dioxide: An Update on Market Experience," *Energy and Resource Economics*, March 1995, *5*:2, 115–29.

Rutledge, Gary L., and Christine R. Vogan, "Pollution Abatement and Control Expenditures, 1972–92," *Survey of Current Business*, May 1994, *74*, 36–49.

Simpson, David, "Environmental Policy, Innovation and Competitive Advantage." Resources for the Future Discussion Paper No. 95–12, 1995.

Simpson, David, and Robert L. Bradford, "Taxing Variable Cost: Environmental Regulation as Industrial Policy," *Journal of Environmental Economics Management*, [May 1996, *30*:3, 282–300].

Ulph, Alistair, "Environmental Policy and International Trade: A Survey of Recent Economic Analysis," Milan, Italy: Nota di Lavoro *53*:94, Fondazione Eni Enrico Mattei, 1994.

U.S. Department of Commerce (Bureau of the Census), "Pollution Abatement Costs and Expenditures, 1993," Current Industrial Reports; MA200(93)-1, Washington, D.C.: U.S. Government Printing Office, 1994.

U.S. Environmental Protection Agency, *Environmental Investments: The Cost of a Clean Environment*. Washington, D.C.: U.S. Environmental Protection Agency, 1990.

U.S. General Accounting Office, "Allowance Trading Offers an Opportunity to Reduce Emissions at Less Cost," document, GAO/RCED-95–30, 1994.

III

The Benefits of Environmental Protection

7 The Contingent Valuation Debate: Why Economists Should Care*

Paul R. Portney

Paul R. Portney is Professor of Economics, Halle Chair in Leadership and Dean, Eller College of Management at the University of Arizona.

The contingent valuation method involves the use of sample surveys (questionnaires) to elicit the willingness of respondents to pay for (generally) hypothetical projects or programs. The name of the method refers to the fact that the values revealed by respondents are contingent upon the constructed or simulated market presented in the survey. A spirited (and occasionally mean-spirited) battle over such methods is currently being waged, involving competing factions within the federal government, economists and lawyers representing business and environmental groups, and interested academics as well. At issue is a seemingly quite specific question: should environmental regulations currently under development at both the Department of the Interior and the Department of Commerce sanction the use of the contingent valuation method in estimating the damage done by spills of oil, chemicals, or other substances covered by federal law? More generally, the debate raises broad questions about what economists have to say about the values that individuals place on public or private goods.

The two papers that follow this one make cases for and against the use of the contingent valuation method. My aim here is to provide an overview of the technique and the debate surrounding it. I also want to suggest why this debate should matter to economists, both professionally and in their roles as citizens and consumers.

"The Contingent Valuation Debate: Why Economists Should Care" by Paul R. Portney. *Journal of Economic Perspectives* 8. 1994. Pp. 3–17. Reprinted by permission of the American Economic Association.

*For helpful comments on earlier drafts of this paper, thanks are due Kenneth Arrow, Richard Carson, Ronald Cummings, Peter Diamond, Rick Freeman, Michael Hanemann, Glen Harrison, Barbara Kanninen, Raymond Kopp, Alan Keuger, Edward Leamer, Robert Mitchell, Richard Schmalensee, Howard Schuman, Carl Shapiro, Robert Solow, and especially Kerry Smith and Timothy Taylor. Taylor's many editorial suggestions improved the paper greatly. Any errors are the author's responsibility alone.

The Origins of the Contingent
Valuation Method

As is often the case, it is useful to start with a bit of history.[1]

The first published reference to the contingent valuation method apparently occurred in 1947, when Ciriacy-Wantrup wrote about the benefits of preventing soil erosion (Ciriacy-Wantrup, 1947). He observed that some of these favorable effects (like reduced siltation of streams) were public goods, and suggested that one way to obtain information on the demand for these goods would be to ask individuals directly how much they would be willing to pay for successive increments. However, he never attempted to implement this idea directly.

It wasn't until almost two decades later that the contingent valuation method began to be applied in academic research. In his efforts to determine the value to hunters and wilderness lovers of a particular recreational area, Davis (1963) designed and implemented the first contingent valuation survey that attempted to elicit these values directly.

As a test for the reasonableness of his findings, Davis compared them with an estimate of willingness-to-pay that was based on the "travel cost" approach. The notion here, first suggested by Hotelling in a letter to the National Park Service in 1947, is that the "price" for visiting a park or other recreational area (even one for which entry is free) will vary according to the travel costs of visitors coming from different places (see also Clawson, 1959). Thus, a natural experiment exists where one can measure the quantity of visits to the park demanded by people at a range of prices (that is, coming from different distances) and estimate a demand curve, consumer surplus, and so on. Davis found that the travel cost method of estimating willingness to pay for visits to a recreation area provided a quite similar answer to his contingent valuation survey.

Natural resource and environmental economics then took an enormous jump when John Krutilla published "Conservation Reconsidered," arguably the most influential paper ever written in that subdiscipline (Krutilla, 1967). In less than ten pages, Krutilla identified the importance of the essentially irreversible nature of the development of natural environments, suggested that the divergence between willingness-to-pay and willingness-to-accept compensation for what he called "grand scenic wonders" may be especially large,[2] pointed to the potentially large economic value of preserving genetic variation, and foreshadowed the apparently growing value of outdoor recreation and wilderness preservation relative to what he referred to as "fabricated goods." Most important for our purposes here, Krutilla raised the possibility in this paper of what is now known as "existence value." This is the value that individuals may attach to the mere knowledge that rare and diverse species, unique natural environments, or other "goods" exist, even if these individuals do not contemplate ever making active use of or benefitting in a

---

[1] For a more elegant and detailed history, see Hanemann (1992).
[2] Hanemann (1991) explores this question in a rigorous way.

more direct way from them. Existence value is sometimes referred to as non-use or passive use value to suggest that the utility derived does not depend on any direct or indirect interaction with the resource or good in question.

Since then, researchers in natural resource and environmental economics (and other branches of economics as well) have made increasing use of contingent valuation techniques to estimate existence values and many other things, as well.[3] For instance, surveys were used to elicit individuals' willingness to pay for such things as a reduction in household soiling and cleaning (Ridker, 1967), the rights to hunt waterfowl (Hammack and Brown, 1974), reduced congestion in wilderness areas (Cicchetti and Smith, 1973), improved visibility in the Southwest (Randall, Ives, and Eastman, 1974), and the value of duck hunting permits (Bishop and Heberlein, 1979), to name but a few. Moreover, contingent valuation methods have been used for the valuation of a large number of non-environmental policies or programs, such as reduced risk of death from heart attack (Acton, 1973), reduced risk of respiratory disease (Krupnick and Cropper, 1992), and improved information about grocery store prices (Devine and Marion, 1979).

But while such studies formed a sort of academic industry, none of them were designed or implemented with litigation in mind. It was not until the late 1980s that contingent valuation studies began to receive the kind of scrutiny routinely devoted to the evidence in high-stakes legal proceedings.

Describing the Methodology

There is no standard approach to the design of a contingent valuation survey. Nevertheless, virtually every application consists of several well-defined elements.[4]

First, a survey must contain a scenario or description of the (hypothetical or real) policy or program the respondent is being asked to value or vote upon. Sticking to environmental issues, this might be a regulatory program that will reduce air pollution concentrations, a land acquisition program to protect wildlife habitats, or a program to reduce the likelihood of oil spills, to name but a few. In some cases, these scenarios are quite detailed, providing information on the expected effects of the program as well as the likely course of events should the program not be adopted. For instance, the scenario might contain an estimate of the reduction in annual mortality risk that would be expected to accompany an improvement in air quality; or it might explain the rate at which an endangered species would be expected to recover if it was given additional protection. In other words, the scenario is

---

[3]For an extraordinary bibliography of papers and studies related to the contingent valuation method a bibliography that includes 1674 entries, see Carson et al. (1994).

[4]For a thorough description of the contingent valuation method, see Mitchell and Carson (1989).

intended to give the respondent a clear picture of the "good" that the respondent is being asked to value.

Next, the survey must contain a mechanism for eliciting value or a choice from the respondent. These mechanisms can take many forms, including such things as open-ended questions ("What is the maximum amount you would be willing to pay for . . . ?"), bidding games ("Would you pay $5 for this program? Yes? Would you pay $10? What about . . . ?") or referendum formats ("The government is considering doing X. Your annual tax bill would go up by Y if this happens. How would you vote?").

Finally, contingent valuation surveys usually elicit information on the socioeconomic characteristics of the respondents (age, race, sex, income, education, marital status, and so on), as well as information about their environmental attitudes and/or recreational behavior, usually with an eye toward estimating a willingness-to-pay function that includes these characteristics as possible explanatory variables. They may also include follow-up questions to see if the respondent both understood and believed the information in the scenario and took the hypothetical decision-making exercise seriously.

Moving to the Policy Arena

When economists attempt to infer values, we prefer evidence based on actual market behavior, whether directly or indirectly revealed. Thus, a technique like the contingent valuation method—wherein values are inferred from individuals' stated responses to hypothetical situations—could readily be expected to stir lively debate in academic seminars and in the pages of economics journals. But why has the controversy over the contingent valuation method spilled over into the "real world," and why has it become so heated?

The answer lies in two federal laws and one very unfortunate accident. These three things have resulted in government agencies bringing lawsuits against a variety of parties in which the former are attempting to recover large sums of money from the latter for lost existence values (among other types of damages) resulting from damages to natural resources. Many regard the contingent valuation method as being the only technique currently capable of providing monetary estimates of the magnitudes of these losses.

The first law is the Comprehensive Environmental Response, Compensation and Liability Act of 1980, also referred to as CERCLA or, more commonly, as the Superfund law. Its primary purposes were to create a mechanism for identifying sites at which hazardous materials posed a threat to human health or the environment, and to establish procedures through which parties that were deemed responsible for the contamination could be identified and made to pay for the cleanup.

But the Superfund law also contains a sleeper provision: it gave government agencies the right to sue for damages to the natural resources for which they were trustees (including lakes, streams, forests, bays, bayous, marshes, land masses, and so on) resulting from discharges of hazardous substances. The Department of the Interior was subsequently directed to write regulations spelling out what kinds of damages were compensable under this section of Superfund and what kinds of techniques would be admissible for damage estimation. Thus did existence values and the contingent valuation method come to meet the real world.

In 1986, the Department of the Interior (DOI) issued these regulations.[5] Oversimplifying somewhat, the regulations specified that lost nonuse values (largely lost existence values) were recoverable under Superfund only if use values were not measurable, and—in a very qualified way—sanctioned the use of the contingent valuation technique to measure damages. In response to a number of legal challenges, in 1989 a federal court of appeals directed DOI to redraft its regulations, specifically instructing the department to give equal weight to use and nonuse values in damage assessments and to treat the contingent valuation method much more seriously as a valuation technique.[6]

To some extent, however, events overtook the Department of the Interior regulations. In March 1989, the supertanker *Exxon Valdez* ran aground on Bligh Reef in Prince William Sound, Alaska, spilling 11 million gallons of crude oil into the sea. Although a number of natural resource damage cases had been brought by individual states and the federal government up to that time, none of the incidents precipitating the suits had nearly the visibility and impact of that spill. Among other things, that accident dramatized the potential economic impact of the DOI regulations. Indeed, if in addition to the out-of-pocket losses suffered by fishermen, resort owners, tour guides, recreationists and others directly and indirectly harmed by the accident, Exxon would be forced to pay also for lost nonuse or existence values, the ante would be raised substantially. This possibility focused the attention of Exxon and many other companies on existence values and the contingent valuation method.

The *Exxon Valdez* spill also caught the attention of Congress. It promptly passed an altogether new law, the Oil Pollution Act of 1990, aimed at reducing the likelihood of future oil spills and providing for damage recovery for any spills that should occur. Under the new law, the Department of Commerce—acting through the National Oceanic and Atmospheric Administration, or NOAA—was directed to write its own regulations governing damage assessment. This became the next battlefield on which to fight about the legitimacy of existence values and the contingent valuation method.

---

[5] See 51 *Federal Register* 27674 (August 1, 1986).
[6] *State of Ohio v. United States Department of Interior*, 880 F. 2d 432 (D.C. Circuit 1989).

The NOAA Panel

The Department of the Interior had worked in relative obscurity when drafting its damage assessment regulations under Superfund. By contrast, NOAA began its parallel task under a spotlight. Environmentalists insisted that the NOAA rules parallel those of Interior, embracing lost existence values as fully compensable damages and identifying the contingent valuation method as the appropriate way to measure them. Not surprisingly, those upon whom these assessments might one day fall—led by the oil companies— pushed hard to exclude existence values and the contingent valuation method from the regulations. Amidst these conflicting pressures, and in recognition of the technical economic nature of the questions at debate, the General Counsel of NOAA, Thomas Campbell, took an unusual step. He asked Nobel laureates Kenneth Arrow and Robert Solow if they would chair a panel of experts to provide advice to NOAA on the following question: is the contingent valuation method capable of providing estimates of lost non-use or existence values that are reliable enough to be used in natural resource damage assessments?[7]

It is important to note that the panel was *not* asked its opinion on the legitimacy of existence values *per se*. This may have been because the court of appeals had earlier ruled, in the case of the Department of the Interior regulations, that lost existence values were to be treated the same as other economic losses in damage assessments; whatever the reason, the panel was asked to confine its attention solely to the potential reliability of the contingent valuation method.

The NOAA panel met eight times between June and November of 1992. This included an extraordinary all-day hearing in August during which it heard statements from 22 experts, including several of the most prominent names in the economics profession, who either extolled the virtues of the contingent valuation method or condemned it. The panel completed its deliberations in December and, on January 11, 1993, submitted its report to NOAA. The report was published in the *Federal Register* on January 15, 1993.[8]

The NOAA panel may have managed to upset everyone with its report. Those opposed to the use of the contingent valuation method were disappointed by what many took to be the "bottom line" of the panel report. This was the phrase, ". . . the Panel concludes that CV studies [applications of the contingent valuation method] can produce estimates reliable enough to be the starting point of a judicial process of damage assessment, including lost passive-use values." Not surprisingly, this conclusion cheered those government agencies, academic researchers, and others wishing to make continued application of the contingent valuation method in their work.

---

[7]In addition to Arrow and Solow, the panel included Edward Learner, Roy Radner, Howard Schuman (a professor of sociology and survey research expert), and myself.

[8]See 58 *Federal Register* 4601 (January 15, 1993).

Nevertheless, the panel reached this conclusion with some reluctance. I believe it fair to say that none of its members would have been comfortable with the use of any of the previous applications of the contingent valuation method as the basis for actual monetary damage awards. (To reiterate, none of these studies was intended for this purpose.) For this reason, the panel established a set of guidelines to which it felt future applications of the contingent valuation method should adhere, if the studies are to produce reliable estimates of lost existence values for the purposes of damage assessment or regulation. Although these guidelines are too numerous to reproduce in their entirety here, seven of the most important are summarized here.

First, applications of the contingent valuation method should rely upon personal interviews rather than telephone surveys where possible, and on the telephone surveys in preference to mail surveys.

Second, applications of the contingent valuation method should elicit willingness to pay to prevent a future incident rather than minimum compensation required for an incident that has already occurred. (Note that the latter would be the theoretically correct measure of damages for an accident that has already taken place.)

Third, applications of the contingent valuation method should utilize the referendum format; that is, the respondents should be asked how they would vote if faced with a program that would produce some kind of environmental benefit in exchange for higher taxes or product prices. The panel reasoned that because individuals are often asked to make such choices in the real world, their answers would be more likely to reflect actual valuations than if confronted with, say, open-ended questions eliciting maximum willingness to pay for the program.

Fourth, applications of the contingent valuation method must begin with a scenario that accurately and understandably describes the expected effects of the program under consideration.

Fifth, applications of the contingent valuation method must contain reminders to respondents that a willingness to pay for the program or policy in question would reduce the amount they would have available to spend on other things.

Sixth, applications of the contingent valuation method must include reminders to respondents of the substitutes for the "commodity" in question. For example, if respondents are being asked how they would vote on a measure to protect a wilderness area, they should be reminded of the other areas that already exist or are being created independent of the one in question.

Seventh, applications of the contingent valuation method should include one or more follow-up questions to ensure that respondents understood the choice they were being asked to make and to discover the reasons for their answer.

These guidelines made a number of proponents of the contingent valuation method quite unhappy. In their view, strict adherence to the panel's guidelines—especially the suggestion that in-person interviews be used to elicit values—would make it very expensive to use the contingent valuation method for damage estimation or regulatory purposes. Moreover, a number of the guidelines seem intended to ensure that applications of the contingent valuation method result in "conservative" estimates of lost existence values—that is, estimates that were more likely to underestimate than to overestimate these values.

The NOAA panel created its long list of requirements because it felt strongly that casual applications of the contingent valuation method should not be used to justify large damage awards, especially in cases where the likelihood of significant lost existence values was quite small. By establishing a series of hurdles for contingent valuation studies to meet, the panel hoped to elevate considerably the quality of future studies and thereby increase the likelihood that these studies would produce estimates that could be relied on for policy purposes.

It should be noted in closing that the NOAA panel report had no special legal standing in NOAA's deliberations. Instead, it was one of literally hundreds of submissions pertaining to the contingent valuation method that NOAA received during the time it was drafting its proposed regulations. Nevertheless, when NOAA published its long-awaited proposed rules on January 7, 1994, it said: "In proposing its standards for the use of CV [contingent valuation] in the damage assessment context, NOAA has relied heavily on the recommendations of the Panel."[9] For instance, the proposed regulations encourage trustees conducting contingent valuation studies to consider using the referendum format, and in-person interviews, as the panel had suggested. In addition, the proposed regulations include a requirement that contingent valuation studies test for the sensitivity of responses to the scope of the damage described in the scenario. The NOAA panel had suggested that if respondents were not willing to pay more to prevent more serious accidents, say, other things being equal, the contingent valuation survey was unlikely to produce reliable results. Interestingly, when the Department of the Interior re-proposed its regulations pertaining to contingent valuation on May 4, 1994, it too included a requirement that contingent valuation studies test for sensitivity to scope.[10] The papers by Diamond and Hausman and also Hanemann in this issue discuss "scope tests" in some detail.

The Importance of the Contingent Valuation Debate

Economists should have a strong interest in the debate surrounding the contingent valuation method. The most obvious reasons have to do with the economic stakes involved; but these are not the only reasons.

---

[9]See 59 *Federal Register* 1062 (January 7, 1994), p. 1143.
[10]See 59 *Federal Register* 2309 (May 4, 1994).

Natural Resource Damage Assessments

Currently, the Department of Commerce (acting through NOAA) is involved in approximately 40 lawsuits in which it is seeking to recover damages for injury to the natural resources for which it is trustee. The Department of the Interior is involved in roughly another 20 cases. The contingent valuation method figures into no more than a dozen of these 60 or so cases, though it could prove to be quite influential in those cases.

To illustrate, consider the case of the Exxon Valdez. In late 1991, Exxon settled the natural resource damage suits brought against it by both the federal government and the State of Alaska for $1.15 billion, payable over 11 years. Yet, a state-of-the-art study done for the State in Alaska in the wake of the accident—one using the contingent valuation method to estimate lost existence values nationally—concluded that these losses alone amounted to nearly $3 billion (Carson et al., 1992). Because the case involving the *Exxon Valdez* was settled out of court, as have all cases involving the contingent valuation method to this point, it is impossible to know whether this study affected the size of the settlement.

It seems highly likely, however, that applications of the contingent valuation method will influence future damage awards or out-of-court settlements. Several of the most heavily regulated industries in the United States are among those affected by either Superfund or the Oil Pollution Act; the chemical and petroleum refining industries are potentially affected by both statutes. This in turn has implications for the amount of deterrence they and others will undertake. If existing state and federal environmental regulations, coupled with the specter of tort liability, already induce something close to the "right" amount of preventive activity by firms in these industries, the possibility of additional liability for lost existence values will push firms beyond the social optimum. On the other hand, if lost existence values are widely accepted as real economic losses that these firms have been ignoring heretofore, the imposition of liability for these losses may move firms closer to the optimum.

These cases alluded to earlier do not provide the only opportunity for damage recovery under Superfund. Currently, there are more than 1,200 sites on EPA's National Priorities List—the list of sites which can be cleaned up using money from the trust fund created for that purpose. Once the appropriate remedy has been selected and implemented at each of these sites, and once liability for the cost of this cleanup has been affixed, the trustees for any damaged resources, such as contaminated groundwater, can bring natural resource damage suits against the responsible parties. In these cases, contingent valuation could be used to estimate possible lost existence values.

New Regulations

Virtually all of the attention that the contingent valuation method has attracted in the policy world has been in the context of natural resource damage assessments under Superfund and the Oil Pollution Act. Neverthe-less, I believe that the most significant applications of the contingent valua-tion method will involve the estimation of the benefits and costs of proposed regulations under Superfund and particularly other environmental laws.

Regulated entities in the United States—private firms, agencies at the federal, state, and local levels, and individuals—currently spend an esti-mated $130 billion annually to comply with federal environmental regula-tions alone (EPA, 1990). This is about 2.2 percent of GDP, a larger fraction than is devoted to environmental compliance expenditures anywhere else in the world. Much less is known about the annual compliance expenditures necessitated by other federal regulatory agencies. However, based on a com-prehensive review of previous analyses, Hopkins (1992) cautiously estimated that annual compliance expenditures for all federal regulation, environmen-tal and otherwise, were in the vicinity of $400 billion.

Under Executive Order 12044 issued by President Carter, Executive Order 12291 issued by President Reagan, and Executive Order 12866 issued by President Clinton, all federal regulatory agencies must make an effort to quantify as many of the benefits and costs of their proposed actions as pos-sible.[11] This is where applications of the contingent valuation method will likely become important.

Imagine, for example, a proposed regulation that would cost a great deal of money but would provide relatively little in the way of direct bene-fits in the areas where environmental quality would improve. In such a case, it may be tempting for the regulatory agency to justify its proposed action by alleging that individuals throughout the country derive a psycho-logical benefit (an existence value) from knowing that environmental qual-ity has been improved in the affected areas—even though there will be no environmental improvements in the areas in which they live. A contingent valuation study might be produced to support this assertion, and might make the difference as to whether the proposal passes a benefit-cost test.

There is no reason why existence values should be unique to environ-mental policy, either. For instance, I might derive utility from knowing that factories are safer as a result of Occupational Safety and Health Adminis-tration regulations, that pharmaceuticals carry less risk because of the oversight of the Food and Drug Administration, and that swimming pool slides are safer because of the vigilance of the Consumer Product Safety Commission. All this may be so even though I do not work in a factory, take prescription drugs, or have a swimming pool. In other words, individuals may have existence values for many different "goods," and the inclusion of such values in a regulatory analysis could markedly alter the decision-making calculus.

---

[11]Strangely enough, this requirement holds true even when the agency is not allowed to engage in benefit-cost balancing in setting certain kinds of standards. For example, the key sections of many environmental statutes forbid balancing benefits and costs, although such trade-offs are per-mitted in other parts of these laws and are even required in some other laws (Portney, 1990).

Which leads me to what I believe has been an important and largely overlooked point in the debate about existence values and the contingent valuation method. To this point, proponents of the technique have envisioned its being used to estimate lost existence values and other *benefits* of proposed regulatory programs. Thus, the business community tends to oppose such methods because it believes the methods will only be used to support expansive regulation and large damage awards.

But sauce for the goose is surely sauce for the gander. Since costs are the duals of benefits, I see no reason why the contingent valuation method cannot or should not be used for the estimation of regulatory costs as well as benefits.

Consider a hypothetical regulation that would increase costs for a number of petroleum refineries and would force several others to shut down. For the purposes of the required benefit-cost analysis, the EPA would usually count as costs the annual capital cost of the equipment installed by the refineries that would remain in operation, plus any additional annual operating and maintenance costs they would incur. An unusually thorough analysis might occasionally include the (generally temporary) loss of or reduction in income of the workers whose jobs would be lost as a result of the regulation. But typically, the extent of the cost analysis is limited to out-of-pocket expenditures for new pollution control equipment or cleaner fuels.

With contingent valuation available to measure lost existence values, the matter is surely more complicated than this.[12] If I derive some utility from the mere existence of certain natural environments I never intend to see (which I do), might I not also derive some satisfaction from knowing that refineries provide well-paying jobs for hard-working people, even though neither I nor anyone I know will ever have such a job? I believe I do. Thus, any policy change that "destroys" those jobs imposes a cost on me—a cost that, in principle, could be estimated using the contingent valuation method.

Since regulatory programs will always impose costs on someone—taking the form of higher prices, job losses, or reduced shareholder earnings—lost existence values may figure every bit as prominently on the cost side of the analytic ledger as the benefit side. To my knowledge, however, no business organization has commissioned an application of the contingent valuation method to ascertain the empirical significance of these potential additional costs, nor has any academic independently undertaken one.

If the concept of existence value comes to be more broadly interpreted in economics, as I have suggested above that it should, and *if* the contingent valuation method comes to be regarded as a reliable way to measure these values, then applied benefit-cost analysis may be forever changed. It

---

[12]Even without the concern raised by contingent valuation, a number of questions can be raised about the very straightforward cost analysis described here. For example, Hazilla and Kopp (1990) have shown that if one takes a general equilibrium approach to social cost estimation, very different results are obtained when compared to those from a traditional partial equilibrium analysis. This calls into question previous estimates of regulatory compliance costs (see also Jorgenson and Wilcoxen, 1990).

is already difficult to conduct such analyses for government programs that impose hard-to-value, non-pecuniary costs on individuals, that change the distribution of income (either at a point in time or between generations), that affect mortality or morbidity, and that involve the preservation of genetic resources.

Imagine now the difficulty of doing applied benefit-cost analysis when virtually every citizen in the United States is potentially benefitted or injured by virtually every possible program. In principle, at least, it will become extraordinarily difficult to draw bounds around those likely to gain and lose so as to facilitate valuation.

In practice, this problem may be somewhat less daunting. Perhaps it will turn out that existence values apply on the benefit side only in cases of truly unique natural environments like the Grand Canyon, irreplaceable "assets" like the Declaration of Independence, or programs that substantially improve the lives of many beneficiaries. On the other side of the ledger, perhaps only policy changes that inflict massive economic harm on certain groups of people or certain regions will generate losses among those not directly affected by the policy. If so, applied benefit-cost analysis may survive intact, but this empirical question is one that economists ought to be interested in answering.

Putting Theory into Practice

A final set of reasons for economists to care about the contingent valuation debate have less to do with policy consequences, and more to do with how contingent valuation is affecting economic theory and the practice of empirical economics.

Whatever its shortcomings, the contingent valuation method would appear to be the only method capable of shedding light on potentially important values. Some environmental benefits can be measured in indirect ways. For example, the benefits of air quality improvements can manifest themselves in residential property values; enhanced workplace health and safety may be reflected in wage rates; improvements in recreational opportunities may be revealed in reduced travel costs. But there is simply no behavioral trace through which economists can glean information about lost existence values.

The only likely candidate for such information that I am aware of is voluntary contributions to national or international conservation organizations. But these groups typically provide their contributions with a mixture of public and private goods (an attractive magazine or calendar, for example), which makes it almost impossible to determine how much of one's contribution represents a willingness to pay for the pure preservation of unique natural area or genetic resources. In addition, many contributors to these organizations visit (make *active* use of) the protected areas, thus making it difficult to separate active from passive use values. Finally, the public good nature of the benefits of preservation means that there will be a tendency to underprovide on account of free riding.

According to proponents of the contingent valuation method, asking people directly has the potential to inform about the nature, depth, and economic significance of these values. Economists who hold this position readily admit that direct elicitation of these values will require the skills of other social scientists, including survey research specialists, cognitive psychologists, political scientists, marketing specialists, sociologists, and perhaps even philosophers. In fact, the critical scrutiny directed at the contingent valuation method has led some economists to think more deeply about cognitive processes, rationality, and the nature of preferences for *all* goods, public or private. We may, in other words, come out of this debate with an improved theory of preference and choice.

Another (and related) reason to care about the contingent valuation method debate has to do with the importance of encouraging the development of new analytical techniques. Here the parallels to experimental economics seem to me to be instructive. It was not so long ago that Vernon Smith, Charles Plott and a handful of other economists began to create artificial markets in "laboratory" settings. One purpose was to see whether hypotheses about market equilibration derived from theoretical models were borne out in laboratory settings. Since that time, experimental methods have been used to inform real-word policy-making, including, among other cases, the allocation of airport landing slots by the Civil Aeronautics Board, the auction of T-bills by the Department of Treasury, the sale of air pollution emission allowances by the Environmental Protection Agency, and the design of natural gas contracts by the Federal Energy Regulatory Commission.

Yet despite its increasing acceptance in the economics profession, and its apparent usefulness to decision makers, experimental economics has not had an easy go. Its early critics claimed that the "artificiality" of the laboratory setting rendered meaningless the findings of experimental studies. And it is my impression (but only that) that some journal editors have been reluctant to embrace papers based on experimental studies. To this day, some critics still have grave doubts about its utility.

This seems to me not unlike the state of play regarding the contingent valuation method today. Its detractors have argued that the technique is not only currently unable to provide reliable estimates of lost existence values, but also that it will never be able to do so. On the other hand, at least some proponents of the contingent valuation method appear to believe that even casual applications can produce results reliable enough to be used as the basis for potentially significant damage awards. Both views were rejected by the NOAA panel.

The present struggle is over whether some middle ground exists. There do exist quite careful and thorough applications of the contingent valuation method, with the work of Carson et al. (1992) on the *Exxon Valdez* oil spill being the best example. I am reluctant to assert that even this study is sufficient to justify monetary penalties. But the estimates from that study are convincing enough to me to suggest that the contingent valuation method should be the object of further research and lively intellectual debate.

Conclusion

Whether the economics profession likes it or not, it seems inevitable to me that contingent valuation methods are going to play a role in public policy formulation. Both regulatory agencies and governmental offices responsible for natural resource damage assessment are making increasing use of it in their work. This has now been reinforced by the Department of the Interior and NOAA–proposed regulations sanctioning the use of the contingent valuation method. Surely, it is better for economists to be involved at all stages of the debate about the contingent valuation method, than to stand by while others dictate the way this tool will be used.

REFERENCES

Acton, Jan, "Evaluating Public Progress to Save Lives: The Case of Heart Attacks," RAND Research Report R-73-02. Santa Monica: RAND Corporation, 1973.

Bishop, Richard, and Thomas Heberlein, "Measuring Values of Extramarket Goods: Are Indirect Measures Biased?," *American Journal of Agricultural Economics*, December 1979, *61*, 926–30.

Carson, Richard, et al., *A Contingent Valuation Study of Lost Passive Use Values Resulting From the Exxon Valdez Oil Spill*, Report to the Attorney General of the State of Alaska, prepared by Natural Resource Damage Assessment, Inc., La Jolla, California, 1992.

———, *A Bibliography of Contingent Valuation Studies and Papers*. La Jolla, California: Natural Resources Damage Assessment, Inc., 1994.

Cicchetti, Charles J., and V. Kerry Smith, "Congestion, Quality Deterioration, and Optimal Use: Wilderness Recreation in the Spanish Peaks Primitive Area," *Social Science Research*, 1973, *2*, 15–30.

Ciriacy-Wantrup, S. V., "Capital Returns from Soil Conservation Practices," *Journal of Farm Economics*, November 1947, *29*, 1181–96.

Clawson, Marion, "Methods of Measuring the Demand for and Value of Outdoor Recreations," Reprint no. 10, Resources for the Future, Washington, D.C., 1959.

Davis, Robert, *The Value of Outdoor Recreation: An Economic Study of the Maine Woods*, doctoral dissertation in economics, Harvard University, 1963.

Devine, D. Grant, and Bruce Marion, "The Influence of Consumer Price Information on Retail Pricing and Consumer Behavior," *American Journal of Agricultural Economics*, May 1979, *61*, 228–37.

Environmental Protection Agency, *Environmental Investments: The Cost of a Clean Environment*, Report no. EPA-230-12-90-084, 1990.

Hammack, Judd, and Gardner Brown, *Waterfowl and Wetlands: Toward Bioeconomic Analysis*. Baltimore: Johns Hopkins University Press, 1974.

Hanemann, W. Michael, "Willingness to Pay and Willingness to Accept: How Much Can They Differ?," *American Economic Review*, June 1991, *81*, 635–47.

———, "Preface: Notes on the History of Environmental Valuation in the U.S." In Navrud, Stale, ed., *Pricing the Environment: The European Experience*. London: Oxford University Press, 1992, 9–35.

Hazilla, Michael, and Raymond Kopp, "Social Cost of Environmental Quality Regulations: A General Equilibrium Analysis," *Journal of Political Economy*, August 1990, *98*, 853–73.

Hopkins, Thomas, "The Costs of Federal Regulation," *Journal of Regulation and Social Costs*, March 1992, *2*, 5–31.

Jorgenson, Dale, and Peter Wilcoxen, "Environmental Regulation and U.S. Economic Growth," *RAND Journal of Economics*, Summer 1990, *21*, 314–40.

Krupnick, Alan, and Maureen Cropper, "The Effect of Information on Health Risk Valuation," *Journal of Risk and Uncertainty*, February 1992, *2*, 29–48.

Krutilla, John, "Conservation Reconsidered," *American Economic Review*, September 1967, *356*, 777–86.

Mitchell, Robert, and Richard Carson, *Using Surveys to Value Public Goods: The Contingent Valuation Method*. Washington, D.C.: Resources for the Future, 1989.

Portney, Paul, *Public Policies for Environmental Protection*. Washington, D.C.: Resources for the Future, 1990.

Randall, Alan, Berry Ives, and Clyde Eastman, "Bidding Games for Valuation of Aesthetic Environmental Improvements," *Journal of Environmental Economics and Management*, 1974, *1*, 132–49.

Ridker, Ronald, *The Economic Cost of Air Pollution*. New York Praeger, 1967.

8　Valuing the Environment through Contingent Valuation*

W. Michael Hanemann

W. Michael Hanemann is Chancellor's Professor of Agricultural and Resource Economics, University of California, Berkeley.

The ability to place a monetary value on the consequences of pollution discharges is a cornerstone of the economic approach to the environment. If this cannot be done, it undercuts the use of economic principles, whether to determine the optimal level of pollution or to implement this via Pigovian taxes or Coase-style liability rules. Sometimes, the valuation involves a straightforward application of methods for valuing market commodities, as when sparks from a passing train set fire to a wheat field. Often, however, the valuation is more difficult. Outcomes such as reducing the risk of human illness or death, maintaining populations of native fish in an estuary, or protecting visibility at national parks are not themselves goods that are bought and sold in a market. Yet, placing a monetary value on them can be essential for sound policy.

The lack of a market to generate prices for such outcomes is no accident. Markets are often missing in such cases because of the nonexcludable or nonrival nature of the damages: for those affected by it, pollution may be a public good (or bad). The public good nature of the damages from pollution has several consequences. It explains, for example, why the damages are sometimes large—only a few people may want to own a sea otter pelt, say, but many may want this animal protected in the wild. It also explains why market prices are inappropriate measures of value. In the presence of externalities, market transactions do not fully capture preferences. Collective choice is the more relevant paradigm.

This is precisely what Ciriacy-Wantrup (1947) had in mind when he first proposed the contingent valuation method. Individuals should be interviewed and "asked how much money they are willing to pay for successive additional quantities of a collective extra-market good." If the individual

"Valuing the Environment through Contingent Valuation" by W. Michael Hanemann. *Journal of Economic Perspectives* 8. 1994. pp. 19–43. Reprinted by permission of the American Economic Association.

*I want to thank Richard Carson, Jon Krosnick, Robert Mitchell, Stanley Presser and Kerry Smith for their helpful comments, and Nicholas Flores and Sandra Hoffmann for excellent assistance. I also thank the editors, without whom this paper would be far longer.

values are aggregated, "the result corresponds to a market-demand schedule" (p. 1189). Thus, surveys offered a way to trace the demand curve for a public good that could not otherwise be gleaned from market data. Schelling (1968) made a similar point in his paper on valuing health. While the price system is one way to find out what things are worth to people, he wrote, another way is to ask people, whether through surveys or votes. Answering surveys may be hypothetical, but no more than buying unfamiliar or infrequent commodities. "In any case, relying exclusively on market valuations and denying the value of direct enquiry in the determination of government programs would depend on there being for every potential government service, a close substitute available in the market at a comparable price. It would be hard to deduce from first principles that this is bound to be the case" (pp. 143–4).

Schelling's point was not that indirect methods using market transactions have no role, but rather that they cannot always be counted on to provide a complete measure of value. Analysts can often capture some effects of a change in air quality or a change in risk to human health through a hedonic analysis that looks for evidence to property values or wage rates (Rosen, 1974). But people may also value those items in ways not reflected in wages or property values. Similarly with averting expenditures and household production models (Freeman, 1993), which rely on the demand for market commodities that are complements to, or surrogates for, the non-market good. If people value that good at least partly for reasons unrelated to their consumption of the complementary private goods, those methods capture just part of people's value—what is called the "use value" component, following Krutilla (1967).[1] They fail to measure the "non-use value" or "existence value" value component, which contingent valuation can capture.

An alternative is to turn to the political system, for example using collective choice models to estimate demands for local public goods (Oates, 1994). However, Cropper (1994) suggests this is unlikely to be useful for the environment because, in the United States, there are few cases where local governments actually set environmental quality. Moreover, as Chase (1968) noted, the method contains an element of circularity: a major reason for the spread of benefit-cost analysis is legislators' desire to obtain information on the public's value for government programs. While it may sometimes be desirable to leave the assessment of value to the legislative process, it is not obvious that this is always so. Measuring liability for damages from pollution is an example. In some cases one wants to ascertain how the public values something, and contingent valuation may be the only way to measure this short of a plebiscite.

Ciriacy-Wantrup (1947) recognized that surveys are not foolproof. The degree of success depends on the skill with which the survey is designed and implemented. But it was time, he felt, that economics took advantage of developments in social psychology and the newly emerging academic field of survey research: "Welfare economics could be put on a more realistic

---

[1]For a formal definition, see Hanemann (1994a).

foundation if a closer cooperation between economics and certain young branches of applied psychology could be established" (p. 1190). This finally occurred in the 1980s, and contingent valuation came of age. Two landmarks were an EPA conference in 1984 that brought together leading practitioners, other economists, and psychologists to assess the state-of-the-art (Cummings et al., 1986), and the publication of what has become the standard reference on contingent valuation, Mitchell and Carson (1989), which puts it in a broader contest involving elements from economics, psychology, sociology, political science, and market research.

Contingent valuation is now used around the world (Navrud, 1992; Bateman and Willis, [2000]), both by government agencies and the World Bank for assessing a variety of investments. A recent bibliography lists 1600 studies and papers from over 40 countries on many topics, including transportation, sanitation, health, the arts and education, as well as the environment (Carson et al., 1994c). Some notable examples are Randall, Ives and Eastman (1974) on air quality in the Four Corners area, the first major nonuse value study; Brookshire et al. (1982) on air pollution in Southern California; Carson and Mitchell (1993) on national water quality benefits from the Clean Water Act; Smith and Desvousges (1986) on cleaning up the Monongahela River, Jones-Lee, Hammerton and Phillips (1985) on highway safety; Boyle, Welsh and Bishop (1993) on rafting in the Grand Canyon; Briscoe et al. (1990) on drinking water supply in Brazil; and the study on the *Exxon Valdez* oil spill I helped conduct for the State of Alaska (Carson et al., 1992).

This paper focuses generally on the use of contingent valuation to measure people's values for environmental resources, rather than specifically on natural resource damages. It will describe how researchers go about conducting reliable surveys. It then addresses some common objections to surveys and, lastly, considers the compatibility between contingent valuation and economic theory.

Conducting Reliable Surveys

In all research, details matter. How a contingent valuation survey is conducted is crucial. While there is no panacea, various procedures have been developed in recent years that enhance the credibility of a survey and make it more likely to produce reliable results. These touch all aspects, including sampling, instrument development, formulation of the valuation scenario, questionnaire structure, and data analysis. The main ways of assuring reliability are summarized here.

Suppose one approached people in a shopping mall, made them put their bags down for a moment, and asked them what was the most they would be willing to pay for a sea otter in Alaska or an expanse of wilderness in Montana. This is how the President of American Petroleum Institute and other critics have characterized contingent valuation (DiBona, 1992). The essence of their argument is summarized in titles such as "Ask a Silly Question" and "Pick a Number" (Anon., 1992; Bate, 1994). It does not require any unusual perspicacity to see that this approach is unlikely to produce reliable results. For precisely this reason, it is *not* what good contingent valuation researchers do, and it is *not* what was recommended by the NOAA Panel on Contingent Valuation (Arrow et al., 1993) described in Portney's paper in this issue.

Serious surveys of the general public avoid convenience sampling, such as stopping people in the street; they employ statistically based probability sampling.[2] They also avoid self-administered surveys, such as mail surveys or questionnaires handed out in a mall, because of the lack of control over the interview process. For a major study, the NOAA Panel recommended in-person interviews for their superior reliability. Furthermore, interviews should occur in a setting that permits respondents to reflect and give a considered opinion, such as their home. Unless the study deals with consumer products, shopping malls are a poor choice. Indeed, the only contingent valuation study where people were stopped for a few minutes in a mall was one performed for Exxon (Desvousges et al., 1992).

The crux is how one elicits value. The two key developments have been to confront subjects with a specific and realistic situation rather than an abstraction, and to use a closed-ended question which frames the valuation as voting in a referendum.

A common temptation is to characterize the object of valuation in rather general terms: "What would you pay for environmental safety?" "What would you pay for wilderness?" The problem is that these are abstractions. People's preferences are not measured in the abstract but in terms of specific items. "Paying for wilderness" is meaningless; what is meaningful is paying higher taxes or prices to finance particular actions by somebody to protect a particular wilderness in some particular manner. Therefore, one wants to confront respondents with something concrete. Moreover, one should try to avoid using counterfactuals. "What would you pay not to have had the *Exxon Valdez* oil spill?" is utterly hypothetical because one cannot undo the past. By contrast, "What would you pay for this new program that will limit damage from any future oil spills in Prince William Sound?" offers something that is tangible.

The goal in designing a contingent valuation survey is to formulate it around a specific commodity that captures what one seeks to value, yet is plausible and meaningful. The scenario for providing the commodity may be real; if not, the key is to make it seem real to respondents. They are not actually making a payment during the interview, but they are expressing their intention to pay. The vaguer and less specific the commodity and payment mechanism, the more likely respondents are to treat the valua-

---

[2]DiBona's scenario actually was the practice in the 1930s when most surveys were "brief encounters" on the street or in stores (Smith, 1987). The 1940s saw the adoption of probability sampling, standardized survey techniques, longer and more complex survey instruments, and in-depth focused interviews (Merton and Kendall, 1946).

tion as symbolic. To make the payment plausible, one needs to specify the details and tie them to provision of the commodity so this cannot occur without payment. There should be a clear sense of commitment; for example, if the program is approved, firms will raise prices, or the government taxes, so there is no avoiding payment once a decision is made.[3]

Until the mid-1980s, most contingent valuation surveys used some version of an open-ended question, like "What is the most you would be willing to pay for . . . ?" Since then, most major contingent valuation studies have used closed-ended questions like "If it cost $x, would you be willing to pay this amount?" or "If it cost $x, would you vote for this?" Different people are confronted with different dollar amounts. Plotting the proportion of "yes" responses against the dollar amount traces out the cumulative distribution function of willingness-to-pay.[4]

Of course, if people carried utility functions engraved in their brains, the question format would not matter. But they don't, and it does matter. In this country, posted prices are the norm rather than bargaining. In market transactions people usually face discrete choices: here is an item, it costs $x, will you take it? Similarly in voting. Moreover, there is abundant evidence that respondents find the open-ended willingness-to-pay question much more difficult to answer than the closed-ended one; for market and nonmarket goods alike, people can generally tell you whether they would pay some particular amount, but they find it much harder to know what is the *most* that they would possibly pay. Indeed, the experience with open-ended willingness-to-pay questions for market goods is that people are more likely to tell you what the good costs than what it is worth to them. In addition to being less realistic and harder to answer, the open-ended format creates incentives which are different from those in the closed-ended format. With the open-ended format, as with an oral auction, there are strategic reasons for stating less than one's full value—a theoretical result strongly supported by experimental evidence. This is not so with a closed-ended format; there, the NOAA Panel held, there is no strategic reason for the respondent to do other than answer truthfully.[5]

For these reasons, the NOAA Panel considered the closed-ended format combined, where possible, with a voting context the most desirable for contingent valuation: "The simplest way to approach the valuation problem," it held, "is to consider a contingent valuation survey as essentially a self-contained referendum in which respondents vote to tax themselves for a particular purpose" (p. 20). This is a rather different conception of contingent valuation from asking silly questions of passers-by.

---

[3]To underscore this, the interviewer may tell respondents that the government uses surveys like this to find out whether taxpayers are willing to pay for new programs it is considering.

[4]The methodology here is to assume a random utility model for individual preferences. This can be estimated using standard techniques for binary choices. Bishop and Heberlein (1979) were the first to use this format; the link with utility theory was developed in Hanemann (1984).

[5]With auctions, it is well documented that formal matters and that oral auctions generate lower prices than posted-price auctions. Why the surprise when the same holds true for open- versus closed-ended payment questions?

In his introduction to this symposium, Portney describes other ways to make a contingent valuation questionnaire more reliable: providing adequate and accurate information; making the survey balanced and impartial; insulating it from any general dislike of big business; reminding respondents of the availability of substitutes, and of their budget constraint; facilitating "don't know" responses; allowing respondents to reconsider at the end of the interview. Several steps can be taken to eliminate any perception of interviewer pressure. At the outset, the interviewer can assure respondents that there are no "right" answers. Before asking the voting question, to legitimate a negative response, the interviewer could say something like: "We have found that some people vote for the program and others vote against. Both have good reasons for voting that way," and then list some reasons for saying "no."[6] Another possibility is if the interviewer does not actually see the respondents' votes, for example by having them write on a ballot placed in a sealed box.

A recent innovation, considered essential by the NOAA Panel, is a "debriefing" section at the end of the survey. This checks respondents' understanding and acceptance of key parts of the contingent valuation scenario. For example, was the damage as bad as described? Did you think the program would work? Did you think you really would have to pay higher taxes if the program went through? This also probes the motives for their answer to the willingness-to-pay question. What was it about the program that made you decide to vote for it? Why did you vote no? Moreover, throughout the survey, all spontaneous remarks by the respondent are recorded verbatim as they occur. After the survey, the interviewer is debriefed and asked about the circumstances of the interview, how attentive the respondent was, whether the respondent seemed to understand the questions and appeared confident in his responses. In this way, one creates a rich portrait of the interview. This information can be exploited in the data analysis. One can monitor for the misunderstandings, measure statistically how they affected respondents' willingness-to-pay, and adjust accordingly. For example, if a subject who voted "yes" appeared to be valuing something different than the survey intended, this case can be dropped or the "yes" converted to a "no."

With any data, different statistical procedures can produce different results. The closed-ended format raises several statistical issues, for example, one might summarize the willingness-to-pay distribution by using its mean, or its median, or another quantile. The mean is extremely sensitive to the right tail of the distribution; that is, to the responses of the higher bidders. For this reason, if the mean is to be used, a nonparametric or bounded influence approach is highly recommended for fitting the willingness-to-pay distribution. The median, by contrast, is usually very robust (Hanemann, 1984). Another issue is that the choice of dollar bids

---

[6]For example, the interviewer might note that some people prefer to spend the money on other social or environmental problems instead, or they find the cost is more than they can afford or than the program is worth, or they cannot support the program because it would benefit only one area (Carson et al., 1992).

affects the precision with which the parameters of the willingness-to-pay distribution are estimated; significant improvements can be achieved by using optimal experimental designs (Kanninen, 1993). Statistical techniques can also be used to probe for yea-saying or other response effects, and correct for them if they are present (Hanemann and Kanninen, [2001]).

While none of these alone is decisive, taken together they are likely to produce a reliable measure of value. Apart from the expense of in-person interviews, they are all eminently feasible.[7] Other essential ingredients are relentless attention to detail and rigorous testing of the instrument, usually in collaboration with survey experts, so that the researcher understands exactly how it works in the field and is sure it communicates what was intended.

It is no coincidence that the handful of studies that Diamond and Hausman select from the contingent valuation literature in their companion paper in this issue violate most of these precepts, as do the Exxon surveys reported in Hausman (1993). None uses in-person interviews. Many are self-administered. Most use open-ended questions. None is cast as voting.[8] Many ask questions with a remarkable lack of detail.[9] Several seem designed to highlight the symbolic aspects of valuation at the expense of substance.[10] The Exxon surveys were designed and fielded in great haste, with little pretesting, just at a time when federal agencies were gearing up for natural resource damage regulations.[11] The only way to justify this is to make the tacit assumption that, if contingent valuation is valid, details of its implementation should not matter. This is fundamentally wrong: measurement results are not invariant with respect to measurement practice in *any* science.

---

[7]Is there an acceptable alternative to in-person surveys? The NOAA Panel felt mail surveys have significant problems rendering them unsuitable. Telephone surveys avoid these problems, but preclude the use of visual aids and need to be short The most promising alternative is a mail/telephone combination in which an information package is mailed to respondents who are then interviewed by phone (Hanemann, Loomis and Kanninen, 1991). This permits an extensive phone interview which seems to provide many of the benefits of an in-person survey at much lower cost.

[8]Two studies Diamond and Hausman cite as showing a lack of commitment in contingent valuation, Seip and Strand (1992) and Duffield and Patterson (1991), used open-ended questions about payment to an environmental charity. Most of Seip and Strand's subjects who were followed up afterwards said that they had been expressing their willingness-to-pay for environmental problems generally, rather than the particular environmental group. Careful pretesting would have discovered this beforehand.

[9]This is notably a problem in Diamond et al. (1993).

[10]Including Kahneman and Ritov (1993), Kahneman and Knetsch (1992), and Kemp and Maxwell (1993). The last two employs a "top-down" procedure in which respondents are given details of the item only *after* they value it. They are first confronted with something broad, like "preparedness for disasters." After stating their willingness-to-pay for the broad category, they are told what it comprises and asked their willingness-to-pay for *one* of those components. Then, they are told what *this* comprises, and so on. The *change* in the *quantity* of any item is never specified.

[11]Hanemann (1994a,b) critiques these studies.

Objections to Surveys

McCloskey (1985, p. 181) observes that economists generally dislike surveys: "Economists are so impressed by the confusions that might possibly arise from questionnaires that they have turned away from them entirely, and prefer the confusions resulting from external observation." In this section, I discuss four common objections to surveys.

Surveys Are Vulnerable to Response Effects

Small changes in question wording or order sometimes cause significant changes in survey responses (Schuman and Presser, 1981). Since virtually all data used in economics come from surveys (including experiments, which are a form of survey), and all surveys are vulnerable to response effects, it is important to understand why these arise and how they can be controlled. A consensus is beginning to emerge based on insights from psychology and linguistics. Answering survey questions requires some effort, usually for no apparent reward. Respondents must interpret the meaning of the question, search their memory for pertinent information, integrate this into a judgment, and communicate the judgment to the interviewer. Although some are motivated to make the effort, others may become impatient, disinterested, or tired. Instead of searching for an accurate and comprehensive answer, they satisfice, just aiming for some response that will be accepted. Furthermore, interviews are interactions governed by social and linguistic norms that shape assumptions and expectations. Viewing respondents as satisficing agents following norms of conversation has proved helpful in interpreting survey data, explaining response effects, and designing more effective surveys (Groves, 1989; Krosnick, 1991).

Not all response phenomena are equally intractable. Some, such as order effects (for example, bias towards the first item in a list), can be detected and controlled, either by choosing the sequence that produces a conservative result or by randomizing the order of items across interviews.

A second type of effect is where there is a shift in meaning. This is substance, not noise. For example, similar words turn out to mean different things: "allow" is not the same as "not forbid," nor "higher prices" the same as "higher taxes."[12] Or there are framing effects, where subjects respond differently to situations the researcher saw as equivalent. It has been shown through debriefings that the subject perceived the situations as substantively different, because either the researcher induced an unintended change in meaning or context, or the subjects made inferences that went

---

[12]And different words can mean the same thing, as in the movie *Annie Hall* where Woody Allen and Diane Keaton are asked by their psychiatrists how often they have sex. He says: "Hardly ever, maybe three times a week." She says: "Constantly, I'd say three times a week." With consumer expenditure surveys, Miller and Guin (1990) attest that life imitates art.

beyond the information given (Frisch, 1993).[13] In each case, the shift in meaning is a source of error only if the researcher is unaware of it. Through rigorous testing with cognitive techniques, the researcher can come to understand exactly what the instrument means to people, and what they mean in response.[14]

A third phenomenon arises from the inherent difficulty of the task assigned the respondent. In recalling past events or behavior, for example, respondents resort to rounding, telescoping (time compression) and other inferential strategies that yield inaccurate reports of magnitudes and frequencies.[15] Bradburn et al. (1987) emphasize that factual and attitudinal surveys share many similar cognitive processes and errors. There is no easy solution for recall errors. This continues to be a problem for many data used by economists,[16] though not for contingent valuation data since there is no recall.

One cannot avoid the fact that surveys, like all communication, are sensitive to nuance and context and are bound by constraints of human cognition. One tries to detect discrepancies and repair them, but they cannot be entirely ruled out. It is important to keep a sense of proportion. As far as I know, nobody has stopped using data from the Current Population Survey, Consumer Expenditure Survey, Monthly Labor Survey, or Panel Study on Income Dynamics because there are response effects in such surveys. The same should apply to contingent valuation surveys.

The Survey Process Creates the Values

It has been asserted that contingent valuation respondents have no real value for the item, but just make one up during the course of the interview: the process creates the values that it seeks to measure. Debriefings can identify whether subjects were inattentive or unfocused and offered hasty or ill-considered responses, and these can be discarded if desired. But, the issue raised here is more fundamental. Diamond and Hausman feel they know

---

[13]When there is incomplete information in a survey, respondents may go ahead and make their own assumptions. Consequently, the researcher loses control over his instrument. Diamond et al. (1993) is a contingent valuation example.

[14]On testing by federal survey agencies, see Tanur (1992). Lack of adequate testing can explain some notable violations of procedural invariance—respondents saw cues or meaning which the researcher didn't intend and failed to detect. An example is the base rate fallacy where "when no specific information was given, prior probabilities are properly utilized; when worthless evidence is given prior probabilities are ignored" (Tversky and Kahneman, 1974). A norm of conservation is to present information one believes relevant. That this was the expectation of subjects could have been detected through debriefings. On violations of conversational norms in base-rate experiments, see Krosnick, Li and Lehman (1990).

[15]Some pronounced telescoping errors are to be found in the Alaska recreation survey conducted by Hausman, Leonard and McFadden (1994).

[16]Juster and Stafford (1991) and Mathiowetz and Duncan (1988) discuss biases in labor supply estimates due to problems with bunching and misreporting in Current Population Survey data. Atkinson and Micklewright (1983) discuss errors in Family Expenditure Survey reports of income and its components. Other inconsistencies between micro- and macro-data sets for the household sector are discussed in Maki and Nishiyama (1993).

real preferences when they see them, and they do not see them in contingent valuation. Based on the debriefing statements in Schkade and Payne (1993) that show most subjects, faced with an open-ended willingness-to-pay question, think about either what the item could cost or what they have spent on something remotely similar, Diamond and Hausman conclude that these people are just making up their answer rather than evincing "true economic preferences." But, what are "true economic preferences?" If a subject responds thoughtfully to a question about voting to raise taxes for a public good, by what criterion is that not a valid preference?

It is true that economists often assume consumer choice reflects an individual's global evaluation of alternatives, a "top-down" or "stored-rule" decision process. The stored-rule notion traces back to Hobbes and the English empiricists who conceived of cognition in terms of storing and retrieving "slightly faded copies of sensory experiences" (Neisser, 1967). Wilson and Hodges (1992) call this the "filing cabinet" concept of the mind. It long dominated not only economics but also psychology. But it is now being abandoned in the face of accumulating evidence from the neurosciences (Rose, 1992) and elsewhere that all cognition is a constructive process—people construct their memories, their attitudes, and their judgments. The manner of construction varies with the person, the item, and the context. A general principle is that people are cognitive misers: they tend to resolve problems of reasoning and choice in the simplest way possible. This is the emerging consensus not only in survey research, but also in social psychology, political psychology, and market research (Martin and Tesser, 1992; Sniderman, Brody and Tetlock, 1991; Payne, Bettman and Johnson, 1988).

For non-habituated and complex consumer choices, people often make "bottom-up" decisions; that is, they make up a decision rule at the moment they need to use it (Bettman, 1988). Olshavsky and Granbois (1979, p. 98) found that "for many purchases a decision process never exists, not even on first purchase." Bettman and Zins (1977) found that grocery shoppers construct a choice heuristic "on the spot" about 25 percent of the time; bottom-up construction of preferences occurred especially for meat and produce "as might be expected, since consumers cannot really rely on brand name for most choices of this type," less often for beverages and dairy products "where either strong taste preferences may exist or only a limited number of brands are available" (p. 81). This calls to mind a remark by Robert Solow that the debriefings in Schkade and Payne "sound an awful lot like Bob Solow in the grocery store." I suppose critics of contingent valuation would consider that Solow does not have true economic preferences, or that he has true economic preferences when buying milk but not meat.

The real issue is not whether preferences are a construct but whether they are a *stable* construct. While this surely varies with circumstances, the evidence for contingent valuation is quite strong. There is now a number of test-retest studies in the contingent valuation literature, and these show both consistency in value over time and a high correlation at the individual level (Carson et al., 1994b). These levels of consistency are comparable to the most stable social attitudes such as political party identification.

Ordinary People Are Ill-Trained for Valuing the Environment

If, as the NOAA Panel suggests, the goal of a contingent valuation survey is to elicit people's preferences as if they were voting in a referendum, then prior-experience or training are irrelevant. These are not a criterion for voting.[17] Nor is their absence an argument against contingent valuation per se. Through direct questioning, one can readily identify which respondents knew of the issue before the interview, or before the oil spill, and determine whether they hold different values from those who did not. How one proceeds in calculating aggregate willingness-to-pay is something that can be decided separately from the survey. Who has standing, and whose values should count, are questions that we as economists have no special competence to judge.

Survey Response Can't Be Verified

There are three ways to validate contingent valuation results: replication, comparison with estimates from other sources, and comparison with actual behavior where this is possible. Replication is useful even on a small scale both to see if results hold up and to check whether the instrument is communicating as intended. This is the single best way for a researcher to determine whether somebody's survey instrument works as claimed.

When contingent valuation measures direct use values, it may be possible to make a comparison with estimates obtained through indirect methods. Knetsch and Davis (1966) conducted the first test, comparing contingent valuation and travel demand estimates (a method described in Portney's paper) of willingness-to-pay for recreation in the Maine woods. The difference was less than 3 percent. There are now over 80 studies, offering several hundred comparisons between contingent valuation and indirect methods. The results are often fairly close; overall, the contingent valuation estimates are slightly *lower* than the revealed preference estimates and highly correlated with them (Carson et al., 1994a).

The ideal is direct testing of contingent valuation predictions against actual behavior. There are about ten such tests in the literature. Diamond

---

[17]Voter ignorance is a constant refrain for Diamond and Hausman. They use it to form a syllogism: voters are ill-informed, contingent valuation is like a referendum, therefore contingent valuation respondents are ill-informed. Both parts are false. Contingent valuation researchers take pains to ensure their samples are representative and their questionnaires intelligible, informative, and impartial, thus avoiding the vagaries of turnout and biased advertising in election campaigns. This is why political scientists are becoming interested in "deliberate polling"—in effect, extended contingent valuation surveys (Fishkin, 1991). Many analysts see a substantial core of rationality in voter behavior. Cronin (1989) finds Magleby's (1984) assessment of voter ignorance in referenda overblown. Fiorina (1981) and McKelvey and Ordeshook (1986) emphasize how campaign protagonists use signals to inform voters. Lupia (1993) analyzes the insurance reform battle in the 1988 California ballot and finds that informational "short cuts" enabled poorly informed voters to act as though they were well informed. What Sniderman (1993) calls "the new look in public opinion research" stresses how ordinary citizens use the information at hand to make sense of politics.

and Hausman mention only five of these. The ones not mentioned yield results quite favorable to contingent valuation.

Bohm (1972) conducted the first test, where subjects in Stockholm were asked their willingness-to-pay to see a new TV program. In five treatments, the program was shown if the group raised 500 Kr, with actual payment based in various ways on stated willingness-to-pay. A sixth treatment asked subjects what was the highest amount they would have given *if* they had been asked to pay an individual admission fee. The mean response was 10.2 Kr (about $2) when the group was asked a hypothetical question, versus an overall average of 8.1 Kr when the group actually paid. The difference between contingent valuation and noncontingent valuation means was not statistically significant in four of the five cases.

Bishop and Heberlein (1990) conducted a series of experiments with hunters who had applied for a deer-hunting permit in a favored game preserve run by the state of Wisconsin. The most relevant for current practice is an experiment in which they wrote to two groups of hunters offering to sell them a permit at a specified price. In one case, this was a real offer; in the other, it was asked as a hypothetical question. Estimated willingness-to-pay was $31 in the real sale versus $35 in the hypothetical sale, a statistically insignificant difference.

Dickie, Fisher and Gerking (1987) offered boxes of strawberries door-to-door at different prices. One treatment was a real offer—the household could buy any number of boxes at this price. The other asked how many boxes they *would* buy if these were offered at the given price. The resulting two demand curves were not significantly different. The parameter estimates were actually more robust over alternative model specifications for the hypothetical than the actual data (Smith, 1994).

Carson, Hanemann and Mitchell (1986) tested the accuracy of voting intentions in a water quality bond election in California in 1985. Closed-ended contingent valuation questions were placed on the Field California Poll a month before the vote, using different figures for the household cost. Adjust for "don't know" responses, the predicted proportion of yes votes at the actual cost was 70–75 percent. The ballot vote in favor was 73 percent.

Cummings, Harrison and Rutström (1993) offered subjects small commodities at various prices. For one group, it was a real sale. A second group was first asked a hypothetical contingent valuation question—this item is not actually for sale but, if it were, would you buy it now? The experimenter then announced that, after all, she *would* sell the item, but they should feel free to revise their answer. When juicers were the item, 11 percent actually bought them in the real sale; with the second treatment, 41 percent said they would but it if it were on sale, but then only 16 percent did. The 41 percent and 11 percent are significantly different. With calculations, 21 percent would buy in the hypothetical sale, versus 8 percent in the real sale. One wonders whether some respondents interpreted the question as "*if you needed a juicer,* would you buy this one?" Smith (1994) shows that the calculator responses do not generate a downward sloping demand curve for either the actual or hypothetical data. The experimental procedure contained nothing to emphasize commitment or counteract yea-saying in the hypothetical treatment. Cummings and his colleagues have recently added wording like the "reasons to say no" mentioned earlier. In one case, this reduced the hypothetical yes for calculators from 21 percent to 10 percent, not significantly different from the real 8 percent; in another there was no effect (Cummings, 1994).

Other contingent valuation tests have used open-ended payment questions, with predictable difficulties. Boyce et al. (1989) measured willingness-to-pay and willingness-to-accept for a house plant, with mixed results; Neill et al. (1994) measured willingness-to-pay for a map and a picture, with negative results. Both confound the issue by comparing contingent valuation responses to an experimental auction, begging the question of whether auction behavior understates willingness-to-pay. Duffield and Patterson (1991) and Seip and Strand (1992) compare actual and hypothetical contributions to an environmental cause. Diamond and Hausman focus on these studies because they showed a significant difference. But, soliciting an intention to make a charitable donation is a poor test of contingent valuation, because it invites less commitment than soliciting an intention to vote for higher taxes. To make things worse, Seip and Strand used members of the environmental group as the interviewers in their hypothetical treatment, thus increasing pressures for compliance. They compared hypothetical phone responses with responses to an actual mail solicitation. Duffield and Patterson compared hypothetical mail solicitations from the University of Montana with actual mail solicitations from the Nature Conservancy. In both studies, the difference in survey administration introduces a confounding factor which undermines the comparison.[18]

A cleaner test is provided by Sinden (1988) who conducted a series of 17 parallel experiments soliciting actual and hypothetical monetary donations to a fund for assisting soil conservation or controlling eucalypt dieback. In all 17 cases, there was no statistical difference between actual and hypothetical willingness-to-pay.

Thus, there is some substantial evidence for the validity of contingent valuation survey responses, although more studies are certainly needed. Many existing studies do not incorporate the refinements in contingent valuation method, described earlier, that emphasize realism and commitment. In this respect, the test by Carson, Hanemann and Mitchell (1986) points in the right direction because it deals directly with expression of voting intentions. The positive results in that study are consistent with other evidence showing that polls in this country reliably indicate public sentiment at the time they are taken, and polls close to an election are generally accurate pre-

---

[18]The problem with mail surveys is that people may think the survey is junk mail and throw it out unopened. Duffield and Patterson made no allowance for the difference in sponsor identity on the envelope, which could explain the difference in response rates (Schuman, 1992). Response rates apart, the pattern of contributions was similar in the two treatments. Seip and Strand made no allowance for the fact that phone and mail solicitations generally have different response rates. Infosino (1986) found a sales rate three times higher with telephone than mail in an AT&T marketing effort.

dictors of the outcome.[19] Kelley and Mirer (1974) found voting intentions correctly predicted the actual vote in four presidential elections for 83 percent of those respondents who voted.[20] Surveys of purchase intentions in market research may not be accurate predictors of subsequent purchase behavior, but surveys of voting intentions are.[21]

Contingent Valuation and Economic Theory

Critics of contingent valuation like Diamond and Hausman, and their coauthors in Hausman (1993), reject contingent valuation as a method of economic valuation because the results of contingent valuation studies are inconsistent with economic theory as they see it. These assertions have become quite widely known. However, careful examination shows that in some cases the claims are not supported by the findings in the contingent valuation literature, and in others they rest on unusual notions about what economic theory does or does not prescribe. I briefly review these issues here, leaving a more detailed treatment to Hanemann (1994a).

Diamond and Hausman, and Milgrom (1993), make a number of statements about what is a permissible argument in a utility function. They argue that people should care about outcomes, not about the process whereby these are generated. People should not care whether animals are killed by man or die naturally. They should not care about details of provision or payment for a commodity, only price. Above all, they should value things for purely selfish motives. In their accompanying piece, Diamond and Hausman phrase this argument by saying that respondents should not contemplate "what they think is good for the country," because that reflects "warm glow" rather than "true economic preferences."[22] From this perspective, contingent

---

[19]Diamond and Hausman seem troubled that voters change their minds during the course of an election campaign. They cite a 1976 electricity rate proposition in Massachusetts where support went from 71 percent in February to 25 percent in the November ballot. They fail to mention the reasons. Magleby (1984, p. 147) identifies opposition spending as the chief cause of such opinion reversals, and that certainly occurred in 1976—opponents outspent supporters more than threefold. In May, the Dukakis administration came out against it, as eventually did businesses, the unions, hospitals, colleges, and major newspapers.

[20]Ajzen and Fishbein (1980) offer some reasons to expect a high level of attitude-behavior correspondence for voting in terms of their theory of reasoned action.

[21]One reason for the difference is timing: unlike elections, people generally control the timing of their market purchases. The result is they may end up buying the commodity, but later than they said (Juster, 1964). This is especially likely for durables, the focus of much literature, since their durability permits delay in replacement. This is consistent with findings that purchase intentions are significantly more accurate for nondurables than durables (Ferber and Piskie, 1965); intentions *not* to purchase durables are highly accurate (Theil and Kosobud, 1968); and predictions of the brand selected when the purchase *does* occur tend to be highly accurate (Ajzen and Fishbein, 1980; Warshaw, 1980).

[22]"Warm glow" is simply a red herring. I have seen no empirical evidence that people get a warm glow from voting to raise their own taxes, whether in real life or in a contingent valuation study.

valuation is unacceptable because it picks up existence values; for those to be allowed in a benefit-cost analysis, Milgrom (1993, p. 431) argues, "it would be necessary for people's individual existence values to reflect only their own personal economic motives and not altruistic motives, or sense of duty, or moral obligation."[23]

This criticism hardly comports with the standard view in economics that decisions about what people value should be left up to them. For example, Kenneth Arrow (1963, p. 17) wrote: "It need not be assumed here that an individual's attitude toward different social states is determined exclusively by the commodity bundles which accrue to his lot under each. The individual may order all social states by whatever standards he deems relevant." Or as Gary Becker (1993, p. 386) writes: "[I]ndividuals maximize welfare *as they conceive it*, whether they be selfish, altruistic, loyal, spiteful, or masochistic." When estimating demand functions for fish prior to Vatican II, no economist ever proposed removing Catholics because they were eating fish out of a sense of duty. Nor, when estimating collective choice models, do we exclude childless couples who vote for school bonds because they lack a personal economic motive.

A more substantive matter is how willingness-to-pay varies with factors that could reasonably be expected to influence it. This has been raised in connection with the embedding effect and the income elasticity of willingness-to-pay. Regarding the latter, Diamond and Hausman assert in this issue that the income effects measured in typical contingent valuation surveys are lower than would be expected if true preferences are measured. McFadden and Leonard (1993, p. 185) make the more specific claim that an income elasticity of willingness-to-pay less than unity constitutes grounds for doubting the validity of the contingent valuation method. There is no basis for either assertion. In the literature on the demand for state and local government services in the United States, the income elasticities generally fall in the range 0.3 to 0.6 (Cutler, Elmendorf and Zeckhauser, 1993). With charitable giving by individuals, the income elasticities generally fall in the range of 0.4 to 0.8 (Clotfelter, 1985). The income elasticities in the contingent valuation literature vary with the item being valued, but are generally in the same range (Kriström and Riera, 1994).

The term "embedding effect," introduced by Kahneman and Knetsch (1992), has come to mean several different things. The general notion is captured in the (mis)conception that, with contingent valuation, you get

---

[23]Milgrom (1993) also asserts that using contingent valuation to measure altruistic preferences creates double counting. His analysis has three flaws. First, it depends on the particular specification of the utility function, as Johansson (1992) notes; if the argument of the utility function is another's consumption rather than his utility, there is no double counting. Second, it derives its force from the auxiliary assumption that the respondent *does not realize* that the other people for whom he cares will have to pay, too; this is not a problem in a referendum format. Third, in many contingent valuation studies the object of the altruism is often wildlife—sea otters, for example. Since those creatures are *not* surveyed, the issue of double counting is moot.

the same willingness-to-pay if you value one lake, two lakes, or ten lakes.[24] This combines three distinct notions. One assertion, which arises when the object of preference is thought to be simply the number of lakes, is that willingness-to-pay varies inadequately with changes in the scale or scope of the item being valued. This is a scope effect. Alternatively, if each lake is seen as a separate argument in the utility function, then the assertion is that a given lake has quite different value if it is first, second or tenth in a set of items to be valued—it gets a high value when the first, but it adds little or nothing to total value when second or tenth. This is a sequencing effect. Thirdly, with either preference structure, the willingness-to-pay for a composite change in a group of public goods may be less than the sum of the willingness-to-pay for the individual changes separately. This is a sub-additivity effect.

The question of how willingness-to-pay varies with the scale or scope of the item being valued in a contingent valuation survey has long been considered, starting with Cicchetti and Smith (1973) who elicited hikers' values for trips in a Montana wilderness area and found that the willingness-to-pay for trips where other hikers were encountered on two nights was 34 percent lower than the willingness-to-pay for trips with no encounters. Many other studies have since reported comparable findings using both internal (within-subject) and external (split-sample) scope tests, including meta-analyses by Walsh, Johnson and McKean (1992) covering over 100 contingent valuation studies of outdoor recreation, and Smith and Osborne (1994) on 10 contingent valuation studies of air quality. Carson (1994) reviews 27 papers with split-sample tests of scope and finds a statistically significant effect of scope on willingness-to-pay in 25 of them.

The two exceptions are Kahneman and Knetsch (1992) and Desvousges et al. (1992). Critics of contingent valuation rely heavily on these two studies when asserting the absence of scope effects in contingent valuation.[25] Some of the problems with these two studies have already been noted, including their failure to use a closed-ended voting format, the after-the-fact provision of information in Kahneman and Knetsch's "top-down" procedure, and the use of brief shopping mall intercepts by Desvousges et al.[26] The latter elicited people's willingness-to-pay for preventing the deaths of migratory waterfowl. Three separate versions of the questionnaire said that 2,000, 20,000, and 200,000 out of 85 million birds die each year from

---

[24]Though widely believed, this is a myth. It may be traced to Kahneman (1986), which is usually cited as showing that respondents were willing to pay the same amount to clean up fishing lakes in one region of Ontario as in all of Ontario. His data actually show a 50 percent difference. Moreover, the survey involved a brief telephone interview using an open-ended willingness-to-pay question. It provided no detail on how and when the cleanup would occur. Respondents may not have seen cleaning up *all* the lakes as something likely to happen soon.

[25]Also, in their contingent valuation survey, Diamond et al. (1993, pp. 45–46) mention that, using a Kruskal-Wallis test, they found no difference in willingness-to-pay for three wilderness areas ranging in size from 700,000 to 1.3 million acres. If they had run a simple regression of willingness-to-pay on acreage, they would have found a significant scope effect.

[26]Other questions about Kahneman and Knetsch are raised by Harrison (1992) and Smith (1992).

exposure to waste-oil holding ponds that could be sealed under a new program. Respondents were told that the deaths amounted to *much less than* 1 *percent* of the bird population, to *less than* 1 *percent*, and to *about 2 percent*. If respondents focused on the relative impact on the population, it is hard to believe that they would have perceived any real difference among these percentages. The results of the scope test depend crucially on how much one trims the data to remove what are clearly outliers. With a 10 percent trim, one obtains a highly significant scope effect.[27] At any rate, even if one regards these two studies as highly credible evidence that respondents were insensitive to scope, they certainly do not represent the majority finding in the contingent valuation literature regarding the variation of willingness-to-pay with scope.

How much should willingness-to-pay vary with scope? Diamond (1993) asserts that economic theory requires it to increase *more than proportionately* with the number of bird deaths. The variables in his model are the number of birds originally in the population, q_0, the number at risk of dying, q_R, and the number of those that are saved, q_s. Let $q_F = q_0 - q_R + q_s$. Diamond assumes that people should care only about qF, the ultimate number of birds, not how many were alive initially, at risk, or saved. He also assumes preferences are quasiconcave in q_0. The two assumptions together imply *quasiconvexity* in q_R, which is what makes the elasticity of willingness-to-pay with respect to q_R greater than unity. The conclusion depends critically on the assumption of perfect substitution between q_0, q_s, and $-q_R$. When contingent valuation data disconfirm this, Diamond dismisses the method. Others might be more inclined to believe the data and drop the assumption.[28]

With regard to sequencing and sub-additivity effects, these effects are certainly present in contingent valuation responses, but one expects them to occur, and they can be explained in terms of substitution effects and diminishing marginal rates of substitution. When the quality of one lake improves, you value an improvement in a second lake *less* if the

---

[27]How the survey was administered clearly affected the results. Schkade and Payne (1993) used the same questionnaire as Desvouges et al., but slowed respondents down and made them think about their answer. Their data show a different pattern of willingness-to-pay responses, and a significant relationship between willingness-to-pay and the percentage of birds killed (Haneman, 1994b).

[28]Some, while not sharing Diamond's extreme position on the elasticity of willingness-to-pay, still hold that contingent valuation responses vary inadequately with scale. People's perceptions undoubtedly differ from objective measures of attributes. But this is not just a feature of contingent valuation. In psychophysics, it has been known since the 1880s that there is a general tendency for judgments of magnitude to vary inadequately. Observers standing at a distance overestimate the height of short posts, and underestimate that of tall ones; people reaching quickly for an object overestimate small distances and angles, and underestimate large ones; subjects matching loudness of a tone to a duration overestimate the loudness of short tones, and underestimate the loudness of long ones; people overestimate infrequent causes of death, and underestimate frequent ones; small probabilities are overestimated, large ones underestimated (Poulton, 1989). This "response contraction bias" in judgment or rating is an authentic feature of how people perceive the world, not an artifact of contingent valuation.

lakes are what Madden (1991) calls *R*-substitutes, and *more* if they are *R*-complements. Far from being inconsistent with economic preferences (Diamond et al., 1993, pp. 48–49), sub-additivity is likely to be the norm: while all goods cannot be *R*-complements, Madden shows they *can* all be *R*-substitutes.[29] Similarly, *R*-substitution explains sequence effects: if the lakes are *R*-substitutes, the willingness-to-pay for an improvement in one lake is *lower* when it comes at the end of a sequence of changes in lake improvements than at the beginning while the willingness-to-accept for the change in the lake is *higher* when it comes later in a sequence (Carson, Flores and Hanemann, 1992).[30] It should come as no surprise that the value of one commodity changes when the quantity of another varies: in other words, that willingness-to-pay depends on economic context.[31]

For many economists, the ultimate argument against contingent valuation is that it violates the habitual commitment of the profession to revealed preference. Three points should be noted. First, one must distinguish between private market goods and public goods. Revealed preference is harder to apply to the latter, especially when they are national rather than local public goods (Cropper, 1994). Second, revealed preference is not foolproof, either. It involves an extrapolation from observation of particular choices to general conclusions about preference. One relies on various auxiliary assumptions to rule out factors that might invalidate the extrapolation. Those assumptions are not themselves verifiable if one is restricted to observed behavior. This can sometimes make revealed preference a relatively hypothetical undertaking.[32] Third, there is no reason why observing

---

[29]If the intention of the Diamond et al. (1993) contingent valuation survey was to test the adding-up of willingness-to-pay, it was strangely designed for the purpose. The survey stated that there were 57 federal wilderness areas in the Rocky Mountain states, without identifying them, and said that there now was a proposal to open these to commercial development. In one version, respondents were told that seven unidentified areas had already been earmarked for development, and were asked their willingness-to-pay to protect an eighth area, identified as the Selway Bitterroot Wilderness. In another, respondents were told that eight unnamed areas had been earmarked for development and asked their willingness-to-pay to protect a ninth area, identified as the Washakie Wilderness. In a third version, respondents were told that seven unnamed areas had been earmarked for development and asked their willingness-to-pay to protect two areas identified as Selway and Washakie. In all three cases, respondents were not told the identity or fate of the other 48 or 49 areas. Given that respondents were not indifferent among wilderness areas, as evidenced by the regression mentioned in note 25, I leave it to the reader to decide whether the surveys constitute a sensible basis for testing the adding-up of willingness-to-pay.

[30]In natural resource damages, where willingness-to-accept is the relevant welfare measure, this implies that the usual practice of taking the injured resource as the first item in any possible valuation sequence is a conservative procedure.

[31]The practical implications are that, when one values a program, it be placed in whatever sequence applies under the circumstances, and that one take care when extrapolating results in a benefits transfer exercise because the values might change with the difference in circumstances (Hoehn and Randall, 1989).

[32]Revealed preference estimates are sensitive to the measurement of price, which is often uncertain and precarious for disaggregated commodities (Pratt, Wise and Zeckhauser, 1979; Randall, 1994). The price at which demand falls to zero, needed to estimate consumer's surplus, may lie outside the range of the observed data and be estimated inaccurately (for example, one knows travel cost only for participants, or one believes that participants and nonparticipants have different pref-

people's behavior and asking them about behavioral intentions and motives should be mutually exclusive. Fathoming human behavior is never easy; one should utilize every possible source of information.

Above all, one should take a balanced view of the difficulties with each approach. As Sen (1973, p. 258) wrote, "we have been too prone, on the one hand, to overstate the difficulties of introspection and communication and, on the other, to underestimate the problems of studying preferences revealed by observed behavior." In the debate on contingent valuation, critics have shown a tendency to employ simplistic dichotomies. Surveys of attitudes are fallible and subject to the vagaries of context and interpretation; surveys of behavior are unerring. In the market place, people are well informed, deliberate, and rational. Outside it, they are ignorant, confused, and illogical. As consumers, people can be taken seriously; as voters, they cannot. In particular instances, these assertions may be correct. As generalizations, however, they are a caricature.

Conclusions

When cost-benefit analysis started in the United States in the 1930s, economic valuation was generally perceived in terms of market prices. To value something, one ascertained an appropriate market price, adjusted for market imperfections if necessary, and then used this to multiply some quantity. Two things changed this. The first was the recognition, prompted by the "new welfare economics" of the 1940s and especially Hotelling's paper on public utility pricing, that the appropriate welfare criterion is maximization of aggregate consumers' plus producers' surplus. While market prices can safely be used to value marginal changes for market commodities, the impact of nonmarginal changes is measured by the change in areas under demand and supply curves. The second development was Samuelson's theory of public goods and his finding that their valuation must be based on vertical aggregation of individual demand curves.

Together, these developments led to an important paradigm shift—one that contributed directly to the emergence of nonmarket valuation and is still evident in the current debate on contingent valuation.[33] This shift changed the focus of valuation away from market prices towards demand and supply functions as the underlying repositories of value. These functions are behavioral relations, and the implication of the paradigm shift was

---

erences). This can cause revealed preference to produce a less reliable estimate of use value than contingent valuation (Hanemann, Chapman and Kanninen, 1993). With other variables there may be inadequate variation in the data (for example, attributes are correlated across brands). Hence, revealed preference data alone may yield a less reliable estimate of demand functions than contingent valuation choice data, and one may need to combine both types of data for best results (Adamowicz, Louviere and Williams, 1994).

[33]For an account of the development of nonmarket valuation generally, see Hanemann (1992).

that economics is not just the study of markets, but more generally the study of human preferences and behavior.

The conceptual link to nonmarket valuation is the recognition that, while a demand curve is not observable if there is no market for a commodity, there still exists a latent demand curve that perhaps can be teased out through other means. Indirect methods are one approach to doing this, and contingent valuation is another. In both cases, the details of implementation have a large impact on the quality of the results.

Faced with the assertion that contingent valuation surveys can *never* be a reliable source of information either for benefit-cost analysis or for damage assessment, the NOAA Panel rejected this as unwarranted. Two years later, there is now even more evidence from recent studies and literature analyses to support the Panel's conclusion. However, it would be misleading for me to suggest that contingent valuation surveys can be made to work well in all circumstances. I am sure situations could exist where a contingent valuation researcher might be unable to devise a plausible scenario for the item of interest. Nor would I wish to argue that all contingent valuation surveys are of high quality. The method, though simple in its directness, is in fact difficult to implement without falling into various types of design problems that require effort, skill and imagination to resolve. Each particular study needs to be scrutinized carefully. But the same is true of any empirical study.

While I believe in the feasibility of using contingent valuation to measure people's value for the environment, I do not mean to advocate a narrow benefit-cost analysis for all environmental policy decisions, nor to suggest that everything can or should be quantified. There will be cases where the information is inadequate, the uncertainties too great, or the consequences too profound or too complex to be reduced to a single number. I am well aware of the fallacy of misplaced precision. But this cuts both ways. It also applies to those who suggest that it is better not to measure nonuse values at all than to measure them through contingent valuation. I reply to such critics by quoting Douglass North: "The price you pay for precision is an inability to deal with real-world issues" (*Wall Street Journal*, 7/29/94).

Is expert judgment an alternative to contingent valuation? Experts clearly play the leading role in determining the physical injuries to the environment and in assessing the costs of cleanup and restoration. Assessing what things *are worth* is different. How the experts know the value that the public places on an uninjured environment, without resort to measurement involving some sort of survey, is unclear. When that public valuation is the object of measurement, a well-designed contingent valuation survey is one way of consulting the relevant experts—the public itself.

REFERENCES

Adamowicz, W., J. Louviere, and M. Williams, "Combining Revealed and Stated Preference Methods for Valuing Environmental Amenities," *Journal of Environmental Economics and Management*, 1994, *26*, 271–92.

Ajzen, Icek, and Martin Fishbein, *Understanding Attitudes and Predicting Social Behavior.* New Jersey: Prentice-Hall, Inc., 1980.

Anonymous, "'Ask a Silly Question . . .' Contingent Valuation of Natural Resource Damages," *Harvard Law Review*, June 1992, *105*, 1981–2000.

Arrow, Kenneth J., *Social Choice and Individual Values*, 2nd ed., New Haven: Yale University Press, 1963.

Arrow, Kenneth et al., *Report of the NOAA Panel on Contingent Valuation*, Washington, D.C.: January 1993, p. 41.

Atkinson, A. B., and J. Micklewright, "On the Reliability of Income Data in the Family Expenditure Survey, 1970–1977," *Journal of the Royal Statistical Society* (A), 1983, *146(1)*, 33–53.

Bate, Roger, "Pick a Number: A Critique of Contingent Valuation Methodology and Its Application in Public Policy." Competitive Enterprise Institute, Environmental Studies Program, Washington, D.C., January 1994.

Bateman, Ian, and Ken Willis (eds.). *Valuing Environmental Preferences: Theory and Practice of the Contingent Valuation Method in the US, EC and Developing Countries.* Oxford, UK: Oxford University Press, [2001].

Becker, Gary S., "Nobel Lecture: The Economic Way of Looking at Behavior." *Journal of Political Economy*, June 1993, *101(3)*, 385–409.

Bettman, James R., "Processes of Adaptivity in Decision Making," *Advances in Consumer Research*, 1988, *15*, 1–4.

Bettman, J. R., and M. A. Zins, "Constructive Processes in Consumer Choice," *Journal of Consumer Research*, September 1977, *4*, 75–85.

Bishop, Richard C., and Thomas A. Heberlein, "Measuring Values of Extramarket Goods: Are Indirect Measures Biased?" *American Journal of Agricultural Economics*, December 1979, *61*, 926–30.

———, "The Contingent Valuation Method." In Johnson, Rebecca L., and Gary V. Johnson, eds., *Economic Valuation of Natural Resources: Issues, Theory, and Applications*, Boulder: Westview Press, 1990, 81–104.

Bohm, Peter, "Estimating Demand for Public Goods: An Experiment," *European Economic Review*, 1972, *3*, 111–30.

Boyce, R. R., et al., "Experimental Evidence of Existence Value in Payment and Compensation Contexts." Paper presented at the USDA W-133 Annual Meeting, San Diego, California, February 1989.

Boyle, Kevin J., Michael P. Welsh, and Richard C. Bishop, "The Role of Question Order and Respondent Experience in Contingent-Valuation Studies," *Journal of Environmental Economics and Management*, 1993, *25*, S-80–S-99.

Bradburn, Norman M., Lance J. Rips, and Steven K. Shevell, "Answering Autobiographical Questions: The Impact of Memory and Inference on Surveys," *Science*, April 1987, *236*, 157–61.

Briscoe, John, et al., "Toward Equitable and Sustainable Rural Water Supplies: A Contingent Valuation Study in Brazil," *World Bank Economic Review*, May 1990, *4*, 115–34.

Brookshire, David S., Mark A. Thayer, William D. Schulze, and Ralph C. d'Arge, "Valuing Public Goods: A Comparison of Survey and Hedonic Approaches," *American Economic Review*, 1982, *72*, 165–77.

Carson, Richard T., "Contingent Valuation Surveys and Tests of Insensitivity to Scope." Paper presented at the International Conference on Determining the Value of Nonmarketed Goods: Economic Psychological, and Policy Relevant Aspects of Contingent Valuation Methods, Bad Hamburg, Germany, July 1994.

Carson, Richard T., and Nicholas E. Flores, "Another Look at 'Does Contingent Valuation Measure Preferences: Experimental Evidence'—How Compelling Is the Evidence?" Economics Department, University of California, San Diego, December 1993.

Carson, R., N. Flores, and W. M. Hanemann, "On the Creation and Destruction of Public Goods: The Matter of Sequencing," working paper 690, Agricultural and Resource Economics, University of California, Berkeley, 1992.

Carson, Richard T., Nicholas E. Flores, Kerry Martin and Jennifer Wright, "Contingent Valuation and Revealed Preference Methodologies: Comparing the Estimates for Quasi-Public Goods," Discussion Paper 94-07, University of California, San Diego, May 1994a.

Carson, Richard T., W. Michael Hanemann, and Robert Cameron Mitchell, "The Use of Simulated Political Markets to Value Public Goods," Economics Department, University of California, San Diego, October 1986.

Carson, Richard T., Kerry Martin, Jennifer Wright," A Note on the Evidence of the Temporal Reliability of Contingent Valuation Estimates," working paper, University of California, San Diego, Economics Department, July 1994b.

Carson, Richard T., and Robert Cameron Mitchell, "The Value of Clean Water: The Public's Willingness to Pay for Boatable, Fishable, and Swimmable Quality Water," *Water Resources Research*, 1993, *29*, 2445–54.

Carson, R., et al., *A Contingent Valuation Study of Lost Passive Use Values Resulting from the Exxon Valdez Oil Spill*, Report to the Attorney General of Alaska, Natural Resource Damage Assessment, Inc. La Jolla, CA, November 1992.

Carson, Richard T., et al., *A Bibliography of Contingent Valuation Studies and Papers*, Natural Resource Damage Assessment, Inc., La Jolla, CA, March 1994c.

Chase, S. B., ed., *Problems in Public Expenditure Analysis*, Washington, D.C.: Brookings Institution, 1968.

Cicchetti, Charles J., and V. Kerry Smith; "Congestion, Quality Deterioration, and Optimal Use: Wilderness Recreation in the Spanish Peaks Primitive Area," *Social Science Research*, 1973, *2*, 15–30.

Ciriacy-Wantrup, S. V., "Capital Returns from Soil-Conservation Practices," *Journal of Farm Economics*, November 1947, *29*, 1188–90.

Clotfelter, Charles T., *Federal Tax Policy and Charitable Giving*. Chicago: University of Chicago Press, 1985.

Cronin, Thomas E., *Direct Democracy: The Politics of Initiative, Referendum, and Recall*. Cambridge: Harvard University Press, 1989.

Cropper, Maureen L., "Comments on Estimating the Demand for Public Goods: The Collective Choice and Contingent Valuation Approaches." Paper presented at the DOE/EPA Workshop on "Using Contingent Valuation to Measure Non-Market Values," Herndon, VA, May 19–20, 1994.

Cummings, Ronald G., "Relating Stated and Revealed Preferences: Challenges and Opportunities." Paper presented at the DOE/EPA Workshop on "Using Contingent Valuation to Measure Non-Market Values," Herndon, VA, May 19–20, 1994.

Cummings, Ronald G., David S. Brookshire, and William D. Schulze, et al., eds. *Valuing Environmental Goods: An Assessment of the Contingent Valuation Method*. Totowa, New Jersey: Rowman and Allanheld, 1986.

Cummings, Ronald G., Glenn W. Harrison, and E. E. Ruström, "Homegrown Values and Hypothetical Surveys: Is the Dichotomous Choice Approach Incentive Compatible?" Economics Working Paper Series, B-92-12, Division of Research, College of Business Administration, The University of South Carolina, February 1993.

Cutler, David, Douglas W. Elmendorf, and Richard J. Zeckhauser, "Demographic Characteristics and the Public Bundle," National Bureau of Economic Research, Cambridge, NBER Working Paper No. 4283, February 1993.

Desvousges, William H., et al., *Measuring Nonuse Damages Using Contingent Valuation: An Experimental Evaluation of Accuracy.* North Carolina: Research Triangle Institute Monograph, 1992.

Diamond, P. A., "Testing the Internal Consistency of Contingent Valuation Surveys," working paper, MIT, 1993.

Diamond, Peter A., Jerry Hausman, Gregory K. Leonard, and Mike A. Denning, "Does Contingent Valuation Measure Preferences? Experimental Evidence." In Hausman, J. A., ed., *Contingent Valuation: A Critical Assessment.* New York: North-Holland, 1993, 41–89.

DiBona, Charles J., "Assessing Environmental Damage," *Issues in Science and Technology*, Fall 1992, *8*, 50–54.

Dickie, M. A. Fisher, and S. Gerking, "Market Transactions and Hypothetical Demand Data: A Comparative Study," *Journal of American Statistical Association*, March 1987, *82*, 69–75.

Duffield, John W., and David A. Patterson, "Field Testing Existence Values: An Instream Flow Trust Fund for Montana Rivers." Presented at the American Economics Association Annual Meeting, New Orleans, Louisiana, January 4, 1991.

Ferber, Robert, and Robert A. Piskie, "Subjective Probabilities and Buying Intentions," *Review of Economics and Statistics*, August 1965, *47*, 322–25.

Fiorina, Morris P., *Retrospective Voting in American National Elections.* New Haven: Yale University Press, 1981.

Fishkin, J. S., *Democracy and Deliberation: New Directions for Democratic Reform.* New Haven: Yale University Press, 1991.

Freeman, A. Myrick, *The Measurement of Environment and Resource Values: Theory and Method.* Washington, D.C.: Resources for the Future, 1993.

Frisch, Deborah, "Reasons for Framing Effects," *Organizational Behavior and Human Decision Processes*, 1993, *54*, 399–429.

Groves, Robert M., *Survey Errors and Survey Costs.* New York: John Wiley and Sons, 1989.

Hanemann, W. Michael, "Welfare Evaluations in Contingent Valuation Experiments with Discrete Responses," *American Journal of Agricultural Economics*, August 1984, *66*, 332–41.

———, "Preface: Notes on the History of Environmental Valuation in the USA." In Navrud, Stale, ed., *Pricing the Environment: The European Experience.* Oxford, UK: Oxford University Press, 1992.

———, "Contingent Valuation and Economics," Working Paper No. 697, Giannini Foundation of Agricultural and Resource Economics, University of California, Berkeley, February 1994a. [In] Willis, Ken, and John Corkindale, eds., *Environmental Valuation: New Perspectives*, Wallingford, Oxon, UK: CAB international, [1995].

———, "Strictly for the Birds: A Re-examination of the Exxon Tests of Scope in CV," working paper, Giannini Foundation of Agricultural and Resource Economics, University of California, Berkeley, August 1994b.

Hanemann, W. Michael, and B. J. Kanninen, "Statistical Analysis of CV Data." In Bateman, I., and K. Willis, eds. *Valuing Environmental Preferences: Theory and Practice of the Contingent Valuation Method in the US, EC and Developing Countries*. Oxford: Oxford University Press, [2001].

Hanemann, W. Michael, David Chapman, and Barbara Kanninen, "Non-Market Valuation Using Contingent Behavior: Model Specification and Consistency Tests." Presented at the American Economic Association Annual Meeting, Anaheim, California, January 6, 1993.

Hanemann, W. M., J. Loomis, and B. Kanninen, "Statistical Efficiency of Double-Bounded Dichotomous Choice Contingent Valuation," *American Journal of Agricultural Economics*, 1991, *73*, 1255–63.

Harrison, Glenn W., "Valuing Public Goods with the Contingent Valuation Method: A Critique of Kahneman and Knetsch," *Journal of Environmental Economics and Management*, 1992, *23*, 248–57.

Hausman, J. A., ed., *Contingent Valuation: A Critical Assessment*. New York: North-Holland, 1993.

Hausman, J. A., G. K. Leonard, and D. McFadden, "A Utility-Consistent Combined Discrete Choice and Count Data Model: Assessing Recreational Use Losses Due to Natural Resource Damage," paper presented at the National Bureau of Economic Research, Cambridge, Massachusetts, April 15, 1994

Hoehn, J. P., and A. Randall, "Too Many Proposals Pass the Benefit Cost Test," *American Economic Review*, June 1989, *79*, 544–51.

Infosino, William J., "Forecasting New Product Sales from Likelihood of Purchase Ratings," *Marketing Science*, Fall 1986, *5*, 372–84.

Johansson, Per-Olov, "Altruism in Cost-Benefit Analysis," *Environmental and Resource Economics*, 1992, *2*, 605–13.

Jones-Lee, Michael W., M. Hammerton, and P. R. Philips, "The Value of Safety: Results of a National Sample Survey," *Economic Journal*, March 1985, *95*, 49–72.

Juster, F. Thomas, *Anticipations and Purchases: An Analysis of Consumer Behavior*. Princeton: Princeton University Press, 1964.

Juster, F. Thomas, and Frank P. Stafford, "The Allocation of Time: Empirical Findings, Behavioral Models, and Problems of Measurement," *Journal of Economic Literature*, 1991, *29*, 471–522.

Kahneman, Daniel, "Valuing Environmental Goods: An Assessment of the Contingent Valuation Method: The Review Panel Assessment." In Cummings, R. G., D. S. Brookshire, W. D. Schulze, et al., eds., *Valuing Environmental Goods: An Assessment of the Contingent Valuation Method*. Totowa, New Jersey: Rowman & Allanheld, 1986, 185–94.

Kahneman, Daniel, and Jack L. Knetsch, "Valuing Public Goods: The Purchase of Moral Satisfaction," *Journal of Environmental Economics and Management*, 1992, *22*, 57–70.

Kahneman, Daniel, and Ilana Ritov, "Determinants of Stated Willingness to Pay for Public Goods: A Study in the Headline Method," unpublished, Department of Psychology, University of California, Berkeley, 1993.

Kanninen, B. J., "Optimal Experimental Design for Double-Bounded Dichotomous Choice Contingent Valuation," *Land Economics*, May 1993, *69*, 128–46.

Kelly, S., and T. W. Mirer, "The Simple Act of Voting," *American Political Science Review*, 1974, *68*, 572–91.

Kemp, Michael A., and Christopher Maxwell, "Exploring a Budget Context for Contingent Valuation Estimates." In Hausman, J. A., ed., *Contingent Valuation: A Critical Assessment*. New York: North-Holland, 1993, 217–69.

Knetsch, J. L., and R. K. Davis, Comparisons of Methods for Recreation Evaluation." In Kneese A. V., and S. C. Smith, eds., *Water Research*, Baltimore: Resources for the Future Inc., Johns Hopkins Press, 1966, 125–42.

Kriström, Bengt, and Pere Riera, "Is the Income Elasticity of Environmental Improvements Less Than One?" Paper presented at the Second Conference on Environmental Economics, Ulvöng, Sweden, June 2–5, 1994.

Krosnick, Jon A., "Response Strategies for Coping with the Cognitive Demands of Attitude Measures in Surveys," *Applied Cognitive Psychology*, 1991, 5, 213–36.

Krosnick, Jon A., Fan Li, and Darrin R. Lehman, "Conservational Conventions, Order of Information Acquisition, and the Effect of Base Rates and Individuating Information on Social Judgments," *Journal of Personality and Social Psychology*, 1990, 59, 1140–52.

Krutilla, John V., "Conservation Reconsidered," *American Economic Review*, September 1967, 57, 777–86.

Lupia, Arthur, "Short Cuts versus Encyclopedias: Information and Voting Behavior in California Insurance Reform Elections," working paper, Department of Political Science, University of California, San Diego, April 1993.

Madden, Paul, "A Generalization of Hicksian *q* Substitutes and Complements with Application to Demand Rationing," *Econometrica*, September 1991, 59, 1497–1508.

Magleby, David B., *Direct Legislation, Voting on Ballot Propositions in the United States*. Baltimore and London: The John Hopkins University Press, 1984.

Maki, Atsushi, and Shigeru Nishiyama, "Consistency Between Macro- and Micro-Data Sets in the Japanese Household Sector," *Review of Income and Wealth*, 1993, 39, 195–207.

Martin, Leonard L., and Abraham Tesser, eds., *The Construction of Social Judgments*. New Jersey: Lawrence Erlbaum Associates, chapter 2, 1992, 37–65.

Mathiowetz, Nancy A., and Greg J. Duncan, "Out of Work, Out of Mind: Response Errors in Retrospective Reports of Unemployment," *Journal of Business & Economic Statistics*, 1988, 6, 221–29.

McCloskey, Donald, *The Rhetoric of Economics*. Madison: The University of Wisconsin Press, 1985.

McFadden, Daniel, and Gregory K. Leonard, "Issues in the Contingent Valuation of Environmental Goods: Methodologies for Data Collection and Analysis." In Hausman, J. A., ed., *Contingent Valuation: A Critical Assessment*. New York: North-Holland, 1993, 165–215.

McKelvey, Richard D., and Peter C. Ordeshook, "Information, Electoral Equilibria and the Democratic Ideal," *Journal of Politics*, 1986, 48, 909–37.

Merton, Robert K., and Patricia L. Kendall, "The Focused Interview," *American Journal of Sociology*, 1946, 51, 541–57.

Milgrom, Paul, "Is Sympathy an Economic Value? Philosophy, Economics, and the Contingent Valuation Method." In Hausman, J. A., ed., *Contingent Valuation: A Critical Assessment*. New York: North-Holland, 1993, 417–41.

Miller, Leslie A., and Theodore Downes-Le Guin, "Reducing Response Error in Consumers' Reports of Medical Expenses: Application of Cognitive Theory to the Consumer Expenditure Interview Survey," *Advances in Consumer Research*, 1990, 17, 193–206.

Mitchell, Robert Cameron, and Richard T. Carson, *Using Surveys to Value Public Goods: The Contingent Valuation Method*. Washington, D.C: Resources for the Future, 1989.

Navrud, Ståle, *Pricing the European Environment*. New York: Oxford University Press, 1992.

Neill, Helen R., et al., "Hypothetical Surveys and Real Economic Commitments," *Land Economics*, May 1994, *70*, 145–54.

Neisser, Urlic, *Cognitive Psychology*. Appleton-Century-Crofts, Educational Division, New York: Meredith Corporation, 1967.

Oates, W., "Comments on Estimating the Demand for Public Goods: The Collective Choice and Contingent Valuation Approaches." Paper presented at the DOE/EPA Workshop on Using Contingent Valuation to Measure Non-Market Values, Hemdon, VA, May 19–20, 1994.

Olshavsky, Richard W., and Donald H. Granbois, "Consumer Decision Making—Fact or Fiction?" *Journal of Consumer Research*, September 1979, *6*, 93–100.

Payne, J. W., J. R. Bettman, and E. J. Johnson, "Adaptive Strategy Selection in Decision Making," *Journal of Experimental Psychology Learning, Memory, and Cognition*, 1988, *14*, 534–52.

Poulton, E. C., *Bias in Quantifying Judgments*. Hove, UK: Lawrence Erlbaum Associates, 1989.

Pratt, John W., David A. Wise, and Richard Zeckhauser, "Price Differences in Almost Competitive Markets," *Quarterly Journal of Economics*, May 1979, *93*, 189–212.

Randall, Alan, "A Difficulty with the Travel Cost Method," *Land Economics*, February 1994, *70*, 88–96.

Randall, Alan, Berry C. Ives, and Clyde Eastman, "Bidding Games for Valuation of Aesthetic Environmental Improvements," *Journal of Environmental Economics and Management*, 1974, *1*, 132–49.

Rose, Steven, *The Making of Memory: From Molecules to Mind*. New York Anchor Books, Doubleday, 1992.

Rosen, S., "Hedonic Prices and Implicit Markets: Product Differentiation in Pure Competition," *Journal of Political Economy*, January–February 1974, *82*, 34–55.

Schelling, Thomas, "The Life You Save May Be Your Own." In Chase, S., ed., *Problems in Public Expenditure Analysis*. Washington, D.C.: Brookings Institution, 1968, 143–44.

Schkade, David A., and John W. Payne, "Where Do the Numbers Come From? How People Respond to Contingent Valuation Questions." In Hausman, J. A., ed., *Contingent Valuation: A Critical Assessment*. New York: North-Holland, 1993, 271–303.

Schuman, H., remarks in transcript of Public Meeting of the National Oceanic and Atmospheric Administration, Contingent Valuation Panel, Washington, D.C.: NOAA, Department of Commerce, August 12, 1992, p. 101.

Schuman, H., and S. Presser, *Questions and Answers in Attitude Surveys*. New York: Academic Press, 1981.

Seip, K., and J. Strand, "Willingness to Pay for Environmental Goods in Norway: A Contingent Valuation Study with Real Payment," *Environmental and Resource Economics*, 1992, *2*, 91–106.

Sen, A. K., "Behavior and the Concept of Preference," *Economica*, August 1973, *40*, 241–59.

Sinden, J. A., "Empirical Tests of Hypothetical Biases in Consumers' Surplus Surveys," *Australian Journal of Agricultural Economics*, 1988, *32*, 98–112.

Smith, Tom W., "The Art of Asking Questions, 1936–1985," *Public Opinion Quarterly*, 1987, *51*, 21–36.

Smith, V. Kerry, "Arbitrary Values, Good Causes, and Premature Verdicts," *Journal of Environmental Economics and Management*, 1992, *22*, 71–89.

———, "Lightning Rods, Dart Boards and Contingent Valuation," *Natural Resources Journal*, forthcoming 1994.

Smith, V. Kerry, and William H. Desvousges, *Measuring Water Quality Benefits.* Boston: Kluwer-Nijhoff Publishing, 1986.

Smith, V. Kerry, and Laura Osborne, "Do Contingent Valuation Estimates Pass a 'Scope' Test?: A Preliminary Meta Analysis." Presented at the American Economics Association Annual Meeting, Boston MA, January 5, 1994.

Sniderman, Paul M., "The New Look in Public Opinion Research." In Finifter, Ada W., ed., *Political Science: The State of the Discipline II.* Washington, D.C.: The American Political Science Association, 1993, 219–45.

Sniderman, Paul M., Richard A. Brody, and Phillip E. Tetlock, *Reasoning and Choice, Explorations in Political Psychology.* Cambridge: Cambridge University Press, 1991.

Tanur, Judith M., ed., *Questions about Questions: Inquiries into the Cognitive Bases of Surveys.* New York: Russell Sage Foundation, 1992.

Theil, Henri, and Richard F. Kosobud, "How Informative Are Consumer Buying Intentions Surveys?" *Review of Economics and Statistics*, February 1968, *50*, 50–59.

Tversky, Amos, and Daniel Kahneman, "Judgment under Uncertainty: Heuristics and Biases," *Science*, 1974, *185*, 124–31.

Walsh, Richard G., Donn M. Johnson, and John R. McKean, "Benefits Transfer of Outdoor Recreation Demand Studies: 1968–1988," *Water Resources Research* 1992, *28*, 707–13.

Warshaw, Paul R., "Predicting Purchase and Other Behaviors from General and Contextually Specific Intentions," *Journal of Marketing Research*, February 1980, *17*, 26–33.

Wilson, Timothy D., and Sara D. Hodges, "Attitudes as Temporary Constructions." In Martin L., and A. Tesser, eds., *The Construction of Social Judgments.* New Jersey: Lawrence Erlbaum Associates, chapter 2, 1992, 37–65.

9 Contingent Valuation: Is Some Number Better Than No Number?*

Peter A. Diamond

Jerry A. Hausman

Peter Diamond is Institute Professor, Department of Economics at the Massachusetts Institute of Technology; and Jerry Hausman is John and Jennie S. MacDonald Professor, Department of Economics at the Massachusetts Institute of Technology.

Most economic analyses aim at explaining market transactions. Data on transactions, or potentially collectible data on transactions, are the touchstone for recognizing interesting economic analyses. However loose the connection between a theoretical or empirical analysis and transactions, this connection is the basis of the methodology of judging the credibility and reliability of economic analyses. Generally, individuals do not purchase public goods directly. Lack of data on transactions implies that economists must find other methods to assess surveys asking for valuations of public goods.

To address this problem, we begin with a discussion of the methodology of evaluating contingent valuation surveys. While there is some experimental evidence about small payments for public goods, we work with the assumption that we do not have data on actual transactions for interesting environmental public goods to compare with survey responses of hypothetical willingness-to-pay. This situation creates the need for other standards for evaluating survey responses. Evaluation involves the credibility, bias (also referred to as reliability in the literature), and precision of responses. Credibility refers to whether survey respondents are answering the question the interviewer is trying to ask. If respondents are answering the right question, reliability refers to the size and direction of the biases that may be present in the answers. Precision refers to the variability in responses. Since precision can usually be increased by the simple expedient of increasing the sample size, we will not discuss precision further in this paper. Problems of credibility or of bias are not reduced by increases in sample size. Thus credibility and bias must be evaluated when considering

"Contingent Valuation: Is Some Number Better than No Number?" by Peter A. Diamond and Jerry A. Hausman. *Journal of Economic Perspectives* 8. 1994. Pp. 45–64. Reprinted by permission of the American Economic Association.

*The authors want to thank Bernard Saffran and four editors for helpful comments.

the use of such surveys—in benefit-cost analyses, in the determination of damages after a finding of liability, or as general information to affect the legislative process.[1]

We discuss how to judge the content in contingent valuation surveys together with evidence from surveys that have been done. Surveys designed to test for consistency between stated willingness-to-pay and economic theory have found that contingent valuation responses are not consistent with economic theory. The main contingent valuation anomaly that we discuss is called the "embedding effect," and was first analyzed systematically by Kahneman and Knetsch (1992).[2] The embedding effect is the name given to the tendency of willingness-to-pay responses to be highly similar across different surveys, even where theory suggests (and sometimes requires) that the responses be very different.[3] An example of embedding would be a willingness-to-pay to clean up one lake roughly equal to that for cleaning up five lakes, including the one asked about individually. The embedding effect is usually thought to arise from the nonexistence of individual preferences for the public good in question and from the failure of survey respondents, in the hypothetical circumstances of the survey, to consider the effect of their budget constraints. Because of these embedding effects, different surveys can obtain widely variable stated willingness-to-pay amounts for the same public good, with no straightforward way for selecting one particular method as the appropriate one.

In short, we think that the evidence supports the conclusion that to date, contingent valuation surveys do not measure the preferences they attempt to measure. Moreover, we present reasons for thinking that changes in survey methods are not likely to change this conclusion. Viewed alternatively as opinion polls on possible government actions, we think that these surveys do not have much information to contribute to informed policymaking. Thus, we conclude that reliance on contingent valuation surveys in either damage assessments or in government decision making is basically misguided.

---

[1]With two estimates of an economic value, one can analyze directly whether one is a biased estimate of the other. With nonuse value, the lack of an alternative direct estimate of willingness-to-pay makes it relevant to consider credibility directly, as well as the differences between survey results and behavior in other contexts where transactions data are available.

[2]Another failure of contingent valuation surveys to be consistent with economic preferences is that stated willingness-to-pay is usually found to be much less than stated willingness-to-accept. From economic theory, willingness-to-pay differs from willingness-to-accept only by an income effect. Thus, their values should be extremely close in typical contingent valuation circumstances, where the stated willingness-to-pay is a small share of the consumer's overall budget, and willingness-to-pay amounts show a small income elasticity. For further discussion of this problem with contingent valuation surveys and other problems, see Diamond and Hausman (1993) and Milgrom (1993).

[3]The term embedding came from the research approach of "embedding" a particular good in a more inclusive good, and contrasting the stated willingness-to-pay for the good with that obtained by allocating the willingness-to-pay for the more inclusive good among its components (Kahneman, personal communication).

Judging Surveys of Willingness-to-Pay for Public Goods

A number of bases exist for forming judgments about whether particular respondents are answering the right question and whether the response is roughly correct. One widely accepted basis is by reaching the conclusion that a particular response is simply not credible as an answer to the question the interviewer is trying to ask. It is standard practice in the contingent valuation literature to eliminate some responses as being unreasonably large to be the true willingness-to-pay. Thus trimming responses that are more than, say, 5 percent of income for an environmental public good that contains only nonuse value may be criticized for having an arbitrary cutoff, but not for omitting answers that are believed to be credible. Similarly, it is standard practice to eliminate some responses of zero on the basis that these are "protest zeros," that answers to other questions in the survey indicate that individuals do put a positive value on changes in the level of the public good, and thus zero is not a credible answer.

A widely accepted incredibility test indicates that it is not automatic that the response given is an answer to the question that the interviewer wants answered. But we need to go further in considering how to form a judgment on the survey responses; it is not adequate to assume that any response that is not obviously wrong is an accurate response to the question the survey designer had in mind.

A number of additional bases have been used by people arguing that responses are or are not acceptable. The methods we shall discuss include verbal protocol analysis, the patterns of willingness-to-pay responses across individuals, and across surveys.

In considering the relevance of this evidence for the question of whether survey responses are accurate measures of true preferences, it is useful to have in mind some possible alternative hypotheses of how people respond to such surveys, since the responses are not simply random numbers. Several hypotheses have been put forward as alternatives to the hypothesis that the responses are measures of true economic preferences. Individuals may be expressing an attitude toward a public good (or class of public goods), expressed in a dollar scale because they are asked to express it in a dollar scale (Kahneman and Ritov, 1993). Individuals may receive a "warm glow" from expressing support for good causes (Andreoni, 1989).[4] Individuals may be describing what they think is good for the country, in a sort of casual benefit-cost analysis (Diamond and Hausman, 1993). Individuals may be expressing a reaction to actions that have been taken (for example, allowing an oil spill) rather than evaluating the state of a resource.

Under all of these alternative hypotheses, responses are not an attempt by an individual to evaluate his or her own preference for a public good. For

---

[4]This approach was developed for actual charitable contributions, not survey responses. Kahneman and Knetsch (1992) call it the purchase of moral satisfaction.

example, people doing casual benefit-cost analyses may be reflecting how much they think people generally care about the issue. We think that different hypotheses are likely to be appropriate for different people. Thus the question is not whether the hypothesis of an accurate measurement of preferences is the single best hypothesis, but whether the fraction of the population for whom the hypothesis of accuracy is reasonable is sufficiently large to make the survey as a whole useful for policy purposes.

All of these alternatives are based on what individuals are trying to do; there are further questions of standard survey biases (such as interviewer bias, framing bias, hypothetical bias) and whether people have enough information to express a preference with any accuracy, even if they are attempting to express a preference. Insofar as this understanding is faulty, expressed preferences are not an expression of true economic preferences.

Verbal Protocol Analysis

For verbal protocol analysis, individuals are asked to "think aloud" as they respond to a questionnaire, reporting everything that goes through their minds. Everything the subjects say is recorded on audio tapes that are transcribed and coded for the types of considerations being mentioned. Schkade and Payne (1993) have done such an analysis using a contingent valuation survey that asks for willingness-to-pay to protect migratory waterfowl from drowning in uncovered waste water holding ponds from oil and gas operations.

The transcripts show the inherent difficulty in selecting a willingness-to-pay response and the extent to which people refer to elements that ought to be irrelevant to evaluating their own preferences. If people are trying to report a preference, we would expect them to consider inputs into the forming of their preferences, such as how much they care about birds, how important the number of killed birds are relative to the numbers in the species. Conversely, we would not expect them to report a willingness-to-pay just equal to what they think the program will cost. Respondents verbalized many diverse considerations. Perhaps the most common strategy involved first acknowledging that something should be done and then trying to figure out an appropriate amount. About one-fourth of the sample mentioned the idea that if everyone did his part then each household would not have to give all that much. About one-sixth of the sample made comparisons with donations to charities. About one-fifth of the sample said they just made up a number or guessed an answer. Many respondents seemed to wish to signal concern for a larger environmental issue. This pattern may reflect the unfamiliarity of the task the respondents faced.

These findings strongly suggest that people are not easily in touch with underlying preferences about the type of commodity asked about. The findings do not lend support to the hypothesis that responses are an attempt to measure and express personal preferences. To the extent that individuals consider costs to everyone, the analysis supports the hypothesis of casual benefit-cost analysis. To the extent that individuals look to their own charitable contributions for a guide, the analysis is consistent with hypotheses that explain actual contributions, such as the warm glow hypothesis.

Variation in Willingness-to-Pay across Individuals

If stated willingness-to-pay is a reflection of true preferences, then we would expect certain patterns of answers across different individuals (other things equal). We would expect self-described environmentalists to have larger willingness-to-pay. We would expect individuals with higher incomes to have larger willingness-to-pay. Both results do occur. However, such results do not distinguish among the various hypotheses that were spelled out above since we would expect roughly similar results from any of them. Thus this potential basis for evaluation does not have much bite.[5] We do observe that the income effects that are measured in typical surveys are lower than we would expect if true preferences are measured, lower for example than measured income elasticities for charitable giving.[6]

Variation in Willingness-to-Pay across Surveys

Another approach to forming a judgment is to compare willingness-to-pay responses to different questions, whether in the same or in different surveys.

Multiple Questions. If a survey question reveals a true valuation, it should not matter whether the question is asked by itself or with other questions, nor if asked with any other questions, what the order of questioning is. However, when Tolley et al. (1983) asked for willingness-to-pay to preserve visibility at the Grand Canyon, the response was five times higher when this was the only question, as compared to its being the third such question. Attempts to claim this result to be consistent with preferences have relied on income effects and substitution effects. Neither of these rationalizations for the anomalous results is compelling, as we explain in a moment.

The importance of question order was also shown in a study by Samples and Hollyer (1990) asking for the values of preserving seals and whales. Some respondents were asked for willingness-to-pay to preserve seals first, followed by a question about whales. Others were asked for willingness-to-pay in the reverse order. Seal value tended to be lower when asked after whale value, while whale value was not affected by the sequence of questions.[7] Thus the sum of willingness-to-pay depended on the sequence of the questions

---

[5]The importance of the lack of bite of such considerations comes, in part, from the fact that the contingent valuation study of the Exxon Valdez spill that was done for the state of Alaska (Carson et al., 1992) included such analyses, but none of the more powerful split-sample consistency tests that we discuss below.

[6]The empirical finding of low income elasticities is also inconsistent with the typical finding of a large divergence between willingness-to-pay and willingness-to-accept, discussed in footnote 2.

[7]Samples and Hollyer used dichotomous choice surveys. They estimated that whales were valued at $125 when asked about first, and $142 when second. Seals were valued at $103 when asked

asked. The authors offer an explanation (p. 189) "based on debriefing sessions held with the interviewer."

> Apparently, when respondents valued seals first, they used their behavior in this market situation to guide their responses to whale valuation questions. Since whales are generally more popular than seals, respondents were reluctant to behave more benevolently toward seals compared with humpback whales. Consequently, whale values were inflated in the S-W questionnaire version to maintain a relatively higher value for the humpbacks. This behavioral anchoring effect did not exist in the W-S version, where whales were valued first.

To have the value of preserving both seals and whales depend on the sequence in which the questions are asked is not consistent with the hypothesis that stated willingness-to-pay accurately measures preferences. These results can be interpreted in two ways. One interpretation is that contingent valuation studies that ask two questions rather than one are unreliable. The other interpretation is that the warm glow hypothesis is supported, since having expressed support for the environment in the first question permits a sharp fall in the second response. This effect is not present, however, when such a response would seem illogical to the respondent. More generally, one needs to decide whether a given pattern of responses is a result of survey design issues or a result of the underlying bases of response. This distinction is especially important when the pattern of results appears anomalous with or contradictory to the hypothesis that preferences are accurately measured.

Single Questions and the Embedding Effect. Alternatively, one can ask a single willingness-to-pay question each to different samples. For example, assume that one group is asked to evaluate public good X; a second is asked to evaluate Y; and a third is asked to evaluate X and Y. What interpretations could we make if the willingness-to-pay for X and Y (together) is considerably less than the sum of the willingness-to-pay for X and the willingness-to-pay for Y?[8] One interpretation is that we are seeing an income effect at work. That is, having "spent" for X, one has less income left to purchase Y. Given that the stated willingness-to-pay amounts are very small relative to income and that measured income elasticities are very small, the attempted income effect argument does not explain the differences found.

A second interpretation is to assume that individual preferences have a large substitution effect between X and Y. In some settings the assumption on preferences needed to justify the results is implausible. For example, Diamond et al. (1993) asked for willingness-to-pay to prevent logging in

---

about first and $62 when second. When they asked about both (together) in a single question, the estimated values were $131 and $146 in two surveys.

[8]This approach is similar to the work that was initiated by Kahneman (1986) and done recently by Kahneman and Knetsch (1992), Kemp and Maxwell (1993), Desvousges et al. (1993), Diamond et al. (1993), McFadden and Leonard (1993), Loomis, Hoehn and Hanemann (1990).

one, two, and three particular wilderness areas. Stated willingness-to-pay to preserve two (and three) areas was less than the sum of willingness-to-pay to preserve each of them separately.

At first look, this result appears to be an appropriate substitution effect, since protecting one area results in being less willing to protect another. However, preferences should be defined over wilderness remaining, not over proposals for development that are defeated. If preferences are concave over the amount of wilderness available (or, more generally, if different wilderness areas are substitutes), then willingness-to-pay is larger the smaller the quantity of wilderness remaining. This implies that the willingness-to-pay to preserve two threatened areas should be larger than the sum of willingness-to-pay to preserve each as the lone area threatened with development.[9] Instead, stated willingness-to-pay was roughly the same for preserving one, two or three threatened areas, making the amount for several areas together significantly less than the sum of the amounts for the areas separately. Note that these surveys vary both the number of areas threatened and the number to be preserved. Neither the income effect nor the substitution effect can plausibly explain the embedding effect in this experiment. The hypothesis that this survey is eliciting individual preferences is not consistent with individuals having reasonably behaved preferences. However, from the point of view of the warm glow hypothesis, this pattern makes sense. That is, the warm glow hypothesis is that individuals are primarily reporting an expression of support for the environment, an expression that does not vary much with small changes in the precise environmental change being described.

A similar variation in responses across surveys appears in the study of Desvousges et al. (1993). They described a problem killing 2000, 20,000 and 200,000 birds. The willingness-to-pay to solve this problem was roughly the same in all three cases. Since the number of surviving birds is smaller the larger the problem, concave preferences over surviving birds should have resulted in more than a 100-fold variation in willingness-to-pay across this range.[10] Thus this study shows a contradiction between stated

---

[9]For derivation of the convexity of willingness-to-pay when preferences are concave and the scenario is varied in this way, see Diamond (1993). That paper also contains a number of other implications of preferences for willingness-to-pay that can be used for internal consistency tests.

[10]Proponents of contingent valuation have made several critiques of this study. One critique is that it was a mall stop survey. But similar results followed when the questionnaire was used for the verbal protocol study cited above, which involved subjects coming to be interviewed. Another criticism is that in addition to the absolute numbers, the survey questions described the number of birds at risk as "much less than 1%" of the population, "less than 1%," and "about 2%." Thus, one can wonder whether respondents were paying attention to the absolute numbers which varied 100-fold or the percentages which varied from "much less than 1%" to "about 2%." Interpreting "much less than" as less than half, about 2% is at least a four-fold increase over less than half of 1%. If some people were paying attention to the percentages and some to the absolute numbers, the range should have been between four-fold and 100-fold. If, as Hanemann suggests, respondents did not perceive any real difference between "much less than 1%" and "about 2%," it is noteworthy that they perceived a large difference between zero and "much less than 1%." Moreover, these percentages were selected by the authors since they were the percentages in three actual oil spills: Arthur Kill,

willingness-to-pay and the usual economic assumptions on preferences. Again, the study is consistent with the hypothesis that the responses are primarily warm glow, and so need not vary noticeably over moderate differences in the resource.

Adding-up Test. One difficulty in the approach described above is that the plausibility of the willingness-to-pay patterns depends on assumptions on the plausible (concave) structure of preferences. Another approach to tests of consistency that does not rely on an assumption of concave preferences is to attempt to measure the same preference in two different ways. This test can be constructed by varying the background scenario as well as varying the commodity to be purchased. For example, assume that one group is asked to evaluate public good X; a second group is told that X will be provided and is asked to evaluate also having Y; and a third is asked to evaluate X and Y (together). Now the willingness-to-pay for X and Y (together) should be the same as the sum of the willingness-to-pay for X and the willingness-to-pay for Y, having been given X (the same up to an income effect that can be measured in the survey and that empirically is small).[11] Thus, Diamond et al. (1993) varied the number of wilderness areas being developed as well as the number that could be protected. In this way the sum of two areas separately evaluated (with different degrees of development) should be the same as the value of preserving two areas (apart from a very small income effect). Again, the results of the survey are inconsistent with the responses being a measure of preferences.[12]

Embedding still infects even very recent work done by experienced contingent valuation analysts who were well aware of the problem. Schulze

---

Nestucca, *Exxon Valdez*. This pattern of results is consistent with the responses being dominated by a "warm glow."

[11]Willingness-to-pay is a function of the two vectors giving alternative levels of public goods and the level of income. Thus the willingness-to-pay to improve the environment from z to z'' of someone with income I can be written WTP (z, z'', I). The change from z to z'' can be broken into two pieces, a change from z to z' and a change from z' to z''. From the definition of willingness-to-pay, one has WTP(z, z'', I) = WTP(z, z'', I) + WTP$(z', z'', I - WTP(z, z', I))$.

This adding-up test makes no use of an assumption on the magnitude or sign of income or substitution effects. One could do an adding-up test without the adjustment of income shown in the equation by comparing WTP(z, z'', I) with WTP(z, z', I) + WTP(z, z'', I). This comparison would involve a deviation from exact adding-up because of the income effect. With a willingness-to-pay on the order of $30 and a household income level of $30,000, even an income elasticity of one—higher than the elasticity typically measured in contingent valuation surveys—would lead to a $.03 deviation from exact adding-up. For a formal derivation, see the revised version of Diamond (1993).

[12]In brief response to Hanemann's criticisms of our analysis, we note that he does not address this adding-up test and seems comfortable accepting the idea that the less wilderness preserved, the less people care about any particular area of wilderness. These two tests do not rely on any assumption of different wilderness areas being interchangeable, as indicated by the vector interpretation of z in the previous footnote. In terms of Hanemann's test mentioned in his note 25 of whether willingness-to-pay to protect each of the areas is the same, we note that he did not do the statistical test correctly. Moreover, this reference is an example of Hanemann's trait of ignoring the central criticism while attacking a side issue. In Diamond et al, the focus is on the adding-up test, not a scope test. The adding-up test was clearly rejected.

et al. (1993) asked for willingness-to-pay for partial and complete cleanup of contamination of the Clark Fork National Priorities List sites in Montana. After removing protest zeroes and high responses, the mean stated willingness-to-pay for complete cleanup was $72.46 (standard error of $4.71) while the mean response for a considerably smaller partial cleanup was $72.02 (s.e. $5.10). As part of the survey, respondents were asked whether their responses were just for this cleanup or partly to clean up other sites or basically as a contribution for all environmental or other causes (or other). Only 16.9 percent reported their answers as just for this cleanup; that is, a vast majority of respondents recognized an embedding effect in their own responses. These respondents were asked what percentage of their previous answer was for this cleanup, and the willingness-to-pay responses were adjusted by these percentages. After this adjustment, the mean stated willingness-to-pay for complete cleanup was $40.00 (s.e. $2.62) while the mean response for partial cleanup was $37.15 (s.e. $2.71).

These numbers (and the large fraction of people recognizing that they are embedding) support the hypothesis that the responses are dominated by a warm glow. No reason is offered by the authors for the conclusion that the adjustment they do removes the dominance of warm glow. Neither do they perform an adding-up test such as that described above. This adding-up test could have been done by asking a third sample for willingness-to-pay to extend a "planned" partial cleanup to a complete cleanup. In short, the embedding problem does not appear to be one that contingent valuation practitioners know how to solve.

With a pattern of results that are inconsistent with the usual economic assumptions, two interpretations are always possible: the surveys were defective or the contingent valuation method as currently practiced does not measure with accuracy. One should consider all the surveys that attempt to test for consistency in order to judge which interpretation is likely to be correct. The studies we have described have been criticized as not done well enough to be an adequate test.[13] However, they are the only quantitative tests we are aware of. No comparable comparison tests have been done by proponents of the accuracy of contingent valuation, although the embedding effect has long been recognized.

Differing Payment Vehicles. It is interesting to note what two contingent valuation proponents, Mitchell and Carson (1989), have written about the question that respondents are trying to answer. In discussing the sensitivity of responses to the payment vehicle (the way in which the hypothetical payment is to be collected), they write (pp. 123–24):

---

[13]One can ask whether the patterns of thought reflected in the responses to the questions in any particular survey also occur in other survey settings. Cognitive psychology has found a number of such patterns that are robust. We think that the patterns reflected in these surveys are similarly robust.

> It was earlier assumed that only the nature and amount of the amenity being valued should influence the WTP [willingness-to-pay] amounts; all other scenario components, such as the payment vehicle and method of provision, should be neutral in effect . . . More recently, Arrow (1986), Kahneman (1986), and Randall (1986) have argued against that view, holding that important conditions of a scenario, such as the payment vehicle, should be expected to affect the WTP amounts. In their view, which we accept, respondents in a CV [contingent valuation] study are not valuing levels of provision of an amenity in the abstract; they are valuing a policy which includes the conditions under which the amenity will be provided, and the way the public is likely to be asked to pay for it.

In other words, Mitchell and Carson appear to accept the idea (consistent with the findings about some respondents by Schkade and Payne, 1993) that individuals' responses arise from casual benefit-cost analyses, not solely from an examination of their own preferences over resources. For welfare analysis and damage measurement, benefit-cost studies may be different from preferences. We will return to this issue.

Evaluation of Bias: Calibration

Surveys about behavior often have systematic biases relative to the behavior they ask about. Thus, it is common to "calibrate" the responses—that is, adjust for the biases—as part of using them for predictive purposes. In particular, when using surveys to estimate demand for new products, it is standard practice to use a calibration factor to adjust survey responses in order to produce an estimate of actual demand (Urban, Katz, Hatch, and Silk, 1983). As Mitchell and Carson (1989, p. 178) have written: "Such 'calibration' is common in marketing designed to predict purchases. If a systematic divergence between actual and CV [contingent valuation] survey existed and could be quantified, calibration of CV results could be undertaken."

As some evidence on the need for calibration, comparisons of hypothetical surveys and actual offers often find large and significant differences. These comparisons have been done for private goods (Bishop and Heberlein, 1979; Dickie, Fisher and Gerking, 1987; Neill et al., 1993).[14] Comparisons have also been done for charitable donations (Duffield and Patterson, 1992; Seip and Strand, 1992). These studies find a need to calibrate, with calibration factors involving dividing stated willingness-to-pay by a number ranging from 1.5 to 10.

How this calibration should be extended to the public good context is unclear, since the public good context includes both unfamiliar commodities and unfamiliar transactions. But the lack of study of appropriate cali-

---

[14]On the Dickie, Fisher and Gerking (1987) study, see also the critique by Hausman and Leonard (1992).

bration factors is not a basis for concluding that the best calibration is one-for-one.[15]

Welfare Analysis

If an accurate measure of willingness-to-pay for the pure public good of the existence of an environmental amenity were available, the measured willingness-to-pay would belong in benefit-cost analysis, just like a pure public good based on resource use. Similarly, the measure should be included in the incentives government creates (through fines and damage payments) to avoid damaging an environmental amenity. As we know from the pure theory of public goods, we would simply add individual willingness-to-pay across the population.[16] In this section, we consider the welfare implications of using stated willingness-to-pay as if it were an accurate measure of preferences in the case that the responses are generated by the alternative hypotheses given above.

One set of problems arises even if willingness-to-pay is being measured accurately, if measured willingness-to-pay contains an altruism component. That is, individuals may be willing to pay to preserve an environmental amenity because of their concerns for others (who may be users or also nonusers). Consider what happens if society adds up everyone's willingness-to-pay and compares the sum with the cost of some action. As a matter of social welfare evaluation we might conclude that such altruistic externalities are double counting, since a utility benefit shows up in the willingness-to-pay of both the person enjoying the public good and the people who care about that person. For example, consider the income distribution problem in a three-person economy. If two of the people start to care about each other, is this change in preferences a reason for a government to increase the level of incomes allocated to the two of them? Similarly, we can ask if the government should devote more taxes to cleaning up lakes where neighbors are friendly with each other than to lakes where neighbors do not know (or care about) each other.

Moreover, if altruistic externalities are thought to be appropriately included in the analysis, it is necessary to include all such externalities for accurate evaluation. In particular, if people care about each other's utilities, they care about the costs borne by others as well as the benefits received by

---

[15]In its proposed rules for damage assessment, the National Oceanic and Atmospheric Administration (1994) has proposed a default calibration of dividing by two, in the absence of direct arguments by trustees of natural resources for a different calibration factor.

[16]For the correct use of a benefit-cost calculation, we need to be considering the marginal project for finding the optimum. With many projects under consideration, and a nonoptimal starting point, one does not get the right answer by asking about many projects independently and carrying out all that pass the test (Hoehn and Randall, 1989).

others. An adjustment for altruism must include external costs as well as external benefits if we are to avoid the possibility of a Pareto worsening from an action based on a calculation that appears to be a Pareto improvement (Milgrom, 1993).

A second general problem arises when stated willingness-to-pay may be a poor guess, even though it may be the best guess individuals have of their true willingness-to-pay. Individuals often face the problem of trying to form judgments about the gains from a purchase in settings where the link between the commodity and utility is hard to evaluate. One example is the grade of gasoline to buy, assuming that one wants to minimize cost per mile. In the case of environmental amenities, individuals may have a derived demand based on their beliefs about the relationship between the amenity and variables they really care about. For example, they may care about the survival of a species and not know about the range of natural variation in population size, about the probability of survival as a function of population size, nor about the effect of environmental damage on population size. Such derived preferences may be a poor guide to policy; it may be more informative to have expert evaluation of the consequences of an environmental change than to consult the public directly about environmental damage.

The issues just discussed were based on the hypothesis that stated willingness-to-pay is a measure of an individual preference over an outcome. Under the hypothesis that responses reflect casual benefit-cost evaluations rather than preferences, it would be inappropriate to add any other benefits to those coming from a contingent valuation survey since such benefits are presumably included by the respondents, however imperfectly, in their benefit-cost analyses. But if contingent valuation is just a survey of benefit-cost estimates, rather than preferences, it might be better to have a more careful analysis done by people knowing more about environmental issues and about the principles of benefit-cost analysis. Moreover, if responses are benefit-cost estimates rather than preferences, they do not measure a compensable loss in damage suits.

The embedding effect is supportive of the hypothesis that responses are primarily determined by warm glow. If respondents get pleasure from thinking of themselves as supportive of the environment, the willingness-to-pay for this warm glow is not part of the gain from a *particular* environmental project—unless there are no cheaper ways of generating the warm glow. That is, if an individual wants to see the government do at least one environmental project (or n projects) a year in order to feel "environmentally supportive," the person should support one project, but not any particular project. Moreover, if different samples are asked about different projects, the responses will appear to support many projects, even though the warm glow comes from the desire to support a single project.

An illustration of this view comes from the fact that when individuals are asked simultaneously about many projects, stated willingness-to-pay is far below the sum of stated willingness-to-pay from asking about the projects separately. For example, Kemp and Maxwell (1993) asked one group for willingness-to-pay to minimize the risk of oil spills off the coast of Alaska, and found a mean stated willingness-to-pay of $85 (with a 95 percent confidence interval of ±$44). Then they asked a different sample for willingness-to-pay for a broad group of government programs, followed by asking these people to divide and subdivide their willingness-to-pay among the separate programs. By the time they reached minimizing the risk of oil spills off the coast of Alaska, they found a mean of $0.29 (with a 95 percent confidence interval of ±$0.21).

These findings make little sense if responses are measures of preferences, and considerable sense if the response is primarily a warm glow effect from a desire to express support for protecting the environment. In the latter circumstance, we would expect little warm glow for any single project in a context where respondents are asked about many government projects affecting the environment. Therefore warm glow may need to be purged from stated willingness-to-pay even if (as witnessed by charitable contributions) people really are willing to pay for some warm glow.[17]

A different complication arises if people do not really care about the resource, but care about the activity that might harm a resource. For example, the stated willingness-to-pay to clean up a natural oil seepage might be zero while the stated willingness-to-pay to clean up a man-made oil spill is positive. This outcome is the flip side of the "protest zero," where people state no willingness-to-pay to repair environmental damage that they feel is someone else's responsibility. As noted earlier, it is standard practice to consider this zero not to be an accurate measure of preferences, on the assumption that people care about the resource.

Survey results suggest that many answers are heavily influenced by concern about actions, not resources. For example, Desvousges et al. (1993) find a large stated willingness-to-pay to save small numbers of common birds. The finding seems much more likely to reflect a feeling that it is a shame that people do things that kill birds rather than a preference over the number of birds. Concern over the actions of others is different from concern about the state of the environment. Concern about actions is conventionally part of the basis of punitive damages, but not compensatory damages. That is, deliberately or recklessly destroying the property of others opens one up to liability for compensatory damages for the value of the property destroyed and also punitive damages. On the other hand, the legal system does not compensate people who are upset that others engage in actions such as reading *Lady Chatterley's Lover*. When and how such concerns should affect public policy is a complex issue, one not explored here.

---

[17]In the context of the bird study by Desvousges et al. (1993), Kahneman (personal communication) has proposed to purge the warm glow by extrapolating willingness-to-pay as a function of birds saved back to zero and then subtracting this amount from the estimate of willingness-to-pay at any particular level of birds. This approach involves a curve-fitting extrapolation and the assumption that warm glow is totally insensitive to the magnitude of the problem, an assumption that is probably not completely correct.

One complication from the perspective of benefit-cost analysis is that preferences over acts (as opposed to states of the world) do not provide the consistency that is necessary for consistent economic policy. For example, if people are willing to pay to offset an act, then proposing and not doing an act appears to generate a welfare gain. For example, consider the warm glow from blocking development of a wilderness area. If one proposes two projects and has one blocked, are people better off (from the warm glow) than if one project is proposed and happens? Does this imply that the government would do good by proposing projects that it does not mind seeing blocked? More generally, the relationship of benefit-cost analysis and Pareto optimality has been developed and is understood in a setting where preferences are defined over resources.

We note that under the hypothesis of Kahneman and Ritov (1993), responses to contingent valuation surveys are expressions of attitudes toward public goods that the respondents are required to state in dollar terms. Responses are then not measures of willingness-to-pay and provide no quantitative basis for estimates of environmental damages, although like polls generally, they do alert the government about concerns of the public.

The "Some Number Is Better Than No Number" Fallacy

We began this essay by arguing that stated willingness-to-pay from contingent valuation surveys are not measures of nonuse preferences over environmental amenities. We then considered some of the welfare implications of treating the responses as if they were a measure of nonuse preferences when they were generated by different considerations. We concluded that such welfare analysis would not be a guide to good policy. Our conclusion is often challenged by the common Washington fallacy that even if stated willingness-to-pay is inaccurate, it should be used because no alternative estimate exists for public policy purposes. Put more crudely, one hears the argument that "some number is better than no number."[18] This argument leads to the claim that it is better to do benefit-cost studies with stated willingness-to-pay numbers, despite inaccuracy and bias, rather than use zero in the benefit-cost analysis and adjust for this omission somewhere else in the decision-making process.

To evaluate this argument, one needs a model of the determination of government policy.[19] Ideally, one would like to carry out a number of gov-

---

[18]The history of economic policy awaits an investigation, similar to the famous study of the sociologist R. K. Merton on the history of Newton's "on the shoulders of giants" remark, to trace the lineage of the "some number is better than no number" fallacy.

[19]One can also consider how a social welfare maximizing planner might use the information in contingent valuation surveys. There is useful information if people are expressing preferences that are not otherwise accessible to the planner. However, if the other hypotheses are the correct description of the bases of willingness-to-pay responses, then the planner would not be receiving useful

ernment decisions twice: once using zero in the benefit-cost study, and a second time using stated willingness-to-pay, with associated adjustments of the decision process in recognition of the inclusion or omission of a contingent valuation number. Such a comparison would recognize that much more input goes into government decisions than just the benefit-cost study. That is, the comparison is not between relying on contingent valuation and relying on Congress, but between relying on Congress after doing a contingent valuation study and relying on Congress without doing a contingent valuation study.[20] Thus one is asking whether inclusion of such survey results tends to improve the allocation process, even if the numbers are not reliable estimates of the preferences called for by the theory. Similarly, one can ask whether the combination of fines and damage payments will result in more efficient decisions to avoid accidents with or without a contingent valuation estimate of nonuse value.

Judge Stephen Breyer (1993) has recently reviewed government responses to public perceptions of risk. Since he feels that public perceptions of risk are inaccurate and that Congress is responsive to these public perceptions, Breyer wants to increase the role of administrative expertise in designing public policy to deal with risks. A similar situation seems to exist with respect to contingent valuations of nonuse value. If we conclude that contingent valuation is really an opinion poll on concern about the environment in general, rather than a measure of preferences about specific projects, public policy is likely to do better if the concern is noted but expert opinion is used to evaluate specific projects and to set financial incentives to avoid accidents. One could hope for a more consistent relative treatment of alternative natural resources in this way.

In both economic logic and politics, we expect that using contingent valuation in decision making about the environment would soon be extended to other policy arenas where existence values are equally plausible. We do not expect that policy would be improved by using contingent valuation to affect the levels and patterns of spending for elementary school education, foreign aid, Medicaid, Medicare, AFDC, construction of safer highways, medical research, airline safety, or police and fire services. Yet people have concerns for others in all of these areas that parallel their concern for the environment.

Concern for other people naturally includes concern about their jobs. Thus, in considering rules that limit economic activity to protect the environment, it is as appropriate to include a contingent valuation of existence

---

information. Treating the responses as measures of what they do not measure would mislead such a planner.

[20]The results of a contingent valuation survey are not binding. Thus a respondent who was behaving strategically would select a response that reflected his or her belief in how the results of the survey would affect actual outcomes. Thus we do not understand how the NOAA Panel could conclude that with a dichotomous choice question there is no strategic reason for the respondent to do otherwise than answer truthfully.

value for destroyed jobs as the one for protection of the environment. The fact that jobs may be created elsewhere in the economy does not rule out concern about job destruction per se. These possible extensions of the use of contingent valuation increase the importance of considering the "some number is better than no number" fallacy.

Referenda

We have heard the argument that if referenda are legitimate, so too is contingent valuation. That is, one can consider a contingent valuation survey to be a forecast of how voters would respond to a binding referendum. This perspective raises the same issues considered above. How should we decide how to interpret the bases of how people vote in referenda? Since different bases imply different appropriate uses of the responses, how should voting responses be used for economic analysis? Moreover, the necessity of calibration remains, since no obvious reason exists for people necessarily to vote the same in binding and nonbinding referenda. And, as in the previous section, we can ask whether we think we get better policies with or without such surveys.

It is interesting to consider issues raised by polls about actual referenda, as well as by the referenda themselves. Sometimes polls are accurate predictors of voting outcomes; sometimes, they are not, even when they are taken close to election day. Sometimes, repeated polls about the same referendum find very large changes in expressed intentions as a referendum campaign proceeds.

Magleby (1984) has analyzed statewide polls in California and Massachusetts for which at least three separate surveys were done. In some cases, the polls show roughly the same margin over time. Magleby calls these "standing opinions" and believes that this stability comes from the deep attachment to their opinions that voters hold on some controversial issues such as the death penalty and the equal rights amendment. In some cases, the polls show significant changes in the margin of preferences, but no change in the side that is ahead. Magleby calls these "uncertain opinions." Examples of such votes involve handgun registration and homosexual teachers. In some cases, significant changes in voting intentions occur as the campaign proceeds, with victory in the actual election going to the side that had at one time been far behind. Magleby calls these outcomes "opinion reversals." For example, in a referendum for flat rate electricity, a February poll showed 71 percent in favor, 17 percent opposed, and 12 percent undecided. The actual vote was 23 percent in favor, 69 percent opposed and 7 percent skipping this question. Other examples of such votes are a state lottery and a tax reduction measure. In his analysis of 36 propositions in California, Magleby found that on 28 percent of the issues, voters held standing opinions, on 19 percent voters had uncertain opinions, and on

53 percent he found opinion reversals. That is, in a majority of cases, early opinion polls were not good predictors of election outcomes. Moreover, they were not even good predictors of later opinion polls, after the campaign had run for some time.

It seems to us that responses to contingent valuation questionnaires for a single environmental issue are likely to be based on little information, since there is limited time for presentation and digestion of information during a contingent valuation survey. This conclusion suggests that the results of such surveys are unlikely to be accurate predictors of informed opinions on the same issues if respondents had more information and further time for reflection, including learning of the opinions of others. Such surveys are therefore unlikely to be a good basis for either informed policy-making or accurate damage assessment.

Even if a contingent valuation survey were a good predictor of an actual referendum, one can also question the use of actual referenda to obtain economic values. Considerable skepticism exists about the extent to which voting on a referendum represents informed decision making (see, for example, Magleby, 1984). In the functioning of a democracy, it may be more important to place some powers directly with the voters, rather than with their elected representatives, than to worry about the quality of decision making by voters.[21] However, incorporating contingent valuation survey responses in benefit-cost analyses or judicial proceedings does not seem to have a special role in enhancing democracy. In the looser context of legislative debate, such opinion polls may have a role to play, although the net value of that role is unclear.

NOAA Panel Evaluation of Contingent Valuation

In light of the controversy and the stakes involved, the National Oceanic and Atmospheric Administration recently appointed a prestigious panel to consider the reliability of contingent valuation studies of nonuse values in damage suits.[22] The panel's Report (NOAA, 1993) begins with criticisms of contingent valuation. In discussing the alleged inconsistency of some results with rational choice, the Report states (p. 4604) that: "some form of internal consistency is the least we would need to feel some confidence that the verbal answers correspond to some reality." The Report also addresses the need for rationality (p. 4604).

---

[21]The allocation of a decision directly to the voters, rather than indirectly through the choice of elected representatives, and the form in which referenda are put to voters are both methods of agenda control. In many settings, design of the agenda has large effects on voting outcomes.

[22]Kenneth Arrow (co-chair), Robert Solow (co-chair), Edward Learner, Paul Portney, Roy Radner, and Howard Schuman.

It could be asked whether rationality is indeed needed. Why not take the values found as given? There are two answers. One is that we do not know yet how to reason about values without some assumption of rationality, if indeed it is possible at all. Rationality requirements impose a constraint on the possible values, without which damage judgments would be arbitrary. A second answer is that, as discussed above, it is difficult to find objective counterparts to verify the values obtained in the response to questionnaires.

In discussing "warm glow" effects, the Report recognizes the claim that contingent valuation responses include a warm glow. They write (p. 4605): "If this is so, CV [contingent valuation] responses should not be taken as reliable estimates of true willingness to pay."

The Report states that the burden of proof of reliability must rest on the survey designers. It states (p. 4609) that a survey would be unreliable if there were "[i]nadequate responsiveness to the scope of the environmental insult," as occurred in the embedding examples we have discussed. Unfortunately, the Panel did not elaborate on how to test for reliability.[23] We interpret the view they express to call for testing of the internal consistency of responses to the same survey instrument with different levels of environmental problem and policy successes. The Report cites no existing study that has passed such internal consistency tests.

The Report presents a set of guidelines which would define an "ideal" contingent valuation survey (and are summarized in Portney's paper in this issue). The Report asserts (p. 4610) that studies meeting such guidelines can produce estimates "reliable enough to be the starting point" of a judicial process of damage assessment. The Report offers no reason for reaching this conclusion, although the finding that surveys that do not meet their guidelines may be biased is not a basis for concluding that surveys that do meet their guidelines are not biased. In particular, they state no reason for reaching the conclusion that following their guidelines implies that responses are not dominated by a "warm glow." The Panel does not explicitly call for testing whether a survey done according to their guidelines is reliable. In particular, they do not mention a need to check the internal consistency of responses. Nor do they explain their conclusion that the inconsistencies between stated willingness-to-pay and economic theory come from survey design issues and would go away if the survey had followed their guidelines.

Conclusion

We believe that contingent valuation is a deeply flawed methodology for measuring nonuse values, one that does not estimate what its proponents claim to be estimating. The absence of direct market parallels affects both

---

[23]Nor, we add, do Portney or Hanemann in this symposium.

the ability to judge the quality of contingent valuation responses and the ability to calibrate responses to have usable numbers. It is precisely the lack of experience both in markets for environmental commodities and in the consequences of such decision that makes contingent valuation questions so hard to answer and the responses so suspect.

We have argued that internal consistency tests (particularly adding-up tests) are required to assess the reliability and validity of such surveys. When these tests have been done, contingent valuation has come up short. Contingent valuation proponents typically claim that the surveys used for these tests were not done well enough. Yet they have not subjected their own surveys to such tests. (We note that Hanemann does not address the question of which split-sample internal consistency tests, if any, he thinks a contingent valuation survey needs to pass.) There is a history of anomalous results in contingent valuation surveys that seems closely tied to the embedding problem. Although this problem has been recognized in the literature for over a decade, it has not been solved. Thus, we conclude that current contingent valuation methods should not be used for damage assessment or for benefit-cost analysis.

It is impossible to conclude definitely that surveys with new methods (or the latest survey that has been done) will not pass internal consistency tests. Yet, we do not see much hope for such success. This skepticism comes from the belief that the internal consistency problems come from an absence of preferences, not a flaw in survey methodology. That is, we do not think that people generally hold views about individual environmental sites (many of which they have never heard of); or that, within the confines of the time available for survey instruments, people will focus successfully on the identification of preferences, to the exclusion of other bases for answering survey questions. This absence of preferences shows up as inconsistency in responses across surveys and implies that the survey responses are not satisfactory bases for policy.

REFERENCES

Andreoni, James, "Giving with Impure Altruism: Applications to Charity and Ricardian Equivalence," *Journal of Political Economy*, December 1989, 97, 1447–58.
Bishop, R. C, and T. A. Heberlein, "Measuring Values of Extramarket Goods: Are Indirect Measures Biased?" *American Journal of Agricultural Economics*, December 1979, *61*, 926–30.
Breyer, Stephen, *Breaking the Vicious Circle: Toward Effective Risk Regulation.* Cambridge: Harvard University Press, 1993.
Carson, Richard T., et al., "A Contingent Valuation Study of Lost Passive Use Values Resulting from the Exxon Valdez Oil Spill," A Report to the Attorney General of the State of Alaska, 1992.
Desvousges, W. H., et al., "Measuring Natural Resource Damages with Contingent Valuation: Test of Validity and Reliability. In Hausman, J., ed., *Contingent Valuation: A Critical Assessment.* Amsterdam: North-Holland Press, 1993, 91–164.

Diamond, P. A., "Testing the Internal Consistency of Contingent Valuation Surveys," working paper, MIT, 1993.

Diamond, P. A., and J. A. Hausman, "On Contingent Valuation Measurement of Nonuse Values" In Hausman, J., Ed., *Contingent Valuation: A Critical Assessment.* Amsterdam: North-Holland Press, 1993, 3–38.

Diamond, P. A., J. A. Hausman, G. K. Leonard, and M. A. Denning, "Does Contingent Valuation Measure Preferences? Experimental Evidence." In Hausman, J., ed., *Contingent Valuation: A Critical Assessment.* Amsterdam: North-Holland Press, 1993.

Dickie, Mark, Ann Fisher, and Shelby Gerking, "Market Transactions and Hypothetical Demand Data: A Comparative Study," *Journal of the American Statistical Association,* March 1987, *82,* 69–75.

Duffield, John W., and David A. Patterson, "Field Testing Existence Values: An Instream Flow Trust Fund for Mountain Rivers," mimeo. University of Montana, 1992.

Hausman, J. A., *Contingent Valuation: A Critical Assessment.* Amsterdam: North-Holland Press, 1993.

Hausman, J. A., and G. Leonard, *Contingent Valuation and the Value of Marketed Commodities.* Cambridge: Cambridge Economics, 1982.

Hoehn, John, and Alan Randall, "Too Many Proposals Pass the Benefit Cost Test," *American Economic Review,* June 1989, *79,* 544–51.

Kahneman, Daniel, "Comments on the Contingent Valuation Method." In Cummings, Ronald G., David S. Brookshire, and William D. Schulze, eds., *Valuing Environmental Goods: A State of the Arts Assessment of the Contingent Valuation Method.* Totowa: Rowman and Allanheld, 1986, 185–94.

Kahneman, Daniel, and Jack L. Knetsch, "Valuing Public Goods: The Purchase of Moral Satisfaction," *Journal of Environmental Economics and Management,* January 1992, *22,* 57–70.

Kahneman, Daniel, and Ilana Ritov, "Determinants of Stated Willingness to Pay for Public Goods: A Study in the Headline Method," mimeo. Department of Psychology, University of California, Berkeley, 1993.

Kemp, M. A. and C. Maxwell, "Exploring a Budget Context for Contingent Valuation Estimates," In Hausman, J., ed., *Contingent Valuation: A Critical Assessment,* Amsterdam: North-Holland Press, 1993, 217–70.

Loomis, John, John Hoehn, and Michael Hanemann, "Testing the Fallacy of Independent Valuation and Summation in Multi-part Policies: An Empirical Test of Whether "Too Many Proposals Pass the Benefit Cost Test,'" mimeo, University of California, Davis, 1990.

Magleby, David B., *Direct Legislation, Voting on Ballot Propositions in the United States.* Baltimore and London: The Johns Hopkins University Press, 1984.

McFadden, Daniel, and Gregory K. Leonard, "Issues in the Contingent Valuation of Environmental Goods: Methodologies for Data Collection and Analysis." In Hausman, J., ed., *Contingent Valuation: A Critical Assessment,* Amsterdam: North-Holland Press, 1993.

Milgrom, P., "Is Sympathy an Economic Value?," In Hausman, J., ed., *Contingent Valuation: A Critical Assessment.* Amsterdam: North-Holland Press, 1993, 417–42.

Mitchell, Robert Cameron and Richard T. Carson, *Using Surveys to Value Public Goods.* Washington, D.C.: Resources for the Future, 1989.

National Oceanic and Atmospheric Administration, 1993, "Report of the NOAA Panel on Contingent Valuation," *Federal Register,* 1993, *58,* 10, 4602–14.

National Oceanic and Atmospheric Administration, "National Resource Damage Assessments; Proposed Rules," *Federal Register*, 1994, *59*, 5, 1062–191.

Neill, Helen, R., et al., "Hypothetical Surveys and Real Economic Commitments," Economics Working Paper B-93-01, Department of Economics, College of Business Administration, University of South Carolina, 1993.

Samples, Karl C., and James R. Hollyer, "Contingent Valuation and Wildlife Resources in the Presence of Substitutes and Complements," In Johnson, Rebecca L., and Gary V. Johnson, eds., *Economic Valuation of Natural Resources: Issues, Theory and Applications*. Boulder: Westview Press, 1990, 177–92.

Schkade, D. A., and J. W. Payne, "Where Do the Numbers Come From? How People Respond to Contingent Valuation Questions." In Hausman, J., ed., *Contingent Valuation: A Critical Assessment*. Amsterdam: North-Holland Press, 1993, 271–304.

Schulze, William, D., et al., "Contingent Valuation of Natural Resource Damages Due to Injuries to the Upper Clark Fork River Basin," State of Montana, Natural Resource Damage Program, 1993.

Seip, Kalle, and Jon Strand, "Willingness to Pay For Environmental Goods in Norway: A Contingent Valuation Study With Real Payment," *Environmental and Resource Economics*, 1992, *2*, 91–106.

Tolley, George S., et al., "Establishing and Valuing the Effects of Improved Visibility in the Eastern United States," Report to the U.S. Environmental Protection Agency, Washington, D.C., 1983.

Urban, Glen L., Gerald M. Katz, Thomas E. Hatch, and Alvin J. Silk, "The ASSESSOR Pre-Test Market Evaluation System," *Interfaces*, 1983 *13*, 38–59.

10　*Euthanizing the Value of a Statistical Life**

Trudy Ann Cameron

Trudy Ann Cameron is Raymond F. Mikesell Professor of Environmental and Resource Economics at the University of Oregon.

[*Vizzini has just cut the rope that The Dread Pirate Roberts has been climbing.*]

Vizzini: He didn't fall? INCONCEIVABLE!
Inigo Montoya: You keep using that word. I do not think it means what you think it means.

—motion picture *The Princess Bride* (1987)

Introduction

Many policies and regulations are intended to protect human life and health. To analyze the benefits and costs of these measures, we must address society's willingness to pay (*WTP*) for a variety of health-risk reductions. By convention, economists report estimates of this *WTP* in terms of a unit called a "statistical life."[1]

While some economists may not be particularly familiar with this terminology, they catch on quickly when the "value of a statistical life" (*VSL*) is explained as a marginal rate of substitution between mortality risk and money (i.e., other goods and services). The *VSL* is a ratio in which the numerator is the marginal utility of a small reduction in mortality risk, r,

"Euthanizing the Value of a Statistical Life" by Trudy Ann Cameron. *Review of Environmental Economics and Policy* 4. 2010. Pp. 161–178. Reprinted with permission.

*This is an expanded version of Cameron (2008), a short article that I wrote for the November 2008 Newsletter of the Association of Environmental and Resource Economists (AERE). I am grateful to Rob Stavins for encouraging me to expand upon the points made there and to seek a broader audience for these ideas, and to Lisa Robinson, Kerry Smith, Kip Viscusi, and Richard Zerbe for helpful comments and suggestions. Charlie Kolstad suggested the best title, and Suzanne Leonard's editorial expertise made great improvements to the exposition. My thoughts on this subject have developed during the course of research supported by the US Environmental Protection Agency (R829485), Health Canada (H5431-010041/001/SS), the National Science Foundation (SES-0551009), and the Mikesell Foundation at the University of Oregon. The views expressed in this paper have not been formally reviewed by any of these entities. Any remaining errors are my own.

[1] A statistical life is a unit defined as a cross-sectional aggregate of enough individual tiny fractional risk reductions so that the total risk reduction is 1.0.

and the denominator is the marginal utility of a small change in income, Y.[2] While the *WTP* for an incremental risk change will be small, the numerical value of this *ratio* is very large. For mortality risks (typically the risk of sudden death in the current period), empirical data on the tradeoffs that real people are willing to make often indicate a middle-of-the-road estimate of around $7,000,000.[3]

Although economists understand the *VSL* terminology, noneconomists often have difficulty making sense of this concept. The most recent nationwide explosion of indignation over the *VSL* was "detonated" by a July 10, 2008, Associated Press article by Seth Borenstein, titled "An American life worth less today." The article described a decision by the U.S. Environmental Protection Agency (EPA) to revise downward its standardized estimate of society's *WTP* for aggregate mortality risk reductions from environmental policies (i.e., its estimate of "the *VSL*") from $7.8 million to $6.9 million.[4] While Borenstein interviewed a number of key experts both inside and outside of the EPA, his description of the issues and the data upon which *VSL* calculations are based was oversimplified, forcing readers to invent their own interpretations. And invent, they did.

In the days following publication of the article, which was picked up by local newspapers throughout the country, I collected a large number of comments from a variety of sources, including public comments on news websites. These reactions to the Borenstein article can leave no doubt that the consumers of our research need to be steered away from the mistaken impression that know-nothing bureaucrats presume to decide on behalf of society the intrinsic worth of a human being. The comments also reflect the damage to economists' reputations from the public's misinterpretation of the concept of a *VSL*. More importantly, however, these comments suggest that a significant amount of reputational capital and person-hours at various government agencies is wasted every time another sensational article about the *VSL* appears in the press.

This article is to discuss in detail what is wrong with the "*VSL*" terminology and economists' conventional notion of a *VSL*, and to propose some

---

[2]This is expressed mathematically as $(\partial U/\partial r)/(\partial U/\partial Y)$, which simplifies to $\partial Y/\partial r$, measured in "dollars per unit of risk reduced." Hammitt (2000) provides a very accessible explanation.

[3]The EPA's current recommendation for the value of a statistical life is that "the central estimate of $7.4 million ($2006), updated to the base year of the analysis, be used in all benefits analyses that seek to quantify mortality risk reduction benefits regardless of the age, income, or other population characteristics of the affected population." http://yosemite.epa.gov/ee/epa/eed.nsf/webpages/MortalityRiskValuation.html#currentvsl. A very thorough and detailed description and history of the EPA's *VSL* numbers and recent controversies is provided in Viscusi (2009a). See also comments by Carruthers (2009), Fourcade (2009), and Robinson (2009), and a reply by Viscusi (2009b).

[4]In fact, different offices at EPA use different VSL estimates for different policies. To update its numbers to reflect more recent research on the *VSL*, producing the lower *VSL* identified in the Borenstein article, the EPA Air Office apparently "selected as its preferred *VSL* the midpoint of the 25th percentile of the estimates in Mrozek and Taylor (2002) and the 75th percentile of Viscusi and Aldy (2000). This unusual mathematical formulation creates the illusion of precision but lacks any scientific basis" (Viscusi 2009a, p. 116).

alternative terminology that is both less provocative and more precise. I begin in the next section with a discussion of public misconceptions about "the *VSL*" and then turn to problems with the *VSL* terminology itself. I will contend that the public relations blunder that is "the *VSL*" is largely of our own making, that our profession's steadfast adherence to the term "*VSL*" was as much responsible for the outrage that followed publication of the Borenstein article as was the author's over-simplified description of the EPA decision. I will also argue that we have been too cavalier with specialized terminology, summarizing demand information in the aggregate, rather than in individual units with which people could more readily identify, and failing to realize that many people have fundamental problems with the idea of "monetization."

In the following section, I propose what I view as a viable alternative to "the *VSL*," one that changes our standard unit of measurement and replaces the "*VSL*" with "willingness to swap" (WTS) alternative goods and services for a microrisk reduction in the chance of sudden death (or other types of risks to life and health). Next I take up the issue of the aggregation of risks, which has led to our profession's misguided and misleading pursuit of a single, one-size-fits-all *VSL* and which precludes any assessment of the distributional consequences of risk-reduction policies based on their impacts on individual *net* benefits. I conclude with a discussion of the steps that need to be taken to "euthanize" the *VSL* terminology.

Misconceptions and Criticism of the VSL

Attempts at political damage control quickly followed publication of the Borenstein article. The day after the article appeared, the following remarks were attributed to the office of Senator Barbara Boxer (D-CA):

> The EPA's decision to reduce the value of a human life when they consider the benefits of new environmental regulations is outrageous and must be reversed. . . . EPA may not think Americans are worth all that much, but the rest of us believe the value of an American life to our families, our communities, our workplaces and our nation is no less than it has ever been. This new math has got to go. . . . If these reports are confirmed, I will be introducing legislation to reverse this unconscionable decision at the earliest opportunity.[5]

---

[5]Naively, I wrote immediately to Senator Boxer's office using the online link at her official website. I carefully explained why this issue was something her office might want to be sure they understood better, before she introduced new legislation. However, after hitting the "send" button, I was informed automatically that since I was not a resident of California, Senator Boxer would not be paying any attention to my comments. Viscusi (2009a) describes Senator Boxer's proposed legislation, the "Restoring the Value of Every American in Environmental Decisions Act" (110th Congress, 2d Session, 2008).

About a week later, a follow-up article (Fahrenthold 2008) appeared on the front page of the *Washington Post*, containing the following ideas:

> Someplace else, people might tell you that human life is priceless. In Washington, the federal government has appraised it like a '96 Camaro with bad brakes. . . . the Washington bureaucracy takes on a question usually left to preachers and poets. . . . for the first time, the EPA has used this little-known process to devalue life. . . . By reducing the value of human life, which is really a devious way of cooking the books, . . . To grasp the mind-bending concept of a Blue Book value on life, government officials say it is important to remember that they are not thinking about anyone specific. . . . an unlikely academic field has grown up to extrapolate life's value from the everyday decisions of average Americans. . . . lowering the value of life. In some bureaucratic corners of Washington, it is the kind of phrase that nobody blinks at anymore.

Ordinary people also vented their indignation in a variety of ways, including letters to the editors of newspapers, comments on news media websites, and even in television news satire.[6] The wide array of viewpoints, objections, and emotions is striking, as is the number of ways in which the idea of a *VSL* can be misinterpreted. Some people were clearly struggling to understand, while others were completely dismissive. The comments ranged from pious to political, from witty to sarcastic, and from sad to downright angry. Most importantly, however, the comments revealed widespread confusion and misconceptions about the *VSL* concept.

This is not the first time there has been a misinformed public maelstrom over the *VSL*. For example, back in 2003, it was revealed in the press that the EPA had explored the idea of using a *VSL* estimate for seniors that was about one-third lower than for other adults. Then Administrator of the EPA Christine Whitman faced public outrage about the so-called "senior death discount." Environmental groups mobilized AARP (formerly the American Association of Retired Persons) to protest the outrageous notion that America's seniors should be so callously "devalued."[7] Whitman did not stay long at the helm of the EPA after this controversy.

The protest over the senior death discount seemed to have as its rallying cry: "We seniors absolutely insist on paying just as much as everyone else!" Having been intrigued for some time by the fervor of this protest, I stopped by the AARP exhibit booth at the meetings of the Agricultural and Applied Economics Association (AAEA) in Orlando, Florida, in July 2008, just a few weeks after publication of Borenstein (2008). I asked the AARP representative if she knew the definition of the *VSL*. She had heard the expression, and knew that the government had tried to put a lower value on the lives of seniors and that the EPA had recently been taken to task for having quietly lowered the overall value of human lives in recent years. However, she could

---

[6]The online supplementary materials for this article present a sample of some 90 public comments. See http://www.reep.oxfordjournals.org.

[7]This mobilization may have been somewhat self-serving. Environmental groups seek to maximize environmental quality, while the AARP seeks to maximize the welfare of seniors. The two different objective functions may not always be fully compatible.

not point me to any AARP literature explaining to its membership the concept of the *VSL* and its implications. She was unaware of the Laughland et al. (2007) paper, which explains for a more general audience the role of benefit–cost analysis in regulatory impact analysis, including the implications of using age in the calculations. This paper was prepared for AARP, and yet it had not filtered down to the front lines, let alone to the general membership of the organization.

A Poor Choice of Words

The term *"VSL"* highlights a downside to the economist's habit of eschewing new jargon. This tendency means that we often build technical labels out of commonly used words that we happen to have "lying around the house." For example, anyone who has taught Principles of Economics knows how much time must be spent explaining exactly what *an economist* means by the words "cost" or "profit." These words do not have the same meaning for economists as for the person on the street Noneconomists often make no distinction between "cost" and "price," for example. And when ordinary people use the word "profit," they typically have in mind accounting profit, rather than economic profit.

By cobbling together the terms "value" and "statistical" and "life," we have done a grave disservice to both our profession and the policymakers we are often trying to help via our research and analysis. Let us consider, individually, each of the three main words in *"VSL."*

"Value": By "value," economists mean *WTP* (or sometimes, willingness-to-accept). By using the term "value" to mean *WTP* for risk reductions, we have created considerable confusion in the public's mind because the public often equates "value" with "intrinsic worth."

"Statistical": Economists probably intended the term "statistical" to indicate probabilistic outcomes rather than death with certainty. When summed over enough people, small probabilities of death will yield the expectation of one death in that large group. The trouble is that many intelligent people do not remember much of what they might have once learned about statistics. In fact, their knowledge may be based on one of the most widely purchased introductions to statistics for the general reader: Darrell Huff's (1954) "How to Lie with Statistics."[8] Or perhaps they have heard the catchy quote attributed to Benjamin Disraeli, and popularized in the United States by Mark Twain (1907), that mentions "lies, damned lies, and statistics." By introduc-

---

[8]See a discussion in Steele (2005). Huff's book includes such provocative chapter headings as "The Sample with the Built-in Bias," "The Little Figures That Are Not There," and "How to Statisticulate." The author himself acknowledges in the introduction that "It may seem altogether too much like a manual for swindlers." As a result, many readers may be left with the impression that all statistics are purposely designed to mislead.

ing the adjective "statistical" into our terminology, we may have courted instant skepticism and distrust of the *VSL*.

"*Life*": Noneconomists think we are valuing one whole, distinct, individual, and identifiable "life," when we are actually seeking to value tiny risk reductions for many different people. It was unwise to decide that the units in which to quote *WTP* for mortality risk reductions should be aggregated across enough different people so that the sum of their individual risk reductions equals 1.0. It would have been equally easy to quote *WTP* in terms of the size of the risk reduction that is relevant for the average individual under the policy in question, which would often be some relatively modest number of dollars. Instead, we quote *WTP* in terms of an arbitrarily huge aggregate risk reduction, which many people confuse with one specific life.

A Poor Choice of Units

Quoting the value of risk reductions in units of statistical lives is akin to quoting the price of milk by the tanker-truck load, rather than by the quart. Most people have a sense of what they might be willing to pay for a quart of milk, at least within an order of magnitude (say $2.00). Moreover, they are likely to be relatively familiar (and comfortable) with contemplating their personal tradeoffs concerning the decision to buy a quart of milk. However, few people would react well to a requirement that they instead contemplate the tradeoffs involved with purchasing a $40,000 truckload of milk (especially if it has not been carefully explained that a milk tanker holds 5,000 *gallons*, but that nobody actually expects one individual to buy the whole truckload). This is exactly the same per-unit price as for the quart of milk— just scaled up to a vastly larger quantity than any family would buy on a trip to the grocery store. Any shopper who encountered a price for milk at the supermarket of $40,000 (per 5,000 gallons) would likely be as much dismayed, befuddled, or outraged as many of the people who contemplate $7 million for "the *VSL*."

Ordinary citizens need to be able to consider, dispassionately and objectively, the reasonableness of the evidence on *WTP* for mortality risk reductions. To help them do this, our evidence about *WTP* should be reported in a way that is easier to grasp than the concept of "statistical lives" (e.g., in terms of the sizes of risk reductions that are relevant for a single individual or household). To trained economists, the choice to use "statistical lives" as the units for risk reductions may have seemed inconsequential. However, it appears to have been a very bad choice from the perspective of consumers.

The Concept of "Monetization"

Although it would clearly be an improvement to quote "*WTP* for risk reductions" in terms of individual risk reductions instead of the "*VSL*," the problems of the terminology go even deeper. As economists, we know precisely what we mean by the term *"WTP."* It is the monetized value of the other goods and services that people would be willing to give up in order to get one more unit of the thing in question. As economists, we have also been carefully taught to understand that it is the *real* tradeoffs that matter, and that money merely facilitates transactions. Thus, we need to know what people are willing to give up in terms of the next best use of the resources that would have to be reallocated to provide or create something (like better health or a safer workplace).

When it comes to health-risk reductions, the consumer might have to give up apples or oranges or shoes or cars or any combination of things that would otherwise provide utility if the health-risk reduction in question were not chosen. Because we cannot add apples and oranges, we use prevailing prices and convert these other things to expenditures. What the consumer is willing to swap to obtain a health-risk reduction is measured by the "dollars' worth" of other goods and services he or she would be prepared to do without. This is equivalent to a reduction in income. In our usual fashion, we economists have been stingy with verbiage and describe this process merely as *"WTP"* for a health-risk reduction—or even more briefly as just "monetization."

It is a subtle but very important point that health, itself, is not being directly or arbitrarily monetized. Instead, monetization is the strategy used to convert to a common denominator all those other heterogeneous goods or services willingly forgone to obtain the health improvement. We measure the "amount" of these other things via the expenditure that would be necessary to acquire them, given current prices. In other words, we measure the value of the health improvement to the individual in terms of the "dollars' worth" of other goods and services a consumer would be willing to forgo in exchange for the health improvement.

Unfortunately, we have done too little to educate the general population about what our specialized terms—*VSL, WTP,* and monetization—actually mean. Equally unfortunate is that these terms carry with them a lot of cultural baggage. Economists are able, implicitly, to separate the baggage from the technical meaning, but the general public often cannot.

Cultural Baggage and the Public's Fundamental Discomfort with Monetization

Americans are skittish about the topic of money. It is one of those things that we are not supposed to discuss in polite company. Why is the topic of money viewed as unsavory? Certain biblical phrases and juxtapositions have had great staying power in our popular culture. For example, the term *filthy lucre* is defined as "money; originally, money obtained dishonestly" (Ammer 1997, p. 207). The Latin word *lucrum*, from which *lucre* is derived, means "material gain, profit" or "avarice."

There are several translations of the biblical passage in the New Testament that contains "filthy lucre."[9] One is "Whose mouths must be stopped, who subvert whole houses, teaching things which they ought not, for filthy lucre's sake." This particular verse is sometimes summarized as "False teachers who must be stopped." This is not an auspicious cultural vantage point from which academic economists should be asking people to entertain the concept of "monetization" of statistical lives.

There is also a huge cultural taboo against the notion of "*WTP*" when the lives of human beings are at stake. There appears to be a short cognitive distance between the "*VSL*" and "paying for the life of a human being" or "slavery." All the repugnant moral connotations of slavery are readily transferred to the idea of paying for a human life. Furthermore, we ask individuals to consider paying for their *own* lives, rather than someone else's! This furthers the sense of moral outrage because people presumably feel an even greater sense of entitlement to their *own* lives.

Finally, consider the anxiety and stress engendered by the traditional "stick-'em-up" ultimatum: "Your money or your life!" Only a dangerous criminal would propose such a choice, and one would have to be looking down the barrel of a gun to consider it. The victim in question is being asked to make a tradeoff, albeit in an increment that is vastly larger than any of those relevant for any normal policy analysis. However, these dramatic and extreme instances of tradeoffs between money and risks to life make an indelible impression on people's psyches and add to their fears.

Rebranding the VSL

Savvy marketers have always known that what you call your product will influence people's demand for it. This phenomenon is reflected in the fact that companies will sometimes legally register a clever trademark (i.e., a name, symbol, or other device that identifies a product) before the product itself has even been developed.[10]

In other cases, companies are taken to task for giving a product a name that makes it appear more desirable or effective than can actually be proven. Consider, for example, a homeopathic product for the seasonal flu virus that was once called "Flu Resist™." Several years ago, this product was quietly renamed "Flu Relief™," with no other change in its packaging. Most people would probably pay more to *prevent* (or "resist") influenza than to treat it, so the relabeling presumably reflects an adjustment away from a

---

[9]The website http://bible.cc/titus/1–11.htm appears to be a good source for a variety of parallel translations of the passage in question, Titus 1:11.

[10]Of course, there is an expectation that a good-faith effort to develop the intended product is under way.

name that exaggerated the desirability of the product, toward one that more accurately reflected its clinically proven efficacy.

Just as the labeling of consumer products is an important determinant of buy-in by the public, so too is the labeling of public policies. During the second Bush administration, we were presented with the Clear Skies Initiative and the Healthy Forests Initiative. Who could argue with clear skies or healthy forests? The policies themselves were multifaceted and would involve a variety of reallocations of resources relative to the status quo, so as usual there would be some winners and some losers. However, these policy labels were easy to enunciate and to remember, and both had indisputably positive connotations, even though the labels were rather imprecise descriptions of the policies themselves.

Economists have proven themselves to be appallingly poor marketers when it comes to the "Value of a Statistical Life" or "VSL." A vowel would certainly have been helpful, so that the acronym could have been pronounceable as a word. But at least the concept can be reduced to a three-letter abbreviation. However, compared to "Clear Skies" or "Healthy Forests," our "VSL" label is a marketing disaster. Surely, we can do better. We need a label for this concept that is brief, accurate, and at least perceived as being neutral and logical, if not actually appealing, by the noneconomist public.[11]

While you cannot fix a problem simply by relabeling a product as something it is not, it is entirely appropriate to correct a name to more accurately portray what the product is or does. I am reminded of trying to get an online survey instrument through the Institutional Review Board (IRB) at one of my former universities. As an incentive for participation, I was offering each respondent the chance to win a prize for completing the survey. I described this prize competition as a lottery. The IRB contacted the campus legal counsel about this plan and I was immediately notified that what I proposed was illegal, since only the state could sponsor a lottery. Realizing that the legal definition of a lottery specified that people must pay money to participate, rather than simply devoting their time (another scarce resource) to complete a survey, I changed the wording to specify that the respondent would be "entered to win a prize." The university counsel's office initially refused to accept this remedy because "just calling it something other than a lottery does not make it legal." It took more effort than should have been necessary to convey the point that the prize competition was never a "lottery" in the first place, in the legal sense, and that just *calling* it a lottery should not make it *illegal*.

I use this anecdote to illustrate the point that even if we attempt to improve our terminology for the VSL, any one of the unhappy people who commented on the Borenstein article might leap to the conclusion that we are simply "putting lipstick on a pig." On the contrary, our goal is to prevent the VSL from being mistaken for a bureaucratic attempt to dictate arbitrarily the worth of a human being. Relabeling the concept more carefully,

---

[11]As a product name, VSL seems to be right up there with the appetite suppressant candy called Ayds that was popular prior to the early 1980s.

to describe precisely what it actually means, is entirely appropriate and, in my view, absolutely necessary.

The Concept of a Micromort

Over two decades ago, Howard (1984, 1989) advocated the concept of a micromort (based on "micro" for millionth and "mort" for mortality) to describe a one-in-a-million chance of death.[12] In most of the literature on the economic valuation of mortality risk reductions, it is assumed that *WTP* is proportional to the size of the risk reduction (as it will be, if the marginal *WTP*, *MWTP*, is constant). If this proportionality assumption holds, then we are free to scale the dollar amounts of *WTP* to correspond to *any* arbitrarily sized risk change. The *VSL*, as a ratio that indicates a marginal rate of substitution, is equivalent to a scaling of the monetary value for a modest risk change to a huge 1.00 (or 100 percent) change in mortality risk. In contrast, *WTP* for a micromort would scale the monetary value to a tiny 0.000001 change in the risk of death.

The units we use to measure risk changes (and to value them) should be within a few orders of magnitude of the typical sizes of risk reductions contemplated under proposed environmental policies or regulations. Thus it would make sense to quote *WTP* for mortality risk reductions in 1/1,000,000 units, for example, rather than in 1.00 units (as the *VSL* does). This change in units provides information that is identical to the *VSL*, but with much less potential for misinterpretation by noneconomists. Remember that we have absolutely no reliable large samples of data about how much people would pay to reduce their own risk of death from 1.00 to 0.00. Yet this is exactly what is implied by the choice to scale *WTP* to a 100 percent mortality risk reduction. Our current approach is to observe tradeoffs with respect to small risks, scale them way up to *VSL*s to report them, then scale them right back down again for use with individual risks of sizes that are relevant for policy evaluation. I suggest that we skip the middle step. It is completely unnecessary and is entirely to blame for a whole lot of confusion.

Microrisks as a More Appropriate Unit

There is considerable merit to the notion that we should separate our primary label for the *size* of the risk reduction in question from a secondary label for the *type* of risk to be reduced. We need to be explicit about both size and type.

If we can pry ourselves away from "statistical lives," even the concept of "*WTP* for a micromort" may not be sufficiently general, since it would apply only to *mortality* risk reductions. Environmental policies and regulations also reduce the risk of *morbidity* (sickness). One might consider an analogous *WTP* for a "micromorb" for morbidity risk reductions, but

---

[12]Howard's work was first brought to my attention by Jim Hammitt.

unfortunately this would be rather difficult to enunciate. Howard (1984) has also suggested other nomenclature, such as a "microdisability" for risks that lead to disability rather than death.

Our terminology needs to be broad enough to apply to a wide variety of health-risk reductions. The more-specific terms mentioned earlier could be introduced for special cases of morbidity or disability risks. However, Howard's most generic term is a *microrisk*. Thus we could refer succinctly to a 1/1,000,000 risk reduction as a *microrisk* (μr) reduction for the risk in question. A 1/1,000 risk reduction could be called a *millirisk* (mr) reduction.[13] We could use multiples in between these two terms, if necessary. Mortality rates are often quoted as "per 100,000." Thus a 1/100,000 risk reduction would be "ten microrisks" ($10\mu r$) and a 1/10,000 risk reduction would be "100 microrisks ($100\mu r$)."[14] Although "*WTP* for a microrisk reduction" is based on more-standard scientific terminology, it certainly does not roll off the tongue as easily as "*VSL*." However, it is less misleading and more precise, and would probably be much less confusing to the public.[15]

It is also important to be explicit about the research context that has provided a particular *WTP* estimate and whether this matches the policy context to which it will be applied. *WTP* for any commodity will depend upon the precise attributes of the commodity in question, as should *WTP* for reductions in risks to life and health. Thus it is important to include risk attributes for an estimate of *WTP* for a risk reduction of a given size, for example "a $10.8 *WTP* for a microrisk reduction, based on wage-risk tradeoffs by middle-aged males concerning on-the-job fatalities in the current period." One might easily contend that we should have been using this level of description all along, even with the *VSL* estimates already in the literature.

Avoiding the Idea of "Payment"

As discussed earlier, noneconomists are reluctant to accept the technically accurate economic term known as "*WTP*," presumably because they are uncomfortable with the notion of paying money for their lives or their health. However, policy choice concerns people's willingness to make *tradeoffs*. That is, to gain improvements in their health or longevity, they may have to settle for higher consumer prices, lower wages, lower investment returns, or even higher taxes. These tradeoffs are likely to be unpleasant

---

[13]The abbreviation adheres to the conventions of the National Institute of Standards and Technology for international System of Units (SI) prefixes for multiples and fractions of units.

[14]Ten times something is "deka-" (da) and 100 times something is "hecto-" (h). So, a 1/100,000 risk reduction (ten times a microrisk) could be called a *dekamicrorisk* ($da\mu r$) reduction, and a 1/10,000 risk reduction (one hundred times a microrisk) could be called a *hectomicrorisk* ($h\mu r$). However, this seems like overkill in terms of jargon.

[15]In contexts where one did not wish to digress to explain the definition of a microrisk reduction, one could simply say "a one-in-one-million risk reduction," or "a 0.000001 risk reduction" if sufficient numeracy can be assumed.

because they force the individual to do without something else that he or she would otherwise have been able to afford.

Given the adverse reactions of the general public to the notion of being asked to pay for risk reductions, we may need to eliminate the word "pay" altogether. A more accurate term would be "forgo," since it conveys the sense of a tradeoff (i.e., that something else will have to be given up or done without). Forgone opportunities are thoroughly understood by economists and could likely be understood by the general public as well. However, "willingness to forgo" does not lend itself to a helpful acronym.

Proposed Replacement Terminology

So, we need a synonym for "forgo" that conveys the same sense of "to give up in exchange for." One candidate might be "to relinquish." Another is "to sacrifice." But perhaps the most neutral verb, and the one with the fewest alternative definitions, is "to swap," which means "to trade one thing for another" or "to exchange (one thing) for another." "Swap" was originally a horse trader's term, being a shortened version of the phrase "swap a bargain." The word *swap* evolved from the Middle English word *swappen:* "to strike, strike hands (in bargaining),"[16] and from the Gaelic word *suaip:* "to exchange, to barter" (Mackay 1877, p. 444). The notion of striking hands (which has evolved to a custom of shaking hands) to signify agreement to a willing trade or contract seems very apt for conveying the notion of *WTP* in contexts where money as a medium of exchange may not be a necessary element of the bargain.

Fortunately, the abbreviation "*WTS*" also seems to be relatively neutral.[17] There may be some initial confusion for economists concerning the meaning of the acronym, since "*S*" commonly stands for "supply" or "substitution" or "savings." But we, as economists, are perhaps better equipped to figure out the *WTS* acronym in the relevant context than the general public has been to interpret the "*VSL*."

Willingness-to-Swap for a Microrisk Reduction Will Not Be $3.141592653589793 . . .

Economists also need to push policymakers to acknowledge that "the *VSL*" is not some true-but-unknown fundamental constant of nature that we merely need to measure more accurately. Instead, "the *VSL*" is the result of attempts to find a convenient one-size-fits-all measure of demand for risk reductions—a number that may or may not be appropriate across all different types of risks or all different affected populations. A single universal

---

[16]swap. (n.d.). *Dictionary.com Unabridged.* Random House, Inc. Retrieved October 22, 2009, from Dictionary.com website: http://dictionary.reference.com/browse/swap.

[17]As an acronym, *WTS* seems to have as its closest competition the Westminster Theological Seminary.

VSL number is politically expedient, of course, but it is also likely to be the *wrong* number, unless the risk is "typical" and it affects a population with "typical" demands for protection. I discuss this issue in more detail in the next section.

The Perils of a One-Size-Fits-All VSL

Why do we think we need "the *VSL*"? Policy evaluators have sought a one-size-fits-all measure of *WTP* for risk reductions in the form of "the *VSL*" because, in their assessment of social benefits of risk reductions, they have traditionally jumped the gun and aggregated across different people too soon in the valuation process.

Premature Aggregation

Ideally, our calculation of the overall benefits of risk reductions should remain disaggregated to the individual level through many steps, starting with the identification of individual risk reductions, through multiplication by the corresponding individual *marginal WTP* amount, to produce individual *WTP* for the particular size of risk reduction in question. Individual marginal costs should also be identified, of course, to permit the calculation of individual *net* benefits. Only then, after the distributional consequences of this pattern of net benefits have been examined, should one aggregate individual net benefits across the affected population to yield an initial (equally weighted) measure of overall net social benefits.[18]

In practice, benefit–cost analysts have tended to identify individual physical risk reductions and then jump straight into aggregation. They first sum individual risk reductions across the affected population, which maybe a very large number of people. When the sum of individual risk reductions reaches 1.00, one "statistical life" has been accumulated. For the policy in question, the quantity of interest is then the number of "statistical lives" to be "saved." Of course, no specific life will be saved with certainty by the policy. The actual risk reductions could be on the order of one in 10,000 or even one in a million for each person, which could be viewed by many people as vanishingly small.

Once analysts have calculated the number of statistical lives involved, they need to convert this aggregate risk reduction into an aggregate *WTP* for this public good. Since the units of risk reduction have been established as "statistical lives," a corresponding dollar value "per statistical life" is required. This dollar measure cannot reflect individual preferences or constraints, because all information about individual heterogeneity has been lost due to premature aggregation, across people, of the individual risk

---

[18]Overall net social benefits are expressed as: $\Sigma i \, (MWTP_i - MC_i)\Delta r_i$, where $MWTPi$ = individual marginal willingness to pay, MC_i = individual marginal costs, and Δr_i = individual risk reductions.

reductions associated with the policy. Aggregate *physical* benefits are measured by the number of statistical lives, and thus a measure of the "social" *WTP* for those statistical lives is needed to monetize these benefits. This accounts for the persistent desire for a single one-size-fits-all *VSL*—to permit calculation of social benefits by multiplying just two terms: $(\Sigma_i \Delta r_i) \times VSL$ (where the first term is the aggregate of the individual risk reductions).

Aggregation of risk and then multiplication by the *VSL* may involve minimal bias if everyone faces the same risk reduction and everyone's *WTP* for risk reductions is identical. But the risk reductions promised by a policy may be distributed very unevenly across the population. Likewise, individual marginal *WTP* for risk reductions may vary widely across people. Risk reductions and marginal *WTP* amounts must therefore be recognized as jointly distributed random variables, which are potentially correlated, either positively or negatively. When two random variables are correlated, it is not true that the average of their products is equal to the product of their averages. Yet we are implicitly assuming the absence of any correlation when we multiply an aggregate risk reduction by the *VSL*.[19]

To illustrate the problem with using a *VSL* when risk reductions may be correlated with *WTP*, consider the case of tighter environmental standards. People in areas already in compliance with the new standard may have higher incomes and may experience no risk reductions at all as a result of the policy. People whose neighborhoods are vastly out of compliance may have lower incomes but may, reap large risk reductions via the policy because the new standards are binding. If marginal *WTP* for risk reductions increases with income, this would be a situation where individual marginal *WTP* is negatively correlated with prospective individual risk reductions. This means that the estimated overall social benefits would be *overstated* by simply multiplying a population average *VSL* by the aggregate of individual risk reductions. In contrast, estimated overall social benefits would be *understated* in a case where individual marginal *WTP* amounts were positively correlated with the individual risk reductions to be experienced.[20]

Of course, practitioners must also document policy *costs* in addition to policy benefits. As with marginal *WTP* and risk reductions, individual costs may be correlated with the sizes of individual risk reductions.

---

[19]Elementary statistics tells us that the product of two random variables, X and Y, has an expected value given by $E[XY] = E[X]E[Y]$ only when X and Y are independent. If the two variables are correlated, then the expected value of their product depends on the covariance between the two variables: $E[XY] = E[X]E[Y] + Cov[XY]$. In this case, we may consider individual risk reductions as X and individual marginal *WTP* amounts as Y. The total number of statistical lives involved would then be $nE[X]$, where n is the size of the affected population. We want to know the average value of XY which, when multiplied by n, yields overall social benefits.

[20]These two scenarios correspond to Case D and Case E in the Appendix, which provides [sic] a concrete numerical example of how premature aggregation can produce misleading results when willingness to pay for a risk reduction is correlated with the size of the risk reduction to be experienced.

Disaggregation and Equity Assessment

For policy evaluation, the most important adjunct to the efficiency assessment of a conventional benefit–cost analysis is a careful consideration of the distributional consequences of the policy. If we are interested only in overall net social benefits, it is acceptable to calculate aggregate social benefits and aggregate social costs separately, and then to take their difference to yield net social benefits.[21] However, because the distributions of costs and benefits may differ, equity assessment cannot be done solely in terms of benefits (or solely in terms of costs). Individual *net* benefits must be studied. This means that for equity assessments, it is necessary to focus attention on the distribution of *individual* net benefits before they are aggregated to produce net *social* benefits.[22]

For example, it is possible for a policy to appear progressive in terms of just its benefits. In other words, the policy may confer monetized benefits upon lower-income people, with the benefits representing a larger proportion of income for lower-income people than for higher-income people. However, the same policy may also be highly regressive in terms of its costs. That is, lower-income people may end up paying a larger proportion of their incomes to obtain these benefits than would higher-income people.[23]

Differentiated *VSLs* (Individuation) and Equity Assessment

Sunstein (2004) makes a persuasive case for the individuation of *WTP* estimates—that *WTP* should be differentiated to reflect differences in risks and in affected populations. Recent evidence concerning this heterogeneity in *WTP* is presented in a special issue of the *Journal of Risk and Uncertainty* (see Viscusi 2010).

The main reason many people object to differentiated *VSL* estimates is that "putting different values on the lives of different people" seems unfair. Some constituencies object to *WTP*-based measures because they tend to suggest greater benefits for people with higher incomes. While it is true that the benefits may be relatively greater for high-income groups because of their greater *WTP*, high-income individuals may bear an even greater share of the social costs of the risk reduction policy. This means the policy could still be "progressive," rather than "regressive," in the sense that the *net* benefits from the policy account for a higher proportion of income for the poor than for the rich. Thus, such a policy could still narrow the gap between rich and poor, even if the benefits to the rich are greater when costs are disregarded.

---

[21]That is: $NSB = SB - SC = \Sigma_i (MWTP_i \, \Delta r_i) - \Sigma_i (MC_i \Delta r_i)$, where NSB = net social benefits, SB = overall social benefits, and SC = overall social costs.

[22]Net social benefits are the aggregate of individual net benefits: $NSB = \Sigma_i (MWTP_i - MC_i)\Delta_i$

[23]Zerbe (1974) offers some early discussion of the regressivity of some types of environmental improvements. His paper considers optimal jurisdictions for environmental regulation (which is pertinent to the environmental federalism literature).

Any *VSL* estimate reflects an underlying demand function (where individual demand functions are basic to consumer theory in modern economics), so it is unlikely that any such demand function could imply a *WTP* that is a simple constant that can be applied for all types of individuals and all kinds of risks. As for any other good or service, *WTP* for health-risk reductions will depend upon the specifications and the quantity of the good in question, the individual's income, the prices (or rationed quantities) of substitutes or complements, and the individual's preferences. The distribution across individuals of the *benefits* of some type of publicly provided risk reduction can thus be expected to depend upon (1) the type of risk and the amount by which it is reduced (or perceived to be reduced) for each individual; (2) the individual's income; (3) the availability of other means for each individual to mitigate or compensate for this type of risk; and (4) the individual's subjective disutility from this type of risk, degree of risk aversion, and discount rate in the case of latent risks that will come to bear sometime in the future.

People need to understand that a policy of "equal protection" via risk-reduction policies—which ignores heterogeneous preferences and incomes and employs a single one-size-fits-all *VSL*—is likely to be ethically acceptable only if this protection is purely a gift. Unfortunately, many types of policies and regulations are akin to "unfunded mandates." Thus, in many important policy and regulatory contexts, people will be required to pay for a substantial share of this extra protection themselves, through higher prices or taxes, lower wages, or lower investment returns, even though they may have other priorities for their scarce resources.

Conclusions: "Euthanizing" the *VSL*

At a recent conference sponsored by the MacArthur Foundation,[24] an audience member asked what it would take to increase acceptance of the use of benefit–cost analysis in decisions about the provision of preventive health-care and the reduction of environmental and safety risks. It seems to me that a necessary (although probably not entirely sufficient) condition for broader public acceptance would be for economists to be able to discuss and report their estimated social benefits of environmental, health, or safety policies in a way that neither confuses nor offends noneconomists.

This does not necessarily mean that we must change all our current methods for measuring the tradeoffs that people reveal or state they are willing to make with respect to their own health risks—although there certainly are more-general ways to characterize the types of choices people make with regard to altering their risks of experiencing a wide range of

---

[24]"Unleashing the Power of Social Benefit-Cost Analysis: Removing Barriers," sponsored by the Benefit-Cost Analysis Center at the University of Washington's Evans School of Public Affairs and funded by The John D. and Catherine T. MacArthur Foundation, October 19–20, 2009, Washington, D.C.

adverse future health profiles.[25] However, it does seem necessary for us, as a profession, to stop using the term "*VSL*" to describe the kinds of numbers we develop. I have suggested that a technically correct measure of what people would be willing to trade for reductions in risk of policy-relevant sizes could be described as "*WTS* other goods and services for a microrisk (μr) reduction *in a specified type of risk.*" An abbreviation for this mouthful of terms could be "*WTS(μr)*" or "*WTS$_{\mu r}$*," or simply "*WTS*." Unfortunately, this is not quite as easy to say as "the *VSL*." But we could always make it easier by inserting the "*i*" from "willingness," which would yield "*WiTS.*"

While this proposed minimum change is a small adjustment, it may have a very large effect in terms of public relations. To echo an observation by Howard (1984, p. 408), "Although this change is cosmetic only, we should remember the size of the cosmetic industry."

To properly implement this new terminology, it will also be important to be more specific about our benefits estimates. We should be careful to specify the *nature* of the health threat for which the risk is being reduced, such as "*WTS$_{\mu r}$* (sudden death from heart attack)" or "*WTS$_{\mu r}$* (death 10 years earlier than otherwise, after 5 years of respiratory disease)." The characteristics of the affected individual will also be expected to influence this *WTS* systematically. Thus a complete set of arguments must include the nature of the risk *and* the characteristics of the affected person or subpopulation. If a benefits transfer is being attempted from one context to another, we should be meticulous about noting any differences between the "study" context and the "policy" context for such a transfer.

Finally, when we report our estimates of *WTS$_{\mu r}$*, it will be particularly important to not yield to the temptation to cut corners by simply using "dollars" as the units. We should be meticulous about reporting *WTS$_{\mu r}$* in "dollars' worth of alternative goods and services." This will be especially important in the abstracts, introductions, and conclusions of our papers, from which some readers are likely to glean their initial impressions of our research. This careful terminology will keep in the forefront of people's minds the idea that consumers typically need (or will be asked) to swap other desirable things for policy-sized reductions in some specific type of risk to their life or health.

It is a challenge to change a discipline's long-standing terminology. Even if we start right now, it may take a decade or more before we will cease needing to include a footnote with the instructions: "To achieve a measure that is equivalent to the construct formerly known as 'the value of a statistical life' (or the *VSL*), take the *WTS$_{\mu r}$* measures reported in this table and multiply by 1 million."

It will also take considerable self-discipline to achieve the conversion. The more "experienced" among us are sufficiently set in our ways that it may be nearly impossible to purge the *VSL* terminology from our casual conversations. Canada's experience in converting to the metric system, between

---

[25]Such a more-general approach has recently been proposed and demonstrated in a series of papers based on Cameron and DeShazo (2010).

1975 and 1983, might be a model for what we can expect. Many older Canadians will never be able to think in terms of litres and kilograms, but the "measuring and weighing" curriculum for schoolchildren provides an opportunity for younger Canadians to "think metric" right from the start.

By analogy, a necessary first step toward euthanizing "the *VSL*" (by removing it from our professional vocabulary) would be to ease this unhelpful terminology out of all of our introductory textbooks and our introductory courses. Anyone who has taught this topic knows how easy it is to squander an entire lecture period trying to smooth the ruffled feathers of indignant and idealistic college students who chafe at the idea of monetizing the value of a human being. Students should probably not even encounter the shorthand that is the "*VSL*" (if ever) until they thoroughly understand the underlying necessity for tradeoffs in policy-making, and the real empirical evidence about people's willingness to swap other goods and services for policy-sized risk reductions. In an introductory course, the term should not be introduced at all, and in more-advanced texts, it should warrant no more than a footnote, noting it as an archaic usage. Eliminating the *VSL* terminology would allow those of us who teach to spend scarce lecture time on more substantive concepts, rather than just damage control.

In addition to eliminating "*VSL*" from our introductory texts and classes, it would be helpful to develop a stable of standard and accessible examples of cases where people are commonly observed to make tradeoffs between risk and money. At the time of this writing, for example, the Toyota Motor Company has dealt with the recall of its vehicles for sudden unintended acceleration and brake problems by embarking on a far-reaching sales program that apparently includes zero percent financing and free maintenance. To the extent that Toyota's customers are willing to accept small increases in expected mortality from accidents in exchange for a better deal on the purchase of a Toyota, they are voluntarily trading risks and dollars.

While it may be somewhat inconvenient to move away from the *VSL* terminology, by doing so, economists may be able to gain a much better public response to our hard-earned quantitative results. Moreover, government agencies responsible for policy-making related to public risk reduction could improve their public image by avoiding—like the plague—any references to the *VSL*. Instead, they should be meticulous in using more-precise descriptions akin to what I have proposed here.

Greater public sympathy (i.e., less misplaced public outrage) should enable our research to have greater influence on the development of rational policies. But this can happen only if we make an effort to keep the highly counterproductive terminology of the *VSL* out of our professional writings and our communications with the press and the general public.

Finally, we need to resist the perennial urge to provide single one-size-fits-all estimates for *WTP* for risk reductions. The willingness to swap other goods and services for specific types of risk reductions can be expected to vary with all of the factors that shift other types of demand functions—income, the prices of substitutes and complements, and tastes or preferences regarding the good in question. Thus, it is not appropriate to average WTS estimates, arbitrarily, across a wide variety of risk reductions affecting different populations. Instead, policymakers should seek to match individual WTS estimates as closely as possible to the policy context in which they are to be used. This implies a need for considerably more basic research to help us to better understand the nature of heterogeneity in the WTS.

Appendix: Numerical Example of the Perils of Premature Aggregation

Heterogeneity in risk reductions, combined with heterogeneity in individual WTP for these risk reductions, can produce misleading results if one calculates aggregate benefits prematurely. Premature aggregation means that one first aggregates risk reductions, and then multiplies by an average VSL estimate for the population, rather than first calculating individual WTP for individual risk reductions and then aggregating these WTP measures. Consider the simple numerical example in Table 1. In each of the five cases (A through E), there are one million people in the overall population, divided into two equal-sized groups. In all five cases, based on the data in columns (1) and (2), individual WTP for a microrisk reduction averages $7 across the population. Likewise, based on the data in columns (1) and (3), in all five cases the aggregate risk reduction across the one million people is exactly 1.0 statistical life. Thus if we aggregate the risks first, we will always have one statistical life and if we average the VSLs implied by the average WTP amounts, we will always get $7 million. If we aggregate the risk reductions and the WTP information separately, and then multiply, the social benefits will always be $7 million. But what happens if we do not aggregate prematurely?

In Case A in Table 1, both groups are the same. All one million people in the population share a common WTP for risk reductions that corresponds to a VSL of $7 million (=$7/0.000001), and everyone faces the same size risk reduction (one in a million). Both groups will experience benefits of $3.5 million, so aggregate benefits produced in Case A will be $7 million. If everyone is the same, then, it does not matter whether we aggregate risks and multiply by a VSL, or preserve disaggregated risks and disaggregated WTP amounts and aggregate across the population only after we have multiplied individual risk changes by individual WTP to get individual benefits.

In Case B, individual WTP for risk reductions differs across the two groups (either because incomes differ or because tastes or risk perceptions differ), but the risk reductions faced by the two groups are identical. In Case C, incomes, preferences, and risk perceptions are the same, leading to identical WTP for risk reductions, but there are different-sized risk reductions for each group. In both cases, if we first multiply individual risk reductions by individual WTP to get individual benefits, and then aggregate these benefits, overall benefits will still be $7 million (because there is no correlation between WTP and risk reductions in these two cases).

The results are more interesting for the final two cases, however. In Case D, the group with the *higher* individual WTP faces the *smaller* risk reduction, while the group with the *lower* individual WTP faces the *larger* risk reduction (i.e., WTP is

Table 1 Calculation of benefits without premature aggregation

Cases	(1) Number of people in each group	(2) Individual WTP per 0.000001 risk reduction in each group	(3) Risk reduction for everyone in each group	(4) Benefits by group	(5) Overall benefits
A: Uniform risk reductions	500,000	$7	0.000001	$3.5 million	$7 million
and uniform *WTP*	500,000	$7	0.000001	$3.5 million	
B: Uniform risk reductions	500,000	$2	0.000001	$1 million	$7 million
and differing *WTP*	500,000	$12	0.000001	$6 million	
C: Differing risk reductions	500,000	$7	0.0000005	$1.75 million	$7 million
and uniform *WTP*	500,000	$7	0.0000015	$5.25 million	
D: Risk reductions and	500,000	$12	0.0000005	$1.5 million	$4.5 million
WTP negatively correlated	500,000	$2	0.0000015	$3 million	
E: Risk reductions and	500,000	$2	0.0000005	$0.5 million	$9.5 million
WTP positively correlated	500,000	$12	0.0000015	$9 million	

Note: In all cases, aggregate risk reduction is one statistical life, and the average *VSL* would be $7 million.

negatively correlated with the size of the risk reduction). In this case, if we calculate individual benefits before aggregating, the overall benefit for the low-risk group is $1.5 million and the overall benefit for the high-risk group is $3 million (column 4), for total social benefits of $4.5 million (column 5). Conversely, in Case E, the group with the *lower* individual *WTP* faces the *smaller* risk reduction (i.e., *WTP* is *positively* correlated with the size of the risk reduction). If we again calculate individual benefits before aggregating, the overall benefit for the low-risk group is $0.5 million and the overall benefit for the high-risk group is $9 million (column 4), for total social benefits of $9.5 million (column 5).

The implication of this example is as follows: The conventional strategy—of aggregating physical risk changes into some number of statistical lives, and then multiplying by some one-size-fits-all *VSL*, here yielding benefits of $7 million in all five cases—will tend to (1) overestimate true social benefits if risk reductions and *WTP* are negatively correlated; and (2) underestimate true social benefits if risk reductions and *WTP* are positively correlated. This can lead to biases if individual risk reductions and individual *WTP* amounts are nonuniform in the population and vary together in a systematic fashion.

REFERENCES

Ammer, Christine. 1997. *The American heritage dictionary of idioms: The most comprehensive collection of idiomatic expressions and phrases.* Boston: Houghton Mifflin.

Borenstein, Seth. 2008. AP IMPACT: An American life worth less today. Thursday, July 10, Associated Press. [Available at http://teamstersonline/com/forums/community-lounge/7956-american-life-worth-less-today.html (accessed 6/8/11)].

Cameron, Trudy Ann. 2008. The value of a statistical life: [They] do not think it means what [we] think it means. *AERE Newsletter* 28(2):36–39.

Cameron, Trudy Ann, and J. R. DeShazo. 2010. *Demand for health risk reductions.* Manuscript, Department of Economics, University of Oregon, Eugene.

Carruthers, Bruce G. 2009. Can social science numbers save public policy from politics? *Regulation & Governance* 3:287–90.

Fahrenthold, David A. 2008. Cosmic markdown: EPA says life is worth less. *Washington Post*, Saturday, July 19; p. A01.

Fourcade, Marion. 2009. The political valuation of life. *Regulation & Governance* 3:291–97.

Hammitt, James K. 2000. Valuing mortality risk: Theory and practice. *Environmental Science and Technology* 34:1396–1400.

Howard, Ronald A. 1984. On fates comparable to death. *Management Science* 30:407–22.

———. 1989. Microrisks for medical decision analysis. *International Journal of Technology Assessment in Health Care* 5:357–70.

Huff, Darrell. 1954. *How to lie with statistics (illustrated by Irving Geis).* New York: W. W. Norton and Company.

Laughland, Drew, A. Myrick Freeman III, Calvin Franz, Aylin Sertkaya (Eastern Research Group, Inc.) and Keith D. Lind (AARP Public Policy Institute). 2007. Exploring the role of cost-benefit analysis in government regulations. AARP Working Paper #207–14 (September).

Mackay, Charles. 1877. *The Gaelic etymology of the languages of western Europe and more especially of the English and lowland Scotch of their slang, cant and colloquial dialects.* London: N. Trübner and Co.

Mrozek, Janusz R., and Laura O. Taylor. 2002. What determines the value of life? A meta-analysis. *Journal of Policy Analysis and Management* 21:253–70.

Robinson, Lisa A. 2009. Valuing lives, valuing risks, and respecting preferences in regulatory analysis. *Regulation & Governance* 3:298–305.

Steele, J. Michael. 2005. Darrell Huff and fifty years of how to lie with statistics. *Statistical Science* 20(3):205–9.

Sunstein, Cass R. 2004. Valuing life: A plea for disaggregation. *Duke Law Journal* 54:385–445.

Twain, Mark. 1907. Chapters from *My Autobiography. North American Review*, No. DCXVIII, July 5. Available at [http://www.online-literature.com/twain/my-autobiography/ (accessed 6/8/11)].

Viscusi, W. Kip. 2009a. The devaluation of life. *Regulation & Governance* 3:103–27.

———. 2009b. Reply to the comments on "The devaluation of life." *Regulation & Governance* 3:306–9.

———. 2010. The heterogeneity of the value of statistical life: Introduction and overview. *Journal of Risk and Uncertainty* 40:1–13.

Viscusi, W. Kip, and Joseph E. Aldy. 2003. The value of a statistical life: A critical review of market estimates throughout the world. *Journal of Risk and Uncertainty* 27:5–76.

Zerbe, Richard 0.1974. Optimal environmental jurisdictions. *Ecology Law Quarterly* 4(2):193–245.

IV

The Goals of Environmental Policy: Economic Efficiency and Benefit-Cost Analysis

11 _Is There a Role for Benefit-Cost Analysis in Environmental, Health, and Safety Regulation?_

Kenneth J. Arrow　　**Paul R. Portney**

Maureen L. Cropper　**Milton Russell**

George C. Eads　　**Richard Schmalensee**

Robert W. Hahn　　**V. Kerry Smith**

Lester B. Lave　　**Robert N. Stavins**

Roger G. Noll

Kenneth J. Arrow is Joan Kenney Professor of Economics Emeritus at Stanford University; Maureen L. Cropper is Professor of Economics at the University of Maryland; George C. Eads is Senior Consultant of Charles River Associates, Washington, D.C.; Robert W. Hahn is Tesco Professor of Economics and Professorial Research Fellow of the Sustainable Consumption Institute at the University of Manchester, Senior Visiting Fellow at the Smith School at Oxford University, and Senior Fellow at the Georgetown Center for Business and Public Policy; Lester B. Lave was James Higgins Professor of Economics and Finance, Professor of Urban and Public Affairs, and Professor of Engineering and Public Policy at Carnegie-Mellon University; Roger G. Noll is Emeritus Professor of Economics in the Department of Economics at Stanford University; Paul R. Portney is Professor of Economics, Halle Chair in Leadership and Dean, Eller College of Management at the University of Arizona; Milton Russell is Senior Fellow of the Institute for a Secure and Sustainable Environment and Professor Emeritus in the Economics Department at the University of Tennessee; V. Kerry Smith is Professor of Environmental Economics at the W.P. Carey School of Business at Arizona State University and University Fellow at Resources for the Future; Richard Schmalensee is Howard W. Johnson Professor of Economics and Management at the Massachusetts Institute of Technology (MIT) and Director of the MIT Center for Energy and Environmental Policy Research; and Robert N. Stavins is Albert Pratt Professor of Business and Government at Harvard Kennedy School, Research Associate at the National Bureau of Economic Research, and University Fellow at Resources for the Future.

"Is There a Role for Benefit-Cost Analysis in Environmental, Health, and Safety Regulation?" _Science_, April 12, 1996. Reprinted with permission.

The growing impact of regulations on the economy has led both Congress and the Administration to search for new ways of reforming the regulatory process. Many of these initiatives call for greater reliance on the use of economic analysis in the development and evaluation of regulations. One specific approach being advocated is benefit-cost analysis, an economic tool for comparing the desirable and undesirable impacts of proposed policies.

For environmental, health, and safety regulation, benefits are typically defined in terms of the value of having a cleaner environment or a safer workplace. Ideally, costs should be measured in the same terms: the losses implied by the increased prices that result from the costs of meeting a regulatory objective. In practice, the costs tend to be measured on the basis of direct compliance costs, with secondary consideration given to indirect costs, such as the value of time spent waiting in a motor vehicle inspection line.

The direct costs of federal environmental, health, and safety regulation appear to be on the order of $200 billion annually, or about the size of all domestic nondefense discretionary spending (1). The benefits of the regulations are less certain, but evidence suggests that some but not all recent regulations would pass a benefit-cost test (2). Moreover, a reallocation of expenditures on environmental, health, and safety regulations has the potential to save significant numbers of lives while using fewer resources (3). The estimated cost per statistical life saved has varied across regulations by a factor of more than $10 million (4), ranging from an estimated cost of $200,000 per statistical life saved with the Environmental Protection Agency's (EPA's) 1979 trihalomethane drinking water standard to more than $6.3 trillion with EPA's 1990 hazardous waste listing for wood-preserving chemicals (3, 5). Thus, a reallocation of priorities among these same regulations could save many more lives at the given cost, or alternatively, save the same number of lives at a much lower cost (6).

Most economists would argue that economic efficiency, measured as the difference between benefits and costs, ought to be one of the fundamental criteria for evaluating proposed environmental, health, and safety regulations. Because society has limited resources to spend on regulation, benefit-cost analysis can help illuminate the trade-offs involved in making different kinds of social investments. In this regard, it seems almost irresponsible to not conduct such analyses, because they can inform decisions about how scarce resources can be put to the greatest social good. Benefit-cost analysis can also help answer the question of how much regulation is enough. From an efficiency standpoint, the answer to this question is simple: regulate until the incremental benefits from regulation are just offset by the incremental costs. In practice, however, the problem is much more difficult, in large part because of inherent problems in measuring marginal benefits and costs. In addition, concerns about fairness and process may be important noneconomic factors that merit consideration. Regulatory policies inevitably involve winners and losers, even when aggregate benefits exceed aggregate costs (7).

Over the years, policy-makers have sent mixed signals regarding the use of benefit-cost analysis in policy evaluation. Congress has passed several statutes to protect health, safety, and the environment that effectively preclude the consideration of benefits and costs in the development of certain regulations, even though other statutes actually require the use of benefit-cost analysis (*8*). Meanwhile, former presidents Carter, Reagan, and [George H. W.] Bush and President Clinton have all introduced formal processes for reviewing economic implications of major environmental, health, and safety regulations. Apparently the Executive Branch, charged with designing and implementing regulations, has seen a need to develop a yardstick against which the efficiency of regulatory proposals can be assessed. Benefit-cost analysis has been the yardstick of choice (*9*).

We suggest that benefit-cost analysis has a potentially important role to play in helping inform regulatory decision-making, although it should not be the sole basis for such decision-making. We offer the following eight principles on the appropriate use of benefit-cost analysis (*10*).

1. **Benefit-cost analysis is useful for comparing the favorable and unfavorable effects of policies.** Benefit-cost analysis can help decision-makers better understand the implications of decisions by identifying and, where appropriate, quantifying the favorable and unfavorable consequences of a proposed policy change, even when information on benefits and costs, is highly uncertain. In some cases, however, benefit-cost analysis cannot be used to conclude that the economic benefits of a decision will exceed or fall short of its costs, because there is simply too much uncertainty.

2. **Decision-makers should not be precluded from considering the economic costs and benefits of different policies in the development of regulations. Agencies should be allowed to use economic analysis to help set regulatory priorities.** Removing statutory prohibitions on the balancing of benefits and costs can help promote more efficient and effective regulation. Congress could further promote more effective use of resources by explicitly asking agencies to consider benefits and costs in formulating their regulatory priorities.

3. **Benefit-cost analysis should be required for all major regulatory decisions.** Although the precise definition of "major" requires judgment (*11*), this general requirement should be applied to all government agencies. The scale of a benefit-cost analysis should depend on both the stakes involved and the likelihood that the resulting information will affect the ultimate decision. For example, benefit-cost analyses of policies intended to retard or halt depletion of stratospheric ozone were worthwhile because of the large stakes involved and the potential for influencing public policy.

4. **Although agencies should be required to conduct benefit-cost analyses for major decisions and to explain why they have**

selected actions for which reliable evidence indicates that expected benefits are significantly less than expected costs, those agencies should not be bound by strict benefit-cost tests. Factors other than aggregate economic benefits and costs, such as equity within and across generations, may be important in some decisions.

5. **Benefits and costs of proposed policies should be quantified wherever possible. Best estimates should be presented along with a description of the uncertainties.** In most instances, it should be possible to describe the effects of proposed policy changes in quantitative terms; however, not all impacts can be quantified, let alone be given a monetary value. Therefore, care should be taken to assure that quantitative factors do not dominate important qualitative factors in decision-making. If an agency wishes to introduce a "margin of safety" into a decision, it should do so explicitly (*12*).

   Whenever possible, values used to quantify benefits and costs in monetary terms should be based on trade-offs that individuals would make, either directly or, as is often the case, indirectly in labor, housing, or other markets (*13*). Benefit-cost analysis is premised on the notion that the values to be assigned to program effects—favorable or unfavorable—should be those of the affected individuals, not the values held by economists, moral philosophers, environmentalists, or others.

6. **The more external review that regulatory analyses receive, the better they are likely to be.** Historically, the U.S. Office of Management and Budget has played a key role in reviewing selected major regulations, particularly those aimed at protecting the environment, health, and safety. Peer review of economic analyses should be used for regulations with potentially large economic impacts (*14*). Retrospective assessments of selected regulatory impact analyses should be carried out periodically.

7. **A core set of economic assumptions should be used in calculating benefits and costs. Key variables include the social discount rate, the value of reducing risks of premature death and accidents, and the values associated with other improvements in health.** It is important to be able to compare results across analyses, and a common set of economic assumptions increases the feasibility of such comparisons. In addition, a common set of appropriate economic assumptions can improve the quality of individual analyses. A single agency should establish a set of default values for typical benefits and costs and should develop a standard format for presenting results.

   Both economic efficiency and intergenerational equity require that benefits and costs experienced in future years be given less weight in decision-making than those experienced today. The rate at which future benefits and costs should be discounted to present values will generally not equal the rate of return on private investment. The discount rate should instead be based on how individuals trade off current for future consumption. Given uncertainties in identifying the correct discount rate, it is appropriate to use a range of rates. Ideally, the same range of discount rates should be used in all regulatory analyses.

8. **Although benefit-cost analysis should focus primarily on the overall relation between benefits and costs, a good analysis will also identify important distributional consequences.** Available data often permit reliable estimation of major policy impacts on important subgroups of the population (*15*). On the other hand, environmental, health, and safety regulations are neither effective nor efficient tolls for achieving redistributional goals.

Conclusion. Benefit-cost analysis can play an important role in legislative and regulatory policy debates on protecting and improving health, safety, and the natural environment. Although formal benefit-cost analysis should not be viewed as either necessary or sufficient for designing sensible public policy, it can provide an exceptionally useful framework for consistently organizing disparate information, and in this way, it can greatly improve the process and, hence, the outcome of policy analysis. If properly done, benefit-cost analysis can be of great help to agencies participating in the development of environmental, health, and safety regulations, and it can likewise be useful in evaluating agency decision-making and in shaping statutes.

REFERENCES AND NOTES

1. T. D. Hopkins, "Cost of Regulation: Filling in the Gaps" (report prepared for the Regulatory Information Service Center, Rochester, NY, 1992); Office of Management and Budget, *Budget of the United States Government, Fiscal Year 1996* (Government Printing Office, Washington, DC, 1995).
2. R. W. Hahn, in *Risks, Costs, and Lives Saved: Getting Better Results from Regulation*. R. W. Hahn, Ed. (Oxford Univ. Press, Oxford, and AEI Press, Washington, DC, [1996]).
3. J. F. Morrall, *Regulation 10*, 25 (November–December 1986).
4. These figures represent the incremental direct cost of part or all of proposed regulations relative to specified baselines. For examinations of issues associated with estimating the full costs of environmental protection, see (*16*).
5. Office of Management and Budget, *Regulatory Program of the United States Government: April 1, 1992–March 31, 1993* (Government Printing Office, Washington, DC, 1993).
6. If the goals of a program or the level of a particular standard have been specified, economic analysis can still play an important role in evaluating the costs of various approaches for achieving these goals. Too frequently, regulation has used a one-size-fits-all or command-and-control approach to achieve specified goals. Cost-effectiveness analysis, which identifies the minimum-cost means to achieve a given goal, can aid in designing more flexible approaches, such as using markets and performance standards that reward results.
7. L. Lave, in (*2*).

8. Several statutes have been interpreted to restrict the ability of regulators to consider benefits and costs. Examples include the Federal Food, Drug, and Cosmetic Act (Delaney Clause); health standards under the Occupational Safety and Health Act; safety regulations from the National Highway and Transportation Safety Agency; the Clean Air Act; the Clean Water Act; the Resource Conservation and Recovery Act; the Safe Drinking Water Act; and the Comprehensive Environmental Response, Compensation, and Liability Act. On the other hand, the Consumer Product Safety Act, the Toxic Substances Control Act, and the Federal Insecticide, Fungicide, and Rodenticide Act explicitly allow regulators to consider benefits and costs.

9. In particular cases, such as the phasing out of lead in gasoline and the banning of certain asbestos products, benefit-cost analysis has played an important role in decision-making (17).

10. For a more extended discussion, see (18).

11. In this context, "major" has traditionally been defined in terms of annual economic impacts on the cost side.

12. For example, potentially irreversible consequences are not outside the scope of benefit-cost analysis. The combination of irreversibilities and uncertainty can have significant effects on valuation.

13. For a conceptual overview of methods of estimating the benefits of environmental regulation and a brief survey of empirical estimates, see (19). For examinations of regulatory costs, see (16).

14. For a description of problems that arise when benefit-cost analysis is used in the absence of standardized peer review, see (20).

15. G. B. Christiansen and T. H. Tietenberg, in Handbook of Natural Resource and Energy Economics, A. V. Kneese and J. L. Sweeney, Eds. (North-Holland, Amsterdam, 1985), vol. 1, pp. 345–393.

16. R. Schmalensee, in Balancing Economic Growth and Environmental Goals, M. B. Kotowski, Ed. (American Council for Capital Formation, Center for Policy Research, Washington, DC, 1994), pp. 55–75; A. B. Jaffe, S. R. Peterson, P. R. Portney, R. N. Stavins, J. Econ. Lit. 33, 132 (1995).

17. A. Fraas, Law Contemp. Probl. 54, 113 (1991).

18. K. J. Arrow et al., Benefit-Cost Analysis in Environmental, Health, and Safety Regulation (AEI Press, Washington, DC, 1996).

19. M. L. Cropper and W. E. Oates, J. Econ. Lit. 30, 675 (1992); A. M. Freeman, The Measurement of Environmental and Resource Values (Resources for the Future, Washington, DC, 1993).

20. W. N. Grubb, D. Whittington, M. Humphries, in Environmental Policy Under Reagan's Executive Order: The Role of Benefit-Cost Analysis. V. K. Smith, Ed. (Univ. of North Carolina Press, Chapel Hill, 1984), pp. 121–164.

21. This work was sponsored by the American Enterprise Institute, the Annapolis Center, and Resources for the Future, with funding provided by the Annapolis Center. The manuscript benefited from comments from an editor and a referee, but the authors alone are responsible for the final product.

12   An Eye on the Future

Lawrence H. Goulder
Robert N. Stavins

Lawrence H. Goulder is Shuzo Nishihara Professor in Environmental and Resource Economics and Chair of the Economics Department, Kennedy-Grossman Fellow in Human Biology; and Senior Fellow at the Institute for Economic Policy Research at Stanford University; Research Associate at the National Bureau of Economic Research; and University Fellow at Resources for the Future. Robert N. Stavins is Albert Pratt Professor of Business and Government at Harvard Kennedy School, Research Associate at the National Bureau of Economic Research, and University Fellow at Resources for the Future.

Decisions made today usually have impacts both now and in the future. But in carrying out policy evaluations to help decision-makers, economic analysts typically discount future impacts. In the environmental realm, many of the future impacts are benefits from policy-induced improvements. Thus, in the environmental-policy context, future benefits (as well as costs) are often discounted.

This is controversial, partly because discounting can seem to give insufficient weight to future benefits and thus to the well-being of future generations. But does it actually shortchange the future? As economists, we have often encountered scepticism about discounting, particularly from non-economists. Some of this scepticism seems valid, yet some reflects misconceptions about the nature and purpose of discounting. By examining here how discounting affects the evaluation of environmental policies, we hope to clarify this concept.

It helps to begin by considering the use of discounting in private investments. Here, the rationale stems from the fact that capital is productive—money earns interest. Consider a company deciding whether to invest $1 million in the purchase of a copper mine, and suppose that the most profitable strategy involves extracting the available copper three years from now, yielding revenues (net of extraction costs) of $1,150,000. Would investing in this mine make sense? Assume that the company has the alternative of putting the $1 million in the bank at 5% annual interest. Then, on a purely financial basis, the company would do better with the bank, as after three years it will have $1,157,625 ($1,000,000×(1.05)³), compared with only $1,150,000 if it invests in the mine.

"Eye on the Future" by Lawrence H. Goulder and Robert N. Stavins. *Nature* 419. 2002. Pp. 673–674.

Future Returns

We compared these alternatives by compounding to the future the up-front cost of the project. It is mathematically equivalent to compare the options by discounting to the present the future revenues or benefits from the mine. Discounting offers a quick way to check whether the return on a project is greater or less than the interest rate by taking future revenues and translating them into present units, using the "alternative rate of return" (the bank's rate of interest in our example) as the discount rate. So the discounted revenue in this case is $1,150,000 divided by $(1.05)^3$, or $993,413—less than the cost of the investment. Thus, the project would not earn as much as the alternative of putting money in the bank. If the discounted revenue exceeded the cost of the project, then the project would yield a higher return than the bank, and the company would be better off investing in the mine.

This simple example suggests a general formula to determine whether an investment offers a return that is greater or less than the alternative of putting money in the bank. Suppose a project involves benefits (revenues) and costs over a time span from the present (time 0) to T years from now. Let B_t and C_t refer, respectively, to the benefit and cost t years from now, and let r represent the annual rate of return on a standard investment. The present value of the net benefit (PVNB) is given by

$$\text{PVNB} = \sum_{t=0}^{T} (B_t - C_t)/(1+r)^t$$

If this value is positive, the project will yield a return that is higher than the market interest rate.

Discounting translates future sums of money into equivalent current sums; it undoes the effects of compound interest. It is not aimed at accounting for inflation, as even if there were no inflation it would still be necessary to discount future revenues to account for the fact that a dollar today translates (through interest) into more dollars in the future.

Sums for Society

Can the same kind of thinking be applied to investments made by the public sector for the benefit of society? Consider the following hypothetical public-sector investment: a potential climate policy. Our purpose is to convey key issues in the starkest terms, so we will intentionally oversimplify some aspects of what follows. Suppose that a policy, if introduced today and maintained, would avoid significant damage to the environment and human welfare 100 years from now. The "return on investment" is the avoidance of future damage to the environment and to people's well-being. Suppose that this policy costs $4 billion to implement, and that this cost is borne in its entirety today. Suppose also that the beneficial impacts—avoided damages to the environment—will be worth $800 billion to people alive 100 years from now. Should the policy be implemented?

The answer will depend, of course, on the evaluation criteria used. Consider first the criterion of whether the winners have the potential to compensate the losers and still be no worse off. For this condition to be met, the benefit to the winners, after being translated to equivalent dollars, needs to be larger than the losses of the losers. After compensation from winners to losers, the policy would yield what economists call a "Pareto improvement": some individuals would be better off, and no individual would be worse off.

Are the benefits great enough that the winners could potentially compensate the losers and still be no worse off? Here, discounting is helpful. If, over the next 100 years, the average rate of interest on ordinary investments is 5%, a gain of $800 billion to people 100 years from now is equivalent to $6.08 billion today. (Equivalently, $6.08 billion today, compounded at an annual interest rate of 5%, will become $800 billion in 100 years). The project satisfies the principle of potential compensation if it costs the current generation less than $6.08 billion.

Because the up-front cost of $4 billion is indeed less than this figure, the benefit to future generations is more than enough to offset the cost to the current one. More generally, a positive PVNB means that the policy has the potential to yield a Pareto improvement. More realistic policies involve costs and benefits that occur at all points in time. For these policies, discounting serves the same purpose, as we convert costs and benefits from various periods into their equivalents at a given time (such as the present, for example).

Applying a discount rate does not mean giving less weight to the welfare of future generations. Rather, the process simply converts the (full) values of the impacts that occur at different points of time into common units. In our example, the full benefit to future generations is translated into a current monetary sum, which then allows us to compare this benefit with the full cost to the present generation.

Winners and Losers

Even if one accepts the idea of discounting as a mechanism to translate impacts into equivalent monetary units, one might be uneasy about PVNB analysis, which is based on the potential Pareto improvement (PPI) criterion—whether the winners from a given policy could compensate the losers and still be better off. If a policy's benefits exceed its costs, and compensation is introduced so that no one is worse off, then the attractiveness, of the policy seems clear. But if compensation is not actually made, the appeal seems considerably weaker.

In our climate-policy example, discounted benefits to future generations will exceed the loss to the current generation, so the potential exists for a Pareto improvement—the PPI criterion is met. But if future generations do not actually compensate the present one, is it still appropriate to enact the policy? Perhaps so, but many would argue that if actual compensation cannot be made, a positive PVNB has less merit as an evaluation criterion.

Suppose a proposed climate policy fails the PPI test—the future benefits are not large enough to offset current costs. Do current generations nevertheless have an obligation to undertake the policy? They might. The PPI criterion deserves to be given weight, but in almost all policy evaluations—especially when compensation is not actually carried out—it is important to consider other evaluation criteria, as there are bound to be some cases in which there are compelling reasons for adopting a policy even when the PPI criterion is not satisfied, or for rejecting a policy even when it is.

Should a lower discount rate be used to incorporate considerations of intergenerational equity more fully in the PVNB calculation? Suppose that, when the market interest rate is used for discounting, a policy that would benefit future generations fails to generate a positive PVNB. Using a lower discount rate would give greater weight to future benefits (and costs), possibly making the PVNB positive. Such adjustments are problematic, however: they blur the distinction between the PPI (efficiency) criterion and other legitimate policy-evaluation criteria, such as distributional (in this case, intergenerational) equity. In evaluating policies, it seems better to use the market interest rate so that the PVNB calculation provides a meaningful indication of whether the PPI criterion is satisfied, while at the same time judging intergenerational fairness by direct examination.

Even if one accepts the use of the PPI criterion and discounting in principle, estimates of PVNB are necessarily imprecise. There is uncertainty about the denominator—the discount rate. Theoretically, this should reflect the market interest rate but, of course, future market rates are impossible to predict. There is also considerable uncertainty about the elements in the numerator—the benefits and costs that current and future generations will experience from a policy that is introduced today. This uncertainty is derived both from scientific uncertainty about the biophysical impacts of policies and from uncertainty about future generations' tastes and preferences—how much they will value the biophysical impacts.

Much scepticism about the discounting and, more broadly, the use of benefit-cost analysis, is connected to these uncertainties. Consider the difficulties of ascertaining, for example, the benefits that future generations would enjoy from a regulation that protects certain endangered species. Some of the gain to future generations might come in the form of medical products (such as serums or vaccines) derived from the protected species, but such future impacts are impossible to predict. Moreover, benefits reflect the value that future generations will attach to the protected species—the enjoyment of observing them in the wild or just knowing of their existence. But how can we predict future generations' values? Economists and other social scientists try to infer them through surveys (such as the contingent valuation method) and by inferring preferences from individuals' behaviour. But these approaches are far from perfect, and at best they indicate only the values or tastes of people alive today.

The uncertainties are substantial and unavoidable. They do not invalidate the use of discounting or benefit-cost analysis, but they do oblige analysts to acknowledge them in their policy evaluations. It is crucial to evaluate policies using a range of values for discount rates and for future benefits and costs. We should have less confidence in a project for which the sign of the PVNB is highly sensitive to the discount rate or to small changes in projected future benefits and costs, compared with a project with a PVNB that is not very sensitive to these elements.

The Discounting Debate

The application of discounting to environmental-policy evaluation is controversial, partly because of misunderstanding outside the economics community of what discounting actually does, which is to translate the values of future impacts into equivalent values in today's monetary units. The PPI criterion, which provides the rationale for discounting and calculation of the PVNB, deserves weight in evaluating environmental policies, although it is also important to consider other criteria (such as distributional equity), especially when the potential harm to "losers" is substantial. Moreover, it is crucial to acknowledge any uncertainties about benefits, costs and interest rates. Some may argue that these complications invalidate PVNB calculations, but in our view such calculations—when carefully executed and thoughtfully interpreted—can provide useful information for making environmental-policy decisions.

FURTHER READING

Arrow, K. J. et al. in *Climate Change 1995: Economic and Social Dimensions of Climate Change* (eds. Bruce, J. P. et al.) 125–144 (Cambridge Univ. Press, 1996).
Arrow, K. J. et al. *Science* 272, 221–222 (1996).
Fullerton, D. & Stavins, R. *Nature* 395, 433–434 (1998).
Portney, P. R. & Weyant, J. P. *Discounting and Intergenerational Equity* (Resources for the Future, Washington DC, 1999).
Weitzman, M. L. *J. Environ. Econ. Management* 36, 201–208 (1998).

13 Uncertainty in Environmental Economics*

Robert S. Pindyck

Robert S. Pindyck is Bank of Tokyo-Mitsubishi Professor of Economics and Finance, Sloan School of Management at the Massachusetts Institute of Technology.

Introduction

An introductory course in environmental economics typically teaches students that the design and evaluation of a policy to deal with an environmental problem boils down to cost-benefit analysis. The instructor might proceed as follows. Left to their own, humans (i.e., producers and consumers) do bad things to the environment, such as polluting rivers and lakes, spewing sulfur dioxide into the air, and releasing ozone-depleting chlorofluorocarbons (CFCs). Government intervention—restrictions or taxes on emissions, banning CFCs—prevents some of this destructive behavior, and thereby reduces the amount of environmental damage. But it does so at a cost (e.g., electric power producers must install expensive scrubbers, and air conditioners must be made with a more expensive or less efficient refrigerant). So the policy problem boils down to deciding whether the benefit in terms of less environmental damage is at least as large as the cost of the policy. Of course, the benefits (and often some of the costs) usually occur in the future, and therefore must be expressed in present value terms. So, given a discount rate, it is all quite simple: calculate the present value of the benefits of a policy, subtract the present value of the costs, and see whether the difference (the net present value, or NPV) is positive. And if one is comparing several alternative policies, choose the one with the highest NPV.[1]

The student, however, may start to realize that the problem is in fact more complicated:

• First, we never really know what the benefits from reduced environmental damage will be, or even the amount of environmental damage

"Uncertainty in Environmental Economics" by Robert S. Pindyck. *Review of Environmental Economics and Policy* 1. 2007. Pp. 45–65. Reprinted with permission.

*This article was written for the *Review of Environmental Economics and Policy*. My thanks to Paul Joskow, Charles Kolstad, Suzanne Leonard, Rob Stavins, Martin Weitzman, and an anonymous referee for helpful comments and suggestions.

[1]For a good textbook discussion of cost-benefit analysis applied to environmental policy, see Tietenberg (2006).

that will be reduced by a particular policy. Worse yet, we *cannot know* with much precision what those benefits will be even if we work very hard to find out. Take the case of global warming. Modern meteorological science tells us that the relationships between greenhouse gas (GHG) concentrations, temperatures (regional or global), and climate patterns are inherently stochastic (i.e., partly random). And even if we knew what those changes in temperatures and climate patterns are likely to be, we know even less about their economic and social impact, in part because we do not know how humans will adapt (e.g., by growing different crops or living in different areas). And if you think global warming is an unfair example because of the very long time horizons involved, take the example of acid rain. Although virtually everyone would agree that the acidification of lakes and rivers—as well as the direct effects on human health—from unregulated nitrogen oxide (NO_x) and sulfur oxide (SO_x) emissions is not a good thing, there is very little agreement as to just how bad it is.

- Second, we usually do not know what the current and future costs of a policy will be. In the case of a carbon tax, for example, we do not know how consumers and producers will respond, especially over the long term. For example, to what extent will consumers use less fuel and buy more fuel-efficient cars and heating systems? And will producers develop and adopt more fuel-efficient technologies? Or in the case of NO_x and SO_x emissions, we know the current cost of scrubbers, but we do not know what their cost will be in the future and how installing them will affect electricity prices and demand.

- Third, what discount rate (or rates) should be used to calculate the present values? There is disagreement among economists regarding the "correct" rate that accounts properly for social time preferences and risk. And even if we settled on a conceptual notion of a "correct" rate, for example, society's marginal rate of return on capital, there would still be considerable uncertainty over the actual numbers for current and future discount rates. (The marginal return on capital is difficult to measure, and its future evolution is inherently uncertain.) Furthermore, as we will see, discount rate uncertainty is itself a determinant of the "correct" effective rate that should be used for policy evaluation.

Of course, the student might argue that there is nothing problematic about uncertainty over current and future benefits, costs, and discount rates. If the student had taken a basic course on finance, she would know that firms frequently make capital investment decisions in the face of similar uncertainties over the future cash flows from the investment, and must select discount rates subject to uncertainty over the correct risk premium. She might argue that firms typically base their investment decisions on the expected values of those cash flows, and environmental policy designs can likewise be based on expected values.

The student might also argue that most public policy decisions must be made in the face of uncertainty. Possible changes in our Social Security or Medicare programs must be evaluated in the context of a broad set of uncertainties over future changes in the demographic makeup of the country, changes in incomes, savings rates and costs of living for different demographic groups, and changes in disease prevalence and medical costs, to name a few. Likewise, it is notoriously difficult to predict the effects of changes in tax policy on income, employment, and government tax revenues. Again, what is special about environmental policy?

I would counter that for many environmental problems the uncertainties are greater and more crucial to policy design and evaluation. In particular, three important complications arise that are often crucial for environmental policy, but are usually much less important for most other private and public policy decisions.

1. The first complication is that environmental cost and benefit functions tend to be *highly nonlinear.* In other words, the damage likely to be caused by air or water pollution or by GHG emissions does not increase linearly with the level of pollution or emissions. Instead, the damage might be barely noticeable for low levels of pollution and then become severe or even catastrophic once some (uncertain) threshold is reached. Likewise, the cost of pollution abatement may be very low for low levels of abatement but then become extremely high for higher or total abatement. This means that one cannot simply use expected values; the expected value of the cost or benefit function will be very different from the function of the expected value.

   Furthermore, the precise shapes of the functions are unknown. This is particularly important if we believe that there is a threshold or "tipping point" at which the impact of a pollutant becomes extremely severe, but we do not know where that point is. For example, how large an increase in GHG concentrations—or in mean temperature— would it take for the consequences to be near-catastrophic? And at what point would over-fishing or habitat destruction lead to the collapse or extinction of a fish or animal population? The lack of answers to these questions suggests that environmental policy should be "precautionary" in the sense of favoring earlier and more intense intervention. But just how "precautionary" should the policy be? Should countries agree, for example, to roll back their GHG emissions to the 1930 levels? I do not mean to be facetious. Rather, I want to stress that uncertainty over the existence and/or position of a "tipping point" can be critical to policy timing and design.

2. The second complication is that environmental policies usually involve important *irreversibilities*, and those irreversibilities sometimes interact in a complicated way with uncertainty. There are two kinds of irreversibilities that are relevant for environmental policies, and they work in opposite directions.

First, policies aimed at reducing environmental degradation almost always impose sunk costs on society. These sunk costs can take the form of discrete investments (e.g., coal-burning utilities might be forced to install scrubbers), or they can take the form of expenditure flows (e.g., a price premium paid by a utility that has committed to burning low-sulfur coal). In either case, if future costs and benefits of the policy are uncertain, these sunk costs create an opportunity cost of adopting the policy, rather than waiting for more information about environmental impacts and their economic consequences. This implies that traditional cost-benefit analysis will be biased toward policy adoption.

Second, environmental damage is often partly or totally irreversible. For example, atmospheric accumulations of GHGs are long lasting; even if we were to drastically reduce GHG emissions, atmospheric concentration levels would take many years to fall. Likewise, the damage to ecosystems from higher global temperatures, acidified lakes and streams, or the clear-cutting of forests may be permanent. This means that adopting a policy now rather than waiting has a sunk benefit, that is a negative opportunity cost. This implies that traditional cost-benefit analysis will be biased against policy adoption.

How important are these irreversibilities and what are their implications for policy? The answers depend on the nature and extent of the uncertainties over costs and benefits, and how those uncertainties are likely to get resolved over time. The greater the current uncertainties, and the greater the rate at which they will be resolved, the greater will be the opportunity costs and benefits associated with policy adoption.

3. Third, unlike most capital investment projects and most other public policy problems, environmental policies often involve *very long time horizons*. While NPV calculations for firms' investments rarely go beyond twenty or twenty-five years, the costs and especially the benefits from an environmental policy can extend for a hundred years or more. The problems of global climate change and nuclear waste disposal are well-known examples with long time horizons, but there are also others. For some forests and the ecosystems they contain, clear-cutting and other interventions can have consequences that extend for many decades; likewise for chemical contaminations of land or water supplies. And the extinction of a species is, by definition, forever.

A long time horizon exacerbates the uncertainty over policy costs and benefits. It is hard enough to predict the impact of pollution or the costs of abatement five or ten years from now. Over a fifty-year horizon, the uncertainties are much greater.

A long time horizon also makes discount rate uncertainty much more important. Suppose we are not sure whether the "correct" discount rate for evaluating a policy is two percent or four percent. (Many rates have been used in policy analysis; the OMB has suggested

3 percent and 7 percent for government regulatory analyses.) With a 2 percent discount rate, a $100 benefit fifty years from now is worth about $37 today, but with a 4 percent rate it is worth only $14 today. If the $100 benefit accrues a hundred years from now, its present value is about $14 with the 2 percent rate, but only $2 with the 4 percent rate. Clearly, with discount rates of 4 percent or more, it would be very hard to justify almost any policy that imposes costs today but yields benefits only fifty or a hundred years in the future.

Uncertainty over future discount rates has an important implication for the choice of discount rate that we should use in practices—it makes that rate *lower* than any expected future discount rate. The expected present value of $100 received T years from now is the expected value of $100 / (1+R)^T$, where R is the (uncertain) discount rate (and $1 / (1+R)^T$ is called the *discount factor*). But the expected value of $100 / (1+R)^T$ is *greater than* $100 / (1+R_e)^T$, where R_e is the expected value of R. Furthermore, the longer the time horizon (i.e., the larger the T), the greater is the difference between the expected value of $100 / (1+R)^T$ and $100/(1+R_e)^T$. This means that the effective discount rate that should be used in a present value calculation is *less than* the expected (or average) discount rate.

The remainder of this article discusses the sources and nature of the uncertainties that tend to rise in environmental economics, and how the policy implications of those uncertainties are shaped by the nonlinear nature of benefit and cost functions, by the irreversibilities that are often present, and by long time horizons. The next section explains why benefits and costs are inherently uncertain, and discusses the nonlinear characteristics of environmental benefit and cost functions. I focus in particular on uncertainty over possible "tipping points," that is a threshold resulting in catastrophic environmental damage. The following two sections deal with irreversibilities and the opportunity costs and benefits they create and examine the implications of long time horizons and discount rate uncertainty. The article concludes by summarizing the lessons for policy design, and the areas where much more research is needed.

Despite its title, this article is not intended to be a comprehensive survey of the many aspects of uncertainty in environmental economics, or the vast amount of recent and ongoing research on the topic. This is, after all, an article, not a book, and I have chosen to focus on those areas where I have a research interest, and where I believe some elucidation would be worthwhile.

The Uncertain Nature of Benefits and Costs

I claimed in the previous section that, in comparison to many other public policy problems, environmental problems typically involve uncertainties that are greater and more crucial to policy design and evaluation. Why? As I have already explained, and will discuss in more detail later, environmental policy design must contend with highly nonlinear benefit and cost functions, irreversibilities, and long time horizons. But in addition, environmental problems usually involve three compounding levels of uncertainty—uncertainty over the underlying physical or ecological processes, uncertainty over the economic impacts of environmental change, and uncertainty over technological changes that might ameliorate those economic impacts and/or reduce the cost of limiting the environmental damage in the first place. (By "economic impacts," I mean to include health impacts, lost consumer and producer surplus from degraded air, water, fisheries, and other public goods, as well as lost output resulting directly from changes in climate, resource availability, etc.).

These compounding levels of uncertainty apply to both the benefit and cost sides of policy design and evaluation. For example, the future benefits of reducing GHG emissions depend first on the uncertain relationships between GHG emission levels, GHG concentrations, and resulting temperature distributions (as well as other climatic effects). But those benefits also depend on the uncertain economic impacts of changes in temperature distributions, as well as adaptation to climate changes (e.g., the use of new plant varieties or irrigation methods) that might reduce those economic consequences. The current and future costs of reducing anthropogenic climate change depend on the amount by which GHG emissions would need to be reduced, but that in turn depends on the uncertain relationships between GHG emission levels, concentrations, and climate effects, and the uncertain economic impacts of the climate effects. (It is the economic impacts, broadly construed, that is the policy concern in the first place.) And those costs also depend on unpredictable technological advances in energy conservation, cheaper nonpolluting energy sources, and methods of carbon sequestration.

These uncertainties and their effects on policy are magnified by the often nonlinear nature of benefit and cost functions. Uncertainties over benefits and costs are manifested not only in the form of parameter uncertainty (e.g., uncertainty over the elasticity of emissions with respect to a tax rate on emissions), but also in the form of uncertainty over the shapes of the (nonlinear) benefit and cost functions (e.g., uncertainty over how that elasticity falls as the tax rate is increased). As discussed below, the problem becomes especially severe when there are "tipping points" (i.e., when at some level of environmental damage the consequences become near-catastrophic), but we do not know what that point is.

To make the discussion over benefits and costs more concrete, I will focus on global warming, for which the policy implications of uncertainty have been studied extensively (but certainly not exhaustively). Later I will turn to the nature and implications of uncertainty for a very different environmental policy problem—the regulation of a fishery.

Uncertainty over Benefits

The point of environmental policy is to bring human exploitation of environmental assets closer to socially optimal levels, thereby creating social benefits. We might impose a carbon tax to reduce the future economic impact of global warming because we expect the benefits (a reduced economic impact from reduced warming) to outweigh the costs of the policy. But how soon should we impose a carbon tax, and how large should it be? Putting aside costs for the moment, the answers depend on the specific benefit functions, that is on how the benefits from the tax vary with its size. And the answers also depend on the nature and extent of uncertainty over those benefits.

The benefits over the next hundred years from reducing GHG emissions depend on (1) expected GHG emission levels absent abatement; (2) how rapidly atmospheric GHG concentrations will grow at the given emission levels; (3) how higher GHG concentrations will affect global temperatures; and (4) how large an economic impact we should expect from higher temperatures.[2] The uncertainties are substantial for each step in this chain. Combining the first three steps, if we take the Intergovernmental Panel on Climate Change (IPCC) report (2001) as a benchmark, the projected increase in mean temperature by the end of this century absent an abatement policy ranges from 1.4°C to 5.8°C. This large range should not be surprising. GHG emission levels are hard to predict because they depend on uncertain economic growth and energy intensities, and energy intensities in turn depend on unpredictable changes in energy prices and technologies.[3] And even if emission levels were known, changes in GHG concentrations and temperature depend on a complex physical system (with feedback loops that might be positive or negative) that is poorly understood.

The economic impact of global warming is even harder to predict. A temperature increase in the middle of the IPCC range—say, 2.5°C—would likely be beneficial for some regions of the world (e.g., Russia and Canada), harmful for other regions (e.g., India, Bangladesh, and Southeast Asia), and might have little or no aggregate net impact on other regions (e.g., the United States). Given the long time horizon involved, we would expect people to adapt to the changing temperatures and changing climates generally (e.g., by planting and developing different crops, and by moving from warm and low-lying areas to cooler and higher ones). Studies have shown that potential adaptation is clearly important (e.g., Mendelsohn, Nordhaus, and Shaw [1994]), but it is still difficult to predict to what extent people will adapt and at what cost.

---

[2]I am simplifying the problem for expositional purposes. For example, GHGs include methane as well as CO_2, and the mix matters. Likewise, it is not simply the change in mean temperature that matters, but also the geographic distribution of temperature changes. And, of course, economic impacts can be complex and vary substantially across geographical regions.

[3]Kelly and Kolstad (2001), for example, point out that future GHG emissions depend critically on population and productivity growth, which are uncertain. Lower growth would make global warming less of a problem. On the other hand, lower productivity growth implies a lower discount rate, which, as Pizer (1999) shows, increases the present value of the future benefits from abatement.

A number of studies have attempted to assess the sources and extent of uncertainty over the benefits from reducing GHG emissions. One of the earliest was Nordhaus (1994b), who obtained estimates of the percentage loss in gross world product from a survey of natural scientists and economists. Roughgarden and Schneider (1999) then used the Nordhaus survey results, along with other survey evidence, to back out confidence intervals for a damage function. Pizer (1999) developed an integrated climate-economy model and used it to both assess parameter uncertainty and study its policy implications. His model has nineteen parameters. Six parameters describe economic activity, and are estimated econometrically using historical data, yielding a joint distribution. Uncertainty over the remaining thirteen parameters (describing emissions growth, GHG retention and decay rates, control costs, and long-term population and productivity growth) is based on "subjective analysis." Other studies likewise assess uncertainty using subjective analysis and expert opinion; for an overview, see Heal and Kriström (2002) and Goulder and Pizer (2006).

One could argue that what really matters is the possibility and consequences of temperature increase at or above the upper end of the IPCC range. How likely is a 6°C temperature increase, and what impact would it have? One possible scenario (absent the probability estimates) was depicted by Gore (2006)—large parts of New York City would be under water. (Could New Yorkers adapt? Perhaps.) Clearly, the issue is whether, for some plausible increase in temperature, things could get really bad, to the point where adaptation could not compensate. In other words, is there a tipping point in the benefit function, and if so, where is it? Unfortunately, we do not know.

As of now, very little work has been done to assess the probabilities of catastrophic climate change, or to estimate the point (e.g., the change in mean temperature) at which a catastrophic outcome becomes likely. People have widely differing (and often strongly held) opinions about the likelihood and makings of a catastrophic outcome, but this is just symptomatic of how little we know. There have been studies of the policy implications of catastrophic outcomes, which I will discuss later, but those studies take the outcome and its characteristics as given.[4]

This problem, which I will call "tipping point uncertainty," is not unique to global warming. For example, studies of toxic waste disposal suggest that points could be reached that are catastrophic for land and water use in localized areas. But again, there is considerable uncertainty as to where those points are.

In summary, what do we know about uncertainty over the benefits of environmental policy? As I have tried to show in the case of global warming,

---

[4]For example, Pizer (2003) modifies the DICE model developed by Nordhaus (1994a), replacing the original quadratic relationship between economic damage and temperature change with a function that is much more convex (and varies the degree of convexity). But his focus is on whether price versus quantity is the more effective policy instrument. As he says, "Unfortunately, there is little empirical information concerning either the degree of steepness or the point where the steepness begins."

which has been studied quite extensively, we know very little. We know that there is a good deal of uncertainty, but we are hardly able to quantify it, especially when it comes to tipping points. We would come to a similar conclusion for environmental problems that have received less attention (e.g., acid rain and toxic waste). Given that uncertainty clearly matters (as I will explain in more detail below), we seem to have our work cut out for us.

Uncertainty over Costs

For some environmental problems, particularly those with more limited time horizons, policy costs are better understood and subject to less uncertainty than are the benefits. For example, we have years of experience with limits on SO_x and NO_x emissions from coal-burning power plants. We know the cost (and effectiveness) of scrubbers and of substituting low-sulfur coal, and we can also infer costs from prices of tradable emission allowances. And while the cost function for emission controls is nonlinear (the cost of an incremental reduction in emissions rises rapidly as the emission level becomes very low), there is no "tipping point" problem.

For other environmental problems, however, cost uncertainty can be quite severe. Once again, global warming is a good example. A carbon tax may be the preferred instrument for reducing carbon dioxide (CO_2) emissions, but how large a tax would it take to reduce those emissions in the United States by, say, 20 percent?[5] The answer depends on how responsive fossil fuel demand would be to tax-induced price changes, and this will vary from sector to sector (e.g., transportation versus residential heating). The responsiveness of fossil fuel demand in any sector to price changes in turn depends on the long-run price elasticity of energy demand in the sector, and the long-run elasticity of substitution between fossil and nonfossil energy sources. We have a reasonable understanding of energy demand elasticities, but our knowledge of the long-run elasticity of substitution between fossil and nonfossil energy sources is tenuous at best. The reason is that the ability to substitute from, say, coal to wind power for electricity production depends on the cost and availability of the latter (and that cost will partly depend on its environmental impact). Today, that substitutability is quite limited; what it would be twenty or fifty years from now largely depends on technological change, which is, again, hard to predict.

Another way to look at this is to ask whether (and how fast) the cost difference between fossil-based and alternative energy supplies will converge. Solar, wind, and biomass costs have fallen over the past twenty years, but the differences are still very large. There is reason to think that over the next fifty years, those differences may decline or even disappear as fossil fuel prices rise (because of depletion) and costs of alternative energy

---

[5]We would also need to know how large a tax it would take to reduce emissions in other countries, and for developing countries like China and India, the uncertainties are far greater than for the OECD. Then there is the cost of free riding. How large a tax would be needed for the OECD countries if the larger developing countries did not also agree to reduce emissions?

sources fall (because of technological change and economies of scale). Chakravorty, Roumasset, and Tse (1997) have developed an empirical model of this process that takes into account the depletion of the potentially discoverable reserves of fossil fuels. They project that the world will move towards wide-scale use of solar energy, so that "ninety percent of the world's coal will never be used," and global temperature will rise only about 1.5–2°C over the next century, making the cost of mitigation low indeed. However, since standard errors are missing, one cannot attach confidence intervals to these optimistic forecasts. Other forecasts suggest starkly different results, with fossil fuels remaining the predominant energy source, in the absence of major policy changes.

The basic problem is that, with long time horizons, policy costs depend on technological change, which is inherently difficult to predict. In fact, it is difficult to even characterize the uncertainty over technological change. Thus, for global warming and other long-horizon environmental problems, the cost side of policy is subject to uncertainty over the uncertainty.

Implications for Policy Design

Uncertainties over benefits and costs can affect policy design in at least three fundamental ways. First, they can affect the optimal choice of *policy instrument*, that is whether pollution is best controlled through a price-based instrument (e.g., an emissions tax) or a quantity-based instrument (e.g., an emissions quota). Second, they can affect the optimal *policy intensity*, for example, the optimal size of the tax or the optimal level of abatement. Third, they can affect the optimal *timing of policy implementation*, that is whether it is best to put an emissions tax in place now or wait several years (and thereby reduce some of the uncertainty).

Choice of Policy Instrument. The implications of uncertainty for the optimal choice of policy instrument has been studied extensively, beginning with the seminal article by Weitzman (1974), who showed that in the presence of cost uncertainty, whether a price-based instrument or a quantity-based instrument is best depends on the relative slopes of the marginal benefit function and marginal cost function. If the marginal benefit function is steeply sloped but the marginal cost function is relatively flat, a quantity-based instrument (e.g., an emissions quota) is preferable: an error in the amount of emissions can be quite costly, but not so for an error in the cost of the emissions reduction. The opposite would be the case if the marginal cost function is steeply sloped and the marginal benefit function is flat. Of course, in a world of certainty, either instrument will be equally effective. If there is substantial uncertainty and the slopes of the marginal benefit and cost functions differ considerably, the choice of instrument can be crucial.

Weitzman's original result has been extended in a number of directions. For example, Stavins (1996) showed that a positive correlation between marginal benefits and marginal costs pushes the optimal choice towards a quantity instrument. Often, however, there is no need to choose exclusively between a price and a quantity instrument. A number of studies have shown that, in the presence of uncertainty, "hybrid" policies that combine both instruments generally dominate the use of a single instrument (e.g., Roberts and Spence [1976], Weitzman [1978], and in the context of climate change policy, Pizer [2002] and Jacoby and Ellerman [2004]). The optimal design of a hybrid policy depends not only on the shapes of the benefit and cost functions, but also on the nature and extent of the uncertainties. Our lack of knowledge of the uncertainties (and often the shapes of the functions) means that policy design will be suboptimal at best; much more work is needed to get a better understanding of just how suboptimal.

Policy Intensity. Uncertainties over benefits and costs can also affect the optimal policy intensity, that is the size of an emissions tax or the amount of abatement that should be mandated. If there are no irreversibilities (which are discussed below), then in many cases uncertainty will lead to a *lower* policy intensity.

Suppose the policy instrument is an emissions quota, which we can think of as an amount of abatement between 0 and 100 percent. The greater the abatement, the greater will be the resulting benefit, and the greater will be the cost. However, in many cases we would expect the benefit function to be concave: increasing the abatement from zero to ten percent will have a large incremental benefit, whereas increasing the abatement from 90 to 100 percent is likely to have a much smaller incremental benefit. (This would be the case, for example, if a high level of pollution has serious health effects, so there is a substantial benefit even from reducing emissions by ten percent, whereas a low level of pollution has negligible health effects, so there is very little added benefit in going from a 90 percent to 100 percent emissions reduction.) Likewise, the cost of abatement is usually convex: going from no abatement to a ten percent reduction in emissions is likely to be much less costly than going from a 90 percent reduction to a 100 percent reduction. If the uncertainties over benefits and costs are proportional to the amount of abatement, it follows that the optimal amount of abatement (which equates expected benefits with expected costs) will be lower than in the absence of uncertainty.[6] On the other hand, if there is no cost uncertainty, and the uncertainty over benefits is proportional to the level of emissions (as opposed to the abatement level), the optimal abatement would be higher than in the absence of uncertainty.

One might ask whether the possibility that little or no abatement would lead to a catastrophic outcome might increase the optimal abatement level.

---

[6]Suppose the cost of abatement is $C(A) = c[(1+\varepsilon)A]^2$, where c is a constant, A is the percentage abatement, and ε is random and equal to either -1 or $+1$, each with probability $1/2$, so the expected value of ε is 0. Using this expected value, the cost of abatement is cA^2. However, the expected cost of abatement is $1/2c(0+4A^2) = 2cA^2$. The uncertainty over ε increases the expected cost of abatement, making the optimal amount of abatement smaller.

It is important not to confuse the *expected* benefit from abatement with the *variance* of that benefit. The possibility of a catastrophe will likely increase the expected benefit from any amount of abatement, which, other things being equal, implies a greater optimal abatement level. But if we are interested in the effect of uncertainty alone, we must keep the expected benefit fixed as we increase the variance of the benefit.

Policy Timing. Uncertainty can also affect the optimal timing of policy implementation—but only if there are sunk costs of implementing the policy, and/or the environmental damage from having no policy in place is at least partly irreversible. Depending on the particular situation, it may be optimal to defer the implementation of a policy until we learn more about benefits and costs, or to speed up the implementation to avoid irreversible damage. I will address this implication of uncertainty as I discuss irreversibilities.

Irreversibilities

It has been understood for many years that environmental damage can be irreversible, and that this can lead to a more "conservationist" policy than would be optimal otherwise. To my knowledge, the earliest economic studies to make this point are Arrow and Fisher (1974) and Henry (1974). But, thanks to Joni Mitchell, even noneconomists know that if we "pave paradise and put up a parking lot," paradise may be gone forever. And if the value of paradise to future generations is uncertain, the benefit from protecting it today should include an "option value," which pushes the cost-benefit calculation towards protection.[7] Thus, it might make sense to restrict commercial development in a wilderness area, even if *today* very few people care at all about that wilderness or have any desire to visit it. After all, if it becomes clear over the next few decades that very few people will *ever* care much about that wilderness, we will still have the option to pave it over. But if we exercise the option of paving over the wilderness today, we will lose the flexibility that the option gave us. If the social value of the wilderness rises sharply over time, the social loss from having exercised our option prematurely could be great.

---

[7]"Option value" and "quasi-option value" have been used in the environmental economics literature in different and sometimes confusing ways. Arrow and Fisher (1974) referred to the value of waiting when environmental damage is irreversible as "quasi-option value." The term "quasi-option value" has been adopted by other authors, who use "option value" to refer to the value of delay because of risk aversion. See, for example, Conrad (1980), Freeman (1984), and Hanemann (1989). I will use the term "option value" to refer to any opportunity costs or benefits resulting from irreversibilities and uncertainty. This is consistent with the real options literature, for example, Dixit and Pindyck (1994), and with modern textbook usage, for example, Tietenberg (2006).

There is a second kind of irreversibility, however, that works in the opposite direction: protecting paradise can impose sunk costs on society. If paradise is the wilderness area, restricting development and human access would imply a (permanently) forgone flow of wage and consumption benefits (e.g., from a large ski resort). If paradise is clean air and water, protecting it could imply discrete sunk cost investments in abatement equipment and/or in ongoing flow of sunk costs for more expensive production processes. In both cases, these costs are permanent—we cannot recapture them in the future should we decide that clean air and water are less important then we had originally thought. The point is that this kind of irreversibility would lead to policies that are *less* "conservationist" than they would be otherwise.

The implications of irreversibilities have been explored in a large and growing literature.[8] The important questions relate to the conditions under which irreversibilities matter for policy and the extent to which they matter.

When Do Irreversibilities Matter?

It is important to stress that *these irreversibilities only matter if there is uncertainty*. To understand why, suppose that today we know *precisely* how society will value a pristine wilderness area every year over the next two hundred years, and we also know what would be the annual flow of profits, wages, and consumer surplus over that same period from the conversion of that wilderness into a large commercial resort. Finally, suppose we know the correct discount rates that would apply over that two-hundred-year period. We could then calculate present values and do a simple cost-benefit comparison of the pristine wilderness and the commercial resort. If the comparison favored the resort, we could allow commercial development, knowing that nothing would change in the future that would cause regret and lead to a desire to "undo" the loss of the wilderness. Likewise, if the comparison favored the wilderness, we could prevent commercial development, knowing that nothing would change that would cause regret over the loss of surplus from a resort. Irreversibility would be irrelevant.

The environmental economics literature has also been concerned with the question of when irreversibility begins to matter in terms of affecting current decisions, even if there is uncertainty (e.g., Kolstad [1996b] and Ulph and Ulph [1997]). The short answer is that irreversibility will affect current decisions if it would constrain future behavior under plausible outcomes. Consider global warming, and suppose that benefits and costs are completely linear and there is no risk aversion. Then the relevant constraint is that while we could (at great cost) have zero emissions in the future, we

---

[8]Fisher and Hanemann (1990) and Gollier, Jullien, and Treich (2000) extend the results of Arrow and Fisher (1974) and Henry (1974), as do Scheinkman and Zariphopoulou (2001), but using a continuous-time model. Kolstad (1996b) and Ulph and Ulph (1997) address the conditions under which irreversibilities matter. Implications for the timing of policy adoption are studied in Pindyck (2000, 2002). These are some examples; for a survey, see Heal and Kriström (2002).

cannot have negative emissions.[9] If there is a nonnegligible chance that we might want to have negative emissions in the future, the irreversibility constraint might bind, and should lead to lower emissions today. However, irreversibility could matter even if there is no chance that we would want negative emissions. Suppose, for example, that the cost of reducing emissions rises more than proportionally with the amount of reduction. In that case, we would lower emissions today by an amount of, say, x, so that we could avoid having to lower them in the future by $2x$ at a cost that is more than twice as large.

The presence of uncertainty can affect policy even if there are no irreversibilities, but in a more limited way than if irreversibilities are present. As explained earlier, uncertainty can affect policy because of nonlinear cost or benefit functions, or discount rate uncertainty. For example, suppose the environmental impact of air pollution was completely reversible so that each year society could impose a quota on the pollutant concentration, at a cost proportional to the quota. Suppose also that each year the *actual* concentration equaled the quota plus a zero-mean proportional error. Finally, suppose (realistically) that the adverse health effect of pollution rises more than proportionally with the concentration, so that the benefit loss from a five-percent unexpected increase in the concentration above the mandated quota is greater than the benefit gain from a five-percent unexpected decrease. Compared to the case of no random errors, the optimal quota would then be lower.

But now suppose that the atmospheric accumulation of this pollutant is very long-lived, so that emissions could be reduced but not the accumulation of past emissions. Because each year's actual emissions are partly random, future concentrations would likewise be random, and the variance of those concentrations will grow with the time horizon. In this case, the policy implications of uncertainty are much greater. The reason is that the range of possible future concentrations is far greater, and should those concentrations turn out to be very large, we will be stuck with them—we cannot "undo" the emissions quotas of the past which *ex post* have turned out to be too high. As a result, the optimal policy would call for a smaller quota than would be the case if accumulations of the pollutant were very short-lived.

It is important to be clear about why irreversibility is the key. Returning to our example, the fact that accumulations of the pollutant are long-lived creates a possibility of severe regret, which is not offset by the possibility of very little pollution. A "bad-news principle" is at work here: if future concentrations of the pollutant turn out to be less than expected ("good news"), or if the economic and health impact of the pollution turns out to be less than expected (more "good news"), we could always relax the quota. But if future concentrations and/or the economic and health impact turn out to be greater than expected ("bad news"), there is little we can do to correct

---

[9]This is not precisely correct With near-zero emissions and a carbon sequestration program, effective emissions could be made negative. But as a practical matter, negative emissions are hard to imagine.

the situation. Even if we make our quota much more stringent, it will take many years for the concentrations to fall. It is this possibility of "bad news" that affects current policy, and the greater the uncertainty, the greater that possibility.[10]

In the example above, I focused on the irreversibility of environmental damage, but the optimal policy would also be affected by the irreversibility inherent in the sunk costs of abatement. To understand this, suppose that atmospheric accumulations of this pollutant were very short-lived, but for it to abate, companies would have to install long-lived equipment. Then, if we later learn that the economic and health impact of the pollutant is much less than expected, we will be stuck with the equipment—we cannot "undo" the emission quotas of the past which *ex post* have turned out to be too small. In effect, a "good news principle" would apply: it is the possibility that the harm from the pollutant will turn out to be less than expected ("good news") that would cause regret. As a result, the optimal policy would call for a *lower* mandated abatement than would be the case if the capital equipment used to abate were very short-lived.

How Do Irreversibilities Affect Policy?

We have seen that irreversibilities can interact with uncertainty to affect current policy, sometimes making it more and sometimes less "conservationist." But how important are irreversibilities, and what is their overall effect on policy? If we ignore them, would we be led seriously astray when designing policies to deal with, say, global warming or toxic waste disposal? And would taking them into account make us more or less "conservationist"?

As one would expect, the answers depend on the particular policy problem. Unfortunately, there are very few policy problems for which the effects of irreversibilities have been studied in any detail. Not surprisingly, the problem that has received the most attention in this context is global warming, a problem for which we have a good sense of the irreversibilities involved, and, as discussed earlier, the uncertainties are considerable. But even here we have no clear answers as to the importance of irreversibilities and the overall effect they have on policy. The reason is that to determine the optimal abatement policy for any realistic climate-economy model, one must solve (analytically or numerically) a complex stochastic dynamic programming problem. Thus, researchers have had to make strong simplifying assumptions, and different sets of simplifying assumptions have led to quite different results. This is best seen by summarizing the approaches and results of several of the studies published over the past decade.

One of the most common simplifying assumptions is to limit time to two periods, so the question becomes how much emissions should be reduced

---

[10]This point was introduced by Bernanke (1983), and is discussed in detail in Dixit and Pindyck (1994). The extension to environmental policy (and the "good news principle" discussed below) is in Pindyck (2002).

now versus in the future. This was the approach used by Kolstad (1996b) in one of the earliest studies of the opposing irreversibilities—long-lasting GHG concentrations versus long-lived abatement capital—involved with global warming. He examined how the prospect of more information about the economic impact of GHGs in the second period would affect sunk expenditures on abatement in the first period. Not surprisingly, both irreversibilities can matter, but the net effect on the first-period policy depends on the relative decay or depreciation rates of GHG concentrations and abatement capital, and on the expected benefit of abatement.

In another study, Kolstad (1996a) adapts the Nordhaus (1994a) DICE model by introducing uncertainty—which is reduced as learning occurs—over whether global warming will be a "big" or "little" problem. He calculates the optimal abatement policy over twenty ten-year periods, and finds that only the irreversibility associated with abatement capital matters, so the near-term policy should be less conservationist. The reason is that temperature change from GHG build-up is sufficiently slow so that emissions could always be slightly reduced in the future. Using a two-period model, also with functional forms and parameters taken from the DICE model, Fisher and Narain (2003) likewise find that the investment irreversibility effect is much larger than the GHG irreversibility effect, so that uncertainty over the impact of climate change leads to a reduction in first-period abatement.

In Pindyck (1998, 2000, 2002), I develop continuous-time models in which there is ongoing uncertainty over both the benefits from reduced GHG concentrations and the evolution of those concentrations, concentrations are long-lived, and there are sunk costs of policy adoption. I focus on the timing and size of a single permanent reduction in emissions (with the sunk cost of abatement a quadratic function of the size of the reduction). I find that, for a "reasonable" range of parameters, either kind of uncertainty leads to a higher threshold for policy adoption and a less stringent reduction in emissions. The reason is that policy adoption commits to a reduction in the entire trajectory of future emissions at a large sunk cost, while inaction over any short time interval only involves continued emissions over that interval.[11]

The studies cited above, however, do not consider possible catastrophic impacts of GHG accumulations. Those that do consider catastrophic impacts find that they can lead to earlier and more stringent abatement policies, but only if the likelihood of a catastrophe is strongly linked to the GHG concentration. This ambiguous result is shown clearly in Clarke and Reed (1994),

---

[11]Newell and Pizer (2003b) and Pizer (2005) also develop dynamic models to study optimal policies when GHG concentrations are long-lived (but abatement capital is not). They focus on the choice of policy instrument, and show that, despite the irreversibility, price-based policies (e.g., taxes) are strongly preferred to quantity-based policies (e.g., tradable emission allowances). Kelly and Kolstad (1999) examine the implications of learning (e.g., about parameters of the benefit function). They show that the ability to learn can imply larger emissions now, because a greater GHG concentration provides more information about parameter values. Gollier, Jullien, and Treich (2000) use a two-period model with irreversibility and learning to show how effects of uncertainty depend on the shape of the representative consumer's utility function.

who develop a simple but revealing theoretical model in which consumption causes the emission of an accumulating pollutant (so that reducing emissions requires consuming less), and the catastrophe is a random (Poisson) arrival in which welfare is reduced permanently to zero. The hazard rate could be a constant, or it could be an increasing function of the stock of pollutant. They show that if the hazard rate is a constant, we should accept *more* pollution now, because we will all be dead (or at least have zero welfare) at some point in the future that is unrelated to how much we pollute. On the other hand, if the hazard rate is sufficiently increasing with the stock of pollutant, we should pollute *less* now, because that will lengthen our expected remaining time on the planet. If the hazard rate increases only slowly with the stock of pollutant, the impact on the current level of pollution could go either way.

In related work, Tsur and Zemel (1996) derive optimal abatement policies using a model in which an undesirable (possibly catastrophic) event is triggered when the stock of pollutant reaches a critical level—but that critical level is unknown. This kind of event uncertainty leads to a strongly cautionary behavior: the optimal emissions policy keeps the stock of pollutant within a fixed interval. Finally, Pizer (2003) studies catastrophic outcomes by replacing the quadratic relationship between economic damage and temperature change in the Nordhaus (1994a) DICE model with a more convex function, and varies the degree of convexity. But there are no sunk costs of adoption, and his focus is on whether price versus quantity is the more effective policy instrument.

So, where does this leave us in terms of the policy implications for global warming? The irreversibilities are clear, and the uncertainties are great. Should we adopt a stringent emissions reduction policy now, despite its cost, or go slowly and wait to learn more about the rate of global warming and its likely economic impact? To my knowledge, research to date does not give us the answer. Those studies cited above that ignore possible catastrophic impacts provide some evidence that we should move slowly. Those studies that do consider the possibility of catastrophic impacts suggest a more stringent emissions policy, but the catastrophic impacts in these studies are more or less assumed, rather than inferred from empirical evidence. Once again, we have a good understanding of the economic theory, but a poor understanding of its implementation in practice.

Renewable Resource Management

So far, I have characterized environmental irreversibility in terms of a stock externality—emissions cause the build-up of a pollutant (e.g., GHGs), and it takes a long time for the stock of pollutant to dissipate. But environmental irreversibilities can arise in other ways, such as species extinction or permanent loss of a wilderness area. An interesting area of environmental economics in which irreversibilities and uncertainty arise and interact in ways quite different from, say, global warming, is the management of a renewable resource, such as a fishery.

The regulation of a fishery can be a complex problem even if the resource has a single owner. The problem becomes more complex (and of greater interest to environmental economists) when the resource is common property (i.e., there is open access). In both cases, the problem is how to regulate extraction (fishing) so as to maximize the economic value of the resource. There is a large amount of literature on this topic, but most of the early work assumed that the growth function for the resource stock is known and deterministic, so that the dynamics of the stock can be described by a simple differential equation in which the rate of change of the stock equals the growth function minus the extraction rate. Thus, left to its own, the stock of fish will increase to some natural carrying capacity, but over-fishing will lead to a stock below the optimal level, or even drive the stock permanently to zero.[12] The environmental irreversibility arises because it may take some time for the stock to recover from over-fishing, and it will never recover if it is driven to zero.

Uncertainty enters into the problem because the resource growth function is in fact stochastic, and sometimes highly stochastic. In other words, the rate of change of the resource stock is not a deterministic function of the current stock level minus the rate of extraction. Instead, the stock dynamics must be described by a stochastic differential equation. Furthermore, we often cannot observe the actual resource stock, but can only estimate its value subject to error. The optimal resource management problem then becomes a problem in stochastic dynamic programming, and its solution can be quite complicated.

How do stochastic fluctuations in resource growth affect the optimal regulated extraction rate? As with the global warming problem discussed above, there is no clear answer. Depending on the particular growth function and the characteristics of the extraction cost and resource demand functions, stochastic fluctuations could lead to a higher or lower regulated extraction rate. But there is an analogy with global warming. As a catastrophic outcome becomes a more distinct possibility, the optimal policy becomes more conservationist, that is an increase in the volatility of stochastic fluctuations in the resource stock leads to a reduction in the extraction rate. The reason is that as the stock becomes smaller there is a greater chance for a stochastic decline in the stock to (irreversibly) drive the resource to extinction.[13]

---

[12]For an excellent textbook treatment of renewable resource management and review of the early literature, see Clark (1990).

[13]I make no attempt to survey the literature on renewable resource management under uncertainty, but examples include Pindyck (1984) and, more recently, Singh, Weninger, and Doyle (2006). Weitzman (2002) shows that, even with severe stochastic fluctuations in the resource stock, landing fees dominate quotas as a policy instrument.

Discounting over Long Time Horizons

The role of uncertainty in policy design is especially important for environmental problems that involve long time horizons. First, it is difficult enough to predict the costs and benefits, over the next decade, of reducing air or water pollution. Over a fifty-year horizon, unpredictable technological change, changes in land and water use, and population shifts make the uncertainties over policy costs and benefits far greater. Second, discount rates are inherently uncertain, and a long time horizon makes that uncertainty extremely important. If the discount rate is "high" it will be difficult to justify almost any policy that imposes costs on society today but yields benefits only fifty to a hundred years from now, so the size of the discount rate can be the make or break factor in policy evaluation. Third, uncertainty over future discount rates impacts the choice of the discount rate that we should actually use in practices—it makes that rate *lower* than any expected future rate. I have already discussed the first and second of these three aspects of long-horizon uncertainty, so I will focus here on the third aspect—the fact that discount rate uncertainty reduces the effective discount rate that should be used for policy evaluation.[14]

As explained earlier, this is a straightforward implication of the fact that the discount factor is $1/(1+R)T$, so with R uncertain, the *expected* discount factor is greater than the discount factor calculated using the expected value of R. A simple example might help clarify this. Suppose we want to evaluate the expected present value of a $100 benefit to be received a hundred years from now, but we believe that the "correct" discount rate over the entire hundred years will turn out to be either zero or ten percent, each with probability 1/2. If we apply the expected value of the discount rate, that is five percent, the $100 future benefit will have a present value of less than $1. But in fact the expected present value of the benefit is much higher than $1. If the true discount rate turns out to be zero, the present value would be $100, but if the discount rate turns out to be ten percent, the present value would be close to zero. Thus the expected present value of the $100 benefit is $1/2(\$100)+1/2(\$0)=\$50$. Now we must ask what single discount rate when applied to a $100 benefit received one hundred years from now would yield a present value of $50. The answer is, about 0.7 percent. Thus even though the expected value of the discount rate is five percent, the uncertainty (it could in fact be either zero or ten percent) implies an *effective* discount rate of less than one percent.

Thus, discount rate uncertainty reduces the effective discount rate that should be used to calculate present values. Of course, the size of the reduc-

---

[14]By "effective discount rate," I mean the single rate that could be used in place of the range of possible future rates. The fact that the effective discount rate is reduced by uncertainty over future rates has been discussed in detail by Weitzman (1998) and Newell and Pizer (2003a). To my knowledge, this result was first formally demonstrated by Dybvig, Ingersoll, and Ross (1996), although in a different context.

tion depends on the extent of the uncertainty. In the example I just gave, if the expected value of the discount rate was five percent but the range for the actual rate was between four and six percent, the effective rate would be only slightly less than five percent (4.58 percent, to be precise). This just means that understanding the nature and extent of discount rate uncertainty is a crucial step in doing the actual discounting, and thereby evaluating a policy that is expected to yield long-term benefits.

One approach to evaluating discount rate uncertainty is to estimate the parameters of the stochastic process followed by an appropriate interest rate. To do this, one needs a very long historical time series for the interest rate, which is problematic. Newell and Pizer (2003a) used this "reduced-form" approach by estimating an autoregressive equation for the interest rate using some two hundred years of data on government bond rates. Putting the quality of the data aside, they found uncertainty to have a substantial effect on the discount rate for horizons of one hundred years or more. For example, depending on the particular estimated interest rate equation, they find that the value today of $100 to be received one hundred (two hundred) years from now is only $1.98 ($0.04) using a constant four percent discount rate, but is between $2.61 and $5.09 ($0.10 and $1.54) when uncertainty is taken into account.

Another approach is to note that the tails of the distribution for future interest rates are what really matter, and to try to estimate that part of the distribution. In the long run, changes in real interest rates will come from changes in real economic growth, so what we want is the distribution for future real growth rates and, in particular, the tails of that distribution. For example, the possibility of rare disasters (not necessarily environmental in origin) would yield "fat tails" for the distribution of future real interest rates, and thereby considerably reduce the current effective discount rate. Barro (2005) extrapolates from the wars and depressions experienced by different countries over the past century, and shows that possible disasters can make the effective discount rate close to zero.[15] However, the number of wars and depressions is limited, making it difficult to pinpoint the effective discount rate.[16]

What discount rate, then, should be used to evaluate costs and benefits over long time horizons? The studies mentioned above do not give us a clear

---

[15]Barro's objective is to explain well-known asset-pricing puzzles, one of which is a near-zero real risk-free interest rate. (Another is the large observed risk premium on the market, which seems only to be consistent with an unreasonably high index of risk aversion on the part of investors.) Weitzman (2006) takes another approach to the same set of puzzles. He shows that parameter uncertainty (in terms of both the mean and the variance) with respect to the structure of the economy will lead to fat tails, which likewise imply near-zero real risk-free interest rates, and explain the large observed market risk premium.

[16]In an engaging book, Posner (2004) examines a wide range of possible catastrophic events ranging from flu pandemics to nuclear war to an asteroid hitting the earth. Although his estimates of the probabilities are largely subjective, the number of possible events is large enough and the economic impacts severe enough to make one think that Barro's study is overly optimistic, and the left tail of the real growth rate distribution is quite fat indeed.

answer. However, they do show that the correct rate should decline over the horizon and that the rate for the distant future is probably well below two percent, which is lower than the rates often used for environmental cost-benefit analysis. Thus, costly environmental policies whose benefits will come a hundred years from now may indeed be justifiable.[17]

Conclusions

Uncertainty is central to environmental policy. For most environmental problems, we have very limited knowledge of the underlying physical or ecological processes, the economic impacts of environmental change, and the possible technological changes that might occur and ameliorate the economic impacts and/or reduce policy costs. If costs and benefits were linear and both environmental damage and policy costs were reversible, these uncertainties would not complicate matters much; policies could be based on expected values of costs and benefits at each point in the future. But as I have tried to show, cost and benefit functions tend to be highly non-linear, and both environmental damage and policy costs are often irreversible. As a result, it can be misleading to base policies on expected values of costs and benefits.

Then how should we base a policy? Unfortunately, there are no simple guidelines or rule of thumb for adapting environmental policies to uncertainty, at least not that I am aware of. As we have seen, the irreversibilities associated with environmental damage and policy costs work in opposite directions, so their net effect tends to be model-specific. Recent studies of global warming that ignore catastrophic impacts show a net effect that favors waiting over early action. This result can be turned around in models in which the health and economic impact rises at a sharply increasing rate with the amount of pollutant, for example, if at some level the pollutant could have a catastrophic impact. This would especially be the case if the point at which a catastrophic outcome would occur is unknown. However, even for well-studied problems like global warming, we know very little about the likelihood of catastrophic impacts. Furthermore, most other environmental problems (e.g., deforestation and toxic waste disposal) have received much less attention, so we know even less about the characteristics of the cost and benefit functions in these cases.

We have made greater progress in terms of understanding the discount rates that should be used to evaluate policies for which impacts occur over very long time horizons. The very fact that the marginal return on capital,

---

[17]Also, there is evidence that consumers' subjective discount rates are much higher for short-run than long-run outcomes. For an overview of behavioral approaches to discount rates, see Frederick, Loewenstein, and O'Donoghue (2002). Weitzman (2001) also provides evidence of higher short-run than long-run rates, and shows that economists differ widely in their opinions regarding discount rates. Related discussions are in Gollier (2001, 2002).

and thus real interest rates, are stochastic implies that the effective discount rate should be lower than some kind of average expected rate, and a rate close to zero is not implausible. But what matters is the tail of the distribution, that is the probabilities of one or more severe economic contractions over the next century, and given our (fortunately) limited experience with severe contractions, we are left with ranges of plausible discount rates. And while zero and 2 percent may both be plausible numbers, they can have very different implications when policy benefits occur a hundred years from now.

The good news is that environmental economists have plenty of work to do, and need not plan on early retirement; likewise for physical scientists working on environmental problems. It seems to me that at least one major focus of research should be on the causes and likelihood of severe or catastrophic outcomes, and this will likely involve collaboration between economists and physical scientists. And, while global warming is an important problem, more work is needed on other problems that may eventually turn out to be even more pressing, such as the depletion or degradation of water resources, acid rain, toxic (and nontoxic) waste disposal, and the loss of wilderness and wildlife.

REFERENCES

Arrow, K. J., and A. C. Fisher. 1974. Environmental preservation, uncertainty, and irreversibility. *Quarterly Journal of Economics* 88: 312–19.

Barro, R. J. 2005. Rare disasters and asset markets in the twentieth century. unpublished manuscript, December 2005.

Bernanke, B. S. 1983. Irreversibility, uncertainty, and cyclical investment. *Quarterly Journal of Economics* 98: 85–106.

Chakravorty, U., J. Roumasset, and K. Tse. 1997. Endogenous substitution among energy resources and global warming. *Journal of Political Economy* 105: 1201–34.

Clark, C. W. 1990. *Mathematical Bioeconomics*, 2nd ed. New York: John Wiley.

Clarke, H. R., and W. J. Reed. 1994. Consumption/pollution tradeoffs in an environment vulnerable to catastrophic collapse. *Journal of Economic Dynamics and Control* 18: 991–1010.

Conrad, J. 1980. Quasi-option value and the expected value of information. *Quarterly Journal of Economics* 92: 813–19.

Dixit, A. K., and R. S. Pindyck. 1994. *Investment under Uncertainty*. Princeton, NJ: Princeton University Press.

Dybvig, P. H., J. E. Ingersoll, Jr., and S. A. Ross. 1996. Long forward and zero-coupon rates can never fall. *Journal of Business* 69: 1–25.

Fisher, A. C, and W. M. Hanemann. 1990. Information and the dynamics of environmental protection: the concept of the critical period. *Scandinavian Journal of Economics* 92: 399–414.

Fisher, A. C., and U. Narain. 2003. Global warming, endogenous risk, and irreversibility. *Environmental and Resource Economics* 25: 395–416.

Frederick, S., G. Loewenstein, and T. O'Donoghue. 2002. Time discounting and time preference: A critical review. *Journal of Economic Literature* 40: 351–401.

Freeman, A. M. 1984. The quasi-option value of irreversible development. *Journal of Environmental Economics and Management* 11: 292–94.

Gollier, C. 2001. *The Economics of Risk and Time*. Cambridge, MA: MIT Press.

Gollier, C. 2002. Discounting an uncertain future. *Journal of Public Economics* 85: 149–66.

Gollier, C, B. Jullien, and N. Treich. 2000. Scientific progress and irreversibility: An economic interpretation of the "Precautionary Principle." *Journal of Public Economics* 75: 229–53.

Gore, A. 2006. *An Inconvenient Truth*. Emmaus, PA: Rodale Books.

Goulder, L. H., and W. A. Pizer. 2006. The economics of climate change. NBER Working Paper No. 11923, January 2006.

Hanemann, W. M. 1989. Information and the concept of option value. *Journal of Environmental Economics and Management* 16: 23–37.

Heal, G., and B. Kriström. 2002. Uncertainty and climate change. *Environmental and Resource Economics* 22: 3–39.

Henry, C. 1974. Investment decisions under uncertainty: the irreversibility effect. *American Economic Review* 64: 1006–12.

Intergovernmental Panel on Climate Change (IPCC). 2001. Climate change 2001: The scientific basis. Technical Report.

Jacoby, H. D., and A. D. Ellerman. 2004. The safety valve and climate policy. *Energy Policy* 32: 481–91.

Kolstad, C. D. 1996a. Learning and stock effects in environmental regulation: The case of greenhouse gas emissions. *Journal of Environmental Economics and Management* 31: 1–18.

———. 1996b. Fundamental irreversibilities in stock externalities. *Journal of Public Economics* 60: 221–33.

Kelly, D. I., and C. D. Kolstad. 1999. Bayesian learning, growth, and pollution. *Journal of Economic Dynamics and Control* 23: 491–518.

———. 2001. Malthus and climate change: betting on a stable population. *Journal of Environmental Economics and Management* 41: 135–61.

Mendelsohn, R., W. Nordhaus, and D. Shaw. 1994. Measuring the impact of global warming on agriculture. *American Economic Review* 84: 753–71.

Newell, R. G, and W. A. Pizer. 2003a. Discounting the distant future: How much do uncertain rates increase valuations? *Journal of Environmental Economics and Management* 46: 52–71.

———. 2003b. Regulating stock externalities under uncertainty. *Journal of Environmental Economics and Management* 46: 416–32.

Nordhaus, W. D. 1994a. *Managing the Global Commons*. Cambridge, MA: MIT Press.

———. Expert opinion on climate change. *American Scientist* 82: 45–51.

Pindyck, R. S. 1984. Uncertainty in the theory of renewable resource markets. *Review of Economic Studies* 51: 289–303.

———. 1998. Sunk costs and sunk benefits in environmental policy. MIT Center for Energy and Environmental Policy Research, Working Paper No. 95-003, December 1998.

———. 2000. Irreversibilities and the timing of environmental policy. *Resource and Energy Economics* 22: 233–59.

———. 2002. Optimal timing problems in environmental economics. *Journal of Economic Dynamics and Control* 26: 1677–97.

Pizer, W. A. 1999. Optimal choice of policy instrument and stringency under uncertainty: The case of climate change. *Resource and Energy Economics* 21: 255–87.

———. 2002. Combining price and quantity controls to mitigate global climate change. *Journal of Public Economics* 85: 409–34.

———. 2003. Climate change catastrophes. Resources for the Future Working Paper 03–31, May 2003.

———. 2005. Climate policy design under uncertainty. Resources for the Future Working Paper 05–44, October 2005.

Posner, R. A. 2004. *Catastrophe.* New York: Oxford University Press.

Roberts, M. J., and A. M. Spence. 1976. Effluent charges and licenses under uncertainty. *Journal of Public Economics* 5: 193–208.

Roughgarden, T., and S. H. Schneider. 1999. Climate change policy: Quantifying uncertainties for damages and optimal carbon taxes. *Energy Policy* 27: 415–29.

Scheinkman, J. A., and T. Zariphopoulou. 2001. Optimal environmental management in the presence of irreversibilities. *Journal of Economic Theory* 96: 180–207.

Singh, R., Q. Weninger, and M. Doyle. 2006. Fisheries management with stock growth uncertainty and costly capital adjustment. *Journal of Environmental Economics and Management* 52: 582–99.

Stavins, R. N. 1996. Correlated uncertainty and policy instrument choice. *Journal of Environmental Economics and Management* 30: 218–32.

Tietenberg, T. 2006. *Environmental and Natural Resource Economics*, 7th ed. Boston: Addison-Wesley.

Tsur, Y., and A. Zemel. 1996. Accounting for global warming risks: resource management under event uncertainty. *Journal of Economic Dynamics and Control* 20: 1289–1305.

Ulph, A., and D. Ulph. 1997. Global warming, irreversibility and learning. *Economic Journal* 107: 636–50.

Weitzman, M. L. 1974. Prices vs. Quantities. *Review of Economic Studies* 41: 477–91.

———. 1978. Optimal rewards for economic regulation. *American Economic Review* 68: 683–91.

———. 1998. Why the far-distant future should be discounted at its lowest possible rate. *Journal of Environmental Economics and Management* 36: 201–8.

———. 2001. Gamma discounting. *American Economic Review* 91: 260–71.

———. 2002. Landing Fees vs Harvest quotas with uncertain fish stocks. *Journal of Environmental Economics and Management* 43: 325–38.

———. 2006. Prior-sensitive expectations and asset-return puzzles, unpublished manuscript, November 2006.

14 Cost-Benefit Analysis: An Ethical Critique (with replies)*

Steven Kelman

Steven Kelman is Albert J. Weatherhead III and Richard W. Weatherhead Professor of Public Management at the Harvard Kennedy School.

At the broadest and vaguest level, cost-benefit analysis may be regarded simply as systematic thinking about decision-making. Who can oppose, economists sometimes ask, efforts to think in a systematic way about the consequences of different courses of action? The alternative, it would appear, is unexamined decision-making. But defining cost-benefit analysis so simply leaves it with few implications for actual regulatory decision-making. Presumably, therefore, those who urge regulators to make greater use of the technique have a more extensive prescription in mind. I assume here that their prescription includes the following views:

1. There exists a strong presumption that an act should not be undertaken unless its benefits outweigh its costs.

2. In order to determine whether benefits outweigh costs, it is desirable to attempt to express all benefits and costs in a common scale or denominator, so that they can be compared with each other, even when some benefits and costs are not traded on markets and hence have no established dollar values.

3. Getting decision-makers to make more use of cost-benefit techniques is important enough to warrant both the expense required to gather the data for improved cost-benefit estimation and the political efforts needed to give the activity higher priority compared to other activities, also valuable in and of themselves.

My focus is on cost-benefit analysis as applied to environmental, safety, and health regulation. In that context, I examine each of the above propositions from the perspective of formal ethical theory, that is, the study of what actions it is morally right to undertake. My conclusions are:

"Cost Benefit Analysis: An Ethical Critique" by Steven Kelman. *Regulation*, January 1981. Pp. 33–40. Reprinted with permission.

*"Defending Cost-Benefit Analysis: Replies to Steven Kelman." *Regulation*, March/April 1981. Pp 39–42. Reprinted with permission.

1. In areas of environmental, safety, and health regulation, there may be many instances where a certain decision might be right even though its benefits do not outweigh its costs.

2. There are good reasons to oppose efforts to put dollar values on non-marketed benefits and costs.

3. Given the relative frequency of occasions in the areas of environmental, safety, and health regulation where one would not wish to use a benefits-outweigh-costs test as a decision rule, and given the reasons to oppose the monetizing of non-marketed benefits or costs that is a prerequisite for cost-benefit analysis, it is not justifiable to devote major resources to the generation of data for cost-benefit calculations or to undertake efforts to "spread the gospel" of cost-benefit analysis further.

I

How do we decide whether a given action is morally right or wrong and hence, assuming the desire to act morally, why it should be undertaken or refrained from? Like the Molière character who spoke prose without knowing it, economists who advocate use of cost-benefit analysis for public decisions are philosophers without knowing it: the answer given by cost-benefit analysis, that actions should be undertaken so as to maximize net benefits, represents one of the classic answers given by moral philosophers—that given by utilitarians. To determine whether an action is right or wrong, utilitarians tote up all the positive consequences of the action in terms of human satisfaction. The act that maximizes attainment of satisfaction under the circumstances is the right act. That the economists' answer is also the answer of one school of philosophers should not be surprising. Early on, economics was a branch of moral philosophy, and only later did it become an independent discipline.

Before proceeding further, the subtlety of the utilitarian position should be noted. The positive and negative consequences of an act for satisfaction may go beyond the act's immediate consequences. A facile version of utilitarianism would give moral sanction to a lie, for instance, if the satisfaction of an individual attained by telling the lie was greater than the suffering imposed on the lie's victim. Few utilitarians would agree. Most of them would add to the list of negative consequences the effect of the one lie on the tendency of the person who lies to tell other lies, even in instances when the lying produced less satisfaction for him than dissatisfaction for others. They would also add the negative effects of the lie on the general level of social regard for truth-telling, which has many consequences for future utility. A further consequence may be added as well. It is sometimes said that we should include in a utilitarian calculation the feeling of dissatisfaction produced in the liar (and perhaps in others) because, by telling a lie, one has "done the wrong thing." Correspondingly, in this view, among the positive consequences to be weighed into a utilitarian calculation of truth-telling is satisfaction arising from "doing the right thing." This view rests on an error, however, because it *assumes* what it is the purpose of the calculation to *determine*—that telling the truth in the instance in question is indeed the right thing to do. Economists are likely to object to this point, arguing that no feeling ought "arbitrarily" to be excluded from a complete cost-benefit calculation, including a feeling of dissatisfaction at doing the wrong thing. Indeed, the economists' cost-benefit calculations would, at least ideally, include such feelings. Note the difference between the economist's and the philosopher's cost-benefit calculations, however. The economist may choose to include feelings of dissatisfaction in his cost-benefit calculation, but what happens if somebody asks the economist, "Why is it right to evaluate an action on the basis of a cost-benefit test?" If an answer is to be given to that question (which does not normally preoccupy economists but which does concern both philosophers and the rest of us who need to be persuaded that cost-benefit analysis is right), then the circularity problem reemerges. And there is also another difficulty with counting feelings of dissatisfaction at doing the wrong thing in a cost-benefit calculation. It leads to the perverse result that under certain circumstances a lie, for example, might be morally right if the individual contemplating the lie felt no compunction about lying and morally wrong only if the individual felt such a compunction!

This error is revealing, however, because it begins to suggest a critique of utilitarianism. Utilitarianism is an important and powerful moral doctrine. But it is probably a minority position among contemporary moral philosophers. It is amazing that economists can proceed in unanimous endorsement of cost-benefit analysis as if unaware that their conceptual framework is highly controversial in the discipline from which it arose—moral philosophy.

Let us explore the critique of utilitarianism. The logical error discussed before appears to suggest that we have a notion of certain things being right or wrong that *predates* our calculation of costs and benefits. Imagine the case of an old man in Nazi Germany who is hostile to the regime. He is wondering whether he should speak out against Hitler. If he speaks out, he will lose his pension. And his action will have done nothing to increase the chances that the Nazi regime will be overthrown: he is regarded as somewhat eccentric by those around him, and nobody has ever consulted his views on political questions. Recall that one cannot add to the benefits of speaking out any satisfaction from doing "the right thing," because the purpose of the exercise is to determine whether speaking out *is* the right thing. How would the utilitarian calculation go? The benefits of the old man's speaking out would, as the example is presented, be nil, while the costs would be his loss of his pension. So the costs of the action would outweigh the benefits. By the utilitarians' cost-benefit calculation, it would be *morally wrong* for the man to speak out.

Another example: two very close friends are on an Arctic expedition together. One of them falls very sick in the snow and bitter cold, and sinks quickly before anything can be done to help him. As he is dying, he asks his friend one thing, "Please, make me a solemn promise that ten years from today you will come back to this spot and place a lighted candle here to remember me." The friend solemnly promises to do so, but does not tell a soul. Now, ten years later, the friend must decide whether to keep his promise. It would be inconvenient for him to make the long trip. Since he told nobody, his failure to go will not affect the general social faith in promise-keeping. And the incident was unique enough so that it is safe to assume that his failure to go will not encourage him to break other promises. Again, the costs of the act outweigh the benefits. A utilitarian would need to believe that it would be *morally wrong* to travel to the Arctic to light the candle.

A third example: a wave of thefts has hit a city and the police are having trouble finding any of the thieves. But they believe, correctly, that punishing someone for theft will have some deterrent effect and will decrease the number of crimes. Unable to arrest any actual perpetrator, the police chief and the prosecutor arrest a person whom they know to be innocent and, in cahoots with each other, fabricate a convincing case against him. The police chief and the prosecutor are about to retire, so the act has no effect on any future actions of theirs. The fabrication is perfectly executed, so nobody finds out about it. Is the *only* question involved in judging the act of framing the innocent man that of whether his suffering from conviction and imprisonment will be greater than the suffering avoided among potential crime victims when some crimes are deterred? A utilitarian would need to believe that it is *morally right to punish the innocent man* as long as it can be demonstrated that the suffering prevented outweighs his suffering.

And a final example: imagine two worlds, each containing the same sum total of happiness. In the first world, this total of happiness came about from a series of acts that included a number of lies and injustices (that is, the total consisted of the immediate gross sum of happiness created by certain acts, minus any long-term unhappiness occasioned by the lies and injustices). In the second world the same amount of happiness was produced by a different series of acts, none of which involved lies or injustices. Do we have any reason to prefer the one world to the other? A utilitarian would need to believe that the choice between the two worlds is a *matter of indifference.*

To those who believe that it would not be morally wrong for the old man to speak out in Nazi Germany or for the explorer to return to the Arctic to light a candle for his deceased friend, that it would not be morally right to convict the innocent man, or that the choice between the two worlds is not a matter of indifference—to those of us who believe these things, utilitarianism is insufficient as a moral view. We believe that some acts whose costs are greater than their benefits may be morally right and, contrariwise, some acts whose benefits are greater than their costs may be morally wrong.

This does not mean that the question whether benefits are greater than costs is morally irrelevant. Few would claim such. Indeed, for a broad range of individual and social decisions, whether an act's benefits outweigh its costs is a sufficient question to ask. But not for all such decisions. These may involve situations where certain duties—duties not to lie, break promises, or kill, for example—make an act wrong, even if it would result in an excess of benefits over costs. Or they may involve instances where people's rights are at stake. We would not permit rape even if it could be demonstrated that the rapist derived enormous happiness from his act, while the victim experienced only minor displeasure. We do not do cost-benefit analyses of freedom of speech or trial by jury. The Bill of Rights was not RARGed. As the United Steelworkers noted in a comment on the Occupational Safety and Health Administration's economic analysis of its proposed rule to reduce worker exposure to carcinogenic coke-oven emissions, the Emancipation Proclamation was not subjected to an inflationary impact statement. The notion of human rights involves the idea that people may make certain claims to be allowed to act in certain ways or to be treated in certain ways, even if the sum of benefits achieved thereby does not outweigh the sum of costs. It is this view that underlies the statement that "workers have a right to a safe and healthy work place" and the expectation that OSHA's decisions will reflect that judgment.

In the most convincing versions of nonutilitarian ethics, various duties or rights are not absolute. But each has a *prima facie* moral validity so that, if duties or rights do not conflict, the morally right act is the act that reflects a duty or respects a right. If duties or rights do conflict, a moral judgment, based on conscious deliberation, must be made. Since one of the duties nonutilitarian philosophers enumerate is the duty of beneficence (the duty to maximize happiness), which in effect incorporates all of utilitarianism by reference, a non-utilitarian who is faced with conflicts between the results of cost-benefit analysis and nonutility-based considerations will need to undertake such deliberation. But in that deliberation, additional elements, which cannot be reduced to a question of whether benefits outweigh costs, have been introduced. Indeed, depending on the moral importance we attach to the right or duty involved, cost-benefit questions may, within wide ranges, become irrelevant to the outcome of the moral judgment.

In addition to questions involving duties and rights, there is a final sort of question where, in my view, the issue of whether benefits outweigh costs should not govern moral judgment. I noted earlier that, for the common run of questions facing individuals and societies, it is possible to begin and end our judgment simply by finding out if the benefits of the contemplated act outweigh the costs. This very fact means that one way to show the great importance, or value, attached to an area is to say that decisions involving the area should not be determined by cost-benefit calculations. This applies, I think, to the view many environmentalists have of decisions involving our natural environment. When officials are deciding what level of pollution will harm certain vulnerable people—such as asthmatics or the elderly—while not harming others, one issue involved may be the right of those people not to be sacrificed on the altar of somewhat higher living standards for the rest of us. But more broadly than this, many environmentalists fear that subjecting decisions about clean air or water to the cost-benefit tests that determine the general run of decisions removes those matters from the realm of specially valued things.

II

In order for cost-benefit calculations to be performed the way they are supposed to be, all costs and benefits must be expressed in a common measure, typically dollars, including things not normally bought and sold on markets, and to which dollar prices are therefore not attached. The most dramatic example of such things is human life itself; but many of the other benefits achieved or preserved by environmental policy—such as peace and quiet, fresh-smelling air, swimmable rivers, spectacular vistas—are not traded on markets either.

Economists who do cost-benefit analysis regard the quest after dollar values for nonmarket things as a difficult challenge—but one to be met with relish. They have tried to develop methods for imputing a person's "willingness to pay" for such things, their approach generally involving a search for bundled goods that *are* traded on markets and that vary as to whether they include a feature that is, *by itself,* not marketed. Thus, fresh air is not marketed, but houses in different parts of Los Angeles that are similar except for the degree of smog are. Peace and quiet is not marketed, but similar houses inside and outside airport flight paths are. The risk of death is not marketed, but similar jobs that have different levels of risk are. Economists have produced many often ingenious efforts to impute dollar prices to nonmarketed things by observing the premiums accorded homes in clean air areas over similar homes in dirty areas or the premiums paid for risky jobs over similar nonrisky jobs.

These ingenious efforts are subject to criticism on a number of technical grounds. It may be difficult to control for all the dimensions of quality other than the presence or absence of the non-marketed thing. More important, in a world where people have different preferences and are subject to different constraints as they make their choices, the dollar value imputed to the non-market things that most people would wish to avoid will be lower than otherwise, because people with unusually weak aversion to those things or usually strong constraints on their choices will be willing to take the bundled good in question at less of a discount than the average person. Thus, to use the property value discount of homes near airports as a measure of people's willingness to pay for quiet means to accept as a proxy for the rest of us the behavior of those least sensitive to noise, of airport employees (who value the convenience of a near-airport location) or of others who are susceptible to an agent's assurances that "it's not so bad." To use the wage premiums accorded hazardous work as a measure of the value of life means to accept as proxies for the rest of us the choices of people who do not have many choices or who are exceptional risk-seekers.

A second problem is that the attempts of economists to measure people's willingness to pay for non-marketed things assume that there is no difference between the price a person would require for *giving up* something to which he has a preexisting right and the price he would pay to *gain* something to which he enjoys no right. Thus, the analysis assumes no difference between how much a homeowner would need to be paid in order to give up an unobstructed mountain view that he already enjoys and how much he would be willing to pay to get an obstruction moved once it is already in place. Available evidence suggests that most people would insist on being paid far more to assent to a worsening of their situation than they would be willing to pay to improve their situation. The difference arises from such factors as being accustomed to and psychologically attached to that which one believes one enjoys by right. But this creates a circularity problem for any attempt to use cost-benefit analysis to determine *whether* to assign to, say, the homeowner the right to an unobstructed mountain view. For willingness to pay will be different depending on whether the right is assigned initially or not. The value judgment about whether to assign the right must thus be made first. (In order to set an upper bound on the value of the benefit, one might hypothetically assign the right to the person and determine how much he would need to be paid to give it up.)

Third, the efforts of economists to impute willingness to pay invariably involve bundled goods exchanged in *private* transactions. Those who use figures garnered from such analysis to provide guidance for *public* decisions assume no difference between how people value certain things in private individual transactions and how they would wish those same things to be valued in public collective decisions. In making such assumptions, economists insidiously slip into their analysis an important and controversial value judgment, growing naturally out of the highly individualistic microeconomic tradition—namely, the view that there should be no difference between private behavior and the behavior we display in public social life. An alternative view—one that enjoys, I would suggest, wide resonance among citizens—would be that public, social decisions provide an opportunity to give certain things a higher valuation than we choose, for one reason or another, to given them in our private activities.

Thus, opponents of stricter regulation of health risks often argue that we show by our daily risk-taking behavior that we do not value life infinitely, and therefore our public decisions should not reflect the high value of life that proponents of strict regulation propose. However, an alternative view is equally plausible. Precisely because we fail, for whatever reasons, to give life-saving the value in everyday personal decisions that we in some general terms believe we should give it, we may wish our social decisions to provide us the occasion to display the reverence for life that we espouse but do not always show. By this view, people do not have fixed unambiguous "preferences" to which they give expression through private activities and which therefore should be given expression in public decisions. Rather, they may have what they themselves regard as "higher" and "lower" preferences. The latter may come to the fore in private decisions, but people may want the former to come to the fore in public decisions. They may sometimes display racial prejudice, but support antidiscrimination laws. They may buy a certain product after seeing a seductive ad, but be skeptical enough of advertising to want the government to keep a close eye on it. In such cases, the use of private behavior to impute the values that should be entered for public decisions, as is done by using willingness to pay in private transactions, commits grievous offense against a view of the behavior of the citizen that is deeply engrained in our democratic tradition. It is a view that denudes politics of any independent role in society, reducing it to a mechanistic, mimicking recalculation based on private behavior.

Finally, one may oppose the effort to place prices on a non-market thing and hence in effect incorporate it into the market system out of a fear that the very act of doing so will reduce the thing's perceived value. To place a price on the benefit may, in other words, reduce the value of that benefit. Cost-benefit analysis thus maybe like the thermometer that, when placed in a liquid to be measured, itself changes the liquid's temperature.

Examples of the perceived cheapening of a thing's value by the very act of buying and selling it abound in everyday life and language. The disgust that accompanies the idea of buying and selling human beings is based on the sense that this would dramatically diminish human worth. Epithets such as "he prostituted himself," applied as linguistic analogies to people who have sold something, reflect the view that certain things should not be sold because doing so diminishes their value. Praise that is bought is worth little, even to the person buying it. A true anecdote is told of an economist who retired to another university community and complained that he was having difficulty making friends. The laconic response of a critical colleague—"If you want a friend why don't you buy yourself one"—illustrates in a pithy way the intuition that, for some things, the very act of placing a price on them reduces their perceived value.

The first reason that pricing something decreases its perceived value is that, in many circumstances, non-market exchange is associated with the production of certain values not associated with market exchange. These may include spontaneity and various other feelings that come from personal relationships. If a good becomes less associated with the production of positively valued feelings because of market exchange, the perceived value of the good declines to the extent that those feelings are valued. This can be seen clearly in instances where a thing may be transferred both by market and by non-market mechanisms. The willingness to pay for sex bought from a prostitute is less than the perceived value of the sex consummating love. (Imagine the reaction if a practitioner of cost-benefit analysis computed the benefits of sex based on the price of prostitute services.)

Furthermore, if one values in a general sense the existence of a non-market sector because of its connection with the production of certain valued feelings, then one ascribes added value to any non-marketed good simply as a repository of values represented by the non-market sector one wishes to preserve. This seems certainly to be the case for things in nature, such as pristine streams or undisturbed forests: for many people who value them, part of their value comes from their position as repositories of values the non-market sector represents.

The second way in which placing a market price on a thing decreases its perceived value is by removing the possibility of proclaiming that the thing is "not for sale," since things on the market by definition are for sale. The very statement that something is not for sale affirms, enhances, and protects a thing's value in a number of ways. To begin with, the statement is a way of showing that a thing is valued for its own sake, whereas selling a thing for money demonstrates that it was valued only instrumentally. Furthermore, to say that something cannot be transferred in that way places it in the exceptional category—which requires the person interested in obtaining that thing to be able to offer something else that is exceptional, rather than allowing him the easier alternative of obtaining the thing for money that could have been obtained in an affinity of ways. This enhances its value. If I am willing to say "You're a really kind person" to whoever pays me to do so, my praise loses the value that attaches to it from being exchangeable only for an act of kindness.

In addition, if we have already decided we value something highly, one way of stamping it with a cachet affirming its high value is to announce that it is "not for sale." Such an announcement does more, however, than just reflect a preexisting high valuation. It signals a thing's distinctive value to others and helps us persuade them to value the thing more highly than they otherwise might. It also expresses our resolution to safeguard that distinctive value. To state that something is not for sale is thus also a source of value for that thing, since if a thing's value is easy to affirm or protect, it will be worth more than an otherwise similar thing without such attributes.

If we proclaim that something is not for sale, we make a once-and-for-all judgment of its special value. When something is priced, the issue of its perceived value is constantly coming up, as a standing invitation to reconsider that original judgment. Were people constantly faced with questions such as "how much money could get you to give up your freedom of speech?" or "how much would you sell your vote for if you could?", the perceived value of the freedom to speak or the right to vote would soon become devastated as, in moments of weakness, people started saying "maybe it's not worth *so much* after all." Better not to be faced with the constant questioning in the first place. Something similar did in fact occur when the slogan "better red than dead" was launched by some pacifists during the Cold War. Critics pointed out that the very posing of this stark choice—in effect, "would you *really* be willing to give up your life in exchange for not living under communism?"—reduced the value people attached to freedom and thus diminished resistance to attacks on freedom.

Finally, of some things valued very highly it is stated that they are "priceless" or that they have "infinite value." Such expressions are reserved for a subset of things not for sale, such as life or health. Economists tend to scoff at talk of pricelessness. For them, saying that something is priceless is to state a willingness to trade off an infinite quantity of all other goods for one unit of the priceless good, a situation that empirically appears highly unlikely. For most people, however, the word priceless is pregnant with meaning. Its value-affirming and value-protecting functions cannot be bestowed on expressions that merely denote a determinate, albeit high, valuation. John Kennedy in his inaugural address proclaimed that the nation was ready to "pay any price [and] bear any burden . . . to assure the survival and the success of liberty." Had he said instead that we were willing to "pay a high price" or "bear a large burden" for liberty, the statement would have rung hollow.

III

An objection that advocates of cost-benefit analysis might well make to the preceding argument should be considered. I noted earlier that, in cases where various non-utility-based duties or rights conflict with the maximization of utility, it is necessary to make a deliberative judgment about what act is finally right. I also argued earlier that the search for commensurability might not always be a desirable one, that the attempt to go beyond expressing benefits in terms of (say) lives saved and costs in terms of dollars is not something devoutly to be wished.

In situations involving things that are not expressed in a common measure, advocates of cost-benefit analysis argue that people making judgments "in effect" perform cost-benefit calculations anyway. If government regulators promulgate a regulation that saves 100 lives at a cost of $1 billion, they are "in effect" valuing a life at (a minimum of) $10 million, whether or not they say that they are willing to place a dollar value on a human life. Since, in this view, cost-benefit analysis "in effect" is inevitable, it might as well be made specific.

This argument misconstrues the real difference in the reasoning processes involved. In cost-benefit analysis, equivalencies are established in *advance* as one of the raw materials for the calculation. One determines costs and benefits, one determines equivalencies (to be able to put various costs and benefits into a common measure), and then one sets to toting things up—waiting, as it were, with bated breath for the results of the calculation to come out. The outcome is determined by the arithmetic; if the outcome is a close call or if one is not good at long division, one does not know how it will turn out until the calculation is finished. In the kind of deliberative judgment that is performed without a common measure, no establishment of equivalencies occurs in advance. Equivalencies are not aids to the decision process. In fact, the decision-maker might not even be aware of what the "in effect" equivalencies were, at least before they are revealed to him afterwards by someone pointing out what he had "in effect" done. The decision-maker would see himself as simply having made a deliberate judgment; the "in effect" equivalency number did not play a causal role in the decision but at most merely reflects it. Given this, the argument against making the process explicit is the one discussed earlier in the discussion of problems with putting specific quantified values on things that are not normally quantified—that the very act of doing so may serve to reduce the value of those things.

———————

My own judgment is that modest efforts to assess levels of benefits and costs are justified, although I do not believe that government agencies ought to sponsor efforts to put dollar prices on non-market things. I also do not believe that the cry for more cost-benefit analysis in regulation is, on the whole, justified. If regulatory officials were so insensitive about regulatory costs that they did not provide acceptable raw material for deliberative judgments (even if not of a strictly cost-benefit nature), my conclusion might be different. But a good deal of research into costs and benefits already occurs—actually, far more in the U.S. regulatory process than in that of any other industrial society. The danger now would seem to come more from the other side.

Replies to Steven Kelman

From James V. DeLong, Director of the Center for the Study of Digital Property at the Progress and Freedom Foundation and Principal for the Regulatory Policy Center

Steven Kelman's "Cost-Benefit Analysis—An Ethical Critique" presents so many targets that it is difficult to concentrate one's fire. However, four points seem worth particular emphasis:

(1) The decision to use cost-benefit analysis by no means implies adoption of the reductionist utilitarianism described by Kelman. It is based instead on the pragmatic conclusion that any value system one adopts is more likely to be promoted if one knows something about the consequences of the choices to be made. The effort to put dollar values on noneconomic benefits is nothing more than an effort to find some common measure for things that are not easily comparable when, in the real world, choice must be made. Its object is not to write a computer program but to improve the quality of difficult social choices under conditions of uncertainty, and no sensible analyst lets himself become the prisoner of the numbers.

(2) Kelman repeatedly lapses into "entitlement" rhetoric, as if an assertion of a moral claim closes an argument. Even leaving aside the fundamental question of the philosophical basis of those entitlements, there are two major problems with this style of argument. First, it tends naturally toward all-encompassing claims.

Kelman quotes a common statement that "workers have a right to a safe and healthy workplace," a statement that contains no recognition that safety and health are not either/or conditions, that the most difficult questions involve gradations of risk, and that the very use of entitlement language tends to assume that a zero-risk level is the only acceptable one. Second, entitlement rhetoric is usually phrased in the passive voice, as if the speaker were arguing with some omnipotent god or government that is maliciously withholding the entitlement out of spite. In the real world, one person's right is another's duty, and it often clarifies the discussion to focus more precisely on who owes this duty and what it is going to cost him or her. For example, the article posits that an issue in government decisions about acceptable pollution levels is "the right" of such vulnerable groups as asthmatics or the elderly "not to be sacrificed on the altar of somewhat higher living standards for the rest of us." This defends the entitlement by assuming the costs involved are both trivial and diffused. Suppose, though, that the price to be paid is not "somewhat higher living standards," but the jobs of a number of workers?

Kelman's counter to this seems to be that entitlements are not firm rights, but only presumptive ones that prevail in any clash with nonentitlements, and that when two entitlements collide the decision depends upon the "moral importance we attach to the right or duty involved." So the above collision would be resolved by deciding whether a job is an entitlement and, if it is, by then deciding whether jobs or air have greater "moral importance."

I agree that conflicts between such interests present difficult choices, but the quantitative questions, the cost-benefit questions, are hardly irrelevant to making them. Suppose taking X quantity of pollution from the air of a city will keep one asthmatic from being forced to leave town and cost 1,000 workers their jobs? Suppose it will keep 1,000 asthmatics from being forced out and cost one job? These are not equivalent choices, economically or morally, and the effort to decide them according to some abstract idea of moral importance only obscures the true nature of the moral problems involved.

(3) Kelman also develops the concept of things that are "specially valued," and that are somehow contaminated if thought about in monetary terms. As an approach to personal decision making, this is silly. There are many things one specially values—in the sense that one would find the effort to assign a market price to them ridiculous—which are nonetheless affected by economic factors. I may specially value a family relationship, but how often I phone is influenced by long-distance rates. I may specially value music, but be affected by the price of records or the cost of tickets at the Kennedy Center.

When translated to the realm of government decisions, however, the concept goes beyond silliness. It creates a political grotesquerie. People specially value many different things. Under Kelman's assumptions, people must, in creating a political coalition, recognize and accept as legitimate everyone's special value, without concern for cost. Therefore, everyone becomes entitled to as much of the thing he specially values as he says he specially values, and it is immoral to discuss vulgar questions of resource limitations. Any coalition built on such premises can go in either of two directions: It can try to incorporate so many different groups and interests that the absurdity of its internal contradictions becomes manifest. Or it can limit its membership at some point and decide that the special values of those left outside are not legitimate and should be sacrificed to the special values of those in the coalition. In the latter case, of course, those outside must be made scapegoats for any frustration of any group member's entitlement, a requirement that eventually leads to political polarization and a holy war between competing coalitions of special values.

(4) The decisions that must be made by contemporary government indeed involve painful choices. They affect both the absolute quantity and the distribution not only of goods and benefits, but also of physical and mental suffering. It is easy to understand why people would want to avoid making such choices and would rather act in ignorance than with knowledge and responsibility for the consequences of their choices. While this may be understandable, I do not regard it as an acceptable moral position. To govern is to choose, and government officials—whether elected or appointed—betray their obligations to the welfare of the people who hired them if they adopt a policy of happy ignorance and nonresponsibility for consequences.

The article concludes with the judgment that the present danger is too much cost-benefit analysis, not too little. But I find it hard to believe, looking around the modern world, that its major problem is that it suffers from an excess of rationality. The world's stock of ignorance is and will remain quite large enough without adding to it as a matter of deliberate policy.

From Robert M. Solow, Institute Professor of Economics Emeritus at the Massachusetts Institute of Technology

I am an economist who has no personal involvement in the practice of cost-benefit analysis, who happens to think that modern economics underplays the significance of ethical judgments both in its approach to policy and its account of individual and organizational behavior, and who once wrote in print:

> It may well be socially destructive to admit the routine exchangeability of certain things. We would prefer to maintain that they are beyond price (although this sometimes means only that we would prefer not to know what the price really is).

You might expect, therefore, that I would be in sympathy with Steven Kelman's ethical critique of cost-benefit analysis. But I found the article profoundly, and not entirely innocently, misleading. I would like to say why.

First of all, it is not the case that cost-benefit analysis works, or must work, by "monetizing" everything from mother love to patriotism. Cost-benefit analysis is needed only when society must give up some of one good thing in order to get more of another good thing. In other cases the decision is not problematical. The underlying rationale of cost-benefit analysis is that the cost of the good thing to be obtained is precisely the good thing that must or will be given up to obtain it. Wherever he reads "willingness to pay" and balks, Kelman should read "willingness to sacrifice" and feel better. In a choice between hospital beds and preventive treatment, lives are traded against lives. I suppose it is only natural that my brethren should get into the habit of measuring the sacrifice in terms of dollars forgone. In the typical instance in which someone actually does a cost-benefit analysis, the question to be decided is, say, whether the public should be taxed to pay for a water project—a context in which it does not seem far-fetched to ask whether the project will provide services for which the public would willingly pay what it would have to give up in taxes. But some less familiar unit of measurement could be used.

Let me add here, parenthetically, that I do agree with Kelman that there are situations in which the body politic's willingness to sacrifice may be badly measured by the sum of individuals' willingnesses to sacrifice in a completely "private" context. But that is at worst an error of technique, not a mistaken principle.

Second, Kelman hints broadly that "economists" are so morally numb as to believe that a routine cost-benefit analysis could justify killing widows and orphans, or abridging freedom of speech, or outlawing simple evidences of piety or friendship. But there is nothing in the theory or the practice of cost-benefit analysis to justify that judgment. Treatises on the subject make clear that certain ethical or political principles may irreversibly dominate the advantages and disadvantages capturable by cost-benefit analysis. Those treatises make a further point that Kelman barely touches on: since the benefits and the costs of a policy decision are usually enjoyed and incurred by different people, a distributional judgment has to be made which can override any simple-minded netting out. In addition, Kelman's point that people may put different values on the acquisition of a good for the first time and on the loss of a preexisting entitlement to the same good is not exactly a discovery. He should look up "compensating variation" and "equivalent variation" in a good economics textbook.

Third, Kelman ends by allowing that it is not a bad thing to have a modest amount of cost-benefit analysis going on. I would have supposed that was a fair description of the state of affairs. Do I detect a tendency to eat one's cost-benefit analysis and have it too? If not, what is the point of all the overkill? As a practical matter, the vacuum created by diminished reliance on cost-benefit analysis is likely to be filled by a poor substitute for ethically informed deliberation. Is the capering of Mr. Stockman more to Mr. Kelman's taste?

From Gerard Butters, Former Assistant Director for Consumer Protection at the Bureau of Economics, Federal Trade Commission; John Calfee, Former Resident Scholar at the American Enterprise Institute; and Pauline Ippolito, Associate Director in the Bureau of Economics at the Federal Trade Commission

In his article, Steven Kelman argues against the increased use of cost-benefit analysis for regulatory decisions involving health, safety, and the environment. His basic contention is that these decisions are moral ones, and that cost-benefit analysis is therefore inappropriate because it requires the adoption of an unsatisfactory moral system. He supports his argument with a series of examples, most of which involve private decisions. In these situations, he asserts, cost-benefit advocates must renounce any moral qualms about lies, broken promises, and violations of human rights.

We disagree (and in doing so, we speak for ourselves, not for the Federal Trade Commission or its staff). Cost-benefit analysis is not a means for judging private decisions. It is a guide for decision making involving others, especially when the welfare of many individuals must be balanced. It is designed not to dictate individual values, but to take them into account when decisions must be made collectively. Its use is grounded on the principle that, in a democracy, government must act as an agent of the citizens.

We see no reason to abandon this principle when health and safety are involved. Consider, for example, a proposal to raise the existing federal standards on automobile safety. Higher standards will raise the costs, and hence the price, of cars. From our point of view, the appropriate policy judgment rests on whether customers will value the increased safety sufficiently to warrant the costs. Any violation of a cost-benefit criterion would require that consumers purchase something they would not voluntarily purchase or prevent them from purchasing something they want. One might argue, in the spirit of Kelman's analysis, that many consumers would want the government to impose a more stringent standard than they would choose for themselves. If so, how is the cost-safety trade-off that consumers really want to be determined? Any objective way of doing this would be a natural part of cost-benefit analysis.

Kelman also argues that the process of assigning a dollar value to things not traded in the marketplace is rife with indignities, flaws, and biases. Up to a point, we agree. It *is* difficult to place objective dollar values on certain intangible costs and benefits. Even with regard to intangibles which have been systematically studied, such as the "value of life," we know of no cost-benefit advocate who believes that regulatory staff economists should reduce every consideration to dollar terms and simply supply the decision maker with the bottom line. Our main concerns are twofold: (1) to make the major costs and benefits explicit so that the decision maker makes the trade-offs consciously and with the prospect of being held accountable, and (2) to encourage the move toward a more consistent set of standards.

The gains from adopting consistent regulatory standards can be dramatic. If costs and benefits are not balanced in making decisions, it is likely that the returns per dollar in terms of health and safety will be small for some programs and large for others. Such programs present opportunities for saving lives, and cost-benefit analysis will reveal them. Perhaps, as Kelman argues, there is something repugnant about assigning dollar values to lives. But the alternative can be to sacrifice lives needlessly by failing to carry out the calculations that would have revealed the means for saving them. It should be kept in mind that the avoidance of cost-benefit analysis has its own cost, which can be gauged in lives as well as in dollars.

Nonetheless, we do not dispute that cost-benefit analysis is highly imperfect. We would welcome a better guide to public policy, a guide that would be efficient, morally attractive, and certain to ensure that governments follow the dictates of the governed. Kelman's proposal is to adopt an ethical system that balances conflicts between certain unspecified "duties" and "rights" according to "deliberate reflection." But who is to do the reflecting, and on whose behalf? His guide places no clear limits on the actions of regulatory agencies. Rather than enhancing the connections between individual values and state decisions, such a vague guideline threatens to sever them. Is there a common moral standard that every regulator will magically and independently arrive at through "deliberate reflection"? We doubt it. Far more likely is a system in which bureaucratic decisions reflect the preferences, not of the citizens, but of those in a peculiar position to influence decisions. What concessions to special interests cannot be disguised by claiming that it is degrading to make explicit the trade-offs reflected in the decision? What individual crusade cannot be rationalized by an appeal to "public values" that "rise above" values revealed by individual choices?

15   The Evolving Regulatory Role of the U.S. Office of Management and Budget*

John D. Graham

John D. Graham is Dean, School of Public and Environmental Affairs at Indiana University.

Introduction

On New Year's Eve of 2001, after the disputed Florida recount, I received a call from the Bush–Cheney transition team. They asked me to consider a senior regulatory post in the Office of Management and Budget (OMB), the largest unit within the Executive Office of the President.

The call was a pleasant surprise since I had not been involved in the Bush–Cheney campaign. In fact, I answered gingerly a question about why I made a financial contribution to Elizabeth Dole's short-lived 2000 presidential campaign.

Having taught benefit-cost analysis for seventeen years at the Harvard School of Public Health, the opportunity to practice what I was preaching was intriguing. And my own scholarship on regulation of health risks had called for a more rigorous approach to selecting regulatory priorities, weighing risks, and devising cost-effective solutions (Graham and Wiener 1995; Graham 1997). Thus, I accepted the offer to serve with hopes of advancing the practice of benefit-cost analysis in regulatory policy making.

After going through a meticulous FBI background check, I was nominated in March 2001 to be the president's "regulatory czar"—the administrator of the OMB's Office of Information and Regulatory Affairs (OIRA).

The Senate confirmation process was my introduction to hardball politics in Washington, DC. A coalition of liberal activists opposed my nomination with provocative rhetoric, but their allegations were effectively countered in the confirmation process (U.S. Congress 2001). I was both

"The Evolving Regulatory Role of the U.S. Office of Management and Budget" by John Graham. *Review of Environmental Economics and Policy* 1. 2007. Pp. 171–191. Reprinted with permission.

*The author appreciates helpful comments on an earlier draft from Diana Epstein, Art Fraas, Jennifer Graham, Sue Graham, Jay Griffin, Robert Hahn, James Hammitt, Ryan Keefe, Debra Knopman, John Morrall, Paul Noe, Yuyan Shi, Elizabeth Vandersarl, Jonathan Wiener, an anonymous referee, and the journal's managing editor. Errors and opinions are the author's responsibility.

encouraged and humbled when so many of my academic colleagues, both Democrats and Republicans, voiced support for my nomination. In July 2001, I was confirmed by the Senate and went to work leading fifty career policy analysts at the OIRA.

The OIRA's role in federal regulation has been controversial. Since the early Reagan years, critics have argued that benefit-cost analysis is used by the OMB as a one-sided tool of deregulation to advance the interests of business. A variety of regulatory scholars and proregulation activists have raised concerns about the role of the OIRA, especially as applied to public health, safety, and environmental issues (Andrews 1984; Morrison 1986; Percival 1991; McGarity 1998). Some argue that health protection is an absolute right, even though it is difficult to base such a claim on modern philosophical theories (Schroeder 1986). They also fear a transfer of power from the regulators to the OMB, since the civil servants working at the mission-oriented agencies tend to be more zealous about regulation than the policy analysts at the OMB (McGarity 1991; Moe and Wilson 1994).

As I entered a probusiness Republican administration, I expected that my office would work to stop bad rules and find less costly ways for regulators to achieve worthy public objectives (e.g., environmental protection). And we did so.

My purpose in this article is to disclose a little-known fact: Benefit-cost analysis also caused the OIRA to be a proregulation advocate in the Bush administration. I support this claim by providing specific examples of how and why the OIRA became a voice—usually an effective one—for sensible proregulation initiatives that addressed risks created by business activity.

I begin with a short description of the federal regulatory process, with an emphasis on the basis for the OIRA's participation in agency rule making. I then offer four case studies that illustrate how the OIRA worked with the Department of Health and Human Services (HHS) on labeling foods for trans fat content, the Department of Transportation (DOT) on improving light-truck fuel economy, and the Environmental Protection Agency (EPA) on controlling diesel engine exhaust and reducing air pollution from coal-fired power plants. I conclude with some suggestions about how science and economics can play a stronger role in federal regulation in the years ahead.

The OMB and the Regulators

Federal regulatory agencies develop rules based on legislative authority that has been delegated to them by the U.S. Congress. Since 1981, the Executive Office of the President has insisted that all major new regulations be supported by a benefit-cost analysis, including an analysis of the potential market failure that motivates the need for rule making (Smith 1984). It is now well accepted that based on presidential executive order, the OMB has authority to oversee the regulatory activities of federal agencies to ensure that presidential policies are followed and that economic analysis is undertaken to inform regulatory policy (Kagan 2001; West 2005).

In order to bring discipline to the regulatory approval process, the OMB requires agencies to submit any significant rule making proposal to the OIRA for clearance before it is published in the Federal Register (Blumstein 2001; GAO 2003). The heart of the OMB's power, as administered by the OIRA, is to return a draft rule to an agency for further consideration (OMB 2002). An agency can overrule the OIRA only by a successful appeal to the OMB director (or the president).

The OIRA does not enforce a strict, numeric benefit-cost test. Although the OIRA tracks the numbers carefully, it also considers qualitative claims about possible benefits and costs as well as a variety of nonefficiency arguments (e.g., matters of fairness). For example, a civil rights rule maybe proposed on philosophic grounds that have nothing to do with economic efficiency. Agencies must explain why benefits justify costs, but the justification does not have to be fully monetary. Since there is no rigorous analytic tool for weighing qualitative benefits or fairness claims, the OIRA review of regulations inevitably entails some policy judgment (OMB 2002).

The key limitation on the OIRA's authority is that the OIRA may not compel a regulator to take a position that is inconsistent with the regulator's legislative authority. If the OIRA induces an agency to make such a mistake, the resulting rule is flawed and may be overturned by a federal court. Thus, a complex interaction between economic, legal, and fairness considerations, coupled with interest-group pressures, defines the negotiations between the OIRA and the regulators (McGarity 1991; Morgenstern and Landy 1997).

In the summer of 2001, my boss, OMB director Mitch Daniels (now the governor of Indiana), explained to me his views on why the OMB should oversee the regulators. He said that just as no modern president has permitted a cabinet department to set its own budget without OMB review, no recent president has permitted federal regulators to impose off-budget expenditures—typically "unfunded mandates" on businesses or states—without review by analysts in the Executive Office of the President. Yet Daniels also stressed that the OIRA could do a good job only if it engaged in careful consideration of benefits as well as costs.

In order to demonstrate the OIRA's backbone, Daniels urged me to move quickly to return some bad or poorly reasoned rule making proposals to agencies. I signed more than twenty of these official return letters in my first year on the job (OMB 2002). That is more than the overall number of returns in eight years of the Clinton administration, but a much lower return rate than in the Reagan years (Power and Schlesinger 2002). Once the regulators realized that I was willing to exercise this power, it became far less necessary to use it. We were able to work out problems with an agency in advance, without the need for any public rebuke.

To make it easier for regulators to understand the OIRA's analytic perspective, we published a formal guidance document ("OMB Circular A-4") that outlines what the OIRA expects to see in a regulatory analysis, especially the benefit-cost evaluation. This document, which is available on the OMB's Web site, was finalized only after the OIRA made revisions to a draft document that was subjected to public comment and expert peer review by academics and other scholars on regulatory policy (OMB 2003). I turn now to the four case studies of the OIRA at work with the regulators.

Labeling Foods for Trans Fat Content

Soon after taking office, one of my senior career staff who covered HHS brought to my attention a rule making that was started in the Clinton administration but had never been finished. That was hardly a rare situation, but my economics staff insisted that this rule making was permissible under existing law, and a good idea.

The proposal, which had been drafted by the Food and Drug Administration (FDA), would have compelled food companies to include the trans fat content on the food label, just as calories and saturated fat content are disclosed. The FDA's economists argued that a variety of informational obstacles were preventing the market from responding to the dangers of trans fats. They believed that the new label would not only aid consumer choice but also encourage food processors to reduce the trans fat content of a variety of widely consumed foods. The FDA projected that the annual health benefits of the rule, measured in less heart disease, would far exceed the annual burdens, which included the costs of food processing modifications and labeling changes (FDA 2003).

The key scientific premise was that trans fat consumption is linked to the development of coronary heart disease. To verify this premise, I asked my staff to consult the recent medical literature and reach out to three groups: the Department of Nutrition at the Harvard School of Public Health, the International Life Sciences Institute (a scientific group affiliated with the food industry), and the Center for Science in the Public Interest (a nonprofit advocacy group). All of these consultations reinforced our conviction that the FDA's scientific premise was sound.

When the the OIRA desk officer checked with the FDA, we learned that the rule making was moving at a snail's pace, in part, because a new FDA commissioner had not yet been nominated. In order to accelerate this rule making, we developed a tool which we called the "prompt letter." It was intended to be a polite nudge—a suggestion that an agency give priority to a matter, or alternatively, explain to the OMB in a public reply letter why it should not be a priority (OMB 2002). However, prompt letters are not legally binding on agencies.

The lawyers in the White House disliked the idea. They argued that a prompt letter revealed too much about preliminary thinking inside the executive branch and might be seen as compromising the OIRA's objectivity in the subsequent review of a rule. However, Director Daniels did not find these objections convincing and gave us the go-ahead.

We issued the first the OIRA prompt letter to the FDA in the fall of 2001. FDA responded by finishing the final rule, and trans fat content is now a standard entry on food labels (FDA 2003). As a result of this rule making, grocery store shelves became filled with foods low in trans fat content and a variety of restaurants and food establishments are also taking new steps to reduce trans fat content.

From 2001 to 2006, I signed more than a dozen of these prompt letters, which are posted on the OMB's Web site [http://georgewbush-whitehouse.archives.gov/omb/pubpress/2001-35.html]. Prompt letters were praised as an important innovation by some commentators outside the government (Hahn and Sunstein 2002). They were less popular at the regulatory agencies. With some justification, agencies asked why the OIRA did not simply convey its suggestions to them informally.

Indeed, later in my tenure at the OIRA, my staff persuaded me that we could often achieve the same result we had achieved on trans fats by simply scheduling a meeting with a regulator, where the topic might be a draft prompt letter or a draft return letter. Nonetheless, I favor public prompt letters from the OIRA because they exemplify the transparency in government that I believe will increase public trust in the OIRA (GAO 2003; Graham, Noe and Branch 2006). The public nature of the prompt letters also encourages outside groups to suggest promising topics for prompt letters to the OIRA and serves as an occasional reminder of the need for the OIRA staff to address shortages as well as excesses of regulation.

The development of the prompt letter and its application to FDA's trans fat rule may be an important event in the history of the OIRA, regardless of how many future prompt letters are issued. It reaffirmed in a public way that the OIRA's role is to advance the cause of "smart regulation," which sometimes will lead to more rather than less regulation (OMB 2002). Some scholars have suggested that there should be a presidential executive order to codify the OIRA's power to issue prompt letters (Hahn and Sunstein 2002; Bagley and Revesz 2006).

Curbing Diesel Engine Exhaust

In late 2000, the Clinton administration issued a flood of new regulations, including an ambitious rule under the Clean Air Act to reduce diesel exhaust from heavy-duty trucks operated on roads and highways. The goal was a 90 percent diesel exhaust reduction to be accomplished as refineries reduce the sulfur content of diesel fuel and engine suppliers add modern emission control equipment.

When President Bush took office in 2001, some analysts in the conservative think-tank community saw in the new Republican administration a potential opportunity to delay, modify, or rescind the highway diesel rule (OMB 2001). And, in fact, the new policy officials at the EPA were asked by some industry officials to reconsider the rule.

Deciding Whether to Retain the Highway Diesel Rule

The highway diesel rule was certainly costly, imposing annualized expenses of $3 to $5 billion per year on refineries and engine suppliers (OMB 2002). Those estimates assumed that the industry would experience a steady decline in variable costs over time as refiners learned how to implement desulphurization at a lower cost. The costs were a bitter pill for an industry that had been downsizing for years. In the 1990s, many small refineries struggled to break even.

Despite the significant costs, what impressed me about the rule was the in-depth benefits analysis prepared by the EPA. The rule was projected to prevent, each year, 8,300 premature deaths, 5,500 cases of chronic bronchitis and 361,400 asthma attacks. When the benefits were expressed in monetary units, they were roughly twenty times larger than the estimated costs (OMB 2002). Moreover, EPA scientists indicated that some of the important human health and ecological benefits were not even included in the benefit calculation because of gaps in scientific knowledge or uncertainty about how to express the benefits in monetary units (EPA 2004).

From an economic perspective, the producers, buyers, and users of diesel engines were creating a classic negative externality: the health risks to people breathing diesel exhaust were not fully considered in market transactions.

Much to the dismay of some White House staff, we decided against reopening the highway diesel rule (OMB 2001). In fact, rather than delay or rescind the rule, in 2002 the OIRA began work on a draft prompt letter calling for the EPA to undertake a similar rule making that would reduce exhaust from numerous off-road engines used in construction, agriculture, and mining.

Reducing Exhaust from Off-road Engines

When we met with the EPA informally on the draft prompt, they insisted that there was no need for a prompt because the rule making was already a priority. They were also pleased to learn about the OIRA's proregulation perspective. We therefore agreed to undertake an unprecedented EPA-OMB rule making collaboration, which was announced via press releases in June 2002 by both the EPA and the the OMB.

The complex rule making, which required a 90 percent reduction in diesel exhaust from off-road engines, was completed more quickly than is typical of large EPA rules (EPA 2004). The rule was costly ($1.3 billion per year), but the estimated ratio of monetary benefit to cost was over 20:1.

In the course of this rule making, we asked the EPA to undertake an analysis of benefits to determine how likely it was that benefits would prove to be large or small. The point of this probability analysis was to account for the key scientific uncertainties in the health and environmental sciences.

Interestingly, the analysis revealed that the benefits of the rule exceeded the costs, even when the most pessimistic assumptions were applied to the benefits assessment. This result caused us to ask whether the rule should be made even more stringent. However, a consensus emerged that requiring more than 90 percent sulfur removal raised feasibility concerns and might lead to unintended yet adverse consequences (Graham and Wiener 1995).

The EPA-OMB collaboration did lead to some controversy. We asked whether trading of emissions-control credits should be permitted between off-road and highway engines, since a broader trading regime might make both rules even more cost-effective. The OMB and EPA lawyers agreed that such trading authority might place the entire rule at legal risk, since the Clean Air Act has no express authority for such an expanded trading regime. Disruptive litigation could cause delays in implementation and lack of predictability for firms expected to make large capital investments. So we retreated to a more modest request that trading of credits be permitted among engines of different sizes within the same off-road engine family. The EPA agreed to this request.

As this rule making was nearing a conclusion in 2004, one of the more satisfying moments for me occurred when EPA officials were briefing skeptical White House staff about why the EPA was undertaking a billion-dollar regulation that was not the subject of any statutory deadline from Congress. Participants at the meeting turned to me: I explained that the rule had an impressive benefit-cost case, and the meeting did not last much longer.

Enforcing Diesel Exhaust Rules

Writing stringent rules is not useful if businesses do not believe they will be enforced. In 1999, the EPA and diesel engine suppliers reached a settlement on an enforcement action that alleged that some suppliers had installed computer software that turns off emission controls when a heavy truck is operated on the highway. As part of the settlement, the suppliers agreed to an accelerated compliance schedule for their new, cleaner engines being developed under the 2000 highway diesel rule.

As the accelerated deadline approached in October 2002, several companies informed the EPA that they might need a delay in the effective date; other companies indicated they were ready to go. The EPA made a strong case to us that delay was out of the question, and we agreed.

The following question then arose: How large should the noncompliance penalties be for a manufacturer that offers for sale a noncompliant engine? According to the applicable law, the penalty must be set to ensure that no manufacturer gains a competitive advantage from noncompliance. In addition to potential savings in research and development and equipment costs from noncompliance, the OIRA felt it was critical that any fuel economy gain over the long life of the noncompliant engine be included in the penalty. Thus, the OIRA staff worked closely with EPA staff to produce a rule that imposed large penalties for noncompliance, including the proper discounting of future fuel savings (EPA 2002).

As our policy leaked to the affected companies, the chief of the EPA's clean-air office and I were called to a meeting with members of Congress who were concerned about these noncompliance penalties. EPA was asked why the agency was harassing industry with regulatory fines, especially with such little notice. As the meeting progressed, it became apparent that the members intended to make the EPA the villain. I listened carefully but, without disclosing our thinking, suggested that there were much better targets than this rule for efforts to reduce the burdens of bad regulation. Once again, I was gratified that sound economic thinking prevailed, without any changes to the noncompliance penalties.

After the grilling on Capitol Hill, Director Daniels called me into his office for a briefing. I explained that we needed a policy that rewarded rather than punished innovators in the industry. Daniels offered this advice: "Get the rule out as quickly as possible. Undue delay allows lobbyists to bill more hours as they apply political pressure." That proved to be good advice, which we used on various occasions in the future.

Promoting More Fuel-efficient Vehicles

The run-up of fuel prices in 2001 underscored why the vice president's energy task force, which was devising a national energy policy for the president, was interested in ways to spur conservation of oil. The United States was becoming more heavily dependent on foreign sources of oil (EIA 2005), and the transportation sector was America's biggest source of oil consumption.

The market-failure rationales for oil conservation were a matter of dispute inside the Bush administration. Some analysts argued that the United States was such a large consumer of world oil that we could check the "monopoly" pricing power of OPEC through a concerted program to reduce U.S. oil consumption. Others argued that oil consumption was underpriced because world oil prices do not fully reflect national security concerns or the damages from carbon dioxide emissions that are implicated in global climate change. Still others speculated that consumer decisions about vehicle fuel economy reflected irrationally high discount rates on future gasoline expenses. Although there was no universal agreement as to which market imperfections were most important, there was a broad consensus that a national policy aimed at curbing U.S. oil consumption was required.

Recognizing that cars and light trucks accounted for the majority of oil use in the U.S. transportation sector, the vice president's energy task force made two key recommendations to enhance vehicle fuel economy (White House 2001). First, Congress should offer tax credits to consumers who purchase cars and light trucks with innovative fuel-saving technologies (e.g., hybrid engines). Second, the DOT should reexamine the Corporate Average Fuel Economy program (CAFE), which sets mileage rules for new vehicles, to determine whether CAFE should be reformed or replaced with a more market-based approach to oil savings. Some White House economists argued instead for higher fuel taxes or carbon taxes, but tax hikes were considered political suicide in Congress.

The Science and Politics of CAFE

In 2001, the CAFE program was moribund. Although in 1974 Congress had granted the DOT authority to set mileage rules for cars and light trucks, in 1996 a bipartisan coalition in Congress began adding riders to DOT appropriations bills each year that froze CAFE standards at 27.5 miles per gallon (mpg) for cars and 20.7 mpg for light trucks (SUVs, vans, and pick up trucks). As a result, the combined fuel economy of cars and light trucks was about twenty-five mpg in model year 2004, unchanged from ten years earlier (EPA 2006).

The environmentalists in Congress were arguing for large increases in CAFE standards, but they were outnumbered by members of Congress who feared that large CAFE increases would harm the economy, especially the auto industry. The dispute was less a partisan fight than a regional and interest-group struggle. Leading Democrats such as Carl Levin of Michigan and Dick Gephardt of Missouri opposed large CAFE increases; prominent Republicans such as John McCain of Arizona and Olympia Snowe of Maine favored stricter mileage rules.

A window of opportunity opened in August 2001 when a committee of the National Academy of Sciences released a major study of the CAFE program (NAS 2001). Chaired by Dr. Paul Portney of Resources for the Future, this committee concluded that reform of the CAFE standards could save more energy, reduce safety risks to motorists, and minimize compliance costs. While tighter CAFE standards for cars had saved fuel in the 1980s, NAS found that those same standards had caused adverse safety consequences among motorists due to the downsizing of cars. NAS suggested that size- or weight-based CAFE standards replace the uniform, fleet-wide mileage standards. In order to enhance economic efficiency, NAS also recommended that the separate CAFE programs for domestic cars, imported cars, and light trucks be combined into a single program and that permission be granted for manufacturers to trade CAFE compliance credits.

At about the same time, vehicle manufacturers and the United Auto Workers (UAW) union were beginning to realize what they were up against in California, where the state legislature passed a CAFE-like bill aimed at reducing carbon-dioxide emissions from vehicles sold in California. Other states in the northeast began to follow California's lead. The prospect of a proliferation of state CAFE programs was frightening to all elements of the industry. Reluctantly, industry leaders began to realize that a revitalized federal CAFE program was far better than putting California and various states in charge of national auto policy.

Inside the White House, the president's legislative affairs team was skeptical about whether any CAFE-related proposal could pass the Congress. Despite their reservations, the decision was made to allow the DOT to ask Congress to lift the freeze on CAFE standards and provide the DOT with new regulatory authority to implement the NAS suggestions.

The DOT proposal to reform CAFE went nowhere in the Congress. There was never even a vote on the House or Senate floor concerning the NAS reforms. Why? All of the stakeholders—the environmentalists, UAW, vehicle manufacturers, and consumer groups—were opposed to giving DOT this broad new authority. As one auto lobbyist told me, "The devil you know is better than the devil you don't know." Although Congress would not budge on the NAS reforms, it did lift the freeze on CAFE standards beginning with model year 2004.

Tightening the Mileage Rules

After this legislative debacle, I was asked by the White House to lead an interagency team charged with reforming CAFE administratively. Our charge was to implement as many of the NAS reforms as permitted under existing legal authority. In addition to the DOT, the team included the OIRA, the Department of Energy (DOE), the EPA, the Council of Economic Advisers (CEA), the Council on Environmental Quality, the vice president's office, and the White House policy offices.

We began by tightening mileage standards for light trucks under the existing CAFE framework while emphasizing the need to reform CAFE in the long run (DOT 2003). For model years 2005 through 2007, the DOT gradually increased light-truck mileage rules from 20.7 mpg to 22.2 mpg. Although the rule was estimated to cost the industry (primarily GM and Ford) more than a billion dollars per year, the benefit-cost analysis showed that the net financial impact on consumers would be beneficial, even assuming that fuel prices stayed around $1.50 per gallon through 2020. Although the extra 1.5 mpg may sound small, it represents a savings of more than 4 billion gallons of fuel over the life of the affected vehicles—even accounting for the fact that some consumers drive more miles when their vehicles become more fuel efficient.

A key assumption in the DOT analysis was that both the private and external benefits of fuel savings should be counted. DOT analysts had learned that there was some low-hanging fruit in the engineering of fuel economy, in part because CAFE standards had been frozen for almost a decade and in part because, they speculated, many consumers apply irrationally large discount rates to future fuel savings. The DOT did consider the possibility that tighter mileage standards might reduce new vehicle sales, but this effect was found to be insignificant.

A breakthrough on one of the NAS recommendations occurred in 2003 when the lawyers on the interagency team discovered that the DOT already had the authority to adopt size-based CAFE standards for light trucks (but not for cars). This oddity in the way the 1974 CAFE law was written allowed us to develop stricter, size-based standards for the fastest growing and least fuel-efficient segment of the vehicle market: light trucks.

Using this reform authority, the DOT gradually tightened mpg targets for light trucks from 2008 through 2011. The long-time horizon of the rule making provided a degree of regulatory certainty for vehicle makers and the opportunity to consider more innovative compliance technologies (e.g., hybrid engines and advanced diesel engines).

The DOT projected that the CAFE rule makings covering model years 2005 to 2011 will boost overall light-truck fuel economy to 24.0 mpg by 2011, about 16 percent higher than the level prevailing when President Bush took office (DOT 2006). The DOT also projected that more than ten billion gallons of fuel will be saved. The benefit-cost analysis was favorable, in part because in 2005 the Energy Information Administration raised the long-term fuel-price projection for 2020 from $1.50 per gallon to $2.10 per gallon (EIA 2005). Since private fuel savings are counted in the DOT analysis, a higher projected fuel price causes higher benefit estimates for those technologies that manufacturers do not plan to implement voluntarily.

For the first time in the history of the CAFE program, the DOT set the stringency of the CAFE standards at the point where marginal benefits equaled marginal costs. In setting the mpg targets, no consideration was given to the financial condition of Ford and GM compared to Toyota and the other vehicle manufacturers. Thus, the financial-affordability test used previously by the DOT was replaced by net-benefit maximization, a reform that resulted in stricter standards than would have resulted if the DOT had taken into account the dismal financial condition of GM and Ford.

The Rationale for Size-based Reform

For model years 2008 through 2011, the DOT reformed the CAFE system so that the stringency of a manufacturer's CAFE standard was adjusted based on the size distribution of new vehicles in the company's fleet. Since it is generally easier to achieve good fuel economy in a small rather than a large vehicle, small vehicles were assigned tougher mpg targets than large ones.

The size-based reform had several policy advantages (DOT 2006). Fortunately, at least one of these advantages appealed to each of the main stakeholders.

First, reform reduced the safety concerns raised by NAS because any vehicle downsizing would cause the vehicle to be assigned a stricter mpg target. Instead of downsizing vehicles, which would save fuel by reducing vehicle weight, manufacturers were encouraged to comply by adopting innovative technology. Since the reform was based on a vehicle's dimensions (called "footprint" in the auto business), not weight per se, innovative lightweight materials remained a viable compliance strategy.

Second, the new size metric created a more level playing field for vehicle manufacturers. This was a critical issue to the UAW, GM, and Ford because Toyota and other competitors were beginning to challenge the dominance of Ford and GM in the market for large SUVs and pick up trucks. And in previous years, Toyota had accumulated large amounts of CAFE credits by competing only in the market for smaller SUVs. In other words, if GM and Ford can survive their near-term financial troubles, there is no reason to believe that the size-based CAFE standards for model years 2008 to 2011 will place them at a long-term competitive disadvantage.

Third, the smallest SUVs were subjected to roughly the same mpg targets as large passenger cars. No longer did the designation "light truck" provide more lenient regulatory treatment than the "car" designation. As a result, there was no perverse regulatory incentive for companies to offer SUVs or minivans instead of large sedans or station wagons. And there was no perverse incentive to raise the ground clearance of a vehicle, possibly creating rollover risks, in order to achieve the "light truck" classification.

Finally, reform saved more fuel because all vehicle manufacturers were induced to innovate. Moreover, the scope of the program was expanded to include large passenger SUVs (e.g., the Hummer) that had previously been exempt from mpg standards. The DOT considered the possibility that the size-based formula might encourage companies to offer larger vehicles, but this outcome seemed unlikely due to the cost of larger vehicle platforms and the growing consumer interest in car-like SUVs.

An Appeal to the President

In 2005 there was some last-minute second guessing about CAFE reform. As fuel prices ran over $3.00 per gallon for a brief period and the red ink in Detroit mushroomed, some White House staffers got cold feet about tighter CAFE standards.

The dissenters advocated a return to the CAFE "freeze" of the 1990s based on two arguments. First, "we don't need CAFE anymore," they argued, because high prices at the pump will spur plenty of conservation. Proponents of CAFE reform responded that long-term market prices will not fully account for concerns about energy and national security, the risks of climate change, and possible irrationalities in how consumers weigh fuel savings in purchasing decisions. Second, dissenters argued that tighter CAFE standards might force GM and Ford into Chapter 11 bankruptcy. Proponents of CAFE reform responded that the stringency of CAFE standards should be set based on net benefits, not the financial fortunes of specific companies, especially since the new sized-based structure provided a level playing field for each manufacturer offering a vehicle of a specific size.

The policy debate was waged in the Oval Office in early 2005. President Bush decided to stay with CAFE reform. Indeed, in his 2007 State of the Union message, President Bush called for even stricter mileage standards for both cars and light trucks over the next ten years under a size-based CAFE program informed by benefit-cost analysis.

A Wedge between Consumers and Producers?

The OIRA and the CEA shared a concern that tighter CAFE standards could cause vehicle producers to build vehicles that consumers do not wish to purchase, especially if fuel prices decline more than expected in the years ahead. Since fuel taxes are not likely to be increased, there is a danger that federal regulation will drive a wedge between what consumers want to purchase and what vehicle makers are required to produce under CAFE. The DOT analysis did not account for the utility losses to consumers who might prefer even larger engines, more interior volume, and other fuel-consuming comforts.

As the OIRA and the DOT were completing the CAFE reform proposal in 2005, Congress finally passed consumer tax credits for fuel-efficient vehicles in the comprehensive energy bill. Scheduled to take effect January 1, 2006, the scope of the credits was expanded at our request to include advanced diesel technology as well as hybrids and fuel cells. Although consumer tax credits are far from a perfect response to the potential "wedge," they may stimulate both consumers and producers to have more interest in fuel-saving innovation than would otherwise be the case.

Thus, the portfolio of policies that the OIRA sought is now operating on both the demand and supply side of the market for fuel economy. The recent advances in hybrid engines and advanced diesel technology announced by Honda, Toyota, Ford, GM, Daimler-Chrysler, and BMW have been encouraging. As more experience with these policies accumulates, adjustments may need to be made in response to economic realities.

Reducing Air Pollution from Coal Plants

One of President Bush's unsuccessful legislative proposals, the Clear Skies Initiative, was an ambitious program to replace numerous federal and state clean-air programs with a national "cap-and-trade" program covering the electric utility industry. The idea was to place a cap on total industry emissions of sulfur dioxide, nitrogen dioxide, and mercury but to allow plants to trade emissions credits in order to keep the cost of the program as low as possible, just as had been done in the successful 1990 program to combat acid rain (Stavins 1998). The OIRA assisted the EPA in preparing the benefit-cost analysis for Clear Skies, which called for a 70 percent reduction in the three pollutants over the next fifteen years.

Clear Skies did not move in Congress because it became embroiled in a political dispute about what should be done about the threat of global warming and the possibility of mercury "hot spots" (Vendantam 2005). As the prospects for passage of Clear Skies dwindled, the White House asked the OIRA to work with the EPA on regulations under existing authority to reduce coal plant air pollution.

As a result, two coordinated rule makings were issued in 2005: the Clean Air Interstate Rule (CAIR), which places caps on sulfur dioxide and nitrogen dioxide emissions, and the Clean Air Mercury Rule (CAMR), which places caps on mercury emissions. The caps on sulfur and nitrogen emissions were designed to help states and local communities meet health-based air standards for ozone and particulates. Without passage of Clear Skies, those caps could be applied only in states east of the Mississippi, where long-range transport of coal plant pollution was significant. The fifty-state mercury program was grounded in a rarely used provision of the 1970 Clean Air Act, even though litigation against this creative use of existing authority was expected.

As a package, the two rule makings were quite costly to businesses and consumers: CAIR was projected to cost almost $2 billion per year, while the controls on mercury were projected to cost an additional $750 million per year by 2020 (EPA 2005a,b). The cost of both rules was minimized by the creation of trading markets, where plants facing high costs of control could purchase emissions credits from plants facing low costs of control.

Surprisingly, the benefit-cost case is far weaker for CAMR than for CAIR, even though CAIR is far more costly. This is because the evidence of benefits from mercury removal is quite weak. As a result, the OIRA exerted a proregulation role on CAIR but worked hard to reduce the unnecessary economic burdens that otherwise might have been imposed by CAMR.

CAIR

In regions of the country that do not meet the EPA's health-based air quality standards, it is often impossible to achieve healthy air without greater emissions reductions by sources in upwind states. Using the Clean Air Act's "good neighbor" authority, EPA was empowered to prevent one state from causing air quality problems in a downwind state.

A regional cap-and-trade program for sulfur dioxide and nitrogen dioxide was established for twenty-eight states and the District of Columbia. Under CAIR, overall emissions from power plants in the region were capped to ensure a 50 percent emission reduction by 2009–2010 and a 65–70 percent reduction by 2015 (EPA 2005a).

The public health benefits of CAIR are estimated to be impressive (EPA 2005a). By 2015, the reductions in particle concentrations (due largely to the sulfur controls) are projected to prevent 17,000 premature deaths, 8,700 cases of chronic bronchitis, 22,000 nonfatal heart attacks, 10,500 hospitalizations, 1.7 million lost workdays and 9.9 million days of restricted physical activity. The health benefits from diminished ozone (smog) levels (due to nitrogen controls) are less impressive but still substantial: 2,800 fewer hospital admissions for respiratory illnesses, 280 fewer emergency room visits for asthma, 690,000 fewer days with restricted activity, and 510,000 fewer days where children are absent from school due to illnesses. The number of premature deaths prevented by the nitrogen controls could be as large as 500 per year.

When expressed in monetary units, the total benefits of the overall CAIR rule were estimated to eventually exceed $150 billion per year. The lion's share of these benefits is attributable to the premature deaths prevented by the sulfur controls. Thus the overall ratio of CAIR's benefits to costs was on the order of 75:1.

The OIRA was skeptical of some of these figures. In 2002 we asked the EPA to perform an alternative analysis with a series of less optimistic assumptions. The results were still encouraging. The alternative benefit esti-mate was a factor of ten smaller than the EPA's preferred estimate, but the benefit-cost ratio of CAIR remained favorable.

The OIRA worked with EPA analysts to take a closer look at the incre-mental benefits and costs of controlling sulfur and nitrogen. That inquiry suggested that sulfur emissions reductions beyond 70 percent would be defensible on benefit-cost grounds. Indeed, the OIRA had made the case—unsuccessfully—that the sulfur cap under Clear Skies should be tighter than what was proposed. The benefit-cost case for additional controls on nitrogen dioxide (beyond a 70 percent reduction) was far less clear.

The lawyers on the interagency team argued that the 2015 sulfur cap could not be set more stringently than a 70 percent reduction—even though it made good economic sense to do so—without exposing the rule to legal risk. Reductions larger than 70 percent could not be easily justified in court because additional reductions were not necessary to assist downwind states in achieving the EPA's standard of healthy air. However, as EPA tightens the twenty-four-hour air-quality standard for particulates, a tighter sulfur cap may become legally defensible in the years ahead (Eilperin 2006).

The OIRA also urged EPA to include industrial as well as utility sources of sulfur and nitrogen dioxide in a broader cap-and-trade program or in a tailored trading market for industrial sources. Although there was sub-stantial interest in this suggestion, the poor financial condition of the man-ufacturing sector of the U.S. economy proved to be a formidable obstacle.

CAMR

At the same time that the OIRA was urging the EPA to make CAIR as strin-gent as possible, the OIRA was working hard to make sure that the CAMR rule was not overly stringent. The OIRA was also working against those who believed that no federal mercury rule was necessary.

Mercury in the environment. After mercury is emitted from the stack and deposited (e.g., during periods of rainfall), it is converted into a more toxic form (methyl mercury) and finds its way into water bodies. EPA scien-tists were concerned that people living near power plants might experience health risks from eating large amounts of locally caught fish contaminated with mercury.

The most sensitive individuals are pregnant women because of the neurotoxic effects of methyl mercury on the rapidly growing brain of the fetus. In the 1990s, many states adopted fish advisories aimed at discour-aging pregnant women from ingesting fish that might be contaminated with mercury. Unfortunately, fish advisories are often ignored, sometimes because low-income, subsistence populations rely on locally caught fish for their daily diet.

About 4–8 percent of pregnant women in the United States have been shown to have mercury levels in their blood that exceed the EPA's safe con-centration, the reference level set to protect the fetus and small child (EPA

2005b). Surveys show that these women consume predominantly marine fish. However, there is no evidence that emissions from U.S. power plants are responsible for the elevated mercury levels in marine fish.

The initial thinking at the EPA was that strict mercury controls were necessary at every power plant to ensure that pregnant women living near plants were protected. If an 80–90 percent reduction in mercury emissions had been required at each plant, the cost could have been several billion dollars per year (Gayer and Hahn 2005). Indeed, the engineers from the DOE and the EPA were disputing whether such reductions were even technically feasible (especially for boilers that burn sub-bituminous and lignite coals). The OIRA and the EPA looked hard for a more cost-effective policy alternative.

A promising insight arose from environmental science: The nonelemental forms of mercury (e.g., oxidized and particulate mercury) are most likely to be deposited near plants, while the elemental form—the pure gas— enters the global pool of mercury and can be deposited virtually anywhere in the world. It is very difficult and expensive to control elemental mercury. Some plant-specific controls may be needed to address nonelemental mercury emissions, but a cap-and-trade program is most appropriate for pollutants (such as elemental mercury) that are rapidly dispersed and transported long distances.

Reducing mercury emissions. In the course of the rule making, the EPA and the OIRA discovered that CAIR by itself (i.e., without CAMR) was quite effective in reducing mercury (EPA 2005b) because the same controls used by utilities to reduce sulfur and nitrogen also reduce (nonelemental) mercury. Without CAIR or CAMR, the EPA projected forty-five to forty-seven tons per year of mercury emissions by 2020. CAIR alone was projected to reduce mercury emissions to thirty-four tons by 2020. Thus, at no extra cost, the CAIR rule was projected to cut overall mercury emissions by 26 percent. More importantly, emissions of nonelemental mercury, which tend to deposit locally, were projected to decline by 55 percent (from twenty-two to ten tons per year by 2020) due to CAIR alone.

The EPA's health risk assessment did not demonstrate any significant health risk from 10 tons per year of nonelemental mercury emissions, even among pregnant women who did not follow fish advisories. It is theoretically possible that some risks remained at a small number of plants with unusual conditions, since the EPA models were regional in coverage and did not have fine precision very close to plants. However, under CAMR, rare instances of localized risk can be addressed by state and local regulators.

The EPA and the OIRA ultimately agreed that the case for strict controls at every plant was weak, especially after the effects of CAIR were considered. The policy debate then shifted to whether the United States should make a significant economic investment, beyond CAIR, to further reduce our nation's contribution to the global pool of mercury.

U.S. power plants contribute to the global mercury pool, but the best estimate is that the contribution in recent years was less than 5 percent of the global total (EPA 2005a). Nevertheless, the United States has an interest in stimulating the development of new mercury control technologies that might be used worldwide to reduce the global pool. Based on this rationale, which was outside a traditional benefit-cost framework, the OIRA supported a national cap-and-trade program to reduce the mercury emissions expected to remain after CAIR. The end result is that in 2020, CAMR sets a cap on national mercury emissions from power plants at sixteen tons per year, about a 65 percent reduction from pre-CAIR levels and a 53 percent reduction from post-CAIR levels.

Although the 2020 mercury cap costs about $750 million per year beyond CAIR, it has several qualitative benefits. It stimulates U.S. industry to develop new mercury-control technologies that can reduce emissions of elemental mercury. As new technologies are commercialized, they can be used throughout the world as well as in the United States. As CAMR reduces further the U.S. contribution to the global mercury pool, other countries may be more readily persuaded that they should reduce their contributions to the global pool. CAMR also makes a contribution to reducing nonelemental mercury emissions (from ten to seven tons per year). The combination of CAIR and CAMR reduces nonelemental mercury emissions by 68 percent, providing an extra measure of assurance that pregnant women living downwind of power plants are protected. Although this benefit could not be quantified, CAMR was considered a precautionary investment with a plausible fairness rationale.

Objections to emissions trading. Some commentators object to the idea of allowing power plants to trade mercury allowances (Heinzerling and Steinzor 2004). They argue that "hot spots" may result near plants where owners decide to buy allowances rather than spend capital to control mercury. Of course, this concern is valid only if pregnant women happen to live downwind at points of high deposition where large amounts of locally caught fish are ingested regularly.

OIRA and EPA economists argued that market forces are likely to reduce rather than increase any "hot spots" that now exist. Economies of scale in pollution control are greatest at the largest plants, those that emit the most mercury and have the most local mercury deposition. If the average plant reduces mercury emissions by 70 percent, even larger percentage reductions will occur at the large power plants. Moreover, the permission to trade is likely to cause disproportionate reductions in nonelemental mercury, which is easier and cheaper to control than elemental mercury. If for some unexpected reason "hot spots" do occur at some plants, state and local authorities have adequate authority to set more stringent standards for those plants. In fact, some states are already setting standards that are more stringent than CAMR (Adams 2006).

In the final analysis, the $750 million annual cost of the CAMR rule was supported by the OIRA and the EPA on the basis of qualitative benefits that could not be monetized. The rule should certainly be revisited as more is understood about the benefits and costs of controlling mercury. Some analysts believe a more stringent rule may be supportable by new science indicating mercury intake is related to elevated risks of heart attacks among adults (Rice and Hammitt 2005). The rule may have to be revisited sooner rather than later if it does not survive the barrage of litigation that has been launched against it.

Taking Stock of the OIRA's Proregulation History

The OIRA's proactive stances on trans fats, diesel engine exhaust, vehicle fuel economy, and coal plant pollution were unusual by historic standards. The early years of the OIRA's history were dominated by efforts to reduce regulatory burdens on industry (Morrison 1986; Percival 1991). Yet the OIRA's support of sound rules in the 2001–2006 period was certainly not unprecedented.

In fact, the OIRA's role in diesel exhaust control is reminiscent of the accelerated phase-out of leaded gasoline that occurred early in the Reagan Administration. In that case, industry came to President Reagan's "regulatory relief" task force seeking a delay of the ban on leaded gasoline that President Carter's EPA had issued. Instead the Reagan OIRA was ultimately persuaded to sign on to the opposite course: an acceleration of the lead phase-out. The pivotal input was a careful benefit-cost analysis by EPA analysts, including review and support by the OIRA (McGarity 1991; Gray et al. 1997; Morgenstern and Landy 1997).

In the Clinton years, the OIRA also made important proregulation accomplishments. For example, the OIRA effectively resisted a determined effort by the DOT to weaken the automobile airbag requirement. In the face of public outcry from libertarians and citizens who feared the explosive device, DOT sought the OIRA approval for a modified rule that would have placed a manual on-off switch in every new vehicle produced with an airbag. The OIRA blocked this proposal on the grounds that the safety harms from a misused on-off switch might be vastly greater than the benefits. Once drivers and front-seat passengers were informed about the benefits and risks of airbags and safety belts through a massive education effort, public acceptance of the technology improved considerably (Graham 2001).

What was different about the OIRA in the George W. Bush years was the OIRA's proactive role in the priority-setting process. In addition to serving as an end-of-the-pipeline mechanism for quality control, the OIRA became a determined participant in the formulation stage of policy making.

The OIRA's proregulation accomplishments in the 2001–2006 period also underscore a lesson that has been repeated throughout the OIRA's twenty-five-year history: Careful economic analysis sometimes suggests that more federal regulation is a wiser public policy than less federal regulation (Smith 1984; Mendeloff 1988; McGarity 1991; Breyer 1993; Sunstein 2002).

Regardless of whether the OIRA is working in a conservative or liberal administration, this is an essential feature of "smart regulation" based on science and economics.

The diesel exhaust and coal plant rule makings also highlight why it is important for the OIRA to be capable of scrutinizing claims of benefits as well as costs. In retrospect, one of my best personnel moves at the OIRA was to recruit the office's first toxicologist and epidemiologist, in addition to new specialists in engineering and health policy. The new experts joined the OIRA's economists and statisticians as the office began to delve more deeply into the technical aspects of regulatory benefit estimates (OMB 2002). Although we respected the views of agency experts, we began to ask more penetrating questions about how benefits were determined.

In the diesel exhaust rule making, we did not accept at face value the huge benefit estimates prepared by the EPA in collaboration with their science advisors. We recognized that there was considerable imprecision (and possible bias) in the EPA estimates, and thus instructed the EPA to prepare an alternative benefit analysis based on more pessimistic assumptions. When we learned that even the alternative benefit estimates supported the EPA's policy, we became even more determined advocates of the EPA's position in the White House.

The benefit story was much more complex for pollution from coal plants. After persistent probing of the EPA over several years, we became convinced that tighter controls on sulfur emissions promised much greater benefits than tighter controls on mercury emissions, even though the mass media and some activist groups often portrayed mercury as the worst of all pollutants. The position we advocated needs to be reevaluated in the years ahead as more scientific knowledge is obtained about both sulfur and mercury emissions from coal plants.

The CAFE rule making illustrates why it is important for the OIRA analysts to remain engaged on an important issue, even if the "first-best" policy is rejected. In the George W. Bush administration and in Congress, higher fuel taxes or new carbon taxes were dead on arrival, even though some economists in the administration saw them as the best course for public policy.

Rather than give up on energy conservation, the OIRA worked persistently with multiple agencies, including the CEA, to improve federal fuel economy regulation and create consumer tax credits for purchase of vehicles with innovative fuel-saving technologies. Coupled with the sustained rise of fuel prices, these "second-best" policies appear to be stimulating a market dynamic in favor of more hybrid engines, more advanced diesel technology, and more lightweight construction materials. The resulting technological innovations provide a solid foundation for more ambitious national or international policies to promote energy security and slow the pace of climate change.

Conclusions and Future Directions for Research

Each year, the OMB publishes agency estimates of regulatory costs and benefits. These data show that during my tenure as the OIRA administrator, the overall net benefits from regulation were larger than was experienced in the 1990s (see Table 1). In part, this occurred because we cut the growth rate of costly major rules by 49 percent compared to the 1990s (OMB 2004, 2005, 2007a,b). But we also encouraged rule making with impressive benefits, causing average yearly benefits from major rules to increase 108 percent compared to the 1990s (OMB 2007a,b).

Overall, the quantified net benefit of major rules from 2001 to 2006 increased by 262 percent compared to the 1990s (OMB 2007b). Fewer major rules were issued, but those that were issued had superior benefit-cost justifications. One of the key lessons is that we should judge regulators not by the number of rules they issue but by their overall contribution to social welfare (Sunstein 2002; Adler and Posner 2006).

Reviewing major new rules was a big challenge, but modernizing the sea of existing federal regulations was an even bigger chore (Grain 2005). Since the OMB began to keep records in 1981, an additional 20,000 new federal rules have been adopted (OMB 2007). For the vast majority of these rules, the regulator has never looked back to determine what the rule accomplished or how expensive it was. Thus at the same time that the OIRA worked to enhance the efficiency of new rules, we also instructed regulators to reexamine and streamline about 100 existing regulations, the first serious "look-back" effort since the early Reagan years (OMB 2003, 2004, 2007).

What surprised some, however, was how frequently our office made a *proregulation* argument to regulators, to White House staff, to the vice president's office, and even to the president himself. Before coming to government, I had discovered that public health regulators suffer from a syndrome of paranoia and neglect: excessive regulation of some risks, inadequate regulation of others (Graham 1997). Past practice at the OIRA had focused on the first part of this problem, but the OIRA had not yet begun to tackle the second part, a longstanding concern of progressive regulatory scholars (Breyer 1993; Sunstein 2002; Bagley and Revesz 2006). I am pleased to have begun an effort at the OIRA to address this imbalance.

Unfortunately, the benefit-cost framework for regulatory reform is only as powerful as the tools and data available to implement the framework. Based on my five years of experience overseeing federal regulatory agencies, I have become even more convinced than I was previously of the need for our nation to make expanded research investments in regulatory economics, science, and engineering. The information base on which we made multibillion-dollar decisions was often remarkably slim. Hence, I conclude this article with several examples of the urgent need for research.

First, environmental regulators assume that each statistical life extended by reducing air pollution should be valued at $6 million (EPA 2004, 2005a). This figure was a crucial input to the benefit assessments for both the diesel

Table 1 Total net benefits from major federal rules, 1992–2005
(in billions of 2001 dollars)

Year	Benefits	Costs	Net benefits
1992	81.1	16.3	64.8
1993	7.7	8.1	−0.4
1994	11.4	8.7	2.7
1995	3.1	3.5	−0.4
1996	19.6	2.6	17.0
1997	2.5	2.4	0.1
1998	12.8	5.4	7.4
1999	15.9	8.4	7.5
2000	35.1	17.9	17.2
2001	0.0	−4.8	4.8
2002	4.3	1.9	2.4
2003	3.1	2.5	0.6
2004	52.2	6.8	45.4
2005	74.0	5.6	68.4
2006	26.0	2.5	23.5

Notes: Figures for 1992 and 2000 include rules issued prior to the presidential inauguration in the next year. Based on 134 major federal rules where agencies produced estimates of benefits and costs. All figures are annualized. Sources: OMB 2007a,b.

engine and coal plant rule making. Upon close inspection, the figures used in the benefit assessments were based primarily on the wage premiums that are necessary to attract workers into occupations with elevated risks of traumatic injury (Viscusi and Aldy, 2003). Although environmental economists use the phrase "benefit transfer" to describe this form of extrapolation, it would be more useful if regulatory analysts had some relevant data on the public's economic demand for improved air quality. That is a challenging research question but one that would be very worthwhile to study directly with innovative research designs and hard data.

Second, the estimated air-quality benefits are based on another crucial assumption: that all fine particles are equally toxic, regardless of their size or chemical composition. Yet there are sound toxicological reasons to suspect that sulfates, nitrates, and carbon-containing particles vary considerably in their toxicity at low concentrations. Moreover, the epidemiologic evidence that currently links air pollution and adverse health outcomes has progressed only modestly beyond what Lester Lave and colleagues published in the early 1970s (Lave and Seskin 1970). Much of the recent literature does not make use of the modern econometric tools that are now considered standard in economics. I would like to see the next generation of environmental epidemiology studies be produced by teams of analysts that include physicians, toxicologists, environmental scientists, statisticians, and econometricians. The future stakes in regulatory policy—whether measured in public health or monetary terms—justify new kinds of scientific collaborations.

Finally, we need better economic models of how consumers and producers in the automotive industry will respond to a multiplicity of federal and state regulations, higher fuel prices, tax policies, and a major restructuring of the industry. A key question is what products will arise from a U.S. automotive market with fuel prices below European experience ($4–5 per gallon) but considerably above the U.S. experience of the 1990s ($1–2 per gallon). As energy security and climate change concerns intensify over the next decade, there will be numerous policy proposals aimed at the world transport sector. Unless our economic models of the global auto industry improve considerably, much of this policy making will be based on guesswork. I believe our universities, think tanks, and government policy shops are capable of producing a stronger analytic foundation for future policy making.

REFERENCES

Adams, Rebecca. 2006. State dropout rate high for Bush mercury plan. *Congressional Quarterly Weekly Report* May 29: 1456–57.

Adler, Matthew D., and Eric A. Posner. 2006. *New foundations of cost-benefit analysis*. Cambridge, MA: Harvard University Press.

Andrews, Richard N. L. 1984. Economics and environmental decisions, past and present. In *Economics and environmental decisions: past and present, environmental policy under, Reagan's executive order: The role of benefit-cost analysis*, ed. V. Kerry Smith, 43–85. Chapel Hill: University of North Carolina Press.

Bagley, Nicholas, and Richard L. Revesz. 2006. *Centralized oversight of the regulatory state*. Washington, DC: AEI Joint Center on Regulatory Studies, Related Publication 6–12.

Blumstein, James. 2001. Presidential administration and administrative law: Regulatory review by the executive office of the president; An overview and policy analysis of recent issues. *Duke Law Journal* 51: 851.

Breyer, Stephen. 1993. *Breaking the vicious circle: Toward effective risk regulation*. Cambridge, MA: Harvard University Press.

Crain, W. Mark. 2005. *The impact of regulatory costs on small firms*. Washington, DC: U.S. Small Business Administration.

Eilperin, Juliet. 2006. EPA cuts soot level allowable daily in air. *Washington Post* Sept. 26: A3.

Energy Information Administration. 2005. Annual Energy Outlook.

Gayer, Ted., and Robert Hahn. 2005. The political economy of mercury regulation. *Regulation* 28, no. 2: 26–33.

General Accountability Office. 2003. *OMB's role in reviews of agencies' draft rules and the transparency of those reviews*. Washington, DC: General Accountability Office.

Graham, John D. 1997. *Legislative approaches to achieving more protection against risk at less cost*, 13–58. Chicago: University of Chicago Legal Forum.

———. 2001. Technological danger without stigma: The case of automobile airbags. In *Risk, media and stigma*, ed. James Flynn, Paul Slovic, and Howard Kunreuther, 241–56. London: Earthscan.

Graham, John D., and Jonathan B. Wiener, eds. 1995. *Risk versus risk: Tradeoffs in protecting health and the environment.* Cambridge, MA: Harvard University Press.

Graham, John D., Paul R. Noe, and Elizabeth L. Branch. 2006. Managing the regulatory state: The experience of the Bush administration. *Fordham Urban Law Journal* 33, no. 4: 953–1002.

Gray, George M., Laury Salisman, and John D. Graham. 1997. The demise of lead in gasoline. In *The Greening of Industry,* ed. John D. Graham and Jennifer Kassalow. Cambridge, MA: Harvard University Press.

Hahn, Robert W., and Cass R. Sunstein. 2002. A new executive order for improving federal regulation? Deeper and wider cost-benefit analysis. *University of Pennsylvania Law Review* 150: 1489.

Heinzerling, Lisa, and Rena I. Steinzor. 2004. A perfect storm: Mercury and the Bush administration, Part II. *Environment Law Reporter* 34: 10485–496.

Kagan, Elena. 2001. Presidential administration. *Harvard Law Review* 114: 2245.

Lave, Lester, and Eugene Seskin. 1970. Air pollution and human health. *Science* August 21: 723–33.

McGarity, Thomas O. 1991. *Reinventing rationality: The role of regulatory analysis in the federal bureaucracy.* New York: Cambridge University Press.

———. 1998. A cost-benefit state. *Administrative Law Review* 50: 7–79.

Mendeloff, J. 1988. *The dilemma of toxic substance regulation: How overregulation causes underregulation at OSHA.* Cambridge, MA: MIT Press.

Moe, Terry M, and Scott A. Wilson. 1994. Regulating regulation: The political economy of administrative procedures and regulatory instruments. *Law and Contemporary Problems* Spring: 1–44.

Morgenstern, R. D., and M. K. Landy. 1997. *Economic analysis: benefits, costs, implications.* Washington, DC: Resources for the Future.

Morrison, Alan B. 1986. OMB interference with agency rulemaking: The wrong way to write a regulation. *Harvard Law Review* 99: 1059.

National Academy of Sciences. 2002. *Effectiveness and impact of corporate average fuel economy standards.* Washington, DC.

Percival, Robert V. 1991. Checks without balance: executive office oversight of the environmental protection agency. *Law and Contemporary Problems* Autumn: 127–204.

Power, Stephen, and Jacob M. Schlesinger. 2002. Bush's rules czar brings long knife to new regulations. *Wall Street Journal* June 12: 1.

Rice, Glenn, and James K. Hammitt. 2005. Economic Valuation of Human Health Benefits of Controlling Mercury Emissions from U.S. Coal-Fired Power Plants. Northeast States for Coordinated Air Use Management.

Schroeder, Christopher H. 1986. Rights against risk. *Columbia Law Review* 86, no. 3: 495–562.

Smith, V. Kerry, ed. 1984. *Environmental policy under Reagan's executive order. The role of benefit-cost analysis.* Chapel Hill: University of North Carolina Press.

Stavins, Robert N. 1998. What can we learn from the grand policy experiment? Lessons from SO_2 allowance trading. *Journal of Economic Perspectives* 12, no. 3: 69–88.

Sunstein, Cass R. 2002. *Risk and reason: Safety, law and the environment.* New York: Cambridge University Press.

U.S. Congress. Senate. 2001. Committee on Governmental Affairs. Nominations of Angela B. Styles, Stephen A. Perry, and John D. Graham. 107th Congress, 1st Session. May 17.

U.S. Department of Transportation. 2003. Light truck fuel economy standards for model years 2005–2007. *Federal Register* 68: 16868.

———. 2006. Average fuel economy standards for light trucks: Model years 2008–2011. *Federal Register* 71: 17566.

U.S. Environmental Protection Agency. 2002. *Final technical support document: Nonconformance penalties for 2004 highway heavy duty diesel engines.* Washington, DC: U.S. Environmental Protection Agency.

———. 2004. Control of emissions of air pollution from nonroad diesel engines and fuel. *Federal Register* 69: 38958.

———. 2005a. Rule to reduce interstate transport of fine particulate matter and ozone (Clean Air Interstate Rule). *Federal Register* 70, no. 91: 25162–227.

———. 2005b. Revision of the December 2000 regulatory finding on the emissions of hazardous air pollutants from electric utility steam generating units and the removal of coal- and oil-fired electric utility steam generating units from the section 112(c) list; final rule. *Federal Register* 70, no. 59: 15994.

———. 2006. Light-Duty Automotive Technology and Fuel Economy Trends: 1975 through 2006. EPA420-R-011.

U.S. Food and Drug Administration. 2003. Trans fatty acids in nutrition labeling, nutrient content claims, and health claims. *Federal Register* 68: 41,434.

U.S. Office of Management and Budget. 2001. *Making sense of regulation.* Washington, DC: U.S. Office of Management and Budget.

———. 2002. *Stimulating smarter regulation.* Washington, DC: U.S. Office of Management and Budget.

———. 2003. *Informing regulatory decisions.* Washington, DC: U.S. Office of Management and Budget.

———. 2004. *Progress in regulatory reform.* Washington, DC: U.S. Office of Management and Budget.

———. 2005. *Validating regulatory analysis.* Washington, DC: U.S. Office of Management and Budget.

———. 2007a. *2006 Report to Congress on the costs and benefits of federal regulations.* Washington, DC: U.S. Office of Management and Budget.

———. 2007b. *Draft 2007 report to Congress on the costs and benefits of federal regulations.* Washington, DC: U.S. Office of Management and Budget.

Vendantam, Shankar. 2005. Senate impasse stops "Clear Skies" measure. *Washington Post* March 10: A4.

Viscusi, W. Kip, and Joseph E. Aldy. 2003. The value of statistical life: A critical review of market estimates throughout the world. *Journal of Risk and Uncertainty* 27, no. 1: 5–76.

West, William F. 2005. The institutionalization of regulatory review: Organizational stability and responsive competence at OIRA. *Presidential Studies Quarterly* 35: 76.

White House. 2001. *National energy policy.* Report of the National Energy Policy Development Group.

V

The Means of Environmental Policy: Cost Effectiveness and Market-Based Instruments

16 *Instrument Choice in Environmental Policy**

Lawrence H. Goulder and Ian W. H. Parry

Lawrence H. Goulder is Shuzo Nishihara Professor in Environmental and Resource Economics and Chair of the Economics Department, Kennedy-Grossman Fellow in Human Biology; and Senior Fellow at the Institute for Economic Policy Research at Stanford University; Research Associate at the National Bureau of Economic Research; and University Fellow at Resources for the Future. Ian W. H. Parry is Technical Assistance Advisor on Climate Change and Environmental Policy in the Fiscal Affairs Department of the International Monetary Fund and Senior Fellow at Resources for the Future.

Introduction

The choice of pollution control instrument is a crucial environmental policy decision. With growing momentum for federal legislation to control greenhouse gases, interest among policy makers in the issue of instrument choice has reached a fever pitch. The toolkit of environmental instruments is extensive, and includes emissions taxes, tradable emissions allowances ("cap-and-trade"), subsidies for emissions reductions, performance standards, mandates for the adoption of specific existing technologies, and subsidies for research toward new, "clean" technologies. How to choose among the alternatives?

The choice is inherently difficult because competing evaluation criteria apply. Economists have tended to focus on the criteria of economic efficiency (a policy's aggregate net benefits) and its close relative, cost-effectiveness. Other important criteria are the distribution of benefits or costs (across income groups, ethnic groups, regions, generations, etc.) and the ability to address uncertainties. Some analysts would also include political feasibility as a criterion.

Evaluating the impacts along any one of these dimensions is hard enough. For example, judging alternative instruments in terms of cost-effectiveness alone is difficult, since a comprehensive assessment of cost would include not only the negative impacts on the regulated entity but also

"Instrument Choice in Environmental Policy" by Lawrence Goulder and Ian Parry. *Review of Environmental Economics and Policy* 2. 2008. Pp. 152–174. Reprinted with permission.

*We are grateful to Dallas Burtraw, William Pizer, Suzanne Leonard, Robert Stavins, Tom Tietenberg, and an anonymous referee for very helpful suggestions and comments on an earlier draft.

monitoring and enforcement costs and general equilibrium impacts outside the sector targeted for regulation. Considering several dimensions is harder still. Beyond the theoretical and empirical challenges involved, there is a sobering conceptual reality: the absence of an objective procedure for deciding how much weight to give to the competing normative criteria. As a result, selecting the "best" instrument involves art as well as science.

A basic tenet in elementary textbooks is the "Pigouvian" principle that pollution should be priced at marginal external cost. This principle usually suggests that emissions taxes are superior to alternative instruments. While the Pigouvian insight remains highly valuable, research conducted over the past few decades indicates that it is not always sufficient or reliable because of information problems, institutional constraints, technology spillovers, and fiscal interactions. A more sophisticated set of considerations is required, which at times will justify using instruments other than emissions taxes.

This essay attempts to pull together some key findings in the recent literature and distill lessons for policy makers. A full treatment of the major issues would occupy an entire volume, perhaps several. Our goal is therefore to sketch out key strengths and weaknesses of alternative environmental policy instruments and refer the reader to relevant studies for the details.[1]

A number of issues are beyond the scope of this article. First, we focus exclusively on mandatory policies; voluntary programs as well as information disclosure programs, such as the Toxic Release Inventory and Energy Star, are beyond our scope (for details see Tietenberg and Wheeler 2001 and Lyon and Maxwell 2002). In addition, we concentrate on domestic policy choice, giving relatively little attention to strictly international considerations relevant to instrument choice or policy design (for details see Aldy and Stavins 2007 and Nordhaus 2007). Finally, our approach is largely normative: while we offer a few comments about why certain instruments tend to have greater political success than others, we do not provide an in-depth analysis of the (positive) political economy of environmental regulation (on this, see Keohane, Revesz, and Stavins 1998).

Several general themes emerge from the discussion, including:

- No single instrument is clearly superior along all the dimensions relevant to policy choice; even the ranking along a single dimension often depends on the circumstances involved.

- Significant trade-offs arise in the choice of instrument. In particular, assuring a reasonable degree of fairness in the distribution of impacts, or ensuring political feasibility, often will require a sacrifice of cost-effectiveness.

- It is sometimes desirable to design hybrid instruments that combine features of various instruments in their "pure" form.

---

[1]For other reviews of the literature see Hepburn (2006) and Tietenberg (2006).

- For many pollution problems, more than one market failure may be involved, which may justify (on efficiency grounds, at least) employing more than one instrument

- Potential interactions among environmental policy instruments are a matter of concern, as are possible adverse interactions between policies simultaneously pursued by separate jurisdictions.

The rest of the article is organized as follows. The next section investigates the cost-effectiveness of alternative emissions control instruments using a relatively narrow, traditional notion of cost, while the third section considers broader cost dimensions. Section 4 explores other considerations relevant to the choice among emissions control instruments. Although much of our focus is on policies aimed at reducing emissions, an important role of decision makers is to consider policies that directly promote the invention or deployment of new technologies. Therefore, in Section 5 we briefly discuss the rationale for supplementing emissions control policies with technology-focused policies. Section 6 considers some further environmental and institutional issues that complicate the choice of instrument. The final section summarizes our conclusions about instrument choice and identifies some of the challenges faced by environmental economists working in this area today.

Cost-Effectiveness of Alternative Emissions Control Instruments

We start our discussion with a comparison of the costs of achieving given emissions reductions using different instruments.[2] For now we apply a narrow interpretation of cost, one that encompasses only compliance costs within the firms or industries targeted for regulation.

Minimizing the cost of reducing pollution by a given targeted amount requires equating marginal abatement costs across all potential options and agents for emissions reduction, including:

- *the various abatement channels* available to an individual firm or facility: namely, switching to cleaner inputs or fuels, installing abatement capital (e.g., postcombustion scrubbers), and reducing the overall scale of production.

- *firms or facilities within a production sector*—which may face very different costs of abatement and existing emissions intensities.

- *production sectors*, such as manufacturing and power generation.

---

[2]Although we treat the emissions-reduction target as given and compare the costs of meeting that target with different instruments, in reality the target itself may be endogenous to the choice of instrument, as the selected target may be revised in response to changes in perceptions about the magnitude of abatement costs.

- *households and firms*, where household options might include reducing automobile use or purchasing more energy-efficient appliances or vehicles.

In theory, these conditions are satisfied when all economic actors face a common price, at the margin, for their contributions to emissions (Baumol and Oates 1971). In such circumstances, every firm in every (emissions-producing) sector has an incentive to exploit all of its abatement opportunities until the marginal cost of reducing emissions equals the emissions price, thereby assuring that the first three conditions listed above are satisfied. Moreover, the cost of emissions control and the price paid for remaining emissions will be passed forward into the prices of final goods and services. Consequently, consumers will face prices reflecting the emissions associated with the production of the goods they buy or the services they use. Thus, in keeping with the fourth condition above, their consumption choices will account for their contributions to emissions.[3] Because all agents will be charged the same unit price for their direct or indirect contributions to emissions, the marginal costs of emissions reductions of all agents will be equal.

Maximizing cost-effectiveness requires that all agents face the same price on emissions. The stronger condition of maximizing the efficiency gains from policy intervention implies a particular level for this price: namely, the one that equates the marginal benefits and costs of emissions reductions.

In reality, environmental regulations are rarely comprehensive enough to apply a given emissions price to all economic sectors or agents. For example, the European Union's Emissions Trading Scheme (ETS) currently covers sectors responsible for only about half of the EU's CO_2 emissions. Far more frequently the goal is to maximize cost-effectiveness within a targeted sector or set of industries. Imposing a common emissions price on all agents within the targeted sector or group of industries will minimize costs (narrowly defined) within that group, but generally will not lower costs as much as a more comprehensive program can.

Having offered this brief introduction, we now compare instruments whose main purpose is curbing emissions or effluent (as opposed to directly promoting the invention or deployment of new technologies). These include both *incentive-based instruments* and *direct regulatory instruments* (sometimes called "command-and-control" instruments).[4] The attributes and advantages of each instrument are summarized in Table 1 and discussed in turn below.

---

[3]This holds even when competitive supply curves are upward sloping and firms cannot pass through all the costs of regulation.

[4]We prefer to use "direct regulatory instruments" rather than "command-and-control" instruments, which has a somewhat negative connotation.

Table 1 Attributes of alternative emissions control instruments

	(1) Promotion of lowest-cost combination of input choice, end-of-pipe treatment, and output reduction	(2) Equalizing of marginal emissions reduction costs across heterogeneous firms	(3) Minimization of general equilibrium costs from interactions with broader tax system	(4) Political feasibility (low share of regulatory burden falling on emitters)	(5) Fairness across income groups (limiting disproportionate burden on low-income households)
Emissions control policies					
Emissions tax (revenue-neutral)	*	*	*		*
Subsidy to emissions abatement		*			
Tax on goods associated with emissions		*	*		
Tradable emissions allowances					
Auctioned (revenue-neutral)	*	*	*		*
Freely allocated	*	*		*	*
Mandated abatement technology				*	*
(Non-tradable) performance standard				*	*

Notes

1. The asterisk indicates that a given instrument has an advantage along the dimension in question. It does not mean that other instruments have no impact along that dimension.

2. Other potentially important considerations excluded from the table are:

(a) Ease of monitoring and enforcement;

(b) Ability to maximize efficiency gains under uncertainty; and

(c) Ease of policy adjustment (in terms of stringency, scope, etc.) in face of new information.

These dimensions are not included as column headings because the relative attractiveness of instruments along these dimensions depends critically on the particular circumstances involved.

Incentive-Based Instruments

Incentive-based instruments include emissions taxes, tradable emissions allowances, subsidies for pollution abatement, and taxes on inputs or goods associated with emissions (e.g., a gasoline tax).

Emissions Taxes and Tradable Allowance Systems. What specific instruments might establish a common emissions price? Clearly an emissions tax is one. A system of tradable emissions allowances (or "cap-and-trade") is another, since it also imposes a single emissions price on all covered sources—that is, all firms or facilities must justify their emissions by submitting allowances. This holds whether the allowances are initially distributed through an auction or by free allocation. In either case, an additional unit of emissions implies a cost equal to the allowance price, since it compels the agent either to purchase one extra allowance or to sell one fewer (and forgo revenue). As under the emissions tax, both the costs of abatement and the emissions price are reflected in higher prices of consumer products.

Subsidies for Pollution Abatement. Another potential emissions pricing instrument is a subsidy for pollution abatement, where firms are rewarded for every unit of emissions that they reduce below some baseline level. At the margin, this instrument provides the same incentives as emission taxes or cap-and-trade, since every additional unit of emissions implies a cost to the firm in forgone subsidy receipts. Thus, these subsidies can bring about the same choices for input intensities and end-of-pipe treatment as other emissions pricing policies. However, in practice such subsidies are less cost-effective than emissions taxes or tradable allowances. Since they lower firms' average costs, they provide the wrong incentives regarding the level of output, which leads to excess entry.[5] As a result, to accomplish the same target emissions reductions as under the other two policies, regulators would need to make the marginal price of emissions (the subsidy rate) higher than under the other policies, leading to too much abatement from input substitution or end-of-pipe treatment, and too little from reduced output. This implies higher aggregate costs of achieving a given emissions target.

Taxes on Inputs or Goods Associated with Emissions. Still another pricing instrument is a tax on an input, produced goods, or service associated with emissions. Taxes on gasoline, electricity, or air travel are examples. These taxes may be an attractive option when it is difficult to monitor emissions directly (see below). However, because these taxes do not focus sharply on the externality, they do not engage all of the pollution reduction channels described above, implying a loss of cost-effectiveness. For example, a tax on

---

[5]It is theoretically possible to design a subsidy program that does not lead to excess entry. However, such programs are very difficult to achieve in practice. See Baumol and Oates (1988) for a discussion.

electricity lowers emissions by raising electricity prices, which lowers equilibrium demand and output; but it provides no incentives for clean fuel substitution in power generation or for the adoption of electrostatic emissions scrubbers (a form of postproduction or "end-of-pipe" treatment). Similarly, although a gasoline tax might encourage motorists to drive hybrid or more fuel-efficient vehicles, it provides no incentives for them to drive cars that burn gasoline more cleanly, or for refiners to change the refinery mix to produce a motor fuel that generates less pollution when combusted.

Direct Regulatory Instruments

Compared with emissions taxes and tradable emissions allowances, direct regulations such as technology mandates and performance standards are at a disadvantage in meeting the conditions for cost-minimization. The disadvantages reflect information problems faced by regulators as well as limitations in the ability of these instruments to optimally engage the various channels for emissions reductions.

Technology Mandates. Consider first the impact of a technology mandate—a specific requirement regarding the production process. The mandate may require, for example, that firms install equipment that implies a particular production method. Given the heterogeneity among firms, it is extremely unlikely that a regulator would have enough information to set mandates that maximize cost-effectiveness—i.e., that cause marginal costs of abatement (through input-substitution and end-of-pipe treatment) to be equated across firms. If a single mandate is applied to all firms, cost-effectiveness will be undermined to the extent that firms face different costs for meeting it (Newell and Stavins 2003).[6]

In addition, the technology mandate does not optimally engage all of the major pollution reduction channels. A technology mandate for end-of-pipe treatment generates no incentive to change the production mix towards cleaner inputs, while a mandate stipulating a particular input mix provides no incentive for end-of-pipe treatment. Both types of mandate fail to equate the marginal costs across the different options for reducing emissions per unit of output.

Moreover, these policies do not optimally utilize the output-reduction channel. Although the price of the firm's output will reflect the variable costs of maintaining the new technology, it will not reflect the cost of the *remaining* pollution associated with each unit of output. This implies that the output price will be lower than in the case of emissions pricing, where the output price will reflect both the variable costs from the new technology *and* (since firms must pay for their remaining pollution) the price attached to the pollution associated with each unit of output. Therefore technology

---

[6]For example, it may be a lot less costly for firms that are currently upgrading or constructing new plants to incorporate a new abatement technology than for firms that must retrofit older plants that are not readily compatible with the newly mandated technology.

mandates do not cause firms to reduce pollution sufficiently through reductions in the scale of output. Thus, in order to achieve the overall emissions-reduction target, the regulator would have to require firms to press further on the input-substitution and end-of-pipe channels than would be necessary under emissions-pricing instruments. The lower per-unit private cost and lower output prices might seem to give the technology mandate an advantage. However, because the scale of output is excessive and the other channels are "overexploited," the *aggregate* cost of achieving the emissions-reduction target—private cost per unit of output times aggregate output—is higher under this policy instrument than under emissions pricing (Spulber 1985; Goulder et al. 1999).

Performance Standards. While technology mandates impose requirements directly on the production process, performance standards require that a firm's *output* meet certain conditions. Examples include maximum emission rates per kilowatt-hour of electricity, energy efficiency standards for buildings or household appliances, and fuel-economy requirements for new cars.[7]

Rather than dictate the specific technique for reducing pollution (or improving energy efficiency), performance standards grant firms flexibility in choosing how to meet the standard. For example, power plants can satisfy maximum allowable emission rates through various combinations of fuel-switching and postcombustion scrubbing, and they can meet renewable portfolio standards by relying more on wind, solar, hydro, and possibly nuclear generation. Auto manufacturers can improve fuel-economy through their chosen combinations of reducing vehicle size, using lighter materials, changing car-body design, and advanced engine technologies. Because they offer greater flexibility, performance standards generally are more cost-effective than specific technology mandates.

As with technology mandates, performance standards fail to exploit optimally the output-reduction channel. Again, firms are not charged for their remaining emissions, which implies lower output prices than under a comparable emission pricing policy, and over-reliance on reducing the emissions intensity of production either through input-substitution or post-combustion ("end-of-pipe") treatment. For example, automobile fuel economy standards do not exploit emissions reductions through incentives to reduce vehicle miles of travel (or vehicle "output"). A gasoline tax, in contrast, does provide such incentives. Moreover, cost-effectiveness generally calls for different performance requirements among firms with differing production capabilities. Regulators generally lack the information required to tailor the standards to individual firms. On the other hand, this problem

---

[7]The performance standard described here is a requirement relating to a firm's output Sometimes the term "performance standard" is used to refer to a constraint on inputs. Examples include minimum requirements for renewable fuels in power generation, and California's "low carbon fuel standard," which requires refiners to include a certain minimal percentage of "low carbon" fuel in the motor fuel they sell.

could be addressed by allowing some firms to undercomply, provided that they buy credits from other firms that go beyond the standard.

As shown in columns 1 and 2 of Table 1, the most cost-effective instruments under the narrow definition of "cost" are those that directly price the pollution externality: namely, emissions taxes and tradable emissions permits. Other price instruments are less cost-effective because they fail to exploit optimally all of the major channels for emissions reductions. Direct regulatory instruments also fail to engage optimally all of the major pollution reduction channels and, if nontradable, fail to equate the marginal costs of emissions reductions across heterogeneous firms.

Cost Comparisons

How important, in quantitative terms, are the differences in costs of the various instruments?

Tietenberg (2006) summarizes 14 simulation studies applied to different pollutants and regions. In all but two cases, abatement costs would be 40–95 percent lower under emissions taxes or tradable allowances than under technology mandates, (nontradable) performance standards, and other policies such as requirements that all sources reduce pollution in the same proportion. In the context of reducing gasoline, Austin and Dinan (2005) estimate that policy costs are around 65 percent lower under fuel taxes than more stringent fuel economy regulation (partly because regulation does not exploit opportunities for fuel savings through reduced driving). Palmer and Burtaw (2005), Fischer and Newell (2008), and Newell and Stavins (2003) estimate that, in the power sector, abatement costs would be about 50 percent lower under emissions pricing than under various performance standards.

In the circumstances considered by these studies, incentive-based policies have a large cost advantage. However, this may not be true in all cases. For example, the cost advantage will be modest if there is little heterogeneity among firms so that a single technology mandate can bring marginal abatement costs close to equality. Similarly, if incentive-based instruments only have a small effect on product prices, then the failure to optimally exploit the output reduction channel under direct regulatory approaches will not matter much in practice. And even if output reduction effects are important, the relative cost differences between emissions pricing and direct regulatory instruments may decline sharply as abatement approaches 100 percent (Goulder et al. 1999).

Broader Cost Considerations

This section expands the narrow notion of cost to include administrative costs and the cost impacts from fiscal interactions.

Administrative Costs

A broader notion of "cost" includes the costs of administering a pollution control program, particularly the costs of monitoring and enforcement (Heyes 2000; Stranlund, Chavez, and Field 2002). In some instances, monitoring emissions is very costly or virtually infeasible. For example, it is extremely difficult, if not impossible, to keep track of "nonpoint" sources of water pollution caused by agricultural production. In circumstances where monitoring emissions is exceptionally costly, emissions pricing may lose its status as the most cost-effective option. Mandates for certain farm practices (like grassed water strips to limit chemical runoff, or lagoons and storage tasks to treat waste from large confined animal feeding operations) may be the most practical approach, as these can be monitored via satellite imagery or on-site inspections. And although an automobile's tailpipe emissions could be taxed using information from periodic odometer readings and emissions per mile data from vehicle inspection programs, it is administratively much easier to impose emission per-mile standards on automobile manufacturers. This alternative also avoids privacy concerns about government collection of data on household driving habits.

In some cases, high monitoring costs associated with emissions pricing can be avoided by employing a "two-part" regulatory instrument to approximate (and in some cases duplicate) the impact of emissions pricing. Eskeland and Devarajan (1995) show that a tax on automobile emissions can be closely approximated by combining a mandated emissions-control technology with a tax on gasoline. Intuitively, the technology mandate assures efficient substitution of the "inputs" (engine characteristics) used to produce transport, while the tax on gasoline helps employ the output-scale channel by raising the variable cost of transport (the car's output) to an efficient level. Similarly, if pay-by-the bag for household garbage is difficult to enforce in rural areas where it might encourage illegal dumping, an alternative might be to combine a packaging tax at the retail level with subsidies for household recycling (e.g., Fullerton and Wolverton 2000).[8]

Cost Impacts from Fiscal Interactions

The cost-ranking of emissions control policies is further complicated by general equilibrium impacts—in particular, interactions between these policies and the distortions in labor and capital markets created by the preexisting tax system. Fiscal interactions can substantially augment or reduce the advantages of incentive-based policies, depending on specific policy features. In fact, once fiscal interactions are taken into account, in some circumstances emissions-pricing policies are more costly than direct regulation.

A number of studies emphasize the idea that emissions mitigation policies affect tax distortions in factor markets, particularly those in the labor

---

[8]This combination has much in common with a deposit-refund system. For a discussion of such systems see Bennear and Stavins (2007).

market created by income and payroll taxes (e.g., Goulder et al. 1997). The studies focus on two main connections with factor market distortions. First, under revenue-raising policies such as emissions taxes, fuel taxes, or cap-and-trade systems with auctioned allowances, the revenue can be used to finance reductions in existing factor taxes. This produces a first-order efficiency gain, equal to the increase in labor supply (or capital) times the difference between the gross- and net-of-tax factor price. Although the proportionate increase in economy-wide factor supplies maybe very small, this beneficial "revenue-recycling effect" can be quite large in relative terms. A second effect works in the opposite direction. To the extent that the costs of environmental policies are shifted forward to consumers (in the form of higher prices paid for refined fuels or energy-intensive goods and services), the consumer price level will rise, implying a reduction in real factor returns. This depresses factor supply, and the resulting efficiency loss, termed the "tax-interaction effect," raises the costs of environmental policies.

Prior studies indicate that under fairly neutral conditions the tax-interaction effect outweighs the revenue-recycling effect, though one can stipulate other conditions under which this is not the case.[9] To the extent that the tax-interaction effect dominates, environmental policies involve greater costs than if one ignored the fiscal interactions. For policies that raise no revenue (such as freely allocated emissions permits, performance standards or mandated technologies) or for policies that raise revenue but do not use them in socially productive ways, only the (costly) tax-interaction effect applies.

What do fiscal interactions imply for the choice among environmental policy instruments? First, they imply that the costs of emissions taxes and tradable emissions allowance systems will depend importantly on whether the system is designed to exploit the revenue-recycling effect. Emissions taxes with efficient recycling of the tax revenue have a cost-advantage over emissions taxes in which the revenues are returned as lump-sum transfers (e.g., rebate checks). Similarly, emissions allowance systems that raise revenue (through auctioning of allowances) and apply the revenue to finance tax cuts have a cost-advantage over emissions allowance systems in which the allowances are initially given out for free.

The cost-advantage can be substantial. For example, a $20 per ton tax on CO_2 might raise annual revenues in the near term by roughly $100 billion (the tax would have a modest impact on reducing current emissions, which are around 6 billion tons). If this tax were revenue-neutral, we would put the cost savings over an equivalent incentive-based policy that did not exploit the revenue-recycling effect at about $30 billion a year. In fact, the decision about whether to auction or freely allocate emissions allowances—that is, whether or not to exploit the revenue-recycling effect—can determine whether an emissions allowance program, scaled to generate allowance prices that equal estimated marginal damages from emissions, produces overall efficiency gains (Parry et al. 1999). If it fails to

---

[9]See, for example, Bovenberg and Goulder (2002) and Parry (1998a) for more detail.

exploit the revenue-recycling effect, firms' abatement costs, plus the tax-interaction effect, may exceed the benefits from reduced pollution.

Fiscal interactions also have important implications for the choice between emissions pricing instruments and other environmental policies. For a given pollution reduction, the tax-interaction effect for technology mandates and performance standards is often smaller than for emissions taxes and emission permits. This is because these policies can have a weaker impact on product prices, as they do not charge firms for their remaining emissions. In fact, at least in a homogeneous firm setting, the superiority on cost-effectiveness grounds of (freely allocated) permit systems over technology mandates and performance standards could be overturned because of the greater tax-interaction effect under the market-based policy (Goulder et al. 1999).[10]

In summary, consideration of fiscal interactions tends to favor (revenue-neutral) emissions taxes, other environmentally oriented taxes, and auctioned emissions allowance systems over other policies when tax or auction revenues are used to finance cuts in existing distortionary taxes (Table 1, column 3).

Additional Considerations

This section discusses two other factors that are relevant to the choice among emissions control instruments: the ability of the instrument to address uncertainty, and the nature of its distributional impacts.

The Role of Uncertainty

Uncertainties are unavoidable: policymakers can never perfectly predict the outcome of environmental policies. This is relevant to instrument choice, since the choice of instrument affects both the type of uncertainty that emerges as well as the expected efficiency gains generated. Instruments also differ in their abilities to adjust to new information.

The Nature of Uncertainty under Different Instruments. Under emissions taxes, the price of emissions (the tax rate) is established at the outset. What is uncertain is the aggregate emissions quantity that will result after firms respond to the tax. In contrast, under pure emissions allowance systems, the aggregate emissions quantity is established at the outset by the number of allowances introduced into the market, while the emissions price is uncertain because it is determined by the market *ex ante*.

To reduce the price uncertainty under emissions allowance systems, some have proposed augmenting such systems with provisions for an allow-

---

[10]Abatement subsidies also generate interactions with the tax system. For a discussion of this case, see Parry (1998b).

ance price ceiling or price floor. The idea of establishing a price ceiling has gained considerable attention in discussions of climate change policy. Here a cap-and-trade program is combined with a "safety valve" to enforce a pre-established ceiling price (Burtraw and Palmer 2006; Jacoby and Ellerman 2004; Pizer 2002). Under this policy, if the allowance price reaches the ceiling price, the regulator is authorized to sell whatever additional allowances must be introduced into the market to prevent allowance prices from rising further. Note that while the safety valve reduces price uncertainty, it introduces uncertainty about aggregate emissions. Similarly, it is possible to enforce a price floor by authorizing the regulator to purchase (withdraw from the market) allowances once the allowance price falls to the pre-established floor price.

Potential price volatility of allowance systems can also be reduced by allowing firms to bank permits for future compliance periods when current allowance prices are considered unusually low, and to run down previously banked permits or borrow permits when current allowance prices are considered unusually high.

Other instruments involve uncertainties about emissions prices, quantities, or both. Like an emissions tax, a tax on a goods associated with emissions (for example, a gasoline tax) leaves the quantity of emissions uncertain. Direct regulatory policies leave uncertain the amount to which aggregate emissions will be reduced, although they may indicate limits on emissions at the facility or firm level. Direct regulatory policies also involve uncertainties as to the effective price of emissions; that is, the shadow price of emissions or the marginal cost of abatement implied by the regulations.

Implications of Uncertainty for Expected Efficiency Gains. Maximizing the efficiency gains from pollution control requires that marginal damages from emissions (or marginal benefits from emissions reductions) equal society's (each firm's) marginal costs of emissions reductions. However, a regulator seeking to maximize efficiency gains will not have perfect information about marginal abatement costs, a reflection of the inability of the regulator to know each firm's current capabilities for input-substitution and end-of-pipe treatment. There is even more uncertainty as to future abatement costs, as these will depend on additional variables that are difficult to predict, such as fuel prices and the extent of technological change.

In the presence of abatement cost uncertainty, the choice of instrument affects the expected efficiency gains.[11] In a static context, the relative efficiency impact of a "price" policy such as an emissions tax compared to a "quantity" policy such as an aggregate emissions cap depends on the relative steepness of the aggregate marginal abatement cost curve and the mar-

---

[11]Policymakers are also uncertain about the marginal damage schedule. However, as discussed in Weitzman (1974) and Stavins (1996), this does not have strong implications for instrument choice unless marginal damages are correlated with marginal abatement costs.

ginal damage curve.[12] In a limiting case, where the marginal damage curve is perfectly elastic, expected net benefits are maximized under the emissions tax, with the tax rate set equal to the (constant) marginal damages. In this case the tax automatically equates marginal damages to marginal abatement costs, regardless of the actual location of the marginal abatement cost schedule. In contrast, if an aggregate emissions cap is employed, with the cap set to equate marginal damages with *expected* marginal abatement costs, abatement will be too high *ex post* if marginal abatement costs turn out to be greater than expected, and too low *ex post* if marginal abatement costs are lower than expected. The relative efficiency gains are reversed in the other limiting case: when marginal damages are perfectly inelastic, expected net benefits are maximized under the emissions cap. For intermediate cases, either the tax or the cap could offer higher net benefits, depending on whether the marginal damage curve is flatter or steeper than the marginal abatement cost curve (Weitzman 1974).

These results carry over to a dynamic setting, where environmental damages depend on the accumulated stock of pollution. Some dynamic analyses (see Kolstad 1996; Pizer 2002; Newell and Pizer 2003) suggest that in the presence of uncertainty, a carbon tax (a "price" policy) might offer substantially higher expected efficiency gains than a cap-and-trade system (a "quantity" policy).

Uncertainty and Policy Flexibility. The analyses just discussed do not consider differences across instruments in the speed at which they can adjust to new information. However, an emissions allowance system that includes provisions for the banking and borrowing of allowances might have a slight advantage over emissions taxes in this regard. For example, suppose that, under a carbon cap-and-trade system, new evidence emerges that global warming is occurring faster than projected. Speculators would anticipate a tightening of the future emissions cap, which would instantly shift up the trajectory of current and expected future permit prices, before any adjustment to the future cap is actually made. In contrast, under a carbon tax, it might take some time to enact legislative change in the tax rate in response to new scientific information, which would leave emission control suboptimal during the period of policy stickiness.

Distributional Impacts

The distributional impacts of alternative environmental policies can be considered across numerous dimensions, such as regions, ethnic groups, or generations. Here we focus on two dimensions that have received especially great attention in policy discussions: the distribution between owners of pol-

---

[12]The aggregate emissions cap policy could involve either fixed quotas on individual pollution sources, or a set of tradable emissions allowances, where the total number of allowances in circulation represents the aggregate cap.

luting or energy-intensive industries and other members of society (consumers, taxpayers, workers), and the distribution across households of different incomes. These distributional impacts have important implications not only for fairness or distributive justice but also for political feasibility.

Distribution between Owners of Polluting Enterprises and Other Economic Actors. Since the combustion of fuels is a major contributor to pollution, an important issue is the burden that pollution control policies might impose on industries supplying these fuels as well as industries (such as electricity and metals production) that use these fuels intensively. Depending on specific design features, different instruments can have very different impacts on capital owners in these industries.

Consider first the impacts of a cap-and-trade system. As discussed in Section 2, for a given quantity of allowances, free allocation leads to the same allowance prices and output price increases as does auctioning of allowances. However, the nature of the initial allocation can have a significant effect on the distributional burden from regulation.

An emissions allowance system causes firms to restrict the level of production, thereby causing an increase in the equilibrium output price. Higher output prices potentially generate rents to firms, in much the same way that a cartel enjoys rents by reducing output.

With free allowance allocation, firms enjoy these rents. In contrast, if allowances are introduced through a competitive auction, the rents are bid away as firms compete to obtain the valuable allowances. In this case, what would be firms' rents under free allocation become government revenue instead. This benefits the general taxpaying public to the extent that it reduces the government's need to rely on various existing taxes for revenue; alternatively, the public could benefit from additional government-provided goods or services financed by the auction revenue.

In fact, when allowances are initially given away for free, regulated firms might even enjoy higher profits than in the case of no regulation: the rents might more than fully compensate firms for the costs of complying with the program. Whether this occurs depends on two factors. The first is the elasticity of supply relative to the elasticity of demand for the industry's output. The greater the relative elasticity of supply, the greater the price increase associated with a given free allocation of allowances, and the larger the rents generated to firms. The second is the extent of required abatement: at low levels of abatement, allowance rents are large relative to compliance costs, which implies a greater potential for an overall increase in profit.

Studies of nitrogen oxide allowance trading under the US Clean Air Act (Bovenberg et al. 2005) and potential carbon dioxide allowance trading in the United States (Bovenberg and Goulder 2001; Smith et al. 2002; and Burtraw and Palmer 2007) suggest that the rents from 100 percent free allocation overcompensate firms for program compliance costs. In fact, these studies show that a fairly small share of the allowances—generally less than 30 percent—needs to be freely allocated to enable firms to retain rents sufficient to prevent a loss of profit.[13] It should be noted, however, that these cases involve relatively modest emission reductions. As the extent of abatement increases, the size of the rents, and hence the scope for compensation, declines relative to the compliance burden imposed on regulated industries.

Free allocation can enhance political feasibility because it avoids imposing burdens on highly mobilized producer groups. On the other hand, auctioning has an advantage in terms of cost-effectiveness because it yields revenues that can be used to finance cuts in existing distortionary taxes. From the studies above, it appears that preventing profit losses is consistent with freely allocating a small share of the allowances and auctioning the rest. In this case, the sacrifice in cost-effectiveness relative to the case of 100 percent auctioning would be fairly small. In Bovenberg and Goulder (2001), for example, partial free allocation raises policy costs by 7.5 percent relative to 100 percent auctioning. The sacrifice of cost-effectiveness could be large in some cases, however. In particular, even 100 percent free allowance allocation may not be enough to compensate firms when the proportionate emissions reduction is very large (Bovenberg et al. 2005).

Free allowance allocation is not the only way to prevent profit losses to regulated firms. Profits can also be preserved through an emissions tax system offering inframarginal exemptions to the tax—in this case, the tax applies only to emissions beyond a certain level. Like an emissions allowance system with partial free allocation, this tax policy generates rents, where the rents increase with the scope of the exemptions. Because of these rents, preserving profits may require exempting only a small fraction of the firm's emissions.

Direct regulations do not charge for remaining emissions, and thus might also impose lower burdens on regulated firms. As discussed above, however, the absence of a charge on remaining emissions implies a sacrifice of cost-effectiveness.

To date, technology mandates, performance standards, and permit systems with free allocation are all far more common than emissions taxes or fully auctioned permit systems. This suggests that owners of polluting facilities may have significantly influenced the ultimate instrument choices.

Distribution across Household Income Groups. Fairness in the distribution of cost impacts across households is a major issue for many pollution control policies—particularly those relating to energy industries—since low-income households tend to spend larger shares of their budgets on electric-

---

[13]In the first phase of the European Union's ETS, over 95 percent of the allowances were given away for free, which generated windfall profits to many of the regulated firms (Sijm, Neuhoff and Chen (2006)). Partly in reaction to this, there has been a distinct shift towards greater emphasis on the auctioning of allowances in planned future phases of the ETS, in various climate bills recently introduced in the U.S. Congress, and in the recently established Regional Greenhouse Gas Initiative in the northeast United States.

ity, home heating fuels, gasoline, and other energy-intensive goods (Parry et al. 2006).

Again, the ultimate impacts of revenue-raising policies such as emissions taxes and auctioned emissions allowances depend critically on how the revenues are used. Dinan and Rogers (2002) and Metcalf (2007) examine recycling revenues from carbon taxes or auctioned carbon allowances via tax reductions favoring low-income groups (e.g., payroll tax rebates, higher income tax thresholds, lump-sum transfers). These recycling schemes can help achieve a fairer distributional burden, for example by imposing a more equitable pattern of burden-to-income ratios across different income groups. However, they might not help some elderly or other nonworking households, who may require targeted energy assistance programs.

The choice between free allocation and auctioning of allowances also has distributional implications across household income groups. In particular, free allocation tends to increase the disparity in the burden-to-income ratios between low- and high-income groups, since firms' equity values will rise with the increase in producer surplus, and upper-income groups own a disproportionate share of such equity (Dinan and Rogers 2002). In this regard, direct regulatory policies may have some appeal since they avoid transferring rents from households (through large price increases) to firms.

Conclusions

From the above discussion it should be clear that numerous dimensions are relevant to instrument choice, and that no single instrument is best along all dimensions. For example, as shown in Table 1, tradable allowance systems with free allocation might perform relatively well in terms of political feasibility (column 4) but relatively poorly in terms of minimizing general equilibrium costs or achieving household equity (columns 3 and 5). The opposite applies for (revenue-neutral) emissions taxes or auctioned allowances. Direct regulatory policies have some appeal in terms of distribution (columns 4 and 5) but are generally less cost-effective along the lines indicated by columns 1–3.

Details matter, and the general type of instrument doesn't always indicate the overall implications for cost, fairness, or political feasibility. Emissions taxes and auctioned allowances may lose some of their key attractive properties if accompanying legislation does not require offsetting reductions in other taxes. On the other hand, the political obstacles to these policies might be tempered by providing tax exemptions for some of the infra-marginal emissions, or by reserving a portion of allowances for free allocation. And the differences between emissions taxes and emission permits in the presence of abatement cost uncertainty can be blurred through provisions, such as banking and borrowing, that reduce allowance price volatility.

Technology Policies

The market failure that seems most central to environmental issues is the inability of the market to address externalities from pollution. These include local health costs, damages to ecosystems and the services they provide, costs to terrestrial and marine wildlife, and global damages such as climate change.

However, additional market failures associated with clean technology development can be inextricably linked to environmental problems, and may provide an efficiency rationale for additional instruments beyond those already discussed. In what follows, we briefly examine potential rationales and instruments for promoting technology development, focusing on two general policy objectives: advancing research and development (R&D) and promoting technology deployment.

R&D Policies

Several US states have recently announced the goal of reducing greenhouse gas emissions by 80 percent below their 1990 levels by 2050. Achieving this goal at reasonable cost would require more than substitution among known technological processes: it would necessitate major technological break-throughs. The emissions control policies previously discussed may be inca-pable of bringing about these breakthrough technologies since they provide invention incentives only indirectly—by emissions pricing or by raising the costs of conventional, "dirty" production methods through direct regulation.

Additional policies to promote clean technology R&D are justified on efficiency grounds to the extent that they address market failures beyond the pollution externality. One important failure stems from the inability of inventors or innovators to fully appropriate the returns from the knowledge they create. In particular, other firms might be able to copy a new technology, legally imitate it if the technology is under patent, or otherwise use knowledge about the technology to advance their own research programs. Numerous empirical studies suggest that the (marginal) social return to innovative activity in general might be several times the (marginal) private return (e.g., Griliches 1992; Mansfield 1985; Levin et al. 1988; and Jones and Williams 1998).[14]

This appropriability problem means that incentives for clean technol-ogy R&D will be inefficiently low, even if pollution externalities are appro-priately priced. There is a theoretical and empirical literature comparing the efficiency of alternative environmental policy instruments in promot-ing the development of cleaner technologies (e.g., Jung et al. 1996; Fischer

---

[14]On the other hand, a "common pool" problem can work toward excessive R&D. This problem stems from the failure of a given firm to account for the fact that its own R&D reduces the likelihood that other firms will obtain innovation rents (Wright (1983)). In general, however, this rent-stealing problem appears to be dominated by the appropriability problem (e.g., Griliches (1992)).

et al. 2003; Milliman and Prince 1989). No single instrument can effectively correct market failures from both emissions externalities and the knowledge appropriability problem, however. Indeed, as Fischer and Newell (2008) and Schneider and Goulder (1997) indicate in the climate policy context, achieving a given emissions reduction through one instrument alone involves considerably higher costs than employing two instruments.[15]

The current literature does not single out any particular instrument as most effective in dealing with this problem. The relative effectiveness of subsidies to private R&D, strengthened patent rules, and technology prizes depends on the severity of the appropriability problem, the extent of monopoly-pricing distortions under patents, and asymmetric information between governments and firms about expected research benefits and costs (e.g., Wright 1983). Also, just how much or how fast we should be pushing technology development is difficult to gauge, given uncertainty about the likelihood that research will lead to viable technologies, and the potential for crowding out other socially valuable research (e.g., Nordhaus 2002 and Goulder and Schneider 1999). Basic government research and demonstration projects can help to restore invention efforts to an efficient level. But it is difficult to quantify the efficient level of basic R&D funding toward such projects, though studies suggest that past federal spending on energy R&D to mitigate pollution and improve knowledge has often yielded considerable net benefits (NRC 2001).

Technology Deployment Policies

Once technologies have been successfully developed and are ready for commercialization, should their deployment be pushed by additional policy interventions? Again, further policy inducements are warranted on efficiency grounds only if there are additional market failures that impede the diffusion process. In theory, there are several possibilities.

Appropriability issues could arise in connection with the deployment of new technologies. Specifically, early adopters of a new technology (e.g., cellulosic ethanol production plants) could achieve lower production costs for the new technology over time through learning-by-doing. This would award external benefits to later adopters of the technology and might justify some short-term assistance for adopting the new technology. Since the potential for deployment-related knowledge spillovers may vary greatly depending on

---

[15]Imposing stiffer emissions prices than warranted by environmental externalities alone—instead of complementing Pigouvian pricing with tailored technology policies—is an inefficient way to promote innovation. Not only does this generate excessive short-term abatement but it also fails to differentiate among technologies that may face very different market impediments. For example, alternative automobile fuels and carbon capture and storage technologies might warrant relatively more support than other technologies, to the extent that there are network externalities associated with the new pipeline infrastructure required to transport fuels to gas stations, or emissions associated with underground storage sites.

the product involved, these policies need to be evaluated on a case-by-case basis.

Another potential market failure relates to consumer valuations of energy-efficiency improvements. Some analysts argue that consumers systematically undervalue such improvements. Possible evidence for this is the tendency of consumers to require very short payback periods for durable energy-using equipment—in effect, to apply discount rates significantly above what might be considered the social discount rate.[16] Greene (1998) cites these problems in claiming that there is a role for automobile fuel economy regulations, as a complement to emission pricing instruments. This issue has long been contentious. Solid empirical research is needed to sort out whether there is a significant additional market failure here and therefore whether additional government incentives are justified on efficiency grounds.

Lack of information could also cause consumers to undervalue (or overvalue) improvements in energy-efficiency. As pointed out by Jaffe and Stavins (1994), the market only "fails" if the costs of providing additional information fall short of the benefits. If the market does fail, the most efficient policy response is to subsidize or require the provision of better information to the consumer (e.g., requiring auto dealers to post certified fuel economy stickers on vehicles).

Conclusions about Technology Policies

In sum, there are strong arguments for invoking technology-advancement policies in addition to instruments aimed at curbing emissions or effluent. Multiple market failures justify multiple instruments. Most agree that additional policies are warranted to support basic and applied research, development, and demonstration projects at government, university, and private institutions, though the specific instruments and level of support are less clear. There is less agreement regarding the justification for measures to promote market deployment once new technologies have been successfully developed. Whether such policies are called for seems to depend on the specific industries or processes involved, as well as assumptions about consumer behavior that deserve further empirical testing.

---

[16]Clearly many economists support the idea that the social rate of discount is lower than the market rate of interest (see, for example, Marglin (1963)), which implies that, from the point of view of social welfare, consumers tend to discount the future too heavily in their choices of consumer durables or, more broadly, in their saving decisions. This provides a rationale for government support of broad savings incentives rather than incentives focused only on saving in the form of purchases of energy-efficient durable goods.

Additional Challenges to Instrument Choice

We now consider three issues that further complicate instrument choice: multiple externalities from a single product or service; the potential for interactions among policy instruments; and the possibility of linking instruments across jurisdictions.

Multiple Externalities

One potential attraction of taxes on electricity, gasoline, or other goods related to emissions is that they may reduce demands for goods whose production or consumption involves multiple externalities. For example, by reducing gasoline consumption a gasoline tax helps address externalities from tailpipe emissions, such as local pollution and global climate impacts; and, by increasing the fuel costs per mile driven, the tax deters vehicle use and thereby reduces externalities from traffic congestion and traffic accidents (to the extent that insurance does not internalize accident risks from driving). Thus, this one tax can accomplish several goals. Apart from administrative considerations, the most cost-effective approach is to introduce multiple taxes. Each tax would be set based on the marginal external cost of a different externality, which would yield appropriate incentives to deal with each of the various problems (emissions, congestion, etc.) involved. On the other hand, the use of multiple taxes can involve substantial administrative costs. Policy makers need to weigh such costs against the potential benefits from implementing multiple, sharply focused taxes.

Regulatory Interactions

Preexisting policies may have implications for the choice of emissions control instruments. Prior regulations on electricity pricing provide an example. In the majority of states that retain average-cost pricing for power generation, prices are often below marginal supply cost. This reflects the fact that older, baseload technologies, such as coal and nuclear generation, tend to have lower variable costs than new or marginal technologies, such as natural gas generation. In these circumstances, the price of electricity is not only below social cost (which includes the environmental cost), but below the marginal private supply cost as well.

In this setting, Burtraw et al. (2001) find that the costs of moderately reducing power plant emissions of CO_2 are about two-thirds lower under auctioned permits than under the performance standards. This is because auctioned permits have a greater impact on electricity prices, as firms must pay for remaining emissions under auctioned permits. Thus, in this setting auctioned permits have an advantage by helping to prices closer to marginal social cost. Burtraw et al. also find that auctioned permits are far less costly than freely allocated permits. This reflects the fact that regulated utilities cannot pass forward the market value of freely allocated permits through higher generation prices.

Multiple Jurisdictions, Leakage, and Policy Linkages

Environmental problems are often addressed by several different jurisdictions and multiple levels of government. This can also have implications for instrument choice.

One important issue is "emissions leakage," where increases in emissions outside of a given jurisdiction offset the reductions promoted within the jurisdiction. Leakage can occur in at least two ways. First, new regulations within one jurisdiction can raise production costs, causing polluting firms to relocate to another jurisdiction. Second, new regulations imposed by one jurisdiction can shift consumer demands away from (higher priced) goods produced within that jurisdiction, leading to increased demands and emissions elsewhere. Although the use of any instrument that raises costs can generate leakage, some instruments might cause more leakage than others. In this regard, certain direct regulatory instruments such as renewable portfolio standards could be superior to cap-and-trade in preventing leakage associated with a shift in demands. In particular, they might minimize a shift from electricity generated within a jurisdiction (e.g., California) to electricity generated elsewhere (outside of California). This is because direct regulatory instruments do not charge for inframarginal emissions and thus are likely to have a weaker impact on within-jurisdiction electricity prices, implying less leakage. This advantage would have to be weighed against any disadvantages in terms of general cost-effectiveness.

Another important consideration is the potential for policy linkages across jurisdictions. If political constraints force environmental policies to be made by governments whose jurisdictions are narrower than what is efficient, the situation can be improved through linkages across regional programs. For example, the cost-effectiveness of various governments' cap-and-trade systems to reduce greenhouse gases can be enhanced by linking the systems, as this yields a broader market and an equating of marginal abatement costs across regions. (Similarly, harmonizing carbon taxes across jurisdictions enhances cost-effectiveness.) In this regard, the relative attractiveness of different instruments to one jurisdiction may depend importantly on the extent to which these instruments mesh with policies previously implemented by other jurisdictions. Thus, in the United States, the fact that 10 northeastern states have already committed themselves to a joint cap-and-trade system (the Regional Greenhouse Gas Initiative) increases the attractiveness of cap-and-trade to other states.

Conclusions

Environmental economists should take pride in the substantial body of literature on instrument choice that has emerged since the work of the "founding fathers" (e.g., Kneese and Bower 1984) in the 1960s. Beyond providing insights into the implications of existing regulatory approaches, environmental economists have helped devise new instruments for combating pollution, and their analyses have had a significant and growing impact on public policy. Moreover, many of the insights concerning environmental policy instruments are relevant to instrument choice or policy design in other areas, including forestry and fisheries, agriculture, transportation, substance abuse, and health.

Notwithstanding our claim that no single instrument is superior to all others in all settings, the analyses in the instrument choice literature have made a strong case for the wider use of flexible, incentive-based policies. They have also helped establish the idea that environmental taxes and auctioned allowances are a particularly efficient potential source of government revenue. Flexible incentive-based instruments that only existed on paper a few decades ago—such as emissions allowance banking and a "safety valve"—are now becoming part of the regulatory landscape. Economists' calls for increased auctioning (rather than free allocation) of allowances are being heeded in the EU's recent proposals for its Emissions Trading Scheme (Commission of the European Communities 2008), as well as in plans for the Regional Greenhouse Gas Initiative in the northeastern United States.

Despite these achievements, significant challenges remain. Discussions of alternative instrument choices often leave something to be desired. Many analyses disregard administrative, legal, or institutional issues relevant to policy costs, or focus exclusively on cost-effectiveness. As emphasized above, a broad range of criteria deserves consideration. In addition, many studies ignore details about market structure or producers' objectives that can influence the relative effectiveness of various instruments.

Government (as opposed to market) failure represents a further challenge. Winston (2007) offers many examples of government intervention in markets where the evidence of a market failure is tenuous at best. Even when there is a clear rationale for policy intervention, inefficient instruments (such as ethanol mandates) may be employed at the expense of far more cost-effective alternatives (such as fuel taxes and CO_2 taxes). Government failures are due in part to the influence of powerful interest groups. Such influence is more a difficulty with the political process than an economics problem. Nevertheless, economists can contribute to improved political outcomes by devising new policy instruments that do a better job reconciling cost-effectiveness and distributional goals (such as avoiding large, near-term burdens on highly mobilized stakeholders). They can also improve the prospects for sound policy by becoming more effective in communicating key research insights to policymakers.

REFERENCES

Aldy, Joseph E., and Robert N. Stavins. 2007. *Architectures for Agreement: Addressing Global Climate Change in the Post-Kyoto World.* Cambridge: Cambridge University Press.

Austin, David, and Terry Dinan. 2005. Clearing the air: The costs and consequences of higher CAFE standards and increased gasoline taxes. *Journal of Environmental Economics and Management* 50: 562–82.

Baumol, William J., and Wallace E. Oates. 1971. The use of standards and prices for protection of the environment. *Swedish Journal of Economics* 73: 42–54.

Bennear, Lori S., and Robert N. Stavins. 2007. Second-best theory and the use of multiple policy instruments. *Environmental and Resource Economics* 37: 111–29.

Bovenberg, A. Lans, and Lawrence H. Goulder. 2001. Neutralizing the adverse industry impacts of CO_2 abatement policies: what does it cost? In *Behavioral and Distributional Effects of Environmental Policy*, eds. C. Carraro and G. Metcalf, pp. 45–85. Chicago: University of Chicago Press.

Bovenberg, A. Lans, and Lawrence H. Goulder. 2002. Environmental taxation and regulation. In *Handbook of Public Economics*, eds. A. Auerbach and M. Feldstein. New York: North-Holland.

Bovenberg, A. Lans, Lawrence H. Goulder, and Derek J. Gurney. 2005. Efficiency costs of meeting industry-distributional constraints under environmental permits and taxes. *RAND Journal of Economics*. Winter.

Burtraw, Dallas, and Karen Palmer. 2006. *Dynamic Adjustment to Incentive-based Environmental Policy to Improve Efficiency and Performance*. Washington, DC: Resources for the Future.

———. 2007. *Compensation Rules for Climate Policy in the Electricity Sector*. Discussion Paper 07–41. Washington, DC: Resources for the Future.

Burtraw, Dallas, Karen Palmer, Ranjit Bharvirkar, and Anthony Paul. 2001. *The Effect of Allowance Allocation on the Cost of Carbon Emission Trading*. Discussion Paper 01–30. Washington, DC: Resources for the Future.

Commission of the European Communities. 2008. 20 20 by 2020: Europe's Climate Change Opportunity. *Communication from the Commission to the European Parliament, the Council, The European Economic and Social Committee, and the Committee of the Regions*.

Dinan, Terry M., and Diane L. Rogers. 2002. Distributional effects of carbon allowance trading: How government decisions determine winners and losers. *National Tax Journal* LV: 199–222.

Eskeland, Gunnar S., and Shantayanan Devarajan. 1995. Taxing bads by taxing goods: Toward efficient pollution control with presumptive charges, In *Public Economics and the Environment in an Imperfect World*, eds. A. Lans Bovenberg and Sijbren Cnossen, pp. 61–112. Boston: Kluwer Academic Publishers.

Fischer, Carolyn, and Richard G. Newell. 2008. Environmental and technology policies for climate mitigation. *Journal of Environmental Economics and Management* 55(2): 142–62.

Fischer, Carolyn, Ian W. H. Parry, and William Pizer. 2003. Instrument choice for environmental protection when technological change is endogenous. *Journal of Environmental Economics and Management* 45: 523–45.

Fullerton, Don, and Ann Wolverton. 2000. Two generalizations of a deposit-refund system. *American Economic Review* [90(2): 238–42] (May).

Goulder, Lawrence H., Ian W. H. Parry, Roberton C. Williams III, and Dallas Burtraw. 1999. The cost-effectiveness of alternative instruments for environmental protection in a second-best setting. *Journal of Public Economics* 72(3): 329–60.

Goulder, Lawrence H., Ian W. H. Parry, and Dallas Burtraw. 1997. Revenue-Raising vs. Other approaches to environmental protection: The critical significance of pre-existing tax distortions. *RAND Journal of Economics* 28(4 Winter): 708–31.

Goulder, Lawrence H., and Stephen H. Schneider. 1999. Induced technological change and the attractiveness of CO_2 emissions abatement policies. *Resource and Energy Economics* 21: 211–53.

Greene, David L. 1998. Why CAFE worked. *Energy Policy* 26:595–614.

Griliches, Zvi. 1992. The Search for R&D Spillovers. *Scandinavian Journal of Economics* 94(Suppl): S29–S47.

Hepburn, Cameron. 2006. "Regulating by Prices, Quantities or Both: An Update and an Overview." *Oxford Review of Economic Policy.* 22:226–47.

Heyes, Anthony. 2000. Implementing environmental regulation: enforcement and compliance. *Journal of Regulatory Economics* 17: 107–29.

Jacoby, H. D., and A. D. Ellerman. 2004. The safety valve and climate policy. *Energy Policy* 32(4): 481–91.

Jaffe, Adam B., and Robert N. Stavins. 1994. The energy paradox and the diffusion of conservation technology. *Resource and Energy Economics* 15(2): 43–64.

Jones, Charles I., and John C. Williams. 1998. Measuring the social return to R&D. *Quarterly Journal of Economics* 113:1119–35.

Jung, C., K. Krutilla, and R. Boyd. 1996. Incentives for advanced pollution abatement technology at the industry level: An evaluation of policy alternatives. *Journal of Environmental Economics and Management* 30:95–111.

Keohane, Nathaniel O., Richard L. Revesz, and Robert N. Stavins. 1998. The choice of regulatory instrumetns in environmental policy. *Harvard Environmental Law Review* 22(2): 313–67.

Kneese, Allen V., and Blair T. Bower. 1984. *Managing Water Quality: Economics, Technology, Institutions.* Washington, DC: Resources for the Future.

Kolstad, Charles D. 1996. Learning and stock effects in environmental regulation: the case of greenhouse gas emissions. *Journal of Environmental Economics and Management* 31:1–18.

Levin, Richard C., Alvin K. Klevorick, Richard R. Nelson, and Sidney G. Winter. 1988. Appropriating the returns from industrial research and development. Special issue on Microeconomics, *Brookings Papers on Economic Activity* 3: 783–820.

Lyon, Thomas, and John W. Maxwell. 2002. Voluntary approaches to environmental protection: a survey. In *Economic Institutions and Environmental Policy: Past, Present and Future*, eds. Maurizio Franzini and Antonio Nicita. Aldershot, Hampshire, UK: Ashgate Publishing Ltd.

Mansfield, Edwin. 1985. How fast does new industrial technology leak out? *Journal of Industrial Economics* 34: 217–33.

Marglin, Stephen A. 1963. The social rate of discount and the optimal rate of investment. *Quarterly Journal of Economics* 95: 95–111.

Metcalf, Gilbert E. 2007. A proposal for a U.S. carbon tax swap: An equitable tax reform to address global climate change. Discussion Paper 2007–12. The Hamilton Project. Washington, DC: The Brookings Institution.

Milliman, S. R., and R. Prince. 1989. Firm incentives to promote technological change in pollution control. *Journal of Environmental Economics and Management* 17: 247–65.

Newell, Richard G., and William A. Pizer. 2003. Discounting the distant future: how much do uncertain rates increase valuations? *Journal of Environmental Economics and Management* 46: 52–71.

Newell, Richard G., and Robert N. Stavins. 2003. Cost heterogeneity and potential savings from market-based policies. *Journal of Regulatory Economics* 23:43–59.

Nordhaus, William D. 2002. Modeling induced innovation in climate-change policy. In *Technological Change and the Environment*, eds. Arnulf Grubler, Nebojsa Nakicenovic, and William Nordhaus, pp: 182–209. Washington, DC: Resources for the Future.

———. 2007. To tax or not to tax: alternative approaches to slowing global warming. *Review of Economics and Policy* 1(1): 26–44.

NRC. 2001. *Energy Research at DOE: Was It Worth It?* Washington, DC: National Academy Press.

Palmer, Karen, and Dallas Burtraw. 2005. Cost-effectiveness of renewable electricity policies. *Energy Economics* 27: 873–94.

Parry, Ian W. H. 1998a. The double dividend: When you get it and when you don't. *National Tax Association Proceedings* 1998: 46–51.

———. 1998b. A second-best analysis of environmental subsidies. *International Tax and Public Finance* 5(2): 153–70.

Parry, Ian W. H., Roberton C. Williams III, and Lawrence H. Goulder. 1999. When can carbon abatement policies increase welfare? The fundamental role of distorted factor markets. *Environmental Economies and Management* 37(1): 52–84.

Parry, Ian W. H., Hilary Sigman, Margaret Walls, and Roberton C. Williams III. 2006. The Incidence of pollution control policies. In *The International Yearbook of Environmental and Resource Economics 2006/2007*, eds. Tom Tietenberg and Henk Folmer, pp. 1–42. Northampton, MA: Edward Elgar Publishers.

Pizer, William A. 2002. Combining price and quantity controls to mitigate global climate change. *Journal of Public Economics* 85: 409–34.

Schneider, Stephen H., and Lawrence H. Goulder. 1997. Achieving low-cost emissions targets. *Nature* 389 (6846): 13–14, September 4.

Sijm, J., K. Neuhoff, and Y. Chen. 2006. CO_2 Cost pass-through and windfall profits in the power sector. *Climate Policy* 6(1): 49–72.

Smith, Anne E., Martin E. Ross, and Montgomery W. David. 2002. Implications of trading implementation design for equity-efficiency tradeoffs in carbon permit allocations. Working Paper. Washington, DC: Charles River Associates.

Spulber, Daniel F. 1985. Effluent regulation and long-run optimality. *Journal of Environmental Economics and Management* 12: 103–16.

Stavins, Robert N. 1996. Correlated uncertainty and policy instrument choice. *Journal of Environmental Economics and Management* 30: 218–32.

Stranlund, J. K., C. A. Chavez, and B. C. Field. 2002. Enforcing emissions trading programs: theory, practice, and performance. *Policy Studies Journal* 30(3): 343–61.

Tietenberg, Tom. 2006. *Emissions Trading: Principles and Practice*. Washington, DC: Resources for the Future.

Tietenberg, Tom, and David Wheeler. 2001. Empowering the community: Information strategies for pollution control. In *Frontiers of Environmental Economics*, eds. Henk Folmer, H. Landis Gabel, Shelby Gerking, and Adam Rose, pp. 85–120. Cheltenham, UK: Edward Elgar Publishers.

Weitzman, Martin L. 1974. Prices vs. quantities. *Review of Economic Studies* 41: 477–91.

Winston, Clifford. 2007. Government failure versus market failure: Microeconomics policy research and government performance. Washington, DC: Brookings Institution.

Wright, Brian D. 1983. The Economics of invention incentives: patents, prizes, and research contracts. *American Economic Review* 73(4): 691–707.

17 What Can We Learn from the Grand Policy Experiment? Lessons from SO₂ Allowance Trading*

Robert N. Stavins

Robert N. Stavins is Albert Pratt Professor of Business and Government at Harvard Kennedy School, Research Associate at the National Bureau of Economic Research, and University Fellow at Resources for the Future.

Economists consistently have urged the use of "market-based" or "economic-incentive" instruments—principally pollution taxes and systems of trade-able permits—to address environmental problems, rather than so-called "command-and-control" instruments, such as design standards, which require the use of particular technologies, or performance standards, which prescribe the maximum amount of pollution that individual sources can emit. At least in theory, a well-designed pollution tax (Pigou, 1920) or trade-able permit system (Crocker, 1966; Dales, 1968; Montgomery, 1972) will minimize the aggregate cost of achieving a given level of environmental protection (Baumol and Oates, 1988), and provide dynamic incentives for the adoption and diffusion of cheaper and better pollution control technologies (Milliman and Prince, 1989).

Despite such advantages, market-based environmental instruments have been used far less frequently than command-and-control standards. In particular, while taxes have been imposed on certain products that are linked to pollution, like gasoline and chemicals, this has typically been done as a way of raising revenue, such as with gas taxes to fund highway construction or chemical taxes to fund cleanup of Superfund toxic waste sites, rather than as incentive devices intended to reduce externalities (Barthold, 1994). But over the past 25 years, the political process has gradually become more receptive to market-oriented environmental tools. Beginning in the 1970s, the Environmental Protection Agency (EPA) offered states the option of employing variants of tradeable permits for the control of localized air

"What Can We Learn from the Grand Policy Experiment? Lessons from SO₂ Allowance Trading" by Robert N. Stavins. *Journal of Economic Perspectives*, Vol. 12, No. 3. Pp. 69–88, Summer 1998.

*I am indebted to Peter Zapfel for excellent research assistance, and Elizabeth Bailey, Dallas Burtraw, Brad De Long, Denny Ellerman, Lawrence Goulder, Robert Hahn, Paul Joskow, Alan Krueger, Richard Schmalensee, and (especially) Timothy Taylor for valuable comments on a previous version of this article. Any remaining errors are my own.

pollutants. Tradeable-permit systems were used in the 1980s to phase leaded gasoline out of the market and to phase out ozone-depleting chlorofluoro-carbons (CFCs). But by far the most ambitious application of these instruments has been for the control of acid rain under Title IV of the Clean Air Act amendments of 1990, which established a sulfur dioxide (SO_2) allowance trading program intended to cut nationwide emissions of SO_2 by 50 percent below 1980 levels by the year 2000.

This essay seeks to identify lessons that can be learned from this grand experiment in economically-oriented environmental policy. Since the SO_2 allowance trading program became binding only in 1995, it might seem premature to search for lessons for future policy. This would be true, were one to consider this policy experiment in isolation. But the SO_2 allowance trading program did not emerge into a policy vacuum; rather, it is but one step in the evolution of market-based environmental policies. Considered in this context, the time is ripe not only for an interim appraisal, but for reflection on what we have learned.

I begin with a brief description of the SO_2 allowance trading system and its performance, relying on the accompanying article by Richard Schmalensee and his colleagues to provide details. I then address questions of positive political economy; for example, given the historical support for command-and-control environmental policy instruments, why was allowance trading adopted for acid-rain control in 1990? Subsequently, I consider normative lessons for the design and implementation of market-oriented environmental policies, and offer some conclusions.

The SO_2 Allowance Trading System and Its Performance

Title IV of the Clean Air Act amendments of 1990 sought to reduce SO_2 emissions by 10 million tons from 1980 levels. The first phase of SO_2 emissions reduction was achieved in 1995, with a second phase of reduction to be accomplished by the year 2000.[1] In Phase I, individual emissions limits were assigned to the 263 most SO_2-emissions intensive generating units at 110 electric utility plants operated by 61 electric utilities, and located largely at coal-fired power plants east of the Mississippi River. EPA allocated each affected unit, on an annual basis, a specified number of allowances related to its share of heat input during the baseline period from 1985–87, plus bonus allowances available under a variety of provisions. After January 1, 1995, these units could emit sulfur dioxide only if they had adequate allowances to cover their emissions. Under Phase II of the program, beginning January 1, 2000, almost all fossil-fuel electric power plants will be brought within the system.

---

[1]The law also sought to reduce nitrogen oxide (NO_x) emissions by 2 million tons annually from 1980 levels. A proposal for trading between SO_2 and NO_x was eliminated by Congress.

Cost-effectiveness is promoted by permitting allowance holders to transfer their permits among one another, so that those who can reduce emissions at the lowest, cost have an incentive to do so and sell their allowances to those for whom reducing the cost would be greater. Allowances can also be "banked" for later use. The anticipated result is that marginal abatement costs will be equated across sources, thus achieving aggregate abatement at minimum total cost. In addition to the private market for bilateral trades, an annual auction of allowances withheld from utilities (about 3 percent of total allowances) was established by EPA, with revenues distributed to utilities on the basis of their original allocations. Also, utilities can offer allowances for sale at the annual government-sponsored auction. Finally, compliance is encouraged by a penalty of $2,000 per ton of emissions that exceed any year's allowances, along with a requirement that such excesses be offset the following year.

The SO_2 allowance trading program has performed successfully. Targeted emissions-reductions have been achieved and exceeded; in fact, because of excess reductions in 1995 and 1996 (and because of bonus allowances distributed by the government), utilities have built up an allowance bank of more than six million tons (U.S. Environmental Protection Agency, 1997). Total abatement costs have been significantly less than what they would have been in the absence of the trading provisions. Trading volume has increased over the life of the program, with EPA having recorded more than four million tons of allowance transfers in 1996 among economically unrelated parties (U.S. Environmental Protection Agency, 1997). This robust market has resulted in cost savings of up to $1 billion annually, compared with the cost of command-and-control regulatory alternatives that were considered by Congress in prior years (Kennedy, 1986).

Prospective analysis in 1990 suggested that the program's benefits would approximately equal its costs (Portney, 1990), but recent analysis indicates that benefits will exceed costs by a very significant margin (Burtraw, Krupnick, Mansur, Austin and Farell, 1997). Although the original motivation of the acid-rain control program was to reduce acidification of forest and aquatic ecosystems, the bulk of the benefits result from reduced human risk of premature mortality through reduced exposure to sulfates.

Positive Political Economy Lessons

To understand why the SO_2 allowance trading system was adopted in its particular form in 1990, it is useful to examine first the factors that led to the dominance of command-and-control over market-based instruments in the previous 20 years. To do this, I consider the demand for environmental policy instruments by individuals, firms, and interest groups, and their supply by the legislature and regulatory agencies. This "political market" framework is developed by Keohane, Revesz and Stavins (1997).

Why Have Command-and-Control Instruments Dominated Environmental Regulations?

The short answer is that command-and-control instruments have predominated because all of the main parties involved had reasons to favor them: affected firms, environmental advocacy groups, organized labor, legislators, and bureaucrats.

On the regulatory demand side, affected firms and their trade associations tended to prefer command-and-control instruments because standards can improve a firm's competitive position, while often costing a firm less than pollution taxes or tradeable permits. Command-and-control standards are inevitably set up with extensive input from existing industry and trade associations, which frequently obtain more stringent requirements for new sources and other advantages for existing firms. In contrast, auctioned permits and pollution taxes require firms to pay not only abatement costs to reduce pollution to some level, but also regulatory costs associated with emissions beyond that level, in the form either of permit purchases or tax payments. Because market-based instruments focus on the quantity of pollution, not on who generates it or the methods used to reduce it, these instruments can make the detailed lobbying role of trade associations less important.

For a long time, most environmental advocacy groups were actively hostile towards market-based instruments, for several reasons. A first reason was philosophical: environmentalists frequently portrayed pollution taxes and tradeable permits as "licenses to pollute." Although such ethical objections to the use of market-based environmental strategies have greatly diminished, they have not disappeared completely (Sandel, 1997). A second concern was that damages from pollution—to human health and ecological well-being—were difficult or impossible to quantify and monetize, and thus could not be summed up in a marginal damage function or captured by a Pigovian tax rate (Kelman, 1981). Third, environmental organizations have opposed market-based schemes out of a fear that permit levels and tax rates—once implemented—would be more difficult to tighten over time than command-and-control standards. If permits are given the status of "property rights," then any subsequent attempt by government to reduce pollution levels further could meet with demands for compensation.[2] Similarly, increasing pollution tax rates may be unlikely because raising tax rates is always politically difficult. A related strategic issue is that moving to tax-based environmental regulation would shift authority from environment committees in the Congress, frequently dominated by pro-environment legislators, to tax-writing committees, which are generally more conservative (Kelman, 1981).[3]

---

[2]This concern was alleviated in the SO_2 provisions of the Clean Air Act Amendments of 1990 by an explicit statutory provision that permits do not represent property rights.

[3]These strategic arguments refer, for the most part, to pollution taxes, not to market-based instruments in general. Indeed, as I discuss later, one reason some environmental groups have come

Finally, environmental organizations have objected to decentralized instruments on the grounds that even if emission taxes or tradeable permits reduce overall levels of emissions, they can lead to localized "hot spots" with relatively high levels of ambient pollution. In cases where this is a reasonable concern, it can be addressed in theory, through the use of "ambient permits" or through charge systems that are keyed to changes in ambient conditions at specified locations (Revesz, 1996). Despite the extensive theoretical literature on such ambient systems going back to Montgomery (1972), they have never been implemented, with the partial exception of a two-zone trading system in Los Angeles under the new RECLAIM program.

Organized labor has also been active in some environmental policy debates. In the case of restrictions on clean air, organized labor has taken the side of the United Mine Workers, whose members are heavily concentrated in eastern mines that produce higher-sulfur coal, and have therefore opposed pollution-control measures that would increase incentives for using low-sulfur coal from the largely nonunionized (and less labor-intensive) mines in the Powder River Basin of Wyoming and Montana. In the 1977 debates over amendments to the Clean Air Act, organized labor fought to include a command-and-control standard that effectively required scrubbing, thereby seeking to discourage switching to cleaner western coal (Ackerman and Hassler, 1981). Likewise, the United Mine Workers opposed the SO_2 allowance trading system in 1990 because of a fear that it would encourage a shift to western low-sulfur coal from non-unionized mines.

Turning to the supply side of environmental regulation, legislators have had a number of reasons to find command-and-control standards attractive. First, many legislators and their staffs are trained in law, which predisposes them to favor legalistic regulatory approaches. Second, standards tend to help hide the costs of pollution control (McCubbins and Sullivan, 1984), while market-based instruments generally impose those costs more directly. Compare, for example, the tone of public debates associated with proposed increases in gasoline taxes with those regarding commensurate increases in the stringency of the Corporate Average Fuel Economy standards for new cars.

Third, standards offers greater opportunities for symbolic politics, because strict standards—strong statements of support for environmental protection—can readily be combined with less visible exemptions or with lax enforcement measures. As one recent example of this pattern (albeit from the executive rather than the legislative branch), the Clinton administration announced with much fanfare in June 1997 that it would tighten regulations of particulates and ambient ozone, but the new requirements do not take effect for eight years! Congress has frequently prescribed administrative rules and procedures to protect intended beneficiaries of legislation by constraining the scope of executive intervention (McCubbins, Noll and Weingast, 1987). Such stacking of the deck is more likely to be

---

to endorse the tradeable permits approach is that it promises the cost savings of taxes, without the drawbacks that environmentalists associate with tax instruments.

successful in the context of command-and-control legislation, since market-based instruments leave the allocation of costs and benefits up to the market, treating polluters identically.[4] Of course, the underlying reason why symbolic politics works is that voters have limited information, and so respond to gestures, while remaining relatively unaware of details.

Fourth, if politicians are risk averse, they will prefer instruments that involve more certain effects.[5] The flexibility inherent in market-based instruments creates uncertainty about distributional impacts and local levels of environmental quality. Typically, legislators in a representative democracy are more concerned with the geographic distribution of costs and benefits than with comparisons of total benefits and costs. Hence, aggregate cost-effectiveness—the major advantage of market-based instruments—is likely to play a less significant role in the legislative calculus than whether a politician is getting a good deal for constituents (Shepsle and Weingast, 1984). Politicians are also likely to oppose instruments that can induce firms to close and relocate, leading to localized unemployment. Although there will be winners as well as losers from such relocation, potential losers are likely to be more certain of their status than potential gainers.

Finally, legislators are wary of enacting programs that are likely to be undermined by bureaucrats in their implementation. And bureaucrats are less likely to undermine legislative decisions if their own preferences over policy instruments are accommodated. Bureaucratic preferences—at least in the past—were not supportive of market-based instruments, on several grounds: bureaucrats were familiar with command-and-control approaches; market-based instruments do not require the same kinds of technical expertise that agencies have developed under command-and-control regulation; and market-based instruments can imply a scaled-down role for the agency by shifting decision-making from the bureaucracy to the private sector. In other words, government bureaucrats—like their counterparts in environmental advocacy groups and trade associations—might be expected to oppose market-based instruments to prevent their expertise from becoming obsolete and to preserve their human capital. More recently, however, this same incentive has helped lead EPA staff involved in the SO_2 trading program to become strong proponents of trading for other air pollution problems.

---

[4]But the Congress has nevertheless tried. Joskow and Schmalensee (1998) examine Congressional attempts along these lines in the SO_2 allowance trading program.

[5]"Legislators are likely to behave as if they are risk averse, even if they are personally risk neutral, if their constituents punish unpredictable policy choices or their reelection probability is nearly unity" (McCubbins, Noll and Weingast, 1989, p. 437).

Why Has the Chosen Form of Market-Based Approaches Always Been Freely Allocated Tradeable Permits?

Economic theory suggests that the choice between tradeable permits and pollution taxes should be based upon case-specific factors, but when market-based instruments have been adopted in the United States, they have virtually always taken the form of tradeable permits rather than emission taxes. As already noted, taxes that are related to sources of pollution, like gasoline taxes, serve primarily as revenue-raising instruments, rather than environmental taxes designed to reduce an externality.[6] Moreover, the initial allocation of such permits has always been through free initial distribution, rather than through auctions, despite the apparent economic superiority of the latter mechanism in terms of economic efficiency (Fullerton and Metcalf, 1997; Goulder, Parry, and Burtraw, 1997; Stavins, 1995). The EPA does have an annual auction of SO_2 allowances, but this represents less than 2 percent of the total allocation (Bailey, 1996). While the EPA auctions may have helped in establishing the market for SO_2 allowances, they are a trivial part of the overall program (Joskow, Schmalensee and Bailey, 1996).

Again, many actors in the system have reasons to favor freely allocated tradeable permits over other market-based instruments. On the regulatory demand side, existing firms favor freely allocated tradeable permits because they convey rents to them. Moreover, like stringent command-and-control standards for new sources, but unlike auctioned permits or taxes, freely allocated permits give rise to entry barriers, since new entrants must purchase permits from existing holders. Thus, the rents conveyed to the private sector by freely allocated tradeable permits are, in effect, sustainable.

Environmental advocacy groups have generally supported command-and-control approaches, but given the choice between tradeable permits and emission taxes, these groups strongly prefer the former. Environmental advocates have a strong incentive to avoid policy instruments that make the costs of environmental protection highly visible to consumers and voters; and taxes make those costs more explicit than permits.[7] Also, environmental advocates prefer permit schemes because they specify the quantity of pollution reduction that will be achieved, in contrast with the indirect effect of pollution taxes. Overall, some environmental groups have come to endorse the tradeable permits approach because it promises the cost savings of

---

[6]This pattern holds in Europe, as well. There, environmental taxes have been far more prevalent than tradeable permits, but the taxes employed have typically been two low to induce pollution abatement (Cansier and Krumm, 1997).

[7]For this same reason, private industry may strategically choose to endorse a pollution tax approach, in the hope that consequent public opposition will result in the setting of a less stringent environmental goal. This may seem farfetched, but it appears to be precisely what happened in the closing days of the 1990 Clean Air Act debate in the U.S. Senate. When it had become clear that a 10 million ton SO_2 allowance trading system was about to be passed, electric utilities suddenly proposed an SO_2 emissions tax as an alternative policy instrument.

pollution taxes, without the drawbacks that environmentalists associate with environmental tax instruments.

Freely allocated tradeable permits are easier for legislators to supply than taxes or auctioned permits, again because the costs imposed on industry are less visible and less burdensome, since no money is exchanged at the time of the initial permit allocation. Also, freely allocated permits offer a much greater degree of political control over the distributional effects of regulation, facilitating the formation of majority coalitions. Joskow and Schmalensee (1998) examined the political process of allocating SO_2 allowances in the 1990 amendments, and found that allocating permits on the basis of prior emissions can produce fairly clear winners and losers among firms and states. An auction allows no such political maneuvering.

Why Was a Market-Based Approach Adopted for SO_2 Emissions in 1990?

By the late 1980s, there had already been a significant shift of the political center toward a more favorable view of using markets to solve social problems. The Bush administration, which proposed the SO_2 allowance trading program and then championed it through an initially resistant Democratic Congress, deserves much of the credit here. The ideas of "fiscally responsible environmental protection" and "harnessing market forces to protect the environment" fit well with its quintessentially moderate Republicanism. (The Reagan administration enthusiastically embraced a market-oriented ideology, but demonstrated little interest in employing actual market-based policies in the environmental area.) More broadly, support for market-oriented solutions to various social problems had been increasing across the political spectrum as early as the Carter administration, as evidenced by deliberations and action regarding deregulation of the airline, telecommunications, trucking, railroad, and banking industries. Indeed, by 1990, the phrase "market-based environmental policy" had evolved from being politically problematic to politically attractive. Even leading liberal environmental advocates like Rep. Henry Waxman began to characterize their clean air proposals as using "economic-incentive mechanisms," even if the actual proposals continued to be of the conventional, command-and-control variety.

Given the historical opposition to market-oriented pollution control policies, how can we explain the adoption of the SO_2 allowance trading program in 1990? More broadly, why has there been increased openness to the use of market-based approaches?

For economists, it would be gratifying to believe that increased understanding of market-based instruments had played a large part in fostering their increased political acceptance, but how important has this really been? In 1981, Steven Kelman surveyed Congressional staff members, and found that Republican support and Democratic opposition to market-based environmental policy instruments was based largely on ideological grounds, with little awareness or understanding of the advantages or disadvantages of the various instruments. What would happen if we were to replicate Kelman's (1981) survey today? My hypothesis is that we would find increased support from Republicans, greatly increased support from Democrats, but insufficient improvements in understanding to explain these changes.[8] So what else has mattered?

One factor has surely been increased pollution control costs, which have led to greater demand for cost-effective instruments. By 1990, U.S. pollution control costs had reached $125 billion annually, nearly a tripling of real costs from 1972 levels (U.S. Environmental Protection Agency, 1990). In the case of SO_2 control, it was well known that utilities faced very different marginal abatement costs and would want to use varying abatement methods, because of differences in the ages of plants and their proximity to sources of low-sulfur coal. EPA estimates in the late 1980s were that a well-functioning tradeable-permit program would save 50 percent on costs that would otherwise exceed $6 billion annually if a dictated technological solution were implemented (ICF, 1989).

A second factor that was important in the 1990 Clean Air Act debates was strong and vocal support for the SO_2 allowance trading system from parts of the environmental community, particularly the Environmental Defense Fund (EDF), which had already become a champion of market-based approaches to environmental protection in other, less nationally prominent domains, such as water marketing in California. By supporting allowance trading, EDF solidified its reputation as a pragmatic environmental organization willing to adopt new strategies involving less confrontation with private industry, and distinguished itself from other groups (Keohane, Revesz and Stavins, 1997). When the memberships (and financial resources) of other environmental advocacy groups subsequently declined with the election of the environment-friendly Clinton-Gore administration, EDF continued to prosper and grow (Lowry, 1993).

A third key factor in 1990 was the fact that the SO_2 allowance trading program was designed to reduce emissions, not simply to reallocate them cost-effectively. In 1990, EDF was able to make powerful arguments for tradeable permits on the grounds that the use of a cost-effective instrument would make it politically feasible to achieve greater reductions in SO_2 emissions than would otherwise be possible. Market-based instruments are most likely to be politically acceptable if they can achieve environmental improvements which otherwise are not politically or economically feasible. It is not coincidental that the earlier (and successful) lead and chlorofluorocarbon permit trading programs also aimed at reducing emissions, while EPA's attempts to reform local air quality regulation through its Emissions Trading Program without incremental improvements in air quality have been troubled and halting.

---

[8]But there has been some increased understanding of market-based approaches to environmental protection among policymakers and their staffs, due in part to the economics training that is now common in law schools, and the proliferation of schools of public policy.

Fourth, many of the economists involved in the deliberations regarding the SO_2 allowance system took the approach of accepting—implicitly or otherwise—a political goal of reducing SO_2 emissions by 10 million tons. Rather than debating the costs and benefits of that goal, they simply focused on the cost-effective means of achieving it. Separating the benefit-cost calculation about the goals from the instruments used to achieve the goal was important to avoid splintering support for an SO_2 trading program. As evidenced by the failed Republican attempts at "regulatory reform" in 1996, the notion of using explicit benefit-cost calculations as the basis for judging regulations remains highly controversial in political circles. Of course, even if the strategy worked out well in the SO_2 case, there are limitations to the wisdom of separating ends and means: one risks designing a fast train to the wrong station.

Fifth, it is important to note that acid rain was effectively an unregulated problem until the SO_2 allowance trading program of 1990. Hence, there were no existing constituencies for the status quo approach, because there *was* no status quo approach. The demand for a market-based instrument is likely to be greatest and the political opportunity costs of legislators providing support are likely to be least when the status quo instrument is essentially nonexistent. This implies that we should be more optimistic about introducing such market-based instruments for "new" problems, such as global climate change, than for existing, highly regulated problems, such as abandoned hazardous waste sites.

Finally, a caveat is in order. The adoption of the SO_2 allowance trading program for acid rain control—like any major innovation in public policy—can partly be attributed to a healthy dose of chance that placed specific persons in key positions, in this case at the White House, EPA, the Congress, and environmental organizations. Within the White House, among the most active and influential enthusiasts of market-based environmental instruments were Counsel Boyden Gray and his Deputy John Schmitz; Domestic Policy Adviser Roger Porter; Council of Economic Advisers (CEA) Member Richard Schmalensee; CEA Senior Staff Economist Robert Hahn; and Office of Management and Budget Associate Director Robert Grady. At EPA, Administrator William Reilly—a "card-carrying environmentalist"—enjoyed valuable credibility with environmental advocacy groups; Deputy Administrator Henry Habicht was a key supporter of market-based instruments; and Assistant Administrator William Rosenberg was an early convert. In the Congress, Senators Timothy Wirth and John Heinz provided high-profile, bipartisan support for the SO_2 allowance trading system and, more broadly, for a variety of market-based instruments for environmental problems through their "Project 88" (Stavins, 1988). Within the environmental community, EDF Executive Director Fred Krupp, Senior Economist Daniel Dudek, and Staff Attorney Joseph Goffman worked closely with the White House to develop the allowance trading proposal.

Normative Lessons

Within the context of 30 years of federal environmental regulation, characterized by sporadic but increasing reliance on market-based policy instruments, I consider normative lessons from the design and implementation of the SO_2 allowance trading system for design and implementation of tradeable permit systems, analysis of prospective and adopted systems, and identification of new applications.

Lessons for Design and Implementation of Tradeable Permit Systems

The performance of the SO_2 allowance trading system to date provides valuable evidence for environmentalists and others who have been resistant to these innovations that market-based instruments can achieve major cost savings while accomplishing their environmental objectives (Ellerman et al., 1997; U.S. General Accounting Office, 1995). Likewise, we have seen that the system can be implemented without a surge of lawsuits, partly because it was well designed (Burtraw and Swift, 1996) and partly because issues of distributional equity were handled through a congressionally imposed allocation. The system's performance also offers lessons about the importance of flexibility, simplicity, the role of monitoring and enforcement, and the capabilities of the private sector to make markets of this sort work.

In regard to flexibility, tradeable permit systems should be designed to allow for a broad set of compliance alternatives, in terms of both timing and technological options. Allowing flexible timing and intertemporal trading of the allowances—that is, "banking" allowances for future use—has played a very important role in the program's performance (Ellerman et al., 1997), much as it did in the lead rights trading program a decade earlier (Kerr and Maré, 1997). The permit system was based on emissions of SO_2, as opposed to sulfur content of fuels, so that both scrubbing and fuel-switching were feasible options. Moreover, one of the most significant benefits of the trading system was simply that technology standards requiring scrubbing of SO_2 were thereby avoided. This allowed midwestern utilities to take advantage of lower rail rates (brought about by railroad deregulation) to reduce their SO_2 emissions by increasing their use of low-sulfur coal from Wyoming and Montana, an approach that would not have been possible if scrubber requirements had been in place. Also, a less flexible system would not have led to the technological change that may have been induced in scrubber performance and rail transport (Burtraw, 1996; Ellerman and Montero, 1996; Bohi and Burtraw, 1997). Likewise, the economic incentives provided by the trading system have led to induced process innovations in the form of bundling of allowances with coal supplies (Doucet and Strauss, 1994) and the installation of emission reduction technology in exchange for generated allowances (Dudek and Goffman, 1995). The flexibility of the allowance trading system accommodates the dynamic market changes that are occurring because of electric utility deregulation, allowing shifts in industry structure and production methods while assuring that total emissions do not increase.

In regard to simplicity, a unique formula for allocating permits based upon historical data is relatively difficult to contest or manipulate. More generally, trading rules should be clearly defined up front, without ambiguity. For example, there should be no requirements for prior government approval of individual trades. Such requirements hampered EPA's Emissions Trading Program in the 1970s, while the lack of such requirements was an important factor in the success of lead trading (Hahn and Hester, 1989). In the case of SO_2 trading, the absence of requirements for prior approval has reduced uncertainty for utilities and administrative costs for government, and contributed to low transactions costs (Rico, 1995).

Considerations of simplicity and the experience of the SO_2 allowance system also argue for using absolute baselines, not relative ones, as the point of departure for tradeable permit programs. The difference is that with an absolute baseline (so-called "cap-and-trade"), sources are each allocated some number of permits (the total of which is the "cap"); with a relative baseline, reductions are credited from an unspecified baseline. The problem is that without a specified baseline, reductions must be credited relative to an unobservable hypothetical—what the source would have emitted in the absence of the regulation. A hybrid system—where a cap-and-trade program is combined with voluntary "opt-in provisions"—creates the possibility for "paper trades," where a regulated source is credited for an emissions reduction (by an unregulated source) that would have taken place in any event (Montero, 1997). The result is a decrease in aggregate costs among regulated sources, but this is partly due to an unintentional increase in the total emissions cap (Atkeson, 1997). As was experienced with EPA's Emissions Trading Program, relative baselines create significant transaction costs by essentially requiring prior approval of trades as the authority investigates the claimed counterfactual from which reductions are calculated and credits generated (Nichols, Farr and Hester, 1996).

The SO_2 program has also brought home the importance of monitoring and enforcement provisions. In 1990, environmental advocates insisted on continuous emissions monitoring (Burtraw and Swift, 1996), which helps build market confidence (McLean, 1995). The costs of such monitoring, however, are significant. On the enforcement side, the Act's stiff penalties have provided sufficient incentive for the very high degree of compliance that has been achieved.

Another normative lesson is linked with positive issues. Above we emphasized the political advantages of freely allocated permit systems, as employed with SO_2. But the same characteristic that makes such allocation attractive in positive political economy terms—the conveyance of scarcity rents to the private sector—also makes free allocation problematic in normative, efficiency terms (Fullerton and Metcalf, 1997). Goulder, Parry, and Burtraw (1997) estimate that the costs of SO_2 allowance trading would be 25 percent less if permits were auctioned rather than freely allocated, because auctioning yields revenues that can be used to finance reductions in pre-existing distortionary taxes. Furthermore, in the presence of some forms of transaction costs, the post-trading equilibrium—and hence aggregate abatement costs—are sensitive to the initial permit allocation (Stavins, 1995). For both reasons, a successful attempt to establish a politically viable program through a specific initial permit allocation can result in a program that is significantly more costly than anticipated.

Finally, the SO_2 program's performance demonstrates that the private sector can fulfill brokerage needs, providing price information and matching trading partners, despite claims to the contrary when the program was enacted. Entrepreneurs have stepped in to make available a variety of services, including private brokerage, electronic bid/ask bulletin boards, and allowance price forecasts. The annual EPA auctions may have served the purpose of helping to reveal market valuations of allowances, but bilateral trading has also informed the auctions (Joskow, Schmalensee and Bailey, 1996).

Lessons for Analysis of Tradeable Permit Systems

When assessing trading programs, economists have typically employed some measure in which gains from trade are estimated for moving from conventional standards to marketable permits. Aggregate cost savings are the best yardstick for measuring success, not number of trades or total trading volume (Hahn and May, 1994).

The challenge for analysts is to compare realistic versions of both tradeable permit systems and "likely alternatives," not idealized versions of either. It is not enough to analyze static gains from trade (Hahn and Stavins, 1992). For example, the gains from banking allowances should also be modeled (unless this is not permitted in practice). It can also be important to allow for the effects of alternative instruments on technology innovation and diffusion (Milliman and Prince, 1989; Jaffe and Stavins, 1995; Doucet and Strauss, 1994; Dudek and Goffman, 1995), especially when permit trading programs impose significant costs over long time horizons (Newell, Jaffe and Stavins, 1997).

More generally, it is important to consider the effects of the pre-existing regulatory environment. The level of pre-existing factor taxes can affect the total costs of regulation (Goulder, Parry and Burtraw, 1997). Also, because SO_2 is both a transboundary precursor of acid rain and a local air pollutant regulated under a separate part of the Clean Air Act, "local" environmental regulations have sometimes prevented utilities from acquiring allowances rather than carrying out emissions reductions (Conrad and Kohn, 1996). Moreover, because electricity generation and distribution have been regulated by state commissions, a prospective analysis of SO_2 trading should consider the incentives these commissions may have to influence the level of allowance trading.[9]

A set of theoretical arguments suggests that state public utility commissions may have incentives to erect such barriers. Coal interests in some midwestern and eastern states, where high-sulfur coal is mined, were opposed to the concept of allowance trading because it would permit utilities to switch to cleaner western coal. Hence, it is reasonable to suspect that those same interests would pressure state regulatory commissions to erect direct or indirect barriers to trading (Bohi and Burtraw, 1992; Burtraw, 1996). However, the only rigorous analysis that has been carried out of this contention suggests that such pressures have not, if applied, been effective (Bailey, 1996). In any event, it is clear that state regulatory commissions have not encouraged utilities to engage in allowance trading, either (Bohi, 1994). The commissions have been reactive, rather than proactive in terms of accounting and tax treatment of allowance transactions (Rose, 1997), restricting themselves to reviewing and approving plans submitted by utilities. Only the Georgia Public Service Commission has actively ordered utilities in its jurisdiction to monitor the allowance market and purchase allowances when prices are below compliance costs.

It has also been suggested that many electric utilities have been reluctant to consider new options, which is consistent with their reputation as firms that seek to minimize risk, rather than cost (Rose, 1997), but this may change due to the heightened role of competition brought about by electricity deregulation. Also, long-term contractual precommitments have tied many utilities to plans conceived before allowance trading was an option (Coggins and Swinton, 1996). Finally, some utilities may be reluctant to make serious investments in allowances in the face of future regulatory uncertainty (U.S. Energy Information Administration, 1997).

Issues such as these must be taken into account in the analysis of any pollution control program, whether it is market-oriented or command-and-control in nature.

Lessons for Identifying New Applications

Market-based policy instruments are now considered for each and every environmental problem that is raised, ranging from endangered species preservation to what may be the greatest of environmental problems, the greenhouse effect and global climate change. Our experiences with SO_2 trading—and with the earlier programs of lead and chlorofluorocarbon trading—offer some guidance to the conditions under which tradeable permits are likely to work well, and when they may face greater difficulties.

First, SO_2 trading is a case where the cost of abating pollution differs widely among sources, and where a market-based system is therefore likely

---

[9]Also, rate-of-return regulation that employs capital investments as a baseline might be expected to lead electric utilities to bias their SO_2 compliance choices toward investments in scrubbers, for example, and away from allowance transactions (Averch and Johnson, 1962).

to have greater gains, relative to conventional, command-and-control regulations (Newell and Stavins, 1997). It was clear early on that SO_2 abatement cost heterogeneity was great, because of differences in ages of plants and their proximity to sources of low-sulfur coal. But where abatement costs are more uniform across sources, the political costs of enacting an allowance trading approach are less likely to be justifiable.

Second, the greater the degree to which pollutants mix in the receiving airshed or watershed, the more attractive a tradeable emission permit (or emission tax) system will be, relative to a conventional uniform standard. This is because taxes or tradeable permits can lead to localized "hot spots" with relatively high levels of ambient pollution. This is a significant distributional issue. Some acid-rain receiving states have attempted to erect barriers to those trades that could increase deposition within their borders.[10] It can also become an efficiency issue, if damages are nonlinearly related to pollutant concentrations.

Third, the efficiency of a tradeable permit system will depend on the pattern of costs and benefits. If uncertainty about marginal abatement costs is significant, and if marginal abatement costs are quite flat and marginal benefits of abatement fall relatively quickly, then a quantity instrument, such as tradeable permits, will be more efficient than a price instrument, such as an emission tax (Weitzman, 1974). Furthermore, when there is also uncertainty about marginal benefits, and marginal benefits are positively correlated with marginal costs (which, it turns out, is a relatively common occurrence for a variety of pollution problems), then there is an additional argument in favor of the relative efficiency of quantity instruments.[11]

Fourth, tradeable permits will work best when transaction costs are low, and the SO_2 experiment shows that if properly designed, private markets will tend to render transaction costs minimal. Finally, considerations of political feasibility point to the wisdom of proposing trading instruments when they can be used to facilitate emissions reductions, as was done with SO_2 allowances and lead rights trading. Policy instruments that appear impeccable from the vantage point of Cambridge, Massachusetts, but consistently prove infeasible in Washington, D.C., can hardly be considered "optimal."

Many of these issues can be illuminated by considering a concrete example: the current interest in applying tradeable permits to the task of cutting carbon dioxide (CO_2) emissions to reduce the risk of global climate change. It is immediately obvious that the number and diversity of sources

---

[10]For example, as recently as the summer of 1997, legislation emerged in the New York State legislature that would penalize utilities for selling allowances to companies "accused of exacerbating New York's acid rain problem" (*Boston Globe*, June 26, 1997, on-line). Under the legislation, if a trade were found to be "detrimental to environmentally sensitive areas," the Public Service Commission would be directed to impose a fine three times the value of the trade.

[11]One generator of stochastic shocks that frequently affects both marginal benefits and marginal costs—with the same sign—is the weather. For further explanation and specific examples, see Stavins (1996).

of CO_2 emissions due to fossil fuel combustion are vastly greater than in the case of SO_2 emissions as a precursor of acid rain, where the focus can be placed on a few hundred electric utility plants (Environmental Law Institute, 1997).

Any pollution-control program must face the possibility of "emissions leakage" from regulated to unregulated sources. This could be a problem for meeting domestic targets for CO_2 emissions reduction, but it would be a vastly greater problem for an international program, where emissions would tend to increase in nonparticipant countries. This also raises serious concerns with provisions in the Kyoto Protocol for industrialized countries to participate in a CO_2 cap-and-trade program, while non-participant (developing) nations retain the option of joining the system on a project-by-project basis, an approach commonly known as "joint implementation." As emphasized earlier, provisions in tradeable permit programs that allow for unregulated sources to "opt in" can lower aggregate costs by substituting low-cost for high-cost control, but may also have the unintended effect of increasing aggregate emissions beyond what they would otherwise have been. This is because there is an incentive for adverse selection: sources in developing countries that would reduce their emissions, opt in, and receive "excess allowances" would tend to be those that would have reduced their emissions in any case.

To the limited degree that any previous trading program can serve as a model for the case of global climate change, some attention should be given to the tradeable-permit system that accomplished the U.S. phaseout of leaded gasoline. The currency of that system was not lead oxide emissions from motor vehicles, but the lead content of gasoline. So too, in the case of global climate, great savings in monitoring and enforcement costs could be had by adopting *input* trading linked to the carbon content of fossil fuels. This is reasonable in the climate case, since—unlike in the SO_2 case—CO_2 emissions are roughly proportional to the carbon content of fossil fuels and scrubbing alternatives are largely unavailable, at least at present. On the other hand, natural sequestration of CO_2 from the atmosphere by expanding forested areas is available (even in the United States) at reasonable cost (Stavins, 1997) and is explicitly counted toward compliance with the targets of the Kyoto Protocol. Hence, it will be important to combine any carbon trading (or carbon tax) program with a carbon sequestration program, possibly denominated by forested areas.

In terms of carbon permit allocation mechanisms, auctions would have the advantage that revenues could be used to finance reductions in distortionary taxes. Although free allocation of carbon permits might meet with less political resistance, such free allocation could increase regulatory costs enough that the sign of the efficiency impact would be reversed from positive to negative net benefits (Parry, Williams and Goulder 1997).

Finally, developing a tradeable permit system in the area of global climate change would surely bring forth an entirely new set of economic, political, and institutional challenges, particularly with regard to enforcement problems (Schmalensee, 1996; Stavins, 1998). But it is also true that the diversity of sources of CO_2 emissions and the magnitude of likely abatement costs make it equally clear that only a market-based instrument—some form of carbon rights trading or (probably revenue-neutral) carbon taxes—will be capable of achieving the domestic targets that may eventually be forthcoming from international agreements.

Conclusion

Given that the SO_2 allowance-trading program became fully binding only in 1995, we should be cautious when drawing conclusions about lessons to be learned from the program's development or its performance. A number of important questions remain. For example, little is known empirically about the impact of trading on technological change. Also, much more empirical research is needed on how the pre-existing regulatory environment affects the operation of permit trading programs. Moreover, all the successes with tradeable permits have involved air pollution: acid rain, leaded gasoline, and chlorofluorocarbons. Our experience (and success rate) with water pollution is much more limited (Hahn, 1989), and in other areas, we have no experience at all. Even for air pollution problems, the tremendous differences between SO_2 and acid rain, on the one hand, and the combustion of fossil fuels and global climate change, on the other, indicate that any rush to judgement regarding global climate policy instruments is unwarranted.

Despite these and other uncertainties, market-based instruments for environmental protection—and, in particular, tradeable permit systems—now enjoy proven successes in reducing pollution at low cost. Such cost effectiveness is the primary focus of economists when evaluating public policies, but the political system clearly gives much greater weight to distributional concerns. In the Congressional deliberations that led up to the Clean Air Act amendments of 1990, considerable pressures were brought to bear to allow less switching from high-sulfur to low-sulfur coal to benefit regions dependent on high-sulfur coal mining. Such provisions would have increased compliance costs for midwestern coal-burning utilities (U.S. Congressional Budget Office, 1986), encouraged political pressures for nationwide cost sharing, and greatly reduced the cost-effectiveness of the system. In this way, individual constituencies, each fighting for its own version of distributional equity, negate efficiency and cost effectiveness. In the pursuit of obtaining nicely shaped pieces of the proverbial pie, we all too often end up with a systematically smaller pie. That this did not happen in 1990 was the exception, not the rule.

There are sound reasons why the political world has been slow to embrace the use of market-based instruments for environmental protection, including the ways economists have packaged and promoted their ideas in the past: failing to separate means (cost-effective instruments) from ends (efficiency); and treating environmental problems as little more than "externalities calling for corrective taxes." Much of the resistance has also been due, of course, to the very nature of the political process and the incentives it provides to both politicians and interest groups to favor command-and-control methods instead of market-based approaches.

But despite this history, market-based instruments have moved center stage, and policy debates look very different from the time when these ideas were characterized as "licenses to pollute" or dismissed as completely impractical. Of course, no single policy instrument—whether market-based or conventional—will be appropriate for all environmental problems. Which instrument is best in any given situation depends upon characteristics of the specific environmental problem, and the social, political, and economic context in which the instrument is to be implemented.

REFERENCES

Ackerman, Bruce A., and William T. Hassler, *Clean Coal/Dirty Air*. New Haven: Yale University Press, 1981.

Atkeson, Erica, "Joint Implementation: Lessons from Title IV's Voluntary Compliance Programs," Working Paper 97–003, MIT Center for Energy and Environmental Policy Research, May 1997.

Averch, Harvey, and Leland L. Johnson, "Behavior of the Firm under Regulatory Constraint," *American Economic Review*, 1962, *52*, 1053–69.

Bailey, Elizabeth M., "Allowance Trading Activity and State Regulatory Rulings: Evidence from the US Acid Rain Program," Working Paper 96–002, MIT Center for Energy and Environmental Policy Research, March 1996.

Barthold, Thomas A., "Issues in the Design of Environmental Excise Taxes," *Journal of Economic Perspectives*, Winter 1994, *8*:1, 133–51.

Baumol, William J., and Wallace E. Oates, *The Theory of Environmental Policy*. Second edition. New York: Cambridge University Press, 1988.

Bohi, Douglas R., "Utilities and State Regulators Are Failing to Take Advantage of Emissions Allowance Trading," *The Electricity Journal*, March 1994, 7:2, 20–27.

Bohi, Douglas R., and Dallas Burtraw, "Utility Investment Behavior and the Emission Trading Market," *Resources and Energy*, April 1992, *14*:1/2, 129–53.

Bohi, Douglas R., and Dallas Burtraw, "SO_2 Allowance Trading: How Do Expectations and Experience Measure Up?" *Electricity Journal*, August/September 1997, 67–75.

Burtraw, Dallas, "The SO_2 Emissions Trading Program: Cost Savings Without Allowance Trades," *Contemporary Economic Policy*, April 1996, *14*, 79–94.

Burtraw, Dallas, Alan Krupnick, Erin Mansur, David Austin, and Deidre Farrell, "The Costs and Benefits of Reducing Acid Rain," Discussion Paper 97-31-REV, Resources for the Future, Washington, D.C., September 1997.

Burtraw, Dallas, and Byron Swift, "A New Standard of Performance: An Analysis of the Clean Air Act's Acid Rain Program," *Environmental Law Reporter News & Analysis*, August 1996, *26*:8, 10411–423.

Cansier, Dieter, and Raimund Krumm, "Air Pollutant Taxation: An Empirical Survey," *Ecological Economics*, 1997, *23*:1, 59–70.

Coggins, Jay S., and John R. Swinton, "The Price of Pollution: A Dual Approach to Valuing SO_2 Allowances," *Journal of Environmental Economics and Management*, January 1996, *30*:1, 58–72.

Conrad, Klaus, and Robert E. Kohn, "The US Market for SO_2 Permits: Policy Implications of the Low Price and Trading Volume," *Energy Policy*, 1996, *24*:12, 1051–59.

Crocker, Thomas D., "The Structuring of Atmospheric Pollution Control Systems." In Harold Wolozin, ed. *The Economics of Air Pollution*. New York: Norton, 1966.

Dales, John H., *Pollution, Property, and Prices*. Toronto: University of Toronto Press, 1968.

Doucet, Joseph A., and Todd Strauss, "On the Bundling of Coal and Sulphur Dioxide Emissions Allowances," *Energy Policy*, September 1994, *22*:9, 764–70.

Dudek, Daniel J., and Joseph Goffman, "The Clean Air Act Acid Rain Program: Lessons for Success in Creating a New Paradigm," 85th Annual Meeting of the Air & Waste Management Association, 95-RA120.06, San Antonio, Texas, 1995.

Ellerman, A. Denny, and Juan Pablo Montero, "Why are Allowance Prices so Low? An Analysis of the SO_2 Emissions Trading Program," Working Paper 96–001, MIT Center for Energy and Environmental Policy Research, February 1996.

Ellerman, A. Denny, Richard Schmalensee, Paul J. Joskow, Juan Pablo Montero, and Elizabeth M. Bailey, *Emissions Trading under the U.S. Acid Rain Program: Evaluation of Compliance Costs and Allowance Market Performance*. Cambridge, MA: MIT Center for Energy and Environmental Policy Research, October 1997.

Environmental Law Institute, "Implementing an Emissions Cap and Allowance Trading System for Greenhouse Gases: Lessons from the Acid Rain Program," Research Report, Washington, D.C., September 1997.

Fullerton, Don, and Gilbert Metcalf, "Environmental Controls, Scarcity Rents, and Pre-Existing Distortions," NBER Working Paper 6091, July 1997.

Goulder, Lawrence H., Ian W. H. Parry, and Dallas Burtraw, "Revenue-Raising vs. Other Approaches to Environmental Protection: The Critical Significance of Pre-Existing Tax Distortions," *RAND Journal of Economics*, Winter 1997, *28*:4, 708–31.

Hahn, Robert W., "Economic Prescriptions for Environmental Problems: How the Patient Followed the Doctor's Orders," *Journal of Economic Perspectives*, Spring 1989, *3*:2, 95–114.

Hahn, Robert W., and Gordon L. Hester, "Marketable Permits: Lessons for Theory and Practice," *Ecology Law Quarterly*, 1989, *16*:2, 361–406.

Hahn, Robert W., and Carol A. May, "The Behavior of the Allowance Market: Theory and Evidence," *The Electricity Journal*, March 1994, *7*:2, 28–37.

Hahn, Robert W., and Robert N. Stavins, "Economic Incentives for Environmental Protection: Integrating Theory and Practice," *American Economic Review*, 1992, *82*, 464–68.

ICF, Inc., "Economic Analysis of Title V (Acid Rain Provisions) of the Administration's Proposed Clean Air Act Amendments (H.R. 3030/S. 1490)." Prepared for the U.S. Environmental Protection Agency, Washington, D.C., 1989.

Jaffe, Adam B., and Robert N. Stavins, "Dynamic Incentives of Environmental Regulations: The Effects of Alternative Policy Instruments on Technological Diffusion." *Journal of Environmental Economics and Management*, November 1995, *29*:3, S43–S63.

Joskow, Paul L., and Richard Schmalensee, "The Political Economy of Market-Based Environmental Policy: The U.S. Acid Rain Program," *Journal of Law and Economics*, April 1998, *41*, 89–135.

Joskow, Paul L., Richard Schmalensee, and Elizabeth M. Bailey, "Auction Design and the Market for Sulfur Dioxide Emissions," National Bureau of Economic Research Working Paper No. 5745, Cambridge, MA, September 1996.

Kelman, Steven P., *What Price Incentives?* Boston: Auburn House, 1981.

Kennedy, David M., *Controlling Acid Rain, 1986*. Case Study C15-86-699.0. Cambridge, MA: John F. Kennedy School of Government. Harvard University, 1986.

Kerr, Suzi, and David Maré, "Efficient Regulation Through Tradeable Permit Markets: The United States Lead Phasedown," Department of Agricultural and Resource Economics, University of Maryland, College Park, Working Paper 96–06, January 1997.

Keohane, Nathaniel O., Richard L. Revesz, and Robert N. Stavins, "The Positive Political Economy of Instrument Choice in Environmental Policy." In Paul Portney and Robert Schwab, eds. *Environmental Economics and Public Policy*. London: Edward Elgar, Ltd., 1997.

Lowry, Robert C, "The Political Economy of Environmental Citizen Groups," unpublished Ph.D. thesis, Harvard University, 1993.

McCubbins, Matthew D., Roger G. Noll, and Barry R. Weingast, "Administrative Procedures as Instruments of Political Control," *Journal of Law, Economics and Organization*, 1987, *3*, 243–77.

———, "Structure and Process, Politics and Policy: Administrative Arrangements and the Political Control of Agencies," *Virginia Law Review*, 1989, *75*, 431–82.

McCubbins, Matthew and Terry Sullivan, "Constituency Influences on Legislative Policy Choice," *Quality and Quantity*, 1984, *18*, 299–319.

McLean, Brian J., "Lessons Learned Implementing Title IV of the Clean Air Act," 85th Annual Meeting of the Air & Waste Management Association, 95-RA120.04, San Antonio, Texas, 1995.

Milliman, Scott R., and Raymond Prince, "Firm Incentives to Promote Technological Changes in Pollution Control," *Journal of Environmental Economics and Management*, 1989, *17*, 247–65.

Montgomery, W. David, "Markets in Licenses and Efficient Pollution Control Programs," *Journal of Economic Theory*, 1972, 395–418.

Montero, Juan-Pablo, "Volunteering for Market-Based Environmental Regulation: The Substitution Provision of the SO_2 Emissions Trading Program," Working Paper 97–001, MIT Center for Energy and Environmental Policy Research, January 1997.

Newell Richard G., Adam B. Jaffe, and Robert N. Stavins, "Environmental Policy and Technological Change: The Effects of Economic Incentives and Direct Regulation on Energy-Saving Innovation," paper presented at the 1997 Allied Social Science Association meeting, New Orleans, January 1997.

Newell, Richard G., and Robert N. Stavins, "Abatement Cost Heterogeneity and Potential Gains from Market-Based Instruments." Working paper, John F. Kennedy School of Government, Harvard University, June 1997.

Nichols, Albert L., John G. Farr, and Gordon Hester, "Trading and the Timing of Emissions: Evidence from the Ozone Transport Region," National Economic Research Associates, Cambridge, Massachusetts, Draft of September 9, 1996.

Parry, Ian, Roberton Williams, and Lawrence Goulder, "When Can Carbon Abatement Policies Increase Welfare? The Fundamental Role of Distorted Factor Markets," Working paper, Resources for the Future and Stanford University, September 1997.

Pigou, Arthur Cecil, *The Economics of Welfare*. London: Macmillan and Company, 1920.

Portney, Paul R., "Policy Watch: Economics and the Clean Air Act," *Journal of Economic Perspectives*, Fall 1990, *4*:4, 173–81.

Revesz, Richard L., "Federalism and Interstate Environmental Externalities," *University of Pennsylvania Law Review*, 1996, 144, 2341.

Rico, Renee, "The U.S. Allowance Trading System for Sulfur Dioxide: An Update of Market Experience," *Environmental and Resource Economics*, March 1995, 5:2, 115–29.

Rose, Kenneth, "Implementing an Emissions Trading Program in an Economically Regulated Industry: Lessons from the SO$_2$ Trading Program." In R. Kosobud, and J. Zimmermann, eds. *Market Based Approaches to Environmental Policy: Regulatory Innovations to the Fore*. New York: Van Nostrand Reinhold, 1997.

Sandel, Michael J., "It's Immoral to Buy the Right to Pollute," *New York Times*, December 15, 1997, p. A29.

Schmalensee, Richard, "Greenhouse Policy Architecture and Institutions," MIT Joint Program on the Science and Policy of Global Change, Report 13, November 1996.

Shepsle, Kenneth A., and Barry R. Weingast, "Political Solutions to Market Problems," *American Political Science Review*, 1984, 78, 417–34.

Stavins, Robert N., "Transaction Costs and Tradable Permits," *Journal of Environmental Economics and Management*, September 1995, 29, 133–48.

Stavins, Robert N., "Correlated Uncertainty and Policy Instrument Choice," *Journal of Environmental Economics and Management*, 1996, 30, 218–32.

Stavins, Robert N., "The Costs of Carbon Sequestration: A Revealed-Preference Approach." Working paper, John F. Kennedy School of Government, Harvard University, November 1997.

———, "Policy Instruments for Climate Change: How Can National Governments Address a Global Problem," *The University of Chicago Legal Forum*, forthcoming 1998.

———, ed., *Project 88—Harnessing Market Forces to Protect Our Environment: Initiatives for the New President*. A Public Policy Study sponsored by Senator Timothy E. Wirth, Colorado, and Senator John Heinz, Pennsylvania. Washington, D.C.: December 1988.

U.S. Congressional Budget Office, *Curbing Acid Rain: Costs, Budget, and Coal-Market Effects*. Washington, D.C., 1986.

U.S. Energy Information Administration, "The Effects of Title IV of the Clean Air Act Amendments of 1990 on Electric Utilities: An Update," DOE/EIA-0582, March 1997, Washington, D.C.

U.S. Environmental Protection Agency, *Environmental Investments: The Cost of a Clean Environment*. Washington, D.C: U.S. Environmental Protection Agency, 1990.

———, "1996 Compliance Record: Acid Rain Program," EPA 430-R-97-025, June 1997, Office of Air and Radiation, Washington, D.C.

U.S. General Accounting Office, "Air Pollution: Allowance Trading Offers an Opportunity to Reduce Emissions at Less Cost," GAO/RCED-95-30, Washington, D.C, 1995.

Weitzman, Martin L., "Prices vs. Quantities," *Review of Economic Studies*, 1974, 41, 477–91.

18   *It's Immoral to Buy the Right to Pollute (with replies)**

Michael J. Sandel

Michael J. Sandel is the Anne T. and Robert M. Bass Professor of Government at Harvard University.

At the conference on global warming in Kyoto, Japan, the United States found itself at toggerheads with developing nations on two important issues: The United States wanted those countries to commit themselves to restraints on emissions, and it wanted any agreement to include a trading scheme that would let countries buy and sell the right to pollute.

The Administration was right on the first point, but wrong on the second. Creating an international market in emission credits would make it easier for us to meet our obligations under the treaty but undermine the ethic we should be trying to foster on the environment.

Indeed, China and India threatened to torpedo the talks over the issue. They were afraid that such trading would enable rich countries to buy their way out of commitments to reduce greenhouse gases. In the end, the developing nations agreed to allow some emissions trading among developed countries, with details to be negotiated next year.

The Clinton Administration has made emission trading a centerpiece of its environmental policy. Creating an international market for emissions, it argues, is a more efficient way to reduce pollution than imposing fixed levels for each country.

Trading in greenhouse gases could also make compliance cheaper and less painful for the United States, which could pay to reduce some other country's carbon dioxide emissions rather than reduce its own. For example, the United States might find it cheaper (and more politically palatable) to pay to update an old coal-burning factory in a developing country than to tax gas-guzzling sports utility vehicles at home.

Since the aim is to limit the global level of these gases, one might ask, what difference does it make which places on the planet send less carbon to the sky?

"It's Immoral to Buy the Right to Pollute" by Michael Sandel. *New York Times*, December 15, 1997. Reprinted by permission of the author.

  *"Replies to Michael Sandel: Emissions Trading Will Lead to Less Pollution." *New York Times*, December 17, 1997. Reprinted by permission of the author.

  *"Emissions Trading Will Lead to Less Pollution; Sacrifice Isn't Required" by Michael Leifman. *New York Times*, Dec. 15, 1997. Reprinted by permission of the author.

It may make no difference from the standpoint of the heavens, but it does make a political difference. Despite the efficiency of international emissions trading, such a system is objectionable for three reasons.

First, it creates loopholes that could enable wealthy countries to evade their obligations. Under the Kyoto formula, for example, the United States could take advantage of the fact that Russia has already reduced its emissions 30 percent since 1990, not through energy efficiencies but through economic decline. The United States could buy excess credits from Russia, and count them toward meeting our obligations under the treaty.

Second, turning pollution into a commodity to be bought and sold removes the moral stigma that is properly associated with it, if a company or a country is fined for spewing excessive pollutants into the air, the community conveys its judgment that the polluter has done something wrong. A fee, on the other hand, makes pollution just another cost of doing business, like wages, benefits and rent.

The distinction between a fine and a fee for despoiling the environment is not one we should give up too easily. Suppose there were a $100 fine for throwing a beer can into the Grand Canyon, and a wealthy hiker decided to pay $100 for the convenience. Would there be nothing wrong in his treating the fine as if it were simply an expensive dumping charge?

Or consider the fine for parking in a place reserved for the disabled. If a busy contractor needs to park near his building site and is willing to pay the fine, is there nothing wrong with his treating that space as an expensive parking lot?

In effacing the distinction between a fine and a fee, emission trading is like a recent proposal to open carpool lanes on Los Angeles freeways to drivers without passengers who are willing to pay a fee. Such drivers are now fined for slipping into carpool lanes; under the market proposal, they would enjoy a quicker commute without opprobrium.

A third objection to emission trading among countries is that it may undermine the sense of shared responsibility that increased global cooperation requires.

Consider an illustration drawn from an autumn ritual: raking fallen leaves into great piles and lighting bonfires. Imagine a neighborhood where each family agrees to have only one small bonfire a year. But they also agree that families can buy and sell their bonfire permits as they choose.

The family in the mansion on the hill buys permits from its neighbors—paying them, in effect, to lug their leaves to the town compost heap. The market works, and pollution is reduced, but without the spirit of shared sacrifice that might have been produced had no market intervened.

Those who have sold their permits and those who have bought them, come to regard the bonfires less as an offense against clean air than as a luxury, a status symbol that can be bought and sold. And the resentment against the family in the mansion makes future, more demanding forms of cooperation more difficult to achieve.

Of course, many countries that attended the Kyoto conference have already made cooperation elusive. They have not yet agreed to restrict their emissions at all. Their refusal undermines the prospect of a global environmental ethic as surely as does our pollution trading scheme.

But the United States would have more suasion if these developing countries could not rightly complain that trading in emissions allows wealthy nations to buy their way out of global obligation.

Replies to Michael J. Sandel

From Steven Shavell, Professor of Law and Economics at Harvard Law School

Michael J. Sandel ("It's Immoral to Buy the Right to Pollute," Op-Ed, Dec. 15) discounts the great benefits of trade in pollution rights and advances flawed arguments against it.

Suppose a rich country like the United States would have to spend $50 billion annually to reduce its carbon dioxide emissions by some amount, whereas China could reduce its emissions by this same amount more cheaply, at a cost of $5 billion (say, by installing simple smoke scrubbers in its coal-burning factories).

If trade in emissions credits were allowed, both China and the United States would be better off.

The United States could pay China $30 billion for the right to emit carbon dioxide. This would make China $25 billion better off: it would receive $30 billion and spend only $5 billion to prevent the emissions. The United States would pay $30 billion rather than spend $50 billion to abate the emissions.

And trade would probably lead ultimately to less pollution. When countries know that they can make profits or that ceilings on pollution are easier to meet, they will be more likely to agree to reduce the total amount of permitted pollution over time.

From Robert N. Stavins, Albert Pratt Professor of Business and Government at Harvard Kennedy School, Research Associate at the National Bureau of Economic Research, and University Fellow at Resources for the Future

The ink is barely dry on the Kyoto protocol, but Michael J. Sandel argues that the agreement's emissions trading provisions, supported by the Clinton Administration, will foster "immoral" behavior (Op-Ed, Dec. 15).

Replies to editorial, by Steven Shavell, Robert N. Stavins, Sanford Gaines, Eric Maskin, and Michael Leifman from *New York Times*, December 17, 1997.

Was it immoral when the United States used a tradable permit system among refineries to phase leaded gasoline out of the market in the 1980's more rapidly than anyone had anticipated and at a savings of $250 million a year?

Is it now immoral that we are reducing acid rain by half through a tradable permit system among electrical utilities, reducing emissions (sulfur dioxide) faster than anyone had predicted and saving up to $1 billion a year for electricity consumers? Is that why the Environmental Defense Fund and others have worked so tirelessly and effectively to implement these emissions-trading programs?

From Sanford E. Gaines, Professor of Law at the University of Houston

Michael J. Sandel (Op-Ed, Dec. 15) invokes the moral argument against emissions trading in the context of reducing greenhouse gas emissions. Maintaining a moral stigma on pollution makes sense for hazardous substances where polluters have choices, for reducing the pollution. But global warming is not such a situation. Does Mr. Sandel really believe he is behaving immorally when he cooks his dinner, switches on a light or turns on a computer to write an Op-Ed article? These activities result in emissions of carbon dioxide. Or is it his utility that should be stigmatized, perhaps for not using nuclear power?

To reduce greenhouse gas emissions, producers and consumers alike need to adopt new technologies. That's a perfect situation to use the power of the market. Mr. Sandel should reserve his moral outrage for those who don't even want the chance to buy the right to pollute because they refuse to accept that the planet can no longer afford cheap energy.

From Eric S. Maskin, Professor, School of Social Science, Institute for Advanced Study at Princeton University

Michael J. Sandel (Op-Ed, Dec. 15) neglects an important distinction in his argument against tradable emissions credits. The examples he gives of immoral acts—throwing beer cans into the Grand Canyon or parking in spots reserved for the disabled—are discrete choices: one can do them or not do them, and society can therefore reasonably ban them outright.

But virtually any manufacturing activity entails the creation of some pollution. So the question is not will we pollute, but rather how much. Further, if there is to be pollution, shouldn't we try to trade it off against its economic consequences? Such a trade-off is facilitated by tradable rights.

From Michael Leifman, Environmental Policy Consultant

Michael J. Sandel's Dec. 15 Op-Ed article displays a misunderstanding of environmental policy and of global warming. He argues that trading emissions credits undermines "the ethic we should be trying to foster on the environment."

What ethic does Mr. Sandel have in mind, other than his misplaced wish for a "spirit of shared sacrifice"? Why should environmental progress be accompanied by sacrifice?

He asserts that a fee (that is, the cost of buying emissions credits) rather than a fine (for noncompliance) "makes pollution just another cost of doing business." Exactly! There is no better way to incorporate environmental ethos into a company than to link the costs of pollution to the bottom line.

Mr. Sandel argues that without fines, there is no moral stigma associated with pollution. Maybe so, but is it better to feel guilty about polluting or to reduce pollution cost effectively?

VI

Economics of Natural Resources

19   *On the Empirical Significance of the Hotelling Rule*

John Livernois

*John Livernois is Professor of Economics and Chair of the Economics
Department at the University of Guelph.*
Department of Economics, University of Guelph; E-mail: live@uoguelph.ca

Introduction

The origins of the field of nonrenewable resource economics can be traced
to Harold Hotelling's (1931) "The Economics of Exhaustible Resources."
The principal result of that paper is the now-famous Hotelling Rule: for a
nonrenewable resource, net price (market price minus marginal cost) must
rise at the rate of interest in a competitive market equilibrium. This basic
rule forms the theoretical core of the economics of nonrenewable resources,
is present in one form or another in every modern paper on nonrenewable
resource economics, and is the conceptual and theoretical framework used
by economists to understand and model the long-run evolution of prices
and supplies for nonrenewable resources.

But what do we know about the empirical relevance of the Hotelling
Rule? What practical insights has it provided for understanding what we
have observed so far in nonrenewable resource markets? Does it help us
understand the supply behavior of extractive firms and industries? The purpose of this article is to address these questions by reviewing the empirical
evidence thus far and evaluating the empirical significance of the Hotelling
Rule.

In the next section, I provide some intuition and additional background
on the Hotelling Rule. This is followed by a discussion of the empirical evidence on market prices for nonrenewable resources. Next, I investigate the
significance of technological change and market structure in influencing
observed trends in prices. This is followed by an examination of the literature on empirical tests of the Hotelling Rule and a discussion of the Hotelling Valuation Principle (HVP). The final section draws conclusions about
the empirical significance of the Hotelling Rule.

"On the Empirical Significance of the Hotelling Rule" by John Livernois. *Review of Environmental
Economics and Policy* 3. 2009. Pp. 22–41. Reprinted with permission.

The Hotelling Rule: Intuition, Background, and Definitions

The intuition behind the Hotelling Rule is straightforward. Net price has to rise at the rate of interest as a condition of equilibrium; otherwise, the present value of the net price that could be received from selling in some periods would be higher than in other periods. In this case, mine owners would not be indifferent about when to extract and sell their resources. Another way to understand the Hotelling Rule is as a condition of intertemporal arbitrage that ensures that the last unit extracted in any time period earns the same return (in present value terms).

Hotelling's seminal article was a response to the conservation movement's claims that unregulated private markets would lead to the overexploitation of nonrenewable resource stocks, so it was natural for him to focus on the intertemporal allocation issue. Hotelling argued that the socially optimal rate of exploitation of a nonrenewable resource over time is achieved in a competitive market equilibrium, provided that the social discount rate equals the interest rate and that there are no sources of market failure such as externalities or incomplete property rights. Nearly 80 years later, the economics literature continues to focus on the intertemporal allocation aspects of nonrenewable resource supply and rely heavily on Hotelling's original insights.

The literature uses a number of names to refer to the concept of "net price": scarcity rent, shadow price, royalty, marginal user cost, and in the language of optimal control theory, the costate variable. In this article, I will use the term "scarcity rent." I will also use the term "interest rate" because that is what Hotelling used. However, the term "discount rate" is a commonly used substitute.

Hotelling recognized that he had constructed a highly stylized and, in some ways, overly simplified model of mining. For example, he pointed out that his basic model fails to capture the tendency for extraction costs to rise as a resource is extracted. This can occur both within an individual deposit, as the firm digs deeper or as pressure declines in a petroleum reservoir, and for the industry as a whole, as firms tend to use up the lowest-cost deposits first. This tendency for extraction costs to rise is often referred to as the degradation effect or the stock effect of extraction. When the Hotelling Rule is modified to incorporate this effect, scarcity rent rises less rapidly because current extraction now has an additional negative effect: it degrades the quality of remaining reserves—or raises the cost of future extraction. This implies that scarcity rent will rise less rapidly than the rate of interest in a competitive equilibrium. In fact, if the degradation effect is strong enough, scarcity rent may eventually decline.

This modification to the Hotelling model has significant implications for the way we think about depletion. It is not the finiteness of the exhaustible resource but rather the rising cost of extracting what is left that becomes the constraining factor. Economists recognize that we will probably never physically exhaust any exhaustible resource. Instead, economic exhaustion will occur when the cost of further extraction becomes higher than the market is willing to pay. Indeed, at this point, the scarcity rent itself becomes zero.

The Hotelling Rule, with and without these modifications, remains the underlying theoretical framework for our understanding of how markets for nonrenewable resources will evolve. Its most important empirical implication is that market price must rise over time in real terms, provided that costs are time-invariant. In the benchmark case of zero marginal cost and perfect competition, market price itself will rise at the rate of interest. With positive but time-invariant marginal cost, market price must rise at a rate proportional to but less than the rate of interest. When degradation effects are present, market price still rises over time even though scarcity rent may eventually decline to zero (Livernois and Martin 2001). Under imperfect competition, scarcity rent must still rise at the rate of interest, or slower if degradation effects are present; however, market price will typically start higher and rise less rapidly than under perfect competition.

Several other modifications and extensions to the basic Hotelling model have appeared in the literature that include factors such as imperfect competition, the presence of a backstop technology, different types of risk, durability of the mineral, recycling, and exploration. I will briefly discuss these extensions below as needed to facilitate the evaluation of the empirical literature.[1]

Empirical Evidence on Market Prices

Although the Hotelling model and the Hotelling Rule have been extended in many directions, the essential idea remains the same: in a market equilibrium, current price reflects both the marginal cost of extraction and the scarcity rent. In the basic model, there is a clear prediction that prices will rise over time to reflect both rising scarcity and a rising marginal extraction cost. What does the empirical literature tell us about prices?

Early Analyses of Mineral Resource Prices

The first systematic analysis of long-run trends for nonrenewable resource prices was conducted by Barnett and Morse (1963), who used price data from 1870 to 1957 for several commodities. Their interest was not in testing the Hotelling model per se, but rather in examining the hypothesis of increasing scarcity for natural resources. The concern was that rising resource scarcity, as reflected in rising costs and prices, would place a drag on economic prosperity and indeed growth. What they found was surprising. Despite the fact that mineral resources had been subject to exploitation

---

[1]For a more thorough discussion, see Krautkraemer (1998); and Gaudet (2007).

for decades at increasingly rapid rates, mineral prices, in real terms, showed no discernible rising trend over the time period.

With the advantage of more sophisticated statistical techniques and a data set that spanned the period 1900 to 1973, Smith (1979) reevaluated Barnett and Morse's (1963) conclusions. He found no statistically stable time trend, either upwards or downwards, in the price index for minerals as a whole over this period and concluded that it was impossible to make inferences about changes in scarcity without detailed analysis of individual mineral commodities.

Evidence of *U*-Shaped Price Paths

Slade (1982) did this more detailed analysis, looking for trends in the prices of eleven major metals and fuels (aluminum, copper, iron, lead, nickel, silver, tin, zinc, coal, natural gas, and petroleum) from 1870 to 1978. She found that many of the price series seemed to bottom out in the 1960s but began to turn upwards in the 1970s. To reconcile these findings with the Hotelling Rule, Slade (1982) developed a modified version of the model in which both cost-increasing degradation effects and cost-reducing technological change are present. Since marginal cost can fall over time if the effect of technological change is greater than the degradation effect, Slade concluded that the price of the nonrenewable resource can fall initially, even if the Hotelling Rule is satisfied. However, Slade found that eventually the cost-reducing effect of technological change is overcome by the cost-increasing effects of depletion and/or the price-increasing effects of the Hotelling Rule, which means price will turn upwards. Overall, her model predicts that *U*-shaped price paths are consistent with the Hotelling Rule.

Another theoretical explanation for *U*-shaped price paths has been suggested by Pindyck (1978a); Livernois and Uhler (1987); and Swierzbinski and Mendelshohn (1989a). When exploration is added to the Hotelling model, even in a deterministic manner so that future discoveries are fully anticipated, the process of building up and then running down proven reserves can lead to a *U*-shaped price path. Deshmukh and Pliska (1980); Arrow and Chang (1982); Lasserre (1984); Swierzbinski and Mendelsohn (1989b); and Cairns and Quyen (1998) have shown that when discoveries are not fully anticipated, price jumps or falls occur as revisions to the expected stock of remaining reserves are made. If, as one might predict, the largest finds and the largest number of finds occur early,[2] then this might add further weight to the prediction of *U*-shaped price paths.

---

[2]Even if exploration were completely random, the probability of finding large or any deposits would likely be larger simply because there are more of them early on.

Evidence of Unit Roots

Slade's theoretical analysis and empirical findings of U-shaped price paths seemed to provide reassuring evidence that Hotelling's predictions were being borne out by the data. However, subsequent research has cast doubt on the statistical robustness of these empirical findings. Indeed, the empirical literature on price trends from this point forward concentrated on sorting out whether the statistical properties of these time-series data are stationary over time. Stationarity in a time series is important: it means we can confidently predict that its statistical properties will be the same in the future as in the past. If a U-shaped trend fits well using historical data (as in Slade's analysis), we can be confident that it is not just an artifact of the time period analyzed, but in fact provides a robust inference about the trend that prices are following.

The most commonly used statistical test to determine if a time series is stationary is the unit-root test.[3] Berck and Roberts (1996) performed this test for most of the commodity prices studied by Slade (1982), but with the advantage of thirteen additional years of data (1870–1991). They found evidence of unit roots in most of the price series and concluded that the U-shaped trend is not stationary. This implies that there is no statistical basis for concluding that prices have bottomed out and are starting to turn upwards.[4] Berck and Roberts (1996) found evidence that the year-to-year changes in prices were themselves stationary time series.[5] However, they were unable to find conclusive evidence from their analysis of these time-series data that price changes were tending to become positive during the sample period.

Ahrens and Sharma (1997) take the story to the next level with their analysis of annual price data from 1870 to 1990 for the same set of eleven nonrenewable resources studied by Slade (1982). They argue that Berck and Roberts (1996) might have been wrong to conclude that unit roots were present in these price series. They cite Perron's (1989) finding that if a structural break is present in the price series but is not controlled for, tests are biased against rejecting the hypothesis of a unit root. After allowing for structural breaks at critical points such as the Great Depression (1929) and the outbreak (1939) and end (1945) of World War II, they reject the hypothesis of a unit root for six of the eleven commodity price series, which casts a doubt on Berck and Roberts' (1996) results. Going one step further with the same data and the same time period (1870–1990), Lee, List, and Stra-

---

[3] A unit root is present if the coefficient on the lagged value of the dependent variable (such as price) in a regression equation is equal to 1. This means that the effect of past shocks never wears off, so the dependent variable does not revert to a stationary value or, if a trend is controlled for, as in the case at hand, never reverts to a stable trend.

[4] A time series is said to have a stationary trend, or to be "trend-stationary," if it has a tendency to return to the trend, even after being subjected to random shocks. In subsequent papers, Slade (1988) and Agbeyegbe (1989) found similar evidence.

[5] This is also referred to as a "difference-stationary" time series.

zicich (2006) allow structural breaks to be determined endogenously for each of the eleven price series and are able to reject the hypothesis of a unit root in all eleven cases. Their results imply that the price series are indeed trend-stationary after all, but only between the endogenously determined structural breaks. They find more downward than upward trends in the eleven price series. But these trends are punctuated by both upward and downward jumps at the structural break points, making it impossible to draw any general conclusions about whether prices are rising or falling.[6]

Problems with Using Price Indices

There are two potential problems associated with deflating nominal resource prices by a price index, an approach used in all of the studies discussed above. The first is that recent research has shown that standard price deflators overestimate the true extent of inflation for three reasons: first, price indices underestimate the extent to which consumers and producers are able to substitute away from goods or inputs that increase in price; second, price indices do not incorporate the introduction of new (and presumably more effective) goods and inputs except with a lag; and third, price indices do not adjust for improvements in the quality of goods or inputs. Using recent estimates in the literature of the size of the inflation bias to adjust the standard deflators downwards, Svedberg and Tilton (2006) find that the adjusted real price of copper follows a statistically significant rising trend from 1870 to 2000, whereas it falls over time using the unadjusted deflators. The second problem is that the standard deflation procedure implicitly assumes that nonrenewable resource prices adjust fully to changes in the general price level. Moazzami and Anderson (1994) argue that this is implausible in the short run and should be a tested hypothesis in the long run. Otherwise researchers could potentially create a specification error that could indeed be responsible for the nonstationarity found in the inflation-adjusted price-series data discussed above. Using the same data as Slade (1982) but with additional years of data, Moazzami and Anderson allow for short-run deviations from the long-run hypothesized trend and test whether the long-run relationship holds. They find that (a) most nominal resource prices do fully adjust to changes in the price index but only in the long run and (b) the data support the hypothesis of a U-shaped trend for most of the price series. Both the Moazzami and Anderson (1994); and the Svedberg and Tilton (2006) studies raise important questions about the measurement of relative prices for nonrenewable resources that deserve further attention before any firm conclusions can be drawn about upward or downward price trends.

---

[6]See Figure 1 in Lee, List, and Strazicich (2006) for plots of the eleven price-series data with the structural breaks and fitted trends.

Conclusions about Nonrenewable Resource Prices

Notwithstanding the measurement issues raised above, the findings in Lee, List, and Strazicich (2006) reflect the current state of knowledge concerning the empirical performance of nonrenewable resource prices. What do their findings tell us? First, there is no common pattern across the eleven commodity price series. Second, no price series unambiguously rises over time; only zinc comes close because it appears to have rising trends interrupted by two downward corrections. Third, one could argue that the price series for natural gas, petroleum, and possibly nickel have the look of a V-shaped (rather than a U-shaped path) and fourth, most prices are falling toward the end of the sample period (1990).

This last conclusion begs the question about what would happen if the analysis were extended to account for what has happened in commodity markets since 1990. This is clearly a question that needs to be addressed, and factoring recent data into a time-series analysis is a potentially fruitful area for future research. While such an analysis is beyond the scope of this article, I offer some observations here. Looking at the price data for the eleven commodities since 1990, one would have to conclude that the downward trends Lee, List, and Strazicich (2006) found in the period immediately preceding 1990 continued for the next decade or so. However, after 2001, all of the prices (with the exception of coal) have shown dramatic increases. For example, the annual average growth rates of prices in real terms (relative to the producer price index) from 2001 to 2007 have been 38 percent for aluminum, 36 percent for nickel, 32 percent for lead, 26 percent for copper, 22 percent for zinc, 19 percent for iron ore, 18 percent for tin and silver, and 16 percent for crude oil (UNCTAD and U.S. Energy Information Administration). These are very rapid growth rates indeed over a six-year period and the markets show no sign of abating as this article goes to press.

Does this mean nonrenewable resource prices have finally turned upward for good? Not likely. Although the Hotelling Rule tells us that nonrenewable resource prices will indeed eventually turn upwards, it cannot justify growth rates in prices as high as those observed recently. This, combined with the observation that commodity prices are highly volatile, suggests that it would be unwise to expect that prices will continue to rise unabated.

The Role of Technological Change in Price Trends

How significant is the role of technological change in explaining the declining relative price paths that have been observed for nonrenewable resources? To cause nonrenewable resource prices to fall relative to a price index, technological change would have to affect nonrenewable resource prices more than it affects the overall index of prices in the economy, and it would have to do this in the presence of cost-increasing degradation effects. Thus, it is a tall order for technological change alone to explain falling real nonrenewable resource prices.

Cost Effects of Technological Change

It is difficult to isolate the effect of technological improvements on costs in nonrenewable resource industries because we are only able to observe the net effect of technological improvement and resource degradation. However, a small number of studies have attempted to isolate the effects of technological change. Lasserre and Ouellette (1988) measured changes in total factor productivity (TFP) for the asbestos industry in Canada while controlling for changes in the quality of the resource as measured by ore grade. They found that the pure effect of technological improvement would have been a 76-percent increase in TFP from 1953 to 1982, an increase similar to what occurred in the textile sector, which was used as a comparable, nonresource sector. However, the net effect was only a 13-percent increase in TFP because of the effect of resource degradation. Schmitz (2005), on the other hand, found evidence of substantial improvements in productivity, including a doubling of labor productivity, in the iron ore industries in the Great Lakes Region. This occurred over a very short period of time in the early 1980s and resulted primarily from reorganization of work practices to meet rising competition from Brazilian exporters. In a very innovative study, Cuddington and Moss (2001) used data on the number of technological diffusions observed per year to isolate the effect of technological change on nonrenewable resource costs. They estimated that finding costs for natural gas would have risen by about 22 percent per year had it not been for technological change. Instead, gas-finding costs rose only by about 2.7 percent per year. It appears that the effect of technological change on finding costs for natural gas, while large, was not enough to outweigh the effects of degradation. Managi et al. (2004) advanced the Cuddington et al. methodology by using the relative importance of specific innovations as expressed by industry experts, rather than the raw number of innovations, as the control for technological change. Using a detailed micro-level data set for offshore oil and gas production in the Gulf of Mexico from 1947 to 1998, they found that technological change more than compensated for the effect of degradation. However, productivity growth in the industry averaged 0.2 percent per year, which was lower than the U.S. national average of 0.7 percent.

The evidence above suggests that technological change alone is not a sufficient explanation for falling real resource prices. If technological change were the only explanation, then nonrenewable resource prices should not have fallen relative to nonresource good prices (as measured by the producer price index). Even though the net effect of degradation and technological change often appears to be cost reducing, it is seldom as large as the effect of technological change on nonresource costs. Thus there is clearly more to the explanation for falling prices than technological change.

Other Factors That Affect Price Trends

Three other significant factors contribute to the explanation of falling prices. First, technological innovations occur at all stages of getting a natural resource product to market, from geophysical exploration to on-site drilling and mapping, development, extraction, and processing. The studies examined above all looked at the impact of technological change on a single stage. As shown in Lin and Wagner (2007), the net effects of technological change combined over all stages in nonrenewable resource production are potentially much larger than the above evidence would suggest. Lin and Wagner (2007) construct a model based on Slade's (1982) analysis that allows them to formally test the hypothesis that the opposing effects of technological improvement and resource degradation exactly offset one another. Using data on extraction costs and prices for a number of mineral commodities from 1970 to 2004, they are unable to reject the hypothesis, which is consistent with their finding of no discernible trend in real prices over this period.

A second factor is that technological innovation can change not only contemporaneous extraction costs, but expected future costs as well. This would lead to an upward reevaluation of the economically recoverable reserves and, hence, a downward adjustment to the value of scarcity rent. The point is that technological change can affect nonrenewable resource prices through at least two channels, first via its effect on current cost and second via its effect on scarcity rent (because of its effect on expected recoverable reserves). In the nonresource sector, technological change can operate only through the first channel. A third, and also unique, channel through which technological change may operate is by reducing the supply price of backstop technologies, which would lead to a further reduction in the current price of the nonrenewable resource.

The third factor is nonrenewable resource discoveries that are not anticipated. It is obvious that major unanticipated discoveries would have a significant downward effect on scarcity rent and hence market price. It is therefore surprising that one cannot find evidence of this in the economics literature or even attempts to determine the extent to which major discoveries could help explain observed prices over time for nonrenewable resources. This impact could be significant and warrants research. For example, Adelman (1993) reports that in 1987, the U.S. Geological Survey estimated that there was no more than a 5-percent probability that world's oil reserves remaining to be discovered and developed were as much as 222 billion barrels. Yet, I calculate that the world's oil production alone since 1988 has been 478 billion barrels and recent estimates of existing world proved reserves are in excess of 1,000 billion barrels (U.S. Energy Information Administration).

A Simulated Price Path for a Nonrenewable Resource

I conclude this section with a report on a simple experiment. I simulated the price path predicted by the basic Hotelling model after augmenting it to include some of the factors discussed above. In particular, I assumed fully

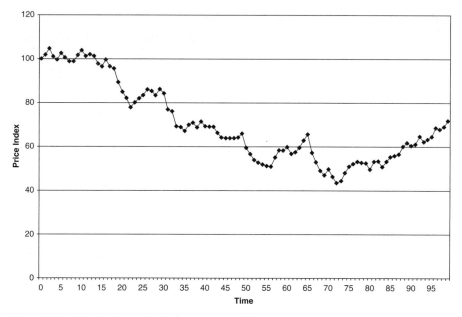

Figure 1 Simulated price path for a nonrenewable resource.

Source: Author's calculations.

anticipated technological change that reduces marginal cost over time at a decreasing rate. I assumed four unanticipated increases in recoverable reserves, which I modeled by extending the expected time to depletion, which in turn reduced the current value of scarcity rent. Finally, I added a small random error term with a zero mean to capture temporary supply and demand shocks.

Figure 1 shows the result of this Hotelling price equation simulated over 100 periods. If an econometrician were presented with the first fifty or sixty data points in this series, he or she would be hard pressed to find anything resembling what we would expect to see from a world in which the Hotelling Rule is operating. However, when we see the whole picture, we detect something resembling a *U*-shaped price path of the kind hypothesized by Slade (1982). Price eventually turns upward (though not smoothly) because unanticipated discoveries peter out, and because the effect of rising scarcity rent eventually dominates the effect of technological change. Overlaying this long-run trend are frequent short-run fluctuations caused by the random error term and less frequent but larger shocks caused by revisions to the expected stock of reserves remaining, which in turn leads to market corrections in scarcity rent and hence market price. The point is, without much effort and without resorting to a complicated modification of the Hotelling model, it is possible to generate price paths that do not look unlike the ones we have observed empirically.

The Role of Market Structure in Price Trends

The discussion so far has focused on the Hotelling Rule in the context of perfect competition, an assumption that may not be realistic for a number of nonrenewable resource industries. How is the empirical significance of the Hotelling Rule affected by the presence of imperfect competition? In particular, would it change what we expect to observe and could it contribute to the explanation of flat or falling real prices?

I will limit the discussion here to what I view as being the most salient point.[7] First, it is a well-known result that under pure monopoly resource price starts higher and rises less rapidly. Under oligopoly, behavior can range from being similar to pure monopoly to being similar to perfect competition. For example, Salant (1976) shows that although the presence of a competitive fringe may constrain the ability of a dominant firm/cartel to diverge from a competitive pricing rule, the dominant firm will ensure that its reserves outlast the competition's so that it eventually becomes a pure monopolist. At the other extreme, even industries that have all the markings of imperfect competition, such as the U.S. copper industry prior to 1978, may actually not behave much differently from what would be predicted by a competitive model (see Agostini 2006). In between these two extremes, the literature offers a rich set of results that can provide insights into the supply behavior of extractive firms. For example, Loury (1986) constructs a theory of "oil"igopoly and with it derives a number of predictions about supply behavior that are distinct from those predicted by a competitive equilibrium. Polasky (1992) tests these predictions and finds that the observed pattern of production for hundreds of U.S. oil companies in 1983 and 1984 and seventy-three countries from 1979 to 1989 is consistent with Loury's "oil"igopoly theory. Polasky's results show that the Hotelling model, recast within the context of oligopoly, provides useful insights into the understanding of observed extraction patterns for the oil industry across firms and nations. However, none of these models of imperfect competition helps to explain the empirical phenomenon that prices for nonrenewable resources have not been rising.

Pindyck (1978b), on the other hand, shows that the optimal pricing strategy for a cartel such as OPEC is *U*-shaped. Price is set high initially to exploit the short-run inelastic demand faced by the cartel. It is then allowed to decline, as demand becomes more elastic over time, until it eventually begins rising again to reflect the rising scarcity rent. Although Pindyck's results are consistent with the observed fall in oil prices after their peak in 1980, this is probably not a strategy OPEC could employ too many times. Salant (1979) analyzes a model in which a monopolist supplier of a nonrenewable resource faces potential competition from a backstop technology

---

[7]Gaudet (2007) provides an excellent, thorough survey of the effect of market structure on nonrenewable resource prices.

if price rises above a critical level. In this model, it is optimal for the monopolist to engage in what Salant calls a dynamic limit pricing strategy. This involves holding price constant over a possibly lengthy interval of time at a level just below the critical level, even though scarcity rent continues to rise. One can imagine that this is a pricing strategy a monopolist might employ to deter not only backstop supply, but also entry of higher cost sources of nonrenewable supply. Thus, this model may provide some rationale for nonincreasing resource prices.

Incorporating elements of market power into the Hotelling model has the potential to improve its ability to provide insight into the behavior of extractive firms. It also has the potential to provide insight into pricing strategies such as the two discussed above that might at first appear inconsistent with the predictions of the Hotelling Rule. Overall, however, one still has to appeal to the forces of technological change and unanticipated discoveries to reconcile the strong empirical evidence on nonrenewable resource price trends with theoretical predictions.

Direct Tests of the Hotelling Model

Looking for trends in market prices is an indirect way of testing the Hotelling Rule. After all, the Hotelling Rule is really about scarcity rent, and scarcity rent is just one among many factors that influences supply and price. A more direct test of the Hotelling Rule would be to compare the actual path of scarcity rent with the theoretical prediction. This is quite difficult, however, because scarcity rent is not usually observable and modern extensions of Hotelling's model have shown that the Hotelling Rule becomes much more complex when factors such as resource quality degradation are taken into account. Let me discuss the second issue first.

Impact of Resource Quality Degradation

The basic Hotelling model predicts that scarcity rent rises at the rate of interest. However, after incorporating the tendency for extraction costs to rise as the resource is depleted (the degradation effect), some recent papers have argued that scarcity rent eventually falls to zero at the point at which economic exhaustion occurs (Heal 1976; Solow and Wan 1976; Levhari and Liviatan 1977; Hanson 1980; and Chakravory and Roumasset 1990). Others argue that scarcity rent rises over time (Long 1979; and Krulce 1993), while still others argue that the path of scarcity rent is indeterminate and, hence, so is the predicted path of market price (Fisher 1981; and Farzin 1992). Livernois and Martin (2001) reconcile these apparently contradictory findings by showing that if the extraction cost function satisfies conventional regularity conditions, the path of scarcity rent is unambiguously nondecreasing.[8] Of course, there is no guarantee that extractive cost functions satisfy these regularity conditions in practice, so there is no guarantee that scarcity rent can be predicted to be monotonically rising. This complicates empirical testing, in the sense that the observation of either a rising or a falling scarcity rent would still not be sufficient evidence to support the Hotelling Rule. Instead, in order to control for degradation effects, it becomes necessary to estimate structural models that are based on an assumed cost function. Inevitably, this makes the test a joint test of the structural model and the Hotelling Rule.

Nonobservability of Scarcity Rent

The first issue—that scarcity rent is not usually observable—presents a more serious problem. Researchers have for the most part been forced to estimate the value of scarcity rent at each point in time by some indirect method. The estimated time series for scarcity rent is then tested to see if it conforms to the path predicted by the Hotelling Rule. Obviously, tests of this nature are only as good as the initial estimates of scarcity rent. In practice, it is difficult to distinguish scarcity rent from rents due to market power and short-run capacity constraints (Krautkraemer 1998), which of course reduces the credibility of any direct test of the Hotelling Rule in which scarcity rent is estimated.

Evidence from the Canadian Nickel Industry

The Canadian nickel industry has figured prominently in the empirical literature on the Hotelling Rule. Cairns (1981) used data for the Canadian nickel industry to estimate a value for scarcity rent. He assumed an exponential tonnage-grade model for the resource and a cost function that depends on grade. Cairns used the results of Levhari and Liviatan (1977), who show that, assuming the resource will never be physically exhausted, scarcity rent consists only of the degradation cost (the present-valued sum of all increases in future costs caused by a marginal degradation of the current stock of ore). Cairns found that, even with strong assumptions, scarcity rent is no more than 5 percent of the metal's value. This is perhaps not surprising given that known nickel reserves in Canada in the 1970s, as he noted, were of the order of 70 times the extraction rate.

Stollery (1983) argued that the nickel industry was ideal for testing the Hotelling Rule because world's nickel supply from the 1950s to 1970s was dominated by a single Canadian firm, the International Nickel Corporation (INCO), so that it was the unquestioned price leader. This made it possible "to study demand, costs, reserves and discovery rates of INCO alone for determination of world nickel prices without having to resort to a complex

---

[8]Specifically, it must be jointly convex in its two arguments: the rate of extraction and the stock of remaining reserves.

oligopoly model." Stollery (1983) estimated the demand curve facing INCO, from which he calculated marginal revenue, and a constant-elasticity-of-substitution (CES) cost function for extraction, from which he calculated marginal cost. Scarcity rent was calculated by subtracting the estimated marginal cost from marginal revenue for each year in the sample (1947–1974). Stollery concluded that scarcity rent, while positive, was a small fraction of output price, a result that is consistent with Cairns' (1981) results. However, a plot over time of his estimated scarcity rent shows it growing fairly steadily, suggesting that Stollery's results may well be consistent with the predicted Hotelling Rule path.

Although Stollery's estimated scarcity rent rose over time, so did the market price. In fact, Cairns (1986) noticed that the estimated scarcity rent seemed to be a fairly constant share of market price. This led him to suggest that Stollery's results were also consistent with a static monopoly-pricing rule under which price equals marginal cost plus a constant markup, a hypothesis neither Cairns (1985) nor Stollery (1985) was subsequently able to reject. Ellis and Halvorsen (2002) investigated this conjecture further. One of the main innovations in their paper was to develop a methodology that allowed them to identify what portion of the wedge between price and marginal cost is due to market power and what portion is due to scarcity rent. What they found was that there was a substantial wedge between price and marginal cost in the Canadian nickel industry, but that most of it was due to market power. In fact, their econometric results found a user cost of about the same magnitude as Cairns'. Using the same data, Lee (2007) estimates values for the scarcity rent for nickel that are consistent with those cited above. However, he finds that the path of his estimated scarcity rent is not consistent with what is predicted by the Hotelling Rule.

The evidence on the Canadian nickel industry seems to point to the conclusion that there is a positive scarcity rent but that it is small and, in fact, relatively insignificant compared to the rent that is due to INCO's market power. Although on balance the evidence does not clearly reject or support the Hotelling Rule, it does suggest that scarcity rent was not an empirically significant determinant of market price.

More Empirical Evidence Concerning Scarcity Rent

Farrow (1985) used proprietary monthly data from an underground mine from January 1975 to December 1981 to derive estimated monthly values for scarcity rent.[9] He then tested whether these estimated values obey the Hotelling Rule by running a regression of the change in scarcity rent on a number of explanatory variables, including scarcity rent. According to the Hotelling Rule, the percentage change in scarcity rent should equal the interest rate, after controlling for other factors such as the degradation effect. Therefore, the estimated value of the coefficient on scarcity rent in his regression

---

[9]More specifically, he estimated a cost function and used it to derive monthly predicted values for marginal cost, which in turn were subtracted from the market price.

should equal the interest rate. Although Farrow tried many variants of the model to capture the effects of various constraints and characteristics of the underground mine, he consistently estimated a negative coefficient value for the interest rate, a clear rejection of the Hotelling Rule.[10]

Young (1992) used panel data on fourteen Canadian copper mines to test the Hotelling model and found that the evidence "corroborates the findings of Farrow (1985) that when firm-level data are examined, they are not consistent with Hotelling's rule." Halvorsen and Smith (1991) estimate scarcity rent in a highly aggregated model of the Canadian metal mining industry and also strongly reject the Hotelling Rule.

Impact of Risk Adjustments

Gaudet and Howitt (1989); Gaudet and Khadr (1991); and Gaudet (2007) show that in the presence of risk, it is necessary to further refine the Hotelling Rule. Holding a mineral asset is risky, and therefore the equilibrium rate of return required by investors in order to hold the asset will include a risk premium. Whether the risk premium is positive or negative depends on how the return on holding the resource is correlated with other assets. Gaudet (2007) points out that it is theoretically possible that if the risk premium is sufficiently negative (because of a strong negative covariance between the rate of change of scarcity rent and the rate of change of consumption), the risk-adjusted Hotelling Rule could imply flat or even decreasing scarcity rent. Slade and Thille (1997) test a risk-adjusted Hotelling Rule using Young's (1992) panel data on fourteen Canadian copper mines. They note that the variance of the price of copper is nearly 100 times its mean, indicating that risk is clearly an important feature in that industry. They find that adjusting the Hotelling Rule for risk leads to improved results over those obtained by Young (1992). In fact, they are unable to reject the risk-adjusted Hotelling Rule; however, they caution readers not to view these results as confirmation of the Hotelling Rule because their statistical test has very little power to reject, and the degree of risk diversification implied by their estimates is too large. Nevertheless, the addition of risk to the Hotelling model clearly improved its empirical performance.

Young and Ryan (1996) also test a risk-adjusted Hotelling Rule but this time using industry-level data for lead, zinc, copper, and silver mining in Canada. Although they find plausible evidence for positive risk premia, it is "not sufficient to completely reconcile such a model with historical price and cost data." They attribute the weak results to problems in obtaining appropriate data.

---

[10]However, as Farrow notes, he actually is rejecting jointly the model used to estimate scarcity rent and the degradation effect along with the Hotelling Rule.

An Empirical Test: Stumpage Prices for Old-Growth Forests

One serious weakness in all the empirical literature discussed above is the lack of data on scarcity rent. To address this weakness, Livernois, Thille, and Zhang (2006) use data on stumpage price bids for old-growth forests in the U.S. Pacific Northwest as a proxy for scarcity rent. Because these old-growth forests are several hundred years old, they are effectively a nonrenewable resource. Private logging firms bid for the right to harvest tracts of old-growth forestland at regularly scheduled public auctions. The winning bid, called the stumpage price, is what the winning firm is willing to pay per unit harvested. As such, these bids are a reasonable proxy for scarcity rent. Livernois, Thille, and Zhang (2006) develop and test a modified Hotelling Rule that accounts for the opportunity cost of land occupied by standing timber. According to this modified rule, stumpage prices should evolve over time in a predictable manner. The modified Hotelling Rule is the basis for the empirical test. The initial regression model used to test the Hotelling Rule is analogous to Farrow's (1985), in that the key coefficient should have an estimated value equal to the interest rate. Whereas Farrow obtained negative values for this coefficient using mineral data, the analysis of the old-growth timber data produces a value of 8.6 percent for the implied interest rate, which is a credible value. In further versions of the model, a number of approaches are used to represent the risk-adjusted discount rate, including the Capital Asset Pricing Model, but the Hotelling Rule still cannot be rejected. Unfortunately, the power of the tests is again low, which is probably due in large part to the high degree of volatility in the stumpage price data. Nevertheless, these results are by far the most favorable yet seen in the empirical literature on the Hotelling Rule.

Why does the Hotelling Rule perform empirically so much better for old-growth stumpage prices than for mineral commodities? The first and most obvious reason is that in the case of old-growth stumpage prices, direct observations are available and are good proxies for scarcity rent. There may be a second reason that has to do with the fact that for old-growth forests the expected stock of recoverable "reserves" and the expected quality of remaining "reserves" probably did not change much from the beginning to the end of the sample. In mining, firms are likely to be updating both of these expectations as they learn about their resource base, which means scarcity rent will be updated too. Without an ability to control for these kinds of revisions as learning takes place, the *ex post* empirical performance of the Hotelling Rule is likely to continue to be only moderately good at best.

In fact, this is the same conclusion reached by Swierzbinski and Mendelsohn (1989b). They model exploration as producing both information and discoveries, with information leading to revised expectations about the likely success of future exploration. They show that the forecasted mean rate of change in scarcity rent is given by the Hotelling Rule. However, the true or *ex post* mean rate of change typically differs from the Hotelling prediction due to the unanticipated changes in expectations caused by the arrival of information. On the basis of this theoretical result, Swierzbinski and Mendelsohn (1989b) argue that *ex post* tests of the Hotelling Rule are not likely to prove successful, but that *ex ante* tests that exploit the predictive power of the Hotelling Rule are likely to be more successful. This leads us to our next topic: a discussion of *ex ante* direct tests of the Hotelling Rule.

The Hotelling Valuation Principle

One testable implication of the basic Hotelling Rule is what Miller and Upton (1985a) termed the Hotelling Valuation Principle, which says that the *ex ante* market value of the reserves of a nonrenewable resource is predicted by the current net price multiplied by the amount of reserves. In the basic Hotelling model with a constant unit cost, profit in any period is just the net price multiplied by the quantity extracted. Since the present value of net price is constant over the life of the mine, the present value of total profit over the life of the mine is just the total reserves extracted multiplied by the current net price.

The elegance of the HVP is that only the current values of price and marginal cost are required to predict the market value of the stock of reserves, even though those reserves will be exploited over many years to come. Thus the HVP provides a simple and convenient method for valuing a firm's or a nation's stock of nonrenewable reserves, which makes it useful in Green National Income Accounting or for investors wanting to determine the market value of a firm's natural capital.

In principle, the HVP can be tested by regressing the observed market value of in situ reserves per unit on observed contemporaneous values of net price, followed by a test of the hypotheses that the intercept term is 0 and the estimated coefficient on net price is equal to 1. Miller and Upton (1985a) showed that the theoretical relationship between market value of reserves and net price becomes more complicated in a Hotelling model that has been augmented to allow for extraction costs that rise with the rate of extraction and resource depletion. The implication is that the estimated intercept term no longer needs to equal 0. However, the estimated coefficient on net price should still be equal to 1, and that remains the important hypothesis test. Since the prices at which in situ reserves change hands are rarely made public, Miller and Upton (1985a) calculate these values using published stock market prices for a sample of U.S. domestic oil- and gas-producing companies after making adjustments for the firms' nonresource assets and liabilities. They find that the estimated coefficient on net price is not statistically different from 1 and conclude that the HVP performs well by accounting for a significant portion of the observed variations in market values. For this reason, the Miller–Upton paper is often cited as the most successful test of the Hotelling Rule.

Subsequent research has produced less favorable results. For example, Watkins (1992) finds that the HVP significantly overestimates the observed values of oil and gas reserves. Even Miller and Upton (1985b), using an updated data set, find that the estimated coefficient on net price falls from about 0.9 in their first study to 0.5. Adelman (1993) argues that the evidence from a number of his studies on actual sales of reserves shows that the unit value of reserves fluctuates around a value of 0.5. He adds that a general rule of thumb among petroleum firms is that the "in-ground value of a developed reserve is one-third of wellhead price, or about one-half of price (net of operating costs, royalties and taxes)." Adelman concludes that, on the basis of the evidence, the "Hotelling Rule and the Hotelling Valuation Principle are thoroughly discredited."

Davis and Cairns (1999), on the other hand, show that it is not the Hotelling model per se that is discredited, but rather that in its highly simplified form it does not capture some of the critical physical constraints under which oil and gas extraction occur. They modify the basic Hotelling model to reflect that (a) the production rate of oil or gas is governed by reservoir pressure which tends to decline with cumulative production, (b) the market price of oil does not rise fast enough to make the producer's net price rise as rapidly as the discount rate, and (c) firms are faced with regulatory constraints on production rates. The authors then derive what they call a Hotelling-type valuation principle and conclude that current net price remains a sufficient statistic to calculate the unit value of reserves; however, they show that their modifications generate a coefficient on net price that is less than 1, and suggest that a value of 0.5 is implied by reasonable parameter values for the model.

The HVP has also been tested for nonfuel nonrenewable resources. Cairns and Davis (1998) use gold reserves transaction data and find that the intercept is 0, but the coefficient on net price is significantly less than 1 (about 0.7). They again attribute the failure of the HVP to its overly simplified model of the production process. They argue that firms have far less flexibility to adjust extraction rates up or down than is implied by the basic Hotelling Rule and develop a "reformulation of the Hotelling Valuation Principle" that takes some of the special characteristics of hard-rock mining into account. Their reformulated rule turns out to be consistent with the data.

One conclusion we can draw from the literature discussed above is that the simple HVP often overestimates the market value of reserves by as much as a factor of 2. The implication is that the simple HVP will overvalue a nation's nonrenewable resource assets in national income accounting. However, the case of old-growth timber may be an exception. Berck and Bentley (1997) use the HVP to estimate the "enhancement" to the value of remaining timber land that occurred as a result of the U.S. government's inclusion of a considerable stock of old-growth timber land in the Redwood National Park in California in 1968 and 1978. While Berck and Bentley did not formally test the HVP in this context, they were unable to reject parameter restrictions implied by the Hotelling Rule in their econometric model of supply and demand. This, combined with the favorable results in Livernois, Thille, and Zhang (2006), suggests that it may be more fruitful to use old-growth forestry data rather than mineral data to test the HVP.

Conclusions

The purpose of this article has been to evaluate the empirical significance of the Hotelling Rule by reviewing the evidence on the behavior of market prices over time, the evidence on the effects of technological change, direct tests on scarcity rent itself, and the performance of the HVP.

Based on the empirical evidence, I have found that overall one cannot conclude that the Hotelling Rule has been a significant force governing the evolution of observed price paths for nonrenewable resources. It appears that other factors, notably technological change, revisions to expectations regarding the resource base, and market structure, have had a more significant influence on the evolution of prices. On the other hand, nothing we have observed in the evolution of prices is inconsistent with the Hotelling Rule. But if the Hotelling Rule is only one among many supply-side factors that influences price, all kinds of price paths are possible. Only by controlling for these other supply factors do we have a credible chance of refuting or supporting the Hotelling Rule. This is an important though difficult area for further empirical research.

Direct tests of the Hotelling Rule to evaluate whether scarcity rent follows its predicted path have been mostly unsuccessful, with one or two exceptions. As I have argued, this is perhaps not surprising as *ex post* tests are not likely to be successful unless one is able to control for the revisions to expectations regarding the quantity and quality of the resource base in response to new information. The fact that *ex ante* tests have also been largely unsuccessful is a cause for concern. However, as Cairns and Davis (1998) point out, when we conduct these tests at the level of the individual mine or a small segment of the industry, the physical and technical constraints under which extraction occurs become critical. The existence of these constraints does not necessarily invalidate the conceptual message of the Hotelling Rule, but does make it extremely difficult to uncover evidence that the Hotelling Rule is operating.

Finally, one can ask whether suppliers of nonrenewable resources really do make supply decisions in the way that is assumed in a Hotelling-type model. Pindyck (1981) asks whether other behavioral assumptions such as bounded rationality (which may imply the use of rules of thumb for making extraction and pricing decisions) or even myopic optimization would provide a better basis for explaining observed resource prices and supply behavior. Cairns (1986) says that mining firms do not make any effort to factor scarcity rent considerations into their determination of output and, if applicable, price. Rather, he argues, other considerations, such as fluctuating markets, technological change, and cost control, tend to dominate their thinking. Slade (1988) points out that "in the medium run (several decades) price uncertainty and volatility overwhelm any deterministic trends." Indeed, if one puts oneself in the shoes of a mine operator, factors such as extreme price volatility, the requirement to raise large amounts of capital, and the importance of delineating the ore body, for example, are probably far more immediate concerns than scarcity rent.

The empirical evidence seems to suggest that scarcity rent may actually have been the least important determinant of price so far. Yet the Hotelling Rule continues to be a central feature of models of nonrenewable resource markets in the literature. Does this mean that there has been a misplaced emphasis in the literature? I don't think so. The Hotelling Rule, or some variant of it, is a consequence of any model which assumes that mining firms think not just about the present but also about the future, and that they wish to maximize the value of their assets. Although mining firms may not be conscious of scarcity rent, at least not in the literal sense, that does not mean that rationality is an unreasonable behavioral assumption. In the end, however, the proof is in the pudding—or in the empirical testing. Unfortunately, the empirical evidence to date has not provided overwhelming support for the Hotelling Rule.

REFERENCES

Adelman, Morris A. 1993. Modelling world oil supply. *Energy Journal* 14: 1–32.

Agbeyegbe, Terence D. 1989. Interest rates and metal price movements: Further evidence. *Journal of Environmental Economics and Management* 16: 184–92.

Agostini, Claudio A. 2006. Estimating market power in the US copper industry. *Review of Industrial Organization* 28: 17–39.

Ahrens, W. Ashley, and Vijaya R. Sharma. 1997. Trends in natural resource commodity prices: Deterministic or stochastic? *Journal of Environmental Economics and Management* 33: 59–74.

Arrow, Kenneth J., and Sheldon Chang. 1982. Optimal pricing, use and exploration of uncertain natural resource stocks. *Journal of Environmental Economics and Management* 9: 1–10.

Barnett, Harold J., and Chandler Morse. 1963. *Scarcity and Growth: The Economics of Natural Resource Availability*. Baltimore: Johns Hopkins University Press for Resources for the Future.

Berck, Peter, and William R. Bentley. 1997. Hotelling's theory, enhancement, and the taking of the Redwood National Park. *American Journal of Agricultural Economics* 79: 287–98.

Berck, Peter, and Michael Roberts. 1996. Natural resource prices: Will they ever turn up? *Journal of Environmental Economics and Management* 31: 65–78.

Cairns, Robert D. 1981. An application of depletion theory to a base metal: Canadian nickel. *Canadian Journal of Economics* XIV: 635–48.

———.1985. Nickel depletion and pricing: Further considerations. *Journal of Environmental Economics and Management* 12: 395–6.

———.1986. More on depletion in the nickel industry. *Journal of Environmental Economics and Management* 13: 93–8.

Cairns, Robert D., and Graham A. Davis. 1998. On using current information to value hard-rock mineral properties. *Review of Economics and Statistics* 80: 658–63.

Cairns, Robert D., and Nguyen Van Quyen. 1998. Optimal exploration for and exploitation of heterogeneous mineral deposits. *Journal of Environmental Economics and Management* 35: 164–89.

Chakravorty, U., and J. Roumasset. 1990. Competitive oil prices and scarcity rents when the extraction cost function is convex. *Resources and Energy* 12: 311–20.

Cuddington, John T., and Diana L. Moss. 2001. Technological change, depletion, and the US petroleum industry. *American Economic Review* 91: 1135–48.

Davis, Graham A., and Robert D. Cairns. 1999. Valuing petroleum reserves using net price. *Economic Inquiry* 37: 295–311.

Deshmukh, Sudhakar, and Stanley R. Pliska. 1980. Optimal consumption and exploration of nonrenewable resources under uncertainty. *Econometrica* 48: 177–200.

Ellis, Gregory, and Robert Halvorsen. 2002. Estimation of market power in a non-renewable resource industry. *Journal of Political Economy* 110: 883–99.

Farrow, Scott. 1985. Testing the efficiency of extraction from a stock resource. *Journal of Political Economy* 93: 452–87.

Farzin, Y. H. 1992. The time path of scarcity rent in the theory of exhaustible resources. *Economic Journal* 102: 813–30.

Fisher, Anthony C. 1981. *Resource and Environmental Economics*. Cambridge: Cambridge University Press.

Gaudet, Gérard. 2007. Natural resource economics under the rule of Hotelling. *Canadian Journal of Economics* 40: 1033–59.

Gaudet, Gérard, and Peter Howitt. 1989. A note on uncertainty and the Hotelling Rule. *Journal of Environmental Economics and Management* 16: 80–86.

Gaudet, Gérard, and Ali M. Khadr. 1991. The evolution of natural resource prices under stochastic investment opportunities: An intertemporal asset-pricing approach. *International Economic Review* 32: 441–55.

Halvorsen, Robert, and Tim R. Smith. 1991. A test of the theory of exhaustible resources. *Quarterly Journal of Economics* 106: 123–40.

Hanson, D. A. 1980. Increasing extraction costs and resource prices: Some further results. *Bell Journal of Economics* 11: 335–42.

Heal, Geoffrey. 1976. The relationship between price and extraction cost for a resource with a backstop technology. *Bell Journal of Economics* 7: 371–78.

Hotelling, Harold. 1931. The economics of exhaustible resources. *Journal of Political Economy* 39(2): 137–75.

Krautkraemer, Jeffrey A. 1998. Nonrenewable resource scarcity. *Journal of Economic Literature* XXXVI: 2065–2107.

Krulce, D.L. 1993. Increasing scarcity rent: A sufficient condition. *Economics Letters* 43: 235–38.

Lasserre, Pierre. 1984. Reserve and land prices with exploration under uncertainty. *Journal of Environmental Economics and Management* 11: 191–201.

Lasserre, Pierre, and Pierre Ouellette. 1988. On measuring and comparing total factor productivities in extractive and non-extractive sectors. *Canadian Journal of Economics* XXI: 826–34.

Lee, Myunghun. 2007. Measurement of the *in situ* value of exhaustible resources: An input distance function. *Ecological Economics* 62: 490–95.

Lee, Junsoo, John A. List, and Mark C. Strazicich. 2006. Non-renewable resource prices: Deterministic or stochastic trends? *Journal of Environmental Economics and Management* 51: 354–70.

Levhari, David, and N. Liviatan. 1977. Notes on Hotelling's economics of exhaustible resources. *Canadian Journal of Economics* 10: 177–92.

Lin, Cynthia C.-Y., and Gernot Wagner. 2007. Steady-state growth in a Hotelling model of resource extraction. *Journal of Environmental Economics and Management* 54: 68–83.

Livernois, John, and Patrick Martin. 2001. Price scarcity rent, and a modified r per cent rule for non-renewable resources. *Canadian Journal of Economics.* 34: 827–45.

Livernois, John, Henry Thille, and Xianqiang Zhang. 2006. A test of the Hotelling Rule using old-growth timber data. *Canadian Journal of Economics* 39: 163–86.

Livernois, John, and Russell Uhler. 1987. Extraction costs and the economics of nonrenewable resources. *Journal of Political Economy* 95: 195–203.

Long, N.V. 1979. Two theorems on generalized diminishing returns and their applications to economic analysis. *Economic Record* 55: 58–63.

Loury, Glenn C. 1986. A theory of 'Oil'Igopoly: Cournot equilibrium in exhaustible resource markets with fixed supplies. *International Economic Review* 27: 285–301.

Managi, Shunsuke, James J. Opaluch, Di Jin, and Thomas A. Grigalunas. 2004. Technological change and depletion in offshore oil and gas. *Journal of Environmental Economics and Management* 47: 388–409.

Miller, Merton H., and Charles W. Upton. 1985a. A test of the Hotelling valuation principle. *Journal of Political Economy* 93: 1–25.

———.1985b. The pricing of oil and gas: Some further results. *Journal of Finance* 40: 1009–20.

Moazzami, B., and F. J. Anderson. 1994. Modelling natural resource scarcity using the error-correction approach. *Canadian Journal of Economics* XXVII: 801–12.

Perron, Pierre. 1989. The great crash, the oil price shock, and the unit root hypothesis. *Econometrica* 57: 1361–1401.

Pindyck, Robert S. 1978a. The optimal exploration and production of nonrenewable resources. *Journal of Political Economy* 86: 841–61.

———.1978b. The gains to producers from the cartelization of exhaustible resources. *Review of Economics and Statistics* 6: 238–51.

———.1981. Models of resource markets and the explanation of resource price behaviour. *Energy Economics* 130–39.

Polasky, Stephen. 1992. Do oil producers act as 'oil'igopolists? *Journal of Environmental Economics and Management* 23: 216–47.

Salant, Stephen W. 1976. Exhaustible Resources and Industrial Structure: A Nash-Cournot Approach to the World Oil Market. *Journal of Political Economy* 84: 1079–93.

Salant, Stephen. 1979. Staving off the backstop: Dynamic limit pricing with a kinked demand curve. In *Advances in the economics of energy and resources,* ed. Robert Pindyck, vol. 2. Greenwich, CT: JAI Press.

Schmitz, James A. Jr. 2005 What determines productivity? Lessons from the dramatic recovery of the U.S. and Canadian iron ore industries following their early 1980s crisis. *Journal of Political Economy* 113: 582–625.

Slade, Margaret E. 1982. Trends in natural-resource commodity prices: An analysis of the time domain. *Journal of Environmental Economics and Management* 9: 122–37.

———.1988. Grade selection under uncertainty: Least-cost last and other anomalies. *Journal of Environmental Economics and Management* 15: 189–205.

Slade, Margaret E., and Henry Thille. 1997. Hotelling confronts CAPM: A test of the theory of exhaustible resources, *Canadian Journal of Economics* XXX: 685–708.

Smith, V. Kerry. 1979. Natural resource scarcity: A statistical analysis. *The Review of Economics and Statistics* 61: 423–27.

Solow, Robert and F.Y. Wan. 1976. Extraction costs in the theory of exhaustible resources. *Bell Journal of Economics* 7: 359–70.

Stollery, K. R. 1983. Mineral depletion with cost as the extraction limit: A model applied to the behavior of prices in the nickel industry. *Journal of Environmental Economics and Management* 10: 151–65.

———.1985. User costs versus markups as determinants of prices in the nickel industry: Reply. *Journal of Environmental Economics and Management* 12: 397–400.

Svedberg, Peter, and John E. Tilton. 2006. The *real*, real price of nonrenewable resources: Copper 1870–2000. *World Development* 34: 501–19.

Swierzbinski, Joseph E., and Robert Mendelsohn. 1989a. Exploration and exhaustible resources: The microfoundations of aggregate models. *International Economic Review* 30: 175–86.

———.1989b. Information and exhaustible resources: A Bayesian analysis. *Journal of Environmental Economics and Management* 16: 193–208.

UNCTAD (United Nations Conference on Trade And Development). *Handbook of statistics.* [www.unctad.org/Templates/Webflyer.asp?intItemID = 1397&docID = 10193 (accessed 6/10/11)].

United States Energy Information Administration [2008]. Official energy statistics of the US government.

Watkins, G. C. 1992. "The Hotelling principle": Autobahn or cul de sac? *Energy Journal* 13: 1–24.

Young, Denise. 1992. Cost specification and firm behaviour in a Hotelling model of resource extraction. *Canadian Journal of Economics* XXV: 41–59.

Young, Denise, and David L. Ryan. 1996. Empirical testing of a risk-adjusted Hotelling model. *Resource and Energy Economics.* 18: 265–89.

20   Understanding Oil Price Behavior through an Analysis of a Crisis

Leonardo Maugeri

Leonardo Maugeri is Senior Executive Vice President, Strategies and Development, Eni; e-mail: leonardo.maugeri@eni.it.

Introduction

Another petroleum boom-and-bust cycle has left its mark on the beginning of the new century. After hovering around $18–$20 per barrel through most of the 1990s, oil prices collapsed to $10 in 1998 and 1999, before beginning a climb that led to a record-shattering $147 per barrel in New York on July 11, 2008. However, this was followed by a steady decline that turned into a rout after the onset of the global economic crisis in mid-September, driving down the price of crude oil to as low as $32 per barrel in December 2008, less than a quarter of what it had been just four months earlier.

The rapid rise in the price of oil and its sudden and dramatic fall caught many industry analysts and experts by surprise, as has been the case with many earlier boom-and-bust cycles. This raises once again a fundamental question about the oil industry: Why is it so difficult to come up with reasonable predictions about the price of oil?

The root of the problem is the extreme complexity of the oil market, which involves a multitude of interacting players, intricate and unsatisfactory models used to set prices, complicated interactions between crude oil and its derivative products, and unique geopolitical pressures that shape the industry. These complexities are unknown to the vast majority of policymakers and the media, who tend to view the world of oil simplistically and in terms of stereotypes.

A second problem, even less understood, plagues the oil market: the scarcity of reliable current data about the industry. The daily flow of information about oil demand, supply, inventories, and reserves is qualitatively suspect, consisting of estimates rather than reliable facts, and the product of a system that has not yet managed to produce accurate real-time numbers.

A third problem that has clouded our understanding of the petroleum industry is the long-standing and widespread misperception that in the

"Understanding Oil Price Behavior through an Analysis of a Crisis" by Leonardo Maugeri. *Review of Environmental Economics and Policy* 3. 2009. Pp. 147–166. Reprinted with permission.

face of constantly growing demand, oil supplies will dwindle and then abruptly decline in the future. Despite having been disproved by history on many occasions, this myth persists even as economic and geologic studies repeatedly challenge it.

Throughout the history of the oil industry, these three elements have often worked together to create a distorted psychology among the industry's players. The objective of this article is to try to bring some clarity to these issues, utilizing the most recent boom-and-bust cycle as an analytical paradigm. In examining the evolution of this cycle, I will highlight those characteristics that I consider most critical to understanding the oil market.

The central argument of this article is that, as with most commodities, the price of oil is basically a function of perceived current and future *effective spare production capacity* (ESC), which is the unused production capacity that can be immediately brought to market, with no restriction of any kind. ESC is different from *potential spare capacity* (PSC), which is the overall production capacity available at any given moment, but which may not be available to consumers because of wars, geo-political considerations, or other reasons.

Low ESC on the upstream side of the oil industry (i.e., exploration and production of oil) has historically coincided with low spare capacity in the downstream sector (i.e., oil refining, services, equipment) and a shortage of the skilled people needed to support a new phase of intensive investments. Thus, if spare capacity (in all sectors of the industry) grows at a lower rate than demand, then, sooner or later, the market is bound to see price increases. The picture worsens if, due to negative perceptions concerning the status of the world's oil reserves, the market believes that there is limited or no potential to rebuild spare capacity in the future. Over time, the relationship between oil's ESC and oil price behavior has repeatedly proven to be critical, and it explains why oil prices started rising after 2000. However, ESC alone cannot fully explain the extent of the price movements after 2000.

Other important factors—above all, the interaction between ESC and market expectations—are affected by the level of ESC and help to determine the price of oil. Here again, history has shown that a low level of ESC and a widespread perception of barriers to rebuilding it in the future tend to foster a pessimistic market psychology about the future equilibrium between demand and supply that eventually becomes self-fulfilling, as reflected in the three oil shocks of the last 35 years (1973, 1979–80, 2004–2008). Although geopolitical tensions affecting oil producers may amplify this negative psychology, they are generally not sufficient to ignite a full-blown crisis.

With this background in mind, in the next section I examine how a very low level ESC—of oil production, skilled people, equipment, and oil services—ignited the boom cycle at the beginning of the new century, which occurred simultaneously with a similar boom for most raw materials. I also explain the key interaction between production capacity and geopolitical events. This is followed by a description of the problems of poor data quality and misleading forecasts, particularly by the International Energy

Agency (IEA), and how they shaped the mistaken view that the dramatic price upsurge was primarily a demand-driven phenomenon, and helped ignite the crisis by supporting a self-reinforcing wave of negative expectations among market operators and experts. Next I discuss the misleading perception that the world is running out of oil and briefly explain some basic concepts about oil reserves and resources. Then I examine two issues that have played a significant role in the deterioration of the oil market, particularly during the most recent crisis: the lack of spare capacity in the refining sector, and the growing discrepancy between the qualities of crude oil that are available and the specific qualities demanded by different regional markets. The complex role that financial oil markets currently play in establishing the price of oil is discussed in the following section. Next I express doubts about the ability of the Organization of the Petroleum Exporting Countries (OPEC) to structurally influence oil prices. This is followed by a description of how all the factors that fed the oil price boom faded during the second half of 2008, leading to the dramatic plunge in prices. I conclude with an attempt to dispel some of the conventional wisdom about the future of oil prices and a warning about the risk of paralysis in the development of "green energy" programs in the face of instability and extreme volatility in oil prices. I suggest that a major global effort is required to solve the key problems that have historically plagued the oil market, condemning it to periodic boom-and-bust cycles that have first fed, and then killed, the prospects for making our lives less carbon intensive and more environmentally friendly.

The Roots of the Crisis: The Oil Boom (2000–2008)

The high price the world began paying for oil in 2000 has its roots in the low prices of the previous two decades, which discouraged research and the development of new capacity. This same phenomenon characterized all types of raw materials, triggering a new boom cycle for virtually all commodities after a long, bearish period.

The Bearish Period

The bearish period began in 1982–1983 and lasted through the end of the 1990s. During that period, the demand for commodities grew at a very modest rate relative to the expanded production capacity that had been developed during the previous commodities boom of 1968–1982. As a result, prices remained depressed, leading to the shutting down of development projects already underway, and discouraging efforts to find new deposits or open new mines. In the case of oil, an excess of supply kept the price of crude at an average of between $18 and $20 per barrel, and twice—in 1986 and again in 1998–1999—caused price crashes that brought the price of oil below $10 per barrel.

It was the law of supply and demand at work. That is, as long as supply outstripped demand, prices stayed low. In those days, few noticed that gold, uranium, and copper mines were closing down; already discovered oil fields were being kept out of production; arable land was being left fallow in the absence of government subsidies; commodity stockpiles were being reduced to avoid the high cost of maintaining them; there were massive layoffs of geologists and engineers; refineries, processing plants, and other infrastructure were being shut down; and investment in infrastructure and equipment was declining. These factors worked together to eliminate excess production capacity both upstream and downstream throughout the industry. As a consequence, when the demand for many commodities, including oil, began to pick up again, shortages developed and market forces produced dramatic price increases.

The Bullish Oil Market

After bottoming in 1998–1999, oil prices started to recover, due mainly to a rare success by OPEC in imposing production cuts. But the key turnaround occurred between 2002 and 2003. Due to production shortfalls driven by

Figure 1 Upstream and downstream capital cost indexes (2000QI = 100).

Source: IHS CERA (2008).

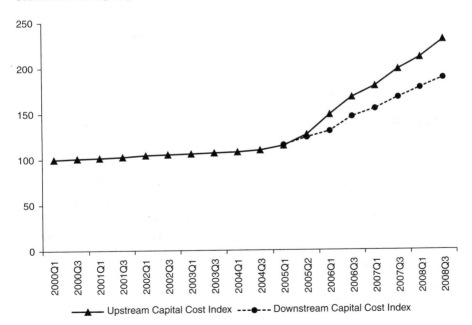

political events in Iraq, Venezuela, and Nigeria, ESC fell to less than 3 million barrels per day (mbd), or less than 4 percent of global oil consumption (CERA 2008).

In 2004, global oil consumption jumped by more than 3 mbd (IEA 2008a), the largest increase since the 1970s, reflecting a new era of accelerated global economic growth, led by China and other emerging economies. Even without such a massive one-time rebound of demand, the lack of ESC would have on its own made for a bullish oil market. Investments in new oil production started rebounding as well, but it was too late. Moreover, as will be discussed in more detail later, by then the idea of a coming age of oil scarcity had penetrated deeply into the market, adding anxiety to what was already a negative mindset. Skilled personnel, engineering and construction services, and equipment for oil exploration and production were also in short supply, a problem shared with the refining system. As a result, as shown in Figure 1, exploration and production costs more than doubled between 2003 and 2008 (CERA 2008).

The Role of Geopolitics

Even during a period of heavy investment in raw materials, there is a long delay before new production capacity comes on line. It takes an average of 8–10 years for a new oil field to become productive, which leads to an additional complication: When supplies of a commodity barely meet demand, the price of that commodity becomes very vulnerable to any potential disruption of available supply, whether it is caused by real or perceived factors. The oil market is particularly vulnerable to such disruptions, ranging from normal maintenance shutdowns, to acts of God (e.g., hurricanes in the Gulf of Mexico), but—above all—geopolitical events.

Since 2000, political problems or decisions involving at least three major oil producers—Iraq, Nigeria, and Venezuela—have resulted in significantly reduced ESC. Furthermore, the mere perception of possible impending threats to the stability of a major producer, especially Iran, which was perceived to be the target of a potential U.S. military attack, added anxiety to a market that was already deprived of its safety margin.

The Crucial Role of ESC

It is essential that the raw materials sector—like any other industrial sector—maintain a cushion of idle production capacity that can be quickly activated when needed. This spare capacity is the key to any commodity's price: When spare capacity is low, price tends to rise, and vice versa. History has shown that an ESC that is lower than 3–4 percent of global oil consumption can trigger a dramatic price rise, that an ESC in the range of 5–6 percent of global demand can provide a cushion of comfort and security sufficient to keep prices under control, and that an ESC that is higher than 6 percent of global consumption may cause a rapid fall in oil prices, particularly in the case of declining demand.

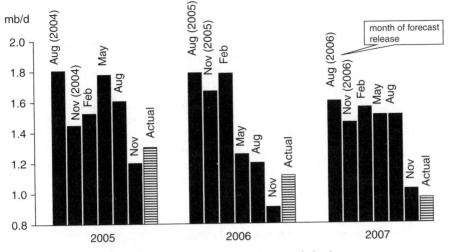

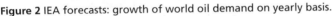

Figure 2 IEA forecasts: growth of world oil demand on yearly basis.

Source: International Energy Agency, Oil Market Report (2005–2007).

Just before the global financial crisis exploded in September 2008, the ESC in the petroleum sector stood at about 2 mbd, or less than 3 percent of worldwide consumption. Consequently, the mere possibility of sudden production losses in one country or another sent tremors of concern through the markets, making it even more susceptible to any new negative developments or perceptions down the road.

The Role of Poor Data and Misleading Forecasts in Shaping Expectations

In order to understand the historical behavior of oil prices and their movements during the recent crisis, one must examine the consistently poor quality of the data and forecasts concerning the oil industry. Poor data and forecasts have plagued the oil market since its inception (Smil 2003). For example, they played a major role in fanning the oil panic of the 1970s, when most analyses and forecasts failed to recognize that there was much more oil available than was widely believed, despite the 1973 Arab oil embargo, the 1979 Iranian Revolution, and the 1979–1980 Iraq-Iran War (Maugeri 2006).

Lack of Reliable Data

As Professor Morris Adelman (1995) has pointed out, following the 1973 Arab oil embargo, there was never any shortfall of supply. What made the crisis possible was panic, which was fed by the lack of reliable data

(Adelman 1995). Unfortunately, the problem of obtaining reliable data is still far from being solved. China and many other developing countries have never adopted a comprehensive system for collecting data about their oil and energy consumption, inventories, etc. Moreover, many advanced countries are slow to report oil consumption data, and even OPEC resorts to secondary sources to assess its own members' actual production. As a result, accurate data for current global oil consumption and inventories tend to emerge with a delay of one to two years. This means that today's figures are only uncertain estimates, subject to change in the future (Mabro 2005). In an attempt to address this problem, in 2001 several organizations, including the IEA and OPEC, launched the Joint Oil Data Initiative (JODI). However, there has yet to be a significant improvement in data quality.

Inaccurate Forecasts: Sources and Impacts

Poor data complicate the work of analysts and make current forecasts of demand, consumption, and prices grossly inaccurate. Unfortunately, the IEA, whose mission is to collect and analyze oil industry data and trends on behalf of the industrialized nations, has failed to fulfill its mission during the recent oil crisis. More specifically, as shown in Figure 2, from 2005 onward, the IEA has made several mistakes in its projections, consistently overestimating demand and underestimating supply, and suggesting a possible production crunch in a few years (IEA 2005–2009). In January 2008, the IEA essentially restated a forecast it had made six months earlier, predicting that demand for petroleum would grow by 2 mbd during 2008 (IEA

Figure 3 IEA forecasts: growth of world oil demand on yearly basis (2008 vs. 2007).

Source: International Energy Agency, Oil Market Report (2008).

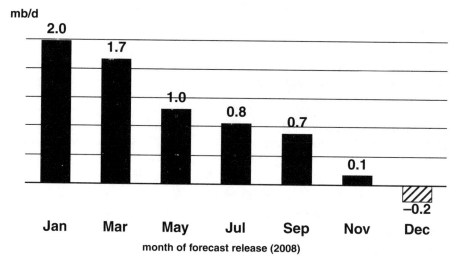

2005–2009), which is equivalent to the daily output of a producer such as Kuwait. This forecast encouraged the perception that demand would rise much faster than production, providing support for the idea that prices would continue to rise. However, starting in February, the IEA gradually revised its projections downward (see Figure 3), and finally stated in December 2008 that demand would, in fact, drop by 200,000 barrels per day in 2008 (IEA 2005–2009).

The IEA is the primary source for current data about oil, as well as for projections about future oil supply and demand. It provides the raw material for the databases and planners at major banks, oil companies, and even oil-producing countries. Thus its forecasts have a pervasive, and often perverse, influence on the expectations—and hence the psychology—of the markets and industry analysts and operators.

A Demand-Driven Phenomenon?

In spite of the IEA's misrepresentation of the world's demand-supply equilibrium, global oil demand grew at a modest average annual rate of 1.7 percent from 2001 through 2007, which was only slightly higher than the rate of 1.4 percent during the 1991–2000 period (IEA 2008a).

The higher oil demand, especially in 2004, was a reflection of not only strong global economic expansion after many years of relative stagnation, but also two distorting factors. The first factor was the easy credit available in many advanced economies, which allowed families and businesses to maintain profligate consumption levels that would not otherwise have been possible. The second factor was the administrative manipulation of energy prices in many developing countries through subsidies, most notably in China, which kept retail prices of gasoline and other petroleum products artificially low, and below market levels (Brown 2008; CERA 2008).

Moreover, the average annual rate of increase in demand during the period was dominated by two years, 2003 and 2004. The rate of growth was 2.1 percent (equivalent to 1.6 mbd) in 2003 and spiked to about 3 mbd (+ 3.7 percent) in 2004, the largest annual increase since the 1970s (IEA 2008a). This was the only real "demand shock" during the period, due to a worldwide expansion of oil consumption. In the following years, oil demand grew much more slowly than in 2004—1.7 percent in 2005, 1.3 percent in 2006, and 1.1 percent in 2007 (IEA 2008a)—which are even lower rates than during the sluggish 1990s. With the exception of 2007, during this time period oil production always rose more than demand in absolute terms.

Given these trends, it is inaccurate to describe the 2000–2008 oil price boom as being demand-driven. Rather, it was driven at least partly by incorrect *expectations* about demand. The IEA bears the lion's share of the responsibility for fostering these expectations.

Running Out of Oil? The Truth about World Oil Reserves

Another inaccurate notion that has once again taken root in the last few years and has contributed to shaping a negative market psychology is the so-called "peak oil theory," which assumes there will be an early decline in production due to the inevitable dwindling of the world's oil reserves. Unfortunately, the public and, above all, policymakers and the media, appear to have forgotten that this is the fourth time we have been warned that the world will run out of oil soon.

False Alarms

The first warning about the impending demise of U.S. oil reserves (now the largest known reserves in the world) was sounded during World War I. The next came during World War II, and once again dealt with the United States. The third warning came in the 1970s, when the doomsday prediction of an oil peak in 1985–1986 followed by growing scarcity was put forth by the most influential institutions of the time, among them the newly created IEA, the Central Intelligence Agency (CIA), the Rockefeller Foundation, Exxon, BP, and many other oil companies, think tanks, professors, and analysts (Maugeri 2006).

All of these institutions and individuals were proven wrong. Instead of "peak oil production" being reached in 1986, a massive wave of overproduction flooded the market, triggering a dramatic collapse of oil prices, as has always happened in the wake of past alarms about impending oil scarcity (Yergin 1991).

Compounding the confusion and myth-making about the future of world oil production, a small coterie of doomsayers has continued to predict an approaching production peak, despite all the evidence to the contrary, while constantly shifting the timeframe for the demise of global oil production (Maugeri 2006). First they said it would happen in 1989, then 1992, then 1994, and so forth. These predictions have always been wrong. Yet these same doomsayers now predict that peak oil production will come in this decade or a little later, and the world is once again accepting these misguided predictions (Maugeri 2006). These predictions have contributed to the market's negative psychology in this decade, spreading the belief that no new significant increase of production capacity is possible, and supporting once again an upward spiral of oil prices.

The Peak Oil Theory

The "Peak Oil Theory" was first formulated by American geologist M. King Hubbert, who came up with a predictive model in 1956 (Hubbert 1956). Hubbert believed that if the geological structure of an oil field is well known, then it is possible to predict the rise and fall of its production. He assumed that production would follow a smooth bell curve. Thus, if a field was showing signs of peaking, one could predict that its production was about to fall at the same rate at which it had risen. Hubbert's 1956 prediction that U.S. oil production in the lower forty-eight states would peak in 1972 proved remarkably accurate, and so the Hubbert camp was born.

Since then, the Hubbert camp has tried to apply Hubbert's theory to the rest of the world. However, while the bell curve may have accurately described production trends in the case of the United States—which by 1956 was already the most heavily surveyed and tapped oil region in the world—the increase in knowledge about the subsoil, the spread of new technologies, and new discoveries have shown time and again that peak production can be increased and delayed. Thus, the decline phase of the bell curve can be shifted to the right, which limits the applicability of Hubbert's theory.

Oil Fundamentals

To understand why we are not running out of oil, it is helpful to briefly review the fundamentals of oil resources, quality, production, transformation, and consumption.

While it is irrefutable that oil resources are finite, it is equally true that no one knows just how finite they are, and trying to assess their order of magnitude is impossible (Adelman and Watkins 2008). An additional complication is the difference among "resources," "recoverable resources," and "reserves" as applied to oil and other raw materials.

The term "resources" refers to the overall stock of a certain mineral in simple physical terms, without any associated economic value and/or estimate of the likelihood of its ever being extracted. Only a part of the existing stock of a resource is both technically and economically exploitable, and this is defined as "recoverable resources." Finally, the part of "recoverable resources" that can be produced and marketed right now is called "reserves."

Today, all major sources estimate the world's oil reserves at about 1.2 trillion barrels (e.g., Oil and Gas Journal 2007; BP 2008; Eni 2008), enough to supply oil at current consumption rates for 39 years. There are an additional 1.4 trillion barrels of recoverable oil resources, which extends the limit to 86 years (USGS 2000). The world's total oil resources, called Original Oil in Place, are estimated at about 7–8 trillion barrels, of which only one trillion barrels have already been consumed (USGS 2000; IEA 2005).

These estimates do not take into account the so-called unconventional oils, such as bitumen-like ultra-heavy oils, tar sands, and shale oils. These resources are estimated at 9 trillion barrels, and conservative estimates put recoverable resources of unconventional oil, located mainly in Canada, Venezuela, and Russia, at 1.3 trillion barrels (USGS 2003; WEC 2007).

These figures indicate that world oil resources are huge, with proven reserves accounting for only a fraction of the total amount. Moreover, only one-third of the world's sedimentary basins—those that may contain hydrocarbons—have been thoroughly explored so far.

Since many of the largest and most productive oil basins in the world are approaching their production limits with currently available conventional technology, the doomsayers view their impending depletion as evidence supporting the peak oil theory. In fact, only a modest fraction of known world reserves of oil is being exploited today: On average, no more than 35 percent of the oil contained in known oil fields worldwide can be recovered with existing technologies (Maugeri 2006), which means that most oil reserves remain untapped.

Oil Recovery Technologies

To maximize oil recovery, the industry has developed a range of techniques that can be grouped into two categories: improved oil recovery (IOR) and enhanced oil recovery (EOR). Thanks to the combined use of both IOR and EOR technologies, the recovery rate can be made to exceed 60 percent or even more. However, the high cost of EOR technologies makes them economically unviable when oil prices are low, and low oil prices ruled the market for most of the twentieth century. What's more, even in times of high oil prices, EOR had to compete with more attractive options, such as exploration campaigns for finding new fields or less costly IOR technologies. In today's context of higher oil prices and—above all—limited access to resources (around 94 percent of global oil reserves is directly controlled by producing countries), the industry faces challenges that strongly support EOR research and development, and wider use of EOR methods would greatly enhance the world's supply of recoverable oil.

Although advances in technology can extend the economic life of a field and thus reduce the costs of exploration, development, and production, one must be careful not to accept as gospel the numbers about proven reserves, which are evolving estimates. As noted above, these estimates tend to increase over time even without new discoveries due to improved knowledge and new technologies for exploring and exploiting resources, and different price scenarios that make it economically viable to drill where previously it was not. This is why most oil fields have produced much more than the initial estimates of their reserves, and even more than the estimates of their original oil in place, a phenomenon geologists call "reserve growth" (Downey, Threet, and Morgan 2002).

Yet, because the application of advanced technology depends crucially on oil price expectations, for many years it was not perceived to be wise to tap new areas or invest in new technologies because the price of oil was too low. Moreover, this misperception amplified the extent of the 2000–2008 oil price boom, feeding the misguided expectation that ever-increasing prices were the reflection of a world that was running out of oil.

The Influence of the Oil Refining System on Prices

One specific factor that may influence the direction of oil prices, and that played a significant role in the most recent crisis, is the structure of the oil refining sector. Petroleum is not a homogeneous product. Rather, it comes in a very wide range of types and qualities. The two most important characteristics that determine petroleum quality are its density and sulfur content. Higher-quality oils are characterized by low density and low sulfur content, and command the highest prices.

The wide variety of crude oils challenges the downstream side of the industry, since each type of oil yields different quantities of final products, such as gasoline, diesel, jet kerosene, and fuel oil, according to a basic principle: The higher the oil quality, the higher the quantity of high value-added products (e.g., gasoline, diesel fuel) that can be produced in a "simple" refinery (i.e., one that has only primary distillation units). This type of plant cannot significantly change the standard yield of a given oil supply and will always leave behind a high percentage of heavy fuel oil with high sulfur content. This percentage increases or decreases depending on the type of crude processed by the refinery; it is lower when light crude is processed, but grows substantially as the quality of crude oil becomes heavier. In order to handle a wider range of crude oils and squeeze out a better mix of high value-added products, the refining system has to be upgraded with "deep conversion" units, which dramatically reduce the amount of residual oils. However, additional kinds of processing units are required to eliminate sulfur from oil products.

All this underscores a basic characteristic of the market: Refiners do not require generic "oil," but rather those specific types of crudes that are suitable both for their plants and for the specific demand for oil products in their markets. This means that although the world may be awash with oil, refiners may not be able to find the kind of oil they need. This is what has happened in the last few years, due to several factors. First, the world's refining system was too rigid after two decades of inadequate investments, and it was particularly short of deep conversion capacity. Second, nearly all growth in oil products demand since the second half of the 1990s was for light products, while demand for fuel oil decreased as a result of a flurry of new regulations for improving the quality of oil products. Third, after 2004, much of the growth in crude oil supply consisted of heavy and sour crude oils (CERA 2006).

This deep market imbalance had already emerged by 2000 and 2001, but it became critical after 2004, at a time when around 80 percent of available crudes were of medium-heavy density with high sulfur content. This, in turn, spurred intense competition among simple refiners to get light and sweet crudes, such as Brent and West Texas Intermediate (WTI), in order to optimize the output of light products and minimize heavy fuel oil production. Moreover, the world perceived that most of OPEC's ESC was not of the right quality, because it consisted partly of heavy oils rich in sulfur that did not fit with the existing structure of the world's refining system. All of these factors worked together to push oil prices up.

The Role of the Financial Oil Markets

The influence on oil price movements of the so-called "paper barrel," the financial market based on futures, options, and other financial derivatives that have oil prices as their underlying factor, is an extremely complicated issue. This financial market's exponential growth over the last decade has raised questions about whether the actions of financial market operators may have played a major role in inflating oil prices to levels lacking any rational explanation. This issue has even triggered an investigation by the Commodity Futures Trading Commission (CFTC), whose final findings had still not been issued at the time this article was written.

Mechanics of the Market

To better understand the role of the financial oil market in oil price movements, one needs to understand the mechanics of this market. As with other raw materials, the main *raison d'être* of the financial oil market is to offer commercial operators instruments for managing their risks, with price volatility at the top of the list. The contracts traded in these markets—in lots of 1,000 barrels per contract—do not involve physical delivery of actual crude, but are simple financial transactions. This is why the product traded here is generally referred to as a "paper barrel."

Transactions mostly involve commercial operators such as oil, airline, and refining companies, which make up the bulk of the market. But purely financial operators also play a role, trying to speculate on price movements. Expiration dates for futures contracts start at one month, and run to three years in London and as long as five years in New York, but the vast majority run for one, two, or three months. In financial market terminology, an operator is "long" when he buys futures contracts and "short" when he sells them.

There are two regulated financial oil markets in the world, each based on a specific benchmark crude. On the New York Mercantile Exchange (NYMEX), the benchmark is WTI crude, whereas London's Intercontinental Exchange Futures (ICE) is based on Brent crude. However, the operations of these two markets represent only one part of global futures transactions in oil. A substantial part takes place through nonstandardized bilateral contracts in the so-called over-the-counter markets, which are not regulated. Information on those operating in these markets and their activities is patchy and opaque. According to some estimates, the volume of activity in these unregulated markets is several times greater than the volume of trading on the official markets (Levin 2008).

Recent Trends in the Financial Oil Market

The importance of the oil futures markets has grown exponentially in the past decade, partly because of the growing problems with the reliability of prices on the spot market, the physical market where real barrels of oil are traded every day. As production of the traditional spot market benchmarks—Brent and WTI—has decreased, the continued reliance on them as market indicators has led to problems and distortions in the market. The meager volumes of these crudes available on the market each day created the possibility that a single transaction involving, for instance, a single cargo of Brent could be manipulated or "squeezed," sending the wrong message to the whole market. As a result, for several reasons, financial markets appeared to offer a more reliable alternative for setting the correct price: Many more operators with differing interests (physical and financial operators), much more information, and much more liquidity. In other words, these markets seemed much more reliable and less prone to price manipulation than the spot market.

The other factor that spurred the massive growth of the "paper barrel" was the huge increase in financial instruments, hedge funds, and purely financial operators that has taken place since the 1990s, along with the generalized flight to commodities that occurred in the early years of the new century.

As a consequence of all these factors, the number of daily average positions on oil futures at the NYMEX increased from 272,262 in 1990 to 468,109 in 2000 to their peak of 1,393,664 in 2007 (CFTC 2008). Since every contract is for a standard quantity of 1,000 barrels, more than 1.4 billion "paper barrels" were traded daily on the NYMEX alone during the bullish days of 2007, even though worldwide physical consumption of oil was less than 85 million barrels per day.

According to many, this extraordinary demand for "paper barrels" hid a massive speculation, which was one of the main reasons for the dramatic oil price increase. However, it is difficult to prove this conclusion. While it is beyond the scope of this article to present a detailed analysis of the relationship between the financial oil market and oil prices, Fattouh (2005) provides an excellent review of both the theoretical and empirical literature on the relationship between the futures markets and the dynamics of crude oil prices. However, he concludes that these papers offer no general consensus, and sometimes even reach opposite conclusions.

More recently, an analysis by Ripple (2008) contradicts the general view that speculators have been uniquely "long" in futures markets, which is the prerequisite for them to drive prices only upward. Ripple notes, for example, that both commercial and noncommercial traders maintained considerable long and short positions in 2007–2008. The commercial traders tended to be "net short." Thus, for the market to balance, these net short positions had to be offset by net long positions by the noncommercial traders. Moreover, spread trading (e.g., maintaining both long and short positions in different maturities) dominated the activity of noncommercials. Hence, Ripple (2008) concluded that constraining the activity of noncommercials could significantly reduce the availability of risk mitigation and market liquidity services for commercials, and that the cost of such services would probably increase. Unfortunately, the available data and existing analyses do not allow us to reach a clear-cut conclusion about this issue.

After many years of experience in the oil industry, my personal view is that even if noncommercial operators play a relatively small role in the financial oil market, they could still influence its evolution while working on its margin. Moreover, considering what has transpired in the oil markets in the last few years, public authorities should investigate the role performed by some financial institutions, such as investment banks. Some of these institutions may have been tainted by conflicts of interest, as, while on the one hand they disseminated their analyses and recommendations about the future trends and prices of the oil market, on the other they traded oil futures and other derivatives.

While it has not been proved, the more likely role of financial markets is that as a group the global financial markets may have amplified the upward trend of oil prices, but that such a role would have been impossible without the misleading analyses and forecasts that distorted perceptions about the future of oil. In other words, my hunch is that fundamentals (e.g., low spare capacity, both current and expected) along with incorrect expectations shaped the behavior of all operators in the financial markets, including noncommercial operators (speculators), who tended to follow, rather than anticipate, price movements.

The Limited Influence of OPEC

Among the many factors that are usually considered to be major determinants of oil price behavior, there is one whose role I believe should be reconsidered: OPEC.

No single country or group of countries is really in command of oil supply, which means that no one can really control the price of oil. Despite the view often expressed by the media, OPEC can only *indirectly* influence the price of oil, by fixing its production quotas to avoid oversupplying the market. This theoretical power, however, is strongly limited by the tendency of several of its members to not comply with the ceilings, a behavior that has historically hampered the cartel's effectiveness (Mabro 2005).

During most of OPEC's existence, a major factor behind the overproduction of oil and the subsequent price collapses has been OPEC members' efforts to break the organization's rules by selling extra oil under the table. Thus, for example, OPEC's stated production cuts failed to stop prices from falling in the early 1980s because its members secretly sold oil in excess of their quotas (Mabro 1986; Skeet 1988). OPEC was also unable to boost oil prices in the 1990s despite several attempts to do so (Parra 2004; Maugeri 2006).

In any case, a little less than 60 percent of global oil production is controlled by producers outside OPEC, who can take advantage of OPEC cutbacks to increase their own sales. And, because OPEC members' production costs are generally lower than those of many other countries, when OPEC succeeds in restraining its own supply to sustain prices, it only helps much less competitive production to come on-stream.

Thus, it is a mistake to view OPEC as an effective cartel, or even as a cartel at all.

Why Did the Oil Bubble Burst?

The first signs that oil demand was not living up to its projected growth appeared in the fourth quarter of 2007, as growth in production began to outstrip growth in demand, with new production coming on line despite the dire forecasts of supporters of the "peak oil theory."

Ignoring Early Signs of a Problem

The market, which had been shaped by inaccurate forecasts, ignored these early signs and still looked for a robust increase in global demand during 2008, which renewed concern about the adequacy of future supplies. Euphoria continued to dominate the market, together with concern about the future stability of some major producers, especially Iran, as rumors spread about the possibility of U.S. military action.

The disconnect between perception and reality and the absence of timely data probably explain why, in January 2008, oil prices broke the $100 per barrel barrier for the first time in history, and kept climbing until July 11, when WTI set an all-time record of $147 per barrel. After that peak was reached, prices began to drop. Yet no one seemed aware that something was changing, that in reality the market was oversupplied and ESC was growing faster than expected, mainly as a result of past investments.

In fact, until September 2008, the market psychology was still shaped by forecasts that envisaged ever-rising prices. A typical, though perhaps extreme, reflection of this mindset came on September 15, 2008, the same day as the "official" start of the U.S. financial crisis (with the announcement of Lehman Brothers' bankruptcy), when the cover of *Fortune* magazine announced "Here Comes $500 Oil."

Impact of the Global Financial Crisis

Only the outbreak of the financial and economic crisis in mid-September swept away the misperceptions about the oil market and made the reality clear, just as the first conclusive data were published showing the malaise already underway in the oil market. In October, the U.S. Energy Information Administration (EIA) indicated that the United States had registered an oil "demand destruction" not seen for decades, with an average drop of about 1 million barrels per day (or 5 percent of total U.S. consumption) between January and September 2008 (EIA 2008). Between September 10 and October 10, U.S. oil consumption dropped by 1.8 million barrels per day (EIA 2008). It was the first time since 1983 that demand had gone down in the United States, which single-handedly consumes 25 percent of the world's oil.

A similar scenario unfolded in other industrialized countries, starting in 2007. Apparently oil demand had only been growing in China and other developing countries, but at rates substantially lower than in the past. By 2008 most emerging economies had started to eliminate or ease price controls and subsidies on petroleum products as they had become unsustainable for their budgets. China appears to have supported global demand at least through the August 2008 Olympic Games, building up substantial stockpiles to avoid the possibility of a sudden shortage tarnishing the image of a new and vital China.

However, by October, fresh data began to show that supply growth had strongly outperformed oil consumption since at least August, probably accounting for the accumulation of about 100 million barrels of additional inventories not previously appearing in the IEA's official statistics.

Thus, all of a sudden, the drop in demand made existing production capacity too big (i.e., higher than 5–6 percent of global consumption), triggering a new market psychology that placed strong additional downward pressure on prices. Projections of future consumption increases were slashed as the financial crisis spread, casting a dark shadow over the prospects for global economic growth in the coming years. Refining was also negatively affected as consumption dropped, spare capacity surged in the three main regions of the world (North America, Europe, and the Asia-Pacific), and refinery utilization rapidly dropped to below 90 percent. To make matters worse, new refining capacity was expected to come on stream shortly as a result of large investments made since the beginning of the decade, particularly in Asia and the Middle East. Meanwhile, speculators faded away (CFTC 2008).

Finally, the November 2008 election of Barack Obama as president of the United States was generally perceived as the opening of a new era in American foreign policy, eliminating the fear of an imminent U.S. attack against Iran. By December, prices were down to about one-fourth of their record level in July.

The Problem of Demand Elasticity

While all the factors above help explain the reversal in oil prices, none of them offers a rational explanation for why that reversal was so sudden and dramatic. In the absence of rigorous data and analytical tools capable of measuring the effect of each of these factors in prompting the oil crash, what we are left with is an observation, based on historical experience, about the impact of the price of oil on demand.

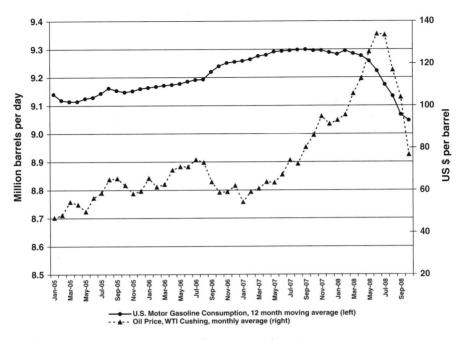

Figure 4 Oil price and U.S. motor gasoline consumption.

Source: Energy Information Administration, Department of Energy (2008); Platt's (2008).

Because of the built-in inertia in consuming markets, it can take years before the ever-rising oil prices lead to a substantial reduction in oil consumption. This means that demand is quasi-inelastic relative to price over the short to medium term. In fact, during the 1970s and in the last decade, it took 7–8 years before demand declined in the face of continuously rising prices. What is more, as we have seen, easy credit and large subsidies pushed oil demand artificially high in the early 2000s, making it even more resilient in the face of rising prices (CERA 2008).

Historical experience seems to show that even if high oil (and other raw materials) prices can be slow to affect the global economy, it would be a mistake to think, as many did during the crisis, that the demand for oil has now become inelastic relative to the price of crude over the long term. Understanding at what level the price of oil starts to affect demand, and even economic growth, is still a matter of debate (and requires more rigorous analysis). Empirically, I believe we can assume that the erosion in demand began somewhere within the range of $75–$100 per barrel, which is also shown by the decline of U.S. gasoline consumption in 2007 and 2008 (see Figure 4). Coincidentally, this matches, in real terms, the peak average yearly price of $34 per barrel prevailing in 1980, which was the height of the second oil shock of the 1970s.

Conclusions: What Does the Future Hold?

Today's conventional wisdom holds that the drop in prices will be short-lived, and will have an extremely negative impact on the future, sparking cutbacks in the investment needed to create new sources of supply. The result will be supply shortages when—in a few years—demand picks up again, spurred by low prices and an end to the financial crisis. I believe I was among the first to present this view in 2006, when I predicted that the rise in oil prices would end during this decade, most likely with a sudden and dramatic drop (Maugeri 2006). I also maintained that an early drop in prices could stop the investment boom then underway, and ultimately lead to yet another shortage-driven crisis (Maugeri 2006). I still believe that this theory is correct, but with several caveats.

Toward a Sustainable Price Level

The first caveat is that we need to identify a sustainable price level that will lead to the kind of investment flow needed to build adequate production capacity, since the price of a barrel of oil must take into account the cost of producing it.

Several industry observers have suggested that the cost today of producing the most expensive barrel needed to meet global demand—the "marginal barrel"—is around $75–$80 per barrel, including a 10 percent return for the producer. However, this assessment is misleading for several reasons.

As we have seen, between 2003 and 2008, oil exploration and production costs more than doubled, driven by the increase in the cost of steel, as well as engineering and construction services, and skilled workers. Thus, while the $75–$80 reference price may represent an acceptable snapshot of past trends, it is not necessarily in line with future costs. As demand for oil plunges, most production costs will plunge as well, due to the decline in demand (and thus price) for steel, engineering and construction services, and skilled personnel, because oil companies tend to cut back, almost overnight, on all production costs when prices decrease so abruptly. It will take time, but such a parallel plunge is inevitable.

As a result, the marginal costs of producing additional crude will be lower, and the industry's cost basis will be lower as well. Putting it another way, the most expensive Canadian oil barrel, which cost around $32–$35 in 2001, almost tripled to around $80 in 2008, not because the producing source had changed, but because the structure of costs had changed, accompanied by an increase in taxes.

It is certainly true that "easy" and "cheap" oil is bound to disappear, and that dealing with new oil basins in frontier areas, such as the Arctic Sea or the ultradeep offshore of Brazil or the Gulf of Mexico, will cost much more. It will also cost much more to revive production from the oldest and largest oil basins in the world, due to the cost of the advanced technologies required to increase their production levels.

Yet, in the longer term, the "learning curve" connected with the development of challenging new areas and the use of advanced technologies will ultimately allow for a lower cost structure, as happened, for example, with the development of North Sea oil in the 1970s, which at the time was considered the most challenging and expensive new oil frontier in the world from an environmental and technological point of view. Meanwhile, in the shorter term (two years from now), we should consider two factors that may further depress the oil market.

First is the size and length of the economic crisis, which may slash oil consumption even more than expected, particularly if—as I fear—there are massive layoffs, and companies around the world are forced out of business. Second, in 2009 and 2010, new production capacity will become available as a result of past investments, which were spurred by past high prices. This new capacity will further weaken a market that will already be too liquid.

As a consequence, unless OPEC succeeds in dealing with such upsurges in capacity, it is hard to imagine that prices will recover significantly. In fact, I believe only a major political crisis could do it.

In the longer term, however, it is reasonable to assume that the price of oil will be much higher than the $18–$20 per barrel registered in the last 15 years of the twentieth century. But it is difficult to say how much higher, without knowing the kind of cost structure that will evolve, how other variables will behave, and especially what the effective demand for oil will be.

The Future of Oil Demand

The second caveat deals with the future demand for oil. Of course, future oil demand will depend on the level of global economic growth, especially for the emerging economies. This basic linkage (i.e., between economic growth and oil demand) tends to permeate most current analyses, whose common assumption is quite simple: Once the world's economic situation recovers, oil demand will again rise rapidly.

However, this view fails to take into account what history has shown, which is that in the wake of an energy crisis, advanced industrial societies tend to introduce structural changes that alter their energy consumption model, usually by increasing the efficiency of energy use. Emerging economies, in turn, may take advantage of new and more efficient devices and technologies developed by advanced countries to build up or develop their own energy systems in order to become more efficient themselves.

As a result of laws and regulations imposed during the 1970s to boost energy efficiency and conservation, per capita oil consumption, and its impact on GDP, is much lower today in the industrialized countries than it was in the 1970s. Europe, Japan, and Australia recorded their peak oil consumption in the 1990s, and have seen a steady, if uneven, reduction since then. The United States is the only advanced country where the demand for oil has been steadily increasing from 1984 until the present, making it the most wasteful consumer of energy in the developed world: Before the recent financial and economic crisis, every U.S. citizen consumed around

26 barrels of oil per year, more than twice the 12 barrels per year consumed by the average Western European (Eni 2008). True, per capita consumption in the United States has fallen since the 1970s, when it peaked at 32 barrels per year. But this improvement in energy efficiency has been modest in comparison to America's ever-growing appetite for energy.

Nevertheless, it is likely that even the United States is nearing the end of this era of profligate consumption. In the coming decade, the United States could see a decline in consumption whose steepness will depend on the toughness of the policies pursued by the Obama administration. A new attitude toward climate change and environmental pollution now seems to dominate the U.S. political agenda, and if the United States embarks on a serious program of energy efficiency, I think that it is realistic to assume that in ten years the country could reduce its oil consumption by as much as 20 percent, or 4 million barrels per day, from its 2007 peak. That's equivalent to Iran's entire current production.

By the same token, the European Union finally established the European Policy on Energy (EPE) in December 2008. With its aggressive 2020 targets of energy efficiency, carbon dioxide (CO_2) emission cuts, and increase in the use of renewable energy sources, the EPE should further reduce Europe's already declining consumption of oil.

Thus, the demand for petroleum will continue to grow only in developing countries, led by China and India. What we need to determine is how these two countries, and others like them, can improve their energy efficiency. Much of India and China's infrastructure dates back to a time when no attention was paid to energy efficiency. It was only around 2000 that this became a matter of urgent concern in planning new power stations, transportation systems, and even in urban planning.

Considering all these elements, I would not be surprised to see a lower than expected rate of increase in global oil demand once the economic crisis has passed. The key to the evolution of future demand will be the balance between declining demand in industrialized countries and rising demand in emerging economies.

Role and Concerns of Oil Producers

The third caveat, which, in a way, may undermine the previous two, is that we cannot exclude from our analyses the producing countries and their legitimate concerns about their role in the future. While the industrialized world is concerned about the security of supply and prices, the producers worry about the security of demand. If the producers become convinced that in the coming decades the world's thirst for oil will diminish, why should they make investments to increase production?

If their investment programs were to be cut back, the supply of crude would shrink, resulting in inevitable price increases followed by drastic drops. In other words, it would be a serious mistake to ignore the producers' legitimate concerns about the future, because their actions could condemn the oil market to extreme volatility and new boom-and-bust cycles.

Some Proposals for Reform

Unfortunately, history has shown that a low price of oil or too much uncertainty about its future behavior are the worst enemies of research and development of alternative sources of energy and efforts to improve energy efficiency. Because of a new global awareness and sensibility about the seriousness of environmental and climatic problems, it seems safe to assume that at least some of the programs to improve energy efficiency and develop new energy sources will survive the crash of oil and other fossil fuel prices. But the risk remains that such programs may be curtailed and consumer acceptance of new and costlier forms of energy may wane because of the economic crisis.

All of this suggests a need for increased efforts to bring greater transparency and stability to the oil market. Changes are needed to prevent poor data and inadequate analytical and forecasting tools from sending the wrong signals into the market, which in turn create distorted realities.

I believe the time is right to establish a new world agency for energy—a sort of Global Energy Agency—whose main task would be to collect transparent data on demand, supply, inventories, production capacity build-up, etc., for all countries. This would address the main limitation of the IEA, which was established by the advanced countries in the wake of the first oil shock to ensure their security of supply, and today is still made up of only those countries.

It would also be advisable to explore new models for trying to reduce oil price volatility. Neither those based on supply and demand for "physical barrels," nor those derived from "paper barrel" trading, have proven satisfactory. The key issue here is how to encourage or reward the creation of spare capacity. One possible option would be to establish a Global Oil Stabilization Fund, financed by a minimum excise tax paid by consumers, to support those producers who are keen to create new spare capacity. This fund could be managed by an independent body, like the Global Energy Agency proposed above, that would be in charge of channeling the funds and certifying the creation of spare capacity. Another option would be the creation of a specific market for spare capacity, financed by the fund described above, where both producers who create spare capacity and consumers who cut their energy consumption could be remunerated.

I recognize that such proposals are very complex and difficult to implement in practice, in particular because of political constraints. Nevertheless, they are efforts worth pursuing, because if the oil market continues to swing between boom-and-bust cycles, it will be much harder for a true energy revolution—one that causes a real transition toward a greener global energy mix—to take place.

REFERENCES

Adelman, Morris A. 1995. *The genie out of the bottle: World oil since 1970*. Cambridge, MA: MIT Press.

Adelman, Morris, and Campbell Watkins. 2008. Reserve prices and mineral resource theory. Special issue in honor of Campbell Watkins, *The Energy Journal*, pp. 1–16.

BP. 2008. *BP statistical review of world energy*. London: BP.

Brown, Derek. 2008. The subsidises' dilemma. *Petroleum Economist*.

CERA (Cambridge Energy Research Associates). 2006. *Oil market dichotomy: Loosening upstream, tight downstream*. Cambridge, MA: CERA.

———. 2008. *"Recession Shock": The impact of the economic and financial crisis on the oil market*. Cambridge, MA: CERA.

CFTC (U.S. Commodity Futures Trading Commission). 2008. *Commitments of traders*. Historical reports. [Available at www.cftc.gov (accessed 6/10/11)].

Downey, Marian W., Jack C. Threet, and William A. Morgan, eds. 2002. *Petroleum provinces of the twenty-first century*. Tulsa, OK: American Association of Petroleum Geologists.

EIA (Energy Information Administration). 2008. Weekly Petroleum Status Report. October 10. [Available at www.eia.gov/pub/oil_gas/petroleum/data_publications/weekly_petroleum_status_report/historical/2008/2008_10_16/wpsr_2008_10_16.html (accessed 6/10/11)].

Eni. 2008. *World oil &gas review*. Rome: Eni.

Fattouh, Bassam. 2005. The origins and evolution of the current international oil pricing system: A critical assessment. In *Oil in 21st century*, Special limited edition, ed. Robert Mabro. Vienna: OPEC.

Hubbert, Marion King. 1956. Nuclear energy and the fossil fuels. In *Proceedings of spring meeting of the American Petroleum Institute*. Washington, DC: American Petroleum Institute.

IEA (International Energy Agency), www.iea.org.

———. 2005–2009. Oil market report. Paris: IEA. [Available at http://search.atomz.com/search/?sp_a=sp10029401&sp_f=ISO-8859-1&sp_q=%22Oil+market+report%22+%2B2005-2009&sp-p=all (accessed 6/10/11)].

———. 2008a. Monthly oil data services. [Available at http://catsearch.atomz.com/search/catsearch?sp-q=%22Monthly+oil+data+services%22+%2B2008&sp-a=sp10029401&sp-p=all&sp-f=ISO-8859-1 (accessed 6/10/11)].

IEA (International Energy Agency). 2008b. World energy outlook. Paris: IEA. [Available at www.worldenergyoutlook.org/2008.asp (accessed 6/10/11)].

IHS. [(for subscribers only) www.ihs.com/products/oil-gas-information/index.aspx?pu=1&rd=ihs_com (accessed 6/10/11)].

JODI. www.jodidata.org.

Levin, Carl. 2008. United States Senate Floor Speech on the Introduction of the Over-the-Counter Speculation Act, S. 3255. [July 11. Available at http://levin.senate.gov/newsroom/press/release/?id=d664b559-bac5-4581-958f-b1ae289a7a7e (accessed 6/10/11)].

Mabro, Robert, ed. 1986. *OPEC and the world oil market: The genesis of the 1986 price crisis*. Oxford: Oxford University Press, Oxford Institute for Energy Studies.

Mabro, Robert. 2005. The international oil price regime: Origins, rationale, and assessment. *Journal of Energy Literature* Vol. XI, No. 1.

Maugeri, Leonardo. 2006. *The age of oil: The mythology, history, and future of the world's most controversial resource*. Westport, CT: Praeger.

———.2006. Two cheers for expensive oil. *Foreign Affairs* 85(2): 149–61.

Oil and Gas Journal. 2007. Worldwide look at reserves and production. *Oil & Gas Journal* December 24, pp. 24–25.

Parra, Francisco. 2004. *Oil politics: A modern history of petroleum.* London: I. B. Tauris.

Ripple, Ronald D. 2008. Have oil futures traders driven up the market? *Oil & Gas Journal* 136: 37.

Skeet, Ian. 1988. *OPEC: Twenty-five years of prices and politics.* Cambridge: Cambridge University Press.

Smil, Vaclav. 2003. *Energy at the crossroads: Global perspectives and uncertainties.* Cambridge, MA: MIT Press.

USGS (United States Geological Survey). 2000. *World petroleum assessment, 2000.* [Available at http://pubs.usgs.gov/dds/dds-060/ (accessed 6/10/11)].

———. 2003. *Heavy oil and natural bitumen—strategic petroleum resources,* ed. Richard F. Meyer and Emil D. Attanasi. Reston, VA: United States Geological Survey. [Available at http://pubs.usgs.gov/fs/fs070-03/fs070-03.html (accessed 6/10/11)].

Yergin, Daniel. 1991. *The prize: The epic quest for oil, money and power.* New York: Simon & Schuster.

WEC (World Energy Council). 2007. *Survey of energy resources 2007.* [Available at www.worldenergy.org/publications/survey_of_energy_resources_2007/default.asp. (accessed 6/10/11)].

21   *The Economics of Managing Scarce Water Resources* *

Sheila M. Olmstead

Sheila M. Olmstead is Associate Professor of Environmental Economics, School of Forestry and Environmental Studies, Yale University and Visiting Scholar, Resources for the Future.

Introduction

Recent events, news articles in the popular press, and research outside the field of economics have raised alarming questions about the sufficiency of global freshwater supplies and the potentially devastating impacts of current and future water shortages. For example, the 2008 Beijing Olympics drew attention to the problems of pollution and water shortages in China, where massive infrastructure projects are planned to address water scarcity in a country that holds 7 percent of the world's water supply but 20 percent of its people. High-profile droughts in the U.S. Southwest and Southeast, two of the country's fastest-growing regions, have focused attention on the issue of scarce water supplies in the United States. In many parts of the world, annual water use regularly exceeds annual surface water streamflow and is maintained only by depleting groundwater sources, so-called groundwater "mining" (Gibbons 1986). In India, for example, groundwater supplies are being rapidly depleted for agricultural irrigation, drinking water, and industrial use.

Climate change may affect both the long-term availability and the short-term variability of water resources in many regions. Potential regional impacts of climate change could include increased frequency and magnitude of droughts and floods, and long-term changes in mean renewable water supplies through changes in precipitation, temperature, humidity, wind intensity, duration of accumulated snowpack, nature and extent of vegetation, soil moisture, and runoff (Solomon et al. 2007). Behavioral changes associated with climate change, such as changes in demand for heating and cooling, will also affect water scarcity.

While economists have studied water resource management for many decades, they have responded in a nonalarmist fashion to the concerns

"The Economics of Managing Scarce Water Resources" by Sheila M. Olmstead. *Review of Environmental Economics and Policy* 4. 2010. Pp. 179–198. Reprinted with permission.

*I am grateful to Hilary Sigman and Karen Fisher-Vanden for comments on an earlier draft, and to an anonymous referee whose helpful suggestions improved the manuscript. All remaining errors and omissions are my own.

raised above about water scarcity. Perhaps economists have responded in this way because these concerns remind us of debates in the 1970s about the limits to growth posed by nonrenewable energy and mineral resources, in which economists' disagreement with those in other disciplines boiled down to the failure of the "limits" models to incorporate the effects of substitution and technological change. In the "limits to growth" debate, economists had the empirical evidence on their side. Many of the same economic principles can be applied to the problem of water scarcity—for example, as prices rise, demand falls (through conservation in various forms), and desalination is a potential "backstop technology."

There are, however, some important differences between the issues in the limits-to-growth debate and the problem of water scarcity. First, the barriers to efficient water use and allocation are, in large part, socially constructed. Unlike energy prices, water prices typically are not determined in markets and do not reflect resource scarcity. Allocation mechanisms are highly political, and even when faced with significant scarcity, management institutions are reluctant to raise prices. In contrast, most energy resources are privately owned, and the profit motive provides sufficient incentives for owners to consider scarcity in their dynamic extraction decisions. Second, typical property rights structures for both renewable and nonrenewable water resources ignore important spatial and temporal externalities and public goods. In many arid regions, for example, the marginal value of water left instream to support public goods may exceed its value in agricultural and other uses (Creel and Loomis 1992). In contrast, estimates of the external costs of energy consumption and production are small relative to energy market prices (Parry and Small 2005). In addition, the welfare implications of insufficient access to clean drinking water supplies in terms of human health are demonstrably very large.

This article, the second in a two-part series on the economics of water,[1] surveys selected contributions of economic research to the management of scarce water resources. The next section surveys the literature on the estimation of demand for water in both diverted uses (urban, agricultural, and industrial) and instream (recreation, habitat preservation). This is followed by discussions of efficient water pricing and water allocation and marketing across sectors. Next comes what is known about the economic efficiency and distributional impacts of large-scale water projects such as dams for irrigation and hydroelectric power. This is followed by an examination of water conservation from the perspective of efficiency and cost-effectiveness. Conclusions are offered in the final section.

---

[1]Water quality and water scarcity are inextricably linked (e.g., abundant water supplies have little value if pollution makes them unsuitable for wildlife, recreation, drinking, irrigation, or industrial use). Although the issues are not easily separated, the first article in this series (Olmstead 2010) surveys the literature on the economics of water quality.

Estimation of Water Demand

In nearly all markets for goods and services, scarce resources are allocated through prices, which transmit information about relative scarcity and value in use. However, in the case of water, as with many other scarce natural resources, true markets are rare. Prices for water are administratively determined, through mechanisms that are often political and rarely take economic value into account. Water prices, therefore, do not respond automatically to short-term and long-term changes in supply.

Prices set by public officials are one potential lever for managing water demand when resources are scarce. Good estimates of the price elasticity of water demand are critical to any such effort—water managers must understand how demand will respond to changes in price. Thus, much of the economics literature on water demand has focused on the econometric estimation of demand parameters, including price elasticity. Demand estimates can also be used to measure the value of water in both its diverted and instream uses. A substantial literature on the price elasticity of water demand has existed since the 1960s (see, e.g., Howe and Lineweaver 1967), although this literature has been somewhat thin over the last decade. This section summarizes the literature on diverted (residential, agricultural, industrial) and instream demands for water.

Water Demand for Diverted Uses

The water demand function for the residential sector must include marginal prices, income, and proxies for household preferences, including household characteristics. Residential demand functions also typically control for factors such as season and weather. The literature indicates that residential water demand is inelastic at current prices. For example, in a meta-analysis of 124 estimates generated between 1963 and 1993, Espey et al. (1997) obtained an average price elasticity of −0.51, a short-run median estimate of −0.38, and a long-run median estimate of −0.64. Likewise, in a meta-analysis of almost 300 price elasticity studies conducted between 1963 and 1998, Dalhuisen et al. (2003) obtained a mean price elasticity of −0.41. Studies have found that the residential price elasticity may increase when price information is posted on water bills (Gaudin 2006), and that it may be higher under increasing-block prices (IBPs) than under uniform volumetric prices (Olmstead et al. 2007).[2]

Recent work has focused on estimating demand under IBPs, an increasingly common water price structure. The classic problem of endogenous prices in demand estimation arises from the simultaneous shifting of demand and supply, making it difficult to distinguish between price and quantity changes that are due to supply (i.e., cost) shocks and changes due to

---

[2]Under IBPs, the marginal water price increases with consumption, so the price schedule takes the form of a staircase ascending from left to right.

shifts in demand. IBPs present a different simultaneity concern. When marginal prices rise with consumption, price and quantity demanded are positively correlated. This has often been handled econometrically by using average rather than marginal prices to estimate price elasticities, or in some other way creating a linear approximation to the full price schedule (Nieswiadomy and Cobb 1993; Martínez-Espiñeira 2002). Other common approaches to estimating residential water demand include instrumental variables (IV) models[3] (e.g., Agthe et al. 1986; Deller et al. 1986; Nieswiadomy and Molina 1988, 1989) and discrete/continuous choice (DCC) models[4] (e.g., Hewitt and Hanemann 1995; Pint 1999; Olmstead et al. 2007; Olmstead 2009).

Unlike residential demand, water demand for industry and agriculture must be modeled as part of the general production process for the particular set of outputs generated with water and nonwater inputs. In both the agricultural and industrial sectors, water demand data can be difficult to obtain. Water supply in these sectors may or may not be metered, and is often free, especially where firms access raw water sources outside piped networks.

Estimating the value of water in industrial use requires isolating the value of the marginal product of water. Industrial price elasticity estimates for water tend to be higher than residential estimates and vary by industry. The literature contains only a handful of industrial elasticity estimates. Griffin (2006) reports the results of five studies (covering 1969–1992), which have elasticity estimates ranging from –0.15 for some two-digit SIC codes (Renzetti 1992a) to –0.98 for the chemical manufacturing industry (Ziegler and Bell 1984). A study of 51 French industrial facilities estimates an average demand elasticity of –0.29 for piped water, with a range of –0.10 to –0.79, depending on industry type (Reynaud 2003).

Farmers who withdraw water directly from surface sources usually incur an energy cost to convey water for irrigation, but do not typically pay a volumetric charge for the water itself. Many agricultural water demand curves are estimated for groundwater, using energy costs for pumping to construct a water price variable. Prices can also be obtained if farms purchase water from irrigation districts or other water management institutions. While the economics literature contains many estimates of agricultural water demand elasticity, the available data are rarely of sufficient quality to estimate demand functions. Other techniques commonly applied for the agricultural sector include mathematical programming (see Scheierling et al. 2006), field experiments, and hedonic methods[5] (see Colby 1989; Young 2005). A recent meta-analysis of 24 U.S. agricultural water demand studies performed between 1963 and 2004 suggests a mean price elasticity of –0.48

---

[3]An IV model first estimates observed marginal prices as a function of a set of variables ("instruments") correlated with price, but uncorrelated with the error in the demand equation. Fitted prices from this first stage are regressors in the second-stage demand equation.

[4]The DCC model is a maximum likelihood model in which each observation of water demand is treated as if it could have occurred at any marginal price in the price schedule. The demand parameter estimates maximize the likelihood of observing the data.

[5]Hedonic methods isolate the portion of agricultural land prices that can be attributed to water supply of a particular quality and quantity.

(Scheierling et al. 2006), although estimates vary widely and, unlike in the industrial and residential sectors, often approach zero. Estimates were found to be higher for regions where water is scarce and prices are higher.

Water Demand for Instream Uses

There is a rich economics literature on the value of improvements in water quality.[6] Recently, the value of increasing the *quantity* of water that is left instream, rather than diverted for irrigation, industry, or municipal use, has also received attention from economists.[7] There is now a substantial literature that quantifies the marginal value of surface water left instream for recreation, riparian and wetlands restoration, and other purposes in many different parts of the world. In some cases, economists have compared these values to estimates of the marginal value of water used for irrigation, often the largest competitor for scarce water. Estimating the value of instream water for recreational use or ecosystem maintenance often requires nonmarket methods such as recreational demand models, contingent valuation (CV),[8] and hedonic housing models.

Several studies have used CV surveys to estimate the benefits to local populations of resuming or increasing flows in dry or degraded rivers, which may affect several ecosystem services. Overall, these studies have found that local populations may have substantial willingness to pay for restoring these flows. For example, in Sonora, Mexico, where the Yaqui River no longer reaches the Gulf of California, residents of one local city have demonstrated a willingness to pay for restoring flows to the delta, though it is unclear which potential ecosystem service improvements are actually valued by respondents (Ojeda et al. 2008). In the United States, studies estimate a favorable benefit/cost ratio for riparian restoration projects along the Little Tennessee River in North Carolina (Holmes et al. 2004), and net benefits to purchasing water leases and farmland easements to restore a section of the Platte River near Denver, Colorado (Loomis et al. 2000). Another CV analysis suggests that there may be significant benefits to restoring flows in the Ejina River in China, which currently runs dry during the peak irrigation season (Zhongmin et al. 2003). According to a recent study (Dadaser-Celik et al. 2009), restoring flows to the Sultan Marshes in Turkey would generate significant benefits to local residents in terms of animal grazing, plant harvesting, ecotourism, and wastewater treatment. Finally, hedonic housing studies in the United States suggest that home-

---

[6]See Olmstead (2010) for a detailed review of this literature.

[7]The value of increasing instream flow highlights an area where the economics of water quality and water quantity are not easily separated. For example, one obvious direct water quality benefit of increasing streamflow is greater capacity for dilution and assimilation of pollution.

[8]CV is a survey method in which economists elicit respondents' willingness to pay for changes in the status quo (such as an increase in instream flow) by asking carefully structured questions.

owners in arid regions have a significant willingness to pay for proximity to healthy riparian systems.[9]

The recreational benefits of increasing instream flow have also been estimated. Spatial and temporal dimensions appear to be particularly important for recreational demand (e.g., the economic value of water instream for recreational fishing varies seasonally and spatially). Estimates for the United States suggest that the marginal value of water for local and downstream fishing exceeds the marginal value of water for irrigation in 51 of the 67 river basins with significant irrigation, but the values are highest in the arid Southwest, where the effects on fishing of marginal changes in streamflow are greatest (Hansen and Hallam 1991). Studies of the marginal value of additional instream flows for whitewater rafting indicate that recreational rafters have significant value for additional units of flow during low-flow periods, but little value for additional increments when flows are adequate to support rafting (Daubert and Young 1979; Leones et al. 1997).

Studies have also estimated comprehensive values for multiple recreational benefits from increasing instream flow. One study found that increasing water supplies to 14 wildlife management areas in California's San Joaquin Valley, which would improve wildlife viewing, fishing, and waterfowl hunting, would have estimated benefits that exceed the marginal value of water for agriculture in the region for the same period (Creel and Loomis 1992).

Unlike the value of water withdrawn for residential, industrial, and agricultural activity, water instream is associated with nonuse value, as well as use value. For example, individuals may hold significant value for the maintenance of flow in surface water systems that support endangered species habitat (Loomis 1987).

While agricultural and urban withdrawals are often the causes of declines in instream flow, deforestation and land development may play a role as well. Economists have estimated the marginal value of alterations in water flows from these activities. For example, Pattanayak and Kramer (2001a, 2001b) demonstrate that the preservation of tropical forests in Manggarai province, Indonesia, boosts agricultural production by increasing baseflow,[10] and estimate a positive and significant elasticity of agricultural profits with respect to baseflow (for coffee and rice). In the case of land development, urbanization has negative impacts on groundwater recharge, which reduces urban areas' ability to withstand drought. Thus it may be efficient to tax the increase in impermeable surface area that results from urbanization (Cutter 2007).

---

[9]See Bark et al. (2009) and Bark-Hodgins and Colby (2006) for analyses for Arizona.

[10]Because forests can be either net demanders or net suppliers of water, this analysis is not relevant to all forested watersheds (Pattanayak and Kramer 2001a).

Efficient Water Pricing

This section discusses the issue of efficient water pricing in the absence of markets. The literature indicates that urban water prices in many countries lie well below efficient prices (Munasinghe 1992; Renzetti 1999; Brookshire et al. 2002; Timmins 2003; Sibly 2006), with significant economic costs (Renzetti 1992b; Russell and Shin 1996b). In most cases, the efficient piped water price is the long-run marginal cost (LRMC) of supply.[11] LRMC reflects the full economic cost of water supply—the cost of transmission, treatment, and distribution; some portion of the capital cost of current reservoirs and treatment systems, as well as future facilities necessitated by current patterns of use; and the opportunity cost of both the use and nonuse value of water for other potential purposes.

The LRMC maybe greater than short-run average cost, because LRMC reflects the cost of new supply acquisition, and new supplies are typically more costly to develop than current supplies (Hanemann 1997). In addition, the efficient price of nonrenewable groundwater supplies must include Hotelling rents, which account for the fact that using up nonrenewable water today will leave less for tomorrow.[12] This means that pricing all units of water at LRMC may cause utility revenues to exceed current expenses, sometimes by a wide margin (Moncur and Pollock 1988; Hall 2000). Since water utilities are usually rate-of-return regulated, the efficient way to address this issue would be to rebate net revenues from a uniform volumetric price in some lump-sum fashion. Instead, water utilities often adopt IBPs, charging something approaching LRMC for "marginal" uses (lawn-watering and the like), while meeting rate-of-return constraints through the manipulation of block cutoffs and inframarginal prices. Even if the highest-tier price in an IBP schedule does reflect LRMC, welfare losses result from subsidies to consumers facing lower-tier prices on the margin.[13]

Pricing by Informal Sector Suppliers

The urban poor in developing countries obtain water service from a wide variety of provider types, including public and private piped water monopolies in the formal sector, and informal sector suppliers such as standpipe operators, water trucks, and households with connections to piped water supply that resell water to unconnected households. In most cities in developing countries, more than half the population obtains basic water service from suppliers other than the official utility (Solo 1998). Yet economists

---

[11]In some cases, charging a short-run marginal cost may be efficient (see Russell and Shin 1996a).

[12]The price of renewable water resources should also include Hotelling rents when allowable withdrawals are limited due to both physical scarcity and legal constraints from sharing with other users (Brookshire et al. 2002).

[13]A uniform marginal price with a rebate has distributional advantages over IBPs in developing countries, where large families and piped water connections shared by multiple households tend to push poor households into the upper tiers of an increasing block tariff (Boland and Whittington 2000).

have paid little attention to the subject of informal sector water supply, where volumetric water prices can be many times the volumetric rates of piped systems (Strand and Walker 2005).

Informal sector suppliers may provide water service to households that would otherwise not have access, representing an optimal response to prevailing economic conditions. It is also possible, however, that the high volumetric rates charged by urban informal sector providers results from their exercise of market power. Water sources, such as standpipes and hydrants, maybe sufficiently far apart that they give rise to local monopolies, as households are unwilling or unable to travel beyond their closest source. Rents may also arise from corruption or collusion. For example, in Jakarta, significant price-cost margins arose due to a limited number of public taps, as well as rents appropriated by public and private officials (Lovei and Whittington 1993). In Onitsha, Nigeria, tanker truck operators have been observed to be marking up prices by 500 to 1,000 percent over cost (Whittington et al. 1991), and in India, large landowners with tubewells exercise monopoly power in pricing irrigation water for their tenant farmers (Jacoby et al. 2004).

Whatever the source, the exercise of market power raises prices for households in the market and rations some households out of the market, forcing them to resort to raw water sources or other unsafe options. Given the significant welfare implications of expanding access to clean drinking water, analysis of pricing in informal water markets in developing countries is an important area for future research.

Privatization of Water Supply

Recently there has been much discussion in the popular press, as well as academic journals, concerning privatization of drinking water access in developing countries.[14] Economists have analyzed several empirical questions concerning privatization of water supply and its effect on poor households, pricing, and water utility efficiency. Regarding the effect on poor households, significant reductions in child mortality were achieved through the privatization of piped water supply in Buenos Aires, Argentina (Galiani et al. 2005). Although the causal mechanism by which this welfare improvement was achieved is unclear, the number of poor households connected to piped supplies increased post-privatization. Following the introduction of private sector participation, the share of households connected to piped water and sewerage increased in Argentina, Bolivia, and Brazil, but similar improvements were observed in control regions where public management was retained, so the improvements cannot be causally attributed to privatization (Clarke et al. 2009). Private water supply corporations in the Texas/Mexico border region that are not subject to price regulation by municipalities or state agencies appear to be more likely to connect poor

---

[14]For reviews of the popular and noneconomics academic literature on social conflicts over privatization, see Finnegan (2002) and Perreault (2005).

communities than are public suppliers (Olmstead 2004). Thus far, the empirical evidence does not support the argument commonly made outside the economics literature that private water suppliers are less likely than public suppliers to serve poor households.

Efficiency and Pricing: Private versus Public Monopolies

Recent reviews of the literature provide support for the hypothesis that private infrastructure owners operate more efficiently than public ones across a variety of sectors (Megginson and Netter 2001). However, the provision of piped water and sanitation is one of only a few remaining natural monopolies—are private monopolies really more efficient than public ones?

Recent studies provide conflicting answers to this question. For example, estimates for the United Kingdom suggest little improvement in productivity when public management was replaced by privatized water and sewerage providers (Saal and Parker 2001). In the United States, an efficiency advantage has been estimated for private providers, but only among operators of small water utilities; large utilities appear to be run more efficiently by public providers (Bhattacharyya et al. 1995). Estache and Rossi (2002) find no difference in the efficiency of public and private water utilities among 50 firms in 29 Asian countries.

In theory, the prices of private water suppliers could be either higher or lower than those of public suppliers, depending on the cost savings (if any) achieved by private operators, profits earned, and the interaction of private operators' cost savings and profit-taking with water price regulation. Empirical evidence suggests that in both France (Chong et al. 2006) and Spain (Martínez-Espiñeira et al. 2009) prices are higher, on average, when utilities are managed in whole or in part by private investors. Prices also increased in the United Kingdom after water sector privatization (Saal and Parker 2001).

Water Allocation and Marketing across Sectors

To the extent that prices do not accurately reflect the economic value of water in various uses (and water instream, like many public goods, lacks an observable measure of social value), allocation of scarce water across sectors is likely inefficient. In theory, the development of markets (i.e., permitting voluntary, mutually beneficial trades) can result in water moving to its highest-valued uses, and the potential gains from water trading have attracted the attention of economists for many decades (Hartman and Seastone 1970; Vaux and Howitt 1984; Saliba and Bush 1987).[15]

---

[15]Water marketing is not the only way that water can be reallocated across sectors to address inefficiencies in the current allocation of supplies. Other potential allocation mechanisms include: administrative transfers, forfeiture and abandonment proceedings under state law, public agency

Informal water markets are common. For example, in India and Pakistan, farmers who can afford large groundwater wells with diesel or electric pumps sell water to smaller farmers who cannot afford such infrastructure, with payment taking the form of cash, labor, or share farming (Bjornlund and McKay 2002). However, given the potential gains from trade, formal, intersectoral water markets have been slow to develop (Easter et al. 1998). This may be because the transaction costs for water marketing can be quite high. These costs include the costs of physical infrastructure necessary for transporting water from sellers to buyers, search costs (i.e., identifying willing buyers and sellers), and the legal costs of creating and enforcing contracts and obtaining regulatory permission. Carey et al. (2002) find that transaction costs reduce trading and favor trades among closely affiliated farms, that trades external to local networks are, on average, larger than local trades in the presence of transaction costs, and that the gains from trade decrease with transaction costs, especially for smaller networks of farms. Nonetheless, many studies have demonstrated potential and realized net benefits from trading, in areas as diverse as south Texas (Chang and Griffin 1992), southern Italy and Spain (Pujol et al. 2006), north-central Chile (Hearne and Easter 1997), Morocco (Diao and Roe 2003), and southeast Australia (Bjornlund and McKay 2002).

The Largest Markets

The largest intra- and inter-sectoral water markets have developed in Chile, Australia, and the American West. Chile's 1981 National Water Code established freely tradable water rights separate from land rights. Significant trading has taken place in north-central Chile, but transactions have been quite rare in other parts of Chile (though more common in arid regions and during droughts), perhaps due to constraints posed by physical geography, infrastructure, legal and administrative complications, and cultural resistance by farmers (Bauer 2004). Chile's water code deals inadequately with externalities. Consumptive rights are rights to full use of the water, with no return flows required.

Australia's Murray-Darling river basin covers 14 percent of the total Australian land area and supports major agricultural production. Until 1980, withdrawal rights for irrigation in the basin were essentially unlimited. Water trading was introduced in South Australia in 1983, in New South Wales in 1989, and in Victoria in 1991. Permanent interstate transfers are not allowed, and there are significant limitations on inter-regional sales, but intra-regional trading is active. A cap on water use in the basin was enacted in 1997. Trade appears to have led to both higher-value agricultural production and more efficient irrigation technologies (Bjornlund and McKay 2002).

---

exercise of eminent domain, legal challenges to existing water allocation, legislative settlements of conflicting claims (at the federal and state levels), and redesign of large-scale water projects to favor different sets of users (Colby 1990).

In the American West, relative prices provide signals of the potential for gains from water trading. Farmers in Arizona's Pima County pay $27 per acre-foot, and water customers in the nearby city of Tucson pay $479–$3267 per acre-foot (Brewer et al. 2008). In Texas' Rio Grande Valley, the value of water in agriculture has been estimated at $300–$2,300 per acre-foot, and in urban uses at $6,500–$21,000 per acre-foot (Griffin and Boadu 1992). While these prices and values are for different commodities (raw water versus treated, piped water), the sharp differences in marginal water values across sectors are also products of inefficient pricing, historic water rights allocations, and subsidized irrigation projects (Wahl 1989).

A recent study of water marketing in twelve western states between 1987 and 2005 suggests that prices are higher, on average, for agricultural to urban transfers than for transfers between agricultural producers, and that this difference is growing over time (Brewer et al. 2008). Water right sales are increasingly more common than short- and long-term leases, and states with the most urban growth appear to engage in the most water trading.

An economic analysis of water market prices suggests that the significant price dispersion apparent in U.S. western markets may be due to the fact that water is a complex, multidimensional commodity (both legally and hydrologically); there are few potential traders in many markets, and they may be of disparate size; and the information flows and linkages in such markets may be insufficient to allow prices to converge (Colby et al. 1993). Statistical estimates of the relationship between water market transaction prices and the characteristics of individual transactions in New Mexico support these hypotheses. For example, water rights of higher seniority (which are more likely to be honored in dry years than junior rights) tend to trade at higher prices, higher volume trades result in lower per-unit prices (suggesting economies of scale), and rights allowing more flexibility in the place and purpose of use command higher prices (Colby et al. 1993). A more recent study of trades in Arizona, Colorado, and New Mexico water markets suggests that water prices are lower in wetter periods (supply shifting out) and that income growth (demand shifting out) drives up prices, findings that are consistent with standard economic theory (Brookshire et al. 2004). In addition, areas with higher-valued agricultural productivity tend to have a lower quantity of water traded (Brookshire et al. 2004).

Many of the low observed prices for agricultural irrigation water in the United States result from federal subsidies. It is interesting to examine the interaction of these subsidies with water markets. If the benefits of historical irrigation projects were capitalized into the land prices prevailing at that time, historical landowners reaped windfall profits from federal projects if they sold their land (Sax 1965). This means that current landowners, while they may have paid for water rights when they purchased their properties, essentially receive a "second wave" of windfall profits when they sell water to U.S. cities today. This raises interesting distributional questions for future research.

Externalities and Water Markets

One of the biggest challenges to welfare improvement from water marketing is dealing adequately with externalities and public goods. The externalities to nonrenewable groundwater extraction in common property settings are well studied (Provencher and Burt 1993), and these externalities complicate water marketing in regions where groundwater is an important resource (Hanak 2005). Return flows present another important externality. For example, irrigation water not lost to evapotranspiration either recharges groundwater aquifers or augments surface water flows; water transferred to coastal cities may be returned to the ocean through offshore wastewater outfall systems (and urban uses, in general, have a higher consumptive component). The spatial component of water withdrawals and return flows is, therefore, an important consideration in water trading, just as the location of emissions is an important consideration in market-based approaches to water quality regulation. When instream flows have value, water market outcomes can be Pareto optimal only when transferable diversion and consumption rights are established, return flow coefficients are established to identify the location of each diverter's return, and institutional mechanisms are established to create a market presence for instream flow values (Griffin and Hsu 1993).

There may also be important positive externalities to water trading. Agricultural drainage may be highly polluted, particularly in arid regions where salinity and drainage problems arise from long-term irrigation. Water marketing in such regions allows farmers to sell water to other users, thus reducing farmers' incentives to apply irrigation water in excess of crop requirements (to leach accumulated salts out of the soil) and producing external water quality benefits (Dinar and Letey 1991; Weinberg et al. 1993).

Efficiency of Large-Scale Water Projects

The effects of inefficient pricing have been exacerbated in many countries by large-scale, publicly subsidized water projects for irrigation, flood control, hydropower, and urban and rural water supply.

Water Projects in the United States

Water development projects in the American West were among the earliest formal subjects of benefit-cost analysis by economists. In the numerous case studies of federal irrigation projects examined by Wahl (1989), historical and current subsidies exceed 85 percent of construction costs. These subsidies take many forms, including interest-free repayment by farmers, below-market interest rates, deferral of payments without interest, and the basing of irrigators' repayment requirements on federal estimates of ability to pay rather than willingness to pay. Disregard for important externalities, such as effects on instream flow and water quality (particularly salinity), and risks related to dam safety, represent additional implicit subsidies.

Although new federal water projects are less common today, recent research suggests that newer projects may also be inefficient. For example, an economic analysis of the Central Arizona Project, which was completed in 1987 and provides water to the city of Phoenix, suggests that the project was built 86 years too early, with a deadweight loss of more than $2.6 billion, and that exploiting groundwater sources to delay its construction would have been more efficient (Holland and Moore 2003). Further research suggests that the national welfare losses might have been reduced very significantly had the project been constructed by a private, rather than a public, institution (Holland 2006). While these types of projects generally have significant net costs at the national level, they result in significant net benefits locally. For example, the Central Arizona Project's net benefit to Arizona was almost $1 billion, and the timing was almost optimal from the state's perspective (Holland and Moore 2003).

Water Projects in Developing Countries

Developing countries, particularly India, China, and Brazil, have increasingly pursued large-scale water projects as tools for development and poverty reduction. By 2000, at least 45,000 large dams had been constructed worldwide for the purposes of water development or energy supply, and nearly one-half of the world's rivers had at least one large dam (World Commission on Dams 2000). Until recently, the welfare impacts of such projects received little formal attention from economists. Designing studies to assess the development impacts of large-scale infrastructure projects is complicated by several statistical issues, most importantly the possibility of endogenous placement of such projects.

The benefits typically cited for large-scale water projects include agricultural development and rural poverty alleviation, through reduced influence of weather shocks for farmers and the introduction of hydropower. In a study of India, Duflo and Pande (2007) show that dam construction leads to significant increases in irrigated area and agricultural production in downstream districts. But dams do not significantly impact agricultural production in the districts in which they are constructed, and they appear to increase the vulnerability of farmers in these districts to rainfall shocks. Duflo and Pande (2007) also find that dams increase rural poverty in the districts where they are located and decrease poverty downstream, and that the effects of upstream poverty increases outweigh the downstream benefits, offering evidence that the projects are not, on average, welfare-improving. However, their analysis does not measure the benefits of electricity generation from dams. Lipscomb et al. (2008) assess the impacts in Brazil of electrification through the construction of hydropower dams, and find that electrification in a county raises the value of the housing stock, increases employment, raises average incomes, reduces the poverty head count ratio (i.e., the fraction of a population with incomes below the official poverty threshold set by the national government), and raises the county's UNDP Human Development Index score (which is an index comprising measures of life expectancy, education, and GDP). Given the amount spent worldwide on such projects (by countries as well as multilateral lending institutions), developing a better understanding of the welfare impacts of large water projects in developing countries is a critical area for future research.

Impacts of Dam Removal

With increasing values for instream water (for recreational use; habitat for fish, birds, and other wildlife), some industrialized countries have been considering the welfare impacts of dam removal. A study of the removal of the Edwards dam and alteration of two other dams on Maine's Kennebec River in 1999 (undertaken largely to encourage the return of anadromous fish to the river above the dam sites) finds that the project may have increased property values (Lewis et al. 2008). There is also some evidence that local property values may be more favorably affected by frontage along free-flowing rivers than by frontage along the lakes created by small dams along those rivers, suggesting that the removal of small dams may improve property values (Provencher et al. 2008).

Recreational use of rivers may also increase after dams are removed. A study of recreational use of the Lower Snake River by Pacific Northwest households (Loomis 2002) suggests that the gain in river recreation after the removal of four dams exceeds the loss in reservoir recreation (since removing dams eliminates the reservoirs created behind them). However, the study also found that in this case recreational benefits alone are not sufficient to justify the costs of dam removal. Another study found that a federal requirement that two hydroelectric dams on the Manistee River in Michigan switch from peak-flow to run-of-river flow operation had net benefits when electricity production costs, air quality benefits, and recreational fishing benefits due to habitat improvements are taken into account (Kotchen et al. 2006). Households may also have substantial nonuse value for dam removal when it benefits endangered species populations, as demonstrated for salmon and steelhead runs in the Pacific Northwest (Loomis 1996). While economic models may be sufficient to estimate the impacts of dam removal on recreational uses, property values, and other implicit market effects, understanding whether dam removal is a cost-effective strategy for habitat recovery or species preservation requires close cooperation between economists and natural scientists (Halsing and Moore 2008).

Economics of Water Conservation

Water conservation generally refers to the *technical* water savings that can be achieved through a particular technology or policy intervention. An economic definition of water conservation, however, requires that the benefits of a technology or policy exceed its costs (Bauman et al. 1984). Even when water prices and allocation across sectors are inefficient, water managers can choose policy instruments to reduce water consumption that minimize the cost of achieving such reductions. Decades of theoretical and empirical economic analysis suggest that market-based environmental policies are more cost-effective than prescriptive policies. Cost-effective water conservation policies would typically require raising water prices in some form or another, rather than implementing technology standards or rationing policies, the two most common prescriptive, or command-and-control (CAC), approaches (Olmstead and Stavins 2009). This section discusses what the literature shows about the effectiveness of CAC and price-based approaches for reducing water consumption.

Technology Standards

Technology standards are common policy instruments for long-run water conservation. However, estimates of the actual water savings from technology standards have often been smaller than expected due to behavioral changes that partially offset the benefit of greater technical efficiency—the well-known "rebound effect" from studies of energy efficiency standards (Greening et al. 2000). For example, in a recent field trial, when randomly selected households had their top-loading clothes-washers replaced by front-loading models, their average clothes-washing increased by 5.6 percent, perhaps due to the cost savings associated with increased efficiency (Davis 2008). The U.S. federal plumbing fixture standards, passed as part of the National Energy Policy Act of 1992, may also have seen a significant rebound effect (Wallander 2009).

Few empirical economic analyses have estimated the welfare losses from water conservation technology standards. However, using data from 13 groundwater-dependent California cities, Timmins (2003) compared a mandatory low-flow appliance regulation with a modest water price increase and found that under all but the least realistic of assumptions, prices were more cost-effective than technology standards in reducing groundwater aquifer lift-height in the long run.

Rationing Policies

Rationing policies for short-run water conservation are ubiquitous. For example, during a 1987–1992 drought in California, 65–80 percent of urban water utilities implemented outdoor watering restrictions (Dixon et al. 1996). In 2008, 75 percent of Australians lived in communities with some form of mandatory water use restrictions (Grafton and Ward 2008). However, rationing policies are not efficient. Grafton and Ward (2008) find that mandatory water restrictions in Sydney, Australia, in 2004–2005, resulted in economic losses of $235 million, about $150 per household, or one-half the average household water bill in Sydney in that year. Brennan et al. (2007) also demonstrate that outdoor watering restrictions generate efficiency losses. An experimental study simulating water consumption from a common pool predicts that consumer heterogeneity generates economic losses from CAC water conservation policies (Krause et al. 2003).[16]

Other studies demonstrate that replacing rationing policies with price increases can substantially reduce the economic cost of achieving short-run water consumption reductions. For example, Collinge (1994) shows that a municipal water trading system can reduce costs significantly over a CAC approach. Empirical studies provide additional evidence supporting price-based policies. For example, a study of 11 urban areas in the United States and Canada compared residential outdoor watering restrictions with drought pricing in the short run (Mansur and Olmstead 2007). The study found that for an aggregate demand reduction equivalent to a two-day-per-week outdoor watering restriction, a market-clearing price would result in gains of about $92 per household per summer, about 30 percent of what the average household in the study sample spent each year on water. Brennan et al. (2007) arrived at similar short-run conclusions: the economic costs of a two-day-per-week sprinkling restriction in Perth, Australia (relative to a price-based approach), are just under $100 per household per season, while the costs of a complete outdoor watering ban range from $347–$870 per household per season. Although nonprice conservation programs can reduce water consumption,[17] both economic theory and the emerging empirical estimates suggest that using price increases to reduce demand, and allowing consumers to adjust their end-uses of water, is more cost-effective than implementing nonprice demand management programs.

Conclusion

This article has reviewed the contributions of economics to the literature on managing scarce water resources. In assessing this literature, we have considered the estimation of water demand in diverted uses and instream uses, water pricing, water allocation and marketing across sectors, the efficiency of large-scale water infrastructure projects, and water conservation.

---

[16] A CV study suggests that Colorado towns with a high probability of water supply shortages are not willing to pay to reduce the probability of water restrictions, and that a city with a low probability of water restrictions may be willing to accept compensation, through reduced water bills, for an increased probability of water restrictions (Howe et al. 1994).

[17] For example, public information campaigns, retrofit subsidies, water rationing, and mandatory water use restrictions had negative and statistically significant impacts on average monthly residential water use in California during the 1990s, and the more stringent policies had stronger effects than voluntary policies and education programs (Renwick and Green 2000).

Since water is not commonly exchanged in markets, and prices are set by water managers and, in some cases, politicians, research on the economics of water demand and the estimation of price elasticities have made price a more useful potential lever for managing water demand. The welfare gains from water marketing across sectors and the significant potential welfare losses from large-scale water infrastructure projects have also been highlighted by economic research over the past three decades. Unfortunately, the results of this research do not appear to have had a strong effect on water policy, as there are many examples of inefficient water allocation and water projects that have been constructed at net social loss. The influence of standard economic principles on the choice of water conservation policies also appears to have been relatively weak, since technology standards and water rationing remain the most common approaches.

Should economists be more actively involved in the debate about the sufficiency and quality of global water supplies to support growing populations and increasing water demand? As mentioned in the introduction, in some ways the debate reflects principles similar to those in earlier debates over the limits posed by natural resource scarcity (i.e., that substitution possibilities and technological change mitigate scarcity). Moreover, there is an important additional factor supporting the economic optimists in the water debate that was lacking in the earlier energy resources debate. That is, since water prices have historically been far below efficient prices, water price increases in the agricultural, municipal, and industrial sectors may go a long way toward ameliorating the problem of water shortages.

However, as competing demands for water exceed supply in more and more regions of the world, economics clearly has much to contribute to the design of water policy. The significant potential welfare gains from providing clean drinking water to the 1.1 billion people worldwide who currently lack it suggest the need for economists to strengthen both their research focus and their engagement in domestic and international policy decisions regarding water supply, pricing in the formal and informal sectors, and privatization. As water resources are increasingly diverted for municipal and agricultural purposes, the marginal value of water left instream rises. Although over the last decade economists have increasingly focused on estimating values for instream public goods, additional estimates of instream values and methods for reliable benefits transfer will be critical inputs to public policy decisions regarding future water allocation. Further economic research on water market structures, externalities, and distributional impacts may also help reduce the significant legal and institutional constraints on trading and improve the welfare impacts of trading where it is already taking place. Given the prevalence of current and planned large-scale water projects worldwide, which are being justified on development grounds, there is also a need for further work by economists to examine these projects' costs, benefits, and distributional impacts.

REFERENCES

Agthe, Donald E., R. Bruce Billings, John L. Dobra, and Kambiz Raffiee. 1986. A simultaneous equation demand model for block rates. *Water Resources Research* 22:1–4.

Antwander, Lars, and Teofilo J. R. Ozuna. 2002. Can public sector reforms improve the efficiency of public water utilities? *Environment and Development Economics* 7:687–700.

Bark, R. H., D. E. Osgood, B. G. Colby, G. Katz, and J. Stromberg. 2009. Habitat preservation and restoration: Do homebuyers have preferences for quality habitat? *Ecological Economics* 68:1465–75.

Bark-Hodgins, Rosalind, and Bonnie G. Colby. 2006. An economic assessment of the Sonoran Desert Conservation Plan. *Natural Resources Journal* 46:709–25.

Bauer, Carl J. 2004. Results of Chilean water markets: Empirical research since 1990. *Water Resources Research* doi:10.1029/2003WR002838.

Baumann, Duane D., John J. Boland, and John H. Sims. 1984. Water conservation: The struggle over definition. *Water Resources Research* 20:428–34.

Bhattacharyya, Arunava, Thomas R. Harris, Rangesan Narayanan, and Kambiz Raffiee. 1995. Specification and estimation of the effect of ownership on the economic efficiency of the water utilities. *Regional Science and Urban Economics* 25:759–84.

Bjornlund, Henning, and Jennifer McKay. 2002. Aspects of water markets for developing countries: Experiences from Australia, Chile, and the US. *Environment and Development Economics* 7:769–95.

Boland, John J., and Dale Whittington. 2000. The political economy of water tariff design in developing countries: Increasing block tariffs versus uniform price with rebate. In *The Political Economy of Water Pricing Reforms*, ed. Ariel Dinar, 215–35. New York: Oxford University Press.

Brennan, Donna, Sorada Tapsuwan, and Gordon Ingram. 2007. The welfare costs of urban outdoor water restrictions. *Australian Journal of Agricultural and Resource Economics* 51:243–61.

Brewer, Jedidiah, Robert Glennon, Alan Ker, and Gary Libecap. 2008. Water markets in the West: Prices, trading, and contractual forms. *Economic Inquiry* 46:91–112.

Brookshire, David S., Bonnie Colby, Mary Ewers, and Philip T. Ganderton. 2004. Market prices for water in the semiarid West of the United States. *Water Resources Research* doi:10.1029/2003WR002846.

Brookshire, David S., H. Stuart Burness, Janie M. Chermak, and Kate Krause. 2002. Western urban water demand. *Natural Resources Journal* 42:873–98.

Carey, Janis, David L. Sunding, and David Zilberman. 2002. Transaction costs and trading behavior in an immature water market. *Environment and Development Economics* 7:733–50.

Chang, Chan, and Ronald C. Griffin. 1992. Water marketing as a reallocative institution in Texas. *Water Resources Research* 28:879–90.

Chong, Eshien, Freddy Huet, Stéphane Saussier, and Faye Steiner. 2006. Public-private partnerships and prices: Evidence from water distribution in France. *Review of Industrial Organization* 29:149–69.

Clarke, George R. G., Katrina Kosec, and Scott Wallsten. 2009. Has private participation in water and sewerage improved coverage? Empirical evidence from Latin America. *Journal of International Development* 21:327–61.

Colby, Bonnie G. 1989. Estimating the value of water in alternative uses. *Natural Resources Journal* 29:511–27.

———. 1990. Enhancing instream flow benefits in an era of water marketing. *Water Resources Research* 26:1113–20.

Colby, Bonnie G., Kristine Crandall, and David B. Bush. 1993. Water right transactions: Market values and price dispersion. *Water Resources Research* 29:1565–72.

Collinge, Robert A. 1994. Transferable rate entitlements: The overlooked opportunity in municipal water pricing. *Public Finance Quarterly* 22:46–64.

Creel, Michael, and John Loomis. 1992. Recreation value of water to wetlands in the San Joaquin Valley: Linked multinomial logit and count data trip frequency models. *Water Resources Research* 28:2597–606.

Cutter, W. Bowman. 2007. Valuing groundwater recharge in an urban context. *Land Economics* 83:234–52.

Dadaser-Celik, Filiz, Jay S. Coggins, Patrick L. Brezonik, and Heinz G. Stefan. 2009. The projected costs and benefits of water diversion from and to the Sultan Marshes (Turkey). *Ecological Economics* 68:1496–506.

Dalhuisen, Jasper M., Raymond J. G. M. Florax, Henri L. F. de Groot, and Peter Nijkamp. 2003. Price and income elasticities of residential water demand: A meta-analysis. *Land Economics* 79:292–308.

Daubert, John T., and Robert A. Young. 1979. Economic benefits from instream flow in a Colorado mountain stream. Colorado Water Resources Research Institute Completion Report No. 91.

Davis, Lucas W. 2008. Durable goods and residential demand for energy and water: Evidence from a field trial. *RAND Journal of Economics* 39:530–46.

Deller, Steven C, David L. Chicoine, and Ganapathi Ramamurthy. 1986. Instrumental variables approach to rural water service demand. *Southern Economic Journal* 53:333–46.

Diao, Xinshen, and Terry Roe. 2003. Can a water market avert the "double-whammy" of trade reform and lead to a "win-win" outcome? *Journal of Environmental Economics and Management* 45:708–23.

Dinar, Ariel, and J. Letey. 1991. Agricultural water marketing, allocative efficiency, and drainage reduction. *Journal of Environmental Economics and Management* 20:210–23.

Dixon, Lloyd S., Nancy Y. Moore, and Ellen M. Pint. 1996. *Drought Management Policies and Economic Effects in Urban Areas of California, 1987–1992.* Santa Monica, CA: RAND Corporation.

Duflo, Esther, and Rohini Pande. 2007. Dams. *Quarterly Journal of Economics* 122:601–46.

Easter, K. William, Mark W. Rosegrant, and Ariel Dinar, eds. 1998. *Markets for water: Potential and performance.* Dordrecht: Kluwer Academic.

Espey, Molly, James Espey, and W. Douglass Shaw. 1997. Price elasticity of residential demand for water: A meta-analysis. *Water Resources Research* 33:1369–74.

Estache, Antonio, and Martín A. Rossi. 2002. How different is the efficiency of public and private water companies in Asia? *World Bank Economic Review* 16:139–48.

Finnegan, William. 2002. Leasing the rain. *The New Yorker.* April 8.

Galiani, Sebastian, P. Gertler, and E. Schargrodsky. 2005. Water for life: The impact of the privatization of water supply on child mortality. *Journal of Political Economy* 113:83–120.

Gaudin, Sylvestre. 2006. Effect of price information on residential water demand. *Applied Economics* 38:383–93.

Gibbons, Diana C. 1986. *The Economic Value of Water.* Washington, DC: Resources for the Future.

Grafton, R. Quentin, and Michael Ward 2008. Prices versus rationing: Marshallian surplus and mandatory water restrictions. *Economic Record* 84:S57–65.

Greening, Lorna A., David L. Greene, and Carmen Difiglio. 2000. Energy efficiency and consumption—The rebound effect—A survey. *Energy Policy* 28:389–401.

Griffin, Ronald C. 2006. *Water Resource Economics: The Analysis of Scarcity, Policies, and Projects.* Cambridge, MA: MIT Press.

Griffin, Ronald C., and Shih-Hsun Hsu. 1993. The potential for water market efficiency when instream flows have value. *American Journal of Agricultural Economics* 75:292–303.

Griffin, Ronald C., and Fred O. Boadu. 1992. Water marketing in Texas: Opportunities for reform. *Natural Resources Journal* 32:265–88.

Hall, Darwin C. 2000. Public choice and water rate design. In *The political economy of water pricing implementation*, ed. Ariel Dinar, pp. 189–212. New York: Oxford University Press.

Halsing, David L., and Michael R. Moore. 2008. Cost-effective management alternatives for Snake River Chinook salmon: A biological-economic synthesis. *Conservation Biology* 22:338–50.

Hanak, Ellen. 2005. Stopping the drain: Third-party responses to California's water market, *Contemporary Economic Policy* 23:59–77.

Hanemann, W. Michael. 1997. Prices and rate structures. In *Urban water demand management and planning*, ed. D. Baumann, J. Boland, and W. M. Hanemann, pp. 137–79. New York: McGraw-Hill.

Hansen, LeRoy T., and Arne Hallam. 1991. National estimates of the recreational value of streamflow. *Water Resources Research* 27:167–75.

Hartman, L. M., and D. Seastone. 1970. *Water transfers: Economic efficiency and alternative institutions.* Baltimore: Johns Hopkins University Press.

Hearne, Robert R., and K. William Easter. 1997. The economic and financial gains from water markets in Chile. *Agricultural Economics* 15:187–99.

Hewitt, Julie A., and W. Michael Hanemann. 1995. A discrete/continuous choice approach to residential water demand under block rate pricing. *Land Economics* 71:173–92.

Holland, Stephen P. 2006. Privatization of water-resource development. *Environmental and Resource Economics* 34:291–315.

Holland, Stephen P., and Michael R. Moore. 2003. *Cadillac Desert* revisited: Property rights, public policy and water-resource depletion. *Journal of Environmental Economics and Management* 46:131–55.

Holmes, Thomas P., John C. Bergstrom, Eric Huszar, Susan B. Kask, and Fritz Orr III. 2004. Contingent valuation, net marginal benefits, and the scale of riparian ecosystem restoration. *Ecological Economics* 49:19–30.

Howe, Charles W., and F. P. Lineweaver. 1967. The impact of price on residential water demand and its relation to system demand and price structure. *Water Resources Research* 3:13–32.

Howe, Charles W., Mark Griffin Smith, Lynne Bennet, Charles M. Brendecke, J. Ernest Flack, Robert M. Hamm, Roger Mann, Lee Rozaklis, and Karl Wunderlich. 1994. The value of water supply reliability in urban water systems. *Journal of Environmental Economics and Management* 26:19–30.

Jacoby, Hanan G., Rinku Murgai, and Saeed Ur Rehman. 2004. Monopoly power and distribution in fragmented markets: The case of groundwater. *Review of Economic Studies* 71:783–808.

Kotchen, Matthew J., Michael R. Moore, Frank Lupi, and Edward S. Rutherford. 2006. Environmental constraints on hydropower: An ex-post benefit-cost analysis of dam relicensing in Michigan. *Land Economics* 82:384–403.

Krause, Kate, Janie M. Chermak, and David S. Brookshire. 2003. The demand for water: Consumer response to scarcity. *Journal of Regulatory Economics* 23:167–91.

Leones, Julie, Bonnie Colby, Dennis Cory, and Liz Ryan. 1997. Measuring regional economic impacts of streamflow depletions. *Water Resources Research* 33:831–38.

Lewis, Lynne Y., Curtis Bohlen, and Sarah Wilson. 2008. Dams, dam removal, and river restoration: A hedonic property value analysis. *Contemporary Economic Policy* 26:175–86.

Lipscomb, Molly, A. Mushfiq Mobarak, and Tania Barham. 2008. Returns to electricity: Evidence from the quasi-random placement of hydropower plants in Brazil. Working Paper, Yale School of Management.

Loomis, John B. 1987. The economic value of instream flow: Methodology and benefit estimates for optimum flows. *Journal of Environmental Management* 24:169–79.

———. 1996. Measuring the economic benefits of removing dams and restoring the Elwha River: Results of a contingent valuation survey. *Water Resources Research* 32:441–47.

———. 2002. Quantifying recreation use values from removing dams and restoring free-flowing rivers: A contingent behavior travel cost demand model for the Lower Snake River. *Water Resources Research* doi:10.1029/2000WR000136.

Loomis, John, Paula Kent, Liz Strange, Kurt Fausch, and Alan Covich. 2000. Measuring the total economic value of restoring ecosystem services in an impaired river basin: Results from a contingent valuation survey. *Ecological Economics* 33:103–17.

Lovei, Laszlo, and Dale Whittington. 1993. Rent-extracting behavior by multiple agents in the provision of municipal water supply: A study of Jakarta, Indonesia. *Water Resources Research* 29:1965–74.

Mansur, Erin T., and Sheila M. Olmstead. 2007. The value of scarce water: Measuring the inefficiency of municipal regulations. NBER Working Paper No. 13513.

Martínez-Espiñeira, Roberto, Maria A. García-Valiñas, and Francisco González-Gómez. 2009. Does private management of water supply services really increase prices? An empirical analysis in Spain. *Urban Studies* 46:923–45.

Martínez-Espiñeira, Roberto. 2002. Residential water demand in the northwest of Spain. *Environmental and Resource Economics* 21:161–87.

Megginson, William L., and Jeffrey M. Netter. 2001. From state to market: A survey of empirical studies on privatization. *Journal of Economic Literature* 39:321–89.

Moncur, James E. T., and Richard L. Pollock. 1988. Scarcity rents for water: A valuation and pricing model. *Land Economics* 64:62–72.

Munasinghe, Mohan. 1992. *Water supply and environmental management: Developing world applications.* Boulder, CO: Westview Press.

Nieswiadomy, Michael L., and David J. Molina. 1988. Urban water demand estimates under increasing block rates. *Growth and Change* 19:1–12.

———. 1989. Comparing residential water demand estimates under decreasing and increasing block rates using household data. *Land Economics* 65:280–89.

Nieswiadomy, Michael L., and S. L. Cobb. 1993. Impact of pricing structure selectivity on urban water demand. *Contemporary Policy Issues* 11:101–13.

Ojeda, Monica Ilija, Alex S. Mayer, and Barry D. Solomon. 2008. Economic valuation of environmental services sustained by water flows in the Yaqui River Delta. *Ecological Economics* 65:155–66.

Olmstead, Sheila M. 2004. Thirsty *colonias*: Rate regulation and the provision of water service. *Land Economics* 80:36–150.

———.2009. Reduced-form vs. structural models of water demand under non-linear prices. *Journal of Business and Economic Statistics* 27:84–94.

———.2010. The economics of water quality. *Review of Environmental Economics and Policy* 4(1):44–62.

Olmstead, Sheila M., and Robert N. Stavins. 2009. Comparing price and non-price approaches to urban water conservation. *Water Resources Research* doi:10.1029/2008WR007227.

Olmstead, Sheila M., W. Michael Hanemann, and Robert N. Stavins. 2007. Water demand under alternative price structures. *Journal of Environmental Economics and Management* 54:181–98.

Parry, Ian, and Kenneth A. Small. 2005. Does Britain or the United States have the right gasoline tax? *American Economic Review* 95:1276–89.

Pattanayak, Subhrendu K., and Randall A. Kramer. 2001a. Pricing ecological services: Willingness to pay for drought mitigation from watershed protection in eastern Indonesia. *Water Resources Research* 37:771–78.

———. 2001b. Worth of watersheds: A producer surplus approach for valuing drought mitigation in Eastern Indonesia. *Environment and Development Economics* 6:123–46.

Perreault, Thomas. 2005. State restructuring and the scale politics of rural water governance in Bolivia. *Environment and Planning A* 37:263–84.

Pint, Ellen M. 1999. Household responses to increased water rates during the California drought. *Land Economics* 75:246–66.

Provencher, Bill, and Oscar Burt. 1993. The externalities associated with the common property exploitation of groundwater. *Journal of Environmental Economics and Management* 24:139–58.

Provencher, Bill, Helen Sarakinos, and Tanya Meyer. 2008. Does small dam removal affect local property values? An empirical analysis. *Contemporary Economic Policy* 26:187–97.

Pujol, Joan, Meri Raggi, and Davide Viaggi. 2006. The potential impact of markets for irrigation water in Italy and Spain: A comparison of two study areas. *Australian Journal of Agricultural and Resource Economics* 50:361–80.

Renwick, Mary E., and Richard D. Green. 2000. Do residential water demand side management policies measure up? An analysis of eight California water agencies. *Journal of Environmental Economics and Management* 40:37–55.

Renzetti, Steven. 1992a. Estimating the structure of industrial water demands: The case of Canadian manufacturing. *Land Economics* 68:396–404.

———.1992b. Evaluating the welfare effects of reforming municipal water prices. *Journal of Environmental Economics and Management* 22:147–63.

———.1999. Municipal water supply and sewage treatment: Costs, prices, and distortions. *Canadian Journal of Economics* 32:688–704.

Reynaud, Arnaud. 2003. An econometric estimation of industrial water demand in France. *Environmental and Resource Economics* 25: 213–32.

Russell, Clifford, and Boo-Shig Shin. 1996a. An application and evaluation of competing marginal cost pricing approximations. In *Marginal cost rate design and wholesale water markets, advances in the economics of environmental resources*, vol. 1, ed. Darwin C. Hall. Greenwich, CT: JAI Press.

————.1996b. Public utility pricing: Theory and practical limitations. In *Marginal cost rate design and wholesale water markets, advances in the economics of environmental resources*, vol. 1, ed. Darwin C. Hall, pp. 123–39. Greenwich, CT: JAI Press.

Saal, David S., and David Parker. 2001. Productivity and price performance in the privatized water and sewerage companies of England and Wales. *Journal of Regulatory Economics* 20:61–90.

Saliba, Bonnie Colby, and David B. Bush. 1987. *Water markets in theory and practice*. Boulder, CO: Westview Press.

Sax, Joseph L. 1965. Selling reclamation water rights: A case study in federal subsidy policy. *Michigan Law Review* 64:13–46.

Scheierling, Susanne M., John B. Loomis, and Robert A. Young. 2006. Irrigation water demand: A meta-analysis of price elasticities. *Water Resources Research* doi:10.1029/2005WR004009.

Sibly, Hugh 2006. Efficient urban water pricing. *Australian Economic Review* 39:227–37.

Solo, T. M. 1998. *Water and sanitation services for the urban poor: Small-scale providers, typology, and profiles*. Washington, DC: UNDP–World Bank Water and Sanitation Program.

Solomon, Susan, Dahe Qin, Martin Manning, Melinda Marquis, Kristen Avery, Melinda M. B. Tignor, Henry LeRoy Miller, and Zhenlin Chen, eds. 2007 *Climate change 2007: The physical science basis*. Contribution of Working Group I to the Fourth Assessment Report of the IPCC. Cambridge: Cambridge University Press.

Strand, Jon, and Ian Walker. 2005. Water markets and demand in Central American cities. *Environment and Development Economics* 10:313–35.

Timmins, Christopher. 2003. Demand-side technology standards under inefficient pricing regimes: Are they effective water conservation tools in the long run? *Environmental and Resource Economics* 26:107–24.

Vaux, H. J., and Richard E. Howitt. 1984. Managing water scarcity: An evaluation of interregional transfers. *Water Resources Research* 20:785–92.

Wahl, Richard W. 1989. *Markets for federal water: Subsidies, property rights, and the Bureau of Reclamation*. Washington, DC: Resources for the Future.

Wallander, Steven. 2009. The water conservation potential of the federal plumbing fixture efficiency standards. Working Paper, Yale School of Forestry and Environmental Studies.

Weinberg, Marca, Catherine L. Kling, and James E. Wilen. 1993. Water markets and water quality. *American Journal of Agricultural Economics* 75:278–91.

Whittington, Dale, Donald T. Lauria, and Xinming Mu. 1991. A study of water vending and willingness to pay for water in Onitsha, Nigeria. *World Development* 19:179–98.

World Commission on Dams. 2000. *Dams and development: A new framework for decision-making*. London: Earthscan Publications.

Young, Robert A. 2005. *Determining the economic value of water: Concepts and methods*. Washington, DC: Resources for the Future.

Zhongmin, Xu, Cheng Guodong, Zhang Zhiqiang, Su Zhiyong, and John Loomis. 2003. Applying contingent valuation in China to measure the total economic value of restoring ecosystem services in Ejina region. *Ecological Economics* 44:345–58.

Ziegler, Joseph A., and Stephen E. Bell. 1984. Estimating demand for intake water by self-supplied firms. *Water Resources Research* 20:4–8.

VII

Corporate Social Responsibility and the Environment

22 Corporate Social Responsibility through an Economic Lens*

Forest L Reinhardt, Robert N. Stavins, and Richard H. K. Vietor

Forest L. Reinhardt is John D. Black Professor of Business Administration at Harvard Business School; Robert N. Stavins is Albert Pratt Professor of Business and Government at Harvard Kennedy School, Research Associate at the National Bureau of Economic Research, and University Fellow at Resources for the Future; and Richard H. K. Vietor is Paul Whiton Cherington Professor of Business Administration and Senior Associate Dean for the Asian Initiative at Harvard Business School.

Introduction

Business leaders, government officials, and academics are focusing more and more attention on the concept of "corporate social responsibility" (CSR). The central issue is the appropriate role of business. Everyone agrees that firms should obey the law. But beyond the law—beyond full compliance with environmental regulations—do firms have additional moral or social responsibilities to (voluntarily) commit resources to environmental protection?

One of the challenges of examining the concept of CSR is simply identifying a consistent and sensible definition from among a bewildering range of concepts and definitions that have been proposed in the literature.[1] We adopt a simple definition originally offered by Elhauge (2005): sacrificing profits in the social interest. This definition has the merit of being consistent with some of the most useful prior perspectives (Graff Ziven and Small 2005; Portney 2005; Reinhardt 2005), while focusing the discussion on the most interesting normative and positive questions.

"Corporate Social Responsibility Through an Economic Lens." National Bureau of Economics Research Working Paper series. #13989 May, 2008.

*Exceptionally valuable research assistance was provided by Matthew Ranson, and our research benefited greatly from conversations with William Alford, Max Bazerman, Robert Clark, Joshua Margolis, and Mark Roe. The authors are grateful to Suzanne Leonard, Charlie Kolstad, and an anonymous referee for valuable comments on a previous version of the manuscript, but all remaining errors are our own.

[1]See reviews by Wood and Jones (1996) and Mohr, Webb, and Harris (2001).

423

Of course, questions regarding sacrificing profits in the social interest apply beyond the environmental sphere. The academic debate over the legality of sacrificing profits in the public interest appears to have begun in 1932 with opposing articles (Dodd 1932; Berle 1932) in a *Harvard Law Review* symposium on "For Whom Are Corporate Managers Trustees?" The debate in economics began more recently, with Milton Friedman's 1970 article, "The Social Responsibility of Business Is to Increase Its Profits," in the *New York Times Magazine*. Since then, the debate has continued, and CSR has received considerable attention from both scholars and the public, especially in the environmental protection area.

The purpose of this article, which is part of a three-article symposium on Corporate Social Responsibility and the Environment,[2] is to introduce and provide an overview of the major issues related to CSR, synthesize what is known about CSR in the environmental arena, and thereby identify where the greatest uncertainties remain. To this end, we address four key questions about the issue of firms sacrificing profits in the social interest.[3] *May* they do so within the scope of their fiduciary responsibilities to their shareholders? *Can* they do so on a sustainable basis, or will the forces of a competitive marketplace render such efforts and their impacts transient at best? *Do* firms, in fact, frequently or at least sometimes behave this way, reducing their earnings by voluntarily engaging in environmental stewardship? And finally, *should* firms carry out such profit-sacrificing activities? In other words, is this an efficient use of social resources?

This article is organized as follows. We begin by examining legal thinking about whether firms *may* sacrifice profits to benefit individuals other than their shareholders, and then look at the legality of CSR in the United States and other countries. Next, we draw on theories of industrial organization and management to identify circumstances under which firms *can* sacrifice profits without being punished by market forces. We then turn to positive questions about whether firms actually *do* engage in CSR. Here we review and synthesize empirical evidence to assess whether some firms truly exceed full compliance with the law, and if so, whether their "socially responsible" actions actually sacrifice profits. To address our fourth question, *should* firms—from a societal perspective—be carrying out such activities, we examine CSR in a normative light and consider economic arguments on both sides of the issue. The final section summarizes our findings and offers some conclusions.

---

[2]The other two articles in the symposium, by Lyon and Maxwell (forthcoming) and Portney (forthcoming), discuss CSR from the theoretical and empirical perspectives, respectively.

[3]These four questions were originally identified by Hay, Stavins, and Vietor (2005).

May Firms Sacrifice Profits in the Social Interest?

The prevailing view among most economists and business scholars is that corporate directors have a fiduciary duty to maximize profits for shareholders. While this view underlies many economic models of firm behavior, its legal basis is actually not very strong. The judicial record, although supportive of a duty to maximize profits for shareholders, also leaves room for the possibility that firms may sacrifice profits in the public interest. The courts' deference towards the judgment of businesspeople—the "business judgment rule"—prevents many public-minded managerial actions from being legally challenged.

The Legal Purpose of the Corporation

The most widely accepted position on the legal purpose of the corporation—known as shareholder primacy (Springer 1999; Fisch 2006; Ehrlich 2005)—was articulated by Milton Friedman in 1970:

> In a free-enterprise, private-property system, a corporate executive is an employee of the owners of the business. He has direct responsibility to his employers. That responsibility is to conduct the business in accordance with their desires, which generally will be to make as much money as possible while conforming to the basic rules of the society, both those embodied in law and those embodied in ethical custom (Friedman 1970).

A more subtle version of the shareholder primacy argument is the "nexus of contracts" approach (Jensen and Meckling 1976; Easterbrook and Fischel 1991), which views the corporation as a nexus of legal contracts between the suppliers of various factors of production, who agree to cooperate in order to generate monetary returns. These agreements specify that in exchange for their contributions, the owners of most factors of production—labor, land, intellectual property rights, etc.—will receive set payments with little risk. Shareholders—the suppliers of capital—accept the residual financial risk of doing business, and in return receive the residual profits. Since shareholders have no contractual guarantee of a fixed payment from the firm's activities, any profits that are diverted towards other activities, such as pursuit of "the social good," come directly out of their pockets (Butler and McChesney 1999). Thus, from this perspective, CSR is close to theft.

A second view of the role of the corporation is found in the team-production model (Blair and Stout 1999), which views the corporation as the solution to the moral hazard problem that arises when the owners of factors of production must make firm-specific investments but fear they will not be rewarded *ex post*. To solve this problem, the board of directors of the corporation functions as a neutral "mediating hierarch" that allocates residual profits to all of the factors of production (team members) according to their relative contributions.[4] Under the team-production model, sacrificing profits in the social interest is legal, as long as the profits are allocated to a deserving factor of production.

A third view of the purpose of the corporation is the "operational discretion" model, which holds that the law grants corporate managers discretion to comply with social and moral norms, even if doing so reduces shareholder profits (Elhauge 2005). The judiciary's unwillingness to second-guess matters of business judgment has the practical effect of shielding managers who choose to sacrifice profits in the public interest.

A fourth and final position is the "progressive view" that the corporation is organized for the benefit of society at large, or at the very least, corporate directors have fiduciary responsibilities that extend to a wide variety of stakeholders (Sheehy 2005; Gabaldon 2006). Under this view, sacrificing profits in the public interest is entirely legal. The progressive view, however, is not well rooted in either statutes or case law (Clark 1986).

The Legality of CSR in the United States

In the United States, a variety of legal requirements define the responsibilities of the corporation (and its board of directors) to shareholders and other stakeholders. However, as discussed below, these requirements are limited in practice.

Corporate Responsibilities to Shareholders and Other Stakeholders. Although corporations in the United States are granted the "legal fiction of separate corporate personality," a corporation's decisions are made by its board of directors, or by executives who have been delegated decision-making authority (Clark 1986). To ensure that directors and managers do not act negligently or subvert corporate resources for their own benefit, the legal system imposes fiduciary duties of care and loyalty.

The duty of loyalty requires directors to act "in good faith and in the best interests of the corporation" (Scalise 2005), and places limitations on the motives, purposes, and goals that can legitimately influence directors' decisions (Cox and Hazen 2003). The duty of care complements the duty of loyalty by requiring managers to "exercise that degree of skill, diligence, and care that a reasonably prudent person would exercise in similar circumstances" (Clark 1986, p. 123). Violation of fiduciary duties can result in personal liability for directors (Scalise 2005). Legal formulations of fiduciary duties typically refer to the "best interests of the corporation," but whether the corporation's "best interests" include only its shareholders or a wider set of constituents is not immediately clear (Cox and Hazen 2003). The prevailing opinion is that fiduciary duties are owed to shareholders (Blomquist 2006), but a minority supports the view that corporations can be managed in part for the benefit of other stakeholders (Lee 2005).

---

[4]For example, many US states have enacted statutes that permit corporate directors to consider the interests of stakeholders other than shareholders.

Every US state recognizes the right of businesses to make charitable contributions. Seven states allow charitable donations regardless of corporate benefit, and nineteen other states allow donations that benefit the business or advance the public welfare (Choper, Coffee, and Gilson 2004). Statutes in the remaining 24 states (including Delaware) include similar language, but without legal clarification about whether donations are permitted when they do not benefit the firm (Donohue 2005).[5]

State corporate statutes grant corporations legal powers similar to those of people, and allow corporations to participate in lawful activities (Clark 1986). As a result, corporations presumably have the power (but not necessarily the *right*) to undertake CSR activities (Donohue 2005). Corporations can write their own corporate charters to explicitly authorize themselves to participate in CSR. For example, the *New York Times* is incorporated to pursue objectives other than profit maximization (Donohue 2005).

These statutory requirements and judicial precedents place limits on the actions of corporations and their boards. But an important judicial construct—the business judgment rule—creates substantial deference to firms' managerial decisions.

The Business Judgment Rule. The business judgment rule "acts as a presumption in favor of corporate managers' actions" (Branson 2002). It requires courts to defer to the judgment of corporate managers, as long as their decisions satisfy certain basic requirements related to negligence and conflict of interest. The basic premise is that since corporate managers are far more skilled at making business judgments than courts, allowing courts to second-guess managers' decisions would create potentially large transactions costs (Elhauge 2005).

The business judgment rule makes fiduciary duties difficult to enforce, and it effectively grants managers discretion to "temper business decision making with their perceptions of social values" (Clark 1986; Fisch 2006; Scalise 2005; Blair and Stout 1999).[6] As a practical matter, as long as managers can plausibly claim that their actions are in the long run interests of the firm, it is almost impossible for shareholders to challenge the actions of managers who act in the public interest.

The business judgment rule also offers managers protection from accusations of conflict of interest, primarily because it does not recognize most nonfinancial incentives as conflicts (Elhauge 2005; Branson 2002). Corporate managers' decisions can be regarded as irrational—and thus not protected by the business judgment rule—only if they "go so far beyond

---

[5]In addition, twenty-nine states have statutes that allow managers to consider the interests of non-shareholders such as employees, customers, suppliers, creditors, and society at large (Springer 1999).

[6]For example, Clark cites the 1968 case of *Shlensky v. Wrigley*, in which the Illinois Court of Appeals allowed William Wrigley, Jr., the president and majority shareholder of the Chicago Cubs, to refuse to install lights at Wrigley Field because of his belief that night games would be bad for the surrounding neighborhood (1986).

the bounds of reasonable business judgment that their only explanation is bad faith" (Blomquist 2006, p. 699). Donohue (2005) cites the extreme example of a Delaware court that ruled that the business judgment rule protected the 1989 decision by Occidental Petroleum to spend $120 million, slightly less than half of the company's yearly net profit, on an art museum named after its 91-year-old CEO, Armand Hammer.

So, are firms in the United States prohibited from sacrificing profits in the public interest? And if so, is the prohibition enforceable? The answers to these two questions appear to be "maybe" and "no," respectively. "While case law falls short of unequivocally mandating shareholder wealth maximization, it also falls short of unambiguously authorizing the pursuit of non-shareholder interests other than instrumentally for the benefit of the shareholders" (Lee 2006, p. 557). And as long as managers claim some plausible connection to future profitability, the business judgment rule grants them substantial leeway to commit corporate resources to projects that benefit the public.

The Legality of CSR in Other Countries

With their cultural traditions of social democracy or firm loyalty to employees, most European countries and Japan have legal systems that differ from the system in the United States. The legal systems in these other countries place a greater emphasis on stakeholder participation, and sometimes codify this by legalizing various forms of profit-sacrificing behavior. Europeans have sought to incorporate CSR into their investment climate, both at the institutional and individual level (Sutton 2004), and in strong social democracies, such as Germany and France, stakeholders (particularly employees) have much stronger legal positions than in the United States (Roe 2000). Corporations in Europe and Asia are also more likely to have a few large shareholders, who may take social responsibilities seriously, particularly those towards employees (Roe 2000). This contrasts with the pattern of highly dispersed share ownership in the United States.

Industrialized Countries. Common law industrialized countries, primarily former British possessions, share many legal features with the United States. Corporations in these countries have similar board structures, face similar legal requirements, and even share some legal precedents. In such countries, CSR is discouraged, but permitted. Under Australian corporate law, for example, corporate managers are required to make decisions in the best interest of the corporation, while a statutory business judgment rule grants managers considerable discretion (Corfield 1998). Likewise, Canadian law requires that directors and officers of corporations act in the best interests of the corporation, but the director is not permitted to ignore the collective interests of shareholders (Borok 2003). The United Kingdom's legal system permits corporate managers to engage in socially beneficial activities, as long as there is a plausible rationale that the activities are in shareholders' interests (Lynch-Fannon 2007).

In contrast with common law jurisdictions, countries with civil law systems tend to place a greater emphasis on stakeholder participation in corporate governance. Corporate boards often include employee representatives, and cultural traditions emphasize loyalty to employees. In these countries, more forms of CSR are permissible. In France, corporate directors have both a duty of care and a duty of loyalty (Fanto 1998). Although there has been a shift towards more investor friendly laws, the French legal code explicitly allows directors to make decisions based on the interests of all constituencies. German law does not even give management an explicit obligation to maximize shareholder value (Marinov and Heiman 1998), and large German corporations have a two-tiered board structure that encourages the board to consider the interests of parties other than shareholders (Corfield 1998).

Japanese corporate law is similar to corporate law in the United States, in that directors have duties of care and loyalty, which, if violated, can be grounds for shareholder lawsuit. But Japanese corporations have a strong tradition of CSR oriented towards their employees. In years with high profits, large corporations usually retain their earnings and reinvest them for the benefit of employees (Miwa 1999). The shares of many firms are owned by banks who handle firms' credit or by important business partners (Corfield 1998). These shareholder-creditors have financial goals that are similar to those of long-term employees, particularly in terms of corporate stability and minimizing risk (Roe 2000).

Developing Countries and Multinational Enterprises. Corporate law in developing countries has a number of special characteristics. First, the corporate legal system is often new. As a result, businesses have little experience complying with the law, and there are fewer judicial precedents mapping out the law's boundaries. Second, legal institutions in developing countries are often weak. Regulations can go unenforced; agency problems can be a serious issue; and members of the judiciary may be corrupt. Third, the operations of multinational corporations in these countries can lead to conflicts between the interests of home and host states.

Thus, both the laws governing CSR and the degree to which those laws are enforced may vary substantially across developing countries. Assuming that the laws in most developing countries allow some scope for managerial activity that may sacrifice profits, the question remains whether firms can do so in view of competitive pressures in the markets for their outputs and inputs. It is to this question that we now turn.

Can Firms Sacrifice Profits in the Social Interest?

Just because the legal system may allow firms to sacrifice profits in the social interest does not mean that firms *can* do so on a sustainable basis in the face of competitive pressures. Under what conditions is it economically feasible for firms to sacrifice profits in the social interest? Before turning to this question, we address a somewhat broader question: under what conditions might it be sustainable for firms to produce goods and services, such as public goods, that benefit individuals other than their customers (Lyon and Maxwell 2004; Vogel 2006)?

We identify six conditions that would facilitate the production of such goods and services. All six of these conditions involve government intervention, imperfect competition, or both. First is the imposition of regulatory constraints that require a firm as well as its competitors to carry out some socially beneficial actions. Second is the possibility that such production is not costly to the firm. For example, restaurants frequently donate leftover food to homeless shelters. The third condition is that the socially beneficial actions may reduce a firm's business expenses by an amount greater than the cost of the actions themselves. For example, installation of energy-saving (climate friendly) technologies may generate long-term cost savings that outweigh upfront costs. Fourth, in some cases socially beneficial actions may yield an increase in revenue. It is easy to think of goods and services that are differentiated along environmental lines, such as clothing made of organic cotton, or wood from forests managed in accordance with some principles of sustainability. Socially beneficial actions could also generate goodwill, improving a firm's reputation and sales. Fifth, firms may choose to go beyond full compliance with environment, health, or safety laws in order to improve their position in current or future regulatory negotiations. By doing so, they may be able to deflect or influence future regulation or deflect enforcement of existing regulation. Sixth, some firms may use overcompliance to spur future regulation, which would provide a competitive advantage over less adaptable firms.

We now turn to our more restrictive definition of CSR and address the question raised above: under what conditions is it economically feasible for firms to sacrifice profits in the social interest?

When Is It Feasible for Firms to Engage in Profit-Sacrificing CSR?

In some cases firms undertake CSR actions voluntarily, while in others they engage in CSR only under pressure from market participants or other social forces. In practice, it is difficult to discern voluntary from "reluctant" CSR. Whether CSR initiatives are voluntary or reluctant, their economic sustainability depends on the market pressures and social expectations confronted by the firm (Borck, Coglianese, and Nash 2006).

Voluntary CSR. The first possibility—that stakeholders voluntarily sacrifice profits—is what some observers would think of as the "purest form" of CSR. The primary economic agents who could fund such activities are shareholders and employees.

Some shareholders may be willing to subsidize firms' profit sacrificing behavior. Stock issued by socially responsible firms is a composite commodity, which combines a financial investment product with a charitable giving vehicle (Graff Zivin and Small 2005). When investors purchase the stock, they may be motivated by self-interest or by altruistic motives. As long as investors are willing to fund CSR activities, firms can participate in them. But whether investors are willing to accept lower returns may depend on whether the firm already enjoys an economic position that allows it to obtain rents, such as through natural monopolies, niche markets, imperfect information, regulatory distortions, anti-takeover laws, and other market imperfections.[7] In this case, investors sacrificing profit may still earn returns above the market norm.

Willingness to accept below market returns may depend on whether investors hold stakes in publicly—or privately—held companies. Investors with large private holdings are more likely to take an interest in their companies' activities and be able to influence the companies' actions. Whether this additional interest and influence would have a positive or negative influence on CSR is an open question.

Evidence suggests that some individuals are willing to pay more for socially responsible goods (Jensen et al. 2002). The existence of such "ethical investors" could—in principle—have consequences for firms that do not participate in CSR activities (Heinkel, Kraus, and Zechner 2001). For example, if ethical investors' choices increase the cost of capital for "irresponsible" firms, some of these firms might be forced to adopt more socially responsible practices. If the share price differential becomes sufficiently large, these firms may decide to participate in CSR activities to increase their own stock price (Heinkel, Kraus, and Zechner 2001; Graff Zivin and Small 2005). But the effect of green investors on the cost of capital may be small. Because irresponsible firms will generate higher returns (relative to their stock price), investors in these firms will accumulate capital more quickly than socially responsible investors, and over time may dominate the capital market. This would lead to a decrease in the cost of capital for irresponsible businesses (Heinkel, Kraus, and Zechner 2001).

Employees may sacrifice part of the returns to labor to further the social good. This could occur explicitly if employees are given the opportunity to use their own salary [sic] and benefits to fund CSR projects. For example, some executives may be able to channel part of their compensation towards the cost of CSR activities, or lawyers may be able to donate their time to pro bono work. Employees may also fund CSR implicitly, such as when a firm works in a field that employees perceive as socially responsible (e.g., providing services to the elderly, remediating oil spills). Employees may be willing to accept less than the fair market value of their labor (as determined by the wage they would receive for working in a less socially responsible

---

[7]Firms have strong economic incentives to take advantage of any market power available to them. If a firm maintains market power, it can—in principle—pass on the costs of CSR to its suppliers and/or customers. For example, regulated public utilities, which are granted geographic monopolies on specific conditions such as provision of universal service, may decide to engage in CSR activities and use the firm's monopoly power to pass resulting costs on to consumers.

industry), because they are compensated in other ways through the knowledge that their work benefits society at large (Frank 1996).

Unfortunately, empirical evidence on CSR and wages is inconclusive. Most revealed preference studies show that wages are lower at non-profit firms than at for-profit firms, but this non-profit wage penalty disappears in econometric analyses that control for worker and firm-specific characteristics (Francois 2004). If non-profit status is a proxy for social responsibility, then socially responsible firms may not enjoy a significant discount on labor prices. This conclusion is supported by findings that CEO compensation at firms listed in the Domini Social Index (DS 400) is not significantly different from CEO compensation at other firms in similar industries (Frye, Nelling, and Webb 2006).

Reluctant CSR. Corporate decisions are actually made by individual managers and directors, not by the "firm" *per se*. Those decisions often further the interests of profit-minded shareholders, but not always. Investors may have little choice but to accept some degree of CSR profit-sacrificing activities. It may be less costly to accept a degree of principal-agent "slack" than to eliminate it completely, because managers who are excessively constrained may be ineffectual.

Investors may also be forced to accept profit-sacrificing activities that are the result of external constraints. This maybe particularly relevant in the developing world, where environmental regulatory standards lag behind those of industrialized countries. For example, equipment purchased from industrialized countries may incorporate pollution control technology that meets standards considerably stricter than those in effect in a developing country (Jaffe et al. 1995).

The magnitude of the profits that managers can sacrifice against investors' wishes depends on the structure of managers' compensation and the strength of shareholder oversight. Principal/agent problems can be costly. Managers have been observed to "satisfice" profits, that is, they seek to achieve an adequate rate of return for shareholders and then divert the firms' resources to their personal ends (Choper, Coffee, and Gilson 2004; Clotfelter 1985).

Unsustainable CSR. Under many conditions, firms that participate in costly CSR activities will have to raise prices, reduce wages and other costs, accept smaller profits, or pay smaller dividends—and accept the economic consequences. For example, a firm's stock price may decline until it is proportional to returns, and attracting new capital may be difficult because returns are below market averages. Other short-term economic consequences may include loss of market share, increased insurance costs, increased borrowing costs, and loss of reputation. In the long term, the firm may face shareholder litigation, corporate takeover, or closure. Such consequences simply illustrate the general proposition and observation that (financially) inefficient firms tend to disappear (Alchian 1950; Altman 1999).

This process of economic survival of the fittest suggests that firms that engage in unsustainable CSR may find themselves being pushed out of business. The forces of globalization only increase this pressure. Given the seemingly inevitable outcome of this process, why would any firm choose to participate in unsustainable CSR activities? First, principal/agent problems may lead managers to make decisions that commit the firm to short-term CSR actions, even if those activities will not be continued in the long run. Second, managers may misjudge the potential profitability of certain actions, leading them to invest in actions that benefit society but harm the firm's bottom line. Neither the managers' probability assessments nor their motivations are transparent to outside observers, making it very difficult to distinguish between them (Baron 2006).

Economic, Structural, and Organizational Constraints

A variety of factors influence the economic actors who make decisions about engaging in CSR activities. These factors include managerial incentive and monitoring constraints, and organizational structure and culture.

Whether or not firms are able and likely to engage in CSR depends on managers' incentives and constraints, which in turn are determined by managers' preferences, ethical beliefs, contracts, and goals. The most direct incentives managers face are their employment agreements. For managers whose compensation is designed to align their incentives with those of shareholders, sacrificing profits means reducing their own compensation. In the United States, chief executive officers (CEOs) are usually paid in a mixture of stocks, stock options, and salary, with their compensation linked to explicit measures of the firm's performance (Prendergast 1999). But the relationship between compensation and firm performance may be close to flat at some levels of firm performance, which means CEOs may be able to trade off compensation against CSR activities at a rate they judge acceptable.

Organizational culture may also be significant (Howard-Grenville, Nash, and Coglianese 2006). Organizational identity influences how individuals within the firm view the purpose of the firm, what it stands for, and its future goals. Organizational self-monitoring affects how an organization interacts with outside stakeholders. Firms that are more self-conscious about their image may expend greater effort to communicate and interact in "socially appropriate" ways than other firms, even if their core values related to socially beneficial behavior are similar.

Other factors may also affect whether firms can sacrifice profits in the social interest. For example, firm size appears to matter, with evidence that larger firms can sacrifice proportionately more profits (Adams and Hardwick 1998). Further, public visibility may increase pressure on firms to participate in CSR activities: firms in notoriously "dirty" industries may find themselves under heavy pressure from public advocacy groups to reduce their emissions or to participate in offsetting activities (Brown, Helland, and Kiholm Smith 2006). Finally, firms cannot participate in CSR if their work provides no scope for it. CSR activities are simply much more plausible for firms in certain industries (Porter and Kramer 2006).

Do Firms Sacrifice Profits in the Social Interest?

As described above, there are specific circumstances in which firms can sacrifice profits in the social interest without suffering serious adverse economic consequences. Whether they actually do so is another matter. This section discusses empirical evidence about the existence of such profit-sacrificing behavior.

Before interpreting the evidence, it is important to be aware of several challenges to making inferences about CSR. First, it is difficult to test whether firms' actions actually go beyond ordinary compliance with environmental regulations. Data on environmental performance are typically very limited, and because of the difficulty of observing appropriate counterfactuals, it is difficult to demonstrate that firms sacrifice profits. Whole industries often engage in CSR together, leaving behind no comparison group. Even when firms act individually, it is difficult to know whether unobservable characteristics explain differences in both socially responsible activity and profitability. Studies that link profitability to CSR practices are particularly vulnerable to this problem. For example, because many high-technology companies have low pollutant emissions (in contrast with firms engaged in electricity generation, heavy manufacturing, or resource extraction), the high-tech boom in the 1990s created a perceived but spurious correlation between market measures of "socially responsible business practices" and stock returns. Furthermore, as discussed above, there are a variety of ways in which firms can profit from investments in socially beneficial projects. Finally, the effects of many actions differ in the short versus the long term, with a short-term decrease in profits followed by a more-than-compensatory increase in the long-term profits. Thus, demonstrating that an action has truly sacrificed profits in the social interest is exceptionally difficult.

Of course, distinguishing between motivations and outcomes is even more difficult. Although most firms are likely motivated by a combination of social and financial concerns, managers may cite social responsibility as the motive for actions that were actually driven by profitability. Or managers may use profitability to justify socially responsible business choices, even when those choices result in smaller profits (Baron 2006).

Do Firms Overcomply?

A first step in evaluating whether firms participate in CSR is to determine whether they overcomply with regulations or participate in other costly activities that benefit society. We consider five sources of evidence: voluntary government programs, voluntary industry initiatives, voluntary action by individual firms, corporate charitable donations, and shareholder resolutions.

Voluntary Government Programs. In principle, the willingness of a firm to participate in a voluntary government program could be evidence of CSR activity. A variety of studies have evaluated the determinants of participation in voluntary government programs (e.g., Borck, Coglianese, and Nash 2006). Several patterns emerge. First, larger firms are more likely to participate in voluntary programs. Second, participation is more likely for firms that either produce final goods or experience more pressure from NGOs and consumers. Third, firms with higher emissions or poor compliance records are more likely to participate in voluntary programs. And fourth, participation may be positively influenced by factors such as industry association membership, R&D expenditures, organizational culture, and managerial discretion. However, there is no consensus that voluntary government programs have generated environmental benefits net of the opportunity cost of the resources required to implement them.

Voluntary Industry Initiatives. In addition to voluntary programs administered by governments, industry associations have created voluntary initiatives. For example, the Responsible Care program, established in 1989 by the US Chemical Manufacturers Association, requires participating facilities to adopt ten guiding principles and six codes of management practices related to the environmental and social dimensions of community interactions, facility management, and customer and supplier interactions. By and large, the program was ineffective because it did not provide strong incentives for compliance (King and Lenox 2000). Similarly, the Institute of Nuclear Power Operations (INPO) was created in the wake of the 1979 reactor meltdown at Three Mile Island, a nuclear power plant in Pennsylvania. A third example is Sustainable Slopes, a voluntary program for reporting and encouraging improved environmental performance at ski resorts. The evidence indicates that firms took advantage of positive publicity, although the actual environmental benefits are debatable (Rivera and de Leon 2004).

In general, industry-sponsored programs exhibit the same kinds of participation patterns as government-administered voluntary programs. That is, larger firms, more prominent firms, and firms with poorer environmental records are more likely to participate. Again, there is no systematic evidence of positive environmental impacts net of social costs.

Voluntary Action by Individual Firms. An indicator of firm participation in independently developed CSR activities is whether firms adopt CSR plans, environmental management systems, or other plans that seek to encourage socially beneficial decision making within the firm. These plans often have the nominal goal of taking a holistic management approach towards compliance with environmental and safety laws, contractual and voluntary environmental obligations, management of environmental and social impacts and risk, and other issues (Clark 2005). These systems may benefit firms by allowing them to manage the business aspects of environmental and social issues, but they may also serve as a mechanism for firms to improve environmental quality or otherwise benefit society.

One such mechanism is ISO 14001, an international standard that provides guidelines for monitoring environmental outputs, controlling environmental processes, and improving environmental performance (US Environmental Protection Agency 2006). To demonstrate that its environmental management system complies with the standard, a business (or any other organization) must receive a third-party audit. Capital intensity, intensity of competition, and dependence on overseas markets are all positively associated with voluntary compliance with the standard (Chapple et al. 2001).

The best source of evidence about whether firms participate in CSR activities on their own initiative is independent studies of socially responsible actions. Perhaps surprisingly, many studies of individual beyond-compliance behavior analyze firms in developing countries (e.g., Hartman, Huq, and Wheeler 1995; Hettige et al. 1996; Pargal and Wheeler 1996; Blackman and Bannister 1998; Dasgupta, Hettige, and Wheeler 2000). One possible reason for this focus is that firms in industrialized countries are subject to a wide range of environmental regulations that make it difficult to judge whether their actions are legally required, risk-averting, or voluntarily beyond compliance. In contrast, in the developing world, pollution regulations maybe poorly enforced or even nonexistent, making it easier to identify individual beyond-compliance behavior.

Corporate Charitable Contributions. Evidence of corporations making financial contributions to charity supports the general hypothesis that corporations can and do commit corporate resources to CSR. Average contributions as a percent of net income before taxes increased, from less than 0.5 percent in the 1930s to 1.1 percent in the 1960s and 1970s (Harris and Klepper 1976). In general, CEOs and other high-level corporate officers have a high degree of control over the amount and destination of corporate charitable contributions, even if their company has established a separate charitable foundation (Kahn 1997). But charitable giving can be curtailed by debtholders (Brown, Helland, and Kiholm Smith 2006; Adams and Hardwick 1998). Overall, the evidence shows that charitable giving is more likely when financial and monitoring constraints are weak. Corporate charitable giving is also sensitive to firm income and marginal tax rates (Clotfelter 1985).

Shareholder Resolutions. Shareholders sometimes request that corporations comply with ethical or other requirements. In 2005, the shareholders of public US corporations proposed 348 resolutions on social and environmental issues, of which 177 reached a proxy vote (Social Investment Forum 2006). On average, these resolutions have received support from 10–12 percent of all votes cast. Of the 25 social policy resolutions in the United States that gained the highest percentage of votes during the years 2003–2005, only six gained a majority of all votes cast. But winning even a modest share of votes in a shareholder resolution can influence management policies.

Is There Evidence of Profit-Sacrificing Behavior?

According to our strict definition of CSR, beyond-compliance behavior is a necessary but not sufficient condition for CSR because, under some conditions, such behavior can be profitable. One way to measure the profit sacrificed by socially responsible companies would be to calculate the difference in profitability between firms that do and do not participate in socially responsible activities. In fact, a large literature, consisting of at least seventeen review articles, has explored this relationship.[8]

The most recent and comprehensive review is by Margolis, Elfenbein, and Walsh (2007). In a meta-analysis of the results from 167 studies of the relationship between financial performance and socially responsible business practices (ignoring the mechanism and direction of causality), they find that 27 percent of the analyses show a positive relationship, 58 percent show a non-significant relationship, and 2 percent show a negative relationship.[9] Margolis, Elfenbein, and Walsh argue that the evidence indicates that CSR, in general, has little effect on profitability. However, they note that there is stronger evidence to suggest some causality in the opposite direction: companies that are profitable are more likely to engage in more CSR activities.

The finding that there is little relationship between CSR and profitability is consistent with a market equilibrium in which firms invest in socially responsible projects until the marginal returns decline to the overall market rate of return. In this situation, investing in CSR is not profitable (in the sense that it does not generate economic rents), but neither is it a losing proposition. Instead it means that for most firms, CSR "pays for itself."

These conclusions require a number of caveats. First, when evaluating studies of the relationship between social responsibility and profitability, it is important to keep in mind that not all companies that are classified as socially responsible actually sacrifice profits. Many operate in industries, such as software development, that by their very nature have little environmental or social impact. Second, many of the measures of CSR used in such studies are not consistent with CSR as we define it in this article. Thus, measured effects on profitability may have more to do with advertising, charitable contributions, or other tangentially relevant factors than with CSR.

In summary, evidence on sacrificing profits in the social interest is lacking. The bulk of the available evidence suggests that most firms view socially responsible actions in the same way that they view more traditional business activities, such as advertising and R&D. Instead of altruistically sacrificing profits, they engage in a more limited—but more profitable—set of socially

---

[8]See, for example, Aupperle, Carroll, and Hatfield 1985; Wood and Jones 1996; Griffin and Mahon 1997; Orlitzky, Schmidt, and Rynes 2003.

[9]Thirteen percent did not report a sample size that could be used to test significance.

beneficial activities that contributes to their financial goals. Hence, although proponents of sustainable business practices may argue that being environmentally responsible will inevitably lead to higher profits in the long term, the relationship between socially responsible activities and profitability may be best characterized as *some* firms will generate long-term profits from *some* socially responsible activities *some* of the time (Reinhardt 2000).

Should Firms Sacrifice Profits in the Social Interest?

Even if firms may, can, and do sacrifice profits in the social interest, an important normative question remains, namely, *should* they? In other words, is it really in the broadly defined social interest for firms to carry out such activity? There are two main approaches to answering this question. First, we can compare firms' actual CSR choices with the CSR alternatives available to them. For any firm, such alternatives include a broad range of projects addressing various private and public issues, costing different amounts, and resulting in varying degrees of environmental protection and profitability. For example, a power plant could reduce its emissions of carbon dioxide, sulfur dioxide, or particulate matter; switch to a renewable source of fuel; implement a job training program to benefit local community members; make a donation to a charitable organization; or take any number of other "socially responsible" actions. The question of interest here is whether firms' actual CSR choices are likely to be optimal relative to available alternatives.

A second approach takes a public policy perspective, where a comparison is made between allowing CSR (i.e., permitting firms to sacrifice profits in the social interest) and prohibiting CSR (i.e., requiring firms exclusively to maximize profits for shareholders). To evaluate these two approaches, we employ a variety of criteria, including social welfare and legal, political, and social considerations.

Social Welfare

In the context of CSR, the social welfare criterion suggests that: (1) firms should invest in projects that produce the highest level of social welfare; and (2) it is preferable to allow CSR if aggregate welfare is likely to be higher when CSR is allowed than when it is prohibited.

The benefits of CSR include direct welfare gains to individuals, such as asthmatics living near a power plant that voluntarily reduces its emissions. More broadly, if firms voluntarily internalize externalities, a more efficient allocation of resources may result. Of course, there is no reason, *ex ante*, to anticipate that firms will reduce externality-producing activities to efficient levels.

The direct costs of CSR are the loss of consumer surplus resulting from firms producing less output at higher cost and hence at higher prices. In addition, shareholders receive reduced financial returns. On the other hand, some shareholders may gain utility from the knowledge that their profits have been invested in socially responsible projects.

There are a number of reasons to believe that firms do not make socially optimal CSR investments, in the sense of choosing activities that generate the greatest net social benefits, subject to budgetary constraints. This is because firms' CSR decisions are influenced by a number of factors that are unrelated to social benefits and costs.

First, firms' CSR investment choices are influenced by managers' personal preferences and firm characteristics. For example, some managers may favor building art museums, while others favor the provision of affordable housing. This idiosyncratic element of personal preference is particularly likely if principal/agent issues drive CSR (Butler and McChesney 1999). Similarly, firms' choices about CSR activities are affected by the nature of their industry, firm size, technical capabilities, and relevant expertise, geographic location, and existing regulatory limits. To the extent that these factors are unrelated to the social benefits and costs of CSR, their influence on firm decisions about CSR may result in social inefficiency.

Second, although firms may be well informed about the private costs of CSR, they may have little experience evaluating its social benefits, leading them to choose inefficient levels of environmental protection effort. Third, firms may fail to consider alternative mechanisms to achieve their social goals. For example, firms may be able to achieve higher social returns by donating profits to charities, which are dedicated exclusively to the task of improving social welfare and thus presumably are well suited to the task. If this is the case, then firms that fund CSR activities effectively "crowd out" their own donations to more efficient charities (Graff Zivin and Small 2005). Finally, choice of CSR activity is affected by the firm's ability to sacrifice profits. Firms that are the most profitable are also the most able to sacrifice profits in the public interest. However, the opportunity cost of sacrificing profits may also be greatest for these firms, assuming they could otherwise invest the resources in their businesses and earn similarly high returns.

Although there are reasons to doubt the optimality of firms' decisions about CSR, there are also reasons to believe that firms' CSR investment decisions may increase welfare. First, firms have access to private information about their current and future pollution activities, including control costs. Such information can lead firms to identify better policies than less well-informed government agencies. Second, firms have relevant expertise and operational capacity. Third, government policies are driven by a variety of objectives, only one of which may be maximizing social welfare. Hence, compared with the counterfactual of prohibiting CSR but leaving government policy otherwise unchanged, allowing CSR may generate higher net social benefits.

Many types of potential CSR activities—from reducing particulate emissions to preserving open space—are mandated to some degree by federal, state, or local laws and regulations. To the extent that such regulations require a level of environmental protection that is below the socially optimal level, additional corporate investment in these activities can increase social welfare (if incremental social benefits exceed incremental social costs). In addition, there may be socially responsible activities that address environmental issues that are unregulated but of significant scientific or political concern (e.g., global climate change). In such cases (i.e., in the absence of government policies), CSR activities may lead to positive net social benefits. However, given that it appears to be relatively rare for firms to actually sacrifice profits in the social interest, the overall net welfare flow from CSR, whether positive or negative, is unlikely to be large.

Legal, Political, and Social Considerations

Although legality is not synonymous with social desirability (as evidenced by the legality of many socially undesirable activities), some observers would surely identify legality as a normative criterion by which to judge many actions. In the second section, we argued that in the United States and other common law countries, sacrificing profits in the social interest is not strictly legal, although in practice CSR is not prohibited because of the business judgment rule and problems of enforcement.

One argument that can be made against CSR is that it is not a democratic process. There is no particular reason to believe that society should prefer firms' choices and priorities to the choices and priorities of a democratic government. Some observers might also argue that corporations already dominate too many aspects of modern life, and that it would be undesirable for them to control the supply of public goods as well.

Under a broader interpretation of the idea of social responsibility, however, it can be argued that businesses have a moral commitment to hold themselves to higher ethical standards and to engage in activities that benefit society. In fact, in a poll of citizens' attitudes towards the responsibility of businesses in 23 developed and developing countries, public opinion seems to support the notion that corporations in the West should "set higher ethical standards and help build a better society." In countries such as China and Kazakhstan, however, the notion that corporations should "make profits, pay taxes, create jobs, and obey all laws" dominates (Environics International Ltd. 1999).

The Special Case of Developing Countries

Given that economic, social, and environmental conditions in developing countries are so different from those in industrialized countries, one would expect the answers to normative questions about CSR to also be different. For example, environmental regulations in the developing world are often not well enforced. Hence, many relatively cost-effective interventions that have already been implemented in industrialized countries may still be available to businesses that operate in the developing world. This suggests that CSR could lead to significant gains in net social welfare.

Other concerns about CSR arise in the developing country context. Precisely because legal and contractual systems often operate poorly in developing countries, it is important to prevent activities that could erode the basis for future economic growth. Thus, strong investor protections may be particularly desirable in developing economies (Marinov and Heiman 1998) to help buttress the political viability of privatization and market-based systems. Allowing managers to divert profits to socially responsible projects means giving managers substantial discretion. However, there is also the risk that this discretion could tempt managers to use corporate resources for personal gain.

Summary and Conclusions

This article has examined the concept of firms sacrificing profits in the social interest in the environmental realm. In this section, we summarize our answers to the four questions posed at the outset: *May* they do so within the scope of their fiduciary responsibilities to their shareholders? *Can* they do so on a sustainable basis? *Do* firms behave this way? And, finally, *should* firms carry out such profit-sacrificing activities?

Our starting point for examining the first question—may they—was the prevailing view among economists and business scholars that corporate directors nave a fiduciary duty to maximize profits for shareholders. Surprisingly, the legal basis for this view is not very strong. Although the judicial record is supportive of a duty to maximize profits for shareholders, it leaves room for firms to sacrifice profits in the public interest. Moreover, the "business judgment rule" effectively protects many public-minded managerial actions from successful legal challenge.

Are firms in the United States prohibited from sacrificing profits in the public interest? And if so, is the prohibition enforceable? The answers to these two sub-questions appear to be "maybe" and "no," respectively. US corporate law is consistent with the shareholder primacy model, but as long as managers claim some plausible connection to future profitability, the business judgment rule grants them leeway to commit corporate resources to projects that benefit the public.

Just because the legal system may allow firms to sacrifice profits in the social interest does not mean that firms *can* do so on a sustainable basis in the face of competitive pressures. Under many conditions, firms that participate in costly CSR activities will have to raise prices, reduce wages and other costs, accept smaller profits, or pay smaller dividends—and accept the economic consequences. After taking such measures, a firm's stock price may decline until proportional to returns, and attracting new capital may be difficult because returns are below market averages. Other short-term economic consequences may include loss of market share, increased insurance costs, increased borrowing costs, and loss of reputation. In the long term, the firm may face shareholder litigation, corporate takeover, or closure.

This process of economic survival of the fittest suggests that firms that engage in unsustainable CSR may find themselves being pushed out of business. Given the seemingly inevitable outcome of this process, why would any firms choose to participate in unsustainable CSR activities? First, the firms that engage (or say they engage) in CSR are often active in markets that are imperfect or distorted by government intervention, so that they are protected from Friedman's evolutionary imperatives. Second, principal/agent problems may lead managers to make decisions that commit the firm to short-term CSR actions, even if those activities will not be continued in the long run.

Despite a large and growing literature on CSR, evidence of firms actually sacrificing profits in the social interest is lacking. The bulk of the available evidence suggests that most firms view socially responsible actions in the same way that they view more traditional business activities. Instead of altruistically sacrificing profits, they engage in a more limited—but more profitable—set of socially beneficial activities that contributes to their financial goals.

Although proponents of sustainable business practices may argue that being environmentally responsible will inevitably lead to higher profits in the long-term, the relationship between socially responsible activities and profitability may be best characterized as *some* firms will generate long-term profits from *some* socially responsible activities *some* of the time.

Is it in the social interest for firms to engage in CSR? More to the point, should governments allow such activity? To the extent that existing regulations require a level of environmental protection that is below the socially optimal level, additional corporate investment in CSR activities may increase social welfare. In this context, CSR should be viewed as a complement to, rather than a substitute for, increasingly effective government regulation.

REFERENCES

Adams, Mike, and Phillip Hardwick. 1998. An analysis of corporate donations: United Kingdom evidence. *Journal of Management Studies* 35(5): 641–54.

Alchian, A. A. 1950. Uncertainty, evolution, and economic theory. *Journal of Political Economy* LVIII: 211–21.

Altman, Morris. 1999. The methodology of economics and the survivor principle revisited and revised: Some welfare and public policy implications of modeling the economic agent. *Review of Social Economy* 57(4): 427–49.

Aupperle, Kenneth, Archie Carroll, and John Hatfield. 1985. An empirical examination of the relationship between corporate social responsibility and profitability. *Academy of Management Journal* 28(2): 446–63.

Baron, David P. 2006. *Business and Its Environment*, 5th ed. Upper Saddle River, NJ: Prentice-Hall.

Berle, A. A. Jr. 1932. For whom corporate managers are trustees: A note. *Harvard Law Review* 45(8): 1365–72.

Blackman, Allen, and Geoffrey Bannister. 1998. (A community pressure and clean technology in the informal sector: An econometric analysis of the adoption of propane by traditional Mexican brickmakers. *Journal of Environmental Economics and Management* 35(1): 1–21.

Blair, Margaret M., and Lynn A. Stout. 1999. A team production theory of corporate law. *Virginia Law Review* 85(March): 247.

Blomquist, Robert. 2006. Six thinking hats for the lorax: Corporate responsibility and the environment. *Georgetown International Environmental Law Review* 18(4): 691–705.

Borck, Jonathan, Cary Coglianese, and Jennifer Nash. 2006. Why do they join? An exploration of business participation in voluntary environmental programs. In *Beyond Compliance: Business Decision Making and the US EPA's Performance Track Program."* Regulatory Policy Program Report RPP-10. Cambridge, MA: John F. Kennedy School of Government, Harvard University.

Borok, Tuvia. 2003. A modern approach to redefining in the best interests of the corporation. *Windsor Review of Legal and Social Issues* 15(March): 113.

Branson, Douglas M. 2002. The rule that isn't a rule—The business judgment rule. *Valparaiso University Law Review* 36(Summer): 631.

Brown, William, Eric Helland, and Janet Kiholm Smith. 2006. Corporate philanthropic practices. *Journal of Corporate Finance* 12(5): 855–77.

Butler, Henry N., and Fred S. McChesney. 1999. Why they give at the office: Shareholder welfare and corporate philanthropy in the contractual theory of the corporation. *Cornell Law Review* 84(July): 1195.

Chapple, Wendy, Andrew Cooke, Vaughn Gait, and David Paton. 2001. The determinants of voluntary investment decisions. *Managerial and Decision Economics* 22(8): 453–63.

Choper, Jesse H., John C. Coffee, and Ronald J. Gilson. 2004. *Cases and materials on corporations*, 6th ed. London: Little, Brown & Co.

Clark, Matthew. 2005. Corporate environmental behavior research: Informing environmental policy. *Structural Change and Economic Dynamics* 16(3): 422–31.

Clark, Robert. 1986. *Corporate Law.* Boston, MA: Little, Brown.

Clotfelter, Charles. 1985. *Federal Tax Policy and Charitable Giving.* Chicago: University of Chicago Press.

Corfield, Andrea. 1998. The stakeholder theory and its future in Australian corporate governance: A preliminary analysis. *Bond Law Review* 10(2): 213.

Cox, James, and Thomas Hazen. 2003. Corporations. New York: Aspen Publishers.

Dasgupta, Susmita, Hemamala Hettige, and David Wheeler. 2000. What improves environmental compliance? Evidence from Mexican industry. *A Journal of Environment Economics and Management* 39(1): 39–66.

Dodd, E. Merrick Jr. 1932. For whom are corporate managers trustees? *Harvard Law Review* 45(7):1145–63.

Donohue, John. 2005. Does greater managerial freedom to sacrifice profits lead to higher social welfare? In *Environmental Protection and the Social Responsibility of Firms*, eds. Bruce Hay, Robert Stavins, and Richard Vietor. Washington, DC: Resources for the Future.

Easterbrook, Frank, and Fischel Daniel. 1991. *The economic structure of corporate law.* Cambridge, MA: Harvard University Press.

Ehrlich, Craig. 2005. Is Business ethics necessary? *DePaul Business & Commercial Law Journal* 4(Fall): 55.

Elhauge, Einer. 2005. Corporate managers' operational discretion to sacrifice corporate profits in the public interest. In *Environmental Protection and the Social Responsibility of Firms*, eds. Bruce Hay, Robert Stavins, and Richard Vietor. Washington, DC: Resources for the Future.

Environics International Ltd. 1999. The millennium poll on corporate social responsibility: Executive briefing. Available at www.globescan.com/news_archives/ MPExec Brief.pdf (accessed 6/13/11).

Fanto, James A. 1998. The role of corporate law in French corporate governance. *Cornell International Law Journal* 31:31.

Fisch, Jill E. 2006. Measuring efficiency in corporate law: The role of shareholder primacy. *Iowa Journal of Corporation Law* 31(Spring): 637.

Francois, Patrick. 2004. Making a difference: Labor donations in the production of public goods. CMPO, University of Bristol, Working Paper Series No. 04/093.

Frank, Robert. 1996. Can socially responsible firms survive in a competitive market? In *Codes of Conduct: Behavioral Research into Business Ethics*, eds. David Messick and Ann Tenbrunsel, 214–27. New York: Russell Sage Foundation.

Friedman, Milton. 1970. The social responsibility of business is to increase its profits. *New York Times Magazine*. September 13.

Frye, Melissa B., Edward Nelling, and Elizabeth Webb. 2006. Executive compensation in socially responsible firms. *Corporate Governance: An International Review* 14(5): 446–55.

Gabaldon, Theresa A. 2006. Like a fish needs a bicycle: Public corporations and their shareholders. *Maryland Law Review* 65:538.

Graff Zivin, Joshua, and Arthur Small. 2005. A Modigliani–Miller theory of altruistic corporate social responsibility. *B. E. Journals in Economic Analysis and Policy: Topics in Economic Analysis and Policy* 5(1): 1–19.

Griffin, Jennifer, and John Mahon. 1997. The corporate social performance and corporate financial performance debate: Twenty-five years of incomparable research. *Business and Society* 36(1): 5–31.

Harris, James, and Anne Klepper. 1976. Corporate philanthropic public service activities. New York: The Conference Board.

Hartman, Raymond, Mainul Huq, and David Wheeler. 1995. Why paper mills clean up: Determinants of pollution abatement in four Asian countries. World Bank Policy Research Department Working Paper 1710.

Hay, Bruce L., Robert N. Stavins, and Richard H. K. Vietor. 2005. The four questions of corporate social responsibility: May they, can they, do they, should they? In *Environmental Protection and the Social Responsibility of Firms*, eds. Bruce Hay, Robert Stavins, and Richard Vietor. Washington, DC: Resources for the Future.

Heinkel, Robert, Alan Kraus, and Josef Zechner. 2001. The effect of green investment on corporate behavior. *Journal of Financial and Quantitative Analysis* 36(4): 431–49.

Hettige, Hemamala, Mainul Huq, Sheoli Pargal, and David Wheeler. 1996. Determinants of pollution abatement in developing countries: Evidence from South and Southeast Asia. *World Development* 24(12): 1891–1904.

Howard-Grenville, Jennifer Nash, and Cary Coglianese. 2006. Constructing the license to operate: Internal factors and their influence on corporate environmental decisions. In *Beyond Compliance: Business Decision Making and the US EPA's Performance Track Program*. Regulatory Policy Program Report

RPP-10. Cambridge, MA: John F. Kennedy School of Government, Harvard University.

Jaffe, Adam B., Steven R. Peterson, Paul R. Portney, and Robert N. Stavins. 1995. Environmental regulation and the competitiveness of US manufacturing: What does the evidence tells us? *Journal of Economic Literature* 33:132–63.

Jensen, Kim, Paul Jakus, Burt English, and Jamey Menard. 2002. Willingness to pay for environmentally certified hardwood products by Tennessee consumers. Study Series No. 01–02. Department of Agricultural Economics, University of Tennessee.

Jensen, Michael, and William Meckling. 1976. Theory of the firm: Managerial behavior, agency costs and ownership structure. *Journal of Financial Economics* 3(4): 305–60.

Kahn, Faith Stevelman. 1997. Pandora's box: Managerial discretion and the problem of corporate philanthropy. *UCLA Law Review* 44(February): 579.

King, Andrew, and Michael Lenox. 2000. Industry self-regulation without sanctions: The chemical industry's responsible care program. *Academy of Management Journal* 43(4): 698–716.

Lee, Ian B. 2006. Efficiency and ethics in the debate about shareholder primacy. *Delaware Journal of Corporate Law* 31: 533.

Lee, Ian B. 2005. Corporate law, profit maximization, and the responsible shareholder. *Stanford Journal of Law, Business, and Finance* 10(Spring): 31.

Lynch-Fannon, Irene. 2007. The corporate social responsibility movement and law's empire: Is there a conflict? *Northern Ireland Legal Quarterly* 58(1).

Lyon, Thomas, and John Maxwell. 2004. *Corporate Environmentalism and Public Policy*. Cambridge, UK: Cambridge University Press.

Lyon, Thomas, and John Maxwell. Corporate Social Responsibility and the Environment: A Theoretical Perspective. *Review of Environmental Economics and Policy* doi:10.1093/reep/ren004.

Margolis, Joshua, Hillary Elfenbein, and James Walsh. 2007. Does it pay to be good? A meta-analysis and redirection of research on the relationship between corporate social and financial performance. Working Paper, Harvard Business School.

Marinov, Boris, and Bruce Heiman. 1998. Company law and corporate governance renewal in transition economies: The Bulgarian dilemma. *European Journal of Law and Economics* 6: 231–61.

Miwa, Yoshiro. 1999. CSR: Dangerous and harmful, though maybe not irrelevant. *Cornell Law Review* 84(July): 1227–54.

Mohr, Lois, Deborah Webb, and Katherine Harris. 2001. Do consumers expect companies to be socially responsible? The impact of corporate social responsibility on buying behavior. *Journal of Consumer Affairs* 35(1): 45–72.

Orlitzky, Marc, Frank Schmidt, and Sara Rynes. 2003. Corporate social and financial performance: A meta-analysis. *Organization Studies* 24(3): 403–41.

Pargal, Sheoli, and David Wheeler. 1996. Informal regulation of industrial pollution in developing countries: Evidence from Indonesia. *Journal of Political Economy* 104(6): 1314–27.

Porter, Michael, and Mark Kramer. 2006. The link between competitive advantage and corporate social responsibility. *Harvard Business Review* 84(12): 78–92.

Portney, Paul. 2005. Corporate social responsibility: An economic and public policy perspective. In *Environmental Protection and the Social Responsibility of Firms*, eds. Bruce Hay, Robert Stavins, and Richard Vietor. Washington, DC: Resources for the Future.

Portney, Paul R. The (Not So) New Corporate Social Responsibility: An Empirical Perspective. *Review of Environmental Economics and Policy* doi: 10.1093/reep/ren003.

Prendergast, Candice. 1999. The provision of incentives in firms. *Journal of Economic Literature* 37(March): 7.

Reinhardt, Forest. 2000. Down to earth. Boston, MA: Harvard Business School Press.

Reinhardt, Forest. 2005. Environmental protection and the social responsibility of firms: Perspectives from the business literature. In *Environmental Protection and the Social Responsibility of Firms*, eds. Bruce Hay, Robert Stavins, and Richard Vietor. Washington, DC: Resources for the Future.

Rivera, Jorge, and Peter deLeon. 2004. Is Greener Whiter? Voluntary environmental performance of western ski areas. *Policy Studies Journal* 32(3): 417–37.

Roe, Mark. 2000. Political preconditions to separating ownership from corporate control. *Stanford Law Review* 53(December): 539.

Scalise, Elisa. 2005. The code for corporate citizenship: States should amend statutes governing corporations and enable corporations to be good citizens. *Seattle University Law Review* 29(Fall): 275.

Sheehy, Benedict. 2005. Scrooge the reluctant stakeholder: Theoretical problems in the shareholder-stakeholder debate. *University of Miami Business Law Review* 14(Fall/Winter):193.

Social Investment Forum. 2006. 2005 Report on socially responsible investing Trends in the United States: Ten year review. Washington, DC: Social Investment Forum.

Springer, Jonathan. 1999. Corporate law, corporate constituency statues: Hollow hopes and false fears. In *New York University School of Law Annual Survey of American Law* 1999: 85.

Sutton, Michele. 2004. Between a rock and a judicial hard place: Corporate social responsibility reporting and potential legal liability under *Kasky v. Nike*. *University of Missouri-Kansas City School of Law Review* 72(Summer): 1159.

US Environmental Protection Agency. 2006. Environmental management systems/ISO 14001—Frequently Asked Questions. Available at www.epa.gov/owm/iso14001/isofaq.htm (accessed 6/13/11).

Vogel, David. 2006. *The Market for Virtue*. Washington, DC: Brookings Institution Press.

Wood, Donna, and Raymond Jones. 1996. Research in corporate social performance: What have we learned? In *Corporate Philanthropy at the Crossroads*, eds. Dwight Burlingame and Dennis Young. Bloomington: Indiana University Press.

23 The (Not So) New Corporate Social Responsibility: An Empirical Perspective*

Paul R. Portney

Paul R. Portney is Professor of Economics, Halle Chair in Leadership and Dean, Eller College of Management at the University of Arizona.

Introduction

It is virtually impossible to open the business section of the *New York Times,* the *Wall Street Journal,* the *Economist,* or any business publication today without seeing mention of measures being taken by some company to become more "socially responsible." Although such measures can take many forms, generally they entail *voluntary* actions by firms to reduce their energy consumption and/or discharges of air, water or other forms of pollution; make their products safer or healthier; improve working conditions for their employees, either at home or abroad; or contribute in some way, either financially or in-kind, to the communities in which their facilities are located. In some cases, of course, companies may engage in outright philanthropy at the national or even international level, as when airfreight companies made planes available at no charge to airlift emergency supplies to the victims of Hurricane Katrina, or when pharmaceutical companies supplied free or below-cost drugs to AIDS victims in Africa. Merely citing such examples is a reminder of just how often we see stories about corporate social responsibility (CSR).

The word "voluntary" in the previous paragraph is important. This is because we can't have a serious discussion about CSR unless we focus on the things companies do that go beyond what is required under prevailing laws and regulations. To be sure, as economists from Adam Smith to Milton Friedman have pointed out, even companies that do nothing more than observe all the rules still do extraordinarily *useful* things by providing the goods and services their customers want while at the same time creating jobs for their employees and outlets for personal savings. But if CSR is to

"The (Not So) New Corporate Social Responsibility: An Empirical Perspective" by Paul R. Portney. *Review of Environmental Economics and Policy* 2. 2008. Pp. 261–275. Reprinted with permission.

*For then very helpful comments on a previous version, I thank Chris Portney, Robert Stavins, Suzy Leonard, and an anonymous referee.

mean anything at all, it ought to be reserved for those activities that go beyond legal requirements.

For this reason, I have previously defined CSR to mean "a consistent pattern, at the very least, of private firms doing more than they are required to do under applicable laws and regulations governing the environment, worker safety and health, and investments in the communities in which they operate" (Portney 2005).[1] With the benefit of hindsight, I would have added to this definition efforts by companies to make their products safer than required and would have clarified, also, that by "private firms" I meant not only those that are privately owned, but also those that are publicly traded. I might also have added something about corporate governance. A number of firms have undertaken efforts to make their governance policies more transparent (especially those that relate to executive compensation) and their boards of directors more accountable to shareholders. For some, such efforts are an integral component of CSR. Nevertheless, the definition above is the one I will use throughout this article.

It is important to note that this definition is not restrictive enough for certain observers, because it includes beyond-compliance activities that may also add to a firm's stream of profits. For instance, Elhague (2005) argues that the only actions on the part of corporations that are worthy of mention in the same breath as CSR are those that are "profit sacrificing," that is, those expenditures or investments that the company knows will *not* recoup their costs. As I will argue below, such actions may in some sense be the most interesting to consider, let alone being the most controversial. Nevertheless, the point here is that if we confine our discussion of CSR only to those cases where a corporation *knows* it is sacrificing profits, then that discussion will be an awfully short one, indeed.

Based on my definition of CSR, it would appear that beyond-compliance activities are almost the norm today. Researchers have shown this to be the case in the environmental arena (e.g., Burtraw and Mansur 1999). Moreover, it is difficult to find any decent-sized company that does *not* have some type of philanthropic program. This does not mean, of course, that all firms are in compliance with all applicable laws and regulations all the time, or that every company gives to the communities in which it has facilities. To the contrary, there are numerous reports of environmental or workplace safety violations (e.g., the series of mining disasters in the United States in 2007), though this is principally because these are far more newsworthy than reports of "still another year of compliance at XYZ Corp." It may even be the case that firms that do much more than required in certain areas—occupational safety and health, for instance—cut things close in others, such as their environmental emissions or other standards. Nevertheless, examples of CSR, at least as defined here, abound.

---

[1]This article draws heavily on the earlier one, though it also updates and extends it in several respects.

This article is part of a three-article symposium on Corporate Social Responsibility and the Environment. The article by Reinhardt, Stavins, and Vietor (2008) introduces and examines the key issues and questions that surround environmental CSR, while the article by Lyon and Maxwell (2008) discusses the theoretical literature that has emerged on this topic. The purpose of the current article is to raise and attempt to answer four questions. First, why do firms engage in CSR? Second, what does the empirical evidence reveal about the impact of CSR? Third, how new is the CSR phenomenon? Fourth, and finally, how should we feel about CSR as it is being practiced today? To give away the story a bit, I believe that while CSR gets far more attention today than it has in the past (even allowing for the fact that in the past these activities lacked such a sexy name), it is not all that new. Rather, I will argue, what have changed are incomes, relative prices, and tastes, and it is the changes in these staples of demand that have prompted firms to engage in activities that take them well above and beyond what they are required to do by law. What is also new today, it is fair to say, is that firms are engaged in "rebranding" in order to get even more mileage from their beyond-compliance endeavors. I conclude with an admonition about heaping too much praise on firms that engage in beyond-compliance activities, whether they be profit-maximizing or profit-sacrificing.

Why Do Firms Engage in CSR?

Corporate executives offer a handful of reasons for why they engage in CSR activities (Holliday, Schmiedheiny, and Watts, 2002). These reasons are presented and discussed below.

To Curry Favor with Customers

The first reason for undertaking CSR activities has to do with the belief that beyond-compliance behavior will help companies curry favor with their current and potential future customers. This is particularly true for firms in the food and consumer products businesses. Thus, for instance, McDonald's Corp. publishes a seventy-page "Corporate Responsibility Report" that details its support for sustainable fisheries as well as a "fork to farm" supply-chain management strategy that emphasizes humane farming, cattle growing, and food processing. In addition, of course, McDonald's contributes significantly to and helps raise additional support for Ronald McDonald House Charities. It does all this in part to avoid the harm to its business that could result, for instance, from a boycott of its restaurants by, say, People for the Ethical Treatment of Animals. Companies like the Body Shop, Patagonia, Coca-Cola, Starbucks, Nike, Whole Foods, and Ben & Jerry's, to mention but a few, all tout their records on environmental sustainability, worker safety or community philanthropy in order to differentiate themselves from their competitors and ensure brand loyalty.

Of course, firms can also find themselves on the defensive on such issues more often than they would like. This is best illustrated by the recent travails of well-known toymakers Mattel and Toys 'R Us. In the former case, Mattel had to recall millions of toys, either because they contained magnets that could be swallowed by children, or because they were contaminated with lead paint applied at the Chinese factories where they were manufactured and painted. Toys 'R Us had to deal with a similar problem—lead-paint contamination on children's bibs, again imported from China.

CSR efforts are not confined to food and consumer products companies. For instance, home-improvement stores such as Home Depot, Lowe's, and Wal-Mart all push the energy efficiency of the appliances they sell and often the fact that the wood they sell has been certified as sustainably grown and harvested. Wal-Mart, in fact, has reached beyond touting the environmental benefits and sustainability of its products to commit itself to reducing the energy consumption of its stores through the installation of partially passive solar lighting and heating. Costco is doing the same. Even for consumer durables such as cars, CSR is now the rage. It was once the case that only the Swedish carmakers Volvo and Saab bragged about the safety features of their cars, and only Volkswagen boasted of its fuel economy. Now the crashworthiness ratings assigned to vehicles by the National Highway Traffic Safety Administration have become a regular feature of automakers' advertising, and even General Motors touts the number of models it sells that get better than thirty miles per gallon.

Finally, environmental marketing has now extended to perhaps the longest-lived of all consumer durables—housing. Builders of new homes, condominiums, and apartments have begun touting the "green construction" of their products, promoting their efforts to ensure passive solar lighting and heating, the energy efficiency of appliances and lights, water conservation, and the use of recycled materials in floors, wallboard, and carpets. Green design has also crept into commercial construction for private and public office buildings, university facilities, and even factories. In fact, in some areas, a sort of competition has emerged to see which buildings can attain the US Green Building Council's highest rating for Leadership in Energy and Environmental Design. A "Platinum" rating is a boon to builders trying to appeal to environmentally conscious buyers or tenants.

It would be a mistake, though, to conclude that CSR is practiced only by firms that sell their goods and services directly to the public. In fact, one of the biggest changes in the CSR landscape over the past decade has been the efforts to push beyond-compliance behavior up the supply chain to parts manufacturers and distributors and even to the producers of the raw materials at the very front end. Indeed, Tiffany's commitment to avoid "conflict diamonds" is akin to that of home-supply stores to sell only wood that comes from sustainable forestry. Increasingly, those who sell intermediate products to final manufacturers are themselves pressured to make their wares in socially responsible ways.

To Encourage Employee Loyalty and Goodwill

A second reason why firms say they engage in CSR has to do with the loyalty and goodwill they believe it engenders among their employees. This connection is an easy one to understand because most people would rather work for an employer that is highly respected than one that is widely reviled. Business magazines regularly publish annual lists of the "best places to work," places whose attributes often include offering benefits such as flexible work schedules, free day- or elder-care, time off for employees to volunteer for charitable causes, generous reimbursement for employees' education, and coverage for domestic partners. Again, according to corporate managers, such actions are good from the company's standpoint because they reduce costly employee turnover, increase productivity, and facilitate the recruitment of new employees.

To Attract Investors

Still another reason firms often go beyond what they are required to do by environmental or job safety regulators, or engage in community philanthropy, is that they believe it will make them attractive to potential investors— whether they be individuals, money managers or large mutual funds. This might be because the investors' values are aligned with those of the corporate leaders, or because the investors believe that beyond-compliance behavior will be rewarded with above-average returns in the market.

About one thing there can be no doubt. "Socially responsible investing" is growing. In 2005, nearly 10 percent of the more than $20 trillion invested under professional management was in funds run by managers who based their stock selection at least in part on companies' commitments to CSR. Moreover, over the past decade, the number of funds that use CSR "screens" has grown more quickly than those that do not. By 2005, the number of socially screened mutual funds had risen to two hundred and contained nearly $180 billion.[2]

To Promote Community Goodwill

A fourth reason for CSR has to do with the goodwill it can engender in the communities in which companies have their customers, headquarters, and/ or operating facilities. This can be extended to national or international philanthropy, as well, for companies that operate across the country or the world. Managers emphasize that a "good neighbor" policy is advantageous when a company wishes to expand a facility or when it becomes embroiled in a local dispute or runs into legal trouble. Because of Enron's considerable corporate philanthropy in Houston and elsewhere, as well as that of its CEO, Ken Lay, the company was slow to be condemned early in its painful

---

[2]There are a number of websites devoted to socially responsible investing, the best of which include [http://ussif.org] and, of particular interest to researchers, http://www.sristudies.org.

demise. However, all the philanthropy in the world could not make up for the high-level corporate misconduct that was eventually revealed.

To Improve Relationships with Regulators

A final reason why firms might engage in CSR has to do with their relationship with the agencies that regulate them. For instance, as Lyon and Maxwell (2004) have argued, the Environmental Protection Agency (EPA) or the Occupational Safety and Health Administration (OSHA) might be slower to impose new standards on firms that have elected to go beyond the prevailing standard of conduct. Similarly, *if* a firm is overcomplying because it has technology that allows it to do so for little extra cost, and *if* the regulator decides to set a more stringent standard for the whole industry based on the accomplishments of the overcomplier, that firm may derive a competitive advantage. For example, DuPont's decision in the late 1980s to abandon chlorofluorocarbons as aerosol propellants over 10 years and support a ban on their further production was surely based in part on its early development of alternative, non-ozone-depleting propellants that its competitors had to purchase from them.

To Improve the Bottom Line

If there is one theme that runs through these explanations for why firms engage in CSR, it is that CSR appears to be good for companies' bottom lines. Customers will be more loyal and/or will be willing to pay more for the goods and services of companies whose CSR records are exemplary. This is true not just in final product markets but even in the markets for intermediate goods and raw materials. Similarly, employees will be less likely to "job hop" and will be more productive when working for an employer with a beyond-compliance ethic. By the same logic, individuals maybe more prone to invest their funds in individual stocks, in mutual funds, or with money managers who employ one or another of the screens that help distinguish CSR practitioners, just as communities and possibly even regulators may give more favorable treatment to such firms.

It is important to observe that while very few top-level managers would be likely to say so (for reasons to be discussed below), firms may sometimes engage in beyond-compliance behavior that does not immediately, or perhaps ever, pay off on the bottom line. Occasionally, for example, executives say they feel an obligation to society in return for the corporate charter to operate that they have been given. In other words, it may be a bit of a straw man to suggest that all CSR behavior is motivated entirely by expected profitability. Nevertheless, the explanation almost always given for CSR is a straightforward "It's good business."

What Does the Empirical Evidence Reveal about the Impact of CSR?

If CSR is, in fact, good for business, it would be nice to be able to point to some strong evidence that supports this point. However, such evidence is scant. To be sure, there are many examples of companies that have launched "green marketing" (i.e., CSR in the hope of increased profits) campaigns. In addition to those identified above, General Electric now bills itself as the company with "Ecomagination" and BP has morphed from staid, old British Petroleum into the new "Beyond Petroleum." In both of these cases, it is difficult to tell whether there was any significant change in corporate philosophy, or whether these companies have merely attempted to give new names to their familiar activities. After all, although GE sells wind and natural-gas turbines as well as commercial nuclear reactors that could replace carbon-intensive coal in electricity generation, they did this well before their Ecomagination campaign began. And while BP has invested money in some alternative forms of energy, it still derives the overwhelming share of its revenues and net income from the sale of gasoline.

A true test of the success of green marketing will probably never come, because it would require the difficult if not impossible task of attributing changes in a company's revenues to specific marketing activities. But a recent assessment of the *environmental* impact of green marketing and consumerism (Makower 2006) suggests that the movement has not amounted to very much at all. Moreover, this assessment came not from one of those eager to debunk modern environmentalism, but rather from one who might be called the father of green marketing and consumerism. In a recent blog, Joel Makower, who wrote *The Green Consumer* seventeen years ago, concluded, "The green marketplace remains barely a blip on the screen for most consumer brands and retailers" (Makower 2006).

Similarly, it is difficult to find empirical evidence that supports the hypothesis that companies that engage in CSR activities have more productive employees and/or less employee turnover. This is partly because data on firm-level productivity and turnover are difficult to come by.[3] However, even if such data were available, empirical analysis related to CSR is challenging because of the lack of agreement on how CSR should be measured. This is in rather sharp contrast to measures of firm-level economic performance, where things such as total shareholder return, earnings per share, or economic value added are commonly used to compare and rank firms' economic performance.

---

[3]One exception is Toyota, which recently reported that employees in its Torrance, CA, customer service office were absent 14 percent less after they moved to an environmentally friendly building (Carlton, 2007).

Impacts of CSR on Investors and Investments

This brings us back to the third reason managers give for engaging in CSR: that it increases the likelihood that their shares (if publicly traded) will appeal to investors. Evidence on this matter is easier to come by. On one level, of course, the data cited above—that there are a great many funds that screen for one or another manifestation of CSR and that, collectively, they contain more than $2 trillion in assets—prove the point. Moreover, money invested in these funds has been growing at a faster rate than money invested in more traditional funds.

Whether the stocks of firms engaged in CSR activities will continue to be attractive to investors in the future depends importantly, though not exclusively, on whether CSR funds perform as well as traditional funds. If they do, we can expect them to grow even faster in the future than they have in the past. Even those investors who are agnostic about CSR would presumably shift money from traditional funds into those screening for CSR if they could earn higher returns there (holding volatility constant). Even if green funds underperform more traditional ones, however, they could continue to grow if more and more investors make CSR a part of their investment philosophy.

But why would even an environmentally conscious investor not direct his money into a better-yielding conventional fund, and then use the proceeds to contribute to the charity or causes of his choice? Baron (2007) provides several reasons. In an interesting recent article, he develops a theoretical model of both investor and entrepreneurial behavior in which he explores this as well as other issues. In this model, an individual investor's willingness to buy stock in a CSR firm depends on the extent to which CSR is a perfect substitute for private philanthropy; when they are perfect substitutes, Baron shows that the market value of CSR firms will be the same as traditional firms. However, individuals may also choose to buy stock in CSR firms for tax reasons. In this case, if the firm and the investor would give to the same causes, then it is more efficient for the firm to do so because the investor is spared the tax he would have to pay on dividends issued to him by the firm. Finally, Baron shows that charitably minded investors may choose CSR firms over traditional ones because of scale economies or other efficiencies the former may have, for example, in ascertaining the quality of competing good causes. Baron shows one other important thing: if CSR firms are clear from the time they are created that they will give part of their profits to good causes, then the costs associated with profit-sacrificing activities will be borne by the entrepreneurs who launch these firms rather than by their shareholders. It is only when a traditional firm is "hijacked" by a CSR do-gooder that the costs are borne by the shareholders.

What about the empirical question, though? Do funds that screen for CSR outperform those that do not? There is a quite large and rapidly growing literature on the impact of CSR (or corporate social performance, as it is sometimes called) on the financial performance of firms, so large that it has been surveyed sixteen times. The two websites identified in the previous section are good places to look for lists of the individual studies, abstracts of many of these studies, and even awards that some of these papers have won.[4] But the best source of information about empirical work on CSR can be found in a very recent and extraordinarily thorough meta-analysis (Margolis, Elfenbein, and Walsh 2007). Based on reasonably uniform criteria, the authors identified 167 studies for inclusion in their analysis. The studies in their sample use one or more of nine different types of measures of corporate social performance and two different types of financial performance measures.

Because of the comprehensiveness of Margolis, Elfenbein, and Walsh (2007), it is not necessary to present another literature survey. Nevertheless, it may be useful to briefly discuss several of the challenges posed by empirical work in this area. Consider first the challenge that socially responsible funds face in selecting individual stocks to hold. This can be a relatively simple matter if, for instance, mutual funds screen in part on the basis of the products companies sell. Perhaps the most common screen in socially responsible investing is to exclude the stocks of tobacco companies. Many funds also exclude companies that sell alcohol (even though a glass or two of wine each day is positively and statistically significantly associated with increased longevity), firearms, weapons for the military, and also gambling equipment and services. Some funds screen out companies if they do business in countries whose policies are opposed by those who manage the fund (e.g., Sudan, Zimbabwe, Libya, Tibet, Kazakhstan).

It becomes more challenging if funds wish to screen stocks based on their corporate governance practices. Firms that are relentlessly and successfully focused on shareholder return may be secretive in their deliberations, reluctant to elect outside directors, and unwilling to release any but the most basic information about executive compensation. Other firms may be paragons of transparency and responsive to shareholder demands, yet do a very poor job of rewarding those shareholders. Nevertheless, for funds wishing to screen companies on their governance, a number of organizations have sprung up over the past several decades to help them do so. For instance, the Corporate Library provides information on and evaluations of corporations' board members and practices to individual and institutional investors and also to academics wishing to study, for example, the possible effects of various governance practices on financial performance. The Investors Responsibility Research Center does the same thing. Those fund managers wishing a less demanding screen may simply choose to exclude companies that do not sign on to a list of principles of good governance and/or environmental practice (the CERES or Sullivan Principles, for instance) or that do not belong to organizations committed to one or another measure of environmental improvement (the Pew Center for Global Climate Change or the Carbon Disclosure Project, for example).

---

[4]One award, the annual Moskowitz Prize—originally awarded by the Social Investment Forum and now by the Center for Responsible Business at UC Berkeley's Haas School of Business—is given to the best paper on the subject of socially responsible investing.

Linking CSR and Environmental Performance

Analysis becomes more complicated still if one wishes to see whether firms that have outstanding environmental records are also likely to have a better financial performance than those firms with less outstanding environmental records. Here the problem is that any firm's overall environmental record depends upon its emissions of air and water pollutants (which number in the hundreds), its generation of solid and hazardous wastes, its water and raw materials use, its efforts to recycle, the volume and composition of materials used in its packaging, and so on. The truth is that any given firm might do very well on one or even a number of these counts, but less well on others. How then does one summarize a firm's environmental record as neatly as its financial performance? Until now, many studies purporting to link environmental and financial performance have used one measure of the former—the rate at which firms have reduced their emissions of substances on EPA's Toxic Release Inventory (or TRI). Why? For the simple reason that those data are readily available. Unfortunately, the TRI does not include the most common air pollutants, including fine particulate matter—thought to be the pollutant most strongly associated with premature mortality and morbidity. Nor does it reflect other important dimensions of a firm's environmental performance.

Evaluating the Relationship between CSR and Financial Performance

Another problem bedevils attempts to compare the performance of CSR versus traditional funds, a problem that is not uncommon in applied econometrics and is referred to as sample-selection bias. Two recent studies illustrate this problem. The first is an article showing that firms that ranked high in terms of corporate governance (i.e., those that conferred on shareholders a variety of rights) earned higher returns than those doing less well in the governance rankings (Gompers, Ishii, and Metrick 2003). This article also showed that hedge funds counting on the stock prices of good-governance firms going up and those of poor-governance firms going down outperformed those not factoring governance into stock selection. A second article (Bebchuck, Cohen, and Ferrell 2004) reached similar conclusions using a somewhat different measure of governance, one that focuses on how entrenched firms' managers are. Especially the first of these two articles has been cited as evidence that firms must take CSR (corporate governance, in this case) seriously if they are to remain attractive to investors.

Recently, however, both studies were the subject of careful reanalysis (Johnson, Moorman, and Sorescu 2007). At the risk of oversimplification, this reanalysis hypothesized that the findings in the two earlier studies might have been affected by a bias in the construction of the good-governance and poor-governance samples. If, for example, the good-governance sample included relatively more firms from the pharmaceutical industry, say, while the poor-governance sample included more from the chemical industry, the results would be biased if one of those industries outperformed the other during the sample period. A better test, in other words, would be one in which these possible industry effects were controlled for statistically. That is just what Johnson, Moorman, and Sorescu (2007) tried to do by using data at an even finer level of disaggregation than in the earlier studies (SIC 3-digit rather than 2-digit data). Once these corrections were made, they found that "governance quality has no impact on long-term abnormal stock returns. The significant results documented by Gompers, Ishii, and Metrick and by Bebchuck, Cohen, and Ferrell are artifacts of either asset pricing model mis-specification or unexpected industry performance."

Telle (2006) came to a similar conclusion. Using plant-level data from Norway, he first regressed plants' financial performance, as indicated by their returns on sales, on the number of employees and measures of the plants' capital stock and environmental performance. The environmental performance measures included an estimate by the Norwegian government of the risk associated with each facility, as well as an index of multiple pollutants. Like many earlier studies, Telle found that good environmental performance was positively and statistically associated with good financial performance in a simple model. However, hypothesizing that these results might be subject to the same industry effects that were later investigated by Johnson, Moorman, and Sorescu (2007), he corrected for them and found that the positive association all but disappeared when he controlled for the industry effects. Such findings are not uncommon in the empirical CSR literature.

Conclusions about the Empirical CSR Literature

It may be best to let interested readers plow on their own through the many studies linking CSR to financial performance. But because Margolis, Elfenbein, and Walsh (2007) have already examined this literature so thoroughly, I would like to give them the last words on this topic here. In discussing their findings, they say, "After thirty-five years of research, the preponderance of evidence indicates a mildly positive relationship between corporate social performance and corporate financial performance" (p. 22). They go on to say, "[Varied results] suggest that more lucrative financial impact might attend investments other than [corporate social performance], providing better returns on the next marginal dollar of corporate spending" (p. 23). Finally, and perhaps most tellingly, they say, ". . . We wonder whether ongoing research efforts [in this area] might be better devoted to other questions" (p. 28).

It is impossible to resist making a last point about the relationship between socially responsible stock funds and their financial performance. If it can be said that there is an "antichrist" among CSR investors, it must surely be the fiendishly named Vice Fund (NASDAQ: Vicex). This fund holds *only* the stocks of companies that are screened out of virtually every socially responsible investment fund—that is, companies that make tobacco products and alcoholic beverages, sell weapons to the military, or operate gambling casinos (Morrissey 2007). The Vice Fund received Morningstar's Five Star rating for the 3-year period 2003–2006, during which time it outperformed the S&P 500 during every benchmark period. It was in the upper quintile for the Lipper one-, two- and three-year rankings as of July 2007, and, according to Lipper, during the past three years it was in the top 3 percent of all funds that contained the stocks of small, medium, and large companies. Of course, this does not make the case against socially responsible investing any more than one strong performance by a CSR fund makes the case for it. But it is a useful (and also entertaining) reminder that there are multiple paths to riches.

How New Is CSR?

Among those who write about CSR, from either an academic or a journalistic perspective, there is often a tendency to suggest that it is a relatively recent phenomenon. However, this is really not the case. Following a brief and admittedly anecdotal discussion of the respects in which CSR has always been with us, I will identify and explain what I believe *is* new about how companies and consumers approach it.

What Is "Old" about CSR?

Two examples—one well-known and one less so—illustrate the types of efforts that have always been made to appeal to customers through environmental and/or social responsibility. For more than 120 years, Johnson & Johnson has been manufacturing health-care products and medical devices for adults and children. Nearly seventy years ago, CEO Robert Wood Johnson wrote a one-page "credo" for the company that spells out its commitments to its customers and also its employees, neighbors, suppliers, and shareholders; it reads like comparable statements by other companies written in the past five or ten years. Moreover, in 1982, CEO James Burke reinforced the public perception that Johnson & Johnson "walked the walk" and actually lived by its credo by the way he handled the corporate crisis surrounding the tampering with the company's Tylenol product and the seven resulting deaths. Nearly forty years ago, in 1971, two entrepreneurs started the Recycled Paper Greetings (RPG) company, which was aimed at customers wishing to both remember friends' and relatives' birthdays and help reduce the harvesting of timber. While this was well before recycling was considered a civic and personal virtue, over time this strategy has helped RPG to become the third-largest greeting-card company in the United States.

What about companies' efforts years ago to appeal to their employees? Here even more examples come immediately to mind. For instance, the consumer products company S.C. Johnson and Son has for the better part of a century treated its workers extraordinarily benevolently, and has turned up perennially on the list of "Best Places to Work."[5] Similarly, for many years IBM offered its employees the closest thing in the corporate world to a lifetime employment guarantee, due in part to the belief that this would ensure a more stable and dedicated workforce.

The same can be said about the longevity of corporate philanthropy— that is, donating to or making investments in the communities in which companies do business. One of the best-known examples of this, perhaps, was Texaco's (now part of the oil company Chevron) remarkable sixty-four-year sponsorship of the [Saturday] afternoon radio and, later, television broadcasts from New York's Metropolitan Opera. Early on in this effort Texaco received thousands of letters each week thanking them for their sponsorship, presumably from people who were also now more likely to buy Texaco's gasoline because of the company's CSR activity. A modern-day analogue is Archer Daniels Midland's underwriting of *The News Hour with Jim Lehrer* each weeknight on Public Broadcasting Service stations around the country. For many years, virtually every major company in the country, and many small- and mid-sized ones, has championed a variety of good causes. However, it is only in the past ten years or so that they have begun to tout this support in their advertising, on their websites or in a regular CSR report.

What Is New about CSR?

What then *has* changed about CSR, it is fair to ask. For one thing, firms are now acutely aware that they can take advantage of their good works—be they environmental, occupational, or philanthropic—and actively seek to do so. In fact, noted business strategist and consulting guru Michael Porter, with coauthor Michael Kramer, has suggested recently in the *Harvard Business Review* that companies can build an entire business strategy around social responsibility by seeking out areas in which they can be profitable by doing socially useful things (Porter and Kramer, 2006).[6] Things are also different today in that firms are expected to do more good or, at the very least, to be much more forthcoming about the good they have always done.

This is not the only reason why we read so much more about CSR, though. Other things have changed, too, that push firms in the direction of more voluntary environmental protection, energy conservation, and investments in the communities in which they do business. But these agents for change are not so much metaphysical as they are the staples of economics— tastes, incomes, and relative prices.

---

[5]Incidentally, this same company elected to remove chlorofluorocarbons as spray propellants in its household products well before the Montreal protocol in 1989 established a ban on their use in the US.

[6]I save for later whether such things are any more socially responsible than selling tennis shoes.

For instance, can anyone really believe that the wave of investments in commercial or industrial energy efficiency across corporate America of late (think Wal-Mart and Costco, for instance) is due to anything other than the increase in energy prices the country has experienced over the past decade? Is General Motors touting the fact that it has ten models that get more than thirty miles per gallon solely because it has seen the true light of sustainability and as a result has decided to eschew the production of SUVs and other gas guzzlers? Of course not. General Motors is responding to the fact that gasoline prices have doubled nominally in the five-year period 2002–2007, thus making its potential customers much more conscious of the importance of fuel economy.

Focusing on energy prices first, incidentally, provides still another reminder that energy conservation has been fashionable since long before CSR was a glint in the eyes of its proponents. The most significant reduction in energy use in the United States has not come recently, but rather during the 1978–1983 period—in the wake of the two major runups in world oil prices, prompted by the oil embargoes of the 1970s. During that time, petroleum use per dollar of GDP produced fell by more than a quarter and has remained well below 1978 levels ever since.

Petroleum is not the only natural resource that has become relatively scarcer. So, too, has water, and with it have appeared signs in most hotel rooms informing guests that, "in the interests of environmental stewardship," the hotel will gladly not wash every towel every night unless the guest so requests. Similarly, the builders and owners of green office buildings, condominiums, dormitories, golf courses, and even factories (e.g., Ford Motor Company's legendary Rouge plant in Dearborn, MI) now routinely tout low-flow appliances or processes and, where possible, the reuse of waste water. This is better understood, I believe, as a response to higher prices rather than the attainment of a higher environmental consciousness.

Prices are not the only factors pushing us in the direction that CSR advocates would have us go. Estimates of the income elasticity of demand for environmental protection[7] show that the level of environmental quality that people desire grows in proportion to or even faster than the growth in their income, at least until relatively high income levels are reached. Even then, of course, the demand for environmental quality may still be very high; the eventual "plateauing" of environmental quality is likely due to the rapidly increasing marginal costs of environmental quality at very high levels. This moderates the tendency to devote more and more of one's income to environmental quality.

More than incomes and relative prices have changed, however. Even controlling for these factors, it does appear that people's tastes have changed and that they now pay more attention to environmental issues than they did in the past. And while it is hard to separate out all the factors that influence

---

[7]Such estimates are typically based on cross-country comparisons of per-capita incomes and air quality—the so-called "environmental Kuznets curve."

people's decisions as business managers, consumers or investors, I am willing to concede that people think more about the long-term natural resource and environmental consequences of their economic decisions than they did previously. Moreover, if this is so, future generations of corporate managers, consumers, and investors may be even more inclined than their current counterparts to consider environmental factors when making their economic decisions.

This leaves one final question to be explored, albeit briefly: Is this a good thing?

How Should We Feel about Today's CSR?

On its face, this is surely an odd-sounding question: after all, who could object to a company behaving in a socially responsible way? But suppose a publicly traded firm engages *only* in those overcompliance or philanthropic activities that it expects to result in more loyal customers, more productive workers, more willing investors, or more tolerant regulators. That is, the firm practices what we might call profit-maximizing CSR. Is this particular firm really any more deserving of praise than a firm that engages in no beyond-compliance behavior because it has determined that the marginal cost of doing so exceeds the marginal revenue product? I find it hard to answer this question in the affirmative. To be sure, we may admire firms that find ways to turn emissions reductions, workplace accident prevention, or donations to good causes into more robust financial performance. I myself do, in fact. But if such beyond-compliance actions are undertaken solely for bottom-line reasons, how are those firms any more commendable than others whose profit-maximizing calculus leads them to do no more than the law requires?

What about those publicly traded firms that reduce their environmental emissions, make their workplaces safer, eliminate the risks associated with their products, or give generously to the communities in which they operate even when they know that such actions are unlikely to pay off in the long run from a purely financial standpoint? Surely, these firms are behaving in a socially responsible way, aren't they? Maybe, maybe not.

For example, if a company makes clear from its founding that it has both financial *and* social objectives (e.g., Whole Foods or Google), its shareholders know from the outset that *their* well-being is not the only criterion the company will use in making its decisions; presumably shareholders factor this in when deciding how much to pay for the company's stock. Here there is alignment between the shareholders' and the managers' interests and there is no reason to object to the managers' actions, so long as they do not stray too far from what is described in their corporate charter. But I suspect that much of the profit-sacrificing CSR that exists today is practiced by firms that came late to the game, perhaps as a result of an acquisition or perhaps because of a new generation of managers who bring their own social agenda to the company. In these cases, it seems more than fair to ask why the firm, instead of engaging in what its managers feel are good works, doesn't instead pay higher dividends to (or buy back outstanding shares of stock from) its current shareholders—letting the shareholders decide for themselves what causes they might wish to support. Good deeds done with other people's money, in other words, shine less brightly.

The discussion above may seem to suggest that there is a clear line in managers' (or shareholders') minds that indicates exactly where CSR stops being profit maximizing and starts becoming purely philanthropic. That is a gross oversimplification, of course, and a firm's managers should be and generally are given great discretion in determining where that line lies. While it may be troubling to contemplate a CEO giving her shareholders' money to her favorite cause, it is equally troubling to contemplate a world in which each and every step along the CSR continuum is litigated by shareholders and decided by judges. Moreover, in a highly competitive world, firms that are too generous with their shareholders' money will find it difficult to raise capital and will be at an operating disadvantage relative to those firms that engage in only profit-maximizing CSR. This too will limit excessive corporate giveaways. Despite these qualifications, it seems fair to me to scrutinize quite carefully companies' CSR activities.

Summary and Conclusions

It is hard to deny that firms engage in CSR, defined as systematic overcompliance with environmental, occupational safety, and health or consumer product safety regulations, or that they frequently make philanthropic contributions at the local, regional, national, or even international levels. Moreover, the explanation almost always given for these actions is that "it's good for business," because such CSR activities ingratiate firms with one or more of their customers, employees, neighbors, shareholders, or regulators. It is much harder, however, to determine whether CSR really is "good for business" because the empirical evidence on strategic CSR is quite mixed. Some studies suggest that CSR is associated with above average financial performance, while others find no such effect. As indicated above, the most careful review of this evidence suggests that CSR may have a small positive effect on firms' bottom lines, but that it may not be worth pursuing in light of other uses for firms' funds. Perhaps the one thing that investigators can agree on in this area is that rigorous empirical tests are hampered by the absence of a good measure of firms' environmental performance.

While it is tempting to ascribe the growing interest in CSR to a new ethic or commitment to sustainability, it is consistent with another explanation as well: firms and individuals are responding to changing prices and higher incomes, as they always have. It seems likely that tastes have also changed. But at least part—and perhaps the biggest part—of any new behaviors being observed is due to traditional economic adjustments.

Finally, how we ought to regard those firms that practice CSR is less clear than one might expect. If firms are engaged in socially responsible activities for purely profit-maximizing reasons, we might be pleased that they can make money while doing good things. However, I would argue that we should not necessarily hold them in any higher regard than those firms that have not found it to be in their (or their shareholders') interests to go above and beyond. Even in those cases where the actions of publicly traded firms are purely altruistic (that is, they hold no prospect for returns that would justify the actions), it is not clear to me that we ought to admire them. In fact, unless these companies have made clear from the outset that they would be guided by social as well as financial returns, it is fair to argue that they would do better to return any monies spent on overcompliance or philanthropy to their shareholders so they can choose and support their own favorite causes.

REFERENCES

Baron, David. 2007. Corporate social responsibility and social entrepreneurship. *Journal of Economics and Managerial Strategy* 16: 683–717.

Bebchuck, Lucian, Alma Cohen, and Allen Ferrell. 2004. What matters in corporate governance? Harvard Law School John M. Olin Center Discussion Paper No. 491. [Available at http://papers.ssrn.com/so13/papers.cfm?abstract_id=593423 (accessed 6/14/11)].

Burtraw, Dallas, and Erin Mansur. 1999. Environmental effects of SO_2 trading and banking. *Environmental Science and Technology* 33: 3489–94.

Carlton, Jim. 2007. Citigroup tries banking on the natural kind of green. *New York Times*, September 5, B1, B7.

Elhague, Einer. 2005. Corporate managers' operational discretion to sacrifice corporate profits in the public interest. In *Environmental Protection and the Social Responsibility of Firms*, ed. Bruce L. Hay, Robert N. Stavins, and Richard K. Vietor, pp. 13–76. Washington, DC: Resources for the Future.

Gompers, Paul A., Joy L. Ishii, and Andrew Metrick. 2003. Corporate governance and equity prices. *Quarterly Journal of Economics* 118: 107–55.

Holliday, Chad, Stephan Schmidheiny, and Philip Watts. 2002. *Walking the Talk*. San Francisco: Better-Koehler.

Johnson, Shane, Theodore Moorman, and Sorescu Sorin. 2007. A reexamination of corporate governance and equity prices. [Available at http://papers.ssrn.com/sol3/papers.cfm?abstract_id=687207 (accessed 6/14/11)].

Lyon, Thomas P., and John W Maxwell. 2004. *Corporate Environmentalism and Public Policy*. Cambridge: Cambridge University Press.

Lyon, Thomas P., and John W Maxwell. 2008. Corporate social responsibility and the environment: A theoretical perspective. *Review of Environmental Economics and Policy* 10.1093/reep/ren004.

Makower, Joel. 2006. Where are all the good, green products? Available at http://makower.typepad.com/joel_makower/2006/10/where_are_all_t.html (accessed 6/14/11).

Margolis, Joshua D., Hillary A. Elfenbein, and James P Walsh. 2007. Does it pay to be good? A meta-analysis and redirection of research on the relationship between corporate social performance and financial performance. (Mimeograph).

Morrissey, Janet. 2007. At least on Wall Street, wages of sin beat those of virtue. *New York Times* September 14.

Porter, Michael E., and Mark R Kramer. 2006. Strategy and society: The link between competitive advantage and corporate social responsibility. *Harvard Business Review* December: 78–101.

Portney, Paul R. 2005. Corporate social responsibility: An economic and policy perspective. In *Environmental Protection and the Social Responsibility of Firms*, ed. Bruce L. Hay, Robert N. Stavins, and Richard K. Vietor, pp. 107–31. Washington, DC: Resources for the Future.

Reinhardt, Forest L., Robert N. Stavins, and Richard H. K Vietor. 2008. Corporate social responsibility through an economic lens. *Review of Environmental Economics and Policy* 10.1093/reep/ren008.

Telle, Kjetil. 2006. It pays to be green—a premature conclusion? *Environmental and Resource Economics* 35: 195–220.

VIII

Global Climate Change

24   *Designing Climate Mitigation Policy**

Joseph E. Aldy, Alan J. Krupnick, Richard G. Newell,
Ian W. H. Parry, and William A. Pizer

*Joseph E. Aldy is Assistant Professor of Public Policy at Harvard Kennedy
School, Nonresident Fellow at Resources for the Future, and Faculty
Research Fellow at the National Bureau of Economic Research; Alan J.
Krupnik is Research Director, Senior Fellow, and Director, Center for Energy
Economics and Policy at Resources for the Future; Richard. G. Newell is
Gendell Associate Professor of Energy and Environmental Economics at
Duke University; Ian W. H. Parry is Technical Assistance Advisor on
Climate Change and Environmental Policy in the Fiscal Affairs Department
of the International Monetary Fund and Senior Fellow at Resources for the
Future; and William A. Pizer is Deputy Assistant Secretary for Environ-
ment and Energy International Affairs at the U.S. Treasury Department.*

*This paper provides (for the nonspecialist) a highly streamlined
discussion of the main issues, and controversies, in the design of
climate mitigation policy. The first part of the paper discusses how
much action to reduce greenhouse gas emissions at the global level is
efficient under both the cost-effectiveness and welfare-maximizing
paradigms. We then discuss various issues in the implementation of
domestic emissions control policy, instrument choice, and incentives
for technological innovation. Finally, we discuss alternative policy
architectures at the international level. (JEL Q54, Q58)*

1.   Introduction

Global warming is one of the most critical, and also most daunting, challenges facing policymakers in the twenty-first century, (e.g., World Bank
2010). Assessing a globally efficient time path for pricing or controlling
greenhouse gas (GHG) emissions is difficult enough, with huge scientific
uncertainties, disagreement over the ultimate goals of climate policy, and
disagreement over which countries should bear most responsibility for
emissions reductions. On top of this, domestic policy design is inherently
difficult because of multiple, and sometimes conflicting, criteria for policy

---

"Designing Climate Mitigation Policy." Discussion Paper, May 2009. Resources for the Future.

*The authors are grateful to Carolyn Fischer, Roger Gordon, Charles Kolstad, Knut Rosendahl,
Kenneth Small, and Brent Sohngen for helpful comments and to Michael Eber for research assistance.

467

evaluation. And at an international level, there are multiple approaches to coordinating emissions control agreements. What should be a rational policy response for such an enormously complex problem?

This paper attempts to provide some broad answers to this question, and to pinpoint the main sources of controversy, by pulling together key findings from diverse literatures on mitigation costs, damage valuation, policy instrument choice, technological innovation, and international climate policy. Given that our target audience is the broader economics profession (rather than the climate specialist), our discussion is highly succinct and avoids details.

We begin with the broadest issue of how much action to price or to control GHGs is warranted in the near and longer term at a global level. There are two distinct approaches to this question. The cost-effectiveness approach acknowledges that policymakers typically have some ultimate target for limiting the amount of projected climate change or atmospheric GHG accumulations, and the question is what policy trajectory might achieve alternative goals at minimum economic cost, accounting for practical constraints, such as incomplete international coordination. The other approach is to weigh the benefits and costs of slowing climate change, which introduces highly contentious issues in damage valuation, dealing with extreme climate risks, and intergenerational discounting.

The second part of the paper deals with issues in the implementation of climate policy. At a domestic (U.S.) level, these include a comparison of alternative emissions control instruments and how they should be designed to simultaneously promote administrative ease and minimize efficiency costs in the presence of other policy distortions, abatement cost uncertainty, and possible distributional constraints. We also discuss the extent to which additional policies are warranted to promote the development and deployment of emissions-saving technologies. And we briefly summarize emerging literature on alternative international policy architectures. A final section discusses key areas for future research.

2. Policy Stringency

2.1. Emissions Pricing to Stabilize Global Climate

The cost-effectiveness approach to global climate policy uses models of the economic and climate system (known as integrated assessment models) to estimate the emissions price trajectory that minimizes the discounted worldwide costs of emissions abatement, subject to a climate stabilization target and possibly other, practical constraints like delayed developing country participation. These models range from bottom-up engineering-economic models with considerable detail on adoption and use of energy technologies to computable general equilibrium models with a more aggregated and continuous structure that better represents demand responses, capital dynamics, and factor substitution. Many models are hybrids containing substantial technological detail in the energy sectors and more aggregate representation in others. Typically the suite of existing and emerging technologies is taken as given, although some models capture induced innovation through learning-by-doing and a few have incorporated R&D-based technological change (e.g., Lawrence H. Goulder and Koshy Mathai 2000).

The choice of model structure is generally less important than assumptions about future baseline data and technology options. Future mitigation costs are highly sensitive to business-as-usual (BAU) emissions, which depend on future population and GDP growth, the energy-intensity of GDP, and the fuel mix. They also depend on the future availability and cost of emissions-saving technologies like nuclear and renewable power, carbon capture and storage, and alternative transportation fuels. Considerable uncertainty surrounds all of these factors.

Given the difficulty of judging which models give the most reliable predictions, we discuss a representative sample of results, beginning with studies that assume emissions reductions are efficiently allocated across countries and time, and use the least expensive technological options (this is known as "where, when, and how" flexibility). The results, summarized in table 1, are from the U.S. Climate Change Science Program (CCSP, Product 2.1A), based on results from three widely regarded models (see Leon E. Clarke et al. 2007 for details), and from the Stanford Energy Modeling Forums EMF-21 study (reported in Francisco C. de la Chesnaye and John P. Weyant 2006) based on sixteen models.

2.1.1. Reference Scenarios. Global CO_2 emissions from fossil fuels have grown from about 2 billion (metric) tons in 1900 to current levels of about 30 billion tons and, in the absence of mitigation policy, are projected to roughly triple 2000 levels by the end of the century (table 1). The huge bulk of the projected future emissions growth is in "non–Annex 1" (nonindustrial) countries—CO_2 emissions from these countries have just overtaken those from "Annex 1" (industrial) countries.[1] These rising emissions trends reflect growing energy demand from population and real income growth outweighing energy- and emissions-saving technological change—traditional fossil fuels still account for around three-quarters of global primary energy consumption by 2100 (Clarke et al. 2007, table TS1).[2]

---

[1] The 1990 UN Framework Convention on Climate Change grouped countries into either Annex 1 or non–Annex 1 according to their per capita income at that time. Only Annex 1 countries agreed to reduce emissions under the 1997 Kyoto Protocol.

[2] Land-use changes currently contribute about an additional 5.5 billion tons of CO_2 releases (primarily through deforestation in developing countries for agriculture and timber) though these sources are projected to grow at a much slower pace than fossil fuel emissions (Intergovernmental Panel on Climate Change 2007). Land-use CO_2 emissions are not priced in the models in table 1.

TABLE 1 Least-Cost Policies to Stabilize Global Climate

CCSP[a]	2025 MERGE	2025 Mini-CAM	2025 IGSM	2050 MERGE	2050 Mini-CAM	2050 IGSM	2100 MERGE	2100 Mini-CAM	2100 IGSM
Global CO_2 emissions, relative to 2000									
Reference	1.27	1.46	1.70	1.59	1.98	2.59	3.42	3.21	3.45
450 CO_2 stabilization	0.92	0.97	0.86	0.53	0.57	0.64	0.24	0.39	0.55
550 CO_2 stabilization	1.25	1.35	1.22	1.32	1.56	1.20	0.79	0.71	0.81
CO_2 concentration, ppm[b]									
Reference	422	430	436	485	507	544	711	746	875
450 CO_2 stabilization	412	416	408	434	440	430	426	456	451
550 CO_2 stabilization	421	427	421	478	490	472	535	562	526
CO_2 price, \$/ton[c]									
450 CO_2 stabilization	41	36	88	157	127	230	166	173	1,651
550 CO_2 stabilization	3	6	26	10	19	67	127	115	475
% reduction in world GDP[d]									
450 CO_2 stabilization	0.8	0.5	2.6	1.8	1.6	5.4	1.4	1.4	16.1
550 CO_2 stabilization	0.0	0.0	0.7	0.2	0.2	1.8	0.7	1.0	6.8
U.S. CO_2 emissions, relative to 2000									
Reference	1.25	1.10	1.40	1.27	1.20	2.00	1.63	1.34	2.93
450 CO_2 stabilization	0.79	0.83	0.88	0.42	0.43	0.54	0.02	0.27	0.40
550 CO_2 stabilization	1.24	1.05	1.04	1.02	0.98	1.13	0.29	0.37	0.59
EMF-21[e]	*lower end*	*median*	*upper end*	*lower end*	*median*	*upper end*	*lower end*	*median*	*upper end*
Global CO_2 emissions, relative to 2000									
Reference	1.33	1.48	1.64	1.64	1.88	2.23	2.11	2.93	3.52
550 CO_2 stabilization	1.17	1.25	1.41	1.13	1.25	1.41	0.66	0.90	1.25
CO_2 price, \$/ton[c]									
550 CO_2 stabilization	3	13	21	12	33	99	31	92	166
% reduction in world GDP[d]									
550 CO_2 stabilization	0.1	0.1	0.8	0.2	0.6	3.1	0.3	5.1	8.2
U.S. CO_2 emissions, relative to 2000									
Reference	1.19	1.26	1.38	1.31	1.65	1.97	0.95	1.85	2.29
550 CO_2 stabilization	1.05	1.14	1.22	0.76	1.02	1.26	0.36	0.53	1.05

Notes: [a]Results are from the Integrated Global Systems Model (IGSM), the Model for Evaluating Regional and Global Effects (MERGE), and MiniCAM Model. See Clarke et al. (2007) for details.
[b]The models stabilize concentrations of all GHGs, rather than CO_2 alone (i.e., the CO_2-equivalent concentration level is higher than the CO_2 concentration). Actual CO_2 concentrations may temporarily overshoot the long run targets.
[c]In year 2000 dollars or thereabouts.
[d]GDP losses are not broken out by region in the models. Losses include those from pricing CO_2 and other GHGs on an equivalent basis. The figures do not account for the benefits of reduced climate change.
[e]Modeling results from Stanford's Energy Modeling Forum, reported in de la Chesnaye and Weyant (2006). The results are from sixteen models for CO_2 prices and twelve models for GDP. Lower and upper ends correspond to lower and upper two-thirds of model results. Atmospheric CO_2 concentrations are not reported.

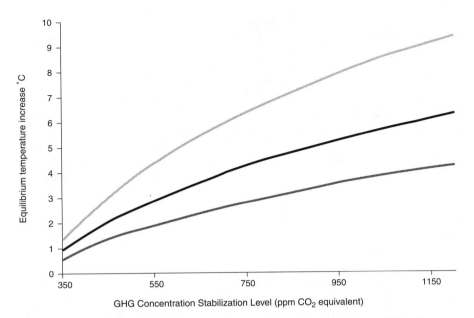

Figure 1 Steady State Warming above Preindustrial Temperatures from Stabilization at Different GHG Concentrations

Note: The black curve indicates the central case projection and the grey curves indicate the 66 percent confidence interval.
Source: International Panel on Climate Change (2007), table 10.8.

About 55 percent of CO_2 releases are immediately absorbed by the upper oceans and terrestrial biosphere while the remainder enters the atmosphere and is removed by the ocean and terrestrial sinks only very gradually (Intergovernmental Panel on Climate Change 2007). The longer term rate of removal of CO_2 from the atmosphere is around 1 percent a year (i.e., CO_2 has an expected atmospheric residence time of about a century), and even this very gradual decay rate might decline as oceans become more saturated with CO_2 Stabilizing atmospheric CO_2 concentrations over the very long term essentially requires elimination of fossil fuel and other GHG emissions.

Atmospheric CO_2 concentrations increased from preindustrial levels of about 280 parts per million (ppm) to 384 ppm in 2007, and are projected to rise to around 700–900 ppm by 2100 (table 1). Accounting for non-CO_2 GHGs, such as methane and nitrous oxides from agriculture, and expressing them on a lifetime warming equivalent basis, the CO_2-equivalent concentration is about 430 ppm (Intergovernmental Panel on Climate Change 2007). Total GHG concentrations in CO_2 equivalents are projected to reach 550 ppm (i.e., about double preindustrial levels) by around mid century.

Globally averaged surface temperature is estimated to have risen by 0.74°C between 1906 and 2006, with most of this warming due to rising atmospheric GHG concentrations, as opposed to other factors like changes in solar radiation, volcanic activity, and urban heat absorption (Intergovernmental Panel on Climate Change 2007). Figure 1, from Intergovernmental Panel on Climate Change (2007), shows the projected long run warming associated with different stabilization levels for atmospheric CO_2-equivalent concentrations (the climate system takes several decades to fully adjust to changing concentration levels, due to gradual heat diffusion processes in the oceans). If CO_2-equivalent concentrations were stabilized at 450, 550, and 650 ppm, mean projected warming over pre-industrial levels is 2.1, 2.9, and 3.6°C respectively. Figure 1 also indicates "likely ranges" of warming about the mean projection, which refer to an approximate 66 percent confidence interval, based on sensitivity analysis from scientific models—for example, the likely warming range for 550 ppm CO_2-equivalent stabilization is 1.9–4.4°C. The fundamental concern is that warming might greatly exceed these ranges due to poorly understood feedbacks not represented in these models, such as heat-induced releases of methane stored under the oceans and in the permafrost.

2.1.2. Least-Cost Pricing. Most economic analysis has focused on climate stabilization targets that are approximately consistent with limiting atmospheric CO_2 concentrations to either 450 or 550 ppm (with other GHGs included, CO_2-equivalent concentrations stabilized at approximately 530 and 670 ppm respectively). The studies in table 1 examine globally cost-effective pricing of all GHGs that are approximately consistent with these goals.[3]

Across the models and stabilization scenarios in table 1, CO_2 emissions prices (in year 2000 dollars) rise steadily (beginning around year 2012) at approximately 5 percent a year, where this figure is the consumer discount rate plus the atmospheric CO_2 decay rate (Stephan C. Peck and Y. Steve Wan 1996). However, one striking feature in table 1 is the considerable price variation across models within a stabilization scenario, reflecting different assumptions about future BAU emissions growth and future costs of carbon-saving technologies. The other striking feature is the dramatic differences between the 550 and 450 ppm CO_2 stabilization targets. In the 550 ppm case, CO_2 prices are $3–26 and $10–99 per ton in 2025 and 2050 respectively, with global emissions 17–41 percent and 13–56 percent *above* 2000 levels at these dates, respectively. In the 450 ppm case, CO_2 prices are 3–16 times those in the 550 ppm case to mid century, while emissions are 3–14 percent and 36–47 percent *below* 2000 levels in 2025 and 2050 respectively.[4]

Although GDP losses maybe an unreliable proxy for efficiency losses we discuss them here as they are the least common denominator reported by

---

[3]The C-8 countries recently adopted a target of limiting projected warming to 2°C above preindustrial levels. This would require ultimately stabilizing CO_2-equivalent concentrations at 450 ppm, which is considerably more stringent than the 450 ppm CO_2 target discussed here. In fact, with current technologies, it is difficult to see how the more stringent target could be achieved (even allowing for transitory overshooting), given that current concentration levels are already approaching this target.

[4]Some analysts express prices per ton of carbon rather than CO_2. To convert to $ per ton of carbon, multiply by the ratio of molecular weights, $44/12 = 3.67$.

the modeling groups. Under the 550 ppm CO_2 target, most models project global GDP losses (from reducing both CO_2 and non-CO_2 GHGs) of less than 1 percent out to 2050, though some models suggest GDP losses could reach 2–3 percent by this date. In present value terms, these losses amount to about $0.4–12 trillion out to 2050 when applied to a world GDP that is $60 trillion and growing (Richard G. Newell 2008, p. 12). Under the 450 ppm CO_2 target, GDP losses are about 1.0–2.5 percent and 1.5–5.5 percent in 2025 and 2050 respectively or about $8–43 trillion in present value from 2010 to 2050.

Under both 450 and 550 ppm CO_2 stabilization scenarios, the energy system is transformed over the next century (though at very different rates), through energy conservation, improved energy efficiency, and particularly reductions in the carbon intensity of energy. Most of the emissions reductions in the first two to three decades occur in the power sector, largely through the progressive replacement of traditional coal plants by coal with carbon capture and storage, natural gas, nuclear, and renewables (wind, solar, and biomass). However, the projected fuel mix is highly sensitive to speculative assumptions about the relative costs and availability of future technologies. For example, there are considerable practical obstacles to the expansion of nuclear power (because of safety issues), renewables (because sites are typically located far from population centers), and carbon capture and storage (because of the difficulty of assigning sub-surface property rights).[5]

As for U.S. CO_2 emissions, in the BAU case they increase by about 30–100 percent above 2000 levels (of approximately 6 billion tons) by mid century (table 1). Under the 550 CO_2 ppm target, emissions initially rise, then fall to roughly 2000 levels by 2050, and fall rapidly thereafter. Under the 450 ppm target, U.S. emissions are rapidly reduced to roughly half 2000 levels by 2050.[6] U.S.-specific GDP losses are not reported in the studies in table 1, but allocating a quarter of the global cost to the United States (based on its share in global GDP) implies a present value cost to the United States through mid century of about $0.1–3 trillion (0–1 percent of the present value of GDP) for the 550 ppm target and $2–11 trillion (1–3 percent of present value GDP) for the 450 ppm target.[7]

---

[5]The transition away from coal reflects not only the range of substitution possibilities in the power sector, but also the disproportionately large impact of emissions pricing on coal prices. A $10 price per ton of CO_2 in the United States would increase 2007 coal prices to utilities by about 60 percent, wellhead natural gas prices by 9 percent, retail electricity and crude oil prices each by 7 percent, and gasoline prices by 3 percent (from Clarke et al. 2007, table TS5, and www.eia.gov).

[6]As of 2009, proposed climate policies in the United States embody emission reduction targets approximately equivalent to about of 80 percent below 2000 levels by 2050. However, actual reductions in U.S. CO_2 emissions would be about 60 percent if provisions to use domestic and international emission offsets were fully exploited.

[7]U.S.-specific models project emissions price ranges that are broadly consistent with those in table 1. For example, analyses by Sergey Paltsev et al. (2007), U.S. Environmental Protection Agency (2008), U.S. Department of Energy, Energy Information Administration (2008a), and CRA International (2008) project emissions prices of around $40–90 per ton of CO_2 in 2025 for climate legislation that would reduce U.S. CO_2 emissions by about 20 percent below 2000 levels by that date.

2.1.3. *Deviations from Least-Cost Pricing.* Aside from the uncertainty surrounding modeling assumptions, a key qualification to the studies in table 1 is that they assume globally efficient abatement policies. More likely, particularly given the "common but differentiated responsibilities" recognized in the Kyoto Protocol, participation in global mitigation efforts among major developing country emitters will be delayed, causing marginal abatement costs to differ across regions. For a given climate stabilization scenario, to what extent does this affect worldwide abatement costs and appropriate policies in developed countries?

James A. Edmonds et al. (2008) explore these issues assuming Annex 1 countries agree to impose a harmonized emissions price starting in 2012, China joins the agreement at a later date, and other countries join whenever their per capita income reaches that of China at the time of Chinas accession. In one scenario, they assume new entrants immediately face the prevailing Annex 1 emissions price, while in another the emissions price for late entrants converges gradually over time to the Annex 1 price. The analysis accounts for emissions leakage, that is, the increase in emissions in nonparticipating countries due to the global relocation of energy-intensive firms, and increased use of fuels elsewhere as decreased demand in participating countries lowers world fuel prices.

Under the 550 ppm CO_2 target, even if China joins between 2020 and 2035, the implications for Annex 1 policies can be significant but are not that striking. Compared with the globally efficient policy, near-term Annex 1 emissions prices rise from between a few percent to 100 percent under the different scenarios, and discounted global abatement costs are higher by 10–70 percent. However, under the 450 ppm CO_2 target, essentially all of the foregone earlier reductions in non–Annex 1 countries must be offset by additional early reduction in Annex 1 countries (rather than more global abatement later in the century). This can imply dramatically higher near-term Annex 1 emissions prices, especially with longer delay and lower initial prices for late entrants. Under these scenarios, discounted global abatement costs are about 30–400 percent higher than under globally efficient pricing, and near and medium term emissions prices can be an order of magnitude larger with China's accession delayed till 2035.

A further key point from Edmonds et al. (2008) is the potentially large shift in the global incidence of abatement costs, underlying the disincentives for early developing country participation. In the globally efficient policy, without any international transfer payments, developing countries bear about 70 percent of discounted abatement costs out to 2100, while they bear "only" 17–34 percent of global abatement costs when Chinas accession occurs in 2035 and new entrants face lower starting prices.

Finally, insofar as possible pricing non-CO_2 GHGs is also important. According to modeling results in de la Chesnaye and Weyant (2006), GDP costs are 20–50 percent larger when only CO_2, as opposed to all, GHGs are priced, for the same overall limit on atmospheric CO_2-equivalent concentrations. This reflects opportunities for large-scale, low-cost options for non-

CO_2 abatement in the first half of this century, though practical difficulties in pricing other GHGs are not factored into the models.

2.1.4. *Summary*. There is a large difference in the appropriate starting prices for GHG emissions, depending on whether the ultimate objective is to limit atmospheric CO_2 concentrations to 450 or 550 ppm—targets that are approximately consistent with keeping the eventual, mean projected warming above preindustrial levels to 2.7 and 3.7°C respectively (assuming non-CO_2 GHGs are also priced). The 450 ppm target implies emissions prices should reach around $40–90 per ton of CO_2 by 2025, while the 550 ppm target implies prices should rise to $3–25 by that date. Securing early and widespread participation in an international emissions control regime can also be critical for containing costs under the 450 ppm target, while under the 550 ppm target there is greater scope for offsetting the effect of delayed participation through greater emissions reductions in the latter half of the century. Given the considerable difference in GDP losses at stake between the two targets ($8–43 trillion in present value under cost-effective pricing out to 2050 compared with $0.4–12 trillion), it is important to carefully assess what starting prices might be justified by avoiding climate change damages.

2.2. Welfare-Maximizing Emissions Pricing

2.2.1. Marginal Damage Estimates. Estimates of the marginal damages from current emissions begin with a point estimate of total contemporaneous damages from warming, usually occurring around 2100. Total damage estimates from a number of studies are roughly in the same ballpark for a given amount of warming. According to representative estimates in figure 2, damages are in the range of about 1–2 percent of world GDP for a warming of 2.5°C above preindustrial levels, though some estimates are close to zero or even negative (the prospects for negative costs diminishes with greater warming). For warming of about 4.0°C, damage estimates are typically in the order of 2–4 percent of world GDP. However, similarities in aggregate impacts mask huge inconsistencies across these studies, which reach strikingly different conclusions about the size of market and nonmarket damage categories and expected catastrophic risks.

Very few studies attempt to value the damages from more extreme warming scenarios, given so little is known about the physical impacts of large temperature changes. Two exceptions are William D. Nordhaus and Joseph Boyer (2000) and Nicholas Stern (2007) who put expected total damages at 10.2 and 11.3 percent of world GDP, for warming of 6.0°C and 7.4°C respectively, though these figures are necessarily based on extrapolations and subjective judgment. Again, there is little consistency across the estimates. In Nordhaus and Boyer (2000), catastrophic risks and market damages account for about 60 and 40 percent of total damages respectively, with nonmarket impacts roughly washing out (for example, the gains from leisure activities offset losses from the disruption of ecosystems and settlements). In

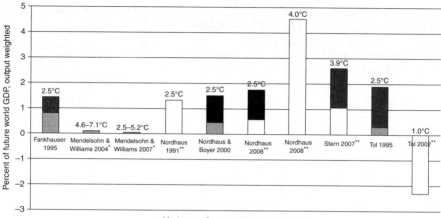

Figure 2 Selected Estimates of Contemporaneous World GDP Damages from Global Warming Occurring around 2100

Notes: * Only market damages were estimated in these studies. The above figure is the midpoint of a range of damage estimates.
** Market/nonmarket impacts are not precisely delineated in these studies.

contrast, nonmarket impacts account for about half of Stern's overall damage estimate.

Marginal damage estimates are based on assumptions about emissions/concentration relationships, climate adjustment and sensitivity, damages from climate change (inferred from a point estimate of total damages using functional form assumptions), and discount rates. Richard S. J. Tol (2009) conducts several meta-analyses of marginal damage estimates, reporting median estimates of $4.1–20.2 per ton of CO_2 (individual studies are not independent however, as they often draw from the same sources and from each other). Although individual estimates are highly divergent, most are on the low side (see also Stephen C. Newbold et al. 2009). Especially striking is the difference between Stern (2007) at $85 and Nordhaus (2008) at $8 per ton of CO_2—a difference largely dependent on discount rate assumptions (see below).[8]

There is some consensus that marginal damages grow at around 2–3 percent a year in real terms (approximately the rate of growth in output potentially affected by climate change) or about half the rate as under cost-effective emissions pricing. Marginal damages rise with the extent of warm-

---

[8] Some of the differences in marginal damage estimates reflect different assumptions about the year for which emissions are being priced, and about the extent of future warming. Most estimates of near-term Pigouvian taxes (i.e., marginal damages from the globally optimized emissions trajectory) are similar to marginal damage estimates at BAU emissions levels. One exception is Stern (2007, p. 344) where marginal damages are considerably reduced when aggressive climate stabilization goals are achieved.

ing (suggesting a faster rate of increase), but an offsetting factor is that warming is a concave (logarithmic) function of atmospheric concentrations. Although CO_2 concentrations ultimately reach 650 ppm in the twenty-second century in Nordhaus's (2008) optimal policy, constraining CO_2 concentrations to 550 ppm affects, only modestly, the emission price trajectory to 2050. Thus, optimal near and medium term emissions prices in Nordhaus (2008) are in the same ballpark with those for cost-effective stabilization of CO_2 concentrations at 550 ppm, while starting prices in Stern (2007) are broadly consistent with cost-effective prices to stabilize CO_2 concentrations at 450 ppm, or lower.

2.2.2 Controversies in Marginal Damage Assessment.
Differences in marginal damage estimates are largely explained by fundamentally different approaches to discounting rather than differences in total damages from a given amount of warming (Nordhaus 2007). However, the valuation of catastrophic and noncatastrophic damages is also highly contentious.

Discounting. The *descriptive* approach to discounting argues that we can do no better than using observed market rates, typically assumed to be about 5 percent.[9] According to this approach, market rates reveal individuals' preferences, as best we understand them, about trade-offs between early and later consumption within their lifecycle, as well as their ethical or intergenerational preferences. And they reflect the return earned by a broad range of private and public investments—the opportunity cost against which other, even intergenerational, investments ought to be measured. Proponents of the descriptive approach view discounting at market rates as essential for meaningful, consistent policy analysis and to avoid highly perverse implications in other policy contexts.

In contrast, the *prescriptive* approach argues that market rates cannot be used when looking across cohorts (rather than within individuals' lifetimes). Instead, the discount rate (r) is decomposed as follows: $r = \rho + x \cdot \eta$, where ρ is the pure rate of time preference, x is the growth rate in consumption, and η is the elasticity of marginal utility with respect to consumption. In Stern (2007), for example, $\rho=0.1$, $x=1.3$, and $\eta=1$, implying $r=1.4$. Choosing a value for ρ, the rate at which the utility of future generations is discounted just because they are in the future, is viewed as a strictly ethical judgment. And ethical neutrality, in this approach, essentially requires setting the pure rate of time preference equal to zero. Discriminating against people just because they are in the future is viewed as being akin to discriminating against people in the present generation just because they live in different

---

[9]There are many market rates, from the long-term pretax real return to equities (about 7 percent) to the after-tax return to government bonds (about 2 percent). Converting all values into their consumption equivalents, and discounting at the consumption rate of interest, narrows the possible range of choice (e.g., Robert C. Lind 1982). In fact, Ellen R. McGrattan and Edward C. Prescott (2003) suggest that the divergence in effective rates of return is actually small, with an average real debt return during peacetime over the last century of almost 4 percent and the average equity return somewhat under 5 percent.

countries (Geoffrey Heal 2009). There is also controversy over the appropriate value for η, which is almost as important as ρ. For example, Partha Dasgupta (2007) argues for using a value of 2 to 4 on normative grounds, while Anthony B. Atkinson and Andrea Brandolini (2010) suggest a value below unity is plausible, based on observed government behavior.[10]

Catastrophic Risks. Although Nordhaus and Boyer (2000) and Stern (2007) include catastrophic risks in their damage assessments, the numbers are best viewed as highly speculative placeholders. Nordhaus and Boyer (2000) put the annual willingness to pay to avoid catastrophic risks at 1.0 and 6.9 percent of world GDP, for warming levels of 2.5 and 6.0°C respectively, based on subjective probabilities (from an expert elicitation survey) for these warming levels permanently wiping out about a third of world GDP. In his central case, Stern (2007) assumes the chance of catastrophic climate change is zero up to a warming of about 5°C, beyond which the annualized risk of regional GDP losses of 5–20 percent rises by about 10 percent for each additional 1°C of warming.

Martin L. Weitzman (2009a) takes a radically different perspective. He shows that, if the probability of increasingly catastrophic outcomes falls more slowly than marginal utility in those outcomes rises (with diminished consumption), then the certainty-equivalent marginal damage from current emissions becomes infinite. These conditions apply if the probability distribution for climate sensitivity is a fat-tailed t-distribution (i.e., approaches zero at a less than exponential rate) and utility is a power function of consumption. Although marginal utility is probably not unbounded, Weitzman shows that with probabilities of a 20°C temperature change inferred from Intergovernmental Panel on Climate Change (2007), and assuming this temperature change would lower world consumption to 1 percent of its current level, expected catastrophic damages could easily dwarf noncatastrophic damages (even with these impacts delayed a century or more and discounted at market rates).[11]

There are several responses to the Weitzman critique. One is that, most likely, the probability distribution for climate sensitivity may have thin rather than fat tails. If the distribution is thin-tailed, Newbold and Adam Daigneault (2009) and Robert S. Pindyck (2008) find that damage risks from extreme global warming are typically under 3 percent of consumption (rather than infinitely large).

---

[10]Besides ethical arguments, Thomas Sterner and U. Martin Persson (2008) argue for discounting the nonmarket impacts of climate change (e.g., ecosystem loss) at below market rates. This is because the value of nonmarket goods (which are essentially fixed in supply) rises over time relative to the value of market goods (for which supply increases along with demand), assuming market and nonmarket goods are imperfect substitutes for one another.

[11]The Intergovernmental Panel on Climate Change report provides probability distributions from twenty-two scientific studies. Combining these distributions, Weitzman (2009a) suggests that there is a 5 percent and 1 percent probability that eventual warming from a doubling of CO_2 equivalent concentrations will exceed 4.5°C and 7.0°C respectively. However, making an (extremely crude) adjustment for the possibility of feedback effects he infers a distribution where the probability of eventual temperature change exceeding 10°C and 20°C is 5 percent and 1 percent respectively.

Second, setting a modest emissions price now does not preclude the possibility of a mid-course correction, involving a rapid phase-down in global emissions, should future learning reveal we are on a catastrophic trajectory (e.g., Gary W. Yohe and Tol 2009). This argument assumes policymakers can avoid the catastrophe—it breaks down if this would require *reversing* previous atmospheric accumulations because an abrupt climate threshold has been crossed.

Finally, a costly, rapid stabilization of GHG concentrations is a highly inefficient way to address the very small probability of extreme outcomes, if a portfolio of last-resort technologies could be successfully developed and deployed, if needed, to head off the catastrophe. These include "air capture" technologies for atmospheric GHG removal and "geo-engineering" technologies for modifying global climate.[12] Moreover, these R&D efforts can be led by one or several countries, avoiding the challenges endemic in organizing a rapid emissions phasedown among a large number of emitting countries with widely differing interests. Nonetheless, public R&D into last-resort technologies (virtually nonexistent at present) is highly contentious. One objection is that advancing last-resort technologies could undermine support for emissions mitigation efforts. Another is that geo-engineering (though not air capture) could have extreme downside risks (e.g., from overcooling the planet or radically altering precipitation patterns) that may be difficult to evaluate prior to widespread deployment. Whether effective institutions could be developed to prevent unilateral deployment of climate modification technologies prior to rigorous assessment of their risks is also unclear (e.g., Scott Barrett 2008; David G. Victor 2008).

In short, the implications of extreme catastrophic risks for emissions pricing are highly controversial. So long as there is some positive likelihood, no matter how small, that the climate sensitivity function is fat-tailed then catastrophic risks can still swamp noncatastrophic impacts. Mid-course policy corrections may come too late to prevent a catastrophe, given that it may take several decades for the full warming impacts of previous atmospheric accumulations to be realized. And the future viability of last-resort technologies is highly uncertain at present. All of these issues—the nature and extent of damages from extreme warming, the feasibility of future, mid-course policy corrections, and the efficient balance between mitigation and investment in last-resort technologies—are badly in need of economic analysis.

Noncatastrophic Impacts. Although on a different scale than catastrophic risks, controversies abound in the valuation of noncatastrophic damages. These include agricultural impacts, costs of increased storm intensity and protecting against rising sea levels, health impacts from heatwaves and the possible spread of vector-borne disease, loss of ecosystems,

---

[12]Besides rapid reforestation programs, air capture might involve bringing air into contact with a sorbent material that binds chemically with CO_2 and extraction of the CO_2 from the sorbent for underground, or other, disposal. Geo-engineering technologies include, for example, deflection of incoming solar radiation through shooting particles into the stratosphere or blowing oceanic water vapor to increase the cover of reflective clouds.

and so on. Box 1 provides a very brief summary of attempts to value these damage categories (see Michael Eber and Alan J. Krupnick 2009 for a more detailed discussion). However, due to the rapid outdating of prior research, daunting methodological challenges, and the small number of economists working on aggregate damage assessment, the valuation literature remains highly inconsistent and poorly developed, as a few examples illustrate (W. Michael Hanemann 2008).

Damage assessments (like those in figure 2) assume losses in consumer and producer surplus in agricultural markets are equivalent to anything from a net gain of about 0.1 percent to a net loss of 0.2 of world GDP for warming of about 2.5°C occurring in 2100. However more recent, country-specific evidence suggests that output losses could be a lot larger than those assumed in the damage assessments to infer welfare costs to agriculture. For example, William R. Cline (2007) suggests total losses of agricultural output in developing countries in the order of 30 percent, while Raymond Guiteras (2008) estimates agricultural losses of 30–40 percent for India. Even for the United States, Wolfram Schlenker, Hanemann, and Anthony C. Fisher (2005) suggest that the output of individual crops could fall by up to 70 percent by 2100. Similarly, recent evidence on ice melting suggests that sea level rises over the next century may be more extreme than the 25–60 cm assumed in most previous damage assessments (box 1). And estimated ecosystem losses of about 0.1–0.2 percent of world GDP seem inconsistent with Andreas Fischlin et al.'s (2007) projection that 20–30 percent of the world's species (an enormous amount of natural capital) faces some (though possibly slight) extinction risk.

More generally, scientific models cannot reliably predict local changes in average temperature, temperature variability, and precipitation, all of which are critical to crop yields. The baseline for impact assessment decades from now is highly sensitive to assumptions about regional development (including the ability to adapt to climate change), future technological change (e.g., into climate- and flood-resistant crops), and other policies (e.g., attempts to eradicate malaria or integrate global food markets). Controversies surround the valuing of nonmarket effects (e.g., the value of mortality in poor countries, how much people in wealthy countries value ecosystem preservation in poor countries). There is scant evidence on additional risks, such as extreme local climate change (e.g., from shifting monsoons and deserts) and broader health effects (e.g., malnutrition from food shortages, the net effects of milder winters and hotter summers, and diarrhea if droughts reduce safe drinking water supplies). Most of the impact assessment literature is based on extrapolations from U.S. studies—country-specific studies that account for local factors (e.g., ability to adapt farm practices to changing climate) have only recently begun to emerge. Finally, worldwide results mask huge disparities in regional burdens, and there is disagreement on how to aggregate impacts across regions with very different per capita income.[13]

---

[13]Most studies aggregate regional impacts using weights equal to the region's share in world GDP or world population. More generally, use of distributional weights can increase total damage estimates up to about 300 percent (e.g., David Pearce 2005).

Box 1. Valuation of Noncatastrophic Climate Damages
(for Warming of 2.5°C or Thereabouts Occurring around 2100)

Agriculture. Estimates of consumer and producer surplus losses in agricultural markets from predicted changes in regional temperature and precipitation use evidence on crop/climate sensitivity from laboratory experiments and on regressions of land values or farm performance on climate variables (e.g., Adams et al. 1990; Reilly et al. 2001; Mendelsohn et al. 1994, 2001). Laboratory studies can control for confounding factors like soil quality and the fertilizing effect of higher CO_2 concentrations, while regression analyses account for farm level adaptation (e.g., changes in crop variety and planting/harvesting dates). Worldwide agricultural impacts have been built up using extrapolations from U.S. studies, adjusting for differences in local agricultural composition and climate, and, more recently, country-specific evidence that captures local factors like adaptive capability. Studies show a pattern of gains in high latitude and temperate regions (like Russia), where current temperatures are below optimum levels for crop growth, counteracting damages in tropical regions, where current temperatures are already higher than optimal.

Sea Level. The annualized costs of future global sea level rises, due to thermal expansion and melting of sea ice, have been estimated using projections of which coastal regions will be protected, engineering data on the costs of dikes, sea walls, beach replenishment, etc., and estimated losses from abandoned or degraded property in unprotected areas. Some studies assume efficient behavior by local policymakers in their choice of which areas to protect and at what time, while others assume all currently developed areas will be protected (Yohe 2000). Nordhaus (2008) also includes an estimate of property losses from increased storm intensity due to greater wind speed and waves coming off a higher water level. Whether storm frequency will increase with more humid air is uncertain (IPCC 2007). Worldwide sea level impacts have been extrapolated from U.S. evidence, adjusting for the fraction of local land area in close proximity to the coast, though recently there have been some local studies that account for the slope and elevation of coastal land and prospective population growth (e.g., Ng and Mendelsohn 2005 on Singapore). Overall, estimates are relatively modest, for example they amount to 0.32 of world GDP in Nordhaus (2008).

Some scientists project that sea levels could increase by several meters by 2100 (Hansen 2007) rather than the 25–60cm projected by IPCC (2007). This would have major impacts on New York, Boston, Miami, London, Tokyo, Bangladesh, the whole of the Netherlands, and so on, and would completely inundate several small island states. Based on extrapolations from sea level protection costs in Holland, the global costs of this more extreme sea level rise may be at least an order of magnitude or more greater than for a moderate sea level rise, especially if coastal protection cannot be constructed expeditiously (Nicholls et al. 2008; Olsthoorn et al. 2008). Another possibility is that warming may cause changes in ocean circulation patterns. However, IPCC (2007) projects that warming from climate change will dominate any cooling effect on Europe from a weaker Gulf Stream.

Other market sectors. Studies suggest other market impacts are relatively minor. With most forests along the increasing part of the inverted-U relation between

(continued)

forest productivity and temperature, Sohngen et al. (2001) find positive overall
impacts from warming on global timber markets. Most studies find a net loss for
the energy sector, as increased costs for space cooling dominate savings in space
heating (e.g., Mendelsohn and Neumann 1999). Impacts on water availability also
tend to be negative, as increased evaporation reduces freshwater supplies, and
the value of these losses is compounded with greater demand for irrigation (Mendelsohn and Williams 2007).

Health. There have been some attempts to quantify future health damages. For
example, using statistical evidence on climate and disease, Nordhaus and Boyer
(2000) put health risks from the possible spread of vector-borne diseases like
malaria at 0.10 percent of world GDP. Broader health risks are even more speculative. According to McMichael et al. (2004), there were 166,000 excess deaths
worldwide in 2000 from climate change to date. Of these, "only" 16 percent were
from malaria, 46 percent reflected greater malnutrition due to food shortages,
another 28 percent more diarrhea cases as droughts reduce safe drinking water
supplies and concentrate contaminants, while 7 percent were from temperature extremes (most in Southeast Asia). However, malnutrition projections are
extremely sensitive to assumptions about whether, over the next century, currently vulnerable regions develop, become more integrated into global food markets, and are able to adopt hardier crops. And increased incidence of water-borne
illness might be counteracted by future development and adoption of water purification systems. Monetizing mortality effects is also contentious as there are
very few direct estimates of the value of a statistical life for poor countries.

Ecosystems. All aspects of future climate change are potential stressors to natural systems. Combining projections of ecosystems at risk from climate change
with evidence on the medicinal value of plants and willingness to pay for species
and habitat preservation, Fankhauser (1995) and Tol (1995) put the value of ecosystem loss in 2100 at 0.21 and 0.13 percent of world GDP respectively. Nordhaus
and Boyer (2000) put the combined risks to natural ecosystems and climate-sensitive human settlements at 0.17 percent of world GDP in 2100, assuming the
capital value of vulnerable systems is 5–25 percent of regional output, and an
annual willingness to pay equal to 1 percent of capital value. These estimates are
highly speculative, given that very little is known about ecological impacts and
how people value large scale (as opposed to marginal) ecosystem loss.

2.2.3 *Further Issues Posed by Uncertainty*

Finally, we touch on some additional complications for emissions pricing posed by uncertain discount rates, risk aversion, and irreversibility.

In damage valuation, the time path of future discount rates is usually
taken as given. However, the discount *factor* applied to damages is a convex
function of the future discount rate, so discount rate uncertainty (for a
given expected value) increases the certainty-equivalent discount factor

(Weitzman 1998). Newell and William A. Pizer (2003) estimated that discount rate uncertainty (inferred from U.S. historical evidence) almost doubles estimates of marginal emissions damages.

Leaving aside extreme risks, should marginal damage estimates include a risk premium? This would be appropriate if the marginal utility of consumption, net of climate damages, were larger in high-damage outcomes, in which case a mean-preserving increase in the spread of possible damages outcomes would increase expected disutility. However, if gross consumption is greater in high-damage scenarios (for example, because rapid productivity growth leads to both high consumption and high emission rates), then the marginal utility of consumption *net* of damages is lower, and possibly even lower than marginal utility in low-damage states. Simulations by Nordhaus (2008, chapter 7) suggest this might in fact be the case, implying the risk premium is actually negative, though empirically small. On the other hand, we do not know what the probability distribution over damage outcomes is. If policymakers are averse to such ambiguity this may, under certain conditions, imply a higher near term price on emissions, though how much higher is difficult to quantify (Andreas Lange and Nicolas Treich 2008).

Returning to the issue of irreversibility and future learning, is there an option value (which should be reflected in the emissions price) gained from delaying atmospheric GHG accumulations until more is known about how much damage they will cause? Option values arise if such delay increases the potential future welfare gains from responding to new information about damage risk (Pindyck 2007). If damages are linear in GHG concentrations, changes in the inherited concentration level do not affect marginal damages from additional, future accumulations. In this case, the welfare effects of policy interventions at different time periods are decoupled (at least from the damage side), and there is no option value. If instead, damages are convex in atmospheric GHG accumulations the prospect of future learning *reduces* the optimal near-term abatement level, to the extent that the damages from near-term emissions can be lowered through greater abatement in future, high-damage scenarios. Moreover, to the extent that current abatement involves (nonrecoverable) sunk investments in emissions-saving technologies, there is another source of option value, from delaying long-lived emissions-saving investments until more is known about the benefits of emissions reductions (Charles D. Kolstad 1996a). For these reasons, theoretical analyses suggest that the prospect of future learning justifies *less* near-term abatement (Kolstad 1996b; Fisher and Urvashi Narain 2003; Pindyck 2007). However, as already noted, the critical exception to this is when there is a possibility of crossing a catastrophic threshold in atmospheric concentrations *prior* to future learning, which is essentially nonreversible given the nonnegativity constraint on future emissions.

2.2.4 Summary. Most estimates of near-term marginal damages are in the order of $5–25 per ton of CO_2. This range is in the same ballpark as near-term emissions prices consistent with least-cost stabilization of atmospheric CO_2 concentrations at 550 ppm. These prices represent a lower bound on appropriate policy stringency. Much higher prices (that are consistent with 450 ppm, or even more stringent, CO_2 stabilization targets) can be implied by low discount rates and, possibly, extreme catastrophic risks (depending on the shape of the climate sensitivity distribution). Thus, whether moderate or aggressive emissions pricing is currently warranted largely hinges on one's view of discounting, whether radical mid-course corrections in response to future learning about catastrophes are feasible, and the prospects for development of last-resort technologies.

3. Policy Design

3.1. Choice among, and Design of, Domestic Emissions Control Instruments

Debate over the choice of instrument for a nationwide carbon control program is no longer about the superiority of market-based approaches over traditional forms of regulation (like technology mandates) but rather between the two market-based alternatives, emissions taxes and cap-and-trade systems.[14] In a world where the emissions externality is the only market distortion, and there is no uncertainty, either instrument could achieve the first-best outcome, if the emissions cap at each date equals the emissions that would result under the Pigouvian tax. Whether allowances are auctioned or given away for free has distributional consequences but does not affect efficiency in this setting, so long as firm behavior does not influence their future allowance allocations. If firms were free to bank and borrow emissions allowances, the policies would still be equivalent, if the permit trading ratios across different time periods were equivalent to the ratio of Pigouvian emissions taxes at those dates (Catherine Kling and Jonathan Rubin 1997).

The equivalence between the two instruments potentially breaks down in the presence of preexisting tax distortions, when distributional impacts are a concern, and when there is uncertainty. Despite these complications, to a large extent permit systems can be designed to mimic the effect of a tax, and vice versa, and therefore the choice of instrument per se is less important than whether the chosen instrument is well designed (Goulder

---

[14] Market-based instruments equalize marginal abatement costs across all abatement opportunities within the firm, across heterogeneous firms, across production sectors, and across households and firms, by establishing an economy-wide emissions price (J. H. Dales 1968; Allen V. Kneese and Blair T. Bower 1968; William J. Baumol and Wallace E. Oates 1971; W. David Montgomery 1972). In contrast, for example, a requirement that all electric utilities generate a fraction of their power from renewables will not achieve any of these efficiency conditions. Some opportunities at the firm level (e.g., substituting natural gas and nuclear power for coal), are not exploited; marginal costs will differ across heterogeneous power companies; household electricity prices will not reflect the cost of the remaining (unpriced) emissions; and abatement opportunities outside of the power sector are unexploited. For a [sic] broad reviews of the literature on environmental policy instrument choice, see Cameron Hepburn (2006) and Goulder and Ian W. H. Parry (2008).

2009). Aside from policy stringency, key design features relate to the point and scope of regulation, the allocation of policy rents, and possible provisions to limit price volatility.

3.1.1 *Point of Regulation.* Either a CO_2 tax or cap-and-trade system can be imposed upstream where fuels enter the economy (the minemouth for coal or wellhead for oil and natural gas) according to a fuel's carbon content or, as in the European trading program, to downstream emitters at the point where fuels are combusted. Upstream systems would require monitoring some 2,000–3,000 entities in the United States or European Union, while downstream systems would apply to 10,000 or more power plants and large industrial smokestacks (Daniel S. Hall 2007).[15] For a given total emissions reduction, the estimated economic costs of downstream programs out to 2030 are not dramatically larger than those for comprehensive upstream systems—about 20 percent larger according to Goulder (2009)—even though downstream programs cover only about half of total U.S. and EU CO_2 emissions. This is because the huge bulk of low-cost abatement opportunities are (initially) in the power sector. Moreover, the infeasibility of monitoring emissions from vehicles, home heating fuels, and small-scale industrial boilers in a downstream system can be largely addressed through supplementary midstream measures targeted at refined transportation and heating fuels, which further narrows the cost discrepancy between upstream and downstream systems.

There are a couple of other notable differences between the two systems. One is that upstream programs must be combined with a crediting system to encourage development and adoption of carbon capture and storage technologies at coal plants and industrial sources. (The tax credit should equal the amount of carbon sequestered, as measured by continuous emission monitoring systems, times the emissions price). The other is that, at least for the United States where many states retain cost-of-service regulation, the opportunity cost of freely allocated emissions allowances to electric utilities in a downstream system may not be passed forward into higher generation prices. As a result, incentives for electricity conservation could be a lot weaker, resulting in a significant loss of cost-effectiveness, compared with upstream programs or downstream programs with full allowance auctioning (Dallas Burtraw et al. 2001).

3.1.2 *Scope of Regulation.* Domestic programs that fail to cover embodied carbon in products imported from countries with suboptimal or no emissions controls may cause significant emissions leakage. The problem is most relevant for downstream, energy-intensive firms competing in global markets (e.g., chemicals and plastics, primary metals, petroleum refining),

---

[15]If introduced at the same points in the economy, CO_2 taxes and cap-and-trade systems are likely to have very similar administrative costs. Under cap-and-trade, costs also include those from administering trading markets, as well as the transactions costs of the trades themselves, though these are relatively small (Robert N. Stavins 1995).

where reduced production at home may be largely offset by increased production in other countries with higher emissions intensity than in the United States. According to some models, as much as 15–25 percent of economy-wide U.S. CO_2 reductions could be offset by extra emissions elsewhere, although the majority of the leakage stems from changes in global fuel prices rather than relocation of footloose capital (Sujata Gupta et al. 2007; Mun S. Ho, Richard Morgenstern, and Jhih-Shyang Shih 2008; Carolyn Fischer and Alan K. Fox 2007, 2009). Possible policy responses to the latter source of leakage include imposing taxes, or permit requirements, according to embodied carbon in product imports (and symmetrical rebates for exporters) or to subsidize the output of leakage-prone industries (e.g., through output-based allocations of free emissions allowances). However, all these approaches may run afoul of international trade obligations.

Certain non-CO_2 GHGs are easily monitored (e.g., vented methane from underground coalmines, fluorinated gases used in refrigerants and air conditioners) and could be directly integrated into a CO_2 mitigation program through taxes, or permit trading ratios, reflecting their relative lifetime warming potential. Other gases are far more difficult to monitor, and are better incorporated, insofar as possible, through offset provisions, where the onus falls on the individual entity to demonstrate valid reductions relative to a credible baseline. For example, methane from landfills and livestock waste might be collected, using an impermeable cover, and flared or used in onsite power generation, while nitrous oxide might be reduced through changes in tilling and fertilizer use (e.g., Shih et al. 2006; Hall 2007).

Finally, CO_2 abatement through forest carbon sequestration (e.g., from reducing deforestation, reforesting abandoned cropland and harvested timberland, modifying harvest practices to reduce soil disturbance) appears to be relatively cost effective. According to Stavins and Kenneth R. Richards (2005), as much as 30 percent of U.S. fossil fuel CO_2 emissions might be sequestered at a cost of up to about $20 per ton of CO_2. Coupling a domestic mitigation program with offset provisions for forest carbon sequestration will require measuring regional forest inventories to establish baselines, monitoring changes in forest use (through remote sensing and ground-level sampling) relative to the baseline, and inferring the emissions implications of these changes based on sampling of local tree species and age. However, even if these monitoring challenges can be overcome, further problems remain. One is that, without an international program covering major forested countries, domestic reductions can be offset through emissions leakage via changes in world timber prices (Brian C. Murray, Bruce A. McCarl, and Heng-Chi Lee 2002 estimate the international leakage rate could be anywhere from less than 10 percent to over 90 percent depending on the type of activity and location in the United States). Another is that sequestered carbon in trees is not necessarily permanent if trees are later cut down, decay or burn, requiring assignment of liability to either the offset buyer or seller for the lost carbon.

3.1.3 *Allocation of Policy Rents.* In their traditional form, emissions taxes raise revenues for the government, while cap-and-trade systems create rents for firms receiving free allowance allocations. However, through allowance auctions, cap-and-trade systems can generate comparable revenues to a tax, while rents can be provided under a tax through inframarginal exemptions for emissions or carbon content. Under either instrument, the fraction of policy rents accruing to the government rather than private firms, and how revenues are used, are extremely important for efficiency and distributional incidence.

Fiscal Linkages. The implications for emissions control policies of pre-existing tax distortions in factor markets have received considerable attention in the broader environmental economics literature (e.g., A. Lans Bovenberg and Goulder 2002), though these distortions are typically not integrated into energy–climate models. This raises two issues: to what extent is there a cost saving from policies that raise revenues and use them to offset distortionary taxes like income and payroll taxes, and to what extent do models that ignore prior tax distortions produce inaccurate estimates of policy costs?

The efficiency gain from recycling revenues in other tax reductions (relative to returning them lump sum or leaving policy rents in the private sector) is simply the amount of revenue raised times the marginal excess burden of taxation. Although there is uncertainty over behavioral responses in factor markets, a typical assumption is that the marginal excess burden of income taxes (with revenue returned lump sum) is around $0.25 for the United States, or perhaps as high as $0.40 if distortions in the pattern of spending created by tax preferences (e.g., for employer medical insurance or homeownership) are taken into account. For modest carbon policies, the efficiency gain from revenue recycling can be large relative to the direct efficiency cost of the policy, or Harberger triangle under the marginal abatement cost schedule. For example, if a $30 tax on U.S. CO_2 emissions (currently about 6 billion tons) reduces annual emissions by 10 percent, the Harberger triangle is $9 billion, while the revenue-recycling benefit is roughly $40–65 billion per year.

However, this does not necessarily mean that revenue-neutral CO_2 taxes or auctioned allowance systems, produce a "double dividend" by reducing the costs of the broader tax system, in addition to slowing climate change. There is a counteracting, "tax-interaction" effect (e.g., Goulder 1995). Specifically, the (policy-induced) increase in energy prices drives up the general price level, which reduces real factor returns, and thereby (slightly) reduces factor supply and efficiency. Most analytical and numerical analyses of environmental tax shifts find that the tax-interaction effect exceeds the revenue-recycling effect, implying no double dividend, and that abatement costs are actually higher due to the presence of preexisting tax distortions. A rough rule of thumb from these models is that the costs of revenue-neutral emissions taxes are about 15 percent greater, due to interactions with prior tax distortions, implying the optimal tax is 15 percent lower than the Pigouvian tax (e.g., Bovenberg and Goulder 2002).

However, the cost increase is far more substantial for policies that do not exploit the revenue recycling effect (i.e., cap-and-trade with free allowance allocation or CO_2 taxes with revenues not used to increase economic efficiency). According to formulas derived in Goulder et al. (1999), the increase exceeds 100 percent when the emissions reduction is below 30 percent.[16]

More generally, there are many ways that carbon policy revenues might be used, such as funding technology programs, climate adaptation projects, deficit reduction, energy efficiency programs, rebates to electricity consumers, and any number of complex adjustments to the tax system, though the efficiency implications of these recycling options are often not well understood. Although in recent years there has been more interest in permit auctions, in some cases it is unclear how the revenues will be spent.[17] Unless legislation accompanying carbon policies specifies offsetting reductions in other distortionary taxes, there is ambiguity to what extent this shift implies a reduction in the overall costs of carbon policies.

Distributional Considerations. The distributional impacts of emissions control policies are potentially important for both equity and feasibility.

On equity grounds the difference between (revenue-neutral) CO_2 taxes/auctioned allowances, and allowance systems with free allocation to firms, can be quite striking. Under the latter policy, permit rents are reflected in higher firm equity values, and therefore (through dividend and capital gains income) ultimately accrue to shareholders, who are concentrated in upper income groups. Terry Dinan and Diane Lim Rogers (2002) estimated that, for a 15 percent reduction in CO_2 emissions, U.S. households in the lowest-income quintile would be worse off on average by around $500 per year, while households in the top-income quintile reap a net gain of around $1,000 (i.e., increased stockholder wealth overcompensates this group for higher energy prices). This inequitable outcome could be avoided under emissions taxes and auctioned allowance systems if revenues were recycled in income tax reductions tilted toward the poor (e.g., Gilbert E. Metcalf 2009).

---

[16]There are some caveats here. One is that the proportionate increase in abatement costs may be much smaller in other countries if tax wedges in factor markets are smaller than those in the United States, or if labor markets are dominated by institutional wage setting (e.g., Francesco Bosello, Carlo Carraro, and Marzio Galeotti 2001). Another is that the tax-interaction effect is weaker if, due to regulated pricing and/or infra-marginal rents on coal technologies that bear some of the burden of emissions pricing, there is incomplete pass through of emissions prices into electricity prices (Antonio M. Bento and Mark Jacobsen 2007; Parry 2005). Finally, the revenue-recycling effect can dominate the tax-interaction effect when tax preferences cause significant distortions or when a large share of revenues are used to cut taxes on capital as opposed to labor (see Parry and Bento 2000 and Bovenberg and Goulder 1997 respectively).

[17] For example, in the first two phases of the European Union's CO_2 trading program (2005–07 and 2008–12), over 95 percent of the allowances were given away free to existing emissions sources. However, partly in response to the large windfall profits earned by power companies, the plan is to transition to full allowance auctions for that sector by 2020, with the decision on how to use revenues largely left to the member states (Jos Sijm, Karsten Neuhoff, and Yihsu Chen 2006; Commission of the European Communities 2008). In the Regional Greenhouse Gas Initiative in the United States, covering power sector CO_2 emissions from ten Northeastern and Mid-Atlantic states, allowances are auctioned with revenues earmarked for energy efficiency and other clean technology programs.

As regards feasibility, compensation for adversely affected industries may be part of the political deal-making needed to first initiate, and progressively tighten, emissions controls (e.g., A. Denny Ellerman 2005). Compensation, through free allowance allocation or tax relief, may be required for both formally regulated sectors and downstream sectors vulnerable to higher energy prices (e.g., energy-intensive firms competing in global markets). However, given the tension between providing industry compensation, and the fiscal and (household) equity reasons for raising revenue, it is important to know how much compensation is needed to keep firms whole. At least for a moderately scaled CO_2 permit system, only about 15–20 percent of allowances are needed to compensate energy intensive industries for their loss of producer surplus, so the huge bulk of the allowances could still be auctioned (Bovenberg and Goulder 2001, Anne E. Smith, Martin T. Ross, and Montgomery 2002). Although there are reasons for phasing out compensation over time, firms may still be amenable to this if they receive excess compensation in the early years of the program (e.g., Stavins 2007).[18]

3.1.4 *Price Volatility.* Another reason CO_2 taxes and cap-and-trade systems may produce different outcomes stems from uncertainty over future abatement costs reflecting, for example, uncertainty over energy prices, technological advances, and substitutes for fossil fuels.

Price versus Quantity Instruments in their Pure Form. If the goal is welfare maximization, abatement cost uncertainty strongly favors emissions taxes over cap-and-trade systems in their pure form. This is most easily seen in a static setting where the marginal benefits from abatement are constant. In this case, a Pigouvian emissions tax automatically equates marginal benefits to marginal abatement costs, regardless of the position of the marginal abatement cost schedule. In contrast, when emissions are capped to equate marginal benefits with expected marginal abatement costs, ex post abatement will either be too high or too low depending on whether the marginal abatement cost schedule is higher or lower than expected (Weitzman 1974; Marc J. Roberts and Michael Spence 1976; Yohe 1978).

This basic result carries over to a dynamic context with a sequence of annual (Pigouvian) taxes or emissions caps, and where environmental damages depend on the accumulated atmospheric stock of emissions. Here, we have strong reasons to believe that the marginal benefits from global emissions reductions are essentially constant, as abatement in any one year has minimal impact on the atmospheric stock. In fact, with abatement cost uncertainty, simulation analyses suggest that discounted welfare gains under (globally imposed) CO_2 taxes might be several times those under

---

[18]One reason for phasing out allowance allocations is that they must initially be based on a firm's historical emission rates (prior to program implementation), which maybe viewed as increasingly unfair as firms grow or contract at different rates, or change their fuel mix, over time. However, any updating of baselines based on firm performance will likely introduce distortions in firm behavior (Knut Einar Rosendahl 2008). Free allowance allocation may also retard the exit of inefficient firms from an industry if firms lose their rights to future allocations when they go out of business.

(equivalently scaled) permits (e.g., Pizer 2002; Michael Hoel and Larry Karp 2002). A qualification to this is that the welfare advantage of taxes is less pronounced if abatement cost shocks persist over time and the emissions cap can be adjusted in response to those shocks (e.g., Karp and Jiang-feng Zhang 2005; Newell and Pizer 2003).

Stabilizing Allowance Prices. Emissions price volatility under cap-and-trade systems can be contained by allowing firms to bank permits when permit prices (and marginal abatement costs) are low, and borrow permits from future periods when prevailing prices are high. In fact, if banking and borrowing were completely unlimited and costless, expected allowance prices would rise at the interest rate, and the system would be largely equivalent to that of an emissions tax growing at the interest rate. Alternatively, through establishing appropriate ratios for trading permits across time, the allowance price trajectory could mimic the growth in marginal emissions damages over time (e.g., Kling and Rubin 1997).

In fact, most existing cap-and-trade systems (e.g., the federal SO_2 and regional CO_2 programs in the United States and the European Union's CO_2 program) now incorporate banking and borrowing provisions, though in response to concerns about default risk, borrowing is penalized through unfavorable trading ratios and/or quantitative limits. Harrison Fell, Ian A. MacKenzie, and Pizer (2008) estimate that banking and borrowing provisions contained in leading U.S. federal climate proposals obtain about one quarter to one half of the cost savings from emissions taxes over equivalent cap-and-trade systems without these provisions.

An alternative approach is to limit price volatility through a "safety valve," where the government sells additional permits at a fixed price to prevent allowance prices from rising above a ceiling price (e.g., Henry D. Jacoby and Ellerman 2004). Expected welfare under this policy is maximized by essentially designing it to mimic a Pigouvian tax—that is, setting the safety valve price equal to marginal emissions damages and the emissions cap tight enough so the safety valve binds nearly all the time (Pizer 2002). Intermediate cases (with higher safety valve prices and/or less stringent caps) generate intermediate welfare gains between those of the pure tax and emissions quota. A further alternative is a collar which combines a price ceiling with a price floor. This approach encourages additional abatement when allowance prices are low (to offset reduced abatement when allowance prices are high) and avoids the potentially harmful impacts of the price ceiling only on incentives to invest in emissions-saving technologies. According to Fell, MacKenzie, and Pizer (2008) the annualized cost savings between emissions taxes and fixed emissions quotas in the United States would be about $4 billion for an emissions price of around $20 per ton of CO_2, with safety valves and price collars yielding intermediate cost savings.

One final twist in instrument choice is that the price flexibility afforded by a cap-and-trade system with (unhindered) allowance borrowing and banking could actually be advantageous from a social welfare perspective, when there is learning about future damages and emissions taxes can only be adjusted at discrete intervals (Murray, Newell, and Pizer 2009).[19] Under the former policy, new information about damages will be immediately reflected in the time path of current and expected future allowance prices, as speculators anticipate an adjustment of future emissions targets in response to that information. In contrast, it may take some time before emissions taxes can be adjusted to reflect new information, leaving emissions prices suboptimal during the period of policy stickiness.

3.2 *Promoting Technology Development and Diffusion*

Several studies have demonstrated the central role that the availability and cost of advanced energy technologies plays in determining the future costs of GHG emission targets (e.g., Clarke et al. 2006; Edmonds, Joseph M. Roop, and Michael J. Scott 2000; Kenneth Gillingham, Newell, and Pizer 2008). For example, Clarke et al. (2006) found that if ambitious goals for technology development are achieved, this can reduce discounted global abatement costs by 50 percent or more. Establishing a price on CO_2 emissions is the single most important policy for encouraging the innovation that might bring about advanced technology development. However, additional measures to promote applied R&D, more basic research, and technology deployment, may be justified to the extent they address market failures at different stages of the innovation process.

3.2.1 *R&D Policy.* One market failure stems from the inability of private sector inventors or innovators to fully appropriate spillover benefits to other firms that might copy a new technology, imitate around the technology if it is under patent, or otherwise use knowledge about the technology to advance their own research programs (Adam B. Jaffe, Newell, and Stavins 2003). Numerous empirical studies suggest that technology spillovers cause the (marginal) social return to (commercial) R&D to be several times the (marginal) private return.[20]

---

[19]Uncertainty over the marginal benefit schedule, in the absence of learning, would not affect the choice between emissions taxes and cap-and-trade because, on average, cumulated emissions reductions, and hence expected environmental benefits, are the same under both instruments (e.g., Stavins 1996).

[20]For example, Zvi Griliches (1992), Edwin Mansfield (1985), Charles I. Jones and John C. Williams (1998). Although there is a possibility of excessive competition for a given amount of innovation rent, analogous to the excessive competition for open-access resources, this problem is generally thought to be dominated by the imperfect appropriability effect (Griliches 1992). In fact, the problem of suboptimal innovation incentives may be especially severe for GHG-saving technologies, compared with commercial technologies. For example, skepticism over long-term commitments to emissions pricing, and the desirability of retaining policy discretion to respond to future scientific knowledge, undermines the durable and substantial incentives needed for encouraging GHG-saving technology investments with high upfront costs. Limited patent lifetimes may also discourage firms from launching R&D programs until a high enough emissions price is established (Reyer Gerlagh, Snorre Kvendokk, and Rosendahl 2008).

Still, efficiency gains from correcting the R&D market failure appear to be smaller than those from correcting the CO_2 emissions externality (Parry, Pizer, and Fischer 2003).

The appropriability problem implies that R&D incentives will be sub-optimal, even under Pigouvian emissions pricing. One response would simply be to set emissions prices at a level higher than warranted by exter-nalities. However, this would generate efficiency losses from excessive short-term abatement, and would not differentiate incentives across tech-nologies that might face very different market impediments. In fact, no single instrument—either emissions pricing or R&D incentives—can effec-tively correct both the emissions externality and the knowledge appropri-ability problem: using one instrument alone may involve considerably higher costs than employing two complementary instruments (Fischer and Newell 2008; Goulder and Stephen H. Schneider 1999).

Unfortunately, available literature provides limited guidance on the design of complementary R&D instruments. It is not clear which instru-ment among, for instance, research subsidies, strengthened patent rules, or technology prizes, is most efficient, as this depends on the magnitude of technology spillovers, the scope for monopoly pricing under patents, and asymmetric information between governments and firms about the expected benefits and costs of research (e.g., Brian Davern Wright 1983). And just how much applied R&D in the energy sector should be expanded is difficult to estimate, given uncertainty over the productivity of research and the risk of crowding out socially valuable research elsewhere in the economy (e.g., Nordhaus 2002; Goulder and Schneider 1999).

3.2.2 Basic Research. Appropriability problems are most severe for more basic research, which is largely conducted by universities, other nonprofits, and federal labs, mostly through central government funding. While it is not practical to assess the efficient allocation of funding across individual pro-grams, Newell (2008, p. 32) suggests that a doubling of U.S. federal climate research spending (currently about $4 billion a year) is likely warranted, based on plausible assumptions about the rate of return on such spending. To avoid crowding out, this should be phased in to allow a progressive expansion in supply of college graduates in engineering and science.

3.2.3 Deployment Policy. In principle there are several possibilities for market failures at the technology deployment stage. For example, through learning-by-doing early adopters of a new technology (e.g., a cellulosic etha-nol plant or solar photovoltaic installations) may lower production costs for later adopters (e.g., Arthur van Benthem, Gillingham, and James Sweeney 2008). But, since the potential for these spillovers may vary greatly depend-ing on industry structure, the maturity of the technology, etc., any case for early adoption subsidies needs to be considered on a case-by-case basis.

Another possible market failure is consumer undervaluation of energy efficiency, which has been a key motivation for regulations governing auto fuel economy and household appliances. However, although there is an empirical literature suggesting that households discount savings from energy efficiency improvements at much higher rates than market rates, whether this is evidence of a market failure as opposed to hidden costs or borrowing constraints remains an unsettled issue (e.g., Gillingham, Newell, and Karen Palmer 2009). Other market imperfections might include asymmetric information between project developers and lenders, network effects in large integrated systems, and incomplete insurance markets for liability associated with specific technologies. However, because solid empirical evidence is lacking, little can be said about the seriousness of all these market failure possibilities, and whether or not they might warrant additional policy interventions.

3.3 *International Policy Design*

Proposed architectures for international emissions control regimes can be loosely classified into those based on bottom-up versus top-down (i.e., internationally negotiated) approaches and cap-and-trade systems versus systems of emissions taxes (e.g., Joseph E. Aldy and Stavins 2007). There is disagreement over which type of architecture is most desirable, and most likely to emerge in practice. In the bottom up approach, norms for participation might evolve from small groups of countries launching regional programs that progressively expand and integrate, or by explicit linking of domestic cap-and-trade programs (e.g., Carraro 2007; Judson Jaffe and Stavins 2008; Victor 2007). Alternatively, countries might regularly pledge emissions reductions with periodic reviews by a formal institution (e.g., Thomas Schelling 2007; Pizer 2007). Here we focus on top-down approaches, given that advocates of rapid climate stabilization tend to favor internationally binding commitments.

The most daunting challenge is designing an architecture that encourages participation among some three or four dozen of the world's largest GHG emitters—the Kyoto framework failed to do this as non–Annex 1 countries, including China, Brazil, South Africa, Mexico and Indonesia, had no emissions control obligations, while the United States withdrew from the agreement.[21] Broad participation is needed—at least over the longer term and possibly also the near term under a stringent climate stabilization target (see above)—to promote the cost-effectiveness of any international agreement, and limit concerns about international competitiveness and emissions leakage. Participation of developing countries through the Clean Development Mechanism (CDM), as at present, does not reduce global emissions—it only lowers the cost to developed countries of meeting their emissions goals by allowing firms to purchase (lower cost) emissions reductions elsewhere on a project-by-project basis. Moreover, there is considerable concern that some CDM credits may not represent truly additional reductions, due the difficulty of establishing a baseline against which reductions can be measured, in which case the CDM serves to *increase* global emissions

---

[21]China's CO_2 emissions now exceed those for the United States, while India's exceed those of Japan (U.S. Department of Energy, Energy Information Administration 2008b, table A10). In fact, fifty non–Annex 1 countries now have per capita income greater than that of the poorest Annex 1 countries.

(e.g., Andrew Keeler and Alexander Thompson 2008; Rosendahl and Jon Strand 2009).

To be successful, each country must perceive an emissions control agreement as equitable in terms of sharing the burden of global mitigation costs. Usually this means that industrial countries bear a disproportionately greater cost burden due to their higher per capita income and greater contribution to historical GHG accumulations. However, as noted above, under a globally cost-effective pricing agreement with no side-payments, developed countries may bear two-thirds or more of discounted global abatement costs over the next century. Negotiations are further hampered, under a Kyoto type of framework, by the need to agree on emissions quotas for every participating country, and to periodically renegotiate these quotas, which can be contentious if economies expand at different rates during interim periods.

Jeffrey Frankel (2008) offers a global cap-and-trade proposal that addresses equity through imposing no cost burden on developing countries in the early years, and subsequently a cost burden comparable to those previously borne by others at a similar stage of economic development. Global cost effectiveness is preserved, and emissions leakage avoided, by establishing a harmonized emissions price through immediately incorporating all countries into the global trading system, with low-income countries initially allocated emissions caps equal to their projected emissions. Effectively, the pattern of stringent and lax quota allocations among developed and developing countries creates a system of side payments from developed countries (who are net permit buyers) which compensates developing countries (who are net permit sellers) for the costs of their emissions reductions. Furthermore, negotiations are greatly simplified by the establishment of simple formulas that automatically start reducing developing country quotas once their per capita income, or per capita emissions, cross certain thresholds.

A globally harmonized CO_2 tax can be designed to essentially replicate this cap-and-trade system, so there appears to be little reason, in this regard, for preferring one instrument over the other. Instead of agreeing on a global emissions cap, and how it adjusts over time, countries would need to agree on a harmonized tax rate, and how this rate is increased over time. And instead of negotiating over rules relating quota allocations to the evolution of per capita income (or emissions) over time, countries would need to agree on rules for explicit side payments related to a country's per capita income (or emissions).

However, under either the cap-and-trade or tax-based approach, there is an obvious tension between compensating developing nations and policy stringency. For example, Jacoby et al. (2008) estimate that, under a global policy that stabilizes CO_2 concentrations at (approximately) 450 ppm, compensation for developing countries would entail (explicit or implicit) side payments by the United States of $200 billion in 2020 (or ten times current U.S. development assistance), which calls into question the credibility of such compensation schemes. Even with less than full compensation, the international transfers are of unprecedented scale. A critical lesson here is to keep down compensation to the minimum amount needed to entice developing country participation. In this regard, granting these countries initial quota allocations equal to their BAU emissions is wasteful, as it provides roughly twice the compensation needed to cover abatement costs (in the absence of other distortions, excess compensation is the integral between the emissions price and the marginal abatement cost curve).

As regards verification of policies, one potential problem with an emissions tax is that countries may undermine its effect through reductions in other energy taxes. In principle, countries might be pressured to adjust their emissions tax rate to offset changes in other energy tax provisions, based on periodic reviews of country tax systems, and progress on emissions reductions, by an independent agency like the International Monetary Fund. Measuring other energy tax provisions in terms of their equivalent tax (or subsidy) on CO_2 would be contentious however, because of opaque systems of tax preferences for energy investments, the possible role of energy taxes in correcting other externalities like local pollution and road congestion, and the possibility of non-tax regulations that further penalize or subsidize energy (e.g., fuel economy standards, energy price regulations). On the other hand, most countries have established tax ministries that would be able to implement a new tax on (the carbon content of) fossil fuels. In contrast, many developing countries may lack the capacity to enforce permit requirements and property rights due to weak environmental agencies and judicial institutions.

Finally, although not incorporated in most energy/climate models, the forest sector appears to offer some of the easiest and least expensive opportunities for cutting CO_2 emissions. For example, under a 550 ppm CO_2 stabilization target, Massimo Tavoni, Brent Sohngen, and Valentina Bosetti (2007) estimate that forest sinks can contribute one-third of total abatement by 2050 and thereby decrease the required price on CO_2 emissions by around 40 percent. This is mainly achieved through avoided deforestation in tropical forests, though it could be sustained in the second half of the century through aforestation and enhanced forest management. Emission credits for slowed deforestation were not permitted under the 1997 Kyoto framework, but since then analysts have become somewhat more optimistic about the feasibility of integrating deforestation into an international emissions control regime, despite the practical challenges noted above (e.g., Ruth DeFries et al. 2006). However, broad participation in any agreement among major tropical forest regions would be critical to avoid the risk of serious emissions leakage.

3.4 *Summary*

A revenue-neutral CO_2 tax has multiple desirable properties from an efficiency standpoint. Although allowances can be auctioned, and emissions price volatility contained, why implement a more elaborate cap-and-trade system if its purpose is to largely mimic the advantages of a tax? A likely answer is that political factors appear to favor the latter instrument (e.g., Goulder 2009). Emissions taxes, at least in the United States, appear to be highly unpopular, while cap-and-trade systems are popular among environmental advocates given their focus on binding emissions targets and they also have active supporters in the financial sector, who see them as opportunities to make money. But whichever instrument is chosen, getting the design details right is critical for cost-effectiveness—especially broad coverage of emissions, raising and efficiently using revenues, and containing price variability.

While most analysts agree that mitigation policies should be supplemented with additional policies to promote basic and applied research into emissions-saving technologies at government, university, and private institutions, the level of support and the specific instruments that should be employed are far less clear. And there is little consensus about the case for further policy intervention at the technology deployment stage—this depends on the specifics of the industries or processes involved and assumptions about consumer behavior that are in need of further study.

At an international level, the choice between cap-and-trade and emissions taxes is also nuanced. Either system can be globally cost-effective and accommodate transfers to developing countries. And while cap-and-trade systems are immune to the possibility of offsetting changes in the broader energy tax system, they may face larger implementation obstacles in developing countries. The biggest problem in transitioning away from the CDM toward an integrated global emissions trading system is the possibility of a large gap between the compensation that might be demanded by developing countries in exchange for their participation and the amount of compensation that developed countries are willing to provide—a gap that could be especially large under rapid atmospheric stabilization targets. Finally, integration of carbon forest sequestration into international emissions control agreements is potentially important for containing the burden of mitigation costs.

4. Research Priorities

While a great deal has been learned about climate policy design over the last couple of decades, much economic analysis remains to be done.

Energy/climate models provide some rough bounds on near-term emissions pricing trajectories, and associated GDP losses, implied by climate stabilization scenarios, and the range of uncertainty may narrow as more is learned about the costs of new technologies and behavioral responses to emissions pricing. Nonetheless, there are many research priorities in this area, such as trying to narrow disagreement over BAU emissions assumptions (e.g., through better population projections); improving the representation of endogenous technological change, prior policy distortions, and possible market power in world oil and natural gas markets; quantifying the benefits of major technological breakthroughs to guide R&D efforts; and further exploring the cost and distributional implications of deviations from globally efficient emissions pricing.

Some of the biggest challenges facing climate economists are to develop, and apply, methodologies for valuing the wide array of market and non-market impacts across different regions, time periods, and scenarios for climate change (ecological, health, and extreme sea level impacts in particular, are poorly understood). However, in terms of shedding more light on whether there is a solid economic basis for aggressive, as opposed to more moderate, near-term emissions pricing, the most critical issues in need of study appear to be the nature and magnitude of damage risks from extreme warming scenarios and the extent to which the possibility of future, mid-course corrections, and deployment of last-resort technologies, in response to future learning, lowers the near-term emissions price. More research on discount rates might also be valuable, especially in trying to reconcile different approaches (e.g., Wilfred Beckerman and Hepburn 2007).

On the design of domestic mitigation schemes, one topic badly in need of study, given the potentially large revenues from carbon policies, is the efficiency and distributional implications of the diverse array of options for revenue use. Additional research priorities include the design of practical, and cost-effective, provisions to address international emissions leakage and incorporate incentives for abatement of non-CO_2 GHGs and forest carbon sequestration.

As regards complementary technology policy, research is needed on both the appropriate level, and the relative efficiency, of alternative instruments to encourage applied R&D, as well as the amount and composition of basic energy R&D. Empirical research is also needed to ascertain whether or not there are additional market failures that justify further policy intervention at the technology deployment stage. Even if the empirical basis for such market failures is weak, research is still needed on the interactions, and possible redundancies, between all kinds of increasingly prevalent climate and energy-related regulatory interventions. For example, in the transportation sector this would include interactions between carbon policies, fuel taxes, fuel economy standards, low-carbon fuel standards, hybrid vehicle purchase subsidies, and subsidies and mandates for renewable fuels. In the power sector it would include interactions with regulations governing the efficiency of buildings, appliances, and lighting and inducements for renewable and other low-carbon fuels.

Finally, a critical issue at an international level is the design of rules for accession and graduated responsibilities for developing countries that are widely perceived as being fair. At the same time, agreements should minimize deviations from cost-effective emissions pricing as well as minimizing the risks of excessive transfers to developing countries.

REFERENCES

Adams, Richard M., Cynthia Rosenzweig, Robert M. Peart, Joe T. Ritchie, Bruce A. McCarl, J. David Glyer, R. Bruce Curry, James W. Jones, Kenneth J. Boote, and L. Hartwell Allen. 1990. "Global Climate Change and US Agriculture." *Nature*, 345(6272): 219–24.

Aldy, Joseph E., and Robert N. Stavins, eds. 2007. *Architectures for Agreement: Addressing Global Climate Change in the Post-Kyoto World*. Cambridge and New York: Cambridge University Press.

Atkinson, Anthony B., and Andrea Brandolini. 2010. "On Analyzing the World Distribution of Income." *World Bank Economic Review*, 24(1): 1–37.

Barrett, Scott. 2008. "The Incredible Economics of Geoengineering." *Environmental and Resource Economics*, 39(1): 45–54.

Baumol, William J., and Wallace E. Oates. 1971. "The Use of Standards and Prices for Protection of the Environment." *Swedish Journal of Economics*, 73(1): 42–54.

Beckerman, Wilfred, and Cameron Hepburn. 2007. "Ethics of the Discount Rate in the Stem Review on the Economics of Climate Change." *World Economics*, 8(1): 187–210.

Bento, Antonio M., and Mark Jacobsen. 2007. "Ricardian Rents, Environmental Policy and the 'Double-Dividend' Hypothesis." *Journal of Environmental Economics and Management*, 53(1): 17–31.

Bosello, Francesco, Carlo Carraro, and Marzio Galeotti. 2001. "The Double Dividend Issue: Modeling Strategies and Empirical Findings." *Environment and Development Economics*, 6(1): 9–45.

Bovenberg, A. Lans, and Lawrence H. Goulder. 1997. "Costs of Environmentally Motivated Taxes in the Presence of Other Taxes: General Equilibrium Analyses." *National Tax Journal*, 50(1): 59–87.

Bovenberg, A. Lans, and Lawrence H. Goulder. 2001. "Neutralizing the Adverse Industry Impacts of CO_2 Abatement Policies: What Does It Cost?" *In Behavioral and Distributional Effects of Environmental Policy*, ed. Carlo Carraro and Gilbert E. Metcalf, 45–85. Chicago and London: University of Chicago Press.

Bovenberg, A. Lans, and Lawrence H. Goulder. 2002. "Environmental Taxation and Regulation." In *Handbook of Public Economics, Volume 3*, ed. Alan J. Auerbach and Martin Feldstein, 1471–1545. Amsterdam; London and New York: Elsevier Science, North-Holland.

Burtraw, Dallas, Karen Palmer, Ranjit Bharvirkar, and Anthony Paul. 2001. "The Effect of Allowance Allocation on the Cost of Carbon Emission Trading." Resources for the Future Discussion Paper 01-30.

Carraro, Carlo. 2007. "Incentives and Institutions: A Bottom–Up Approach to Climate Policy." In *Architectures for Agreement: Addressing Global Climate Change in the Post-Kyoto World*, ed. Joseph E. Aldy and Robert N. Stavins, 161–72. Cambridge and New York: Cambridge University Press.

de la Chesnaye, Francisco C., and John P. Weyant, eds. 2006. "Multi-greenhouse Gas Mitigation and Climate Policy." *Climate Policy*, (Special Issue).

Clarke, Leon E., James A. Edmonds, Henry D. Jacoby, Hugh M. Pitcher, John M. Reilly, and Richard G. Richels. 2007. *Scenarios of Greenhouse Gas Emissions and Atmospheric Concentrations*. Washington, D.C.: U.S. Climate Change Science Program.

Clarke, Leon E., Marshall Wise, M. Placet, R. C. Izaurralde, Joshua Lurz, S. H. Kim, S. J. Smith, and A. M. Thomson. 2006. "Climate Change Mitigation: An

Analysis of Advanced Technology Scenarios." Richland, Wash.: Pacific Northwest National Laboratory.

Cline, William R. 2007. *Global Warming and Agriculture: Impact Estimates by Country*. Washington, D.C.: Center for Global Development.

Commission of the European Communities. 2008. "20 20 by 2020: Europe's Climate Change Opportunity." Commission of the European Communities, Communication from the Commission to the European Parliament, the Council, the European Economic and Social Committee and the Committee of the Regions.

CRA International. 2008. "Economic Analysis of the Lieberman–Warner Climate Security Act of 2007 Using CRA's MRN–NEEM Model." http://216.133.239.2/pdf/040808_crai_presentation.pdf.

Dales, J. H. 1968. *Pollution, Property and Prices: An Essay in Policy-Making and Economics*. Toronto: University of Toronto Press.

Dasgupta, Partha. 2007. "The Stern Review: Accounting for Well-Being." *Journal of the Foundation for Science and Technology*, 19(4): 16–17.

DeFries, Ruth, Frédéric Achard, Sandra Brown, Martin Herold, Daniel Murdiyarso, Bernhard Schlamadinger, and Carlos de Souza. 2006. "Reducing Greenhouse Gas Emissions from Deforestation in Developing Countries: Considerations for Monitoring and Measuring." Global Terrestrial Observing System Report 46.

Dinan, Terry, and Diane Lim Rogers. 2002. "Distributional Effects of Carbon Allowance Trading: How Government Decisions Determine Winners and Losers." *National Tax Journal*, 55(2): 199–221.

Eber, Michael, and Alan J. Krupnick. 2009. "Valuing Climate Damages." Unpublished.

Edmonds, James A., Leon E. Clarke, Joshua Lurz, and Marshall Wise. 2008. "Stabilizing CO_2 Concentrations with Incomplete International Cooperation." *Climate Policy*, 8(4): 355–76.

Edmonds, James A., Joseph M. Roop, and Michael J. Scott. 2000. "Technology and the Economics of Climate Change Policy." Arlington: Pew Center on Global Climate Change.

Ellerman, A. Denny. 2005. "US Experience with Emissions Trading: Lessons for CO_2 in Emissions Trading." In *Emissions Trading for Climate Policy: US and European Perspectives*, ed. Bemd Hansjurgens, 78–95. Cambridge and New York: Cambridge University Press.

Fankhauser, Samuel. 1995. *Valuing Climate Change: The Economics of the Greenhouse*. London and Sterling, Va.: Earthscan Publications.

Fell, Harrison, Ian A. MacKenzie, and William A. Pizer. 2008. "Prices versus Quantities versus Bankable Quantities." Resources for the Future Discussion Paper 08-32.

Fischer, Carolyn, and Alan K. Fox. 2007. "Output-Based Allocation of Emissions Permits for Mitigating Tax and Trade Interactions." *Land Economics*, 83(4): 575–99.

Fischer, Carolyn, and Alan K. Fox. 2009. "Combining Rebates with Carbon Taxes: Optimal Strategies for Coping with Emissions Leakage and Tax Interactions." Resources for the Future Discussion Paper 09-12.

Fischer, Carolyn, and Richard G. Newell. 2008. "Environmental and Technology Policies for Climate Mitigation." *Journal of Environmental Economics and Management*, 55(2): 142–62.

Fischlin, Andreas, Guy F. Midgley, Jeff Price, Rik Leemans, Brij Gopal, Carol Turley, Mark Rounsevell, Pauline Dube, Juan Tarazona, and Andrei Velichko. 2007. "Ecosystems, Their Properties, Goods, and Services." In *Climate Change 2007: Impacts, Adaptation and Vulnerability*, ed. Martin Parry, Osvaldo Canziani, Jean

Palutikof, Paul van der Linden, and Clair Hanson, 211–72. Contribution of Working Group II to the Fourth Assessment Report of the Intergovernmental Panel on Climate Change. Cambridge and New York: Cambridge University Press.

Fisher, Anthony C, and Urvashi Narain. 2003. "Global Warming, Endogenous Risk, and Irreversibility." *Environmental and Resource Economics*, 25(4): 395–416.

Frankel, Jeffrey. 2008. "An Elaborated Proposal for Global Climate Policy Architecture: Specific Formulas and Emission Targets for All Countries in All Decades." Harvard Project on International Climate Agreements Discussion Paper 08-08.

Gerlagh, Reyer, Snorre Kverndokk, and Knut Einar Rosendahl. 2009. "Optimal Timing of Climate Change Policy: Interaction between Carbon Taxes and Innovation Externalities." *Environmental and Resource Economics*, 43(3): 369–90.

Gillingham, Kenneth, Richard G. Newell, and Karen Palmer. 2009. "Energy Efficiency Economics and Policy." *Annual Review of Resource Economics*, 1: 597–620.

Gillingham, Kenneth, Richard G. Newell, and William A. Pizer. 2008. "Modeling Endogenous Technological Change for Climate Policy Analysis." *Energy Economics*, 30(6): 2734–53.

Goulder, Lawrence H. 1995. "Environmental Taxation and the Double Dividend: A Readers Guide." *International Tax and Public Finance*, 2(2): 157–83.

Goulder, Lawrence H. 2009. "Carbon Taxes vs. Cap and Trade." Unpublished.

Goulder, Lawrence H., and Koshy Mathai. 2000. "Optimal CO_2 Abatement in the Presence of Induced Technological Change." *Journal of Environmental Economics and Management*, 39(1): 1–38.

Goulder, Lawrence H., and Ian W. H. Parry. 2008. "Instrument Choice in Environmental Policy." *Review of Environmental Economics and Policy*, 2(2): 152–74.

Goulder, Lawrence H., Ian W. H. Parry, Roberton C. Williams, and Dallas Burtraw. 1999. "The Cost-Effectiveness of Alternative Instruments for Environmental Protection in a Second-Best Setting." *Journal of Public Economics*, 72(3): 329–60.

Goulder, Lawrence H., and Stephen H. Schneider. 1999. "Induced Technological Change and the Attractiveness of CO_2 Abatement Policies." *Resource and Energy Economics*, 21(3–4): 211–53.

Griliches, Zvi. 1992. "The Search for R&D Spillovers." *Scandinavian Journal of Economics*, 94(Supplement): S29–47.

Guiteras, Raymond. 2008. "The Impact of Climate Change on Indian Agriculture." Unpublished.

Gupta, Sujata, Dennis A. Tirpak, Nicholas Burger, Joyeeta Gupta, Niklas Höhne, Antonina Ivanova Boncheva, Gorashi Mohammed Kanoan, Charles D. Kolstad, Joseph A. Kruger, Axel Michaelowa, Shinya Murase, Jonathan Pershing, Tatsuyoshi Saijo, and Agus Sari. 2007. "Policies, Instruments and Cooperative Arrangements." In *Climate Change 2007: Mitigation*, ed. Bert Metz, Ogunlade Davidson, Peter Bosch, Rutu Dave, and Leo Meyer, 745–808. Contribution of Working Group III to the Fourth Assessment Report of the Intergovernmental Panel on Climate Change. Cambridge and New York: Cambridge University Press.

Hall, Daniel S. 2007. "Mandatory Regulation of Non-traditional Greenhouse Gases: Policy Options for Industrial Process Emissions and Non-CO_2 Gases." In *Assessing U.S. Climate Policy Options*, ed. Raymond J. Kopp and William A. Pizer, 183–88. Washington, D.C.: Resources for the Future.

Hansen, J. E. 2007. "Scientific Reticence and Sea Level Rise." *Environmental Research Letters*, 2(2): 1–6.

Heal, Geoffrey. 2009. "Climate Economics: A Meta-review and Some Suggestions for Future Research." *Review of Environmental Economics and Policy*, 3(1): 4–21.

Hepburn, Cameron. 2006. "Regulation by Prices, Quantities, or Both: A Review of Instrument Choice." *Oxford Review of Economic Policy*, 22(2): 226–47.

Ho, Mun S., Richard Morgenstern, and Jhih-Shyang Shih. 2008. "Impact of Carbon Price Policies on U.S. Industry." Resources for the Future Discussion Paper 08-37

Hoel, Michael, and Larry Karp. 2002. "Taxes versus Quotas for a Stock Pollutant." *Resource and Energy Economics*, 24(4): 367–84.

Intergovernmental Panel on Climate Change. 2007. *Climate Change 2007: The Physical Science Basis*. Contribution of Working Group I to the Fourth Assessment Report of the IPCC. Cambridge and New York: Cambridge University Press.

Jacoby, Henry D., Mustafa H. Babiker, Sergey Paltsev, and John M. Reilly. 2008. "Sharing the Burden of GHG Reductions." Massachusetts Institute of Technology Joint Program on the Science and Policy of Global Change Report 167.

Jacoby, Henry D., and A. Denny Ellerman. 2004. "The Safety Valve and Climate Policy." *Energy Policy*, 32(4): 481–91.

Jaffe, Adam B., Richard G. Newell, and Robert N. Stavins. 2003. "Technological Change and the Environment." In *Handbook of Environmental Economics, Volume 1, Environmental Degradation and Institutional Responses*, ed. Karl-Göran Maler and Jeffrey R. Vincent, 461–516. Amsterdam; Boston and London: Elsevier Science, North-Holland.

Jaffe, Judson, and Robert N. Stavins. 2008. "Linking a U.S. Cap-and-Trade System for Greenhouse Gas Emissions: Opportunities, Implications, and Challenges." AEI Center for Regulatory and Market Studies Working Paper 08–01.

Jones, Charles I., and John C. Williams. 1998. "Measuring the Social Return to R&D." *Quarterly Journal of Economics*, 113(4): 1119–35.

Karp, Larry, and Jiangfeng Zhang. 2005. "Regulation of Stock Externalities with Correlated Abatement Costs." *Environmental and Resource Economics*, 32(2): 273–99.

Keeler, Andrew, and Alexander Thompson. 2008. "Industrialized-Country Mitigation Policy and Resource Transfers to Developing Countries: Improving and Expanding Greenhouse Gas Offsets." Harvard Project on International Climate Agreements Discussion Paper 08-05.

Kling, Catherine, and Jonathan Rubin. 1997. "Bankable Permits for the Control of Environmental Pollution." *Journal of Public Economics*, 64(1): 101–15.

Kneese, Allen V., and Blair T. Bower. 1968. *Managing Water Quality: Economics, Technology Institutions*. Baltimore: Johns Hopkins University Press.

Kolstad, Charles D. 1996a. "Fundamental Irreversibilities in Stock Externalities." *Journal of Public Economics*, 60(2): 221–33.

Kolstad, Charles D. 1996b. "Learning and Stock Effects in Environmental Regulation: The Case of Greenhouse Gas Emissions." *Journal of Environmental Economics and Management*, 31(1): 1–18.

Lange, Andreas, and Nicolas Treich. 2008. "Uncertainty, Learning and Ambiguity in Economic Models on Climate Policy: Some Classical Results and New Directions." *Climate Change*, 89(1–2): 7–21.

Lind, Robert C. 1982. "A Primer on the Major Issues Relating to the Discount Rate for Evaluating National Energy Options." In *Discounting for Time and Risk in Energy Policy*, ed. Robert C. Lind, 21–94. Washington, D.C.: Resources for the Future.

Mansfield, Edwin. 1985. "How Rapidly Does New Industrial Technology Leak Out?" *Journal of Industrial Economics*, 34(2): 217–23.

McGrattan, Ellen R., and Edward C. Prescott. 2003. "Average Debt and Equity Returns: Puzzling?" *American Economic Review*, 93(2): 392–97.

McMichael, Anthony, Diarmid Campbell-Lendrum, Sari Kovats, Sally Edwards, Paul Wilkinson, Theresa Wilson, Robert Nicholls, Simon Hales, Frank Tanser, David Le Sueuer, Michael Schlesinger, and Natasha Andonova. 2004. "Global Climate Change." In *Comparative Quantification of Health Risks: Global and Regional Burden of Disease Attributable to Selected Major Risk Factors*, ed. Majid Ezzati, Alan D. Lopez, Anthony Rodgers, and Christopher J. L. Murray, 1543–1650. Geneva: World Health Organization.

Mendelsohn, Robert, Ariel Dinar, and Apurva Sanghi. 2001. "The Effect of Development on the Climate Sensitivity of Agriculture." *Environment and Development Economics*, 6(1): 85–101.

Mendelsohn, Robert, William D. Nordhaus, and Daigee Shaw. 1994. "The Impact of Global Warming on Agriculture: A Ricardian Analysis." *American Economic Review*, 84(4): 753–71.

Mendelsohn, Robert, and James E. Neumann. 1999. *The Impact of Climate Change on the United States Economy*. Cambridge and New York: Cambridge University Press.

Mendelsohn, Robert, and Larry Williams. 2004. "Comparing Forecasts of the Global Impacts of Climate Change." *Mitigation and Adaptation Strategies for Global Change*, 9(4): 315–33.

Mendelsohn, Robert, and Larry Williams. 2007. "Dynamic Forecasts of the Sectoral Impacts of Climate Change." In *Human-Induced Climate Change: An Interdisciplinary Assessment*, ed. Michael E. Schlensinger, Haroon Kheshgi, Joel B. Smith, Francisco C. de la Chesnaye, John M. Reilly, Tom Wilson, and Charles Kolstad, 107–18. Cambridge and New York: Cambridge University Press.

Metcalf, Gilbert E. 2009. "Designing a Carbon Tax to Reduce U.S. Greenhouse Gas Emissions." *Review of Environmental Economics and Policy*, 3(1): 63–83.

Montgomery, W. David. 1972. "Markets in Licenses and Efficient Pollution Control Programs." *Journal of Economic Theory*, 5(3): 395–418.

Murray, Brian C., Bruce A. McCarl, and Heng-Chi Lee. 2002. "Estimating Leakage from Forest Carbon Sequestration Programs." Research Triangle Institute International Working Paper 02–06.

Murray, Brian C., Richard G. Newell, and William A. Pizer. 2009. "Balancing Cost and Emissions Certainty: An Allowance Reserve for Cap-and-Trade." *Review of Environmental Economics and Policy*, 3(1): 84–103.

Newbold, Stephen C., and Adam Daigneault. 2009. "Climate Response Uncertainty and the Benefits of Greenhouse Gas Emissions Reductions." *Environmental and Resource Economics*, 44(3): 351–77.

Newbold, Stephen C., Charles Griffiths, Chris Moore, and Ann Wolverton. 2009. "The 'Social Cost of Carbon' Made Simple." Unpublished.

Newell, Richard G. 2008. "A U.S. Innovation Strategy for Climate Change Mitigation." Brookings Institution Discussion Paper 2008–15.

Newell, Richard G., and William A. Pizer. 2003. "Regulating Stock Externalities under Uncertainty." *Journal of Environmental Economics and Management*, 45(2 Supplement 1): 416–32.

Ng, Wei-Shiuen, and Robert Mendelsohn. 2005. "The Impact of Sea Level Rise on Singapore." *Environment and Development Economics*, 10(2): 201–15.

Nicholls, Robert J., Richard S. J. Tol, and Athanasios T. Vafeidis. 2008. "Global Estimates of the Impact of a Collapse of the West Antarctic Ice Sheet: An Application of FUND." *Climatic Change*, 91(1–2): 171–91.

Nordhaus, William D. 1991. "To Slow or Not To Slow: The Economics of the Greenhouse Effect." *Economic Journal*, 101(407): 920–37.

Nordhaus, William D. 2002. "Modeling Induced Innovation in Climate-Change Policy." In *Technological Change and the Environment*, ed. Arnulf Grübler, Nebojsa Nakicenovic and William D. Nordhaus, 182–209. Washington, D.C.: Resources for the Future; Laxenburg: International Institute for Applied Systems Analysis.

Nordhaus, William D. 2007. "A Review of the Stern Review on the Economics of Climate Change." *Journal of Economic Literature*, 45(3): 686–702.

Nordhaus, William D. 2008. *A Question of Balance: Weighing the Options on Global Warming Policies*. New Haven and London: Yale University Press.

Nordhaus, William D., and Joseph Boyer. 2000. *Warming the World: Economic Models of Global Warming*. Cambridge and London: MIT Press.

Olsthoorn, Alexander A., Peter van der Werff, Laurens M. Bouwer, and David Huitema. 2008. "Neo-Atlantis: The Netherlands under a 5-m Sea Level Rise." *Climatic Change*, 91(1–2): 103–22.

Paltsev, Sergey, John M. Reilly, Henry D. Jacoby, Angelo C. Gurgel, Gilbert E. Metcalf, Andrei P. Sokolov, and Jennifer F. Holak. 2007. "Assessment of U.S. Cap-and-Trade Proposals." Massachusetts Institute of Technology Joint Program on the Science and Policy of Global Change Report 146.

Parry, Ian W. H. 2005. "Fiscal Interactions and the Costs of Controlling Pollution from Electricity." *RAND Journal of Economics*, 36(4): 849–39.

Parry, Ian W. H., and Antonio M. Bento. 2000. "Tax Deductions, Environmental Policy, and the 'Double Dividend' Hypothesis." *Journal of Environmental Economics and Management*, 39(1): 67–96.

Parry, Ian W. H., William A. Pizer, and Carolyn Fischer. 2003. "How Large Are the Welfare Gains from Technological Innovation Induced by Environmental Policies?" *Journal of Regulatory Economics*, 23(3): 237–55.

Pearce, David. 2005. "The Social Cost of Carbon." In *Climate-Change Policy*, ed. Dieter Helm, 99–133. Oxford and New York: Oxford University Press.

Peck, Stephan C., and Y. Steve Wan. 1996. "Analytic Solutions of Simple Optimal Greenhouse Gas Emission Models." In *Economics of Atmospheric Pollution*, ed. Ekko C. van Ierland and Kazimierz Górka, 113–22. New York and Berlin: Springer-Verlag.

Pindyck, Robert S. 2007. "Uncertainty in Environmental Economics." *Review of Environmental Economics and Policy*, 1(1): 45–65.

Pindyck, Robert S. 2008. "Uncertainty, Extreme Outcomes, and Climate Change Policy." Paper presented at the 2008 NBER Summer Institute.

Pizer, William A. 2002. "Combining Price and Quantity Controls to Mitigate Global Climate Change." *Journal of Public Economics*, 85(3): 409–34.

Pizer, William A. 2007. "Practical Global Climate Policy." In *Architectures for Agreement: Addressing Global Climate Change in the Post-Kyoto World*, ed. Joseph E. Aldy and Robert N. Stavins, 280–314. Cambridge and New York: Cambridge University Press.

Reilly, John M., ed. 2001. *Agriculture: The Potential Consequences of Climate Variability and Change for the United States*. Cambridge and New York: Cambridge University Press.

Roberts, Marc J., and Michael Spence. 1976. "Effluent Charges and Licenses under Uncertainty." *Journal of Public Economics*, 5(3–4): 193–208.

Rosendahl, Knut Einar. 2008. "Incentives and Prices in an Emissions Trading Scheme with Updating." *Journal of Environmental Economics and Management*, 56(1): 69–82.

Rosendahl, Knut Einar, and Jon Strand. 2009. "Simple Model Frameworks for Explaining Inefficiency of the Clean Development Mechanism." World Bank Policy Research Working Paper 4931.

Schelling, Thomas. 2007. "Epilogue: Architectures for Agreement." In *Architectures for Agreement: Addressing Global Climate Change in the Post-Kyoto World*, ed. Joseph E. Aldy and Robert N. Stavins, 343–49. Cambridge and New York: Cambridge University Press.

Schlenker, Wolfram, W. Michael Hanemann, and Anthony C. Fisher. 2005. "Will U.S. Agriculture Really Benefit from Global Warming? Accounting for Irrigation in the Hedonic Approach." *American Economic Review*, 95(1): 395–406.

Shih, Jhih-Shyang, Dallas Burtraw, Karen Palmer, and Juha Siikamäki. 2006. "Air Emissions of Ammonia and Methane from Livestock Operations: Valuation and Policy Options." Resources for the Future Discussion Paper 06-11.

Sijm, Jos, Karsten Neuhoff, and Yihsu Chen. 2006. "CO_2 Cost Pass-through and Windfall Profits in the Power Sector." *Climate Policy*, 6(1): 49–72.

Smith, Anne E., Martin T. Ross, and W. David Montgomery. 2002. "Implications of Trading Implementation Design for Equity–Efficiency Trade-Offs in Carbon Permit Allocations." Charles River Associates Working Paper.

Sohngen, Brent, Robert Mendelsohn, and Roger Sedjo. 2001. "A Global Model of Climate Change Impacts on Timber Markets." *Journal of Agricultural and Resource Economics*, 26(2): 326–43.

Stavins, Robert N. 1995. "Transaction Costs and Tradeable Permits." *Journal of Environmental Economics and Management*, 29(2): 133–48.

Stavins, Robert N. 1996. "Correlated Uncertainty and Policy Instrument Choice." *Journal of Environmental Economics and Management*, 30(2): 218–32.

Stavins, Robert N. 2007. "A U.S. Cap-and-Trade System to Address Global Climate Change." Brookings Institution Discussion Paper 2007–13.

Stavins, Robert N., and Kenneth R. Richards. 2005. "The Cost of U.S. Forest-Based Carbon Sequestration." Arlington, Va.: Pew Center on Global Climate Change.

Stern, Nicholas. 2007. *The Economics of Climate Change: The Stern Review*. Cambridge and New York: Cambridge University Press.

Sterner, Thomas, and U. Martin Persson. 2008. "An Even Sterner Review: Introducing Relative Prices into the Discounting Debate." *Review of Environmental Economics and Policy*, 2(1): 61–76.

Tavoni, Massimo, Brent Sohngen, and Valentina Bosetti. 2007. "Forestry and the Carbon Market Response to Stabilize Climate." Fondazione Eni Enrico Mattei Working Paper 81.

Tol, Richard S. J. 1995. "The Damage Costs of Climate Change toward More Comprehensive Calculations." *Environmental and Resource Economics*, 5(4): 353–74.

Tol, Richard S. J. 2002. "Estimates of the Damage Costs of Climate Change. Part 1: Benchmark Estimates." *Environmental and Resource Economics*, 21(1): 47–73.

Tol, Richard S. J. 2009. "The Economic Effects of Climate Change." *Journal of Economic Perspectives*, 23(2): 29–51.

U.S. Department of Energy, Energy Information Administration. 2008a. *Energy Market and Economic Impacts of S. 2191, the Lieberman–Warner Climate Secu-*

rity Act of 2007. U.S. Department of Energy, Energy Information Administration Report SR/OIAF/2008-01.

U.S. Department of Energy, Energy Information Administration. 2008b. *International Energy Outlook 2008.* Washington, D.C.: U.S. Department of Energy, Energy Information Administration.

U.S. Environmental Protection Agency. 2008. *EPA Analysis of the Lieberman–Warner Climate Security Act of 2008 (S. 2191).* Washington, D.C.: U.S. Environmental Protection Agency Office of Atmospheric Programs.

Van Benthem, Arthur, Kenneth Gillingham, and James Sweeney. 2008. "Learning-by-Doing and the Optimal Solar Policy in California." *Energy Journal*, 29(3): 131–51.

Victor, David G. 2007. "Fragmented Carbon Markets and Reluctant Nations: Implications for the Design of Effective Architectures." In *Architectures for Agreement: Addressing Global Climate Change in the Post-Kyoto World*, ed. Joseph E. Aldy and Robert N. Stavins, 133–60. Cambridge and New York: Cambridge University Press.

Victor, David G. 2008. "On the Regulation of Geoengineering." *Oxford Review of Economic Policy*, 24(2): 322–36.

Weitzman, Martin L. 1974. "Prices vs. Quantities." *Review of Economic Studies*, 41(4): 477–91.

Weitzman, Martin L. 1998. "Why the Far-Distant Future Should Be Discounted at Its Lowest Possible Rate." *Journal of Environmental Economics and Management*, 36(3): 201–08.

Weitzman, Martin L. 2009a. "On Modeling and Interpreting the Economics of Catastrophic Climate Change." *Review of Economics and Statistics*, 91(1): 1–19.

Weitzman, Martin L. 2009b. "Reactions to the Nordhaus Critique." Unpublished.

World Bank 2010. *World Development Report 2010: Development and Climate Change.* Washington, D.C.: World Bank.

Wright, Brian Davern. 1983. "The Economics of Invention Incentives: Patents, Prizes, and Research Contracts." *American Economic Review*, 73(4): 691–707.

Yohe, Gary W. 1978. "Towards a General Comparison of Price Controls and Quantity Controls under Uncertainty." *Review of Economic Studies*, 45(2): 229–38.

Yohe, Gary W. 2000. "Assessing the Role of Adaptation in Evaluating Vulnerability to Climate Change." *Climatic Change*, 46(3): 371–90.

Yohe, Gary W., and Richard S. J. Tol. 2009. "Precaution and a Dismal Theorem: Implications for Climate Policy and Climate Research." In *Risk Management in Commodity Markets: From Shipping to Agriculturals and Energy*, ed. Hélyette Geman, 91–100. Hoboken, N.J.: Wiley.

25 Critical Assumptions in the Stern Review on Climate Change

William Nordhaus

William Nordhaus is Sterling Professor of Economics at Yale University.

In November 2006, the British government presented a comprehensive study on the economics of climate change (*1*),[1] the Stern Review. It painted a dark picture for the globe[.] "[I]f we don't act, the overall costs and risks of climate change will be equivalent to losing at least 5% of global GDP [gross domestic product] each year, now and forever. If a wider range of risks and impacts is taken into account, the estimates of damage could rise to 20% of GDP or more." The Stern Review recommended urgent, immediate, and sharp reductions in greenhouse-gas emissions.

These findings differ markedly from economic models that calculate least-cost emissions paths to stabilize concentrations or paths that balance the costs and benefits of emissions reductions. Mainstream economic models definitely find it economically beneficial to take steps today to slow warming, but efficient policies generally involve modest rates of emissions reductions in the near term, followed by sharp reductions in the medium and long term (*2–5*).

A standard way of showing the stringency of policies is to calculate the "carbon tax," or penalty on carbon emissions. A recent study by the author estimates an optimal carbon tax for 2005 of around $30 per ton carbon in today's prices, rising to $85 by the mid=21st century and further increasing after that (*5*). A similar carbon price has been found in studies that estimate the least-cost path to stabilize CO_2 concentrations at two times preindustrial levels (*2*). The sharply rising carbon tax reflects initially low, but rising, emissions-reduction rates. We call this the climate-policy ramp, in which policies to slow global warming increasingly tighten or ramp up over time. A $30 carbon tax may appear to be a modest target, but it is at least 10 times the current globally averaged carbon tax implicit in the Kyoto Protocol (shown as Stern assumptions).

What is the logic of the ramp? In a world where capital is productive and damages are far in the future (see chart above), the highest-return investments today are primarily in tangible, technological, and human capital. In the coming decades, damages are predicted to rise relative to

"Critical Assumptions in the Stern Review on Climate Change" by William Nordhaus. *Science* 317, No. 5835. 2007. Pp. 201–202. Reprinted with permission.

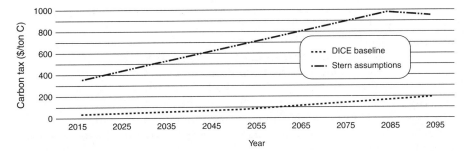

Comparing the optimal carbon tax under alternative discounting assumptions. The Dynamic Integrated model of Climate and the Economy (DICE model) (5) integrates the economic costs and benefits of greenhouse-gas (GHG) reductions with a simple dynamic representation of the scientific and economic links of output, emissions, concentrations, and climate change. The DICE model is designed to choose levels of investment in tangible capital and in GHG reductions that maximize economic welfare. It calculates the optimal carbon tax as the price of carbon emissions that will balance the incremental costs of abating carbon emissions with the incremental benefits of lower future damages from climate change. Using the DICE model to optimize climate policy leads to an optimal carbon tax in 2005 of around $30 per ton carbon (shown here as "DICE baseline"). If we substitute the Stern Review's assumptions about time discounting and the consumption elasticity into the DICE model, the calculated optimal carbon tax is much higher and rises much more rapidly (shown as "Stern assumptions").

output. As that occurs, it becomes efficient to shift investments toward more intensive emissions reductions and the accompanying higher carbon taxes. The exact timing of emissions reductions depends on details of costs, damages, learning, and the extent to which climate change and damages are nonlinear and irreversible.

The Stern Review proposes to move the timetable for emissions reductions sharply forward. It suggests global emissions reductions of between 30 and 70% over the next two decades, objectives consistent with a carbon tax of around $300 per ton today, or about 10 times the level suggested by standard economic models.

Given that the Stern Review embraces traditional economic techniques such as those described in (2–5), how does it get such different results and strategies? Having analyzed the Stern Review in (6) (which also contains a list of recent analyses), I find that the difference stems almost entirely from its technique for calculating discount rates and only marginally on new science or economics. The reasoning has questionable foundations in terms of its ethical assumptions and also leads to economic results that are inconsistent with market data.

Some background on growth economics and discounting concepts is necessary to understand the debate. In choosing among alternative trajectories for emissions reductions, the key economic variable is the real return on capital, r, which measures the net yield on investments in capital, education, and technology. In principle, this is observable in the marketplace. For example, the real pretax return on U.S. corporate capital over the last four decades has averaged about 0.07 yr⁻¹. Estimated real returns on human capital range from 0.06 yr⁻¹ to >0.20 yr⁻¹, depending on the country and time period (7). The return on capital is the "discount rate" that enters into the determination of the efficient balance between the cost of emissions reductions today and the benefit of reduced climate damages in the future. A high return on capital tilts the balance toward emissions reductions in the future, whereas a low return tilts reductions toward the present. The Stern Review's economic analysis recommended immediate emissions reductions because its assumptions led to very low assumed real returns on capital.

Where does the return on capital come from? The Stern Review and other analyses of climate economics base the analysis of real returns on the optimal economic growth theory (8, 9). In this framework, the real return on capital is an economic variable that is determined by two normative parameters. The first parameter is the time discount rate, denoted by ρ, which refers to the discount on future "utility" or welfare (not on future goods, like the return on capital). It measures the relative importance in societal decisions of the welfare of future generations relative to that of the current generation. A zero discount rate means that all generations into the indefinite future are treated the same; a positive discount rate means that that the welfare of future generations is reduced or "discounted" compared with nearer generations.

Analyses are sometimes divided between the "descriptive approach," in which assumed discount rates should conform to actual political and economic decisions and prices, and the "prescriptive approach," where discount rates should conform to an ethical ideal, sometimes taken to be very low or even zero. Philosophers and economists have conducted vigorous debates about how to apply discount rates in areas as diverse as economic growth, climate change, energy, nuclear waste, major infrastructure programs, hurricane levees, and reparations for slavery.

The Stern Review takes the prescriptive approach in the extreme, arguing that it is indefensible to make long-term decisions with a positive time discount rate. The actual time discount rate used in the Stern Review is 0.001 yr⁻¹, which is vaguely justified by estimates of the probability of the extinction of the human race.

The second parameter that determines return on capital is the consumption elasticity, denoted as η. This parameter represents the aversion to the economic equality among different generations. A low (high) value of η implies that decisions take little (much) heed about whether the future is richer or poorer than the present. Under standard optimal growth theory, if time discounting is low and society cares little about income inequality, then it will save a great deal for the future, and the real return will be low. This is the case assumed by the Stern Review. Alternatively, if either the time discount rate is high or society is averse to inequality, the current savings rate is low and the real return is high.

This relation is captured by the "Ramsey equation" of optimal growth theory (8, 9), in which the long-run equilibrium real return on capital is determined by $r = \rho + \eta g$, where g is the average growth in consumption per capita, ρ is the time discount rate, and η is the consumption elasticity. Using the Stern Review's assumption of $\rho = 0.001$ yr^{-1} and $\eta = 1$, along with its assumed growth rate ($g^+ = 0.013$ yr^{-1}) and a stable population, yields an equilibrium real interest rate of 0.014 yr^{-1}, far below the returns to standard investments. It would also lead to much higher savings rates than today's. This low rate of return is used in the Stern Review without any reference to actual rates of return or savings rates.

The low return also means that future damages are discounted at a low rate, and this helps explain the Stern Review's estimate that the cost of climate change could represent the equivalent of a "20% cut in per-capita consumption, now and forever." When the Stern Review says that there are substantial losses "now," it does not mean "today." In fact, the Stern Review's estimate of the output loss "today" is essentially zero. We can illustrate this using the Stern Review's high-climate scenario with catastrophic and non-market impacts. For this case, the mean losses are 0.4% of world output in 2060, 2.9% in 2100, and 13.8% in 2200. This is reported as a loss in "current per capita consumption" of 14.4%.

How do damages that average around 1% over the next century turn into 14.4% cuts "now and forever"? The answer is that, with the low interest rate, the relatively small damages in the next two centuries get overwhelmed by the high damages over the centuries and millennia that follow 2200. In fact, if the Stern Review's methodology is used, more than half of the estimated damages "now and forever" occur after 2800.

What difference would it make if we used assumptions that are consistent with standard returns to capital and savings rates? For example, take the Stern Review's near-zero time discount rate with a high inequality aversion represented by a consumption elasticity of $\eta = 3$. This combination would yield real returns and savings rates close to those observed in today's economy and dramatically different from those shown in the Stern Review. The optimal carbon tax and the social cost of carbon decline by a factor of ~10 relative to these consistent with the Stern Review's assumptions, and the efficient trajectory looks like the policy ramp discussed above. In other words, the Stern Review's alarming findings about damages, as well as its economic rationale, rest on its model parameterization—a low time discount rate and low inequality aversion—that leads to savings rates and real returns that differ greatly from actual market data. If we correct these parameterizations, we get a carbon tax and emissions reductions that look like standard economic models.

The Stern Review's unambiguous conclusions about the need for urgent and immediate action will not survive the substitution of assumptions that are consistent with today's marketplace real interest rates and savings rates. So the central questions about global-warming policy—how much, how fast, and how costly—remain open.

REFERENCES

1. N. Stern, *The Economics of Climate Change: The Stern Review* (Cambridge Univ. Press, Cambridge, UK, 2007).
2. J. Weyant, Ed., *Energy Econ.* 26 (4), Special Issue on EMF 19, pp. 501–755 (2004).
3. W. D. Nordhaus, J. Boyer, *Warming the World: Economic Modeling of Global Warming* (MIT Press, Cambridge, MA, 2000).
4. R. S. J. Tol, *Energy Policy*, 33, 2064–2074 (2005).
5. W. D. Nordhaus, "The Challenge of Global Warming: Economic Models and Environmental Policy" (Yale Univ., New Haven, CT, 2007); available at [http://nordhaus.econ.yale.edu/dice_mss_072407_all.pdf (accessed 6/17/11)].
6. W. D. Nordhaus, *J. Econ. Lit.*, in press; available at http://nordhaus.econ.yale.edu/recent_stuff.html.
7. K. J. Arrow *et al.*, *Climate Change 1995—Economic and Social Dimensions of Climate Change*, J. Bruce, H. Lee, E. Haites, Eds. (Cambridge Univ. Press, Cambridge, 1996), pp. 125–144.
8. F. Ramsey, *Econ. J.* 38, 543 (1928).
9. T. C. Koopmans, *Acad. Sci. Scripta Maria* 28, 1 (1965).

26 Climate Change: Risk, Ethics, and the Stern Review

Nicholas Stern and Chris Taylor

Nicholas Stern is IG Patel Professor of Economics and Government and Chair of the Grantham Research Institute on Climate Change and the Environment at the London School of Economics. Chris Taylor is an economist at the United Kingdom Government—HM Treasury.

Any thorough analysis of policy on climate change must examine scientific, economic, and political issues and many other relationships and structures and must have ethics at its heart. In a Policy Forum in this issue of *Science*, Nordhaus (*1*) suggests that our results as described in the Stern Review (*2*) stem almost entirely from ethical judgments. This is not correct. In addition to revisiting the ethics, we also incorporated the latest science, which tells us that, for a given change in atmospheric concentration, the worst impacts now appear more likely. Further, the science also now gives us a better understanding of probabilities, so we could incorporate explicit risk analysis, largely overlooked in previous studies. It is risk plus ethics that drive our results.

The most direct way to look at the problem of constructing an economic response to climate change is to look at the individual impacts of climate change alongside the cost of reducing emissions and then to ask whether it is worth paying for mitigation. However, we do not have the kind of information that would enable formally attaching numbers to all consequences, weighting them, and adding them all up with any plausibility. Thus, economists attempt aggregations of impacts and costs using very simplified aggregate modeling and, in the process, throw away much that is of fundamental importance to a balanced judgment.

The central estimate of mitigation costs for stabilizing emissions below 550 ppm CO_2 equivalent is 1% of gross domestic product (GDP) per annum (*2*). The basic question is thus whether it is worth paying 1% of GDP to avoid the additional risks of higher emissions. The modeling in the Stern Review is valuable in identifying some key drivers of costs and benefits in terms of economic modeling approaches, scientific variables, and ethical considerations. However, excessive focus on the narrow aspects of these simplistic models distorts and often exaggerates their role in policy decisions. They cannot substitute for the detailed risk and cost analysis of key effects.

Our sensitivity analysis shows that our main conclusions—that the costs of strong action are less than the costs of the damage avoided by that actions—are robust to a range of assumptions. These assumptions concern (i) model structure and inputs (including population, structure of the damage function, aversion to irreversible consequences, future conditions, and the rise in price of environmental goods relative to consumption goods) and (ii) value judgments (attitudes to risk and inequality, the extent to which future generations matter, and intra-generational income distribution and/or regional equity weighting).

Some credible assumptions about the rate at which climate change will result in damage would lead to cost estimates that are much higher; our modeling approach has been cautious. Some modelers are very optimistic about economic growth and social rates of return for the next centuries. However, they appear to overlook that such rapid growth is likely to lead to greater emissions and, hence, the more rapid onset of climate change.

The ethical approach adopted in our analysis focuses on the ethics of allocation between richer and poorer people and between those born at different times. Ramsey (3) developed the standard social welfare discounting formula $r = \eta g + \rho$, where r is the consumption discount rate, η is the elasticity of the social benefits attained (also called the social marginal utility), g is per-capita consumption growth rate, and ρ is the time discount rate (also called the pure rate of time preference). The equation arises from comparing the social value of a bit of consumption in the future with a unit now and asking how it falls over time, the definition of a discount rate.

Traditionally, the discount rate has been applied to policies and projects involving small changes with direct benefits and costs over less than one generation (say a few decades at most), which means that people are feeling the impact of their decisions in their own lives. However, climate change is an intergenerational policy issue, and thus, we must see ρ as a parameter capturing discrimination by date of birth. For example, applying a 2% pure time discounting rate ($\rho = 2$) gives half the ethical weight to someone born in 2008 relative to someone born in 1973. Surely, many would find this difficult to justify.

In addition, the discounting formula described above depends on the path of future growth in consumption. Climate change involves potentially very large changes and can reduce future growth in consumption, so the discount rate applied in a world with climate change will be less than that in a world without, all else being equal. Moreover, this logic can be extended so that the uncertainty around climate impacts is taken into account. For every possible scenario of future climate change, there will be a specific average discount rate, depending on the growth rate of consumption in that scenario (4). Thus, to speak of "the discount rate" is misguided.

Using $\eta = 1$ implies that a given social benefit will be valued more highly by a factor of five for someone with one-fifth the resources of someone else. Some commentators have suggested that higher values should be used. Using $\eta = 2$ would mean that an extra benefit to the person who is poorer by a factor of five would have a value 25 times that to a richer person. In a transfer from the richer individual to the poorer one, how much would you be prepared to lose in the process and still regard it as a beneficial transfer? In the case of $\eta = 2$, as long as less than 96% is lost, it would be seen as beneficial and, for $\eta = 1$, less than 80%. Although it is a tenable ethical position, those who argue for η as high as 2 should be advocating very strong redistribution policies.

In the case of $\eta = 3$ in Nordhaus' example, over 99% could be lost and a transfer would still be beneficial. Does he advocate huge increases in transfers from rich to poor in the current generation?

A value of unity for η is quite commonly invoked, but higher values of ρ are sometimes used in cost-benefit analysis. Indeed, there are a number of reasons why a smaller-scale project such as a new road or railway may not be as valuable—or relevant at all—in several years time as circumstances change. However, avoiding the impacts of climate change (the value of a stable climate, human life, and ecosystems) is likely to continue to be relevant as long as the planet and its people exist.

Further, as people become richer and environmental goods become scarcer, it seems likely that, rather than fall, their value will rise very rapidly, which was an issue raised in chapter 2 of our review and has been investigated in later analyses (5). And the flow-stock nature of greenhouse gas accumulation, plus the powerful impact of climate change, will render many consequences irreversible. Thus, investing elsewhere and using the resources to compensate for any later environmental damage may be very cost-ineffective.

Many of the comments on the review have suggested that the ethical side of the modeling should be consistent with observable market behavior. As discussed by Hepburn (6), there are many reasons for thinking that market rates and other approaches that illustrate observable market behavior cannot be seen as reflections of an ethical response to the issues at hand. There is no real economic market that reveals our ethical decisions on how we should act together on environmental issues in the very long term.

Most long-term capital markets are very thin and imperfect. Choices that reflect current individual personal allocations of resource may be different from collective values and from what individuals may prefer in their capacity as citizens. Individuals will have a different attitude to risk because they have a higher probability of demise in that year than society. Those who do not feature in the market place (future generations) have no say in the calculus, and those who feature in the market less prominently (the young and the poor) have less influence on the behaviors that are being observed.

The issue of ethics should be tackled directly and explicitly through discussion (7). No discussion of the appropriateness of particular value judgments can be decisive. Alternative ethical approaches should be explored: Within the narrow confines of the modeling, sensitivity analysis does this. There is also scope for further work attempting to disentangle the roles of risk aversion and inequality aversion that are conflated (via η) in this modeling. Furthermore, we should go beyond the narrow framework of social welfare functions to consider other ethical approaches, including those involving rights and sustainability.

We note briefly that Nordhaus misrepresents the Stern Review on the subject of taxes. He argues that we propose a tax of $85 per ton of carbon dioxide, which equates to $312 per ton of carbon. This was our estimate of the marginal environmental cost of each extra carbon emission (the "social cost of carbon," hereafter SCC) under business-as-usual, with no policies to reduce emissions. To identify this with a recommended tax makes two mistakes. First, any estimate of the SCC is path-dependent. In chapter 13 of the Stern Review, we justify our proposed policy goal of stabilizing emissions between 450 and 550 ppm CO_2 equivalent. In this range, we estimate the social cost of carbon to be between $25 per ton of carbon dioxide (450 ppm) and $30 per ton (550 ppm), and so the proposed package of policies should be broadly consistent with this range. Second, in distorted and uncertain economies, any tax should be different from an SCC (8). Stabilization between 450 and 550 ppm is equivalent to reductions of around 25 to 70% in 2050. Nordhaus claims erroneously that the review suggests reductions on this scale over the next two decades. The Stern Review is also clear that prices should increase over time, although perhaps not as sharply as Nordhaus suggests.

The ethical approach in Nordhaus' modeling helps drive the initial low level of action and the steepness of his policy ramp. As future generations have a lower weight they are expected to shoulder the burden of greater mitigation costs. This could be a source of dynamic inconsistency, because future generations will be faced with the same challenge and, if they take the same approach, will also seek to minimize short-term costs but expect greater reductions in the future as they place a larger weight on consumption now over the effects on future generations (thus perpetuating the delay for significant reductions).

We have argued strongly for an assessment of policy on climate change to be based on a disaggregated approach to consequences—looking at different dimensions, places, and times—and a broad ethical approach. Nevertheless, our modeling sensitivity analysis demonstrates that the treatment of risk and uncertainty and the extent to which the model responds to progress in the scientific literature, are of roughly similar importance in shaping damage estimates as our approach to ethics and discounting. It is these three factors that explain higher damage estimates than those in the previous literature.

Given the centrality of risk, scientific advance, and ethics, in our view, the question should really be why, with some important exemptions, did the previous literature pay inadequate attention to these issues?

There was much structural caution in our approach. We left out many risks that are likely to be important, for example, the possibility of strong disruption of carbon cycles by changes to oceans and forests. It is possible that risks and damages are higher than we estimated. But one thing is clear: however unpleasant the damages from climate change are likely to appear in the future, any disregard for the future, simply because it is in the future, will suppress action to address climate change.

REFERENCES AND NOTES

1. W. Nordhaus, *Science* **317**, 201 (2007).
2. N. Stern, *The Economic of Climate Change: The Stern Review* (Cambridge Univ. Press, Cambridge, 2006).
3. F. P. Ramsey, *Econ. J.* **38**, 543 (1928).
4. In the review's modeling, the g in the discount rate is specific to the growth path in each of the thousands of model runs in the Monte Carlo analysis of aggregated-impact cost estimates.
5. T. Sterner, U. M. Persson, "An even sterner review: Introducing relative prices into the discounting debate," Working draft, May 2007; www.hgu.gu.se/files/nationalekonomi/personal/thomas%20sterner/b88.pdf
6. C. Hepburn, "The economics and ethics of Stern discounting," presentation at the workshop the Economics of Climate Change, 9 March 2007, University of Birmingham, Birmingham, UK; www.economics.bham.ac.uk/maddison/Cameron%20Hepburn%20Presentation.pdf
7. N. Stern, "Value judgments, welfare weights and discounting," Paper B of "After the Stern Review: Reflections and responses," 12 February 2007, Working draft of paper published on Stern Review Web site. [Available at http://webarchive.nationalarchives.gov.uk/+/http://www.hm-treasury. gov.uk/stern_review_report.htm (accessed 6/17/11)].
8. N. Stern, "The case for action to reduce the risks of climate change," Paper A of "After the Stern Review: Reflections and responses," working draft of paper published on Stern Review Web site, 12 February 2007. [Available at http://webarchive.nationalarchives.gov.uk/+/http://www.hm-treasury. gov.uk/stera_review_report.htm (accessed 6/17/11)].

27   Market-based Policy Options· to Control U.S. Greenhouse Gas Emissions*

Gilbert E. Metcalf

Gilbert E. Metcalf is Professor of Economics, Tufts University, Medford, Massachusetts, and Research Associate, National Bureau of Economic Research, Cambridge, Massachusetts. His e-mail address is (gilbert.metcalf@tufts.edu).

Growing concentrations of greenhouse gases raise the specter of large-scale climate change and global warming over the next hundred years. Atmospheric concentrations of carbon dioxide have risen from a preindustrial level of 280 parts per million to the current level of over 380 parts per million. Because greenhouse gases persist in the atmosphere for many hundreds of years, the current levels of emissions will have a significant effect on atmospheric concentrations for centuries to come. Scientists are sounding an increasingly urgent call for action to reduce emissions. For background on the science of climate change and the consequences of inaction see, for example, the Intergovernmental Panel on Climate Change (2007) and Stern (2007).

Carbon dioxide is by far the dominant greenhouse gas. The other major greenhouse gases are methane, nitrous oxides (NO_x), hydrofluorocarbons, perfluorocarbons, and sulfur hexafluoride. These gases can be converted into a common unit by the use of "global warming potentials," which provide a multiple for the extent to which emissions of other gases affect climate over a 100-year period relative to CO_2. These conversion factors range widely across greenhouse gases. For example, based on the Third Assessment Report of the Intergovernmental Panel on Climate Change (IPCC), methane's "global warming potential" is 21 while sulfur hexafluoride's is 23,900. A global warming potential of 21 means that one ton of methane has the same global warming impact over 100 years as does 21 tons of carbon dioxide emissions. With nearly 95 percent of carbon dioxide emissions generated by fossil fuel combustion, the major focus of efforts to reduce greenhouse gas emissions has been on energy use. Table 1 shows U.S. emissions of greenhouse gases by sector in 2006.

Historically, the United States has tended to use "command and control" regulatory approaches to control pollutants. This approach includes

"Market-based Policy Options to Control U.S. Greenhouse Gas Emissions" by Gilbert E. Metcalf. *Journal of Economic Perspectives* 23, No. 2, 2009. Pp. 5–27. Reprinted with permission.

*I thank Don Fullerton, Rob Stavins, and Timothy Taylor for useful comments.

requirements to use best available technology or other specific technology mandates. The most significant existing regulations for reduction of carbon emissions are probably the Corporate Average Fuel Efficiency (CAFE) standards, originally enacted in 1978, which mandate minimum fleet mileage standards for motor vehicles sold in the United States. After being tightened in 2007, CAFE mandates a fleet efficiency of 35 miles per gallon by the year 2020 for cars and light trucks. (For a fuller discussion of CAFE standards, the interested reader might start with Portney, Parry, Gruenspecht, and Harrington in the Fall 2003 issue of this journal.)[1]

Other programs to reduce greenhouse gas emissions have attempted to promote alternative technologies. An example of technology-promoting rules, only enacted at the state level so far, are "renewable portfolio standards" that set a target that some share of electricity be produced by renewable sources. Such requirements are similar to production and investment tax credits for renewable energy, as I analyze in Metcalf (2007a), in providing incentives to particular technologies rather than a general incentive to reduce emissions.

All of these regulatory approaches to reducing carbon emissions raise issues of sectoral inefficiency. For example, fuel economy standards force the automotive sector to bear a disproportionate share of the cost of reducing greenhouse gas emissions, when most studies suggest that the cost of reducing greenhouse gas emissions in the transport sector is quite high compared with other sectors of the economy.

But perhaps the most practical concern with any of the current regulatory approaches is that they are not reducing greenhouse gas emissions. U.S. greenhouse gas emissions have risen by nearly 15 percent since 1990. Emissions of energy-related carbon dioxide are projected to rise by a further 16 percent between 2006 and 2030 (U.S. Energy Information Administration, 2008). If the United States is to reduce its emissions of greenhouse gases, it will need to take far more dramatic steps.

For economists, the obvious choice is to move toward market-based environmental mechanisms that put a price on greenhouse gas emissions. The two main approaches are a carbon tax and a cap-and-trade system of marketable permits for emissions. These market-based approaches are superior to regulatory approaches in a number of dimensions. They ensure that all polluters, regardless of industrial sector, face the same marginal cost of abatement—a necessary condition for efficiency. They provide the right incentive to shift the larger pollution reductions from firms or sectors with high marginal abatement costs to those with low marginal abatement costs. Pricing pollution also encourages innovation, given the potential for reducing pollution at lower cost with new technology, and thus reduces the price that needs to be paid for emissions of greenhouse gases.

---

[1] A potentially significant regulatory approach at the state level is California's low-carbon fuel standard put in place by Governor Arnold Schwarzenegger in 2007. Holland, Knittel, and Hughes (2009) note that such a policy could in fact lead to an increase in emissions, and that even if the standard does reduce emissions, a low-carbon fuel standard is a particularly costly approach.

Table 1 U.S. Greenhouse Gas Emissions by Sector in 2006

Sector	Emissions	Share
Electricity	2,378	34%
Transportation	1,970	28%
Industry	1,372	19%
Agriculture	534	8%
Commercial	395	6%
Residential	345	5%
Total	**7,054**	

Source: U.S. Environmental Protection Agency (2008), Table ES-2.
Note: Emissions are measured in millions of metric tons of CO_2e (carbon dioxide equivalent). The total in the bottom row includes emissions from U.S. territories not included in the other row entries.

This paper begins by looking at some design issues that confront any policy for putting a price on greenhouse gases. I introduce the specific policy instruments of 1) taxing greenhouse gas emissions and 2) a cap-and-trade program. I then offer some comparisons of the two options along various dimensions: How well can they deal with uncertainty in costs of abating pollution? What are their implications for industry rents and government revenue? Do they differ in ease of administration? How would they be linked to existing programs, including those in other countries? I conclude with some observations on the likely directions of climate change policy in the United States. A note on terminology: Since carbon makes up the vast bulk of greenhouse gas emissions, it is standard practice to refer to the price of carbon (permit price or tax rate) rather than the price of greenhouse gas emissions. Other greenhouse gases can be denominated in units of carbon so nothing is lost in this terminology. Despite the use of this terminology, a carbon tax or cap-and-trade system can (and should) extend to greenhouse gases beyond carbon.

Design Issues

Any policy instrument for putting a price on greenhouse gas emission—whether a tax or a cap-and-trade system—faces several central design issues.

Upstream or Downstream?

The first question concerns the point at which the policy should be administered. For fossil fuels, for example, a carbon pricing policy can be imposed where the fuel is burned or at some earlier stage of production. Unlike the case of water pollution, where changes in production processes can result in less pollution, changes in processing and different uses of carbon fuels do not affect total emissions of carbon. Emissions per ton of lignite coal, for example, are essentially constant, and so the carbon price on this coal could be applied at the power plant where the coal is burned, on the railroad or pipeline that transports the coal, or on the producer of the coal (either the firm that mines it or the company that imports it).

A carbon price imposed on fossil fuel users is termed a *downstream* system while a price imposed on producers is an *upstream* system. Implementing the price upstream reduces the number of firms that must be included in the pricing system. In contrast, a comprehensive downstream system would include each factory using fossil fuels, gas stations where gasoline is sold to drivers, and oil and gas distributers. Cambridge Energy Research Associates (2006) estimates that millions of point sources would fall under an inclusive downstream carbon pricing system.

What Greenhouse Gases Should Be Covered?

Putting a price on fossil fuels used for energy production covers 80 percent of greenhouse gas emissions, as shown in Table 2. Some non-fossil fuel emissions would be relatively easy to bring into a carbon pricing system. For example, carbon pricing could be applied fairly easily to nonenergy carbon emissions from iron, steel, and cement production. In the case of cement production, for example, carbon emissions result from the production of "clinker," an intermediate product, which is a combination of lime and silica-containing materials. The quantity of CO_2 released during production is directly proportional to the lime content of the clinker and so carbon pricing could be imposed on clinker production. There are 118 cement plants in the United States owned by 39 companies. These large, stationary sources of emissions would be relatively easy to bring into a carbon pricing system. Concentrated production or use of hydrofluorocarbons, perfluorocarbons, and sulfur hexafluoride also suggest it should be relatively straightforward to address these emissions in a carbon pricing policy.

In contrast, releases of nitrous oxides through agricultural soil management are more difficult to incorporate into a carbon pricing scheme, because actual emissions vary according to factors like the granularity of the soil and cannot be measured directly. Roughly 20 percent of nitrous oxide emissions arise from the use of artificial fertilizers, but a policy that raises the price of nitrogen-based fertilizers could easily encourage practices that raise other greenhouse gas emissions. Higher fertilizer prices, for example, create incentives to substitute toward manure which raises the demand for livestock and, therefore, possibly increase emissions from livestock.

In Metcalf and Weisbach (2008), my coauthor and I discuss other significant emissions sources and conclude that roughly 90 percent of U.S. greenhouse gas emissions could be brought into a carbon tax base (or a cap-and-trade system) at relatively low cost. Paltsev et al. (2007) provide an

Table 2 Major Greenhouse Gas Sources in 2006

Rank	Source	Gas	MMT CO₂e	Share	Cumulative Share
1	Fossil fuels	CO_2	5,637.0	79.9%	79.9%
2	Agricultural soil management	N_2O	265.0	3.8%	83.7%
3	Nonenergy use of fuels	CO_2	138.0	2.0%	85.6%
4	Landfills	Methane	132.0	1.9%	87.5%
5	Enteric fermentation	Methane	126.2	1.8%	89.3%
6	Ozone depleting substance substitutes	HFC	110.4	1.6%	90.8%
7	Natural gas systems (methane)	Methane	102.4	1.5%	92.3%
8	Coal mining	Methane	58.5	0.8%	93.1%
9	Iron and steel production	CO_2	49.1	0.7%	93.8%
10	Cement manufacturing	CO_2	45.7	0.6%	94.5%
11	Manure management	Methane	41.4	0.6%	95.1%

Source: Metcalf and Weisbach (2008) based on data from U. S. Environmental Protection Agency (2008).
Note: Emissions are measured in millions of metric tons (MMT) of CO₂e (carbon dioxide equivalent). Enteric fermentation takes place in the digestive systems of ruminant animals such as cows.

analysis of carbon pricing that suggests significant efficiency gains arise from including non-CO₂ gases in the policy scheme. This reflects the relatively lower cost of reducing non-CO₂ emissions in the short run.

Other Issues: Carbon Capture, Price, and Policy Integration

Any policy to put a price on greenhouse gas emissions needs to ensure that the price does not apply to emissions that are captured and stored permanently. This includes fossil fuels used as feedstocks in manufacturing activities, in which the carbon is permanently stored in the product. It also applies to fuels that are burned in plants where carbon capture and storage is utilized—technologies that remove carbon from the exhaust streams and store it underground, either locally or after transportation to a storage site, for many centuries.

Sequestration is especially important for coal. The United States has one-third of the world's reserves of coal (BP, 2008). Nearly all the coal consumed in the United States is used to produce electricity, accounting for over half of electricity production domestically. China also has large coal reserves (13 percent of the world total). It is unlikely that either country will willingly set aside these inexpensive energy resources despite concerns about the climate. This fact gives greater urgency to the need for technological and regulatory advances in carbon sequestration.

Proposals for carbon pricing that have been floated in the United States have prices that start in the neighborhood of $15 to $20 per ton of CO_2, or its equivalent from other gases, and then rise over time. Ideally, the price would be set equal to the marginal damages of emissions, but no consensus exists on an estimate of the marginal damages and hence the optimal carbon price (as Tol discusses in this issue). Price trajectories in most federal proposals for carbon taxes or cap and trade are linked directly or indirectly to a desired reduction in aggregate emissions over the first half of this century.

Finally an important design consideration will be how to integrate U.S. policy with current or proposed policies in other countries and at the state or regional level in the United States. I discuss this theme below.

A Tax on Greenhouse Gas Emissions

Since carbon makes up the vast bulk of greenhouse gas emissions, a tax on greenhouse gas emissions is generally referred to as a carbon tax. An upstream carbon tax applied to fossil fuels, along with the carbon equivalent in certain other greenhouse gases, is relatively straightforward to administer, because nearly all of the firms that would be subject to the tax already pay taxes on the products that would be subject to the carbon tax.

The tax would need to be combined with a crediting mechanism to provide a rebate of taxes paid on emissions that are sequestered at a downstream location. Electric utilities that burn coal in an advanced boiler with carbon capture and storage technology, for example, should be allowed a (perhaps tradable) tax credit for sequestered carbon. Credits for certain land-use activities, including forestry sequestration, could also be considered for credit eligibility. In this way, sectors not covered by the carbon tax could receive payments for approved carbon-reducing activities.

We have some experience with the use of carbon taxes in different parts of the world; indeed, because a carbon tax is in large measure a tax on energy use, we can also draw on information from the extensive use of energy taxes throughout the world. Finland passed the first carbon tax in 1990, followed soon after by Sweden, Denmark, the Netherlands, and Norway. Finland's tax rate is currently €20 (equivalent to $26) per ton of CO_2 and applies to liquid fuels and coal. A reduced rate is applied to natural gas, and electricity is not subject to the tax. Finland's carbon tax is a surtax on existing energy taxes and was increased 13 percent at the beginning of 2008. The tax raises roughly €500 million annually.

Bruvolle and Larsen (2004) estimate that Norway's carbon tax reduced greenhouse gas emissions (carbon dioxide, methane, and nitrous oxides) by 2 percent in 1999 relative to what emissions would have been in the absence of the tax. To put this in perspective, emissions of these gases grew by nearly 16 percent during the decade despite the tax being put in place in 1991. While the maximum carbon tax rate in Norway was $51 per ton of carbon dioxide equivalent, or CO_2e, various sectors were taxed at lower rates or exempted from the tax altogether. Bruvolle and Larsen estimate that 64 percent of emissions were subject to the tax and that the tax rate averaged across all emissions was $21 per ton. The authors estimate that a comprehensive carbon tax set at $21 per ton would have reduced emissions in Norway by approximately 14 percent.

The story in Sweden is similar. It passed a carbon tax in 1991 with an initial rate of SKr250 per ton CO_2 (roughly $10 per ton of CO_2). Sweden's tax is indexed for inflation and was recently raised by SKr60 per ton of CO_2. However, Sweden's tax has only limited effect, because it is not applied to fuels used in electricity production and the rate is cut in half for fuels used by industry. Also, deeper reductions are allowed to energy-intensive industries (Johansson, 2000). The exclusion of the electricity sector in the case of Sweden is not nearly as significant as it might appear because Sweden generates most of its electricity from hydro and nuclear power. The United States, in contrast, generates over half of its electricity from coal. The carbon tax raised SKr 24.7 billion in 2006, roughly 1.75 percent of general government tax collections (including Social Security contributions) (Swedish Tax Agency, 2008, Table 17). Norway is similar to Sweden in that its carbon tax raises a significant amount of revenue (roughly 1.7 percent of total tax revenues), is differentiated across fuel types, and exempts significant sectors from taxation.

The province of Quebec in Canada put in place a carbon tax designed to raise roughly $200 million Canadian in 2008 (Tomesco, 2007). This modest tax amounts to 0.8 cents per liter of gasoline (3 cents per gallon). The tax is levied on fuel distributors and applies to gasoline, diesel, natural gas, and electricity from fossil fuels. As such, it is a limited tax on greenhouse gas emissions. In 2008, the province of British Columbia enacted a broad-based carbon tax with an initial rate of $10 (Canadian) per ton of CO_2, to be raised by $5 per ton per year for the following four years (Ministry of Finance, Province of British Columbia, 2008). The tax applies to virtually all fossil fuels, with revenues earmarked for tax reductions as a revenue neutral reform. The tax went into effect in July 2008. It is too soon to evaluate the effects of either of these taxes.

Stern (2007) identifies three defects in the way that most countries have implemented carbon taxes to date. First, numerous exemptions have been provided to industry, which add significant complexity to the tax and weaken the incentives to reduce carbon emissions. Second, tax rates across different fuels typically do not reflect the carbon emissions arising from their use. Third, countries imposing a carbon tax have not attempted to harmonize their tax rates. This pattern is particularly striking in the Scandinavian countries that all implemented carbon taxes in the early 1990s. The provincial tax in British Columbia has taken a more comprehensive approach, though a tax at a sub-national level in isolation has more symbolic than substantive value.

Clearly, the early steps toward a carbon tax have been tentative and limited in nature. Most carbon taxes were not comprehensive in coverage. Despite this, some countries have collected relatively significant amounts of revenue from the tax—Sweden and Norway in particular.

Finally, one might argue that the United States and many other countries have an implicit carbon tax in place in the form of taxes on motor vehicle fuels. The average federal and state tax rate on gasoline in the United States equals 45 cents per gallon (American Petroleum Institute, 2009). In contrast, a number of European countries including Germany, the Netherlands, and the United Kingdom face tax rates on gasoline above $3.00 per gallon (Metcalf, 2009). The average gas tax in the United States is equivalent to a carbon tax rate of $50 per ton of CO_2 while a European tax rate of $3.00 is equivalent to a carbon tax rate of about $340 per ton of CO_2. Driving has a number of other externalities than global climate change from carbon emissions (congestion, tailpipe pollution, health problems, and others) that can be addressed with some form of a gasoline tax. Parry and Small (2005) consider the range of externalities associated with driving and conclude that the U.S. tax rate on gasoline is roughly half its optimal level. The tax in the United Kingdom, in contrast, is roughly twice its optimal level.

High gas taxes in Europe have contributed to reductions in driving and the production of more fuel-efficient vehicles. But a gas tax is not a substitute for a carbon tax. First, the tax covers at most one-third of U.S. carbon dioxide emissions because it excludes from coverage industrial oil use as well as coal and natural gas. Second, taxes on gasoline were put in place for a variety of reasons, ranging from concerns over driving-related externalities to a desire to fund highway construction. A carbon tax would address an externality not accounted for in the political calculations that entered into the existing gas tax.

Cap-and-Trade Program

In its simplest form, a cap-and-trade program sets an aggregate limit on emissions and creates permits for this amount. The government can issue the permits for free to regulated firms or other entities (for example, like state governments), auction the permits, or use some combination of free distribution and auctions. Regulated firms must surrender permits equal in value to the emissions for which their activities are responsible. The permits may be bought and sold so that firms with high costs of emissions abatement may purchase permits from firms with low abatement costs. With a well-functioning permit trading market, the permit price reflects the opportunity cost at the margin of a firm's emissions. Equating marginal costs across all firms emitting greenhouse gases is a necessary condition for efficiency. While a carbon tax fixes the price of emissions and leaves the market to determine the equilibrium quantity, the cap-and-trade program fixes the quantity of emissions and leaves the market to determine the price.

We now have some experience with cap-and-trade programs that can inform a decision on how best to design a program to control greenhouse gas emissions; this subject is usefully discussed in Stavins (2003). The first significant use of cap and trade was the sulfur dioxide (SO_2) trading program for electric utilities established under the Clean Air Act Amendments of 1990. The trading program was designed to reduce SO_2 emissions by ten million tons and nitrogen oxide emissions by two million tons from 1980 levels. Phase I of the program from 1995 to 2000 covered 263 generating units in 110 plants, most of which were large coal-fired facilities east of the Mississippi River. Phase II beginning in 2000 expanded the coverage of the program to most electric generating facilities with capacity of 25 MW or greater and tightened the caps further. Permit trading appears to have reduced the cost of achieving lower SO_2 emissions on the order of 50 percent Ellerman, Joskow, Schmalensee, Montero, and Bailey (2000) present an analysis of cost savings; also see Schmalensee, Joskow, Ellerman, Montero, and Bailey (1998) and Stavins (1998).

Other trading programs include the Regional Clean Air Incentives Market (RECLAIM) program to reduce nitrogen oxide and sulfur dioxide emissions in the Los Angeles region that began in 1994. A regional trading system in nitrogen oxides for the northeastern states began in 1999—the Northeast Ozone Transport Region—allows trading for covered sources. However, these U.S.-based programs are all relatively small-scale in comparison to the projected size of a national cap-and-trade system for carbon emissions.

On January 1, 2005, 25 countries in Europe embarked on a major policy experiment in the use of market-based instruments to control greenhouse gas emissions. The European Union's Emissions Trading Scheme is a cap-and-trade program in which country-by-country caps on carbon emissions were set for energy—intensive industries and the utility sector, and permits for emissions were issued. The program does not include the transportation sector.

Carbon permits can be traded within and across countries in the European Union. Ellerman, Buchner, and Carraro (2007) describe the design and allocation process in the first phase of the program from 2005 to 2007, which was designed as a trial run to work out the kinks in large-scale trading. The experience in this period illustrates both the strengths and challenges of a carbon pricing system.

First, prices exhibited considerable volatility. Permit prices fell sharply in April 2006 on the release of information indicating that the permit allocations had been overly generous. The December 2008 futures price fell from a peak of €32.25 on April 19, 2006, to €22.15 on April 26, 2006, and to €17.80 on May 12, 2006. Prices rebounded briefly but drifted downward for much of the rest of 2006. Volatility in the Phase I permits was even higher, as shown in Figure 1. These permit prices fell from €31.50 on April 19 to €9.80 on May 15, before rebounding briefly.

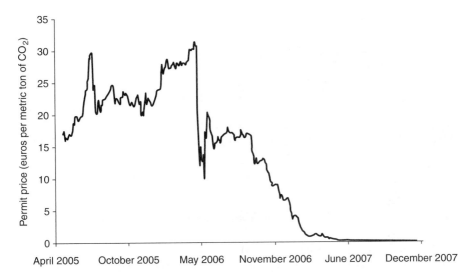

Figure 1 Permit Price for Carbon Emissions, Phase 1 of the European Union's Emissions Trading Scheme

Source: European Climate Exchange (2008).

Second, the experience in Phase I of the EU Emissions Trading Scheme illustrates the importance of allowing trading across time periods. Permits from Phase I were not allowed to be used in Phase II of the program—running from 2008 to 2012. The inability to save permits for future use, along with the overallocation of permits in the first phase, drove the permit price essentially to zero by the middle of 2007. Allowing permits to be saved for use in later years is known as "banking" and contributes considerably to the efficiency of a trading program. Given the long-lived nature of most major greenhouse gases, it is relatively immaterial whether a ton of carbon dioxide is released into the atmosphere today or in 15 years.[2] Banking allows firms to make inexpensive reductions now in excess of their required reductions and so smooth their adjustment costs as permit prices rise in the future with tightening restrictions on emissions. Banking also drives up the price of current permits, thereby sending a signal through the market that long-run capital investments to reduce emissions will be profitable.

Third, Phase I illustrated the lead-time required to implement a cap-and-trade program. The Kyoto Protocol was signed in 1997 and the trading system went into effect in 2005. During this time, a system of national allocations was established and measuring, monitoring, and verification systems put in

---

[2]The majority of carbon emissions released today will be removed from the atmosphere within 100 years, but roughly one-fifth will persist for many centuries (Intergovernmental Panel on Climate Change, 2007).

place. Once all this was up and running, permit price volatility declined over time as markets thickened. For example, average volume rose from a half million contracts in 2005 to nearly seven million contracts in the first three quarters of 2008.

One concern has been the European practice of giving the emissions permits to firms at no cost. An alternative would be to auction them. Proposals for cap-and-trade programs in the United States have increasingly called for auctioning a significant share of the permits with proceeds used for a variety of initiatives including green spending and tax reductions. I discuss this point further below.

The first instance of a carbon cap-and-trade system in which all of the permits will be auctioned has just gotten underway in the U.S. Northeast with the Regional Greenhouse Gas Initiative (RGGI). Ten states in the Northeast and Middle Atlantic regions have committed to capping carbon emissions from electric power plants 25 MW or greater in size at 2009 levels between 2009 and 2014 and then reducing emissions by 2.5 percent per year for the next four years. Proceeds from the auctions will fund energy efficiency and renewable investments in the region. Covered facilities under RGGI account for roughly one-quarter of greenhouse gas emissions in the region.

The first RGGI auction took place in September 2008 and the market clearing price for emissions was $3.07 per ton of carbon dioxide. Given the slowdown in the region's economy since the cap was established, widespread concern exists that the cap may not bind (Daley, 2008). While it is possible that the reason the cap may not bind at a high price is because utilities are undertaking aggressive efforts to reduce emissions, it is more likely that the cap was initially set at a relatively high level. This raises a general point that cap-and-trade programs are only effective at reducing emissions significantly if the caps are set at levels substantially below the business-as-usual emission levels.

Cap-and-trade systems have appealed to policymakers in the United States, both because they appear to offer greater certainty about the quantity of emissions and also because they do not explicitly place a price on emissions. However—as noted above—setting a cap is not the same as reducing emissions. Also, cap and trade is an indirect pricing instrument raising the possibility of large price swings for the permits. The permit price volatility experienced in the European cap-and-trade program is not unique. Permit prices for the California Regional Clean Air Incentives Market (RECLAIM) rose abruptly from under $5,000 per ton of nitrous oxides (NO_x) to nearly $45,000 per ton in the summer of 2000. Permit prices in EPA's Acid Rain Program rose to nearly $1,600 per ton SO_2 in late 2005 from a price of roughly $900 at the beginning of the year. NO_x prices in the Northeast states' Ozone Transport Commission jumped to nearly $8,000 per ton in early 1999 before falling back to more typical levels between $1,000 and $2,000 per ton. Unexpectedly high permit prices erode political support for the program and led in the RECLAIM market to a relaxation of the permit cap in response to the high prices.

Concerns with the potential volatility of carbon prices have led a number of analysts to propose hybrid systems combining elements of price and quantity systems (for example, Pizer, 2002; Stavins, 2007). The simplest hybrid is the "safety valve" approach in which a cap-and-trade system is implemented with a provision allowing firms to purchase an unlimited number of permits at a set price—thus setting a ceiling on the price of permits. A cap-and-trade system which reaches its binding safety valve price level in effect becomes a carbon tax. Even in the absence of an explicit safety valve, we should not assume that the caps in a cap-and-trade law are fixed. After all, Congress serves as the ultimate safety valve if it finds carbon prices rise to unacceptable levels.

Variations have been proposed on the basic safety valve approach. For example, Murray, Newell, and Pizer (2008) propose a variant on a safety valve system by limiting the number of allowances that the government could sell. A fixed allowance reserve that caps the number of allowances the government could sell balances the desire to manage costs under a permit system with a commitment to limiting emissions. Burtraw and Palmer (2006) note that a safety valve lowers the expected permit price and can discourage investment in new technologies to reduce emissions. They recommend combining a safety valve with a price *floor* to maintain the same expected permit price as would occur in the absence of a safety valve. The risk of low permit prices in the future will tend to reduce returns to investments in innovative technologies to reduce carbon emissions.

Allowing banking and borrowing of emission permits can reduce short-term volatility. Recall the experience in Europe with the transition from Phase I to Phase II of its permit system. If firms had been allowed to bank permits between the two phases, permit prices would not have gone to zero in Phase I and prices in Phase II would have been slightly lower at the beginning of the second phase.

Assessing the Options

Nearly all economists agree that upstream implementation of a carbon pricing policy is preferable to a regulatory approach and that all fossil fuels should be included in such a policy. How many of the additional greenhouse gases should be included in the system or how to bring them in may differ across proposals depending on views about how feasible it is to measure and incorporate them. However, carbon taxes and cap-and-trade systems do differ along a number of key dimensions.

Emissions with Uncertainty in Abatement Costs

If marginal costs of abating carbon are known with certainty, the same emissions outcome can be achieved with either a price mechanism like a carbon tax or a quantity mechanism like a cap-and-trade system. However, if the marginal abatement cost curve is uncertain, then the two approaches are no longer equivalent. This follows from an application of Weitzman's (1974) framework of optimal instrument choice under uncertainty.

Figure 2 illustrates the idea behind Weitzman's (1974) model. The horizontal axis measures reductions in emissions of some pollutant (A). The downward sloping curve is the marginal benefits (MB) curve for reducing emissions of this pollutant. This line reflects the social benefits of pollution reduction. From the polluter's point of view, the marginal benefit of abatement is zero. The upward sloping curve measures the marginal cost of abatement (MC). The vertical axis measures marginal costs and benefits in dollars per ton of abatement. In the absence of policy, the firm would undertake no abatement activities. In Figure 2A, we can increase abatement activity either by setting a tax on emissions or by capping emissions at some limit. If a tax is levied, then the firm's private marginal benefit of emissions abatement equals the tax rate (T*). If a cap on emissions is set, then the firm is required to engage in a certain amount of abatement activity (A*). If the tax is set assuming marginal cost and benefit curves MC and MB respectively, abatement amounts of A* will occur. Conversely, if abatement of A* is required, then the shadow price of the cap will equal T*.

Now imagine that the tax or cap on emissions is set assuming the marginal benefit curve MB but the actual marginal benefit curve is MB'. The firm will continue to abate to A* whether it faces a tax or an emissions cap. The cap requires A* of abatement and the tax leads the firm to choose A* in abatement to maximize profits. The two policies will result in equally inefficient outcomes with deadweight loss given by the shaded triangle in the figure. The first observation from Weitzman's model is that uncertainty in the marginal benefit curve will not affect the optimal choice between taxes and pollution caps.

Next consider uncertainty over the marginal abatement cost curve, illustrated in Figure 2B. T* and A* are set assuming marginal benefits and costs of MB and MC. If MC' is the actual marginal abatement cost curve then the tax will lead to A** of abatement with deadweight loss given by the small dark triangle whereas the cap requires A* of abatement leading to deadweight loss represented by the larger lightly shaded triangle. As drawn, the pollution cap has greater deadweight loss than does the tax. As Weitzman demonstrates, this difference is driven by the relative slopes of the marginal benefit and cost curves. If the marginal benefit curve is flatter than the marginal cost curve, then the tax will lead to lower expected deadweight loss than the cap. The intuition is straightforward: We would like the private cost of emissions (either the tax or shadow price of the cap) to reflect the marginal damages of pollution (or equivalently the marginal benefits of abatement). With a relatively flat marginal benefit MB curve, the tax is more likely to be "close" to marginal damages than will the shadow price of a cap. Conversely, if the MB curve is very steep, this suggests that the pollutant has some threshold effect that drives damages up sharply if abatement is set too low. In that case, society is better off with a cap to ensure that a sufficient level of abatement occurs.

A: Uncertainty over the Marginal Benefits of Abatement

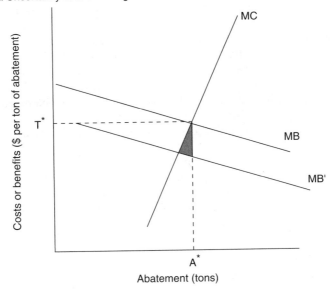

B: Uncertainty over the Marginal Costs of Abatement

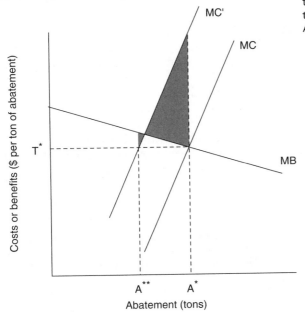

Figure 2 Uncertainty over the Marginal Benefits or the Marginal Costs of Abatement

Greenhouse gases are a pollutant where a stock builds up over time, and so the analysis is a bit more complicated, but the intuition carries over to a large extent. With a stock pollutant that persists in the atmosphere for a very long time, marginal damages from emissions in any given year are essentially constant. A flat MB curve favors the tax approach. This insight is borne out by a number of analyses that have found that taxes dominate cap-and-trade systems for a broad range of parameter values consistent with scientific understanding of the global warming problem (for example, Hoel and Karp, 2002; Karp and Zhang, 2005; Newell and Pizer, 2003).

The analyses described above assume a policy choice is made at one point in time and then is not altered as new information is received. This is a limitation of the Weitzman model as Congress is likely to review allowance targets under a cap-and-trade system and tax rates under a carbon tax as new information becomes available. With frequent updating, the efficiency differences are reduced and—in the limit with continual updating—the two instruments once again have identical efficiency consequences.[3]

Rents and Revenue

A U.S. carbon pricing policy has the potential to raise significant revenue. The U.S. Department of State (2007) projects greenhouse gas emissions of 8,115 million metric tons in 2012. Energy-related carbon dioxide emissions are projected under the business-as-usual scenario to be 6,318 tons. Assuming a modest reduction in emissions from a carbon pricing policy—either a tax or cap-and-trade system with auctioned permits applied just to energy-related CO_2 emissions—such a program could raise roughly $90 billion annually for a carbon price of $15 per ton.

Of course, a cap-and-trade system only raises revenue if the permits are sold by the government. Historically, permits in other U.S. cap-and-trade programs have been given away to industry as part of a process of obtaining political support for the system. The EU Emissions Trading Scheme also has given the permits away for free. To be fair, prior U.S. cap-and-trade programs were an order of magnitude smaller than any potential carbon cap-and-trade program. Thus, given the revenues involved, auctioning permits in those programs was simply not that important. As noted above, the RGGI program in the U.S. Northeast has committed to 100 percent auctioning of permits.

---

[3]The inefficiency described above is distinct from the inefficiency that arises from distortionary taxes. Set aside the uncertainty described above for the moment. In the absence of other distortions in the economy, a tax set at the marginal damages of pollution (or a cap-and-trade system with shadow price of emissions equal to marginal damages) would be efficient. With pre-existing distortions, however, a carbon tax leads to lower pollution damages but also generates its own deadweight loss (this is known as the "tax interaction effect"). The important point for instrument choice is that a carbon tax and a cap-and-trade system that lead to the same price on emissions have equivalent distortionary impacts through the tax interaction effect. The argument that taxes are distortionary does not favor cap-and-trade systems. They are equally distortionary on this dimension.

In addition to the loss of substantial revenue, freely allocated permits may undermine the key goal of discouraging the consumption of carbon-intensive energy. Although retail competition for electricity exists in many states (primarily in the Northeast), a large proportion of electricity consumers still operate in markets subject to state-level regulation (Joskow, 2006). It is unclear if regulators will allow regulated utilities to pass through the cost of carbon emissions permits in the form of higher electricity prices for customers if the permits are given without charge to the utilities. In that case, carbon emissions permits would have no effect in reducing electricity demand—although they would still encourage utilities to find alternative sources or fuels for electricity that use less carbon.

In deregulated markets, utilities that are freely given permits will likely raise the price of electricity because the marginal cost of production would then include the opportunity cost of giving up permits they could have sold. This increase in the price without any commensurate increase in the utilities' real costs will generate windfall profits. This pattern unfolded during the first allocation period of the European Union's Emissions Trading Scheme and led to controversy and discussion of re-regulation. Such windfall profits are simply the realization of the value of freely given permits to the electric utilities and reflect the fact that complete grandfathering overcompensates energy industries for losses they incur through the imposition of carbon pricing. In their analysis of a possible U.S. cap-and-trade system, Bovenberg and Goulder (2001) find that grandfathering more than 4 percent of permits in the coal industry and 15 percent in the oil and gas industry overcompensate[s] these industries for their losses. Utilities actually lose relatively little from permit costs because these costs are largely passed forward to final consumers in the form of higher energy prices.

The issue of revenue from carbon pricing also raises the question of distributional effects. Table 3 presents results from a distributional analysis of carbon pricing on U.S. households using data from the 2003 Consumer Expenditure Survey. Most analyses of energy taxes suggest that they are shifted forward to consumers in the form of higher energy prices. I measure the effect on household purchases of a $15 per ton carbon price taking into account the direct effect (higher cost of energy purchases) as well as the indirect effect (higher cost of goods and services due to increase in energy costs of production). I describe this methodology in detail in Metcalf (1999) and have used it (Metcalf, 2007b) to evaluate carbon tax reforms. Dinan and Rogers (2002) also use this methodology to evaluate permit allocation under cap-and-trade programs in the United States.

The first column of Table 3 illustrates that carbon pricing by itself is regressive. Low-income households spend over 3 percent of their income in higher costs for goods and services for the carbon price. The share of income going to pay the carbon price falls to just under 1 percent for the highest-income groups. I also report results for two different ways in which carbon revenues could be returned to households. First, I consider a reform detailed in Metcalf (2007b) where an environmental earned income tax credit is provided to workers capped at a level that makes the reform revenue-

Table 3 Income Distribution and Carbon Pricing

Income group (decile)	Carbon pricing alone	With revenue returned to households	With revenue returned to energy producers	Carbon pricing lifetime measure
	Mean tax change as a percentage of disposable income			
1 (lowest)	−3.4	−0.7	−1.8	−1.2
2	−3.1	−1.0	−0.6	−1.2
3	−2.4	−0.2	−0.6	−1.2
4	−2.0	0.1	−0.4	−1.2
5	−1.8	0.1	−0.5	−1.3
6	−1.5	0.3	−0.5	−1.2
7	−1.4	0.2	−0.2	−1.2
8	−1.2	0.2	−0.2	−1.1
9	−1.1	0.0	0.1	−1.0
10 (highest)	−0.8	0.0	0.5	−0.9

Sources: Metcalf (2007b) for annual income measures; Hassett, Mathur, and Metcalf (2009) for the lifetime income measure.
Note: Table 3 presents results from a distributional analysis of carbon pricing on U.S. households using data from the 2003 Consumer Expenditure Survey. I measure the effect on household purchases of a $15 per ton carbon price taking into account the direct effect (higher cost of energy purchases) as well as the indirect effect (higher cost of goods and services due to increase in energy costs of production). See text for details. The lowest decile includes households in the 5th to the 10th percentiles.

neutral. For a $15 per ton carbon price in 2003, the cap is $560 per worker. This reform, reported in column 2, eliminates most of the regressivity of the carbon price, and modest variations in this reform can make the net transfer distributionally neutral or progressive as desired. In contrast, a return of revenue to energy producers (or equivalently free distribution of permits to energy producers) leads to a distinctly regressive outcome (column 3). Clearly, how carbon revenues are used has significant distributional implications.

The analysis in the first three columns of Table 3 takes an annual income incidence approach. A large body of research shows that the distributional impact of taxes can look very different if we use a lifetime incidence approach (for example, Davies, St-Hilaire, and Whalley, 1984; Poterba, 1989, 1991; and others). Drawing on work described in Hassett, Mathur, and Metcalf (2009), the last column of Table 3 shows that the regressivity of carbon pricing is blunted significantly if one uses a lifetime measure of income in the incidence analysis. The annual income and lifetime income approaches are two ends of a spectrum. People clearly take future income into account when making consumption decisions today; on the other hand, it is unlikely that most people are full lifetime-income optimizers. We can think of the annual and lifetime income incidence measures as bracketing the true distributive effect.

Finally, let me note another distributional concern: that certain sectors are disproportionately affected by a carbon price. This concern is particularly relevant for the coal industry. We should not protect coal from carbon pricing, but we may wish to provide transitional assistance in this industry. The cost should not be that great. The value added by the coal industry (labor compensation, owners' profits, and indirect business taxes) totaled $11 billion in 2005. If the share of labor compensation in coal mining value added is unchanged from 1997, when labor accounted for one-half the value added in coal mining, the maximum potential loss to labor is $6.5 billion annually. This puts an upper limit on the losses to this sector; actual losses will be less, since coal production will not disappear. Moreover, as time goes on, participants in this industry can begin to make adjustments to move into other sectors. Thus, any transitional assistance should be temporary in nature with particular attention paid to those factors that are least able to make a transition to new jobs (for example, older workers).

Administration

How quickly could a carbon pricing system be put in place? A carbon tax would be implemented through the Internal Revenue Service and could piggyback on existing energy taxes. For example, coal producers already pay an excise tax to fund the Black Lung Trust Fund and oil producers pay a tax to fund the Oil Spill Trust Fund. The United States also has precedents for refundable credits for CO_2 sequestration activities in ethanol tax credits in the federal gas tax.

The United States also has a model for running an upstream carbon cap-and-trade program in the SO_2 trading program described earlier, which has been administered by the Environmental Protection Agency. However, the experience from establishing cap-and-trade systems suggests considerable lead-time is required to establish allocations (Congressional Budget Office, 2008).

Linkage with Existing Programs

Any federal carbon pricing scheme would have to be linked to existing programs. Linkage issues arise in three contexts: cap-and-trade programs in other countries; sub-federal cap-and-trade programs; and other carbon policies in other countries. My discussion of these issues draws on Stavins (2007).

Consider first linkage with cap-and-trade programs in other countries. A U.S. cap-and-trade system would need to decide whether permits could be purchased from foreign cap-and-trade programs. If so, would there be limits on the number of permits that could be used? A cap-and-trade bill reported to the floor of the U.S. Senate in 2007 provided for the use of permits from other trading programs up to 5 percent of allowed emissions. Next, the United States would have to decide whether it would demand reciprocity, in which case foreigners could purchase U.S. emissions permits.

Full harmonization across countries has the potential to bring down the costs of achieving domestic caps given the greater flexibility in reducing emissions in a harmonized program. On the other hand, if the price for permits are [sic] set as a result of extensive international trading, then no individual country will control the price paid for its own domestic emissions. Moreover, full harmonization has the potential to degrade the quality of domestic permits to the extent that some foreign governments have lax standards for measuring, monitoring, and verifying emission reductions in their countries. U.S. firms could end up buying permits from other countries based on the promise of significant reductions in those countries that are never realized.

Strictly speaking, one cannot link a foreign cap-and-trade system with a domestic carbon tax. But we can connect the two systems by harmonizing the price of carbon in the two systems. A commitment to keep permit prices and tax rates within some range ensures that "leakage"—the movement of economic activity from countries that price carbon to those that don't—remains a second-order issue. A useful component of a global agreement to address greenhouse gas emissions would be an agreement on a price path for carbon emissions, which would still leave the decision on instrument choice to each country.

Next is the question of linkage of a national U.S. cap-and-trade program with U.S. state or regional programs. For example, would electric utilities in the Northeast states subject to RGGI be required to surrender federal as well as RGGI permits for their emissions? Stavins (2007) recommends that the federal program pre-empt state and regional programs to avoid confusion and administrative complexity. Presumably pre-emption would be combined with some mechanism to convert existing permits in the state or regional program into federal permits. Similarly, a federal carbon tax could, though need not, preempt state and regional cap-and-trade programs.

Finally, what to be done about countries that do not have a carbon pricing policy? Concerns about leakage of economic activity have largely focused on the possible loss of jobs to China, India, and other emerging developing countries if the U.S. adopts some form of carbon pricing and these countries don't. However, it should be noted that a large fraction of U.S. energy-intensive imports come from countries that currently have or are likely to have a carbon pricing policy (Houser and Bradley, 2008).

If the United States adopted a carbon tax, the natural mechanism to address imports from countries that do not have comparable carbon policies is through a border tax adjustment. Imported fossil fuels from countries with low or no carbon prices would be subject to the tax at the border. To reduce incentives for shifting carbon-intensive manufacturing to countries that do not impose a carbon price, the United States should also apply the carbon tax to the embodied carbon in certain carbon-intensive imports. In Metcalf and Weisbach (2008), my coauthor and I describe this modified origin approach in more detail.

Whether this policy would be administratively feasible, desirable, and legal under rules of the World Trade Organization are matters of some debate. It would clearly be administratively complex to collect a carbon tax on the carbon embedded in *all* imports. But the United States could apply a border tax adjustment to a small number of carbon-intensive imports like steel, aluminum, paper, chemicals, and cement. While it would be desirable to tax the imports on their actual carbon content, this content will vary from country to country, and so it may be more practical to set the tax adjustment at a level based on average domestic content. Countries could apply for a variance from the average rate by providing documentation that their exports to the United States have a lower carbon content.

Trade economists are generally skeptical of any proposal to apply tariffs on imports for social reasons. The essential and legitimate concern is that social policy might be used as a cover for protectionist policies. World Trade Organizations rules are clear that, in general, taxes on imports are permissible so long as the tax is on the product, rather than the processes and production methods. However, WTO has explicitly built into its rules exemptions for health and the environment (Article XX).[4] As long as the proposed border tax adjustment treats domestic production and imports equivalently, it would be hard to argue that a border tax adjustment has protectionist implications.

An argument could be made that a border tax adjustment based on U.S. content circumvents the processes and production methods issue entirely. The issue, however, will only be resolved once a country implements a carbon tax with a border tax adjustment.

Similar issues arise with any policies to address leakage of economic activity to other jurisdictions in a cap-and-trade system. Stavins (2007) recommends requiring permits to be surrendered by importers of a selective number of carbon-intensive products. Similar issues of legality under the World Trade Organization rules, and of measurement of carbon content to determine the number of allowances to be surrendered upon import, arise with this system as with a carbon tax.

Conclusion

Nearly all economists on both sides of this instrument choice debate agree that a comprehensive carbon pricing policy using either a carbon tax or a cap-and-trade system strongly dominates a sectoral-based command-and-control regulatory approach on efficiency and distributional grounds. We can expand the pricing system beyond energy-related carbon emissions to capture something on the order of half of the other greenhouse gases at reasonable cost. Economists seem to be reaching agreement on some other points as well. Whether the United States implements a tax or permit system, it should put the point of compliance as far upstream as possible to

---

[4]Frankel (2005) argues that the language of the WTO's ruling on the U.S. ban on shrimp imports from countries not protecting endangered sea turtles also opens the door to the regulation of processes and production methods. Also see Frankel (2008).

reduce administrative costs. The country also needs to have a forthright discussion of the revenues that will be (or could be) generated with carbon pricing, with a particular focus on minimizing adverse impacts on low-income households. Finally implementing a carbon price—either through a tax or permit system—provides an opportunity to end current energy subsidies and regulatory programs that would no longer be needed with a meaningful carbon price.

In closing, let me address a common criticism of U.S. action on climate change. If the United States—or the United States along with other developed countries—reduces greenhouse gas emissions without participation by developing countries, it is observed that all we will have accomplished is a shift of production of carbon-intensive manufacturing to the developing world and no consequent drop in emissions. In short, global participation in greenhouse gas reductions is essential for solving this global problem. While this point is absolutely correct, it does not imply that the United States and other developed countries should not act before obtaining international agreement to reduce emissions. It is hard to imagine how we can get major developing countries to commit to greenhouse gas reduction if the United States, as the world's richest country, does not commit to significant greenhouse gas reductions.

While a U.S. program to reduce emissions of greenhouse gases is likely a necessary condition for a comprehensive international agreement to reduce emissions, it is by no means a sufficient condition. The United States could commit to a policy that includes border tax adjustments for carbon-intensive imports from countries that do not have a substantive emissions program and perhaps provide a timetable for commitment by major carbon emitting nations to join an international agreement. If, for example, China and other major emitting nations do not commit to significant emission reductions within the next 15 years, the U.S. and other developed nations could even promise to remove their tax or trading systems.

A U.S. carbon pricing scheme—whether in the form of a comprehensive carbon tax or cap-and-trade systems—will be an enormous undertaking. It could end up covering emissions on the order of six billion metric tons of CO_2 equivalent—which would be roughly three times the annual covered emissions under the 2008–2012 phase of the EU's Emissions Trading Scheme. Nonetheless, it is time for the United States to enact a meaningful policy to reduce greenhouse gas emissions. Without the participation and leadership of the world's richest country and one of the leading emitters of greenhouse gases, it is difficult to imagine how the world can ever make meaningful progress on slowing and eventually stopping global warming.

REFERENCES

American Petroleum Institute. 2009. "Motor Fuel Taxes." http://www.api:org/ [(accessed 6/17/11)].
Bovenberg, A. Lans, and Lawrence Goulder. 2001. "Neutralizing the Adverse Industry Impacts of CO_2 Abatement Policies: What Does It Cost?" In *Distributional*

and Behavioral Effects of Environmental Policy, ed. C. Carraro and G. E. Metcalf, 45–85. Chicago: University of Chicago Press.

BP. 2008. "BP Statistical Review of World Energy June 2008." London: BP p.l.c.

Bruvolle, Annegrete, and Bodil Merethe Larsen. 2004. "Greenhouse Gas Emissions in Norway: Do Carbon Taxes Work?" *Energy Policy*, 32(4): 493–505.

Burtraw, Dallas, and Karen Palmer. 2006. "Dynamic Adjustment to Incentive Based Policy to Improve Efficiency and Performance." Washington, DC: Resources for the Future.

Cambridge Energy Research Associates. 2006. "Design Issues for Market-Based Greenhouse Gas Reduction Strategies." Washington, DC: CERA.

Congressional Budget Office. 2008. "Policy Options for Reducing CO_2 Emissions." Washington, DC: Congressional Budget Office.

Daley, Beth. 2008. "Emissions Down, but Lasting Efforts May Suffer." In *The Boston Globe*, January 3.

Davies, James B., France St-Hilaire, and John Whalley. 1984. "Some Calculations of Lifetime Tax Incidence." *American Economic Review*, 74(4): 633–49.

Dinan, Terry, and Diane Lim Rogers. 2002. "Distributional Effects of Carbon Allowance Trading: How Government Decisions Determine Winners and Losers." *National Tax Journal*, 55(2): 199–221.

Ellerman, A. Denny, Barbara Buchner, and Carlo Carraro. 2007. *Allocation in the European Emissions Trading Scheme*. Cambridge: Cambridge University Press.

Ellerman, A. Denny, Paul L. Joskow, Richard Schmalensee, Juan-Pablo Montero, and Elizabeth M. Bailey. 2000. *Markets for Clean Air. The U.S. Acid Rain Program*. Cambridge: Cambridge University Press.

Frankel, Jeffrey. 2005. "Climate and Trade: Link between the Kyoto Protocol and WTO." *Environment*, 47(7): 8–19.

Frankel, Jeffrey. 2008. "Global Environmental Policy and Global Trade Policy." Cambridge: Harvard Project on International Climate Agreements.

Hassett, Kevin A., Aparna Mathur, and Gilbert E. Metcalf. 2009. "The Incidence of a U.S. Carbon Tax: A Lifetime and Regional Analysis." *The Energy Journal*, 30(2): 157–79.

Hoel, Michael, and Larry Karp. 2002. "Taxes versus Quotas for a Stock Pollutant." *Resource and Energy Economics*, 24(4): 367–84.

Holland, Stephen P., Christopher R. Knittel, and Jonathan E. Hughes. 2009. "Greenhouse Gas Reductions under Low Carbon Fuel Standards?" *American Economic Journal: Economic Policy*, 1(1): 106–46.

Houser, Trevor, and Rob Bradley. 2008. "Leveling the Carbon Playing Field." Washington, DC: World Resources Institute.

Intergovernmental Panel on Climate Change. 2007. "Climate Change 2007—The Physical Science Basis, Contribution of Working Group I to the Fourth Assessment Report of the IPCC." Cambridge University Press.

Johansson, Bengt. 2000. "Economic Instruments in Practice 1: Carbon Tax in Sweden." OECD. http://www.oecd.org/dataoecd/25/0/2108273.pdf [(accessed 6/17/00)].

Joskow, Paul L. 2006. "Markets for Power in the United States: An Interim Assessment." *The Energy Journal*, 27(1): 1–36.

Karp, Larry, and Jiangfeng Zhang. 2005. "Regulation of Stock Externalities with Correlated Abatement Costs." *Environmental and Resource Economics*, 32(2): 273–99.

Metcalf, Gilbert E. 1999. "A Distributional Analysis of Green Tax Reforms." *National Tax Journal*, 52(4): 655–81.

Metcalf, Gilbert E. 2007a. "Federal Tax Policy towards Energy." *Tax Policy and the Economy*, Vol. 21 (in NBER Book Series Tax Policy and the Economy), 145–84. MIT Press.

Metcalf, Gilbert E. 2007b. "A Proposal for a U.S. Carbon Tax Swap: An Equitable Tax Reform to Address Global Climate Change." Discussion Paper 2007–12, Hamilton Project, Brookings Institution.

Metcalf, Gilbert E. 2009. "Environmental Taxation: What Have We Learned in This Decade?" In *Tax Policy Lessons from the 2000s*, ed. A. Viard, 7–34. Washington, DC: AEI Press.

Metcalf, Gilbert E., and David Weisbach. 2008. "The Design of a Carbon Tax." Tufts University and the University of Chicago.

Ministry of Finance, Province of British Columbia. 2008. "B.C.'S Revenue-Neutral Carbon Tax." http://www.bcbudget.gov.bc.ca/2008/backgrounders/backgrounder _carbon_tax.htm [(accessed 6/17/11)].

Murray, Brian C., Richard G. Newell, and William A. Pizer. 2008. "Balancing Cost and Emissions Certainty: An Allowance Reserve for Cap-and-Trade." Cambridge, MA: National Bureau of Economic Research.

Newell, Richard G., and William A. Pizer. 2003. "Regulating Stock Externalities under Uncertainty." *Journal of Environmental Economics and Management*, 45(2): 416–32.

Paltsev, Sergey, John M. Reilly, Henry D. Jacoby, Angelo C. Gurgel, Gilbert E. Metcalf, Andrei P. Sokolov, and Jennifer F. Holak. 2007. "Assessment of U.S. Cap-and-Trade Proposals." Cambridge, MA: MTT Joint Program on the Science and Policy of Global Change.

Parry, Ian, and Kenneth A. Small. 2005. "Does Britain or the United States Have the Right Gasoline. Tax?" *American Economic Review*, 95(4): 1276–89.

Pizer, William A. 2002. "Combining Price and Quantity Controls to Mitigate Global Climate Change." *Journal of Public Economics*, 85(3): 409–34.

Portney, Paul R., Ian W. H. Parry, Howard K. Gruenspecht, and Winston Harrington. 2003. "Policy Watch: The Economics of Fuel Economy Standards." *Journal of Economic Perspectives*, 17(4): 203–217.

Poterba, James. 1989. "Lifetime Incidence and the Distributional Burden of Excise Taxes." *American Economic Review*, 79(2): 325–30.

Poterba, James. 1991. "Is the Gasoline Tax Regressive?" *Tax Policy and the Economy*, Vol. 5 (in NBER Book Series Tax Policy and the Economy), 145–64. MIT Press.

Schmalensee, Richard, Paul L. Joskow, A. Denny Ellerman, Juan Pablo Montero, and Elizabeth M. Bailey. 1998. "An Interim Evaluation of Sulfur Dioxide Emissions Trading." *The Journal of Economic Perspectives*, 12(3): 53–68.

Stavins, Robert N. 1998. "What Can We Learn from the Grand Policy Experiment? Lessons from SO$_2$ Allowance Trading" *The Journal of Economic Perspectives*, 12(3): 69–88.

Stavins, Robert N. 2003. "Experience with Market-Based Environmental Policy Instruments." In *Handbook of Environmental Economics. Vol. 1. Environmental Degradation and Institutional Responses*, ed. R. N. Stavins, K.-G. Maler, and J. R. Vincent, 355–435. Amsterdam: Elsevier Science, North-Holland.

Stavins, Robert N. 2007. "Proposal for a U.S. Cap-and-Trade System to Address Global Climate Change: A Sensible and Practical Approach to Reduce Greenhouse Gas Emissions." Washington, DC: The Hamilton Project.

Stern, Nicholas. 2007. *The Economics of Climate Change: The Stern Review*. Cambridge: Cambridge University Press.

Swedish Tax Agency. 2008. "Taxes in Sweden 2007: An English Translation." Stock-holm: Swedish Tax Agency. [Available at www.skatteverket.se/download/18.23 3f91f71260075abe8800097303/10408.pdf (accessed 6/17/11)].

Tomesco, Frederic. 2007. "Quebec Approves Carbon Tax to Cut Greenhouse Gases." Bloomberg.com. [Available at www.bloomberg.com/apps/news?pid=newsarchive &refer=canada&sid=ahB7G9DC_HSI (accessed 6/17/11)].

U.S. Environmental Protection Agency. 2008. *Inventory of U.S. Greenhouse Gas Emissions and Sinks: 1990–2006*. [Available at www.epa.gov/climatechange/ emissions/downloads/08_CR.pdf (accessed 6/17/11)].

U.S. Department of State. 2007. *Fourth Climate Action Report to the UN Framework Convention on Climate Change*. Washington, DC: Department of State. [Available at www.state.gov/g/oes/rls/rpts/car4/index.htm (accessed 6/17/11)].

U.S. Energy Information Administration. 2008. "Annual Energy Outlook 2008." Report No. DOE/EIA-0383 (2008). Washington, DC: U.S. Energy Information Administration.

Weitzman, Martin. 1974. "Prices vs. Quantities." *Review of Economic Studies*, 41(4): 477–91.

IX

Sustainability, the Commons,
and Globalization

28 Sustainability: An Economist's Perspective

Robert M. Solow

Robert M. Solow is Institute Professor of Economics Emeritus at the Massachusetts Institute of Technology.

This talk is different from anything else anyone has heard at Woods Hole; certainly for the last two days. Three people have asked me, "Do you plan to use any transparencies or slides?" Three times I said, "No," and three times I was met with this blank stare of disbelief. I actually have some beautiful aerial photographs of Prince William Sound that I could have brought along to show you, and I also have a spectacular picture of Michael Jordan in full flight that you would have liked to have seen. But in fact I don't need or want any slides or transparencies. I want to talk to you about an idea. The notion of sustainability or sustainable growth (although, as you will see, it has nothing necessarily to do with growth) has infiltrated discussions of long-run economic policy in the last few years. It is very hard to be against sustainability. In fact, the less you know about it, the better it sounds. That is true of lots of ideas. The questions that come to be connected with sustainable development or sustainable growth or just sustainability are genuine and deeply felt and very complex. The combination of deep feeling and complexity breeds buzzwords, and sustainability has certainly become a buzzword. What I thought I might do, when I was invited to talk to a group like this, was to try to talk out loud about how one might think straight about the concept of sustainability, what it might mean and what its implications (not for daily life but for your annual vote or your concern for economic policy) might be.

Definitions are usually boring. That is probably true here too. But here it matters a lot. Some people say they don't know what sustainability means, but it sounds good. I've seen things on restaurant menus that strike me the same way. I took these two parts of a definition from a UNESCO document: ". . . every generation should leave water, air and soil resources as pure and unpolluted as when it came on earth." Alternatively, it was suggested that "each generation should leave undiminished all the species of animals it found existing on earth." I suppose that sounds good, as it is meant to. But I believe that kind of thought is fundamentally the wrong

"Sustainability: An Economist's Perspective" by Robert M. Solow. *National Geographic Research and Exploration* 8. 1992. Pp. 10–21. Reprinted with permission.

way to go in thinking about this issue. I must also say that there are some much more carefully thought out definitions and discussions, say by the U.N. Environment Programme and the World Conservation Union. They all turn out to be vague; in a way, the message I want to leave with you today is that sustainability is an essentially vague concept, and it would be wrong to think of it as being precise, or even capable of being made precise. It is therefore probably not in any clear way an exact guide to policy. Nevertheless, it is not at all useless.

Pretty clearly the notion of sustainability is about our obligation to the future. It says something about a moral obligation that we are supposed to have for future generations. I think it is very important to keep in mind—I'm talking like a philosopher for the next few sentences and I don't really know how to do that—that you can't be morally obligated to do something that is not feasible. Could I be morally obligated to be like Peter Pan and flap my wings and fly around the room? The answer is clearly not. I can't have a moral obligation like that because I am not capable of flapping my arms and flying around the room. If I fail to carry out a moral obligation, you must be entitled to blame me. You could properly say unkind things about me. But you couldn't possibly say unkind things about me for not flying around the room like Peter Pan because you know, as well as I do, that I can't do it.

If you define sustainability as an obligation to leave the world as we found it in detail, I think that's glib but essentially unfeasible. It is, when you think about it, not even desirable. To carry out literally the injunction of UNESCO would mean to make no use of mineral resources; it would mean to do no permanent construction or semi-permanent construction; build no roads; build no dams; build no piers. A mooring would be all right but not a pier. Apart from being essentially an injunction to do something that is not feasible, it asks us to do something that is not, on reflection, desirable. I doubt that I would feel myself better off if I had found the world exactly as the Iroquois left it. It is not clear that one would really want to do that.

To make something reasonable and useful out of the idea of sustainability, I think you have to try a different kind of definition. The best thing I could think of is to say that it is an obligation to conduct ourselves so that we leave to the future the option or the capacity to be as well off as we are. It is not clear to me that one can be more precise than that. Sustainability is an injunction not to satisfy ourselves by impoverishing our successors. That sounds good too, but I want you to realize how problematic it is—how hard it is to make anything precise or checkable out of that thought. If we try to look far ahead, as presumably we ought to if we are trying to obey the injunction to sustainability, we realize that the tastes, the preferences, of future generations are something that we don't know about. Nor do we know anything very much about the technology that will be available to people 100 years from now. Put yourself in the position of someone in 1880 trying to imagine what life would be like in 1980 and you will see how wrong you would be. I think all we can do in this respect is to imagine people in the future being much like ourselves and attributing to them, imputing to them, whatever technology we can "reasonably" extrapolate—

whatever that means. I am trying to emphasize the vagueness but not the meaningless of that concept. It is not meaningless, it is just inevitably vague.

We are entitled to please ourselves, according to this definition, so long as it is not at the expense (in the sense that I stated) of future well-being. You have to take into account, in thinking about sustainability, the resources that we use up and the resources that we leave behind, but also the sort of environment we leave behind including the built environment, including productive capacity (plant and equipment) and including techno-logical knowledge. *To talk about sustainability in that way is not at all empty.* It attracts your attention, first, to what history tells us is an impor-tant fact, namely, that goods and services can be substituted for one another. If you don't eat one species of fish, you can eat another species of fish. Resources are, to use a favorite word of economists, fungible in a certain sense. They can take the place of each other. That is extremely important because it suggests that we do not owe to the future any particular thing. There is no specific object that the goal of sustainability, the obligation of sustainability, requires us to leave untouched.

What about nature? What about wilderness or unspoiled nature? I think that we ought, in our policy choices, to embody our desire for unspoiled nature as a component of well-being. But we have to recognize that different amenities really are, to some extent, substitutable for one another, and we should be as inclusive as possible in our calculations. It is perfectly okay, it is perfectly logical and rational, to argue for the preserva-tion of a particular species or the preservation of a particular landscape. But that has to be done on its own, for its own sake, because this landscape is intrinsically what we want or this species is intrinsically important to preserve, not under the heading of sustainability. Sustainability doesn't require that any *particular* species of owl or any *particular* species of fish or any *particular* tract of forest be preserved. Substitutability is also impor-tant on the production side. We know that one kind of input can be substi-tuted for another in production. There is no reason for our society to feel guilty about using up aluminum as long as we leave behind a capacity to perform the same or analogous functions using other kinds of materials— plastics or other natural or artificial materials. In making policy decisions we can take advantage of the principle of substitutability, remembering that what we are obligated to leave behind is a generalized capacity to cre-ate well-being, not any particular thing or any particular natural resource.

If you approach the problem that way in trying to make plans and make policies, it is certain that there will be mistakes. We will impute to the future tastes that they don't have or we will impute to them technologi-cal capacities that they won't have or we will fail to impute to them tastes and technological capacities that they do have. The set of possible mistakes is usually pretty symmetric.

That suggests to me the importance of choosing robust policies when-ever we can. We should choose policies that will be appropriate over as wide a range of possible circumstances as we can imagine. But it would be wrong for policy to be paralyzed by the notion that one can make mistakes.

Liability to error is the law of life. And, as most people around Woods Hole know, you choose policies to avoid potentially catastrophic errors, if you can. You insure whenever you can, but that's it.

The way I have put this, and I meant to do so, emphasizes that sustainability is about distributional equity. It is about who gets what. It is about the sharing of well-being between present people and future people. I have also emphasized the need to keep in mind, in making plans, that we don't know what they will do, what they will like, what they will want. And, to be honest, it is none of our business.

It is often asked whether, at this level, the goal or obligation of sustainability can be left entirely to the market. It seems to me that there is no reason to believe in a doctrinaire way that it can. The future is not adequately represented in the market, at least not the far future. If you remember that our societies live with real interest rates of the order of 5 or 6 percent, you will realize that that means that the dollar a generation from now, thirty years from now, is worth 25 cents today. That kind of discount seems to me to be much sharper than we would seriously propose in our public capacity, as citizens thinking about our obligation to the future. It seems to me to be a stronger discount than most of us would like to make. It is fair to say that those people a few generations hence are not adequately represented in today's market. They don't participate in it, and therefore there is no doctrinaire reason for saying, "Oh well, ordinary supply and demand, ordinary market behavior, will take care of whatever obligation we have to the future."

Now, in principle, government could serve as a trustee, as a representative for future interests. Policy actions, taxes, subsidies, regulations could, in principle, correct for the excessive present-mindedness of ordinary people like ourselves in our daily business. Of course, we are not sure that government will do a good job. If often seems that the rate at which governments discount the future is rather sharper than that at which the bond market does. So we can't be sure that public policy will do a good job. That is why we talk about it in a democracy. We are trying to think about collective decisions for the future, and discussions like this, not with just me talking, are the way in which policies of that kind ought to be thrashed out.

Just to give you some idea of how uncertain both private and public behavior can be in an issue like this, let me ask you to think about the past, not about the future. You could make a good case that our ancestors, who were considerably poorer than we are, whose standard of living was considerably less than our own, were probably excessively generous in providing for us. They cut down a lot of trees, but they saved a lot and they built a lot of railroad rights-of-way. Both private and publicly they probably did better by us than a sort of fair-minded judge in thinking about the equity (whether they got their share and we got our share or whether we profited at their expense) would have required. It would have been okay for them to save a little less, to enjoy a little more and given us a little less of a start than our generation has had. I don't think there is any simple generalization that will serve to guide policy about these issues. There is every reason to discuss economic policy and social policy from this point of view, and anything else is likely to be ideology rather than analysis.

Once you take the point of view that I have been urging on you in thinking about sustainability as a matter of distributional equity between the present and the future, you can see that it becomes a problem about saving and investment. It becomes a problem about the choice between current consumption and providing for the future.

There is a sort of dual connection—a connection that need not be intrinsic but is there—between environmental issues and sustainability issues. The environment needs protection by public policy because each of us knows that by burdening the environment, by damaging it, we can profit and have some of the cost, perhaps most of the cost, borne by others. Sustainability is a problem precisely because each of us knows or realizes that we can profit at the expense of the future rather than at the expense of our contemporaries and the environment. We free-ride on each other and we free-ride on the future.

Environmental policy is important for both reasons. One of the ways we free-ride on the future is by burdening the environment. And so current environmental protection—this is what I meant by a dual connection—will almost certainly contribute quite a lot to sustainability. Although, I want to warn you, not automatically. Current environmental protection contributes to sustainability if it comes at the expense of current consumption. Not if it comes at the expense of investment, of additions to future capacity. So, there are no absolutes. There is nothing precise about this notion but there are perhaps approximate guides to public policy that come out of this way of reasoning about the idea of sustainability. A correct principle, a correct general guide is that when we use up something—and by we I mean our society, our country, our civilization, however broadly you want to think—when we use up something that is irreplaceable, whether it is minerals or a fish species, or an environmental amenity, then we should be thinking about providing a substitute of equal value, and the vagueness comes in the notion of value. The something that we provide in exchange could be knowledge, could be technology. It needn't even be a physical object.

Let me give you an excellent example from the recent past of a case of good thought along these lines and also a case of bad thought along these lines. Commercially usable volumes of oil were discovered in the North Sea some years ago. The two main beneficiaries of North Sea oil were the United Kingdom and Norway. It is only right to say that the United Kingdom dissipated North Sea oil, wasted it, used it up in consumption and on employment. If I meet Mrs. Thatcher in heaven, since that is where I intend to go, the biggest thing I will tax her with is that she blew North Sea oil. Here was an asset that by happenstance the U.K. acquired. If the sort of general approach to sustainability that I have been suggesting to you had been taken by the Thatcher government, someone would have said, "It's okay we are going to use up the oil, that's what it is for, but we will make sure that we provide something else in exchange, that we guide those resources, at least in large part, into investment in capacity in the future." That did not happen. As I said, if you ask where (and by the way the curve of production from the North Sea fields is already on the way down; that asset is on its way to exhaustion) it went, it went into maintaining consumption in the United Kingdom and, at the same time, into unemployment.

Norway, on the other hand, went about it in the typical sober way you expect of good Scandinavians. The Norwegians said, here is a wasting asset. Here is an asset that we are going to use up. Scandinavians are also slightly masochistic, as you know. They said the one thing we must avoid is blowing this; the one thing we must avoid is a binge. They tried very hard to convert a large fraction of the revenues, of the rentals, of the royalties from North Sea oil into investment. I confess I don't know how well they succeeded but I am willing to bet that they did a better job of it than the United Kingdom.

This brings me to the one piece of technical economics that I want to mention. There is a neat analytical result in economics (mainly done by John Hartwick of Queen's University in Canada) which studies an economy that takes what we call the rentals, the pure return to a non-renewable resource, and invests those rentals.[1] That is, it uses up a natural asset like the North Sea oil field, but makes a point of investing whatever revenues intrinsically inhere to the oil itself. That policy can be shown to have neat sustainability properties. In a simple sort of economy, it will guarantee a perpetually constant capacity to consume. By the way, it is a very simple rule, and it is really true only for very simple economies; but it has the advantage, first of all, of sounding right, of sounding like justice, and secondly, of being practical. It is a calculation that could be made. It is a calculation that we don't make and I am going to suggest in a minute that we should be making it. You might want to do better. You might feel so good about your great-grandchildren that you would like to do better than invest the rents on the non-renewable resources that you use up. But in any case, it is, at a minimum, a policy that one could pursue for the sake of sustainability. I want to remind you again that most environmental protection can be regarded as an act of investment. If we were to think that our obligation to the future is in principle discharged by seeing that the return to non-renewable resources is funnelled into capital formation, any kind of capital formation—plant and equipment, research and development, physical oceanography, economics or environmental investment—we could have some feeling that we were about on the right track.

Now I want to mention what strikes me as sort of a paradox—as a difficulty with a concept of sustainability. I said, I kind of insisted, that you should think about it as a matter of equity, as a matter of distributional equity, as a matter of choice of how productive capacity should be shared between us and them, them being the future. Once you think about it that way you are almost forced logically to think about equity not between peri-

[1]John M. Hartwick, "Substitution among exhaustible resources and intergenerational equity," *Review of Economic Studies* 45(2): 347–543 (June 1978).

ods of time but equity right now. There is something inconsistent about people who profess to be terribly concerned about the welfare of future generations but do not seem to be terribly concerned about the welfare of poor people today. You will see in a way why this comes to be a paradox. The only reason for thinking that sustainability is a problem is that you think that some people are likely to be shortchanged, namely, in the future. Then I think you really are obligated to ask, "Well, is anybody being short-changed right now?"

The paradox arises because if you are concerned about people who are currently poor, it will turn out that your concern for them will translate into an increase in current consumption, not into an increase in investment. The logic of sustainability says, "You ought to be thinking about poor people today, and thinking about poor people today will be disadvantageous from the point of view of sustainability." Intellectually, there is no difficulty in resolving that paradox, but practically there is every difficulty in the world in resolving that paradox. And I don't have the vaguest notion of how it can be done in practice.

The most dramatic way in which I can remind you of the nature of that paradox is to think about what it will mean for, say, CO_2 discharge when the Chinese start to burn their coal in a very large way; and, then, while you are interested in moral obligation, I think you should invent for yourself how you are going to explain to the Chinese that they shouldn't burn the coal, even living at their standard of living they shouldn't burn the coal, because the CO_2 might conceivably damage somebody in 50 or 100 years.

Actually the record of the U.S. is not very good on either the intergenerational equity of the intra-generational equity front. We tolerate, for a rich society, quite a lot of poverty, and at the same time we don't save or invest a lot. I've just spent some time in West Germany, and there is considerably less apparent poverty in the former Federal Republic than there is here; and at the same time they are investing a larger fraction of their GNP than we are by a large margin.

It would not be very hard for us to do better. One thing we might do, for starters, is to make a comprehensive accounting of rents on non-renewable resources. It is something that we do not do. There is nothing in the national accounts of the U.S. which will tell you what fraction of the national income is the return to the using up of non-renewable resources. If we were to make that accounting, then we would have a better idea than we have now as to whether we are at least meeting that minimal obligation to channel those rents into saving and investment. And I also suggested that careful attention to current environmental protection is another way that is very likely to slip in some advantage in the way of sustainability, provided it is at the expense of current consumption and not at the expense of other forms of investment.

I have left out of this talk, as some of you may have noticed until now, any mention of population growth; and I did that on purpose, although it might be the natural first order concern if you are thinking about sustainability issues. Control of population growth would probably be the best available policy on behalf of sustainability. You know that, I know that, and

I have no particular competence to discuss it any further; so I won't, except to remind you that rapid population growth is fundamentally a Third World phenomenon, not a developed country phenomenon. So once again, you are up against the paradox that people in poor countries have children as insurance policies for their own old age. It is very hard to preach to them not to do that. On the other hand, if they continue to do that, then you have probably the largest, single danger to sustainability of the world economy.

All that remains for me is to summarize. What I have been trying to say goes roughly as follows. Sustainability as a moral obligation is a general obligation not a specific one. It is not an obligation to preserve this or preserve that. It is an obligation, if you want to make sense out of it, to preserve the capacity to be well off, to be as well off as we. That does not preclude preserving specific resources, if they have an independent value and no good substitutes. But we shouldn't kid ourselves, that is part of the value of specific resources. It is not a consequence of any interest in sustainability. Secondly, an interest in sustainability speaks for investment generally. I mentioned that directing the rents on non-renewable resources into investment is a good rule of thumb, a reasonable and dependable starting point. But what sustainability speaks for is investment, investment of any kind. In particular, environmental investment seems to me to correlate well with concerns about sustainability and so, of course, does reliance on renewable resources as a substitute for non-renewable ones. Third, there is something faintly phony about deep concern for the future combined with callousness about the state of the world today. The catch is that today's poor want consumption not investment. So the conflict is pretty deep and there is unlikely to be any easy to way resolve it. Fourth, research is a good thing. Knowledge on the whole is an environmentally neutral asset that we can contribute to the future. I said that in thinking about sustainability you want to be as inclusive as you can. Investment in the broader sense and investment in knowledge, especially technological and scientific knowledge, is an environmentally clean an asset as we know. And the last thing I want to say is, don't forget that sustainability is a vague concept. It is intrinsically inexact. It is not something that can be measured out in coffee spoons. It is not something that you could be numerically accurate about. It is, at best, a general guide to policies that have to do with investment, conservation and resource use. And we shouldn't pretend that it is anything other than that.

Thank you very much.

REFERENCES

World Commission on Environment and Development, *Our Common Future* (The Brundtland Report). Oxford: Oxford University Press, 1987.

World Conservation Union, *Caring for the Earth*. Gland, Switzerland, 1991; see especially p. 10.

World Resources Institute, *World Resources 1992–93: Toward Sustainable Development*. New York: Oxford University Press, 1992. See especially Ch. 1.

29 A General Framework for Analyzing Sustainability of Social-Ecological Systems

Elinor Ostrom[1,2]*

Elinor Olstrom is Arthur F. Bentley Professor of Political Science and Senior Research Director, Workshop in Political Theory and Policy Analysis at Indiana University, Bloomington.

A major problem worldwide is the potential loss of fisheries, forests, and water resources. Understanding of the processes that lead to improvements in or deterioration of natural resources is limited, because scientific disciplines use different concepts and languages to describe and explain complex social-ecological systems (SESs). Without a common framework to organize findings, isolated knowledge does not cumulate. Until recently, accepted theory has assumed that resource users will never self-organize to maintain their resources and that governments must impose solutions. Research in multiple disciplines, however, has found that some government policies accelerate resource destruction, whereas some resource users have invested their time and energy to achieve sustainability. A general framework is used to identify 10 subsystem variables that affect the likelihood of self-organization in efforts to achieve a sustainable SES.

The world is currently threatened by considerable damage to or losses of many natural resources, including fisheries, lakes, and forests, as well as experiencing major reductions in biodiversity and the threat of massive climatic change. All humanly used resources are embedded in complex, social-ecological systems (SESs). SESs are composed of multiple subsystems and internal variables within these subsystems at multiple levels analogous to organisms composed of organs, organs of tissues, tissues of cells, cells of proteins, etc. (*1*). In a complex SES, subsystems such as a

"A General Framework for Analyzing Sustainability of Social Ecology Systems" by Elinor Ostrom. *Science* 325, No. 5939. 2009. Pp. 419–422. Reprinted with permission.

[1]Workshop in Political Theory and Policy Analysis, Indiana University, Bloomington, IN 47408, USA. [2]Center for the Study of Institutional Diversity, Arizona State University, Tempe, AZ 85287, USA.
*E-mail: ostrom@indiana.edu

resource system (e.g., a coastal fishery), resource units (lobsters), users (fishers), and governance systems (organizations and rules that govern fishing on that coast) are relatively separable but interact to produce outcomes at the SES level, which in turn feed back to affect these subsystems and their components, as well other larger or smaller SESs.

Scientific knowledge is needed to enhance efforts to sustain SESs, but the ecological and social sciences have developed independently and do not combine easily (2). Furthermore, scholars have tended to develop simple theoretical models to analyze aspects of resource problems and to prescribe universal solutions. For example, theoretical predictions of the destruction of natural resources due to the lack of recognized property systems have led to one-size-fits-all recommendations to impose particular policy solutions that frequently fail (3, 4).

The prediction of resource collapse is supported in very large, highly valuable, open-access systems when the resource harvesters are diverse, do not communicate, and fail to develop rules and norms for managing the resource (5). The dire predictions, however, are not supported under conditions that enable harvesters and local leaders to self-organize effective rules to manage a resource or in rigorous laboratory experiments when subjects can discuss options to avoid overharvesting (3, 6).

A core challenge in diagnosing why some SESs are sustainable whereas others collapse is the identification and analysis of relationships among multiple levels of these complex systems at different spatial and temporal scales (7–9). Understanding a complex whole requires knowledge about specific variables and how their component parts are related (10). Thus, we must learn how to dissect and harness complexity, rather than eliminate it from such systems (11). This process is complicated, however, because entirely different frameworks, theories, and models are used by different disciplines to analyze their parts of the complex multilevel whole. A common, classificatory framework is needed to facilitate multidisciplinary efforts toward a better understanding of complex SESs.

I present an updated version of a multilevel, nested framework for analyzing outcomes achieved in SESs (12). Figure 1 provides an overview of the framework, showing the relationships among four first-level core subsystems of an SES that affect each other as well as linked social, economic, and political settings and related ecosystems. The subsystems are (i) resource systems (e.g., a designated protected park encompassing a specified territory containing forested areas, wildlife, and water systems); (ii) resource units (e.g., trees, shrubs, and plants contained in the park, types of wildlife, and amount and flow of water); (iii) governance systems (e.g., the government and other organizations that manage the park, the specific rules related to the use of the park, and how these rules are made); and (iv) users (e.g., individuals who use the park in diverse ways for sustenance, recreation, or commercial purposes). Each core subsystem is made up of multiple second-level variables (e.g., size of a resource system, mobility of a resource unit, level of governance, users' knowledge of the resource system) (Table 1), which are further composed of deeper-level variables.

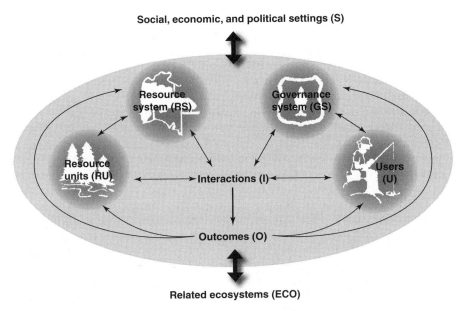

Figure 1 The core subsystems in a framework for analyzing social-ecological systems.

This framework helps to identify relevant variables for studying a single focal SES, such as the lobster fishery on the Maine coast and the fishers who rely on it (*13*). It also provides a common set of variables for organizing studies of similar SESs such as the lakes in northern Wisconsin (e.g., why are the pollution levels in some lakes worse than in others?) (*14*), forests around the world (e.g., why do some locally managed forests thrive better than government-protected forests?) (*15*), or water institutions (e.g., what factors affect the likelihood that farmers will effectively manage irrigation systems?) (*16*). Without a framework to organize relevant variables identified in theories and empirical research, isolated knowledge acquired from studies of diverse resource systems in different countries by biophysical and social scientists is not likely to cumulate.

A framework is thus useful in providing a common set of potentially relevant variables and their subcomponents to use in the design of data collection instruments, the conduct of fieldwork, and the analysis of findings about the sustainability of complex SESs. It helps identify factors that may affect the likelihood of particular policies enhancing sustainability in one type and size of resource system and not in others. Table 1 lists the second-level variables identified in many empirical studies as affecting interactions and outcomes. The choice of relevant second or deeper levels of variables for analysis (from the large set of variables at multiple levels) depends on the particular questions under study, the type of SES, and the spatial and temporal scales of analysis.

To illustrate one use of the SES framework, I will focus on the question: When will the users of a resource invest time and energy to avert "a tragedy of the commons"? Garrett Hardin (17) earlier argued that users were trapped in accelerated overuse and would never invest time and energy to extract themselves. If that answer were supported by research, the SES framework would not be needed to analyze this question. Extensive empirical studies by scholars in diverse disciplines have found that the users of many (but not all) resources have invested in designing and implementing costly governance systems to increase the likelihood of sustaining them (3, 6, 7, 18).

A theoretical answer to this question is that when expected benefits of managing a resource exceed the perceived costs of investing in better rules and norms for most users and their leaders, the probability of users' self-organizing is high (supporting online material text). Although joint benefits may be created, self-organizing to sustain a resource costs time, and effort can result in a loss of short-term economic gains. These costs, as well as the fear that some users will cheat on rules related to when, where, and how to harvest, can lead users to avoid costly changes and continue to overharvest (6). Accurate and reliable measures of users' perceived benefits and costs are difficult and costly to obtain, making it hard to test theories based on users' expected net benefits.

Multiple variables that have been observed and measured by field researchers are posited to affect the likelihood of users' engaging in collective action to self-organize. Ten second-level variables (indicated by asterisks in Table 1) are frequently identified as positively or negatively affecting the likelihood of users' self-organizing to manage a resource (3, 6, 19, 20). To explain why these variables are potentially important for understanding sustainability and, in particular, for addressing the question of when self-organization activities will occur, I briefly discuss how they affect perceived benefits and costs.

Size of resource system (RS3):

For land-related resource systems, such as forests, very large territories are unlikely to be self-organized given the high costs of defining boundaries (e.g., surrounding with markers or fences), monitoring use patterns, and gaining ecological knowledge. Very small territories do not generate substantial flows of valuable products. Thus, moderate territorial size is most conducive to self-organization (15). Fishers who consistently harvest from moderately sized coastal zones, lakes, or rivers are also more likely to organize (13) than fishers who travel the ocean in search of valuable fish (5).

Productivity of system (RS5)

A resource system's current productivity has a curvilinear effect on self-organization across all sectors. If a water source or a fishery is already exhausted or apparently very abundant, users will not see a need to manage for the future. Users need to observe some scarcity before they invest in self-organization (*19*).

Predictability of system dynamics (RS7)

System dynamics need to be sufficiently predictable that users can estimate what would happen if they were to establish particular harvesting rules or no-entry territories. Forests tend to be more predictable than water systems. Some fishery systems approach mathematical chaos and are particularly challenging for users or government officials (*21*). Unpredictability at a small scale may lead users of pastoral systems to organize at larger scales to increase overall predictability (*22, 23*).

Resource unit mobility (RU1)

Due to the costs of observing and managing a system, self-organization is less likely with mobile resource units, such as wildlife or water in an unregulated river, than with stationary units such as trees and plants or water in a lake (*24*).

Number of users (U1)

The impact of group size on the transaction costs of self-organizing tends to be negative given the higher costs of getting users together and agreeing on changes (*19, 20*). If the tasks of managing a resource, however, such as monitoring extensive community forests in India, are very costly, larger groups are more able to mobilize necessary labor and other resources (*25*). Thus, group size is always relevant, but its effect on self-organization depends on other SES variables and the types of management tasks envisioned.

Table 1. Examples of second-level variables under first-level core subsystems (S, RS, GS, RU, U, I, O and ECO) in a framework for analyzing social-ecological systems. The framework does not list variables in an order of importance, because their importance varies in different studies. [Adapted from (*12*)]

Social, economic, and political settings (S)
S1 Economic development. S2 Demographic trends. S3 Political stability.
S4 Government resource policies. S5 Market incentives. S6 Media organization.

Resource systems (RS)	*GS1 Government organizations*
RS1 Sector (e.g., water, forests, pasture, fish)	GS1 Government organizations
RS2 Clarity of system boundaries	GS2 Nongovernment organizations
RS3 Size of resource system*	GS3 Network structure
RS4 Human-constructed facilities	GS4 Property-rights systems
RS5 Productivity of system*	GS5 Operational rules
RS6 Equilibrium properties	GS6 Collective-choice rules*
RS7 Predictability of system dynamics*	GS7 Constitutional rules
RS8 Storage characteristics	GS8 Monitoring and sanctioning processes
RS9 Location	

Resource units (RU)	*Users (U)*
RU1 Resource unit mobility*	U1 Number of users*
RU2 Growth or replacement rate	U2 Socioeconomic attributes of users
RU3 Interaction among resource units	U3 History of use
RU4 Economic value	U4 Location
RU5 Number of units	U5 Leadership/entrepreneurship*
RU6 Distinctive markings	U6 Norms/social capital*
RU7 Spatial and temporal distribution	U7 Knowledge of SES/mental models*
	U8 Importance of resource*
	U9 Technology used

Interactions (I) → *outcomes (O)*

I1 Harvesting levels of diverse users	O1 Social performance measures (e.g., efficiency, equity, accountability, sustainability)
I2 Information sharing among users	
I3 Deliberation processes	
I4 Conflicts among users	O2 Ecological performance measures (e.g., overharvested, resilience, bio-diversity, sustainability)
I5 Investment activities	
I6 Lobbying activities	
I7 Self-organizing activities	O3 Externalities to other SESs
I8 Networking activities	

Related ecosystems (ECO)
ECO1 Climate patterns. ECO2 Pollution patterns. ECO3 Flows into and out of focal SES.

---

*Subset of variables found to be associated with self-organization.

Leadership (U5)

When some users of any type of resource system have entrepreneurial skills and are respected as local leaders as a result of prior organization for other purposes, self-organization is more likely (*19, 20*). The presence of college graduates and influential elders, for example, had a strong positive effect on the establishment of irrigation organization in a stratified sample of 48 irrigation systems in Karnataka and Rajasthan, India (*16*).

Norms/social capital (U6)

Users of all types of resource systems who share moral and ethical standards regarding how to behave in groups they form, and thus the norms of reciprocity, and have sufficient trust in one another to keep agreements will face lower transaction costs in reaching agreements and lower costs of monitoring (*20, 26, 27*).

Knowledge of the SES (U7)

When users share common knowledge of relevant SES attributes, how their actions affect each other, and rules used in other SESs, they will perceive lower costs of organizing (*7*). If the resource system regenerates slowly while the population grows rapidly, such as on Easter Island, users may not understand the carrying capacity of the resource, fail to organize, and destroy the resource (*28*).

Importance of resource to users (U8)

In successful cases of self-organization, users are either dependent on the RS for a substantial portion of their livelihoods or attach high value to the sustainability of the resource. Otherwise, the costs of organizing and maintaining a self-governing system may not be worth the effort (*3, 7, 15*).

Collective-choice rules (GS6)

When users, such as the Seri fishers in Mexico (*29*) and forest user groups in Nepal (*30*), have full autonomy at the collective-choice level to craft and enforce some of their own rules, they face lower transaction costs as well as lower costs in defending a resource against invasion by others (*5*).

Obtaining measures for these 10 variables is the first step in analyzing whether the users of one or more SESs would self-organize. Data analysis of these relationships is challenging, because the impact of any one variable depends on the values of other SES variables. As in most complex systems, the variables interact in a nonlinear fashion (8–10). Furthermore, although the long-term sustainability of SESs is initially dependent on users or a government to establish rules, these rules may not be sufficient over the long run (7, 18).

If the initial set of rules established by the users, or by a government, are not congruent with local conditions, long-term sustainability may not be achieved (8, 9, 18). Studies of irrigation systems (16, 26), forests (25, 31), and coastal fisheries (13) suggest that long-term sustainability depends on rules matching the attributes of the resource system, resource units, and users. Rules forbidding the harvest of pregnant female fish are easy to monitor and enforce in the case of lobster, where eggs are visibly attached to the belly, and have been important in sustaining lobster fisheries (13). However, monitoring and enforcing these rules have proven more difficult in the case of gravid fish, where the presence of internal eggs is harder to assess.

Comparative studies of rules used in long-surviving resource systems governed by traditional societies document the wide diversity of rules used across sectors and regions of the world (21). Simple blueprint policies do not work. For example, the total allowable catch quotas established by the Canadian government for the west coast of Canada led to widespread dumping of unwanted fish, misrepresentation of catches, and the closure of the groundfishery in 1995 (32). To remedy this initial failure, the government reopened the fishery but divided the coastal area into more than 50 sectors, assigned transferable quotas, and required that all ships have neutral observers onboard to record all catches (32).

Furthermore, the long-term sustainability of rules devised at a focal SES level depends on monitoring and enforcement as well their not being overruled by larger government policies. The long-term effectiveness of rules has been shown in recent studies of forests in multiple countries to depend on users' willingness to monitor one another's harvesting practices (15, 31, 33, 34). Larger-scale governance systems may either facilitate or destroy governance systems at a focal SES level. The colonial powers in Africa, Asia, and Latin America, for example, did not recognize local resource institutions that had been developed over centuries and imposed their own rules, which frequently led to overuse if not destruction (3, 7, 23).

Efforts are currently under way to revise and further develop the SES framework presented here with the goal of establishing comparable databases to enhance the gathering of research findings about processes affecting the sustainability of forests, pastures, coastal zones, and water systems around the world. Research across disciplines and questions will thus cumulate more rapidly and increase the knowledge needed to enhance the sustainability of complex SESs. Quantitative and qualitative data about the core set of SES variables across resource systems are needed to enable scholars to build and test theoretical models of heterogeneous costs and benefits between governments, communities, and individuals and to lead to improved policies.

REFERENCES AND NOTES

1. E. Pennisi, *Science* **302**, 1646 (2003).
2. R. B. Norgaard, *Conserv. Biol.* **22**, 862 (2008).
3. National Research Council, *The Drama of the Commons* (National Academies Press, Washington, DC, 2002).
4. L. Pritchett, M. Woolcock, *World Dev.* **32**, 191 (2004).
5. F. Berkes *et al.*, *Science* **311**, 1557 (2006).
6. E. Ostrom, R. Gardner, J. Walker, *Rules, Games, and Common-Pool Resources* (Univ. of Michigan Press, Ann Arbor, MI, 1994).
7. F. Berkes, C. Folke, Eds., *Linking Social and Ecological Systems* (Cambridge Univ. Press, Cambridge, 1998).
8. M. A. Janssen, *Complexity and Ecosystem Management* (Edward Elgar, Cheltenham, UK, 2002).
9. J. Norberg, G. Cumming, Eds., *Complexity Theory for a Sustainable Future* (Columbia Univ. Press, New York, 2008).
10. S. A. Levin, *Ecology* **73**, 1943 (1992).
11. R. Axelrod, M. D. Cohen, *Harnessing Complexity* (Free Press, New York, 2001).
12. E. Ostrom, *Proc. Natl. Acad. Sci. U.S.A.* **104**, 15181 (2007).
13. J. Wilson, L. Yan, C. Wilson, *Proc. Natl. Acad. Sci. U.S.A.* **104**, 15212 (2007).
14. W. A. Brock, S. R. Carpenter, *Proc. Natl. Acad. Sci. U.S.A.* **104**, 15206 (2007).
15. A. Chhatre, A. Agrawal, *Proc. Natl. Acad. Sci. U.S.A.* **105**, 13286 (2008).
16. R. Meinzen-Dick, *Proc. Natl. Acad. Sci. U.S.A.* **104**, 15200 (2007).
17. G. Hardin, *Science* **162**, 1243 (1968).
18. T. Dietz, E. Ostrom, P. Stern, *Science* **302**, 1907 (2003).
19. R. Wade, *Village Republics: Economic Conditions for Collective Action in South India* (ICS, San Francisco, CA, 1994).
20. J.-M. Baland, J.-P. Platteau, *Halting Degradation of Natural Resources* (Oxford Univ. Press, New York, 2000).
21. J. M. Acheson, J. A. Wilson, R. S. Steneck, in *Linking Social and Ecological Systems*, F. Berkes, C. Folke, Eds. (Cambridge Univ. Press, Cambridge, 1998), pp. 390–413.
22. P. N. Wilson, G. D. Thompson, *Econ. Dev. Cult. Change* **41**, 299 (1993).
23. E. Mwangi, *Socioeconomic Change and Land Use in Africa* (Palgrave MacMillan, New York, 2007).
24. E. Schlager, W. Blomquist, S. Y. Tang, *Land Econ.* **70**, 294 (1994).
25. A. Agrawal, in *People and Forests: Communities, Institutions, and Governance*, C. C. Gibson, M. A. McKean, E. Ostrom, Eds. (MIT Press, Cambridge, MA, 2000), pp. 57–86.
26. P. B. Trawick, *Hum. Ecol.* **29**, 1 (2001).
27. E. Ostrom, *Understanding Institutional Diversity* (Princeton Univ. Press, Princeton, NJ, 2005).
28. J. A. Brander, M. S. Taylor, *Am. Econ. Rev.* **88**, 119 (1998).
29. X. Basurto, *J. Soc. Nat. Resour.* **18**, 643 (2005).
30. H. Nagendra, *Proc. Natl. Acad. Sci. U.S.A.* **104**, 15218 (2007).
31. E. Ostrom, H. Nagendra, *Proc. Natl. Acad. Sci. U.S.A.* **103**, 19224 (2006).

32. C. W. Clark, *The Worldwide Crisis in Fisheries: Economic Models and Human Behavior* (Cambridge Univ. Press, Cambridge, 2006).
33. G. C. Gibson, J. T. Williams, E. Ostrom, *World Dev.* **33**, 273 (2005).
34. E. Coleman, B. Steed, *Ecol. Econ.* **68**, 2106 (2009).
35. Supported in part by NSF grants BCS-0624178 and BCS-0601320. I thank T. K. Ahn, R. Axtell, X. Basurto, J. Broderick, E. Coleman, C. Eavey, B. Fischer, C. A. González, E. Jameson, B. de Leon, D. Porter, M. Schlueter, D. Sprinz, and J. Walker for comments and suggestions.

30 The Problem of the Commons: Still Unsettled after 100 Years*

Robert N. Stavins

Robert N. Stavins is Albert Pratt Professor of Business and Government at Harvard Kennedy School, Research Associate at the National Bureau of Economic Research, and University Fellow at Resources for the Future.

The problem of the commons is more important to our lives and thus more central to economics than a century ago when Katharine Coman led off the first issue of the American Economic Review. *As the US and other economies have grown, the carrying capacity of the planet—in regard to natural resources and environmental quality—has become a greater concern, particularly for common-property and open-access resources. The focus of this article is on some important, unsettled problems of the commons. Within the realm of natural resources, there are special challenges associated with renewable resources, which are frequently characterized by open-access. An important example is the degradation of open-access fisheries. Critical commons problems are also associated with environmental quality. A key contribution of economics has been the development of market-based approaches to environmental protection. These instruments are key to addressing the ultimate commons problem of the twenty-first century—global climate change. (JEL Q15, Q21, Q22, Q25, Q54)*

As the first decade of the twenty-first century comes to a close, the problem of the commons is more central to economics and more important to our lives than a century ago when Katharine Coman led off the first issue of

"The Problem of the Commons: Still Unsettled After 100 Years" by Robert N. Stavins. *American Economic Review* 101. 2011. Pp. 81–108.

*I am grateful to Lori Bennear, Maureen Cropper, Denny Ellerman, Lawrence Goulder, Robert Hahn, Geoffrey Heal, Suzi Kerr, Charles Kolstad, Gilbert Metcalf, William Nordhaus, Wallace Oates, Sheila Olmstead, Robert Pindyck, Andy Reisinger, James Sanchirico, Richard Schmalensee, Kerry Smith, Robert Stowe, Martin Weitzman, and Richard Zeckhauser for very helpful comments on a previous version of this article; and Jane Callahan and Ian Graham of the Wellesley College Archives for having provided inspiration by making available the archives of Katharine Coman (1857–1915), professor of history, then economics, and first chair of Wellesley College's Department of Economics. Any and all remaining errors are my own.

the *American Economic Review* with her examination of "Some Unsettled Problems of Irrigation" (Coman 1911). Since that time, 100 years of remarkable economic progress have accompanied 100 years of increasingly challenging problems.

As the US and other economies have grown, the carrying capacity of the planet—in regard to both natural resources and environmental quality—has become a greater concern. This is particularly true for common-property and open-access resources. While small communities frequently provide modes of oversight and methods for policing their citizens (Elinor Ostrom 2010), as the scale of society has grown, commons problems have spread across communities and even across nations. In some of these cases, no overarching authority can offer complete control, rendering commons problems more severe. Although the type of water allocation problems of concern to Coman (1911) have frequently been addressed by common-property regimes of collective management (Ostrom 1990), less easily governed problems of open access are associated with growing concerns about air and water quality hazardous waste, species extinction, maintenance of stratospheric ozone, and—most recently—the stability of the global climate in the face of the steady accumulation of greenhouse gases.

Whereas common-property resources are held as private property by some group, open-access resources are nonexcludable. This article focuses exclusively on the latter, and thereby reflects on some important, unsettled problems of the commons.[1] It identifies both the contributions made by economic analysis and the challenges facing public policy. Section I begins with natural resources, highlighting the difference between most nonrenewable natural resources, pure private goods that are both excludable and rival in consumption, and renewable natural resources, many of which are nonexcludable (Table 1). Some of these are rival in consumption but characterized by open access. An example is the degradation of ocean fisheries. An economic perspective on these resources helps identify the problems they present for management and provides guidance for sensible solutions.

Section II turns to a major set of commons problems that were not addressed until the last three decades of the twentieth century—environmental quality. Although frequently characterized as textbook examples of externalities, these problems can also be viewed as a particular category of commons problems: pure public goods, that are both nonexcludable and nonrival in consumption (Table 1). A key contribution of economics has been the development of market-based approaches to environmental protection, including emission taxes and tradable rights. These have poten-

---

[1]Ostrom has made key contributions to our understanding of the role of collective action in common-property regimes, as she does in her article in this issue of the *Review* (Ostrom 2011). With her ably covering that territory, my focus is exclusively on situations of open access. As Daniel W. Bromley (1992) has noted, the better characterizations might be common property *regimes* and open-access *regimes*, because it is the respective institutional arrangements—as much as the resources themselves—that define the problems. However, I use the conventional characterizations because of their general use in the literature. Although my focus is on the natural resources and environmental realm, similar problems—and related public policies—arise in other areas, such as the allocation of the electromagnetic spectrum for uses in communication (Roberto E. Muñoz and Thomas W. Hazlett 2009).

Table 1—A Taxonomy of Common Problems in the Natural Resource and Environment Realm

	Excludable	Nonexcludable
Rival	*Pure private goods* Most nonrenewable natural resources (Fossil fuels & minerals) Some privatized renewable resources (Aquaculture)	*Renewable natural resources* *characterized by open access* (Ocean fishing) Some nonrenewable resources (Ogallala Aquifer)
Nonrival	*Club goods* (Water quality of municipal pond)	*Pure public goods* (Clean air greenhouse gases and climate change)

tial to address the ultimate commons problem of the twenty-first century, global climate change. Section III concludes.

Several themes emerge. First, economic theory—by focusing on market failures linked with incomplete systems of property rights—has made major contributions to our understanding of commons problems and the development of prudent public policies. Second, as our understanding of the commons has become more complex, the design of economic policy instruments has become more sophisticated, enabling policy makers to address problems that are characterized by uncertainty, spatial and temporal heterogeneity, and long duration. Third, government policies that have not accounted for economic responses have been excessively costly, often ineffective, and sometimes counterproductive. Fourth, commons problems have not diminished. While some have been addressed successfully, others have emerged that are more important and more difficult. Fifth, environmental economics is well positioned to offer better understanding and better policies to address these ongoing challenges.

I. The Problem of the Commons and the Economics of Natural Resources

Despite their finite supply in the earth's crust (and despite decades of doomsday predictions),[2] reserves of mineral and fossil fuel resources have not been exhausted. Price signals reflecting relative (economic) scarcity have stimulated exploration and discovery, technological progress, and supply substitution. Hence, the world of nonrenewable natural resources is characterized more by smooth transitions (Robert M. Solow 1991; William D. Nordhaus 1992) than by overshoot and collapse. Reserves have increased, demand has changed, substitution has occurred, and—in some cases—recycling has been stimulated. As a result, for much of the past century, the economic scarcity of natural resources had not been increasing, but decreasing (Harold J. Barnett and Chandler Morse 1963). Late in the twentieth century,

---

[2]See, for example. Donella H. Meadows et al. (1972).

increasing scarcity may have set in for a subset of nonrenewable resources, although the time trends are far from clear (V. Kerry Smith 1980; Junsoo Lee, John A. List, and Mark C. Strazicich 2006; John Livernois 2009).

The picture is quite different if we turn from nonrenewable natural resources—minerals and fossil fuels—to renewable natural resources (including many forests and most fisheries), which have exhibited *monotonically increasing scarcity.* The irony is obvious: many nonrenewable natural resources, which are in finite supply, have not become more scarce over time, and *none* has been exhausted; but renewable natural resources, which have the capacity to regenerate themselves, have in many cases become more scarce, and in some cases have indeed been exhausted, that is, become extinct.

This irony can be explained by the fact that while most nonrenewable natural resources are characterized by well-defined, enforceable property rights, many renewable resources are held as common property or open access (Table 1). Whereas scarcity is therefore well reflected by markets for nonrenewable natural resources (in the form of "scarcity rent," the difference between price and marginal extraction cost, originally characterized by Harold Hotelling in 1931 as "net price"),[3] such rents are dissipated for open-access resources, a reality well illustrated by the bioeconomics of open-access fisheries.

A. Biology

Since the middle of the nineteenth century, open-access fishery stocks of numerous species have been depleted beyond sustainable levels, sometimes close to the edge of extinction. The basic biology and economics of fisheries—descendent from the Gordon-Schaefer model (H. Scott Gordon 1954; Anthony Scott 1955; M. B. Schaefer 1957; Colin W. Clark 1990)—makes clear why this has happened.

In the upper panel of Figure 1, a logistical growth function plots the time rate of change of the fishery stock (dS/dt) on the vertical axis against the stock's mass (S) on the horizontal axis:

$$(1) \qquad F(S_t) = \delta S_t \left[1 - \frac{S_t}{K} \right].$$

where δ is the intrinsic growth rate of the stock, and K is the carrying capacity of the environment. As the size of the stock increases, its rate of growth increases until scarce food supplies and other consequences of

---

[3]This is not to suggest that the market rate of extraction of nonrenewable natural resources always matches the dynamically efficient rate. Under any one of a number of conditions, markets may lead to inefficient rates of extraction: imperfect information; noncompetitive market structure (the international petroleum cartel); poorly defined property rights (ground water); externalities in production or consumption (coal mining and combustion); or differences in market and social discount rates.

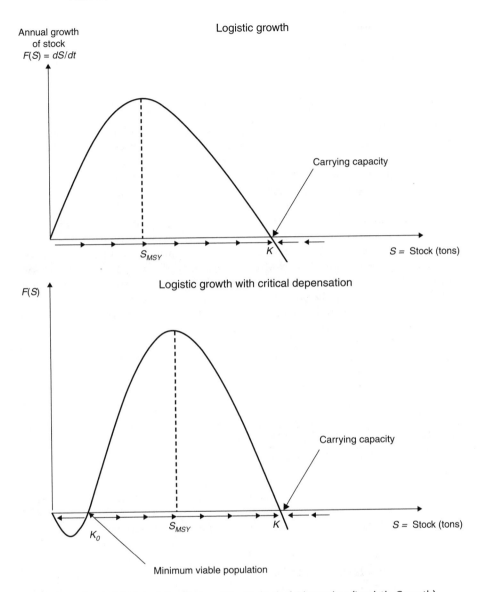

Figure 1 A Simple Model of the Fishery: The Biological Dimension (Logistic Growth)

crowding lead to decreasing growth rates. The maximum growth rate is achieved at S_{MSY}, where the "maximum sustainable yield" (*MSY*) occurs. A stable equilibrium is found where the rate of growth transitions from positive to negative, a level of the stock described by biologists as the "carrying capacity" or "natural equilibrium" of the fishery. Another stable equilibrium is found at the origin—exhaustion (extinction).

The likelihood of extinction is particularly acute when the natural growth function of a species exhibits "critical depensation," illustrated in the lower panel of Figure 1:

$$(2) \qquad F(S_t) = \delta S_t \left[1 - \frac{S_t}{K} \right] \left[\frac{S_t}{K_0} - 1 \right].$$

where K_0 is the minimum viable population level. Below this critical level of the stock, the natural rate of growth is negative. Hence there are three equilibria: extinction (the origin); the carrying capacity; and the minimum viable population. This reflects the reality that the large habitat ranges that exist for some species, such as whales and some species of birds, means that relatively small numbers are insufficient for mating pairs to yield birth rates that exceed the natural rate of loss to predators and disease.

This third equilibrium is unstable. Once the population falls below this critical level, it will proceed inevitably to extinction (unless "artificial" actions are taken, such as confined breeding of the California condor, man-made habitats for the whooping crane, or "zoos in the wild" for giant pandas in China). In the nineteenth century, hunters did not shoot down each and every passenger pigeon, but nevertheless, the species was driven to extinction. A similar pattern has doomed other species. A contemporary case in point could be the blue whale (Michael A. Spence 1974), the largest animal known to have existed. Harvesting has been prohibited under international agreements since 1965, but it is unclear whether stocks have rebounded, although numbers have been increasing in one region. Across species, there is a mixed picture. Stocks of some whale species are believed to be above and others below their respective minimum viable population (International Whaling Commission 2010).

B. Bioeconomics

A much greater threat to renewable natural resources than this unusual and unstable biological growth function is the way many of these resources are managed: as common property or open access. To see this, we add some basic economics to the biology of the fishery (Figure 2). First, a change in the stock of a fishery can be due not only to its biological fundamentals, but to harvests, that is, fishing:

$$(3) \qquad \frac{dS}{dt} = \dot{S}_t = F(S_t) - q_t$$

where q_i is the harvest rate at time t.[4]

The harvest is a function of the stock and the level of effort, E_i, by firms (fishing boats and crews). Abstracting from dynamics, we can identify the

---

[4]If equation (3) is replaced by a stochastic differential equation—to characterize uncertainty inherent in the biological growth function—then even lower harvest rates than otherwise can lead to extinction (Robert S. Pindyck 1984).

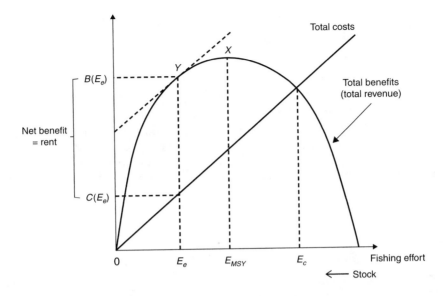

Figure 2 A Simple Model of the Fishery: The Economic Dimension

static efficient sustainable yield (that is, we ignore discounting over time, which is all that distinguishes this from the dynamically efficient sustainable yield), without loss of key insights. To keep things simple for the graphics, three assumptions are employed: (a) there is perfectly elastic demand, that is, the price of fish is constant, not a function of the quantity sold; (b) the marginal cost of a unit of fishing effort is constant; and (c) the quantity of fish caught per unit of effort is proportional to the size of the stock. With these assumptions, the relationship between effort and harvest is:

(4) $$q_t(S_t, E_t) = \alpha_t\, S_t\, E_t,$$

where α_t is a proportional "catchability coefficient." And profits, π_t, are given by:

(5) $$\pi_t = p_t q_t(S_t, E_t) - \alpha_t E_t$$

where p_t, is the market price of fish and c is the marginal cost of fishing effort. In the steady state, harvest is equal to growth:

(6) $$F(S_t) = q_t,$$

and so from equations (1) and (2):

(7) $$\delta S_t \left[1 - \frac{S_t}{K} \right] = \alpha_t S_t E_t$$

Solving for S and substituting into equation (4) yields steady-state harvest as a function of effort:

$$(8) \qquad q_{SS} = \alpha_t E_t K \left[1 - \frac{\alpha_t E_t}{\delta} \right].$$

With this, total revenue at the steady-state (or sustainable) level, equivalent to pq, is indicated in Figure 2 as the total benefits of fishing as a function of effort level. When effort exceeds level E_{MSY}, total fish catch and revenues decline. Total cost is equivalent to the constant marginal cost of effort, c, multiplied by the effort level. Hence, the efficient level of effort, E_e, is where net benefits—the difference between total revenue and total cost—are maximized, namely where marginal benefits equal marginal costs. Clearly the maximum sustainable yield is not the efficient harvest level (but would be if fishing were costless).

C. The Consequences of Open Access

What happens in actual markets with open access, which historically has characterized much of commercial fishing around the world (as well as markets for a number of other renewable natural resources)? At the efficient level of effort, E_e, each boat would make profits equal to its share of scarcity rent, $B(E_e)$ minus $C(E_e)$, but with open access these profits become a stimulus for more capital and labor to enter the fishery. Each fisherman considers his marginal revenue and marginal extraction cost, but—without firm property rights—scarcity rent is ignored, and each has an incentive to expend further effort (including more entry) until profits in the fishery are driven to zero: effort level E_c in Figure 2, where marginal cost is equal to *average* revenue rather than equal to *marginal* revenue. Thus, with open access, it is rational for each fisherman to ignore the asset value of the fishery, because he cannot appropriate it; all scarcity rent is dissipated (Scott 1955).

Because no one holds title to fish stocks in the open ocean, for example, everyone races to catch as much as possible. Each fisherman receives the full benefit of aggressive fishing—a larger catch—but none pays the full cost, an imperiled fishery for everyone. One fisherman's choices have an effect on other fishermen (of this generation and the next), but in an open access fishery—unlike a privately held copper mine—these impacts are not taken into account.

These consequences of open access—predicted by theory—have been validated repeatedly with empirical data. A study of the Pacific halibut fishery in the Bering Sea estimated that the efficient number of ships was nine, while the actual number was 140 (Daniel D. Huppert 1990).[5] An examination of the New England lobster fishery found that in

---

[5]These fisheries are actually "regulated open-access fisheries," because they are subject to restrictions (James N. Sanchirico and James E. Wilen 2007), as explained below.

1966 the efficient number of traps set would have been about 450,000, while the actual number was nearly one million. Likewise, an analysis of the North Atlantic stock of minke whale found that the efficient stock size was about 67,000 adult males, whereas the open-access stock had been depleted to 25,000 (Erik S. Amundsen, Trond Bjørndal, and Jon M. Conrad 1995). In terms of social costs, an analysis of two lobster fisheries in eastern Canada found that losses due to unrestricted entry amounted to about 25 percent of market value of harvests, due mainly to excess deployment of resources for harvest, with fishery effort exceeding the efficient level by some 350 percent (J. V. Henderson and M. Tugwell 1979).

Under conditions of open access, two externalities may be said to be present. One is a contemporaneous externality (as with any public good) in which there is overcommitment of resources: too many boats, too many fishermen, and too much effort as everyone rushes to harvest before others. The other is an intertemporal externality in which overfishing reduces the stock and hence lowers future profits from fishing.

A classic time path of open-access fisheries has been repeated around the world. First, a newly discovered resource is open to all comers; eventually, large harvests and profits attract more entry to the fishery; boats work harder to maintain their harvest; despite increased efforts, the harvests decline; and this leads to greater increases in effort, resulting in even greater declines in harvest, resulting in essential collapse of the fishery. This pattern has been documented for numerous species, including the North Pacific fur seal (Wilen 1976) and the Northern anchovy fishery (Jean-Didier Opsomer and Conrad 1994), as well as Atlantic cod harvested by US and Canadian fishing fleets in the second half of the twentieth century (Figure 3).

Although open access drives the stock below its efficient level, it normally does not lead to the stock being exhausted (except possibly under critical depensation, as explained above), because below a certain stock level, the benefits of additional harvest are simply less than the additional costs. This is at the heart of a fundamental error in what is probably the most frequently cited article on common-property and open-access resources, Garrett Hardin's "The Tragedy of the Commons" (1968):

> Picture a pasture open to all . . . A rational herdsman concludes that the only sensible course for him to pursue is to add another animal to his herd. And another; and another . . . Each man is locked into a system that compels him to increase his herd without limit—in a world that is limited. Ruin is the destination toward which all men rush, each pursuing his own best interest in a society that believes in the freedom of the commons. Freedom in the commons brings ruin to all (Hardin 1968, 1244).

As Partha Dasgupta (1982) subsequently wrote: "It would be difficult to locate another passage of comparable length and fame containing as many errors as the one above." Ruin is not the outcome of the commons, but rather

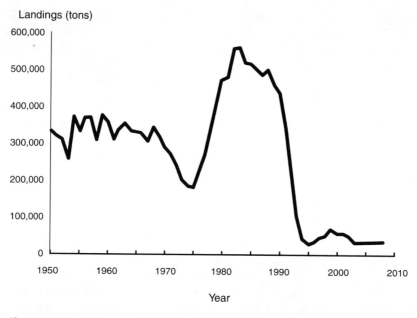

Figure 3 Annual Harvest of Atlantic Cod, 1950–2008

Source: United Nations Food and Agriculture Organization 2010.

excessive employment of capital and labor, small profits for participants, and an excessively depleted resource stock.[6] Those are bad enough.

D. *Alternative Policies for the Commons Problem*

The most obvious solution to a commons problem—in principle—may be to enclose it, that is, put in place fee-simple or other well-defined property rights to limit access.[7] In the case of a natural fishery, this is typically not feasible, but it is if species are immobile (oysters, clams, mussels), can be confined by barriers (shrimp, carp, catfish), or instinctively return to their place of birth to spawn (salmon, ocean trout). Such fish farming (aquaculture) is feasible and profitable with a limited but important set of commercial species (Table 1). Presently, approximately one-third of global fisheries production is supplied by commercial aquaculture, much of it in Asia (United Nations Food and Agriculture Organization 2007).

---

[6]The annual loss due to rent dissipation in global fisheries has been estimated to be on the order of $90 billion (Sanchirico and Wilen 2007).

[7]Recall that my focus is on open access, not common property. Arrangements of various kinds can and do serve to limit access to common-property resources (Ostrom 2010). An example in the fisheries realm would be the informal groups of lobster harvesters ("gangs") in coastal Maine that seek to restrict access to identified areas (James M. Acheson 2003).

Because aquaculture remains confined to a limited set of commercial species (and environmental concerns may preclude expansion), there has been a history of government attempts to regulate open-access fisheries through other means. The most frequent regulatory approach has been to limit annual catches (with the target typically being the maximum sustainable yield, not the efficient level of effort) through restrictions on allowed technologies, closure of particular areas, or imposition of limited seasons. These regulatory approaches have the effect of raising the marginal cost of fishing effort, in effect pivoting up the total cost function in Figure 2 until it intersects the benefit function at point X, thereby achieving the fishing effort associated with maximum sustainable yield, E_{MSY}, or potentially to point Y, thereby achieving the efficient effort level, E_e.

Marginal costs increase because each new constraint causes fishermen to reoptimize. In response to constraints on technology, areas, or season, fishermen employ excessively expensive methods (overcapitalization) to catch a given quantity of fish. Technology constraints can lead to the employment of more labor; area closures can lead to the adoption of more sophisticated technologies; and reduced seasons result in the use of more boats. Although the harvest may be curtailed as desired, the net benefits to the fishery are essentially zero. Costs go up for fishermen (as resources are squandered). Social efficiency is not achieved, nor is it approached.

A dramatic example is provided by New York City's once thriving oyster fishery. In 1860, 12 million oysters were sold in New York City markets. By 1880, production was up to 700 million oysters per year. "New Yorkers rich and poor were slurping the creatures in oyster cellars, saloons, stands, houses, cafes, and restaurants . . ." (Elizabeth Royte 2006). It became clear that the oyster beds were being depleted. First the city restricted who could harvest oysters, then when they were permitted to do so. Eventually, the city limited the use of dredges and steam power. Nevertheless, in 1927, the last of the city's oyster beds closed (a casualty not only of open access to the oyster habitats, but also of the use of the city's harbors as another sort of commons, namely as a depository for the city's sewage).

The economic implications of conventionally regulated open-access fisheries are typically worse than those that occur under unregulated open-access conditions (Frances R. Homans and Wilen 1997; Martin D. Smith and Wilen 2003). Overcapitalization is greater, as is the consequent welfare loss. Such situations with conventional open-access fisheries regulation are commonplace: overfishing occurs, the fishery stock is depleted, the government responds by regulating the catch, thereby driving up the cost of fishing, fishermen complain that they cannot make a profit, and harvests continue to fall. Is there a better way?

From an economic perspective, the most obvious way of assuring that harvest levels are maintained at an efficient level while providing incentives for cost reductions is a tax on fish harvests. Such an efficient tax, which increases marginal costs, rotates the total costs line in Figure 2 until it intersects total benefits at point Y, and thereby brings about E_e, similar to conventional regulation. The tax that would accomplish this would be equal to the difference between $B(E_e)$ and $C(E_e)$. Despite the apparent graphical similarity with the conventional regulatory outcome, this approach is efficient, because rather than destroying the rents through higher resource costs, the tax transfers the rents from the private to the public sector. Hence, the social net benefits of the tax approach are identical to those under the efficient outcome.

There is a problem, however. For the fishermen, these transfers are very real costs. The rent that would be received by a sole owner is received by the government instead. Any fishermen who might want the fishery to be managed efficiently will surely object to this particular approach. So, is there some way that the catch can be restricted to the efficient level, with real resource costs minimized, but without transferring the rents from fishermen to the government?

One answer is a system of individual transferable quotas (ITQs), by which the government sets the overall, annual allowable catch (equal to the efficient catch for the fishery), allocates this catch to fishermen in the form of quotas that entitle holders to catch a specified quantity of fish per year, and allows the fishermen to transfer (buy and sell) the quotas.[8] As we examine in more detail below in the context of tradable "pollution allowances," the quotas in the fishery will flow to those that gain the most net benefit from them due to lower costs. Hence, cost-reducing technologies and management are encouraged (as with a tax), but rents are retained by the fishing industry.[9]

Such ITQ systems have been used successfully in some 150 major fisheries of 170 species in seventeen countries—some with very significant fishing industries, such as Australia, Canada, Iceland, and New Zealand (Richard G. Newell, Sanchirico, and Suzi Kerr 2005). In fact, New Zealand regulates virtually its entire commercial fishery this way. Since 1986, the system has been effective, largely eliminating overfishing, restoring stocks to sustainable levels, and increasing fishermen's profits. Several ITQ systems are in operation in the United States, including ones for Alaska's Pacific halibut and Virginia's striped-bass fisheries.

In addition to reducing catches in an efficient manner, these systems have been found to improve safety by reducing incentives for fishermen to go out (or stay out) when weather conditions are dangerous. Further, because ITQ systems eliminate the motivation for government to limit the duration of the fishing season, supplies available to consumers improve in quality. Since fishermen own shares of the assets under an ITQ system, the total allowable catch is self-enforcing, in the sense that all participants have incentives to report anyone not complying with the rules.

The example of the Pacific halibut fishery is illuminating (Huppert 1990, 2005; Homans and Wilen 1997). Open access had led to a gradually

---

[8]Martin L. Weitzman (2002) has shown that an optimal "landing fee" (tax on fish caught) can be superior to an optimal ITQ system when particular forms of biological (stock) uncertainty are present.

[9]If the government chose to auction the quotas, rather than distribute them freely, the distributional result would be the same as with the tax.

diminishing stock throughout the 1970s. In an effort to reduce the harvest, the season was first reduced from 125 days in 1975 to 25 days in 1980, and then to just 2 days in 1994. The result, of course, was more effort expended in a shorter time. Overcapitalization of the fishery was rampant. By 1994, crews remained out for the entire 48 hours of the season, leading to high rates of injury—and even mortality. Due to the rushed fishing, the by-catch (of other species) was exceedingly high, as was so-called "ghost fishing" from abandoned nets. Fresh halibut became a rarity, because nearly all of the catch had to be frozen; much of it decayed on docks due to insufficient processing capacity. Furthermore, the regulatory approach failed even to limit the catch, with the targeted total allowable catch exceeded in two out of three years (Homans and Wilen 1997).

An ITQ system was established in 1995. The season length increased from two days to more than 200 days (United States National Research Council 1999). Safety problems were diminished, by-catch was reduced by 80 percent, ghost fishing losses fell by 77 percent, and the quality of fish in the market increased. From 1994 to 1999, the number of fishing vessels decreased by 10 percent, while the value of the harvest increased by 34 percent. Total allowable catch has not been exceeded since the inception of the program.

In 2006, a group of scientists projected that at existing rates of ocean fisheries depletion, all commercial fisheries would collapse by the middle of the century (Boris Worm, et al. 2006). Two years later, Christopher Costello, Steven D. Gaines, and John Lynham (2008) compiled a global database of fisheries management and catch statistics for more than 11 thousand fisheries from 1950 to 2003. They concluded that, where implemented, ITQ systems had halted and reversed trends toward collapse.[10]

All of the approaches described above can be used in the context of inland bodies of water and within countries' exclusive economic zones—200 miles from coastlines, where the richest and most important ocean fisheries are located. But in the open ocean, beyond the 200-mile limit, international negotiation and regulation is required (as with whaling), and the challenges become much greater (Bromley 1992), a generic problem that is taken up below.

II. Environmental Quality as a Problem of the Commons

In the late twentieth century, concerns about the commons expanded well beyond renewable, open-access resources to include environmental degra-

---

[10]To be precise, Costello, Gaines, and Lynham (2008) compared systems with caps to systems without; they were unable to distinguish between cap and trade (ITQ) and caps without trade; see Geoffrey Heal and Wolfram Schlenker (2008). As economic understanding of fisheries has advanced, more sophisticated policy instruments have been developed, such as those intended to address the spatial and dynamic features of these resources (Smith, Sanchirico, and Wilen 2009).

dation, that is, the use of common airsheds, watersheds, and land masses as repositories of pollution and waste. For much of the past 90 years, economists have thought of environmental pollution as a classic—indeed, textbook—example of a negative externality, that is, an unintentional consequence of production or consumption that reduces another agent's profits or utility (Arthur C. Pigou 1920). A separate but related strand of literature—stemming from Ronald Coase's work (1960)—has identified environmental pollution essentially as a public-good problem, that is, a problem of incomplete property rights.

Both perspectives identify the problem as one of the commons, but they lead to somewhat different policy prescriptions: emission taxes versus tradable emission rights. Both prescriptions can facilitate cost-effective environmental protection, and the respective economic literatures together constitute what is arguably the most important contribution of environmental economics to public policy—the notion and means of getting the prices right, that is, the development of market-based approaches to environmental protection.

A. Cost Effectiveness

Whereas much of normative economics has focused on questions of efficiency (maximizing net benefits), discussions in the environmental policy realm have tended to employ a more modest criterion—cost effectiveness (minimizing costs of achieving some given objective)—largely because of the difficulty of measuring the benefits of environmental protection.[11] To be more precise, by cost effectiveness I mean that allocation of control efforts among pollution sources that results in an aggregate abatement target being achieved at the lowest possible cost, that is, the allocation that satisfies the following cost-minimization problem:

$$(9) \qquad \min_{r_i} C = \sum_{t=1}^{N} c_i(r_i),$$

$$(10) \qquad \text{s.t.} \sum_{i=1}^{N} [u_i - r_i] \leq E$$

$$(11) \qquad \text{and } 0 \leq r_i \leq u_i,$$

where r_i is reductions in emissions (abatement or control) by source i ($i = 1$ to N); $c_i(r_i)$ is the cost function for source i; C is aggregate cost of control; u_i

---

[11]Despite the tendency for environmental standards to be set based on political and other considerations, economists have sought to inform policy through the comparison of benefits and costs. Considerable progress has been made in developing better methods for estimating the benefits of environmental protection (A. Myrick Freeman III 2003) for use in normative analysis (Nicholas Kaldor 1939; John R. Hicks 1939), sometimes under conditions of uncertainty (Weitzman 1974). A concise survey is provided by Richard L. Revesz and Stavins (2007).

is uncontrolled emissions by source i; and E is the aggregate emissions target imposed by a regulatory authority.

If the cost functions are convex, then necessary and sufficient conditions for satisfaction of the constrained optimization problem posed by equations (9) through (11) are:

(12)
$$\frac{\partial o_i(r_i)}{\partial r_i} - \lambda \geq 0$$

(13)
$$r_i \left[\frac{\partial o_i(r_i)}{\partial r_i} - \lambda \right] = 0$$

where λ is a Lagrange multiplier that reflects the shadow price of emissions. Equations (12) and (13) together imply the crucial condition for cost effectiveness: that all sources that exercise some degree of control experience the *same marginal abatement cost* (William J. Baumol and Wallace E. Oates 1988). Thus, when considering alternative environmental policy instruments, a key question is whether instruments are likely to result in marginal abatement costs being equated across sources.[12]

Conventional approaches to regulating the environment—frequently characterized as command and control—allow relatively little flexibility in the means of achieving goals. Such policy instruments tend to force firms to take on similar shares of the pollution-control burden, regardless of the cost, sometimes by setting uniform standards for firms, the most prevalent of which are technology- and performance-based standards.

Where there is significant heterogeneity of costs—which is a common feature of pollution abatement—command-and-control methods will not be cost effective. In reality, costs can vary enormously due to production design, physical configuration, age of assets, and other factors. Holding all firms to the same target will be unduly expensive.

In principle, governments could employ nonuniform performance standards to bring about the cost-effective allocation of control responsibility, but to develop such a set of source-specific standards, the government would need to know the marginal abatement cost functions of all sources within its jurisdiction, information that is generally not available to governments. Is there a means by which the government can achieve the cost-effective allocation of control responsibility among pollution sources, but without needing to have information about source-level control costs?

---

[12]The model of cost effectiveness I employ is of a uniformly mixed flow pollutant, that is, a pollutant for which the location of emissions has no effect on the location of damages and which does not accumulate in the environment. Little additional insight is gained but much is sacrificed in terms of transparency and tractability by modeling a more complex nonuniformly mixed stock pollutant.

B. *Pigou and Environmental Taxation*

For some 40 years prior to Coase (1960), the sole economic response to the problem of externalities was that the externality in question should be taxed. In principle, a regulator could ensure that emitters would internalize the damages they caused by charging a tax on each unit of pollution equal to the marginal social damages at the efficient level of pollution (Pigou 1920). Such a system makes it worthwhile for firms to reduce emissions to the point where their marginal abatement costs are equal to the common tax rate. Hence, marginal abatement costs will be equated across sources, satisfying the condition for cost effectiveness (equations 12 and 13). Whenever abatement costs differ across emitters, conventional policies would not be cost-effective, but a uniform Pigouvian tax would be. This is true both in the short term, and in the long term by providing incentives for the innovation (Newell, Adam B. Jaffe, and Stavins 1999) and diffusion (Jaffe and Stavins 1995) of low-cost abatement technologies.

The conventional wisdom is that pollution taxes have been rarely, if ever, employed. This is not strictly correct if one defines environmental tax systems broadly (Stavins 2003). In this spirit, these systems can be divided into those for which behavioral impacts are central to their design and performance; and those for which anticipated behavioral impacts are secondary, at best. Within the first set, effluent charges have been employed—typically for water pollution and at low levels with minimal behavioral effects—in a number of European and other nations. Beyond that, deposit-refund systems—in which front-end charges are combined with refunds payable when particular behavior is carried out—have been used in 10 US states for beverage containers and 11 states for motor vehicle batteries, as well as in dozens of other countries for these and other products. In addition, various forms of tax differentiation—tax cuts, credits, and subsidies—intended to encourage environmentally desirable behavior are common in Europe, the United States, and many other countries (Stavins 2003).

Why have true Pigouvian taxes been used infrequently, despite their theoretical advantages (Allen V. Kneese and Charles L. Schultze 1975; Don Fullerton 1996)? First, it is difficult to identify the appropriate tax rate. For social efficiency, it should be set equal to the marginal benefits of cleanup at the efficient level of cleanup, but policy makers are more likely to think in terms of a desired level of cleanup, and they do not know beforehand how firms will respond to a given level of taxation. A more important political problem posed by pollution taxes is associated with their distributional consequences for regulated sources. Despite the fact that such systems minimize aggregate social costs, these systems are likely to be *more* costly than comparable command-and-control instruments *for regulated firms*, because firms both incur their abatement costs and pay taxes on their residual emissions (James M. Buchanan and Gordon Tullock 1975). In practice, some of these costs will be passed on to consumers, but many firms may still be worse off under a tax.

Is there a way the government can achieve its pollution-control targets cost effectively, but eliminate the abatement uncertainty inherent in the Pigouvian tax approach, and—more important, politically—eliminate the distributional impacts on regulated firms?

C. *Coase and Tradable Rights*

Following Coase (1960), it became possible to think about solving the problem of pollution as one of clarifying poorly defined property rights. If resources such as clean air and water could be recognized as a form of property, whose corresponding rights could be traded in a market, private actors could allocate the use of this property in a cost-effective way. Some 40 years ago, Thomas D. Crocker (1966) and J. H. Dales (1968) each proposed a system of transferable discharge permits that could provide such a market solution: the regulator need only designate the total quantity of emissions allowed (the cap), distribute rights corresponding to this total, and allow individual sources of emissions to trade the permits until an optimal allocation had been reached. This was the fundamental thinking behind what has come to be known as "cap and trade."[13]

Under this approach, an allowable overall level of pollution is established by the government (not necessarily at the efficient level), and allocated among firms in the form of allowances. Firms that keep their emissions below their allotted level may sell their surplus allowances to other firms or use them to offset excess emissions in other parts of their operations. Under these conditions, it is in the interest of each source to carry out abatement up to the point where its marginal control costs are equal to the market-determined price of tradable allowances. Hence, the environmental constraint is satisfied, and marginal abatement costs are equated across sources, satisfying the condition for cost effectiveness (equations 12 and 13).[14]

The unique cost-effective equilibrium is achieved independent of the initial allocation of allowances (W. David Montgomery 1972).[15] This independence property is of central political importance and is the primary reason why cap-and-trade systems have been employed in representative democracies, where distributional issues are of paramount importance in

---

[13]Cap-and-trade systems should not be confused with "emission reduction–credit" or "offset" systems, whereby permits are assigned when a source reduces emissions below some baseline, which may or may not be readily observable.

[14]In theory, a number of factors can adversely affect the performance of a cap-and-trade system, including: concentration in the permit market (Robert W. Hahn 1984), concentration in the product market (David A. Malueg 1990), transaction costs (Stavins 1995), nonprofit maximizing behavior, such as sales or staff maximization (John T. Tschirhart 1984), the preexisting regulatory environment (Douglas Bohi and Dallas Burtraw 1992), and the degree of monitoring and enforcement (Juan-Pablo Montero 2007). Some of these also affect the performance of pollution taxes.

[15]This property is likely to be violated under specific, but relatively infrequent conditions (Hahn and Stavins 2010).

mustering support for a policy. In principle, the government can set the overall emissions cap—whether on the basis of economic efficiency or, more likely, some other grounds—and then leave it up to the legislature to allocate the available number of allowances among sources to build a constituency of support for the initiative *without* reducing the system's environmental performance or driving up its cost.[16] This should be contrasted with most public policy proposals—environmental or otherwise—for which the normal course of events is that the political machinations that are necessary to develop sufficient legislative support reduce the effectiveness of the policy and/or drive up its costs.

Cap and trade has been used in the United States and Europe, as well as other countries (Stavins 2003). In the 1980s, leaded gasoline was phased out of the US market with a program similar to cap and trade among refineries, saving about $250 million per year compared with a program without trading (US Environmental Protection Agency 1985), and providing measurable incentives for cost-saving technological change (Kerr and Newell 2003). Since 1995, under the Clean Air Act amendments of 1990, a sulfur dioxide (SO_2) allowance trading program has reduced emissions by half, saving $1 billion per year compared with a conventional approach (Stavins 1998; Curtis Carlson et. al 2000).[17] Most recently, Australia, Canada, Europe, Japan, New Zealand, and the United States have turned their attention to employing cap and trade to address the ultimate problem of the commons.

D. *The Ultimate Commons Problem: Global Climate Change*

Anthropogenic emissions of greenhouse gases[18]—including carbon dioxide (CO_2) from fossil-fuel combustion and land-use changes (Stavins 1999)—are likely to change the earth's climate in ways that will have serious environmental, economic, and social consequences (Martin Parry et al. 2007). The atmospheric concentration of CO_2 increased from the preindustrial value of about 280 parts per million (ppm) to 379 ppm by 2005 (Rajendra K. Pachauri and Andy Reisinger 2008). These increased concentrations of CO_2 and other greenhouse gases (GHGs) have been accompanied by increases in global mean temperatures measured over land and oceans (Figure 4).

Although the 2008–2009 global recession slowed emissions growth significantly, global atmospheric GHG concentrations (in CO_2-equivalent terms) are likely to double well before the end of the century, leading to an

---

[16]Experience has validated the political importance of this property. For example, in the Senate debate over the Clean Air Act Amendments of 1990, "bonus allowances" were awarded to electricity generators in Ohio, which were going to incur particularly high costs because of their reliance on high-sulfur coal (Paul L. Joskow and Richard Schmalensee 1998); the result was the key support of Senator John Glenn (D-Ohio) for the legislation.

[17]As with fisheries, greater economic understanding of the complexities of environmental problems has led to the development of more sophisticated policy instruments, such as in recognizing the spatial heterogeneity of some pollution problems (Nicholas Z. Muller and Robert Mendelsohn 2009).

[18]The major anthropogenic greenhouse gases in the atmosphere are carbon dioxide (CO_2), methane (CH_4), nitrous oxide (N_2O), and various halocarbons.

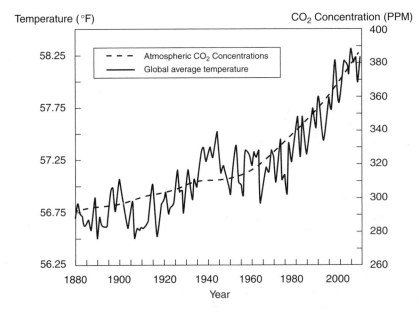

Figure 4 Global Temperature and Carbon Dioxide Concentrations, 1880–2010

Notes: Global annual average temperature measured over land and oceans. The dark dashed line shows atmospheric CO_2 concentrations in parts per million (PPM).
Source: US National Aeronautics and Space Administration 2010.

average global temperature increase of 1.8 to 4.0°C (3.2 to 7.2°F), relative to 1980–1990 levels, depending upon the quantity of future emissions and the relationship between GHG concentrations and warming (Pachauri and Reisinger 2008). But increased temperatures—which might be welcome in some places—are only part of the story.

The most important anticipated consequences of climate change are changes in precipitation, decreased snowpack, glacier melting, droughts in mid to low latitudes, decreased cereal crop productivity at lower latitudes, increased sea level, loss of islands and coastal wetlands, increased flooding, greater storm intensity, species extinction, and spread of infectious disease. Climate change will also bring longer growing seasons to higher latitudes and some health benefits to temperate areas, such as fewer deaths from cold exposure. However, it is anticipated that such benefits will be greatly outweighed by negative impacts (Parry et al. 2007).

These biophysical impacts will have significant economic, social, and political consequences. Estimates of economic impacts of unrestrained climate change vary, with most falling in the range of 1 to 3 percent of world GDP per year by the middle of the current century (with large regional differences), assuming 4°C warming (Parry et al. 2007; Nordhaus 2010a). The best estimates of marginal damages of emissions (by midcentury) are in the range of $75 to $175 per ton of CO_2, in today's dollars (Nordhaus 2008;

United States Environmental Protection Agency 2008). In order to have a 0.50 probability of keeping temperature increases below 2°C (a long-term goal acknowledged by most national governments), it would be necessary to stabilize atmospheric concentrations at 450 ppm, which in principle could be achieved by cutting global emissions 60 to 80 percent below 2005 levels by 2050 (Metz et al. 2007), a task that currently appears to be politically impossible, despite its apparent economic and technological feasibility. Of course, economic feasibility does not necessarily imply economic desirability, normally thought of as requiring a comparison of anticipated benefits and costs.[19]

Climate change is a commons problem of unparalleled magnitude along two key dimensions: temporal and spatial (Christopher Robert and Richard Zeckhauser 2010). In the temporal domain, it is a stock, not a flow problem, with greenhouse gases remaining in the atmosphere for decades to centuries. In the spatial domain, greenhouse gases uniformly mix in the atmosphere, and so the nature, magnitude, and location of damages are independent of the location of emissions. Hence, for any individual political jurisdiction, the direct benefits of taking action will inevitably be less than the costs, producing a free-rider problem, and thereby suggesting the importance of international—if not global—cooperation (Nordhaus 2010b).

Despite the apparent necessity of international cooperation for the achievement of meaningful GHG targets, the key political unit of implementation—and decision making—for any international climate policy will be the sovereign state, that is, the nations of the world. Therefore, before turning to the topic of international cooperation, it is important to ask what economics has to say about the best instruments for national action. In both cases, I limit my attention to the means—the instruments—of climate policy, although economists have and will continue to make important contributions to analyses of the ends—the goals—of climate policy.

There is widespread agreement among economists (and a diverse set of other policy analysts) that economy-wide carbon pricing will be an essential ingredient of any policy that can achieve meaningful reductions of CO_2 emissions cost effectively, at least in the United States and other industrial-

---

[19]Such a comparison of anticipated benefits and costs presents challenges to economics. It has been argued that long duration, great uncertainty, and potentially unlimited liability to the planet characterize anthropogenic climate change. Hence, it is important to consider the risk of extreme outcomes, that is, catastrophic consequences with small but nonnegligible probabilities, in addition to—and some would argue, instead of—conventionally defined expected values of abatement costs and benefits (Weitzman 2009). At the heart of this concern is the possibility that the economic consequences of fat-tailed structural uncertainty will outweigh the economic effects of temporal discounting, because (under specific conditions regarding the structure of uncertainty and preferences) there will be an infinitely large expected loss from low-probability, high-consequence events (Weitzman 2010). Although it cannot be said that there is agreement regarding the specific analysis that is appropriate (Stern 2007; Lawrence Summers and Zeckhauser 2008; Nordhaus forthcoming; Pindyck forthcoming; Weitzman forthcoming), there is considerable agreement that benefit-cost analysis based exclusively on conventional expected values is of less use in this realm than in others and that the primary (economic) argument for limiting increases in GHG concentrations is to provide insurance against catastrophic climate risks.

ized countries (Gilbert E. Metcalf 2009; Louis Kaplow 2010).[20] The ubiquitous nature of energy generation and use and the diversity of CO_2 sources in a modern economy mean that conventional technology and performance standards would be infeasible and—in any event—excessively costly (Newell and Stavins 2003). There is somewhat less agreement among economists regarding the choice of specific carbon-pricing policy instruments, with some tending to support carbon taxes (N. Gregory Mankiw 2006; Nordhaus 2007; Metcalf 2007) and others cap-and-trade mechanisms (A. Denny Ellerman, Joskow, and David Harrison 2003; Stavins 2007; Nathaniel Keohane 2009).

These two instruments—carbon taxes and carbon cap and trade—may be said to derive respectively from the externality (Pigou 1920) and property-rights (Coase 1960) perspectives. But, in truth, the two approaches are more similar than different. A carbon tax would directly place a price on carbon (most likely upstream, where fossil fuels—coal, petroleum, and natural gas—enter the economy), with quantities of carbon use and CO_2 emissions adjusting in response. An upstream carbon cap-and-trade system would constrain the quantity of carbon entering the economy through allowances on the carbon content of the three fossil fuels, with prices emerging indirectly from the market for allowances. Either instrument can be designed—in principle—to be equivalent to the other in distributional terms. If allowances are auctioned, a cap-and-trade system looks much like a carbon tax from the perspective of regulated firms. Likewise, if tax revenues are refunded in particular ways, a carbon tax can resemble cap and trade with free allowances.

What may appear to be key differences between the two instruments fade on closer inspection. First, a carbon tax would raise revenues that can be used for beneficial public purposes, such as for cutting distortionary taxes, thereby lowering the social cost of the overall policy (A. Lans Bovenberg and Lawrence H. Goulder 1996). Given the need for government revenues, this is an important attribute of taxes. But, an auction mechanism under cap-and-trade can do precisely the same. Second, it might appear that cap-and-trade systems offer greater opportunities to protect the profits of regulated firms (through free allocation of allowances). However, the same can be accomplished under a tax regime through inframarginal tax exemptions.

Third, an important question is the relative effect of the two approaches on technological innovation. A series of theoretical explorations have found that a tax and a cap-and-trade system with auctioned allowances are equivalent in their incentives for carbon-saving innovation (Scott R. Milliman

---

[20]Carbon pricing is necessary but not sufficient, because other market failures limit the impacts of price signals (Jaffe, Newell, and Stavins 2005). One example is the well-known principal-agent problem that constrains incentives for energy-efficiency investments by either landlords or tenants in renter-occupied properties. Another is the public-good nature of research and development, whereby firms capture only a share of the benefits of the information their research produces. Both argue for specific public policies that would complement a carbon-pricing regime.

and Raymond Prince 1989; Chulho Jung, Kerry Krutilla, and Roy Boyd 1996), or at least that neither system dominates (Carolyn Fischer, Ian W. H. Parry, and William A. Pizer 2003).[21]

Fourth, there is the simplicity of a carbon tax, in which firms would not need to manage and trade allowances, and the government would not need to track allowance transactions and ownership. However, experience with cap-and-trade systems indicates that the actual costs of trading institutions have not been significant. And whether a policy as important as a national carbon tax would turn out to be "simple" in its design and implementation is at least open to question.

Fifth, there is resistance to new taxes. In their simplest respective forms (a carbon tax without revenue recycling, and a cap-and-trade system without auctions), a carbon tax is more costly than a cap-and-trade system to the regulated sector, because with the former firms incur both abatement costs and the cost of tax payments to the government. This might argue politically against the tax approach, but now that cap and trade has been demonized—in US politics, at least—as "cap and tax," this difference has surely diminished.

That said, there are some real differences between these two approaches. First, there is the reality of abatement cost uncertainty under a cap-and-trade system versus emissions uncertainty under a tax regime. From an economic perspective, it makes sense to allow emissions (of a stock pollutant) to vary from year to year with economic conditions that affect aggregate abatement costs.[22] This happens automatically with a carbon tax. With a cap-and-trade system, such temporal flexibility needs to be built in through provisions for banking and borrowing of allowances. Furthermore, a tax approach eliminates the potential for short-term price volatility, which can exist under a cap-and-trade system.

Second, there are fears of market manipulation, a relevant argument against the use of cap-and-trade systems in a developing-country context. In industrialized countries, however, appropriate regulatory oversight can address such concerns. Third, there has been considerable experience with the use of cap-and-trade systems, as noted above, but virtually no experience with Pigouvian taxes for pollution control. It should be noted, however, that there is abundant experience with a wide variety of taxes to accomplish a diverse set of social objectives.

Fourth, cap-and-trade systems generate a natural unit of exchange for international harmonization and linkage: allowances denominated in units of carbon content of fossil fuels (or CO_2 emissions). Hence, it is easier

---

[21]The optimal system in this regard is a hybrid instrument, that is, a cap-and-trade system with a price collar (Thomas A. Weber and Karsten Neuhoff 2010).

[22]Because climate change is a function of the accumulated GHGs in the atmosphere, it is reasonable to anticipate that the marginal damage (benefit) function has a smaller slope (in absolute value) than the marginal cost function, and that the more efficient instrument under conditions of uncertainty about abatement costs will be a price instrument, rather than a quantity instrument, such as cap and trade (Weitzman 1974; Newell and Pizer 2003).

to harmonize with other countries' carbon mitigation programs, which are more likely to employ cap-and-trade than tax approaches (Judson Jaffe, Matthew Ranson, and Stavins 2009). However, through appropriate mechanisms, international linkage can include carbon tax systems (Metcalf and David Weisbach 2010).

Fifth and finally, there is a fundamental political-economy difference. Cap and trade leaves distributional issues up to politicians, and thereby provides a straightforward means to compensate burdened sectors. Of course, this political advantage is also an economic disadvantage in that it invites rent-seeking behavior. In any event, the compensation associated with free distribution of allowances based on historical activities can be mimicked under a tax regime through the assignment of specific tax exemptions. A real difference is that the cap-and-trade approach avoids likely battles over tax exemptions among vulnerable industries and sectors that would drive up the costs of the program, as more and more sources (emission-reduction opportunities) are exempted from the program, thereby simultaneously compromising environmental performance. Instead, a cap-and-trade system leads to battles over the allowance allocation, but these do not raise the overall cost of the program nor affect its climate impacts (Montgomery 1972).

Remaining differences between carbon taxes and cap and trade can diminish with implementation. Hybrid schemes that include features of taxes and cap-and-trade systems blur distinctions. The government can auction allowances in a cap-and-trade system, thereby reproducing many of the properties of a tax approach. Mechanisms that deal with uncertainty in a cap-and-trade system also bring it close to a tax approach, including a cost containment mechanism that places a cap or collar on allowance prices, banking that creates a floor under prices, and borrowing that provides flexibility similar to a tax. To some degree, the dichotomous choice between taxes and cap and trade can be a choice of design elements along a policy continuum (Weisbach 2010).

Because of the similarity between the two approaches to carbon pricing, it has been argued that the key questions that should be used to decide between these two policy approaches are: which is more politically feasible; and which is more likely to be well designed (Jason Furman, et al. 2007). To some degree, responses to these questions have been provided by the political revealed preference of individual countries, with the world's most significant climate policy employing a cap-and-trade system to constrain Europe's CO_2 emissions—the European Union Emission Trading Scheme (EU ETS).[23] Although the system had its share of problems in its pilot phase, it has functioned as anticipated since then (Ellerman, Frank J. Convery, and Christian de Perthuis 2010). This is despite the fact that the 2008–2009 recession led to significantly lower allowance prices and hence

---

[23]One factor which is said to have influenced the choice of cap and trade over a tax approach was the fact that fiscal measures—such as a carbon tax—require unanimity in the Council of the European Union, whereas most other measures require only a majority.

fewer emission reductions than anticipated (Richard N. Cooper 2010b).[24] In addition, New Zealand has launched a GHG cap-and-trade system, and Australia and Japan have considered doing likewise for CO_2. Canada has indicated that it will launch a domestic system when and if the United States does so, but domestic US politics slowed developments in 2010.[25]

Even as domestic climate policies move forward in some countries but not others, it is clear that due to the global commons nature of the problem, meaningful international cooperation will eventually be necessary. The Kyoto Protocol (1997) to the United Nations Framework Convention on Climate Change (1992) will expire in 2012, and is, in any event, insufficient to the long-term task, due to the exclusion of developing countries from responsibility. Although the industrialized countries accounted for the majority of annual CO_2 emissions until 2004 (and the majority of annual GHG emissions until 2000), that is no longer the case. China has surpassed the United States as the world's largest emitter, and most growth in CO_2 emissions in the coming decades will come from countries outside of the Organization of Economic Cooperation and Development (OECD), with emissions in nearly all OECD countries close to stable or falling (Figure 5).

A wide range of potential paths forward are possible (Joseph E. Aldy, Scott Barrett, and Stavins 2003), including: top-down international agreements involving targets and timetables that involve more countries as they become more wealthy (Jeffrey Frankel 2010), harmonized national policies, such as domestic carbon taxes (Cooper 2010a), and bottom-up, loosely coordinated national policies, such as the linkage of regional and national cap-and-trade systems through bilateral arrangements (Jaffe, Ranson, and Stavins 2009). The most promising alternatives can—in principle—achieve reasonable environmental performance cost effectively by including not only the currently industrialized nations, but also the key emerging economies (Aldy and Stavins 2009).

Political feasibility is another matter, partly due to countries' asymmetric situations (Edward A. Parson and Zeckhauser 1995). The United States and other industrialized countries have come to insist that the large, emerging economies—China, India, Brazil, Korea, Mexico, and South Africa—begin to take on proportionate shares of the mitigation burden, while some of those emerging economies plus most developing countries insist that the rich countries go first, and possibly compensate developing countries for climate damages (due to cumulative emissions from the industrialized

---

[24]Note that the lower allowance prices and fewer reductions that occur with cap and trade during a recession are an economic virtue, i.e., countercyclicality.

[25]With political stalemate in Washington, attention has turned to subnational policies, including the Regional Greenhouse Gas Initiative in the Northeast and California's Global Warming Solutions Act (Assembly Bill 32). These subnational policies will interact in a variety of ways with federal policy when and if a federal policy is enacted. Some of these interactions would be problematic, some benign, and some could be positive (Goulder and Stavins 2010).

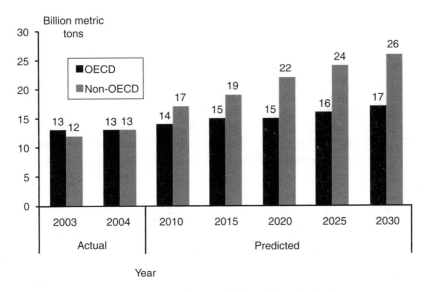

Figure 5 Energy-Related World Carbon Dioxide Emissions by Region

Source: US Energy Information Administration 2010.

world). At a minimum, developing countries want their mitigation and adaptation to be financed by the wealthier countries, but such large financial transfers are unlikely.

Given the spatial and temporal nature of this global commons problem, political incentives around the world are to rely upon others to take action. Since sovereign nations cannot be compelled to act against their wishes, successful cooperation—whether in the form of international treaties or less formal mechanisms—must create internal incentives for compliance, along with external incentives for participation. Because no single approach guarantees a sure path to ultimate success, the best strategy to address this ultimate commons problem may be to pursue a variety of approaches simultaneously. The difficulties inherent in addressing the climate problem cannot be overstated.[26] As Coman (1911) observed a cen-

---

[26]It might be asked whether a useful precedent is provided by the successful regime put in place under the Montreal Protocol on Substances That Deplete the Ozone Layer (1987) to address another global commons problem—stratospheric ozone depletion linked with emissions of chlorofluorocarbons (CFCs) and hydrochlorofluorocarbons (HCFCs) (Barrett 2003, 2007). It is expected that the ozone layer (which protects the planet from harmful ultraviolet radiation) will recover by 2050 (World Meteorological Organization 2007). However, the differences between stratospheric ozone depletion and global climate change explain why this success provides little precedent for addressing global climate change: (1) the cost of reducing CFC and HCFC production and use was extremely small relative to the cost of weaning economies away from fossil-fuel use: (2) substitutes for CFCs and HCFCs were readily available; and (3) production of these compounds was limited to a small set of countries.

tury ago, appropriate regimes to govern the commons—though some-times theoretically clear—may nevertheless be very difficult to achieve in practice.

III. Conclusions

Problems of the commons are both more widespread and more important today than when Coman wrote about unsettled problems in the first issue of the *Review* 100 years ago. A century of economic growth and globaliza-tion have brought unparalleled improvements in societal well-being, but also unprecedented challenges to the carrying capacity of the planet. What would have been in 1911 inconceivable increases in income and population have come about and have greatly heightened pressures on the commons, particularly where there has been open access to it.

The stocks of a variety of renewable natural resources—including water, forests, fisheries, and numerous other species of plant and animal—have been depleted below socially efficient levels, principally because of poorly defined property-right regimes. Likewise, the same market failures of open access—whether characterized as externalities, following Pigou, or public goods, following Coase—have led to the degradation of air and water quality, inappropriate disposal of hazardous waste, depletion of stratospheric ozone, and the atmospheric accumulation of greenhouse gases linked with global climate change.

Over this same century, economics—as a discipline—has gradually come to focus more and more attention on these commons problems, first with regard to natural resources, and more recently with regard to envi-ronmental quality. Economic research within academia and think tanks has improved our understanding of the causes and consequences of exces-sive resource depletion and inefficient environmental degradation, and thereby has helped identify sensible policy solutions. Conventional regula-tory policies, which have not accounted for economic responses, have been excessively costly, ineffective, or even counterproductive. The problems behind what Hardin (1968) characterized as the "tragedy of the commons" might better be described as the "failure of commons regulation." As our understanding of the commons has become more complex, the design of economic policy instruments has become more sophisticated.

Problems of the commons have not diminished, and the lag between understanding and action can be long. While some commons problems have been addressed successfully, others continue to emerge. Some—such as the threat of global climate change—are both more important and more diffi-cult than problems of the past. Fortunately, economics is well positioned to offer better understanding and better policies to address these ongoing chal-lenges. As the first decade of the twenty-first century comes to a close, natu-ral resource and environmental economics has emerged as a productive field of our discipline and one that shows even greater promise for the future.

REFERENCES

Acheson, James M. 2003. *Capturing the Commons: Devising Institutions to Manage the Maine Lobster Industry*. Lebanon. NH: University Press of New England.

Aldy, Joseph E., and Robert N. Stavins. 2009. *Post-Kyoto International Climate Policy: Summary for Policymakers*. New York: Cambridge University Press.

Aldy, Joseph E., Scott Barrett, and Robert N. Stavins. 2003. "Thirteen Plus One: A Comparison of Global Climate Policy Architectures." *Climate Policy*, 3(4): 373–97.

Amundsen, Eirik S., Trond Bjørndal, and Jon M. Conrad. 1995. "Open Access Harvesting of the Northeast Atlantic Minke Whale." *Environmental and Resource Economics*, 6(2): 167–85.

Barnett, Harold J., and Chandler Morse. 1963. *Scarcity and Growth: The Economics of Natural Resource Availability*. Baltimore, MD: Johns Hopkins University Press.

Barrett, Scott. 2003. *Environment and Statecraft: The Strategy of Environmental Treaty-Making*. New York: Oxford University Press.

Barrett, Scott. 2007. *Why Cooperate? The Incentive to Supply Global Public Goods*. New York: Oxford University Press.

Baurnol, William J., and Wallace E. Oates. 1988. *The Theory of Environmental Policy*. 2nd Ed. New York: Cambridge University Press.

Bohi, Douglas, and Dallas Burtraw. 1992 "Utility Investment Behavior and the Emission Trading Market." *Resources and Energy*, 14(1–2): 129–53.

Bovenberg, A. Lans, and Lawrence H. Goulder. 1996. "Optimal Environmental Taxation in the Presence of Other Taxes: General-Equilibrium Analyses." *American Economic Review*, 86(4): 985–1000.

Bromley, Daniel W. 1992. "The Commons, Common Property, and Environmental Policy." *Environmental and Resource Economics*, 2(1): 1–17.

Buchanan, James M., and Gordon Tullock. 1975. "Polluters' Profits and Political Response: Direct Controls versus Taxes." *American Economic Review*, 65(1): 139–47.

Carlson, Curtis, Dallas Burtraw, Maureen Cropper, and Karen L. Palmer. 2000. "Sulfur Dioxide Control by Electric Utilities: What Are the Gains from Trade?" *Journal of Political Economy*, 108(6): 1292–1326.

Clark, Colin W. 1990. *Mathematical Bioeconomics: The Optimal Management of Renewable Resources*. 2nd Ed. New York: Wiley.

Coase, Ronald. 1960. "The Problem of Social Cost." *Journal of Law and Economics*, 3(10): 1–44.

Coman, Katharine. 1911. "Some Unsettled Problems of Irrigation." *American Economic Review*, 1(1): 1–19.

Cooper, Richard N. 2010a. "The Case for Charges on Greenhouse Gas Emissions." In *Post-Kyoto International Climate Policy: Implementing Architectures for Agreement*, ed. Joseph E. Aldy, and Robert N. Stavins, 151–78. New York: Cambridge University Press.

Cooper, Richard N. 2010b. "Europe's Emissions Trading System." Harvard Project on International Climate Agreements Discussion Paper 10–40.

Costello, Christopher, Steven D. Gaines, and John Lynham. 2008. "Can Catch Shares Prevent Fisheries Collapse?" *Science*, 321(5896): 1678–81.

Crocker, Thomas D. 1966. "The Structuring of Atmospheric Pollution Control Systems." In *The Economics of Air Pollution*, ed. Harold Wolozin, 61–86. New York: W. W. Norton and Co.

Dales, J. H. 1968. "Land, Water, and Ownership." *Canadian Journal of Economics,* 1(4): 791–804.

Dasgupta, Partha. 1982. *The Control of Resources.* Cambridge, MA: Harvard University Press.

Ellerman, A. Denny, Frank J. Convery, and Christian de Perthuis, ed. 2010. *Pricing Carbon: The European Union Emissions Trading Scheme.* New York: Cambridge University Press.

Ellerman, A. Denny., Paul L. Joskow, and David Harrison. 2003. *Emissions Trading in the US: Experience, Lessons, and Considerations for Greenhouse Gases.* Arlington, VA: Pew Center on Global Climate Change.

Fischer, Carolyn, Ian W. H. Parry, and William A. Pizer. 2003. "Instrument Choice for Environmental Protection When Technological Innovation Is Endogenous." *Journal of Environmental Economics and Management.* 45(3): 523–45.

Frankel, Jeffrey. 2010. "An Elaborate Proposal for a Global Climate Policy Architecture: Specific Formulas and Emission Targets for All Countries in All Decades." In *Post-Kyoto International Climate Policy: Implementing Architectures for Agreement,* ed. Joseph E. Aldy, and Robert N. Stavins, 31–87. New York: Cambridge University Press.

Freeman, A. Myrick, III. 2003. *The Measurement of Environmental and Resource Values: Theory and Methods.* 2nd Ed. Washington, DC: Resources for the Future.

Fullerton, Don. 1996. "Why Have Separate Environmental Taxes?" In *Tax Policy and the Economy,* Vol. 10, ed. James M. Poterba, 33–70. Cambridge, MA: MIT Press.

Furman, Jason, Jason E. Bordoff, Manasi A. Deshpande, and Pascal J. Noel. 2007. *An Economic Strategy to Address Climate Change and Promote Energy Security.* Hamilton Project Strategy Paper. Washington, DC: Brookings Institution.

Gordon, H. Scott. 1954. "The Economic Theory of a Common-Property Resource: The Fishery." *Journal of Political Economy,* 62(2): 124–42.

Goulder, Lawrence H., and Robert N. Stavins. 2010. "Interactions between State and Federal Climate Change Policies." National Bureau of Economic Research Working Paper 16123.

Hahn, Robert W. 1984. "Market Power and Transferable Property Rights." *Quarterly Journal of Economics,* 99(4): 753–65.

Hahn, Robert W., and Robert N. Stavins. 2010. "The Effect of Allowance Allocations on Cap-and-Trade System Performance." National Bureau of Economic Research Working Paper 15854.

Hardin, Garrett. 1968. "The Tragedy of the Commons." *Science,* 162(3859): 1243–48.

Heal, Geoffrey, and Wolfram Schlenker. 2008. "Sustainable Fisheries." *Nature,* 455(7216): 1044–45.

Henderson, J. V., and M. Tugwell. 1979. "Exploitation of the Lobster Fishery: Some Empirical Results." *Journal of Environmental Economics and Management.* 6(4): 287–96.

Hicks, John R. 1939. "The Foundations of Welfare Economics." *Economic Journal,* 49(196): 696–712.

Homans, Frances R., and James E. Wilen. 1997. "A Model of Regulated Open Access Resource Use." *Journal of Environmental Economics and Management,* 32(1): 1–21.

Hotelling, Harold. 1931. "The Economics of Exhaustible Resources." *Journal of Political Economy,* 39(2): 137–75.

Huppert, Daniel D. 1990. "Managing Alaska's Groundfish Fisheries: History and Prospects." Unpublished.

Huppert, Daniel D. 2005. "An Overview of Fishing Rights." *Reviews in Fish Biology and Fisheries*, 15(3): 201–15.

International Whaling Commission. 2010. "Status of Whales." International Whaling Commission. http://iwcoffice.org/conservation/status.htm. (accessed 6/20/11).

Jaffe, Adam B., and Robert N. Stavins. 1995. "Dynamic Incentives of Environmental Regulations: The Effects of Alternative Policy Instruments on Technology Diffusion." *Journal of Environmental Economics and Management*, 29(3): S43–63.

Jaffe, Adam B., Richard G. Newell, and Robert N. Stavins. 2005. "A Tale of Two Market Failures: Technology and Environmental Policy." *Ecological Economics*, 54(2–3): 164–74.

Jaffe, Judson, Matthew Ranson, and Robert N. Stavins. 2009. "Linking Tradable Permit Systems: A Key Element of Emerging International Climate Policy Architecture." *Ecology Law Quarterly*, 36(4): 789–808.

Joskow, Paul L., and Richard Schmalensee. 1998. "The Political Economy of Market-Based Environmental Policy: The U.S. Acid Rain Program." *Journal of Law and Economics*, 41(1): 37–83.

Jung, Chulho, Kerry Krutilla, and Roy Boyd. 1996. "Incentives for Advanced Pollution Abatement Technology at the Industry Level: An Evaluation of Policy Alternatives." *Journal of Environmental Economics and Management*, 30(1): 95–111.

Kaldor, Nicholas. 1939. "Welfare Propositions of Economics and Interpersonal Comparisons of Utility." *Economic Journal*, 49(195): 549–52.

Kaplow, Louis. 2010. "Taxes, Permits, and Climate Change." National Bureau of Economic Research Working Paper 16268.

Keohane, Nathaniel O. 2009. "Cap and Trade, Rehabilitated: Using Tradable Permits to Control U.S. Greenhouse Gases." *Review of Environmental Economics and Policy*, 3(1): 42–62.

Kerr, Suzi, and Richard G. Newell. 2003. "Policy-Induced Technology Adoption: Evidence from the U.S. Lead Phasedown." *Journal of Industrial Economics*, 51(3): 317–43.

Kneese, Allen V., and Charles L. Schultze. 1975. *Pollution, Prices and Public Policy.* Washington, DC: Brookings Institution Press.

Lee, Junsoo, John A. List, and Mark C. Strazicich. 2006. "Non-Renewable Resource Prices: Deterministic or Stochastic Trends?" *Journal of Environmental Economics and Management*, 51(3): 354–70.

Livernois, John. 2009. "On the Empirical Significance of the Hotelling Rule." *Review of Environmental Economics and Policy*, 3(1): 22–41.

Malueg, David A. 1990. "Welfare Consequences of Emission Credit Trading Programs." *Journal of Environmental Economics and Management*, 18(1): 66–77.

Mankiw, N. Gregory. 2006. "The Pigou Club Manifesto." http://gregmankiw.blogspot.com/2006/10/pigou-club-manifesto.html. [(accessed 6/20/11)].

Meadows, Donella H., Dennis L. Meadows, Jørgen Randers, and William W. Behrens, III. 1972. *The Limits to Growth.* New York: Universe Books.

Metcalf, Gilbert E. 2007. "A Proposal for a U.S. Carbon Tax Swap: An Equitable Reform to Address Global Climate Change." Brookings Institution Hamilton Project Discussion Paper 2007–12.

Metcalf, Gilbert E. 2009. "Market-Based Policy Options to Control U.S. Greenhouse Gas Emissions." *Journal of Economic Perspectives*, 23(2): 5–27.

Metcalf, Gilbert E., and David Weisbach. 2010. "Linking Policies when Tastes Differ: Global Climate Policy in a Heterogeneous World." Harvard Project on International Climate Agreements Discussion Paper 2010–038.

Metz, Bert, Ogunlade Davidson, Peter Bosch, Rutu Dave, and Leo Meyer, ed. 2007. *Climate Change 2007: Mitigation of Climate Change. Working Group III Contribution to the Fourth Assessment Report of the Intergovernmental Panel on Climate Change*. New York: Cambridge University Press.

Milliman, Scott R., and Raymond Prince. 1989. "Firm Incentives to Promote Technological Change in Pollution Control." *Journal of Environmental Economics and Management*, 17(3): 247–65.

Montero, Juan-Pablo. 2007. "Tradable Permits with Incomplete Monitoring: Evidence from Santiago's Particulate Permits Program." In *Moving to Markets in Environmental Regulation: Lessons from Twenty Years of Experience*, ed. Jody Freeman, and Charles D. Kolstad. 147–70. New York: Oxford University Press.

Montgomery, W. David. 1972. "Markets in Licenses and Efficient Pollution Control Programs." *Journal of Economic Theory*, 5(3): 395–418.

Muller, Nicholas Z., and Robert Mendelsohn. 2009. "Efficient Pollution Regulation: Getting the Prices Right." *American Economic Review*, 99(5): 1714–39.

Muñoz, Roberto E., and Thomas W. Hazlett. 2009. "A Welfare Analysis of Spectrum Allocation Policies." *RAND Journal of Economics*, 40(3): 424–54.

Newell, Richard G., and William A. Pizer. 2003. "Regulating Stock Externalities under Uncertainty." *Journal of Environmental Economics and Management*, 45(2S): 416–32.

Newell, Richard G., and Robert N. Stavins. 2003. "Cost Heterogeneity and the Potential Savings from Market-Based Policies." *Journal of Regulatory Economics*, 23(1): 43–59.

Newell, Richard G., Adam B. Jaffe, and Robert N. Stavins. 1999. "The Induced Innovation Hypothesis and Energy-Saving Technological Change." *Quarterly Journal of Economics*, 114(3): 941–75.

Newell, Richard G., James N. Sanchirico, and Suzi Kerr. 2005. "Fishing Quota Markets." *Journal of Environmental Economics and Management*, 49(3): 437–62.

Nordhaus, William D. Forthcoming. "Tail Events and Economic Analysis." *Review of Environmental Economics and Policy*.

Nordhaus, William D. 1992. "Lethal Model 2: The Limits to Growth Revisited." *Brookings Papers on Economic Activity*, 23(2): 1–43.

Nordhaus, William D. 2007. "To Tax or Not to Tax: Alternative Approaches to Slowing Global Warming." *Review of Environmental Economics and Policy*, 1(1): 26–44.

Nordhaus, William D. 2008. *A Question of Balance: Weighing the Options on Global Warming Policies*. New Haven, CT: Yale University Press.

Nordhaus, William D. 2010a. "Economic Aspects of Global Warming in a Post-Copenhagen Environment." *Proceedings of the National Academy of Sciences*, 107(26): 11721–26.

Nordhaus, William D. 2010b. "Some Foundational and Transformative Grand Challenges for the Social and Behavioral Sciences: The Problem of Global Public Goods." Unpublished.

Opsomer, Jean-Didier, and Jon M. Conrad. 1994. "An Open-Access Analysis of the Northern Anchovy Fishery." *Journal of Environmental Economics and Management*, 27(1): 21–37.

Ostrom, Elinor. 1990. *Governing the Commons: The Evolution of Institutions for Collective Action*. Political Economy of Institutions and Decisions series. New York: Cambridge University Press.

Ostrom, Elinor. 2010. "Beyond Markets and States: Polycentric Governance of Complex Economic Systems." *American Economic Review*, 100(3): 641–72.

Ostrom, Elinor. 2011. "Reflections on 'Some Unsettled Problems of Irrigation.'" *American Economic Review*, 101(1): 49–63.

Pachauri, Rajendra K., and Andy Reisinger, ed. 2008. *Climate Change 2007: Synthesis Report. Contribution of Working Groups I, II and III to the Fourth Assessment Report of the Intergovernmental Panel on Climate Change*. Geneva: Intergovernmental Panel on Climate Change.

Parry, Martin, Osvaldo Canziani, Jean Palutikof, Paul van der Linden, and Clair Hanson, ed. 2007. *Climate Change 2007: Impacts, Adaptation and Vulnerability. Contribution of Working Group II to the Fourth Assessment Report of the Intergovernmental Panel on Climate Change*. New York: Cambridge University Press.

Parson, Edward A., and Richard J. Zeckhauser. 1995. "Equal Measures or Fair Burdens: Negotiating Environmental Treaties in an Unequal World." In *Shaping National Responses to Climate Change: A Post-Rio Guide*, ed. Henry Lee, 81–114. Washington, DC: Island Press.

Pigou, Alfred C. 1920. *The Economics of Welfare*. London: MacMillan.

Pindyck, Robert S. Forthcoming. "Fat Tails. Thin Tails, and Climate Change Policy." *Review of Environmental Economics and Policy*.

Pindyck, Robert S. 1984. "Uncertainty in the Theory of Renewable Resource Markets." *Review of Economic Studies*, 51(2): 289–303.

Revesz, Richard L., and Robert N. Stavins. 2007. "Environmental Law." In *Handbook of Law and Economics, Volume 1*. Handbooks in Economics, Vol. 27, ed. A. Mitchell Polinsky, and Steven Shavell, 499–589. New York: Elsevier Science.

Robert, Christopher, and Richard Zeckhauser. 2010. "The Methodology of Positive Policy Analysis." Harvard Kennedy School Faculty Research Working Paper 10–041.

Royte, Elizabeth. 2006. "The Mollusk That Made Manhattan." *New York Times, Sunday Book Review*, March 5.

Sanchirico, James N., and James E. Wilen. 2007. "Global Marine Fisheries Resources: Status and Prospects." *International Journal of Global Environmental Issues*, 7(2–3): 106–18.

Schaefer, M. B. 1957. "Some Considerations of Population Dynamics and Economics in Relation to the Management of the Commercial Marine Fisheries." *Journal of the Fisheries Research Board of Canada*, 14(5): 669–81.

Scott, Anthony. 1955. "The Fishery: The Objectives of Sole Ownership." *Journal of Political Economy*, 63(2): 116–24.

Smith, Martin D., and James E. Wilen. 2003. "Economic Impacts of Marine Reserves: The Importance of Spatial Behavior." *Journal of Environmental Economics and Management*, 46(2): 183–206.

Smith, Martin D., James N. Sanchirico, and James E. Wilen. 2009. "The Economics of Spatial-Dynamic Processes: Applications to Renewable Resources." *Journal of Environmental Economics and Management*, 57(1): 104–21.

Smith, V. Kerry. 1980. "The Evaluation of Natural Resource Adequacy: Elusive Quest or Frontier of Economic Analysis?" *Land Economics*, 56(3): 257–98.

Solow, Robert M. 1991. "Sustainability: An Economist's Perspective." The Eighteenth J. Seward Johnson Lecture to the Marine Policy Center, Woods Hole Oceanographic Institution, Woods Hole, MA, June 14.

Spence, A. Michael. 1974. "Blue Whales and Applied Control Theory." In *Systems Approaches and Environmental Problems*, ed. Hans W. Gottinger, 97–174. Göttingen, Germany: Vandenhoeck & Ruprecht.

Stavins, Robert N. 1995. "Transaction Costs and Tradeable Permits." *Journal of Environmental Economics and Management*, 29(2): 133–48.

Stavins, Robert N. 1998. "What Can We Learn from the Grand Policy Experiment? Lessons from SO_2 Allowance Trading." *Journal of Economic Perspectives*, 12(3): 69–88.

Stavins, Robert N. 1999. "The Costs of Carbon Sequestration: A Revealed-Preference Approach." *American Economic Review*, 89(4): 994–1009.

Stavins, Robert N. 2003. "Experience with Market-Based Environmental Policy Instruments." In *Handbook of Environmental Economics, Volume 1: Environmental Degradation and Institutional Responses*. Handbooks in Economics, Vol. 20, ed. Karl-Göran Mäler and Jeffrey R. Vincent, 355–435. Amsterdam: North-Holland.

Stavins, Robert N. 2007. "A U.S. Cap-and-Trade System to Address Global Climate Change." Brookings Institution Hamilton Project Discussion Paper 2007–13.

Stavins, Robert N. 2008. "Addressing Climate Change with a Comprehensive US Cap-and-Trade System." *Oxford Review of Economic Policy*, 24(2): 298–321.

Stern, Nicholas. 2007. *The Economics of Climate Change: The Stern Review.* New York: Cambridge University Press.

Summers, Lawrence, and Richard Zeckhauser. 2008. "Policymaking for Posterity." *Journal of Risk and Uncertainty*, 37(2–3): 115–40.

Tschirhart, John T. 1984. "Transferable Discharge Permits and Profit-Maximizing Behavior." In *Economic Perspectives on Acid Deposition Control*, ed. Thomas D. Crocker, 157–72. Boston: Butterworth.

United Nations Food and Agriculture Organization. 2007. *The State of World Fisheries and Aquaculture 2006.* Rome: FAO Fisheries and Aquaculture Department.

United Nations Food and Agriculture Organization. 2010. Global Capture Production: US and Canadian Atlantic Cod. http://www.fao.org/fishery/statistics/global-capture-production/en (accessed 6/20/11).

United States Energy Information Administration. 2009. *International Energy Outlook 2009.* Washington, DC: United States Department of Energy.

United States Environmental Protection Agency. 1985. *Costs and Benefits of Reducing Lead in Gasoline: Final Regulatory Impact Analysis.* Schwartz, Joel, Hugh Pitcher, Ronnie Levin. Bart Ostro, and Albert L. Nichols. Washington, DC: United States Environmental Protection Agency.

United States Environmental Protection Agency. 2008. "Technical Support Document on Benefits of Reducing GHG Emissions." http://www.eenews.net/public/25/10084/features/documents/2009/03/11/document_gw_04.pdf [(accessed 6/20/11)].

United States National Aeronautics and Space Administration. 2010. Global Land-Ocean Temperature Index. http://data.giss.nasa.gov/gistemp/tabledata/GLB.Ts+dSST.txt (accessed 6/20/11).

United States National Research Council. 1999. *Sharing the Fish: Toward a National Policy on Individual Fishing Quotas.* Washington: DC: National Academy Press.

Weber, Thomas A., and Karsten Neuhoff. 2010. Carbon Markets and Technological Innovation. *Journal of Environmental Economics and Management*, 60(2): 115–32.

Weisbach, David. 2010. "Instrument Choice is Instrument Design." In *U.S. Energy Tax Policy*, ed. Gilbert Metcalf, 113–58. New York: Cambridge University Press.

Weitzman, Martin L. Forthcoming. "Fat-Tailed Uncertainty and the Economics of Climate Change." *Review of Environmental Economics and Policy.*

Weitzman, Martin L. 1974. "Prices vs. Quantities." *Review of Economic Studies,* 41(4): 477–91.

Weitzman, Martin L. 2002. "Landing Fees vs. Harvest Quotas with Uncertain Fish Stocks." *Journal of Environmental Economics and Management,* 43(2): 325–38.

Weitzman, Martin L. 2009. "On Modeling and Interpreting the Economics of Catastrophic Climate Change." *Review of Economics and Statistics,* 91(1): 1–19.

Weitzman, Martin L. 2010. "GHG Targets as Insurance against Catastrophic Climate Damages." Harvard Project on International Climate Agreements Discussion Paper 10–42.

Wilen, James E. 1976. "Common Property Resources and the Dynamics of Overexploitation: The Case of the North Pacific Fur Seal." University of British Columbia Programme in Natural Resource Economics Working Paper 3.

World Meteorological Organization. 2007. *Scientific Assessment of Ozone Depletion, 2006.* Geneva, Switzerland: World Meteorological Organization.

Worm, Boris, Edward B. Barbier, Nicola Beaumont, J. Emmett Duffy, Carl Folke, Benjamin S. Halpern, Jeremy B. C. Jackson, et al. 2006. "Impacts of Biodiversity Loss on Ocean Ecosystem Services." *Science,* 314(5800): 787–90.

31   *The Environment and Globalization**

Jeffrey A. Frankel

Harpel Professor of Capital Formation and Growth at Harvard Kennedy School

Introduction

At the Ministerial meeting of the World Trade Organization in Seattle in November 1999, some protestors wore turtle costumes while launching the first of the big anti-globalization demonstrations. These demonstrators were concerned that international trade in shrimp was harming sea turtles by ensnaring them in nets. They felt that a WTO panel had, in the name of free trade, negated the ability of the United States to protect the turtles, simultaneously undermining the international environment and national sovereignty.

Subsequently, anti-globalization protests became common at meetings of multinational organizations. Perhaps no aspect of globalization worries the critics more than its implications for the environment. The concern is understandable. It is widely (if not universally) accepted that the direct effects of globalization on the economy are positive, as measured by Gross Domestic Product. Concerns rise more with regard to "non-economic" effects of globalization.[1] Of these, some, such as labor rights, might be considered to be a subject properly of national sovereignty, with each nation bearing the responsibility of deciding to what extent it wishes to protect its own labor force, based on its own values, capabilities, and politics. When we turn to influences on the environment, however, the case for countries sticking their noses into each other's business is stronger. We all share a common planet.

Pollution and other forms of environmental degradation are the classic instance of what economists call an externality. This term means that individual people and firms, and sometimes even individual countries, lack the

---

"The Environment and Globalization" by Jeffrey Frankel from *Globalization: What's New*, edited by Michael Weinstein, Council of Foreign Relations, 2004. Reprinted with permission.

*The author would like to thank Steve Charnovitz, Dan Esty, Don Fullerton, Rob Stavins, and Michael Weinstein for useful comments; Anne Lebrun for research assistance; and the Savitz Research Fund for support.

[1]The quotation marks are necessary around "non-economic," because economists' conceptual framework fully incorporates such objectives as environmental quality, even though pollution is an externality that is not measured by GDP. For further reading on how economists think about the environment, see Hanley, Shogren, and White (1997) or Stavins (2000).

incentive to restrain their pollution, because under a market system the costs are borne primarily by others, rather than by themselves. The phrase "tragedy of the commons" was originally coined in the context of a village's shared pasture land, which would inevitably be over-grazed if each farmer were allowed free and unrestricted use. It captures the idea that we will foul our shared air and water supplies and deplete our natural resources unless somehow we are individually faced with the costs of our actions.

A central question for this chapter is whether globalization helps or hurts in achieving the best tradeoff between environmental and economic goals. Do international trade and investment allow countries to achieve more economic growth for any given level of environmental quality? Or do they undermine environmental quality for any given rate of economic growth? Globalization is a complex trend, encompassing many forces and many effects. It would be surprising if all of them were always unfavorable to the environment, or all of them favorable. The highest priority should be to determine ways in which globalization can be successfully harnessed to promote protection of the environment, along with other shared objectives, as opposed to degradation of the environment.[2]

One point to be emphasized here is that it is an illusion to think that environmental issues could be effectively addressed if each country were insulated against incursions into its national sovereignty at the hands of international trade or the WTO. Increasingly, people living in one country want to protect the air, water, forests, and animals not just in their *own* countries, but also in *other* countries as well. To do so international cooperation is required. National sovereignty is the obstacle to such efforts, not the ally. Multilateral institutions are a potential ally, not the obstacle.

In the course of this chapter, we encounter three ways in which globalization can be a means of environmental improvement. So the author hopes to convince the reader, at any rate. Each has a component that is new.

First is the exercise of *consumer power*. There is the beginning of a worldwide trend toward labeling, codes of corporate conduct, and other ways that environmentally conscious consumers can use their purchasing power to give expression and weight to their wishes. These tools would not exist without international trade. American citizens would have little way to dissuade Mexican fishermen from using dolphin-unfriendly nets if Americans did not import tuna to begin with. The attraction of labeling is that it suits a decentralized world, where we have both national sovereignty and consumer sovereignty. Nevertheless, labeling cannot be a completely laissez faire affair. For it to work, there need to be some rules or standards. Otherwise, any producer could inaccurately label its product as environmentally pure, and any country could unfairly put a pejorative label on imports from

---

[2]The literature on trade and the environment is surveyed in Dean (1992, 2001) and Copeland and Taylor (2003b).

rival producers. This consideration leads to the second respect in which globalization can be a means of environmental improvement.

International environmental issues require international cooperation, a system in which countries interact under a set of *multilateral rules* determined in multilateral negotiations and monitored by multilateral institutions. This is just as true in the case of environmental objectives, which are increasingly cross-border, as of other objectives. It is true that in the past, the economic objectives of international trade have been pursued more effectively by the GATT and other multilateral organizations than have environmental objectives. But multilateral institutions can be made a means of environmental protection. This will sound like pie-in-the-sky to the many who have been taken in by the mantra that recent WTO panel decisions have overruled legislative efforts to protect the environment. But the WTO has actually moved importantly in the environmentalists' direction in recent years.

The front lines of multilateral governance currently concern—not illusory alternatives of an all-powerful WTO versus none at all—but rather questions about how reasonably to balance both economic and environmental objectives. One question under debate is whether countries are to be allowed to adopt laws that may be trade restricting, but that have as their objective influencing other countries' processes and production methods (PPMs), such as their fishermen's use of nets. While the issue is still controversial, the WTO has moved clearly in the direction of answering this question in the affirmative, that is, asserting in panel decisions countries' ability to adopt such laws. The only "catch" is that the measures cannot be unnecessarily unilateral or discriminatory. The environmentalist community has almost entirely failed to notice this major favorable development, because of confusion over the latter qualification. But not only is the qualification what a reasonable person would want, it is secondary to the primary issue of countries' rights under the trading system to implement such laws. By ignoring their victory on the main issue, environmentalists risk losing the opportunity to consolidate it. Some players, particularly poor countries, would love to deny the precedent set in these panel decisions and to return to a system where other countries cannot restrict trade in pursuit of PPMs.

Third, countries can learn from others' experiences. There has recently accumulated *statistical evidence* on how globalization and growth tend to affect environmental objectives on average, even without multilateral institutions. Looking for patterns in the data across countries in recent decades can help us answer some important questions. Increased international trade turns out to have been beneficial for some environmental measures, such as SO_2 pollution. There is little evidence to support the contrary fear that international competition in practice works to lower environmental standards overall. Rather, globalization can aid the process whereby economic growth enables people to demand higher environmental quality. To be sure, effective government regulation is probably required if this demand is ever to be translated into actual improvement; the environment cannot take care of itself. But the statistical evidence says that high-income countries do indeed eventually tend to use some of their wealth to clean up the environment, on average, for measures such as SO_2 pollution. For the increasingly important category of global environmental externalities, however, such as emission of greenhouse gases, regulation at the national level is not enough.

These three new reasons to think that globalization can be beneficial for the environment—consumer power, multilateralism, and cross-country statistical evidence—are very different in nature. But in each case what is striking is how little the facts correspond to the suspicions of critics that turning back the clock on globalization would somehow allow them to achieve environmental goals. The rise in globalization, with the attempts at international environmental accord and quasi-judicial oversight, is less a threat to the environment than an ally. It is unfettered national sovereignty that poses the larger threat.

This chapter will try to lay out the key conceptual points concerning the relationship of economic globalization and the environment and to summarize the available empirical evidence, with an emphasis on what is new. We begin by clarifying some basic issues, such as defining objectives, before going on to consider the impact of globalization.

Objectives

It is important to begin a consideration of these issues by making clear that both economic income and environmental quality are worthy objectives. Individuals may disagree on the weight that should be placed on one objective or another. But we should not let such disagreements lead to deadlocked political outcomes in which the economy and the environment are both worse off than necessary. Can globalization be made to improve the environment that comes with a given level of income in market-measured terms? Many seem to believe that globalization necessarily makes things worse. If Mexico grows rapidly, is an increase in pollution inevitable? Is it likely, on average? If that growth arises from globalization, rather than from domestic sources, does that make environmental damage more likely? Less likely? Are there policies that can simultaneously promote *both* economic growth and an improved environment? These are the questions of interest.

Two Objectives: GDP and the Environment

An extreme version of environmental activism would argue that we should turn back the clock on industrialization—that it is worth deliberately impoverishing ourselves—if that is what it takes to save the environment. If the human species still consisted of a few million hunter-gatherers, human-made pollution would be close to zero. Thomas Malthus, writing in the early 19th century, predicted that geometric growth in population and in the economy would eventually and inevitably run into the natural resource limits of the carrying capacity of the planet.[3] In the 1960s, the Club of Rome picked up where Malthus had left off, warning that environmental disaster was coming soon. Some adherents to this school might favor the deliberate reversal of industrialization—reducing market-measured income below current levels in order to save the environment.[4]

But environmental concerns have become more mainstream since the 1960s. We have all had time to think about it. Most people believe that both a clean environment and economic growth are desirable, that we can have a combination of both, and it is a matter of finding the best tradeoff. Indeed, that is one possible interpretation of the popular phrase "sustainable development."

To evaluate the costs and benefits of globalization with regard to the environment, it is important to be precise conceptually, for example to make the distinction between effects on the environment that come *via* rapid economic growth and those that come *for a given level* of economic output.

We have a single concept, GDP, that attempts to measure the aggregate value of goods and services that are sold in the marketplace and that does a relatively good job of it. Measurement of environmental quality is much less well advanced. There are many different aspects of the environment that we care about, and it is hard to know how to combine them into a single overall measure. It would be harder still to agree on how to combine such a measure with GDP to get a measure of overall welfare. Proponents of so-called green GDP accounting have tried to do exactly that, but so far the enterprise is very incomplete. For the time being, the best we can do is look at a variety of separate measures capturing various aspects of the environment.

A Classification of Environmental Objectives

For the purpose of this chapter, it is useful to array different aspects of the environment according to the extent to which damage is localized around specific sources, as opposed to spilling out over a geographically more extensive area.

The first category of environmental damage is pollution that is *internal* to the household or firm. Perhaps 80 percent (by population) of world exposure to particulates is indoor pollution in poor countries—smoke from indoor cooking fires—which need not involve any externality.[5] There may be a role for dissemination of information regarding long-term health impacts that are not immediately evident. Nevertheless, what households

---

[3]Malthus was an economist. A contemporary commentator reacted by calling economics the dismal science. This description has stuck, long after ecology or environmental science broke off as independent fields of study, fields that in fact make economists look like sunny optimists by comparison.

[4]Meadows et al. (1972), and Daly (1993). For a general survey of the issues, see Esty (2001).

[5]Chaudhuri and Pfaff (2002) cite Smith (1993, p. 551).

in such countries are primarily lacking is the economic resources to afford stoves that run on cleaner fuels.[6] In the case of internal pollution, higher incomes directly allow the solution of the problem.

Some other categories of environmental damage pose potential externalities, but could be internalized by assigning property rights. If a company has clear title to a depletable natural resource such as an oil well, it has some incentive to keep some of the oil for the future, rather than pumping it all today.[7] The biggest problems arise when the legal system fails to enforce clear divisions of property rights. Tropical forest land that anyone can enter to chop down trees will be rapidly over-logged. Many poor countries lack the institutional and economic resources to enforce laws protecting such resources. Often corrupt arms of the government themselves collude in the plundering. Another example is the dumping of waste. If someone agreed to be paid to let his land be used as a waste disposal site, voluntarily and without hidden adverse effects, economics says that there would not necessarily be anything wrong with the arrangement. Waste has to go somewhere. But the situation would be different if the government of a poor undemocratic country were to agree to be paid to accept waste that then hurt the environment and health of residents who lacked the information or political clout to participate in the policy decision or to share in the benefits.

A second category, *national externalities,* includes most kinds of air pollution and water pollution, the latter a particularly great health hazard in the third world. The pollution is external to the individual firm or household, and often external to the state or province as well, but most of the damage is felt within the country in question. Intervention by the government is necessary to control such pollution. There is no reason why each national government cannot undertake the necessary regulation on its own, though the adequacy of economic resources to pay the costs of the regulation is again an issue.

A third category is *international externalities.* Increasingly, as we will see, environmental problems cross national boundaries. Acid rain is an example. In these cases, some cooperation among countries is necessary. The strongest examples are purely *global externalities:* chemicals that deplete the stratospheric ozone layer, greenhouse gases that lead to global climate change, and habitat destruction that impairs biological diversity. Individual countries should not expect to be able to do much about global externalities on their own. These distinctions will turn out to be important.

---

[6]Some health risks in industrial production are analogous. Workers in every country voluntarily accept dangerous jobs, e.g., in mining, because they pay better than other jobs that are available to someone with the same set of skills.

[7]Even when property rights are not in doubt and there is no externality, a common environmental concern is that the welfare of future generations does not receive enough weight, because they are not here to represent themselves. From the economists' viewpoint, the question is whether the interest rate that enters firms' decisions incorporates the correct *discount rate.* This topic is beyond the scope of this chapter, but Goulder and Stavins (2002) provide a concise survey.

The Relationship between Economic Production and the Environment

Scholars often catalog three intermediating variables or channels of influence that can determine the aggregate economic impacts of trade or growth on the environment.

- First is the *scale* of economic activity: For physical reasons, more out put means more pollution, other things equal. But other things are usually not equal.

- Second is the *composition* of economic activity: Trade and growth can shift the composition of output, for example, among the agricultural, manufacturing, and service sectors. Because environmental damage per unit of output varies across these sectors, the aggregate can shift.

- Third are the *techniques* of economic activity: Often the same commodity can be produced through a variety of different techniques, some cleaner than others. Electric power, for example, can be generated by a very wide range of fuels and techniques.[8] To the extent trade or growth involves the adoption of cleaner techniques, pollution per unit of GDP will fall.

The positive effects of international trade and investment on GDP have been fairly well established by researchers, both theoretically and empirically. The relationship between GDP and the environment is not quite as well understood and is certainly less of a constant relationship. The relationship is rarely monotonic: Sometimes a country's growth is first bad for the environment and later good. The reason is the three conflicting forces that were just noted. On the one hand, when GDP increases, the greater scale of production leads directly to more pollution and other environmental degradation. On the other hand, there tend to be favorable shifts in the composition of output and in the techniques of production. The question is whether the latter two effects can outweigh the first.

The Environmental Kuznets Curve

A look at data across countries or across time allows some rough generalization as to the usual outcome of these conflicting effects. For some important environmental measures, a U-shaped relationship appears: At

---

[8]The most important alternatives are

- coal-fired plants (the dirtiest fuel, though there is a little scope for mitigating the damage, through low-sulphur coal, scrubbers, and perhaps someday new carbon-sequestration technologies);

- petroleum products (not quite as dirty);

- solar (very clean, but much more expensive); and

- hydro and nuclear (very clean with respect to pollution, but controversial on other environmental grounds).

relatively low levels of income per capita, growth leads to greater environmental damage, until it levels off at an intermediate level of income, after which further growth leads to improvements in the environment. This empirical relationship is known as the environmental Kuznets curve. The label is by analogy with the original Kuznets curve, which was a U-shaped relationship between average income and inequality. The World Bank (1992) and Grossman and Krueger (1993, 1995) brought to public attention this statistical finding for a cross section of countries.[9] Grossman and Krueger (1995) estimated that SO_2 pollution peaked when a country's income was about \$5,000–\$6,000 per capita (in 1985 dollars). Most developing countries have not yet reached this threshold.

For countries where a long enough time series of data is available, there is also some evidence that the same U-shaped relationship can hold across time. The air in London was far more polluted in the 1950s than it is today. (The infamous "pea soup" fogs were from pollution.) The same pattern has held in Tokyo, Los Angeles, and other cities. A similar pattern holds typically with respect to deforestation in rich countries: The percentage of US land that was forested fell in the 18th century and first half of the 19th century but rose in the 20th century.[10]

The idea behind the environmental Kuznets curve is that growth is bad for air and water pollution at the initial stages of industrialization, but later on reduces pollution, as countries become rich enough to pay to clean up their environments. The dominant theoretical explanation is that production technology makes some pollution inevitable, but that demand for environmental quality rises with income. The standard rationale is thus that, at higher levels of income per capita, growth raises the public's demand for environmental quality, which can translate into environmental regulation. Environmental regulation, if effective, then translates into a cleaner environment. It operates largely through the techniques channel, encouraging or requiring the use of cleaner production techniques for given products, although regulation might also have a composition effect: raising the

---

[9]Grossman and Krueger (1993, 1995) found the Kuznets curve pattern for urban air pollution (SO_2 and smoke) and several measures of water pollution. Selden and Song (1994) found the pattern for SO_2, suspended particulate matter (PM), NO_x, and carbon monoxide. Shafik (1994) found evidence of the U shape for deforestation, suspended PM, and SO_2, but not for water pollution and some other measures. Among more recent studies, Hilton and Levinson (1998) found the U-shaped relationship for automotive lead emissions and Bradford, Schlieckert and Shore (2000) found some evidence of the environmental Kuznets curve for arsenic, COD, dissolved oxygen, lead, and SO_2, while obtaining more negative results in the cases of PM and some other measures of pollution. Bimonte (2001) found the relationship for the percentage of land that is protected area, within national territory. Harbaugh, Levinson, and Wilson (2000) pointed out that the relationship is very sensitive with respect, for example, to functional form and updating of the data set. The evidence is generally against the proposition that the curve turns down in the case of CO_2 (e.g., Holtz-Eakin and Selden, 1995), as is discussed later.

[10]Cropper and Griffiths (1994) find little evidence across countries of an EKC for forest growth. But Foster and Rosenzweig (2003) find supportive evidence in the time series for India.

price of polluting goods and services relative to clean ones and thus encouraging consumers to buy more of the latter.[11]

It would be inaccurate to portray the environmental Kuznets curve as demonstrating—or even claiming—that if countries promote growth, the environment will eventually take care of itself. Only if pollution is largely confined within the home or within the firm does that Panglossian view necessarily apply.[12] Most pollution, such as SO_2, NO_x, etc., is external to the home or firm. For such externalities, higher income and a popular desire to clean up the environment are not enough. There must also be effective government regulation, which usually requires a democratic system to translate the popular will into action (something that was missing in the Soviet Union, for example), as well as the rule of law and reasonably intelligent mechanisms of regulation. The empirical evidence confirms that the participation of well-functioning democratic governments is an important part of the process. That is at the national level. The requirements for dealing with cross-border externalities are greater still.

Another possible explanation for the pattern of the environmental Kuznets curve is that it works naturally via the composition of output. In theory, the pattern could result from the usual stages of economic development: the transition from an agrarian economy to manufacturing, and then from manufacturing to services. Services tend to generate less pollution than heavy manufacturing.[13] This explanation is less likely than the conventional view to require the mechanism of effective government regulation. If the Kuznets curve in practice resulted solely from this composition effect, however, then high incomes should lead to a better environment even when externalities arise at the international level, which is not the case. No Kuznets curve has yet appeared for carbon dioxide, for example. Even though emissions per unit of GDP do tend to fall, this is not enough to reduce overall emissions, in the absence of a multilateral effort.

Regulation

It will help if we clarify one more fundamental set of issues before we turn to the main subject, the role of globalization per se.

It is logical to expect environmental regulation to cost something, to have a negative effect on measured productivity and income per capita.

---

[11]Theoretical derivations of the environmental Kuznets curve include Andreoni and Levinson (2001), Jaeger and Kolpin (2000), Selden and Song (1995), and Stokey (1998), among others.

[12]Chaudhuri and Pfaff (2002) find a U-shaped relationship between income and the generation of indoor smoke, across households. In the poorest households, rising incomes mean more cooking and more indoor pollution. Still-higher incomes allow a switch to cleaner fuels. Individual families make the switch on their own, as they gain the wherewithal to do so. Government intervention is not required.

[13]Arrow et al. (1995), Panayotou (1993).

"There is no free lunch," Milton Friedman famously said. Most tangible good things in life cost something, and for many kinds of regulation, if effective, people will readily agree that the cost is worth paying. Cost-benefit tests and cost-minimization strategies are economists' tools for trying to make sure that policies deliver the best environment for a given economic cost or the lowest economic cost for a given environmental goal. Taxes on energy, for example, particularly on hydrocarbon fuels, are quite an efficient mode of environmental regulation (if the revenue is "recycled" efficiently). Fuel efficiency standards are somewhat less efficient. (Differentiated CAFE standards for vehicles, for example, probably encouraged the birth of the SUV craze.) And crude "command and control" methods are less efficient still. (Government mandates regarding what specific technologies firms must use, for example, deny firms the flexibility to find better ways to achieve a given goal.) Some environmental regulations, when legislated or implemented poorly, can impose very large and unnecessary economic costs on firms, and workers, and consumers.

Occasionally policy measures have both environmental and economic benefits. Usually these "win-win" ideas constitute the elimination of some previously existing distortion in public policy. Many countries have historically subsidized the use of coal. The United States subsidizes mining and cattle grazing on federal land, and sometimes logging and oil drilling as well, not to mention water use. Other countries have substantial subsidies for ocean fishing. Elimination of such subsidies would improve the environment and save money at the same time—not just for the federal budget, but for people's real income in the aggregate as well. Admittedly the economists' approach—taxing gasoline or making ranchers pay for grazing rights—is often extremely unpopular politically.

Another idea that would have economic and environmental benefits simultaneously would be to remove all barriers against international trade in environmental equipment and services, such as those involved in renewable energy generation, smokestack scrubbing, or waste treatment facilities. There would again be a double payoff: the growth-enhancing effect of elimination barriers to exports (in a sector where the United States is likely to be able to develop a comparative advantage), together with the environment-enhancing effect of facilitating imports of the inputs that go into environmental protection. A precedent is the removal of barriers to the imports of fuel-efficient cars from Japan, which was a clear case of simultaneously promoting free trade and clean air.

A different school of thought claims that opportunities for saving money while simultaneously saving the environment are common rather than rare. The *Porter hypothesis* holds that a tightening of environmental regulation stimulates technological innovation and thereby has positive effects on both the economy and the environment—for example, saving money by saving energy.[14] The analytical rationale for this view is not

---

[14]Porter and van der Linde (1995).

always made clear. (Is the claim that a change in regulation, regardless in what direction, stimulates innovation, or is there something special about environmental regulation? Is there something special about the energy sector?) Its proponents cite a number of real-world examples where a new environmental initiative turned out to be profitable for a given firm or industry. Such cases surely exist, but there is little reason to think that a link between regulation and productivity growth holds as a matter of generality. The hypothesis is perhaps better understood as making a point regarding "first mover advantage." That is, if the world is in the future to be moving in a particular direction, such as toward more environmentally friendly energy sources, then a country that innovates new products and new technologies of this sort before others do will be in a position to sell the fruits to the latecomers.

Effects of Openness to Trade

The central topic of this chapter is the implications of trade for the environment. Some effects come via economic growth, and some come even for a given level of income. In both cases, the effects can be either beneficial or detrimental. Probably the strongest effects of trade are the first sort, via income. Much like saving and investment, technological progress, and other sources of growth, trade tends to raise income. As we have seen, higher income in turn has an effect on some environmental measures that is initially adverse but, according to the environmental Kuznets curve, eventually turns favorable.

What about effects of trade that do not operate via economic growth? They can be classified in three categories: systemwide effects that are adverse, systemwide effects that are beneficial, and effects that vary across countries depending on local "comparative advantage."

Race to the Bottom

The *"race to the bottom"* hypothesis is perhaps the strongest basis for fearing that international trade and investment specifically (rather than industrialization generally) will put downward pressure on countries' environmental standards and thus damage the environment across the global system. Leaders of industry, and of the unions whose members are employed in industry, are always concerned about competition from abroad. When domestic regulation raises their costs, they fear that they will lose competitiveness against firms in other countries. They warn of a loss of sales, employment, and investment to foreign competitors.[15] Thus domestic pro-

---

[15]Levinson and Taylor (2001) find that those U.S. industries experiencing the largest rise in environmental control costs have indeed also experienced the largest increases in net imports.

ducers often sound the competitiveness alarm as a way of applying political pressure on their governments to minimize the burden of regulation.[16]

To some, the phrase "race to the bottom" connotes that the equilibrium will be a world of little or no regulation. Others emphasize that, in practice, it is not necessarily a matter of globalization leading to environmental standards that actually decline over time, but rather retarding the gradual raising of environmental standards that would otherwise occur. Either way, the concern is that, to the extent that countries are open to international trade and investment, environmental standards will be lower than they would otherwise be. But how important is this in practice? Some economists' research suggests that environmental regulation is not one of the more important determinants of firms' ability to compete internationally. When deciding where to locate, multinational firms seem to pay more attention to such issues as labor costs and market access than to the stringency of local environmental regulation.[17]

Once again, it is important to distinguish (1) the fear that globalization will lead to a race to the bottom in regulatory standards from (2) fears that the environment will be damaged by the very process of industrialization and economic growth itself. Opening national economies to international trade and investment could play a role in both cases, but the two possible channels are very different. In the first case, the race to the bottom hypothesis, the claim is that openness undermines environmental standards even for a given path of economic growth. This would be a damning conclusion from the standpoint of globalization, because it would imply that by limiting trade and investment in some way, we might be able to attain a better environment for any given level of GDP. In the second case, the implication would be that openness affects the environment only in the way that investment, or education, or productivity growth, or any other source of growth affects the environment, by moving the economy along the environmental Kuznets curve. Trying to restrict trade and investment would be a less attractive strategy in this case, because it would amount to deliberate self-impoverishment.

---

[16]What is competitiveness? Economists tend to argue that concerns regarding international competitiveness, if interpreted as fears of trade deficits, are misplaced, which would seem to imply they should not affect rational policy-making. (Or else, to the extent competitiveness concerns can be interpreted as downward pressure on regulation commensurate with cost considerations, economists figure that they may be appropriate and efficient.) But Esty and Gerardin (1998, pp. 17–21) point out that competitiveness fears, under actual political economy conditions, may inhibit environmental regulation even if they are not fully rational. Ederington and Minier (2002) find econometrically that countries do indeed use environmental regulation to reduce trade flows—that they tend to adopt less stringent environmental regulations for their import-competing industries than for others.

[17]Jaffe, Peterson, Portney and Stavins (1995), Grossman and Krueger (1993), Low and Yeats (1992), and Tobey (1990). Other empirical researchers, however, have found more of an effect of environmental regulation on direct investment decisions: Lee and Roland-Hoist (1997) and Smarzynska and Wei (2001). Theoretical analyses include Copeland and Taylor (1994, 1995, 2001) and Liddle (2001).

Gains from Trade

While the possibility that exposure to international competition might have an adverse effect on environmental regulation is familiar, less widely recognized and more surprising is the possibility of effects in the beneficial direction, which we will call the "gains from trade hypothesis." Trade allows countries to attain more of what they want, which includes environmental goods in addition to market-measured output.

How could openness have a positive effect on environmental quality, once we set aside the possibility of accelerating progress down the beneficial slope of the environmental Kuznets curve? A first possibility concerns technological and managerial innovation. Openness encourages ongoing innovation.[18] It then seems possible that openness could encourage innovation beneficial to environmental improvement well as economic progress. A second possibility is an international ratcheting up of environmental standards.[19] The largest political jurisdiction can set the pace for others. Within the United States, it is called the "California effect": When the largest state sets high standards for auto pollution control equipment, for example, the result may be similar standards in other states as well. The United States can play the same role globally.

Multinational corporations (MNCs) are often the vehicle for these effects. They tend to bring clean state-of-the-art production techniques from high-standard countries of origin, to host countries where they are not yet known, for several reasons:

> First, many companies find that the efficiency of having a single set of management practices, pollution control technologies, and training programmes geared to a common set of standards outweighs any cost advantage that might be obtained by scaling back on environmental investments at overseas facilities. Second, multinational enterprises often operate on a large scale, and recognise that their visibility makes them especially attractive targets for local enforcement officials . . . Third, the prospect of liability for failing to meet standards often motivates better environmental performance . . . (Esty and Gentry 1997, p. 161)

The claim is not that all multinational corporations apply the highest environmental standards when operating in other countries. Rather the claim is that the standards tend on average to be higher than if the host country were undertaking the same activity on its own.[20]

Corporate codes of conduct, as under the U.N. Global Compact promoted by Kofi Annan, offer a new way that residents of some countries can

---

[18]Trade speeds the absorption of frontier technologies and best-practice management. This explains why countries that trade more appear to experience a sustained increase in growth rather than just the one-time increase in the level of real income predicted by classical trade theory.

[19]E.g., Vogel (1995), Braithwaite and Drahos (2000), Porter (1990, 1991) and Porter and van der Linde (1995). This ratcheting up may be more effective for product standards than for standards regarding processes and production methods.

[20]Esty and Gentry (1997, pp. 157, 161, 163) and Schmidheiny (1992).

pursue environmental goals in other countries.[21] Formal international cooperation among governments is another way that interdependence can lead to higher environmental standards rather than lower.[22]

Furthermore, because trade offers consumers the opportunity to consume goods of greater variety, it allows countries to attain higher levels of welfare (for any given level of domestically produced output), which, as before, will raise the demand for environmental quality. Again, if the appropriate institutions are in place, this demand for higher environmental quality will translate into effective regulation and the desired reduction in pollution.

Attempts to Evaluate the Overall Effects of Trade on the Environment

If a set of countries opens up to trade, is it on average likely to have a positive or negative effect on the environment (for a given level of income)? Which tend in practice to dominate, the unfavorable "race to the bottom" effects or the favorable "gains from trade" effects? Econometrics can help answer the question.

Statistically, some measures of environmental quality are positively correlated with the level of trade. Figure 1 shows a rough inverse correlation between countries' openness to trade and their levels of SO_2 pollution. But the causality is complex, running in many directions simultaneously. One would not want to claim that trade leads to a cleaner environment, if in reality they are both responding to some other third factor, such as economic growth or democracy.[23]

Eiras and Schaeffer (2001, p. 4) find: "In countries with an open economy, the average environmental sustainability score is more than 30 percent higher than the scores of countries with moderately open economies, and almost twice as high as those of countries with closed economies." Does this mean that trade is good for the environment? Not necessarily. It might be a result of the Porter hypothesis—environmental regulation stimulates productivity—together with the positive effect of income on trade. Or it might be because democracy leads to higher levels of environmental regulation, and democracy is causally intertwined with income and trade. As noted, democracy raises the demand for environmental regulation. Figure 1 suggests that the relationship between SO_2 concentrations and openness remains clear even if one controls for the beneficial effect of democracy. But there remain other possible third factors.

A number of studies have sought to isolate the independent effect of openness. Lucas et al. (1992) studied the toxic intensity implied by the composition of manufacturing output in a sample of 80 countries and found

---

[21]Ruggie (2002).

[22]Neumayer (2002). Multilateral environmental agreements (MEAs) are discussed in a subsequent section.

[23]Barrett and Graddy (2000) is one of several studies to find that an increase in civil and political freedoms significantly reduces some measures of pollution.

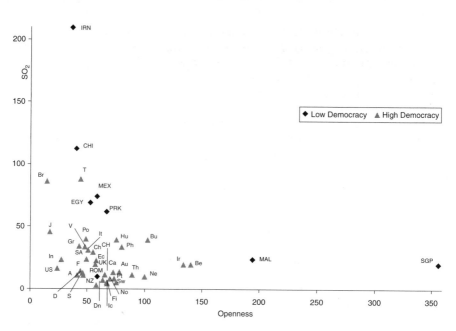

Figure 1 Openness vs SO₂ Concentrations, in Low- vs High-Democracy Regimes, 1990

that a high degree of trade-distorting policies increases pollution in rapidly growing countries. Harbaugh, Levinson, and Wilson (2000) report in passing a beneficial effect of trade on the environment, after controlling for income. Dean (2002) found a detrimental direct effect of liberalization for a given level of income, via the terms of trade, though this is outweighed by a beneficial indirect effect via income. Antweiler, Copeland, and Taylor (2001) and Copeland and Taylor (2001, 2003a) represent an extensive body of empirical research explicitly focused on the effects of trade on the environment. They conclude that trade liberalization that raises the scale of economic activity by 1 percent works to raise SO₂ concentrations by ¼ to ½ percent via the scale channel, but that the accompanying technique channel reduces concentrations by 1¼ to 1½, so that the overall effect is beneficial.

None of these studies makes allowances for the problem that trade may be the *result* of other factors rather than the cause. Antweiler et al. point out this potential weakness.[24] Frankel and Rose (2003) attempt to disentangle the various causal relationships. The study focuses on exogenous variation in trade across countries attributable to factors such as geographical location. It finds effects on several measures of air pollution

---

[24]A few authors have sought to address some aspects of the problem of endogeneity. Levinson (1999) shows that controlling for endogeneity of environmental regulation can change results, in his study of hazardous waste trade. Dean (2002) treats income as endogenous in her study of the effect of trade liberalization on water pollution across Chinese provinces. But the existing research does not directly address the problem that trade may be simultaneously determined with income and environmental outcomes.

(particularly SO_2 and NO_x concentrations), for a given level of income, that are more good than bad. This suggests that the "gains from trade" effects may be at least as powerful as the "race to the bottom" effect. The findings are not as optimistic for other measures of environmental quality, however, particularly emissions of CO_2.

Differential Effects Arising from Comparative Advantage

So far we have considered only effects that could be expected to hold for the average country, to the extent that it is open to international trade and investment. What if the environment improves in some open countries and worsens in others? An oft-expressed concern is that, to the extent that countries are open to international trade and investment, some will specialize in producing dirty products and export them to other countries. Such countries could be said to exploit a comparative advantage in pollution. The prediction is that the environment will be damaged in this set of countries, as compared to what would happen without trade. The environment will be *cleaner* in the second set of countries, those that specialize in clean production and instead import the dirty products from the other countries. Leaving aside the possibility of a race to the bottom effect, the worldwide environment on average might even benefit somewhat, just as aggregate output should benefit, because of the gains from trade. But not everyone would approve of such a bargain.

What determines whether a given country is expected to be in the set of economies specializing in clean or dirty environmental production? There are several possible determinants of comparative advantage.

Endowments and comparative advantage. First, trade patterns could be determined by endowments of capital and labor, as in the standard neoclassical theory of trade, attributed to Heckscher, Ohlin, and Samuelson. Assume manufacturing is more polluting than alternative economic activities, such as services. (If the alternative sector, say agriculture, is instead just as polluting as manufacturing, then trade has no overall implications for the environment.) Since manufacturing is capital intensive, the country with the high capital/labor ratio—say Japan—will specialize in the dirty manufactured goods, while countries with low capital/labor ratios—say China—will specialize in cleaner goods.

For example, Grossman and Krueger predicted that NAFTA might reduce overall pollution in Mexico and raise it in the United States and Canada, because of the composition effect: Mexico has a comparative advantage in agriculture and labor-intensive manufacturing, which are relatively cleaner, versus the northern comparative advantage in more capital intensive sectors. This composition effect runs in the opposite direction from the usual worry, that trade would turn Mexico into a pollution haven as a result of high demand for environmental quality in the United States. That theory is discussed in the next section, below.

Second, comparative advantage could be determined by endowments of natural resources. A country with abundant hardwood forests will tend to export them if given the opportunity to do so. Here there cannot be much doubt that trade is indeed likely to damage the environment of such countries. True, in theory, if clear property rights can be allocated and enforced, someone will have the proper incentive to conserve these natural resources for the future. In practice, it seldom works this way. Poor miners and farmers cannot be kept out of large tracts of primitive forest. And even if there were clear property rights over the natural resources, private firms would not have the correct incentives to constrain external side effects of logging and mining, such as air and water pollution, soil erosion, loss of species, and so on. Government regulation is called for, but is often stymied by the problems of inadequate resources, at best, and corruption, at worst.

Pollution havens. Third, comparative advantage could be deliberately created by differences in environmental regulation itself. This is the pollution haven hypothesis. The motivation for varying levels of regulation could be differences in demand for environmental quality, arising, for example, from differences in income per capita. Or the motivation could be differences in the supply of environmental quality, arising, for example, from differences in population density.

Many object to an "eco dumping" system according to which economic integration results in some countries exporting pollution to others, even if the overall global level of pollution does not rise.[25] They find distasteful the idea that the impersonal market system would deliberately allocate environmental damage to an "underdeveloped" country. A chief economist of the World Bank once signed his name to an internal memo with economists' language that read (in the summary sentence of its most inflammatory passage) "Just between you and me, shouldn't the World Bank be encouraging *more* migration of the dirty industries to the LDCs?" After the memo was leaked, public perceptions of the young Larry Summers were damaged for years.

There is a little empirical evidence, but not much, to support the hypothesis that countries that have a particularly high demand for environmental quality—the rich countries—currently specialize in products that can be produced cleanly and let the poor countries produce and sell the products that require pollution.[26] For the specific case of SO_2, the evidence appears to be, if anything, that trade leads to a reallocation of pollution from the poor country to the rich country, rather than the other way

---

[25]The desire to "harmonize" environmental regulation across countries, and the arguments against it, are analyzed by Bhagwati and Srinivasan (1996).

[26]Suri and Chapman (1998) find that middle-income countries' growth only leads to lower domestic pollution if they increase imports of manufactures. Muradian, O'Connor, and Martinez-Alier (2001) find evidence that the imports of rich countries embody more air pollution than their exports. Ederington, Levinson and Minier (2003) find that pollution abatement costs are relevant for only a small sub-set of trade: imports from developing countries in sectors that are especially mobile geographically.

around.[27] This is consistent with the finding of Antweiler, Copeland, and Taylor (2001) that trade has a significantly less favorable effect on SO_2 emissions in rich countries than in poor countries. Their explanation is that rich countries have higher capital/labor ratios, capital-intensive industries are more polluting, and this factor-based pollution-haven effect dominates the income-based pollution-haven effect.

Does Most U.S. Trade and FDI Take Place with Low-Standard Countries?

To listen to some American discussion of globalization, one would think that the typical partner in U.S. trade and investment is a poor country with low environmental or labor standards. If so, it would help explain the fear that opening to international trade and investment in general puts downward pressure on U.S. standards. In fact, less than half of U.S. trade and investment takes place with partners who have lower wages and lower incomes than we do. Our most important partners have long been Canada, Japan, and the European Union (though Mexico has now become important as well). These trading partners sometimes regard *the United States* as the low-standard country.

Does Economic Globalization Conflict with Environmental Regulation?

There is a popular sense that globalization is a powerful force undermining environmental regulation. This can be the case in some circumstances. The "race to the bottom" phenomenon can potentially put downward pressure on the regulatory standards of countries that complete internationally in trade and investment. But, as an argument against globalization, it leaves much out.

First is the point that, for most of us, environmental quality is one goal, but not the only goal. As already noted, we care also about income, and trade is one means of promoting economic growth. The goals often need to be balanced against each other.

Environmental concerns can be an excuse for protectionism. If policymakers give in to protectionist arguments and erect trade barriers, we will enjoy less growth in trade and income. We will not even necessarily end up with a better environment. Import-competing corporations (or their workers), in sectors that may themselves not be particularly friendly to the environment, sometimes seek to erect or retain barriers to imports in the name of environmental protection, when in reality it is their own pocketbooks

---

[27]Frankel and Rose (2003). We do not find significant evidence of other pollution-haven effects, based on population density or factor endowments, or for other pollutants.

they are trying to protect. In other words, environmentalism is an excuse for protectionism.

Often, the problem is less sinister, but more complex. To see how the political economy works, let us begin with the point that most policy debates are settled as the outcome of a complicated mix of multiple countervailing arguments and domestic interest groups on both sides. Most of the major viewpoints are in some way represented "at the table" in the federal government decision-making process. In the case of environmental measures, there are often adversely affected industry groups sitting across the table from the environmentalists, and they have an effect on the final political outcome. But when the commodity in question happens to be produced by firms in foreign countries, then that point of view largely disappears from the table around which the decision is made. If the issue is big enough, the State Department may weigh in to explain the potential costs facing foreign countries. But, understandably, the foreigners receive less weight in the policy process than would the identical firms if they were American. The result is that the environmental policies that are adopted on average can discriminate against foreign firms relative to domestic firms, without anyone ever deliberately having supported a measure out of protectionist intent.

One possible example is the strong opposition in Europe to genetically modified organisms (GMOs). A Biosafety Agreement was negotiated in Montreal, January 29, 2000, in which the United States felt it had to agree to label grain shipments that might in part be bio-engineered and to allow countries to block imports of GMOs.[28] In some ways, these negotiations might serve as a useful model for compromise in other areas.[29] But why have Europeans decided so definitively that they want to keep out genetically modified varieties of corn, despite the emergence of little or no scientific evidence against them as of yet, where American consumers are far less agitated? Is it because Europeans are predisposed to have higher standards for environmental issues? Perhaps.[30] An important part of the explanation, however, is that Monsanto and other U.S. technology companies and U.S. farmers are the ones who developed the technology and produce the stuff, not European companies or European farmers. Thus it is American producers, not Europeans, who stand to lose from the European squeamishness. European agriculture need not consciously launch a cam-

---

[28]*The Economist*, February 5, 2000. So far, the United States has been reluctant to bring the GMO case to the WTO, out of a fear that the outcome might be a political failure even if a legal success. As Victor and Runge (2002, 112–113) argue, the Europeans were sufficiently traumatized in the 1990s by a series of scandals in the regulation of their food, such as the UK government's failure to stop "Mad Cow" disease, that an attempt by the United States to use the WTO dispute settlement process to pry the European market open for GMOs would be counterproductive, regardless of the scientific evidence. But the United States may go ahead anyway.

[29]Environmental NGOs were allowed inside the meeting hall, a new precedent. *FT*, February 1, 2000.

[30]But it is interesting that some health issues have gone the other way. The United States has in the past cared more about feared carcinogens than Europeans. The United States requires cheese to be pasteurized, and the EU does not (Vogel, 1995).

paign against GMOs. All that the European movement needed was an absence around the table of producers who would be adversely affected by a ban. But the result is to reduce trade, hurt American producers, and benefit European farmers.

Whatever the source of different perceptions across countries, it is important to have a set of internationally agreed rules to govern trade and if possible a mechanism for settling disputes that arise. That is the role of the WTO. The need for such an institution does not vanish when environmental issues are a part of the dispute. Certainly if one cares at all about trade and growth, then one cannot automatically sign on to each and every campaign seeking to block trade on environmental grounds. But even if one cares solely about the environment, claims need to be evaluated through some sort of neutral process. One can be easily misled; corporations make dubious claims to environmental motivations in, for example, seeking federal support of "clean coal" research or ethanol production. Most of the time, there is no substitute for investigating the details and merits of the case in question. One should not presume that an interest group's claims are right just because that group happens to be of one's own nationality.

The Impossible Trinity of Global Environmental Regulation

The concerns of anti-globalizers can be understood by means of a trilemma of regulation, called the principle of the "impossible trinity of global governance" (see Figure 2). In designing a system of global governance, three kinds of goals are desirable. First, *globalization* is desirable, other things equal, for its economic benefits if nothing else. Second, *regulation* is desirable when it comes to externalities like pollution or other social goals not adequately addressed by the marketplace. Third, national *sovereignty* is desirable, because different countries have different needs or preferences and also because nations take pride in their political independence. The principle of the impossible trinity points out that it is feasible to design a system with any two of these attributes, but not with all three.

The three attributes are represented as the sides of the triangle in the accompanying figure. The lower left corner represents a system of complete laissez faire. The private market is given responsibility for everything. With no government regulation, there is nothing to coordinate internationally, and thus no loss in national sovereignty. If another country wants to make the mistake of heavy-handed intervention, that is its affair. One can imagine Friederich von Hayek, Ayn Rand, or Milton Friedman favoring the laissez faire corner.

The lower right corner represents a system of regulation at the global level. While there are not many "world federalists" around today, a proposal to establish a powerful world environment organization would be a step in this direction.

The top corner represents isolationism. Only if countries cut themselves off from trade, investment, and other international interactions can they

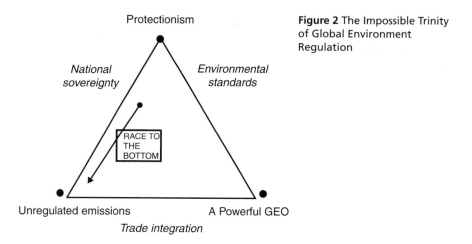

Protectionism

National sovereignty

Environmental standards

RACE TO THE BOTTOM

Unregulated emissions

A Powerful GEO

Trade integration

Figure 2 The Impossible Trinity of Global Environment Regulation

preserve complete national sovereignty, while practicing whatever kind of regulation they wish. Two candidates in the year 2000 U.S. presidential election, Ralph Nader and Pat Buchanan, seemed to want to move in this direction.

The environmental concerns created by globalization can be understood in terms of this diagram. The process of international economic integration is moving the United States and most other countries downward in the graph, toward the bottom side of the triangle. As a result, globalization is creating a growing conflict between the needs of environmental regulation and the demands of national sovereignty, or so goes the theory. National sovereignty has been winning, which means that the movement has been toward the lower left corner. The claim is that globalization has undermined the ability of sovereign governments to impose the level of environmental standards they would like.

Although the impossible trinity can be a useful way to think about the potential for globalization to undercut national environmental regulation, it can be very misleading in some contexts. There are two main reasons for this. First, even for environmental externalities that are largely confined within countries, such as local air pollution, there is little empirical evidence that the "race to the bottom" hypothesis in fact holds, i.e., that international trade and investment in fact put significant downward pressure on environmental regulation in the aggregate. Indeed, international trade and activities of multinational corporations may sometimes put upward pressure on environmental standards. Second, and more importantly, some environmental issues spill over across national borders even in the absence of international trade and investment, making it difficult for individual countries to address them through independent regulation.

Environmental Concerns Cross National Borders

Even those who do not care about trade at all should appreciate the role of international agreements and institutions. The reason is the increasing importance of major sources of environmental damage that cross national borders and that would do so even if there were no such thing as international trade. Some externalities have long spilled over from each country to its neighbors—such as SO_2 pollution, which is responsible for acid rain, or water pollution, which flows downriver. They can be addressed by negotiations between the two countries involved (e.g., United States and Canada). An increasing number of environmental externalities are truly global, however. The best examples are greenhouse gases. A ton of carbon dioxide creates the same global warming potential regardless where in the world it is emitted. Other good examples of direct global externalities are stratospheric ozone depletion, depletion of ocean fish stocks, and threats to biodiversity.

Even localized environmental damage, such as deforestation, is increasingly seen as a valid object of international concern. A distinction is traditional between trade measures that target specific undesirable products, such as asbestos, and those that target *processes and production methods*, such as the use of prison labor in the manufacture of the commodity in question. It is clear that a country concerned about its own health or environment has the right to tax or ban products that it regards as harmful, so long as it does not discriminate against foreign producers. Indeed, such bans are less liable to become a vehicle for surreptitious protectionism than are attempts to pass judgment on other countries' production methods that are unrelated to the physical attributes of the product itself. But is it legitimate for importing countries also to discriminate according to how a given product was produced? Some ask what business is it of others whether the producing country wants to use its own prison labor, or cut down its own forests, or pollute its own environment?[31]

Often an international externality can be easily identified. Forests absorb carbon dioxide (a process called "sequestration," or creating carbon sinks), so logging contributes to global climate change. An endangered species may contain a unique genetic element that someday could be useful to international scientists. Desertification can lead to social instability and political conflict, which can in turn produce problems for international security. Thus environmental damage in one country can have indirect effects on others.

But foreign residents increasingly care about localized environmental damage as well, even when they live far away and even when there is no evident link to their interests. The idea of "non-use value" is that many people place value on keeping, for example, a river canyon unspoiled, even

---

[31]See Charnovitz (2002a) on the history, law, and analysis of PPMs, and for other references. He argues that the public failure to understand environment-friendly developments in the late 1990s within GATT/WTO jurisprudence regarding PPMs is now an obstacle to further progress (e.g., in the WTO Committee on Trade and Environment, pp. 64, 103–104).

if they know they will never see it. While the methodology of estimating the value according to what people say they would pay ("contingent valuation") is fraught with problems, the basic principle of non-use value is now widely accepted. This means that citizens in one country may have a stake in whether another country dams up a gorge, kills its wildlife, or pollutes its air and water.

Reversing Globalization Would Not End the Tension of Regulation vs. Sovereignty

Thus, for an increasingly important set of environmental issues, the idea that individual countries could properly address the issues if left on their own is myth. If countries do not cooperate through multilateral institutions, each will be tempted to free ride on the efforts of others, and little will get done. Globalization and multilateral institutions are not the obstacle—and the appeal of national sovereignty is not an ally—in international efforts to protect the environment. Rather, environmentalists need global agreements and global agencies if they are going to get other countries to do the things they want them to do. It is the appeal of national sovereignty that is the obstacle.

The mistake of blaming all ills on globalization and multilateral institutions such as the WTO has yielded some very strange bedfellows. Environmentally concerned protestors have been treating labor unions and poor countries as comrades in arms, proud of the fact that a disparate set of groups have supposedly been brought together by a shared opposition to globalization. But in fact, some of these groups are on the other side of the environmental issue. U.S. labor unions are strong opponents of the Kyoto Protocol on Global Climate Change. Poor countries tend to be strong opponents of international environmental agreements in general. Both groups cite national sovereignty in support of their positions. It is particularly puzzling that some environmentalists see pro-sovereignty supporters as natural allies, when so many environmental problems can be addressed only by means of multilateral institutions that in fact infringe on national sovereignty.

If labor unions and environmentalists can come together on an issue, that is fine. *But they have to agree on that issue.* They should share something more than an emotional antipathy to some particular multilateral institution: They should want the institution to move in the same direction, not opposite directions. They don't have to get into fine details, if they don't want to. But if, for example, one group thinks that the proper response to globalization is that the multilateral institutions should exercise less invasion of national sovereignty in the pursuit of environmental regulation and the other thinks the institutions should exercise more invasion of national sovereignty in that pursuit, then they are in truth hardly allies.

International Agreements and Institutions

Environmentalists are keen to interject themselves into the WTO. Those who live in the world of international trade negotiations tell those who live in the environmentalist world that their concerns may be valid, but that they should address them outside the WTO, in their own, separate, negotiations and their own multilateral agencies.[32]

Multilateral Environmental Organizations

The one multilateral organization dedicated to environmental issues in general, the United Nations Environmental Program, is universally considered small and weak, even by the standards of UN agencies. Some may favor beefing it up. Most feel that it is not fixable, that—to begin with—it would have to be based somewhere like Geneva in order to be taken seriously, not in Nairobi as now. On these grounds, some have proposed a new, powerful, multilateral world environment organization.[33] Daniel Esty (1994) proposed that it be called the Global Environmental Organization, providing the appropriate acronym GEO. But the source of the problem is not some accident of bureaucratic design history or geography. The problem, rather, is that there is very little support among the world's governments for a powerful multilateral agency in the area of the environment. They fear infringement on their sovereignty.

One can say that in concentrating their fire on the WTO, environmental activists are adopting a strategy of taking the multilateral trading system hostage. They envy the relative success of the WTO system. They are aware that international environmental treaties, even if successfully negotiated and ratified, may be toothless. The agreements made at Rio de Janeiro in 1992 are an example. The activists would ideally like to adopt trade sanctions as a means of enforcement, as does the WTO itself.

Such proposals do not explain attempts to take globalization hostage more broadly, for example by demonstrations at WTO ministerial meetings. There is nothing in the WTO to block multilateral environmental treaties from adopting penalties against relevant trade with non-members. Indeed, the Montreal Protocol on stratospheric ozone depletion has such trade controls, ran into no problems under international trade rules, and is generally considered to have been successful in achieving its goals. Admittedly there is strong resistance to using trade to overcome the free rider problem. Most governments do not favor international environmental agreement that are so aggressive as to include trade sanctions. Again, the failure does not mean that globalization and global institutions like

---

[32]The most prominent and articulate spokesman of the viewpoint opposing linkage between trade and unrelated issues is Jadgish Bhagwati (2000).

[33]Charnovitz (2002b) surveys the proposals. Juma (2000) argues in opposition, on the grounds that decentralized agreements can do the job better.

the WTO are the problem. More likely it is the other way around: Globalization is the ally, and national sovereignty is the obstacle.

Bilateral and Regional RTAs

Regional and bilateral agreements, such as the European Union or the Australia–New Zealand Closer Economic Relationship, have incorporated environmental components more often than have multilateral agreements. Whether because of cultural homogeneity or the small numbers involved, a group consisting of a few neighbors is usually readier to contemplate the sort of "deep integration" required for harmonization of environmental standards than are negotiators in groups with more than 100 diverse members, such as the WTO.

In the public debate over the North American Free Trade Agreement, one of the most prominent concerns of opponents was the pollution that had already accompanied industrialization in northern Mexico, particularly among the maquilladoras along the border, which in turn was a result of the ability to trade with the United States. The final agreement departed from previous U.S. trade agreements, and those in most other parts of the world, by taking into account environmental concerns, at least in a small way. The preamble includes environmentally friendly language, such as a stipulation that the NAFTA goals are to be pursued "in a manner consistent with environmental protection and conservation." Chapter 7B allows the member countries to continue adopting sanitary and phyto-sanitary standards. Chapter 9 allows countries to set whatever environmental standards they want, provided only that they do not discriminate or discourage trade unnecessarily.[34]

Nevertheless, environmental groups were unhappy with the subsequent outcome. Proposed side agreements, for example, to establish a bank to finance environmental cleanup along the border received a lot of attention during Bill Clinton's presidential campaign and during the subsequent NAFTA ratification campaign. Followup after the NAFTA went into effect in 1994, however, was disappointing.

Meanwhile, provisions under Chapter 11, which governs direct investment, have turned out to be important. On the one hand, the text reads "the Parties recognize that it is inappropriate to encourage investment by relaxing domestic health, safety or environmental measures." On the other hand, protection of the rights of investors has confirmed some environmentalists' fears particularly a case brought by a Canadian company called Metalclad under the dispute settlement mechanism. Under a clause that forbids a signatory from taking measures "tantamount to nationalization or expropriation" of firms from other member countries, Metalclad in August 2000 won a judgment from a NAFTA tribunal against local Mexican regulators' attempt to close its hazardous waste disposal plant without compensation.

---

[34]Hufbauer, Esty, Orejas, Rubio, and Schott (2000).

The finding that Mexican regulation had denied a foreign firm fair and equitable treatment was potentially an important precedent under the NAFTA.[35] But it would be strange, even from a pro-business viewpoint, if an American or Canadian firm were extensively protected against regulatory "takings" in Mexico when it would not be in its country of origin.

The NAFTA experience reinforced environmentalists' concerns with trade agreements. They urged the U.S. government to bring environmental issues inside trade negotiations, for example, forbidding parties in trade agreements from relaxing environmental regulation in order to seek competitive advantage. A preferential trading arrangement negotiated by the United States at the end of the Clinton Administration, the Jordan-U.S. free trade agreement, incorporated such environmental provisions directly in the text, rather than as a side agreement, a precedent that was hoped to establish a "template" or precedent for future agreements. In addition, an executive order now requires that the government prepare an "environmental impact statement" whenever negotiating new trade agreements in the future, to guard against possible inadvertent side effects adverse to the environment.[36]

The Failed Multilateral Agreement on Investment

The first time that NGOs using Internet-age methods successfully mobilized to block a major multilateral economic agreement was not in Seattle in 1999, but rather the preceding campaign against the Multilateral Agreement on Investment (MAI). Efforts to agree on rules governing cross-border investment tend to founder as soon as the circle of countries is broadened beyond a small regional grouping. The MAI was an attempt to negotiate such rules among the industrialized countries, at the OECD (Organization for Economic Cooperation and Development). Notwithstanding the weakness of the negotiated text and the seeming obscurity of the issue, environmentalist and other NGOs were energized by claims that the MAI would handcuff countries' regulatory efforts, and the MAI was not ratified.

The WTO and Some Panel Cases

In the postwar period, the vehicle for conducting the multilateral negotiations that succeeded in bringing down trade barriers in many countries was the General Agreement on Tariffs and Trade. An important outcome of the Uruguay Round of negotiations was the replacement of the GATT organization with a real agency, the World Trade Organization, which came into existence in 1995. One reason why the change was important is that the new institution featured a dispute settlement mechanism, whose findings were

---

[35]*Ibid.* pp. 8–14.

[36]The executive order was issued by President Clinton in 1999. But President George W. Bush announced he would continue to abide by it, e.g., in preparing possible free-trade agreements with Singapore, Chile, and the Americas. Martin Crutsinger, AP 4/21/2001 [e.g., *Boston Globe*].

to be binding on the member countries. Previously, a party that did not like the ruling of a GATT panel could reject it.

Why do so many environmentalists apparently feel that the still-young WTO is a hostile power? Allegations concern lack of democratic accountability and negative effects on the environment. It is difficult to see how these allegations could apply to the process of setting WTO rules themselves. Regarding the alleged lack of democracy, the GATT and WTO are in principle one-country one-vote bodies that make decisions by consensus. Clearly in practice, some countries—particularly the United States—matter far more than others. But consider what it would mean to make this process more democratic. It would presumably mean giving less weight to U.S. views and more to the views, for example, of India, the world's most populous democracy. But, given India's preferences and its aversion to "eco-imperialism," this would indisputably mean giving *less* attention in the WTO to environmental goals, not more.

The allegation that the GATT and WTO are hostile to environmental measures could conceivably arise from the core provisions of the GATT, which prohibit a member country from discriminating against the exports of another, in favor of "like products" made either by a third country (that is the Most Favored Nation provision of Article I) or by domestic producers (the national treatment provision of Article III). But Article XX allows for exceptions to the non-discrimination principle for environmental reasons (among others), provided that the measures in question are not "a means of arbitrary or unjustifiable discrimination" or a "disguised restriction on international trade." (Umbrella clauses allow countries to take actions to protect human, animal or plant life or health, and to conserve exhaustible natural resources.).

Under the GATT, there was ambiguity of interpretation as to what was to happen when Article XX conflicted with the non-discrimination article. To clarify the matter, in the preamble of the articles agreed at Marrakech establishing the WTO, language was added specifying that its objectives were not limited to promoting trade but included also optimal use of the world's resources, sustainable development, and environmental protection. Environmental objectives are also recognized specifically in the WTO agreements dealing with product standards, food safety, intellectual property protection, etc.

The protests are in a sense a puzzle. It would be easy to understand a political campaign in favor of the WTO taking a more aggressive pro-environment stance. But how does one explain the common view in the protest movement that the WTO currently is actively harmful to the environment?

When members of the protest movement identify specifics, they usually mention the rulings of WTO panels under the dispute settlement mechanism. The panels are quasi-judicial tribunals, whose job is to rule in disputes whether parties are abiding by the rules that they have already agreed to. Like most judicial proceedings, the panels themselves are not intended to be democratic. The rulings to date do not show a pattern of having been dominated by any particular country or interest group. There have been three or four fairly prominent WTO panel rulings that concern the environment in some way. Most within the environmentalist and NGO community have at some point acquired the belief that these rulings told the United States, or other defendant country, that their attempts to protect the environment must be repealed. The mystery is why this impression is so widespread, because it has little basis in fact.

The four WTO cases that will be briefly reviewed here are Canadian asbestos, Venezuelan reformulated gasoline, U.S. hormone-fed beef, and Asian shrimp and turtles. We will also touch on the Mexican tuna-dolphin case. Each of the cases involves an environmental measure that the producer plaintiff alleged to have trade-distorting effects. The complaints were not based, however, on the allegation that the goal of the measure was not valid or that protectionism was the original motivation of the measure. In most of the cases, the allegation was that discrimination against foreigners was an incidental, and unnecessary, feature of the environmental measure.

Canadian asbestos. One case is considered a clear win for the environmentalists. The WTO appellate body in 2001 upheld a French ban on asbestos products, against a challenge by Canada, which had been exporting to France. This ruling made real the WTO claim that its charter gives priority to health, safety, and environmental requirements, in that for such purposes GATT Article XX explicitly allows exceptions to the Most Favored Nation and national treatment rules.[37]

Venezuelan reformulated gasoline. In the reformulated gasoline case, Venezuela successfully claimed that U.S. law violated national treatment, i.e., discriminated in favor of domestic producers (with regard to whether refineries were allowed to use individual composition baselines when measuring pollution reduction). The case was unusual in that the intent to discriminate had at the time of passage been made explicit by U.S. administration officials seeking to please a domestic interest group. If the WTO had ruled in the U.S. favor, it would have been saying that it was fine for a country to discriminate needlessly and explicitly against foreign producers so long as the law came under an environmental label. Those who oppose this panel decision provide ready-made ammunition for the viewpoint that environmental activism is a false disguise worn by protectionist interests.

The United States was not blocked in implementing its targets, under the Clean Air Act, as commonly charged. Rather, the offending regulation was easily changed so as to be nondiscriminatory and thus to be permissible under the rules agreed by members of the WTO. This case sent precisely the right message to the world's governments, that environmental measures should not and need not discriminate against foreign producers.

---

[37]*New York Times*, July 25, 2000.

Hormone-fed beef. What happens if the commodity in question is produced entirely, or almost entirely, by foreign producers, so that it cannot be conclusively demonstrated whether a ban, or other penalty, is or is not discriminatory? The WTO has attempted to maintain the rule that such measures are fine so long as a scientific study has supported the claimed environmental or health benefits of the measure. In the hormone-fed beef case, the WTO ruled against an EU ban on beef raised with growth hormones because the EU conspicuously failed to produce a science-based risk assessment showing that it might be dangerous. It thus resembles the case of the EU moratorium on GMOs.

These are genuinely difficult cases. On the one hand, where popular beliefs regarding a scientific question vary widely, a useful role for a multilateral institution could be to rule on the scientific merits. Or, at least, a useful role could be, as under the current WTO procedures, to rule on whether the country seeking to impose the regulation has carried out internally a reasonable study of the scientific merits. This logic suggests overruling the EU bans. On the other hand, the world may not be ready for even this mild level of loss of national sovereignty. If a nation's intent is to protect its health or environment, even if the measure has little scientific basis and even if its primary burden would fall on foreign producers, perhaps ensuring that the ban does not unnecessarily discriminate among producing countries is the best that can be done.

Despite the WTO ruling on hormone-fed beef, the Europeans did not cancel the ban. Their strategy, which they justify with the name "precautionary principle," is to continue to study the matter before allowing the product in. The precautionary principle, as the Europeans apply it, says to prohibit new technologies that have not yet been proven safe, even if there is no evidence that they are dangerous.[38] A compromise would be to allow imports of American beef subject to labeling requirements, as in the Montreal agreement on GMOs, thus letting the consumer decide.

Shrimp-turtle. Perceptions regarding the WTO panel ruling on a dispute about shrimp imports and the protection of sea turtles probably vary more widely than on any other case. The perception among many environmentalists is that the panel ruling struck down a U.S. law to protect sea turtles that are caught in the nets of shrimp fishermen in the Indian Ocean. (The provision was pursuant to the U.S. Endangered Species Act.) In reality, the dispute resembled the gasoline case in the respect that the ban on imports

---

[38]Does the precautionary principle derive from risk aversion? Someone should point out that risk aversion in the presence of uncertainty is not necessarily sufficient to justify it. For poor residents of developing countries, the risk may be higher from drought or pests or disease in their crops, or from existing pesticides, than from the new GMOs that are designed to combat them more safely. Does the precautionary principle say that society should persist with what is natural and traditional, even if the current state of scientific evidence suggests a better, artificial, substitute? Then Asian men concerned about maintaining virility should continue to buy powdered rhino horn rather than switching to Viagra. (Gollier, 2001, offers another economist's perspective on the precautionary principle.)

from countries without adequate regulatory regimes in place was unnecessarily selective and restrictive. The WTO panel and appellate body decided that the U.S. application of the law, in a complex variety of ways, was arbitrarily and unjustifiably discriminatory against the four plaintiff countries (Asian shrimp suppliers). The United States had unilaterally and inflexibly banned shrimp imports from countries that did not have in place for all production a specific turtle-protection regime of its own liking, one that mandated Turtle Excluder Devices.[39]

The case could in fact be considered a victory for the environmentalists, in that the WTO panel and the appeals body in 1998 explicitly stated that the United States could pursue the protection of endangered sea turtles against foreign fishermen. The United States subsequently allowed more flexibility in its regulation and made good-faith efforts to negotiate an agreement with the Asian producers, which it could have done in the first place. The WTO panel and appellate body in 2001 found the new U.S. regime to be WTO compliant.[40] The case set a precedent in clarifying support for the principle that the WTO rules allow countries to pass judgment on other countries' processes and production methods, even if it means using trade controls to do so, provided only that the measures are not unnecessarily discriminatory.[41]

Tuna-dolphin. In an earlier attempt to protect another large flippered sea animal, the United States (under the Marine Mammal Protection Act) had banned imports of tuna from countries that allowed the fishermen to use nets that also caught dolphins. Mexico brought a case before the GATT, as this pre-dated the WTO, and the GATT panel ruled against the U.S. law. Its report was never adopted. The parties instead in effect worked out their differences bilaterally, "out of court." The case could be considered a setback for trade-sensitive environmental measures, at least unilateral ones, but a setback that was to prove temporary. That the GATT ruling in the tuna case did not affirm the right of the United States to use trade bans to protect the dolphins shows how much the environmentalist cause has progressed under the WTO, in the subsequent gasoline, shrimp-turtle, and asbestos cases.

---

[39]For example, the Asian suppliers had been given only four months' notice, thus discriminating against them and in favor of Caribbean suppliers. (The U.S. measure has also been pronounced unnecessarily restrictive in another sense: the majority of suppliers in India raise shrimp by aquaculture, where no sea turtles are endangered. Jadgish Bhagwati, *Financial Times*, December 21, 1999.)

[40]Charnovitz (2002a, pp. 98–99).

[41]For a full explanation of the legal issues, see Charnovitz (2002a). Also Michael Weinstein, "Greens and Globalization: Declaring Defeat in the Face of Victory," *New York Times*, April 22, 2001. Charnovitz and Weinstein (2001) argue that the environmentalists fail to realize the progress they have made in recent WTO panel cases and may thereby miss an opportunity to consolidate those gains. It is not only environmentalists who are under the impression that the GATT rules do not allow PPMs. Some developing countries also claim that PPMs violate the GATT. The motive of the first group is to fight the GATT, while the motive of the second group is to fight PPMs.

A system for labeling tuna in the U.S. market as either "dolphin safe" or not was later found consistent with the GATT. The American consumer response turned out to be sufficiently great to accomplish the desired purpose. Since 1990, the major companies have sold only the dolphin-safe kind of tuna. The moral is not just that the goal of protecting the dolphins was accomplished despite globalization in its GATT incarnation. The moral is, rather, that *globalization was instrumental in the protection of the dolphins.* The goal could not have been accomplished without international trade, because American citizens would have had no effective way of putting pressure on Mexico. Leaving the U.S. government free to regulate its own fishermen would not have helped.[42]

Multilateral Environmental Agreements

When it comes to global externalities such as endangered species, stratospheric ozone depletion, and global climate change, it is particularly clear that the problem cannot be addressed by a system where each country pursues environmental measures on its own. Multilateral negotiations, agreements, and institutions are required. Furthermore, the point is not simply that global regulatory measures are necessary in any effort to combat the effects of economic globalization. If countries had industrialized in isolation, without any international trade or investment among them, they would still be emitting greenhouse gases, and we would still need a globally coordinated response.

Multilateral environmental agreements (MEAs), even if they involve trade-restricting measures, are viewed more favorably under the international rules than unilateral environmental measures. Leaving aside the Law of the Sea, the Basel Convention on Hazardous Wastes, and a large number of relatively more minor agreements, three MEAs merit particular mention.

The Convention on International Trade in Endangered Species (CITES) was negotiated in 1973. Although it lacks the teeth that many would like, it was notable as a precedent establishing that MEAs are compatible with the GATT even if they restrict trade. An interesting issue relevant for species protection is whether a plan of using animals to support the economic livelihood of local residents can be a more sustainable form of protection than attempts to leave them untouched altogether.

The Montreal Protocol on Substances that Deplete the Ozone Layer is the most successful example of an MEA, as it has resulted in the phasing out of most use of CFCs (chlorofluorocarbons) and other ozone-depleting

---

[42]Thomas Friedman, *New York Times*, December 8, 1999, p. A31. Presumably, in the absence of the opportunity to export to the United States, Mexican fisherman would not have caught as many tuna for the domestic market alone, which would have limited the dolphin casualties somewhat. It is not known whether the much-reduced number of dolphins still killed under the current system is less than in the hypothetical no-trade case. But working through the channel of voting power represented by U.S. imports was surely a better way to have accomplished the goal. Telling Mexican fisherman they must remain poor and telling American consumers that they couldn't eat tuna would have been a less satisfactory solution to the problem.

chemicals. The success of this agreement is partly attributable to the enforcement role played by trade penalties: the protocol prohibits trade in controlled substances with countries that do not participate. This created the necessary incentive to push those developing countries that otherwise might have been reluctant into joining. If substantial numbers of countries had nevertheless remained outside the protocol, the trade controls would have also accomplished the second objective—minimizing *leakage*, that is, the migration of production of banned substances to non-participating countries.[43] The protocol was helped to succeed in that there were a relatively small number of producers. It also helped that there turned out to be good substitutes for the banned substances, though that was not known until the ban was tried.[44] One might say it also helped bolster the principle that PPM-targeted measures were not necessarily incompatible with the GATT: the agreement threatened non-participants not only with a ban on trade in ozone-depleting chemicals themselves, but also a potential ban on trade in goods manufactured with such chemicals in the sense that governments were required to determine the feasibility of such a ban. But it never went further than that.

The Kyoto Protocol on Global Climate Change, negotiated in 1997, is the most ambitious attempt at a multilateral environment agreement to date. This is not the place to discuss the Kyoto Protocol at length. The task of addressing climate change while satisfying the political constraints of the various factions (particularly, the United States, EU, and developing countries) was an inherently impossible task. Most economists emphasize that the agreement as it was written at Kyoto would impose large economic costs on the United States and other countries, while making only a minor dent in the problem. The Clinton Administration's interpretation of the protocol insisted on so-called flexibility mechanisms, such as international trading of emission permits, to bring the economic costs down to a modest range.[45] This interpretation was rejected by the Europeans at the Hague in November 2000. Without the flexibility mechanisms, the United Sates would be out of the protocol, even if the subsequent administration had been more environmentally friendly than it was. (Ironically, now that European and other

---

[43]Brack (1996).

[44]Parson (2002).

[45]The author was one of the few economists sympathetic to the Clinton Administration policy on the Kyoto Protocol. Two claims: (1) Quantitative targets a la Kyoto are the "least impossible" way politically to structure an international agreement (see Frankel, 2003, for my response to the arguments of Cooper, 1998, Nordhaus, 2001, and Schelling, 2002, against assignment of quantitative targets). And (2) Bill Clinton's approach—signing the treaty but announcing his intention not to submit for ratification unless the Europeans agreed to unrestricted international trading of emission permits and unless developing countries agreed to participate in the system—was the least impossible way, subject to the existing political constraints, of demonstrating U.S. willingness to address climate change. It was our hope that when the world is ready to make a more serious attempt, it will build on the good aspects of the Kyoto Protocol, particularly the role for international permit trading and other flexibility mechanisms.

countries are trying to go ahead without the United States, they are finding that they cannot manage without such trading mechanisms.)

Even most of those who for one reason or another do not believe that Kyoto was a useful step, however, must acknowledge that multilateral agreements will be necessary if the problem of global climate change is to be tackled. The current U.S. administration has yet to face up to this. The point for present purposes is that a system in which each country insists, based on an appeal to national sovereignty, that it be left to formulate environmental policies on its own, would be a world in which global externalities like greenhouse gas emissions would not be effectively addressed.

Summary of Conclusions

The relationship between globalization and the environment is too complex to sum up in a single judgment—whether "good" or "bad." In many respects, global trade and investment operate like other sources of economic growth. They tend to raise income as measured in the marketplace. On the one hand, the higher scale of output can mean more pollution, deforestation, and other kinds of environmental damage. On the other hand, changes in the composition and techniques of economic activity can lower the damage relative to income. Although it is not possible to generalize universally about the net effect of these channels, it is possible to put forward general answers to some major relevant questions.

- A key question is whether openness to international trade undermines national attempts at environmental regulation, through a "race to the bottom" effect. This no doubt happens sometimes. But there is little statistical evidence, across countries, that the unfavorable effects on average outweigh favorable "gains from trade" effects on measures of pollution, such as SO_2 concentrations. If anything, the answer seems to be that favorable effects dominate.

- Perceptions that WTO panel rulings have interfered with the ability of individual countries to pursue environmental goals are poorly informed. In cases such as Canadian asbestos, Venezuelan gasoline, and Asian shrimp, the rulings have confirmed that countries can enact environmental measures, even if they affect trade and even if they concern others' processes and production methods, provided the measures do not unnecessarily discriminate among producer countries.

- People care about both the environment and the economy. As their real income rises, their demand for environmental quality rises. Under the right conditions, this can translate into environmental progress. The right conditions include democracy, effective regulation, and externalities that are largely confined within national borders and are therefore amenable to national regulation.

- Increasingly, however, environmental problems do in fact spill across national borders. The strongest examples are pure global externalities such as global climate change and ozone depletion. Economic growth alone will not address such problems, in a system where each country acts individually, due to the free rider problem. International institutions are required. This would be equally true in the absence of international trade.

- Indeed, trade offers a handle whereby citizens of one country can exercise a role in environmental problems of other countries that they would otherwise not have. Consumer labeling campaigns and corporate codes of conduct are examples.

- Many aspects of the environment that might have been considered purely domestic matters in the past, or that foreign residents might not even have known about, are increasingly of concern to those living in other countries. It again follows that if the issues are to be addressed, then multilateral institutions are the vehicle and expressions of national sovereignty are the obstacle, not the other way around. Indeed, if one broadens the definition of globalization, beyond international trade and investment, to include the globalization of ideas and of NGO activities, then one can see the international environmental movement as itself an example of globalization.

REFERENCES

Andreoni, James, and Arik Levinson. 2001. "The Simple Analytics of the Environmental Kuznets Curve," NBER Working Paper no. 6739. *Journal of Public Economics* 80, May, 269–286.

Antweiler, Werner, Brian Copeland, and M. Scott Taylor. 2001. "Is Free Trade Good for the Environment?" NBER Working Paper No. 6707. *American Economic Review* 91, no. 4, September, 877–908.

Arrow, K., R. Bolin, P. Costanza, P. Dasgupta, C. Folke, C. S. Holling, B. O. Jansson, S. Levin, K. G. Mäler, C. Perrings, and D. Pimentel. 1995. "Economic Growth, Carrying Capacity, and the Environment," *Science* 268, April 28, 520–521.

Barrett, Scott, and Kathryn Graddy. 2000. "Freedom, Growth, and the Environment," *Environment and Development Economics* 5, 433–456.

Bhagwati, Jadgish. 2000. "On Thinking Clearly About the Linkage Between Trade and the Environment," in *The Wind of the Hundred Days: How Washington Mismanaged Globalization*, Cambridge: MIT Press.

Bhagwati, Jadgish, and T. N. Srinivasan. 1996. "Trade and the Environment: Does Environmental Diversity Detract from the Case for Free Trade," in *Fair Trade and Harmonization*, Vol. 1: *Economic Analysis*, Jadgish Bhagwati and Robert Hudec eds. Cambridge: MIT Press, pp. 159–223.

Bimonte, Salvatore. 2001. "Model of Growth and Environmental Quality, A New Evidence of the Environmental Kuznets Curve," Universita degli Studi di Siena, Quaderni, no. 321, April.

Brack, Duncan. 1996. *International Trade and the Montreal Protocol*, London: The Royal Institute of International Affairs and Earthscan Publications, Ltd.

Bradford, David, Rebecca Schlieckert and Stephen Shore. 2000. "The Environmental Kuznets Curve: Exploring a Fresh Specification," NBER Working Paper no. 8001. Forthcoming, *Topics in Economic Analysis and Policy.*

Braithwaite, John, and Peter Drahos. 2000. *Global Business Regulation,* UK: Cambridge University Press.

Charnovitz, Steve. 2002a. "The Law of Environmental 'PPMs' in the WTO: Debunking the Myth of Illegality," *Yale Journal of International Law* 27, no. 1, Winter, pp. 59–110.

Charnovitz, Steve. 2002b. "A World Environment Organization," *Columbia Journal of Environmental Law* 27, no. 2, 323–362.

Charnovitz, Steve, and Michael Weinstein. 2001. "The Greening of the WTO," *Foreign Affairs* 80, no. 6, 147–156.

Chaudhuri, Shubham, and Alexander Pfaff. 2002. "Economic Growth and the Environment: What Can We Learn from Household Data?" Columbia University, February.

Cooper, Richard. 1998. "Why Kyoto Won't Work," *Foreign Affairs,* March/April.

Copeland, Brian, and M. Scott Taylor. 1994. "North-South Trade and the Environment," *Quarterly Journal of Economics* 109, 755–787.

Copeland, Brian, and M. Scott Taylor. 1995. "Trade and the Environment: A Partial Synthesis," *American Journal of Agricultural Economics* 77, 765–771.

Copeland, Brian, and M. Scott Taylor. 2001. "International Trade and the Environment: A Framework for Analysis," NBER Working Paper No. 8540, October.

Copeland, Brian, and M. Scott Taylor. 2003a. *Trade and the Environment: Theory and Evidence,* Princeton: Princeton University Press.

Copeland, Brian, and M. Scott Taylor. 2003b. "Trade, Growth and the Environment." NBER Working Paper No. 9823, July.

Cropper, Maureen, and Charles Griffiths. 1994. "The Interaction of Population Growth and Environmental Quality," *American Economic Review* 84, no. 2, May, 250–254.

Daly, Herman. 1993. "The Perils of Free Trade," *Scientific American,* November, 51–55.

Dean, Judy. 1992. "Trade and the Environment: A Survey of the Literature," in Patrick Low, ed., *International Trade and the Environment.* World Bank Discussion Paper No. 159.

Dean, Judy. 2001. "Overview," in *International Trade and the Environment,* J. Dean, ed., International Library of Environmental Economics and Policy Series, (UK: Ashgate Publishing).

Dean, Judy. 2002. "Does Trade Liberalization Harm the Environment? A New Test," *Canadian Journal of Economics* 35, no. 4, 819–842 November.

Dua, Andre, and Daniel Esty, 1997, *Sustaining the Asia Pacific Miracle: Environmental Protection and Economic Integration,* Institute for International Economics: Washington DC.

Ederington, Josh, and Jenny Minier. 2002. "Is Environmental Policy a Secondary Trade Barrier? An Empirical Analysis," University of Miami; *Canadian Journal of Economics,* forthcoming.

Ederington, Josh, Arik Levinson, and Jenny Minier. 2003. "Footloose and Pollution-Free," NBER Working Paper No. 9718, May.

Eiras, Ana, and Brett Schaefer. 2001. "Trade: The Best Way to Protect the Environment," *Backgrounder,* The Heritage Foundation no. 1480, September 27.

Esty, Daniel. 1994. *Greening the GATT: Trade, Environment, and the Future,* Washington, DC: Institute for International Economics.

Esty, Daniel. 2001. "Bridging the Trade-Environment Divide," *Journal of Economic Perspectives*, Summer 15, no. 3, 113–130.

Esty, Daniel, and Bradford Gentry. 1997. "Foreign Investment, Globalisation, and the Environment," in *Globalization and the Environment*, Tom Jones ed. Paris: Organization for Economic Cooperation and Development.

Esty, Daniel, and Damien Giradin. 1998. "Environmental Protection and International Competitiveness: A Conceptual Framework," *Journal of World Trade* 32, no. 3, June, 5–46.

Esty, Daniel, and Michael Porter. 2001. "Measuring National Environmental Performance and Its Determinants," Yale Law School and Harvard Business School, April.

Foster, Andrew, and Mark Rosenzweig. 2003. "Economic Growth and the Rise of Forests," *Quarterly Journal of Economics* 118, issue 2, May, 601–638.

Frankel, Jeffrey. 2003. "You're Getting Warmer: The Most Feasible Path for Addressing Global Climate Change Does Run Through Kyoto," Fondazione Eni Enrico Mattei, Milan, Italy; forthcoming in *Trade and the Environment in the Perspective of the EU Enlargement*, edited John Maxwell, with Marialuisa Tamborra, London: Edward Elgar Publishers, Ltd.

Frankel, Jeffrey, and Andrew Rose. 2003. "Is Trade Good or Bad for the Environment? Sorting Out the Causality," RWP03-038, Kennedy School, Harvard University, September. Revised version of NBER Working Paper 9201. *Review of Economics and Statistics*, forthcoming.

Gollier, Christian. 2001. "Should We Beware the Precautionary Principle?" *Economic Policy* 33, October, 303–327.

Goulder, Lawrence, and Robert Stavins. 2002. "An Eye on the Future," *Nature*, 419, October 17, 673–674.

Grossman, Gene, and Alan Krueger. 1993. "Environmental Impacts of a North American Free Trade Agreement," in *The U.S.-Mexico Free Trade Agreement*, Peter Garber, ed., Cambridge MA: MIT Press.

Grossman, Gene, and Alan Krueger. 1995. "Economic Growth and the Environment," *Quarterly Journal of Economics*, 110, no. 2, May 1995, pp. 353–377.

Hanley, Nick, Jason Shogren, and Ben White, *Environmental Economics in Theory and Practice*, New York: Oxford University Press, 1997.

Harbaugh, William, Arik Levinson, and David Wilson. 2000. "Reexamining the Empirical Evidence for an Environmental Kuznets Curve," NBER Working Paper No. 7711, May.

Hilton, F. G. Hank, and Arik Levinson. 1998. "Factoring the Environmental Kuznets Curve: Evidence from Automotive Lead Emissions," *Journal of Environmental Economics and Management* 35, 126–141.

Holtz-Eakin and T. Selden. 1995. "Stoking the Fires? CO_2 Emissions and Economic Growth," *Journal of Public Economics* 57, May, 85–101.

Hufbauer, Gary, Daniel Esty, Diana Orejas, Luis Rubio, and Jeffrey Schott. 2000. *NAFTA and the Environment: Seven Years Later*, Policy Analyses in International Economics No. 61, Washington, DC: Institute for International Economics, October.

Jaeger, William, and Van Kolpin. 2000. "Economic Growth and Environmental Resource Allocation," Williams University and University of Oregon, August 22.

Jaffe, Adam, S. R. Peterson, Paul Portney, and Robert Stavins. 1995. "Environmental Regulation and the Competitiveness of U.S. Manufacturing: What Does the Evidence Tell Us?" *Journal of Economic Literature* 33, 132–163.

Juma, Calestous. 2000. "The Perils of Centralizing Global Environmental Governance" *Environment* 42, no. 9, November, 44–45.

Lee, Hiro, and David Roland-Holst, "The Environment and Welfare Implications of Trade and Tax Policy," *Journal of Development Economics*, February 1997, 52, 65–82.

Levinson, Arik. 1999. "State Taxes and Interstate Hazardous Waste Shipments," *American Economic Review* 89, no. 3, June.

Levinson, Arik, and M. Scott Taylor. 2001. "Trade and the Environment: Unmasking the Pollution Haven Effect," Georgetown University and University of Wisconsin.

Liddle, Brantley. 2001. "Free Trade and the Environment-Development System," *Ecological Economics* 39, 21–36.

Low, P., and A. Yeats. 1992. "Do 'Dirty' Industries Migrate?" in *International Trade and the Environment*, P. Low ed., 89–104. Geneva: World Bank, 1992.

Lucas, Robert E. B., David Wheeler, and Hememala Hettige. 1992. "Economic Development, Environmental Regulation and the International Migration of Toxic Industrial Pollution: 1960–1988," in Patrick Low, editor, *International Trade and the Environment*, World Bank Discussion Papers no. 159 (The World Bank: Washington DC).

Meadows, Donella, Dennis Meadows, Jorgen Randres, and William Behrens. 1972. *The Limits to Growth*, New York: Universe Books.

Muradian, Roldan, Martin O'Connor, and Joan Martinez-Alier. 2001. "Embodied Pollution in Trade: Estimating the 'Environmental Load Displacement' of Industrialised Countries," FEEM Working Paper No. 57, July, Milan.

Neumayer, Eric. 2002. "Does Trade Openness Promote Multilateral Environmental Cooperation?" *The World Economy* 25, no. 6, 812–832.

Nordhaus, William. 2001. "After Kyoto: Alternative Mechanisms to Control Global Warming," American Economic Association, Atlanta, GA, January 4.

Panayotou, Theo. 1993. "Empirical Tests and Policy Analysis of Environmental Degradation at Different Stages of Development," Working Paper WP238, Technology and Employment Programme (Geneva: International Labor Office).

Parson, Edward. [2003]. *Protecting the Ozone Layer: Science, Strategy, and Negotiation in the Shaping of a Global Environmental Regime* [New York.] Oxford University Press.

Porter, Michael. 1990. *The Competitive Advantage of Nations*. New York: The Free Press, Macmillan.

Porter, Michael. 1991. "America's Green Strategy," *Scientific American*, April.

Porter, Michael, and Claas van der Linde. 1995. "Toward a New Conception of the Environment-Competitiveness Relationship," *Journal of Economic Perspectives* 9, No. 4.

Ruggie, John. 2002. "Trade, Sustainability and Global Governance," *Columbia Journal of Environmental Law* 27, no. 297–307.

Schelling, Thomas. 2002. "What Makes Greenhouse Sense?" *Foreign Affairs* 81, no. 3, May/June.

Schmidheiny, Stephan. *Changing Course: A Global Business Perspective on Development and the Environment*. Cambridge: The MIT Press, 1992.

Selden, Thomas, and Daqing Song. 1994. "Environmental Quality and Development: Is There a Kuznets Curve for Air Pollution Emissions," *Journal of Environmental Economics and Management* 27, 147–162.

Selden, Thomas, and Daqing Song. 1995. "Neoclassical Growth, the J Curve for Abatement, and the Inverted U Curve for Pollution," *Journal of Environmental Economics and Management* 29, 162–168.

Shafik, Nemat. 1994. "Economic Development and Environmental Quality: An Econometric Analysis," *Oxford Economic Papers* 46, 757–773.

Smarzynska, Beata, and Shang-Jin Wei. 2001. "Pollution Havens and Foreign Direct Investment: Dirty Secret or Popular Myth?" NBER Working Paper No. 8465, September.

Smith, Kirk. "Fuel Combustion, Air Pollution Exposure, and Health: The Situation in Developing Countries," *Annual Review of Energy and Environment*, 1993, 18, 529–566.

Stavins, Robert. 2000. *Economics of the Environment: Selected Readings*, 4th ed, Norton.

Stokey, Nancy. 1998. "Are There Limits to Growth," *International Economic Review* 39, no. 1, February, 1–31.

Suri, Vivek, and Duane Chapman. 1998. "Economic Growth, Trade and Energy: Implications for the Environmental Kuznet Curve," *Ecological Economics* 25, 2, May, 147–160.

Tobey, James A. 1990. "The Effects of Domestic Environmental Policies on Patterns of World Trade: An Empirical Test," *Kyklos* 43, 191–209.

Victor, David, and C. Ford Runge. 2002. "Farming the Genetic Frontier," *Foreign Affairs* 81, no. 3 pp. 107–121.

Vogel, David. 1995. *Trading Up: Consumer and Environmental Regulation in a Global Economy*, Cambridge: Harvard University Press.

World Bank. 1992. *Development and the Environment*, World Development Report.

X

*Economics and Environmental
Policy Making*

32 The Choice of Regulatory Instruments in Environmental Policy*

Nathaniel O. Keohane

Richard L. Revesz

Robert N. Stavins

Nathaniel O. Keohane is Special Assistant to the President on Energy and Environmental Issues, National Economic Council. Richard L. Revesz is Dean and Lawrence King Professor of Law, New York University Schools of Law; Robert N. Stavins is Albert Pratt Professor of Business and Government at Harvard Kennedy School, Research Associate at the National Bureau of Economic Research, and University Fellow at Resources for the Future.

I. Introduction

The design of environmental policy requires answers to two central questions: (1) what is the desired level of environmental protection?; and (2) what policy instruments should be used to achieve this level of protection? With respect to the second question, thirty years of positive political reality in the United States has diverged strikingly from the recommendations of normative economic theory. The purpose of this Article is to explain why.

Four gaps between normative theory and positive reality merit particular attention. First, so-called "command-and-control" instruments (such as design standards requiring a particular technology's usage, or performance standards prescribing the maximum amount of pollution that a source can emit)[1] are used to a significantly greater degree than "market-based" or

"The Choice of Regulatory Instruments in Environmental Policy." *Harvard Environmental Law Review,* Vol. 22, No. 2, Pp. 313–367. 1998. Reprinted with permission.

*Helpful comments on a previous version of the Article were provided by: David Charny, Cary Coglianese, John Ferejohn, Don Fullerton, Robert Hahn, James Hamilton, Robert Keohane, David King, Lewis Kornhauser, Robert Lowry, Roger Noll, Kenneth Shepsle, and Richard Stewart. Financial support was provided by the Dean's Research Fund, John F. Kennedy School of Government, and the Filomen D'Agostino and Max E. Greenberg Research Fund at the New York University School of Law. The authors alone are responsible for any errors.

[1]Performance standards could specify an absolute quantity of permissible emissions (that is, a given quantity of emissions per unit of time), but more typically these standards establish allowable emissions in proportional terms (that is, quantity of emissions per unit of product output or per unit of a particular input). This Article uses the term "standard" to refer somewhat generically to

"economic-incentive" instruments (principally pollution taxes or charges[2] and systems of tradeable permits[3]), despite economists' consistent endorsement of the latter.

At least in theory, market-based instruments minimize the aggregate cost of achieving a given level of environmental protection,[4] and provide dynamic incentives for the adoption and diffusion of cheaper and better control technologies.[5] Despite these advantages, market-based instruments have been used far less frequently than command-and-control standards.[6] For example, the cores of the Clean Air Act ("CAA")[7] and Clean Water Act ("CWA")[8] consist of federally prescribed emission and effluent standards, set by reference to the levels that can be achieved through the use of the "best available technology."[9]

Second, when command-and-control standards have been used, the required level of pollution abatement has generally been far more stringent for new pollution sources than for existing ones, possibly worsening pollution by encouraging firms to keep older, dirtier plants in operation.[10]

---

command-and-control approaches. Except where stated otherwise, the Article refers to proportional performance standards.

[2]The development of the notion of a corrective tax on pollution is generally credited to Pigou. See generally Arthur Cecil Pigou, *The Economics of Welfare* (1920).

[3]John Dales initially proposed a system of tradeable permits to control pollution. See generally John H. Dales, *Pollution, Property, & Prices* (1968). David Montgomery then formalized this system. See generally W. David Montgomery, "Markets in Licenses and Efficient Pollution Control Programs," 5 *J. Econ. Theory* 395 (1972). However, much of the literature can be traced back to Ronald Coase. See Ronald H. Coase, "The Problem of Social Cost," 3 *J.L. & Econ.* 1, 39–44 (1960).

[4]As is well known, a necessary condition for the achievement of such cost-minimization is that the marginal costs of abatement be equal for all sources. See William J. Baumol & Wallace E. Oates, *The Theory of Environmental Policy* 177 (1988). In theory, pollution taxes and systems of marketable permits induce this effect, at least under specified conditions.

[5]Market-based systems can provide continuous dynamic incentives for adoption of superior technologies, since under such systems it is always in the interest of firms to clean up more if sufficiently inexpensive cleanup technologies can be identified. See Scott R. Milliman & Raymond Prince, "Firm Incentives to Promote Technological Change in Pollution Control," 17 *J. Envtl. Econ. & Mgmt.* 247, 257–61 (1989); Adam B. Jaffe & Robert N. Stavins, "Dynamic Incentives of Environmental Regulation: The Effects of Alternative Policy Instruments and Technology Diffusion," 29 *J. Envtl. Econ. & Mgmt.* S43, S43–S46 (1995).

[6]Office of Tech. Assessment, Tech. Assessment Board of the 103d Congress, *Environmental Policy Tools: A User's Guide* 27–28 (1995).

[7]See 42 U.S.C. § 7411(a),(b) (1994).

[8]See 33 U.S.C. §§ 1311(b), 1316 (1994).

[9]We use this label as a generic one. The various statutory schemes employ somewhat different formulations. See, e.g., 33 U.S.C. § 1311(b)(1)(A) (1994) ("best practicable control technology"); id. § 1311(b)(2)(A) ("best available technology"); id. § 1316(a)(1) ("best available demonstrated control technology"); 42 U.S.C. § 7411(a)(1) (1994) ("best system of emission reduction"); id. § 7479(3) ("best available control technology").

[10]New plants ought to have somewhat more stringent standards because their abatement costs are lower, although such standards should be linked with actual abatement costs, not with the proxy of plant vintage. When new source standards are sufficiently more stringent, however, they can give rise to an "old-plant" effect, precluding plant replacements that would otherwise take place. See Matthew D. McCubbins et al., "Structure and Process, Politics, and Policy: Administrative Arrangements

The federal environmental statutes further these disparities by bifurcating the regulatory requirements that apply to new and existing sources. For example, under the Clean Air Act, emission standards for new sources are set federally, whereas the corresponding standards for existing sources are set by the states.[11] Similarly, the CAA's Prevention of Significant Deterioration ("PSD") program,[12] which applies to areas with air that is cleaner than the National Ambient Air Quality Standards ("NAAQS"),[13] imposes additional emission standards only on new sources.[14] The Clean Water Act sets effluent limitations for both new and existing sources, but these limitations are governed by different statutory provisions.[15]

Third, in the relatively rare instances in which they have been adopted, market-based instruments have nearly always taken the form of tradeable permits rather than emission taxes,[16] although economic theory suggests that the optimal choice between tradeable permits and emission taxes is dependent upon case-specific factors.[17] Moreover, the initial allocation of such

---

and the Political Control of Agencies," 75 *Va. L. Rev.* 431, 467 (1989); Richard B. Stewart, "Regulation, Innovation, and Administrative Law: A Conceptual Framework," 69 *Cal. L. Rev.* 1259, 1270–71 (1981). Empirical evidence shows that differential environmental regulations lengthen the time before plants are retired. See Michael T. Maloney & Gordon L. Brady, "Capital Turnover and Marketable Pollution Rights," 31 *J.L. & Econ.* 203, 206 (1988); Randy Nelson et al., "Differential Environmental Regulation: Effects on Electric Utility Capital Turnover and Emissions," 75 *Rev. Econ. & Stat.* 368, 373 (1993).

[11]Compare 42 U.S.C. § 7411(a), (b) (1994) (defining federal standards for new sources) with id. § 7410(a) (requiring state plans for existing sources).

[12]See 42 U.S.C. §§ 7470–7479 (1994).

[13]See id. § 7471.

[14]See id. § 7475(a).

[15]Compare 33 U.S.C. § 1316 (1994) (prescribing standards for new sources) with id. § 1311(b) (setting standards for existing sources).

[16]Taxes (so-called unit charges) have been used in some communities for municipal solid waste collection. See Office of Tech. Assessment, supra note 6, at 119–21. Gasoline taxes serve primarily as revenue-raising instruments, rather than environmental (Pigouvian) taxes per se. Interestingly, the European experience is the reverse: environmental taxes are far more prevalent than tradeable permits, although the taxes employed have typically been too low to induce much pollution abatement. See Richard B. Stewart, "Economic Incentives for Environmental Protection: Opportunities and Obstacles" 42 (1996) (unpublished manuscript, on file with New York University). A more comprehensive positive analysis of instrument choice than we provide here would seek to explain this difference between the European and U.S. experiences.

[17]With perfect information, tradeable permits sold at auction have the same effect as a tax. Under conditions of uncertainty, the relative efficiency of tradeable permits and fixed tax rates depends upon the relative slopes of the relevant marginal benefit and marginal cost functions. See Martin L. Weitzman, "Prices v. Quantities," 41 *Rev. Econ. Stud.* 477, 485–90 (1974); Gary W. Yohe, "Towards a General Comparison of Price Controls and Quantity Controls Under Uncertainty," 45 *Rev. Econ. Stud.* 229, 238 (1978); Robert N. Stavins, "Correlated Uncertainty and Policy Instrument Choice," 30 *J. Envtl. Econ. & Mgmt.* 218, 219–25 (1996).

In theory, a hybrid system that incorporates aspects and attributes of both a simple linear tax or a simple tradeable permit system will be preferable, under conditions of uncertainty, to either alone. See Marc J. Roberts & Michael Spence, "Effluent Charges and Licenses Under Uncertain," 5 *J. Pub. Econ.* 193, 196–97 (1976); Louis Kaplow & Steven Shavell, "On the Superiority of Corrective Taxes to Quantity Regulation" 12–14 (National Bureau of Econ. Research Working Paper No. 6251, 1997).

permits has been through "grandfathering," or free initial distribution based on existing levels of pollution,[18] rather than through auctions, despite the apparently superior mechanism of auctions.[19] Despite diversity of available market-based instruments (taxes, revenue-neutral taxes, auctioned permits, and grandfathered permits)[20] and the numerous tradeoffs that exist in normative economic terms, the U.S. experience has been dominated by one choice: grandfathered permits.

Notably, the acid rain provision of the Clean Air Act allocates, without charge, marketable permits for sulfur dioxide emissions to current emitters.[21] Similarly, grandfathered marketable permits are created by the offset

---

[18]Mandated by the Clean Air Act amendments of 1990, the sulfur dioxide ("SO_2") allowance program (a tradeable permit program to reduce acid rain) provides for annual auctions in addition to grandfathering. However, such auctions involve less than three percent of the total allocation. See Elizabeth M. Bailey, "Allowance Trading Activity and State Regulatory Rulings: Evidence from the U.S. Acid Rain Program" 4 (Mass. Inst. of Tech. Working Paper No. MIT-CEEPR 96-002, 1996). These auctions have proven to be a trivial part of the overall program. See Paul L. Joskow et al., "Auction Design and the Market for Sulfur Dioxide Emissions" 27–28 (National Bureau of Econ. Research Working Paper No. 5745, 1996).

[19]With perfect information and no transactions costs, trading will result in the economically efficient outcome independently of the initial distribution of permits. See W. David Montgomery, "Markets in Licenses and Efficient Pollution Control Programs" 5 *J. Econ. Theory* 395, 409 (1972); Coase, supra note 3, at 15; Robert W. Hahn & Roger G. Noll, "Designing a Market for Tradeable Emission Permits." in *Reform of Environmental Regulation* 120–21 (Wesley Magat ed., 1982). Under more realistic scenarios, however, there are compelling arguments for the superiority of auctioned permits. First, auctions are more cost-effective in the presence of certain kinds of transactions costs. See Robert N. Stavins, "Transaction Costs and Tradeable Permits," 29 *J. Envtl. Econ. & Mgmt.* 133, 146 (1995). Second, the revenue raised by an auction mechanism can be used to finance a reduction in some distortionary tax. See Lawrence H. Goulder et al., "Revenue-Raising vs. Other Approaches to Environmental Protection: The Critical Significance of Pre-Existing Tax Distortions" 1 (National Bureau of Econ. Research Working Paper No. 5641, 1996). Instruments that restrict pollution production (such as tradeable permits) can create entry barriers that raise product prices, reduce the real wage, and exacerbate preexisting labor supply distortions. However, this effect can be offset if the government auctions the permits, retains the scarcity rents, and recycles the revenue by reducing distortionary labor taxes. See Don Fullerton & Gilbert Metcalf, "Environmental Regulation in a Second-Best World" 6, 25 (1996) (unpublished manuscript, on file with authors). Third, auctions provide greater incentives for firms to develop substitutes for regulated products, by requiring firms to pay for permits rather than giving them rents. See Robert W. Hahn & Albert M. McGartland, "The Political Economy of Instrument Choice: An Examination of the U.S. Role in Implementing the Montreal Protocol, " 83 *Nw. U. L. Rev.* 592, 604 (1989). Fourth, the revenue raised by auctions may provide administrative agencies with an incentive to monitor compliance. See Bruce A. Ackerman & Richard B. Stewart, "Reforming Environmental Law," 37 *Stan. L. Rev.* 1333, 1344–46 (1985). Fifth, grandfathering, if accepted as general practice, could lead unregulated firms to increase their emissions in order to maximize the pollution rights that they obtain if there is a transition to a market-based system. See Donald N. Dewees, "Instrument Choice in Environmental Policy," 21 *Econ. Inquiry* 53, 62–63 (1983).

[20]In a straightforward scheme of effluent taxes, a constant tax is levied on each unit of pollution. In a revenue-neutral framework, the tax revenues are then rebated to the payors, by some method other than the amount of their pollution. In marketable permit schemes, the initial allocation can be performed through an auction, or through grandfathering. In a deterministic setting and abstracting from a set of other issues, a revenue-neutral emission tax can be designed which is equivalent to a grandfathered tradeable permit system. Likewise, under such conditions, a simple emission tax will be roughly equivalent to an auctioned permit system.

[21]See 42 U.S.C. § 7651(b) (1994). The amount of the allocation is capped in Phase I, which is currently in effect, at 2.5 pounds of sulfur dioxide per million BTUs of fuel input consumed. In

mechanism of the nonattainment provision of the CAA.[22] This mechanism permits existing sources to reduce their emissions and sell the resulting reduction to new sources attempting to locate in the area.[23]

Fourth and finally, there has been a conceptual gap between prior and current political practice. In recent years, the political process has been more receptive to market-based instruments,[24] even though they continue to be a small part of the overall portfolio of existing environmental laws and regulations. After being largely ignored for so long, why have incentive-based instruments begun to gain acceptance in recent years?

Commentators have advanced various explanations for the existence of these four gaps between normative theory and positive reality. While some explanations emerge from formal theories, others take the form of informal hypotheses, purporting to explain certain aspects of environmental policy, but not as a part of a formal theory of political behavior. This Article reviews, evaluates, and extends these explanations. Moreover, this Article places these disparate explanations within the framework of an equilibrium model of instrument choice in environmental policy, based upon the metaphor of a political market.

Informed by intellectual traditions within economics, political science, and law, this framework organizes and synthesizes existing theories and empirical evidence about observed departures of normative prescription from political reality. The scope of the Article, however, is limited in a number of respects. The emphasis is on the control of pollution rather than the management of natural resources. The Article treats Congress, rather than administrative agencies, as the locus of instrument choice decisions; it views legislators (rather than regulators) as the "suppliers" of regulation.[25] Moreover, the Article focuses exclusively on the choice among the policy instruments used to achieve a given level of environmental protection, ranging

---

Phase II, which goes into effect in the year 2000, the cap will be 1.2 pounds of sulfur dioxide per million BTUs of fuel input consumed. See Paul L. Joskow & Richard Schmalensee, "The Political Economy of Market-based Environmental Policy: The 1990 U.S. Acid Rain Program," 41 *J.L. & Econ.* [37–83] April 1998) (manuscript at 94–95, on file with authors).

[22]See 42 U.S.C. § 7503(a)(1)(A) (1994).

[23]See id. at § 7503(c)(1).

[24]Beginning in the 1970s, the U.S. Environmental Protection Agency ("EPA") allowed states to implement trading schemes, as alternatives to command-and-control regulation, in their State Implementation Plans under the Clean Air Act. See Robert W. Hahn, "Economic Prescriptions for Environmental Problems: How the Patient Followed the Doctor's Orders," *J. Econ. Persp.*, Spring 1989, at 95, 101. More significantly, tradeable permit systems were used in the 1980s to accomplish the phasedown of lead in gasoline. See Suzi Kerr & David Maré, "Efficient Regulation Through Tradeable Permit Markets: The United States Lead Phasedown" 3–6 (U. Md. C. Park Working Paper No. 96–06, 1997). Moreover, such systems facilitated the phasedown of ozone-depleting chlorofluo-rocarbons ("CFCs") and are projected to cut nationwide SO_2 emissions by 50% by the year 2005, see Office of Air Radiation, U.S. Environmental Protection Agency, *1995 Compliance Results: Acid Rain Program* 10–11 (1996), as well as achieving ambient ozone reductions in the northeast and imple-menting stricter local air pollution controls in the Los Angeles metropolitan region.

[25]We do not intend, however, to deny the importance of executive branch departments and administrative agencies, such as the EPA. For example, the intra-firm emission trading programs of the 1970s were largely the direct creation of EPA.

from tradeable permits to taxes to standards. It does not explore the related issues of how the level of protection is chosen or enforced. Nor does it address why Congress chooses to delegate authority to administrative agencies in the first place.[26] Finally, the Article's outlook is positive, not normative: it seeks to understand why the current set of tools exists, rather than which tools are desirable.

Part II of the Article reviews the relevant intellectual traditions in economics, political science, and law. Part III presents the key features of our equilibrium framework. Part IV considers the demand for environmental policy instruments, while Part V examines the supply side. Finally, Part VI presents some conclusions.

II. Intellectual Traditions

Positive theories of policy instrument choice find their roots in the broader study of government regulation, a vast literature which has been reviewed elsewhere.[27] For the purposes of this Article, the literature can be divided into three approaches for explaining government regulation: demand-driven explanations, supply-driven explanations, and explanations incorporating the interaction between demand and supply.

A. Demand-Side Analyses

Explanations that focus heavily on the demand for regulation are grounded largely in economics. Not surprisingly, economists have generally concentrated on the demand for economic (rather than social) regulation, devoting most attention to the interests of affected firms. The "economic theory of regulation," initiated by George Stigler[28] and developed further by Richard Posner,[29] Sam Peltzman,[30] and Gary Becker,[31] suggests that much regulation is not imposed on firms but rather demanded by them, as a means of harnessing the coercive power of the state to restrict entry, support prices,

---

[26]See generally Morris P. Fiorina, "Legislative Choice of Regulatory Forms: Legal Process or Administrative Process?," 39 *Pub. Choice* 33 (1982).

[27]See generally Thomas Romer & Howard Rosenthal, "Modern Political Economy and the Study of Regulation," in *Public Regulation: New Perspectives on Institutions and Policies* 73 (Elizabeth E. Bailey ed., 1987).

[28]See generally George J. Stigler, "The Theory of Economic Regulation," 2 *Bell J. Econ.* 3 (1971).

[29]See generally Richard A. Posner, "Theories of Economic Regulation," 5 *Bell J. Econ.* 335 (1974).

[30]See generally Sam Peltzman, "Toward a More General Theory of Regulation," 19 *J.L. & Econ.* 211 (1976).

[31]See generally Gary S. Becker, "A Theory of Competition among Pressure Groups for Political Influence," 98 *Q.J. Econ.* 371 (1983).

or provide direct cash subsidies.[32] A related strand of literature has likewise emphasized rent-seeking behavior.[33]

In a number of these economic analyses, the supply side (i.e., the political process itself) is virtually ignored.[34] One paper typifying this demand-driven approach has examined private industry's preferences for regulation and has simply assumed that those policy preferences will prevail.[35] Similarly, another model of the resource allocation decisions of competing interest groups has assumed that the policy outcome depends solely on the relative pressures exerted by interest groups.[36]

Even when they model political processes, economic explanations of regulation have often remained driven by the demand of firms. In Stigler's analysis[37] and Peltzman's elaboration,[38] the state enacts the program of the industry (or, more generally, of the interest group) offering the most resources to the governing party; in other words, regulation goes to the "highest bidder."[39] Thus, private industry will tend to be regulated where and when the benefits to firms from government regulation are highly concentrated, but the costs are widely dispersed.[40] The "government" simply acts to maximize an exogenous "political support function" and thus caters to the more powerful group. Following a conceptually similar tack, another model pictures a single policymaker's decision as

---

[32]Stigler's influential paper has been characterized as breaking with a previously dominant view (among economists) that regulation is initiated to correct market imperfections. See Stigler, supra note 28, at 3; see also Posner, supra note 29, at 343. It is worth nothing that as far back as E.E. Schattschneider, political scientists recognized the importance of economic interests among groups pressuring Congress. See E.E. Schattschneider, *Politics, Pressures, and the Tariff* 4 (1935). The "capture theory of regulation" in political science was already well developed by the time of Stigler's work. Stigler's main contribution was less his recognition that economic interests will seek favorable regulation than his introduction of that insight into the economics literature and his application of economic models of behavior (i.e., treating political parties as resource maximizers) to explain policy formulation.

[33]See generally James M. Buchanan & Gordon Tullock, *The Calculus of Consent* (1962); Gordon Tullock, "The Welfare Cost of Tariffs, Monopolies, and Theft," 5 *W. Econ. J.* 224 (1967).

[34]See generally Jean-Jacque Laffont & Jean Tirole, *A Theory of Incentives in Procurement and Regulation* (1993); Romer & Rosenthal, supra note 27.

[35]See James M. Buchanan & Gordon Tullock, "Polluters' Profits and Political Response: Direct Controls Versus Taxes," 65 *Am. Econ. Rev.* 139, 142 (1975).

[36]See Becker, supra note 31, at 392.

[37]See Stigler, supra note 28, at 12.

[38]See Peltzman, supra note 30, at 214.

[39]The Stigler-Peltzman model is essentially a policy auction. See Stigler, supra note 28, at 12–13; Peltzman, supra note 30, at 212.

[40]Peanut regulation provides an excellent example of the effect of concentrated benefits and diffuse costs. Quotas, import restrictions, and price supports combined in 1982–1987 to transfer an average of $255 million a year from consumers to producers, with a deadweight loss of $34 million. The annual cost to each consumer was only $1.23; each peanut farmer, on the other hand, gained $11,100. Peanut farmers clearly had an incentive to preserve the program, while any individual consumer had little to gain from dismantling it. See W. Kip Viscusi et al., *Economics of Regulation and Antitrust* 331 (1995).

responding to a weighted sum of industry interests and environmental interests.[41]

Political actors are included in these analyses, but they are treated as economic agents reacting somewhat mechanically to the resources or the demands of interest groups. In many cases, as in the Stigler-Peltzman model, they have no interest other than collecting political contributions. Moreover, government is treated as a monolith, controlled by a single political party, with regulatory agencies and legislatures combined into a single unit. These accounts leave no room for constituency pressures, variation among legislators, slack between legislative direction and the actions of administrative agencies, or other supply-side phenomena.

B. Supply-Side Analyses

By contrast, political scientists and economists studying the supply side of regulation (and of legislation more generally) have focused on the voting behavior of legislators and the institutional structure of the legislature. The approach typically used by political scientists to explain voting behavior is based upon interview and survey data. On the basis of these sources, Congressmen are seen to be most influenced by colleagues and constituents in deciding how to vote.[42] An alternative approach analyzes roll-call data to estimate the relative importance of ideology, constituent interests, and interest groups in legislative voting.[43] One study found that legislators base their votes not only on the economic interests of their constituents (as the economic theory of regulation assumes), but also on their ideologies.[44] Some scholars, notably Michael Munger and his colleagues, have sought to explain voting behavior by explicitly linking it to campaign contributions.[45] However, just as the Stigler-Peltzman model incorporates politicians but remains fundamentally demand-driven, their approach acknowledges the role of interest groups but is driven by supply-side factors. Some mention is made of the costs to legislators of supplying legislation to interest groups,

---

[41]See generally Robert W. Hahn, "The Political Economy of Environmental Regulation: Towards a Unifying Framework," 65 *Pub. Choice* 21 (1990).

[42]See John W. Kingdon, *Congressmen's Voting Decisions* 17 (1989).

[43]See generally Joseph P. Kalt & Mark A. Zupan, "Capture and Ideology in the Economic Theory of Politics," 74 *Am. Econ. Rev.* 279 (1984); James B. Kau & Paul H. Rubin, "Self-Interest, Ideology, and Logrolling in Congressional Voting," 22 *J.L. & Econ.* 365 (1979); Sam Peltzman, "Constituent Interest and Congressional Voting," 27 *J.L. & Econ.* 181 (1984).

[44]See Kalt & Zupan, supra note 43, at 298. Their econometric analysis has been criticized by John Jackson and John Kingdon. See John E. Jackson & John W. Kingdon, "Ideology, Interest Group Scores, and Legislative Votes," 36 *Am. J. Pol. Sci.* 805, 806 (1992).

[45]See generally Arthur T. Denzau & Michael C. Munger, "Legislators and Interest Groups: How Unorganized Interests Get Represented," 80 *Am. Pol. Sci. Rev.* 89 (1986); see also Kevin B. Grier & Michael C. Munger, "Comparing Interest Group PAC Contributions to House and Senate Incumbents, 1980–1986," 55 *J. Pol.* 615, 625–40 (1993).

but the models focus on estimating a "supply price" determined solely by the characteristics of legislators.[46]

A second line of inquiry on the supply side has investigated the role of institutional structure in the legislature. The policy outcome in Congress depends not only on the voting preferences of individual legislators, but also on features such as decision rules, the order of voting, and especially the powers of committees (and their chairmen) to control the agenda of the legislature.[47] Further, expectations of subsequent problems of overseeing implementation of regulatory policy by administrative agencies may influence legislators in their choice of regulatory procedures and instruments.[48]

C. Equilibrium Analyses

Compared to the above, relatively few works have taken an equilibrium approach by considering the interaction of the supply and demand for regulation. Those considering such linkages have typically focused on the role of campaign contributions. Several researchers have modeled campaign contributions from profit-maximizing firms to vote-maximizing politicians,[49] where candidates choose optimal policy positions that balance the need to get votes (by moving towards the policy preferences of voters) and the need to secure campaign funds (by moving towards the preferences of contributors).[50] In a similar vein, some analysts have employed game-theoretic models to link campaign contributions by interest groups and policy positions adopted by legislators.[51]

One group considered legislative outcomes directly, modeling the determination of campaign contributions, legislators' floor votes, and constituents' votes, but without advancing a theoretical model of legislative behavior.[52] Another research has explicitly considered the interaction of interest group

---

[46]In empirical studies of interest group contributions, a number of researchers seem to have in mind a "market model" of interest group contributions to legislators where interest groups offer campaign contributions and votes in return for political support. See Jonathan I. Silberman & Garey C. Durden, "Determining Legislative Preferences on the Minimum Wage: An Economic Approach," 84 *J. Pol. Econ.* 317, 328 (1976); Garey C. Durden et al., "The Effects of Interest Group Pressure on Coal Strip-Mining Legislation," 72 *Soc. Sci. Q.* 239, 249 (1991).

[47]See generally Kenneth A. Shepsle & Barry R. Weingast, "Positive Theories of Congressional Institutions," 19 *Legis. Stud. Q.* 149 (1994) (reviewing recent literature on congressional institutions).

[48]See Matthew D. McCubbins et al., "Administrative Procedures as Instruments of Political Control," 3 *J.L. Econ. & Org.* 243, 252–53 (1987); McCubbins et al., supra note 10, at 481.

[49]See generally Uri Ben-Zion & Zeev Eytan, "On Money, Votes, and Policy in a Democratic Society," 17 *Pub. Choice* 1 (1974).

[50]Bental and Ben-Zion extend the model to consider the case where politicians derive utility from adopting a platform close to their personal policy preferences. See Benjamin Bental & Uri Benzion, "Political Contribution and Policy—Some Extensions," 24 *Pub. Choice* 1, 1–4 (1975).

[51]See David Austen-Smith, "Interest Groups, Campaign Contributions, and Probabilistic Voting," 54 *Pub. Choice* 123, 128–34 (1987).

[52]See James B. Kau et al., "A General Equilibrium Model of Congressional Voting," 97 *Q.J. Econ.* 271, 288–89 (1982).

demand and the legislative supply of policy instruments.[53] In his model, the choice of regulatory instrument is the equilibrium of a game between interest groups (who choose how much to allocate to lobbying in support of their preferred instrument) and legislators (who vote for the instrument that maximizes their support, taking into account the contributions from the interest groups).

Despite the relative scarcity of equilibrium models of positive political economy, the metaphor of a "political market" has frequently been employed in the public choice literature. The works using the market metaphor seem to have had three distinct markets in mind. One market is the market for votes *within* a legislature: legislators are at once demanders and suppliers of votes as they engage in vote trading and logrolling.[54] Other market models focus on the distribution of wealth resulting *from* legislation: the demanders are the beneficiaries of legislation and the suppliers are the losers, with politicians serving as brokers between the two groups.[55] This Article employs what is perhaps the most prevalent conception of the "political market," one which focuses on the exchange between legislators and constituents or interest groups.[56]

The remainder of this Article develops a new model of a political market involving legislators, constituents, and interest groups in the context of instrument choice in environmental policy. This market framework supplements existing work by simultaneously considering the demand for regulation, the supply of regulatory options, and the equilibrium outcome, that is, the choice of policy instrument in the legislature. In this way, the Article strives to synthesize prior research from the demand side and supply side, using it as a foundation for our own equilibrium framework. This Article also seeks to suggest a richer sense of the supply side than is found in existing equilibrium models,[57] incorporating legislator

---

[53]See Jose Edgardo L. Campos, "Legislative Institutions, Lobbying, and the Endogenous Choice of Regulatory Instruments: A Political Economy Approach to Instrument Choice," 5 *J.L. Econ. & Org.* 333, 348–49 (1989).

[54]In a "logroll," or vote trade, several legislators might arrange to vote for each others' bills, so that each legislator secures her most preferred outcome in return for supporting other legislators' bills (which she may oppose only slightly if at all). For example, a series of public works projects might prompt a logroll, since each in the series matters a great deal to the representative whose district receives the funds, but is insignificant to other legislators.

[55]See *Public Choice Theory* at xviii (Charles K. Rowley ed., 1993).

[56]In previous work, the identity of demanders and suppliers has varied; the market has been in electoral votes (with legislators "paying" for votes with legislation) and in legislation (with voters paying for the policies with their votes). Peltzman, for one, was clear that the demanders were constituents and the suppliers legislators: "[t]he essential commodity being transacted in the political market is a transfer of wealth, with constituents on the demand side and their political representatives on the supply side." See Peltzman, supra note 30, at 212. In this Article's framework, the market is in units of effective political support (for particular public policies).

[57]See, e.g., Campos, supra note 53, at 338–48.

ideology as well as a fuller description of the opportunity costs of supplying legislation.[58]

III. A Market Framework for Examining Instrument Choice

To develop a framework within which various existing positive political economy theories can be synthesized, consider a "political market" embodied in a legislature and focused on a single "commodity," namely legislators' support for a given instrument in a specific policy context.[59] A schematic view of this political market is provided in Figure 1. Demand for various degrees of support comes from diverse interest groups, including environmental advocacy organizations, private firms, and trade associations. The currency in this market takes the form of resources (monetary and other contributions, and/or endorsements or other forms of support) that can facilitate legislators' reelections. The aggregation of these individual demands is not a simple sum, because the public good nature of regulation means that interest groups can free-ride on the demands of others.

Next, it is assumed that each individual legislator seeks to maximize her expected utility, which involves the satisfaction that comes from being a member of the legislature, now and in the future. The result is the legislator's political-support supply function, the shape of which is determined by her ideological predisposition, her perception of her constituents' preferences, and the increasing opportunity cost of providing additional support for the policy instrument (in terms of expended effort, foregone future electoral votes in her home district, and discomfort associated with departures from her ideology). Since each legislator supplies units of a homogeneous product called "effective support" (at differing costs), the individual legislators' supply functions combine to yield an aggregate supply function at the level of the legislature.

Thus, for each instrument, a competitive equilibrium in the legislature is given by the intersection between the aggregate political-support

---

[58]As noted above, Congress is seen as the locus of policy instrument choice. Extending the framework to cover regulatory agencies and the courts would introduce several interesting but complex issues. For regulatory agencies, for example, it is important to deal with issues such as the principal-agent relationship between the agency and Congress; the degree and nature of congressional oversight; the possibly conflicting goals of the agency head and career bureaucrats; the objective function of the bureaucrats (for example, job security, power, protection of expertise); and the way in which policy demands provide payoffs to the agency.

[59]"Specific policy context" simply refers to the fact that the demand for instruments and the supply of instrument options are both linked to the specific environmental problems for which the instruments are being considered. Also, as discussed below, the legislature in this framework selects a policy instrument from among a range of options, including alternative policy instruments plus the status quo.

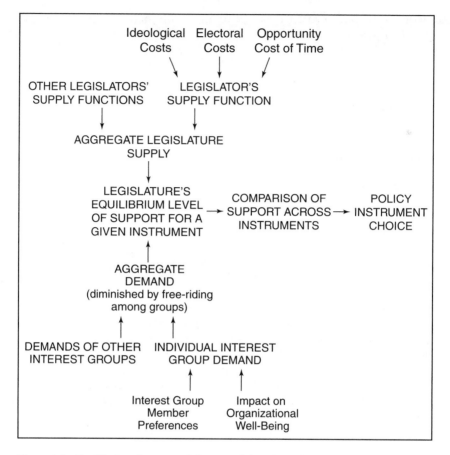

Figure 1 An Equilibrium Framework for Examining the Political Market

supply function and the aggregation of relevant demands.[60] Levels of effective support provided by individual members of the legislature are hence equivalent to the amounts they are willing to provide at the competitive equilibrium "price," the points of intersection of their supply functions with the infinitely elastic demand they face. The aggregate support is simply the sum over legislators of their individual levels of effective support. The legislative outcome, i.e., the choice of a policy instrument, then depends upon the relative degrees of support generated for alternative policy instruments.

---

[60]It is implicitly assumed that the effective support provided by individual legislators can be observed. This is a reasonable assumption in many but not all situations. Future work should explicitly incorporate this uncertainty.

The following sections describe the political market's commodity and currency, and then turn to more detailed expositions of the origins of regulatory demand and supply, respectively. Finally, the Article discusses the nature of political market equilibria and the legislative outcomes that result.

A. The Political Market's Commodity and Currency

Each legislator supplies some degree of support for a given regulatory instrument. Interest groups seek to secure support from legislators in the political market. The commodity of support is seen to be *homogeneous* among legislators. That is, the support produced by one legislator is equivalent to (a perfect substitute for) support produced by any other legislator. This commodity may be characterized as "effective support."[61] It is a measure of impact (output), not of effort (input).

To be sure, different legislators require different amounts of effort to produce a unit of effective support. These variations in productivity are due to such factors as the size and effectiveness of members' staffs, their seniority, their committee assignments, and their leadership positions, including committee chairs. Moreover, a legislator's effort may encompass a much larger range of activities than simply voting for a given instrument: among other things, a legislator might hold hearings, attend committee markup meetings, draft or sponsor legislation, insert statements into committee reports,

---

[61]It might be argued that interest groups ultimately care about votes, which at the level of an individual legislator reduces to a binary variable. But there are several reasons to focus on support, rather than on votes alone. First, this approach facilitates comparisons among several instruments, since the outcome of the legislative process is the instrument that garners the most effective support. Second, empirical analysis has largely failed to link campaign contribution with legislators' votes, see Richard L. Hall & Frank W. Wayman, "Buying Time: Moneyed Interests and the Mobilization of Bias in Congressional Committees," 84 *Am. Pol. Sci. Rev.* 797, 813 (1990), while campaign contributions have been found to be highly correlated with legislators' participation in committees, itself closely linked with the notion of "effective support[.]" See Grier & Munger, supra note 45, at 641; Jonathan I. Silberman & Garey C. Durden, "Determining Legislative Preferences on the Minimum Wage: An Economic Approach," 84 *J. Pol. Econ.* 317, 326–27 (1976). Third, the fate of most prospective legislation is determined before it reaches the floor for a vote. The agenda-setting powers of committees make them virtual arbiters of whether or not bills reach the floor for voting. See Kenneth A. Shepsle & Barry R. Weingast, "The Institutional Foundations of Committee Power," 81 *Am. Pol. Sci. Rev.* 85, 87 (1987). Once a bill reaches the floor, norms of deference may lead many members of Congress to follow committee recommendations, either because of implicit logrolls among committees, see Barry R. Weingast & William J. Marshall, "The Industrial Organization of Congress, or, Why Legislatures, Like Firms, Are Not Organized as Markets," 96 *J. Pol. Econ.* 132, 157–58 (1988), or because of recognition of committees' greater expertise. See Kingdon, supra note 42, at 133.

Votes of committee members are usually less critical than the intensity of members' support. See Richard L. Hall, "Participation and Purpose in Committee Decision Making," 81 *Am. Pol. Sci. Rev.* 105, 105–06 (1987); David R. Mayhew, *Congress: The Electoral Connection* 92 (1974). Hence, securing the support of a relatively small number of legislators (each of whom is a highly efficient producer of effective support) may be the primary goal of interest groups, even though the groups ultimately care about the outcome of floor votes. This reality is captured by the above framework, with its focus on levels of "effective support."

propose amendments, seek to influence colleagues, or make behind-the-scenes deals.[62]

The political currency in this market is seen as the resources necessary for the legislator's reelection: not only votes, but also monetary and other contributions.[63] An environmental interest group, for example, may publicly endorse a candidate for office, or may volunteer time and effort to mobilize votes in a legislator's district. Other forms of "payment" to legislators (such as time spent drafting legislation or policy information for the legislator) are also valued by a legislator seeking reelection, since association with the interest group may increase the legislator's support, and the time saved by the legislator may be spent on activities that generate home district votes. Incorporating home district votes, financial contributions, and nonmonetary contributions in the currency of "resources," the model adopts a monetary numeraire for convenience.

B. Origins of Demand for Environmental Policy Instruments

The Article now explores the nature of demand by firms and individuals, dividing the latter category into three overlapping groups (consumers, workers, and environmentalists), and then considers the role of interest groups in the political market.[64]

1. Firms and Individuals. Firms are affected by environmental regulation through the costs they incur to produce goods and services. Consider a price-taking firm[65] that wishes to maximize its profit from producing a sin-

---

[62]One set of researchers describes the range of services legislators can offer interest groups. See Denzau & Munger, supra note 45, at 91. Another group analyzes a similar measure of legislator participation, which they call "political support effort." See Silberman & Durden, supra note 61, at 318. Notably, these models generally treat as an output what in this framework is an input: namely, the effort exerted by the legislator to produce effective support. The above framework incorporates differences among legislators in effectiveness and productivity into the supply side (production of effective support) rather than the demand side (demand of interest groups for support from different legislators). For further discussion of the ways in which members of Congress participate in policy making, especially in committee, see Hall, supra note 61, at 106–08; Richard L. Hall, *Participation in Congress* 40–48 (1996); Hall & Wayman, supra note 61, at 804–15.

[63]Monetary contributions can be used to finance advertising campaigns, literature production and distribution, and other activities that increase the probability of a legislator being reelected.

[64]Of course, individuals and interest groups also play a role on the "supply side" of the political market by affecting legislators' electoral prospects. Individuals vote, while interest groups may spend resources to influence that vote directly (for example, by disseminating information about a legislator's voting record on an issue). Stated in terms of our framework, individuals and interest groups not only exhibit a demand function, but also may also shift legislators' supply functions. See infra Part III.C. This Article attempts to draw a conceptual distinction between these two facets of individual and interest group involvement.

[65]In a competitive market economy, individual firms cannot independently set the price that they will charge (only monopolists can do this); rather, they must accept or "take" the price given by the competitively determined supply-demand equilibrium, and then decide how much to supply at that price.

gle product and that employs a set of factors in its production, each of which has some cost associated with it. One of these input factors is the set of relevant features of the regulatory environment. In seeking to maximize profits, the firm chooses levels of all its inputs, including the efforts it puts into securing its desired regulatory environment. By solving this maximization problem, the firm derives its demand functions for all its inputs, including its demand for the environmental policy instrument. In this simple model, individual firms have a decreasing marginal willingness to pay to secure particular policy instruments.[66] At a minimum, a firm's demand for a policy instrument is a function of output and input prices, including the "price of legislators' support."[67]

The choice of environmental policy instruments can also have an effect on individuals. For example, individuals can be affected by the level of environmental quality that results from the use of a particular instruments,[68] or by the costs of environmental protection as reflected in the prices of the goods and services they buy. Individuals might even derive some direct utility from knowing that a particular type of policy instrument was employed. These effects can be reflected in a utility function, which the consumer maximizes subject to a budgetary constraint. The result is a set of demand functions for all private and public goods, including demand functions for any environmental policy instruments that affect the individual's utility either directly or indirectly. Thus, like firms, individuals can have a decreasing marginal willingness to pay to secure particular policy instruments.[69] Their demand for a policy instrument is a function of their income and of the relative prices of relevant goods, including the price of securing support for their preferred instrument.

---

[66]The maximized objective function is the firm's profit function. Hotelling's Lemma (a basic microeconomic theorem) establishes that the factor demand functions are downward sloping as long as the profit function is convex.

[67]This stylized framework implicitly assumes that firms are profit-maximizing (or cost-minimizing) atomistic units, and thus that there is no significant principal-agent slack between managers and shareholders. There is little doubt that this assumption departs from reality in many cases, but we leave its investigation to future research.

[68]Although attention has been restricted at the outset to the policy instruments used to achieve a given level of protection, the choice of cost-effective instruments can lead to the adoption of more stringent environmental standards, as noted below.

[69]The maximized utility function is the individual's indirect utility function. By Roy's Identity (a basic microeconomic truism), the demand functions are derived as downward sloping, as long as the utility functions has the usual properties. It is possible that over a certain region the demand function will be increasing. For example, a unit of support for an instrument will be virtually worthless at very low levels of support, since adoption of that instrument will be extremely unlikely. Assume, however, that the demand function is decreasing over the politically relevant range, in which adoption of the instrument is a realistic possibility. It might be argued that if a legislature were composed of a single legislator and there was perfect information, demand functions for political support would (in the case of support relevant for voting) be a step function with a single step: interest groups would have no willingness-to-pay below some level of (adequate) support, and no willingness-to-pay above a sufficient level of support. But in a multi-member body, more support from individual legislators can always be worth something, and if there is uncertainty about how much support is sufficient, the demand function is likely to be downward sloping over at least some range.

Moreover, individuals can be categorized as "consumers," "environmentalists," and "workers"; these three categories are neither mutually exclusive nor exhaustive. Individuals are "consumers" to the degree that the choice of environmental policy instrument affects them through its impact on the prices of goods and services, "environmentalists" to the degree that they are affected by the impact of instrument choice on the level of environmental quality, and "workers" to the degree that they are affected by environmental policy through its impact on the demand for labor, and hence their wages.

2. Interest Groups. Because there are significant costs of lobbying and because the target of demand (i.e., the public policy) is a public good,[70] an individual and even a firm will receive relatively small rewards for any direct lobbying efforts. For individuals, the marginal costs of lobbying are likely to outweigh the perceived marginal benefits over much of the relevant range of lobbying activity, such that individuals will undersupply lobbying, hoping instead to free ride on the efforts of others. Although some large firms maintain offices in Washington, D.C., to facilitate direct lobbying of Congress, most of the demand for public policies from both firms and individuals is transmitted through organized interest groups.

The free-riding problem standing in the way of individual lobbying efforts can also be a significant obstacle to the formation of interest groups.[71] For an interest group to organize, it must overcome the free-riding problem by offering its members enough benefits to make the costs of membership worthwhile. For a citizen group, such as an environmental advocacy organization, these benefits are likely to include: "material incentives," such as newsletters, workshops, or gifts, "solidary incentives," namely the benefits derived from social interaction; and "purposive incentives," such as the personal satisfaction derived from membership in an organization whose activities one supports.[72]

Among citizen groups, taxpayer and consumer organizations may face greater free-riding problems than environmental groups:[73] their lobbying actions are likely to have an even wider range of potential beneficiaries;

---

[70]Regulation may not always be nonexclusive. Loopholes, narrowly applying clauses in statutes, and bureaucratic exemptions can all afford special treatment for some firms or narrowly defined categories of consumers. This possibility may provide enough incentive for some individual firms to lobby.

[71]See Mancur Olson, *The Logic of Collective Action: Public Goods and the Theory of Groups* 43–44 (1965).

[72]See Lawrence S. Rothenberg, *Linking Citizens to Government: Interest Group Politics at Common Cause* 66 (1992); James Q. Wilson, *Political Organizations* 33–35 (1995).

[73]Notably, labor unions are able to overcome free-riding problems through mandatory dues payments. See Olson, supra note 71, at 76; Wilson, supra note 72, at 119. To the extent that these funds are used for lobbying efforts, unions might be expected to be especially well-represented in the political arena. Yet, since unions dedicate most of their campaign contributions to securing favorable labor policy, unions as a group have only rarely been influential (or even active) in environmental policy debates.

they may be able to offer fewer material incentives; and they lack the compelling moral mission that may drive the purposive incentives motivating members of environmental groups.

To overcome their own set of free-rider problems, trade associations can offer a range of benefits to member firms that nonmembers do not enjoy, including: influence over policy goals; information on policy developments; reports on economic trends; and participation in an annual convention.[74] Compared with citizen groups, trade associations may have significant advantages in overcoming free-riding: they are usually smaller, making the contributions of each member more significant; and even substantial annual dues may be negligible costs for member firms.[75] Hence, private industry interests may be over-represented in the political process relative to citizen groups.

Importantly, interest groups do not simply aggregate the political demands of their members. Indeed, an interest group's utility maximization function may diverge significantly from those of its members as a result of a principal-agent problem: the members (and donors) are principals who contract with their agent—the interest group (or, more precisely, its professional staff)—to represent their views to the legislature.[76] As in many such contractual relationships, the output exerted by the agents may not be directly observable or controllable by the principal. This principal-agent problem is probably far more serious for environmental advocacy groups than for private industry trade associations.[77]

Principal-agent slack between what the members want and what the interest group actually does arises because the organization's staff has its own self interests. A trade association, for example, may not only want to maximize the profits of its member firms; it may also seek to expand its membership or to increase revenue from member dues. Similarly, the objective function of an environmental group may include not only the level of environmental quality, but also factors such as membership size, budget,

---

[74]See Olson, supra note 71, at 139–41.

[75]See Wilson, supra note 72, at 144.

[76]In the typical principal-agent relationship, the principals (in this case, the firms) know their own interests and wish to ensure that the agent (here the trade association) acts in accordance with those interests. It is conceivable, however, that interest group staff may be leading the charge for policy changes that will benefit member firms, while those firms remain largely ignorant about the policy issues at stake. See Raymond A. Bauer et al., *American Business and Public Policy* 331 (1963).

[77]An environmental organization may have a hundred thousand members or more scattered across the country, paying scant attention to the operational proprieties of the organization (let alone the details of its day-to-day activities). Trade associations, on the other hand, may be dominated by a large producer, with an incentive to monitor the association's activities, and their boards of directors may be made up of executives from member firms. Moreover, trade associations have many fewer members, and therefore the stake of each in the organization is greater, and monitoring is more likely to be worthwhile. On the other hand, trade associations have their own set of problems. Among these are the possible necessity of obtaining an expression of consensus from member firms prior to undertaking specific lobbying efforts.

and reputation among various constituencies that affect the organization's health and viability.[78]

With these competing interests and constraints in mind, an interest group must decide how to allocate its scarce resources as it lobbies the legislature for its preferred outcome. The total benefits to an interest group of the legislature's support for an instrument rise with the degree of support offered, but there are increasing marginal returns. As in the case of individuals and firms, a unit increased in support when the legislature is already very favorably disposed to one's position is worth less than a unit increase in support by a lukewarm or previously unsupportive legislature. This characteristic produces a downward-sloping demand function: an interest group's marginal willingness-to-pay for support decreases as the legislature's total support increases.

C. Origins of Supply of Environmental Policy Instruments

The Article now considers a legislator who derives utility from a number of relevant interests: making public policy, doing good things for the country or for her district, satisfying ideological beliefs, having prestige and the perquisites of office, and so on. To continue getting utility from these factors, the legislator must be reelected. Assuming that legislators seek to maximize their expected utility, a legislator will choose her level of support for a proposed policy instrument based on the effort required to provide that support, the inherent satisfaction she derives from providing that level of support, and the effects her position will likely have on her chances of reelection.[79]

Accordingly, the legislator's supply function consists of three components: (1) the opportunity cost of efforts required to provide a given degree of support for a policy instrument; (2) the psychological cost of supporting an instrument despite one's ideological beliefs;[80] and (3) the opportunity cost (in terms of reduced probability of reelection) of supporting an instrument not favored by one's electoral constituency in terms of reduced probability of reelection.[81]

---

[78]One researcher treats the agency problem in environmental groups extensively, arguing that, because members and patrons cannot observe the outputs or effort of their agents directly, they must instead make funding and membership decisions based on a group's inputs: its expenditures on lobbying, member materials, advertising, and fund raising. See Robert C. Lowry, "The Political Economy of Environmental Citizen Groups" 94–96 (1993) (unpublished Ph.D. dissertation, Harvard University) (on file with the Harvard University Library).

[79]This notion of legislators' goals is consistent with other descriptions of Representatives as having three basic objectives: reelection, influence within the House, and good public policy. See Richard F. Fenno, Jr., *Home Style: House Members in Their Districts* 137 (1978). In our framework, "influence within the House" and "good public policy" are combined in "being a legislator." If the legislator wishes to continue to be a legislator in the future, she will also value reelection.

[80]If supporting the instrument is consistent with one's ideological beliefs, then this is a "negative cost," i.e., a benefit.

[81]This is also a "negative cost" (benefit) if supporting the instrument is consistent with one's constituents' positions.

The first component emerges from the individual legislator's productivity in providing support. As indicated in Figure 2, the legislator's input is "effort"[82] and the relevant output is "effective support." Some legislators may produce "effective support" more efficiently with a given amount of effort thanks to the size and effectiveness of their staffs, their seniority in the legislature, and their membership and leadership on relevant committees. By placing a value on the opportunity cost of time and effort, an opportunity cost function can be derived (Figure 3), and from that, the related marginal opportunity cost of effort, represented by the upward-sloping line emanating from the origin in Figure 4.[83]

Next, assuming that a legislator derives disutility from acting inconsistently with her ideology, the psychological cost of supporting a policy inconsistent with one's ideological beliefs can be introduced into the framework. As suggested above, this cost would be negative (a benefit) if one were ideologically predisposed to favor the particular policy. In either case, it is conceivable that these marginal psychological costs might be increasing or decreasing (in absolute value) with the degree of support, but for ease of presentation we portray this marginal cost as constant in Figure 4. In this case, the legislator's ideology has no effect on the slope of the combined marginal cost function; rather, ideology shifts the function upwards (for inconsistency with ideology) or downwards (for consistency with ideology).

Finally, the framework incorporates the third component of the legislator's supply function: the opportunity cost corresponding to the reduced probability of reelection given the support of an instrument not favored by one's electoral constituency. Lost votes from constituents unhappy with the legislator's position would directly affect the legislator's chances of reelection, whereas protest and grassroots efforts by interest groups unhappy with the legislator's position could indirectly affect constituents' assessment of the legislator.[84] Again, this is a "negative cost" if supporting the instrument is consistent with one's constituents' positions.[85] As with ideological costs,

---

[82]This includes the use of other resources, but may be thought of as being denominated in units of time.

[83]In the face of the overwhelming claims on her time and resources—both in Washington and in her home districts—a member's time and effort carries a significant opportunity cost. See Bauer, supra note 76, at 412–13; Kingdon, supra note 42, at 216; Fenno, supra note 79, at 141. Effort invested in providing support for one bill could have been spent working on other legislation that would satisfy ideological goals, reflect voters' objectives, and/or attract votes, dollars, and other resources; or visiting the home district and supplying constituency services such as help in dealing with the bureaucracy. See Denzau & Munger, supra note 45, at 92–96; Grier & Munger, supra note 45, at 618. Note that the marginal cost function is assumed in the figure to be linear, simply to keep the explication simple.

[84]Members of Congress tend to take into account the preferences of the people who voted for them, i.e., their "supporting coalition," see Kingdon, supra note 42, at 60, or their "reelection constituency," see Fenno, supra note 79, at 8. A conservative legislator whose reelection constituency is anti-regulatory, for example, will not be affected by a minority group of environmentalists calling for command-and-control regulation.

[85]Departing from the preferences of constituents reduces the probability of the legislator's reelection. This reduced probability can be evaluated in terms of the resources required to maintain a constant probability of reelection.

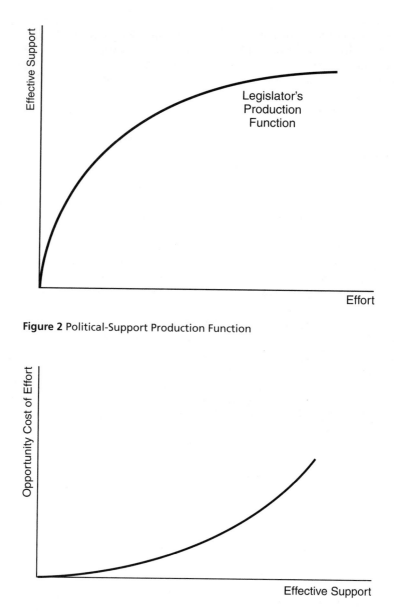

Figure 2 Political-Support Production Function

Figure 3 Political-Support Cost Function

although these marginal electoral opportunity costs could be increasing or decreasing with the level of the legislator's support, they are drawn as constant (and positive) in Figure 4, to keep things simple.[86]

---

[86]Figure 4 represents both ideological costs and electoral costs as being positive; support for the policy is essentially inconsistent both with the legislator's own ideology and her constituents'

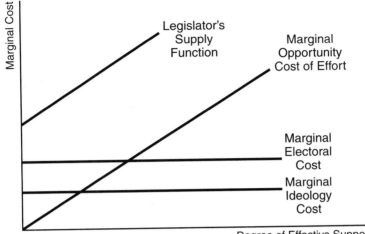

Figure 4 Opportunity Costs and the Supply of Political Support by an Individual Legislator

Accordingly, the overall (individual) marginal cost function, or the legislator's supply-of-support function, is simply the vertical summation of these three components: opportunity costs of effort, ideological costs, and constituency costs (Figure 4). The amount of support for a policy instrument that a legislator would supply in the absence of any contributions helpful to advancing the member's goals (including her reelection) is represented in Figure 5 as the "preferred point," the intersection of the supply function with the horizontal axis. In this framework, the legislator can be induced to offer progressively greater degrees of support from this preferred point through offers of "political compensation" that offset the legislator's respective opportunity costs.

Thus, the legislator has an upward-sloping marginal opportunity-cost or supply function, beginning at her preferred degree of support along the horizontal axis. The intersection of the supply function with the horizontal axis can take place at either a positive or a negative degree of support (see S_1 and S_3, respectively, in Figure 5). A politician who is strongly opposed to a given instrument will have a supply function with a negative intercept on the horizontal axis (and a positive intercept on the vertical axis). For such a legislator, a positive, non-marginal shadow price[87] of political compensation is

---

preferences. It is not inconceivable that these could be of opposite sign, but in a representative democracy, that would be the exception, not the rule. As stated by one author, "If your conscience and your district disagree too often,' members like to say, 'you're in the wrong business.'" Fenno, supra note 79, at 142.

[87]The shadow price refers to the implicit price or the marginal valuation of the good or service in question.

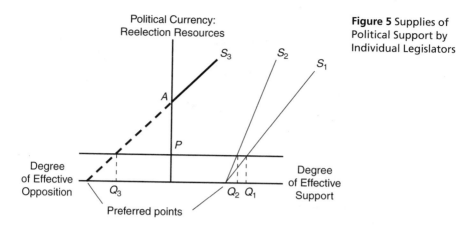

Political Currency:
Reelection Resources

Figure 5 Supplies of
Political Support by
Individual Legislators

required for any positive degree of support to be forthcoming (see point A in Figure 5).

The legislator's supply function is affected by several exogenous factors. First, an exogenous increase in the negative impact of a given instrument on a legislator's constituents (for example, the construction in the legislator's district of a new factory that would have to pay pollution taxes) may increase the legislator's opportunity costs of supporting that instrument. Conversely, an exogenous increase in the benefits of an instrument to the legislator's constituents (for example, the expansion of a firm in the district that produced a mandated abatement technology) would decrease the legislator's opportunity costs.

Second, the position of the legislator's political party is also relevant. Parties supply funds and organizational support in reelection campaigns. Moreover, leadership posts in the party offer opportunities for increased effectiveness in the legislature. Obviously, parties are likely to be more generous with legislators who are loyal.[88]

Third, the actions of other legislators will have a bearing on the costs of supplying support thanks to the possibilities for vote trading. For example, one legislator may care a great deal about the chosen level of environmental protection, while having only a slight preference for standards over taxes; another legislator may care less about the exact level but have a strong preference for taxes over standards, given her own market-oriented ideology. In a logroll, both legislators could gain from vote trading, with such a logroll affecting both legislators' costs of supplying support for a given instrument.

---

[88]Party leaders may conceivably also become effective demanders for policy instrument support by offering various resources to legislators in exchange for support, in which case the parties are essentially functioning as interest groups.

Fourth and finally, it is both the intent and the consequence of some lobbying activities to shift legislators' supply functions. In other words, in addition to being the primary demanders for alternative forms of regulation, organized interest groups can also play a role in determining the position and shape of legislators' supply functions. Lobbyists might attempt to: affect a legislator's ideologically based perception of the merits of a proposed policy instrument;[89] affect a legislator's perceptions of her constituents' policy preferences;[90] and/or affect a legislator's effort-support production function through provision of information or technical support.[91]

D. Formation of Equilibria and Legislative Outcomes

Up to this point, this Article has focused on the origins of supply and demand for a single policy instrument. However, in many contexts, there will be a *set* of possible instruments considered for achieving a given policy goal: for example, a standard, a tax, and a system of tradeable permits. In addition, there will exist the possibility of doing nothing, i.e., maintaining the status quo. Hence if N alternative instruments are under consideration, then there will be N + 1 possible choices of action.[92] Each option can define a "political market" for effective support.[93] On the demand side, each policy instrument may have an associated set of interest groups seeking to secure support for it. Moreover, on the supply side, each policy instrument gives rise to its own set of legislator supply functions.[94]

The legislative outcome is the choice of one of the N + 1 alternatives arising from the interactions of interest groups' demands for and legislators' supplies of support for alternative instruments. The degree of aggregate support for each instrument results from an equilibrium established in the legislature, and the outcome in the legislature favors the policy instrument with the greatest degree of total support.

The following sections examine the component parts of this process. First, the nature of the aggregation of demand for a policy instrument across interested individuals and groups, and the aggregation of supplies of support for a policy instrument across members of the legislature, is considered. Then, the formation of equilibria in the legislature for alternative policy

---

[89]See Kingdon, supra note 42, at 141–42.

[90]See David Austen-Smith & John R. Wright, "Counteractive Lobbying," 38 *Am. J. Pol. Sci.* 25, 29–30 (1994).

[91]See Bauer, supra note 76, at 354–57.

[92]The choice set of instruments is simply taken as given. Important questions remain regarding how it is determined, but these are beyond the scope of this Article.

[93]An interest group can demand and a legislator can supply support for more than one instrument. Although this may at first seem counterintuitive, recall that each legislator's supply function for a given instrument may include the possibility of opposition.

[94]A single legislator may be more efficient at producing support for one instrument than for another and may even have different ideological attitudes towards different instruments. Moreover, the preferences of her reelection constituency may vary across instruments.

instruments and the consequent choice of political outcome is examined. Finally, alternative approaches to modeling this political market are discussed.

1. Aggregation of Demand for Policy Instrument Support. Typically, more than one interest group will be pressing for support from the legislature. How is such interest group demand to be aggregated? In the classic model associated with Stigler[95] and Peltzman,[96] the "winner takes all": the highest bidder wins and gains control over regulation. In another model, competing interest groups participate in a zero-sum game along a single dimension: one group is taxed, the other subsidized, and each tries to improve its lot at the expense of the other.[97] In an actual legislature, interest groups may be opposed to one another or aligned in support of the same instrument.

The most obvious approach for aggregating the demand functions of interest groups might be simply to sum, at each level of willingness-to-pay, the degrees of support that each group demands at that price. Such demand aggregation makes sense for private goods, but the support the legislature provides is essentially a public good. Hence, an efficient approach might involve taking a given level of support and vertically summing what each interest group is (marginally) willing to pay for that degree of support. But such an efficient approach is unlikely to reflect positive reality, as long as free-rider problems among interest groups exist. Therefore, the aggregate demand thus calculated represents the upper bound of actual aggregate demand, that is, the demand experienced in the absence of free-riding.

2. Aggregation of Supply of Policy Instrument Options. In this framework, the degree of support by individual legislators is denominated in terms of homogenous units of "effective support," with differences among legislators already incorporated into the underlying production functions with respect to individual marginal opportunity costs of effort (as well as individual marginal ideological and electoral costs). Therefore, the legislature's supply function can be derived by horizontally summing the supply functions of individual legislators. As noted above, some legislators' supply functions may extend to the left of the vertical axis (for example, S_3 in Figure 5), corresponding to opposition to the instrument in question. Therefore, when the individual legislator supply functions are horizontally added, the aggregate supply function for the legislature represents the relevant net supply of support. Like the supply function for an individual legislator, the aggregate supply function for some instruments may intersect the vertical axis at a positive price.

---

[95]See Stigler, supra note 28, at 12–13.
[96]See Peltzman, supra note 30, at 212.
[97]See Becker, supra note 31, at 373–76.

3. Equilibrium Support in the Legislature for a Policy Instrument. The model treats the legislature as a competitive market for the support of policy instruments. Given the homogeneity of the commodity demanded and supplied, the number of members in the two houses of Congress, and the number of active interest groups, perfect competition is a reasonable first approximation. Under that assumption, the equilibrium, aggregate level of "effective support" provided for the policy instrument is the level for which aggregate supply equals aggregate demand (Q* in Figure 6). This level is associated with a shadow price (P in Figure 6) representing the aggregate marginal willingness to pay for support in the legislature's equilibrium.

There are two cases of interest in which the aggregate supply and demand functions do not intersect in the politically relevant positive orthant, the northeast part of the graph where both price and quantity are positive. In one case, the demand function intersects the horizontal axis to the left of the legislature's "aggregate preferred point" (see the gap between points B and E_A in Figure 7). In that instance, the maximum support demanded in aggregate by interest groups (at zero price) is lower than the amount that the legislature would provide on its own. In this case of "excess supply," it is reasonable to assume that the legislature would provide support at its preferred point (E_A). With the likelihood of free-riding among interest groups, it would not be surprising if the aggregate demand by interest groups often fell short of the support a strongly committed legislature would provide absent any lobbying. In the above case, the competitive equilibrium price is zero, with each legislator providing support at her own preferred point.

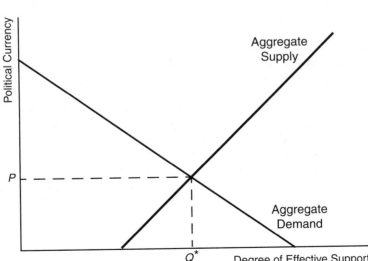

Figure 6 Aggregate Demand and Aggregate Supply of Political Support and the Formation of a Legislative Equilibrium

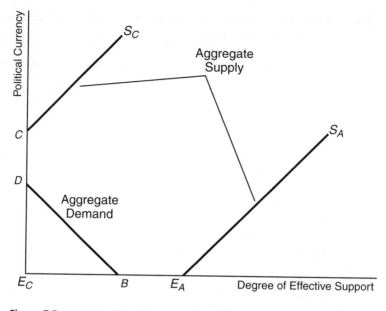

Figure 7 Degenerate Cases in the Political Market

A second special case arises when a legislature so strongly opposes a policy that its upward-sloping aggregate supply function intersects the vertical axis at a positive price (point C in Figure 7). In this case, the supply function could conceivably lie entirely above the interest groups' aggregate demand function. The political price that such a legislature would require for a positive degree of support is simply greater than the interest groups' overall reservation price for obtaining such support (point D in Figure 7).

In this competitive political market framework, an individual legislator will tend to supply support for a particular policy instrument up to the point where her marginal opportunity costs of doing so are equivalent to the infinitely elastic demand for support she faces from interest groups, represented by the horizontal line through the point P in Figure 5 (derived with the equilibrium in Figure 6). Thus, a set of legislators with supply functions represented by S_1, S_2, and S_3 (Figure 5), would provide effective support of Q_1, Q_2, and Q_3, respectively.

The legislator with supply function S_3 provides a negative level of support, i.e., opposition. An interest group might benefit from contributing to this legislator in the hope of reducing her degree of active opposition,[98] just

---

[98]Hall and Wayman examine legislator participation in committees, and argue that interest groups give contributions to "hostile" legislators in order to reduce their participation, i.e., their opposition. See Hall & Wayman, supra note 61, at 803.

as it can benefit by increasing the support of a "friendly" legislator. It would take a level of demand (and political compensation) equivalent to point A in Figure 5 to move this same legislator to a position of inaction or indifference. On the other hand, legislators such as those represented by S_1 and S_2 in Figure 5 derive benefits (negative costs) from supporting an instrument, no matter what the position of relevant interest groups. Not surprisingly, such friendly legislators supply even greater levels of support in response to interest group demand.

4. Legislative Outcomes. The previous section discussed the equilibrium level of support for a policy instrument by a single legislator. The next step, then, is to ask how these individual levels of support translate into policy outcomes. One could imagine summing the individual levels of support across legislators to find the aggregate support for an instrument. Such an approach is insufficient, however, because it ignores institutional processes (for example, various kinds of voting rules) that influence collective decisions. In moving from individual support to policy outcomes, therefore, the analysis must take institutional features of the legislature into account.

First, the committee structure of Congress (especially in the House of Representatives) gives different legislators widely different levels of influence over policy.[99] Thus, legislators vary greatly in the effectiveness of the support they can supply for a given instrument. However, with the framework's focus on degrees of *effective* support, this reality is already incorporated (through the political support production functions) and has no effect on the appropriate aggregation; it remains one of simple summation of individual equilibria.

Second, legislative outcomes are affected by voting rules. The number of votes necessary for passage (taking into account the veto power of the executive) determines the level and distribution of support needed to pass a bill.[100] Furthermore, the order of voting on amendments and the nature of

---

[99]Norms of deference, backed up by repeated interactions and the threat of retaliation, give members of committees and subcommittees significant influence over policies under their jurisdiction. See Shepsle & Weingast, supra note 61, at 88–89; Weingast & Marshall, supra note 61, at 158. Agenda-setting or "gate keeping" powers give committees the right to send bills to the floor or table them in committee. Standing committees are also heavily represented on the conference committees that are established to reconcile differences between the chambers before final passage. Power is particularly concentrated in the hands of committee chairs, who hold sway over the committees' agendas and the bills reported to the floor. Given the importance of committee composition, policy outcomes may differ markedly from the preferences of the legislature as a whole; given low committee turnover and the importance of seniority, the status quo may persist long after support in the full legislature has ebbed. See Kenneth A. Shepsle & Barry R. Weingast, "Political Solutions to Market Problems," 78 *Am. Pol. Sci. Rev.* 417, 429 (1984).

[100]In the U.S. Congress, a bill needs a bare majority in the House of Representatives, but may have to clear a higher hurdle in the Senate to bring closure to debate. If the President vetoes the bill, of course, two-thirds majorities in both houses are required to enact legislation.

the final vote also affect the outcome.[101] The question is then how support translates into votes. Whereas the model's "degree of support" is a continuous variable, it produces a binary variable: a vote. Any empirical implementation of this framework would need to address this linkage.[102] For the purposes of this Article, focus can be confined to the reality that, in general, the policy instrument chosen will be the alternative garnering the greatest aggregate support.

5. Alternative Equilibrium Frameworks. Alternative conceptual frameworks of the political market are possible. One potential approach would give greater emphasis to the differences existing among individual legislators in terms of the nature of support they can provide. Thus, instead of quantifying support in terms of perfectly homogenous units of "effective support," the "uniqueness" of support from any single legislator (particularly from powerful members of the legislature) would be interpreted as leading to a set of monopoly political markets, rather than to a single competitive political market.

At one extreme, each member of the legislature is assumed to be a monopoly supplier of her unique type of support and is thus facing a downward-sloping demand for her support. As such, there would exist a set of monopoly equilibria, one for each member of the legislature. In their respective equilibria, each member equates her marginal cost (individual supply function) with the "marginal revenue" function associated with the policy demands she faces, and determines her equilibrium (and utility-maximizing) level of support.

The extreme case of multiple monopoly suppliers appears less reasonable than the perfectly competitive case as an approximation of political reality. However, it does illustrate the potential for alternative models of imperfect competition that may be superior for capturing important characteristics of political markets. Various models of cooperative and noncooperative oligopoly might capture significant elements of legislative relationships.[103] Such explorations will not be dealt with here. Instead, in order to develop a conceptual framework within which existing political economy theories can be organized and synthesized, the basic competitive framework is examined further.

---

[101]If modified by successful amendments, a bill will be considered in opposition to the status quo in the final vote. This arrangement favors the status quo and requires that each bill be compared ultimately with the status quo rather than with other alternatives.

[102]Discrete-choice econometric models theoretically based on the existence of an unobserved latent variable are obvious candidates.

[103]For example, the respective roles played by committee chairs and members may be modeled as a monopolist operating in the context of a competitive fringe.

IV. Demand for Environmental Policy Instruments

Demand-side explanations for the choice among environmental policy instruments can be separated into four sectors of regulatory demand: firms, environmentalists, labor, and consumers.

A. Firms

Firms tend to demand the policy instruments promising the highest profits (or the lowest losses) from regulation. While all environmental regulation imposes costs of compliance on firms, not all instruments impose the same costs to achieve a given regulatory goal. Positive political economy explanations of firm demand for environmental regulation can be divided into three principal categories: firm preferences for particular instruments given lower aggregate costs of compliance compared to the industry as a whole; the presence of rents and entry barriers; and differential costs of compliance across firms in a given industry.[104]

1. Lower Aggregate Costs to an Industry as a Whole. All else being equal, firms will tend to prefer regulatory instruments with lower aggregate costs for the industry as a whole. As market-based approaches are likely more cost-effective than command-and-control instruments, the above would suggest that private industry as a whole would generally prefer market-based approaches. However, a crucial distinction exists between the aggregate cost for society and the aggregate cost for private industry. By definition, cost-effective instruments minimize costs to society; they may however vary in proportion of costs imposed on polluters. Accordingly, the use of market-based instruments does not guarantee that firms' compliance costs will be less than the compliance costs of command-and-control regulation.

It would then follow that firms would oppose regulatory instruments that shift a greater cost burden onto industry. For instance, the virtually unanimous opposition by private industry to pollution taxes results from the fact that, under such schemes, firms pay not only their private costs of compliance, but also the costs of tax payments to the government for any

---

[104]There are other plausible explanations for firms' preferences. Firms may simply support the continuation of the status quo, which is generally the command-and-control approach, because replacing familiar policies with new instruments can mean that existing expertise within firms becomes less valued. See Steven P. Kelman, *What Price Incentives?* 118–22 (1981); Stewart, supra note 16, at 40. For example, lobbyists—the agents in a principal-agent relationship—may be rationally expected to resist the dissipation of their human capital. See Robert W. Hahn & Robert N. Stavins, "Incentive-based Environmental Regulation: A New Era from an Old Idea," 18 *Ecology L.Q.* 1, 24 (1991). It has also been suggested that market-based instruments may be opposed simply because they are not well understood, and there is at least anecdotal evidence that this has been the case. See Kelman at 96, above; W.P. Welch, "The Political Feasibility of Full Ownership Property Rights: The Case of Pollution and Fisheries," 16 *Pol'y Sci.* 165, 175 (1983). Such lack of understanding can also affect the supply side, and we discuss this later.

residual emissions.[105] Similarly, under tradeable permit schemes, firms bear equivalent costs if the initial distribution of the permits is through an auction. In contrast, under a tradeable permit scheme with grandfathered permits, existing firms do not bear any cost for their residual emissions.[106]

The above suggests that private industry as a whole would prefer grandfathered permits *and* standards to other instruments, since grandfathered permits are cost-effective and the burden placed on industry (at least on existing firms) is minimized. Emissions standards are usually worse for industry in terms of the total-cost criterion, but are likely to be preferred by firms to auctioned permits or taxes.

2. Generation of Rents and Erection of Entry Barriers. Certain types of regulation can actually augment firms' profits through the generation of rents and the erection of entry barriers. In general, firms earn rents if a regulatory instrument drives price above average cost. Assume the case of a command-and-control standard that sets an allowable level of aggregate pollution for each firm, where firms can meet the standard only by reducing output.[107] Assume further that the industry is initially made up of many identical firms, each facing an identical demand, with classical average and marginal cost functions. In the absence of regulation, each firm would produce at the intersection of its marginal and average cost curves, making zero profits. The environmental standard reduces total production and therefore raises price along the aggregate demand curve. If the environmental restriction is not exceptionally severe, the new price will be above average cost for all firms. Firms, therefore, earn rent: the difference between the price they receive for their product and their cost of production. If entry is prohibited, existing firms will continue earning rents into the future; even if not, rents will last until enough new firms enter to reestablish competitive equilibrium at the new price. Hence, in the above model, firms may prefer standards to no regulation at all, and firms will prefer standards to taxes, since a tax charges for a resource that otherwise would be free.[108]

---

[105]On this point, see Kelman, supra note 104, at 120; see also Frank S. Arnold, *Economic Analysis of Environmental Policy and Regulation* 227 (1995); Robert W. Crandall, *Controlling Industrial Pollution* 70 (1983); Robert W. Hahn & Roger G. Noll, "Environmental Markets in the Year 2000," 3 *J. Risk Uncertainty* 351, 359 (1990). Actually, firms pay less than the full amount of the tax, since a share is passed on to consumers.

[106]Grandfathering distributes the rents from permits to firms that participate in the initial allocation, in contrast with an auction. See Donald N. Dewees, "Instrument Choice in Environmental Policy," 21 *Econ. Inquiry* 53, 59 (1983); Gary W. Yohe, "Polluters' Profits and Political Response: Direct Control Versus Taxes: Comment," 66 *Am. Econ. Rev.* 981, 981 (1976).

[107]See James M. Buchanan & Gordon Tullock, "Polluters' Profits and Political Response: Direct Control Versus Taxes," 65 *Am. Econ. Rev.* 139, 140 (1975).

[108]Even if the restriction is severe enough to impose losses on firms, they will prefer standards to taxes, which impose new costs. In the long run, under a tax scheme, firms will exit the industry until a new zero-profit equilibrium is reached; in the short term, firms will lose money. The tax reduces each firm's present value of income, whether it remains in the industry or exits. Firms will therefore oppose the introduction of pollution taxes.

Firms, however, are not limited to the single response of cutting output. They can also reduce emissions by adopting new technologies or by changing their input mix. In this more general and realistic scenario, depending on the stringency of the standards and other factors, command-and-control standards can still have the effect of providing rents to regulated firms.[109] Here, too, under certain conditions, firms may prefer command-and-control standards to no regulation at all.[110]

It is important to note that the enhanced industry profitability resulting from rents will be sustainable over the long term *only* in the presence of entry restrictions. Thus, firms regulated by a rent-generating instrument, such as command-and-control standards, will benefit if that instrument is linked to a mechanism that imposes barriers to entry. In theory, such a mechanism might prohibit new entry outright; a more politically feasible approach would impose higher costs on new entrants.[111]

The above body of theory explains why private firms (and their trade associations) may have a strong preference for command-and-control standards, which may create rents, and especially for considerably more stringent command-and-control standards for new pollution sources, which create barriers to entry.[112] The indication that firms would support this form of regulation begins to explain the prevalence of such instruments in U.S. environmental law. Furthermore, the theory indicates that, under certain conditions, the regulated industry would be better off than without regulation.

Although the theoretical arguments are strong, there are no conclusive empirical validations of these demand-side propositions. Direct empirical tests of firm demand for regulatory instruments (such as analyses of resources devoted to lobbying for such instruments as a function of firms'

---

[109]See Michael T. Maloney & Robert E. McCormick, "A Positive Theory of Environmental Quality Regulation," 25 *J.L. & Econ.* 99, 105 (1982).

[110]Pollution restrictions raise both the average and marginal cost curves. Each firm will produce at the level where restricted marginal cost intersects the per-firm demand curve. If the minimum average cost under regulation is to the left of this point, the price (marginal cost) will exceed average cost, and firms will earn rents. Maloney and McCormick identified three conditions that are sufficient for regulation to enhance producer profits: (1) output under regulation corresponds to some cost-minimizing level of output in the absence of regulation; (2) pollution increases with output; and (3) average costs increase more at higher levels of output under regulation. See id. at 104. The necessary and sufficient condition for higher profits is that the intersection of average and marginal cost under regulation lie to the left of the firm's demand curve.

[111]See Stigler, supra note 28, at 3, 5; Eric Rasmusen & Mark Zupan, "Extending the Economic Theory of Regulation to the Form of Policy," 72 *Pub. Choic* 167, 187–89 (1991).

[112]Other barriers to entry result, for example, from the permitting requirements for new sources under the PSD and non-attainment programs under the Clean Air Act, as well as by non-attainment programs' offset requirements for new sources. The positive significance of scarcity rents as a major explanation for the prevalence of particular forms of environmental regulation has important normative implications as well. This is because, in the presence of pre-existing tax distortions, the distribution of these rents can have efficiency implications. See Fullerton & Metcalf, supra note 19, at 44–45. It is ironic that the mechanism that facilitates political acceptance of some environmental policies (transmission of scarcity rents to the regulated sector) may also undo some or all of the welfare gains that would have been forthcoming.

stakes in an issue) are virtually nonexistent. Instead, most empirical work in this area simply seeks to measure the benefits an industry receives under regulation. Thus, the work examines not instrument demand itself, but rather the presumed product of such demand.[113]

The above discussion also provides a positive political economy explanation for why market-based instruments have virtually always taken the form of grandfathered tradeable permits, or at least why private firms should be expected to have strong demands for this means of permit allocation. In tradeable permit schemes, grandfathering not only conveys scarcity rents to firms, since existing polluters are granted valuable economic resources for free, but also provides entry barriers, in that new entrants must purchase permits from existing holders.[114]

The preceding discussion does not provide a compelling explanation for the prevalence of command-and-control standards over grandfathered tradeable permits. In principle, either instrument could provide sustainable rents to existing firms. The theory needs to be extended to explain this phenomenon.

3. Differential Costs across Firms in an Industry. An alternative explanation for the landscape of environmental policy instruments arises from the existence of differential costs of environmental compliance across firms. Due to this heterogeneity, a firm may support policy instruments that impose costs on it, as long as those costs affect it less than the industry average, giving it a competitive advantage.[115] For example, firms which could reduce lead content at relatively low costs (thanks to large refineries) tended to support the gradeable permit system by which the leaded content of gasoline was reduced in the 1980s,[116] while firms with less efficient, smaller refineries were vehemently opposed.[117] Other empirical work, however, has cast doubt

---

[113]Several researchers employed financial market event analysis in two regulatory cases to test whether the value of regulated firms (measured by stock market prices) was positively affected by the announcement of regulation, as the economic theory of regulation would suggest. They found that cotton dust standards promulgated by the U.S. Occupational, Safety, and Health Administration ("OSHA") raised the asset value of cotton producers, which is consistent with the notion that regulation increased firms' profits by creating rents. See Maloney & McCormick, supra note 109, at 122. However, a more comprehensive study reached the opposite conclusion. See John S. Hughes et al., "The Economic Consequences of the OSHA Cotton Dust Standards: An Analysis of Stock Market Price Behavior," 29 *J.L. Econ.* 29, 58–59 (1986).

[114]One research group provided anecdotal evidence for rent-seeking in the decision making process over EPA's implementation of the Montreal Protocol restricting the use and production of CFCs. See Hahn & McGartland, supra note 19, at 601–10. They argue that a rent-seeking model explains the positions of large producers supporting grandfathered tradeable permits and opposing other implementation schemes, including an auction proposal. See id.

[115]See Robert A. Leone & John E. Jackson, *Studies in Public Regulation* 231, 247 (Gary Fromm ed. 1981); Sharon Oster, "The Strategic Use of Regulatory Investment by Industry Sub-groups," 20 *Econ. Inquiry* 604, 606 (1982).

[116]See Kerr & Maré, supra note 24, at 31.

[117]See Small Refiner Lead Phasedown Task Force v. EPA, 705 F.2d 506, 514 (D.C. Cir. 1983) (discussing small refineries' opposition). Another example of such intra-industry differentials, and the resulting splintering of lobbying strategy, occurred when the National Coal Association ("NCA")

on the proposition that firms advocate instruments based on inter-industry or intra-industry transfers.[118]

Another form of cost differential arises as a result of barriers to entry. It is important to maintain the distinction between the entry of new firms and the expansion of existing firms. Entry barriers from environmental regulation generally apply to both situations. Within an industry, firms with no plans to expand would derive greater benefit from entry barriers, potentially discouraging further growth by their competitors.

Conversely, firms with ambitious expansion plans relative to their existing operations would benefit from weaker barriers. Such firms would also try to structure barriers in a manner giving them an advantage relative to newcomers. For example, the "bubble" program of the Clean Air Act creates barriers that are less onerous for existing firms because firms are allowed to engage in intra-firm emissions trading.[119] Under this program, a firm can reduce the emissions of an existing source by an amount at least equal to the emissions of the new source, instead of having to take the more costly step of meeting the command-and-control standard otherwise applicable to new sources.[120] The CAA's banking policies, which allow intra-firm trading across time periods, also make expansion by an incumbent easier than entry by a new firm.

The mechanism for allocating tradeable permits might also produce different winners and losers within an industry. Under a grandfathering scheme that allocates permits on the basis of emissions at the time of the scheme's establishment, firms investing in pollution abatement prior to regulation stand to lose relative to their more heavily polluting competitors.[121] Although such investing and expanding firms might conceivably prefer the allocation of permits by means of an initial auction,[122] smaller firms often

divided over the question of scrubber requirements in clean air legislation. A universal scrubber requirement would have preserved demand for eastern coal, which had higher sulfur content than its cleaner western competition. The NCA split between eastern and western coal producers and stayed out of the debates leading up to the 1977 Clean Air Act Amendments. See Bruce A. Ackerman & William T. Hassler, *Clean Coal/Dirty Air* 31 (1981). Similarly, the largest producers of CFCs (DuPont and Imperial Chemical Industries) supported a ban on CFCs mainly because they were the firms best able to develop substitutes. See Kenneth A. Oye & James H. Maxwell, "Self-Interest and Environmental Management," in *Local Commons and Global Interdependence: Heterogeneity and Cooperation in Two Domains* 191, 198 (Robert O. Keohane & Elinor Ostrom eds., 1995).

[118]Several researchers found that legislators with a paper producer in their districts voted against water pollution control legislation, regardless of whether the producer stood to gain or lose relative to its competitors. See Leone & Jackson, supra note 115, at 247. These authors note that firms may oppose regulation out of uncertainty concerning how the legislation will be implemented, since cost predictions depend on subsequent rulemaking decisions by administrative agencies. Id. at 248.

[119]See 51 Fed. Reg. 43,814, 43,830 (1986). The bubble program typically permits only geographically contiguous trades. Thus, even among existing firms with expansion plans, the benefits of the program depend on where the expansion is contemplated.

[120]Inter-firm trading (as opposed to only intra-firm trading) would eliminate this advantage. See 51 Fed. Reg. 43,814, 43,847–48 (1986).

[121]See Hahn & Noll, supra note 105, at 359.

[122]Some supporting evidence is provided by the establishment of a market in takeoff and landing slots at the nation's busiest airports. Since 1968, peak-hour takeoffs and landings have been

prefer grandfathering out of concern that auctions will be dominated by larger players.[123]

B. Environmental Organizations

As noted above, the utility of an environmental advocacy group will probably be affected by both the organization's well-being and the level of environmental quality. First, organizational well-being may be measured partly by budgetary resources, which are a function of donor contributions. This financial concern can affect an organization's demand for specific policy instruments if such support attracts members, persuades donors to make contributions, or, more broadly, increases the visibility and prestige of the organization. Hence, an organization's demand for a given policy instrument is likely to be affected by several factors, all else being equal: the likelihood that the instrument will be chosen by policymakers;[124] the degree to which the organization is clearly identified with supporting the instrument; the magnitude of potential funding gains from distinguishing the organization from other environmental groups; and the ability to offer donors and members a compelling environmental quality argument in support of the instrument.

A prominent example is provided by the Environmental Defense Fund's ("EDF") enthusiastic and effective support of the SO_2 allowance trading system adopted as part of the Clean Air Act Amendments of 1990. With the Bush Administration eager to back up the President's claim of being "the environmental President," and with key senior staff in the Administration having strong predispositions to the use of market-based approaches, the proposal had a strong chance of success. EDF had already become a cham-

---

restricted at LaGuardia, John F. Kennedy, O'Hare, and Washington National Airports. Until 1986, these slots were allocated by a scheduling committee composed of the airlines using a given airport. In that year, the Federal Aviation Administration ("FAA") replaced the committee allocation system with a system of grandfathered tradeable permits. See "Government Policies on the Transfer of Operating Rights Granted by the Federal Government: Hearings before the Subcomm. on Aviation of the House Comm. on Pub. Works and Transp." 99th Cong. 2–4 (1985) (statement of Rep. Norman Y. Mineta). In the months before the proposal was to go into effect, Congress held hearings and considered whether to overrule the FAA. At the hearings, large airlines, which already held most of the slots, supported grandfathering. See, e.g., id. at 55–56 (statement of Robert L. Crandall, CEO, American Airlines); id. at 96 (statement of Steven G. Rothmeier, CEO, Northwest Airlines). In contrast, upstart airlines looking to expand but having few slots, such as People Express, Republic, and Western, vigorously opposed grandfathering, calling for a large percentage of existing slots to be auctioned or distributed by lottery. See, e.g., id. at 71 (statement of Robert E. Cohn, CEO, People Express); id. at 372 (statement of A.B. Magary, Marketing VP, Republic Airlines).

[123]See Hahn & McGartland, supra note 19, at 606. Similarly, since the transition to a grandfathered-permits system is likely to involve less uncertainty than an auction, it might receive disproportionate support from risk-averse firms. Id. at 605.

[124]There is an important distinction between advocacy groups' strategic and tactical decisions. An environmental organization's strategic decision to express demand for a policy instrument and get it on the agenda for consideration tends to be positively related to perceived probability of success, whereas the tactical decision to express demand for an instrument already on the agenda may well be negatively related to probability of success.

pion of market-based approaches to environmental protection in other, less nationally prominent, domains. Now it faced an opportunity to strengthen that position and solidify its reputation as a pragmatic environmental organization willing to adopt new strategies involving less confrontation with private industry. By supporting tradeable permits, EDF could seize a market niche in the environmental movement, distinguishing itself further from other groups. Importantly, EDF was able to make a powerful argument for tradeable permits on environmental, as opposed to economic, grounds: the use of a cost-effective instrument would make it politically possible to achieve greater reductions in sulfur dioxide emissions than would otherwise be the case.[125]

EDF is an outlier in this realm. Most environmental advocacy groups have been relatively hostile towards market-based instruments. This should not be terribly surprising. Because of their interest in strengthening environmental protection, environmental organizations might be expected to prefer command-and-control approaches to market-based schemes for philosophical, strategic, and technical reasons. On philosophical grounds, environmentalists have portrayed pollution taxes and tradeable permits as "license[s] to pollute."[126] Moreover, they have voiced concerns that damages from pollution—to human health and to ecological well-being—are so difficult or impossible to quantify and monetize that the harm cannot be calculated through a marginal damage function or captured by a Pigouvian tax rate.[127]

Second, environmental organizations may oppose market-based schemes on strategic grounds. Once implemented, permit levels and tax rates may be more difficult to alter than command-and-control standards. If permits are given the status of "property rights," an attempt to reduce pollution levels in the future may meet with "takings" claims and demands for government compensation.[128] This concern, however, can be alleviated by an explicit statutory provision (like that contained in the acid rain provisions of the Clean Air Act Amendments of 1990) stating that permits do not represent property rights,[129] or by "sunset" provisions that specify a particular period of time during which a permit is valid.

Likewise, in the case of pollution taxes, if increased tax rates become desirable in response to new information about a pollutant or about the response of firms to the existing taxes, adjustment may be unlikely because raising tax rates is politically difficult. Furthermore, taxes have long been treated as "political footballs" in the United States (or as in the recent case of efforts to reduce gasoline taxes). Hence, environmental organizations

---

[125]See Hahn & Stavins, supra note 104, at 33 n. 180.

[126]See Kelman, supra note 104, at 44. This criticism overlooks the fact that under conventional command-and-control regulations, firms receive these same licenses to pollute for free. See Hahn & Stavins, supra note 104, at 37.

[127]See Kelman, supra note 104, at 54–55.

[128]See Hahn & Noll, supra note 105, at 359.

[129]See 42 U.S.C. § 765b(f) (1994).

might oppose pollution taxes out of fear that they would be reduced or eliminated over time. A related strategic reason for environmentalists' opposition of tax instruments is that a shift from command-and-control to tax-based environmental regulation would shift authority from environment committees in the Congress, frequently dominated by pro-environment legislators, to tax-writing committees, which are generally more conservative.[130]

Third, environmental organizations may object to decentralized instruments on technical grounds. Although market-based instruments are theoretically superior in terms of cost-effectiveness, problems may arise in translating theory into practice.[131] For example, an emission tax or trade-able permit scheme can lead to localized "hot spots" with relatively high levels of ambient pollution.[132] While this problem can be addressed in theory through the use of permits or charge systems that are denominated in units of environmental degradation, the design of such systems might be perceived as excessively cumbersome.[133]

C. Labor

Since unions generally seek to protect jobs, they might be expected to oppose instruments likely to lead to plant closings or other large industrial dislocations. Under a tradeable permit scheme, for example, firms might close their factories in heavily polluted areas, sell permits, and relocate to less polluted areas, where permits are less expensive.[134] In contrast, command-and-control standards have generally been tailored to protect aging plants. The threat of factory dislocation is a likely explanation of support from northern, urban members of Congress for the PSD policy in clean air regulation, which has discouraged movement of industry out of urban areas in the northeast into high-quality air sheds in the South and West.[135] Depending on the tradeoffs between job creation and preservation effects, labor might support stricter command-and-control standards for new sources.[136]

---

[130]See Kelman, supra note 104, at 139–42. Note that these strategic arguments refer, for the most part, to pollution taxes, not to market-based instruments in general. Indeed, one reason environmental groups such as EDF have endorsed the tradeable permits approach is that it promises the cost savings of taxes without the drawbacks that environmentalists associate with tax instruments.

[131]See Robert W. Hahn & Robert L. Axtell, "Reevaluating the Relationship Between Transferable Property Rights and Command-and-Control Regulation," 8 *J. Reg. Econ.* 125, 126–27 (1995).

[132]See Richard L. Revesz, "Federalism and Interstate Environmental Externalities," 144 *U. Pa. L. Rev.* 2341, 2412 (1996).

[133]See id. at 2412–14.

[134]See Hahn & Noll, supra note 105, at 358.

[135]See, e.g., Crandall, supra note 105, at 127–29 (1983); B. Peter Pashigian, "Environmental Regulation: Whose Self-Interests Are Being Protected?," 23 *Econ. Inquiry* 551, 552–53 (1985).

[136]There are other examples of labor concern over the choice of environmental policy instruments. In the 1977 debates over amendments to the Clean Air Act, eastern coal miners' unions fought to include a command-and-control standard that effectively required scrubbing, thereby seeking to ensure continued reliance on cheap, high-sulfur coal from the east, over cleaner western coal. See Ackerman & Hassler, supra note 117, at 31. Likewise, in the debates over the SO_2 allowance trading system in the 1990 amendments to the CAA, the United Mine Workers opposed the system because it would create incentives for the use of low-sulfur coal from largely non-unionized mines

D. Consumers

To the extent that consumer groups have preferences among environmental policy instruments, one might expect them to favor those instruments that minimize any increases in the prices of consumer goods and services; this would seem to suggest cost-effective (hence, market-based) instruments over command-and-control.[137] In practice, however, these groups typically have not expressed strong demand for environmental policies. As mentioned above, free-riding and limited information are likely to present greater obstacles for consumer organizations than for environmental groups, especially on environmental issues. Thus demand from consumer groups for environmental policy instruments is likely to be muted. Moreover, environmental policy may lie outside the core concerns of consumer groups' constituents. Indeed, when consumer groups do get involved, it may be on "consumer health and safety" issues, where their interests are aligned with those of environmentalists. Calls for cost-effective policies might also be voiced by taxpayer organizations, but again, the minutiae of instrument choice lie outside the scope of these groups' primary concerns. Hence, environmental groups are unlikely to face significant opposition from other public interest organizations.

V. Supply of Environmental Policy Instruments

There are several plausible positive political economy explanations for the nature of the supply of environmental policy instruments. First, legislators and their staffs are thought to be predisposed by their predominantly legal training to favor command-and-control approaches to regulation.[138] Similarly, legislators may need to spend time learning about unfamiliar policy instruments before they can provide substantial support, thereby giving rise to a status quo bias in favor of the current regime of command-and-control regulation.[139] Both these effects may become weaker in the coming

---

in Wyoming's Powder River Basin over high-sulfur coal from eastern, unionized mines. See "Clean Air Reauthorization: Hearing Before the Subcomm. on Energy and Power of the House Comm. on Energy and Commerce," 101st Cong. 455–56 (1989) (statement of Richard L. Trumka, President, United Mine Workers).

[137]It is also possible to distinguish among types of market-based instruments and types of command-and-control instruments, given that any environmental policy instrument that generates privately retained scarcity rents (such as new source performance standards, grandfathered tradeable permits, and others) also raises consumer prices, relative to a policy that does not generate such rents. See Fullerton & Metcalf, supra note 19, at 44.

[138]See Allen V. Kneese & Charles L. Schulze, *Pollution, Prices, and Public Policy* 116–17 (1975).

[139]See id. at 114–15. This argument assumes that a legislator (or at least her staff) needs to understand an instrument in order to support it. Although such understanding might not be a precondition for voting in favor of the instrument, it is more important for other forms of support, such as insertion of a statement into the legislative history, efforts to get a bill through committee, or attempts to persuade other legislators. Moreover, a lack of understanding may hurt the legislator in her reelection campaign if the press or an opponent seeks to make it an issue. Thus, the greater the prominence of an

years, as a result of the increasing understanding of economics among lawyers as well as among legislators and their staffs.[140]

Second, ideology plays a significant role in instrument choice. A conservative lawmaker who generally supports the free market might be predisposed to support market-based instruments; a legislator with more faith in government and less faith in the private sector might, all else being equal, prefer a command-and-control approach. A 1981 survey of congressional staff members found that support and opposition to effluent charges was based largely on ideological grounds.[141] For example, Republicans who supported the concept of pollution charges offered assertions such as "I trust the marketplace more" or "less bureaucracy" is desirable, without any real awareness or understanding of the economic arguments for market-based programs.[142] Likewise, Democratic opposition was largely based upon analogously ideological factors, with little or no apparent understanding of the real advantages or disadvantages of the various instruments.[143]

Third, constituents react to their perceptions of the costs and benefits to themselves and others of a particular policy, regardless of the real costs and benefits.[144] The more visible the benefits, the greater the demand for an instrument; the more visible the costs, the greater the opposition and thus the political costs to the legislator. The importance of perceived costs and benefits is a consequence of the limited information most voters have about the details of public policy.[145] Hence, politicians are likely to prefer command-and-control instruments because they tend to hide the cost of regulation in

---

issue, the more important it will be for a legislator to have a compelling rationale for her position. Responding to this need, interest groups may supply legislators with justifications for supporting given policies. See, e.g., Fenno, supra note 79, at 141–43; Kingdon, supra note 42, at 46–48.

[140]See Hahn & Stavins, supra note 104, at 31, 36. Thus, outreach efforts by economists and others may be thought to have both demand-side and supply-side effects. On the demand side, increased understanding of market-based instruments may have increased the demand for these instruments by various interest groups. On the supply side, increased understanding reduces learning costs for legislators. Since both effects translate into rightward shifts of the respective functions, the outcome is unambiguous in terms of increased degrees of support.

Economists have also played a sometimes significant role as advocates of market-based instruments on efficiency grounds, not only in aspects of environmental policy (such as the U.S. acid rain program) but also in other policy areas, such as the allocation of airport landing spots and the broadcast spectrum. Economists therefore might be seen as acting as "policy entrepreneurs" outside of the interest group-politician nexus (i.e., outside of the strict supply-and-demand framework posited here). See id. at 41.

[141]See Kelman, supra note 104, at 100.

[142]See id. at 100, 104.

[143]See id. at 100–01.

[144]See, e.g., Matthew D. McCubbins & Terry Sullivan, "Constituency Influences on Legislative Policy Choice," 18 Quantity & Quality 299, 301–02 (1984); Robert W. Hahn, "Jobs and Environmental Quality. Some Implications for Instrument Choice," 20 Pol'y Sci. 289, 299 (1987).

[145]A rational voter will choose to remain ignorant on most issues, because the costs of gathering information are likely to outweigh the nearly insignificant benefits from voting knowledgeably. See Anthony Downs, An Economic Theory of Democracy 212–13 (1957). In contrast, organized interest groups with large stakes in an issue are likely to be well-informed and thus overrepresented in the political process. These issues raised by asymmetric information are particularly relevant to instrument choice, because votes on instrument choice are often much more technical than votes on policy goals, and therefore attract even less attention from average voters. See generally James T.

the price increases passed on to consumers.[146] In contrast, though they impose lower total costs, market-based instruments generally impose those costs directly, in the form of effluent or permit charges.[147] Grandfathered permits fare better on the visibility criterion than auctioned permits or taxes, because no money is exchanged at the time of the initial allocation.[148]

Fourth, voters' limited information may also lead politicians to engage in symbolic politics: the use of superficial slogans and symbols to attract constituent support, even when the policies actually implemented are either ineffectual or inconsistent with the symbols employed. Such symbolism offers the legislator political benefits at little opportunity cost. Command-and-control instruments are likely to be well suited to symbolic politics, because strict standards, as strong statements of support for environmental protection, can be readily combined with less visible exemptions.[149] Congress has on several occasions passed environmental laws with strict compliance standards, while simultaneously including lax or insufficient enforcement measures.[150] Tradeable permits and taxes do not offer the powerful symbolic benefits of declaring strict standards. Moreover, it may be difficult to have market-based instruments which simultaneously "exempt" certain parties or which are "loosely" enforced.[151]

Fifth, if politicians are risk averse, they will prefer instruments involving more certain effects.[152] With respect to environmental policy instruments, uncertainty is likely to arise with respect to the distribution of costs and benefits among the affected actors and to the implementation of the legislative decision by the bureaucracy. The flexibility inherent in permits and taxes creates uncertainty about distributional effects and local levels of

---

Hamilton, "Taxes, Torts, and the Toxics Release Inventory: Congressional Voting on Instruments to Control Pollution." 35 *Econ. Inquiry* 745 (1997).

[146]See McCubbins & Sullivan, supra note 144, at 306. The point that politicians prefer, all else being equal, regulatory instruments with "invisible" associated costs is related to the more general notion that legislators may seek to disguise transfers to special interests. See Stephen Coate & Stephen Morris, "On the Form of Transfers to Special Interests," 103 *J. Pol. Econ.* 1210, 1212 (1995).

[147]The potential government revenue offered by auctions and taxes is likely to be politically attractive. See Hahn & McGartland, supra note 19, at 608–09.

[148]One commentator emphasized the importance of observable costs and benefits in explaining why Wisconsin chose a largely state-funded pollution-credit program over an effluent charge. See Hahn, supra note 144, at 299. The instrument offered visible job creation, by favoring the construction of new facilities, at the expense of diffuse, less visible costs to widely distributed third parties. In contrast, the market-based alternative would have appeared to sacrifice jobs while its cost-saving benefits would have been less evident. See id. at 299–300.

[149]See Hahn & Noll, supra note 105, at 361. Of course, the reliance on voter ignorance may be countered by better informed interest groups.

[150]See id.

[151]But see Joskow & Schmalensee, supra note 21 (examining Congressional attempts to confer benefits on particular firms within the context of the SO_2 allowance trading program).

[152]See Matthew D. McCubbins et al., "Structure and Process, Politics and Policy: Administrative Arrangements and the Political Control of Agencies," 75 *Va. L. Rev.* 431, 437 n.22 (1989) ("Legislators are likely to behave as if they are risk averse, even if they are personally risk neutral, if their constituents punish unpredictable policy choices or their reelection probability is nearly unity.")

environmental quality.[153] Typically, legislators are more concerned with the distribution of costs and benefits than with a comparison of total benefits and costs.[154] For this reason, aggregate cost-effectiveness, perhaps the major advantage of market-based instruments, is likely to play a less significant role in the legislative calculus than whether a politician is getting the best deal possible for her constituents.[155] Moreover, politicians are likely to oppose instruments (such as tradeable permit schemes) that may induce firms to close business and relocate elsewhere, leading to localized unemployment.[156] Although there will be winners as well as losers from such relocation, potential losers are likely to be more certain of their status than potential gainers. This asymmetry creates a bias in favor of the status quo.[157]

Sixth, command-and-control instruments offer Congress greater control with respect to the implementation of legislative outcomes by administrative agencies. To ensure that the interests of the winning coalition are protected in implementation, Congress may effectively prescribe administrative rules and procedures that favor one group over another.[158] In theory, such a practice protects intended beneficiaries of legislation by constraining the scope of subsequent executive intervention in implementation.[159] If stacking the deck is an important aspect of policymaking, it is more likely to be successful in the context of command-and-control legislation. Market-based instruments leave the allocation of costs and benefits up to the market, treating polluters identically.[160] Standards, on the other hand, open up possibilities for stacking

---

[153]See Matthew D. McCubbins & Talbot Page, "The Congressional Foundations of Agency Performance," 51 *Pub. Choice* 173, 178 (1986).

[154]See Hahn & Stavins, supra note 104, at 38–41.

[155]See Kenneth A. Shepsle & Barry Weingast, "Political Solutions to Market Problems," 78 *Am. Pol. Sci. Rev.* 417, 418–20 (1984).

[156]See Hahn & Noll, supra note 105, at 358. Tradeable permits are more likely to be adopted in cases where the industry to be regulated is relatively dispersed and has relatively homogeneous abatement costs. See id. at 363–64. But such homogeneity also means that the gains from a market-based approach are more limited.

[157]The Clean Air Act Amendments of 1977 provide an example of legislation built upon such compromises. See id. at 361–62. Stringent standards for urban non-attainment areas were offset by industry-specific exemptions and by measures preventing relocation of urban factories to less polluted areas, the so-called PSD policy described above. See id. at 361. The winning coalition would likely not have held up under a tradeable permit scheme, which would have allowed rust belt firms to purchase pollution permits from firms in cleaner areas and thus to relocate. See id. On the other hand, a tradeable permit scheme that prevented interregional trading could presumably have protected northern factory jobs just as well.

For the same reason, grandfathering of tradeable permits is more widely to attract a winning coalition than auctions, since grandfathering allows leeway in rewarding firms and distributing the costs and benefits of regulation among jurisdictions. Several prominent researchers have examined the political process of allocating SO_2 emissions permits in the 1990 amendments to the Clean Air Act. See Joskow & Schmalensee, supra note 21. Their focus was on empirically measuring the role of interest group politics and rent-seeking in how those permits were allocated, but another point is made clear by their work: allocating permits by grandfathering can produce fairly clear "winners: and "losers" among firms and states. See id. An auction, on the other hand, would allow no such political maneuvering.

[158]See McCubbins et al., supra note 152, at 244.

[159]See id. at 261–62.

[160]See Hahn & Noll, supra note 105, at 362.

the deck, by building protections in favor of particular constituencies.[161] For example, Congress might favor industry by placing the burden of proof in standard-setting on the administrative agencies, or alternatively help out environmental groups by including citizen-suit provisions allowing legal action to impel standards enforcement.

Seventh, bureaucrats are less likely to undermine the legislative decision if their preferences over policy instruments are accommodated. Administrative decisionmakers are likely to oppose decentralized instruments on several grounds: they are familiar with command-and-control approaches; market-based instruments may not require the same kinds of technical expertise that agencies have developed under command-and-control regulation; and market-based instruments imply a scaled-down role for the agency by shifting decisionmaking from the bureaucracy to private firms, undermining the agency's prestige and its staff's job security.[162]

VI. Conclusions

This Article has attempted to synthesize the seemingly diverse trends of the positive political economy literature by viewing them as relating to component parts of a political market framework. In this framework, interest groups have demands for particular instruments. Legislators, in turn, provide political support for such instruments. The demands of the various interest groups are aggregated, as are the supplies of support from individual legislators. The interaction of such aggregate demand and supply produce a legislature's equilibrium level of aggregate support, with each member simultaneously determining her effective support level. The effective support levels of the various legislators are combined, in an institutional context, to produce the legislature's choice of policy instrument.

This framework is far from complete, since it focuses on the decisions of individual legislators, while leaving unanswered those questions of how individual (and continuous) legislator support translates into binary votes and how such support or votes are aggregated to the level of the legislature. For example, the model does not deal with the nature of competition among legislators, only briefly considers the role that congressional committees and other institutions play in structuring and influencing instrument choice, and does not explain how instrument choices are framed. Likewise, this is only a competitive legislative model as a first approximation; alternative approaches were discussed briefly. These issues represent promising avenues for extending this framework and building a workable model of instrument choice.

This Article takes a modest step toward a unified framework for positive analysis of policy instrument choice. This framework may permit greater

---

[161]See id.

[162]See Hahn & Stavins, supra note 104, at 14, 21.

understanding than approaches that focus almost exclusively on one component of the problem at a time. Thus, for example, if one considers only the benefits that a particular industry derives from a proposed regulatory program, one might conclude that a program will be forthcoming if the benefits are sufficiently high. Attention to questions of supply shows why this might not be the case. If the legislature prefers the status quo to the instrument demanded by the interest group, and if the legislature's aggregate supply function is sufficiently inelastic, there may be no equilibrium under which the legislature provides positive support for the demanded instrument. Indeed, the supply function of such a legislature might be above the industry demand function everywhere in the politically relevant domain. Similarly, whether a large shift in the demand for a particular instrument resulting from exogenous factors causes a comparable shift in the actual support provided by the legislature depends on the elasticity of supply. There will be relatively little change in equilibrium support if supply is inelastic, but a far larger change if supply is elastic.

This framework helps us to organize and synthesize available explorations of the four gaps which introduced the Article: three gaps between economic prescription and political reality and one gap between past and current political practices. With respect to the first—the predominance of command-and-control over market-based instruments despite the economic superiority of the latter—firms are likely to prefer command-and-control standards to auctioned permits and taxes. Standards produce rents, which can be sustainable if coupled with sufficiently more stringent requirements for new sources. In contrast, auctioned permits and taxes require firms to pay not only abatement costs to reduce pollution to a specified level, but also costs of polluting up to that level. Environmental interest groups are also likely to prefer command-and-control instruments, for philosophical, strategic, and technical reasons.

On the supply side, command-and-control standards are likely to be supplied more cheaply by legislators for several reasons: the training and experience of legislators may make them more comfortable with a direct standards approach than with market-based approaches; the time needed to learn about market-based instruments may represent significant opportunity costs; standards tend to hide the costs of pollution control while emphasizing the benefits; and standards may offer greater opportunities for symbolic politics. Finally, at the level of the legislature, command-and-control standards offer legislators a greater degree of control over the distributional effects of environmental regulation. This feature is likely to make majority coalitions easier to assemble, because legislative compromise is easier in the face of less uncertainty, and because the winning coalition can better guarantee that its interests will be served in the implementation of policy.

The second gap—that when command-and-control standards have been used, the standards for new sources have been far more stringent than those for existing sources, despite the potentially perverse incentives of this approach—can also be understood in the context of this market framework. Demand for new source standards comes from existing firms, which seek to erect entry barriers to restrict competition and protect the rents created by command-and-control standards. In turn, environmentalists often support strict standards for new sources because they represent environmental progress, at least symbolically. On the supply side, more stringent standards for new sources allow legislators to protect existing constituents and interests by placing the bulk of the pollution control burden on unbuilt factories.

Many of these same arguments can also be used to explain the third gap—the use of grandfathered tradeable permits as the exclusive market-based mechanism in the United States, despite the disadvantages of this allocation scheme. Like command-and-control standards, tradeable permits create rents; grandfathering distributes those rents to firms, while auctioning transfers the rents to government. Moreover, like stringent command-and-control standards for new sources, but unlike auctioned permits or taxes, grandfathered permits give rise to entry barriers. Thus, the rents conveyed to the private sector by grandfathered tradeable permits are, in effect, sustainable.

Moreover, grandfathered tradeable permits are likely to be less costly for legislators to supply. The costs imposed on industry are less visible and less burdensome for grandfathered permits than for auctioned permits or taxes. Also, grandfathered permits offer a greater degree of political control over the distributional effects of regulation, facilitating the formation of majority coalitions. In both these respects, grandfathered permits are somewhat analogous to command-and-control standards.

The fourth and final gap—between the recent rise of the use of market-based instruments and the lack of receptiveness such schemes had encountered in the past—can be credited to several factors. These include: the increased understanding of and familiarity with market-based instruments; niche-seeking by environmental groups interested in both environmental quality and organizational visibility; increased pollution control costs, which create greater demand for cost-effective instruments; attention to new, unregulated environmental problems without constituencies for a status quo approach; and a general shift of the political center toward a more favorable view of using the market to solve social problems. Overall, the image is one of both demand and supply functions for market-based instruments shifting rightward, leading to greater degrees of political support for these market-based instruments over time.[163]

Although some of the current preferences for command-and-control standards simply reflects a desire to maintain the regulatory status quo, the aggregate demand for a market-based instrument is likely to be greatest (and the opportunity costs of legislator support is likely to be least) when the

---

[163]It is also possible that changes in some of the institutional features identified above have affected individual legislators' degrees of support. For example, changes may have occurred that led to particular legislators taking on important committee positions, thus changing their production functions, and hence their opportunity costs.

environmental problem has not previously been regulated.[164] Hence, the prospects may be promising with respect to the introduction of such market-based instruments for new problems, such as global climate change, rather than for existing, regulated problems, such as abandoned hazardous waste sites.

Such a market framework can generate empirical work on the positive political economy of instrument choice for environmental regulation. So far, most of the academic work in this area has been theoretical; very few arguments have been subjected to empirical validation. Several of the existing empirical studies have addressed the question of why firms might support particular instruments, rather than whether firms actually provide such support. No empirical studies have constructed demand functions by determining how much firms actually are willing to pay (in the form of lobbying expenses and campaign contributions, for example) to secure particular outcomes. Similarly, no work has sought to determine the nature of demand by interest groups other than industry. In particular, the motives of environmental organizations merit more consideration. This Article discussed the possible self-interested motives of such organizations, and how their demands for particular policy instruments may be motivated by niche-seeking. Whether their expenditures in the political process comport with this theory remains essentially untested.

On the supply side, substantial impediments to empirical work remain. Existing studies have primarily attempted to determine the factors that affect legislative votes on particular programs.[165] In recent years, however, Congress has enacted a greater proportion of legislation by voice vote, rather than recorded vote. There has also been a shift from votes on comparatively narrow bills to votes on omnibus bills, which make it virtually impossible to determine a legislator's actual position with respect to specific components. Thus, the relative dearth of new data makes it difficult to perform studies of legislative voting behavior.

Legislative voting studies also share a substantial problem: distinguishing votes that reflect a legislator's true views about a bill from votes cast as part of an implicit or explicit logrolling trade, in which a legislator votes in favor of a program that she otherwise opposes in order to obtain a more valuable quid pro quo.[166] Moreover, as argued above, a vote constitutes only one component of the support that a legislator can extend to a bill. But the other components of support are less well suited to quantitative analysis.[167] Thus, in some cases, the best way to explore empirically the supply side of the equilibrium framework may be through detailed case

---

[164]See Hahn & Stavins, supra note 104, at 42.

[165]See generally Hamilton, supra note 145; see also Pashigan, supra note 135, at 551–54.

[166]Compare Kau & Rubin, supra note 43, at 380–81 (attempting to measure the importance of logrolling with a conditional probability model that examined votes as a function of one another) with Jackson & Kingdon, supra note 44, at 807 (criticizing aspects of Kau and Rubin study).

[167]A pattern of votes on a series of amendments may be used as a proxy for a continuous underlying support variable, overcoming this problem. See Silberman & Durden, supra note 61, at 322–27. Such series of closely related votes, however, are rarely available, particularly in the case of instru-

studies of the legislative decisionmaking process.[168]

The market model will, in the end, be an imperfect and incomplete description of political behavior. But there are real advantages to considering instrument choice within this framework, and from developing more fully the details of the market model and its implications. The ultimate test of the usefulness of such a framework will be the extent to which it enables reliable predictions of the choices legislatures make, and the extent to which it facilitates the design of policy instruments that are both economically rational and politically successful.

---

ment choice. A different approach has examined the relationship between campaign contributions and degrees of participation in committee activities. See Hall & Wayman, supra note 61, at 805–09.

[168]See generally Ackerman & Hassler, supra note 117.

33 Environmental Policy since Earth Day I: What Have We Gained?*

A. Myrick Freeman III

A. Myrick Freeman III is William D. Shipman Research Professor of Economics, Emeritus, Bowdoin College, Brunswick, Maine.

Earth Day I, which occurred on April 22, 1970, is an appropriate starting point for an examination of the economic benefits and costs that have been realized through United States environmental policy. There were federal laws on the books dealing with air and water pollution prior to that date. But those laws placed primary responsibility for the implementation and enforcement of pollution control requirements on the states, and by 1970, they had not accomplished very much.

The first Earth Day reflected a major increase in public awareness of and concern about environmental problems. It was followed in relatively quick succession by the passage of the Clean Air Act of 1970, the formation of the Environmental Protection Agency (EPA) in December 1970, and the passage of the Federal Water Pollution Control Act of 1972, now known as the Clean Water Act. In these two acts, much more stringent pollution control objectives were established, and responsibility for establishing and enforcing pollution control requirements was shifted largely to the federal government.[1] The next ten years saw the enactment of the Safe Drinking Water Act (1974), the Toxic Substances Control Act (1976), the Resource Conservation and Recovery Act (1976), the Comprehensive Environmental Response, Compensation and Liability Act (known as Superfund) (1980) and major amendments to the Federal Insecticide, Fungicide and Rodenticide Act (1972).

Broadly speaking, the goals of environmental policy can be based either on a balancing of benefits and costs (economic efficiency) or on

---

"Environmental Policy Since Earth Day I: What Have We Gained?" by Myrick A. Freeman. *Journal of Economic Perspectives* 16. 2002. Pp. 125–146. Reprinted by permission of the American Economic Association.

*I am grateful to J. Clarence Davies, Lauren E. Freeman, Robert W. Hahn, DeWitt John, Paul R. Portney, V. Kerry Smith, Robert Stavins, David Vail and the editors of this journal for helpful comments and suggestions.

[1]For discussion of the context in which the Clean Air Act of 1970 and the Federal Water Pollution Control Act of 1972 were passed and the goals and aims of these acts, see Portney (2000) and Freeman (2000), respectively.

some other goal, such as safety, protection of human health, protection of ecosystems or the achievement of technically feasible levels of emissions control. Economic efficiency in environmental policy requires that the marginal benefit of environmental improvement in each dimension be set equal to its marginal cost and that each environmental improvement be achieved at least cost.

In the first two major environmental laws of the early 1970s—the Clean Air Act and the Federal Water Pollution Control Act—Congress explicitly rejected the economic approach to goal setting. With regard to clean air, it emphasized protecting human health. With regard to clean water, it emphasized achieving fishable and swimmable water quality. However, more recently, Congress has written implicit or explicit economic efficiency criteria into three major environmental laws: the Toxic Substances Control Act of 1976, the Federal Insecticide, Fungicide and Rodenticide Act of 1976 and the Safe Drinking Water Act Amendments of 1996. Moreover, as a result of a series of executive orders by presidents of both parties stretching back to the Nixon administration, there has been an expanding set of requirements for federal agencies to perform economic assessments of all major proposed regulations, including an assessment of their benefits and costs (Smith, 1984; Morgenstern, 1997; Hahn, 1996, 1998, 2000). These assessments are commonly referred to as "regulatory impact assessments."

In this paper, I will review the available information on trends in the major indicators of performance of the clean air and water laws over the past three decades and what can be said about the roles of these laws in explaining these trends. My main focus will be on what these improvements are worth to people (their benefits) and what they have cost. In aggregate, federal environmental laws are imposing significant costs on the American society. The most recent comprehensive EPA survey of the annual costs of compliance with existing environmental laws, done in 1990, estimated costs in the year 1990 to be about $152 billion, rising to perhaps $225 billion in 2000 (U.S. Environmental Protection Agency, 1990).[2] (All dollar values presented in this paper are expressed in 2000 prices.) Are the benefits of these far-reaching environmental laws commensurate with their costs?

---

[2]Unfortunately, the EPA has not updated its 1990 analysis, and I know of no other recent, comprehensive and credible estimate of total compliance costs for more recent years. Moreover, some analysts have substantial reservations about the methods used by the EPA to project compliance costs forward from 1990; they suspect that the costs for 2000 were substantially overestimated (Paul Portney, personal communication, July 26, 2001).

The Clean Air Act

The goals of the Clean Air Act of 1970 are expressed in two major sets of provisions. First, Congress specified that EPA should establish the maximum allowable concentrations in the air for the six major "conventional" air pollutants: sulfur dioxide, nitrogen oxides, particulate matter, carbon monoxide, ozone and lead. These air quality standards were to be set so as to "protect human health . . . allowing an adequate margin of safety. . . ." This language and the absence of any reference to cost have generally been interpreted as meaning that the cost of attaining the standard was not to be taken into account in setting the standard.

The second major provision regarding goals in the original Clean Air Act was the establishment of specific tailpipe emissions standards for new cars, to be met originally by 1975 and 1976. These standards entailed reductions of 84 percent to 90 percent in emissions per mile traveled from the then current uncontrolled levels. These reduction targets were based on a crude calculation of what would be required to reduce the concentrations of these pollutants to levels where no adverse health effects were expected (Seskin, 1978; Tietenberg, 2000, p. 427). In subsequent amendments to the Clean Air Act, these tailpipe emissions standards have been further tightened, but these revisions have not been based on any explicit consideration of human health or cost.

Emissions and Air Quality

To assess the effects of the Clean Air Act on emissions and air pollution levels, it is not enough to show downward trends in measures of pollution. It is necessary to compare what emissions and air quality would have been in the absence of the act with what has actually been observed. As part of a retrospective analysis of the benefits and costs of the Clean Air Act, EPA developed a model of the United States economy to generate estimates of emissions of five major air pollutants both with the act and what they would have been in the absence of the regulations promulgated under the act (U.S. Environmental Protection Agency, 1997a). Figure 1 shows the actual estimated emissions of total suspended particulate matter for the country as a whole from 1950 to 1990 (labeled "Trends") along with the predicted emissions under the "Control" (the law passed) and "No-control" (the law didn't pass) scenarios. It shows that emissions actually declined from 1950 to 1970 and that the decline accelerated during the first decade of the Clean Air Act. Also, during the 20 years covered by the act, actual and predicted emissions were approximately equal. Finally, it shows that an increasing trend in emissions was expected to occur from 1970 to 1990 in the absence of the controls imposed by the act. The two principal sources of the projected increases were electric utilities and motor vehicles.

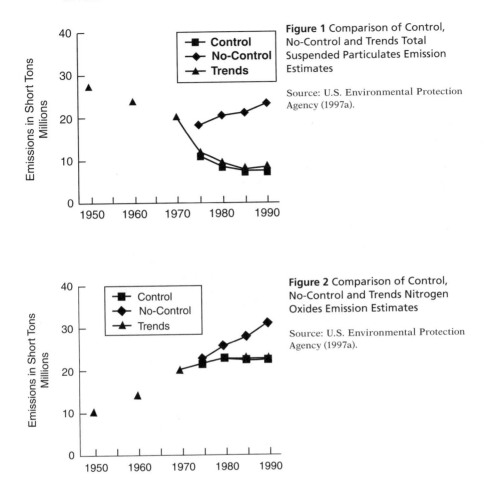

Figure 1 Comparison of Control, No-Control and Trends Total Suspended Particulates Emission Estimates

Source: U.S. Environmental Protection Agency (1997a).

Figure 2 Comparison of Control, No-Control and Trends Nitrogen Oxides Emission Estimates

Source: U.S. Environmental Protection Agency (1997a).

Figure 2 shows similar estimates of actual, control and no-control emissions of nitrogen oxides from 1950 to 1990. Actual emissions were increasing over the period 1950 to 1980 and were approximately constant from 1980 to 1990. EPA projected that in the absence of the act, the rising trend of emissions would have continued throughout the period. EPA has generated similar figures for emissions trends for sulfur dioxide, volatile organic compounds and carbon monoxide (U.S. Environmental Protection Agency, 1997a). In all cases, the analysis shows that the act had a significant effect in reducing emissions. These data suggest that the observed decreases in the national average concentrations of these pollutants can reasonably be attributed to the Clean Air Act. For more discussion of emissions and air quality, see Portney (2000) or U.S. Environmental Protection Agency (1998).

A similar modeling exercise undertaken for the prospective analysis of the benefits and costs of the Clean Air Act Amendments of 1990 projected emissions of the major air pollutants both with and without the amendments for the years 2000 and 2010 (U.S. Environmental Protection Agency, 1999). These projections show substantial decreases in the predicted emissions of volatile organic chemicals, nitrogen oxides and sulfur dioxide.

Benefits and Costs

At the time that the original Clean Air Act was being considered by Congress in the late 1960s, no comprehensive assessments existed of the likely benefits and costs of the act—nor of any alternative changes in air pollution policy. In the ten years or so after its enactment, a number of studies were done of specific benefits from cleaner air, including health, reduced materials damage, public amenities and higher crop yields. In 1982, I published a review and synthesis of the available studies and compared my best estimate of the aggregate benefits realized as of 1978 with the costs as estimated by the Council on Environmental Quality (Freeman, 1982).[3] My estimate of benefits was based on the assumption that in the absence of the act, total emissions would have remained at the 1970 level. I considered costs and benefits separately for mobile sources—primarily motor vehicles—and for stationary sources—primarily industrial and power plants. I provided both best estimates and subjective uncertainty bounds, which were substantial.

As Table 1 shows, I found that the control of stationary sources was yielding substantial net benefits, but the emissions standards for automobiles were not. Almost 80 percent of the benefits were in the form of improvements to human health; and most of that category was due to reductions in premature mortality associated with airborne particulates. At that time, there was a great deal of controversy about the possible link between particulates and premature mortality. Now the evidence for such a link is substantially stronger, although controversy continues.

In Section 812 of the Clean Air Act Amendments of 1990, Congress expressed its concern over the economic consequences of the original Clean Air Act by directing EPA to undertake a "comprehensive analysis of the impact of this Act on the public health, economy, and the environment. . . ." This report is known as the "Retrospective Analysis." Congress also required that EPA publish an update of the original analysis and projections of future benefits and costs every two years thereafter. These reports are known as the "Prospective Analyses." Finally, Congress directed EPA to establish an independent panel of experts to review the methodologies, data and findings of the assessment.[4]

---

[3]For further discussion of these estimates, see Portney (1990).

[4]In the interest of full disclosure, I served on this panel, which is known as the Advisory Council on Clean Air Compliance Analysis, from its inception in 1992 until 2000.

Table 1 Benefits and Costs of the Clean Air Act as of 1978
(in billions of 2000 dollars per year)

	Mobile Sources	*Stationary Sources*	*Total*
Benefits	$ 0.8	$56.5	$57.3
Costs	$20.1	$23.8	$43.8

Source: Freeman (1982).

The EPA released its Retrospective Analysis (U.S. Environmental Protection Agency, 1997a) some six years after the deadline for publication. EPA modeled economic activity and the resulting emissions in the United States over the period 1970–1990 both with the Clean Air Act and under the assumption of no requirements other than those already in place in 1970. It estimated the monetary values of the reductions in the adverse effects of pollution brought about by the act. These effects included premature mortality, chronic bronchitis, other respiratory health effects, reductions in IQ associated with elevated blood lead levels in children, reductions in visibility, and damages to materials and crops.

Table 2 shows that in this analysis, the estimated benefits exceeded the costs by a ratio of about 28:1, 45:1 and 48:1 in the three years selected. The EPA also carried out Monte Carlo Analyses of benefits and reported sensitivity analyses of various categories of benefits under alternative assumptions. Even the 95 percent lower bound on benefits was an order of magnitude greater than the estimated costs. However, the EPA estimates understate the true uncertainty. The analysis of uncertainty in benefits considered only statistical uncertainties in the estimation of impacts and valuations. It did not include model uncertainties or uncertainties in estimates of emissions and changes in air quality. Also, there was no treatment of uncertainty in the cost estimates.

How plausible are these EPA figures? The EPA's estimates of average annual benefits are an order of magnitude higher than my estimates in 1982. Four factors account for most of this difference: the higher values used by EPA for the value of reducing the risk of premature mortality (based on more recent evidence); greater sensitivity of mortality to particulate matter exposures (again based on more recent evidence); different assumptions about air pollution levels in the absence of the act; and the inclusion of additional years with improved air quality.

The whole stream of benefits estimated by the EPA from 1970 to 1990 comes to $30 trillion (brought forward at 5 percent per year in 2000 dollars). Lutter and Belzer (2000) think that this amount is implausibly high, pointing out that this is "roughly the aggregate net worth of all U.S. households in 1990" (see also Portney, 2000, p. 110). But that comparison is somewhat misleading. A more accurate description would be to say that as of 1970 (the starting point of the Retrospective Analysis), the present value of the stream

Table 2 Benefits and Costs of the Clean Air Act for Selected Years
(in billions of 2000 dollars per year)

	1975	*1980*	*1990*
Benefits[a]	$468	$1,225	$1,644
Costs			
Mobile Sources[b]	$7.2	$7.7	$8.8
Stationary Sources[b]	$8.1	$16.7	$23.5
Other[c]	$2.7	$2.9	$2.0
Total	$18.0	$27.4	$34.3

[a]Table I-5.
[b]Table A-9.
[c]Table A-9; monitoring, enforcement and R&D costs by governments.
Note: Column totals may not match due to rounding.
Source: U.S. Environmental Protection Agency (1997a).

of future benefits from the Clean Air Act from 1971 to 1990 was about 20 percent of the present value of the future stream of personal income in the United States over that time. Many might feel that this amount is still too high. But I would argue that it is not wildly implausible that people would be willing to give up 20 percent of their income to avoid the increase in air pollution emissions that the EPA had projected for 1970 to 1990 and instead to experience the falling emissions and improving air quality associated with the act.

The EPA report does not provide separate estimates of the benefits of controlling mobile and stationary sources nor of the costs of eliminating lead in gasoline so that program-specific benefits and costs can be compared.[5] But some interesting lessons can still be learned. First, 75 percent of the total benefits claimed by EPA come from reducing premature mortality associated with fine particles,[6] and another 8 percent of the total benefits

---

[5]This was one of the major criticisms of both the Retrospective and Prospective Reports by the Council. See the Council letters to the Administrator, U.S. Environmental Protection Agency, Science Advisory Board (1997, 1999) available at ⟨http://www.epa.gov/sab/fisclrpt.htm⟩. See also Lutter and Belzer (2000).

[6]Since reductions in mortality figure so importantly in the estimates of the benefits of environmental policies described in this paper, it is useful to say a few words about how the monetary value of these benefits is calculated. The typical approach is to translate individuals' willingness to pay for a small reduction in the risk of death into a value per statistical life protected. This number is the average individual's willingness to pay for a small risk reduction divided by the change in risk. For example, if the average person had a willingness to pay of $50 for a reduction in the risk of death of 0.00001, the value of a statistical life would be $5 million. For a population of 100,000, there would be on average one fewer death per year; and the sum of the individuals' willingness to pay for the risk reduction would be $5 million. For further discussions of the issues involved in the economics of valuation of lifesaving policies and reviews of recent estimates of this value, see Viscusi (1992) and U.S. Environmental Protection Agency (1999).

come from reduced incidence of chronic bronchitis from the same cause. Since fine particles come mostly from stationary sources, the analysis shows that the benefits of stationary source controls on the emissions of fine particles and their precursors (oxides of sulfur and nitrogen) very substantially outweigh the costs. Second, the benefits of eliminating lead in gasoline are about 8 percent of the total, and they accrue primarily after 1985. Even if all of the mobile source control costs were attributed to removing lead, the benefits of lead removal would substantially outweigh the costs, and probably no more than 10 percent of the mobile source control costs reported here are associated with the lead program (U.S. Environmental Protection Agency, 1985). Finally, even if all of the remaining categories of benefits (primarily other respiratory health effects and crop damages) were attributed to controlling mobile source emissions other than lead, their costs would substantially exceed benefits.

The EPA has now published its first Prospective Analysis, which estimates the benefits and costs associated with the Clean Air Act Amendments of 1990 (U.S. Environmental Protection Agency, 1999). It also shows total benefits well in excess of costs. However, the only explicit comparison of benefits and costs for a specific program is for Title VI, which limits emissions of stratospheric ozone-depleting substances such as chlorofluorocarbons. For this title, annual benefits are estimated at $33 billion over the next 75 years compared to annual costs of only $1.8 billion. Even if one looks at only the lower end of the 95 percent confidence interval for benefits, benefits for this title would exceed costs by nearly a factor of four (Table 8-4).

The EPA's estimate of the benefits of Title VI might be biased upward for several reasons. Reducing fatalities from melanoma (a form of skin cancer) is a major component of the benefits of controlling ozone depleting substances, but there is substantial uncertainty about the relationship between ultraviolet radiation and melanoma (U.S. Environmental Protection Agency, Science Advisory Board, 1999). Also, the analysis assumes no changes in behavior to reduce exposure to ultraviolet radiation as a way of mitigating the effects of stratospheric ozone depletion. It further assumes no improvements in cure rates for melanoma due to expanded early detection programs or improved treatment. On the other hand, benefits are understated to the extent that there might be significant ecological impacts due to ultraviolet radiation that are difficult to predict and evaluate in economic terms.

For the remaining parts of the Clean Air Act Amendments of 1990, aggregate benefits exceed costs by 4 to 1. But the 95 percent lower bound on benefits is less than the estimated costs. Moreover, as in the case of the Retrospective Analysis study, the true uncertainties are understated.

Again, it is possible to get some sense of the relative costs and benefits of the stationary source and mobile source programs by digging into the numbers. Title II establishes the emissions standards for vehicles, the reformulated gasoline and clean vehicle requirements and the requirements for inspection and repair of vehicles. The annual costs of Title II in 2010 are predicted to be almost $12 billion (U.S. Environmental Protection Agency, 1999, Table 8-3). Of the estimated $145 billion in annual benefits for that year, about $139 billion are attributed to the health benefits of controlling particulate matter emissions (U.S. Environmental Protection Agency, 1999, Table H-5). Even if *all* of the remaining $6 billion in benefits could be attributed to reductions in ozone concentrations due to Title II (and they cannot be), the total cost of Title II would be twice its benefits.

But even this comparison is too crude to be of much help to policymakers, since it does not identify which components of this complex set of legislative mandates and regulations are to blame for the negative net benefits of the Title II program as a whole. What is needed is an analysis that breaks out both benefits and costs for the specific components of this program (U.S. Environmental Protection Agency, Science Advisory Board, 1999).

All of this discussion takes the numbers in these two reports at face value. But it should be no surprise that the numbers themselves are quite controversial. The most controversial feature of the analysis is the relationship between particulate matter and premature mortality used by the EPA in calculating benefits (Crandall, 1997; Lutter and Belzer, 2000; Portney, 2000). The EPA's analysis implies that about 10 percent of all mortality in the United States is associated with particulate air pollution, which, at a glance, looks high. However, the EPA predictions do have some reputable evidence behind them. They are based on a long-term cohort epidemiology study that tracked more than 500,000 subjects from 151 cities over an eight-year period (Pope et al., 1995); and an earlier, smaller study from six cities estimated an even stronger relationship between premature mortality and particulate matter (Dockery et al., 1993). More recently, the Health Effects Institute reanalyzed the data from both studies and confirmed the results (Krewski et al., 2000). The association between premature mortality and particulate matter is also consistent with a number of studies of the relationship between daily mortality rates and daily changes in air pollution. For further discussion of these issues, see U.S. Environmental Protection Agency (1997a, 1999).

Another point of controversy in these EPA studies is the value placed on reducing premature mortality. EPA used a value per life saved of $6.3 million, drawn from an analysis of a set of estimates based mostly on the wage-risk tradeoffs revealed in labor markets. The sample mean willingness to pay for a reduction in risk from the labor market studies is for a roughly 40 year-old healthy worker with a substantial remaining life expectancy. But a major fraction of the people at risk of death due to elevated particulate matter is much older, typically 70 and above. The life years to be saved are much fewer for the group experiencing the greatest reduction in the risk of premature mortality. It can be argued that the willingness to pay to reduce the risk of death for people in this group would be less than that of a typical 40-year-old.

Another issue involves the omission of indirect or general equilibrium effects in the estimate of costs. The EPA's cost estimate is the sum of annual direct expenditures on operation and maintenance and the amortized capital investments in pollution control equipment. Not included are the indirect costs that arise through general equilibrium effects in labor and capital markets that are already distorted by income and other taxes (Parry and Oates, 2000). These indirect costs could increase estimated costs by 25 percent to 35 percent (U.S. Environmental Protection Agency, Science Advisory Board, 1999).

While taking note of the issues raised here as well as of other matters, the panel that was established by Congress to review these studies characterized them as "serious, careful stud[ies] that, in general, employ[ed] sound methods and data" and produced conclusions that were "generally consistent with the weight of available evidence" (U.S. Environmental Protection Agency, Science Advisory Board, 1997, 1999).

Another way to assess the welfare implications of the Clean Air Act is to examine the regulatory impact assessments for specific regulations promulgated under the act. Hahn (2000) looked at 136 of these regulatory impact assessments carried out between 1981 and mid-1996 from eight different agencies, including those for 45 rules promulgated or proposed by EPA under the Clean Air Act. He put the regulatory impact assessments on a comparable footing by standardizing the discount rate (at 5 percent) and the valuation of reductions in premature mortality (at $5.6 million per statistical life). For the Clean Air Act, he found that in aggregate, the 35 final rules actually promulgated were estimated to produce net benefits of about $660 billion in present value terms. Almost two-thirds of this total is due to one regulation that substantially reduced the lead content of gasoline in 1985. Only 19 of the 35 rules had significant positive net benefits when evaluated separately. Similar results held for the proposed rules. Hahn argued that regulatory agencies in general are likely to overstate benefits and understate costs in these analyses, so that the true picture would be less favorable than his analysis shows.

The New Air Quality Standards for Particulate Matter and Ozone

The most significant recent policy choice made under the Clean Air Act is the revision to the air quality standards for particulate matter and ozone. The EPA is required to review the scientific evidence and consider revisions to each standard every five years. In 1996, the EPA proposed a significant tightening of these standards. In 1997, it released its regulatory impact assessment for the proposed standards. The proposal is interesting for both the legal and economic issues it raised.

The legal requirement that standards be set so as to protect human health with an adequate margin of safety can only be satisfied if the relationship between the concentration of the pollutant and the health effect has a threshold, as illustrated by function A in Figure 3. If there is no threshold, as with function B, reductions in concentrations all the way down to zero (or at least to the background environmental level) will increase the degree of protection against adverse health effects. For ozone and particulate matter, the scientific consensus is that there is no threshold (U.S. Environmental Protection Agency, Science Advisory Board, 1995; 1996). So how can the EPA comply with the mandate of the Clean Air Act?

The EPA promulgated revised standards for particulates and ozone that were above the zero or background level in July 1997. Affected groups, including the American Trucking Associations, appealed these standards to the U.S. Circuit Court. In *American Trucking Associations v. Browner* (No. 97-1441), the U.S. Circuit Court (1999) stated that "the only concentration for ozone and PM that is utterly risk free . . . is zero," "For EPA to pick any non-zero level it must explain the degree of imperfection permitted," and "EPA . . . has failed to state intelligibly how much is too much." The court also ruled that since the Clean Air Act provided no clear basis for deciding how much air pollution to allow, it was an unconstitutional delegation of legislative power. At the same time, the appeals court rejected the plaintiffs' claim that the Clean Air Act allows the EPA to take costs into account in setting air quality standards. Both parties appealed this ruling to the Supreme Court.

Of course one intelligible way to say "how much is too much" is to take costs into account and to balance costs against benefits either formally or informally. In fact, the AEI-Brookings Joint Center for Regulatory Studies (2000) submitted a friend-of-the-court brief in the case signed by 39 prominent economists, including Kenneth Arrow, Milton Friedman and Robert Solow, arguing that point. However, in *Whitman v. American Trucking Associations* (No. 99-1257), the U.S. Supreme Court (2001) ruled that the Clean Air Act does preclude consideration of costs in setting air quality standards and that the limits on the EPA's discretion in setting standards are no more vague than in other statutes that have withstood judicial scrutiny. While this

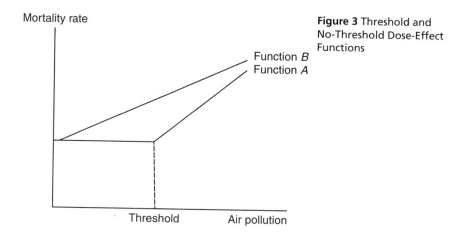

Figure 3 Threshold and No-Threshold Dose-Effect Functions

decision leaves the EPA's new standards for particulates and ozone intact, it also leaves the EPA with no guidance about how close to zero to set its pollution standards in future revisions. The U.S. Supreme Court decision has set up an awkward situation in which the EPA is required by the executive order to carry out what is, in effect, a benefit-cost analysis of alternative levels for the standards, but is bound by law to ignore the cost side of the analysis when making its decisions.

Despite this anomalous situation, the regulatory impact assessments done for the particulate and ozone standards are illuminating. The EPA reported estimates of benefits and costs of both partial attainment and full attainment of the proposed standards. This was because they could not identify control technologies that were capable of achieving the proposed standards in all parts of the country. The full attainment costs were based on the assumption that additional control technologies would become available at costs not to exceed about $10,000 per ton of emissions controlled. Although the EPA argued on the grounds of technological optimism that full attainment costs were likely overstated, it seems more likely that the costs are underestimated.

The EPA reported "low-end" and "high-end" estimates of costs and benefits, but did not report a best estimate or expected value. Neither did they incorporate uncertainties in the cost estimates. The results for partial attainment are shown in Table 3. The substantial net benefits for the proposed particulate matter standard come primarily in the form of reduced risk of premature mortality, and, as noted above, there is controversy over the magnitude of this relationship. However, if the EPA's numbers are taken at face value, there is the additional question of whether an even stricter standard might be justified on the basis of marginal benefits vs. marginal costs. The EPA did do an assessment of the benefits and costs of partial attainment of a more strict standard for particulates, but they only reported the high-end value for benefits. The high-end analysis showed positive marginal net benefits. However, the best estimate of marginal net benefits is not reported, leaving open the possibility that they might be negative.

According to the EPA numbers, the net benefits of the proposed ozone standard could be positive. But the high-end estimate of benefits is based on a recent study that shows an association between elevated ozone levels and premature mortality. This finding is even more controversial than the particulate mortality relationship and has not been found consistently in other studies. If ozone does not cause premature mortality, then the proposed ozone standard does not appear to pass a benefit-cost test. Many analysts believe that the EPA substantially underestimated the costs of partial attainment of the ozone standard (for example, Krupnick, 1997). Thus, even the high-end positive net benefits are in doubt.

Table 3 The Annual Benefits and Costs of Partial Attainment of the Proposed Air Quality Standards by PM$_{2.5}$ and Ozone *(in 2000 dollars)*

	Benefits	*Costs*	*Net Benefits*
PM$_{2.5}$	\$25 to \$137 billion	\$11.3 billion	\$13.7 to \$126 billion
Ozone	\$0.5 to \$2.8 billion	\$1.4 billion	−\$0.9 to \$1.4 billion

Note: PM$_{2.5}$ is fine particles less than 2.5 microns in diameter.
Source: U.S. Environmental Protection Agency (1997b).

The Clean Water Act

The original version of the Clean Water Act became law in 1972 and established national goals for water pollution policy: the attainment of fishable and swimmable waters by July 1, 1983, and the elimination of all discharges of pollutants into navigable waters by 1985. The means selected for achieving this goal were a system of technology-based standards to be established by the EPA and applied to discharges from all industrial and municipal (especially sewage treatment plant) sources. These standards were to define the maximum quantities of pollutants that each source would be allowed to discharge. The standards were to be based strictly on technological factors, such as what kind of pollution abatement equipment was available, rather than on water quality objectives. Under the act, regulators did not need to estimate the capacity of bodies of water to assimilate pollutants nor to consider the relationship between individual dischargers and water quality. The act called for the same effluent standards to be applied to all dischargers within classes and categories of industries, rather than a plant-by-plant determination of allowable discharges on the basis of water quality considerations.

Economics played only a minor role in this process, in the sense that the requirement to use the best feasible technology was accompanied by phrases such as "at reasonable cost." But the relationship between benefits and costs played no explicit role in determining what levels of pollution abatement would be required under the act.

Accomplishments of the Clean Water Act

Bingham et al. (1998) used a model of pollution discharges and water quality across the United States to predict how much the water quality of our rivers improved because of the Clean Water Act as of the mid-1990s, compared with a baseline that assumed no additional controls on discharges with the passage of the act. The improvement in the number of river miles meeting water quality standards for various uses is relatively small. The number of river miles meeting standards for swimming, fishing and boating increased by only 6.3 percent, 4.2 percent and 2.8 percent, respectively.

In a review of this and other evidence on accomplishments of the Clean Water Act 1972, Freeman (2000) suggests that average water quality was not too bad in 1972 and has improved only modestly since then. However, certain local areas that were quite bad in 1972 have been cleaned up dramatically. Although the Clean Water Act has done a good job on "point sources" of pollution from factories and sewage treatment plants, it has done little to address "nonpoint sources" of water pollution, like runoff from urban and agricultural areas, which seem to be increasing.

Benefits and Costs

At the time of the passage of the original version of the Clean Water Act in 1972, no assessment of the benefits and costs of its major provisions existed. During the next decade, a number of studies of various categories of benefits were carried out, especially for water-based recreation. None of these studies would meet modern standards of benefit-cost assessment. They did not, for the most part, model the relationship between reductions in discharges and improvements in water quality, nor did they establish scenarios for what water quality would have been in the absence of the provisions of the act. Nevertheless, in 1982, I reviewed a number of these studies, synthesized their results and compared them with the limited information available on the costs of water pollution control under the act (Freeman, 1982). I concluded that the total costs of meeting the 1983 and 1985 targets were very likely in excess of the benefits.

The Bingham et al. (1998) study described above also provided estimates of the benefits of the predicted water quality improvements attributable to the Clean Water Act. It used estimates of willingness to pay for various levels of improved water quality from a contingent valuation study by Carson and Mitchell (1993) to calculate the benefits of attaining water quality targets for each river.[7] Total willingness to pay for the United States urban population was about $9.9 billion per year. This figure counts only benefits of in-stream uses and the pleasure received from the control of conventional pollutants. It does not include benefits for improvements in water quality in lakes, ponds, estuaries, and marine waters, benefits from the control of toxic discharges, or benefits associated with diversionary uses of water, such as municipal water supply.

However, the EPA estimates that the annual costs of water pollution control in 1990 were about $59.7 billion per year (U.S. Environmental Protection Agency, 1990). This is not directly comparable to the estimate of willingness to pay, since the years are different and the willingness to pay covers only some of the benefits of cleaner water. However, the rough magnitude of these

---

[7]In a contingent valuation study, values of environmental protection are determined from responses to hypothetical survey questions about willingness to pay for specified improvements in environmental quality. For discussion of these methods, see Portney (1994) and the exchange between Diamond and Hausman (1994) and Hanemann (1994) in the *Journal of Economic Perspectives*.

estimates tends to support the conclusion that the Clean Water Act does not appear to have achieved benefits commensurate with its costs.

The assessments of specific regulations promulgated under the Clean Water Act are consistent with this conclusion. Hahn's (2000) study of the regulatory impact assessments carried out between 1981 and 1996 shows that for the eight final rules analyzed, aggregate benefits were about 5 percent of aggregate costs. The same conclusion held for the four proposed rules that were analyzed. Earlier, Hahn (1996, p. 215) had reported that only one of the rules analyzed between 1990 and mid-1995 had positive net benefits.

The Federal Insecticide, Fungicide and Rodenticide Act, the Toxic Substances Control Act and "Unreasonable Risk"

In 1972, Congress amended the Federal Insecticide, Fungicide and Rodenticide Act to allow pesticides to be registered for use so long as the EPA found that they would not "cause unreasonable adverse effects on the environment," "taking into account the economic, social, and environmental costs and benefits" of use. The second phrase, which is part of the definition of "unreasonable adverse effects," is clearly a call to balance benefits against costs in making decisions. In 1976, Congress enacted the Toxic Substances Control Act, which included authorization to regulate the production and use of existing and new chemicals if the EPA finds that they pose an "unreasonable risk of injury to health or the environment." Because of its legislative history and the earlier language in the Federal Insecticide, Fungicide and Rodenticide Act, the Toxic Substances Control Act has also generally been interpreted as allowing a balancing of benefits and costs (Shapiro, 1990; Augustyniak, 1997).

The evidence on costs and benefits of the rules promulgated under these two acts is somewhat limited, but there are two main pieces of evidence. The first comes from Hahn's (2000) study of rules proposed or promulgated between 1981 and mid-1996. There were only six major rules promulgated during this time period under these acts. Their total present value of costs of almost $24 billion yielded only a little more than $0.3 billion in identified *and* monetized benefits. Hahn (2000, p. 44) reported that in most cases the EPA either identified benefits without quantifying them or did not identify any benefits.

The second piece of evidence is an analysis of EPA decision making under these two acts carried out by Van Houtven and Cropper (1996). This study looked at 245 decisions made between 1975 and 1989 about whether an existing pesticide could be reregistered for use. These decisions involved 19 active ingredients that are known or suspected carcinogens. The authors estimated a model to predict the probability that a specific use of an ingredient would be banned. Explanatory variables included expected numbers of cancer cases avoided for food consumers, those who apply the pesticide, and those who mix or load it, and the estimated costs of the ban. They found that the coefficients on cancer cases avoided for those who apply the pesticide and costs were both significant and of the expected sign, indicating that the EPA was considering both costs and benefits in its decisions. However, the average cost per cancer case avoided by banning uses was more than $70 million. Even if all pesticide-induced cancers were fatal, this cost is an order of magnitude larger than the value of statistical lifesaving typically used in analyses of benefits of regulation. This indicates that if a benefit-cost analysis of the whole package of decisions was done with a reasonable value of statistical life (say in the range of $3 million to $6 million), the program would fail unless other categories of benefits were quite large. However, it remains possible that certain individual decisions could pass a benefit-cost test.

Van Houtven and Cropper (1996) also conducted a similar analysis of EPA decisions under the Toxic Substances Control Act regarding banning the use of asbestos in a number of products. This analysis showed an even higher cost per cancer case avoided, suggesting that costs exceeded benefits here as well.

However, these studies give an incomplete picture of the impacts of these two laws. These laws, with their requirements for prior approval of new chemicals and pesticides, no doubt had a preventive effect that went beyond the specific approvals or denials of applications for uses. It is likely that some manufacturers chose not to develop some potential chemicals and apply for approvals on the expectation that the applications would be denied. To the extent that those potential chemicals would have had social costs that exceeded social benefits, the laws brought unmeasured economic benefits.[8] But it is also possible that these laws discouraged the development of some chemicals that would have been socially beneficial.

The Safe Drinking Water Act

The Safe Drinking Water Act was first enacted in 1974. It directed the EPA to establish safe standards for drinking water supplied by public water systems above a certain small size. These standards take the form of maximum allowable concentrations for chemical and microbial contaminants. In the first ten years after the passage of the act, the EPA promulgated only one maximum allowable concentration. Congress responded in 1986 by amending the act to include a listing of 83 contaminants and the requirement that maximum allowable concentrations be established for these contaminants within three years. While the EPA was not able to meet the three-year deadline, the task is now essentially complete.

---

[8]I am indebted to J. Clarence Davies for suggesting this point.

For these water quality standards, are the benefits in the forms of improved human health and reduced risk of disease commensurate with costs of meeting these standards? The EPA was not required by law to address this question, and I know of no comprehensive assessment of this question. However, some revealing partial evidence is available.

A study of the results of the Safe Drinking Water Act done for the EPA by Raucher et al. (1993) sheds some light on the subject. Their analysis was limited to contaminants posing a risk of cancer. They first reported costs and cancer deaths avoided for the program as a whole. The result is a cost per cancer death avoided of about $4.7 million. This value compares favorably with the value of statistical life used by the EPA in several recent assessments ($6.3 million), which suggests that the benefits of the maximum allowable concentrations for carcinogens exceed the costs.

The authors then reported costs and deaths avoided for the ten most cost-effective contaminants (primarily volatile organic compounds). The cost per death avoided for these contaminants was an even more favorable $2.9 million, well below the EPA's value of statistical life. However, from these data it is possible to estimate the cost per life saved associated with the maximum allowable concentrations for the remaining carcinogens (more than 60 substances). This amount is a very high $127 million per death avoided, suggesting that the costs for these maximum allowable concentrations substantially exceeded their benefits. However, this calculation does ignore any benefits associated with reducing health effects other than cancer for these substances and also ignores the benefits and costs of reducing exposures to those substances that do not cause cancer.

Hahn's (2000) analysis of regulatory impact assessments carried out between 1981 and 1996 includes five final rules and three proposed rules under the Safe Drinking Water Act. Both the proposed and final rules taken as a group show aggregate benefits exceeding costs. But almost all of the benefits of the final rules are attributable to only one rule—regarding lead in drinking water (see also Levin, 1997). Again, it is thus possible to infer that the benefits are less than the costs for the other rules.

Amendments to the Safe Drinking Water Act in 1996 directed EPA to undertake an economic analysis of future proposed maximum allowable concentrations to determine if the benefits justify the costs and to adjust the maximum allowable concentrations in light of this analysis as necessary. Thus, the Safe Drinking Water Act joined the Federal Insecticide, Fungicide and Rodenticide Act and Toxic Substances Control Act as the only environmental laws that explicitly call for consideration of benefits and costs. The EPA has now finalized a rule for a maximum allowable concentration for radon.[9] As Hahn and Burnett (2001) point out, the EPA's own data show a benefit-cost ratio of only about 0.3 for this rule, and deficiencies in the EPA's analysis likely result in an overestimate of the benefits of the rule.

---

[9]In the closing days of the Clinton administration, the EPA established a new, more strict maximum allowable concentration for arsenic. But within weeks of taking office, the Bush administration withdrew the rule for further study and review of the scientific and economic bases for the standard.

The Comprehensive Environmental Response, Compensation and Liability Act: Superfund

The Comprehensive Environmental Response, Compensation and Liability Act, commonly known as Superfund, was enacted in 1980 to provide for the cleanup of hazardous waste sites already in existence. Thanks to the Superfund Amendments and Reauthorization Act of 1986, more stringent cleanup requirements are in place today. The primary focus of the cleanup requirements is the protection of human health. The EPA investigates contaminated sites, estimates risks to health, and for those sites deemed to pose a risk to health, establishes a remediation plan based on criteria set forth in the act. Remediation plans are not subjected to a benefit-cost analysis.

Hamilton and Viscusi (1999a, b) have carried out a comprehensive analysis of the risks, costs and cost-effectiveness of the remediation plans for a selected sample of 150 Superfund sites in 1991–1992. The best single indicator of the relationship between the benefits and costs of remediation at these sites is Hamilton and Viscusi's estimates of the cost per cancer case avoided by the selected remediation plan. They found that for the 145 sites for which data are available, the mean cost is about $3.5 million per case avoided. Making the assumption that all cancers are fatal, this implies that a benefit-cost analysis using a value of anything above $3.5 million per death avoided would show that the program was economically justified. However, this result occurs because the aggregate data are dominated by a relatively small number of sites with low costs per cancer case avoided. About 70 percent of the sites have estimated costs per case avoided that are greater than about $112 million, implying that unless there are significant benefits in such categories as avoiding noncancer health effects and ecological and natural resource effects, the majority of the remediation plans are not economically justified, at least not at their present scope and degree of cleanup.

Conclusions

We have looked at the available evidence concerning the benefits and costs of the six major environmental laws enacted or substantially amended since Earth Day I: the Clean Air Act, the Clean Water Act, the Federal Insecticide, Fungicide and Rodenticide Act, the Toxic Substances Control Act, the Safe Drinking Water Act and the Comprehensive Environmental Response, Compensation and Liability Act. It is not a particularly useful exercise to attempt to aggregate all of the benefit and cost data reviewed here to arrive at a total net benefit estimate to try to see whether environmental regulation as a whole has been positive or negative. There have been some winners and some losers. The important question is what changes can we make to the current set of policies to improve the net benefits.

Among the winners in terms of net economic benefits are the following: the removal of lead from gasoline; controlling particulate matter air pollution; reducing the concentration of lead in drinking water under the Safe Drinking Water Act; the setting of maximum allowable concentrations on some volatile organic compounds under the Safe Drinking Water Act; the cleanup of those hazardous waste sites with the lowest cost per cancer case avoided under Superfund; and probably also the control of emissions of chlorofluorocarbons. These winners share the common characteristics of involving threats to human health, especially mortality, and widespread exposures of people. Even in the case of lead, which is primarily known for its toxic effect on nervous systems, a major portion of the monetizable benefits of controlling lead comes from the reduction in hypertension and the associated risk of cardiovascular disease in adults.

The environmental rules that appear to be losers in terms of net economic benefits include the following: mobile source air pollution control; much of the control of discharges into the nation's waterways, with the exception of some lakes and rivers that were especially polluted; and many of the regulations, standards and cleanup decisions taken under the Federal Insecticide, Fungicide and Rodenticide Act, the Toxic Substances Control Act, the Safe Drinking Water Act and Superfund.

Before turning to the policy implications of these findings, we need to identify some qualifications and caveats. All benefit-cost analyses have uncertainties and omissions. For example, there may be important effects of pollutants on human health that have so far escaped detection. If this is the case, present estimates of the health benefits of environmental cleanup are biased downward. Also, omitted benefits could include the protection of ecological systems and their services, preservation of biodiversity and what are called "nonuse" or "existence" values, meaning the value that people place on a cleaner environment as a goal in itself. Many natural scientists argue that ecosystem and biodiversity values are not given sufficient attention by economists (for example, Daily, 1997). But there is very limited evidence concerning the effects of present-day environmental policy decisions on ecological systems and biodiversity and these values were not a principal focus of most of the environmental laws considered here.

On the cost side, it is sometimes argued that costs are systematically overestimated because of the inability to anticipate the technological improvements in pollution control, process change and input substitution that are stimulated by the requirements of the regulations themselves (for example, Porter, 1991; Porter and van der Linde, 1995). On the other hand, Hahn (1996) argues that agencies have systematic incentives to underestimate costs and to overestimate benefits. Harrington, Morgenstern and Nelson (2000) found a limited number of cases of underestimation of costs but for half of the rules they studied, they found overestimation of costs to be the case. Moreover, at least the most extreme versions of technological optimism regarding pollution control are not supported by the evidence (Palmer, Oates and Portney, 1995; Jaffe et al., 1995).

The first and perhaps most important policy implication of this analysis is to emphasize that virtually all environmental policies and programs could be improved by making them more cost-effective, that is, by finding ways to reduce the costs of attaining given targets.

One method to improve cost-effectiveness is to replace command and control policy instruments with market-based incentives, such as tradeable emissions permits, emission taxes and deposit-refund systems. The potential for effluent taxes, fuel taxes and tradeable permits to improve cost-effectiveness is especially relevant for water and mobile source air pollution control. For further discussion of the present potential of market-based environmental tools, see Stavins (2000), Portney (2000) and Freeman (2000). The cost-effectiveness of regulatory programs can also be improved by scaling back or eliminating specific regulations and standards where the costs per unit of measurable performance (for example, cost per cancer case avoided) are high and adopting more strict standards where costs per unit of performance are low. See, for example, Hahn (1996, 2000), Hamilton and Viscusi (1999b) and Raucher et al. (1993).

Another way to improve the economic performance of environmental policy is to give more weight to the comparison of benefits and costs, especially at the margin, in making environmental choices. As we have seen, some laws preclude balancing of costs and benefits in setting standards. But even where balancing is allowed or required—as in the Federal Insecticide, Fungicide and Rodenticide Act, the Toxic Substances Control Act and the Safe Drinking Water Act—the economic performance of environmental regulation has been spotty at best. Standards and regulations have been adopted even when realistic assessments show that the benefits are less than the costs. At a minimum, this result should make one skeptical of the argument that environmental regulatory agencies have been "captured" by polluting interests. Indeed, Hahn (1996) has argued that the substantial number of cases where environmental costs exceed benefits is evidence that regulatory agencies have been successful in increasing their power and expanding their budgets and roles in the American economy.

However, there are alternative explanations for what appears to be over-regulation. One is that there may be benefits of regulation that economics has not been able to identify and quantify. It may be that these benefits are recognized by environmental decision makers and by the voters who apparently support these policies. Another way to put this is to argue that the American people, by their willingness to continue to support environmental programs that show measurable benefits that are less than costs, are revealing that they are willing to pay more for these environmental improvements than the amount captured by conventional measures of benefits.

Another possibility is that voters believe that at least for the policies they support, the costs are borne by others, the "black hat polluters." If this is the case, then the challenge for policymakers is to describe the opportunity costs of excess regulation to those who actually bear them and commit themselves to maintaining or improving standards in those areas where benefits demonstrably exceed costs. A public perception that the benefits of environmental protection can be realized while costs are borne by others will sooner or later collide with the reality that for the more intractable of our environmental problems—for example, the pollution and congestion externalities associated with private automobile transportation—we all will have to pay for any benefits we expect to receive.

It is difficult to know whether the American public would support a set of environmental policies that is economically rational by conventional measures. The challenge for policymakers may be to build credibility for cost-benefit analysis by making a public commitment to maintaining or improving environmental standards in those areas where benefits demonstrably exceed costs. By offering vocal support for environmental policies that do provide net benefits, and perhaps giving the benefit of the doubt to cases where the measureable net benefits are close to zero, policymakers may be able to build credibility when they need to argue that certain regulations have opportunity costs in excess of their benefits.

REFERENCES

AEI-Brookings Joint Center for Regulatory Studies. 2000. "Brief *Amici Curiae* in American Trucking Associations, Inc., et al. v. Carol Browner." July 21. Available at http://www.aei.brookings.org/publications/briefs/brief_00_01.pdf.

Augustyniak, Christine M. 1997. "Asbestos," in *Economic Analysis at EPA: Assessing Regulatory Impact.* Richard D. Morgenstern, ed. Washington, D.C.: Resources for the Future, pp. 171–203.

Bingham, Tayler H. et al. 1998. *A Benefits Assessment of Water Pollution Control Programs Since 1972.* Revised draft report to the U.S. Environmental Protection Agency. Research Triangle Park, N.C.: Research Triangle Institute.

Carson, Richard T. and Robert Cameron Mitchell. 1993. "The Value of Clean Water: The Public's Willingness to Pay for Boatable, Fishable, and Swimmable Quality Water." *Water Resources Research.* 29:7, pp. 2445–54.

Crandall, Robert W. 1997. "The Costly Pursuit of the Impossible." *The Brookings Review.* Summer, 15:3, pp. 41–47.

Daily, Gretchen C., ed. 1997. *Nature's Services: Societal Dependence on Natural Ecosystems.* Washington, D.C.: Island Press.

Diamond, Peter A. and Jerry A. Hausman. 1994. "Contingent Valuation: Is Any Number Better than No Number?" *Journal of Economic Perspectives.* Fall, 8:4, pp. 45–64.

Dockery, D. W. et al. 1993. "An Association Between Air Pollution and Mortality in Six U.S. Cities." *New England Journal of Medicine.* 329:24, pp. 1753–59.

Freeman, A. Myrick III. 1982. *Air and Water Pollution Control: A Benefit-Cost Assessment.* New York: John Wiley.

Freeman, A. Myrick III. 2000. "Water Pollution Policy," in *Public Policies for Environmental Protection, Second Edition.* Paul R. Portney and Robert N. Stavins, eds. Washington, D.C.: Resources for the Future, pp. 97–149.

Hahn, Robert W. 1996. "Regulatory Reform: What Do the Government's Numbers Tell Us?" in *Risks, Costs, and Lives Saved: Getting Better Results from Regulation.* Robert Hahn, ed. New York: Oxford University Press, pp. 208–53.

Hahn, Robert W. 1998. "Policy Watch: Government Analysis of the Benefits and Costs of Regulation." *Journal of Economic Perspectives.* Fall, 12:4, pp. 201–10.

Hahn, Robert W. 2000. *Reviving Regulatory Reform: A Global Perspective.* Washington, D.C.: AEI-Brookings Joint Center for Regulatory Studies.

Hahn, Robert W. and Jason K. Burnett. 2001. "The EPA's Radon Rule: A Case Study in How Not to Regulate Risks." AEI-Brookings Joint Center for Regulatory Studies Regulatory Analysis 01-01. January.

Hamilton, James T. and W. Kip Viscusi. 1999a. "How Costly is 'Clean'? An Analysis of the Benefits and Costs of Superfund Remediations." *Journal of Policy Analysis and Management.* 18:1, pp. 2–27.

Hamilton, James T. and W. Kip Viscusi. 1999b. *Calculating Risks: The Spatial and Political Dimensions of Hazardous Waste Policy.* Cambridge, Mass.: MIT Press.

Hanemann, W. Michael. 1994. "Valuing Environment Through Contingent Valuation." *Journal of Economic Perspectives.* Fall, 8:4, pp. 19–43.

Harrington, Winston, Richard D. Morgenstern and Peter Nelson. 2000. "On the Accuracy of Regulatory Cost Estimates." *Journal of Policy Analysis and Management.* 19:2, pp. 297–322.

Jaffe, Adam B. et al. 1995. "Environmental Regulation and the Competitiveness of U.S. Manufacturing: What Does the Evidence Tell Us?" *Journal of Economic Literature.* 33:1, pp. 132–63.

Krewski, D. et al. 2000. *Reanalysis of the Harvard Six Cities Study and the American Cancer Society Study of Particulate Air Pollution and Mortality.* Cambridge, Mass.: Health Effects Institute.

Krupnick, Alan J. 1997. "The Proposed NAAQS for PM and Ozone." Testimony before the Subcommittee on Clean Air, Wetlands, Private Property and Nuclear Safety, Committee on Environment and Public Works, U.S. Senate, Washington, D.C.

Levin, Ronnie. 1997. "Lead in Drinking Water," in *Economic Analysis at EPA: Assessing Regulatory Impact.* Richard D. Morgenstern, ed. Washington, D.C.: Resources for the Future, pp. 205–32.

Lutter, Randall and Richard B. Belzer. 2000. "EPA Pats Itself on the Back." *Regulation.* 23:3, pp. 23–8.

Morgenstern, Richard D. 1997. *Economic Analysis at EPA: Assessing Regulatory Impact.* Washington, D.C.: Resources for the Future.

Palmer, Karen, Wallace E. Oates and Paul R. Portney. 1995. "Tightening Environmental Standards: The Benefit-Cost or the No-Cost Paradigm?" *Journal of Economic Perspectives.* Winter, 9:1, pp. 129–32.

Parry, Ian W.H. and Wallace E. Oates. 2000. "Policy Analysis on the Presence of Distorting Taxes." *Journal of Policy Analysis and Management.* 19:4, pp. 603–13.

Pope, C.A. et al. 1995. "Particulate Air Pollution as a Predictor of Mortality in a Prospective Study of U.S. Adults." *American Journal of Respiratory and Critical Care Medicine.* 151:3, pp. 669–74.

Porter, Michael E. 1991. "America's Green Strategy." *Scientific American.* 264:4, p. 168.

Porter, Michael E. and Claas van der Linde. 1995. "Toward a New Conception of the Environment-Competitiveness Relationship." *Journal of Economic Perspectives.* Fall, 9:4, pp. 97–118.

Portney, Paul R. 1990. "Air Pollution Policy," in *Public Policies for Environmental Protection.* Paul R. Portney, ed. Washington, D.C.: Resources for the Future, pp. 27–96.

Portney, Paul R. 1994. "The Contingent Valuation Debate: Why Economists Should Care." *Journal of Economic Perspectives*. Fall, 8:4, pp. 1–17.

Portney, Paul R. 2000. "Air Pollution Policy," in *Public Policies for Environmental Protection, Second Edition*. Paul R. Portney and Robert N. Stavins, eds. Washington, D.C.: Resources for the Future, chapter 4.

Portney, Paul R. 2001. Personal Communication. July 26.

Raucher, Robert S. et al. 1993. *An Evaluation of the Federal Drinking Water Program under the Safe Drinking Water Act as Amended in 1986*. Prepared for the American Water Works Association by RCG/Hagler, Bailly, Inc., Boulder, Colo.

Seskin, Eugene P. 1978. "Automobile Air Pollution Policy," in *Current Issues in U.S. Environmental Policy*. Paul R. Portney, ed. Baltimore, Md.: Johns Hopkins University Press, pp. 68–104.

Shapiro, Michael. 1990. "Toxic Substances Policy," in *Public Policies for Environmental Protection*. Paul R. Portney, ed. Washington, D.C.: Resources for the Future, pp. 195–241.

Smith, V. Kerry, ed. 1984. *Environmental Policy Under Reagan's Executive Order: The Role of Benefit-Cost Analysis*. Chapel Hill, N.C.: University of North Carolina Press.

Stavins, Robert N. 2000. "Market-Based Environmental Policies," in *Public Policies for Environmental Protection, Second Edition*. Paul R. Portney and Robert N. Stavins, eds. Washington, D.C.: Resources for the Future, chapter 3.

Tietenberg, Tom. 2000. *Environmental and Natural Resource Economics, Fifth Edition*. Reading, Mass.: Addison-Wesley.

U.S. Circuit Court of Appeals. 1999. *American Trucking Associations v. Browner*. No. 97-1441, May 26.

U.S. Environmental Protection Agency. 1985. *Costs and Benefits of Reducing Lead in Gasoline*. Washington, D.C.: Office of Policy Analysis.

U.S. Environmental Protection Agency. 1990. *Environmental Investments: The Cost of Clean Environment*. Washington, D.C.: Office of Policy Analysis.

U.S. Environmental Protection Agency. 1997a. *The Benefits and Cost of the Clean Air Act: 1970–1990*. Washington, D.C.: Office of Policy Analysis.

U.S. Environmental Protection Agency. 1997b. *Regulatory Import Assessment for Particulate Matter and Ozone NAAQS and Proposed Regional Haze Rule*. Washington, D.C.: Office of Policy Analysis.

U.S. Environmental Protection Agency. 1998. *National Air Quality and Emissions and Trends Report*. Research Triangle Park, N.C.: Office of Air Quality Planning and Standards.

U.S. Environmental Protection Agency. 1999. *The Benefits and Cost of the Clean Air Act: 1990–2010*. Washington, D.C.: Office of Policy Analysis.

U.S. Environmental Protection Agency, Science Advisory Board, Clean Air Science Advisory Committee. 1995. *Letter to Honorable Carol Browner, Administrator of U.S. EPA (EPA-SAB-CASAC-LTR-96-002)*. Washington, D.C.: U.S. Environmental Protection Agency.

U.S. Environmental Protection Agency, Science Advisory Board, Clean Air Science Advisory Committee. 1996. *Letter to Honorable Carol Browner, Administrator of U.S. EPA (EPA-SAB-CASAC-LTR-96-003)*. Washington, D.C.: U.S. Environmental Protection Agency.

U.S. Environmental Protection Agency, Science Advisory Board, Advisory Council on Clean Air Act Compliance Analysis. 1997. *Letter to Honorable Carol Browner, Administrator of U.S. EPA (EPA-SAB-COUNCIL-LTR-97-008)*. Washington, D.C.: U.S. Environmental Protection Agency.

U.S. Environmental Protection Agency, Science Advisory Board, Advisory Council on Clean Air Act Compliance Analysis. 1999. *Letter to Honorable Carol Browner, Administrator of U.S. EPA (EPA-SAB-COUNCIL-ADV-00-002).* Washington, D.C.: U.S. Environmental Protection Agency.

U.S. Supreme Court. 2001. *Whitman v. American Trucking Associations.* No. 99-1257, February 27, 2001.

Van Houtven, George and Maureen L. Cropper. 1996. "When is a Life Too Costly to Save? The Evidence from U.S. Environmental Regulations." *Journal of Environmental Economics and Management.* 30:3, pp. 344–68.

Viscusi, W. Kip. 1992. "The Value of Risks to Life and Health." *Journal of Economic Literature.* 31:4, pp. 1912–46.

34 *The Impact of Economics on Environmental Policy*

Robert W. Hahn[1]

Robert W. Hahn is Tesco Professor of Economics and Professorial Research Fellow of the Sustainable Consumption Institute at the University of Manchester, Senior Visiting Fellow at the Smith School at Oxford University, and Senior Fellow at the Georgetown Center for Business and Public Policy.

1. Introduction

Many scholars dream about having their ideas put into practice. Yet, when the dream becomes a reality, it frequently feels different—in large part because of the gulf between the ivory tower and the real world. Environmental economists have seen their ideas translated into the rough-and-tumble policy world for over two decades. They have played an important role in shaping some key aspects of policy. They have, for example, witnessed the application of economic instruments to several environmental issues, including preserving wetlands, lowering lead levels, and curbing acid rain. Despite a few notable successes, the influence of economists on environmental policy to date has been modest.

I will focus on two related, but distinct phenomena—the increasing interest in using incentive-based mechanisms, such as tradable permits, to achieve environmental goals, and the increasing interest in using analytical tools such as benefit–cost analysis in regulatory decision making.[2] For purposes of this essay, an economic instrument is defined as any instrument that is expected to increase economic efficiency relative to the status quo. This broad definition includes traditional incentive-based mecha-

"The Impact of Economics on Environmental Policy" by Robert W. Hahn. *Journal of Environmental Economics and Management* 39. 2000. Pp. 375–399. Reprinted with permission.

[1]The views in this paper reflect those of the author and do not necessarily represent the views of the institutions with which he is affiliated. The helpful comments of Dallas Burtraw, Maureen Cropper, Henry Lee, Anne Sholtz, and Robert Stavins are gratefully acknowledged. Petrea Moyle and Fumie Yokota provided valuable research assistance.

[2]Other tools include cost-effectiveness analysis and risk-risk analysis. By risk-risk analysis, I mean an evaluation of potential increases in health risks that may arise from efforts to combat a targeted health risk. Such an evaluation can help decision makers compare policies [50]. Farmers, for example, may increase the use of an equally toxic alternative pesticide if use of the original pesticide is restricted or banned to prevent drinking water contamination. For a more detailed description of risk-risk analysis, see Graham and Wiener [34].

nisms, process reforms, and economic analysis that is used as a basis for designing more efficient policies.[3]

Economists can influence environmental policy in several ways. One is by advocating the use of particular tools for achieving better environmental outcomes through research, teaching, and outreach to policy makers. Another is by analyzing the benefits and costs of regulations and standards, which may demonstrate the inefficiencies of the goals themselves. A third way is by analyzing how decisions are made—by examining the political economy of environmental regulation.[4] Each of these approaches can eventually have an impact on the different branches of government.

My thesis is that economists and economic instruments are playing an increasingly important role in shaping environmental, health and safety regulation. Although the role of economics is becoming more prominent, it does not follow that environmental policy will become more efficient. This apparent inconsistency can be explained by the political economy of environmental policy. I argue that economists need to do more than simply develop good ideas to influence policy. They need to understand how the political process affects outcomes, and actively market the use of appropriate and feasible economic instruments for promoting more efficient environmental policy.

Section 2 provides background on U.S. laws and regulations. Section 3 highlights the use of economic instruments in environmental policy.[5] Section 4 examines critical factors leading to the increased prominence of economics in environmental policy and also explains why economic efficiency is rarely central in environmental decision making. Section 5 summarizes the main arguments and suggests ways to enhance the impact of economists on environmental policy.

2. Laws, Regulations, and the Need for Economic Instruments

Most environmental laws cover specific media, such as air, water, and land, and specific problems such as the control of toxic substances and the prevention of oil spills. They give rise to a staggering array of regulations

---

[3]The narrow definition of economic instruments is typically restricted to incentive-based mechanisms, such as emission taxes, deposit-refund schemes, tradable permits, subsidies, and removal of subsidies. Such mechanisms have the potential to achieve environmental outcomes at a lower cost than direct regulation. For a broader perspective on economic instruments that highlights the importance of transaction costs, see Richards [73]. Note that the definition used here explicitly allows for command-and-control regulation to be an economic instrument in situations where it would lead to improvements in economic efficiency.

[4]See, for example, Metrick and Weitzman [55] for an analysis of choices related to biodiversity preservation.

[5]I focus on the United States because that is the country with which I am most familiar; however, I believe the theses advanced in the paper are generally applicable to a wide range of developed countries as well as some developing countries.

requiring firms to obtain permits and meet specific requirements and guidelines. In some cases, firms must gain permission from federal or state authorities before making changes to production processes that have little or no impact on environmental quality.

There are now at least 10 major U.S. federal laws that address environmental quality.[6] The largest in terms of estimated costs are the Clean Air Act (CAA), the Resource Conservation and Recovery Act (RCRA), and the Safe Drinking Water Act (SDWA).[7] According to the first comprehensive government report on the benefits and cost of federal regulation produced by the Office of Management and Budget, the direct cost of federally mandated environmental quality regulations in 1997 is approximately $147 billion (OMB, 1997).[8,9] This is more than half of total federal government spending on all domestic discretionary programs.[10] Estimates of direct and indirect costs using general equilibrium approaches suggest that the costs are substantially higher [40, 44].[11] The benefits from these laws are less certain than the costs. Some estimates suggest that aggregate benefits are in the neighborhood of costs [29, 63]; others suggest that they substantially exceed costs [91].[12]

The aggregate analysis of benefits and costs masks some important information on individual regulations, such as evidence that many environmental regulations would not pass a standard benefit–cost test. For example, more than two-thirds of the federal government's environmental quality regulations from 1982 to 1996 fail a strict benefit-cost test using the

---

[6]Consider the following laws that primarily the EPA administers: the Federal Insecticide, Fungicide, and Rodenticide Act, Clean Water Act, Clean Air Act, Resource Conservation and Recovery Act, Ocean Dumping Act, Safe Drinking Water Act, Toxic Substance Control Act, Comprehensive Environmental Response, Compensation, and Liability Act (Superfund), Emergency Planning and Community Right-to-Know Act, and Pollution Prevention Act. The list would be longer if it included laws not primarily under EPA's jurisdiction, such as the Endangered Species Act.

[7]According to the present value of compliance costs for final regulations published between 1982 and 1996, the CAA is the most burdensome with $192 billion, second is RCRA with $121.6 billion, and third is SDWA with $43.6 billion in 1995 dollars [35].

[8]Direct costs include the costs of capital equipment and labor needed to comply with a standard or regulation. Most of the cost estimates of individual regulations used by the OMB to calculate the aggregate costs only include direct costs, although a few also include indirect net changes in consumer and producer surplus. The OMB derives the aggregate cost estimate by using the EPA's estimate of the federally mandated compliance cost [89] as the baseline estimate for 1988 and adding the incremental costs from EPA's major regulations finalized between 1987 and 1996 [62].

[9]Unless otherwise stated, all dollar figures have been converted to 1997 dollars using the GDP implicit price deflator [19].

[10]The total outlays in 1997 for domestic discretionary programs were $258 billion [6]. This figure does not include expenditures related to national defense or international affairs.

[11]Hazilla and Kopp [40] find that although social costs were below EPA's compliance cost estimates in 1975, they exceeded compliance costs in the 1980's. This result is partially explained by people's substitution of leisure for direct consumption as a result of pollution control regulation, thereby decreasing output over time.

[12]The EPA estimates that the total benefits from the Clean Air Act between 1970 and 1990 are in the range of $5.6 to $49.4 trillion in 1990 dollars, while the direct compliance costs for the same period are $0.5 trillion in 1990 dollars [91]. For an insightful critique of the EPA's estimate, see Lutter [53].

government's own numbers.[13] Indeed, if the government did not implement all major social regulations that failed a benefit–cost test during this period, net benefits would have increased by about $280 billion [35]. Moreover, there is ample room to reallocate expenditures to save more lives at lower cost [31, 57]. A reallocation of mandated expenditures toward the regulations with the highest payoff to society could save as many as 60,000 more lives a year at no additional cost [83].

For over two decades, economists have highlighted two significant problems with the current legal framework in U.S. environmental policy. The first is that the laws are overly prescriptive. Both laws and regulations frequently specify a preferred technology or set of technologies for achieving an outcome. For example, scrubbers were required for some power plants as part of a compromise reached under the 1977 Clean Air Act Amendments [1]. Economists have argued that a more flexible approach, such as an emissions tax, could achieve the same or similar environmental results at much lower cost (see e.g., [12, 86]). A second problem is that, while some statutes now require agencies to at least consider, if not balance, the benefits and costs of regulations, many laws prohibit such balancing [20, 70]. According to the courts interpretation of Section 109 of the Clean Air Act, for example, the Environmental Protection Agency cannot consider the costs of determining national ambient air quality standards for designated pollutants. The result has been that many environmental programs and regulations have been put in place that would not pass a strict benefit–cost test. Both observations suggest that economic instruments could play a critical role in designing more efficient policies.

3. An Overview of Economic Instruments

As noted above, an economic instrument is one that is expected to increase economic efficiency. That definition of economic instruments has the advantage that it includes a wide array of instruments. One drawback is that, unlike the conventional definition, an instrument is not necessarily an economic instrument just because it is incentive-based. For example, an emission fee need not be an economic instrument using my definition if it leads to a reduction in economic efficiency. The definition used here requires the ability to specify a counterfactual—what would have happened in the absence of the application of a particular economic instrument—to determine how the policy would affect efficiency. I offer this definition because it seems natural that we should want economic instruments to improve economic efficiency.

Economists rarely frame the instrument choice problem in such general terms. Instead, they tend to focus on particular mechanisms, such as fees and permits, which are known to have efficiency-enhancing properties

---

[13]Of the 70 final EPA regulations analyzed, monetized benefits exceeded the costs for only 31% [35].

in theory. Below I examine these instruments, but I also consider other instruments, including the increasing role of economic analysis in the formulation of environmental policy.

It is useful to consider two categories of economic instruments for framing policy choices: incentive based mechanisms and process reforms. The two categories are related in the sense that process reforms could help policy makers determine whether to use different types of incentive-based mechanisms. Incentive-based mechanisms include emission fees, tradable permits, deposit-refund schemes, direct subsidies, removal of subsidies with negative environmental impacts, reductions in market barriers, and performance standards.[14] The idea behind such instruments is that they create incentives for achieving particular goals that are welfare enhancing. Generally not included in this category are highly prescriptive technology-based standards. Process reforms include accountability mechanisms and analytical requirements. Accountability mechanisms include peer review, judicial review, sunset provisions, regulatory budgets, and requirements to provide better information to Congress. Analytical requirements include mandates to balance costs and benefits, consider risk–risk tradeoffs, and evaluate the cost-effectiveness of different regulatory alternatives.

The Increasing Use of Incentive-Based Mechanisms

A broad array of incentive-based mechanisms have been used in U.S. federal environmental policy. Table I highlights some of the more important federal applications of fees, subsidies, tradable permits, and the provision of information. These mechanisms have been used for all media in a variety of applications.[15] Perhaps best known in terms of their potential for achieving cost savings are tradable permits. As can be seen from the table, their use has steadily increased over time at the federal level. Moreover, there has been increasing interest in the potential application of economic instruments as well [90].

The table shows that the ideas of economists regarding economic instruments are being taken seriously. President Clinton's 1993 Executive Order 12866 for Regulatory Planning and Review provides a good example. The order directs agencies to identify and assess incentive-based mechanisms, such as user fees and tradable permits, as an alternative to traditional command-and-control regulation, which provides less flexibility in achieving environmental goals.

---

[14]See Stavins [80] for a good overview of instrument types and their application. Kneese and Schultze [48] provide an early treatment of some of the practical issues to consider in shifting to effluent taxes.

[15]This section focuses on efforts to improve environmental quality through pollution control measures, and does not review incentive-based mechanisms used in natural resource management. There are, however, notable initiatives at the state and federal level such as wetlands mitigation banking programs.

Table I Examples of Federal Incentive-Based Programs

Fees/charges/taxes		
Air	1978–	Gas Guzzler Tax
	1990–	Air Emission Permit Fees
	1990–	Ozone Depleting Chemicals Fees
	2005–	Ozone Nonattainment Area Fees
Land	1980–1995	Crude Oil and Chemical Taxes (Superfund)
	NA	Public Land Grazing Fees
Water	NA	National Pollution Discharge Elimination Permit System Fees
Subsidies		
Air	NA	Clean Fuel and Low-Emission Vehicle Subsidies
	NA	Renewable Energy and Energy Conservation Subsidies
Land	1995–	Brownfield Pilot Project Grants
Water	1956–	Municipal Sewage Treatment Construction
Cross media	early 1980's–	Supplemental Environmental Projects for Non-Compliance Penalty Reduction
Tradeable permits		
Air	1974–	Emissions Trading Program
	1978–	Corporate Average Fuel Economy Standards
	1982–1987	Lead Credit Trading
	1988–	Ozone Depleting Chemicals Allowance Trading
	1990–	Heavy-Duty Truck Manufacturers Emissions Averaging
	1992–	Reformulated Gasoline Credit Trading Program
	1992–	Hazardous Air Pollutant Early Reduction Program
	1992–	Greenhouse Gas Emission Reduction Joint Implementation Program
	1994–	Synthetic Organic Chemical Manufacturing Emissions Averaging (NESHAPS)
	1995–	Acid Rain Allowance Trading for SO_2 and NO_x
	1995–	Petroleum Refining Emissions Averaging (NESHAPS)
	1995–	Marine Tank Vessel Loading Operations Emissions Averaging (NESHAPS)
	1998–	Open Market Trading Ozone
	pending	El Paso Region Cross Border Air Emission Trading
	NA	Clean Fuel Vehicle Credit Trading Program
Water	1983	Iron and Steel Industry Effluent "Bubble" Trading System
Other		
Cross media	1986	Emergency Planning and Community Right-To-Know Act

Note: NESHAPS = National Emissions Standards for Hazardous Air Pollutants.
Sources: Anderson and Lohof [3]; Stavins [80].

The use of incentive-based mechanisms at the state level is also growing. Table II shows that many states are exploring a diverse array of incentive-based approaches. There are also many programs at the regional level, such as Southern California's Regional Emissions Clean Air Incentives Market (RECLAIM), that allow polluters to trade emission allowances to achieve air pollution goals.

The interest in using incentive-based mechanisms is also growing in other countries. A survey by the Organization for Economic Co-operation and Development (OECD) showed that, in 1992, 21 OECD countries had various fees and charges for emissions, 20 had fees and charges for specific high pollution products, 16 countries had deposit-refund programs, and 5 countries had a tradable permit program [65]. Although the United States has predominantly used the tradable permits scheme at the federal level, European countries have more often used fees to help achieve their environmental goals. These fees typically have not had a direct effect on pollution because they have not been set at a level that directly affects behavior.[16]

In principle, the use of these mechanisms has the potential to achieve environmental objectives at the lowest cost. Many economic studies have projected cost savings from replacing the traditional command-and-control regulations with more flexible incentive-based regulations. A review of *ex ante* empirical studies on cost savings from achieving least-cost air pollution control pattern shows significant potential gains from incentive-based policies [87]. The ratio of costs from a traditional command-and-control approach to the least-cost policy for the 11 studies reviewed ranged from 1.07 to 22.00, with an average of 6.13. These studies generally assume that a market-based approach will operate with maximum efficiency to achieve the same level of environmental quality at lower cost. In the real world, the counterfactual is less clear. It would be more realistic to compare actual command-and-control policies with actual market-based approaches [37].

An aggregate savings estimate from all current incentive-based mechanisms for air, water, and land pollution control in the United States was developed by Anderson and Lohof [3] using published estimates of potential savings and rough estimates where no studies were available. The authors estimate that in 1992, existing incentive-based programs saved $11 billion over command-and-control approaches, and that they will save over $16 billion by the year 2000. This estimate includes significant state programs in addition to federal initiatives.

Although such an estimate provides a rough picture of the magnitude of potential cost savings, it does not provide an assessment of the actual cost savings. Many of the studies used to compile the estimate are based on *ex ante* simulations that assume incentive-based mechanisms achieve the optimal result. This is rarely the case in practice. Political obstacles frequently lead to markets that have high transaction costs and institutional barriers

---

[16]Revenues from these fees, however, are often used to invest in improvements in environmental quality.

Table II Examples of State/Regional Incentive-Based Programs

Deposit-refund schemes		
Land	1972–	Beverage Container Deposit Systems
	1985–	Maine Pesticide Container Deposit System
	1988–	Rhode Island Tire Deposit
	NA	Lead–Acid Battery Deposit Systems
	NA	Performance Bonds
Fees/charges/taxes		
Air	1989–	Texas Clean Fuel Incentive Charge
	1995–	Congestion Pricing Schemes
	NA	California "Hot Spots" Fees
Land	1993–1995	Advance Product Disposal Fees
	1995–	Minnesota Contaminated Property Tax
	NA	Variable Cost Pricing for Household Waste
	NA	Landfill Operator Taxes
	NA	Hazardous Waste Generation and Management Taxes
	NA	Tire Charges
	NA	Rhode Island "Hard-to-Dispose Materials" Tax
	NA	Fertilizer Charges
	NA	"Pay-as-you-throw" Garbage Disposal Fees
	NA	Wetlands Compensation Fees
	NA	Public Land Grazing Fees
	NA	Wetlands Mitigation Banking
Water	NA	California Bay Protection and Toxic Cleanup Fees
	NA	Stormwater Runoff Fees
Subsidies		
Air	NA	Polluting Vehicle Scrappage Programs
	NA	Clean Fuel and Low-Emission Vehicle Subsidies
Land	1990–	New Jersey Illegal Dumping Information Awards Program
	NA	Recycling Loans and Grants
	NA	Recycling Tax Incentives
	NA	Brownfield Tax Incentives and Loans
Cross media	1990–1992	Louisiana Environmental Scorecard
	NA	Tax Benefits for Pollution Control Equipment
	NA	Loans and Tax-Exempt Bonds for Pollution Control Projects
Treadeable permits		
Air	1987–	Colorado Wood Stove and Fireplace Permit Trading
	1990–	Spokane Grass Burning Permit Trading

(Continued)

Table II (Continued)

	1993–	Texas Emission Credit Reduction Bank and Trading Program
	1994–	Los Angeles Regional Clean Air Incentives Market
	1995–	Massachusetts Emissions Trading for VOC, NO*x*, and CO
	1996–	Delaware Emissions Trading for VOCs and NO*x*
	1996–	Michigan Emissions Trading for VOCs and Criteria Pollutants
	1996–	Wisconsin Emissions Trading for VOCs and NO*x*
	1997–	Illinois Clean Air Market for VOCs
	1999–	OTC/OTAG Regional NO*x* Reduction Program
	pending	New Jersey Emissions Trading
Water	1981–	Wisconsin Fox River Point-to-Point Source Effluent Trading
	1984–	Point-to-Nonpoint Source Effluent Trading

Note: If a state is not specified, multiple states have implemented similar programs.
Source: Anderson and Lohof [3].

that reduce the potential for cost savings. Another problem with the estimation of savings is that it is difficult to assess what would have happened in the absence of a particular program. Even where cost savings are measured based on actual market data, it is not always clear if the program in question can be solely credited with the savings.[17]

There are three general categories of cost savings estimates for incentive-based mechanisms. The first is *ex ante* savings estimates that generally rely on simulations that assume the least cost abatement pattern is achieved.

The second is *ex post* savings estimates that rely on market simulations similar to the *ex ante* estimates. The third is *ex post* savings estimates that use actual data from trades. Although there are a number of *ex ante* simulation studies of potential cost savings from achieving the least-cost pollution abatement scheme for various pollutants, there are relatively few *ex post* assessments of actual incentive-based programs and even fewer *ex post* assessments of actual cost savings. Table III highlights some of the problems with current knowledge of cost savings. The table shows *ex ante* and/or *ex post* estimates of cost savings for five tradable permit programs for air pollution control. I chose these programs since they represent programs where the most information is available; however, as the table shows, there are relatively few assessments of the actual impact of programs.

---

[17]For example, railroad deregulation led to lower than expected prices for sulfur dioxide allowances by reducing the premium for low-sulfur coal [16].

I was not able to find any *ex ante* assessments of the potential savings from the various parts of the Emissions Trading Program designed to reduce the cost of meeting air pollution regulation.[18] Hahn and Hester [36] produced the only comprehensive study of cost savings based on actual trades. They estimated that the program achieved savings on the order of $1.4 to $19 billion over the first 14 years. These savings, however, do not represent the full extent of potential cost savings. The program generally failed to create an active market for emission reduction credits, but it did allow for the environmental goals to be met at a lower cost [36].

Lead trading, on the other hand, comes much closer to the economist's ideal for a smoothly functioning market. The EPA originally projected cost savings of $310 million to refiners from the banking provision of the program between 1985 and 1987 [88]. The actual cost savings may be much higher than anticipated since the level of banking was higher than EPA's expectations. There are no *ex post* estimates of cost savings based on actual trading.

There was at least one *ex ante* study of cost savings using an incentive-based approach to curb the use of ozone-depleting chemicals. Palmer *et al.* estimated that between 1980 and 1990, a price-based incentive policy would save a total of $143 million over a command-and-control approach [30]. The EPA implemented an allowance trading program, and a tax on the ozone depleting chemicals was later added. Although the primary intent of the tax was to raise revenue, it may have been set high enough to have a significant incentive effect. The actual cost savings from the two approaches are unclear since there are no comprehensive *ex post* studies.

There have been some *ex ante* and *ex post* studies of the sulfur dioxide allowance trading program to reduce acid rain. *Ex ante* studies projected savings on the order of $1 billion per year [42]. The magnitude of actual cost savings achieved is estimated to be significantly less.[19]

The pattern of prices provides one indicator of cost savings, assuming that the marginal cost of abatement equals the price and total costs increase as marginal costs increase. In 1990, predictions of SO_2 permit prices were $400 to $1,000 per ton. The estimates from the beginning of the current phase of the program were significantly lower—between $250 and $400 per ton. Today actual SO_2 permit prices are about $90 to $110 per ton.[20] The discrepancy arises for a couple of reasons. First, early analyses did not include all provisions of the final bill such as the distribution of 3.5 million extra bonus allowances. The one estimate that included the extra allowances pre-

---

[18]For examples of early assessments of cost savings from using market-based approaches to achieve particular air pollution goals, see General Accounting Office [30] and Tietenberg [86].

[19]This discussion draws from Stavins [81].

[20]Actual incremental SO_2 abatement costs may be on the order of $200 per ton. Permit prices are lower than abatement costs for three reasons. First, in the 1990 CAA Amendments, allowances are "not property rights," which means that the allowance would have a lower value than if they were a secure property right. Second, public utility commissions place restrictions on some utilities' ability to purchase permits, thus raising their abatement costs. Third, utilities may have believed early high price predictions, and so overinvested in scrubbers.

Table III Estimates of Cost Savings over Command-and-Control Approach

Emission Trading Program (1974–)

ex ante	No comprehensive studies on compliance cost savings.	
ex post	Total cost savings between 1974 and 1989 were between $960 million and $13 billion. "Netting" portion of the program was estimated to have saved $25 million to $300 million in permitting costs and $500 million to $12 billion in emission control costs. "Bubbles" provision of the program was estimated to have saved $300 million from federally approved trades and $135 million from state approved trades (1984 collars).	Hahn and Hester [36]

Lead Credit Trading (1982–1987)

ex ante	Refiners were expected to save approximately $200 million over the period 1985 to 1987 (1983 dollars).	EPA [88]
ex post	None as of 1998.	

Ozone Depleting Chemicals Allowance Trading (1988–)

ex ante	The total compliance cost would be $77 million, or roughly 40% less than a command-and-control approach, between 1980 and 1990 (1980 dollars).	Palmer et al. as reported in GAO [30]
ex post	None as of 1998.	

Sulfur Dioxide Allowance Trading (1995–)

ex ante	$689 million to $973 million per year between 1993 and 2010 or 39 to 44% less than the costs without allowance cost trading (1990 dollars).	ICF[42]
	Annual savings in 2002 is $1.9 billion with internal trading, $3.1 billion with interutility trading or 42 and 68% less than the cost absent trading (1992 dollars).	GAO [31]
ex post	Total annual compliance cost savings in 2010 under the least cost approach is $600 million or 35% less than the command and control approach (1995 dollars).	Carlson et al. [17]
	$225 to $375 million dollars or 25 to 35% of compliance costs absent trading (1995 dollars).	Schmalensee et al. [75]

Table III (Continued)

RECLAIM (1994–)

ex ante	The RECLAIM program is expected to reduce compliance costs by $38.2 million in 1994, $97.8 million in 1995, $46.6 million in 1996, $32.9 million in 1997, $67.7 million in 1998, and $64.0 million in 1999 (1987 dollars). In the early years, the compliance costs are approximately 80% less than under a command-and-control approach, and close to 30% less in the later years.	Johnson and Pekelney [43]
ex post	None as of 1998.	

dicted prices of $170 to $200 per ton. Second, much of the remaining difference between predicted and actual permit prices is due to railroad deregulation, the resulting fall in the price of low-sulfur coal, and the decision to scrub [18, 75].

Although the absolute savings that were projected have not materialized, relative savings are in the range predicted by *ex ante* studies— approximately 25 to 35% of costs absent trading [17]. Interestingly, Burtraw [16] has found that the primary source of cost savings was not directly from trading across utilities, but rather from the flexibility in choosing abatement strategies within utilities, which is consistent with earlier predictions. Therefore, improving the trading program may allow utilities to achieve further cost savings.[21]

The RECLAIM program in Southern California has received much attention over the past few years. The program was expected to produce significant cost savings. The South Coast Air Quality Management District (SCAQMD) had estimated that the program would yield cost savings of $52 million in 1994 [43]. Although the potential savings are sizable and a review of the trading activity to date suggests significant cost savings have been achieved, there are no comprehensive studies that have assessed the actual savings.

As these examples show, the use of these mechanisms has increased and the potential savings are substantial; however, a more detailed review of these applications suggests that their performance has varied widely [36]. The variation in performance of these programs can be explained, in part, by differences in the underlying politics governing the choice and design of these programs. These political forces have led to policies that deviate from the economist's ideal.

---

[21]However, these savings are likely to be less than the savings that accrue from intrautility trading [41].

Although the tradable permit schemes reviewed here did not exhaust cost savings, the programs generally improved environmental quality at a lower cost than alternatives under consideration. In contrast, the purpose of many environmental taxes and fees in the U.S. has been to raise revenue rather than reduce pollution. For example, the Superfund tax levied on crude oil, chemicals, and gross business profits is used to help finance cleanup. When fees have been levied directly on pollution, they have not been large enough to have significant impacts on behavior. Absent adequate incentives from fees, regulators have relied on command-and-control approaches to achieve desired levels of environmental protection. Thus, most environmental fees in the U.S. would not be economic instruments using the definition in this paper.[22]

The incentive-based mechanisms considered above are primarily concerned with issues of cost effectiveness—that is, achieving a given goal at low cost. In contrast, the regulatory analysis considered below addresses the choice of goals.

Moves toward Analyzing the Benefits and Costs of Environmental Regulation

To address the dramatic increase in regulatory activity beginning in the late 1960s, the past five Presidents have introduced mechanisms for overseeing regulations with varying degrees of success. A central component of later oversight mechanisms was formal economic analysis, which included benefit–cost analysis and cost-effectiveness analysis.

As a result of concerns that some environmental regulations were ineffective or too costly, President Nixon established a "Quality of Life" review of selected regulations in 1971. The review process, administered by OMB, required agencies issuing regulations affecting the environment, health, and safety to coordinate their activities. In 1974, President Ford formalized and broadened this review process in Executive Order 11281. Agencies were required to prepare inflationary impact statements of major rules. President Carter further strengthened regulatory oversight in 1978 by issuing Executive Order 12044, which required detailed regulatory analyses of proposed rules and centralized review by the Regulatory Analysis Review Group. This group consisted of representatives from the Executive Office of the President, including the Council of Economic Advisers, and regulatory agencies. A major focus of this review group was on environmental regulations such as the ozone standard, diesel particulate emissions, and heavy-duty truck emissions [92].

Since 1981, Presidents have required agencies to complete a regulatory impact analysis (RIA) for every major regulation. President Reagan's Executive Order 12291 required an RIA for each "major" rule whose annual impact

---

[22]Some fees in Europe, such as Sweden's charge on nitrogen oxides from stationary sources, would be economic instruments [78].

on the economy was estimated to exceed $100 million [77].[23] The aim of this Executive Order was to develop more effective and less costly regulation. President Bush used the same Executive Order. President Clinton issued Executive Order 12866, which is similar to Reagan's order in terms of its analytical requirements but adds and changes some requirements. Generally, Clinton's Executive Order directs agencies to choose the most cost-effective design of a regulation to achieve the regulatory objective, and to adopt a regulation only after balancing the costs and benefits. Clinton's order requires agencies to promulgate regulations if the benefits "justify" the costs. This language is generally perceived as more flexible than Reagan's order, which required the benefits to "outweigh" the costs. Clinton's order also places greater emphasis on distributional concerns.[24] Clinton's order requires a benefit-cost analysis for major regulations as well as an assessment of reasonably feasible alternatives to the planned regulation and a statement of why the planned regulation was chosen instead of the alternatives. Most of the major federal environmental, health, and safety regulations that have been reviewed to date are promulgated by the EPA because those regulations tend to be the most expensive.

The Congress has been slower to support efforts to require the balancing of benefits and costs of major environmental regulations. In 1982 the Senate unanimously passed such a law, but it was defeated in the House of Representatives. The two primary environmental statutes that allowed the balancing of benefits and costs prior to the mid-1990s are the Toxic Substances Control Act and the Federal Insecticide, Fungicide, and Rodenticide Act [27]. Recently, Congress has shown greater interest in emphasizing the balancing of benefits and costs. Table IV reviews recent regulatory reform initiatives, which could help improve environmental regulation and legislation. The table suggests that Congress now shares the concern of the Executive Branch that the regulatory system is in need of repair and could benefit from economic analysis [20]. All reforms highlighted in the table emphasize a trend towards considering the benefits and costs of regulation, although the effectiveness of the provisions is as of yet unclear. Perhaps owing to the politicized nature of the debate over regulatory reform, these reform efforts have come about in a piecemeal fashion, and there is some overlap in the requirements for analysis.[25] These incremental efforts

---

[23]While the definition of "major" has changed somewhat over time, it is currently defined as a regulation that has "an annual effect on the economy of $100 million or more, or adversely affects, in a material way, a sector of the economy, productivity, competition, jobs, the environment, public health or safety, or state, local, or tribal government or communities" (3(f)(1)(EO 12866)).

[24]For instance, Clinton's Principles of Regulation instructs that ". . . each agency shall consider . . . distributive impacts, and equity. On the other hand, Reagan's Executive order instructs agencies merely to identify the parties most likely to receive benefits and pay costs.

[25]There has been some recent interest in Congress in reducing this overlap by establishing a single congressional agency that would have the responsibility for assessing the government regulation. This agency would be similar to the Congressional Budget Office but have responsibility for regulation. It could help stimulate better analysis and review of agency rules by providing an additional source of information.

fall into the two categories of process reforms described earlier in the paper: accountability mechanisms and analytical requirements.

Examples of accountability mechanisms include the provision in the Small Business Regulatory Enforcement Fairness Act of 1996 that requires agencies to submit final regulations to Congress for review. The Telecommunications Act of 1996 requires the Federal Communications Commission to conduct a biennial review of all regulations promulgated under the Act. Congress added regulatory accountability provisions to senate appropriations legislation in 1996, 1997, and 1998 that require the Office of Management and Budget to assess the benefits and costs of existing federal regulatory programs and present the results in a public report. The OMB must also recommend programs or specific regulations to reform or eliminate. The reports represent the most significant recent step towards strengthening the use of economic analysis in the regulatory process.[26]

The addition of analytical requirements has generally received more attention than the addition of accountability mechanisms, partly because of their prominence in the Reagan and Clinton executive orders and partly because of controversy regarding their impact. The variation of the language and the choice of analytical requirement for each of the statutes listed in Table IV reflect the results of the ongoing controversy regarding analytical requirements, which takes place every time Congress debates using them. Some statutes require only cost-effectiveness analysis, some require full-fledged benefit–cost analysis, and some combine some form of benefit–cost analysis with risk–risk analysis.

The Unfunded Mandates Reform Act of 1995 requires agencies to choose the "most cost-effective" alternative and to describe the costs and benefits of any unfunded mandate, but does not require the benefits of the mandate to justify the costs. The Safe Drinking Water Amendments of 1996 require the Administrator of the Environmental Protection Agency to determine whether the benefits justify the costs of a drinking water standard, but the Administrator does not have to set a new standard if the benefits do not justify the costs.[27] Amendments in 1996 to the process through which the Secretary of Transportation sets gas pipeline safety standards, on the other hand, require the Secretary to propose a standard for pipeline safety *only* if

---

[26]Other examples in the policy category include the Paperwork Reduction Act, which sets measurable goals to reduce the regulatory burden, and the Government Performance and Results Act, which establishes requirements for agencies to develop mission statements, performance goals, and measures of performance.

[27]The Amendments also require some form of risk–risk analysis. They require the Administrator of the Environmental Protection Agency to set maximum levels for contaminants in drinking water at a "feasible" level, defined as feasible with the use of the best technology and treatment techniques available, while "taking cost into consideration." The Administrator must ignore the feasibility constraint if the feasible level would result in an increase in the concentration of other contaminants in drinking water or would interfere with the efficacy of treatment techniques used to comply with other national primary drinking water regulations. If the feasibility constraint does not apply, the Administrator must set the maximum level to minimize "the overall risk of adverse health effects by balancing the risk from the contaminant and the risk from other contaminants."

Table IV Recent Regulatory Reform Regulation

Legislation	Description
Unfunded Mandates Reform Act of 1995	Requires the Congressional Budget Office to estimate the direct costs of unfunded federal mandates with significant economic impacts. Direct agencies to describe the costs and benefits of the majority of such mandates. Requires agencies to identify alternatives to the proposed mandate and select the "least costly, most cost-effective, or least burdensome alternative" that achieves the desired social objective.
Small Business Regulatory Enforcement Fairness Act of 1996	Requires agencies to submit each final regulation with supporting analyses to Congress. Congress has 60 days to review major regulations, and can enact a joint resolution of disapproval to void the regulation if the resolution is passed and signed by the President. Strengthens judicial review provisions to hold agencies more accountable for the impacts of regulation on small entities.
Food Quality Protection Act of 1996	Eliminates the Delancy Clause of the Food, Drug, and Cosmetic Act, which set a zero-tolerance standard for pesticide residues on processed food. Establishes a "safe" tolerance level, defined as "a reasonable certainty of no harm." Allows the Administrator of the Environmental Protection Agency to modify the tolerance level if use of the pesticide protects consumers from health risks greater than the dietary risk from the residue, or if use is necessary to avoid a "significant disruption" of the food supply. Amends the Federal Insecticide, Fungicide, and Rodenticide Act by requiring a reevaluation of the safe tolerance level after the Administrator determines during the reregistration process whether a pesticide will present an "unreasonable risk to man or the environment, taking into account the economic, social, and environmental costs and benefits of the use of any pesticide."

(Continued)

Table IV (Continued)

Legislation	Description
Safe Drinking Water Act Amendments of 1996	Amends the procedure to set maximum contaminant levels for contaminants in public water supplies. Adds requirement to determine whether the benefits of the level justify the costs. Maintains feasibility standard for contaminant levels, unless feasible level would result in an increase in the concentration of other contaminants, or would interfere with the efficacy of treatment techniques used to comply with other national drinking water regulations. Requires the Administrator to set contaminant levels to minimize the overall risk of adverse health effects by balancing the risk from the contaminant and the risk from other contaminants in such cases.
Regulatory Accountability Provision of 1996, 1997, and 1998	In separate appropriations legislation in 1996, 1997, and 1998, Congress required the Office of Management and Budget to submit an assessment of the annual benefits and costs of all existing federal regulatory programs to Congress for 1997, 1998, and 2000, respectively. The Office of Management and Budget already must review and approve analyses submitted by agencies estimating the costs and benefits of major proposed rules. The annual report provisions build on this review process.

Source: Hahn [35].

the benefits justify the costs. Other statutes simply require the agency to only consider costs and benefits. The Food Quality Protection Act of 1996 is even more vague. The Act eliminates the Delaney Clause in the Food, Drug, and Cosmetic Act, the zero-tolerance standard for carcinogenic pesticide residues on processed food. Instead, the Administrator of the Environmental Protection Agency must set a tolerance level that is "safe," defined as "reasonable certainty of no harm." While the Food Quality Protection Act does not explicitly require the Administrator to consider benefits and costs when determining safe tolerance levels, the new language suggests increased balancing of costs and benefits relative to the original requirement. While the addition of such language to statutes represents an improvement over the status quo, it is clear that the major aims of the efforts to date have been to require more information on the benefits and costs of regulations and to increase oversight of regulatory activities and agency performance. Ensuring that regulations pass some form of a benefit–cost test has not been a priority.

There is evidence that states are also moving toward the systematic analysis of significant regulatory actions. According to a survey by the National Association on Administrative Rules Review (NAARR) in 1996, administrative law review officials in 27 states noted that their state statutes require an economic impact analysis for all proposed rules, and 10 states require benefit–cost analysis for all proposed rules.[28] Table V highlights efforts in six states. The first section describes efforts to review existing rules and procedures including any measures of success, and the second section describes the analysis requirements for new activities. While the efforts vary in their authority, coverage of activities, and amount of resources, they all place greater emphasis on economic analysis and the review of existing regulations and procedures. In addition, some states have begun to document the success of their efforts; however, the measures have generally been limited to the number of rules reviewed or eliminated. No estimates of actual welfare gains are available.

The use of economic analysis is also increasing in other countries. Although the requirements for analysis and the structure of oversight vary from country to country, there are 18 OECD countries, including the United States, that require some assessment of the impacts of their regulations [66]. Although there is some anecdotal evidence of significant impacts RIAs have had on policy, the OECD study concluded that RIAs generally only have a "marginal influence" on decision making. Just as the review of U.S. federal experience with RIAs in Hahn [35] showed inconsistencies in the quality of the analysis, the same pattern appears to exist in other countries.

The preceding discussion suggests that both incentive-based mechanisms and process reforms are playing a more important role in environmental policy. One key challenge is to better understand the ways in which economics can influence the environmental policy debate.

4. Understanding the Role of Economics and Economists in Shaping the Reforms

This section addresses the avenues through which economists have affected environmental policy, the limited influence of economics on policy, and the likely impact economists will have on future policy.

Avenues of Impact

There are three ways in which economists have influenced the debate over environmental policy—through research, teaching, and outreach.

---

[28]All 50 states, except for Rhode Island, responded to a questionnaire sent by the NAARR [58]. Unfortunately, little is known about the level of compliance with these requirements, the quality of the analysis, and the influence it has on decision making.

Table V State Efforts to Assess the Economic Impacts of Regulation

	Review of existing rules			Analysis of new rules		Requirement that benefits exceed costs
	Initiated	Coverage	Examples of results	Key revisions[a]	Required analysis	
Arizona	1986	Continuous (S)	49% of 1,392 rules reviewed in FY 1996 were identified for modification.	1993	Economic impact (S)	All rules (S)
California	1995	One-time (E)	3,900 regulations were identified for repeal; 1,700 were recommended for modification.	1991–1993, 1997	Economic impact (S, E)	Selected rules (S, E)
Massachusetts	1996	One-time (E)	Of the 1,595 regulations reviewed, 19% were identified for repeal and 44% were identified for modification.	1996	Economic impact (E)	All rules (E)
New York	1995	One-time (E)	In progress.	1995	Economic impact (S, E); Benefit-cost for selected rules (E)	All rules (E)
Pennsylvania	1996	One-time (E)	The Department of Environmental Protection identified 1,716 sections of regulations to be eliminated.	1996	Economic impact for selected rules (S); Benefit–cost for selected rules (E)	All rules (E)
Virginia	1994	Continuous (E)	Of the rules reviewed, 27% were identified for repeal and 40% for modification.	1994	Economic impact (S, E)	None

Note: Authority: E = Executive Order, S = Statute.
Source: Hahn [35].

[a]Many of these states previously had some very limited requirements for analysis of new rules. Important revisions were made through new executive orders and statutory changes to clarify and expand requirements and establish oversight.

The literature on economic instruments is voluminous and growing. There are three key ideas in the literature that have had an important impact on environmental policymaking: first, incentive-based instruments can help achieve goals at a lower cost than other instruments; second, benefit-cost analysis can provide a useful framework for decision making; and third, all policies and regulations have opportunity costs. Those ideas may seem obvious to economists, but they have not always been heeded in policy debates.

Economists have provided a normative framework for evaluating environmental policy and public goods (see, e.g., [9, 74]).[29] The literature on using incentive-based instruments to internalize externalities dates back to Pigou [69], and for tradable permits to Crocker [21] and Dales [24]. The application of benefit–cost analysis to public projects begins with Eckstein [25]. Economists have also been helpful in comparing benefit–cost analysis with other frameworks for assessing the impacts of policies (see, e.g., [50, 67]).

Studies of incentive-based instruments have revealed that there are large potential cost savings from applying those instruments [86]. Moreover, economists have now marshaled some evidence of the potential cost savings of such systems in practice, as shown in Table III.

The second way in which economists have translated their ideas into policy is by educating students who subsequently enter the world of policy and business. Many of those students embrace aspects of the economist's paradigm, in this case, as it applies to environmental policy. Thus, for example, as more students in policy schools, business schools, and law schools are exposed to the idea of pollution taxes and tradable permits, it is more likely that they will consider applying economic ideas to particular problems, such as curbing acid rain and limiting greenhouse gas emissions.

Formal education is part of the process of diffusion from the ivory tower to the policy world. Most major environmental groups, businesses, and agencies involved in environmental policy now have staff members with at least some graduate training in economics. Environmental advocates are more likely to support policies that embrace incentive-based mechanisms, and their advocacy is more likely to be couched in the language of economics. A comparison of today's debate over policy instruments for climate change with earlier debates on emission fees is revealing. In the seventies, emission fees and tradable permits were more likely to be viewed as "licenses to pollute." Today, most policy discussions on climate change identify the need for using incentive-based instruments to achieve goals in a cost-effective manner. The sea change in attitude toward the use of incentive-based instruments represents one of the major accomplishments of environmental economics over the last three decades.

A third, more direct way that economists have translated their ideas into policy is through policy outreach and advocacy. They have become

---

[29]An excellent survey of the academic literature is provided by Cropper and Oates [22].

increasingly effective "lobbyists for efficiency" [47].[30] For example, my colleague, Robert Stavins, developed a very influential policy document that helped affect the course of the debate on acid rain by highlighting the potential for using incentive-based mechanisms [79]. Another example is the letter on climate change policy signed by over 2,500 economists [6]. I have personally been involved in several efforts that developed a consensus among academics to help inform the broader policy community [5, 20]. The impact of such consensus documents, while difficult to measure, should not be underestimated.

To increase their influence on policy, economists may wish to think carefully about how they allocate their time among the activities discussed above. In terms of getting policies implemented effectively, it is generally not sufficient simply to develop a good idea. Some kind of marketing is necessary before the seedling can grow into a tree.

Limitations of Impact: Economics in the Broader Policy Process

Economists, of course, are only one part of the environmental policymaking puzzle. Politics affects the process in many ways that can block outcomes that would result in higher levels of economic welfare. Indeed, one of the primary lessons of the political economy of regulation is that economic efficiency is not likely to be a key objective in the design of policy [10, 59].

Policy ideas can affect interest group positions directly, which can then affect the positions of key decision makers (such as elected officials and civil servants), who then structure policies through the passage of laws and regulations that meet their political objectives. Alternatively, ideas may influence decision makers directly.[31]

Policy proposals can help shape outcomes by expanding the production possibility frontier; however, the precise position on the frontier is determined by several factors. Take, for example, the design of incentive-based instruments for environmental protection (see, e.g., [18, 28, 38]). Several scholars have argued that the actual design of economic instruments typically departs dramatically for political reasons from the "efficient" design of such instruments (see, e.g., [7, 15, 36, 46, 54]). Frequently, taxes have been used to raise revenues rather than to reflect optimal damages [7]. Standards have been made more stringent on new sources than old sources as a way of inhibiting growth in selected regions [1]; and agricultural interests have fought hard against the idea of transferable water rights because of concerns over losing a valuable entitlement. In some cases, the government has argued for a command-and-control approach when affected parties were ready

---

[30]There are also a growing number of economic consultants and part-time consultants that may serve to impede the cause of efficiency [59].

[31]In this discussion, the institutional environment (e.g., the three branches of government and the rules governing each branch) is taken as a given. Obviously, other ideas can affect the structure of those institutions.

to endorse a more flexible market-oriented approach. This was the case, for example, in the debate over restoring the Everglades [68]. In short, rent-seeking and interest group politics have been shown to have a very important impact on the design of actual policy [93].[32]

Political concerns affect not only the design of incentive-based instruments, but also the use and abuse of economic analysis in the political process. Notwithstanding such concerns, some scholars have argued that economic analysis has had a constructive impact on the policy process [27, 56, 71]. In certain instances, research suggests that such optimism is justified; however, one must be careful about generalizing from a small sample. In many situations, analysis tends to get ignored or manipulated to achieve political ends. This is particularly true for environmental issues that have political saliency.[33] At the same time, by exposing such analysis to sunshine and serious reanalysis, there is a hope that politicians may be encouraged to pursue more efficient policies in some instances. My own experience suggests that analysis can help shape the debate in selected instances by making tradeoffs clearer to decision makers.[34]

The key point is that environmental economists should not be too optimistic about implementing some of their most fervently held professional beliefs in the real world. By improving their understanding of the constraints imposed by the political system, economists can help design more efficient policies that have a higher probability of being implemented.[35]

Likely Impact in the Future

To understand the likely impact of economics on environmental policy in the future, it is helpful to understand the reasons for its importance in the past. A simple story is that federal environmental policy was initially designed without much regard to cost in the wake of Earth Day in 1970, which marked the beginning of an acute national awareness of environmental issues. As the costs increased and became more visible, and the goals became more ambitious, the constituencies opposing such regulation on economic grounds grew. Currently, the political (as opposed to economic) demands for environmental quality are high, but the costs are also high in many instances. This is an obvious situation in which economists can help by building more cost-effective mechanisms for achieving goals.

---

[32]In addition, examination of particular rule-making proceedings has shown the relative influence of particular factors in shaping environmental decisions (see, e.g., [23, 53a]).

[33]See, for example, the optimistic account of the cost to the U.S. of reducing greenhouse gases provided by the Council of Economic Advisers [95].

[34]The impact of analysis on policy outcomes is not well understood; however, participants in the process can usually point to special cases where analysis was important. For example, in the clean air debate over alternative fuels, analysis of the cost and benefits of requiring companies to sell a large fraction of methanol-powered vehicles made this option look very unattractive.

[35]For example, in the debate over acid rain, it was clear there would be some implicit or explicit compensation to high sulfur coal interests. The challenge was to develop approaches that would maximize cost savings subject to that constraint.

So far, environmental economists have enjoyed limited success in seeing their ideas translated into practice. That success is likely to continue in the future. In particular, there are likely to be more incentive-based mechanisms, greater use of benefit–cost analysis, and more careful consideration of the opportunity costs of such policies. But that does not mean that the overall net benefits of environmental policy will necessarily increase because the political forces that lead to less efficient environmental policy will be strong.[36]

For those who believe benefit-cost analysis should play a more prominent role in decision making—in particular, the setting of goals—it will be a long, uphill struggle. The recent fight over the Regulatory Improvement Act of 1998 sponsored by Senators Levin and Thompson provides a good example. This bill essentially codifies the Executive Orders calling for benefit-cost analysis of major rules; yet many within the environmental community are strongly opposed, arguing that it could lead to an analytical quagmire [39, 76]. There are at least three reasons such opponents would take this stand: first, because making such claims is good for mobilizing financial support;[37] second, because of concerns that such legislation could help lead to more serious consideration of economics in environmental decision making; third, because opponents are concerned that agencies will misuse cost–benefit analysis and related analytical tools. In particular, there is concern with what will happen if politicians decide that cost is no longer a "four-letter" word—so that benefits and costs can be compared explicitly! Given the limited scope of this bill and the level of resistance encountered thus far, it is clear that the potential for change in the short term is limited.

The problem facing economists who want benefit–cost analysis to play a greater role in decision making is that it is difficult for politicians to oppose environmental laws and regulations simply because they may fail a benefit-cost test. After all, who could be against an environmental policy if it has some demonstrable benefits for some worthy constituency? It is hard to make arguments opposing such regulation in a 10-second soundbite on television.

But economists will continue to make slow progress in the area of balancing benefits and costs. In the short term, they will do so by making arguments about the potential for reallocating regulatory expenditures in ways that can save more lives or trees. Over the longer term, they will build a better information base that clearly shows that many environmental policies will pass a benefit-cost test if they are designed judiciously, but many also will not.

---

[36]Environmentalists have been successful in framing the debate as being either "for" or "against" the environment, making it difficult to introduce the notion of explicit tradeoffs. Their success is likely to continue for the foreseeable future.

[37]The 1994 Republican plan to repeal regulations, for example, breathed new life into the green movement. The highly publicized plan resulted in a dramatic increase in memberships to environmental groups and an increase in donations by active members [85]. To the extent that benefit–costs analysis is perceived as a means to repeal regulations, opposing the use of such tools may have a similar revenue-enhancing effect.

5. Concluding Thoughts

This paper has made a preliminary attempt to assess the impact of economics on environmental policy. There are at least three key points to be made about the nature of this impact. First, the impact often occurs with considerable time lags. Second, the introduction of economic instruments occurs in a political environment, which frequently has dramatic effects on the form and content of policy. Third, economists are not very close to a public policy heaven in which benefit–cost analysis plays a major role in shaping environmental policy decisions that governments view within their domain.

The latter topic concerning the appropriate domain for environmental policy may be one on which the profession contributes a great deal in the future. In particular, it is difficult to determine when it is "appropriate" for a particular level of government to intervene in the development of environmental policy [61, 72]. This is a subject on which there is a great deal of legitimate intellectual and political ferment. At one extreme, free market environmentalists wish to leave most, if not all, choices about such policy to the market [2, 49]. At the other extreme, some analysts believe there is a need for many levels of government intervention, including the design of a global environmental institution (see, e.g., [26]). Achieving some degree of consensus on that issue is likely to be difficult, but not impossible. For example, most economists agree that for global environmental problems, it is difficult to address them effectively without having some kind of international agency or agreement. At the same time, many economists recognize that the arguments suggesting competitive jurisdictions will under-provide environmental amenities is somewhat weaker than was suggested two decades ago (see, e.g., [82]).

Environmental economists will have many opportunities to shape the policy debate in new areas. Examples include international trade and the environment and the development of new taxation systems [11, 33, 45, 84]. One of the critical factors that will affect the rate of diffusion of ideas from environmental economists to the policy world is the *perception* of their success. If, for example, markets for environmental quality are viewed as a successful mechanism for achieving goals by both business and environmentalists, their future in the policymakers' tool chest looks brighter. The same can be said of benefit–cost analysis.

There are many challenges that lie ahead for the environmental economics community. The most important one is becoming more policy-relevant.[38] To achieve that end, economists need to become more problem-driven rather

---

[38]It is possible that the influence of economics on environmental policy in developing countries may be greater because these countries have fewer resources to waste. That is, governments in developing countries may more likely use the tools advocated by economists to develop policies. While there are certainly many applications of economics in environmental policy in developing countries, the general thesis has yet to be demonstrated (see, e.g., [94]). Moreover, judging by the levels of inefficiency of other policies in developing countries, it is unclear why environmental policies may be designed more efficiently (see e.g., [87]).

that [sic] tool-driven. There seems to be a move in this direction, but there are also incentives in the profession that still push it in the opposite direction—most notable publish or perish.

Another challenge for the economics community is to determine how far it is willing to push the paradigm. Some would like government regulations, including environmental regulations, to a least pass a broadly defined benefit–cost test [20]. Others more skeptical about the tool and less skeptical about the outcomes of certain kinds of government intervention think economists and policymakers should not ask benefit–cost analysis to bear too much weight (see, e.g., [14, 50]).

Finally, economists need to get more comfortable with the idea of being lobbyists for efficiency or advocates for policies in which they believe. This comfort level is increasing slowly. Moreover, economists are finding ways to institutionalize their power in certain policy settings. A good example is the Environmental Economics Advisory Committee within the Science Advisory Board at the Environmental Protection Agency. The primary function of that group is to help provide economic guidance to the agency on important regulatory issues. Now economists have a voice.

In sum, the impact of economists on environmental policy to date has been modest. Economists can claim credit for having helped changed the terms of the debate to include economic instruments—no small feat. They can also claim some credit for legislation that promotes greater balancing of costs and benefits. But specific victories of consequence are few and far between. Most of the day-to-day policy that real folks must address involves the activities associated with complying with standards, permits, guidelines and regulations. While economists have said a few intelligent things about such matters, their attention has largely been focused on those parts of environmental policy that they enjoy talking about—areas where theoretical economics can offer relatively clean insights. Perhaps if we expand our domain of inquiry judiciously and continue to teach tomorrow's decisionmakers, we can also expand our influence. Hope springs eternal.

REFERENCES

1. B. A. Ackerman and W. T. Hassler, "Clean Coal/Dirty Air: Or How the Clean Air Act Became a Multibillion-Dollar Bail-out for High-Sulfur Coal Producers and What Should Be Done About It," Yale Univ. Press, New Haven, CT (1981).
2. T. L. Anderson and D. R. Leal, "Free Market Environmentalism," Pacific Research Institute for Public Policy, San Francisco (1991).
3. R. C. Anderson and A. Q. Lohof, "United States Experience with Economic Incentives in Environmental Pollution Control Policy," Environmental Law Institute, Washington DC (1997).
4. R. C. Anderson, A. Carlin, A. McGartland, and J. Weinberger, Cost savings from the use of market incentives for pollution control, in "Market-Based Approaches to Environmental Policy" (R. Kosobud and J. Zimmerman, Eds.), Van Nostrand Reinhold, New York (1997).

5. K. J. Arrow, M. L. Cropper, G. C. Eads, R. W. Hahn, L. B. Lave, R. G. Noll, P. R. Portney, M. Russell, R. Schmalensee, V. K. Smith, and R. N. Stavins, "Benefit-Cost Analysis in Environmental, Health, and Safety Regulation: A Statement of Principles," AEI Press, Washington, DC (1996).

6. K. J. Arrow, D. Jorgenson, P. Krugman, W. Nordhaus, and R. Solow, "The Economist's Statement on Climate Change," Redefining Progress, San Francisco, CA (1997).

7. T. A. Barthold, Issues in the design of environmental excise taxes, *J. Econom. Perspect.* 8, 133–151 (1994).

8. R. H. Bates, "Markets and States in Tropical Africa: The Political Basis of Agricultural Policies," Univ. of California Press, Berkeley, CA (1981).

9. W. Baumol and W. Oates, "The Theory of Environmental Policy," 2nd ed., Prentice-Hall, Englewood Cliffs, NJ (1988).

10. G. Becker, A theory of competition among pressure groups for political influence, *Quart. J. Econom.* 97, 371–400 (1983).

11. J. Bhagwati and T. N. Srinivasan, Trade and the environment: Does environmental diversity detract from the case for free trade?, *in* "Fair Trade and Harmonization: Prerequisites for Free Trade?" (J. Bhagwati and R. Hudec, Eds.), MIT Press, Cambridge, MA (1996).

12. P. Bohn and R. S. Clifford, Comparative analysis of alternative policy instruments, *in* "Handbook of Natural Resource and Energy Economics, Volume I" (A. V. Kneese and J. L. Sweeney, Eds.), pp. 395–460, North-Holland, Amsterdam (1985).

13. A. Bovenberg and L. H. Goulder, Optimal environmental taxation in the presence of other taxes: General equilibrium analysis, *Amer. Econom. Rev.* 86, 985–1000 (1996).

14. D. W. Bromley, The ideology of efficiency: Searching for a theory of policy analysis, *J. Environ. Econom. Management* 19, 86–107 (1990).

15. J. M. Buchanan and G. Tullock, Polluters' profits and political response: Direct controls versus taxes, *Amer. Econom. Rev.* 65, 139–147 (1975).

16. D. Burtraw, "Cost Savings Sans Allowance Trades? Evaluating the SO$_2$ Emission Trading Program to Date," Discussion Paper 95-30-REV, Resources for the Future, Washington, DC (1996).

17. C. Carlson, D. Burtraw, M. Cropper, and K. L. Palmer, "SO$_2$ Control by Electric Utilities: What Are the Gains from Trade?" Discussion Paper, Resources for the Future, Washington, DC [2007].

18. T. N. Cason, Seller incentive properties of EPA's emission trading auction, *J. Environ. Econom. Management* 25, 177–195 (1993).

19. Council of Economic Advisers, "Economic Report of the President," U.S. Government Printing Office, Washington, DC (1998).

20. R. W. Crandall, C. DeMuth, R. W. Hahn, R. E. Litan, P. S. Nivola, And P. R. Portney, "An Agenda for Reforming Federal Regulation," AEI Press and Brookings Institution Press, Washington, DC (1997).

21. T. Crocker, The structuring of atmospheric pollution control systems, *in* "The Economics of Air Pollution" (H. Wolozin, Ed.), pp. 61–86, Norton, New York (1966).

22. M. L. Cropper and W. E. Oates, Environmental economics: A survey, *J. Econom. Lit.* 30, 675–740 (1992).

23. M. L. Cropper *et al.*, The determinants of pesticide regulation: A statistical analysis of EPA decision making, *J. Pol. Econom.* 100, 175–197 (1992).

24. J. H. Dales, "Pollution, Property and Prices," University Press, Toronto (1968).

25. O. Eckstein, "Water-Resource Development: The Economics of Project Evaluation," Harvard Univ. Press, Cambridge, MA (1958).

26. D. C. Esty, "Greening the GATT: Trade, Environment, and the Future," Institute for International Economics, Washington, DC (1994).

27. A. G. Fraas, The role of economic analysis in shaping environmental policy, *Law Contemp. Problems 54*, 113–125 (1991),

28. R. Franciosi, R. M. Isaac, D. E. Pingry, and S. S. Reynolds, An experimental investigation of the Hahn-Noll revenue neutral auction for emissions licenses, *J. Environ. Econom. Management 24*, 1–24 (1993).

29. A. M. Freeman, Water Pollution Policy, *in* "Public Policies for Environmental Protection" (P. R. Portney, Ed.), Resources for the Future, Washington, DC (1990).

30. General Accounting Office, "A Market Approach to Air Pollution Control Could Reduce Compliance Costs without Jeopardizing Clean Air Goals," PAD-82-15, General Accounting Office, Washington, DC (1982).

31. General Accounting Office, "Air Pollution: Allowance Trading Offers an Opportunity to Reduce Emissions at Less Costs," GAO/RCED-95-30, Resources, Community, and Economic Development Division, General Accounting Office, Washington, DC (1994).

32. I. Goklany, Rationing health care while writing blank checks for environmental hazards, *Regulation*, 14–15, (1992).

33. L. Goulder, Environmental taxation and the "double dividend:" A reader's guide. *Int. Tax Public Finance 2*(2), 157–184 (1995).

34. J. D. Graham and J. B. Wiener (Eds.), "Risk vs. Risk: Tradeoffs in Protecting Health and the Environment," Harvard Univ. Press, Cambridge, MA (1995).

35. R. W. Hahn, "Reviving Regulatory Reform: A Global Perspective," AEI Press and Brookings Institution, New York, NY, forthcoming (2000).

36. R. W. Hahn and G. L. Hester, Marketable permits: Lessons for theory and practice, *Ecology Law Quart*, *16*, 361–406 (1989).

37. R. W. Hahn and R. N. Stavins, Economic incentives for environmental protection: Integrating theory and practice, *Amer. Econom. Rev. 82*, 464–468 (1992).

38. K. Hausker, The politics and economics of auction design in the market for sulfur dioxide pollution, *J. Policy Anal. Management 11*, 553–572 (1992).

39. D. Hawkins and G. Wetstone, Regulatory obstacle course, *Washington Post*, A18, March 9 (1998).

40. M. Hazilla and R. J. Kopp, The social cost of environmental quality regulations: A general equilibrium analysis, *J. Polit. Econom. 98*, 853–873 (1990).

41. ICF Resources, Inc., "Economic Environmental, and Coal Market Impacts of SO_2 Emissions Trading under Alternative Acid Rain Control Proposals," prepared for the U.S. Environmental Protection Agency, OPPE, Fairfax, VA (1989).

42. ICF Resources, Inc., "Regulatory Impact Analysis of the Final Acid Rain Implementation Regulations," prepared for the Office of Atmospheric and Indoor Air Programs, Acid Rain Division, U.S. Environmental Protection Agency, Washington, DC, October 19 (1992).

43. S. L. Johnson and D. M. Pekelney, Economic assessment of the regional clean air incentives market: A new emissions trading program for Los Angeles, *Land Econom. 72*, 277–297 (1996).

44. D. W. Jorgenson and P. J. Wilcoxen, Environmental regulation and U.S. economic growth, *Rand J. Econom. 21*, 314–340 (1990).

45. J. P. Kalt, Exhaustible resource price policy, international trade, and intertemporal welfare, *J. Environ. Econom. Management, 17* (1989).

46. N. Keohane, R. Revesz, and R. N. Stavins, The positive political economy of instrument choice in environmental policy, *in* "Environmental Economics and

Public Policy: Essays in Honor of Wallace Oates" (Arvind Panagariya, P. Portney and R. Schwab, Eds.), Edward Elgar, London, 1999, pp. 89–125.

47. S. Kelman, "What Price Incentives? Economists and the Environment," Auburn House, Boston (1981).

48. A. V. Kneese And C. L. Schultze, "Pollution, Prices, and Public Policy," Brookings Institution, Washington, DC (1975).

49. J. E. Krier, The tragedy of the commons, part two, *Harvard J. Law Pub. Policy* *15*, 325–347 (1992).

50. L. B. Lave, "The Strategy of Social Regulation," Brookings Institution, Washington, DC (1981).

51. L. B. Lave, Benefit-cost analysis: Do the benefits exceed the costs? *in* "Risks, Costs, and Lives Saved: Getting Better Results from Regulation" (R. W. Hahn, Ed.), Oxford Univ. Press/AEI Press, New York (1996).

52. R. E. Litan and W. D. Nordhaus, "Reforming Federal Regulation," Yale Univ. Press, New Haven, CT (1983).

53. R. Lutter, "An Analysis of the Use of EPA's Clean Air Benefit Estimates in OMB's Draft Report on the Costs and Benefits of Regulation," Regulatory Analysis 98-2, AEI-Brookings Joint Center for Regulatory Studies, Washington, DC (1998).

53a. W. Magat, A. Krupnick, and W. Harrington, "Rules in the Making: A Statistical Analysis of Regulatory Agency Behavior," Resources for the Future, Washington, DC (1986).

54. M. Maloney and R. E. McCormick, A positive theory of environmental quality regulation, *J. Law Econom.* *25*, 99–123 (1982).

55. A. Metrick and M. L. Weitzman, Conflicts and choices in biodiversity preservation, *J. Econom. Perspectives* *12*(3), 21–34 (1998).

56. R. D. Morgenstern (Ed.), "Economic Analysis at EPA: Assessing Regulatory Impact," Resources for the Future, Washington, DC (1997).

57. J. F. Morrall, A review of the record, *Regulation 10*, 25–34 (1986).

58. National Association of Administrative Rules Review, "The National Association on Administrative Rules Review 1996–97 Administrative Rules Review Directory and Survey," The Council of State Governments, Midwest Office, Lexington, KY (1996).

59. R. G. Noll, The economics and politics of the slowdown *in* regulatory reform, in "Reviving Regulatory Reform: A Global Perspective" (R. W. Hahn, Ed.), Cambridge Univ. Press/AEI Press, New York, forthcoming (1998).

60. R. G. Noll, Economic perspectives on the politics of regulation, in "Handbook of Industrial Organization" (R. Schmalensee and R. Willig, Eds.), North-Holland, Amsterdam (1989).

61. W. E. Oates and R. M. Schwab, Economic competition among jurisdictions: Efficiency enhancing or distortion inducing? *J. Public Econom.* *35*, 333–354 (1988).

62. Office of Management and Budget, "More Benefits, Fewer Burdens" Creating A Regulatory System that Works for the American People," a Report to the President on the Third Anniversary of Executive Order 12866, Office of Management and Budget, Office of Information and Regulatory Affairs, Washington, DC (1996).

63. Office of Management and Budget, "Report to Congress on the Costs and Benefits of Federal Regulations," Office of Management and Budget, Office of Information and Regulatory Affairs, Washington, DC (1997).

64. Office of Management and Budget, "Budget of the United States Government, Fiscal Year 1999: Historical Tables," Executive Office of the President, Office of Management and Budget, Washington, DC (1998).

65. J. B. Opschoor, A. F. de Savornin Lohman, and H. B. Vos, "Managing the Environment: Role of Economic Instruments," Organisation for Economic Co-operation and Development, Paris, France (1994).

66. Organisation for Economic Co-operation and Development, "Regulatory Impact analysis: Best Practices in OECD Countries," Organisation for Economic Co-operation and Development, Paris, France (1997).

67. T. Page, "Conservation and Economic Efficiency: An Approach to Materials Policy," published for Resources for the Future, Johns Hopkins University Press, Baltimore, MD (1977).

68. P. Passell, A free-enterprise plan for an Everglades cleanup, *New York Times*, May 1 (1992).

69. A. C. Pigou, "The Economics of Welfare," Macmillan & Co., London, (1932); 4th ed. (1952).

70. P. R. Portney (Ed.), "Public Policies for Environmental Protection," Resources for the Future, Washington, DC (1990).

71. P. R. Portney, Counting the cost: The growing role of economics in environmental decisionmaking, *Environment 40*, 14–21 (1998).

72. R. L. Revesz, Rehabilitating interstate competition: Rethinking the 'race-to-the-bottom' rationale for federal environmental regulation, *New York Univ. Law Rev. 67*, 1210–1254 (1992).

73. K. R. Richards, "Framing Environmental Policy Instrument Choice, Working Paper, School of Public and Environmental Affairs, Indiana University, Bloomington, Indiana (1998).

74. P. A. Samuelson, The pure theory of public expenditure, *Rev. Econom. Stat. 36*, 387–389 (1954).

75. R. Schmalensee, P. L. Joskow, A. D. Ellerman, J. P. Montero, and E. M. Bailey, An interim evaluation of sulfur dioxide emissions trading, *J. Econom. Perspect., 12*(3) 53–68 (1998).

76. C. Skrzycki, A bipartisan bill runs into a Lott of opposition, *Washington Post*, F01, March 20 (1998).

77. V. K. Smith (Ed.), "Environmental Policy under Reagan's Executive Order: The Role of Cost-Benefit Analysis." Univ. North Carolina Press, Chapel Hill, NC (1984).

78. S. Smith and H. B. Vos, "Evaluating Economic Instruments for Environmental Policy," Organisation for Economic Co-operation and Development, Paris, France (1997).

79. R. N. Stavins (Ed.), "Project 88: Harnessing Market Forces to Protect Our Environment—Initiatives for the New President," Public Policy Study sponsored by Senator Timothy E. Wirth and Senator John Heinz, Washington, DC (1998).

80. R. N. Stavins, "Market Based Environmental Policies," Discussion Paper 98-26, Resources for the Future, Washington, DC (1998).

81. R. N. Stavins, What can we learn from the grand policy experiment: Positive and normative lessons from the SO_2 allowance trading, *J. Econom. Perspect. 12*(3), 69–88 (1998).

82. R. B. Stewart, Pyramids of sacrifice? Problems of federalism in mandating state implementation of national environmental policy, *Yale Law J. 86*, 1196–1272 (1977).

83. T. O. Tengs and J. Graham, The opportunity cost of haphazard social regulation, *in* "Risks, Costs and Lives Saved: Getting Better Results from Regulation" (R. W. Hahn, Ed.), Oxford Univ. Press/AEI Press, Washington, DC (1996).

84. D. Terkla, The efficiency value of effluent tax revenues, *J. Environ. Econom. Management 11*, 107–123 (1984).

85. The *Economist*, The defense of nature (2): Sprouting again, The Economist Newspaper Limited, April 12 (1997).

86. T. Tietenberg, "Emissions Trading: An Exercise in Reforming Pollution Policy," Resources for the Future, Washington, DC (1985).

87. T. Tietenberg, Economic instruments for environmental regulation, *Oxford Rev. Econom. Policy 6*, 17–33 (1990).

88. U.S. Environmental Protection Agency, "Costs and Benefits of Reducing Lead in Gasoline," Final Regulatory Impact Analysis III-2, U.S. Environmental Protection Agency, Office of Policy Analysis, Washington, DC (1985).

89. U.S. Environmental Protection Agency, "Environmental Investments: The Cost of a Clean Environment," U.S. Environmental Protection Agency, Office of Policy, Planning and Evaluation, Washington, DC (1990).

90. U.S. Environmental Protection Agency, "Economic Incentives: Options for Environmental Protection," U.S. Environmental Protection Agency, Policy, Planning and Evaluation, Washington, DC (1991).

91. U.S. Environmental Protection Agency, "The Benefits and Costs of the Clean Air Act: 1970 to 1990," U.S. Environmental Protection Agency, Office of Air and Radiation, Washington, DC (1997).

92. L. J. White, "Reforming Regulation: Processes and Problems," Prentice-Hall, Englewood Cliffs, NJ (1981).

93. B. Yandle, Bootleggers and Baptists in the market for regulation, *in* "The Political Economy of Government Regulation" (J. F. Shogren, Ed.), Topics in Regulatory Economics and Policy Series, Kluwer, Dordrecht/London, Norwell, MA (1989).

94. D. Wheeler, "Pollution Charge Systems in Developing Countries," World Bank, mimeo, Washington, DC (1998).

95. J. Yellen, statement of Janet Yellen, Chair, White House Council of Economic Advisers, before the U.S. Senate Committee on Agriculture, Nutrition, and Forestry on the Economics of the Kyoto Protocol, Washington, DC March 5 (1998).